THE NOISE OF BATTLE

The British Army and the Last Breakthrough Battle West of the Rhine, February-March 1945

So all day long the noise of battle roll'd
Among the mountains by the winter sea …
Such a sleep they sleep – the men I loved.
Morte d'Arthur: Alfred, Lord Tennyson, 1842

We heard the noise of battle but could see nothing.
Lt George Dicks MC, 1 Royal Norfolks, 1 March 1945

Intelligence officers can be confused by what they call 'noise', a mass of irrelevant signals: the amount of evidence is so great and so contradictory that none of it makes sense.
Changing Enemies. The Defeat and Regeneration of Germany: Noel, Lord Annan, 1995

This Book is Dedicated to:

112830 Major Peter Henry Woodthorpe Clarke, MC of Binbrook in Lincolnshire.

He was killed without a mark on his body, aged 23, leading D Company of 2 Lincolns on 2 March 1945 at Winnekendonk, and is buried in the Reichswald (Forest) Military Cemetery, Plot 48.C.3.

Maj-Gen Glyn Gilbert, CB, MC: *Peter was in the last Sandhurst intake and I was in the one before. He was an only child and the godfather of my eldest son. All his service was in the 2nd Battalion. He was a fine cricketer, and I believe played for English Public Schools at Repton. I believe Peter was in for a bar to his MC, but his death precluded the award.*

Maj-Gen Cecil L. Firbank, CBE, DSO and Bar: *He was quite brilliant, and would have gone straight to the top.*

Capt Jack Harrod: *Brought up in a military tradition and with a military heritage, the Regiment was his pride, and the Battalion his joy. To it he devoted his all – a service that was timeless and self-less, combining to a nicety the confidence and exuberance of youth with the thoughtful judgement of a veteran. He was beloved by his fellow officers, and almost worshipped by his men. His name will live in their hearts forever.*

Maj Leslie Colvin, MC, the author's father was deeply affected by Peter's death. The author's brother, born in 1946, is named after him, as is his grandson.

THE NOISE OF BATTLE

The British Army and the Last Breakthrough Battle West of the Rhine, February-March 1945

Tony Colvin

Helion & Company

Helion & Company Limited
26 Willow Road
Solihull
West Midlands
B91 1UE
England
Tel. 0121 705 3393
Fax 0121 711 4075
Email: info@helion.co.uk
Website: www.helion.co.uk
Twitter: @helionbooks
Visit our blog http://blog.helion.co.uk/

Published by Helion & Company 2016
Designed and typeset by Mach 3 Solutions Ltd (www.mach3solutions.co.uk)
Cover designed by Paul Hewitt, Battlefield Design (www.battlefield-design.co.uk)
Printed by Gutenberg Press Limited, Tarxien, Malta

Front Cover: Michael Colvin; a 1995 photograph computer-modified according to the recollections of Eric Houldershaw and John Keenan.
Back Cover: Shoulder flashes of 2 Lincolns and 3 Scots Guards, and a Fallschirmschützenabzeichen der Luftwaffe (Air Force paratrooper badge) – early Assmann Type E.

ISBN 978-1-910777-11-4

A catalogue record for this book is available from the British Library.

Contents

List of Illustrations

List of Maps and Aerial Photographs

Conventions and Abbreviations

Conventions

Dates – eg. 28 February. All are 1945 except when otherwise specified.
Square brackets contain comments by this author.
Map references refer to the contemporary military map which was a copy of the German and has kilometre squares.
* = yards

Abbreviations

A&SD	Argyll & Sutherland Highlanders
AA	anti aircraft
AAF	Auxiliary Air Force
AACC	Army Air Control Centre
AASC	Army Air Support Control
AASL	Anti-Aircraft Search Light
A&SH	Argyll & Sutherland Highlanders
a/c	aircraft
AC	Armoured Carrier
A/CMO	Acting Chief Medical Officer
ACV	Armoured Command Vehicle
AD	Airborne Division
ADGB	Air Defence of Great Britain
Adjt	Adjutant
adm	administration
ADS	Advanced Dressing Station
adv	advance
AEAF	Allied Expeditionary Air Force
AFV	Armoured Fighting Vehicle
AG	Army Group
AGRA	Army Group Royal Artillery
AIF	Australian Imperial Force
aka	also known as
ALB	Air Landing Brigade
ALO	Air Liaison Officer
AMES	American Microwave Early Warning Set
amn	ammunition
AOK	Armeeoberkommando or Field Army Command

AOP	Air Observation Post
AP	armour piercing
APC	Armoured Personnel Carrier
APCBC	AP Capped Ballistic Capped
APCR	Armour Piercing Composite Rigid high density core with lighter-weight full-bore cover
APDS	Armour Piercing Discarding Sabot
APIS	Aerial Photograph Intelligence Section
APW	Armour Protected Weapon
A/Q	Acting Quartermaster Officer
Armd	armoured
arty	artillery
ARV	Armoured Recovery Vehicle
ASSU	Air Support Signals Unit
Assy	assembly
ATB	Army Tank Brigade
ATI	Army Training Instruction
ATK	Anti-Tank
ATM	Army Training Memorandum
ATS	Anti-Tetanus Serum
Aufklärung	Reconnaissance
Ausbildung or aus	training
AVRE	Armoured Vehicle Royal Engineers
AWOL	Absence Without Leave
BAD	British Armoured Division
BAOR	British Army of the Rhine
BAR	Browning Automatic Rifle
barrage	planned artillery shoot usually moving in coordination with the infantry
BATB	British Army Tank Brigade
BC	Battery Commander
BC	Bomber Command of the RAF
BCATP	British Commonwealth Air Training Programme
BCB	British Commando Brigade
Bde	Brigade
BEAF	British Expeditionary Air Force
BESA	light 7.92 mm tank machine gun
BGS	Brigadier General Staff at Corps HQ
bg	bearing
BIB	British Infantry Brigade
BID	British Infantry Division

BIO	Brigade Intelligence Officer
BLA	British Liberation Army, renamed BAOR
Bn	Battalion
BoB	Battle of Britain
Bomb	Bombardier
br	bridge
BRAC	Brigadier, Royal Armoured Corps
BRASCO	Brigade RASC Officer
Brig	brigadier
brhead	bridgehead
Brylcreem Boys	army term for an airman
Brown Job	RAF slang for a soldier
BTB	British Tank Brigade
BTO	Brigade Transport Officer
Bty	Battery
BVRC	Bermuda Volunteer Rifle Corps
CAB	Canadian Armoured Brigade
Cabrank	aircraft circling overhead receiving detailed targeting by a VCP
CAD	Canadian Armoured Division
CAMP	Commander Military Police
Canloan	Canadian officers seconded to the British army
Capt	Captain
cas	casualties
CAS	Close Air Support
CB	Counter Battery
CCP	Casualty Clearance Post
CCS	Casualty Clearing Station
CCS	Combined Chiefs of Staff
CDL	Canal Defence Light
Cdn	Canadian
CG	Coldstream Guards
Ch	Chapter
CIB	Canadian Infantry Brigade
CID	Canadian Infantry Division
CIGS	Chief of the Imperial General Staff
Circus	bomber attacks with fighter escorts to bring up German fighters
CLY	County of London Yeomanry
CM	Counter Mortar
CMO	Commanding Medical Officer
CO	Commanding Officer
Comd, Comnd or Cmd	Command or Commander
comm	communications
conc	concentration pinpoint artillery shoot

Contact Car	VCP with a TR.1143 VHF radio for communication with overhead a/c
Coords	Coordinates
COS	Chief of Staff
Coy	Company
CP	Control Post
Cpl	Corporal
CQMS	Company Quartermaster Sergeant
CRA	Commander Royal Artillery
CRAC	Commander Royal Armoured Corps
CRE	Commander Royal Engineers
CS	Close Support using a mortar not a gun
CSM	Company Sergeant Major
CSO	Central Statistical Office
CTB	Canadian Tank Brigade
D-Day	day specified for the start of an operation
DAA	Deputy Assistant Adjutant
DAK	Deutsche Afrika Korps
DD	Duplex Drive amphibious power
DF	Defensive Fire
dis	disabled or non-functioning
Div	Division
DLI	Durham Light Infantry
DMO	Director of Military Operations
DND	Canadian Department of National Defence
DP	dual purpose
DR	despatch rider
DRAC	Director Royal Armoured Corps
DSAP	Discarding Sabot Armour Piercing
ech	echelon
elev.	elevation
elts	elements
EME	Electrical & Mechanical Engineer
EMF	Experimental Mechanised Force
erk	aircraftman
Erprobung	test
Ersatz or ers	replacement
est	estimated
ETO	European Theatre of Operations
evac	evacuated
Evacuees	naval term for a soldier
FAA	Fleet Air Arm
FAC	Forward Air Controller

fascines	large bundles of wood bound with wire and dropped by AVREs in ditches to allow tanks to cross
FCP	Forward Control Post located at corps with radio communication to the ASSU & overhead a/c
Fd or Fld	Field
FDR	Franklin Delano Roosevelt
FE	Far East
Feldpolizei	Field Police
FF Yeo	Fife & Forfar Yeomanry
FJD	Fallschirmjäger Division or Paratroop Div
FJR	Fallschirmjäger Regt or Paratroop Regt
Flak	Flieger Abschoss Kanone or anti-aircraft gun
FOO	Forward Observation Officer
formn	formation, a combination of units
FPN	Feld Post Nummer Field Post Office Number
fps	feet per second
FR	Field Regiment
FRV	final rendezvous point
FS	Fallschirm or parachute
Funnies	special tanks in 79 BAD
FUP	Forming Up Point
FUSAG	First US Army Group
fwd	forward
GAB	Guards Armoured Brigade
GAD	Guards Armoured Division
GAF	German Air Force or Luftwaffe
GCC	Group Control Centre
Gdsm	Guardsman
Gen	general
GG	Grenadier Guards
GHQ	General HQ
GIB	Guards Infantry Brigade
GID	German Infantry Division
GMD	German Mountain Division
GOC	General Officer Commanding
GP	General Purpose
Gp	Group compromising 3 to 5 Wings
GPS	Global Positioning System
GR	Grenadier Regiment
GS	General Staff
GSO3	Third General Staff Officer or Assistant to Brigade Major
GTB	Guards Tank Brigade
guerre de course	commerce raiding

H-Hour	hour specified for the start of the operation
HD	Highland Division
HE	High Explosive
Heer	German army
HIAG	Hilfsgemeinschaft auf Gegenseitigkeit der Angehörigen der ehemaligen Waffen-SS or Mutual Help Association of Former Waffen SS Members.
Hiwi	Hilfswilliger or volunteer helpers
HJ	Hitler Jugend or Hitler Youth
HKL	Hauptkampflinie or main defensive line
HLPR	High Level Photo Reconnaissance
hr	hour
HVAP	High Velocity Armour Piercing
hy	heavy
IGAF	Imperial German Air Force
inf	infantry
infm	information
instr	instruction
int	intelligence
intel	intelligence
IO	Intelligence Officer
IR	Infantry Regiment
I-tank	infantry tank
IWGC	Imperial War Graves Commission
IWM	Imperial War Museum
Jabo	Jagdbomber or fighter bomber
JG	Jagd Gruppe or fighter group
Jg Pz	Jagd Panzer or tank destroyer
JIC	Joint Intelligence Committee
Kangaroo	turretless tank used as an APC
Kgr	Kampfgruppe or Battle Group
KG	Kampf Gruppe or Bomber Group
kia	killed in action
KOSB	Kings Own Scottish Borderers
Kp	Kompanie or Company
KPD	Kommunist Partei Deutschland or German Communist Party
KRRC	Kings Royal Rifle Corps
KSLI	Kings Shropshire Light Infantry
LAA	Light Anti-Aircraft (Bofors guns)
LAC	Library and Archives Canada
LAC	Leading Aircraftman
Landser	infantryman
LCA	Landing Craft Assault

LCMSDS	Laurier Centre for Military Strategic and Disarmament Studies
L Cpl	Lance Corporal
Ldr	Leader
LEHR	demonstration and experimentation
LF Sqn	Left Flank Squadron
LFH	Leicht Feld Haubitze or Light Field Howitzer
LFH 18	10.5 cm howitzer
LHCMA	Liddell Hart Centre for Military Archives
LIAP	Leave In Addition to Python, given to those with 'only' 2¾ years service overseas
LMG	Light Machine Gun, Bren
LO	Liaison Officer
LOB	Left Out of Battle
LRDG	Long Range Desert Group
Lt	Lieutenant
lt	light
Lt-Col	Lieutenant Colonel
LW	Luftwaffe
LWFD	Luftwaffenfelddivision or Luftwaffe Field Division
Maj	Major
MC	medium case (metal thickness)
ME	Middle East
med	medium
MET	Motorised Enemy Transport
MFAA	Monuments, Fine Arts Archive Programme
mg	machine gun
Mike or M Target	all 24 guns of the Field Regt
MMG	Medium Machine Guns, Vickers
MOD	Ministry/Minister of Defence
MOS	Ministry of Supply
MP	Military Police
MPI	Mean Point of Impact
MRCP	Mobile Radar Control Post
MT	Motorised Transport
MTP	Military Training Pamphlet
Mx	Middlesex Regiment
NA	National Archives
NCO	Non Commissioned Officer
NIH	North Irish Horse
NSDAP	Nationalsozialistische deutsche Arbeitspartei or Nazi
NSG	Nacht Schlacht Gruppe or Night Attack Group
NWE	North West Europe (Theatre of Ops)
NZAB	New Zealand Armoured Brigade

NZIB	New Zealand Infantry Brigade
NZID	New Zealand Infantry Division
O Group	Orders Group
OC	Officer Commanding
OCTU	Officer Cadet Training Unit
offr	officer
OIC	officer in command
OKH	Oberkommando Heer or army high command
OKL	Oberkommando Luftwaffe or LW high command
OKW	Oberkommando Wehrmacht or Armed Forces High Command
OP	Observation Post
Op	Operation
OR	Other Ranks ie not officers
OR	Operational Research
ORB	Order of Battle
ORB	Operations Record Book (RAF War Diary)
p.	page
PAD	Polish Armoured Division
PAK or Pak	Panzer Abschoss Kanone or Anti-tank gun
Pakfront	grouping of anti-tank guns under one commander
Panzerjäger	Tank Destroyer or TD
PBI	Poor Bloody Infantry, said self-mockingly
PBS	Prefabricated Bituminous Surfacing
PD	Panzer Division
PG	Panzer Grenadier
PGD	Panzer Grenadier Division
PGR	Panzer Grenadier Regiment
PIAT	Projectile Infantry Anti Tank
Pionieren	German sappers
Pl	Platoon
PMC	President of the Mess Committee
P Mines	(anti) personnel mines
pnrs	pioneers
Pongos	RAF term for 'brown jobs' or soldiers, (in Congolese, ape is 'mpongo))
posn	position
p.s.c.	Passed Staff College
PSP	Pressed Steel Plate
pt	point
Pte	Private
pty	party
PW	POW or prisoner of war
Python	home or leave for those with 4 plus years service abroad

Pz	Panzer or tank
PzJg	Panzerjäger or tank destroyer
PzJgAbt	Panzerjäger Abteilung or tank destroyer section
QMO	Quartermaster Officer
RA	Royal Artillery
RAAF	Royal Australian Air Force
RAC	Royal Armoured Corps
RAD	Reichs Arbeit Dienst or German Labour Service
ranker	officer promoted from the ranks
RAMC	Royal Army Medical Corps
Ramrod duty	daylight bomber raid
RAP	Regimental Aid Post
RASC	Royal Army Service Corps
RCE	Royal Canadian Engineers
RE	Royal Engineers
Regt	Regiment (British battalion: German brigade)
rep	representative
res	reserve
RF Sqn	Right Flank Squadron
RFB	Rote Frontkampferband or Red Frontfighters
RFC	Royal Flying Corps or British Army Aviation
RHA	Royal Horse Artillery
RHU	Reinforcement Holding Unit
Rhubarb	operations involving fighter-bombers seeking targets of opportunity
RIDG	Royal Inniskilling Dragoon Guards
rly	railway
RMO	Regimental Medical Officer
Rodeo	fighter sweeps over enemy territory
Rover	armed recce seeking targets of opportunity
R/P	Rocket Projectile
rpg	rounds per gun
RN	Royal Navy
RSF	Royal Scots Fusiliers
RSM	Regimental Sergeant Major
R/T	radiotelephone
RTC	Royal Tank Corps
RTR	Royal Tank Regiment
RTU	Return To Unit
RUR	Royal Ulster Rifles
RUSI	Royal United Services Institution
RV	rendezvous point
RWF	Royal Welch Fusiliers
SA	small arms

SA	Sturm Abteilung or Storm Troop
SAA	Small Arms Ammunition
sabot	sub-calibre shell contained within a shoe that dispersed once outside the barrel
SAR	South Alberta Regiment
SASO	Senior Air Staff Officer
SB	Stretcher Bearer
SBG	Small Box Girder bridge
Schnell	fast
Schwerpunkt	axis of attack
sec	section
Serenade Target	US version of a Victor Target
SG	Scots Guards
Sgt	Sergeant
sig	signals
Sitn	situation
SITREP	Situation Report
SL	Start Line
Slidex	code system changed daily
SMT	Square Mesh Track
SP	Self Propelled (Gun)
sp	support
Spandau	MG42, a light machine-gun
SPD	Sozialistische Partei Deutschland or German Socialist Party
sp	support
spetsnaz	special purpose
Sqn	Squadron of 18 aircraft
SSTK	SS Totenkopf
sta	station
StG 44	MP 44 assault rifle
stonk	see concentration
sticky	slow or no movement
str	strength
StuG	Sturmgeschütz or assault gun
sup	supply
Svy	Survey
swanning	unauthorised leisure travel
TA	Territorial Army
Tac	tactical
Tac R	tactical recce
TAF	Tactical Air Force
TB	Tank Brigade
TC	Troop Commander

TC	Traffic Control
TCV	Troop Carrying Vehicles
TD	Tank Destroyer
Tiefangriff	low level attack
tk	tank
TOE	Table of Establishment
tp	troop
tpr	trooper
tpt	transport
trg	training
tk	tank
uc	under command
u/s	unserviceable
Uncle Target	all 72 howitzers of the division
unit	an operationally self-contained entity; eg a battalion or squadron that cannot be sub-divided further and remain self-supporting
USAD	US Armoured Division
USAWC	US Army War College
USII	United Service Institution of India
USID	US Infantry Division
USPIR	US Paratroop Infantry Regiment
USSBS	US Strategic Bombing Survey
USWD	US War Department
VCP	Visual Control Post[1] directing air strikes through communications with overhead a/c
Vernichtungskrieg	war of extermination
Victor Target	all corps guns (150 to 250 guns)
VLR	Very Long Range
VVS	Soviet air force
Wehrkreis	German military District
Wing	formation of 3 to 5 squadrons = Group in USAAF parlance
Wing Co	Wing Commander
WO	War Office
WOSB	War Office Selection Board
WSC	Winston Spencer Churchill
2ic	second in command
5.5	5.5 inch (14 cm) medium howitzer firing 100 lb shell
yd	yard
*	yards

1. Cheval Lallement called it a Visual Control Point.

Acknowledgements

This book was written with the help of many people. I would like to express gratitude to them all.

First to acknowledge are the sixty-seven eyewitnesses and participants who through correspondence and interview made this book possible, and whose story it is. They are: Geoff Kirk, JG Smith and Andrew Wilson of the Buffs; Anna Gellings, Maria Hoogen, Heinrich Kempkes, Maria and Johannes Raadts and Katherina Schmitz who were civilians caught up in the battles; Otto Einert, Erich Freund, Willi Lennartz and Ted Winkler of FJR7; H. Volberg of FJR17; Heinrich Nattkamp of FJR19; Willi Thielecke of FJR22; Hans Kühn of Panzer Jäger Abteilung 33; John Lincoln, Bryan Balsom, George Dicks, Peter Gould and Humphrey Wilson of 1 Royal Norfolk Regiment; Jim Fetterley, Bill Renison, Robbie Robertson, Lionel Roebuck and Reg Rutherford of 2 East Yorkshire Regiment; Bill Banks and Tom Read of 2 Kings Shropshire Light Infantry; Eddie Jones of 1 South Lancashire Regiment; David Bates, John Boys, Joe Collinson, Leslie Colvin, Alfie Curnow, Ken Deer, Cecil Firbank, Darby Houlton-Hart, Glyn Gilbert, Eric Houldershaw, John Hunt, John Keenan, John Pacey, Pat Smith, George Wall, Len Waters and Colin Welch of 2 Lincolnshire Regiment; Rex Fendick of 2 Middlesex Regiment; Harry Illing of 2 Royal Warwickshire Regiment; Richard Hough, A. Laforce, J. Mathys and Desmond Scott of 2 Tactical Airforce; Alan Cathcart, Charles Farrell, Mark Fearfield, Hector Laing, John MacDonald-Buchanan, Robert Runcie and William Whitelaw of 3 Scots Guards; Alec Foucard and Alexis Napier of 4 Coldstream Guards; Robert Boscawen of 1 Coldstream Guards; Tony Edwards, Ivor Norton and Chips Parker-Smith of 33 Field Regiment Royal Artillery; and John Ford of 76 Field Regiment RA.

Archival and other help was provided in Kervenheim and Winnekendonk by Franz Josef Drißen and Georg his son, the Elders family and especially Josef Elders (from whose mother I borrowed a book that was not returned for 32 years), Maria Hoogen, Alois Janssen, Heinrich Kempkes, Hansgerd Kronenberg, Willi and Cilli Klümpen, Bernhard Meiners and Lothar Stanetzky.

Over many years academics and historians have given kindly of their time to read drafts; others have invited me to lectures and workshops, shared their experience, given me contacts and permissions, or offered office services. They include Maj John Ainsworth of the Royal Sussex Regimental Association, Vorsitzender Heinz Bosch of the Historische Verein für Geldern und Umgegend, Professor John Campbell and Professor Dick Rempel of McMaster University, Professor Emeritus Terry Copp of Wilfrid Laurier University, Carlo D'Este, Professor Dominick Graham of the University of New Brunswick, David Fletcher and Stuart Wheeler of the Bovington Tank Museum, Professor Lt Col John A. English of Queen's University, Professor Emeritus Jack Granatstein of York University, Professor Nigel Hamilton of the University of Massachusetts, Professor Geoffrey Hayes of the University of Waterloo, Jonathan Mantle, Ian Martin of the KOSB Regimental Museum, Maj Boris Mollo of the Shropshire Regimental Museum, Professor Richard Overy of Exeter University, Winston Ramsey, Norman Scarfe of Leicester University, Senior Research Historian Richard C. Anderson Jr of the Dupuy Institute, Gerry Chester, Terence Cuneo, Doug Knight, Derek Nudd, Phil Spicer, Ken Tout, Simon Tan and Colin Williams.

The families of veterans have been most helpful: the Alldred family and especially Andrew have worked out the battlefield movements of Jim Alldred and Bob Runcie while Dave Alldred has contributed from his website; Ben Beck, Stephen Clarke, David Dunkelman, Simon Firbank, Dido Farrell, Reginald Fendick, Graham Gilbert, Donald Gordon, Rod Hoffmeister, Alastair MacDonald-Buchanan, Dominic Norman-Rowsell, Andrew Renison and Andrew Smyth.

Major contributors to the text have been Bill Renison, who lent me his original campaign diary and gave permission to quote it verbatim in the Yorkshire Bridge chapter, and Reg Thompson and his mother Mel who permitted me to use verbatim the eyewitness description of the Battle of Kervenheim written by their father and husband, the war correspondent and under-appreciated historian RW Thompson as well as his papers lodged in the Liddell Hart Archive.

Lady Whistler permitted me to quote from her husband's diary held in the West Sussex Record Office.

My late brother, Michael, spent hours in discussion, reading drafts and accompanying me on battlefield visits. The computer-generated picture of the exploding Churchill at Winnekendonk, which is on this book's cover, was created by him with the help of John Keenan and Eric Houldershaw, who replayed the scene from their mind's eye and guided Michael's computer mouse.

Lt Col ffrench-Blake of the School of Infantry kindly invited Michael and me to attend Exercise Phantom Bugle as his guests on 12 December 1984 on Salisbury Plain in winter. It was an unforgettable introduction to armoured soldiering.

My cousin, Flt Lt Piers Colvin at RAF Laarbruch in 1983 entertained my son Jonathan and me in the mess and took us up in a light plane for an aerial photographic tour of the battlefield, whose results were marred unfortunately by misty weather.

Rob Belk has supported the project from the beginning, and personifies the informed readership for whom this book is written.

My family, Helen, Jonathan, Richard, Alex and Ben accepted without demur the consequences of my undertaking this book, and Jenny Pearson spent weeks proof-reading and copy-editing the manuscript to the professional standard expected of a trained Shell secretary and PA.

To all those whose help is not acknowledged, please accept my apologies for the oversight. In mitigation I can refer only to the wear and tear of the period of thirty-three years during which, and the four different houses within which, the book was written, besides failing memory.

This author of course bears sole responsibility for all errors and unsubstantiated opinions.

Topsham, January 2016

Author's Notes

Square brackets contain this author's explanatory notes.

Map references refer to the contemporary military map which was metrical. The area of a map square is one square kilometre. The references are always in the same form and are either 4-figure or 6-figure. A 4-figure reference denotes a square; e.g. 9244 denotes the square between the 92 and 93 Longitude – the vertical lines on the map – and the 44 and 45 Latitude – the horizontal lines. A position referred to as 926443 is 60% of the distance between the 92 and 93 Longitude – and 30% of the distance between 44 and 45 Latitude. The kilometre grid used was the Modified Lambert Projection (conformal conic projection) of the Nord de Guerre Zone Grid. This zone lay between two standard parallels chosen to provide seamless map connections from Normandy to Brandenburg with minimal scale decreases between them. The modern UTM grid (Universal Transverse Mercator) is not in the same place and the references cannot be transferred without significant modification. All have since been replaced by the GPS.

Bibliography All of the books referenced in the text are listed in the Archives, Sources and Bibliography.

Glossary Abbreviations are used extensively in the text and are defined in Conventions & Abbreviations.

Part I

The Battles

1

The Battle of the Rhineland

Often defined as the area between the Maas and the Rhine, the Rhineland was defined by Montgomery as the area between Düsseldorf and Nijmegen. In his lexicon of twelve operations, *Preparation for the Battle of the Rhineland* was Operation 7, and the *Battle of the Rhineland* itself was Operation 9 (See Table 1).

The distance from Normandy to the Baltic is 660 miles, and was covered by 21 AG at an average speed of 2 miles/day. However, during the six-month period from the capture of Groesbeek on 18 September in Operation 5 to reaching the Rhine bank opposite Wesel on 10 March in Operation 9, the average speed fell by over 90% to 300 yards/day, and against a foe that had been beaten and written off in Normandy.

Table 1 Montgomery's operational lexicon[1]

Operation 1	June 1944	The Assault
Operation 2	June/July 1944	Establishment of the initial bridgehead & capture of Cherbourg
Operation 3	July/August 1944	Break-out and advance to the River Seine
Operation 4	August 1944	Crossing of the River Seine
Operation 5	September 1944	Drive on Brussels & Antwerp. Clearance of the Channel Ports. The Battle of Arnhem
Operation 6	September/October 1944	Clearance of the Scheldt Estuary & opening of the Port of Antwerp
Operation 7	October/November 1944	Preparations for the Battle of the Rhineland & Clearance of the west bank of the River Meuse
Operation 8	December 1944	Battle of the Ardennes
Operation 9	January/February 1945	Battle of the Rhineland
Operation 10	March 1945	Battle of the Rhine
Operation 11	April 1945	Advance to the Elbe
Operation 12	May 1945	Drive to the Baltic, & German surrender

The Battle of Arnhem, Operation 5, was delayed by Eisenhower's indecision and indisposition and, when finally approved, the opportunity to 'bounce' the Germans right across the Rhine[2] to enter the North German Plain through Arnhem and over the River Ijssel had evaporated, even had it once existed which is debatable. As consolation prizes, however, the Allies had bridgeheads over the River Maas in Nijmegen and Groesbeek, and over the River Waal in the Island. They now had the choice of striking through the Reichswald or along the east bank of the Rhine. After Arnhem was evacuated on 26 September, XXX Corps began to plan an operation through the Reichswald,

1 BL Montgomery. *Normandy to the Baltic* (London: Hutchinson, 1946), pp. vii-viii.
2 Nigel Hamilton. *Monty: The Field Marshal* (London: Hutchinson, 1986), p. 98.

Map 1 Most of the *Veritable* battlefield from contemporary Sheets 2a and 3a at 1:250,000 scale.

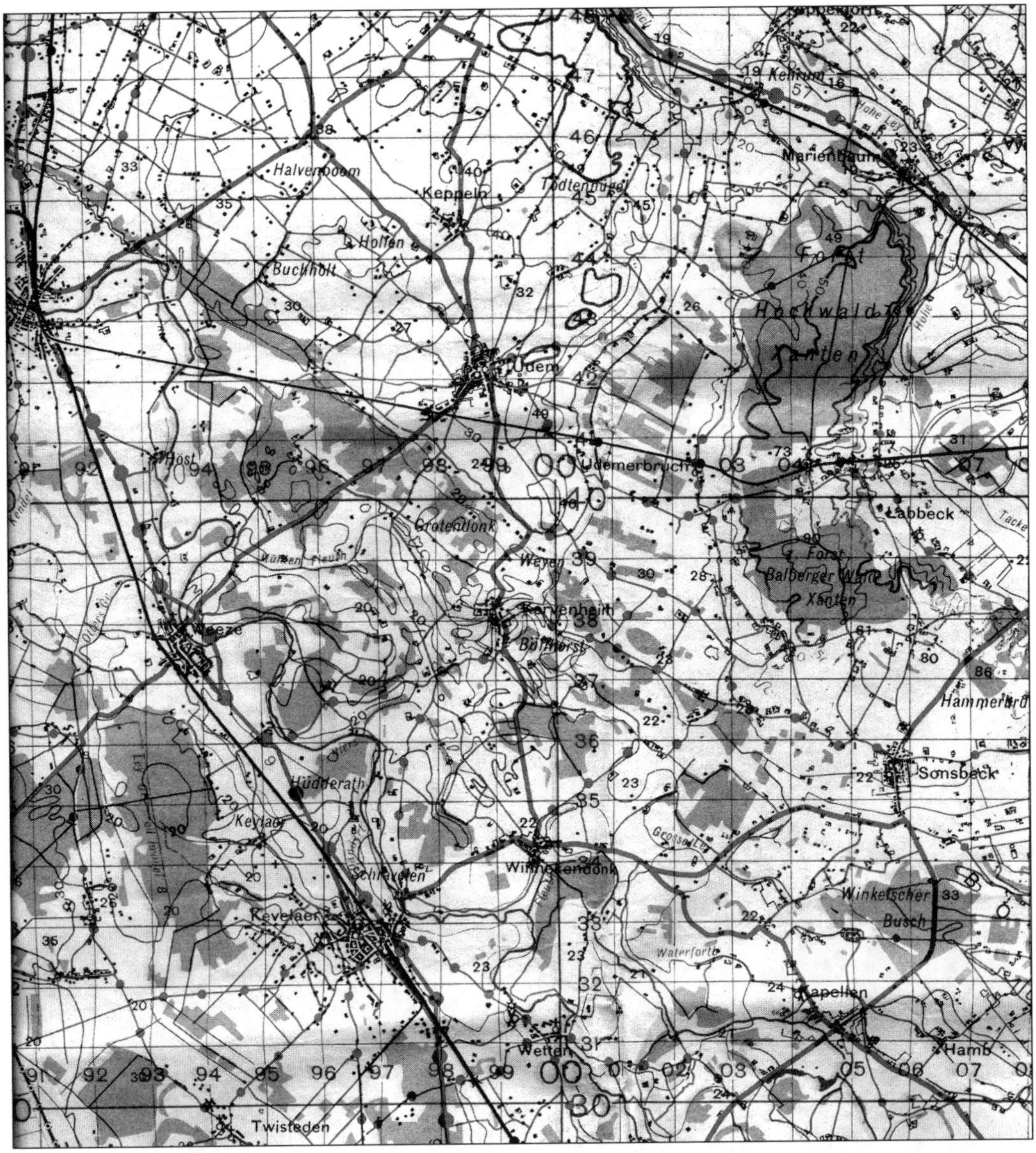

Map 2 Part of the *Veritable* battlefield from contemporary Sheet Q1 Essen at 1:100,000 scale.

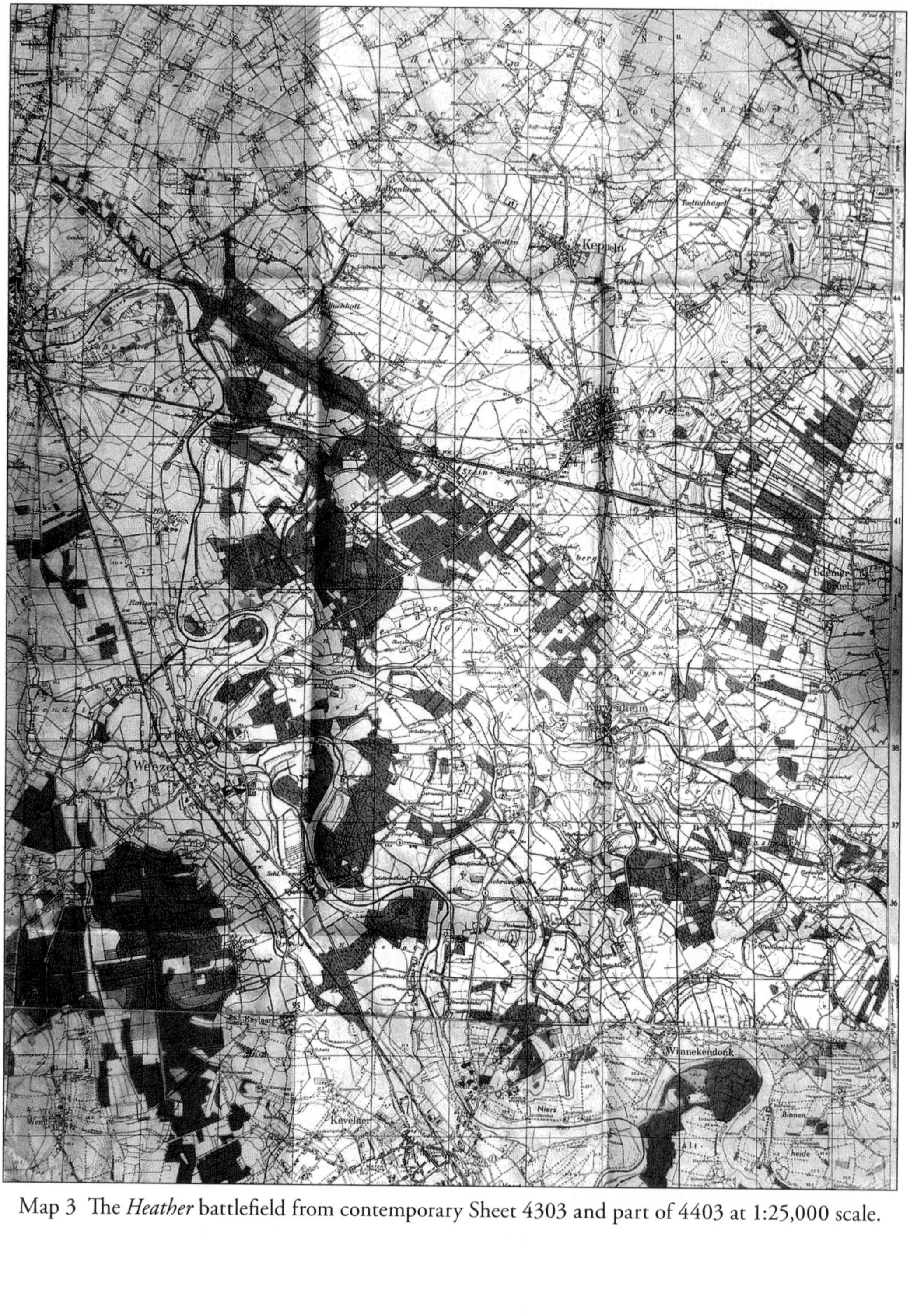

Map 3 The *Heather* battlefield from contemporary Sheet 4303 and part of 4403 at 1:25,000 scale.

The senior commanders of Operations *Veritable* and *Grenade* with Bradley and Dempsey. Presentation of decorations by FM Montgomery and Gen Eisenhower, 1 March 1945, Geldrop, Netherlands. (l.-r. seated) FM Montgomery, Gen Eisenhower, Lt Gen Bradley (l.-r. standing) Gen Crerar, Lt Gen Simpson, Lt Gen Dempsey. (Barney J Gloster/Canada. Dept of National Defence/Library & Archives Canada/ PA-136327)

called *Gatwick*. Horrocks intended to use 43 BID and 3 BID with 6 GTB, and all were moving up when the operation was cancelled.

Gatwick was postponed repeatedly, but remained in the active file. In October priority went where it should always have been, to Operation 6, *The Clearance of the Scheldt Estuary and the Opening of the Port of Antwerp*. In October *Gatwick* morphed into *Valediction* and then *Veritable* in which 1 Canadian Army would combine with 9 US Army's Operation *Grenade* in a pincer movement to clear up the Rhineland, while 12 USAG would seize a bridgehead over the Rhine in early November. American attention shifted south while Canadian plans to clear the Island were aborted by its flooding.

Matters came to a head at the Maastricht conference on 7 December when Eisenhower refused to appoint Montgomery overall commander of a single thrust with 40 divisions through the Ruhr, but confirmed the availability of Simpson's 9 US Army. The Canadians were ordered to be ready for *Veritable* by 1 January. The Americans by then had a surplus of divisions while the British were reduced to breaking up infantry divisions for reinforcements. Patton meanwhile had attempted to battle his way through at Metz where he incurred heavier casualties than at Arnhem and with the same result. The Americans attacked around Aachen and through the Hürtgen Forest, while the French attacked in the far south. All operations were disrupted by the Ardennes Offensive in Operation 8.

Eisenhower reacted to the Offensive by passing command privately from Bradley to Montgomery, revealed shortly before a Press Conference on 7 January 1945 in which Montgomery's reported description of it as a 'very interesting little battle' belittled the Americans. These were the words as remembered by Brig Williams[3] but, according to John Eisenhower, Montgomery called it 'a very interesting and tricky battle'[4] – arrogant and gauche but scarcely belittling. Montgomery was always using 'very interesting'; for example in 1946 he presented a hundred copies of '*Normandy to the Baltic*' to the US Army in order "to facilitate the study by professional soldiers of a very interesting campaign". Neither Bradley nor Patton found the Battle of the Bulge interesting, and wanted Montgomery blamed, as Hamilton[5] explains, for delaying the counter-attack. Montgomery saw no need to react to the Germans and compromise *Veritable*, which he could not mention which further annoyed Bradley. It was not until a conference on 16 January that the *Veritable/Grenade* plans were finalised, with their respective start-dates of 8 and 15 February being settled on 23 January.

In December 1944 the American preponderance in the number of divisions had grown to an overwhelming forty-four to twenty-five Anglo-Canadian-French-Polish divisions, or two-thirds of an overall total of sixty-nine divisions.[6] If Montgomery had refused to back down from his demand to lead forty divisions on Berlin, Eisenhower would have replaced him with Alexander. Montgomery had finally overplayed his hand and thereafter was sidelined.

The waterlogged land between Maas and the Rhine in any February was among the worst places in Europe in which to attempt a mechanised assault relying on speed, and especially in a year of record water levels in the Rhine. For the same reason it was a good location to defend. In August 1944, Montgomery's planners had labelled the route through Wesel as unsuitable in winter. Montgomery still dismissed it on 28 November as a place for winter warfare, writing about *Valediction*; 'There is no intention of launching this operation now, and I have never expressed any wish to do so. All I want you to do is examine it and put the planners on to thinking it out. It will NOT be launched till the spring, i.e. March or later.'[7]

The operation ruled out in August and November was sanctioned in December because it was the only option available to 21 AG and 9 US Army.

Of the five gateways into Germany, shown in Map 4, two were in 21 AG's area of operation. The northern one through Arnhem had been tried disastrously and the Island had since been flooded. The second gateway through Wesel was approachable from two directions of equal distance; Nijmegen through the Reichswald or Deurne over a newly constructed Maas bridge at Wanssum/Well. However, the Deurne-route ran through the Peel Marsh which could not support the traffic of one, let alone nine, divisions. This left the third gateway eventually used by *Grenade* as favourite, leading from the Roer valley to the Rhine around Düsseldorf. This, however, could not be used until the Roer Dams were secured or their water released. The RAF/USAAF failed to destroy the dams, and Bradley showed his contempt for the sidelined Montgomery by delaying his order to Hodges to take them until 4 February, when Eisenhower was forced to intervene and insist on their being taken. Hodges took until 11 February to secure the dams and succeeded only after they had been sabotaged by the Germans to ensure a measured release of water that would make the Roer impassable for two weeks. The fourth and fifth gateways through the Ardennes and Saar were ruled out because the country was difficult, and in any case were too far from the ports.

---

3 Hamilton, *Monty: The Field Marshal*, p. 303.
4 JD Eisenhower. *Bitter Woods* (London: Robert Hale, 1969), p. 113.
5 Hamilton, *Monty: The Field Marshal*, p. 316.
6 CP Stacey. *The Victory Campaign* (Ottawa: DND, 1960), p. 437.
7 Op. Cit., p. 436.

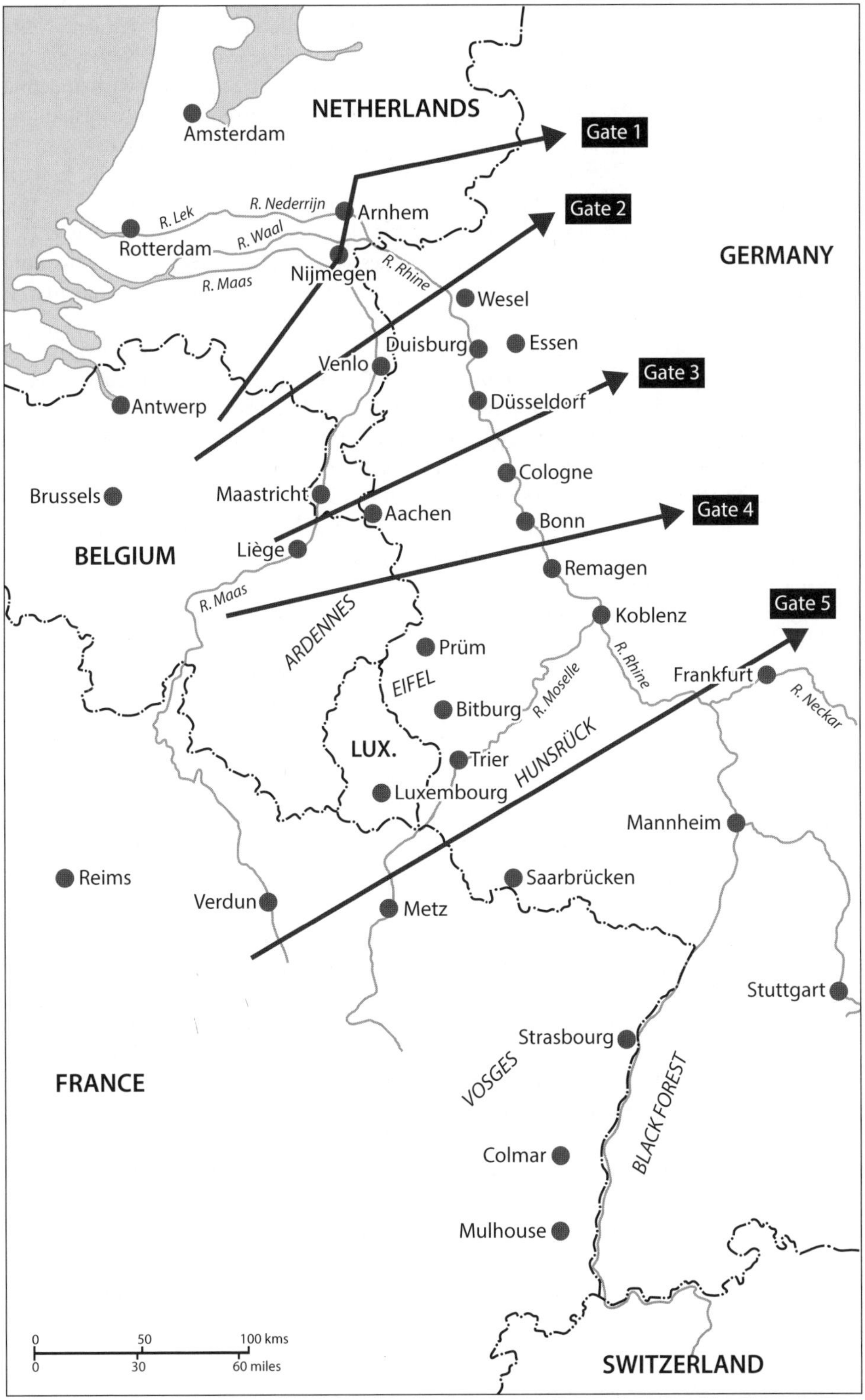

Map 4 The five gateways into Germany.

The Germans had used the fourth route in reverse in both 1940 and 1944, but in neither case was it defended. In January 1945, Bradley was using it but making no progress.

The Canadians were made responsible for the Nijmegen bridgehead on 9 November, on the day that Crerar returned from hospital where he had been since late September with anaemia and internal troubles.[8] He was now responsible for 140 miles of front from Walcheren Island, where resistance had ceased the previous day, to Boxmeer on the Maas opposite the Reichswald. Already a Companion of the Bath, Crerar on 21 November was made a full General, the first time a Canadian held such rank in the field. His reputation has not survived in Canada, where a popular encyclopaedia dismissed him as an excellent staff officer but mediocre commander, and claimed Montgomery had little confidence in him.[9] Chris Vokes said he liked Crerar despite his humourlessness, but added that because he had never commanded in battle he was simply chairman of the board rather than CEO.

The *Veritable* plan, shown in Map 6, was for 15 BID to break through the forward defences at Kranenburg under an artillery barrage of over 1,000 guns, and to open the road to the high ground near Cleve. 43 BID would then pass through to the Materborn area where it would swing down the east side of the Reichswald to capture Goch, helped both by 51 BID attacking south of the Reichswald, and by 53 BID straight through the centre of the Reichswald. GAD was ordered to follow 43 BID through the Materborn feature and to break out in the north to seize the high ground north of Sonsbeck. A mobile column of GAD would then capture the bridge at Wesel which, with luck, would be intact. It was all to happen so quickly that the surprised Germans would have no time for reinforcement.

The Canadians made preparations to attack north, but the Germans were not deceived and believed the offensive would come through Mönchen Gladbach (Gateway 3), although Schlemm claimed he foresaw the thrust through the Reichswald. The Germans lost sight of XXX Corps and in the event were surprised, having only one infantry division and a Paratroop Regiment in the Reichswald. Their parachute reserves and 43 BID collided in the ruins of 'Caenned' Cleve.

Veritable started as a XXX Corps operation on a six-mile front. It was the left arm of a pincer movement whose right hook was Operation *Grenade* attacking from across the River Roer along its length from Jülich to where it joins the Maas at Roermond. The assault through the Reichswald was a large operation that eventually sucked in eleven divisions and half a million men. Initially five divisions were employed forward with two in reserve. These were soon increased to nine divisions in first one and then two corps. Horrocks' XXX Corps began the battle on 8 February. As it approached Goch on 15 February, the capture of which would open a supply route south of the Reichswald, II Canadian Corps took command of the left flank with five divisions on the axis Cleve-Üdem, with Horrocks commanding four divisions on the centre line Cleve-Goch-Weeze-Kevelaer.

The line-up left to right after the injection of 3 BID and 11 BAD became: (see Map 7) II Canadian Corps with 43 BID, 2 CID, 3 CID, 4 CAD & 11 BAD; and XXX Corps with 3 BID, 53 BID, 51 BID & 52 BID, with GAD in reserve. The disposition was complete by 26 February when II Canadian Corps opened *Blockbuster* with the objective of 'destroying the enemy between the Maas and the Rhine,' shortly followed by XXX Corps' *Heather* and *Leek*. *Grenade* was the responsibility of Lt-Gen W. H. (Bill) Simpson's 9 US Army with ten divisions under command in three corps, assaulting with six divisions up and four in reserve.

21 AG was able to reinforce *Veritable* because early in the operation, when flooding forced the postponement of Operation *Grenade*, Montgomery asked the Americans to take over the line between Roermond and Venlo. This released 11 BAD and 52 BID, which were immediately fed

8 Hamilton. *Monty: The Field Marshal*, p.105.
9 James Marsh. *The Canadian Encyclopedia* (Edmonton: Hurtig, 1985).

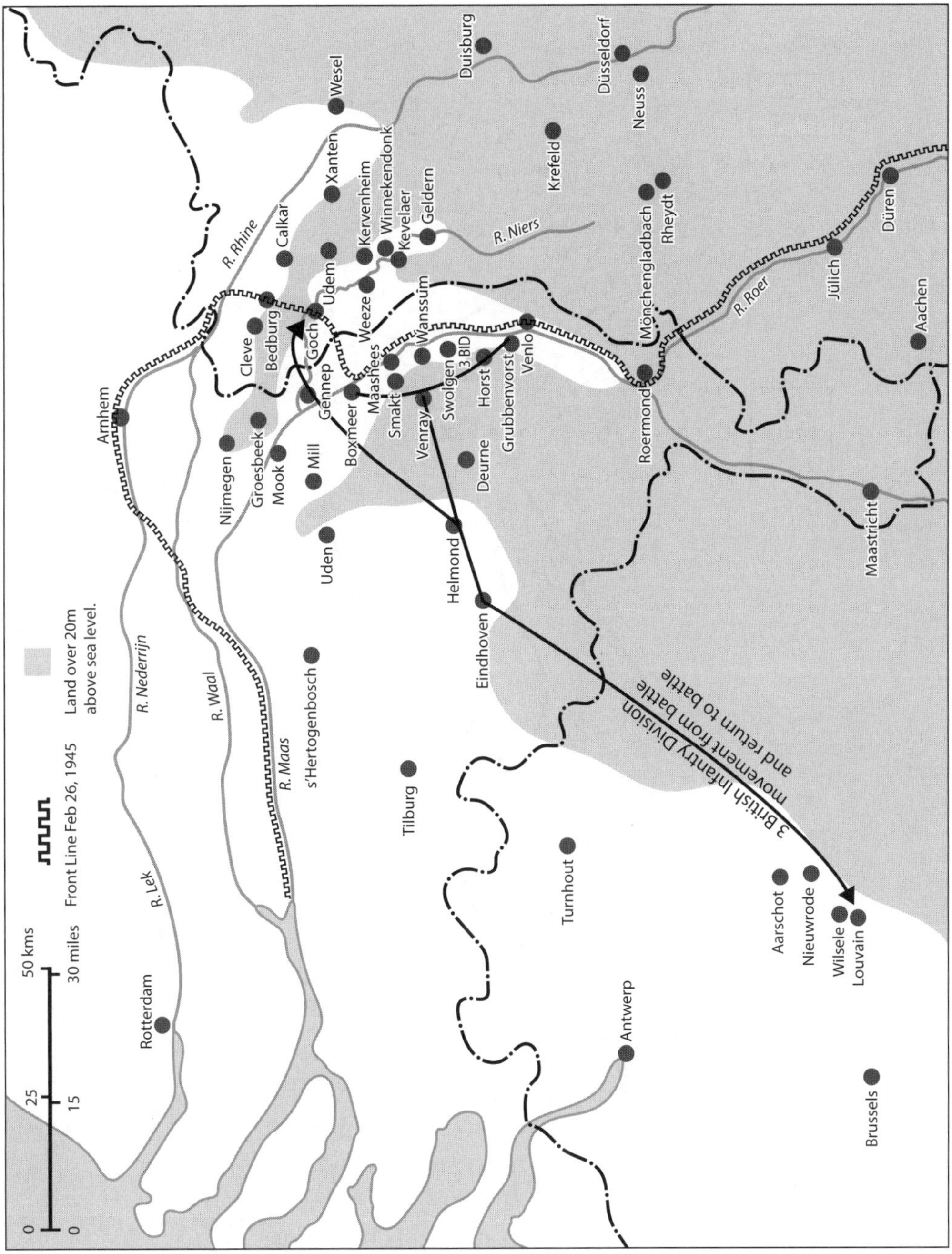

Map 5 3 BID's move from the Maas to Goch, showing the front line on 26 February 1945.

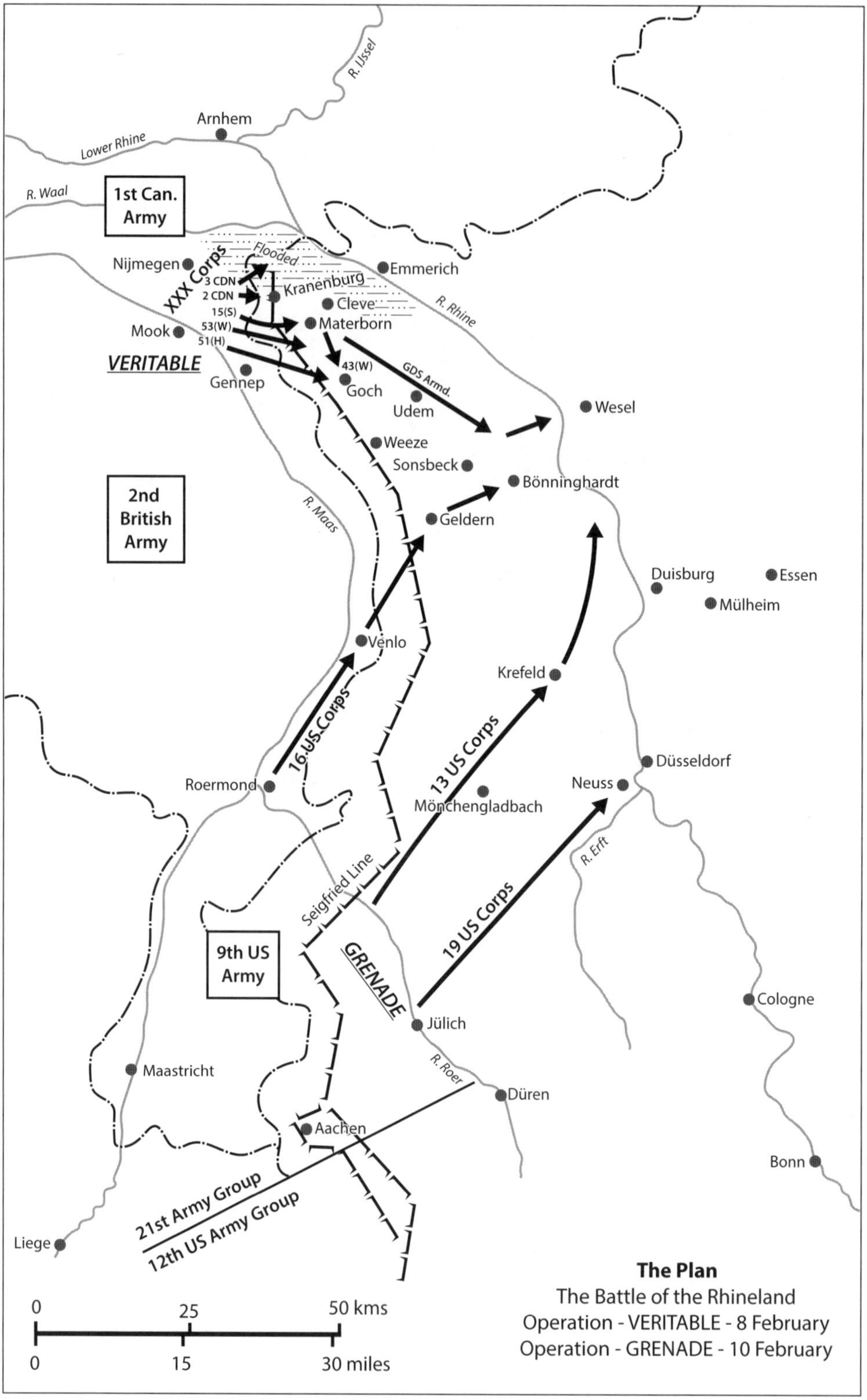

Map 6 The plan for Operations *Veritable* and *Grenade*.

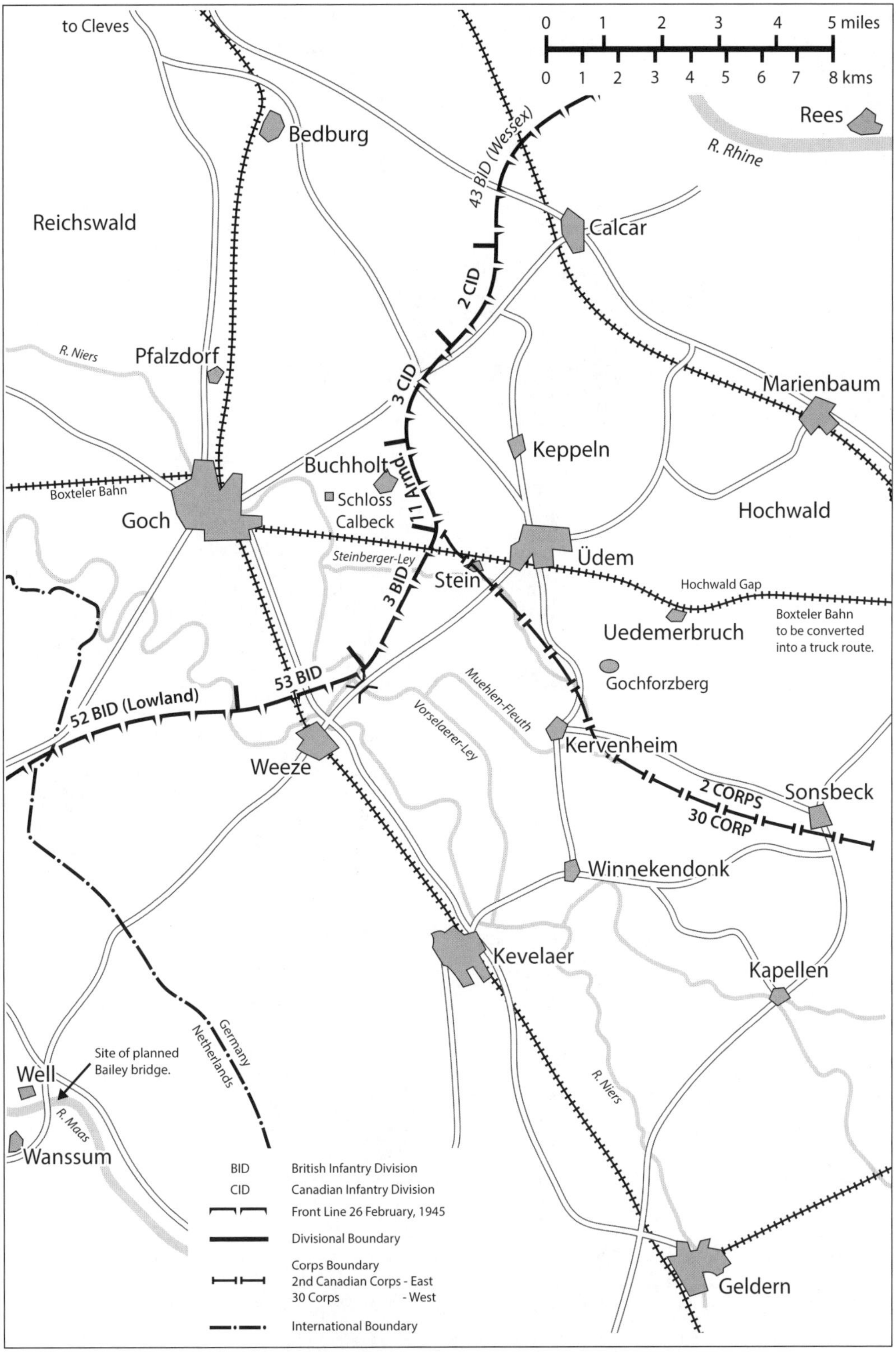

Map 7 21 Army Group's dispositions in the Rhineland on 26 February.

Schloss Calbeck (see Map 7) was the family seat of von Vittinghoff-Schell. It was burnt down in 1799 and rebuilt in 1810 but again destroyed during its capture on 24 February 1945. It was again rebuilt although the garden wing was left as a single storey as pictured here in 1984. 2 Lincolns kicked off Operation *Heather*. In 2001 the missing second storey was added.

The destroyed stairway to the garden entrance.

FJR7 return to the battlefield in the 1980s. Shown standing on the restored stairway to the garden entrance of Schloss Calbeck are (l.-r.) Erwin Becke, Herbert Elkendorf, Werner Bös, Klaus Müller, Erich Freund, Waldemar Böhmer and Dr. Felix Freiherr von Vittinghoff-Schell (1910-1992)

into battle, going respectively to the corps of Simonds and Horrocks. Furthermore, as Goch was captured, 3 BID relieved 15 BID, while 51 BID was squeezed out; both these Scottish divisions then withdrew to prepare for the Rhine crossing.

The complete pincer operation employed 5 corps containing 21 divisions, one third of the total force of 68 divisions available to the Allies, but only half the force of 40 divisions Montgomery had earlier advocated for a narrow thrust to Berlin under his own command. The Germans matched the western allies in number of divisions but they were distributed differently, with more in the Netherlands.

While *Veritable* continued, Simonds issued an unwritten operational order for *Blockbuster*. Horrocks produced written divisional orders; *Heather* for 3 BID and *Leek* for 53 BID. Stacey believed erroneously that *Veritable* was replaced by *Blockbuster, Heather and Leek*, and he split the Battle of the Rhineland into two: *Veritable* lasting from 8 – 21 February (p 460) and *Blockbuster, Heather* and *Leek* from 22 February – 10 March (p 491). This author is indebted to Rex Fendick for pointing out this surprising and egregious error.

Simonds planned *Blockbuster* as a reprise of Operation *Totalise* of 8 August 1944, when he and Cerar had tried to repeat the success of Amiens under Monash and Currie of 8 August 1918, and reminded his army of its anniversary: 'I have no doubt that we shall make the 8th of August 1944 an even blacker day for the German Armies than is recorded against that same date twenty-six years ago.'[10]

Totalise was a massed tank-infantry night assault by two infantry divisions and two armoured brigades (51BID/33BAB and 2 CID/2CAB) in seven columns with support on the flanks from heavy bombers. The columns moved at speed through the German defences on either side of the Falaise Road. In spite of the Germans expecting the onslaught, they moved troops away from the threatened sector under Hitler's orders for the Mortain counter-attack. Phase I in the early hours of 8 August was therefore successful. Phase II, *Tractable*, started later on 8 August and brought in 3 CID, 4 CAD and 1 PAD. It was much less successful, marred by inaccurate and disruptive bombing by medium bombers, by loss of direction by the attackers and by stiff resistance from the aroused defenders.

The similarities between *Blockbuster* and *Totalise* are striking, and for Stacey their affinity was obvious.[11] The similarities were, however, then ignored until recently:[12] the same commanders and force strength; the same surprise use of cruiser tanks; the same use of tank-infantry task-forces in columns either side of a road, using the same Canadian although different British divisions; the same background of slow progress by British commanders; the same demand for bombing of selected targets by heavies, although Harris refused their use in *Blockbuster*; the same division of forces into armoured columns with specific tasks; the same intention to strike in darkness with the same use of artificial moonlight and Bofors' tracer to keep direction; the same early success; the same rivalry with another corps on the right flank (XII Corps in 1944 and XXX Corps in 1945); and the same environment of Americans taking advantage of reduced opposition to make startling gains, while the Anglo-Canadians battled again in relative obscurity.

10 Stacey, *Victory Campaign*, p. 216.

11 Op. Cit., p. 497.

12 There is no reference to *Totalise* in S & D Whitaker. *Rhineland: The Battle To End The War* (Toronto: Stoddart, 1989) even though Denis fought in both; nor in Hubert Essame. *Battle For Germany* (London: Batsford, 1969), and Essame fought in *Blockbuster*; nor in Dominick Graham. *The Price of Command: A Biography of Gen Guy Simonds* (Toronto: Stoddart, 1993). A limited resemblance was identified in John Dickson. *A Thoroughly Canadian General*. (Toronto: University of Toronto Press, 2007), pp. 385, 394; and in John English. *Patton's Peers* (Mechanicsburg: Stackpole, 2009), pp. 47-48.

There are unexplained aspects to *Blockbuster*. In a directive to Simonds and Horrocks on 25 February, Crerar stated that if by D Plus One of *Blockbuster* (27 February) the armoured breakthrough had not been achieved and a re-grouping and further deliberate attack was required, 'the weight of the Canadian Army effort will then be transferred to XXX Corps'.[13]

This was not done in spite of the stated conditions being fulfilled. Two explanations have been proposed; Essame speculated that Montgomery uncharacteristically failed to call off the struggle in the Hochwald Gap and reinforce the success of 3 BID because he wanted to avoid the unintended consequences of breaching Anglo-Canadian confidence by appearing to question Canadian abilities. Nevertheless Essame was baffled by the repeated Canadian attacks against the strongest part of the line and refusal to outflank it, and by the silence of their official history on the matter.[14]

Simonds's biographer, who should have known better because he was there, erroneously lumped together 3 BID and the unsuccessful 11 BAD to conclude that neither was of any use on the right. Simonds was therefore left with only 3 CID to try and outflank the 'Hochwald-Balburger-Hammerbruch feature' on 1 March onwards.[15]

The Whitakers were contemptuous of Crerar and Simonds's reinforcement of failure, but also ignored the magnitude of 3 BID's achievement in breaking through, and the opportunity it gave II Canadian Corps to make an end run behind the defenders on 3 March:

> It was now February 28: D-plus-Two of Operation *Blockbuster*. Crerar's warning that he would shift the weight of the attack to Horrocks's command on the right was being curiously ignored. Essame has suggested that the reason Montgomery refused to call off the ill-fated struggle in the gap and stage a full-scale attack elsewhere instead was to avoid "an Anglo-Canadian breach of confidence". More likely, Simonds, determined to see his plan through, by-passed Crerar's command by using his direct pipeline to Montgomery. Whatever the reason, the folly continued... Nor was the advance of Horrocks's 30 Corps any more galvanised [untrue, but see below]. His four divisions were struggling against the same terrible combination of determined enemy opposition, impossible ground conditions, and reduced air support that were daunting 2 Canadian Corps' advance.[16]

It is in hindsight unfortunate that these weighty soldier-historians – Essame, Whitakers and Graham – failed to interrogate either Simonds (d. 1974), Montgomery (d. 1976), Horrocks (d. 1985), Church Mann (d. 1988) or Stacey (d. 1989) for their views.

As narrated in the following three chapters, on 2 March 1945 3 BID cleared Kervenheim in the morning and broke through the last of the manned defences at Winnekendonk in the evening. Although Winnekendonk involved hard fighting and significant British casualties in a notable feat or arms, Stacey ascribed the success to the approaching Americans. His interpretation has never been corrected and has acquired the status of 'urban myth'. Stacey wrote:

> Meanwhile, the effect of the Ninth Army's drive northward was most notable on the 30th Corps' front, where the tempo of the advance by General Horrocks's divisions showed a quickening which increased from left to right [sic; he meant right to left].[17]

---

13 LAC: 958C.009, D93, 1-0-4/1, Appendix 1: GOC-in-C file.
14 Essame. *The Battle,* pp. 166-67& 176.
15 Graham, *The Price*, pp. 206-207.
16 Whitaker, *Rhineland,* pp. 224 & 229.
17 Stacey, *Victory Campaign*, p. 514.

Stacey's conclusion is repeated to this day. A current battlefield tour guide interprets the cleverly executed German tactical withdrawal from Kervenheim to Winnekendonk that ensured freedom from hot pursuit, as evidence that fear of approaching Americans caused something like panic among the defenders.

> The impact of the American advance was first felt on the British front where 3rd Division and the 6th Guards Tank Brigade had been fighting for every foot of ground. Suddenly they found the enemy gone.'[18]

The Whitakers went much further and imagined Schlemm's reaction to the German defeat at Winnekendonk:

> Still, he (Schlemm) was livid to hear that 250 men from the Panzer Lehr Regiment [sic; he meant the Para Lehr Regiment] had surrendered (in Winnekendonk) after a vicious tank-infantry battle with the 1st [sic] Lincolnshire Regiment and the 3rd Battalion Scots Guards... The morale of the German troops remained – with these few exceptions – high.[19]

This author asked the Whitakers for the source of their reference to Schlemm's state of mind, and was at their Oakville home in 1993 when they searched their files to conclude that they could find none, and that they must have been mistaken.

All three examples are from Canadian historians who have studied deeply the Hochwald deadlock. Their problem was to explain why the neighbouring 3 BID could waltz through Winnekendonk, and Stacey's suggestion seemed reasonable to them that it was because the defenders cleared out to avoid capture by the Americans. British historians, by contrast, have not given the matter much thought, which leaves the field clear for this Anglo-Canadian author to correct the record and answer the question.

There was another factor. Dominick Graham interpreted 3 BID's rôle as secondary to, and supportive of, II Canadian Corps, and believed its freedom of action was constrained by supply shortages resulting from delayed construction of the Well-Wanssum bridge. In these circumstances, he concluded, 3 BID was unlikely to strain every nerve or be, as the Whitackers said above, 'any more galvanised' than 11 BAD and the Canadians.[20] His conclusion is contradicted by the evidence that, to the contrary, 3 BID did both metaphorically and literally strain every nerve to go the extra mile. In hindsight, and considering what little came from their exertions, it might even be possible to claim 3 BID were thereby being busy fools, which does grave (pun intended) disservice to the dead who were doing their duty. For all of these reasons, 3 BID's breakthrough has never before been fully examined.

In 2009 the question was finally asked by John English, but not answered, why Crerar failed to reinforce 3 BID, especially as it would have been administratively simple to do so:

> Crerar's failure to switch the main effort of the First Canadian Army away from the bloodletting in the Hochwald gap remains a mystery. During this time, the advance of the British 30 Corps had picked up speed; the British 3rd Division, next to the boundary with the 2 Canadian Corps, pushed forward three miles per day, capturing Kervenheim on 1 March

18 Terry Copp & Mike Bechthold. *The Canadian Battlefields in Belgium, the Netherlands and Germany* (Waterloo: Laurier Centre for Military etc. Studies, 2011), p. 86.

19 Whitakers, *Rhineland,* p. 266.

20 Graham, *The Price*, p. 203.

> and Winnekendonk the next day. By 3 March, it had reached the deserted Schlieffen Line in front of Kapellen... As field commander, Crerar could have redirected Simonds by placing the British 3rd Division under him and adjusting the inter corps boundary to the Niers River. This would have had the effect of leaving the main effort with the 2 Canadian Corps while giving Simonds both the space and troop resources of the British 11th Armoured and British 3rd Infantry Divisions to take the gap in the rear by executing a southerly turning movement around the Hochwalder and Balberger Wald.[21]

In the 70 years since the Second World War, uncounted millions of words have been expended on it. It is therefore both remarkable and disappointing that despite this degree of attention mysteries persist, which are usually cover-ups in the interest of those with the power to suppress the evidence. The worst example perhaps is the draft peace treaty apparently brought to Britain by Rudolf Hess in 1941. This remains mysterious to this day due probably to a combination of the British Government's misplaced loyalty to the monarchy who have all the important documents in the Royal Archive and immune to FOI, and the fear of having to explain the consequences of its rejection – the deaths of millions of Jews and occupied EU allies.

Several factors make the business of the historian of the Second World War difficult and sometimes impossible. The leaders, and especially Churchill, FDR and Montgomery, dissembled or deceived others or even themselves (depending on how one views their motives)[22] but exercised their power to ensure no evidence inconsistent with their self-serving memoir narratives survived. The worst example from the viewpoint of this book is the absence of any record of what Montgomery discussed with his armour advisers, Hobart and Richards during the NWE campaign. The strong sense of loyalty to the command hierarchy backed by the legal sanctions of the Official Secrets Act ensured that, for example, the Enigma secret persisted until well after Churchill's memoirs had been absorbed by a public lacking competing narratives or access to insights, and when even Alanbrooke's memoirs were bowdlerised. The only insights occurred when Bradley became incensed at Eisenhower's gentlemanly refusal to contradict Montgomery's misrepresentations. Finally, academic and professional historians hold the view that statements unsupported by documentary evidence are mere speculation or 'historical fiction', and are more 'about what you wish had happened rather than what did happen'.[23] There are no norms for evaluating unsatisfactory explanations in the absence of documentary evidence, although a symposium or conference such as that attended by three hundred participants on the occasion of the 50th anniversary of the Battle of Britain, and published as *The Battle Re-thought,* has shown one way to clear the air and advance the subject.

21 AG was an alliance of national forces within SHAEF. There were national tensions not only infamously between British and Americans but also between British and Canadians. Thus Maj-Gen 'Bubbles' Barker, GOC 49 BID, claimed in his diary that his division had done everything in the Le Havre peninsula while the Canadians with their inferiority complex got the credit in spite of not even knowing how to put their troops into battle.[24]

This book addresses the question why as late as March 1945 the western Allies despite overwhelming power and resources could not progress against the Wehrmacht without incurring intolerable losses. The explanation is presented in Chapter 10 and can be summarised here. The tank scandal continued in the House of Commons with Richard Stokes MP contrasting Russian progress with Allied deadlock, complaining of inferior Allied equipment and condemning the

21 English, *Patton's Peers,* pp. 47-48.
22 Carlo D'Este. *Decision in Normandy* (New York: Harper, 1994), pp. 476-501.
23 E-mail comment from Terry Copp on 14 April 2014.
24 Patrick Delaforce. *The Polar Bears* (Stroud: Fonthill Media, 2013), p.152.

pointless and criminal Allied area bombing of Dresden. Churchill, erstwhile tank inventor whose eponymous model was being scrapped by Montgomery, and champion of area bombing, was anxious to identify what ailed 21 AG during his visit to 1 Canadian Army on 3 and 4 March.

This was not just the social event represented by Simonds's biographer.[25] Montgomery was equally determined that Churchill should see and learn nothing of importance. Montgomery recycled the 'Caen hinge strategy' excuse for the deadlock in the Hochwald while *Grenade* made great gains, which had the advantage that the greater the losses in the Hochwald the more convincing the excuse sounded. In this environment of deceit, with tactical incompetence presented again as strategic success (the *Goodwood* excuse), the egregious success of 3 BID in breaking through at Winnekendonk was a potential embarrassment to Montgomery who had no interest in bruiting it or in any way drawing attention to 6 GAB's success with Churchill's eponymous tank. The inordinate slowness of GAD's Shermans in the Hochwald would have been contrasted by Montgomery with that of the speed of American Shermans in *Grenade* to divert attention away from Richard Stokes's damning criticism of that inflammable tank. In effect this book essays the analysis Churchill was prevented even from starting.

After the breakout from Normandy at the beginning of September, there was a vacuum in the high command. Eisenhower was incapacitated with a twisted knee in his isolated Forward HQ near Granville in the Gulf of St Malo, and his bosses were out of touch at Quebec. A supply shortage developed as the advancing armies ran out of fuel and fought each other for priority. Eisenhower's method of command was to receive proposals from subordinates, and to make a decision only when feeling comfortable. He then instructed that person to 'have a go'. It was said by Montgomery to be the American way of command.

This characterisation was at once unkind, untrue and unwise. It is a personal rather than a national trait in a commander; for example Dorman Smith similarly gave advice and brought ideas for Auchinleck to choose from. This method was contrasted by Montgomery with his habit of producing an outline of a master plan for the planners to work up in details. When this was translated into orders, all objections could be dismissed as 'bellyaching'. This process was more efficient only if the master plan was adequate. Unfortunately, Montgomery's arrogant certainties and circle of selected yes-men made this unlikely if not impossible.

Montgomery's lack of structured input and consultation resulted from an absence of self-critical assessment, from repetition of failed methods especially in all-arms, from over-simplification and sometimes from recklessness, as at Arnhem. The major problem was the lack of grounding in effective operational methodology. The plan to seize Caen on D-Day was, as Carlo D'Este has shown, naïve; an ambush of 9 BIB at Carpiquet by 21 Panzer and 12 SS Panzer Divisions on D-Day afternoon could have led to Allied defeat, because no one was given the task of showing exactly how Caen was to be seized and held on D-Day if counter-attacked in force. D'Este interviewed Brig ET Williams, Montgomery's Chief of Intelligence, who noted that Montgomery sometimes showed a disconcerting sense of detachment where he should have been intimately involved. This had occurred at Dieppe, in the Orne bridgehead and most publicly at Arnhem when he failed to involve himself in the airborne/RAF planning.

Far better was the actual and unplanned bite-and-hold result against 21 Panzer's counter-attack on D-Day, when its force was decimated by 17-pdrs on the Periers Ridge. The Allies' lack of intellectual rigour permeated the system from top to bottom. A sensible proposal was made by Montgomery for an encirclement of the Ruhr by a northern thrust crossing the Maas at Venlo and the Rhine at Wesel to meet with Bradley entering Germany through the Aachen 'Gap' and crossing the Rhine at Düsseldorf. The plan went nowhere when Bradley refused his cooperation, preferring

25 Graham, *The Price*, p. 208.

Tilburg, February 1945. Brigadier Church Mann (Chief of Staff 1 Canadian Army) and Air Marshal Teddy Hudleston (AOC 84 Group 2 TAF) with Gen Crerar. Mann was a stern critic of 2 TAF both then and post-war. (Ken Bell/Canada. Dept of National Defence/Library & Archives Canada/PA-1457616)

to support Patton attacking towards the Saar and Frankfurt. Eisenhower would not overrule him. The Allies stretched themselves thin in their belief that German resistance was broken.

Veritable, still called *Valediction*, took final shape at the time of the Maastricht Conference on 7 December. The Canadians had assumed that II Canadian Corps would undertake the operation, and they used Horrocks's outline for *Gatwick*, or *Wyvern* as they called it, which they inherited from XXX Corps at the hand-over in November. On 6 December Montgomery wavered about using the Canadians, telling Crerar that the battle should be under 2 British Army. At the same time in Maastricht, Montgomery, after talking to Whistler, informed Horrocks he would get the five divisions he had requested. On 7 December Montgomery changed his mind and phoned Crerar to tell him it would be a Canadian battle after all and that he would have XXX Corps with up to 5 divisions if needed. However, Montgomery added, if II Canadian Corps fought the battle then XXX Corps would need to be brought in on the right 'for future reasons'.[26] This is taken to mean that Montgomery wanted British troops alongside the Americans in the event of an assault on Berlin.

The target date set by Montgomery was '1 Jan, or as soon thereafter as conditions permit'. The unsuitability of the terrain, which had been uppermost in Montgomery's mind in November, was never again mentioned except in post-facto excuse for taking a month to reach Wesel. The strange idea that the attack would force mobile war on the Germans which they could not support, was

26 Stacey, *Victory Campaign*, p. 438.

emphasised by Crerar on 14 December and by Montgomery two days later on the eve of the German attack through the Ardennes in a mobile battle.

Planning for *Veritable* was undertaken by Crerar's 1 Canadian Army assisted by Horrocks' staff comprising the BGS (Chief of Staff) C. P. Jones, and Brigadier Q (Administration) George Webb (who shared with Horrocks the distinction of being an Olympic athlete). *Gatwick* was updated with the assistance of the Corps Commanders RA and RE and a liaison officer from 83 Group, 2 TAF.

Orders were given out at a Corps conference attended by the Divisional Commanders and the many others involved in the logistical arrangements needed to supply 470,000 troops and 1,000 guns. Crerar gave responsibility for *Veritable* to XXX Corps, and placed 3 CID under Horrocks at Simonds's suggestion. If *Veritable* had gone according to plan a bridgehead would have been established at Wesel within days. Simonds would have wanted his Canadian divisions to be involved in the Rhine crossing since they had been planning for it in the preliminaries during the previous months. 2 CID was added later. On 21 January Montgomery finalised the plans for *Veritable* and *Grenade* subject to ratification by Eisenhower. This was very uncertain since Bradley was attacking through the Ardennes and was demanding the return of Simpson's 9 US Army, using the self-serving argument that any refusal by Eisenhower would be a public expression of lack of confidence in American commanders. It was not until 1 February that Bradley was ordered to stop attacking in the Ardennes and to start helping Simpson secure the Roer dams to permit the start of *Veritable/Grenade* on 8 February.

Christopher Dawnay, Montgomery's Military Assistant, recorded in the campaign diary that in the week of 24 to 31 January Eisenhower was indecisive about continuing Bradley's thrust through the Ardennes until he met George Marshall and was ordered to support *Veritable/Grenade*. The result was a stormy meeting on 1 February when Bradley had no real choice but to accept that *Grenade* was going to happen.[27] In fact it was not Marshall but Brooke who, at the Combined Chiefs meeting in Malta on 31 January, showed Bedell Smith the faults in Eisenhower's appreciation of the situation. This was reported to Eisenhower who was shamed into supporting Montgomery.[28] The historian must conclude that within this hot-bed of national intrigue and inflated egos the priority for each general was to grab what employment and forces he could to trumpet 'his' achievements. Objectivity and regard for the troops, who were suffering heavy casualties, were factors said to be paramount, but in reality received little consideration. Getting to Berlin first involved a race without any rules which every soldier wanted to win. Mark Clark's manipulation of people and events to secure his own entry into Rome and onto the front pages of the newspapers had finally debased the currency of co-operation.

The same factors had been part of the reason for the failure to close the Falaise pocket, because French and US eyes were on the Champs Élysées when they should have been on the capture of Germans. Bradley, Montgomery and Patton each believed he only had the answer. Neither Bradley nor Patton could bear to see Montgomery succeed, while Montgomery, and he should be believed, always claimed that he would serve under Bradley provided a single thrust was mounted. Eisenhower could not decide on a single thrust because it would mean a single commander and a threat to his own position. The way was open for the private deal between Eisenhower and Stalin whereby SHAEF forswore Berlin.

The justification for *Veritable* given to the troops by Crerar included the intentions of the C-in-C to:

> continue operations throughout the winter, allowing the enemy no respite. The Winter campaign for 21 Army Group must be so designed that it leads into, and prepares the way for,

27 Hamilton, *Monty: The Field Marshal*, p. 357.
28 Alan Brooke. *War Diaries 1939-1945* (London: Phoenix, 2002), p. 653.

> the Spring offensive. The governing factors in reaching decisions concerning these operations are:
> a) The selected objectives must be of a decisive nature – this points to the Ruhr
> b) Our operations must force the enemy into engaging in mobile warfare, in which he will be at a disadvantage due to lack of petrol, mechanical transport and tanks.[29]

It is unclear how a 'winter' differs from a 'spring' offensive. It is inconceivable that Montgomery had forgotten his statement that campaigning in the Reichswald could not be considered before March, so it must be concluded that, like Horrocks, he decided to make the best of a bad job and gamble his troops on getting a win.

The alternatives to *Veritable* were to do nothing until the spring when the land dried up, or to move south and support Simpson when the Roer floods subsided. A further possibility was to go with Bradley through the Ardennes or further south. Instead, Montgomery was told by Crerar and Horrocks that with the frost in the ground there was a good opportunity of seizing the bridge at Wesel within days. He had no trouble persuading Eisenhower, and when the thaw started they decided to go ahead in any case, starting on 8 February.

Veritable achieved tactical surprise. 50,000 troops with 500 tanks and 500 special tracked vehicles attacked 11,000 Germans with 36 StuGs, a predominance of five to one. In spite of a sudden thaw, early progress was good, although slower than expected. Cleve was reached a day early on 10 February, Gennep by the 11th but Asperden not until 17 February. The German Parachute and Panzer reserves fought back tenaciously. One infantry division, two parachute divisions, 15 PGR and the 116 PD became engaged, leaving only Panzer Lehr in reserve for two army groups. Then it also became embroiled, leaving only 30,000 men and 70 tanks to hold *Grenade* when it came.

Horrocks, sensing breakthrough, sent in 43 BID, but the Germans fought back around Cleve and a great traffic jam occurred behind the British front. Elstob believed that Horrocks's natural optimism was heightened by a fever of 103 degrees lasting four days.[30]

The water on the Kranenberg road rose inexorably as the snows melted in the hills and mountains all the way to Switzerland; 18 inches were reported in places on 9 February; 2 feet on the following day and 4 feet on 13 February. Only DUKWs could use the roads. During the night of 9/10 February, the Germans carefully destroyed the Roer Dams and, as the river rose, Montgomery had to agree to postpone *Grenade*. Eisenhower was approached and agreed to release two American divisions to the British sector to allow 11 BAD and 52 BID to move into XXX Corps' reserve on 13 February. It was at this same time that the Germans gave priority to stopping *Veritable*, and determined to recapture Cleve. Then the mud took over.

On 10 February Bradley phoned Patton to crow that 'Montgomery's alleged attack is the biggest mistake Ike has made in this war'. He predicted that *Grenade* would be abandoned and the resources switched to help Patton.[31]

Patton was already undertaking 'active defence' and Bradley was tacitly encouraging him to move along the northern bank of the Moselle. 7 US Army cleared the Colmar pocket on the upper Rhine, goading Patton to borrow 10 USAD from SHAEF reserve in an unauthorised and expensive drive for Bitburg and Trier.

The *Veritable* plan called for both Goch and Cleve to be captured by 11 February, when GAD would break out to Sonsbeck. Instead the Germans committed their reserves, the XLVII

29 Stacey, *Victory Campaign*, p. 438.
30 Peter Elstob. *Battle of the Reichswald* (London: Ballantine Books, 1970), p. 97.
31 Op. Cit., p. 116.

Panzer Corps under Heinrich Freiherr von Lüttwitz with Mk IVs, Panthers and Tigers, including Jagd-Panthers.

On 14 February, Crerar decided to divide his front. He rejected Simonds proposal to attack down the east side of the Rhine. Instead Crerar told Horrocks to plan for the capture of Goch and Simonds to work out how to take Calcar. The Germans continued to reinforce their positions, and for the Allies the hardest fighting still lay ahead of them.

The command change was effected on 15 February with the corps boundary following the Steinberger Ley to the west of the Bedburg-Ǘdem road, along the Mǘhlen Fleuth to the east of Kervenheim and then west of the Ǘdem-Sonsbeck road. II Canadian Corps concentrated on Moyland Wood with 46 BIB and 6 GAB temporarily under command, and where the only effective weapon against German paratroopers proved to be flame-throwers, either organically controlled Carrier Wasps or Churchill Crocodiles of 79 BAD. On 16 February, 43 BID broke through at Pfalzdorf and reached the escarpment in front of Goch. Horrocks described this remarkable 8,000-yard advance as the turning point in the Reichswald Battle since it cut the link between the Moyland and Goch defensive positions.

Heavy fighting by the Canadians for Moyland and by three British divisions for Goch was eventually rewarded when the garrison commander, Colonel Matussek was deceived about the direction of the assault. Meindl was prevented from switching FJR7 south from Moyland to Goch in time when the Calcar-Goch road was cut. On 22 February, D+14, Goch was at last clear and after two weeks and 6,000 casualties, of whom 80% were British, the line planned for D Plus Three was reached.

On that same 22 February, 15 BID probed south from Goch, taking Schloss Calbeck on the east bank of the Niers. It was predicted that by 24 February the Roer reservoirs would be empty and the river level would start to fall, but Simpson launched *Grenade* a day earlier on 23 February to achieve surprise. *Leek* began on 24 February, *Blockbuster* on the 26, and *Heather* on the following day.

After helping secure Goch, 53 BID had two days of rest before moving forward again to assault Weeze in *Leek*. Horrocks had been ordered to link up with the Americans on the right, and the road through Weeze to Geldern was his chosen route. FJD6 and FJD8 opposed them. 53 BID started at 1 am on 24 February, the day after *Grenade* kicked off across the Roer. It is 4 miles from Goch to Weeze with the meandering River Niers connecting the two towns and marking the divisional boundary with 15 BID. The Scots had cleared forward through the woods past Schloss Calbeck on the east bank of the Niers the previous day and were awaiting relief by 3 BID.

Horrocks lived in a caravan at main HQ consisting of about a hundred camouflaged vehicles in a wooded area about 400 yards square near an airstrip in the southern end of the Reichswald at 827500. II Canadian Corps was at 885535 near Cleve. Crerar was at Uden in the Netherlands, Montgomery at Geldrop – moving north from Zonhoven on 7 February – and Eisenhower was in the Trianon Palace Hotel in Versailles.

Maj-Gen Ross, GOC 53 BID, had been sent on leave, suffering from insomnia, and his temporary replacement was Brig 'Fish' Elrington (killed on 14 April and replaced by Cecil Firbank of 2 Lincolns). Elrington sent 160 BIB straight down the main road from Goch to Weeze. They married up with their tanks at 6 am, led by 6 Royal Welch Fusiliers, but were held up in Houenhof by 115 GR. An attempt to bypass the defence by attacking the village of Höst on the Niers got nowhere and three times they were beaten off. At 5 pm, 71 BIB took over and 1 HLI made a storming assault through Höst to Rottum, which they took at 9 pm. By 9.45 pm they were 400 yards short of the anti-tank ditch from which they made an assault on Weeze. They attacked a wood with heavy losses and were stopped. At 5.15 am on 25 February, they were told to hold one mile north of Weeze while the Corps artillery supported the start of operation *Blockbuster*. It took five more days to occupy Weeze.

There was a pause as Elrington regrouped, which led Crerar on 25 February to warn Horrocks and Simonds that if the Weeze-Well road could not soon be opened for bridging over the Maas to provide a new supply route, the plan might need rethinking. On this same 25 February, Schlemm told the surprised von Rundstedt that he could afford to release an infantry and two armoured divisions.

The seizure of Yorkshire Bridge by 3 BID's coup-de-main, described in the next chapter, seemed to offer a back-door way into Weeze but provoked a violent reaction from the German defenders. In Operation *Daffodil*, Elrington gave 71 BIB the task of frontal assault on Weeze, sending 158 BIB to the west of the railway line and 160 BIB into 3 BID's area to attack from the east over Yorkshire Bridge. But Weeze did not fall until the night of 1 March, when the German Paratroops abandoned the town to avoid being cut off by 'Robin Force' of 1 E Lancs (158 BIB) which had crossed the Niers nearly 2 miles to the south of Weeze.

Simonds produced no written orders for *Blockbuster*. Stacey, the Canadian Official Historian, in recording the fact made no comment as to how unusual the practice was. Chris Vokes of 4 CAD said there were orders that were normally unwritten, although he did not define which or why, and for the rest urgency and a lack of paper precluded it.[32]

It was *Totalise* all over again with the same commanders and many of the same troops. Simonds had been working on the concept since 14 February and revealed what he wanted together with its name to his GOCs and Brigadiers at a conference on 22 February. He told them that they were going to smash through the German defences and seize Xanten, a distance of about 10 miles. Every available division would be used and the Goch to Wesel railroad, which ran right through the *schwerpunkt* of the Hochwald Gap, would be torn up and the ballast levelled to make a main one-way supply route for lorries.

Matthews' 2 CID was switched to the northern flank and directed at the Calcar-Marienbaum road. It was hoped that the Germans might thereby be deceived about the axis. On their left 43 BID moved up to take Calcar. Chris Vokes' 4 CAD formed the columns which were to seize the Hochwald Gap. 'Tiger Group' under Moncel was made up of the Algonquin Regiment and the South Albertas' Shermans. The remainder of the division was named 'Lion Group' under Jefferson. Their job was to seize the high ground east of Üdem. 'Lion Group' itself was subdivided into five groups, each with a specific part to play: 'Jerry Group' had two squadrons of Shermans, two companies of infantry in Kangaroos and a troop of flails. 'Jock' and 'Cole' were to mop up the opposition, while 'Smith Group' had the task of seizing 'Tiger's' jumping-off point for the Hochwald Gap.

On 4 CAD's right, 3 CID under Dan Spry drove for Keppeln and Üdem, and on their right Pip Roberts' 11 BAD attacked towards Stein to pass south of Üdem along the boundary with XXX Corps' 3 BID.

Three VCs were won in the next four days. Sergeant Aubrey Cousins of Ben Dunkelman's D Company, the Queen's Own Rifles of Canada in 8 CIB, 3 CID, killed 20 Germans and captured as many more before being killed while taking Mooshof on the Goch-Calcar road in the early hours of 26 February. Major F.A. Tilston of the Essex Scottish, 4 CIB, 2 CID, survived his gallant attack to break through the defences into the northern part of the Hochwald near Marienbaum on 1 March, but lost both legs. And around noon on the same day on the eastern outskirts of Kervenheim, Private James Stokes of 2 KSLI, 185 BIB, 3 BID died as will be described in Chapter 3.

Üdem was taken on 27 February and the Algonquins reached Point 73 in the Hochwald Gap on the same day, where the advance met a brick wall of heavy German artillery fire and counter-attacks. Montgomery called it the heaviest concentration of enemy artillery-fire on the

32 Chris Vokes. *My Story* (Ottawa: Gallery Books, 1985), p. 194.

western front. Over 1,000 guns were brought to bear on the unfortunate Canadians, some firing from the eastern bank of the Rhine and only a few miles from the Ruhr. Repeated attempts to fight through the Gap failed. On 28 February, the Lincoln and Welland were sent in to join the Argyll and Sutherlands and the Algonquins. More attempts were made on 1 March when Kervenheim, just 3 miles to the south of the Hochwald Gap, was taken by 3 BID and Weeze fell to 53 BID. The Canadians tried again on 2 March when 24FJR stopped them in the Gap while 3 BID on that day broke clean through the last German defences at Winnekendonk and began to accelerate for Kapellen. On the same day 11 BAD began closing up to Sonsbeck but stopped to let 3 CID take the town. GAD eventually 'swept' through 3 BID to Kapellen on 4 March but were held for two days between Hamb and Bonninghardt. On this same 6 March 3 BID and 3 CID met outside Sonsbeck. On 10 March, Schlemm ordered the bridges at Wesel to be blown as the last of his extraordinary Paratroop Army finally withdrew, their task achieved. On 11 March, XVI US Corps arrived opposite Wesel.

General der Fallschirmtruppe Eugen Meindl on 1 August 1942. (Bundesarchiv Bild i83-2006-01245-503)

General der Fallschirmtruppe Alfred Schlemm. (Bundesarchiv Bild 1011-579-1962-23)

Lt-Col Rowan Coleman of The Lincoln and Welland Regiment, 10 BIB, 4 CID was in the Hochwald Gap on 28 February, and being pressed by an anxious Simonds:

> I spent the whole morning there, where I could see what was happening. The Argylls had been pushed back and had withdrawn and this shellfire was coming down. I didn't move and I told the wireless operator that I was out to lunch if anybody called. I wasn't going to take any calls. This poor guy. He had a terrible time all morning answering calls and telling them that I wasn't available. They were coming from higher and higher authority. He was only a few yards from me. He said, "Sir, I just have to tell you this". He said, "Super Colossal Sunray wants to talk to you". So I said I guess I better answer that one. It was Guy Simonds himself on the blower. I recognised the unmistakeable English accent. I remember being mildly amused and outraged at his breaking security. He said, "Rowan. Is there anything you can do down there?" I said, "Well, I don't think so sir". It was a stalemate for the time being. We were under murderous fire. He said, "You must do something to relieve the pressure down there."[33]

33 GW Hayes. *The Lincs: A History of the Lincoln & Welland Regiment at War* (Alma: Maple Leaf, 1986), p. 104.

Simonds's irresistible military force had met an immoveable object. *Totalise* had worked on its first day because the armoured columns had been able to work around and between the German defences. The conditions for this did not exist in the Hochwald Gap. Not only were the shortcomings of the Shermans in mud and their thin armour brutally exposed, but there was no room to manoeuvre away from the Defensive Fire of the German guns, which had the exact range and could observe the fall of shot. The Germans massed 717 mortars and 1054 guns. And because Simonds concentrated everything he had available and put it in the shop window, he had no fall-back plan or position.

The German defenders were critical of Simonds's tactics. Denis Whitaker interviewed Maj-Gen Heinz Guderian, then chief of staff of 116 PD, who said the Canadians never concentrated their attack on any one front on the same day, allowing the defenders to rush from point to point. General Plocher, GOC 6FJD, believed that if II Canadian Corps had gone round the Hochwald in strength, either to the north or south, they could not have been held for long.[34]

These were the events taking place on the flanks of 3 BID as it entered its first set-piece battle since the furious battle of Overloon in October. In that engagement also it had been supported by 6 GAB, which had been fighting since then in *Blackcock* and in *Veritable* from its beginning. The experience and record of this Brigade were exceptional. The German forces resisting *Heather* were the same Paratroops as were holding up *Leek* and *Blockbuster*, with the same heavy artillery support on call. The Anglo-Canadian forces were all identically trained, equipped and fed, and all were supported by the same artillery and air and by the 'Funnies' of 79 BAD.

The only variable setting *Heather* apart from *Leek* and *Blockbuster* was in the nature of the tank support. Both *Leek* and *Blockbuster* were supported by armoured brigades equipped with the medium Sherman and Cromwell cruiser tanks, operated by units of the Royal Armoured Corps. The school of the apostles of mobility – Liddell Hart, Hobart and the Desert generals – had trained them and with few exceptions such as the South Alberta Regiment they were not trusted by the infantry.

3 BID on the contrary, was supported by the heavy infantry tank, the Churchill, manned by Guardsmen of 6 Tank Brigade – by then renamed an armoured brigade. These Guards enjoyed a unique heritage and set themselves high standards of discipline and performance. They were trained originally as infantry and from this standpoint developed their own approach to tank-infantry co-operation. They operated a vehicle designed solely for the purpose of supporting infantry, and had little or no knowledge of the Royal Armoured Corps' philosophy, and no connection with GAD. Their performance in *Heather* was exceptional if a little patchy given exhaustion from being three weeks in the line.

Personnel of 9th Field Squadron, RCE, lifting Boxteler Bahn rails to make a road for vehicles near the Hochwald, Germany, 2 March 1945. (Capt Jack H Smith/Canada. Dept of National Defence/Library & Archives Canada/PA-192055)

The operational methodology used in *Heather* was quite different from that of the units fighting on either flank, and was reflected in their unique success. These and other matters are discussed in Chapter 10.

In consideration of the wet conditions expected at that time of year, and the need for rapid re-supply of a quick planned breakthrough to Wesel and beyond, Simonds converted the Boxteler Bahn into an all-weather one-way express truck route to the front.

Beginning in 1878, the Boxteler Bahn operated by the NBDS (North Brabant German Railway), provided the

34 Whitaker, *Rhineland*, p. 228.

Another view of converting the Boxteler Bahn into a supply road. (Capt Jack H Smith/Canada. Dept of National Defence/Library & Archives Canada/ PA-192056)

Pedestrians used the route in either direction. The POWs are a mix of paratroops, such as the medic, and Heer from 116 Panzer Division. Above the hooded POW in the fourth row can be seen the Hochwald Gap on the skyline. (Capt Jack H Smith/Canada. Dept of National Defence/Library & Archives Canada/PA-192049)

Sapper M.L. Rogers of the Mechanical Equipment Company, RCE, and Pte R.E. Osborn of the Cameron Highlanders of Ottawa (MG) clearing rubble off a body of a German soldier, Udem, Germany, 2 March 1945. The Paratroopers' resistance was determined. The blade of Rogers's bulldozer is visible bottom left. Sometimes the only way of defeating Paras was to collapse the building on top of them. (Capt Jack H Smith/Canada. Dept of National Defence/Library & Archives Canada/ PA-129758)

fastest connection between London, Berlin and St Petersburg. The North Sea crossing between 1876 and 1927 was between Queenborough in Kent and Flushing (Vlissingen) in the Netherlands. Although both Tsar and Kaiser used the route, it was a commercial failure due to competition by the state railway through the border crossing at Venlo. The Boxteler Bahn was single track with crossing places such as that pictured. It was not rebuilt even in the Netherlands where Uden remains without a train.

2

The Battle of Yorkshire Bridge

Tuesday, 27 February 1945. Weather: cloudy and mild.

Now who will stand on either hand
And keep the bridge with me?
Lord Macaulay: Horatius At The Bridge

The new area was dismal and unattractive, in a thick wood centred upon a monument of gloom called Schloss Calbeck.

Charles Graves: The Royal Ulster Rifles

Troops Employed

British: 3 BID (Whistler) & 6 GAB (Greenacre)
- 8 BIB/4GG; 1 Suffolks/2 Sqn, 2 E Yorks/1 Sqn, 1 S Lancs/3 Sqn
- 9 BIB/3 SG; 2 Lincs/RF Sqn, 1 KOSB/S Sqn, 2 RUR/LF Sqn
- 3 BID Artillery with artillery of GAD, 15 BID, 53 BID, 72 & 79 Medium Regts & 5 AGRA

German: 8 FJD (Wadehn)
- IIIFJR7 – transferred from 2 FJD
- IFJR24 and IIIFJR22 (against bridge)
- IFJR2I and IIIFJR21
- elements of 84 GID
- XII Parachute Assault Gun Brigade
- 7 FJD Artillery and supporting units

Plan

British: Feb 27

0700 – 2 Lincs with 3 SG secure Krüsbeckshof
– 1 Suffolks with 4 GG advance from Saarbrockshof to secure flanks of 2 Lincs & 2 E Yorks

1000 Four Battalions attack to secure line of Üdem-Weeze road on 4,000 yards frontage
– 2 RUR & 1 KOSB with 3 SG pass through 2 Lincs
– 1 S Lancs pass through 1 Suffolks & 2 E Yorks and 4GG attack from their positions
– Yorkshire Bridge to be seized by 2 E Yorks & 4 GG for 53 BID to pass through and outflank Weeze
When possible, 185 BIB take Kervenheim, and 9 BIB take Winnekendonk

Germans: Hold fortified line: Weeze-Kervenheim-Üdem

Actual Outcome 27/2:

0700-0800 hr	2 Lincs took Krüsbeckshof, and 1 Suffolks occupied Babbe, securing startline
1020	1 KOSB & 2 RUR attacked against stiffening opposition which became strong when they reached the road
1000	2 E Yorks & 1 S Lancs began attack. 2 E Yorks seized Yorkshire Bridge. S Lancs had tough time in wood
1530	KOSB & Right Flank 3 SG failed to seize second bridgehead at Wettermannshof/ Aengen Throughout the night Germans counter-attacked with armour against Yorkshire Bridge and wasted IIIFJR22

Actual Outcome 28/2: 7 RWF (53 BID) relieved 2 E Yorks across the bridge

Casualties:

British:	72 killed & missing; 262 wounded; total 334
German:	150 killed & missing; 300 wounded; 547 German P/W, for total losses of about 1,000.

The land where Operation *Heather* was fought lies south east of Goch in the area between Schloss Calbeck and Winnekendonk, with an outrider towards Weeze. It is an extension of the Maas valley, and only 10 to 15 miles as the crow flies from where the rifle companies of 3 BID had spent the winter in waterlogged places on the west bank of the Maas at Swolgen, Wanssum, Smakt and Maashees. The entire battlefield lies between the 17 and 20 metre contours with a few 22 metre eminences like the one just to the north of Yorkshire Bridge. To the north-east is land rising to 81 m in the Hochwald then falling to the flooded Rhine valley normally at 13 m.

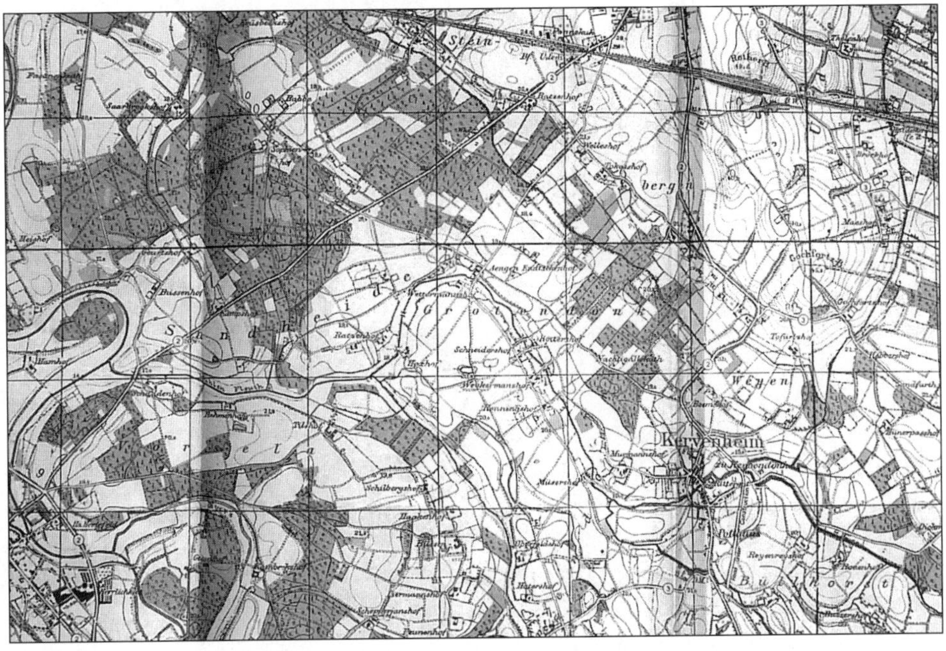

Map 8 The Yorkshire Bridge battlefield, 1:25,000.

Map 9 Aerial photograph taken on 16 February, orientated NE-SW, with Yorkshire Bridge and Schaddenhof in the centre. (NCAP/ncap.org.uk)

The inter-divisional boundaries were watercourses (see Map 7). The western boundary with 53 BID was, for a short distance, the River Niers; then the Kervenheimer Mühlen Fleuth (Millstream), which ran diagonally across the front; and then south again along its tributary, the Vorselaerer Ley. The eastern boundary with 11 BAD, which was also the corps boundary, was the Steinberger Ley until it petered out near Kervenheim. The boundary then jumped across to the Mühlen Fleuth flowing in from the southeast.

In mid-February 1945 the Maas-Niers valley was sodden from the vast quantities of water flowing into the Maas at Roermond from the destroyed Roer dams. The Germans jammed open a sluice gate on the Schwammenauel Dam on 9 February, releasing a relentless flow which raised the level of the Roer by 4 ft and the Maas by 2 ft. It took two weeks until 23 February for the reservoir to empty, and meanwhile Simpson's 9 US Army was immobilised south of the barrier. Perhaps because the resulting wave would destroy the Bailey Bridges over the Maas, the Americans did not breach the captured dam with explosives to release the water all at once. The rising Maas backed up the River Niers, which flows north-west from Mönchen Gladbach through Goch to join the Maas between Gennep and Cuijk where the river banks are only 10 m above sea level. Every soldier remembered the Bailey Bridge at Gennep; 'The bridge over the swamps and the river was the finest and longest military bridge we had ever seen, stretching not only over the Maas but over the swampy wastes on either side.'[1]

The soil of the battlefield is sandy loam atop gravel. Since the war, this gravel has been dredged on a large scale and flooded gravel pits dot the area. A fossilised skeleton of a whale found near Kervenheim showed this was once a delta formed by river-borne erosion from as far away as the Alps. The soil is a poor load carrier and, although quick to drain, offers no resistance to rising ground water. When waterlogged it turns into a kind of quicksand. The towns of Mook, Goch, Kervenheim, Winnekendonk, Geldern and Kevelaer mark the edge of the plain. To their east around Üdem the land rises to 56 metres above sea level and to 81 m in the Hochwald.

The choice of time and place – February fill-dyke black from the absence of frost that recalled the farmer's doggerel verse – *February fill-dyke be it black or be it white; but if it be white it's better to like* – with its water-logged sandy loam famous for its asparagus beds and interspersed with streams and swamps, created extreme problems and misery for the troops. The sappers would find repairing tracks a nightmare; so-called cross-country vehicles like Jeeps, carriers and half-tracks would be useless off the roads and only the new Weasel and to a lesser degree Churchills and Kangaroos, could move across country with some, but never complete, reliability; temporary bridges would sink with no firm ground to support them; German mine craters in the few good roads would take hours to bridge and could not be circumvented; felled trees had to be cleared from tracks sown with the hated schu-mines; guns would be out of range and hours would be spent trying to move them up. The conditions of mud were as severe as anything seen in Flanders in 1917 at the same elevation; the St Julien battlefield in Flanders rose from the Yser Canal at 10 m to Pilckem Ridge and Mouse Trap Farm at 25 m above sea level, but most fighting took place between the 18 to 22 m contours like this battlefield. The result was that artillery ammunition would almost run out; 4.2 inch mortar bombs and Mk VIIIz machine-gun ammunition would be in permanently short supply;[2] wireless sets for infantry and tanks would go "dis" or out of range in the woods and at night, and communications would fail or be so garbled that Yorkshire Bridge was believed to have been lost; the weather would be bitterly cold with snow and sleet; the German artillery would be concentrated in overwhelming numbers and supplied with adequate ammunition almost from the factory door in the Ruhr; the Fallschirmjägers would defend with skill, amply

1 RB Moberly. *Second Battalion the Middlesex Regt* (Cairo: R. Schindler, 1946), p. 108.
2 TNA: WO 171/6241: 2 Middlesex War Diary.

armed with effective infantry weapons like panzerfausts and the superb MG42, while strongly supported by StuG IIIs and IVs, 88s and other PAKs, mortars, nebelwerfers and artillery moving on undamaged roads and able to hide from the diminished 2 TAF. The only thing absent was a daylight threat from the GAF which, however, operated with impunity at night while German defenders were suffering from exhaustion, lack of reinforcement and fuel shortage, causing perhaps a dozen StuGs to be abandoned.

John Keenan of B Coy, 2 Lincolns described these conditions from the squaddie's point of view. His brigade, 9 BIB, moved ten miles as the crow flies from Maashees to the egg-farm, Krüsbeckshof, to 'help First Canadian Army out of a bit of trouble' as he put it:

> On the Maas we found ourselves in trenches that were about 18 inches deep and we were in about 6 inches of water anyway and we were laid down there and the Germans were actually on top of us. I well remember some of our lot were right in the front and the Company commander says, "Well. We're thinking of relieving you". The whole lot of us turned round and said; "It's so ruddy horrible, don't relieve us. Just leave us here. We don't really want anybody else to relieve us, because we're absolutely wet through. We might as well remain wet through and anybody else who's dry might as well remain dry". I remember very clearly shaving in a cup of tea and I was not only taking the beard off my face but about a quarter of an inch of muck which had stuck in my beard at the same time. We were in this situation for three or four days and in the end the company commander said, "To hell with it. You've got to come out!" We came out and he put somebody else in the position. [John and his good-natured section ran the risk of contracting trench foot, aka Non Freezing Cold Injury. It was probably the 2ic, John Boys, who left them for as long as he dared. Had they gone sick despite the application of whale oil preventive, Boys would have been disciplined for neglecting the men's welfare and risking their effectiveness.]
>
> We wound up in this house which was some way behind where we were. In the cellar and the attic was the artillery OP and while we were drying out and one thing and another in this house the Germans got a bead on it. They were aiming at it with a *Minenwerfer*, [actually a *Nebelwerfer]* what we used to call a *Moaning Minnie*. Although I didn't smoke, in the space of about three hours I smoked 50 cigarettes. It was one of those things.
>
> About this time the powers that be decided that the 3rd Division would be withdrawn to rest with the object that we would cross the Rhine as the assault group. Much to our delight we were removed from the front line and taken to Louvain, which is possibly 5 or 6 miles from Brussels. This was some sort of seventh heaven.
>
> Can't remember an awful lot about Louvain. We weren't there as long as we anticipated because the 1st Canadian Army, which was an anomaly because they had a Canadian Army HQ, about two armoured brigades and one Canadian Division. Of course, when it was spoken of on the news that the 1st Canadian Army had taken over the assault on this that and the other, it basically meant what Canadian troops there were plus most of the 2nd British Army, who'd all of a sudden lost their identity and become the 1st Canadian Army and were doing what was necessary. [John was no doubt quoting a notorious editorial in the Daily Telegraph that claimed the Canadian Army was mostly British and Canadian authorities were trying to grab undue credit. This canard was propagated by Brendan Bracken through his control of the National Publishers Association, according to Richard Malone.[3] Canada provided 3 divisions out of the 16 in 21 AG, and 16 divisions merited only one army HQ. The British, however, needed an army group of two armies to maintain influence with the dominant Americans

3 Richard Malone. *A World in Flames* (Toronto: Collins, 1984), p. 186.

who had increased their strength from 49 divisions in January to 61 in March 1945 out of a SHAEF total of 85 divisions. In WWI, 4 Canadian divisions in France justified a corps HQ, and never an army, but Canada needed a national army to impress Quebec, which criticised conscription, blaming their government for trying to maintain an excessive armed force in the field. Many Canadian Francophones supported Mussolini and Vichy France, including the Mayor of Montreal, Camillien Houde CBE, interned from 1940 to 1943, and others like Pierre Elliott Trudeau who wore a German steel helmet. A Governor-General of Quebec, Jean-Louis Roux, resigned in 1996 after revealing that he sported the swastika as a student. Quebec viewed both world wars as imperialist and campaigned against conscription. The Federal Government of Canada had to be seen to act in all things as a sovereign Dominion. Ironically it was supply integration that permitted John's switching in and out of 1 Canadian Army, which was impossible with a separately supplied and differently equipped US army. 1 Canadian Army achieved a theoretical quorum so to speak, by including I Canadian Corps which was prevented from returning from Italy by lack of shipping. Canadians privately liked the idea of commanding the British Army in XXX Corps. Charles Lynch wrote in the Montreal Gazette in 1983, that, 'Crerar had 15 (sic) divisions under command, including the cream of the British army. It was a source of anguish for British correspondents that they had to file despatches datelined 'with the First Canadian Army' when they were writing about the exploits of their own troops, but the Canadians regarded this as sweet revenge for all the years they had been described as Brits'. So in the final analysis John surrendered his identity to appease Quebec over conscription.] They were attacking in the Reichswald Forest. They got in a bit of a mess and the result was that our rest period and the likelihood of us crossing the Rhine as the first assault troops disappeared up the spout and we had to go chasing up to the north of Holland over the border of Germany to attack in the Reichswald Forest. And let no one fool you the Dutch that were on the edge of Germany were possibly more avid Nazis than the Germans themselves. Every house that we passed had *Ein Reich. Ein Volk. Ein Führer.* – or some such slogan on the wall. One might say to be charitable that the Germans had put the slogans there. But they hadn't been put there by the Germans but by the local Dutch.

We went to the Reichswald and it was snowing, or raining, or sleeting. It was pretty horrible. The Germans were fighting on the border and were taking it very hard. Their way of taking it very hard was to make it ruddy hard for us. As I remember events, we arrived in the area, went over a startline, did an attack, never saw any Germans who ran before us. The next day we were booked to attack a place called Kervenheim.[4]

The historian of 2 Middlesex described Germany from his own frank experience as the country of white flags. He thought the locals were hanging out tablecloths and sheets in the same spirit as Swastika flags were flown a few years earlier; it was the thing to do.

The destruction is unbelievable. The white-painted Nazi slogans on the walls seem a little out-of-date. Civilians are liable to be shot if they come out of doors in the front line area. Women are allowed out for two hours a day to fetch water and food. They have to put lists of occupants on the doors of their houses. They huddle, white-faced and bomb-happy, in an airless stinking cellar. They look at you as if you are the Frankenstein of Goebbels' propaganda; they wonder when the raping and murdering is going to start. Some of them put little notices on the doors in their best English – "Old womans. Young childs. Please, have mercy". They are surprised to find that we ignore them completely. In our leisure moments we are much more interested in

4 John Keenan's memoirs tape-recorded in 1994.

> looking at the contents of the houses. It is called 'searching for weapons'; it is chiefly curiosity and souvenir hunting; it is liable to develop into looting after a while. Canadian engineers are building roads the quick way. Just blow a house down and bulldoze it onto the road.[5]

The destruction was frequently unnecessary, indiscriminate and counter-productive. At this time Maj Ronald Balfour of the MFAA was successfully persuading 1 Canadian Army to bulldoze a new road around the mediaeval Steintor in Goch rather than demolish it to allow tanks to travel through the town more easily. Balfour complained of the plundering, with every house forced open and searched including safes and cupboards. He tried to rescue as much as possible and put up warning signs but had no idea of their effect. Balfour was killed by shellfire on 10 March in Cleves while saving an altarpiece from the 14th century Collegiate Church.[6] The historian of 11 BAD complained:

> Nor was our progress made any easier by the activities of our own troops. Operating now for the first time on German soil they set about the task of destroying German towns and villages with undisguised enthusiasm, and the resulting debris frequently delayed traffic for some hours until a passage could be opened.[7]

3 BID relieved 15 BID, setting up camp near Goch, 32 m above sea level on the edge of the long finger-shaped ridge whose base extended across to Calcar with Nijmegen at its tip. The approach march to battle for most of them was downhill through the woods past the 'monument to gloom', Schloss Calbeck, south of which 8 BIB was entrenched in the lower ground. XXX Corps' – 3 BID, 53 BID, 51 BID and 1 BCB – now battled in the Maas flood-plain, while Simonds' II Canadian Corps – 11 BAD, 4 CAD, 3 CID, 2 CID and 43 BID – had the benefit of the higher ground on their left. It does not seem to have done them much good; the going everywhere off-road was indescribably bad.

Barber's 15 BID had been fighting south of Goch for a week and needed to rest and refit. Eyewitness material from both sides of this battle is available. On 20 February, 227 BIB with 6 GAB attacked south past Schloss Calbeck to the railway line against IFJR7 and elements of 15 PGD. The next day 6 RSF of 44 BIB took the lead and advanced 500 yards across the railway line. On 22 February, 46 BIB took up the attack while Panzer Lehr and IFJR7 counter-attacked. The result was stalemate and Panzer Lehr withdrew. 44 BIB made a 2 km advance the next day, 23 February, against IFJR7 and 15 PGD. There was no action on 24 to February when 3 BID took over the line. The Germans also made their changes; IFJR7 and 15 PGD were relieved by IFJR24 and 2FJR24.

On the left flank of 3 BID, 11 BAD of II Canadian Corps was attacking south to Stein on 26 February, staying up on the ridge as right flank of an armoured thrust through the Hochwald to Xanten and Wesel in Operation *Blockbuster*. Right of their centre line was the single-track Goch-Xanten railway, which would immediately be torn up and turned into a single-track supply road for lorries, as described above. On the right flank of 3 BID, 53 BID supported by 8 BAB was assaulting Weeze in Operation *Leek*[8] beginning on 24 February and with orders to push on to Geldern. The intention was to drive south-east astride the river Niers and to cut off Weeze. 4/7 Royal Dragoon Guards supporting 71 BIB were on the right and 13/18 Hussars were in the woods

5 Moberly, *Second Battalion*, pp. 107-8.
6 Claudia Joseph. *The Real Monuments Man* (Mail Online, 26 January 2014).
7 Anon. *Taurus Pursuant, A History of 11th Armoured Div* (Germany: BAOR, 1945), p. 86.
8 Stacey, *Victory Campaign*, p. 491.

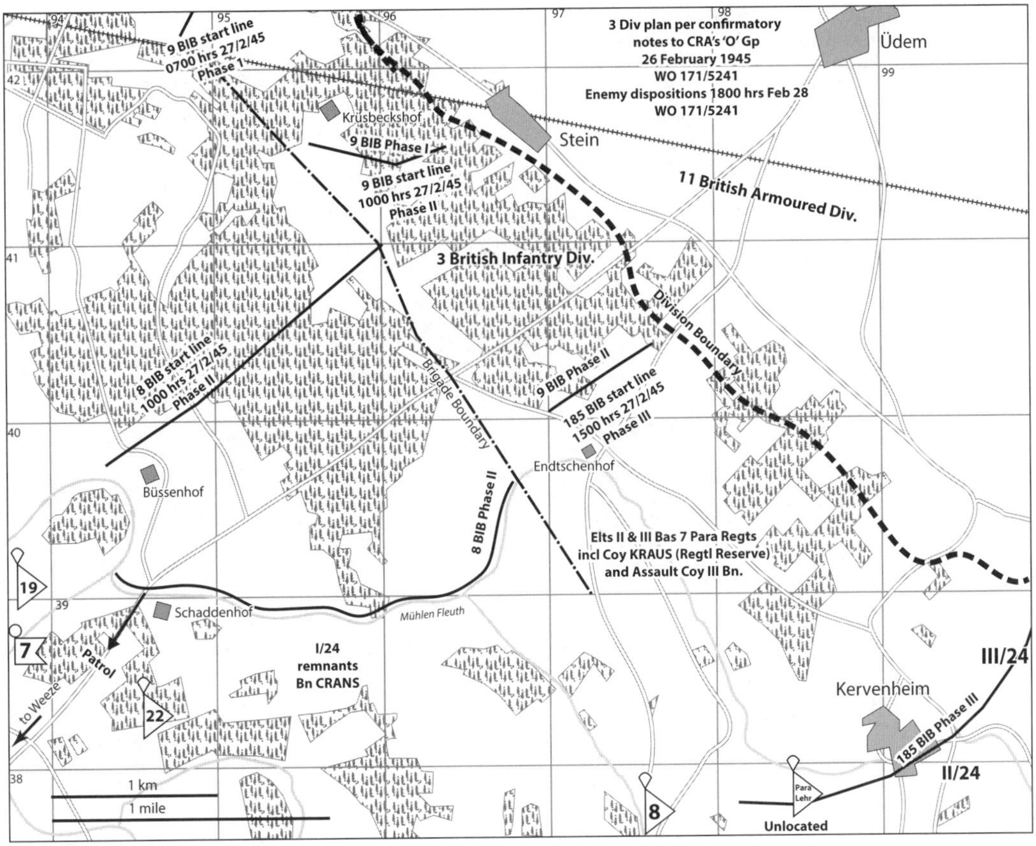

Map 10 3rd Division's three-phase plan for *Heather*.

with 160 BIB on the left. The Sherwood Rangers Yeomanry who had suffered heavy casualties in the previous operation were resting in Cleve, as were 12 KRRC. Going was difficult and the enemy defences were reinforced by Panthers which dominated the Shermans. Some progress was made but, as both flanks of the advance were open, it was decided to call a halt till 51 BID on the right and 3 BID on the left came up level.[9] The capture of Weeze was vital in order to free the lateral road to the Maas and permit the building of a Bailey Bridge between Wanssum and Well for the supply of XXX Corps (see Map 7). To his front, Whistler was informed the Americans were over the Roer and heading towards them in Operation *Grenade*. He was given the support of 6 Guards Armoured Brigade together with units of 79 BAD and augmented artillery.

Whistler had intended to move his Main and Tac HQs from Tilburg 160325 to Pfalzdorf 909458 on 26 February, but at 1445 hrs on 25 February was informed that the Gennep Bailey Bridge would be closed the next day from 1800 to 2000 hrs. He therefore ordered an immediate move and on arrival called an O Group. '1800 hrs. 25 Feb. Div 'O' Gp. Orders given out for Div to secure line rd UDEM 9842-WEEZE 9337 and capture Kervenheim 9938 on 27 Feb 45.'[10] Confirmatory Notes were issued the next day when the CRA held his own O Gp.[11]

9 Anon. *A Short History of the 8th Armoured Brigade* (Hanover: BAOR, 1945), Ch. V.
10 TNA: WO 171/4130: 3 BID War Diary,
11 TNA: WO 171/5241: 2 Middlesex War Diary.

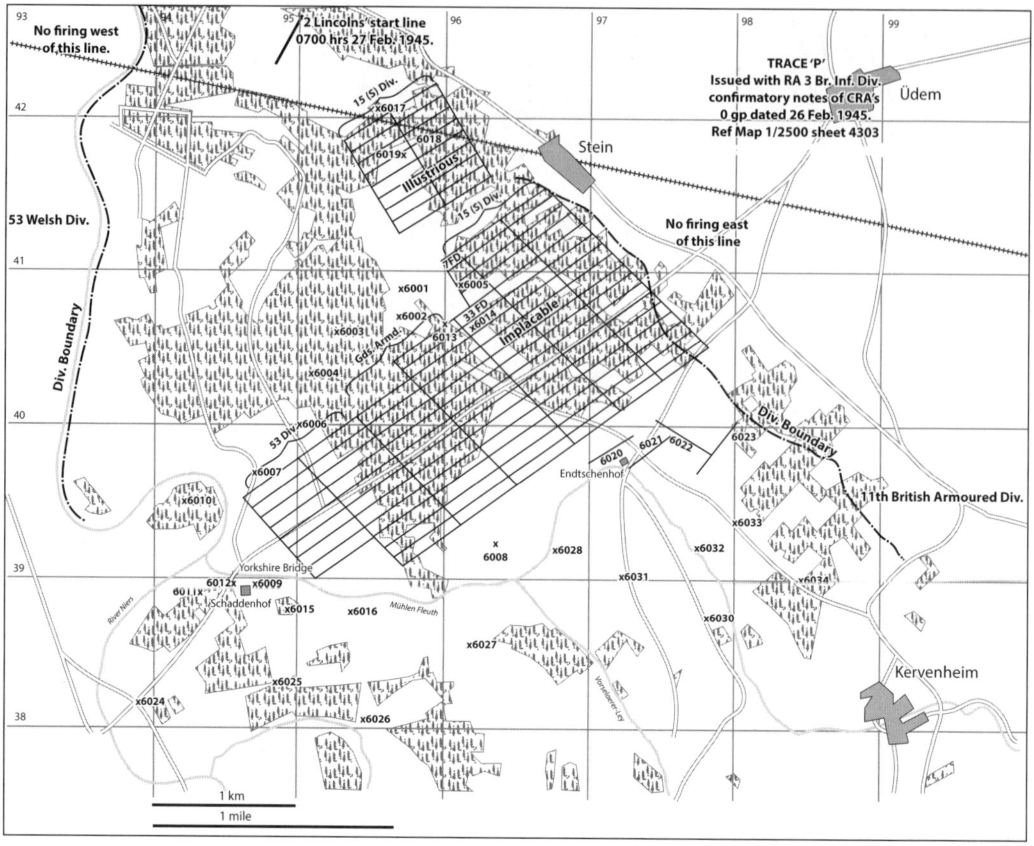

Map 11 The artillery plan for Phases I and II of *Heather*.

The Divisional Plan comprised three phases, with Phase II split in two. Later, when Winnekendonk became in effect Phase IV, it was made the responsibility of 9 BIB:

Phase I: 9 BIB at 7 am to capture the edge of the wood from 955416 – 961415 – 964416
Phase II: 9 BIB at 10 am to secure the edge of the wood from 970400 to 976404
Phase II: 8 BIB at 10 am to secure the Mühlen Fleuth and capture [Yorkshire] bridge at 945390
Phase III: 185 BIB at 3 pm to pass through 9 BIB and capture Kervenheim.

There was no centre line. 'The Division's axes of advance were two soft, saturated sandy tracks leading south-east through the woods'[12] and this, according to Scarfe, led to the tactical surprise of FJR7. The truth is different: FJR 7 was diverted by 11 BAD's night action under Mike Carver.

9 BIB attacked the sector held by 84 GID, whose responsibilities included the defence of Üdem. They were supported by FJR7. From 19 to 24 February, FJR7 had been under command of 15 PGD, which held the sector between the two railway lines running out of Goch to Weeze and Üdem, and straddled the River Niers. 15 PGD went south on 24 February to face the Americans and was replaced by 8FJD, comprising FJR22, FJR24 and FJRLehr, with its original FJR23 transferred to 2FJD. According to the Intelligence Summary of II Canadian Corps, only FJR22/III,

12 Norman Scarfe. *Assault Division* (London: Collins, 1947), p. 207.

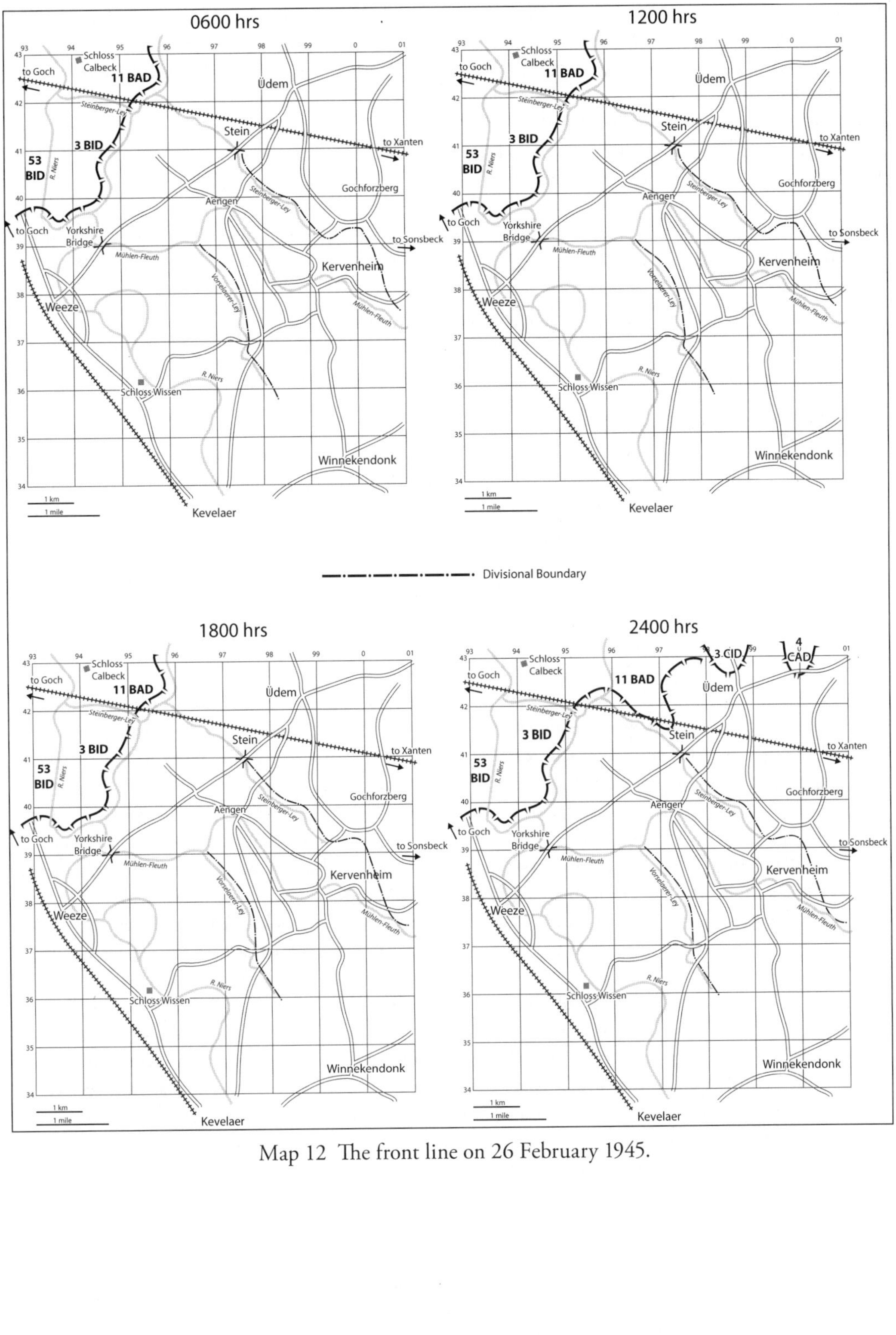

Map 12 The front line on 26 February 1945.

previously known as Battalion Müller, was permanently available to 8FJD. 'The remaining two battalions seem to have become Para Army reserves,' 'shifting allegiance from 6 to 8 Para Division as the situation warrants.'[13] In exchange, FJR7 from 2FJD reinforced 8FJD during these battles. From its HQ near Schloss Wissen, which was also a major field hospital, 8FJD also controlled the last elements of the much-diminished 84 GID, and a Battle Group of the 33 Tank Destroyer Unit armed with Mk IV Tank destroyers, left behind by 15 PGD.

It was 8FJD that now faced 53 BID on its left in Weeze, 3 BID in its centre moving on Kervenheim, and 11 BAD with the Canadian Lion Force on its right at Üdem. The area between Weeze and the Maas was being attacked by 52 BID and defended by FJR19, FJR20 and FJR21 of 7 FJD.

3 BID's Intelligence Summary number 226 was issued per the War Diary at 1300 hrs on 26 February, and number 227 at 0110 hrs the next morning.

3 Br Inf Div Int Summary No 226
1200 hrs 26 Feb.
Part I

Enemy Sitn – Own Front

1. Last night's attack SW of Goch [by 51 BID, see Map 7] was successful & all objectives were taken. BOCKELT 8842, GASDONK 8840, HUM 9040 were captured. Resistance was moderate, but the enemy arty fire was heavy. Elts of 7 Parachute Div were encountered, and 180 Bn was found NE of SIEBENGEWALD 8941.
2. This morning a heavy attack was opened on our left. [II Canadian Corps' Operation *Blockbuster*]. Despite the small enemy spoiling attack earlier in the night good progress has been made, and we have reached the edge of the plateau NE of UDEM at 0146. At the moment of writing enemy tks are counter-attacking in the area. This formation may be either Pz Lehr or 116 Pz Div.
3. As the new attack develops, it can be expected to modify the enemy's dispositions on our front. At the moment there appears to be some four bns of Paratroops holding the line against us, with elts of Parachute Lehr Regt in the South and 7 Parachute Regt further north. Those elements of 84 Div which were previously believed to be facing us are worth very little and have probably been withdrawn. Apart from his inf the enemy will rely largely on his arty to stop our attack, and he has a considerable number of guns between Weeze and Kervenheim. Many of these may be engaged in the ops on our left, and will certainly distract the guns in the HOCHWALD from our sector.
4. The enemy is unlikely to be able to free any res to meet our attack, as what little he has will be fully employed further to the East. A possible arrival is 24 Parachute Regt HUBNER of 8 Parachute Div, but there is evidence that this formation will be called upon to return one or two of the regiments of 7 Parachute Div. The enemy has a small number of SP Atk guns [Jagdpanzer 38(t) Hetzer and Jagdpanzer IV SdKfz 162] which he may use against us. The Paratroops may be expected to offer skilful and dogged resistance making full use of the difficult country which is largely wooded, in some places marshy and intersected by many small waterways. The largest of these streams is the MUHLEN FLEUTH, 24 ft wide along most of its course. Our progress will largely depend upon who possesses the escarpment on our left, the town of UDEM and the feature at 001397.
5. Att at Appendix A is a diagram.

13 LAC: Appendix A to II Canadian Corps Intelligence Summary No 136.

6. Identifications are more than ever important in this battle. Every effort must be made to get back the infm at once. PW will be found mainly without paybooks, but carrying a card entitled 'Grabenausweis', showing the FPN. This number must be passed as quickly as possible. Documents must not be removed.

Appx to Part II

3. Enemy appreciation and intentions
   The enemy appreciation is that the attacking Allied force consists of five divisions [actually seven divisions]. Playing on the current belief that the Allies are pressed for manpower, it is believed that they cannot afford to lose a division. The policy is therefore to defend every possible position and inflict as heavy casualties as possible.
   The most strongly defended position will be the so-called Schlieffen Line (HOCHWALD area). All West Wall workers were sent to the area last week. A considerable amount of Atk and AA weapons are being moved there, or are due to fall back on the position.
   After that line, PW believes the road to KREFELD will be open. Source was Major Grenz. Claimed to be a Polish national, married to a Polish woman and lives in Alsace. Claims was a Polish officer until 1925 when he moved to Germany on business and was accepted as a member of the German officer corps. Promoted to Major in 1944. He also said that the priority of Goering was to reinforce 7 Parachute Div.

3 Br Inf Div Int Summary No 227. 26 Feb, 1945 (Selected extracts)

   1. Identifications during the day have shown that South of the rly GOCH-UDEM, the sector is held by all three battalions 7 Parachute Regt, and North of the rly elts of 1062 GR are in position.[14]

This appreciation was out-of-date even before it was issued. *Blockbuster* began on 26 February at 4.30 am when 2 CID advanced south of Calcar to draw the defenders' attention, while 3 CID crossed their startline at 8.45 am against Keppeln. Progress was slow despite the use of Wasps against anti-tank guns, but Keppeln was occupied by mid afternoon. Meanwhile 4 CAD's Tiger Group had turned south towards Üdem and by 4 pm had taken Todtenhügel, letting Smith Force pass through and take the Katzenberg to the north-east of Üdem after nightfall. FJR7 was pulled out of Kervenheim to the defence of Üdem, with FJR7/I being destroyed north and east of Üdem by Smith Force. 3 CID reached the outskirts of Üdem from the north in the late afternoon, and occupied it between midnight and 4 am on 27 February – the hour at which 2 Lincolns began to move forward in *Heather*. Meanwhile at 6 pm on 26 February, a mixed battle group of 4 KSLI of 159 BIB and the Scots Greys of 4 BAB under Mike Carver, who had been temporarily placed under command of 11 BAD, was released. They thrust south in artificial moonlight from Buchholt through Herringschenhof to Stein as pictured secondhand by Bryan de Grineau and published in *The Illustrated London News*. They occupied Stein at 5 am on 27 February after heavy night fighting against 84 GID, capturing 350 dazed prisoners, four StuGs[15] and two tanks, seen by R.W. Thompson at the HQ of 185 BIB on the following day. They then tried to swing left towards the Gochfortzberg but FJR7 stopped them with armour and PAKs operating out of Kervenheim. Roberts then diverted another mixed battle group of 1 Herefords and 3/4 CLY north through Üdem to take the Gochfortzberg, which they attacked at 2.30 pm and seized at 4.30 pm on 27 February. Meanwhile 7 CIB of 3 CID demonstrated south of Üdem towards Kervenheim, while 11 BAD and 3 CID became entangled as the German defences stiffened and held.

14 TNA: WO171/4130: 3 BID War Diary.
15 Anon, *Taurus Pursuant*, p. 84.

Pip Roberts, GOC 11 BAD, complained of being out of his element in 'the most unpleasant battle I had anything to do with in the whole war.[16] It had been:

> a slow, miserable and costly operation. We had been fighting our way through country where no armoured division could have been expected for one moment to fulfill a natural role. We had been confronted by impenetrable forests, impassable bogs, numerous craters, roadblocks, mines and every form of demolition.[17]

FJR7 was therefore preoccupied with the attacks from the direction of Stein and Üdem when 9 BIB attacked through the woods with tanks at 7 am to secure the Üdem-Weeze road. With 11 BAD occupying the ground to their left front, the advance of 2 Lincolns met no resistance. The Austrians of the 84 GID included 'large numbers of confused stragglers,' according to the Intelligence Summary. They offered sparse and at times only token resistance until the Üdem-Weeze road was reached and the Kervenheim Pakfront, which had by now already slowed 11 BAD, took control under 8 FJD (or perhaps under von Lüttwitz's direct control – see below).

A PW identified 3 Pl of 15 Coy, FJR7 as holding the line of the Üdem-Weeze road at 965403 under command of Capt Lisowski's III Battalion.

> All three pls of 15 Coy left the WAGENINGEN area on 17 Feb and moved in lorries to ÜDEM arriving three days later. 3 Pl came under command of III Bn, and it is probable that the other two pls were suballotted in a similar manner. While at ÜDEM 3 Pl was employed putting up wire obstacles. On 27 Feb 3 Pl was withdrawn to an area believed to have been E985403, [Tokatshof] while PW was probably left at III Bn HQ as runner.[18]

The organisation of 15 Coy was defined by the POW. It comprised 100 men under Lt Richter, and had three platoons under subalterns. Unfortunately only the name of 2/Lt Engelhard, who commanded 1 Platoon, was given. He said each platoon of 33 men had three sections of 10 men each, armed with one MG42, one MP38, 1 cup discharger (the *Schiessbecher* which was a short, rifled barrel that clamped on the end of a rifle to hold an anti-personnel grenade fixed to a rod that was pushed down the rifle barrel, and fired with a special blank cartridge), 2 Panzerfausts (a hollow-charge anti-tank firework in a one-shot launcher) and rifles. It is quite possible that they had acquired an additional MG42 or even two (a machine-gun that fired at 1,000 rpm, and sounded like tearing calico).

Also in the area was FJR7's Assault Coy with 140 men organized in three normal plns and a heavy pln with three sections, two of which contained 9 men with 5 MP44 assault rifles, 1 MG42 and 3 rifles. The third was a Tank Destroyer section with 12 men armed with Panzerfausts and Ofenrohr/Panzerschrecks (re-loadable anti-tank rocket). It was probably these men who did such physical and psychological damage to 4 GG as described below.

> The assault coy of 7 para Regt was formed at BENNEKOM, HOLLAND, E5879 on 18 Feb from approximately 120 men who came from the coys of 7 para Regt. That night the newly formed coy marched via ARNHEM, ISSELBURG, and REES to UDEMERBRUCH A0240, arriving there on about 21 Feb. PW gave the organization of the assault coy, (see above). PW does not believe any tps relieved them in the WAGENINGEN area. The assault

16 Patrick Delaforce. *The Black Bull* (Stroud: Alan Sutton, 1993), p. 201.
17 Anon, *Taurus Pursuant*, p. 86.
18 LAC: Appendix A to II Canadian Corps Intelligence Summary No 136.

> coy took up its final position in the woods E984388.[19] [The woods from which the Norfolks later assaulted Kervenheim].

Although a week earlier StuGs had been operating around Fasanenkath, none was encountered in the woods, which did not suit its tactics or design. The Churchill tank had less trouble, although conditions on much of the battlefield were marginal for it also. Since armour was a key element, it is time to consider the armour used on either side.

The StuG with a short 75-mm L24 gun and 50-mm of frontal armour, was originally designed as mobile artillery to assist marching infantry in their assault on fortified positions. This was in the early days of the Second World War when the rôle of the fast (*schnell)* armoured formations was to bypass fortified areas and exploit miles ahead of the slow army of footsloggers following up to occupy the territory seized by the fast troops. *Blitzkrieg's* success was misunderstood. Its success resulted not from the poor tanks fielded by the Germans, which the Russians derided as 'toys', but on an integrated all-arms operational methodology commanded at the tip by a commander with real-time communications controlling motorised infantry, tanks, artillery and *Stukas* on call as aerial artillery.

Although absent from the Polish campaign, where the caution of the *Landser* was compared unfavourably with the spirit of Langemarck (when the deaths of 2,000 young soldiers at Bixschote in November 1914 were fêted as a victory), it was observed in France that when employed as an infantry weapon the StuG overcame infantry stickiness. Then as Russian superiority in tank numbers and quality developed, the StuG was transformed into a defensive tank destroyer with frontal armour increased to 80-mm and a gun doubled in length to L48. The vehicle was based on both the MkIII and MkIV tank chassis. Its job was to destroy medium tanks in order to separate their accompanying infantry for destruction by the infantry's MG42 and mortars.

The system was transferred unchanged to Italy and Normandy. Fast, low, and effective against a Sherman and the sides of a Churchill, whose 4-inch thick frontal plate was beyond the StuG's capabilities at anything over 500 m, it destroyed enemy armour from carefully pre-selected ambush positions, and usually from a flank. Ideally the positions offered cover from view and were behind a tank obstacle, such as a river, marsh or minefield, to prevent the ambusher from being swarmed. Once the enemy's *Schwerpunkt* was identified, a skilled StuG commander pre-planned with the infantry a series of ambush positions between which his troop could move at speed. Alongside a farmhouse (whose cellar roof was not strong enough to support a StuG in the sitting-room) or inside a barn on hard going with a good field of fire and a concealed path of retreat, the StuG proved a formidable ambush weapon and was particularly well handled in these battles by the XII Parachute Assault Gun Brigade. In the Schloss Calbeck woods, however, its strengths were neutralised and it was at a disadvantage due to narrow tracks, gun overhang and lack of a turret.

Churchills of Right Flank 3 Scots Guards had been operating in the area for a week with 15 BID, and the defenders could expect their reappearance with 3 BID. Schlemm and Meindl would therefore have known that while the 50 mm PAK screen extending from the Hochwald to Winnekendonk could stop the Shermans and Cromwells of 4 CAD and 11 BAD, they were of no use against Churchills and their feared Crocodile flame-thrower derivatives. All the signs showed the Germans received the attack by 3 BID with respect and fielded their best against it. It turned out to be the only Anglo-Canadian division they could not stop.

Whistler's plan was for 185 BIB (2 R Warwick, 1 R Norfolk, 2 KSLI) to be in reserve on 27 February and to move up on the following day to take over the lead and launch an attack on Kervenheim. 3 Recce Regiment was told to be ready to cross Yorkshire Bridge on its capture by 8 BIB (1 Suffolk, 2 E Yorks, 1 S Lancs) and fulfil the recce function for a brigade of 53 BID,

19 Op. Cit.

which was to outflank Weeze and keep between the River Niers and the Vorselaerer Ley. 9 BIB (2 Lincolns, 1 KOSB, 2 RUR) would pass through 185 BIB as soon as Kervenheim was secured, take Winnekendonk and burst out with GAD.

In spite of the odds being strongly in favour of the defenders, the rested 3 BID quickly reached the Üdem-Weeze road, seized Yorkshire Bridge, wrote down FJR22/III in its defence, got a black eye and a VC while taking Kervenheim and then stormed into Winnekendonk in a manner reminiscent of Monash with his unstoppable Anzacs and Canadians of 1918. 3 BID fought three battles to advance 6 miles (9 km) in 4 days – a 50 percent faster average than the 30 miles in 30 days taken to get from Groesbeek to Wesel. Meanwhile the Canadians, in spite of heroism rewarded with two VCs (Sgt Cosens at Mooshof on 26 February and Maj Tiltson near Calcar on 1 March) and their excellent progress on 26 February, became stuck in the Hochwald Gap 3 miles to the north-east of Kervenheim until 3 March, taking severe punishment and leaving hundreds of Shermans and Cromwells disabled, bogged and burnt out in the fields. The CO of the RHLI, Denis Whitaker, won a Bar to his DSO on the Goch-Calcar road, but concluded; 'The Battle of the Hochwald Gap was like the Battle of the Huertgen Forest: the wrong troops used in the wrong place at the wrong time, and a battle that never should have been.'[20]

Extant (in Appendix 1) is the adjutant's numbered copy of 2 Lincolns' operation order for *Heather*, dated 26 February 1945. The Lincolns of 9 BIB were first in and last out of the operation and together with 3 SG the only battalions to go 'over the top' twice. This was the ninth operation order issued in the nine months since D-Day by the adjutant and peacetime schoolmaster, Capt Jack Harrod. His clerk typed and roneoed 25 copies, 19 for internal circulation and 6 for the information of other units, numbering them by hand at Bn HQ located in a house at 926443. On 28 February, as soon as the Lincolns vacated it, the building was occupied by the Regimental HQ of 84 (Sussex) Medium Regt RA. There was competition for undamaged houses, and recces were sent ahead to grab whatever was available, since possession was everything. The first Lincolns arrived on 24 February, relieving 2 Argyll & Sutherland Highlanders who were already out of the line and identified in Jack Brymer's memoir. The official history of 2 Lincolns wrongly identified the unit as 7 A&SH.[21] The coys were located at 917443, 923443, 928442 and 923439.[22]

The Lincolns' attack went as planned so it can be reconstructed in detail from the orders – see Appendix. These were presented in the standard format laid down in the manuals – Information, Intention, Method, Aim, Intercommunication – which ensured quick understanding when read under stress or in bad light. It also meant those dictating the orders in haste remembered to cover every topic. Evidence of such haste or perhaps fatigue is revealed in the duplicate numbering of the second Paragraph. Written orders indicated a settled existence with clerks, typewriters, duplicators, paper and ink, the transport to move them and the time to prepare and disseminate them. By this period of the war, the Germans lacked these things and learned to do without, relying extensively on runners to deliver hand-written or verbal orders at the level of battalion and below, and on radio above it. At all operational levels the British convened O Groups prior to battle and then used wireless and the simple Slidex code.

The Divisional artillery also arrived from Louvain and Mears, the CRA, called the COs of the Fld Regts to an O Group on 26 February. Confirmatory Notes were issued – see Appendix 2. HQRA was in a sandpit near Pfalzdorf north of Goch alongside the Divisional HQ. Mears could call on 336 howitzers, comprising 288 gun-howitzer 25pdrs of four divisions, and 48 medium 5.5 inch howitzers of two regiments. He had 88 howitzers under command, comprising 3 BID's

20 Whitaker, *Rhineland,* p. 235.
21 L Gates. *The History of the Tenth Foot* (Aldershot: Gale & Polden, 1953), p. 250.
22 TNA: WO 171/5231: 2 Lincolns' War Diary.

25pdrs (72 units) and 84 Medium Regiment's 5.5 inch (16 units). The remaining 248 howitzers were in support, being the 25pdrs of three divisions and the 5.5 inch of two medium regiments.The heavy guns – 7.2 inch and 155 mm howitzers – of 5 AGRA were available if required but probably did not fire in support of 3 BID. They were usually tasked for long-distance counter-battery work, and since during this time the Germans amassed a thousand guns to overwhelm the Canadians in the Hochwald and batter the KOSB outside Bruch on 2 March, they never lacked for urgent targets. Barrages were thickened up with 'pepperpots' from 45 divisional 17pdr anti-tank and Bofors 40 mm anti-aircraft guns.

Item 5(e) of the Notes shows how each infantry Brigade was permanently tied with a Field Regiment; 7 Fld Regt with 185 BIB, 33 with 9 BIB and 76 with 8 BIB. The Fld Regts permanently assigned a battery to each infantry battalion, and assigned an FOO at each level. Regiments fired 'at will' in support of their brigade and battalions. All Fld Regts contributed to the artillery barrages worked out by the CRA. 6 GAB was assigned support from 86 Fld Regt from GAD's own artillery but it was out of range for the Kervenheim and Winnekendonk battles and, although slated to fire for the Yorkshire Bridge battle, may not have done so.

3 BID concentrated to the east of Goch with 8 and 9 BIBs up and 185 BIB back in Pfalzdorf in square 9146. 8 BIB concentrated in 9441 south of the railway line and Schloss Calbeck. A plaque today records this railway line was built in the 1870s to link London via Flushing (Vlissingen) with St. Petersburg. The rails taken up by the Canadians were never re-laid. It is now a road between Goch and Üdem, and a walking trail through the Hochwald. The Lincolns were in square 9244, the RUR in 9443 and the KOSB in Buchholt 9444 after moving up from Herent.

> We moved out of Herent at 8 am on the 21st of February, and in bright sunshine, the column wound its way back along the familiar roads of Belgium and Holland – by Diest, Eindhoven, Helmond and St Anthonis – until at Boxmeer we passed into new territory, where already the sights of recent battle became apparent… Late in the afternoon we crossed the River Maas by an enormously long Bailey Bridge and moved on through the villages still plastered with bombastic Nazi slogans… To our left we could see the battered slopes of the Reichswald, which had just been cleared in heavy fighting, and the traffic became more congested as we jolted our way into the Highland Division's transport area. Gradually as ambulances trickled past us, we realised that we were being relentlessly drawn once more into the harsh world of battle. At that time the normal signposts were down, and few of us knew that we had crossed into Germany, until in Asperden we saw the German script on shops and cafés. The houses looked deserted and it was only in the outskirts of Goch, whose factory chimneys stuck up silent and smokeless above the ruin of the town, that we saw our first German civilians scrapping about among the rubble. As we entered the town the column halted in order to pick up our guides, and we found ourselves in the middle of one of the Highland Division's gun areas at the precise moment when a sudden burst of activity began. This completed the work of readjustment: all the old emotions, which for long had been suppressed, suddenly leapt into the foreground of consciousness, and our mood changed utterly from the easy-going nonchalance of Herent into that grim, watchful tension which holds the mind together during action.
>
> We had a few words with the grimy gunners before pushing on, and learned from them that the enemy was still reacting savagely against our capture of Goch and the Reichswald. They also gave us a solemnizing account of the German artillery, and it was in a serious frame of mind that we moved on to the undulating farmlands west of Udem, in the neighbourhood of Bockholt (sic), where we took over from a Battalion of the 15th (Scottish) Division. Our first night in Germany was spent in this area. Quickly we readjusted ourselves to the routine of trench life and appreciatively to the sustained roar of our guns. The enemy was being given no respite and the immense concentration of the British and Canadian artillery, which seemed

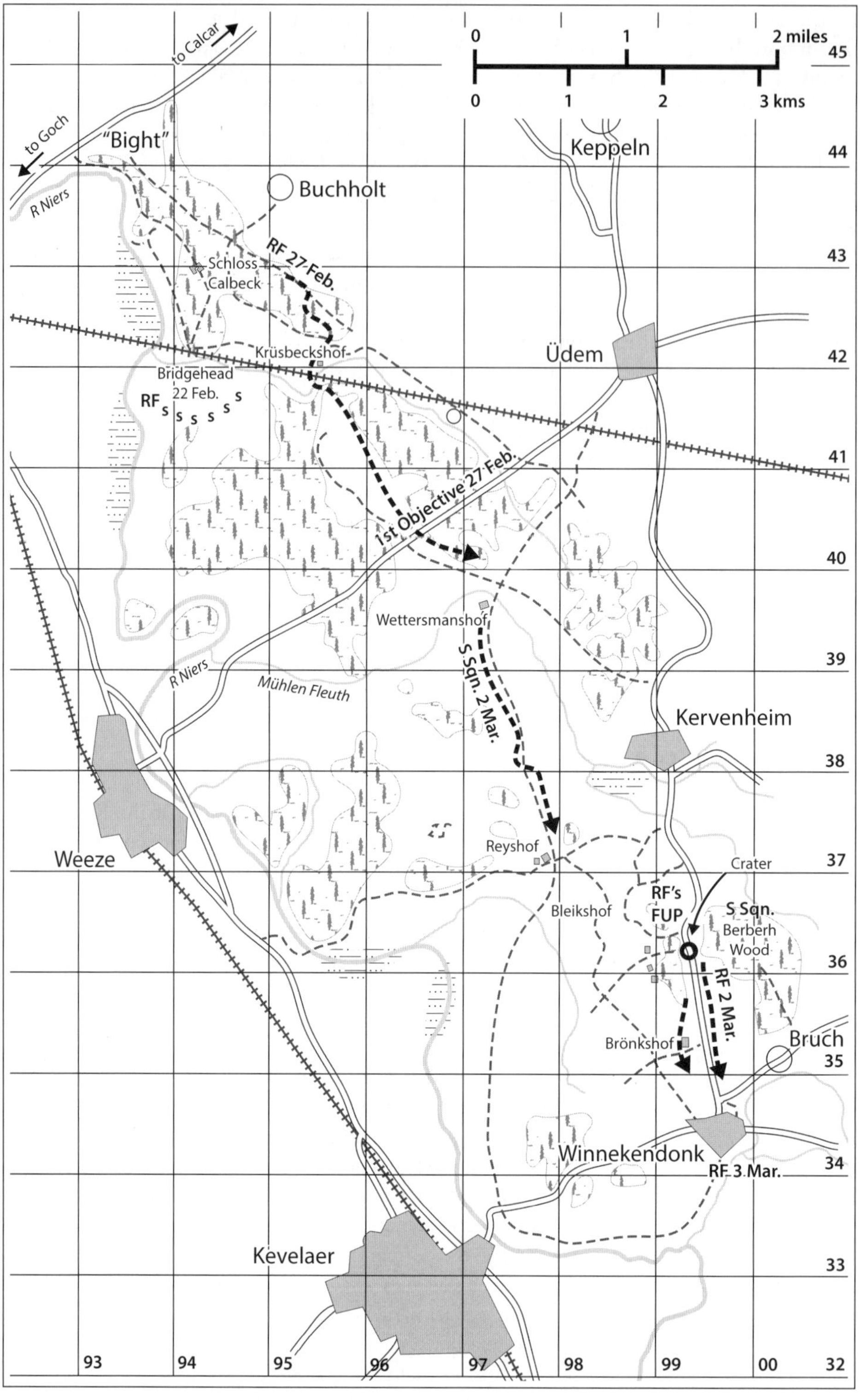

Map 13 Copy of an illustration in 3 SG's War Diary. Krüsbeckshof should be located south of the railway. (TNA WO/171 1258)

> to fill every field between Goch and Gennep, promised the enemy a still more devastating hammering at the start of the next great phase of this crucial Maas-Rhine battle.[23]

3 SG came into support of 9 BIB at 1 pm on 26 February (see Map 13). 6 GAB had been in the area since 19 February fighting in the Schloss Calbeck woods with 15 BID and they knew the area well. Right Flank Sqn was teamed up with 2 Lincolns. At 3 pm there was a commanding officers O Grp at 9 BIB in Schloss Calbeck, 943430, when Maj Cathcart, OC RF and Lt-Col Firbank, CO 2 Lincolns, must have met for the first time. The plan for the following day was issued. From the map Cathcart could see that success depended on the strength and condition of the bridge at 958422. So Capt Pember of 3 SG's Recce, and Lt Brown, a sapper, were sent out on foot at 7 pm to carry out a hazardous patrol that returned at 10.30 pm with an affirmative answer having passed through a Schu minefield in which, the Diary records, 'five lives were subsequently lost'.[24] The *Schu* mine was an anti-personnel mine made of wood and plastic containing 200gr of TNT that exploded at ground level. Mine-detectors operating on the principle of ferrous disturbance of an electro-magnetic field were useless, so Allied troops were issued with rods to find mines by poking for them. The quick solution for uncleared areas was for infantry to follow tank tracks, and the best solution was to use flail tanks, but their availability was controlled by 79 BAD and had to be ordered in advance.

The Diary of 253 Fd Coy RE on 27 February describes the hazardous nature of the sappers' work and the condition of 3 BID's axis of advance:

> lifting mines at 958424 prior to op (4 casualties). Mine clearance cancelled and bulldozer left on track. Recce of br 958422 [Brown and LO from 3 SG]. Br intact but bad going due floods. Track cleared through woods by ARV and AVRE fascines. Mines at 957427 (Lt Quin lost foot). Second D.7 (Armd) blew up. [The Caterpillar D7 was a slow-speed tracked commercial heavy tractor armoured to protect the engine and operator from SA. They were fitted with a blade and winch for grading, road repair and un-ditching vehicles. As the roads collapsed in the woods the quickest repair was to bulldoze trees into the soft-spots]. 1 Pl cleared br at 958422 of mines, clearing pty accompanying leading Coy of 2 Lincolns. Earth roads lasting remarkably well.[25]

At 10.30 pm on 26 February, RF Sqn 3 SG moved out of Goch and harboured in The Bight at 937441. The next morning at 5.15 am, Cathcart moved them up to support the Lincolns:

> but had an extremely difficult journey as the narrow track was completely blocked by AVREs of 11 Armoured Division, coming in the opposite direction on a route to which they had no right. In addition despite RE efforts throughout the night, RF discovered that the prepared tank track was impassable owing to mines and mined vehicles. An unrecced route had to be taken, but luckily proved clear, and the shoot in was successful after a very difficult journey.[26]

The RUR were active in preparing for the first light attack by the Lincolns. On 25 February they established an OP at 949422. This was Pleesenhof which, 'fell on the night of 20/21 February. It had been defended by 1/FJR7 and 5/1051 together with the Flieger Ersatz Bn (airmen replacement

23 WIG Wilson. *A Short History of the 1 KOSB in NWE* (Berwick-Upon-Tweed: *KOSB Museum*), pp. 41-42.
24 TNA: WO 171/ 1258: 3 Scots Guards War Diary.
25 TNA: WO 171/5525: War Diary of 253 Field Company RE.
26 TNA: WO 171/1258: War Diary of 3 Scots Guards.

battalion). A Parachutist destroyed another tank near there and met a hero's death.[27] The RUR watched the battlefield and that night did some active patrolling. The carrier platoon visited the hamlet at 955421 (Eberskath), which the Lincolns were to attack at first light on the 27th. Two sentries were seen. A Coy sent a recce to 957424 close to the bridge which Pember visited the following night, and found signs of enemy occupation at 959423 and 960423. 2 RUR war diary records that a 9 Bde O Group was held at the Lincolns' HQ at 9.15 am on 26 February when the plan was first disclosed. 2 RUR were told that they had to clear the woods to the flank of the Lincoln's attack up to 959422 by 11 pm that night. At 2 pm Capt Baudains (who in 1954 became Army Rifle Champion but was not the only first class shot in the area; Canloan Rex Fendick won the King's Medal in the Canadian Forces in 1948), was sent with a patrol to 958424 coming into contact with the enemy near the railway line killing 1 and capturing 2 POW from 2/1061 PzJag.[28] This is probably a misprint for 2/1062 GR. Div Int Summary No 228 of 27 February reported 90 prisoners from this unit which was part of Fiebig's 84 GID that by then had ceased to be battle-worthy. Darby Hart called them Austrians and happy to surrender.

2 RUR was ordered to secure the Brigade startline and prevent enemy infiltration across it. The startline was a track running across the front and about 200 yards forward of the positions which constituted the Brigade axis of advance. Baudains was sent out to make a reconnaissance of the startline. While moving he came upon the bodies of three men of a British tank unit lying on the track. He crawled forward to them, and looking up for a moment from examining them, he caught a glimpse of a German steel helmet peeping over the top of a bank not 30 feet from him. Throwing himself flat and crawling back to his men, Captain Baudains immediately organised an attack on this position. Covered by 2 in mortar fire, he put in a quick flanking movement and finally charged with three Bren groups firing from the hip, and flushed out two very timid defenders. They proved to be most valuable because on being marched down the track, they indicated with shaking fingers and terrified shouts of "Minen, Minen" that the track was mined. Details of the number and depth of these mines were duly extracted by the Dutch interpreter, Lt Daniëls, and the information passed back'. The RUR attempted to lift the mines during the night in the absence of the Sappers who were busy on the roads.[29]

In regard to Lt Daniëls, each battalion in 3 BID employed a Dutch interpreter from the days of liberating South Brabant. Speaking German and knowing Germans, they were invaluable. They were commissioned with the rank of Lt, paid the going rate and were subject to military discipline. It is not known whether their commission was from the King or the Dutch Queen, or both. Dr. M.J.M. Daniëls from Deurne was attached to 2 Lincolns, and it was his brother who was serving with 2 RUR.

The schu mines were laid on the track 955426, 957425 which the SG would use the next day, after B Squadron I Lothians 'flailed 200 yds East and West of E957424 successfully'.[30] The patrol remained in the area 958424. At 5 pm the Lincolns' O Gp was held and orders issued for the morning attack at 10 am. A and C Coys were told to lead. A Coy's task was to mop up the wood at 968414 and the houses on the west. C Coy was then to pass through with 3 SG in support. Since transport was a problem in the bad conditions, no vehicles were to accompany the battalion except the two Kangaroos and three Weasels of Tac HQ, two Artillery Weasels and the RA troop commander's Sherman tank containing the communications. The RAP was set up in Krüsbeckshof once the Lincolns had captured it.

27 Geldern Stadtsarchiv. *Heimatkalendar 1950.*
28 TNA: WO 171/5279: 2 RUR War Diary.
29 Charles Graves. *Royal Ulster Rifles* (Mexborough: RUR, 1950), p. 154.
30 TNA: WO 171/5318: War Diary of HQ 6 Assault Regiment RE.

The Lincolns kicked off *Heather* as described in Operation Order No 9. They were woken with a substantial hot meal at 3 am on 27 February, and left their concentration area at 4 am for the 3 km march to the SL through the woods. This led them across the rear of Schloss Calbeck but not close enough to see it. The SL was, 'a sunken track screened by bushes from which could be obtained a good view of the objective, a wooded area near a small village.'[31]

Today the startline is a double row of trees overgrown with brush without a track down the middle. It bisects a long open field surrounded by woods. The railway line along their right flank is now the busy Uedemer Strasse. The 'small village' is a farm with barns called Eberskath. The sunken track ran north-east from Schlübeckshof to the woods. The attack was supported by six Churchills (two troops) of RF Sqn on the left 'shooting them in' from the edge of these woods. The other two troops were further into the wood defending the left flank although it had been secured by 11 BAD's capture of Stein two hours earlier.

Rex Fendick was the Canloan (CDN 453) commander of 1 Pl in A Company, 2 Middlesex, which was the Divisional MG Support battalion. His photographs of the events on the first day are unique although of poor quality, and he kept a diary. The following extracts begin at Lubeek in Belgium.

> Saturday, 24 February 1945
> After usual series of cancellations we push off at 1000 hrs – via Diest, Burg Leopold, Eindhoven, Helmond, St Antonis, Boxmeer, Gennep Bridge, Gennep, Goch, to posn. Trip went well but 3 gun carriers got lost in last few miles. 1st Bn [Middlesex, 15 BID] carry on for night, we get a sleep in nice straw and take over in the morning. [Bergmannshof 942459]. Nice day coming up, with bags of planes. Loads of searchlights and moon on Maas. 4000 ft pontoon bridge at Gennep. Quantity of artillery over here is staggering.
>
> Sunday, 25 Feb.
> 3 missing carriers turned up at first light. Took over gun position and moved into house. Pl HQ in good cellar. Mac and I in two-platoon position on call from KOSB and RUR (Indirect). German civilians here – have been kicked out of house – are living in barn next door. Are allowed in 2 hours per day to tend stock. Terrific one opened up at 0345 tonight – never heard anything like it. (Barrage in support of Canadian's attack towards Üdem). Rain most of the night.
>
> Monday 26 Feb.
> More barrage this morning. The 25pr SPs [only armoured divisions had SP 25pdrs, so these would have belonged to 11 BAD] in our back yard shake the place down every time they fire. We will be going on tomorrow. Still wet – the armour moving up have churned the roads up badly. Going into position to do left flank protection for 9 Bde tomorrow morning 0600 hrs. Mac and I did recce this afternoon. Lots of bodies laying around. May have to go forward with 185 Bde later tomorrow. Terrific barrage tonight again. SPs in yard are shaking the house.
>
> Tuesday 27 Feb.
> Reveillez 0400, on carrier 0500. Guns in position 0700, covering road crossing north of ÜDEM. [Probably this is wrong, should have been West of Udem, at 969417.] The first gun position was at about 955425, and the picture on page 170 of my book would have been taken

31 Gates, *History*, p. 251.

Rex Fendick, Canloan 453, outside his dugout with two telephones, whose line snakes away to the right of the picture. (© Reginald Fendick)

The best of the three photograps on pp. 170-71 of Rex Fendick's book, *A Canloan Officer*. It was taken at 958426 on 27 February and showed the carriers of 1 Pln 2 Mx in the wood north of the railway waiting to be called forward to support 9 BIB. (© Reginald Fendick)

> there. The two pictures on page 171 were taken after we left that position, moved out onto the track through the woods and were harboured in an assembly area, waiting for the call for the next move forward. [This would be at about 958426.] Covering left flank of 9 Bde attack. 0800 – report Phase 1 successful – about 30 POWs. That means there is no more [move] for us. Will probably move soon to cover right flank of 185 Bde when they pass through 9 Bde.[32]

As always, the Gunners were well up. Two unpublished accounts by officers of 33 Fld Regt exist. The Regt comprised 680 men and 24 guns and had been twinned with 9 BIB since the beginning of the war. It left Aerschot at 9 am on Saturday, 24 February and arrived in its new position (924448) near Goch at 9 pm. It was deployed and ready by noon on 25 February and shot to register the guns. Jack Brymer's account is given further on in the narrative. A Troop Commander (of 4 guns), Lt. J.S. (Jack) Hunton, recorded:

> 25/26th Feb. I was at the gun end. 300 rounds per gun were dumped on the position in preparation for Operation HEATHER. On the night of the 26 I had to go to an 'O' Gp at the Lincolns HQ and stayed the rest of the time with 'A' Coy. We prepared a walking party for the following morning as we were to be the forward coy. [Sam Larkin's A Coy was the last one on the march to the FUP and followed Pat Smith's B Coy in the attack. It then passed through B Company and led in the occupation of the woods from which KOSB & RUR would attack at 10 am].
>
> 27th Feb. About 0300 hr. we started walking with the leading Coy 'A' arriving at the start point about 0500 hr. L/Bombardier Elliott carried an 18 set [a second man operated it, weight 32 lbs, range R/T 2-5 miles, W/T 4-10 miles, in communication with the battery], Gunner Edwards a 68 set [a longer range version of the 18 set using lower frequencies with range over 5 miles on R/T and over 10 miles for W/T], and Gunner Palmer batteries and rations. After this 4 mile walk, we had to dig in and prepare for the battle beginning at 0700 hr., which was supported by a barrage. Just before we were due to move, the BC contacted me and gave me instructions to travel with the CO, Lt-Col Firbank of the Lincs, as his own set was out of order. By 0800 hr we were on our first objective and by 1200 hr. the Bn had reached the South edge of the wood which was due South of Goch and west of Udem. After the first stage, Bomb. Anderson had a line through and our Weasel and carrier arrived. This was the first time we had used a Weasel and it proved absolutely first class. We went forward in the Weasel and at the railway got heavily shelled. The Weasel broke down and L/Bomb Sheppard took it back. He had done well to get so far, the clutch was not too good. In this operation so far we had taken 150 prisoners. Chips Smith was with us with "A" OP Ivor [Norton] being on leave.[33]

Pat Smith's B Coy led off on the left accompanied by D Coy on the right under Peter Clarke. Following up were A and C Coys, left and right under Sam Larkin and Glyn Gilbert respectively. There was little opposition and 70 prisoners were taken at the cost of 1 officer and 3 other ranks wounded. The prisoners were not Paras but Austrians from 84 GID.

George Wall of D Coy, 2 Lincolns, described the battle and its preliminaries:

32 E-mail from Rex to this author on 7 March 2002, with later additions in round brackets.

33 Personal diary of Lt Jack Hunton.

> We left the area of Louvain or thereabouts in Belgium on the 26th February 1945. I had my 23rd birthday there. We then went on to Goch in Germany. In between Goch and Weeze we had breakfast and moved on. I knew we couldn't be far from the action as you could hear the artillery all night. That took our appetite away. The following morning we made for a wooded area. I knew we were getting close to the action as they told us to be quiet. We were stopped. That meant we had to start digging. As soon as we finished, they said we had to move a few feet and we could see another wood. We were told it was infested with Germans and we were to put in a quick attack. Trembling and scared we did, but found the cupboard bare to our relief. Not quite so – we found a chicken farm with an abundance of eggs [Krüsbeckshof]. We nearly became egg bound. When at the reunion, everybody seems to recollect the egg farm but nothing else. When I ask where it was, all they can tell me is Germany. Even John Gilleard remembers the farm. We stayed there becoming egg bound until 27th Feb.[34]

Lt J.A. Hunt, commanding 17 Pl in D Coy, 2 Lincolns, also described the attack:

> The first attack against the farm Krüsbeckshof again had 17 Pl on the right and comprised a frontal attack through the open ground between the woods rather than through the woods themselves which were ranged for their mortars etc. It was completely successful and a number of prisoners were taken. My own recollection is of a night then spent in the shattered farm buildings in the company of dead dogs, chickens, horses and cows – very unpleasant but we could sleep anywhere in those days.[35]

After taking the objective, which was the start-line for the KOSB and RUR, the Lincolns concentrated around the Krüsbeckshof egg farm with Battalion HQ 300 yards back at 956421. There they remained for the rest of the day and the night in support of KOSB and RUR, coming under command of 8 BIB as the counter-attacks at Yorkshire Bridge mounted and all three of their battalions were engaged. The tenacious stand by 2 E Yorks meant reinforcement by the Lincolns was not needed, and the next day they came under command of 185 BIB to support the capture of Kervenheim since all three of their battalions were then engaged. This constant switching between brigades shows the grip Whistler maintained on the battle and how he fought the three brigades of the division as one unit. An advancing brigade tried to have two battalions up, separated by half a mile, with one battalion behind in support. When all three battalions became engaged, a fourth battalion was switched into support from another brigade.

Following after the Lincolns, the KOSB and RUR moved up to their startline. The CO of the KOSB, Lt-Col R.C. Macdonald, commonly called "Wee Mac", wrote:

> At 7.30 we saw the Lincolns advancing. The barrage made a most heartening and impressive noise. We did not wait long before we were on the move behind the Lincolns, who seemed to be getting on well. As we moved up to cross the stream we saw the first prisoners coming back. There were about sixty of them, formed up in threes, and marching quite smartly to the rear, only looking pretty dazed. The enemy defensive fire had started, but I think the direction of our attack took him by surprise, as it fell mostly on our flanks. The Lincolns' attack was completely successful and enabled the Ulster Rifles and ourselves to form up as planned.[36]

---

34 Letter from George Wall to this author in 1994.
35 Letter from Lt J.A. Hunt to this author in 1983.
36 Scarfe, *Assault Division,* p. 209.

Macdonald failed to mention that it was he who took the bn's first prisoners, and that the battalion had been provided with three Weasels and four Kangaroos to ensure mobility in the mud:

> At 5.30 on a dull morning we moved away from Bockolt (sic) to our assembly area. The news of the armoured attack to the left was excellent, and we were encouraged to hear that the Canadians had taken Udem. As daylight strengthened we negotiated minefields and, on our way to the woods where the Companies formed up, passed large numbers of German prisoners. A certain amount of enemy defensive fire began to land near us and some casualties were caused, but the Germans had not judged our positions correctly and were directing most of their fire into a wood over on our right. The Commanding Officer, much to his embarrassment, when making his reconnaissance for the Kangaroos and other tracked vehicles to reach the assembly area, collected our first two prisoners of the day.[37]

The RUR's Tac HQ left Schloss Calbeck for the FUP at 960418 at 8.30 am, finding the route difficult with trees felled across the tracks. The Germans ringed trees with explosive of the correct charge strength and positioning to fell trees directionally. Wiring the detonators together, rows of trees could be brought down to block the roads, which in those days were usually tree-lined. The FUP was reached at 9.15 am and the barrage began its 100-yd lift every 5 minutes. A slight enemy DF was noticed. At 10 am on schedule, 2 RUR on the left and 1 KOSB on the right crossed the SL at 963416. This was the front edge of the woods between Babbe on the right and the Steinberger Ley on the left, representing the brigade and corps boundaries.

> A barrage of colossal intensity crept forward in front of the advancing troops, and what was left uncompleted was well looked after by the Churchills of the Scots Guards, whose support with Besas and tank guns was so close and effective that the German heads were kept down until the Rifles were right on them. The Germans were completely demoralised and many were captured. Some were youngsters of sixteen who threw off their belts and equipment in disgust when taken; some were old men; and here and there were tough Paratroopers. The advance went forward in an impressive line – A Company, then C Company on the left, D in the centre, and the KOSB on the right. D Company alone claimed eighty prisoners, while in C Company tremendous strides forward were made by Lieutenant Purcell who, at the head of his platoon, captured several posts with great dash and took a large number of prisoners. One batch of them was ignominiously hauled from the cellar of a house [Probably 968414] and two further groups of ten each were taken as the platoon pressed forward to its final objective. The official count of prisoners for this action was 140, but this is only the figure for those who passed back through the battalion's Intelligence Section. Many others in the heat of the battle were passed on to the nearest unit and were put down to ultra-Battalion sources. Altogether, casualties for this operation – most of which were sustained in shelling before the attack began – were two officers and 64 ORs. On the more cheerful side, Lieutenant Purcell was later awarded the MC for his part in this operation.[38]

The KOSB advanced quickly:

> We waited in relative quietness until 10 am, at which hour the guns opened fire and our Companies moved forward, hugging the barrage up to pre-determined report lines, when they

37 Wilson, *A Short History*, p. 43.
38 Graves, *Royal Ulster Rifles*, p. 155.

> sent back word to battalion Headquarters so that control could be maintained. "A" and "D" Companies performed this somewhat tricky, and dangerous operation with complete success, over-running one German position after another before the enemy had recovered from his shock. While these two companies pressed forward through the woods information was received that enemy were holding some farms in the clearing which lay to our left; tanks working forward in this area sent back a call for infantry support and "B" Company was detached for this purpose: energetic and daring leadership by the Platoon Commanders. Aided by a stream of incendiary bullets from the tanks, soon liquidated the paratroopers' resistance in these strongpoints, and more prisoners were sent back. At 11 am the forward Companies reported that the Udem-Weeze road had been successfully cut. This meant that in exactly 50 minutes they had advanced one thousand yards across strongly held enemy territory. Once across the road, there was a ten minutes pause and, when "A" Company moved on again, they raked in a further sixty Germans who were dug in, but too disordered to offer much resistance.[39]

Scarfe identified the platoon that rushed the group of buildings in the clearing capturing the defenders as being led by Lt Simpson and Sgt Jaggers. About the pause, 'a good thing it was, as a German locality about sixty strong were dug in just beyond the main road, and they got the full benefit of the ten minute pause. They were thrown into disorder and the whole lot fell to A Company, who had a fine picnic.'[40]

A Coy RUR reached the wood at 968414 below the hill from Stein and C Coy passed through being the first of the RUR to reach the Üdem-Weeze road at 973408, where there was a house. It was approximately 1.30 pm. A Coy joined them at 973407. A patrol was sent to the bridge at 974409 and found it prepared for demolition with charges laid. The fact it was not blown showed it had lost tactical significance once Üdem was taken. The stream under this bridge marked the inter-corps boundary and the area to its west was being cleared by 11 BAD but against stiffening opposition. C Coy then pushed on across the road through the woods as far as the houses at 976404 which they cleared with prisoners taken. Then they returned and dug in at 973403 taking more prisoners when clearing the house at 974404. B Coy dug in at 974406. By 2 pm all were in position and the CO visited them. A StuG could be seen moving along the road at 975395 in a southeasterly direction towards Kervenheim. Rarely seen when changing its ambush position, this one was on the western side of the Mühlen Fleuth between Wettermannshof and Schneidershof and almost certainly had just ambushed Runcie's troop and stopped the KOSBs' attempt to seize a bridgehead at Wettermannshof, as described below. Tac HQ moved to the house at 973408. At this point shelling began and D Coy was counter-attacked, but the attack dissolved under British DF. For the rest of the afternoon the Germans shelled the dug-in RUR. They had a quiet night and contemplated with satisfaction their haul of 134 POWs, including 2 officers.

3 SG managed to keep up with the infantry in spite of the difficult conditions. Having seen the Lincolns to their objective, RF with great determination managed to get across the stream by the narrow causeway and bridge that Pember had reconnoitered the previous night (see Map 13). Crossing the railway they arrived in time to form up for the second phase with the RUR and KOSB. Right Flank silenced the main opposition coming from the houses on their side of the brigade boundary southwest of Sophienhof. About 300 POWs with officers were captured, and many others killed.

With all the final objectives taken by 1.30 pm, Brigadier Douglas Renny of 9 BIB decided to exploit forward. Instead he overextended himself and earned the uncharacteristic rebuke of

39 Wilson, *A Short History*, p. 43.
40 Scarfe, *Assault Division*, p. 209.

the CO of 3 SG in the war diary. Dunbar was probably only reflecting the general bad odour in which Renny was then held, as described in the chapter on 3 BID. In a proper attempt to maintain momentum and reinforce success, Renny ordered the bridge at Aengen Endtschenhof 973397 seized by *coup de main*. It was about the same time that the next bridge downstream at Schaddenhof was being seized by 2 E Yorks. For Renny this was the only water obstacle remaining before his ultimate objective of Winnekendonk, and its possession offered the chance of outflanking Kervenheim. The Germans were, however, wide-awake and prepared, and in fact had blown the bridge four and a half hours earlier at 11 am, according to Pastor Coenders' report in the next chapter. Had Renny known of the bridge's destruction, he might not have tried to rush its remains.

Renny ordered a company of 1 KOSB, his old regiment, to seize the bridge with the support of two troops of RF. The attempt was ambushed by StuGs. Even though this was only the first day of battle, a shortage of smoke shells soon developed on the British side. The absence of smoke at Kervenheim, where it was ordered, and at Winnekendonk, suggests the entire stock of smoke shells was now fired and could not be replenished.

> The next task to be attempted was to secure a bridgehead across a stream which lay some three hundred yards further on. This involved crossing a stretch of open country with both flanks completely exposed, and in face of Spandau fire from a group of farms across the stream. Ammunition shortage affected the quantity of smoke, which we required to cover the flanks, but at 3.30 pm "C" Company made the attack, with eight tanks [actually 7 with the FOO tank] in support.
>
> Success eluded us at this stage. The tanks quickly bogged in the deep mud, and four of them halted before they even brought their guns to bear. The remainder gave such covering fire as they could, but the steady stream of Spandau fire pinned the infantry down about half way to the objective. At this juncture the smoke ran out and an enemy gun situated on the left British right flank, promptly knocked out three of our tanks, one after the other – from the German point of view a first class performance. It was not possible to continue the attack under these conditions with any prospect of success and, under cover of artillery fire, the Company withdrew to its original position. Even so, the day had been highly successful, and we were well in advance of the unit on our right; our own casualties were twenty eight but we had taken over one hundred and forty prisoners.[41]

Forbes describes the debacle from the point of view of the armour:

> It was now decided that one Company of the KOSBs would push half a mile further south to a point near Wettermannshof and seize a bridgehead over the Muhlen Fleuth. A quick fire-plan was arranged – a concentration of two batteries lasting for ten minutes, but owing to the haste of planning, nearly all the shells fell short, giving trouble to the infantry as they formed up. After this debacle, the tanks and the Infantry left the southern fringes of the wood, only to be met by heavy close-range fire from Spandaus and SP guns situated near Wettermannshof. Two tanks were immediately knocked out, three others became bogged in full view of the enemy and the Infantry suffered heavy casualties. The gunners now redeemed themselves handsomely by laying on an extremely effective smoke screen. This was arranged by the FOO who was forced to bale out of his own tank but immediately jumped into another as it withdrew and, fully exposed to enemy fire, directed the guns.[42]

41 Wilson, *A Short History*, p. 44.
42 Patrick Forbes. *6th Guards Tank Brigade* (London: Sampson Low, Marston, 1947), p. 109.

It is likely that the troop of the StuG ace, Lt. Heinz Deutsch destroyed these tanks. He was operating in support of 8FJD at the time, commanding a platoon of three StuGs in 3 Troop under Krall in Fallschirm-Sturmgeschütz-Brigade 12, nicknamed the Green Devils (GrünTeufel) under Hauptmann Gersteuer.[43] Deutsch was just getting into his stride. His first kill was at St Lô on 13 July 1944 supporting 3FJD, and he was lucky to escape the Falaise Pocket. By 25 February he had destroyed 13 tanks, and his final score of 260 made him top scorer in the west on either side. He was awarded the German Cross in Gold on 5 March and on 15 April became one of only 5,070 bearers of the Ritterkreuz. On 25 February he moved from Weeze to Üdem to counterattack the Canadians at Keppeln and Totenhügel to the east of 3 BID. There he destroyed two Shermans and a Cromwell, conclusively identifying 11 BAD since only they operated Cromwells. Over the next few days, Deutsch stated[44] that he was operating out of Kevelaer. Lothar Hinz of IFJR.22, which had the task of defending the area between Weeze and Kervenheim that included Yorkshire Bridge, met Deutsch in Weeze. Hinz wrote[45] that sometime on 27 February, he and another were assigned to protect Deutsch's troop hidden between the houses on Grafschen Weg in Weeze, facing west. This could have been after Deutsch returned from stopping the advance by shooting up Runcie's troop and the KOSB. Hinz added that during the next morning, 28 February, Deutsch destroyed one of two enemy tanks feeling their way forward towards Weeze from the direction of Kendel-Helsum to the west of Weeze. The range was 800 metres.

The most likely scenario is as follows: the Schwerpunkt of 3 BID was identified, which Schlemm claimed was always easy to do, by mid-morning on 27 February. StuGs were then sent to ambush the leading tanks. 3 BID was clearly heading for Kervenheim and had to drive across the front of Wettermannshof. This did not happen until 3.30 pm, giving Deutsch plenty of time to get into position. Once the engagement was over and their positions compromised, the StuGs withdrew to escape retribution from artillery and Typhoons, and we have seen that the RUR observed one doing so.

Deutsch said that on 1 March he destroyed two Churchills at Kloppermannshof and that both the other StuGs in his troop scored. This identified 3 BID, since neither 8 BAB supporting 53 BID nor 11 BAD or Canadian units operated this equipment. The dates are a problem but, because their war diaries were destroyed, German Fallschirmjäger veterans had no records to consult when writing their memoirs. February with its 28 days was confusing so mistakes were perhaps inevitable. Some of the worst offenders for mis-dating material, by the way, were British war photographers. One German veteran in discussion with this author said all dates should be treated as approximate. As for Kloppermannshof, enquiries over 30 years have failed to identify any farm with that name. However, since the StuGs were committed against the *Schwerpunkten* of 3 and 53 BIDs, only a relatively small number of farms could have been involved. If Kloppermannshof is ruled out, then Wettermannshof is a likely candidate for its replacement, especially as it sounds somewhat similar and has the same number of syllables. Alternatively, the date could be correct and Deutsch was referring to Müsershof or Murmannshof outside Kervenheim about 1 km to the south.

Lt. Bob Runcie commanded the leading troop. He told his official biographer what happened across the Üdem-Weeze road although also mistaking the day.

43 G. Tornau & F. Kurowski. *Sturmartillerie. Fels in der Brandung* (Hamburg: Maximilian-Verlag, 1965), p. 260.
44 Karl Alman. *Sprung in Die Hölle* (Rastatt: Erich Pabel, 1964), p. 235.
45 L Hinz. *Unser Einsatz am Niederrhein* (Der deutsche Fallschirmjäger, Vol. 3, 1973).

> The previous day [actually three days earlier], again we'd gone a bit too far ahead, and were in a wood, and suddenly a whole lot of soldiers came walking either side of my tanks. I thought they were the infantry we were supposed to be supporting. In fact they were Germans whom we'd disturbed, who'd been sleeping there. Anyway they were rounded up and captured. That was one of the times when I felt, I don't think I'm going to get out of this. I think I'm actually going to die. [The wood was the one attacked by the KOSB and RUR to the east of Babbe. It is unlikely the Germans were caught asleep. More likely they were POWs ordered back or they would have killed Runcie. It should be noted Runcie was behind the troops he was supporting].
>
> One of my tanks had been hit then, and it was on fire. And they all came tumbling out, and I said, 'Where's Philip?' And he was stuck – the turret was stuck over the co-driver's lid – and the tank was on fire. It wasn't blazing; it was just smoking. Of course something might have exploded, but you don't think about that sort of thing.
>
> I had to get in first, you see, and then turn the thing round, so that it moved the turret. But he was confused and we still needed to drag him out of the tank and bring him back to us.
>
> And this was still while they were under fire?
>
> 'Well the tank had been knocked out – we'd gone out from the wood – we'd emerged from it – you can see this isn't a well-honed story. We were not under infantry fire, small arms fire, but we were under long-distance anti-tank fire.[46]

Carpenter had asked him if they were still under fire because a previous biographer, Margaret Duggan had so described him; 'With shells falling all around, he jumped from his own tank and ran to turn the turret and drag the co-driver out.'[47] Runcie was the sole source of both accounts separated by 13 years, and yet the later one given to Carpenter is more precise, showing that there was nothing wrong with Runcie's memory.

The distance between the StuGs and Runcie's Churchills was about 500 yards. This was the usual range at which armour engaged in the Second World War. Range on StuGs was calculated with scissors-type optical range-finders but by eye on Churchills. The troop under Deutsch, if it was he, was safe behind the stream after the bridge was blown, and hidden alongside Wettermannshof. The troop commander would have measured the exact range of each feature in advance with his range finder. So when Runcie's troop cleared the trees with the KOSB, where today there is a lake and gravel extraction and the vista is cut by the high embankment of the motorway, the first shots would have been aimed at and struck the 4 inch front armour of the Churchills. If Runcie's Philip was in a Churchill VII, and that is unknown but unlikely, its side armour was 4 inches thick but its frontal armour was 6 inch. The StuG's 75 mm K40 L48 with APCBC PzGr 39 could penetrate 4 inches of sloped but 5½ inches of vertical armour at 500 yards. So at least 18 lbs of red-hot steel, comprising the 12 lb projectile and a 6 lb plug of the Churchill's own armour, would have been driven inside the tank. The shock failed to set off the ammunition, whose explosion could have blown off the turret and killed the entire crew, as happened three days later at Winnekendonk in front of Runcie. But it started a fire forcing evacuation of the tank, and jammed the turret over the driver's hatch.

The Churchill's 75 mm MkV gun firing APCPC could penetrate the StuGs 3 inch of angled armour at ranges of up to 2,000 yards, and 4 inches at 500 yards. Each troop had one Churchill with a 6pdr firing sabot ammunition (APDS), which could do 30% better even than this. It is doubtful whether any Churchill fired at the StuGs on 27 February, and possibly never identified their camouflaged positions before the StuGs withdrew.

---

46 Humphrey Carpenter. *Robert Runcie* (London: Hodder & Stoughton, 1996), p. 80.
47 Margaret Duggan. *Runcie; The Making of an Archbishop* (London: Hodder & Stoughton, 1983), p. 79

The KOSB suffered 28 casualties on 27 February, most of them in this final operation. Dunbar, the SG's CO, commented in the war diary with acerbity: 'A perfect lesson of the folly of attempting too much with too little and without thought to the artillery support.'[48]

The SG's biographer was more philosophical and rebuked Dunbar, although neither suspected the opposition might have come from such an able practitioner as Heinz Deutsch:

> It had been an action which might well have succeeded but, as it turned out, too much had been attempted with too little. War is full of such actions, which are hailed as strokes of genius when they are brought off, and are too harshly criticised when they fail.[49]

Renny, however, told the KOSB that, 'he was well pleased with what the Battalion had done and would have looked upon the capture of the bridgehead as a bonus had we taken it.'[50]

The task of occupying Endtschenhof so that a Churchill bridge-layer could bridge the stream was accomplished the next day by the Warwicks, and is covered in the next chapter. Here we need to reflect on the fact that the advance was held up for two days by a German weapon that in 1945 was at least three years old and in the case of the 88 mm ten years old. All Allied tank crews were anxious about, and some terrified of, debouching from cover or rounding a corner. What they needed were tanks with frontal immunity to the common 75 mm and 88 mm anti-tank guns, which is a major conclusion of this book.

A story is told which could only refer to this episode. When 9 BIB tried, as we have seen, to advance on Kervenheim across the Üdem-Weeze road, they were met with strong resistance. The radio and observation post on top of the church steeple in Kervenheim, whose call sign was 'Caesar', made out the armoured advance 3 km away and warned a battery of mortars located near the rectory. However the signaller was not at his post but flirting with a girl. Loud shouting from the top of the steeple recalled the defaulter and the DF was successfully laid on.[51]

During the afternoon 3 SG's S Squadron was alerted and given notice to move with the object of going through to Kervenheim with the Lincolns, but after the failure of the KOSB's attack this plan was abandoned. S Sqn harboured at 954414. RF were released at 6.45 pm and harboured at 964408. The RUR and KOSB dug themselves in forward of the Udem-Weeze road, and the Lincolns stayed around Krüsbeckshof in support of 8 BIB.

On the right of 3 BID, 8 BIB had also began their operations at first light. The Churchills of 4 GG harboured overnight at Schloss Calbeck, but unable to do a full recce they planned their support from the map. At 7 am, 2 Sqn accompanied 1 Suffolks over the small bridge across the stream at Saarbrockshof, 949412 which had been seized by 2 E Yorks. The leading troop was then held up by the trunks of trees felled by the Germans across the track. When these were moved to one side, two troops advanced. Lt Gray's troop with 18 Pl of D Coy under Sgt Jack Offord, who had taken command when the Pl Cdr and Pl Sgt were wounded, attacked Babbe. Lt Gray's tank was hit by a Panzerfaust and Gray wounded, but despite a minefield and accurate LMG and rifle fire, Lance Sgt J. Offord led a charge that killed several Germans and took 25 men prisoner, earning an MM.[52] The time is not given, but was probably around 8.30 am because the S. Lancashires record that the Suffolks had gained all their objectives by 9 am. This was when

48 TNA. WO 171/1258: 3 Scots Guards War Diary.
49 David Erskine. *The Scots Guards* (London: William Clowes, 1956), p. 408.
50 From an article titled *Operation Heather* in an unknown magazine sent by George Wall.
51 Heinz Bosch. *Der Zweite Weltkrieg Zwischen Maas und Rhein* (Geldern: Verlag des Historischen Vereins, 1977), p. 222.
52 W.N. Nicholson. *The Suffolk Regiment* (Ipswich: East Anglian Magazine, 1948), p. 141.

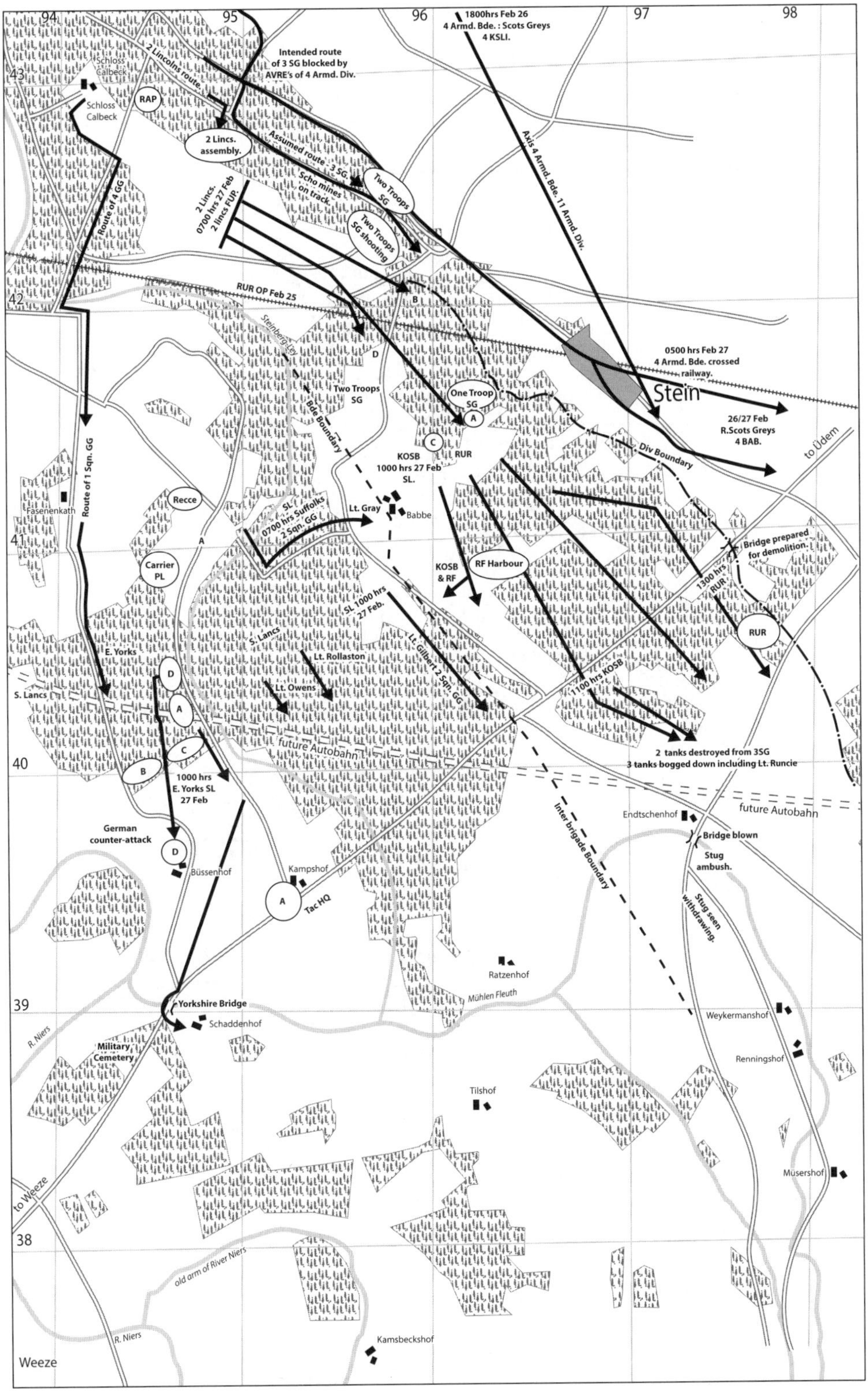

Map 14 The battle on 27 February 1945.

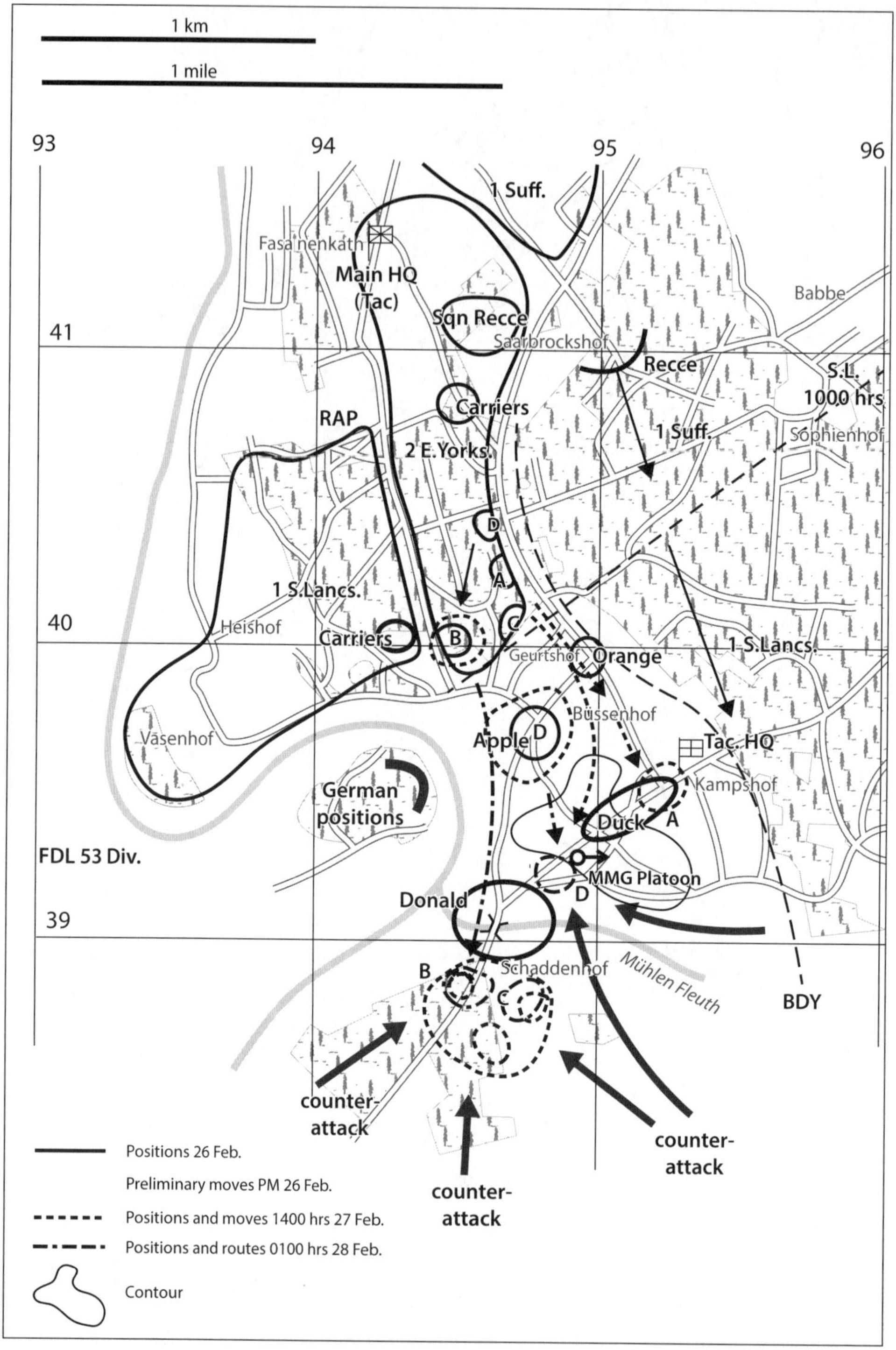

Map 15 The battle of Yorkshire Bridge. (Copied from TNA WO/171 1258)

Advance towards Kervenheim. Prisoners are marched out of the woods. The prisoners were from IIIFJR7, and the troops were 1 Suffolks. They are entering Hovesaat, aka the *Forsthaus*, on 27 February 1945. (© Crown Copyright IWM, B14928 by Sgt Carpenter)

The inside of the same Hovesaat gateway in 2014.

© Crown Copyright IWM, B14929 by Sgt Carpenter. These Parachute Regt prisoners are not to be trusted and are made to face the wall with hands held high.

The same wall at the end of the garden in Hovesaat in 2014.

Veterans of IFJR7 who fought in and around Hovesaat on 25 February, paying their respects to their dead colleagues at the Weeze War Cemetery in 2000. (L.-r.) Erwin Becke, wounded in the eye, married Patricia and took British citizenship; Hubert Elkendorf, left behind in Hovesaat with a bad back wound; Werner Bős, badly wounded in the hip and hospitalized in Troon; Claus Műller, unwounded; Lt Otto Einert, light head wound and only non-POW; Erich Freund, small shrapnel wounds, married Ireene and took British citizenship; Clei Kiehsen, wounded in Brest and evacuated, so did not fight in Hovesaat; Waldemar Bőhmer, wounded and awarded the Iron Cross in Sonsbeck.

FJR7 when arriving from the Netherlands would have looked like these paratroops near Arnhem in 1944. (Bundesarchiv Bild *101I-590-23333-7A*)

1 Suffolks dig in for the night of 26 February facing enemy occupied Schrőershof, 948418. The officer giving the finger in the Canadian manner and amusing his sergeant is probably CDN438 Lt John S Buchanan MM, earned at Dieppe. (IWM B14930 by Sgt Carpenter)

Swazi Waller, CO 1 S Lancs was renowned for a 'complete disregard for enemy fire.' (© Digby Waller)

Capt Eddie Jones, IO 1 S Lancs, was author of an unpublished memoir. (© Eddie Jones)

Sophienhof was taken by Sgt Gilbert's troop of 2 Sqn 4 GG, who then continued on and reached the main road at 11 am and reported a StuG.[53]

> MM Lance Sergeant 5836585 Jack OFFORD 1 Suffolk
> This NCO landed with the Battalion on D Day and has twice been wounded.
>
> During the attack on BABBE Wood in Germany on 27 Feb 45 both the Platoon Comd and Platoon Sjt of 18 Platoon 'D' Company, became casualties. Without hesitation Lance Serjeant Offord took command of 18 Platoon and part of another platoon and put in an attack on a group of houses held by the enemy.
>
> An anti-personnel minefield surrounded the buildings and heavy and accurate MG and rifle fire was directed from them onto 18 Platoon. With great determination, dash and personal courage, Lance Serjeant Offord charged the objective, and, after killing several of the enemy, captured the buildings with twenty five prisoners.
>
> He was wounded by a mine but returned to the battalion a few weeks later.
>
> Thoughout the time he was in North West Europe Lance Serjeant Offord always volunteered for difficult and dangerous patrols, whether of a reconnaissance or fighting nature, and on many occasions gained most valuable information about the enemy. He personally accounted for several enemy on one particular fighting patrol.
>
> The men of 'D' Company have the greatest admiration for the fine leadership, quite dauntless courage and cheerful bearing which this NCO displays on the field of battle.[54] [The citation was not submitted by Goodwin but by his replacement, and not until 5 July 1945. Goulburn and Whistler signed and someone for 1 Corps District on 31 July, being gazetted on 24 January 1946. It was signed neither by Montgomery nor Dempsey, the Army commander.]

1 South Lancashires under Swazi Waller spent the night of 24 February in Tilburg and relieved 6 KOSB at 11.0 pm the next day. Eddie Jones, the battalion IO was at his post at Battalion HQ and watched the leading companies approaching the wood under shellfire.

> Meanwhile the CO and myself had moved forward with his carrier to a position a few yards short of the woods we were to clear, having pulled off the track a few yards to the right, in order to establish Bn. HQ. I could see the track disappearing into the wood, where tree-trunks laid as a corduroy road crossed a marshy area. It was an extremely dangerous position for us, and typical of the CO that he should want to be well forward with his leading troops and in the thick of things. We watched the companies coming up along the track towards us and pass us before entering the wood and I waved to Len Ringham, a younger contemporary of mine at school, who had joined us as a Lieutenant a short while before. Sure enough, before long the enemy artillery, well aware of what was afoot, began firing on the approaches to the wood. I leant with my back against the carrier, looking away from the enemy towards the troops of the Bn advancing, and watched the shells going overhead, rather like following the flight of a golf-ball from a position directly behind the hitter. They were exploding on the track but fortunately beyond our troops. The enemy gradually shortened the range, however, were soon level with us and began dropping them very accurately on the corduroy road across the marshy section. It was no surprise, therefore, when a stray private from another unit, withdrawing from the wood, remarked to the CO as he passed; 'There's one of your officers lying dead on the track just inside the wood'. As we moved forward a few minutes later we found

53 Forbes, *6th Guards,* p. 110.
54 TNA: WO 373/56: L/Sgt Offord's citation.

> it was Maj. Carse. I had last met him in Scotland where he commanded the Divisional Battle School, and he had recently been posted to us and assumed command of C Coy.[55]

No 3 Sqn of the GGs crossed the startline with the South Lancashires.

> At 1025 hours C and B Companies of 1 South Lancs passed through the Suffolks with two troops of the Grenadier guards in support. Felled trees lay across the tracks through the woods and the going was slow, but both companies reached the midway line of the woods before they met serious opposition, but here they were held up by dug-in machine-gun positions and snipers and the supporting tanks were pushed out to bypass the wood, but as soon as they reached the main road beyond they were picked off by bazookas and were unable to give further immediate assistance.
>
> D Company were now thrown into the fight, being ordered to push forward between the two leading companies, and A Company was ordered to work round the right flank. The companies fought their way slowly forward and the leading platoon of A Company succeeded in reaching the main road but were held up again by snipers established across the main road and machine-guns which took them in enfilade. The enemy machine-guns and snipers were skilfully placed and determinedly handled; all attempts to force a way through the woods and on to the line of the main road failed, and in the afternoon the companies consolidated the positions they had won, varying from between 300 and 400 yards short of their objective.
>
> The day's fighting had been costly, especially in officer casualties and the count at the end of the day was as follows: Killed – 5 officers and 25 other ranks. Wounded – 2 officers and 40 other ranks. Missing – 4 other ranks.
>
> The officers who were killed were Major E.A. Carse, MBE, who had only recently joined the battalion and was commanding C Company; Major P. Watson, who had been commanding A Company since the end of June, 1944; Capt F.W. Carmichael; Lt J. Slack; and Lt H.E. Helm. Lts P.F. Owens and J. Addison were wounded. During the day the battalion captured 32 prisoners and on the 28th 6 deserters gave themselves up to B Company.
>
> The enemy had concentrated his opposition against the 1st Battalion attack in the centre, and the troops on either flank had encountered much less stubborn resistance and had been able to reach the line of the Udem-Weeze road and exploit beyond it, and on the afternoon of the 28th the battalion was moved to a concentration area north of the railway, where it spent the night.[56]

The tanks found the going impossible through the thick and swampy woods with tracks leading to impassable bogs. Lt Rolleston's troop led on the right with Lt Owen's troop on the left. Rolleston's tank went up on a mine and he took over his troop corporal's tank. His driver, Guardsman McCulloch was throwing an empty Besa ammunition box out of the hatch when a panzerfaust hit the turret and badly lacerated his hand. He still managed to reverse. Owen lost contact with C Coy and after waiting some time for them, was told to press on to the road where his infantry would be waiting for him.

> This turned out to be an optimistic prediction because as he emerged into a clearing just in front of the road, paratroopers from 7 Para Division [7 Para Regiment] swarmed around his tanks and knocked all three of them with bazookas. Gdns Rule was killed, L/Cpl Yerbury,

55 From an unpublished memoir by Lt-Col Eddie. Jones.

56 BR Mullaly. *The South Lancashire Regiment* (Bristol: White Swan Press, 1952), p. 431.

> Gdsn Howells, Sgt Hanks and Lt Owen were all seriously wounded. The troop was withdrawn by Sgt Hanks (who was subsequently awarded the MM) and a new plan drawn up. It had to be cancelled, however, as the Infantry had suffered so many casualties that they could not mount another attack.[57]

This left an open left flank for Renison of the E Yorks to worry about as he seized Yorkshire Bridge and fought for his survival.

The attempt by tanks and infantry to reach the objective independently resulted in heavy losses to both. Eddie Jones explained:

> I distinctly remember that at the 'O' Group, the Guards officer in charge of the tanks said they were quite prepared to press forward and sit on the objective, provided the infantry arrived quickly, so possibly that was his intention from the start. Unfortunately, as the snipers quickly killed 3 of the 4 Coy commanders (and also accounted for 2 subalterns killed and 2 wounded) the attack lost both leadership and impetus, and slowed down. Thus the tanks and the infantry became separated.[58]

According to the Buffs, 4 GG had asked for Crocodiles to accompany them into the woods, and the Buffs had refused with serious repercussions later in Kervenheim.

Lt-Col J.D.W. (Bill) Renison was CO of 2 E Yorks in 8 BIB. He told this author that Bolo Whistler always referred to him as 'that bloody Scotsman', although he sounded English and came from Liverpool, having served in the Liverpool Scottish TA. He was a rarity, being a Territorial in command of a regular battalion, which made the brass suspicious of him according to two Canloan officers, 192 and 267, Lt Leonard (Robbie) Robertson, MC and Capt Jim Fetterley, MC. They both served with Bill and described him as a methodical man, unorthodox, fair with everybody and very sincere. 'We loved him. In fact Maj. Baker said several times that in Renison we've got the best and for Maj. Baker to say that!' Renison kept a daily diary and wrote it all out in longhand in 1946, illustrating it with his maps and photographs, when he returned home to the Wirral. Bill lent it to this author with permission to publish, and it is quoted extensively in this chapter. It is now lodged in the IWM as Document No. 11327.

In 1946 as Renison wrote up his diary, the Gunner, Norman Scarfe, was completing the official history of 3 BID, *Assault Division*. In it Scarfe called the action at Yorkshire Bridge, which he had supported from a cellar in Goch, an epic. Private Lionel Roebuck was in 13 Platoon, C Coy of 2 E Yorks and was severely wounded at the bridge, almost certainly by one of Scarfe's shells. He typed his experiences in 1985 at the same time as his company commander, Reg Rutherford, with Lt Applebee and the FOO John Ford were being filmed for a projected War Office training film. In addition there are two memoirs published in the 1952 *Heimatkalendar* written by German tenant farmers: Theodor Verheyen of Büssenhof and Anton Mülders of Steinhövelskath. Altogether these eight sources present a picture of the same battle from different points of view.

We pick up Renison's story at 'sparrow-fart' on 24 February, as he travelled in his Jeep from Holland into Germany. This author's comments as always are in square brackets.

> We were a little late in starting owing to the Brigadier [Eddie Goulburn] being held up by a level crossing and, in view of the number of vehicles, we travelled more or less independently. The route was via Tilburg and 's-Hertogenbosch crossing the Maas by the pontoon bridge at

57 Forbes, *6th Guards,* p. 113.
58 Letter to this author from Lt-Col E. Jones of 17 November 1999.

Officers of 2 E Yorks. (L.-r.) Maj Reg Rutherford, Lt Col Bill Renison, Capt Bone, Maj Baker, Clift and Simpson. (© Andrew Renison)

Maj Reg Rutherford receiving the MC at Gimers Monastery on 11 December 1944. (© Crown Copyright IWM, B12764 by Sgt Morris)

Mook. Here we lost everyone else and having failed to memorise the route correctly went by the most obvious road to Gennep and thence straight through the middle of the Reichswald on our way to Bedburg south-east of Cleve, where we had been told we would find 15 Div. HQ. This proved to be totally out of date, but we luckily saw some 15 Div. signs pointing towards Goch and after a slow crawl in endless traffic from Cleve onwards we reached Div. HQ just after the scheduled time of 0930 hr. to find we were the only people who had made the grade. The correct route should have been north from Mook via Groesbeek and into Cleve from the west and this everyone else had taken only to find a one-way road about the whole way with tanks proceeding along it at one mile per hour nose to tail [no doubt GAD]. The result was that the Brigadier, after an abortive call at Bedburg, didn't arrive until about 1330 hr. with the remainder of the Brigade group trickling in about the same time. We filled in the time with breakfast from our own resources and any other meals we could scrounge on the spot, and with getting all the information we could as to the local situation. I found out [from 3 BID Intelligence Summary] that the line at this time was roughly just east of the Goch/Calcar road with a salient pushed out by 46 Bde towards Weeze on the east bank of the River Niers, which was the inter-Div. boundary on the right with 53 Div., who were just south of Goch with their next objective Weeze. We were to relieve 15 Div. on the night of the 25/26th and I gathered from our own GII that 8 Bde were to relieve 46 Bde with 9 Bde on the left and 185 Bde in reserve. It wasn't quite so simple as that as 15 Div. had got a little mixed up, but that was the general idea. Half way through the morning in despair of seeing any of 8 Bde again, I sent off George Kingcome to look for the Brigadier, but he returned without any success. I was able to have a word with General 'Tiny' Barber, a Cameron Highlander, who had been in the Liverpool Scottish at the beginning of the last war and knew my father. The other profitable visit was to the Intelligence office, where we managed to scrounge some maps of the area. 15 Div. were being withdrawn from the battle altogether and going back to our old area around Louvain. The Boche at present were showing no sign of going back behind the Rhine and our policy was obviously to hit hard and go on hitting; Guards Armd Div. were coming up into the battle as well as 3 Div., hence the block on the roads. The ground off the roads was still pretty sticky for armour and the Canadians away on the left flank advancing along the south bank of the Rhine had actually been fighting from island to island in Buffaloes.

The late arrival of the Brigadier spoilt all our recce plans and it was quite obvious that the Bn Cmdrs were going to be very lucky if they saw anything in daylight and it was quite useless the coy cmds arriving before the morning. The Brigadier therefore sent a liaison officer to tell the recce parties to come up as far as Gennep that night and I sent a message to Banger [Maj 'Banger' King, MC 2ic of 2 E Yorks] giving him the rough form and telling the O gp to meet me at 46 Bde HQ on the morning of the 25th.

After getting preliminary orders at Div., we went on to 46 Bde, which was situated at Dormannshof on the Goch/Calcar road about a mile outside Goch (936446) and in The Bight. I was pleased to find Jimmie Bannatyne there as Bde major and arranged for George and me to spend the night there, which saved a lot of bother. We were to take over from a Bn of the Royal Scots – the Bde had all three bns up, the South Lancs on the right with their flank resting on the River Niers, ourselves in the centre with our left refused back along the line of a small stream and the Suffolks continuing the line to the north-east. In front of the South Lancs and ourselves the ground was open to the Udem-Weeze road, but on our left there were thick woods, which continued across the front of the Suffolks. The Boche were in the woods and in the various farms on our front. The Royal Scots HQ was down a long and very indifferent track, cutting through the grounds of the Schloss Calbeck towards Weeze, in the cellar of a very ruined house called Fasanenkath next door to the HQ of the right hand Bn, who had collared by far and away the better of the two available buildings. It was almost

> dark by the time I got down there and it was obviously farcical to attempt any ground recce so I had to content myself with getting the layout from a map. I had a squadron of the Recce Regt dismounted under command as the area I was taking over was rather bigger than that of the Royal Scots; in fact two of our bdes were taking over an area that had been held by all three bdes of 15 Div. 46 Bde had had a stiff fight through the Calbeck woods two days previously and, as they had been in action since the opening days of 'Veritable', their strength was very much lower than ours; they offered however to dig additional slit trenches before our arrival. This was very necessary as the shelling on the forward edges of the woods was heavy and persistent and it had been found useless to attempt to keep open a line of communication as it was repeatedly cut. Movement down to the forward coys was entirely under cover but the axis track was always liable to shelling and any noisy vehicle movement especially of trucks was a sure signal for a stonk to come. The Royal Scots had been bothered particularly by a troop [of M10s] of a Corps SP Antitank Regt who came forward at first light but retired as it got dark to the accompaniment of the Boche artillery. First impressions were certainly not very favourable, but the expectation of a 53 Div. advance on the west bank of the Niers was likely to improve matters a lot.[59]

An anonymous soldier in IFJR7, who was possibly Erich Freund, published his memoirs in the *1950 Heimatkalendar.* He described the battles around Fasanenkath. On 19 February the British broke through from Buchholt and reached the railway line defended by 1051/2 and 1061/2 Regiments of 84 GID. Schloss Calbeck fell. The defenders' command post was established in Gutes Hovesaat and their Bn Tac HQ in Fasanenkath. Hovesaat, which Freund called *Forsthaus*, was attacked across the railway line and on 20 February the British reinforced their positions. On 21 February at 4.07 pm, FJR7 counterattacked but was repulsed with heavy losses. The British attacked Hovesaat all day with intense shelling. Fasanenkath was destroyed with Tac HQ in it. On 23 February a counter-attack by Panzer Lehr along the railway was ordered. Meanwhile the defenders were pushed back and dug defences on the edge of the wood 700 m behind Fasanenkath. On 22 February, FJR7/I fell back further to Geurtshof and Büssenhof and a mixed group including SP crews, who had been forced by lack of petrol to destroy their own StuGs, were attacked by Scottish infantry and tanks. The enemy's attack was repulsed. Panzer Lehr's attack on 23 February never materialised. On 24 February they were ordered to the northeast to attack Rosenhof but the StuG support failed to get across the railway. 26 February should have been a day of rest but the Canadians attacked Üdem and the Germans were pushed back. The anonymous author of the memoirs was captured on 27 February near Lindenhof east of Üdem. Fasanenkath was never rebuilt, and its ruins can be found to this day (in 1994) among the trees.

Bill Renison continued:

> I got back to 46 Bde HQ in time to see the Bde Cmd and gave him my ideas. I was very well entertained by my Scottish hosts and their Brigadier was perfectly charming: he had himself commanded one of the Regular Bns of the Camerons. James kept me well plied with whisky and bedded me down on a camp bed in his own room with a most glorious fug. George [Kingcome] was also well looked after and Rice [Renison's batman] got himself fixed up in the guard room. It was my first night on German soil and I had been surprised to see the people on the farm [Dormannshof] going about their ordinary farmyard tasks in the middle of the Bde HQ vehicles: it was noticeable however that they were all old people or quite young children [meaning that the foreign forced labour had left].

59 Bill Renison's diary.

> The recce parties arrived quite early and after I had given my orders and they had had their breakfasts they were able to get moving with plenty of time to spare. The relief was to take place that night just after last light and the Bn column was expected to arrive about midday after having staged the night in Tilburg. They were coming by the much more direct route from Gennep via Goch. The whole column was to pull off the road into some fields just beside Bde HQ, [Schloss Calbeck] feed there and, after briefing, move straight forward to the relief, whilst the vehicles were taken off to an echelon area a little further back. The recce squadron were parking their vehicles just beside us and the remainder of the Bde were quite close by. As we were well within gun range, it seemed a terrific concentration of men and vehicles if anything were to go wrong.[60]

Lionel Roebuck, a private soldier in 2 E Yorks, was in Nieuwrhode about to go on leave when the Division was ordered forward:

Elsie and Lionel Roebuck, who was severely wounded at Yorkshire Bridge, in 1997.

> We were loaded on the TCVs [Bedford QLT 3-tonners with bench seats sent from XXX Corps] ready in battle gear, for the slow move along the worn roads to reach Tilburg in the late afternoon. There we had a meal, were given a blanket and then billeted on a local family for the night. Tired out after the long, slow drag in the troop transport, there didn't seem much hope for my leave…Wherever we stopped, a friendly liaison was soon made between civilians and the troops. Even language differences were no barrier as the exchange of items was always a good way to get acquainted. A two shilling piece would go a long way when, with a bite, the recipient pronounced it 'Ah, Silder'. Tilburg was no exception as in every house the weary soldiers were made welcome. We were invited into the towns-peoples' homes and given drinks; in return, we gave them cigarettes, sweets and chocolate.
>
> At first light, we moved off again in convoy; the roads were getting worse and we slowed as we reached the wide, swollen river Maas. The vehicles rattled across the planks over the long, low floating bridge at Gennep before the last stretch to Goch. On reaching the first German town of 'no more' (even in the dusk the scenes of utter destruction were shattering, with many bulldozers working to make a road through the debris and to fill in the huge craters) there were few civilians, as the convoy skirted round the north of the town. Even so, we were close enough to see that the central built-up area, of blocked up streets and wrecked buildings, consisted of just huge piles of rubble.

60 Bill Renison's diary.

> We slowly picked our way through the shattered remains of Goch and along the minor roads, then field tracks, as the rumble of battle was heard in the distance. By then it was getting dark and the vehicles stopped to unload their troops for the last time. The sound of exploding shells, already ranging in our direction, was an unwelcome reminder of the battle which lay ahead. We lined up with our mess-tins for the usual thick, warm stew and strong tea which were dished out to us before we started to make our way forward. In the dark we went along a field track leading towards an area of pine-woods where the troops we were to relieve were holding a defence line of slit-trenches.[61]

Renison takes up the story (see Map 15):

> The column pulled in more or less complete and immediately started to prepare a meal. There were luckily a number of Boche vehicle pits in the area, which gave the cookers some shelter, but it was pretty unpleasant for the troops after a long trip in TCVs and about to go forward into a none-too-healthy area. They had had a good night in Tilburg and seemed to have found the local people very friendly. Banger had gone ahead to recce the billets and had his trailer stolen from his parked jeep – by the observance of a small Dutch boy, he had been able to trace the unit of the troops, who had taken it, and found them about to paint out the Div. sign and unit serial number. Needless to say he soon had his trailer back.
>
> It was a poor night for a relief and the approach track was getting very badly churned up with the area just around Bn HQ worse than most other places, but the rifle coys in the pine woods were mostly in sand and fairly dry on the whole. B and C Coys were along the forward edge of the woods with B on the right facing more or less south and A & D Coys were behind C Coy facing eastwards and watching particularly a small bridge over the stream on our left flank. The recce squadron were in the area of Saarbrockshof and responsible for a further bridge and the carrier pl linked up with the recce with A Coy. The carrier pl at this time were rather low in strength owing to a high incidence of UK leave and both its officers were away temporarily on courses. The mortars were dug in some 500 yds behind Bn HQ firing at some 1500 yds range, with the RAP in the cellars of Schloss Calbeck. We only had a skeleton Tac Bn HQ forward as there was very little room for it and Ronnie remained with main HQ at a farm called Heidhausen (945445) just forward of the Goch/Udem road. It was just as well in the light of after events as 9 Bde HQ moved into the area and took up all the accommodation not already occupied by gunners. The relief was completed without any serious incidents, although it proved very difficult in the dark to get the anti-tank guns into position and one of them had to be left until first light in spite of the danger of it being seen getting into position. The Royal Scots told us that they had had some bother from the two farms of Geurtshof and Büssenhof [This is the correct spelling; Renison wrote Buissenhof as it is mistakenly written on the military map] just forward of the woods and that the tracks leading out to these farms had been mined by them.[62]

Roebuck described the arrival:

> We set off carrying weapons, pouches full of grenades plus Bren magazines and an extra 50 rounds bandoleer of .303" ammunition. Each platoon was in a staggered, single file formation with advance party guides leading the way and giving us instructions in quiet subdued voices. German guns were already dropping shells, ranged on the approach tracks, so our presence

61 Lionel Roebuck's memoir.
62 Bill Renison's diary.

had possibly been indicated by the noise made by our transports. Shells started to rain down as we kept moving towards where the 15th Scottish were waiting to be relieved after their last push forward from Goch.

Those in the section just behind mine were caught by a shell bursting in their midst. Cries for help with the dead and wounded were heard, and Edwin Darkwell was one of those who were wounded, but all who were able kept on moving forward, leaving the stretcher-bearers to care for those who could not. The track led up to and through dense pine-woods, continuing on beyond where the most forward troops were well dug in. Their slit-trenches were to the right of the track, spaced out within the twenty-yards strip along the fringe of the wood which bordered on to the open fields.

C Company took over the stretch from the track and 13 Platoon the first part of it. With quiet whispers about the dangers ahead, 'The Scots' went back along the same way their relief had come. Jack Dunne and myself, when taking over a trench on the extreme fringe of the wood, were warned about a farm-house [Geurtshof 950400], some two hundred yards along the track, which was occupied by the Germans. This was to the left of the track as it went forward from the woods and, as dawn broke, we viewed it with some caution. We had been able to sleep through what had been left of the night, sitting down in turn in the bottom of the slit-trench. Having one's head below ground, with a reliable companion on look-out, gave enough sense of security to be able to relax and sleep.[63]

Renison (see Map 10):

On the morning of the 26th the 53rd Div. launched their attack southwards from Goch towards Weeze on the west bank of the river Niers and as was only natural there was a certain amount of shelling by the Boche in reply on our front but on the whole it caused very little damage, though A Coy lost a first class signaller – owing to the bends in the river a lot of the bursts that sounded very close were not actually on our front at all, but there was always the curse of air bursts in the trees and overhead cover was especially necessary in the forward companies. Luckily the Corps SP guns had most of their tanks back for maintenance and we had a minimum of trouble from the noise of their movement. We did however lose an Anti-tank sergeant with a 'Blighty' one from a sniper operating in front of B Coy's area. Our activities were confined to recce patrols for a limited distance into the woods on our left flank which was done without any contact being made though it seemed obvious that there were Boche patrols in or near the same area.

There was an O Gp at Bde [in Schloss Calbeck] about midday and we learnt that the Div. was to attack on the morning of 27 Feb with the object of reaching and cutting the lateral road from Udem to Weeze: two Bdes up, 8 right and 9 left, starting from their present positions. At 0700 hr. the Suffolks on our left and 9 Bde were to attack in order to bring the front line parallel with the Udem road and level with our present front right across the whole frontage of the Div.; during this phase we were to sit tight. Then there would be a pause until 1000 hr. when the barrage would recommence along the entire front and we would kick off with the South Lancs moving through the Suffolks and parallel with us on our left. Our objective was the road and particularly the bridge over a small stream called the Muehlen Fleuth which flowed into the Niers: it was hoped to take this bridge intact or secure a bridgehead sufficient to allow a bridge to be built and a Bde of 53 Div. would be passed through us immediately to allow them to attack Weeze on both sides of the river. The latest reports of their progress

63 Lionel Roebuck's memoir.

on the west bank indicated that things were getting sticky about the area of Rottum more or less parallel with our line where a stream ran out across their front. The Boche defensive fire certainly sounded heavier than anything we had heard since Normandy.

There were two immediate preliminary operations to be carried out. Firstly the South Lancs were moving out their forward coys from our right flank in order to be in a position to move forward through the Suffolks on our left. This left our right very much unprotected and in the air, although the advance of 53 Div. had improved matters a bit. But there was a big loop in the river to our right front with a wood on the far side and it was essential to keep this watched. All I had was the weak carrier pl – adequate with its many guns in daylight but precious thin in the dark. Sgt Hamnett therefore relieved the left forward coy of the South Lancs and came under command of B Coy.

The other move was to ensure that the Suffolks could cross the stream on our left flank without having to fight for their startline and to this end the Recce squadron established without opposition a bridgehead covering the bridge immediately south of their position Saarbrockshof. I hadn't quite realised the importance of this operation and got a sharp rap over the knuckles from the Bde Cmd for not getting the job done quickly enough. The mistake must have been mine, for never have I left any O gp with the intention of my commander made so crystal clear to me as I did that day – the job was to seize that bridge, if possible, intact and to hold it. There was something in the atmosphere in the dark little room where the Brigadier [Eddie Goulburn] gave his orders that I shall always remember – the haze of tobacco smoke, the crowded table with each man's map-board overlapping his neighbours, the asides to supporting arms – but above all the confidence with which the Brigadier told us what the job was and left the method to us. He was always ready to discuss the pros and cons of a method but never dictated. Finally there was the complete sense of co-operation, whether it was making up the fire plan or tying up with the Sappers or tanks; we knew each other well and it made everything else so easy. We had one squadron of the Guards [1 Sqn, 4 GG, commanded by Maj RH Heywood-Lonsdale] in support and I arranged with the Squadron Commander to meet at Tac HQ as soon as possible to recce the ground and to have his troop commanders forward later on to tie up with the coy commanders.

It was very difficult to see much of the ground over which we were going to attack as there was a small ridge about two hundred yards forward of the woods and the ground beyond including the main road and the bridge were in dead ground. The rise was not very great but it was just enough to mask the view. However the tank axis was governed largely by the exits from the woods and it was obvious that Büssenhof and Geurtshof had got to be cleaned up on the way. One source of worry alike to us and to the tanks was the wood in the bend of the river on our right flank which was entirely open and might contain 88s as well as infantry. This had to be dealt with in the fire plan. The ground between us and the main road was open stubble fields practically devoid of cover, but there appeared to be a small triangular copse on the main road dominating the bridge. On our left flank there were thick woods through which the South Lancs were attacking and the degree of interference we encountered from that direction depended on the progress of the South Lancs' advance: in any case we had to be careful that the angle of our fire, especially of tanks, was sufficiently acute to insure that we didn't shoot them up (see Map 15).

I held my O gp in the passage of the wrecked house [Fasanenkath 942413], which housed the Command Post: it was by no means ideal as we were strung out in a long line sitting on the floor and the light was far from good, but the cellar was quite inadequate and outside it was extremely muddy and by no means free from periodical stonks; 53 Div. were still hammering away on the far side of the river. Bn O gps always seemed to assume a gigantic size but the number of supporting arms always helped to swell the total and in this case we had everyone. The plan was to attack with D Coy on the right – objectives Büssenhof, and then the bridge; A on the left – objectives Geurtshof and then Kampshof and the ring contour on the main road. C Coy and B Coy were to remain in reserve to move probably to the triangular copse on the main road and Buissenhof [sic], whilst a pl of Middlesex MMGs came forward also into the copse. Bn HQ was to move off the axis of the main track to Büssenhof. The remains of the HQ remained at Fasanenkath during the attack and Ronnie and Main HQ remained right back as I was told we should be relieved almost immediately by 53 Div. and move back to that area. The doctor set up a tented RAP just behind the woods forward of our present HQ [942406], adjacent to the axis. A troop of tanks was in support of each of A and D Coys and the remainder of the squadron was held to support the attack on the bridge if it should be necessary. The troop cmds were able to tie up with the coy cmds that evening and we arranged for the tanks to be up in good time hoping that the guns on the Suffolks front would muffle the sound of their approach. The infantry was starting from their present positions with the exceptions of D Coy, who were timed to move over to the right flank at the last possible moment to avoid any exposure to Boche DF on the forward edge of the woods.

The fire plan (see Map 11) was complicated owing to the earlier zero hour for the Suffolks on the left and because the barrage when it finally started at ten o'clock across the whole front had to keep further ahead of the South Lancs than of us owing to the air bursts in the trees. The traces did not arrive until early midnight and when they came, I was horrified to find as I checked them through rather drowsily in the Command Post cellar with Burton Pirie that after the initial concentrations on Büssenhof and Geurtshof there was a gap of ten minutes with no fire at all on our front just at the moment we would be crossing the startline. [Renison's problem can be discerned in detail in the CRA's Confirmatory Notes – see Appendix 2. The Code Name for the concentrations on Büssenhof (task 6007) and Geurtshof (task 6006) by 53 BID was HUNTER. This was timed for Z hr +5 mins to Z hr +15 mins. But the E Yorks' barrage, known as Line p, did not begin until Z hr + 25 mins. Thus the worrisome gap of 10 minutes. The trouble was that 7 and 33 Field Regiments were occupied in thickening the barrage around Babbe at that time.] I went round to see Swazi Waller and check up with Hamish Lindsay, his battery commander, that our reading of the traces was correct. There ensued a hectic telephone conversation with Graham Peddie at Bde: it was impossible at this hour to close this horrid gap. This meant altering all the traces before they went out to Coy Cmds.

The South Lancs' cellar [next door in Fasanenkath] was a palatial affair compared with ours, which was just solid bodies by the time we had fitted six and the necessary signals apparatus into it. There was an O gp going on as we arrived but they dispersed whilst I was talking to Swazi taking with them the tin hat I had had since 1939 and leaving me a peculiarly ill-fitting one in exchange. I never recovered my own and had to wear the substitute in default of anything else.

The 27th dawned fine after a dry night and luckily the axis track had dried up quite a lot to allow the movement of transport. The Suffolks' attack went in without very much trouble except in the area of Babbe on their left flank and they were on all their objectives well before our zero hour. We had no last minute changes of plan except the news of immediate relief by 53 Div. and I was rather guarded about passing this bit of optimism on to the troops. It was essential that we got the main track cleared of mines and the sappers and our own pioneers, now commanded by Bill Simpson, were given this as a priority task. Patrols had removed our own 75 grenades [connected to trip wires strung above ground to alert against intruders] during the night and B Coy's patrol had had an uneventful clash with the Boche in so doing. 53 Div. were still pushing forward on our right but progress was very slow and the (to us) all-important loop in the river was still in Boche hands. The Boche was fighting very hard for Weeze, because as we pushed down the bank of the Maas and the American advance from the Roer gathered headway, it was one of the main channels of escape towards the Rhine for all those troops who had been holding the line of the Maas itself. Our attack was coming in behind the Siegfried Line at this point and all along the front we were moving parallel with it.

I went down to the startline about half an hour before zero hour with Burton Pirie, George Kingcome and Laurens, with the tank L.O. following in a Honey tank with my carrier and the gunner OP carrier [These three tracked vehicles contained the communications between: Renison and his HQs and Company Commanders; the gunner OP and the guns; and between the tanks' LO and his Sqn]. Just as we got into the woods we got caught in one bout of shelling and, when it was over, I discovered that we had lost Maynard; it took several minutes to discover him. He had taken cover in a derelict German tank of which there were several lying about, relics of 15 Div.'s attack, and his incurable love of loot had delayed him whilst he looked round to see if there was anything worth taking. A little further on we found that the carriers, which had the wireless sets on board, were not following us and I had to send Laurens back to look for them. While we were waiting for his return, lying at the bottom of the deep tank ruts in the sand, the Boche started sending some heavy stuff into the forward edge of the wood and I found my face bleeding. I picked up from under my nose a fair sized lump of warm metal that presumably had caused the trouble, but discovered that all I had got was a small scratch just under my nose, which was however bleeding profusely. The fragment must luckily have bounced a good many times before it hit me. Laurens eventually rejoined us with the vehicles having found them stuck at a corner, where the Honey tank had failed to take the bend. [Like all US tanks, it had the Cletrac controlled differential transmission giving a fixed radius of turn, which was insufficient here. Far superior was the Churchill's epicyclic differential.] Burton by this time was getting a bit concerned about his communications. I had Hurst and Smith with me with the 18 set.

Jack Pearse and I had had a long discussion with the Bde Signal officer the night before as he was very concerned that we had split our three eleven sets between my command gps, advanced HQ and Ronnie at Main HQ and so appeared to have no reserve. We pointed out to him that I had additional links to Bde on both the gunner and tank nets and that advanced HQ was also connected to Bde by line and to me by 18 set, whilst my 18 set link to the forward coys was duplicated by the FOO's set and by the tank troop cmds. It was an interesting discussion in the light of subsequent events as all methods were fully tested and stood the strain although as usual when working with tanks their frequency was far too close to our 18 set frequency and repeatedly jammed it. Actually my 11 set [a short-range infantry set with a range of 5-10 miles with R/T and W/T introduced in the 1930s] went dis in the FUP and was not used at all throughout the action.[64]

Roebuck:

On the morning of the attack, 27-2-45, the activity started with tanks moving up the track through the wood but not breaking out forward of them. Ginger Smith, a corporal, originally from the PT corps and responsible when possible for the company's physical training, was always keen to be active and keep up his fitness with exercises. He got out of his trench after a cramped night to loosen up and do some press-ups and was about ten to fifteen yards from Jack and myself, behind the front edge of the wood. Suddenly a shot rang out from the direction of Geurtshof, the farm-house about which we had been warned, and Ginger was hit in the knee. He was certainly surprised, but with all the movement, he really had been tempting providence.[65]

64 Bill Renison's Diary.
65 Lionel Roebuck's memoir.

Renison:

> We met D Coy moving through the wood to their FUP and then went on to A Coy and saw Eveleigh just as he was getting on the move. The barrage had already opened on the front of the South Lancs and about 1010 hr. the guns opened up their concentrations on Büssenhof and Geurtshof and the 4.2 mortars [operated by 2 Mx] plastered the wood in the bend of the river. At 1020 hr. the forward coys moved forward as the barrage started and the 4.2s lifted onto the bridge: the Boche started to reply straight away and the front of the woods received attention from some pretty heavy stuff. We had moved into A Coy's HQ dug-out and it wasn't very long before it became apparent that the Boche was holding Geurtshof and was determined to fight it out for possession. Casualties started to come back in numbers larger than the stretcher bearers could cope with and both my carrier and A Coy's carrier were pressed into service to assist the carriers already attached to the RAP: stretchers were the real problem and we established a collecting point at Tac HQ whilst we did our best to fix dressings. Eventually Geurtshof was taken but the cost was heavy. Eveleigh had been killed leading a charge at close quarters and Churnin had received wounds from which he afterwards died in hospital. The tanks lost two vehicles on a minefield surrounding the house, and considerable sniping was experienced from the wood on the left flank where the South Lancs were apparently finding the close country very slow work. Percy Adams took on the remains of the company and succeeded in reaching his objective with only about thirty all ranks left. When they got there, they complained that they were still being fired at from Geurtshof and hadn't got anyone to deal with it themselves. It was probable that this fire was really coming from the woods but I sent forward a platoon of C Coy to make quite certain that the Boche didn't get back into the house. Sgt McGarrell of A Coy did a very fine job of work on the objective in dealing with a Boche spandau that was giving the company a good deal of trouble from the edge of the woods quite close to them: he was subsequently awarded the MM.
>
> In the meantime D Coy were experiencing very much the same opposition on the right and had a considerable number of casualties to start off with from a few suicidally inclined Boche in a small house only just outside the woods themselves [Steinhövelskath, 945398]. They finally had to be silenced by the tanks at short range and the house rushed after the company had tried to outflank it on the left. Even then there was still considerable interference from the right flank and a platoon of B Coy was dispatched to keep this flank quiet in addition to the carrier platoon. Our own 3" mortars were already laid on the wood in the bend of the river to take up, if necessary, where the 4.2"s had left off.
>
> Büssenhof proved just as tough a nut to crack as Geurtshof had and the lie of the land complicated the tank support. The Boche eventually allowed the company to get right into the house and then fought it out with grenades inside. The house itself was well alight and fighting hand to hand was very fierce in the smoke. Eventually the area which comprised a number of buildings was cleared and a number of prisoners sent back to swell the total which A Coy had taken. The company had lost Davidson and David Parkinson killed. As they were reorganising before pushing on to the bridge, the Boche dropped a shell straight inside a roofless barn where Coy HQ and one platoon were taking cover and practically every man was hit including CSM Trowell who was killed. This reduced the strength of the company to very little more than a platoon strong and this was obviously insufficient to take the bridge, if it was defended, and to hold it in any case. D Coy's 18 set had gone dis and my communication with Bob Laird was over the tank net.[66]

66 Bill Renison's Diary.

The biographer of 6 GAB stated that the losses were due to two platoons approaching Büssenhof where white flags were flying. The Germans had then pulled in the flags and killed them. The truth was less sinister.[67] Roebuck quoted German sources for the confusion at Büssenhof.

> The attack…had started out well; the initial artillery fire had cut the German defenders' telephone link with their HQ, so the German supporting artillery fire couldn't initially be brought to bear accurately on their attackers who closed in on the farm. They nevertheless fought off the first attacks until a hand grenade was thrown into the front cellar where the Commander along with a few soldiers, the tenant-farmer Verhayen and some civilians were sheltering. A soldier who picked up the grenade was killed when attempting to throw it out; the others, who were protected by a wall, were unhurt. A red and white flag was then displayed by them to indicate their surrender. This was to avoid further deaths amongst the civilians and themselves, as they felt they were trapped and in an untenable position. As two groups from D Company went forward from out of cover into the open to accept the Germans' surrender, they were fired on by a second group of German soldiers. These were in the rear cellar, and were not aware of the red and white flag being shown by their commander.
>
> This unexpected firing accounted for the death of half the advancing group, the others being wounded. Thus the battle took on a fiercer tone with the Germans given no chance to repeat the false gesture. They were attacked without mercy with grenades and Sten-guns and smoked out of their cellars until they threw down all their arms and clearly surrendered, after severe casualties to soldiers and civilians alike.[68]

The 1952 Heimatkalendar issued by the District Administration (Kreisverwaltung) of Geldern included the following article:

> The 1950 Heimatkalendar carried the story of a soldier from 2 Coy 7FJR who fought around Kalbeck, mainly in the area between Gut Hovesaat, Fasanenkath, Sarrbrockshof, Büssenhof and Geurtshof. The last named farms were only mentioned casually since they were on the edge of the battle area of the unit involved as the remnants of his greatly weakened company fell back on Vorselaer and were relieved by other units.
>
> From 23 to 27 February, 1945 these farms were hotly contested. On 27 February they fell to the Canadians [sic; one third of the officers in the rifle companies of 2 E Yorks were Canloans wearing a Canada flash]. This was the last line of German resistance in Kalbeck. For the enemy they were the chosen startline for the attack on Schaddenhof which lay 100 metres further on and was taken three days later. Schaddenhof was counter-attacked nine times and is close to a wooded area which today, September 10, 1950, was dedicated by Bundespresident Heuss as a military cemetery.
>
> Last year we published a soldier's story. This year we record the experiences of two civilians. Theodor Verheyen, tenant of Büssenhof, and Anton Mülders, who rented Steinhövelskath, remained on their farms and personally experienced the battle. This account of their day-to-day lives places their vivid memories on the record.

67 Forbes, *6th Guards,* p. 110.
68 Lionel Roebuck's memoir.

Theodor Verheyen writes:

'The first enemy impact on Büssenhof happened on the evening of 11 February around 2300 hours. Shortly after the bombers devastated Goch enemy aircraft burnt down the barn and damaged the farmhouse. During the following days as the front came nearer, we were regularly attacked by low-flying aircraft. The artillery shelled different targets on the edge of the wood and on the high ground on that side. Soldiers moved into the farm. They described to us the violence of the fighting in the Kalbeck woods, while the sound of artillery and tank guns and the chattering of infantry weapons could be heard all day long from that same direction. As the threat increased I took my wife and five small children to Vasenhof [938395] which had a secure cellar. I stayed behind on the farm.

For many days the farm was the regimental Tac HQ of Lt-Col Nolte who commanded the infantry regiments engaged in the local battle. At times an artillery FOO was established in the farm and at the same time eight anti-aircraft guns were emplaced. This led to frequent shelling which further damaged the buildings causing casualties among the soldiers.

Subsequently, on 22 February there was comparative peace, but on the next morning the German positions were hammered by an intense artillery concentration. From noon until 1700 hours there was scarcely any let up. This shelling, thickened by fire from tank guns, further damaged Büssenhof. Scarcely had the shelling stopped than the first tanks attacked from out of the wood. Many Canadian (sic) tanks advanced around the farm but were stopped by German DF and retreated back into the wood. The enemy infantry were prevented from advancing by the defensive fire of our soldiers. The heavy shelling of the house and the positions in front of the farm which had lasted for almost nine hours claimed many dead and wounded. An NCO was mortally wounded by a shell splinter while inside the house. For a short while the farm was an RAP. Around evening the unit was relieved by the Paratroops who occupied the house and took up positions in the open fields.

During the following days the fighting died down a little [during the relief of 15 BID]. Once when I took a step out of the farmhouse I was immediately shot at from the wood and received a grazing wound in the knee.

27 February arrived. This was the main day of the battle and brought the destruction of the defences and the end of Büssenhof. About 0800 hr [10 am Allied time] an intense artillery concentration began which was heavier than anything experienced before. The farm received many hits and the stables and the rear of the house were soon set on fire by enemy tracer. All the animals were burnt to death. The violent artillery storm lasted for many hours. Then the tanks attacked. From down in the cellar hole of the house I could see how two tanks broke through the defences in front of the farm and advanced into the front garden. At short range they began to fire into the house.

The Paratroops had barricaded themselves in the ruins of the burnt-out part of the house at the rear of the courtyard (*Hinterhaus*) and were occupying the defences ringing the farm. They had to rely on their infantry weapons and panzerfausts since all communication rearward had been destroyed and no DF could be laid on. The Canadian attack supported by overwhelming firepower was maintained for the next hour. Since no reinforcement or ammunition re-supply was possible the defence gradually weakened. After about five hours of battle a runner came into the cellar which was filled with soldiers and three other civilians apart from myself, and reported that the last of the ammunition was in the process of being expended. Shortly afterwards at about 1330 hours, enemy infantry succeeded in forcing their way into the house and throwing a hand grenade into the cellar. An NCO wireless operator was killed and an artillery FOO severely wounded. The survivors were crouching behind a projecting wall and escaped injury.

A short while later the weak defensive fire upstairs in the house fell silent. There was a pause and then the enemy ordered us out of the cellar. We climbed out as the cellar filled up with drifting, stifling smoke. The destruction of the house had weakened the basement. We went through the open fields to freedom. In the entrance hall lay ten dead Canadians (sic). They had been killed by the defensive fire of the Paratroops who from the ruins of the rear buildings had kept the entrance to the farm covered until they had run out of ammunition. Only then had the surviving Paratroops surrendered.

In the entrance hall the Canadians met us at gunpoint. Outside I looked at my farm which was a smoking pile of rubble. The neighbouring farms were also covered in thick, drifting smoke. From their ruins and from the positions around the houses the Paratroops were hauled out and taken prisoner. We civilians, three young women and myself, had to put our hands on our heads and were led off by four Canadians with drawn sidearms. In front of the farm and in the fields we saw dead and wounded, both German and Canadian. Then we were taken to Fursthaus Kalbeck where we met up with other civilians. We were then taken to the other side of the Niers. A lorry carried us all to Bedburg-Hau where we were interned for nearly six weeks.

The account of Anton Mülders of Steinhövelskath:

I and five relatives remained on the farm during the battle. We didn't want to leave. An advanced dressing station was established in the house for the soldiers wounded in the fighting around Schloss Kalbeck [Fursthaus]. The staff of a tank unit also found quarter in the house.

In the days leading up to 22 February the house and stables were damaged by artillery fire. The high beech hedge right in front of the farm, whose trees were largely destroyed by shell-fire in the course of the fighting, stopped many shells which otherwise would have hit part of the house. During the frequent shelling we stayed in the cellar which remained undamaged for the time being.

On 22 February, German soldiers occupied the farm and the edge of the wood. Around 8 am the following morning the enemy artillery fire thickened into a heavy concentration. At the same time low-flying aircraft strafed the surrounding fields. After many hours the heavy shelling stopped but no one attacked the house and the positions in the beech hedge. During the shelling our soldiers had moved out in the direction of Schaddenhof going through the meadows by the Niers. The staff also left our house. After the artillery concentration had stopped the wounded were transported to the rear.

About an hour later a lone Canadian (sic) came cautiously to the house. After satisfying himself there were no German soldiers around he marched back to the wood which lay on the other side of our field about 100 metres away, where the Canadians had their positions and which we could see from the hay-barn.

By now the shelling had completely stopped. We breathed a sigh of relief as we were sure the war had now ended for us. For a long way around us the countryside was quiet and we went to bed early being deadly tired since we had scarcely slept at all during the past few days. But about 10 pm we were wakened suddenly by the Paratroops who had re-occupied our house and the positions in front of the farm and at the edge of the wood, without the enemy shooting them or even apparently noticing them in spite of their proximity.

Next day around 7 pm the Paratroops made contact with the enemy and destroyed a tank close to the farm. From the Canadian positions the tanks then shelled the house heavily causing severe damage. The cellar entrance became completely buried. We had a lot of trouble finding a way through the ruin of the house which was now on fire. The soldiers managed to put the fire out. Then because of the incessant firing and the presence of soldiers in all the rooms we decided we couldn't stay in the house any more and the five of us hid ourselves away in the potato cellar that was 5 metres long by 1 metre wide. Here like herrings in a barrel we spent the greater part of the next three days. When darkness fell we got provisions for ourselves and took care of the cattle in the stall.

During 25 and 26 February there developed a few skirmishes in the hundred metre wide strip of no-man's land separating the Canadians from our own soldiers. We wondered why the enemy didn't attack the weakly defended positions of our Paratroops. Mind you 27 February showed at last that everything had been painstakingly prepared. About 8 am, the Canadians opened up with an intensity of fire from artillery, tanks and infantry weapons such as we had never experienced before. The shelling reduced the house and cow stalls to ruins and they burnt out. The cattle were consumed in the flames. The heavy shelling continued for many hours. Then the enemy attacked the Paratroops' positions in the smoking ruins of the farmhouse, in the front of the farm and in the beech hedge. The Paratroops had only their infantry weapons to respond with. No DF came from our artillery, and no ammunition could be brought forward. The defenders were lucky the Canadians had 80 metres of open field to cross before they reached the Paratroops' positions.

The battle lasted for many hours. Heavy fighting occurred as the enemy infantry reached the beech hedge in front of the house. Our soldiers were taken in flank and rear from Büssenhof and were taken prisoner. About 2 pm the Paratroops who were still fit for battle expended the last of their ammunition. Finding all possible lines of retreat blocked, they began to surrender.

At the end of the battle we were pulled out of our hiding place by the Canadians and taken away. We were allowed to take only our smallest possessions with us. As we headed towards the transport at Schloss Kalbeck [Fursthaus], we passed the fields that the enemy had crossed and from which they were recovering their dead and wounded. Together with the civilians from the nearby farms, which had all been burned, we were taken to Bedburg-Hau where we were interned for nearly six weeks. When we were allowed to return we found Steinhövelskath nothing but a pile of rubble.[69]

Renison:

C Coy by this time had been warned that they might have to go for the bridge and Reg Rutherford was close to me with his platoon comds ready to move. C Coy were to move up to Geurtshof and then go straight from there to the triangular wood on the road and thence to the bridge. The Boche by this time had turned his artillery onto Geurtshof and Büssenhof and was shelling them pretty hard at intervals. I went up to Geurtshof with Reg and found a certain amount of cover along a bank alongside the track leading forward to Kampshof. As the leading pl left this cover across the bare open stubble the Boche opened up with spandaus from the woods on the left and from the houses beyond the main road ahead. It took some minutes to get the gunners onto this latter target and there was a feeling of uncertainty in C Coy as to whether the Boche were not firing from Kampshof; in fact one platoon deployed to engage it. However I was able to assure them that A Coy were there and they then started to lay a smoke screen with their own 2" mortars to cover their left flank. Once this had become effective the whole company moved across the open faster than anything I have ever seen in battle before or since as Sticky Glew's platoon rushed the bridge and accounted for the post on it before they had time to fire a shot. The bridge was intact and as the platoon arrived a truck was seen to drive off in the direction of Weeze, which was assumed to contain the sappers who should have done the demolition as the bridge was found to be fully prepared for blowing. Just

69 1952 Heimatkalendar sent by Franz Josef Drißen, and translated by this author.

> over the bridge was a farm called Schaddenhof, which the Boche were holding, but Applebee took his platoon through the stream and coming in from the left took the garrison by surprise without much of a fight. The whole operation was conducted with the utmost dash and C Coy's casualties were very small: it seems probable that the Boche were expecting the attack to come from the Büssenhof direction as the contours of the ground prevented them from seeing any movement from our left until the leading troops were quite close to the bridge.[70]

Roebuck:

> The severe losses altered the original plan and the CO warned C Company to be ready to take on the task of storming the road bridge over the Muhlen Fleuth and taking the farm, Schaddenhof, just beyond it. We left our back-stop position in single file and went along the track to Geurtshof, where the two knocked out tanks were. There we lined up, taking cover from the increased shelling against a bank on our right. Our initial aim was to cross the fields to reach a small copse just short of the bridge. A group of prisoners came down the track towards us and Sergeant Nicholson, who was close by me, said, 'Escort them back to the next manned position'. They were quickly taken back and then left with some walking wounded, just inside the fringe of the wood.[71]

In many units this was the cue for the escort to stay with the prisoners and delay his return to the front-line. It was a problem which exercised the officers because it drained front-line strength. It must have been such a factor which tempted the SS and some Allied units to shoot prisoners and be done with them. Roebuck continued:

> On my way back, an A Company casualty, Holiday, who had earlier been shot through his leg by a machine-gun, fell in pain asking me for help. A field-dressing was wrapped around the wound, he was assisted to his feet and told that help was just beyond the edge of the wood. A German soldier then broke cover and, as he ran from behind the farm, I potted at him from over a hedge. He dropped and disappeared from my view.
>
> After being held up by machine-gun fire, the rest of the company had started up the bank and across the open fields under the cover of artillery fire and a smoke screen. I followed up close behind passing by a shell-crater in which Bob Spring, a big Cockney lad who had been the drummer in the band, had two prisoners. They were all smoking cigarettes and it was surprising how quickly, after having done their best to kill one another, acts of friendship were taking place. The usual smell of the Boche, from a chlorine-type bleach with which their uniforms were impregnated, drifted over to me on passing by them. They all looked happy enough to be out of it and alive.
>
> Machine-gun fire was still coming from the left but, while we were in the shelter of the copse, had not much effect. Another smoke-screen was put down and, under its cover, we set off towards the bridge. With little loss, 13 Platoon, led by Lieutenant Glew and Sergeant Nicholson, who later died of wounds received that day, was first over! One section of machine-gunners on the right was soon dealt with by the use of grenades and Sten gun fire. The field of fire from the machine-gunners' reinforced log bunker ran out just before the bridge, so once we, their attackers, were across the bridge we could not be fired on from that position. I

70 Bill Renison's Diary.
71 Lionel Roebuck's memoir.

> was quick to take the dead German machine-gunner's Luger, a good weapon, and one always much sought after.
>
> A German lorry, just along the road to Weeze, started to move off. 'Tabby' Barker shouted to the others to open fire on it as he himself fired his Bren-gun at the departing vehicle. We then moved further along the road [Lionel stated in conversation with this author that he saw 'all the trees along the roadside had a broad collar of explosive material wrapped around the trunk'] to take up a defence position on the right and, about two hundred yards forward of the bridge dug slit-trench defences. We dug about a dozen slit-trenches in a semi-circle and these covered the road and a clearing, and faced towards a bank above which more densely packed trees were growing.[72]

According to Forbes,[73] Lt Minette-Lucas sent Tp Sgt Ingham over the bridge where the tank crushed an 'R' mine attached to aerial bombs. [The Riegel mine, R.Mi.43, was a rectangular steel box, 800 × 95 × 120 mm, containing nearly 9 lb (4 kg). of Amatol/TNT, enough to penetrate the belly armour and destroy a tank but not a bridge]. Ingham continued towards Weeze for 100 yards until ordered back. This information is repeated in the NATO battlefield tour, which concluded that '(T)he situation had been saved just in time by the co-operation between the infantry and armour'.[74] The troop covered the bridge until 6 pm. No one in the infantry, however, saw or heard the tank cross the stream. Lionel Roebuck and the rest of Glew's 13 Platoon were quite clearly first over. They chased away the German Pioneers and dug in 200 yards forward of the bridge near the edge of the present cemetery carpark. The tank seems to have crossed after the infantry and advanced 100 yards without making contact before returning. Since everyone was staring to the front the tank came and went unnoticed. The Churchills then, according to Lionel Roebuck, hung well back and refused all entreaties to join the defenders on the south bank. Nor did Renison know anything of Ingham's exploits, and Scarfe stated categorically that only Ford's OP tank crossed.[75] The historian can take it no further.

Reg Rutherford MC came from the Newland area of Hull, and was a ranker commissioned in the Northamptons before joining his county regiment. Among the first to land on D-day, he was later awarded the MC for dragging a wounded officer from the centre of the road while taking Venraij. A brother was killed crewing an RAF bomber. After the war he worked for Clover diaries in Hull and managed the central engineering works at Scunthorpe Steelworks. He died in 1995. At Yorkshire Bridge, Reg commanded C Coy, and was interviewed for a War Office film that was never completed.

Renison told this author that the film was planned as a WO training film around 1984 for junior leaders whose performance in the Falklands War raised concerns. Roebuck added that the film was the idea of the then GOC 3 BID, Sir David Ramsbotham. When he moved on, the project was dropped. Applebee, Sir John Ford and Reg Rutherford were interviewed. These extracts were transcribed by this author from the sound track of a video supplied by Jim Fetterley.

> *Mr. Rutherford. When the 2nd East Yorkshires launched their attack on 27 February, your company was in reserve. What happened next?*
>
> I got a radio message from the CO, Col Renison, asking me to go to an O Group. When I arrived there I was told that two companies had already been pinned badly down, the attack

72 Lionel Roebuck's memoir.
73 Forbes, *6th Guards*, p. 111.
74 NATO. Battlefield Tour of 1983: 1700.A-1/NAEPPL/83).
75 Scarfe, *Assault Division*, p. 211

had gone astray or lost momentum and that he was asking me then to take on the task of capturing the bridge which was the original objective. The situation was obviously desperate and it required a quick appreciation on my part as the Coy Commander. That appreciation quickly told me that the fire and movement in this particular instance was of little use for the simple reason the companies appeared to be completely pinned down, and appeared to be pinned down from certainly three sides. So I asked the CO to get the maximum artillery support in the form of smoke with a slight mixing of HE, and I decided to use the whole of my company mortars firing smoke with the odd occasion putting in HE as well. [10 Platoon of 2 Middlesex fired 900 bombs from their 4.2 in mortars in support of 2 E Yorks].[76] I told the Company exactly what I required them to do, told them it was a question of moving from A to B as quickly as possible and that having established ourselves across the bridge to consolidate in front of the woods on the far side. I gave the orders quite clearly. I can't remember exactly what the platoon number was, but Lt Glew was in charge of the leading [13] platoon. I was behind the leading platoon with the two other platoons following on. As soon as the smoke was thick enough we set off at the double. The idea was to move as quickly as possible and spring the maximum amount of surprise on the enemy on the bridge. As we reached the bridge we could see the two pits in the centre of the bridge which were obviously holding the explosive charges to blow the bridge, [Scarfe called them four 500 lb bombs, and they were almost certainly aircraft bombs] and we despatched the Germans in those two pits and rushed the farmhouse which was just to the left and across the bridge. We were very very fortunate when we arrived at the farmhouse inasmuch as the ground around the farmhouse formed a natural possibly 4foot high barrier, and the ground on the far side of it was higher. So this gave us a fair amount of cover within the confines of the farmhouse yard itself. I decided to move one platoon covering the bridge itself and looking towards the woods on the right where the enemy still were; one platoon forward of the farmhouse alongside the ridge; and Glew's platoon on the left towards the end of the barn where there was no ridge and part of the ridge that was looking out towards the woods. [In summary, Glew's platoon was right, Applebee's left and the third platoon was in the centre]. And that was the situation when the CO called me in and the arrival at the bridge itself. During the period we received no casualties whatsoever up to establishing ourselves within the confines of that farmyard.

Did you suffer much crossfire during that attack?

Oh yes. The crossfire was there all the time, but being shrouded with smoke it was very haphazard. Many many times it went above our heads.

Did you have any tanks with you?

No tanks whatsoever.

So what was the next thing that happened?

The FOO came up with his tank. I'd had an FOO on foot with me most of the time but then I'm assuming that Capt Ford was senior to this one, and was at a loose end. He had the tank and of course his wireless set was a big boost. It was a very high-powered set compared with the ones that I was carrying and we used the tank exclusively then for communication between ourselves at Company HQ and back to the CO at Battalion HQ. Of course at that time I didn't know where Battalion HQ was. It was not until later that they did tell us that they were, I believe, at Schaddenhof or Büssenhof [Neither. Reg was in Schaddenhof. Bn Tac HQ was in Kampshof] – I'm mixed up with which one it was. We established ourselves in those three positions, but no sooner had we established ourselves than we saw enemy movement in all the woods in front of us and this was where obviously we were going to be

76 Moberly, *Second Battalion,* p. 109.

counter-attacked. At that particular period I asked Capt Ford to bring down DF in those woods in front of us.

And that worked successfully?

That was successful, yes.[77]

Lt. Applebee described his platoon's attack on the Schaddenhof:

How did you attack the farmhouse?

We had with us what, I believe now, were three tanks, I understand were Churchills. And when we reached the road, we were to the left, and the Company Commander sent off platoons to the bridge itself, and I was asked with my platoon to cross a stream and into the farmhouse itself and the farm buildings. We did that, having crossed the stream with barbed wire and little obstacles around, and when we got to the farmhouse and went through it, it was clear. We were not in any direct contact with the enemy at that time – not close to. Having done that we organised ourselves by going through the farmhouse, and I sited the platoon on a sandy, grassy bank 30 to 40 ft in front of the farmhouse. And we covered with the Bren gun fire the open ground immediately in front of that position and further over to the left of that position, which we found very soon was still occupied by German troops.[78]

Renison continued his account:

Reg put his HQ in a good solid Boche dug-out beside Schaddenhof itself and dug in his three platoons in a perimeter covering the approaches to the bridge with Glew's pl about 200 yards forward on the left [Not so. Lionel Roebuck was in Glew's 13 Platoon and wrote; 'we were on the right, where the edge of the German cemetery car park is now'] of the road along the forward edges of a strip of wood. The difficult flank was the right of the road where there was an unbroken stretch of wood running right up to the bridge itself with the river Niers outside it. Communications remained good throughout and John Ford soon had his OP tank across the bridge and settled in beside Rutherford's HQ at the corner of the farm. The DF had already been laid on astride the road in front of the coy position with a further task on a small wood about two hundred yards away to their left: the 4.2" mortars were engaging the far end of the wood towards Weeze to prevent any infiltration by the Boche back towards the bridge from the Weeze direction.

In the meantime Tac HQ had moved forward to Kampshof and installed itself in the capacious cellars there with A Coy dug in round it, mainly behind a big potato pile to the right. The house must have been a Boche gunner OP as we found a wireless set and sundry other relics left behind. [This was confirmed from the German side]. By a wide sweep across the open Burton Pirie and the tank LO were able to bring up their vehicles without getting involved in the mines around Geurtshof and there were two tanks also round the house covering the edges of the woods on our left. The South Lancs at this time were still well behind us and, we discovered later, were finding it pretty slow work in the woods, where their tanks were of very little assistance. After a little difficulty I contacted the Middlesex MG platoon [2 Middlesex with Vickers machine guns and 4.2-in mortars were the Divisional support battalion and on this occasion appear to have freely interpreted their orders. Moberley identified them as '9 Platoon of C Coy

77 WO training film sound-track.
78 WO training film sound-track.

who had consolidated with the East Yorks][79] and got them to move up to the triangular copse on the road behind the bridge, but it was impossible to get in touch with the carrier pl satisfactorily and eventually I sent George Kingcome back to order them to move forward to Büssenhof to bolster up D Coy, leaving B Coy still in their original position in reserve. Unfortunately George got caught in a stonk as he approached Geurtshof and went to ground under an armoured car, unknown to its occupants, who decided things were getting too hot and drove off straight over George's back. His mess tin was squashed quite flat, but it was originally believed that he himself was only slightly injured. However as soon as he had had himself transferred to his wife's General Hospital it was discovered that he was more seriously hurt than he had at first thought and back to the UK he went, once again leaving his wife behind him. [The details of this unlikely human-interest story are unfortunately unknown].

The problem was to get the carrier pl up and to bring forward the Anti-tank guns and, having told Laurens what I wanted he and I set out to go over to D Coy to get things tied up on that flank, things being fairly quiet with us and C Coy having dug in without much interference. Banger had already brought up the rations carriers with a midday meal following hot on the steps of the leading companies as he always did. In fact as A Coy's carrier drew up behind their potato pile, the CQMS threw up his hand with a cry of 'Char's up, chaps', and was immediately sniped through the wrist from the woods ahead.

As Laurens and I were crossing the open we got caught in one of the Boche's periodical stonks and both Laurens and his runner were hit. Banger was passing in a carrier and I managed to attract his attention but Laurens was dead before we got him to the carrier: his runner was not badly hurt and I was able to arrange with Banger to RV the guns and send Sgt Lamb, the ATK pl sgt, up to me. [Laurens therefore had been OC Support Coy.] I found Bob Laird with his company dug in but very thin on the ground, although most of the tank squadron had rallied in the area of Büssenhof. This had its disadvantage as it was attracting more than its fair share of the Boche artillery. Bob had had bad luck in his own digging, as after getting down a couple of feet he had come up against the stone floor of a non-existent building and had to start digging all over again.

There didn't appear to be any trouble from the other side of the river and so I ordered B Coy up to Büssenhof, which had also had its garrison reinforced by the 17-pdr SP [M10 17-pdr SP Gun Achilles] guns of the Corps A/TK troop. Unfortunately John Baker was slightly wounded in the leg in bringing the company up and this left young Terry Russell in command of the company with Sgt Bell as a tower of strength behind him. I saw Terry who had got the company well underground in some Boche trenches round the south and west side of the house: the farm itself was still uninhabitable owing to the fire. The Boche rather obviously was centering his shelling on the farm areas, but once we were underground there was very little damage caused by it. I fixed up with Bob to use B Coy's 18 set when he wanted to and then went back to the Command Post in Kampshof. The ground was getting pretty chewed up round there and the tank LO got his tank well bogged for a while. However the anti-tank guns were up and C Coy were having no real trouble, so I decided to leave the Bn dispositions as they were for the moment with the prospect of 53 Div. relieving us during the night. The South Lancs had reached the line of the main road and had contacted A Coy, but they had not succeeded yet in getting forward across the road to the southern edges of the woods as had been intended and the Boche were certainly still in the houses about 300 yards to our front on this side of the Muehlen Fleuth and we had engaged them with both mortars and artillery [presumably Ratzenhof 964393]. None of this prevented the evening

79 Moberly, *Second Battalion*, p. 109.

meal from coming forward and we had fed before darkness fell. In fact things must have appeared so stabilised further back that a Squadron Commander from the 53rd Recce Regt appeared in the Command Post about 1600 hr. announcing that he was going over the bridge and through C Coy towards Weeze. I suggested that we knew that the Boche weren't so very far up the road and that there wasn't much more daylight in any case and he retired to think things over. Someone must have thought better of it as we never heard any more of his proposed activities.[80]

Roebuck:

Except for the tree roots it had been easy to dig the slit trenches. The afternoon was fine and pleasant. All had become quiet – a little interlude with hardly any shelling – and for a while the war had seemed to just stand still. There was the opportunity to examine the Germans' machine-gun dug-outs; they were strong with log walls and roof, but were no use to us in 13 Platoon as we needed to fire in the opposite direction.

The afternoon wore on with only the occasional sighting of Germans. They had first appeared far over on the other side of the fields on the left of the road, close to the fringes of the woodland cover and too far away from 13 Platoon's position to worry about or to shoot at. Later, others crept nearer, and there was the glimpse of the odd figure within the densely packed trees immediately to our front. My trench was at the end of the semi-circle, the nearest to the road, with its right-hand side close to a tree trunk. 'Tabby' Barker's was further over, across on the other side of it. It was quite natural for me, feeling under threat at the nearness of the Germans, to ask him to come over to give me some support in case they decided to attack from my side.

'Tabby' nipped quickly over. When he had almost reached my trench a shot rang out. He was hit by a bullet which just skimmed over my head catching 'Tabby' in his left leg, just below the hip-joint. I let fly a few shots in the direction of the firing, then applied a field-dressing to the wound. Stretcher-bearers were called for, and 'Tabby' was quickly loaded on to the stretcher and taken away back towards the bridge.

A more vigilant look-out was then kept, and I fired at every movement where it was obvious that the Germans were preparing to make a counter-attack. Artillery fire, called for to shell the enemy position, dropped shells just clear of the defence line. The evening came without the position being rushed. Whenever a move started from the trees, a volley of rifle fire and grenades stopped it. My Mills (36) grenades had been used and a lot of my rifle .303" ammunition. I even resorted to using my Luger pistol.[81]

Renison:

As it was starting to get dark C Coy reported that the Boche was starting to infiltrate through the woods on their right and a little later called down the SOS accompanied by a call for more ammunition. I was under the impression that their carrier had gone up to them as they had called for it some time previously and Banger had sent all the company carriers up. It wasn't until a long time afterwards that we discovered that the carrier had been hit by a shell on the way up and had its suspension broken. The counter-attack [according to Scarfe[82] and

80 Bill Renison's diary.

81 Lionel Roebuck's memoir.

82 Scarfe, *Assault Division,* p. 211.

Bosch[83] the first was IFJR24 but the second was IIFJR22 under Leutnant Schreiber and Pl Cmdr Weinmann. Thielecke, who attacked Schaddenhof, was in IIIFJR22 Wittstock, which is evidence enough] increased in intensity as the darkness fell and the calls for ammunition became more insistent; a party was sent back to the Middlesex in the triangular copse to borrow some more [3,000 rounds were 'borrowed' from the Middlesex][84] and finally the company were reduced to drawing on the small supply in the OP tank; in the Command Post we overheard on the gunner net a voice say 'A hand will come in through the opening; fill it with 303.' [Norman Scarfe in a cellar in Goch heard it also, as reported in his letter to the author]. We got onto the main HQ urging them to send up C Coy's carrier as soon as possible and I ordered Chris Pemberton, whom Banger had brought up from the LOBs to take B Coy up across the bridge and take over the right half of the bridgehead perimeter.[85]

Roebuck:

It became a cat and mouse situation with the Germans just waiting to make their move but, as darkness approached with myself reduced to using just the Luger, it was decided to withdraw to the farm, Schaddenhof, where Company HQ had been installed. Somewhat isolated, on the outlying edge of the defence line, and while not hearing the order to move back, on seeing shadowy figures creeping away in the ghostly light from the search-lights reflected off the clouds above, I decided it was high time to get out. Picking up my gear, rifle and the Luger, I slowly slid out of my slit-trench and stooping low, ran to join up with three others, the last in my platoon to go!

Near the bridge, we crossed over the road to join a track leading to the farm. A row of mature oak-trees was on the left and a banking, in which there were log-reinforced German dug-outs, was on the right. As we neared them the shelling, which had been going on as we ran, got worse. So after we had stacked our packs and webbing gear against one of the oak trees, we piled into one of the dug-outs for shelter. It was an L shape, roofed over, with a narrow entry, the long arm running to the left. I was the first in, with my back against the end of the dug-out, the other three on top of me and there we stayed, reasonably safe, while shells rained down all around our shelter.

Rutherford:

So when did the enemy counter-attacks begin?
Memory probably fails me on this but I seem to think that the time would be around tea-time. But again towards dark the enemy started again and I know that at that particular time the German infantry got right up to the end of the farmhouse. In fact one of the Germans entered the far end of the barn, and I clearly remember the far end of the barn was on fire, with a panzerfaust and he was despatched with either SA or a grenade, I am not quite certain which. But he was lying just within the confines of the door and of course this was reaching the stage of desperation then. At the same time we had fired so much ammunition both in the initial stages of getting onto the bridge and the farmhouse that we were now running very very low of ammunition and I repeatedly called for my carrier which carried the ammunition to be brought up to reinforce our ammunition supplies.

83 Bosch, *Zweite Weltkrieg,* p. 222.
84 Scarfe, *Assault Division,* p. 211.
85 Bill Renison's diary.

And did you get your ammunition?
No, no, and the situation became desperate because the attack continued for a considerable period. I think I must emphasise that during this period and throughout the whole of this period of the counter-attack we had magnificent support from the artillery who were firing continually defensive as near to our positions as was possible. And I'm absolutely certain that but for the artillery barrage we should possibly have been overrun. Now during this period we got an anti-tank gun [small 6pdr, organic to the bn, and easy to conceal. The large and effective 17pdrs were not under battalion control] across the bridge and it was stationed in the forward area overlooking the main Weeze-Uedem road. But unfortunately that gun was of no use to us because at this time no tanks appeared from that direction whatsoever. Eventually when the tanks did come they came from the woods away onto the left and the gun was in the wrong position.

How was the ammunition crisis resolved?
Well first of all we were very very fortunate that we got a certain amount of SA ammunition out of the FOO's tank. We were most grateful for that, but repeated requests to Col Renison eventually brought the Battalion's 2ic over the bridge driving a carrier on his own, and he was obviously sprayed with fire for almost the full length of that road until he reached the bridge, because the copse behind us that was on the far side of the Muhlen Fleuth from where we were sited was full of Germans at that particular time. I'd been led to believe that Middlesex Regt. was coming up to relieve our rear in that respect, but apparently they never did get up or they were ejected from the wood and it remained full of Germans. Now Banger, he came past that wood – he was fired on continuously while he passed that wood – and pulled up in front of the farmhouse in the yard. Now I went out to see Banger. I thanked him most profusely and got as many people as I could to take the ammunition into the farmhouse. And at the same time I gave strict instructions that the German prisoners in that cellar were also to help fill the Bren magazines that we were desperately requiring. Banger King also evacuated two wounded people on the carrier. One was of course one of the FOO's men and the other was one of the worst wounded [Roebuck] out of the farmhouse itself. And there is no doubt about it that we should have been in pretty queer street had not Banger arrived in that carrier. He was a very very wonderful fine fellow as far as I was concerned and a living example… [here the film section ran out].[86]

Applebee:

And did you soon come under counter-attack?
This was during the day-time and not immediately, not very serious counter-attacks. There was fire the whole time but not directly and I think the counter-attack as such did not occur probably until after dark. The building-up to that whilst it was still daylight I did see and reported, so a group of German officers in the open some hundreds of yards away [were] obviously preparing their plan to counter-attack.

And what happened when the counter-attack did come in?
The counter-attack came in after dark. We were under rather intense fire, there's no doubt, and it appeared that a tank together with infantry had got round to the side of the farm-house and the farm buildings and came in from that direction. My sections still on the bank were over-run and the remnants were able to get back to the farmhouse.

86 WO training film's sound-track.

And when you were in the farmhouse how did you organise the defence of that position?
The farmhouse itself had shattered windows and shattered doors and with a cowshed to its left, and all we could do was to mount as far as possible, and remember by that time we were short of ammunition, and we held the front of the house and to the side. We tried to look after the entrance, which was quite wide-open coming in from the cowshed or the farm building on the left. The back of the farmhouse as far as I can remember had no slits or holes knocked into the brickwork so we had no need for a defence there.

And did the enemy manage to get into the buildings or did you keep them out?
The enemy got into the shed at the back and that became rather serious. I was told that Germans were coming in from the end of the farmhouse and as I say we were very short of ammunition but I did get around the connecting doors and was able to throw in a 36-type grenade which seemed to settle them and we had no more direct trouble from that source.[87]

Rutherford:

At what point did you decide to bring the artillery fire down on your own positions?
Well, the Germans were now swarming in from three sides. From the woods to the right of the bridge; forward and down the right hand side of the road; to the left of the bridge and we were being constantly harassed from the spinney in the rear. A tank had rolled up to the farmhouse and asked us to surrender, and it was fairly obvious that a major attack was about to be launched. I would say at this particular stage we were down to possibly 60 men in all in the Company and in spite of the fact that the CO had said he was sending B Company up to reinforce us I had never seen or contacted anyone from B Company. The platoon on the right was constantly under fire, and it was fairly obvious to me that unless we did something desperate we would lose the bridge and certainly be overrun. I was determined that this wasn't going to happen. We'd caught the bridge very very easily. We'd suffered continuously throughout the afternoon and I decided at this stage then that it would be better being in well-fortified positions to bring our own artillery down on us who were in those positions and be able to catch the Germans who were out in the open. I therefore asked the FOO to bring what artillery fire he could to bear down on our own positions. And this of course he did with magnificent effect.

It must have been a very difficult decision to take?
It was difficult yes certainly, but I felt in this particular case that we were so well dug in, that the farmhouse had particularly thick walls, the situation was desperate and required desperate measures and that is why I decided to do it.

And did these measures work?
It worked magnificently. The attack faltered, the tank withdrew and for a short period after that there was quite clearly a period of calm. It was obviously a very successful move and there's all thanks to the artillery for that.

And was your ammunition shortage eventually solved?
Oh yes. That was solved quite clearly by the arrival of the 2ic of the Battalion.

87 WO training film's sound-track.

And how did he reach you?
I had a message from Bn HQ that ammunition was on the way. I was unaware at that time who would be bringing it or what would be bringing it, but I notified the platoon on the bridge to watch out as there was an ammunition carrier coming up. It was fairly obvious we knew he was coming up a considerable time before because he was being fired on as he came up the main Weeze-Uedem road. He came in at a tremendous speed into the farmyard. I came out from Company HQ which was in the dugout just outside the farmhouse and started unloading. I also got as many bods as I could from the farmhouse to unload. We got a lot of the cases of ammunition down to the cellar and I instructed the people down there to see that the prisoners did load the magazines which were desperately required for our light MGs.

So your position was slightly easier after that?
Much easier after we got ammunition. We were then in a position to bring maximum fire to bear on anyone that approached the farmhouse or the vicinity of the farmhouse.

And did the German counter-attacks continue?
They continued but on a reduced dimension for about 5 hours, and then they mounted a sort of last-ditch dimension after about 5 hours. When I say 5 hours I am sort of racking my memory because time was of no consequence in the heat of the battle.[88]

Applebee:

What happened when the enemy tank approached the farmhouse?
The enemy tank on the first occasion without coming round, and it came to be in the close proximity to the front of the farm and the OP tank which was situated between the farmhouse and Company HQ. That tank came round and fired and I believe it was that actual thing that happened, that it fired. It hit our own tank just as I was approaching the door of the farmhouse and I was thrown right the way backwards into the arms of the people behind me. That tank then proceeded, and I can't be sure of timing, but eventually it came around the back of the whole of the farmhouse and the chap in the tank decided to have a bit of fun with us and asked us all to surrender. 'Come on Tommy. Give it up. Not a chance'. We kept quiet and it went away.

That must have been a worrying moment?
It was a worrying moment because there were enemy infantry with the tank and with our own wounded in the farm building as well as German wounded and prisoners I thought that that was nothing at the time as we were short of ammunition.

Mr. Applebee. Can you tell me about your part in the decision to bring artillery fire down onto the company's position?
Yes. The decisions had already been made to bring the fire down closer and closer to the position until it was coming down I think less than 100 yards in front of the farmhouse. However, at that time we were completely surrounded by these Germans with the tank and you could hear this activity all the way round. It was rather like being in a western fort with the Indians dashing around the perimeter. I was then reporting to Maj. Rutherford and he asked whether the situation was such that all our own troops were under cover, as far as I could tell, and whether there was any objection to bringing down the fire to completely

88 WO training film's sound-track.

blanket the farmhouse itself. I checked as far as I could and I was absolutely convinced that none of my own platoon were still alive in their original position, that the Platoon on the far right commanded by Mr. Glew, that was away from where the fire would fall anyway, and those on the bridge had the protection of the bridge. So I thought it was the right thing to do to bring it down. It was up to Maj. Rutherford to decide and he decided then that he would bring the fire down. I think the time, zero hour before it was fixed, and in that time I had to get back into the farmhouse and ensure that all the wounded were down in the cellar, and that everybody except for two or three who would keep a final look out for any intruders were into the cellar at the same time. As the minute arrived we had everybody down in the cellar. So we had our own wounded, we had the German wounded and the remnants of the farm people. And we just sat and waited. That was the position at that time.

What was it like when the artillery fire came down?
It was rather like waiting for the two-minute silence to begin at the Cenotaph only in reverse. We were waiting for the moment and then it appeared that all hell let loose with thumping and thudding and it went on for quite some little time. Luckily the building itself must have been fairly solid because we were not in any way injured and there were no casualties from it as far as we were concerned. But in conclusion I believe that was the end of the battle. I believe that was the final coffin in the nail (sic) of the attack.

Did any of the building catch fire at all?
The barn caught fire in places but not seriously, not enough to burn it down. It wasn't a big conflagration.[89]

Capt John Ford:

Sir John. You weren't originally attached to C Company of the E Yorks in this attack. How did you come to be in the bridgehead?
I had finished my task with D Coy and arrived at the top of the hill where C Coy were beginning to assemble, and saw they hadn't got a powerful wireless such as the one I had in my tank. ['I had lost my carrier a day or two before when it was blown up (and the driver killed) by a bomb planted under a railway line, which the mine-sweepers had missed. It was for that reason I was using my tank on the 27th'].[90] I can't remember I suggested it or whether my CO suggested it, but I went on with them and that is how I came to be there as the senior FOO, although Lt McLean had originally (been), and was still actually, there.

And when you reached the farmhouse how did you organise your observation post?
The location of the farm was roughly a farm with outbuildings, and to the right of the farm, as you looked towards the enemy forward along the road, there was a dugout, and Reg Rutherford the Company Commander chose to make that dugout his Company HQ. So I put the tank immediately outside the dugout almost alongside the door so that the wireless lead could be led from the tank into the dugout, so that I could in fact use the wireless from the dugout without getting out and climbing into the tank.

89 WO training film's sound-track.
90 Letter to this author by Sir John Ford on 25 February 1997. He asked that it be noted here that his knighthood was awarded in 1977 while he was British Ambasador in Jakarta.

And when did the enemy counter-attacks begin to become a nuisance?
Well I can't remember. As far as I can, as it was getting dark the infantry reported there were signs of enemy movement in the wood and that they feared that enemy troops were getting ready to mount a counter-attack. Rutherford asked me to call down SOS fire on the wood to prevent troops forming up to launch a formal attack, and we called down the SOS fire on the wood. Then some time later, and I think it was after dark that reports came through that the infantry were in fact attacking, and we then brought the SOS fire down closer as the pressure on the infantry increased. Some time later in the evening, maybe 8 or 9, maybe later I don't know, Rutherford came to the conclusion that we ought to bring it down even closer and we actually brought the fire down over the field immediately in front of the farmhouse, which meant that shells coming short would be likely to fall in the farm buildings area which we were in. This seemed a reasonable risk to take because at that time we were all either in the dugout or in the actual farm itself where there were thick walls and a cellar, and the Germans attacking were out in the open.

What part did your tank crew play in the activities of the night?
Well they acted because the tank was where it was and the wireless was in the tank. For the early part of the evening two of them were actually in the tank manning the set, and also as the evening wore on, and as we heard sounds of a German AFV of some kind in the wood, we used our tank to fire its HE shells at the front of the wood, and also to use the BESA to spray the front of the wood to try and mask the fact that we were really as weak as we were. [Ford said that none of the RA OP had been trained to fire the main 75 mm tank gun or to perform any part of being a tank crew. They had amused themselves in idle moments by firing the odd HE shell in the direction of the enemy. He remained mystified why the 4 GG Churchill tanks did not join him and the infantry. Their tanks were far better armoured than the Sherman, and there were no 88 mms in the vicinity. He read the Guards' comments that they could not fire their main guns for fear of revealing their position with wonder because it was never a concern of his].[91]

There was a considerable ammunition shortage as well and the 2ic brought up a new load of ammunition. Did you have to adjust the artillery fire at all for that?
I can't recollect that at all. I can recollect some signal coming through from Bn HQ where my Major was to the effect that Banger was on his way but I can't recollect myself doing any adjustment to the artillery fire. It may well be that was done by Maj. Pirie himself at Battalion HQ.

Was there a lot of ammunition expended by the artillery in this operation?
Yes an enormous amount. In fact I always reckoned that perhaps I was the most expensive FOO to the British taxpayer that there was throughout the War, because if I remember rightly the SOS was fired intermittently by my troop of guns for approximately 8 hours. A lot of the time it was fired by the whole Regiment. Some of the time we had Divisional fire and we even had Corps fire, and I think I heard afterwards the figure of something like 450 shells per gun by my troop at the end of the night, [Scarfe wrote that expenditure was 450 rounds per gun of 76 Fld Regt and probably the same for the other two fld regts, while Corps fired 100 rounds per gun].[92] which at the present price of shells is a horrible sum of money. I thought at the time it was most remarkable for the incredibly efficient transport and supply

91 Sir John Ford in a phone conversation with this author on 12 March 1997.
92 Scarfe, *Assault Division,* p. 213.

system which must have applied because my own gunners were absolutely worn out carrying the shells from the deposit where the lorries dumped them to the actual gun position, and the congestion on the roads and the transport facilities must have been a headache of tremendous dimensions.

Your OP tank, was it attacked at all during the night?
Yes it was. During the night the tank we had heard in the wood somehow made its way across the field without our being aware of it, and then sidled up alongside the farm and suddenly appeared round the corner of the farm and fired an HE shell [HE would have been 'up the spout' against men and buildings, with no effect on armour] at point-blank range at my tank hitting it on the mudguard, if you can call it that, facing it without doing any damage beyond denting the tank. Unfortunately my tank crew, seeing this tank suddenly appear at 30 feet range and knowing they had been hit directly and expecting an AP shell to come next, evacuated the tank at once. One of them was shot by infantry who were crouching around by the enemy tank, which had penetrated the area, and that was my senior bombardier who unfortunately died afterwards. And from then on in fact the tank was not manned but the wireless was still running and the extension lead operated so we still had our communications, and we went back into the tank I think later on in the night when the enemy attack had petered out.[93]

Norman Scarfe remembered that night vividly:

I knew of the intensity of the battle, though from the relatively comfortable platform of RHQ, 76 Field Regt., at that time. It was hair-raising listening to Ford and Maclean across the mill-stream on, I suppose, the night of 27 Feb: we were trying to co-ordinate defensive fire but from the shelter of a cellar in Goch.[94]

It was all hands to the pump. The Adjutant of 33 Fld Regt, Capt. J.A. Brymer described the frantic and incessant firing during the night of 27/28th February:

By midday the next day (26th) 9 Bde had completed their relief of 227 Bde of 15 Scottish Div., and ammunition dumps were being built up to a total of 300 rpg in preparation for Op HEATHER. The whole area was extremely soggy and OPs were issued with Weasels as it was considered carriers and tanks would be useless. The attack went well, and at the end of five hours the Infantry were well into the enemy's positions, with 350 Parachute prisoners. [Most prisoners were from 84 GID, although there were some Fallschirmjägers]. The attack was supported by a barrage fired by twelve Field Regts, and the rumble of the guns, including those of 11 Armd and 53 Welsh Divs who were advancing on our left and right respectively, was unceasing. It was during the night that the ammunition holdings, for the only time in the campaign, reached a dangerously low figure. The late afternoon of the 27th had been fairly quiet and, as the regiment was due to move during the evening, a proportion of the stocks of ammunition was carried forward. Major E.V. Hollis, who was attached to the regiment, was acting as FOO with the 2 E Yorks [the only mention of Hollis, whose role in the bridge battle is unknown], who had been attacking on the right of 9 Bde. An equivalent advance had been made, but at about 1930 hr the enemy succeeded in launching a counter-attack across a small

93 WO training film's sound-track.
94 Norman Scarfe in a letter of 27 April 1984.

stream. SA ammunition was practically exhausted and he called for DF. This was continued almost without interruption for four hours. Every time we thought we had finished, HQRA ordered 'Continue DF Rate 1 for further 20 minutes'. Stocks got lower and lower and we eventually moved to our new position [Buchholt at 949439 on 1 March] with about 400 rounds in each Battery. The remainder of the night was an ammunition nightmare, replenishment being made in all sorts of trucks from five separate locations, 10,000 rounds being handled between 0500 and 0900 hr. However the DF did plenty of execution and 80 enemy dead were counted next morning. During these two days the regiment fired 15,849 rounds, an average of 660 rpg.[95]

Renison:

Time passed and C Coy's calls for reinforcement and ammunition became more insistent: Glew's platoon had run almost completely out of ammunition and the whole company had to pull in to a very tight perimeter round Schaddenhof itself – there was a sandy bank about six to eight feet high in a half circle round its south side and into this the company withdrew. Glew, himself wounded, carried out this manoeuvre very gallantly and got back all his wounded; for this he was later mentioned in despatches. The SOS call was insistent and Graham Peddie worked like a Trojan for us at bde stepping up the fire until we had practically the whole of the Corps artillery firing on our front. The tanks were unwilling to launch themselves across the bridge in the dark but cruised up to our side and fired high over C Coy's heads in the direction of Weeze – they agreed to stay forward as long as we needed them instead of returning to a rear rally.[96]

Forbes wrote that as Minette-Lucas's troop withdrew at 6 pm from their covering position at the bridge, two of the tanks became bogged, and their crews were brought back on Ingham's tank to the forward edge of the wood, where the Squadron were in a 'hedgehog' position for all-round defence. Capt Swift and Sgt Quick tried hard to recover these tanks with an ARV, but the mortaring was so accurate that they had to leave them until next day. Monty's Moonlight illuminated the battlefield. At 10.15 pm, Sgt Dillingham and L/Sgt Higgin, who had remained less than 300 yards from the bridge, fired their Besas across the stream but, Forbes wrote, they could not fire HE because it would have been suicidal to let the Germans know that there were still tanks in the vicinity. The guardsmen feared that the Fallschirmjägers would stalk them with panzerfausts in the darkness, and their imagination ran riot:

No 1 Squadron were ordered to send a troop right up to the bridge and Sgt Dillingham was chosen for the task. Near to his position was a farm, and the paratroopers inside kept waving a lantern in front of a window, hoping that the tanks would fire at it, give away their position and thus become easy prey for stalkers. Luckily Sgt Dillingham saw through this trick and held his fire.[97] [The nearest German held farm was Rahmenhof, which was 700 yards to the east and an equal distance south of Kampshof. The story is inexplicable].

95 Brymer's diary. These extracts from Hunton's and Brymer's diaries were supplied by Ivor Norton, who started his home leave on 27 February 1945.
96 Bill Renison's diary.
97 Forbes, *6th Guards*, p. 112.

In Roebuck's view the GG Churchills held back. He based his opinion on the narratives of Rutherford, Ford, Applebee and Russell:

> The tank support had been somewhat weakened in the initial attacks on the enemy-held farms, by the effectiveness of the enemy's mines and Bazooka attacks. However, they were able to give limited support during and after the bridge had been stormed, but were missing in the heat of the counter-attacks on it when C Company was beleaguered. This was because they failed to follow in close support, and (to) push their tanks beyond the small copse, which led to the bridge, for fear of bazooka attacks.[98]

Of course the infantry's job was to protect the tanks against Panzerfausts so the discussion becomes circular. Mutual distrust seems to have characterised tank-infantry relations that night. Lionel Roebuck was hit and severely wounded:

> Later, as the barrage slackened, a call of nature meant my asking the others to back off and let me out to relieve myself. Then, on finding my water-bottle I had a drink from it. The shelling restarted, so I had to rush back to the trench and this time was the last man in, only just under cover of the entrance. A direct hit on the dug-out sent shrapnel crashing through my steel helmet and into my head with such a bang! Taking off my helmet I saw, in the artificial moonlight's silver reflection, a big hole right through it. One of my mates pushed it back on, then I knew nothing more until coming round in military hospital after an operation to remove the bone and splinters!
>
> You have raised the point of the origin of the shell. At that time it could well have been one of ours. There is a reference (by Rutherford and Applebee) that everyone was under cover when our guns brought their fire right down on the position. If there was, we in the dugout were unaware of this. Not that it was going to make any difference. A direct hit is a direct hit with all the consequences. The same applies to the decision to withdraw from our forward defence dug-outs. I didn't hear any order to withdraw, but moved out with the last ones to go.[99]

Willi Thielecke was in IIIFJR22 in the attack on Schaddenhof. He described how he came to be there and what happened:

> I was born in 1923 in Beetzendorf, and on 15 April 1942 was conscripted into Luftwaffe radio intercept. After basic training, I was trained as a radar operator and then a radar mechanic. After passing out I was ordered to report to a Freya radar station in Arras and later one in Evreuse… In mid-August 1944 as the Allies approached we blew up our radar installations and tried to get back to Germany. Near the border of Lorraine we received new radars but were not made operational. So I can say that we were out of work and, as we were Luftwaffe, we volunteered for the paratroops to avoid transferring into the Army. We moved to Gardelegen where paratroops were trained, but we got no jump training. Nevertheless we were all now called Fallschirmjägers even though destined for a ground role. We were posted to Winterswijk in the Netherlands where we were given basic training as infantry before being marched to the front at Roermond [IIIFJR22 was at one time called FJR Wittstock,[100] and

98 Lionel Roebuck in a letter to this author.
99 Letter from Lionel Roebuck.
100 E Busch. *Die Fallschirmjäger-Chronik* (Friedberg: Podzun-Pallas-Verlag, 1983), p. 160.

Wittstock was Willi's CO in 8FJD]. The front line was threatened so we were marched very quickly to Weeze where a bridge had been seized by British troops. We were under orders to re-take that bridge. I remember the words of our platoon commander, Lt Schreiber; 'So boys, now we go very slowly like we go to a funeral', since he must also have seen no sense in what we were ordered to do.

Around midday on 28 February [(sic): he must mean 27 February] an assault detachment of about 20 men was assembled at Rahmenhof to re-take the bridge at Schaddenhof. After a short German artillery barrage we advanced towards Schaddenhof. Passing beyond the small wood that is between Rahmenhof and Schaddenhof we encountered strong resistance from the English soldiers who were occupying Schaddenhof. We were also fired at by a tank that stood to the north of the Mühlen Fleuth. It was impossible for us to advance any further. Thereupon Lt Schreiber sent me with a message to the battalion's Tac HQ in Rahmenhof. The battalion commander, Capt Wittstock? sent me back with the order to defend the position until reinforcements could be sent. We dug in behind a turnip clamp. As reinforcements arrived throughout the night, the fighting got heavier again. Schaddenhof remained in English hands. During the battle our Company Commander, Lt Bruckmüller, I think, was wounded. If I remember correctly, he received a shrapnel wound in his arm. Lt Schreiber took over the Company. In the morning around 5 am on 1 March, [28 February] a retreat to Rahmenhof was ordered so its defence could be organised (the battalion's Tac HQ had meanwhile departed). About 8 am the English attacked with tank support. Since it was impossible to defend ourselves, we surrendered. If I remember correctly, the troops that took us prisoner wore an armband with the word Poland [he remembered they were not British and might be remembering the Canadian Canloan officers in 3 BID]. We were taken back to Schaddenhof, now securely in English hands, while being shelled by German artillery. Behind Schaddenhof we were interrogated for the first time. What was left of our battalion numbered only 40 men, one of whom was an officer, Lt Schreiber, who was now separated from us. In Goch we were collected into a large POW camp for the first time, and new POWs arrived running. 1 March was a rainy day [correct. 27 February was cloudy & mild, 28 February was fair, while 1 March was wet & cold], and we drank rainwater to quench our thirst. The roof of the POW camp was completely destroyed. Consequently the night of 2 March was spent on wet straw. We then went through Holland to Belgium and were held in POW Camps 2226 and 2224 near Ostend where the food was scarce and poor and I lost a great deal of weight. Things changed completely when we were moved to POW Camp 29 in Royston, Hertfordshire. I was discharged in February 1947, and returned home.[101]

Renison continued:

The forming up place for the Boche counter-attack seemed to have shifted from the axis of the road to the triangular wood on C Coy's left and this was receiving particular attention from our guns. But still B Coy had not arrived and as there was no word from them I decided to go over to Büssenhof again and find out what had happened. This meant leaving the Command Post without a Bn officer, but I was quite happy to leave things in the hands of Burton Pirie: we had worked together long enough to know each other's minds and Burton was always an invaluable source of advice and encouragement to me. I never had to make up a fire plan, it was always there ready for me to vet. The whole position however was given a different

101 Edited letters from Willi Thielecke of 21 February and 4 March 2000 to Greg Way of Widewell in Plymouth, and a more detailed letter of 10 October 2002 to this author.

> complexion when the Middlesex pl cmd arrived into the Command Post to say that the Boche had come into the triangular copse where his guns had been and that he had withdrawn the whole pl to a position just between Kampshof and Geurtshof.[102]

The historian of 2 Middlesex wrote:

> Middlesex support for the attack was limited, because 4.2" and Mk.VIIIz ammunition was in very short supply since the Reichswald battle. 10 Platoon fired some 900 bombs in support of the advance (of 8 BIB). 9 Platoon of C Company, who had consolidated with the East Yorks, were in the thick of it, and had to withdraw some distance at one stage of the proceedings. They had two casualties, including Sgt Merritt. 10 Platoon had a very hectic night. They fired all the ammunition of the whole mortar company. Fetching all this ammunition was quite a feat, over the muddy tracks in the wood.[103]

Renison:

> This meant that C Coy was now entirely out in the blue with the Boche on the road behind them. The copse must be retaken. B Coy must get across the bridge and C Coy must get its ammunition: I set off to Büssenhof to find B Coy.
>
> The first person of B Coy I met was Sgt Saxby with his pl, who said that they hadn't been able to reach the bridge, although they didn't appear to have bumped any Boche. I contacted Bob Laird and also saw Payne, C Coy's carrier driver, and discovered what had happened to his vehicle. I then heard over the air that Banger had arrived at the Command Post with a carrier and, in spite of the presence of Boche between him and the bridge, had set off straight away to go to C Coy. With his carrier going flat out down the road and in the face of a fusillade of shots from the copse, Banger crossed the bridge and reached Schaddenhof. [Renison asked Banger how long he needed to deliver the ammunition. He replied, 'About ten minutes good going on the main road'; he did it in five].[104] It is significant of all that Banger meant to the Bn that the only message that came back over the air was 'Banger's here'. With the amn and some wireless batteries delivered and the worst of C Coy's casualties on board [including the badly wounded and unconscious Lionel Roebuck, as Lionel explains below], the carrier came back to Büssenhof and I heard from Banger what was happening. For this and many other acts during this battle Banger received a bar to his DSO and Pte Rippon, the carrier driver, was mentioned in despatches.
>
> I eventually found Chris and it became evident that the company had started off all right but had lost direction and wandered too far to the right and come up against the River Niers instead of the bridge. We did a further recce together and having made quite certain of his direction, I told Chris to take the Company, with the Carrier pl under command to make good the numbers who had been detached in the previous attempt, straight for the bridge disregarding the Boche in the copse completely. When the company were safely past the copse, they were to fire a Verey signal – this was to be the sign for D Coy to attack and retake the copse.[105]

102 Bill Renison's diary.
103 Moberly, *Second Battalion,* p. 109.
104 Scarfe, *Assault Division*, p. 212.
105 Bill Renison's diary.

Roebuck:

> I am aware that Maj. Rutherford has not accepted any company other than C Company being involved. They [D Coy] came forward afterwards to take up position in the German dug-outs close by the bridge. There is some distance from the bridge to the farm and it was dark, so their presence there may not have been noticed by Major Rutherford.[106]

Renison:

> If these manoeuvres came off, I reckoned we should be fairly secure, but I asked Banger to stress with bde the fact that all our goods were in the shop window and there was no further reserve available. The sooner 53 Div. came up behind the better – there were only the tanks to hold Büssenhof if anyone came across the Niers from the right.[107]

The biographer of 6 GAB[108] wrote that a message back to Bn HQ was misunderstood, and news spread of a calamity in the bridgehead. This, according to Forbes, led the Infantry Brigadier to go off and organise a counter-attack with a battalion of 53 BID. Forbes believed the day was saved by the bravery of the infantry and by the arrival of eight tanks under Heywood-Lonsdale and Minette-Lucas, 'who had blazed away with their guns until the enemy withdrew, completely overwhelmed by the combination of Besa and Bren'. A cynic might say these events illustrate Count Ciano's saying that *La vittoria trova cento padri, e nessuno vuole riconoscere l'insuccesso* (Victory has a hundred parents, and defeat is an orphan). Renison continued:

> When I got back to Kampshof, I quite soon heard that B Coy had got across and were digging in in close contact with Rutherford, and D Coy re-established the position in the triangular copse. I then tried to send the Middlesex platoon back to join D Coy but to my intense annoyance was unable to find them anywhere in spite of making a personal recce. It wasn't until early in the morning that I discovered that they had found their proposed position unsuitable and had moved elsewhere without telling me. The one thing that was really worrying me now was a possible attack on A Coy from the left but the South Lancs must have been engaging the full attention of the Boche in this direction as we had no bother except from the constant shelling. Luckily the house was pretty solid.
>
> The sappers had confirmed the condition of the bridge quite soon after C Coy's arrival there. A Young Scots subaltern had strolled up to the Command Post on his own and, having assured himself that we were over, walked quite nonchalantly straight across the front with a long stick in his hand, tested the depth of the water, the width of the stream and the strength of the bridge, and then walked back again. It was a perfect example of complete absorption in the task in hand.
>
> The Boche counter-attacks were maintaining their intensity, and the reports of tanks heard in the distance were now being converted to the actual presence of tanks in the counter-attack [Lionel Roebuck wrote; 'night-time action didn't seem to be much of a worry to them'] and there was even a rumour of Boche tanks on our side of the bridge. The SOS continued in its full intensity and the range was shortened until it seemed to Burton and me to be right on top of the companies, but we left the control to those on the spot, who knew what they

106 Lionel Roebuck's memoir.
107 Bill Renison's diary.
108 Forbes, *6th Guards*, p. 112.

> wanted. The call was now for anti-tank support as our own anti-tank guns had been overrun when C Coy had been forced to pull in from their first perimeter. We all felt very strongly that the mere presence of a British tank over the bridge would have a big morale effect on our own troops, but in spite of every argument and every effort both on my part and on the part of Brigade we failed completely to get the Corps SP guns to commit themselves across the bridge. There were some pretty hard words said and for his sake I am glad that I never met that troop commander.[109]

These were either M10 3 inch SPs, called TDs by the Americans and Wolverines by the British, or 17pdr Achilles, of 198 Anti-Tank Battery (SP) RA. In Mears Confirmatory Notes to CRA's 'O' Group 26 Feb, see above, this unit was 'under command', but refused to take commands from Brigade, according to Renison. This suggests that even when technically 'under command', the crews behaved as if they had the discretion that went with being 'in support'. In fact the M10s would not have survived the heavy DF, since the crews served the guns in an open-topped turret. It was the heavily armoured Churchills of 4 GG that were immune to 25-pdrs and should have been in the Schaddenhof perimeter. Renison again:

> The culminating point was reached when the Boche actually penetrated right up to the walls of Schaddenhof itself with infantry supported by a tank. As they passed the windows of the house the Boche shouted at the troops inside, but were greeted with shouts of defiance, which turned the tank's gun onto the house. One shot actually hit the turret [actually the mud shield] of the OP tank at a few yards' range but was luckily HE and not solid shot. The Boche tank drove over a corner of C Coy's HQ and let light into it before turning away.[110]

Roebuck was unconscious, but heard later that the German tank,

> fired on the OP tank, but without causing serious damage. However, this prompted a quick evacuation from the tank and into the HQ's bunker. With some audacity, the tank commander called out, in English, to those in the farm-house; 'Are you all right in there, Tommee?' Initially no-one replied, but after a few more times it was too much and someone shouted out; 'Of course we bloody well are'. He then called on them to surrender and this was met with a defiant refusal. After he had called again, the tank backed off away from the building and shells were fired…An attempt was made by Sergeant Whitfield to stalk the tank with the hope of knocking it out with the PIAT but tragically he was run down by the tank and killed. For some reason [a PIAT?] the tank was then driven away from the vicinity of the farm, leaving only the infantry to continue with their persistent attacks.[111]

Renison:

> At the east end of the house a battle raged for some time between a party commanded by MacLean, one of the FOOs, and some Boche who had installed themselves in some of the outbuildings armed with panzerfausts. The marks on the walls bore witness to the Boche's efforts. Mac afterwards received an MC for his part in the battle as also did John Ford, who was doing the actual shooting of the guns. At one moment John was off the air for about

109 Bill Renison's diary.
110 Bill Renison's diary.
111 Lionel Roebuck's memoir.

twenty minutes and, when he came through again, Burton asked what had happened. John's reply, which I overheard, was, 'You will realise that it is pretty hot up here and we have to make a dash for it'. Burton asked him to try and cut down his off-periods as much as possible, to which John replied, 'OK – we'll leave our dash to the last possible moment'. At one time everyone was so fully employed that two Boche prisoners were being used to hand up grenades from the cellar. However, try as they might, and they tried mighty hard, the Boche failed to break the two companies and the effect of the continuous gunfire on the troops forming up in the woods must have been appalling. They must have wanted to prevent us getting to Weeze on that side of the river very badly to have sacrificed the number of troops they did. Without the artillery support they received, it is very doubtful whether even the two coys could have held their ground all night.

A minor crisis occurred in the Command Post during the night when the last vestige of oil in our only hurricane lamp burnt out and it looked as if we would have to fall back on torches. However the tank LO came to the rescue by bringing a long lead from his tank down into the cellar and supplying us with electric light from his inspection lamp. Its only snag was the fact that each time anyone came down the stairs he broke the lead.

Early in the morning a recce party from an RWF Bn in 53 Div. came up to arrange the postponed relief. I was discussing the situation with their CO and explaining to him that as we were still being counter-attacked it was difficult to fix anything firm, until things were straightened out a bit. All of a sudden the Boche scored a direct hit on the back corner of the house and to my horror I discovered that they had a full recce party waiting outside with no cover – this was the first I had heard of it. Two of them were killed outright and four others wounded.[112]

The biographer of 53 BID explained:

A party from 6 RWF, who were to relieve 2 East Yorks in the Mühlen Fleuth bridgehead, set off the make a reconnaissance. Just as they had finished the enemy staged a local counter-attack accompanied by heavy artillery fire. They caught the recce party and inflicted heavy losses. Maj E Hughes, Capt L Owen and Capt G Griffith were killed and two other officers seriously wounded. The loss of these experienced officers, following so closely the casualties two days before, was a heavy blow to the battalion.[113]

Renison continued:

It took some time to get an RAP carrier up to get the wounded back and we made them as comfortable as we could in the cellar. The remainder of the party went back to Bde to sort things out, but I did learn that the Bn was now in the woods from which we had started so our tail was not quite so much in the air.

However the Boche still appeared determined to maintain his grip on our side of the bridge and D Coy with only a mere handful left out of their original numbers were unable to prevent the Boche from getting back into the copse on the road and about 0230 hr. Bob Laird came into the Command Post to report that he had been forced out by very much superior numbers and that in the dark he had been unable to reorganise the very few that were left. Most of them must have pulled back to Büssenhof but they were obviously not strong enough to stage another attack and there were no other reserves available to take on the job. All that could

112 Bill Renison's diary.
113 CN Barclay. *History of the 53rd (Welsh) Div* (London: William Clowes, 1956), p. 135.

> be done was to see that the Boche stayed where they were and to ensure this the tanks lined up in front of Büssenhof and at intermittent intervals during the night fired bursts of Besa at the copse to keep the Boche's heads down. Actually we found out later that this was not particularly effective as the road ran on a small embankment, which screened anyone in the copse beyond: two of D Coy turned up in the morning having spent the whole night there looking after two Boche prisoners.[114]

According to Forbes, Sgt Dillingham commanded a troop right by the bridge where they could see Paratroopers waving a lantern in a window tempting the tanks to fire HE and give away their position. Then at 4 am, again according to Forbes, the Germans hurled a furious counter-attack against the bridgehead. Almost at once Dillingham was wounded by a panzerfaust and:

> as the Infantry had been slightly withdrawn, Sgt Higgin and one SP were left to defend the bridge by themselves...until Heywood-Lonsdale ordered them to withdraw.[115]

Renison continued the story:

> About four o'clock the counter-attacks started to ease off and we were able to drop the rate of fire of the artillery, but not before the Divisional Artillery had expended 400 rounds per gun for our benefit and the Corps artillery some 100 r.p.g. I had had a long chat with the Brigadier [Goulburn] over the 18 set to main HQ at about three o'clock, so long in fact that the Intelligence Log simply recorded '0245/0315 hr. Brigadier and CO'. However I was able to give him a pretty good idea of the situation and learnt that Banger was coming up to tell me of 53 Div.'s plans for the morning relief.
>
> Banger arrived to say that A Coy would be relieved almost at once and that a company was coming up to Büssenhof to reoccupy the copse at first light with any assistance that the tanks could give them. Once this was accomplished the relief of B and C Coys would start and we hoped to be clear by about 0900 hr. In view of this I arranged with Banger not to send breakfasts forward but to have them ready for us when we got back. The concentration area was around the level crossing where the axis track crossed the Goch/Udem railway about 2500 yards back. [941422. By this time the railway line, which runs to Xanten through the Hochwald Gap was being taken up and the permanent way converted into a road].
>
> A Coy got out without incident, Shaw having come up from the LOBs to relieve Adams, who had been wounded in the leg early in the day: he had not said anything about it earlier on but was now finding it difficult to walk. I also sent back some of the Tac HQ personnel whom I no longer required with a fresh company in the locality and made room for the Welsh coy HQ in Kampshof. This enabled me to keep in touch with the movements of the rest of their Bn. The copse was duly reoccupied without trouble and two companies moved across the bridge and extended our bridgehead without any opposition other than some desultory shelling of the bridge approaches. With the coming of daylight all efforts by the Boche to retake the bridge had ceased and the doctor after several trips across the bridge with the RAP carriers had succeeded in getting all the casualties back. C Coy had lost their sgt major, Loughram, wounded after he had spent most of the night distributing amn under the most difficult conditions. Pte Russell, one of the HQ runners, was later awarded an immediate MM for his gallantry in assisting with the distribution.

114 Bill Renison's diary.
115 Forbes, *6th Guards*, p. 112.

Even now there was a last minute hitch in the relief, as the Welsh Bde was unwilling to allow us to move back until they had got three coys into the bridgehead. About 0900 hr. B Coy came back but Rutherford asked if he could come out in his own time as the shelling was increasing and there was a suspicion of some interference from across the Niers. He eventually got clear by about midday bringing with him the 6-pdrs, which had been recovered, although one of the Windsor carriers parked in the triangular copse had had a direct hit and was burnt out. I went over to Büssenhof to meet him, but owing to the shelling of that area they crossed the open ground to Geurtshof, only to meet a salvo there as well – fortunately without mishap. I found however that Burton Pirie in pulling his OP tank out from Kampshof had gone up on a mine in spite of taking the precaution of driving down someone else's tracks – there were no casualties except the tank.

Burton and I walked back through the woods together where the rest of the Welsh Brigade were concentrated and called in at the HQ of the Bn, which had relieved us. After their experiences of the night, they had wisely decided that Kampshof was no place for a Bn HQ. Certainly I should never have chosen it as a free choice, but it was rather a case of having shelter thrust upon one. The battle was over and the 53 Div. entered Weeze the following day [untrue; it was the day after, 2 March], but from the haul of prisoners it was apparent that the bulk of the Boche on the Maas had got away through the corridor.

It was difficult to assess what we had been up against but at least two Bns were identified from prisoners and both were Fallschirmjäger Bns. I went into Brigade Tac HQ at Schloss Kalbeck [942430] on my way back and was very warmly greeted by the Brigadier [Goulburn], who reiterated once again his oft-repeated comments on the spirit of the Bn. Our casualties had been heavy: 4 officers and 29 other ranks killed, five officers wounded one of whom died later, 118 Other Ranks were wounded and 4 other ranks were missing. What the Boche's' casualties were, it is of course impossible to tell: we had taken about 150 prisoners and counted at least 85 corpses in the battle area. The proportions of wounded from shellfire in the woods must have been pretty high.

The Bn, with the sole exception of Bn HQ, was dug in in the woods and unfortunately the weather again took a turn for the worse and the tracks became practically impassable with one of the coy areas – so bad that we eventually took them further back to a small cottage. But the morale was tremendous and a visit from General Horrocks, XXX Corps Cmd, was very popular as he chatted quite informally with the troops he met by the roadside. I received the following personal letter from the Div. Cmd:-

Dear Renison.
I am sorry that I have been unable to visit you and your gallant chaps today. I wanted to come and tell you personally how very proud I am of the magnificent fight you made last night.

Will you let all ranks know that I shall come and tell them, as soon as I possibly can, how moved I have been by their very gallant actions.

Yours very sincerely,
L.G. Whistler.

It was a tremendous moment for me to walk round the Bn and read the letter to the troops. It was difficult not to give C Coy the lion's share of the credit, but I hope that in the preceding pages I have given every company due credit for their share in the action's successful outcome: it had been a Bn battle in real truth. It gave the greatest pleasure to all ranks when the Div. Cmd gave orders to the Div. Engineers to place a name board on the bridge bearing the Regimental Crest and the title 'Yorkshire Bridge'.

And even the ranks of Tuscany
Could scarce forbear to cheer.[116]

In reality, the 'ranks of Tuscany' cared nothing about one more bloody defeat in the service of a regime that continues to embarrass most Germans. There was no cheering and the name board quickly vanished and was not replaced. Schaddenhof was rebuilt without a sign of its former importance to either side. Subsequently the original bridge was replaced through the need for road improvement, a fate shared with the more famous Pegasus Bridge outside Caen as late as 1994.

Maj Charles Kenneth King, Banger to everyone, received a bar to his DSO in record time. The citation was written on 28 February by Renison, signed by Goulburn on 1 March, by Whistler on 2 March, by Horrocks on 4 March and by Crerar on 8 March. Montgomery never dated his signature, which was a formality as it was Crerar's decision. Banger's citation:

8 BIB, 3 BID, XXX Corps, 2 E Yorks, S/Maj 32009, Charles Kenneth KING DSO
During the attack NE of WEEZE on 27/28 Feb 45 this offr was acting as second in comd of the Bn. The Bn established a one company bridgehead across the MUHLEN FLEUTH during the afternoon, but were heavily counterattacked immediately after dark by enemy infiltrating through the woods in front of them and to their flanks supported by tanks which in some cases overran the company posns. At the same time the enemy established themselves in a small wood on the rd leading to the bridge from the north and cut the L of C to the fwd coy. Amn had run very low and by 2000 hrs the coy was reduced to the small amount in the RA OP tank. Maj King during the whole operation had been present with ration and amn carriers in the fwd area and under very heavy arty and mortar fire had personally delivered a dinner meal to all fwd coys incl the coy across the bridge. Entirely on his own initiative and with only the most confused infm as to the situation around the bridge, Maj King took the coy amn carrier straight past the enemy position in the wood on the south of the bridge in the face of aimed spandau fire and succeeded in reaching the coy HQ on the south side of the bridge and delivering amn and wireless batteries to the coy. This action restored the amn situation and enabled the coy to re-establish comn. Maj King then returned to Bn Tac HQ with a first-hand knowledge of the position and this knowledge alone enabled a second coy to be moved immediately to reinforce the coy across the bridge. Throughout the entire engagement this officer moved all over the battle area with a complete disregard for his own personal safety and was able to keep Bde fully informed of the tactical situation at first hand. His bravery and initiative were a source of inspiration to all who saw him and his action in bringing forward the amn was responsible more than anything else for enabling the forward coy to hold on to its very small bridgehead.[117]

Intelligence Summary no. 228, issued late on 27 February, reported that 5 enemy officers and 472 other ranks were taken prisoner on that day. Details of their units are given in Appendix 3. Over half were from FJR7 and 1062GR.

3 Br Inf Div Int Summary No 228. 27 Feb, 1945
(Selected extracts)

1. Our attack began at 0700 hrs this morning. It appears that the enemy was expecting to be attacked along the axis of the rd UDEM-WEEZE, and our operation caught him

116 Bill Renison's diary.
117 TNA: WO 373/53: 'Banger' King's Citation.

off guard. Moreover progress of the armour on our left as far as the rly line at 908427 had shaken up the battle groups of 84 Div that were defending the NW approaches at UDEM and pushed large numbers of confused stragglers into our sector. As a result we encountered at first only scattered resistance and made as good speed as the difficult going and random mines allowed. The rd WEEZE-UDEM was reached on a broad front by midday and two vital bridges taken intact – that at 974409, prepared for demolition but not blown, and at 945390. By this time the resistance was stiffening and hard fighting ensued. On the left the woods South of the rd were cleared and patrols went fwd as far as 973397 and 977399. On the right the enemy made skilful use of the uneven wood at 959395 and is still in possession of that area tonight. The latest development has been a spirited counter-attack against our br head 945390, which has been in progress for a considerable time and at one period achieved a small penetration.

2. The identity of the tps encountered has been very much as expected. A total of eight offrs and over 600 men has been taken since last night, including a certain number handed over to us by the formn on our left. It appears that Parachute Bn CRAHS was holding a sector facing NE at BATZENHOF 9741 and II & III Bns of 7 Parachute Regt were holding to the West of Bn CRAHS; II Bn facing North and III Bn with its right flank on the rly facing NW. The other important identification during the day was of 3 Coy 24 Parachute Regt HUBNER. This Bn appears to have been holding the West of the line resting on the River NIERS at 945393. In sp of this inf the enemy used a few tks on the Eastern flank. These are reported to be both Panthers and Tigers. No identification of this tk unit has been made. The enemy possesses SP guns in fair number, but the tk strength of Pz formn now in the area is almost negligible. If the presence of Tigers be confirmed, they must belong to GHQ Hy Tk Bn. The other weapon that the enemy has employed has been his arty, but the volume of fire has been very much lighter than that of the previous few days.
3. The enemy line is probably held by – from East to West – II and III Bns 7 Parachute Regt, not worth more than one Bn together; Bn CRAHS in the wooded area 9438. II and III Bns of the Regt may be found in the front by tomorrow morning. But they constitute the only available res, and will not likely be committed in the line when the safety of two towns – WEEZE and KERVENHEIM – is in jeopardy.
5. Pz Lehr withdrawn to München-Gladbach.
   On our left there has been notable progress. The Cdns have left the plateau and breached the SCHLIEFFEN line at UDEMERBRUCH 0240.
8. It was reported that a German officer was found dead bound and gagged in the area 960432 – apparently the victim of his less than enthusiastic colleagues.[118]

Sir John Ford remembered seeing a lot of British dead in front of the position when the sun came up. In a conversation about whether it would be possible to estimate how many shells were fired at Schaddenhof and its approaches during the long night, Ford answered that it would be no more than a guess. The artillery had other tasks, he said, and although the number of rounds fired per gun is known their targets were not recorded. Nor did the condition of the landscape reveal the tonnage fired, he said, since a lot went into the woods. He recalled that the meadows were not unduly chewed up and were still green with grass. It was not like the Somme, he added.[119] Ten German skeletons were found in the fields in the 1980s, including five in 1989, according

118 TNA: WO 171/4130: 3 British Infantry Division War Diary.
119 Sir John Ford in conversation with this author on 12 March 1997.

to the *Weeze Nachrichten*. It did not report whether the dead had been intentionally buried and forgotten, or were among the missing.

Bosch[120] describes what happened on the German side. Erdmann, GOC 7FJD, was told straight away about the bridgehead and gave orders that the bridge must be retaken at any cost, or at the least destroyed. An attempt at 6 pm by the remnants of I/24 was not pursued because it was under fire. So 7FJD ordered IFJR24 to storm the bridge. Bosch does not explain why FJR22 and FJR24 in Wadehn's 8FJD should have been taking orders from Erdmann, GOC 7FJD, but the reason was surely that Erdmann was responsible for the defence of Weeze. IFJR24 (or IIFJR24) attacked down the west side of the road against Lionel Roebuck's 13 Platoon. IIIFJR22 attacked Schaddenhof. They dug in in the woods south-west of Schaddenhof waiting for darkness without realising how close they were to C Coy of 2 E Yorks, who heard the preparations and brought down a heavy artillery stonk which lasted four hours. At midnight, 9 Coy attacked from Rahmenhof, and in the first attack 2 and 3 Sections were repulsed by the British. But a second attack supported by 10 Section with the heavy weapons support platoon brought success. Sappers and Paratroopers under Lt Schreiber and Platoon Leader Weinmann reached the bridge. The explosives, however, failed to go off and the heavy British machine-gun and mortar fire drove them back. C Coy had an artillery tank controlling the artillery, but ammunition began to get low. The position of C Coy seemed hopeless as their ammunition ran out. Paratroopers crossed the stream and occupied the wood astride the communications. The E Yorkshires' B Coy got lost but later reinforced the bridge, but no one knew where the other side was. C Coy then withdrew into the farmhouse surrounded by Paratroopers. Major King delivered ammunition just in time to avoid surrender. A StuG was sent in after midnight to batter the building, and the British were driven out only to retake it minutes later in a counter-attack. The German coy commander made a mistake in attacking from the south rather than from the north or west, because they were badly mauled by the British defensive fire. IIFJR22 attacked again with the StuG, which opened up the walls and fired down the corridor. A Fallschirmjäger section entered the farmhouse, but none reappeared. At 4 am the Fallschirmjägers consolidated at Rahmenhof, and at 5.30 am the British were reinforced by the RWF of 53 BID. Heavy German machine-gun fire could not prevent their arrival because the Artillery put down a dense smoke screen. The exhausted C and B Coys were then relieved by 53 BID. The Germans then stopped their efforts to destroy the bridge, and fell back to resist 53 BID's Operation *Daffodil*.

Lionel Roebuck described what happened after he was wounded:

> From information which has been gathered over many years, [I can say that] the three others with me in the dug-out, who were never identified despite my many enquiries, had looked after my welfare and got me into the farm-house. It would have been a struggle for them, as my body blocked the only way out of the dug-out. Jimmy Russell MM, who was awarded the decoration for his gallantry that day, had seen me and had helped to bring me in, thinking me a certain 'gonner' because of the wounds and blackness of my face. Arthur, my old school-mate, also looked after me. He had helped them to put my stretcher against a wall inside the farmhouse. So, while the battle raged all around us and in the farm buildings, with grenades, Sten and Bren guns, hand to hand fighting and a Tiger [StuG – Lionel later commented that to most British soldiers all German tanks were Tigers] tank belting shells into the farm walls at close range, I was unconscious and blissfully unaware of all that was happening.
>
> The gallant action of Major 'Banger' King DSO and Bar, when he drove a Bren-Gun Carrier loaded with ammunition through the enemy lines to reach the beleaguered C Company had been my salvation. ...his load of ammunition was quickly taken into the farm-house. Major

120 Bosch, *Der Zweite Weltkrieg*, p. 222.

Reg Rutherford MC, deciding that the RA signaller and myself were the most seriously wounded near at hand, helped to load us on the Bren Carrier for the return trip, back through the hail of fire from the Germans in the copse…Many others died that night who could have lived, had they been got out earlier for the urgent medical attention which they badly needed. Unfortunately, the RA signaller of the OP tank later died of his stomach wounds.[121]

MM 8BIB, 3BID, 30 Corps, 2 E Yorks, Private 4347864 James RUSSELL
During the attack NE of WEEZE on 27 Feb 45, this soldier was acting as Pl runner in the coy ordered to capture and hold the bridge over the MUHLEN FLEUTH. During one enemy counter-attack, when a forward sec had been overrun, Pte Russell volunteered to go out in the face of fierce spandau and schmeiser fire to bring in casualties and actually succeeded in doing so. When ammunition was running out this soldier collected a further supply from another pl, which involved crossing the bridge under heavy fire and went round from man to man distributing the amn. This action alone enabled his pl to beat off a further counter-attack by fire. Later, hearing cries of help from the trees just forward of his position, Pte Russell went out alone to acc who was there and brought in a wounded German. Throughout the entire action this soldier showed such a complete disregard of his own personal safety and such devotion to duty under continuous heavy fire that his whole company were inspired by his coolness and gallantry.[122]

John Ford wrote:

It would be nice if you could mention my signaller's name. He was Bombardier Benny White, a most gallant man. He had been wounded when the carrier was blown up on a mine two days earlier crossing the railway track, and he was suffering from a premonition that he would be killed.[123]

Ford was put in for an immediate DSO by Peddie on 5 March, which was endorsed by Whistler on 6 March, but changed by Horrocks on 15 March to an MC, and signed by Crerar and Montgomery.

MC 8 BIB, 76th (H) Field Regt RA, T/Capt 237535 John Archibald FORD
For sustained gallantry, skill and devotion to duty. On 27 Feb 45 Capt FORD was FOO with 'D' Coy E YORKS Regt which had the important task of securing a bridgehead over the MUHLEN FLEUTH stream, NE of WEEZE. 'D' Coy suffered heavy casualties during the assault of the battalion's immediate objective. It was greatly assisted by Capt FORD who used the weapons of his OP tank to deal with enemy resistance, showing great initiative and courage in doing so. 'C' Coy then passed through 'D' Coy, and Capt FORD accompanied them across the stream. About 2000 hrs the enemy began a series of attacks which lasted until 0600 hrs 28 Feb. It was essential that the bridgehead should be held and Capt FORD so directed the fire of the divisional artillery that the enemy suffered heavy casualties before reaching the infantry localities. Over 80 dead were found in the woods in front of the bridgehead. At one time the infantry were running short of ammunition and Capt FORD used the automatic weapons of his tank with great effect. The Armoured Regt had withdrawn after the capture of the bridgehead, and Capt FORD's Sherman was the only AFV on the position. It

121 Lionel Roebuck's memoir.
122 TNA: WO 373/53 Russell's citation.
123 Letter from John Ford in March 1997.

attracted much attention and was finally hit by an enemy tank at a range of 10 yards. During the whole of this action Capt FORD showed initiative and resource of the highest order, and not only of his handling of the artillery, but also by his magnificent courage and example to those around him, contributed greatly to the capture and successful defence of a vital bridgehead.[124]

Lt Alastair Maclean received an immediate MC from Renison, which was a most unusual procedure, but Maclean had in effect joined and took command of infantry in the best tradition of The Regiment. It was to happen the next day with the Norfolks. Renison wrote and signed the citation which was countersigned by Peddie, OC 76 Fld Regt RA, on 5 March; it went to the CRA, Brig Mears (6 March), to Whistler (7 March), to Horrocks (9 March), to Crerar (11 March) and Montgomery (undated as usual).

MC, 8BIB, 3BID, 76 (H) Fld Regt RA, Lt 293923 Alistair Finlayson MACLEAN
During the attack NE of WEEZE on 27/28 Feb 45, this officer was acting as FOO with a coy of 2 E YORKS ordered to seize the bridge over the MUHLEN FLEUTH. During the approach to the bridge the Coy came under very heavy artillery and aimed MG fire from the left flank while crossing open ground. In a position entirely devoid of any cover Lt MACLEAN with the greatest coolness and disregard for his own personal safety so directed the fire of his guns that the enemy MG was silenced and the Coy enabled to reach its objective with very few casualties. He was then joined by an FOO in a tank [John Ford] and being released form his gunner responsibilities offered his services to the inf coy comd to reinforce the dwindling number of officers and NCOs. From dusk onward the Coy was subjected to continuous counter-attacks and with amn almost expended Lt MACLEAN took a carrying party across the bridge to borrow amn from a MMG pl behind. On his return he took over comd of a force of 15 men and organized the defence of one end of a house [Schaddenhof]. The enemy penetrated into buildings within a few yards of his position but, in spite of repeated attempts to get into the house by the use of bazookas, he and his force beat off every counter attack and were still in position in the morning. This officer by his personal courage and fine leadership inspired the infantry tps under his comd to fight on even when their amn was almost all gone and his example contributed in very great part to the Coy's achievement of holding fast to their bridgehead.[125]

Roebuck:

'Tabby' Barker was one who did survive the night. He had been taken back towards the bridge, down the farm track towards the Regimental Aid Post which was located in one of the German bunkers. He had nearly reached it when a shell exploded nearby, killing both the stretcher-bearers. 'Tabby' had rolled off the stretcher without further injury and managed to crawl into the RAP shelter. Of all those, so badly wounded, who were in the shelter, he was the only one alive next day. When some of the 53rd Welsh Div. came along to relieve them, 'Tabby' heard a voice say; 'It looks as if they're all dead in here'. He was quick to shout out: 'There's one who isn't'.

124 TNA: WO 373/53, Ford's citation.
125 TNA: WO 373/53, Maclean's citation.

> During that harrowing night, one by one, with no attention to their wounds, they had all died. Johnny Vayro, one of the last to go, asked 'Tabby' to hold his hand to give him some comfort and died a few minutes later with 'Tabby' still holding his hand.
>
> My first recollections, after at least two days of unconsciousness, were of brightness and of voices asking questions about sensitivity to touch on my legs and the right side of my body. Someone was lightly stroking me with soft material and pricking me with a sharp point to find out the degree of feeling. Everywhere they touched felt thick and numb. The doctor remarked to a colleague: 'Many splinters and bits of bone have been removed, but the more deeply seated ones have been left and the tracts not followed up'. My visual recollections were of very little. All the time, there was a lapsing in and out of consciousness. My next recollection was of being attended to on an aeroplane and somewhat deliriously asking for assurance about personal possessions – my 1200 Belgium Francs leave money, the Luger pistol and the mechanical flashlight. [The Luger had been taken from the German machine-gunner killed in defending the bridge. Lionel didn't see it again. He had another Luger at home taken from another machine gunner killed on 27 June 1944 at the Château de la Londe. Lionel kept it until in a moment of weakness long after the War he succumbed to police entreaties to surrender unauthorised firearms to Huddersfield Police Station].
>
> The ambulance trip from the aerodrome to hospital was a terrible ordeal for me and the medical attendants must have been really fed up with all the moans and questions about when the seemingly never-ending journey was going to end. This was because of my delirious state and because I was not really aware of what was happening. The journey took me to St Hughes College, which had been taken over as a military hospital. There I was well looked after, making as good a recovery as possible, before being sent off on a long period of convalescence. It was just over twelve months later, on 26-3-46, that I was discharged from the services.[126]

Only 200 yards south west of Yorkshire Bridge, on the right of the road heading towards Weeze, is a German War Cemetery. The following inscription, exactly as written, will be a memorial for all the 'Banger' Kings of both sides who are buried there and in the Reichswald British War Cemetery. It should be noted that the Weeze Cemetery is the only monument for all those from Weeze and district who are buried in the Eastern vastnesses and whose graves were systematically destroyed by the Soviets when obliterating every vestige of Germany's occupation of their country. Only on Russian War Memorials built since 1994 have Germans at last been portrayed, if only as the dragon being lanced by St. Michael.

> After the invasion of the allied forces in Normandy in June 1944 also the Land of the Lower Rhine became a battle area. It was in February/March 1945 when fierce fightings were going to reach their climax. Several times towns, villages and places changed hands. There was a three days lasting fight for almost every house in Weeze and eighty percent of that place were devastated and destroyed.
>
> English and Canadian troops who followed buried the dead soldiers they found, but hundreds remained lying unburied in the woods and fields and under the ruins and debris.
>
> In August 1945 the people who had been evacuated returned home, and although in great distress with their own sorrows and worries they looked after the recovery of the dead and took care of the graves. However, very soon it was obvious that this was a task they alone couldn't fulfill. In 1947 the *Volksbund Deutsche Kriegsgräberfürsorge* (German War Graves Commission) in close co-operation with the municipal authorities of Weeze, began to transfer

126 Extracts from the unpublished memoirs of Lionel Roebuck.

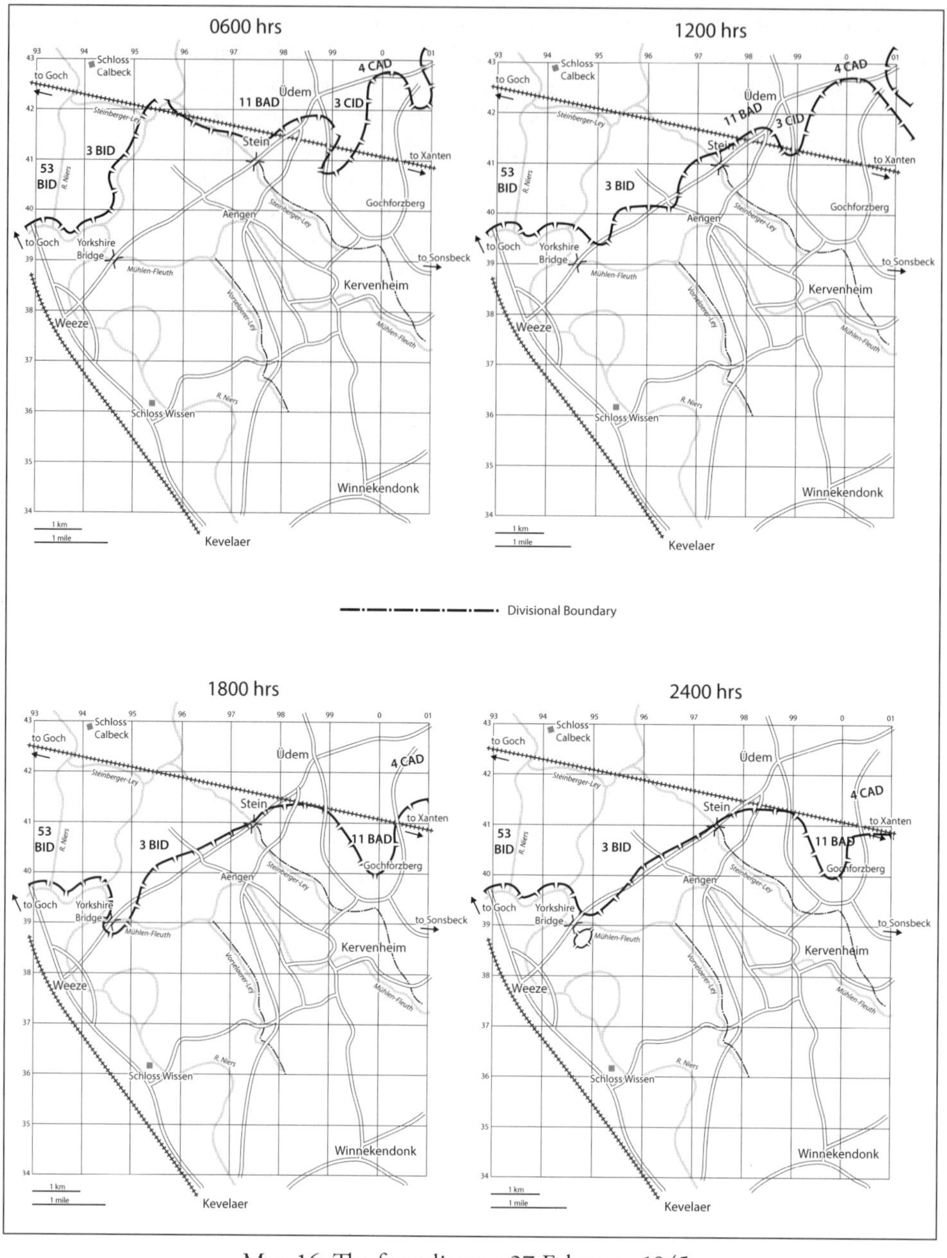

Map 16 The front line on 27 February 1945.

the dead soldiers from their provisional graves to this war cemetery in Weeze in order to give them a perpetual resting place. The family of the count von Loé made available this place the people usually call 'Sandberg' and which changes hand nine times during the heavy fightings. So this place of hard battles had become the last resting place of nearly 2000 dead soldiers.

An arrangement of high crosses made of black basalt lava too, is the centre of the entire cemetery. These three crosses, the one in the middle is about five metres tall, were cut out from a monolith with a weight of 275 tons and comes from a quarry near Gerolstein.

On the right side in front of the arrangement of high crosses there is a butters [sic, buttress] where one can find the cemetery register. All the dead are laid to rest in single graves. Small gravestones in front of the graves show their names. More over the names are shown on plaques which are fixed on the walls in the two small chapels. The tombstones in between tell the names of those who first had been unknown but could be identified later.

The burying place of the nearly 2000 dead who once had their home in all parts of Germany and Austria also comprises the remembrance of the fallen soldiers who had lived in Weeze and lie buried in alien soil. Their names are written on oaken pillars lining the way from the entrance to the arrangement of high crosses.

On 10th September 1950 the war cemetery Weeze was inaugurated and the municipality of Weeze was put in charge of it. Many relatives of the fallen soldiers had come, representatives of the English and Italian War Graves Commissions and numerous visitors from the neighbouring Netherlands attended the inauguration ceremony. The President of the Federal Republic of Germany [Theodor Heuss] said in his speech:

'Many fell as a victim to the dying at the Lower Rhine in 1944/45, and they were sacrificed, as the war was already lost, and many of those lying here knew it was lost. And this is the tragic feeling. They died bound by their duty, and we shall only talk about it with respect of the fate of the individual. A different tone is not allowed'.[127]

Today the area around Yorkshire Bridge, Schaddenhof, Geurtshof, Kampshof and Büssenhof is almost unchanged except for the encroachment of the woods around Geurtshof. In the rest of the Kalbeck area, which is laid out for recreation with bike paths and hiking trails, there has also been restricted development, with four large exceptions. The Goch-Xanten railroad, which Simonds made into his supply road through the Hochwald, is now the D78 road as far as Üdem; the new A57 Autobahn cuts right through the woods where the Grenadier Churchills struggled and its shadow falls where Bob Runcie struggled to free Philip; large lakes have appeared where gravel has been extracted; and the paths and tracks which caused the British sappers so much grief are now paved to a high standard while some are restricted to bicycles and pedestrians. If the visitor can manage to 'look through' these changes, then this is a pleasant battlefield to visit. Respects can be paid to the German dead in the magnificent *Kriegsgräberstätte* just south of Yorkshire Bridge. In the British tradition there is a guest-book in its own cupboard. The British fallen lie in the Reichswald Military Cemetery about 18 km to the northwest in the forest near Cleves. In peace, as in war, divided.

The losses on this day were serious on both sides. The German defenders would have lost over 1,000 men including at least 150 killed and 300 wounded, while 547 prisoners were counted by the British infantry and 600 reported in the Intelligence Summary. British casualties numbered 334, of which 72 were kia and 262 wounded. Two units suffered more than two-thirds or 236 of the total casualties; 2 East Yorkshire with 37 kia and missing, and 123 wounded, for a total of 160; and 1 S Lancashire with 34 kia and missing, and 42 wounded, totalling 76. The S Lancs had 5 officers kia, one more than the E. Yorks.

127 Inscription at the Weeze War Cemetery.

3

The Battle of Kervenheim

Wednesday, 28 February 1945. Weather: fair

Thursday, 1 March 1945. Weather – cold and wet

> *Kervenheim was a sod.*
> Lt-Col Peter Barclay, CO 1 R Norfolk

> *It was only a probing attack. Never a set piece. Should have used more guns and Typhoons.*
> Maj Humphrey Wilson, 2ic 1 R Norfolk

> *The Shropshires are a funny old lot. If somebody has a go at them, they have a go back.*
> Lt 'Ginger' Banks, 2 KSLI

> *(Kervenheim) A piece of ground that to me is one of the richest experiences of my life. Without the infantry, all else is vain. These men are bloody heroes.*
> R.W. Thompson, Sunday Times correspondent

Objectives:
British: To drive through Kervenheim and break out of the Schlieffen Line at Winnekendonk to release GAD to seize the Rhine bridges at Wesel
German: To write down 3 BID, and keep the Rhine crossings open

Troops:
British: 3 BID, 185 BIB: 2 R Warwicks, 1 R Norfolks, 2 KSLI, 2 Lincolns uc
3 Div arty – 72 units 25pdrs
– 198 Bty, 73 Anti-Tk Regt RA with M10 3 inch SP
6 GAB – 4 CG; 1 Sqn/Warwicks; 2 Sqn/KSLI; 3 Sqn/Norfolks
79 BAD – HQ 6 Assault Regiment RE
– C Sqn 141 Regiment RAC (The Buffs) – Crocodiles
– B Sqn 1 Lothian & Border Yeomanry – flails
– A Sqn 49 APC Regiment – Kangaroos
– 284 Assault Sqn RE – AVREs
– 82 Assault Sqn RE – bridgelayers
– 81 Assault Sqn RE – fascines
German: 8FJD, III FJR7 uc, II FJR24 (Müller)
– 7 FJD artillery 105 mm
– XII Assault Gun Brigade StuG III
– Kgr Panzerjäger Abteilung 33 of 15 PGD Jagdpanzer IV

Plan:
British: 28 February, KSLI and Warwicks with CG secure first objective of woods in front of Kervenheim and bridgehead over Mühlen Fleuth at Endtschenhof and Hoxhof. Then Norfolks take Kervenheim and Murmannshof, Warwicks seize Müsershof and KSLI advance on left flank to Mühlen Fleuth in contact with 11 BAD on their left.

German: Defend Kervenheim; use Müsershof, Murmannshof and Boemshof to enfilade the approach to Kervenheim and destroy attack.

Outcome:
KSLI and Warwicks secured first objective on 28 February. Armour vetoed night attack. Early on 1 March, Warwicks were counter-attacked and held off throughout the day leaving left flank open and Müsershof occupied by Germans. Norfolks moved up at 4.30 am and with KSLI attacked at 9 am. Norfolks repulsed on right and held in centre with heavy loss due to bogging of Coldstream tanks, enfilade from Murmannshof and Boemshof, and local counter-attack with armour. At mid-morning D Coy Norfolks with the support of Melikoff's tank entered Kervenheim on the left through a gap in the defences. Melikoff was hit and withdrew. Germans occupied houses by the tower and sealed in the Norfolks. This attracted the attention of Z Company KSLI to the east. With tank support they took the houses and Stokes won the VC. This re-opened access to Kervenheim for A Coy Lincolns and C Coy Norfolks. Brig Matthews declared victory and ordered 2 Lincolns with Churchills and Crocodiles through the village to seize the high ground on the approach to Winnekendonk. One Churchill was destroyed and a Crocodile withdrew. A quiet night followed. The Germans withdrew from Kervenheim and Weeze around 6 am on 2 March.

Conclusion:
3 BID lost 5% casualties (Norfolks 30%) and delayed for 2 days during which 7FJD escaped entrapment. FJR7 lost 30% casualties and 3 StuGs. 3 BID resumed the advance to take Winnekendonk on 2 March.

Casualties:

British:
Norfolks: 45 dead and 124 wounded; Lincolns: 1 dead and 9 wounded; KSLI estimated: 5 killed and 20 wounded; Warwicks: 10 dead and 38 wounded; CG and 141 Regt RAC estimated: 3 dead and 15 wounded: total allied losses 64 killed and 206 wounded for combined loss of 270 and three POWs.

German:
In Murmannshof 9 dead and 5 civilian deaths are recorded. Other losses are unknown but are estimated in total as 95 military deaths and 180 military wounded for a total combined loss of approximately 338.

The British press on the last day of February 1945 reported on the German moves to counter the Anglo-Canadian *Schwerpunkten*:

> **Germans Move Troops South; Maas Front Plugged; Crerar Brings Up More Power.** With the Canadian Army, 28 February. Three main German strong points in the Hochwald area continued to hold out after more than 24 hours' heavy fighting. There is evidence, however,

Map 17 The Kervenheim battlefield, 1:25,000.

Map 18 Aerial photograph of the western part of the Kervenheim battlefield taken on 16 February 1945. (NCAP/ncap.org)

Map 19 Aerial photograph of the eastern part of the Kervenheim battlefield taken on 16 February 1945. (NCAP/ncap.org)

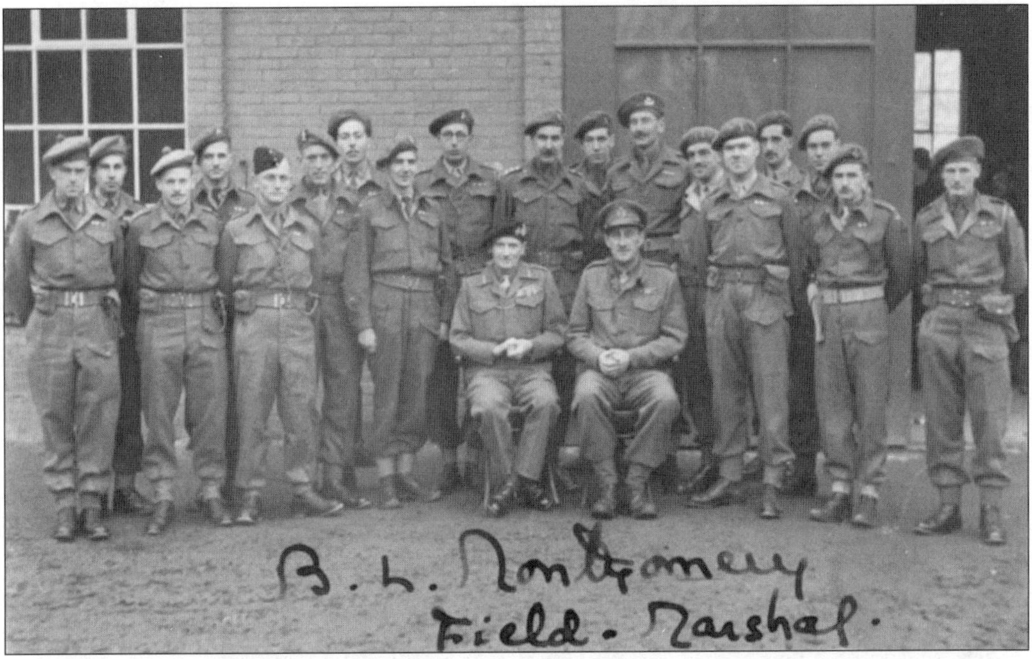

Many of those mentioned in this work were decorated for their bravery in Normandy in two award ceremonies for 3 BID presided over by the seated FM Montgomery and Maj Gen Whistler. This one took place in Gemert in the Netherlands on 18 November 1944, photographed by Sgt Morris. (Standing L.-r.): second Maj Harry Illing, 2 Warwicks; third Lt Col RC MacDonald, 1 KOSB; fourth Capt James R Fetterly, 2 E Yorks & Canloan; fifth Major Leslie Colvin, 2 Lincolns; eighth Capt Len Robertson, 2 E Yorks & Canloan; ninth Lt Col RH Bellamy, 1 R Norfolks; tenth Brig EH Goulburn, OC 8 BIB; eleventh Maj Donald Smith, 1 R Nofolks and killed at Kervenheim; twelth Lt Col DLA Gibbs, 2 Warwicks; seventeenth Maj Jock Aitken, 2 KSLI; eighteenth Lt GA Smith killed at Kervenheim. (© Tony Colvin)

Maj Donald Smith, I R Norfolks at the ceremony on 18 November 1944. He was killed leading C Company's attack on Murmannshof. (© Crown Copyright IWM, B 11869 by Sgt Morris)

The second 3 BID award ceremony was at Gimers Monastery in the Netherlands on 11 December 1944 for those decorated for bravery in the Low Countries, photographed again by Sgt Morris. (L.-r.) top row: third Capt HJ Pacey, 2 Lincolns; middle row: fourth Lt HR Aldridge, 2 KSLI killed at Kervenheim; fifth Lt Terry Rourke, 1 R Norfolks, killed at Kervenheim; sixth Maj Glyn Gilbert, 2 Lincolns; seventh Maj Sam Larkin, 2 Lincolns; eighth Maj Peter Clarke, 2 Lincolns, killed at Winnekendonk; front row: Lt Col Cecil Firbank, 2 Lincolns; second Lt Col RE Godwin, 1 Suffolks; fifth Brig EL Bols, GOC 185 BIB. (© Simon Firbank)

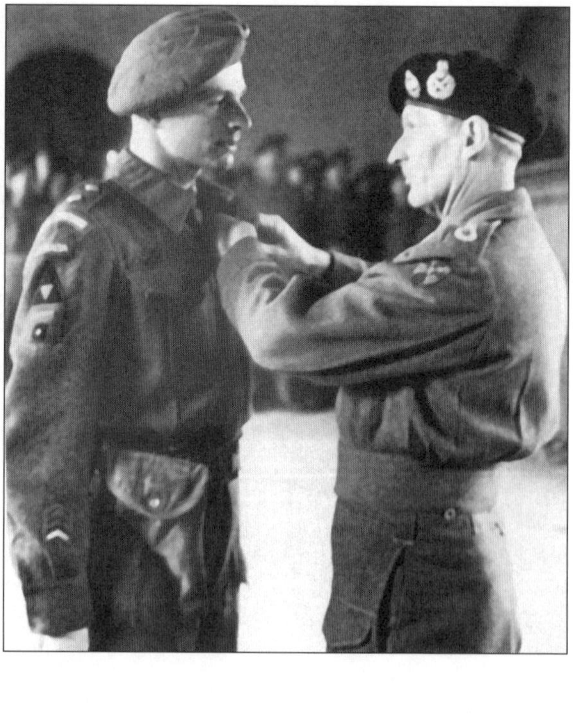

Canloan 267 Jim Fetterley at the ceremony on 18 November. The Canadian flash explains why Germans called 2 E Yorks a Canadian regiment.

> that enemy troops have left the Rhine-Maas front in some strength to meet the threat in the south. The enemy strong points are at Weeze, at Kervenheim, and astride the railway line which runs through a gap in the Hochwald. These "plugs" were thrown in by the Germans where they think our main threats are being made. If these plugs go, then the battle should open up again.
>
> The Hochwald strong point astride the railway consists of dug-in tanks and self-propelled guns behind the Siegfried works through which the Canadians have penetrated. To the west British troops are thrusting in the direction of the Kervenheim strong point, hampered by a system of waterways interfering with tank operations. Other British troops are within 1,000 yards of Weeze.
>
> Altogether it was a day of heavy fighting but no spectacular gains, with Crerar moving more of his striking power into the forward areas for more thrusts.
>
> The Germans counter-attacked today the British bridgehead across the Niers north-east of Weeze, but the [Yorkshire Bridge] bridgehead is still intact after a day of bitter fighting. Another counter-attack was inside the Hochwald Forest with infantry and self-propelled guns. Rocket-firing Typhoons knocked out two of the guns and the attack was broken up and fifty prisoners taken.
>
> The enemy shelled Udem all day. Our own guns have the Rhine ferries at Xanten under fire, and last night blasted then after some movement across the river had been reported.[1]

185 BIB was the last to enter Germany, moving into Divisional reserve around Pfalzdorf (908463) on 26 February. The coming battle would be the first time Brigadier F.R.G. Matthews and Lt-Col Peter Barclay (lately CO 4 Lincolns in 49 BID) exercised their new commands. 1 Royal Norfolk's War Diary commented optimistically that, 'with new commanders came new ideas, always a good thing'. The Norfolks were the last battalion to be engaged, and received the worst mauling. They had been training for the assault crossing of the Rhine in Buffaloes, and the sudden switch was unsettling. The CO later remarked in the war diary after the entry for 28 February:

> At long last our term of River holding is temporarily over. The Bn is badly in need of trg, particularly on a small unit level. Discipline wants tightening up. Young officers trg in adm is noticeably lacking. The latter fortnight of the month has given limited opportunities to brush up these weaknesses. The Buffalo trg was interesting, tho' others will reap the benefit of our experimental labours. Morale of the Bn is splendid.[2]

Lt Col Peter Barclay, CO 1 R Norfolks, pictured postwar. (© John Lincoln)

1 Western Daily Press, 1 March 1945; Manchester Guardian, 1 March 1945.
2 TNA: WO 171/5247: I R Norfolk's war diary.

Peter Barclay could never afterwards speak about Kervenheim. His was a CO's worst nightmare. He probably blamed himself for trusting Brig Matthews who, he quickly realised, was 'another futile operator', and for neglecting training, and he almost certainly blamed 4 CG, and probably 2 Warwicks also for failing to secure his right flank.

Matthews travelled up from Reckheim in Belgium (573605) ahead of his troops to attend an O group at divisional HQ in Pfalzdorf (909458) on 25 February. There he would have learned that 8 and 9 BIBs would secure the Üdem-Weeze road for 185 BIB to pass through and take Kervenheim on 27 February. Matthews then called his three infantry and the armoured battalion commanders – Gibbs (2 Warwicks), Barclay (1 R Norfolks), Daly (2 KSLI) and Smith (4 CG) – and support arms, to a brigade O Group held at 9 am on 26 February. The plan was for the KSLI and Warwicks to pass through the RUR and KOSB of 9 BIB, and at 3 pm on the following day to cross a startline 500 yards forward of the Üdem-Weeze road and advance to secure the startline for the assault on Kervenheim. The KSLI would be on the left, advancing across country between the Steinberger Ley, which was the boundary with 11 BAD, and the Mühlen Fleuth. The Warwicks on the right would make an assault crossing of the Mühlen Fleuth, raising fears of another Molen Beek (a costly battle that occurred on 16 October 1944 between Overloon and Venraij), to advance between the Mühlen Fleuth and the Vorselärer Ley, which was the boundary with 53 BID. The Norfolks would then line up between them for a brigade assault on Kervenheim and the areas on both flanks. The Norfolks were told they would not move to the startline until Matthews gave them the order. The possibility was mooted of a switch to the west of the Mühlen Fleuth to capture Kervenheim from the west.

On 26 February, Matthews moved his HQ from 916437 into Herdhausen 944442, a farm about 1 km northwest of Buchholt. The following day, he relocated to a more convenient farm at Stein 971414 that had recently been taken by Michael Carver's battle-group of 11 BAD in II Canadian Corps. Whistler moved into the farm vacated by Matthews, remaining there until 3 March when he moved into the Schloss in Kervenheim. HQRA 970415 moved in next door to Matthews. 9 BIB moved to Schloss Calbeck 943430 from 934455 on 27 February. The convenience of Stein lay in its proximity to the road being built by Canadian engineers along the line of the railway as a vehicular supply route for the Hochwald offensive.'The stripping of the rails from the railway across the valley gave us an excellent one-way route, the ballast fortunately being crushed rock instead of shale as in Holland.'[3]

At day's end on 26 February, an amendment was issued to orders postponing the start of operations until first light on 28 February, probably because the battalions could not arrive until early on 27 February. The attack planned for 8.30 am on 28 February was postponed until noon because of the heavy counter-attacks at Yorkshire Bridge, and then again to 1.15 pm, and finally to 2.0 pm because of the 'difficulty of 8 and 9 Brigades clearing the woods to the Brigade startline'. The difficulty was only on 8 BIB's front, where the Suffolks were unable to clear the woods to the south and west of the startline until that evening, resulting in the Warwicks' right flank being open during the assault crossing of the Mühlen Fleuth. Indeed R. W. Thompson saw a StuG firing southeast at the Warwicks from these woods during the afternoon. Early on 28 February the plan was changed into a four-battalion operation when 2 Lincolns were transferred into 185 BIB from 9 BIB as reserve battalion uc.

The KSLI's Tac HQ arrived in Pfalzdorf (912465) on 25 February. Their War Diary noted; 'German nationals were found docile and were concentrated in one building of the village'. The rest of the battalion was at Eysden on 26 February, arriving at Pfalzdorf at 3.45 am on 27 February without staging. They spent the day in houses, and that night moved into

3 LAC: II Canadian Corps' War Diary for 28 February 1945.

the concentration area in the woods (954418) to the immediate west of their Tac HQ in Krüsbeckshof (957418), the 'egg farm' captured earlier in the day by the Lincolns. The next morning, February 28, at 7.30 am they moved to their assembly area (962408 to 967411) and then to the startline. This had been moved back 500 yards and was now a section of the Üdem-Weeze road roughly two miles as the crow flies from the centre of Kervenheim. They lined up (between 966404 and 972406) with the Warwicks on their right. The situation on the left was confused because the Herefords of 11 BAD attacking south from Üdem had reached the crest of the Gochfortzberg (000398) on the previous evening, but the area in between them and 3 BID had not been cleared.[4]

The supporting armour, 4 CG, left Cleve at 7 am on 27 February, and motored south through Pfalzdorf to join 185 BIB. They had enjoyed four days of rest after being continuously engaged for 14 days from the start of *Veritable*. While it was safer to serve in a tank, and especially a Churchill, the downside was spending longer periods in the front line. In four days, however, it was possible only to clean up and catch some sleep, with no time for reorganisation. A sympathetic observer from 3 SG, Mark Fearfield, believed the Coldstreamers had suffered the loss of so many officers, mostly from head wounds, that their performance was affected.[5] They were about to suffer more; Michael Harrison killed with a bullet through the head, John Robb wounded with a bullet through the cheek and Alexis Melikoff with Panzerfaust shrapnel in his head, while Christopher Brooks's tank was hit twice by a StuG. In a letter home dated 5 March, a wounded officer in 3 Sqn wrote that of the five of them that came over, four had become victims of enemy action in one way or another.[6] Such losses, while common in the infantry, were unusual in tanks and were the consequence of the TCs commanding with their heads out of the turret.

The squadrons spent the day and the night in a field east of Goch called 'The Bight' among a noisy regiment of 25-pdrs. Then on 28 February, while it was still dark, they drove on to their Forward Assembly Areas behind the Üdem-Weeze road and 'married-up' with their infantry. The Grenadiers had grim stories to tell of the paratroops defending the woods, who would attack tanks with grenades and bazookas in complete scorn of death, and the battalion steeled itself for a hard day's fighting.[7] The Buffs later suspected that 4 GG blamed the losses on them for refusing to take their Crocodile flamethrowers into the woods in their support, and retailed this accusation to 4 CG. It would explain the bad blood between 4 CG and the Buffs, and lead indirectly to Carroll's death in Kervenheim.

Rex Fendick, OC 1 Pln, A Coy, 2 Middlesex was guarding the left flank of 9 BIB's advance on 27 February as we have seen. He was not needed in the event because 11 BAD had cleared the area south and west of Üdem. He correctly predicted that his next task would be in support of 185 BIB.

> Will probably move soon to cover right flank of 185 Bde when they pass through 9 Bde. Had to do two recces in afternoon – 185 Bde show postponed for all of today – next time is 0900 hrs tomorrow. 9 Bde show very successful. Spend night doubled up in slit trench – very uncomfortable and cold. Roads getting very muddy – tanks tearing them up – doubt if we can get forward tomorrow. Heavy cloud but no rain.[8]

4 Delaforce, *Black Bull*, p. 197.
5 Mark Fearfield in conversation.
6 A request by this author to quote from these letters was refused.
7 M. Howard & J Sparrow. *The Coldstream Guards* (Oxford: OUP, 1951), p. 326.
8 Rex Fendick's personal diary.

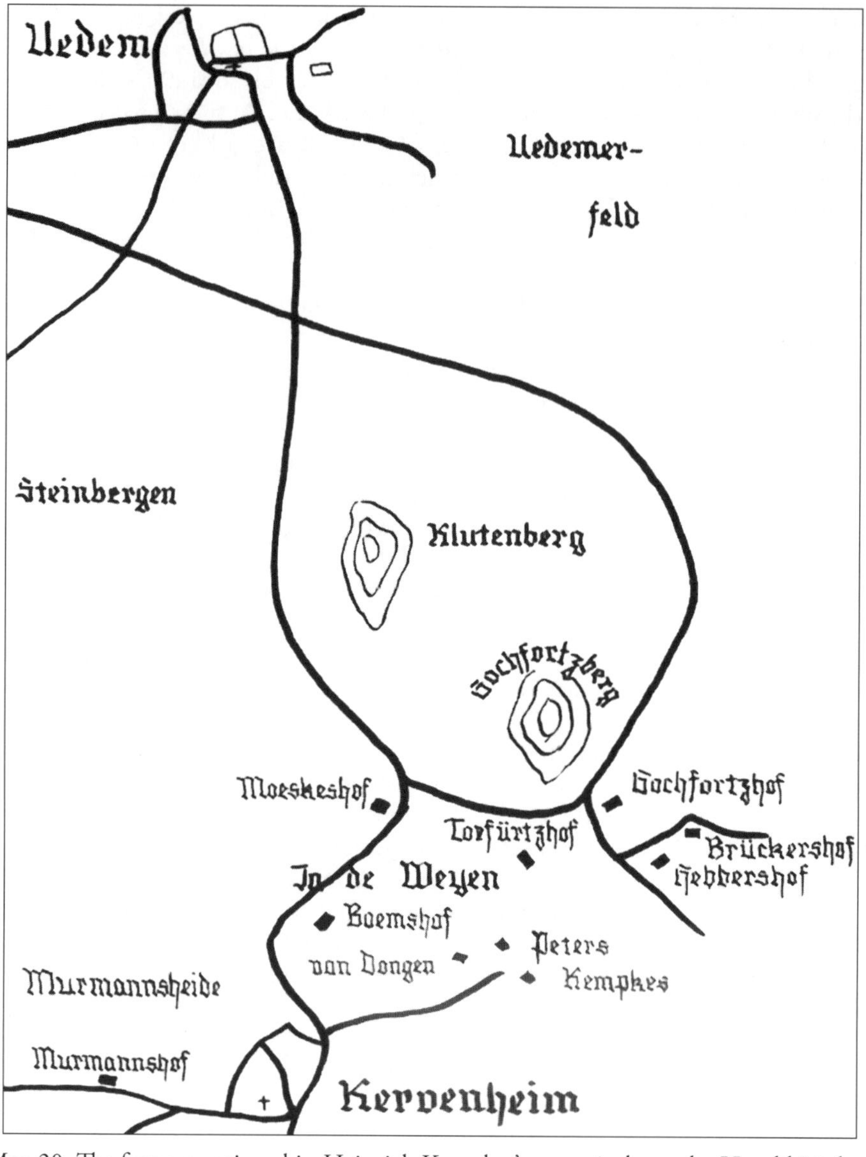

Map 20 The farms mentioned in Heinrich Kempkes's memoir drawn by Harald Löcker. (© Heinrich Kempkes)

Awareness of the deteriorating ground conditions spread right back to Pfalzdorf where GAD was waiting theoretically at two hours' notice to break out.[9]

A 15 year old farmer's son just to the east of Kervenheim in 'De Weyen' at 998386, Heinrich Kempkes, found himself in the middle of a battle.

> On 27 February 1945 Para Lehr of 7FJD established a command post on my parents' farm on the outskirts of Kervenheim [998386]. Sections of this unit took up positions

9 Robert Boscawen of 1 CG, GAD in a phone conversation on 5 December 2003.

in Tofürtzhof [999392] and Gochfortzhof [003395] between Kervenheim and Uedem. A soldier informed me they had left behind several wounded with two medics in Steinbergen to the southwest of Uedem. Towards evening an FOO and a signaller arrived on our farm. The British had already occupied Moeskeshof [995394]. The German artillery then shelled that farm, setting ablaze the farmhouse and stables. A Nebelwerfer battery was emplaced near Hebbershof [004392] to target enemy troop concentrations, and for the first time I heard the terrible howling of its rockets. About midnight we heard the sound of tracked vehicles as three German StuGs took position close to van Dongen and Peters [the neighbouring farms].

Early on 28 February a runner arrived on our farm to inform the lieutenant company commander that two farms were on fire. When the lieutenant asked me, I said it must be Gochfortzhof and perhaps Hebbershof or Brückershof. At 10 am we could see out of our kitchen window 28 enemy tanks on the Gochfortzberg. One of them was knocked out as they drove towards Hebbershof where another AFV was destroyed. That farm house was set alight by Nebelwerfer rockets. My young sister cried and said, "Now the poor Tekath children won't have beds anymore".

A runner who suddenly turned up pointed out to us a German sniper. After nearly every shot two Canadian stretcher bearers carrying a red-cross flag ran over and carried off the dead and wounded. Later near the Hebbershof barn we saw the graves of a Canadian major, a lieutenant, a sergeant and two soldiers with their steel helmets placed on top of the crosses.

Around midday there was an exchange of fire between the StuGs and the British tanks. I could see them near van Dongens. The first British shells fell short. After every shot the StuGs withdrew into cover behind the barns to reload [and change ambush position to avoid retribution]. Van Dongen's stables and sheds were badly damaged. After five minutes the shooting stopped, and a StuG commander came into our cellar to report that a British tank had been knocked out in Tofürtzhof (see photo). In the afternoon the British put down a smoke screen over their lines to cover their tanks while they were dispersed without being observed. A message arrived at the company command post that altogether seven British tanks had been knocked out. (Four were identified by position as being at: Hebbershof, destroyed in flames by Nebelwerfen; across from Tofürtzhof (photo); in the entrance to Tofürtzhof; and across from Moeskeshof knocked out by artillery).

At 4 pm the Germans began a bombardment of the Canadian troops on the Gochfortzberg, who became demoralised and abandoned their targeted positions. Around midnight the StuGs withdrew. A recce patrol established meanwhile that Tofürtzhof had been occupied by the British. The Paratroops in de Weyen were from 14 Coy FJR7.[10]

On 28 February, Fendick moved his platoon westward to open fields near Babbe ahead of the Krüsbeckshof 'egg farm' at about 955414, which had been captured by Sgt Offord of 1 Suffolk the previous day. Their new task was to fire up to their maximum range of 4,500 yards on targets in the wooded areas in 9740 and 9839 on the left flank of the axis of advance on Kervenheim. It was there that Fendick took the pictures of his emplaced guns and of his platoon plucking chickens for the pot.

10 Heinrich Kempkes. *Die Kampfhandlungen und das Ende des Zweiten Weltkriegs im Bereich von Kervenheim* (Geldern: Geldrischen Heimatkalender, 2001), pp. 134-35. A letter from Heinrich Kempkes of 2 November 2014 added the information contained in the round brackets. Translation is by this author.

Helmut Walter, Heinrich Kempkes and Peter Kempkes by an M4 Sherman of 11 British Armoured Division on the lower slopes of the Gochfortzberg at 998391 in 1948. It was destroyed by StuGs operating in and around van Dongens farm in de Weyen on 28 February 1945, watched by Heinrich from his kichen window. Note the shell hole behind Helmut's right elbow. (© Heinrich Kempkes)

Rex Fendick's picture of Vickers machine guns of his platoon of 2 Middlesex firing on 28 February 1945 at Babbe 959410. (© Reginald Fendick)

Rex Fendick's picture of Bob Doyle and helpers preparing chickens taken from the Krűsbeckshof chicken farm at Babbe 959410 on 28 February 1945. (© Reginald Fendick)

Rex Fendick recorded the following in his diary:

> Wednesday 28 Feb
> Reveillez 0400. Clear and cool. Cloudy as sun comes up. Move forward and into Coy position in open field (place called BABBE). Further postponements – hear counter-attack on right (8 Bde) has lost us 200 yds [No details of this counterattack are known. It might have been connected with the gruesome scene of the Churchill tank surrounded by dead Paratroops] and the status quo of the attack. All OK at 1400 hrs. 185 Bde go through – we fire 10 belts [2,500 rounds] over 35 minutes – later another 2 [500 rounds] – later again 5 more [1,250] on direct orders from Brigade. Attack slowed up a little. Typhoons doing terrific job today in spite of cloud. 2000 hrs. Just got down to it when word came to meet Pat [Weston] a few hundred yards back. Mac [McConaghy] and I to join 2 RUR tomorrow, John [Milne)] KOSBs, for new bash on [the anticipated advance to Winnekendonk]. I'm to leave at first light for orders and then call Mac up with the platoons. Terrific barrage on Weeze in night.[11]

Fendick went into more detail in his book.

> I called Tony [Hewitt, OC 'A' Coy] to tell him of our plans for the company gun line, with myself forward with the BN CO [Daly of KSLI] as FOO, but due to the appalling roads, Tony couldn't get forward. So we set up the company gun line in a large open field, with tasks to support attacks towards Kervenheim, and I found myself for a short while by popular agreement, the Unofficial (unpaid) OC, to act as MG Company FOO with the battalion we were supporting. Mac and Milne were at the gun line.

11 Rex Fendick's diary.

I set up in a barn attached to the farmhouse which was Battalion [KSLI] HQ, and tried to keep in touch with the platoons on the gun line through the night by company radio net. But radio always deteriorated badly at night. There were no alarms during the night and at first light I went back to the gun line to warn the company for a move forward. When I returned to the Bn HQ, I found that while I was gone the attached barn in which I had spent the night had taken a direct hit through the centre of the roof by a large calibre shell, and there was little left of the barn. I have always thought that hit was probably a result of the German radio monitoring services having taken bearings on this building, from the heavy radio traffic eminating (sic) from it during the night. [This widely held view that Germans could and did target the sources of radio transmissions has been rejected in a recent history of British WW2 signals as a military urban myth. In such cases this author reserves judgement].

Soon after my arrival back, the CO of the Battalion [Pat Daly of the KSLI] took off in a Kangaroo, and I was part of his recce party. I kept up with him as best I could in my carrier, and he pulled up on the edge of a large open area, at the startline of his battalion's attack (see Map 20). I had called down the fire of our Company's guns on flank targets along the line of his advance, and one of our 4.2" mortar platoons was firing as well. A squadron of Cromwell tanks [Churchills of 2 Sqn, 4 CG under Milbank] was with us on the startline, to move with the front ranks of the assault.

The infantry had about 500 yards to go across completely open ground to a village beyond a fringe of trees on the far side of the open fields. The leading troops moved out in the most perfect order, nicely spaced, with rifles at the high port and bayonets fixed, almost like a Tattoo display. The tanks moved with them at infantry pace. As they moved out into the open, heavy enemy small-arms and HE fire started coming in.

At that moment, a flight of Typhoon rocket-firing aircraft [almost certainly 609 Sqn] came down in line in a steep dive, from behind the objective towards us. They plastered the objective with rockets and MG fire, and pulled out low, directly over our heads. They pulled around and came back again for several passes, each time diving directly towards us at the objective, and pulling out so low over us that it seemed we could reach up and touch them. As soon as the tanks saw them coming down the first time, they all paused and fired coloured smoke from their projectors just in case the pilots were not up on their target recognition.

I sat in my carrier on the startline, close to the battalion CO's Kangaroo [the first reference to a Bn CO having a personal Kangaroo], until the assault was well into the objective, and then I went back to our gun line. There I found that because of the appalling mud and the tracks being demolished by tanks plowing through them, we had been unable to get a carrier back to Coy HQ for replenishment, and we were getting very short of ammunition, with no re-supply possible. However we solved the problem [of food, not ammunition]. There was an abandoned farm nearby [Krüsbeckshof, the 'chicken farm'] with many chickens running loose and, of course, our troops couldn't bear to see them go hungry and neglected. A couple of biscuit-tin brew-cans, plus Bob Doyle's skill as a poulterer, made short work of the chickens, which were very nicely boiled in the tins over an open fire. To go with the boiled chicken, we found potatoes which had been dug up in the autumn and buried in rows in the fields, [in clamps] covered with straw and earth. As we had plenty of mud, I showed the platoon how to pack the spuds in mud jackets and bury them in the coals of our fire. Very good baked potatoes.[12]

12 RF Fendick. *A Canloan Officer* (Nauwigewauk: Reginald F Fendick, 2000), pp. 172-74.

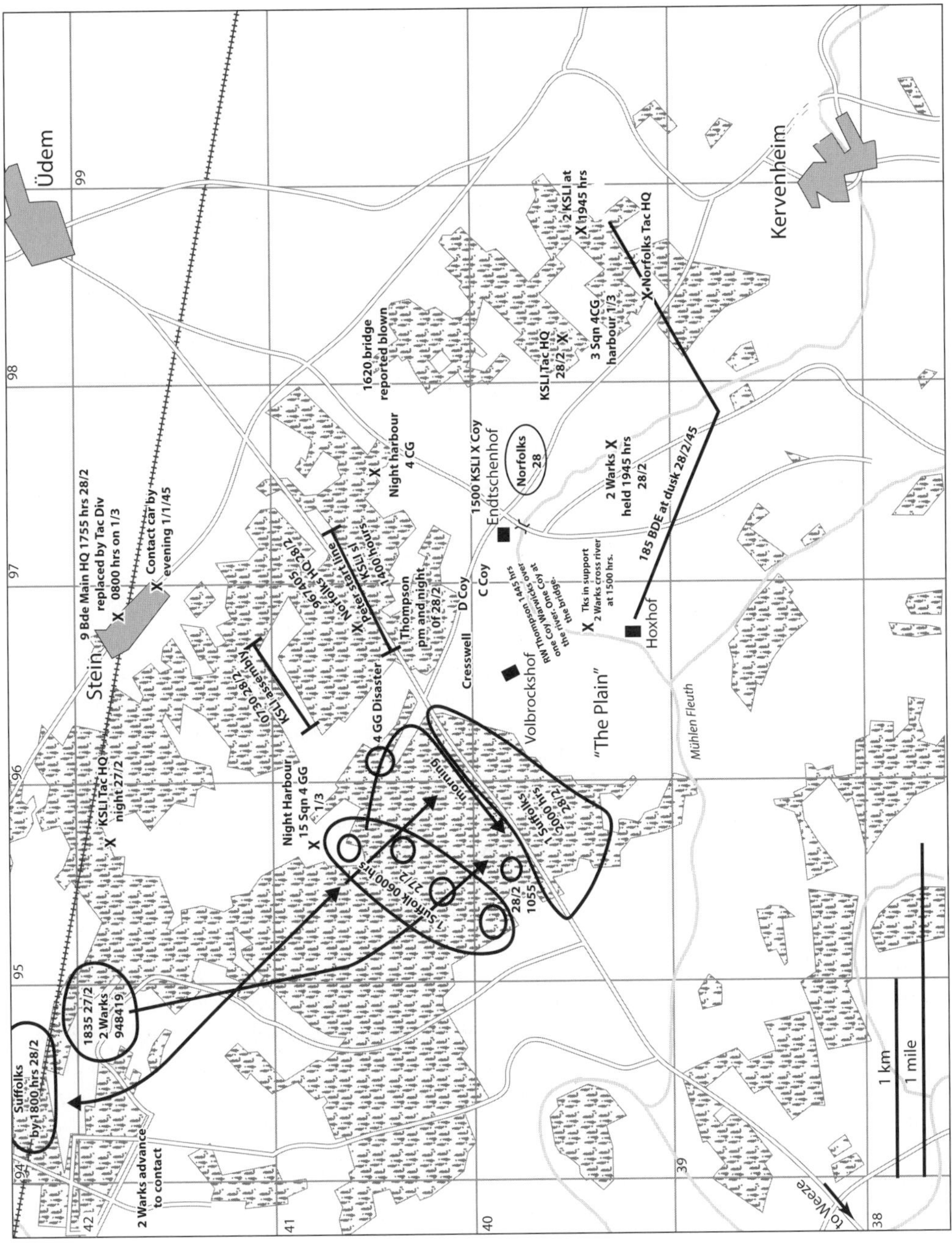

Map 21 The advance to the battle of Kervenheim.

2 KSLI were on the startline at 2 pm, waiting 15 minutes for the barrage to lift. Their official historian unaccountably gives a time of one hour earlier.[13] The inevitable changes to the barrage due to the altered startline and the presence of 53 BID in the westernmost section, have not come to light.

The KSLI advanced with all four companies up under the personal command of their CO, Pat Daly with his Tac HQ. They were supported by all four troops of 2 Sqn CG, one assigned to each coy and accompanied by their HQ tp. Two coys were forward – X right and W left – and two back – Z right and Y left – with the Tac HQ of the CO between them. In Jock Aitken's X Company, L/Sgt Bob Littlar commanded the forward platoon in the absence on leave of the Canloan 320 Lt Georges Bellavance MC.

Littlar was just 20 years old and had been identified as officer material at a WOSB before D-Day.[14] He recalled that during the 15-minute hiatus after 2 pm as they waited for the barrage to lift, the Coldstreamers offered them *cha*. Suddenly, however, the enemy began their defensive bombardment, making the infantry forget tea and return hurriedly to their slit trenches. The Germans often aimed to walk their barrage behind the British barrage in order to kill the attacking infantry. For this they needed to know the startline, which they seem to have figured out or observed in this case, and the rate of advance. They would not, however, know how long the barrage would dwell on its initial line before lifting which was when the infantry would come out of their slit trenches to follow their barrage and become vulnerable. This occurred at 2.10 pm when Pte Alfred Hewett of W Company on the left won the MM. The citation was signed by Daley (8 March), Matthews (8 March), Whistler (10 March), Horrocks (15 March), Crerar (7 April) and Montgomery (undated).

> **MM. 3 BID, XXX Corps, 2nd Bn KSLI, 14753164 Pte Alfred William HEWETT**
> On 28 Feb 45 Pte Hewett was 'W' Coy runner. Seeing that one of the Pls was suffering very heavy casualties from shell and mortar fire, he personally collected two stretchers and rushed forward through intense fire and organized the removal of casualties to cover. The same afternoon Pte Hewett was given the task of giving flank covering fire with a Bren to assist the Coy advance. On his own initiative he worked forward on the flank and engaged enemy strong points, enabling the forward Pls to assault successive points. During this phase he personally assaulted one enemy position and captured two prisoners. In the evening Pte Hewett volunteered for a Patrol into the enemy held town of KERVENHEIM. It was largely due to his dash and initiative that the patrol brought back a prisoner and invaluable information. Pte Hewett's untiring gallantry and initiative were a very real inspiration to the whole Coy.

According to the divisional log, X Company reached Endtschenhof at 3 pm. The KSLI, like this author and even recent German cartographers, almost certainly believed that the map named the farm at the bridge as Aengen and a farm 500 yards away as Endtschenhof. Reality was that Aengen Endtschenhof was and is the farm at the bridge 973398 where the civilian refugee, Pastor R. Coenders was staying with the Deckers family who owned the farm. The farm reached by the KSLI at 3 pm and is not Endtschenhof is unnamed on the map at 977399.

In Endtschenhof itself was staying Pastor Coenders and a sister who had been expelled from Kevelaer. From September to November 1944 there were several moves to evacuate Kevelaer, but most of the population stayed put. At the end of January, however, the Nazis increased the pressure. On 5 February 1945, more than 1,000 men of the Orpo or Green Ordnungspolizei, the

13 GLY Radcliffe. *KSLI: History of the 2nd Battalion* (Oxford, Basil Blackwell, 1947), p. 71.
14 From a series of transatlantic phone calls with Bob Littlar in 2000.

uniformed police under Himmler, arrived and tried to force the population out.[15] All of the priests in Kevelaer, including Coenders, were personally targeted by the Nazi Mayor, Aloys Eickelberg,[16] in retribution for their seditiously anti-Nazi sympathies and because of their influence. The church was strong in Kevelaer as a major site of Marian pilgrimage dating from 1642, and it remained loyal to the outspoken anti-Nazi Bishop Frings of Cologne, who was also a Marian devotee, and Bishop von Galen of Münster, nicknamed *Der Löwe.* He outraged Hitler and the Nazis firstly by revealing their murderous euthanasia programme and then asking publicly if they now intended to euthanize wounded German soldiers. Hitler said in his table talk: 'I am quite sure that a man like Bishop von Galen knows full well that after the war I shall extract retribution to the last farthing'. After the war von Galen attacked the occupying forces for treating all Germans as Nazis – it was illegal for them to fraternize with any German including von Galen himself – for plundering and starving the Germans and failing to protect women against Russian rapists. He was made a cardinal at Christmas 1945.

Coenders wrote a memoir.

> I was forced to leave Kevelaer on 5 February 1945, having until then managed to resist pressure from the Nazis to leave. That morning, however, Police Lieutenant Herbst told me I had until the evening to leave Kevelaer or be arrested. Immediately I asked the Deckers family [of Endtschenhof], who had earlier promised me accommodation in the event I was expelled, kindly to fetch me and Sister. Quickly we packed a few things, and soon after midday a vehicle arrived to take us to Kervendonk. With us travelled Herr Beykirch and his wife, who however were not staying in Kervendonk but were on their way to Kalkar. En route we recited the rosary.
>
> The Deckers received us most affectionately, and provided us with a pleasant room. I must say the Deckers always gave us the best, and denied themselves for our comfort. This was even more considerate given we were not the only guests; German soldiers were billeted there, which meant family members were confined to a small part of the house. After all the harassment we had experienced in Kevelaer, we felt very happy in Kervendonk, especially when father Deckers told us that night: 'When you next hear an aircraft, don't get up (and take shelter) because nothing ever happens here'.
>
> So the first few days in Kervendonk passed in peace and quiet, apart from enemy aircraft that were flying around, but causing no harm except to German vehicles and tanks caught in the open. I celebrated mass in the hospital in Uedem, and afterwards had a good breakfast. Deckers' daughter-in-law was in Uedem hospital, recovering from child-birth.
>
> On Wednesday, 7 February, about 9 o'clock Goch was badly bombed. Sister and I had already retired, but the effects were so dire even as far away as Kervendonk that we went into the kitchen half dressed and very concerned. Windows and doors rattled and every moment we feared the house would collapse. Father Deckers said: 'We must not stay inside but go out'. While danger mounted we had time for only a brief confession before I gave the general absolution [Fearing death, they wanted to be in a state of grace, ie. sanctified by God through the priest. It is described in *Misericordia Dei* of 7 April 2002, how a priest is permitted to give a general absolution without hearing individual confessions when or 'if the danger of death is imminent and there is not time for the priest or priests to hear the confessions of the individual penitents'], and then we all trooped outside, seeking shelter as best we could in ditches,

15 https://de.wikipedia.org/wiki/Kevelaer

16 Martin Willing. *Blutiger Winter* (Blattus Martini: Kevelaerer Enzyklopädie). http://www.blattus.de/buch/Blutiger%20Winter/BlutigerWinter-aufschlag.html, p. 2.

behind hedges, shrubs etc. and finding cover. Outside we found father Deckers who had been absent during the general absolution. Mother Deckers begged me to absolve him also, which I did. After about half an hour silence fell, and we went back to bed. As a precaution we did not undress. A few minutes later there was a new raid, and this time on Kervendonk. In seconds we were all outside again seeking cover. Mother Deckers said: 'Open the barn; we must shelter in the root cellar!' And that became our sanctuary. As soon as the barn door opened, we all rushed into the cellar, praying aloud and expecting the worst. A soldier called Emil, who was late leaving the house, was found dead near the dog kennel. He was buried with full military honours the following Monday, 12 February in the cemetery in Kervenheim. Father Deckers and I attended the funeral which was taken by Pastor Nellis, the Rector of Kervenheim [Franz Nellis (1891-1977) also kept a diary – see below], who gave a very moving graveside address. Franz also had been unable to reach the root cellar but had found shelter elsewhere. We all rejoiced at having survived the bombing unwounded. Father Deckers, who after the raid had gone to the house, now returned, weeping and saying, 'Our home has been hit'. A large bomb had demolished a front corner, and caused such destruction and devastation that the house was uninhabitable. In this emergency our neighbour Wehren, the Ortsbauenführer [the local farmers' leader, and not necessarily a Nazi. He was appointed by the NSDAP under *Gleichschaltung,* ('forcible-coordination' in Richard Evans' translation), as the contact point between NSDAP and Burgermeister. There were 52,000 Ortsbauenführers, of whom about half were Nazis] arrived and offered to put us up in his undamaged home [Schneidershof] 976392. We thankfully accepted, and on the night of 7-8 February, taking only bare essentials that could be rescued, we moved five minutes away to Wehren's. The house held not only the Ortsbauenführer but also the house-owner, Herr Dorsenmagen and his wife from Kleve, and soldiers. Mother Deckers took over the kitchen, bringing necessities from Endtschenhof, and we ate together with the Wehren family. The sleeping accommodation was cramped because there were so many people. Six or seven people slept in our room; the oldest were given beds, while the rest slept on the floor. Snoring was a major problem, and more than once you could hear the cry, 'The – snoring!!!!!' During the day I was royally treated by having a heated room placed at my disposal.

On Friday, 9 February Father Deckers and I silently buried Gretchen's baby, who had died soon after being born, in the children's cemetery in Uedem. Father Deckers was the sole mourner.

Meanwhile the war came ever closer. Planes flew over day and night. Flak was emplaced by the house. The thunder of the guns became ever more terrible. The quiet of the night was often disturbed not only by the snoring but by the shout of the sentry: 'Enemy planes approaching. Take shelter'. In a great rush everybody stumbled out of the house, heading for wherever there was cover, and into father Deckers root cellar if there was time to reach it safely.

On Tuesday 13 February Gretchen and little Maria, her surviving child, left hospital and arrived at Ortsbauernführer Wehren's. She had been advised to find somewhere safer to stay because of frequent air raids on Uedem.

On Wednesday 14 February the entire Deckers family including the guests returned to the Hof (Endtschenhof). The root cellar in the barn had been cleared out and prepared so we could all live and sleep there. Cooking was done initially in the bombed-out kitchen, but because of the danger from aircraft it also was soon moved into the root cellar. The kitchen functioned in spite of the greatest difficulties, and we always fed on time; and not only those living in the Hof, but also relatives, soldiers, and strangers arriving for some reason or on the off-chance were fed. No one left the Hof hungry. The kitchen excelled itself, I must add, when it set up a feeding point in the yard for evacuees directed there by the military government, who paid nothing for the service and contributed nothing in kind. During the evening of 14 February there was an interlude, even a joyful Intermezzo; Gretchen had spent the entire day with the little one waiting for a car to take them to her parents' farm in Kempen. The car never came, and after we had given up hope and gone to bed we got the news that the car had arrived! But it could not drive up to the Hof in the dark, which meant Franz "Prince" had to hitch up the dog-cart and with the ever-present risk of bombing and shelling take Gretchen and the infant to the car. Fortunately everything went without a hitch and no one was injured.

The next two days passed without any noteworthy incident, but on Saturday afternoon, 17 February, Uedem was badly bombed. On Sunday 18 February, I celebrated Mass in Kervenheim. A car gave me a lift part of the way because the Endsche Weg was almost impassable. 19 February was a critical day, and we had to spend the entire day in the cellar. The next day Fraulein Beykirch visited us and brought news from Kevelaer, and in particular that our house was still standing with the 'greenery' removed. She invited us to return to Kevelaer with her. After much discussion this way and that, we decided to stay in Kervendonk partly because of the uncertainty that existed in Kevelaer but also because the Deckers were keen for us to stay and I did not want to leave them in the lurch as things got more dangerous. At this time there was feverish activity around the Hof and nearby, as large and small guns were emplaced. An instruction arrived that the cattle should be driven away. An Unterführer, who I suppose in rank was the equivalent of a Lieutenant, was responsible for overseeing and caring for the cattle while they were removed. The Unterführer stayed with us at the Hof and ate at our table, even though he was, if I am correctly informed, billeted on another Hof. He came from the East and had many stories to tell about his journeys. When I told him I had visited Rome but never Berlin, I realised I had lost his sympathy. He was tall and had long legs so his bed had to be specially prepared, which he did himself. He was with us for a full 8 days and then disappeared; despite all his plans, not one cow was taken from the Deckers or from neighbouring Hofs.

20 February was a 'dies ater', or black day for the Deckers Family. There was widespread shelling which meant we had to stay in the cellar all day as it was too dangerous to go out. Nevertheless, about 9 o'clock in the morning a couple of the loyal farmhands dared to go a couple of hundred metres away from the Hof to the clamp to collect beets for the cows which had been without them for several days. As they reached the clamp, a shell killed Johann and badly wounded Jacob, as well as one of Wehren's servants. The horse with them was killed by shrapnel, and the cart destroyed completely. Soldiers dug a grave at the foot of the Cross that stood in the farmyard, and at 11 the following morning I held a funeral service for the faithful farmhand who had lost his life in an instant. Remember him in reverent prayer!

The day before that a truck full of ammunition had been driven into the barn. Had it exploded we would all have been killed without exception. Father Deckers knew he had to find a Captain who could order the ammunition truck removed. You can imagine how relieved we were when this dangerous vehicle had left. During the night of Tuesday 20 February, many retreating soldiers came by. Conditions became increasingly dangerous for them. Large numbers of enemy aircraft flew overhead and heavily bombed Uedem. That afternoon around 3'o'clock I gave the general absolution.

On Thursday, 22 February there was another terrible artillery bombardment that kept us in the cellar for almost the entire day.

On the following day, Friday 23 February, Ortsbauenführer Wehren left. He had been saying for several days that considering how dangerous Kervendonk had become he wanted to seek safety on the east bank of the Rhine. Father Deckers tried to persuade him to stay right until the time he went. Because the shelling continued all day, he postponed his departure until after dark. Herr Dorsenmagen and wife left with him. They had spent many nights with us in the cellar because the Wehren's house lacked a bomb-proof room. Wehren left his cattle tied up in the stalls, and if Franz had not had pity on them they would have perished miserably.

24 February was a much quieter day. A shot-down aircraft crashed on von Halmann's Hof and set it on fire. The Hof burnt down but none of those living there, including many soldiers, was wounded. The abandoned cattle were later seen wandering about.

The night of Saturday into Sunday was very noisy. Many soldiers withdrew. I did not celebrate mass that Sunday, and those staying at the Deckers had no mass they could attend. During the continuous shelling we had to stay in the cellar where I was unable to say mass, so we held a prayer vigil there instead.

In the night of Sunday to Monday [25-26 February] there was again terrible shelling. None of us could sleep, so we prayed a lot. Luckily our cellar was spared. At the end of the day it quietened down somewhat.

The night of Monday-Tuesday, 26-27 February, was very restless. Practically every hour soldiers arrived going from Hof to Hof seeking information, so father Deckers had to be constantly available. From morning to mid afternoon there was terrible shelling. The following morning (27th) about 11 o'clock the bridge over the Fleuth was blown [to prevent an attempted coup-de-main by Runcie's tp]. We had to stay in the cellar, lying on the floor and keeping quiet, and with prayer we survived the horror. Luckily no one was killed. I found out later that one of the two charges of dynamite installed on the bridge had not been fused. Had they been fused, the detonation would have been worse and the remaining part of the house and barn blown down and perhaps people killed. [It was blown at 11 am as 1 KOSB approached the Uedem-Weeze road 900 metres away. At 3.30 pm a company of 1 KOSB with the support of Runcie's troop of Churchill tanks, tried to seize it in a *coup de main* but were savagely repulsed only 500 m north-east of Endtschenhof – see previous chapter]. If I remember rightly, during this perilous hour we praised the Lord and promised that if the dear God saved us then we would say five Our Fathers and Hail Marys every day for the rest of our lives. During the continuous shelling and the blowing up of the bridge we could not cook. Late in the afternoon we had a cold meal. During the afternoon more farms caught fire and burnt down, von Beckmanns, Wehrens, Köhnens, etc. In Kervenheim a large fire raged. During the afternoon more wounded German soldiers were brought into the cellar. I heard the confession of one of them.

The night of Tuesday-Wednesday, 27-28 February, was fairly quiet. I stayed up on watch until 4 o'clock in the morning, when I handed over to father Deckers. On the morning of 28 February terrible shelling began. Every moment we feared being hit. In this very dangerous situation I gave the general absolution. At midday around 2 o'clock there was more dreadful shelling. All we could do was cower in the cellar trembling in fear of death. Franz lay in front by the door, trying to make out what was going on, and looking out for the expected Englishmen.

About 3 o'clock in the afternoon Franz saw the first Englishmen entering the barn and shouted out 'Hurrah', at which we all came up out of the cellar with our hands up and our hearts beating. The Englishmen were nervous, obviously suspecting there were German soldiers in the cellar who they threatened to shoot. But holding up the Rosary in raised hands we begged: "Nicht schiessen; nicht schiessen". After checking the cellar was empty, they motioned us to move to the other end of the barn. They told us to stand behind a metre high wall of piled sheaves of thrashed corn. We were under guard. The soldiers searched the barn and the house. The English soldiers became friendlier when they realised we were peaceable. They threw cigarettes over to us and asked if they could drink milk from churns

> standing on the threshing floor, to which we naturally agreed, and then they brought us milk to drink. The guard was not strict and we chatted to one another. But we could smell burning, and began to fear the house was on fire. They would not allow us to leave to put out the fire. After half an hour they searched us. We had to show them everything we had in our bags. They took my penknife from me, but let me keep everything else. Father Deckers had to hand over his gold watch. When that was over, we were sent back to the cellar where there was a great smell of burning. It became obvious the house and stables were on fire. Behind the house we had a large cart full of food, clothes, linen etc that would have been needed had we been forced to flee. We begged to be allowed to drag the cart away from the barn but that was not allowed. Flames then consumed the cart with all its valuable contents. Eventually, after much begging and pleading, Franz was allowed out. He chopped through the roof beam connecting the stable to the barn and his superhuman efforts saved the barn at least. Outside there was a terrible scene. The cattle released by the English were wandering around. Nevertheless, many animals including valuable stallions, cows, and bullocks burnt to death. I do not know how many died. But who had set fire to the house? We suspected that German soldiers, who until the last minute were dug-in in slit trenches and shell holes, had torched the house as they retreated. Whether these German soldiers were taken prisoner by the English I know not. That evening the English stayed with us in the cellar. For dinner we had eggs, milk, biscuits, white bread from far away, coffee and cigarettes. [German bread was dark with a high proportion of rye, often baked as *Knäckebrot* or crispbread with a long shelf-life. The unfamiliar English white bread contained durum wheat grown on the Canadian prairies.] During the night the soldiers perched on chairs and slept, so well had it gone for them. They did not molest us. That night there was a dreadful scene outside. All the farms around were ablaze, at least ten or twelve of them. This was a dreadful thing to see, in fact the worst thing I ever saw in the war.[17] [Coenders' story is continued in Chapter 6].

It is likely that the soldiers were from C Coy, 2 Warwicks. R.W. Thompson wrote; '1415 hours. One company of Warwicks over the river [A Coy]. One company at the bridge. Avres and tanks ordered up to river bridge.'[18] At 1 pm the KSLI were reported as being 400 metres to the north-east. Furthermore, the 2 Warwicks war diary stated that C Coy had to fight in houses on the left to reach its objective on the left, which would have been the bridge.[19]

The planned rate of advance for infantry in villages and woods was 100 yards in 5 minutes, and 2½ minutes in open country. At the most it should have taken 100 minutes for the KSLI to cover the 1,500 – 2,000 yards from the Üdem-Weeze road to the point where the KSLI dug in for the night of 28 February. The fact it took three hours was due to heavy shelling and fighting. Bob Littlar says they stopped for long periods. The 4 CG's history fails to distinguish between the KSLI and the Warwicks; after all infantry all looked the same.

> At 2 o'clock …the Coldstream went forward through the woods to attack. It was hard going: from the high ground on the right the enemy could watch every step of the advance, and the infantry had to edge their way forward through a continuous barrage of shell-fire. There was a stream to be crossed [the Mühlen Fleuth at Endtschenhof], but 1 Sqn brought its bridge-layer into action [although 6 GAB had an establishment of three Churchill bridgelayers, this one

17 The account was sent by Frau Käthe Schmitz on 5 March 2013. It is translated by this author with the help of Jenny Pearson & Jens Graul. Part of this account is printed in Bosch. *Der Zweite Weltkrieg*, p. 237, where it is ascribed to Pfarrer Weber.

18 RW Thompson. *Men Under Fire* (London: Macdonald, 1945), p. 78.

19 TNA: WO 171/5280: 2 Warwicks' war diary.

3 March 1945, the destroyed bridge at Endtschenhof was captured by 2 Warwicks on 28 February. An M5 Halftrack is shown crossing the Class 9 bridge (9 ton rating), consisting of two sections of 1939 MkIII FBE (Folding Boat Equipment) resting in the middle on an FBE Trestle, and assembled in situ about 30 yds downstream of the destroyed bridge. Churchills required a Class 40 bridge believed to have been laid later on the ruins of the blown bridge by a Churchill bridgelayer in the vicinity of the tipper lorry. (© Crown Copyright IWM, B 15044, by Sgt Carpenter)

Endtschenhof and the bridge photographed from the A57 motorway bridge in 1994. Beyond is the plain described by RW Thompson. The road crossing right to left connects Krűsbeckshof to Kervenheim and was 3 BID's axis of advance. The road straight ahead crosses the bridge at the bend and ends up in Kevelaer.

> appears to have been part of a composite troop of 2 & 3 tps, 284 Assault Sqn RE, 79 BAD, whose War Diary entry for 27 February, 1945 states; 'Composite troop formed with 4 fascines and bridgelayer and put in support of 185 Brigade for operations on 28th'], and by nightfall the infantry had advanced 2,000 yards to a good position for the attack on Kervenheim.[20]

The infantry crossing the Mühlen Fleuth were 2 Warwicks. They had been at Opgrimby on the Maas practising in Buffaloes for the assault crossing of the Rhine. On 21 February they were warned to make the move to their concentration area near Pfalzdorf 910470 at 2 am on 26 February, travelling via Nijmegen and Cleve. They had a day there before spending the evening of 27 February marching in battle order for 5 miles past Schloss Calbeck to their assembly area at 948419 around Schröershof, arriving at 1835 hrs, according to 3 BID's War Diary. They were immediately behind 1 Suffolks, 'the foremost troops at that time.' It is unclear if they rested there before moving on to their FUP, since Illing stated below that they arrived opposite Hoxhof very late at night and exhausted. Their War Diary complained that:

> There was a certain amount of shelling and great difficulties had to be faced in reconnoitering roads for essential transport from this assembly area to the FUP ready for the attack. The whole of this area was thickly wooded and gun fire had so broken down the trees that they had fallen across the few very bad tracks leading into the woods and there were also a lot of mines about in the verges of the tracks.[21]

The battalion historian wrote that the day's move had gone well, although it, 'was difficult to keep direction in an area of woods, waterlogged clay fields, scattered houses, no roads to speak of'.'[22] The next morning they moved to the FUP behind 1 Suffolk, who at 10.55 am had reached the Üdem-Weeze road at 955397 without further opposition. Losses to the Warwicks had been two killed and three wounded.

Maj. Harry Illing, OC A Coy, 2 Warwicks described his arrival in position on 27 February.

> We assembled before Hoxhof very late at night. [In the wood north of the Üdem-Weeze road, 1,000 yards from Hoxhof across the Mühlen Fleuth.] It was cold, very dark with no moon, and raining. We had been travelling for two days and were dog tired. We dug in quickly for there was periodic shelling. I recall the deep contentment of being able, when my second-in-command took over on duty, to crouch at the bottom of a slit covered by a groundsheet to sleep. Comfort is relative.
>
> At dawn we reconnoitred. [They must have passed through the Suffolks in front of them]. I went forward to the edge of the wood which was to be our forming-up place to give out orders. Our objective was two groups of farm buildings, one dead ahead and the other off to one flank, both on small hills and dominating our approach. [He could see two, but in fact they had to deal with three farms; Hoxhof was ahead behind Ratzenhof, the two straddling the Mühlen Fleuth, with Volbrockshof on the left flank]. The ground was open, the plan was simple: to crash down the maximum artillery fire and 'lean' on it, with one platoon dashing forward to a covering fire position and then two platoons assaulting in echelon, the right platoon going first for the buildings on the flank which could enfilade the approach to the

20 Howard & Sparrow, *Coldstream Guards*, p. 327.
21 TNA: WO 171/5280: 2 Warwicks' war diary.
22 M Cunliffe. *History of The Royal Warwickshire Regt* (London: William Clowes, 1956), p. 151.

> main position and then with that secured an assault onto Hoxhof farm itself. The enemy were good and tough parachutists – no mean opponents.
>
> The first thing that went wrong was that the leading platoon, which at H hour [1400 hr] was to sprint forward to a fire position covering the assault to both objectives, got caught by heavy enemy defensive fire in its forming up place, suffered casualties and disorganization. The other two assaulting platoons therefore had to scramble through and the intended fire platoon collected into a reserve to follow along. The rest was highly successful, the discipline and experience of the soldiers told as we kept right up almost into our own shells and by short section rushes under our own close covering fire got on top of the enemy before they got their heads up out of their trenches. We killed, wounded or captured a half hundred, at a cost of only some twenty.
>
> One of my platoon commanders was a Canadian, a very brave soldier indeed but incorrigible. I went to see his platoon which was consolidating after having secured the farm on the flank [probably Volbrockshof] – he was missing and I was livid. 'Where the hell have you been', 'Oh', said he surprised, 'I was hunting up some eggs', 'aigs' he called them.[23]

He was Lt Don J. Oland, Canloan 183 from Halifax NS. His accent had survived schooling at the Jesuit's Beaumont College in Windsor, Berkshire, where another present on the battlefield that day, Lt-Col J. Drummond of 2 RUR, had also been educated.

> Many CANLOAN officers made determined if not desperate efforts to return to units in action, often to suffer additional wounds or death. Though wounded in Normandy, he (Oland) managed to return to his battalion and played an active part in the advance towards Bremen, capturing for example several prisoners in an attack at the Ems Canal on 10 April. Finally near Bremen he was wounded again and had to have a leg amputated'.[24]

Illing continued:

> This action at Hoxhof was the only occasion in which I nearly had a case of a soldier shooting a prisoner. It was a shock to me particularly as the soldier concerned was a pleasant, cheerful lad and courageous; I just stopped him as with a Bren at the hip, he was about to let loose. The family owning the farm were in safety down in the large, well lit and furnished cellar and got the very rough edge of my tongue. One young Sgt, a splendid fellow, was badly wounded under the arm pit and bleeding profusely. I feared he might die from loss of blood. The stretcher bearers got him to the cellar and cut his jacket to plug the bleeding with the German family protesting at this uninvited invasion of their private cellar, an odd lot.[25]

A neighbour recently wrote; 'The people in Hoxhof are no longer alive. Their son was born in 1948, and he never spoke to his parents about the war. They certainly had a well-lit cellar'.[26] The approach to Hoxhof is now a lake resulting from extensive gravel extraction.

It was probably Don Oland's platoon in A Coy that seized Volbrockshof. Maria Raadts, née Kühnen, showed this author round the rebuilt farm and the original cellar where she was sheltering as a child with her family. She wrote a memoir.

---

23 HC Illing. *No Better Soldier* (Warwick: Royal Warkwickshire Museum, 2001), p. 34.
24 Wilfred J. Smith. *Code Word Canloan* (Toronto: Dundurn Press, 1992), p. 213.
25 Illing, *No Better*, p. 34.
26 Letter from Maria Raadts on 20 November 2014.

> On 28 February 1945 there was firing from the Uedemerstrasse, about a kilometre away, that struck the potato cellar in our barn at about 2 pm. An armour piercing shell (Panzer-Granate) penetrated the cellar wall facing the Kervenheim road and exploded against the opposite wall. The cellar was divided into two rooms and we had been there for a week seeking shelter. Some refugees from Weeze were with us. I was then eight years old, and my father had died two days before Christmas. Now this! Father's brother and mother's sister and my grandfather Kühnen were all killed instantly by the shell. We children had no idea what was happening. Everything was dark and full of smoke. British infantry then stormed the farm. The cellar door was flung open and a hand grenade was thrown in that wounded us two children. Those who could move were then ordered out of the cellar, and went on foot into the unknown, ending up in the Bedburg internment camp. Our wounded remained in the cellar and among them was Dela Kühnen. They were taken in a Jeep to the hospital in Bedburg. Her arm was amputated and shrapnel removed from her stomach. Today she is 80 years old. The three dead Kühnens were buried alongside the farm. Dela and I are the only two Kühnen survivors, a family from the border area between Kalbeck and Kervenheim.[27]

While Illing's A Coy took Hoxhof, Albury's C Coy occupied Endtschenhof while Johnson's B Coy and Bell's D Coy crossed the Fleuth and secured Wettermannshof. B Coy took the river road and had occupied Schneidershof by 5.45 pm.

R.W. Thompson and the Coldstreamer LO, Capt. Cresswell observed the Warwicks' attack as they waited with the Norfolks to be ordered forward. Looking west across the plain, which is best seen today from the embanked Autobahn bridge above Endtschenhof, they could see Ratzenhof and Hoxhof in flames as AVREs placed fascines in the Fleuth to enable the Churchills of 1 Sqn to cross the Fleuth. They could also see the road running south from Endtschenhof towards Kevelaer along which Heinz Deutsch or another troop from XII Fallschirm-Jäger-Sturmgeschutz-Brigade was withdrawing. Cresswell observed a StuG in the woods and called for fire from the medium 5.5s. The infantry defenders were from Unit Kraus of IIIFJR7, according to 3 BID Intelligence Summary No 230:

> EINHEIT KRAUS. Was formed in Coy strength about eight days ago from coy and bn "B" Ech personnel of III/7 Para Regt and any other spare oddments of the bn who had not been in action before. They were held as an emergency reserve some 4 Km EAST of UDEM until 26 Feb when they were put into the line in the area of HOXHOF 9639. Original strength 100-120. The comd is O/LT KRAUS.

Another source states the defenders were 7 Coy FJR7, defending the sector from Hoxhof to Müsershof.[28] This puts them in II/FJR7. (1-4 in IFJR, 5-8 in IIFJR, and 9-12 in IIIFJR.

As the light was going at about 5.45 pm on 28 February, the KSLI entrenched themselves in the woods less than a mile from Kervenheim. Bob Littlar recalled a track to his right leading 800 yards to a farmhouse, which would have been Nachtigallskath, and sending a section to search it. They found some old people who were ordered out, lined up and checked before being released. No enemy was seen although an MG 42 opened up on them from a distance. The KSLI's flanks were in the air with the Warwicks on the right some way back at Schneidershof, and no contact on the left with 11 BAD. That night they dug tight defensive positions with Tac HQ (982395) between the two reserve companies. After dark main HQ's 20 vehicles moved up to within 2,000 yards,

27 Ibid.
28 Letter from Heinrich Kempkes to this author on 4 November 2014.

Volbrockshof, pictured in the 1930s, was RW Thompson's 'farm on the plain', and located 700 m north-east of Endtschenhof. He observed it for several hours and saw its capture. Maria Raadts, née Kuhnen, was in the root cellar with her family and with refugees. The cellar was approached through the door in the barn on the right of the house. An AP shell penetrated the wall behind which they were sheltering with lethal results. (© Maria Raadts)

Maria Raadts, née Kuhnen, at home in Volbrockshof in September 2014. Like many farmhouses in the area, it is now a virtual island in a sea of flooded gravel pits. The landowner is Vittinghoff-Schell of Schloß Calbeck, now Spies von Büllesheim through marriage and a family known to this author in 1946 as the owners of Haus Hall in Ratheim.

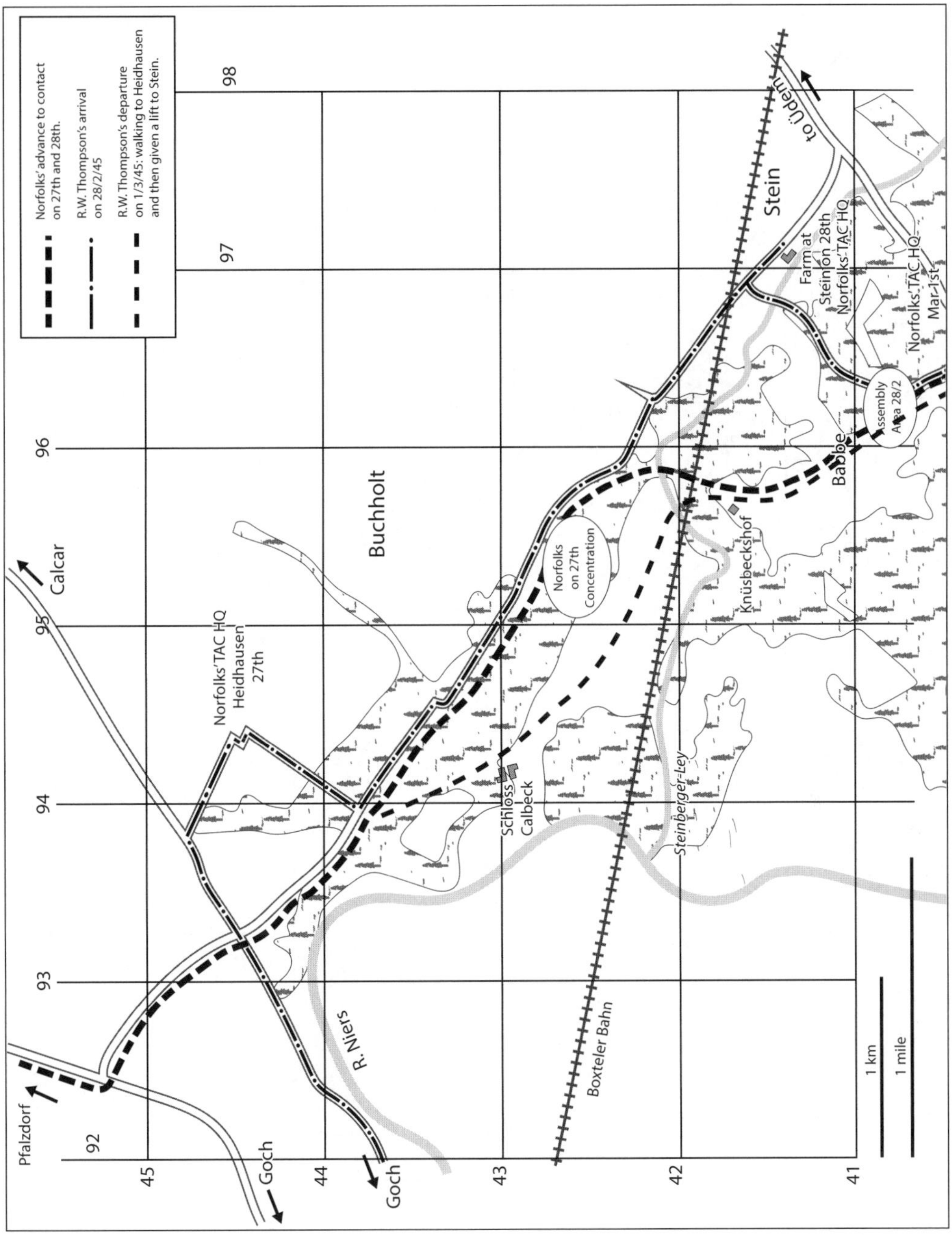

Map 22 Routes taken by 1 R Norfolks and RW Thompson to the battle of Kervenheim.

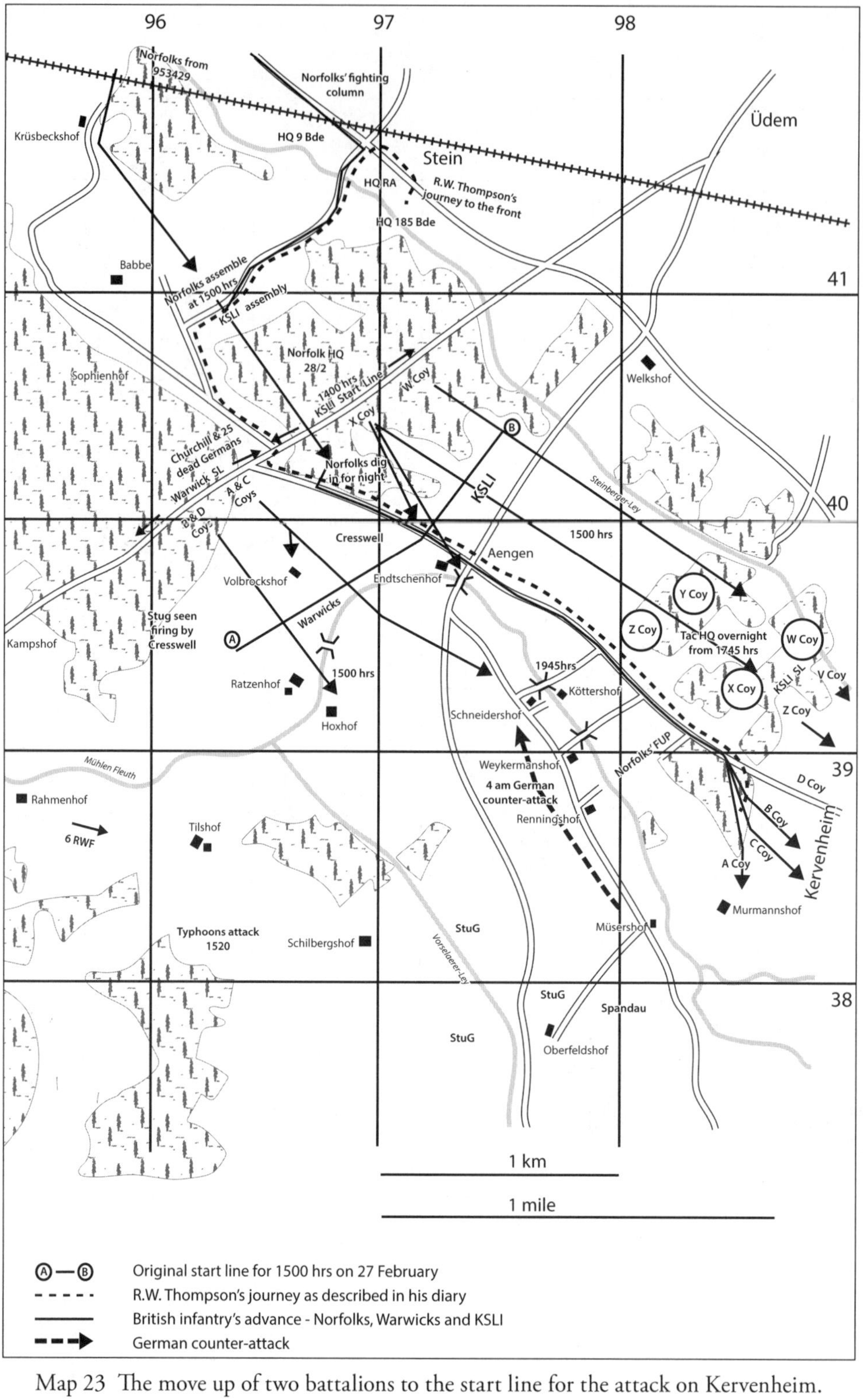

Map 23 The move up of two battalions to the start line for the attack on Kervenheim.

bringing the cooks who served a hot meal at midnight. They had difficulty crossing the Üdem-Weeze road that was jammed with the traffic of 53 BID, whose 6 RWF had crossed Yorkshire Bridge that morning and by then were moving east and south to outflank Weeze.

A suggestion by Hans Kühn of 33 Tank Destroyer Unit, 15 PGD, that Kervenheim was attacked on what must have been 28 February, cannot be discounted. Kühn states below that the attack was made on 28 February after an advance on 27 February supported by Typhoons which is impossible because on that day 84 Gp was grounded by the weather. 28 February was dry and clear, however, while 1 March was wet which was exactly as Kühn described it. In further correspondence, Kühn stated that his account should not be taken literally and that the Churchills attacked at 10 am, which indicates 1 March. Alexis Napier suggested that Kühn hit Harrison of 1 Sqn whose tank was destroyed since no tank in 2 and 3 Sqns CG was destroyed, but Harrison was on the right flank with the Warwicks and out of sight of the factory. Melikoff/Napier said he saw Typhoons bombing in Kervenheim which could well have been Kühn in the half hour before John Lincoln arrived to find the hole in the factory wall exactly as Kühn described it,[29] although no direct corroboration has been found in the British records. There is however a hint that it might be true in an entry in the 3 BID War Diary for 0900 hrs on 28 February; "Contact made with 11 Armd Div on LEFT who were intimately concerned with our ops against KERVENHEIM". Their concern was to outflank the strong opposition at Dickmanns 008378 by using the Sonsbeck road, which was in their area but originated in Kervenheim which was not. Brig Mike Carver was the enterprising but stymied commander, and he might have tried something in Kervenheim. Kühn, however, says the attackers were Churchills and not Shermans operated by Carver.

Soldiering has always been a matter of 'hurry up and wait'. The Norfolks spent 27 and 28 February in a meandering and seemingly interminable 'advance to contact' behind the KSLI and Warwicks. On 27 February they marched for several miles from Pfalzdorf 914466 to the woods a mile east of Schloss Calbeck at 954428, sharing the area with the Lincolns, who were under orders during the night to be ready to move against any German breakthrough at Yorkshire Bridge. The Norfolks were ready and keyed up for action. The original H-Hour had been 3 pm, but enemy resistance caused postponement and they spent the night in the woods. The next day, 28 February, they marched past Krüsbeckshof and Babbe to meet their CO and the war correspondent, RW Thompson in the assembly area recently vacated by the KSLI.

As the Warwicks and KSLI pushed forward on both sides of the Brigade's centre-line, the Norfolks followed up, ready to make a dash for Kervenheim along the brigade axis. They crossed the Üdem-Weeze road and waited in the fields and wood alongside the road on the eastern side of the river. They did not dig in, according to Lt John Lincoln. He described how he carried his entrenching shovel hanging upside down and retained against his back by the crossed over webbing straps that tied down the flap of his small pack. Sometimes the handle hit him behind the knee but the vital implement was out of the way yet immediately to hand. John recalls seeing the occasional soldier carrying the shovel balanced over his shoulder with the handle pushed front-to-rear through the epaulet. No one carried a pick in those stone-less sandy soils where digging-in was quick, and emergency shelter could be obtained in five minutes, except in the woods where roots had to be broken through.

During the afternoon of that interminable 28 February, Lt George Dicks remembers lying down in the open field with the wood behind him and having three hours sleep. He heard the noise of battle but could see nothing. He remembers that a couple of his blokes were detailed to escort two POWs to the rear, and they did not return for two hours. His irritation mounted, but when they reported back there was nothing amiss. Thompson wrote that during the afternoon he

29 This author's correspondence with Kühn and Melikoff (Alexis Napier) in 1997.

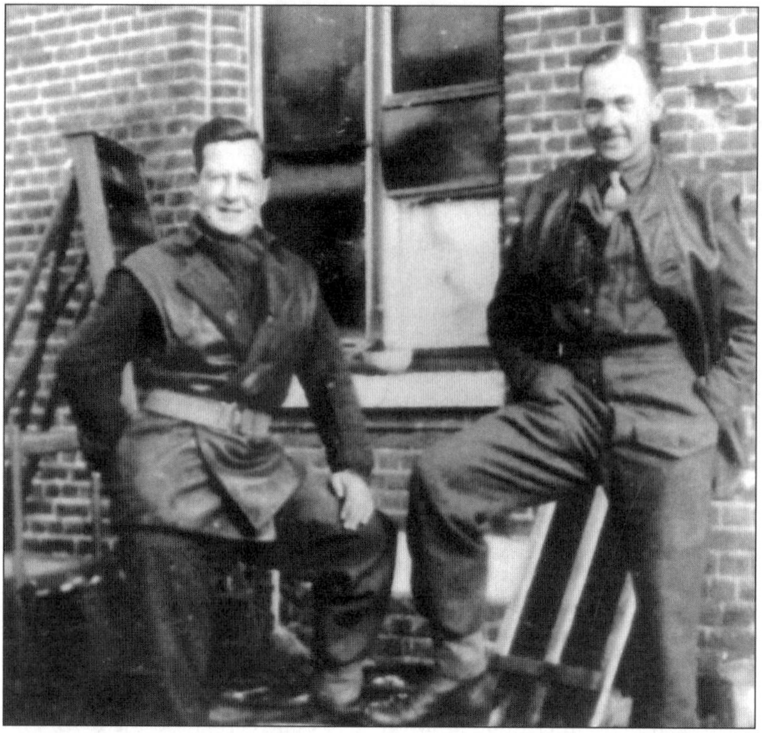

Lt Friar Balsam and Lt George Dicks, 1 R Norfolks in Venraij in October 1944. (© John Lincoln)

shared the roadside ditch with some Norfolks, confirming again that some of the battalion was not entrenched although subject to intermittent shellfire. Lincoln remembers that the battalion was constantly moving and his platoon even moved during the night and again did not dig in, although all who Thompson saw that night were well dug in. The War Diary placed some of the Norfolks at 975397, 200 m east of Endtschenhof alongside the Mühlen Fleuth; George Dicks verbally confirmed being near the stream. Main HQ was in the wood on the west of the Üdem-Weeze road at 975397 with the Churchills harbouring a few hundred yards further back. The War Diary is silent on the point, but Tac HQ must have been in the wood between the Kervenheim and Üdem-Weeze roads at 967403, which is where Thompson would have spent the night. He wrote of being in a wood and west of the village (Endtschenhof).

The German defenders were 7 Coy FJR7, part of IIFJR7, from Hoxhof to Müsershof, west of the Mühlen Fleuth, and 8 Coy, part of III FJR7 from Murmannshof to Kervenheim, east and north of the Fleuth.[30]

The German defensive arrangements turned the approaches to Kervenheim into a zone of beaten cross-fire from the houses in front and from two farms, Müsershof and Murmannshof on the western flank, and Boemshof on the east. The roughly two hundred paratroop defenders were backed by one or perhaps two 88-mms and a troop of three StuGs from XII Para Assault Gun Brigade. They had observers on the higher ground on the west in wireless contact with HQ. There was also a Battle Group of 33 Tank Destroyer Unit of 15 Panzer Grenadier Division armed with Mk IV Tank Destroyers in Kervenheim. They destroyed two Churchills (a Coldstreamer at Endtschenhof and a Buffs' Churchill gun-tank in Kervenheim), led counter-attacks in the town-centre and at the tower and supported the paratroopers in the houses. There was unified command

30 Heinrich Kempkes in a letter on 4 November 2014.

under an unidentified paratroop officer. It could have been Hauptmann Gräfing, since 'Those who escaped mass-capture of the FJ-Lehr-Regt on September 4, 1944 were dispersed among II/FJR25, FJR32, FJ-Btl. Balzereit, FJ-Btl.Crass, FJ-Btl.Gräfing and KG von der Heydte'.[31] II/32FJR was last heard of in Host on 23 February.[32]

> The Para HQ was established in Müsershof together with the wireless that controlled the overall defense. The result [of this wireless traffic] was intense [British] artillery fire [aimed at the source of the transmissions] that finally forced the HQ to retreat [This must be either the regimental or divisional HQ as Müsershof is 1 km west of the centre of Kervenheim].[33]

The Warwicks' advance in the afternoon threatened the German defensive arrangements. They reacted to this threat by counter-attacking and stopping the Warwicks at 977393, between Schneidershof and Weykermanshof, 1,000 yds short of Müsershof and Murmannshof. The 185 Brigade's War Diary at last light puts the Warwicks at Renningshof; 'By dusk the Bde was est on the line HOXHOF 967393 – RENNINGSHOF 978387 – NACHTIGALLSKATH 984391 – SE EDGE OF WOOD 988394.'[34]

The divisional log disagreed, recording at 7.45 pm; '2 KSLI have reached PETER 987394, 2 Warwicks still held up at 977393 and attempt to pass 1 Norfolk through there NOT successful.'[35] This was the only mention made of an attempt to pass the Norfolks through the Warwicks on the West bank of the Mühlen Fleuth, although they were positioned to do so. The Regimental history recorded quite wrongly that 'by nightfall the Battalion was consolidated just outside Kervenheim, ready to complete the attack next morning.'[36]

The Germans were determined to keep the British away from their prepared strongpoints: Műsershof and Murmannshof to the west of Kervenheim, and Boemshof to the east. They took no action against the KSLI on the east, but took concerted action against 2 Warwicks on the west. First to be attacked was A Coy. Harry Illing, its commander in Hoxhof, described what happened:

> That night [28 February to 1 March] we were counter attacked, though I have never been sure that the enemy were not just trying to relieve their own troops in the mistaken belief that they were still in occupation. Suffice it to say that we deciminated (sic) them at close range and those who were not killed or wounded dodged back whence they came pursued by fire of every sort. The cries of their wounded were pitiful and although we were under frequent small arms and mortar fire, my own stretcher bearers with great courage went out from the safety of their own positions to bring them in. Their officer was wounded in a dozen places by fragments of an anti-tank shell; clutched in his hand was a brief case. We opened to check its contents, it contained silk pyjamas, shaving kit and a collection of foreign stamps – this is what really made me doubt he was leading a counter attack![37]

Matthews' orders were given out on 28 February and confirmed in writing. They defined the startline as PETER, codeword for the front edge of the woods facing Kervenheim. The Norfolks were ordered to be dug in on the right of the KSLI on the startline by first light. H Hr was to be

31 H Bliss & B Bosshammer. *Das FJ-Lehr-Regt* (Witzenhausen: Bliss, 1992), p. 399.
32 HG Martin. *History of 15th Scottish Div* (Edinburgh: William Blackwood, 1948), p. 270.
33 *Heimatkalender 1951.*
34 TNA: W0 171/4434: 185 BIB war diary. 1 March coverage was revealingly superficial.
35 TNA: WO 171/4130: 3 BID's war diary.
36 Cunliffe, *History*, p. 151.
37 Illing, *No Better*, p. 35.

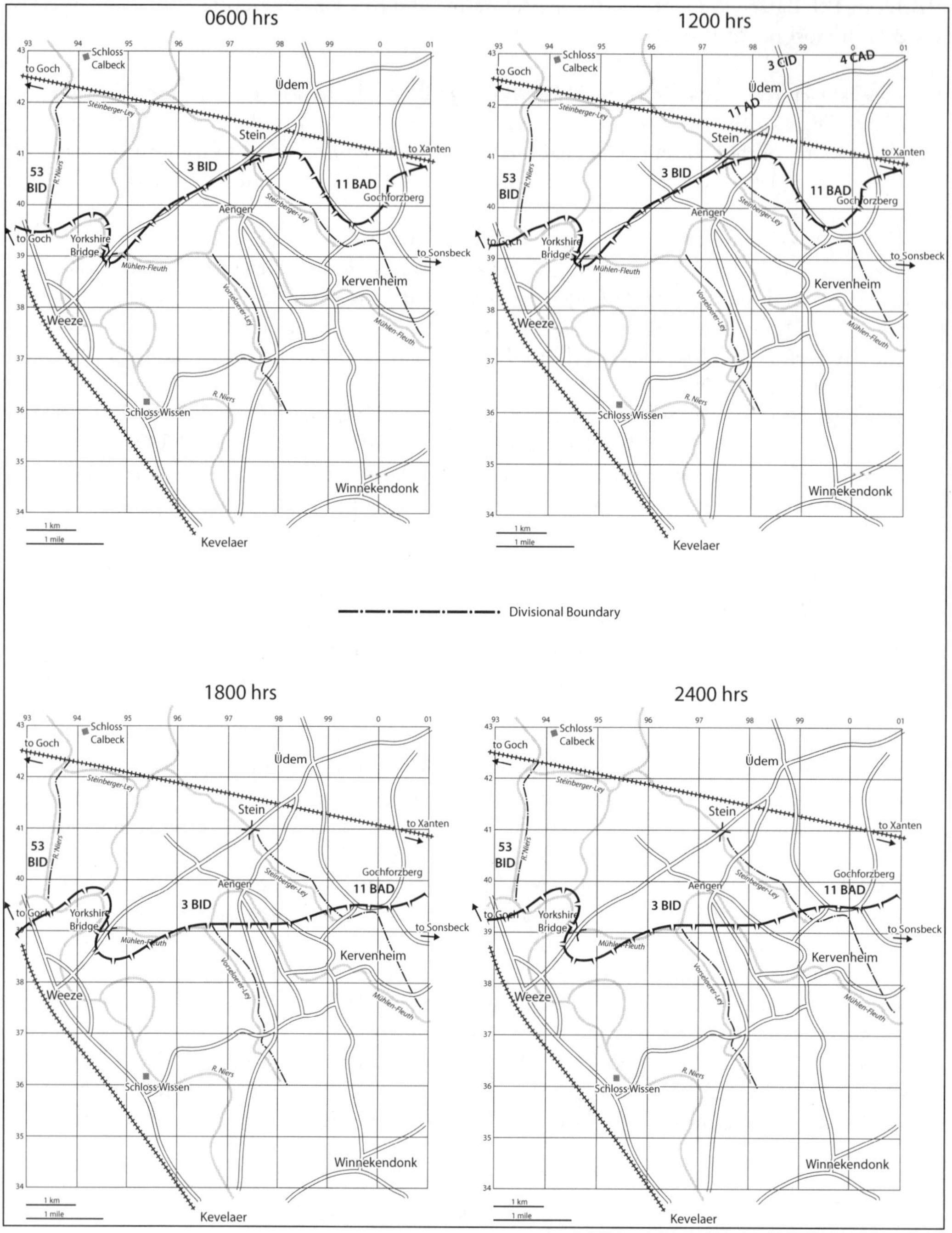

Map 24 The front line during 28 February 1945.

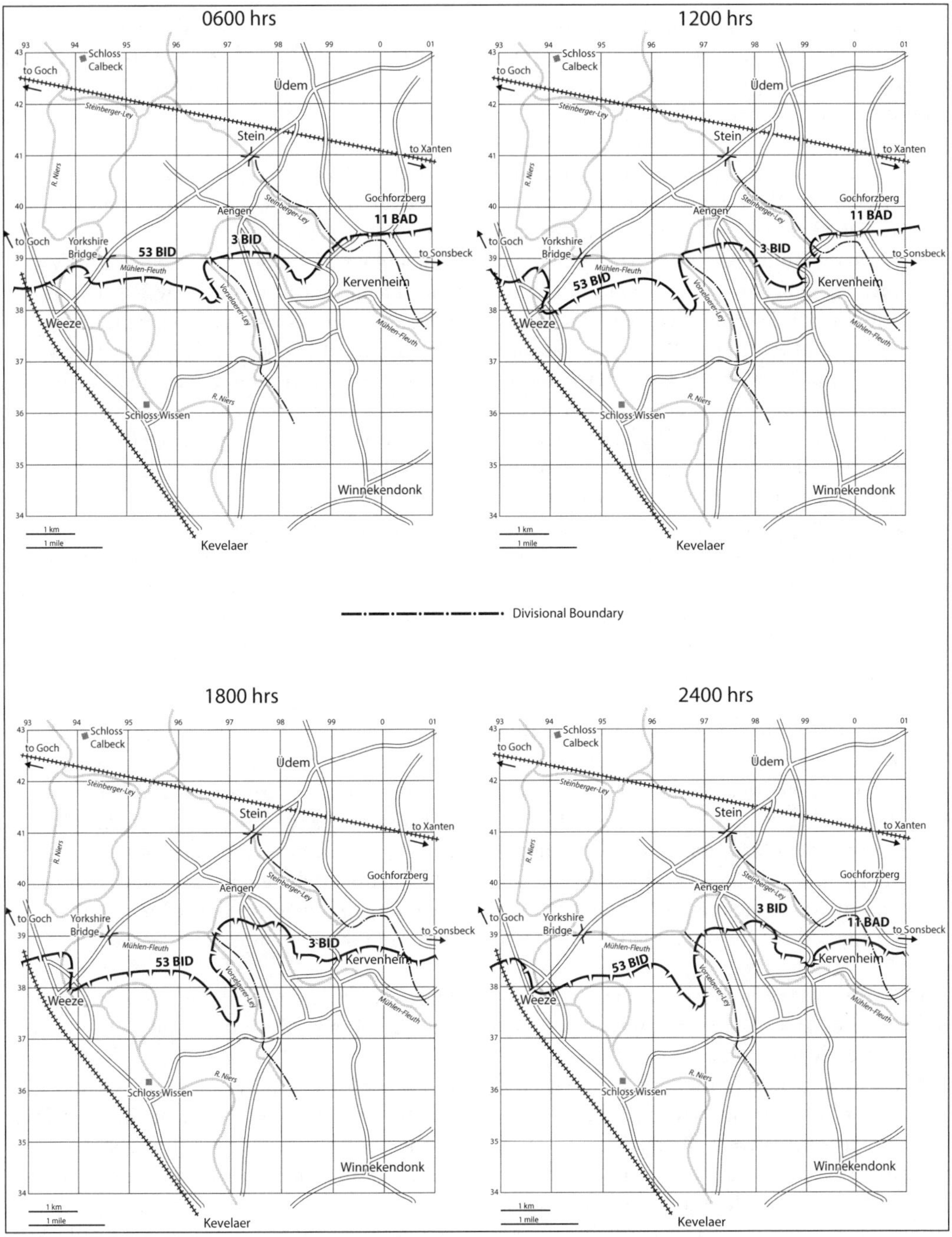

Map 25 The front line during 1 March 1945.

9 am. The Warwicks were to send a fighting patrol into Müsershof (981382) during the Venus Barrage. Matthews lost control of the battle at this moment when he failed to realize the danger to the Norfolks from Müsershof and Murmannshof, and therefore failed to order 2 Warwicks and 1 Sqn 4 CG to take them. A fighting patrol lacked the power to do so, but even that failed to materialize. The biographers of the two units expressed contentment that the battalion stood firm and that the squadron of tanks stood watch, while what the Norfolks required from them both was an all-out attack. Describing the Warwicks:

> The Bn was holding a kind of salient, particularly exposed on the right flank. Its sense of isolation was heightened by roads through the woods. Only by the greatest exertions had the QM (Capt S.J. Williams) and transport officer managed to bring forward a meal the previous evening. At dawn the enemy began to shell and mortar with an ominous intensity. Then a counter-attack, by about 75 Germans with some SP guns, was delivered against B Coy. For a little while the situation was serious, especially for Lt Guest's platoon, which bore the brunt of the attack. But he kept his head, and members of his platoon fought back very effectively. So did Pte C. Cook of the anti-tank platoon, who fired HE over open sights at the advancing infantry. He also succeeded in knocking out an SP. He was awarded the MM. So was Pte R. Duck, a stretcher-bearer who showed bravery of no less testing character when he evacuated casualties under shellfire. A troop of Churchills likewise played its part in defeating the German paratroopers, who withdrew, with considerable losses. But the Bn also suffered casualties; and since the enemy was so active in this neighbourhood, 185 Bde's advance was continued that day by the 2nd KSLI and 1st Norfolk, both of whom lost a good many men in bitter fighting before they eventually drove the enemy from Kervenheim. The 2nd Bn in the meantime was holding firm, under unpleasantly accurate fire. Eight of its other ranks were killed during the day and 31 wounded. Two subalterns, Mavins and Hood, were wounded [as well as Capt Johnson and Maj Albery].[38]

1 Sqn 4 CG with 15 Churchill tanks supported the Warwicks:

> The assault began at 9 o'clock next morning [1 March]. 1 Sqn was still on the right, and Lt Harrison led the way across the new bridge. He had gone only a few hundred yards when he was shot dead by a sniper; a shell from a S.P. gun hit his tank, wounding two of the crew, whom Gdn. Holborough carried back to safety under intense machine-gun fire. The Germans were still directing their guns from the hills on the right, and further advance on this flank was impossible. The squadron withdrew to the bridge, and there remained on the watch.[39]

Unit historians always put a good face on events. The Warwicks and Coldstreamers do not appear to have made any further attempts to put the fighting patrol into Müsershof, and Matthews did not apparently insist on it.

Matthews reaction to the unilateral withdrawal from the bridgehead by 1 Sqn 4 CG is nowhere recorded, while the unit's two historians played down the withdrawal and re-wrote history. Their explanations successively changed from protection of the tanks to conjuring up the genie of force majeure. This was a result, no doubt, of increasing post-war awareness of the high cost paid by 1 Norfolks for the pusillanimity displayed on the western flank. The rationale for withdrawal went through three stages; firstly, the original reason appeared in the 1945 War Diary and would have

38 Cunliffe, *History*, p. 151.
39 Howard & Sparrow, *Coldstream Guards*, p. 327.

come from Hamilton-Stubber; 'As several SPs had been firing at the Sqn, Capt Hamilton-Stubber gave orders for the two leading troops to pull back to the area of the bridge to a more protected position'.[40] Secondly, Forbes in 1947 added a modifying adverb and mentioned smoke; 'Several SPs had been firing at the Squadron and so the Squadron Leader, Captain Hamilton-Stubber, ordered the leading troop to withdraw a short distance under cover of smoke to the bridge which was slightly more protected than the open ground in front.'[41] Thirdly, Howard & Sparrow in 1951 removed mention of protection and smoke and invented force majeure, whose unspoken name was Heinz Deutsch; 'The Germans were still directing their guns from the hills on the right, and further advance on this flank was impossible. The squadron withdrew to the bridge, and there remained on the watch'.[42] Howard & Sparrow made other mistakes on this and the following page; viz that the Germans evacuating Kervenheim were threatened by 53 BID, and that the KOSB took Winnekendonk.

Two troops comprising six tanks had crossed the bridge and five returned. There remained 14 Churchills and a battalion of infantry which Brig Matthews apparently agreed should do nothing all day while the noise of battle raged 2½ kms away. It is a military maxim that those who are able must march towards the sound of the guns. There is no record of Matthews issuing orders to deal with the StuGs. One vehicle they sniped at on the approach road into Kervenheim was a Lincolns' HQ carrier containing the 2ic, Leslie Colvin. He recalled climbing out of it to relieve himself, and on climbing back in the end of his shovel was cleanly removed by an AP round.

The ideal antidote to long-range sniping by StuGs would have been a dive-bomber or an aircraft equipped with an armour-piercing gun. Alternatively, Matthews could have ordered the Medium 5.5 inch howitzers to shell the StuGs and 88s, and brought up the powerful 17pdrs available in quantity at the divisional level in both towed and SPform. StuGs were frightened of both, and 88s were vulnerable to HE shelling. There must have been pointed remarks made at 9 BID's post-battle conference, because Thatcher, who commanded 45 Anti-tank Battery with the 17pdrs, stated enigmatically and surely defensively that '17 Pdr Atk guns are not strictly supposed to be deployed in fwd coy localities but in fact can be made available if required.'[43]

Illing reflected on the battle at home forty years later, avoiding the question of why the Warwicks did not galvanise the tanks into attacking:

> The tanks were not a battle winner, and an infantryman would gladly exchange an extra battery for a troop of tanks. The country was very difficult and although the mines were fewer the tanks were controlled by the Germans. There were times when the tanks were very effective, but often in unconventional places such as in a village firing through a wall. At most other times the tanks only went where the PBI had made it safe for them.[44]

The troop of StuGs on the western flank had an influence out of all proportion to their numbers, which suggests that their ace, Leutnant Heinz Deutsch, was dominating the field again that day. It was probably Deutsch who two days earlier had destroyed Runcie's troop of 3 SG. Indeed his very presence seemed to cow the British. Evidence that it was Deutsch's unit comes from this passage:

> In the early morning hours of 1 March a hard battle broke out near Kloppermannshof in the vicinity of Kevelaer. Two Churchills were bagged which added to Leutenant Deutsch's score.

40 TNA: WO 171/5142: 4 Coldstream Guards war diary.
41 Forbes, *6th Guards*, p. 115.
42 Howard & Sparrow, *Coldstream Guards*, p. 327.
43 Appendix: 9 BID's Post-battle Conference Notes.
44 Harry Illing in conversation with this author in Warwick in 1985.

> The other two StuGs also made kills. Again the enemy tank attack was stopped, and this was repeated on the following day when the StuGs rescued the paratroopers in front of Kevelaer from being overrun.[45]

Searches for Kloppermannshof have failed, and this author concludes that Deutsch was referring to Wettermannshof or Murmannshof and what failed was his memory and the absence of a war diary. The same confusion undoubtedly exists with the dates. Kervenheim was the only battle on 1 March in the 'neighbourhood of,' or '*in der Nähe von*', Kevelaer. The only Churchills attacking that day were with 4 CG, since the Churchills supporting 53 BID north of Weeze were Crocodiles, and Deutsch always specifically mentioned these hated flamethrowers. There is another problem with Deutsch's account; he claimed two Shermans and a Churchill near Kevelaer on 2 March, which is difficult to explain unless he called Pember's Honey at Winnekendonk a Sherman. Intelligence placed Deutsch's 3 Troop under Krall in the sector, even though a prisoner from 2 Troop told interrogators that FJR7 was supported by 2 Troop under Behne; '2 Tp was the only one known to be in our sector and that was in sp of 7 Para Regt. It had lost two LFH 18s. The other tps are thought to be in the sector.'[46] This author believes the balance of probabilities favours the presence of Deutsch at Kervenheim, reinforcing 2 Troop and destroying Harrison.

Illing described how the Warwicks took no further part in the battle for Kervenheim:

> We remained at Hoxhof for twenty-four hours or so under periodic but progressively slackening fire and by next evening [presumably the evening of 1 March] were able to patrol forward. The enemy had gone and so I pushed on a strong patrol for about a mile only to be ordered to bring it back as a new formation was to pass through and capture Kervenheim, the next small town some miles ahead. This they did under cover of heavy artillery fire – I told them the enemy had gone from our immediate front but it made no difference – quite a few of them became casualties from our own shells.
>
> Next day we were ordered to move forward through Kervenheim and capture the next town Kapellen, and my company was detailed to do it… [Illing has the chronology wrong; he was not ordered to take Kapellen until two days later on 3 March].[47]

It is impossible to know Brigadier Matthews's thought-processes on 28 February, although it is clear he was deafened by the noise of conflicting opinions and demands, being out of his depth and without experience. He had made his name as a trainer of troops rather than a commander. If he accepted Kervenheim was defended, which was the view of 1 Canadian Army as reported that day by the Manchester Guardian and the Western Daily Press quoted above, then as it became dark he had options. He could have reinforced the Warwicks with the Lincolns, when they came under command at midnight, and attacked down the western flank that night. He could have sanctioned Barclay's attack on Kervenheim that night with his fresh troops, even forgoing tank support since they refused to fight that night, as Cresswell told Thompson on the 28th:

> 1730 hours. …The Squadron Commander of the tanks [Holdsworth-Hunt] won't want to go in without some light. It's no fun, blind in a tank, Spike [Cresswell] says. I can imagine.
>
> 1815 hours. "We attack", he [Barclay] says. "The tanks will stay with us. Zero 1815." Spike is on the radio with his Squadron Commander, who thinks it's too late…

45 Alman; *Sprung*, p. 236, this author's translation.
46 TNA: WO 171/4130: 3 BID war diary; Div Intel Summary No 231 of 3 March.
47 Illing, *No Better*, p. 35.

Capt ER Cresswell, referred to by RW Thompson as Spike, 4 Coldstream Guards, and receiving his MC in Plön on 12 June 1945. (© Crown Copyright IWM, BU 7827 by Sgt Morris)

Maj Humphrey Wilson, 2ic 1 R Norfolks. (© John Lincoln)

> 1815 hours. The attack seems to be off for tonight.
> 1930 hours. A decision had not yet been reached.
> Midnight. Now things were cut and dried… attack under a barrage at 0900 hours.[48]

There is evidence that 3 Sqn of 4CG, which was assigned to support 1 R Norfolks, was desperately tired. An officer of the Norfolks told this author that he was briefed by a Coldstreamer with a severe facial twitch who appeared to be suffering a nervous breakdown. CG had been fighting almost non-stop since the beginning of *Veritable* three weeks earlier and, despite receiving four days rest, were mentally exhausted. One officer in 3 Sqn had recently reported his troop sergeant and corporal for constantly stopping because of imagined 'mechanical failure' This was referred to in a letter home seen by this author who was refused permission to publish it. Whatever the case might have been, Matthews did not as far as we know support Barclay and argue up to division against the refusal of Holdsworth-Hunt, the OC of 3 Sqn and of Cresswell the LO to fight that night. Division might have received such a request sympathetically given the recent precedent of Carver's successful night attack on the left flank. We shall never know, but Humphrey Wilson, the Norfolks' 2ic, was surely either wrong or acting the good soldier when he wrote anonymously in the Regimental history:

> The C.O., quite rightly, decided to stay put where we were till 0400 hours and get everyone fed and rested, and then move up to a forming-up place under cover of darkness and wait for a proper artillery plan to be put into operation before launching the battalion under this in daylight – a much more satisfactory arrangement.[49]

Matthews probably thought the Warwicks were meeting a local difficulty which they would overcome at first light. It wasn't until the counter-attack before dawn and the retreat of 1 Sqn 4CG that questions would have been raised about the ability of the Warwicks to achieve their objective in time and any proposal to pass the Norfolks through the Warwicks became irrelevant. Matthews would then have considered it too late to change the plan and delay the assault on Kervenheim without risking a rocket from division or even corps with consequences for his chances of promotion.

At this point 3 BID was stretched to the limit. German resistance across the front had firmed, and the high hopes in II Canadian Corps of breaking through the Hochwald Layback in a 'two-day zip' to Wesel had faded. It was at this time that Crerar changed his mind about reinforcing success wherever it happened, and on 1 March told Simonds not to worry about the consequences of a XXX Corps breakout; 'Army Comd indicated that he would keep the main weight behind the 2 Cdn Corps thrust which now to be directed at RHEINBURG, with 30 Corps supporting the thrust.'[50]

Standard practice called for a brigade to advance with two battalions up separated by half a mile or so with its third battalion in reserve. With one fifth of 3 BID no longer combat worthy after the hard fighting of the previous two days (2 E Yorks and 1 S Lancs were re-forming) and with over half of the division committed to the attack on Kervenheim (1 Suffolk, which had just ended its fight to secure part of the startline, 1 Norfolk, 2 KSLI, 2 Warwicks and 2 Lincolns), there remained only the minimum of two battalions with which to take Winnekendonk -1 KOSB and 2 RUR. The transfer of either of these units into 185 BIB would have compromised the

48 Thompson, *Men*, pp. 82-85.
49 The Battalion. *History of 1st Bn the R Norfolk Regt* (Norwich: Jarrold, 1947), p. 44.
50 LAC: HQ II Canadian Corps: War diary.

overall objective of breaking through at Winnekendonk. The chosen option was to carry on with the frontal attack by Norfolks and KSLI and expect them to seize Murmannshof and Boemshof. Müsershof on the west bank of the Mühlen Fleuth was the responsibility of the Warwicks, and if it could not be taken it was to be isolated from the battle by smoke; which in the event failed to be implemented because no one checked whether smoke shells were available. The Norfolk subalterns, Dicks, Balsom and Lincoln all remembered being promised a smoke screen on the right flank, and querying its absence at the time and later.

Evidence for a different interpretation of Matthews' intentions has emerged from Humphrey Wilson's surprising statement in 1985 to this author that Kervenheim was no more than a probing attack or reconnaissance in force. The Warwicks and KSLI each sent a full four companies with a Tac HQ to secure the startline called Peter. For the assault attack on Kervenheim, however, the Warwicks were absent while the Norfolks sent three and the KSLI only two, companies 'over the top'. The COs of the Norfolks and KSLI remained behind the startline with the reserve companies uncommitted. In the other battles examined in these chapters the COs of 2 E Yorks and 2 Lincolns led the whole battalion to the objective, signifying it was a do-or-die effort. This partial commitment was the same also with the tanks. Lt. Prince Alexis Melikoff, now Alexis Napier, commanded 11 Troop in 3 Sqn, and was ordered to leave his troop behind and to follow behind D Coy of the Norfolks into Kervenheim. Napier explained why tank deployment was limited:

> The terrain over which the Royal Norfolks and KSLI were attacking was marshy with the consequent risk of any tank trying to cross it, getting bogged right in front of the enemy positions. My route into Kervenheim was therefore along the road, even though I had to move across the front of the enemy, past the enemy occupied houses by the tower, and then take the turning into Kervenheim. The remaining tanks of No. 3 Squadron gave supporting fire from the wood at the startline, as it would have made little tactical sense for them to follow me along the road – across the enemy's front – exposing the whole squadron to possible enemy anti-tank gun fire. No. 2 Squadron had a similar problem of marshy ground, although Alec Foucard's route took him more directly towards Kervenheim, than mine did.[51]

What Alexis failed to mention was that Alec Foucard led his troop in 2 Sqn through similarly swampy ground nearby on foot and came through with his one tank that in effect won the battle.

Another factor referred to has been the caution exercised by Holdsworth-Hunt, OC 3 Sqn 4CG, in the light of the open landscape and the presence of StuGs. Tom Read of the KSLI believed their reason for attacking with only two companies was cautious uncertainty about the defenders' strength, combined with the desire to limit the risk to the battalion in a bare and open landscape where the defense had the advantage. The narrow battalion frontage was a further consideration. 'It would have been crazy to put all the companies on the battlefield.'[52]

This evidence that it was a probing attack sharply conflicts with the understanding of the Norfolks' veteran junior officers. Wilson's statement was put to the platoon commander, George Dicks, whose military career ended at Kervenheim:

> This is a turn-up for the book! What do you call an attack by two battalions supported by tanks (!) and a creeping barrage. My view and the views of Friar Balsom and John Lincoln is that this was a serious set-piece affair. But perhaps we should defer to the views of a Senior

51 Letter from Alexis Napier (Melikoff) on 4 December 1999.
52 Phone conversation with Tom Read.

> Regular Officer [Humphrey Wilson]. After all he was privy to discussions which mere subalterns knew nothing about.[53]

Despite this semantic confusion, the direct attack on Kervenheim and Murmannshof by the Norfolks received the intimate support of only Melikoff's tank although two took to the field and bogged about half way across.

The Germans were thrown off Yorkshire Bridge and out of Winnekendonk through surprise, but they withdrew from Kervenheim and Weeze in their own time to the next prepared position. The Norfolks acted predictably in Kervenheim and without significant tank support; RW Thompson joked with the crews of tanks unengaged with the enemy throughout that dreadful day. At 2 pm Thompson was told that the battle was won and he departed, although Kervenheim remained occupied by the Germans for another 16 hours. Division was told the Lincolns were sweeping through Kervenheim, while in reality only a small part of Kervenheim was occupied. The War Diary of 9 BIB recorded that at 4 pm the Lincolns were attacking Kervenheim supported by a troop of Crocodiles, when there was one company and one Crocodile. There is a hint of disagreement between Firbank of 2 Lincolns and Barclay of 1 Norfolks about who was fighting the battle. At 9 BIB's post-battle conference, Firbank was told that absent any other instruction, the senior battalion's commander was in command, which meant the CO of the Norfolks' (IX Foot) commanded the Lincolns' (X Foot) CO. All this evidence places the orders given to Alexis Melikoff in a new light. Brig Matthews and Lt Cols Smith, Barclay, Daly, Gibbs and Firbank lost control of the battle which was won by the VC-winning exploits of the KSLI with 2 Sqn, CG. The battle concluded when it did only because the Germans withdrew.

The Lincolns were transferred to 185 BIB at one minute past midnight on 1 March. Updated orders were needed from Brigadiers Mears (CRA) and Matthews. Two barrages, Vinegar and Venus, were planned for the divisional artillery, with Vinegar reinforced by GAD, and a series of concentrations called Vacuum were further reinforced by the artillery of 53 BID, 5 AGRA of XXX Corps and 9 AGRA of II Canadian Corps. The eyewitness, R.W. Thompson, mentioned three barrages but he probably confused the concentration with a barrage. In the event, GAD made no contribution to *Heather.* Its artillery was always included in the planning, but they never actually participated. The orders are reproduced in the appendices.

The Norfolks had the task of taking Kervenheim. Their 2ic, Maj Humphrey Wilson, wrote a description of the battle (map references and farm names have been added by this author):

> By midday on 27th February the battalion had concentrated in the woods south-east of Goch (953429 about 1 km east of Schloss Calbeck). The woods had only just been cleared, and the recently occupied Boche trenches still contained the usual litter left behind. An uneventful day and night were passed – not completely uneventful as the Bn pioneer officer, Lt J.R. Williams, was killed by an 'S' mine whilst recceing and clearing a path for the battalion to follow the next day. [These same mines had troubled the RUR on 26 February. It raises the question whether a mechanism existed for passing on information from one battalion to another. The Pioneer platoon briefed its replacement, but here the Norfolks moved in hours after the RUR had left]. This was a sad blow to all.
>
> Tac HQ of Bde now moved ahead of us [to Stein]. The CO was to stay with the Brigadier whilst the bn was all ready for a move up at a moment's notice. Eventually, at 1300 hrs on 28th Feb, the marching troops moved off to an assembly area about a mile along the Bde axis [actually 2,500 yards]. The tracks and wheels of the fighting echelon were brought round by

53 Letter from the late George Dicks.

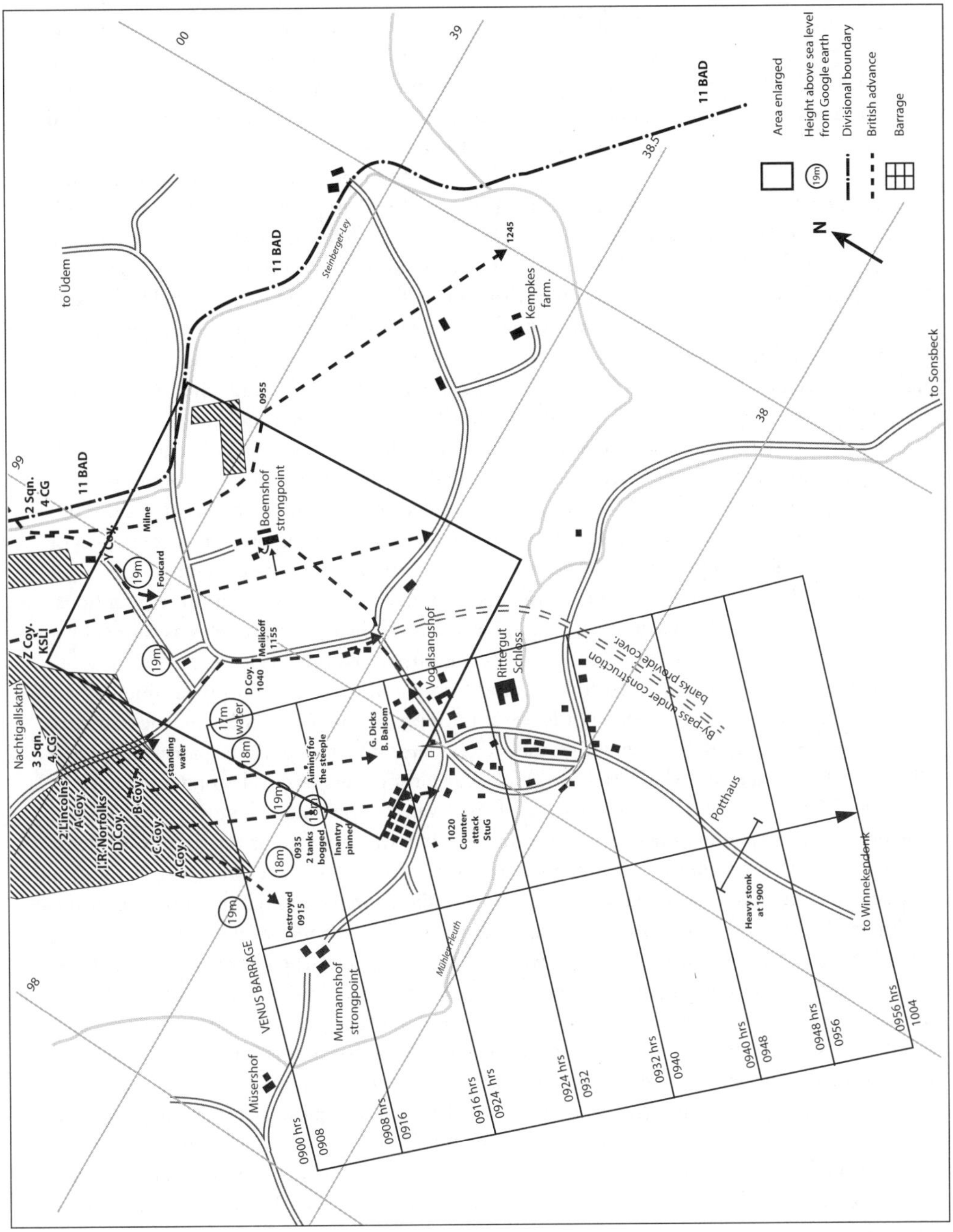

Map 26 The battle of Kervenheim.

the only existing road to meet the marching personnel at a prearranged RV. This worked very well, as the head of the two columns coincided at exactly the right moment. The bde plan was for the KSLI and Warwicks to secure the flanks, and the bn was then to pass through to assault the town of Kervenheim. [The original plan was for all three battalions to take Kervenheim in a sort of three-horse race. KSLI and Warwicks were to secure the start line where the Norfolks would join them in the centre of a three-battalion assault, rather than pass through them alone. Later the plan seems to have become defined in the way Wilson explained it, and this was confirmed by R.W. Thompson; 'The moments the flanks are secure, the Norfolks will go through on the centre line and take the town of Kervenheim.' However, ambiguity persisted. Neither flank was secure in the sense that both had to be fought for, when the Norfolks went over the startline, but the horse-race element persisted and might explain the lack of soul-searching in the Warwicks about the outcome: so their horse fell and another won the cup; big deal! In the event three coys of Norfolks started without even the prospect of a secure right flank where the Germans were strong, and with only half of the KSLI taking the field alongside them]. The bn detail was A Coy right, B Coy centre with C Coy left, and D Coy echeloned behind B Coy. [This is not the line-up recorded by John Lincoln and others, which was from right to left; A Coy, C Coy, B Coy and with D Coy behind in reserve. Map IX, p.161 of *Thank God and the Infantry*. This author concludes that Humphrey made a surprising mistake]. It was hoped to put in the attack that evening, but our flanks were not yet secure and it was still a good thousand yards to the startline through tricky country not properly cleared and very exposed from our right. The CO, quite rightly, decided to stay put where we were till 0400 hrs and get everyone fed and rested, and then move up to the forming-up place under cover of darkness and wait for a proper artillery plan to be put into operation before launching the bn under this in daylight – a much more satisfactory arrangement. [This account is tendentious. It avoids mention of Barclay's desire for a night attack after the evening attack was vetoed by 4 CG. RW Thompson witnessed and reported the argument recounted below].

A patrol was now ordered to go forward and find out all that could be ascertained about positions and strength of the enemy. Lt Rowe led this patrol, and went right into the outskirts of the town, returning after dawn with some very valuable information. [The patrol confirmed the enemy's presence, but what else is unknown]. A most gallant and well-conducted patrol.

At 0415 hrs [on 1 March] a long snake of men wound their way along the track to the assembly area. A spandau opened up on our right but was directed against the Warwicks. Keeping a weather eye and not an unconcerned [Concern was justified. The Warwicks were stopped, and the flank left open] one open on that flank, we continued our advance in the darkness. We did not want to get mixed up in any diversions from our main task or to break one of the most important principles of war i.e. maintenance of the objective. Before dawn on 1st March the bn was dug in complete with command post [98439 Nachtigallskath] in its forming-up place. By 0800 hrs our tanks had arrived and the final link-up was completed. At 0900 hrs the leading coys crossed the startline and the battle was on. The startline was the edge of a wood beyond which lay open fields with no cover of any sort. To the right were two groups of farm buildings [Murmannshof and Müsershof] and it was from these that we suffered our initial set-back. A Coy on the right suffered badly. Maj D.W. Smith, MC, shot clean through the head and killed. [A German civilian described below how after the battle an officer of the Norfolks was very upset over the death of a fellow. The author believes that Humphrey Wilson was that officer and the clue is the detail he provides about the manner of Donald Smith's disfiguring death]. All the platoon commanders were either hit or badly wounded [Lt Terry Rourke MC killed by the blast from one of our own shells, according to acting CSM, George Carr, Lt G Smith MM killed and Lt William Lewis wounded], only the gunner FOO [Capt George Haigh] remaining to control what was left. B Coy on the left had got on a bit better, but were still being troubled by the farther farm on the right [Müsershof]. They did not know exactly how far A Coy had got and called for fire. This was answered by an 'Uncle' target but the enemy still held firm.[54]

Friar Balsom knew Lt G Smith MM well.

He was a most efficient soldier. He had been awarded the MM at Perrier Ridge on 6th August in the same engagement that Cpl Bates won the VC. They were both in 11 Platoon in B Company. At that time I was the only surviving officer in C Company which also had heavy casualties. In the subsequent reorganisation I took over 11 Platoon at the same time as a number of young reinforcements arrived straight from the Norfolks' depot. I had great support from Sgt Smith in creating a new platoon of the old and the new. We were together throughout the autumn campaign in Holland. He was always most helpful and supportive – a little formal/reserved perhaps, but only to be expected when a newcomer/outsider like myself arrives. I was very pleased to support his move to a commission. I had only a few occasions to meet him after he joined A Company.[55]

Lt Terry Rourke was a ranker from the RA in N Africa and was awarded the MC at the Molen Beek. During a period of two days he successfully prepared the bn to cross the brook, although with great loss. CSM Ted Carr fought alongside Rourke both at the Beek and in Kervenheim:

He was a fearless sort of chap. He went into everything with great gusto and without flinching… (At Kervenheim A) Company was almost annihilated, and even now I can still remember seeing Terry Rourke's body. He was laying on the ground as if he had fallen down and gone to sleep. [Shell blast can collapse the lungs or the brain].

Rourke's nephew, Terry Smith wrote in a newspaper article; 'The tragic irony about his death is that, having been wounded, he was killed by one of our own shells falling short.'[56] Lasting memories of Terry live on in Helmond with Carla Coenen-van Hoof who was fifteen when the twenty-two year old Terry was billeted on her family, and with whom he continued to correspond and to send presents until his death.[57]

In 1999 Alois Janssen, who inherited Murmannshof, found a .38 in Enfield No. 2 Mk.II service revolver with a piece of the bakelite grip broken off in a hedge behind Murmannshof that was being grubbed out. It was officer issue, so belonged either to Donald Smith, Terry Rourke or G.A. Smith who may have got behind the defenders in the farm before being killed. Alois also found two graves in his garden in 1966 and 2000. Heinrich Kempkes identified them from a letter he found in the Kevelaer archive containing a diagram of a field cemetery established by the British; the names were Hermann Scheurenbrand, killed by shellfire on 28 February and found in 2000 and Oskar Meilich. In total nine defenders were killed, including five who burned to death in the barn.[58]

Lt William Lewis led 7 Pl in A Coy, against Murmannshof, and survived his wounds.

---

54 Battalion, *History*, pp. 44-45. Humphrey Wilson wrote this and most of the book.

55 Friar Balsom in a letter on 1 March 2000.

56 Steve Snelling. *Terry's trail to honour family hero* (Eastern Daily Press, 20 October 1995), sent by Carla Coenen-van Hoof on 7 November 1999.

57 Ibid.

58 Heinrich Kempkes. *Die verschwundeten Soldatengräber auf dem Murmannshof in Kervendonk.* (Kervenheim: Geschichtsbrief, Nr. 40, 2004.)

Enfield No 2 MkI revolver found by Alois Janssen in a hedge behind Murmannshof, and presented to the author. It would have belonged to one of the three officers of A Company 1 R Norfolks killed in the attack. It has been cleaned of surface rust and a lanyard attached. In exchange Alois received a wartime aerial photograph of his farm. The Enfield was later deactivated by Terry Abrams in Essex. The powder in each shell was viable, and two of the percussion caps still worked.

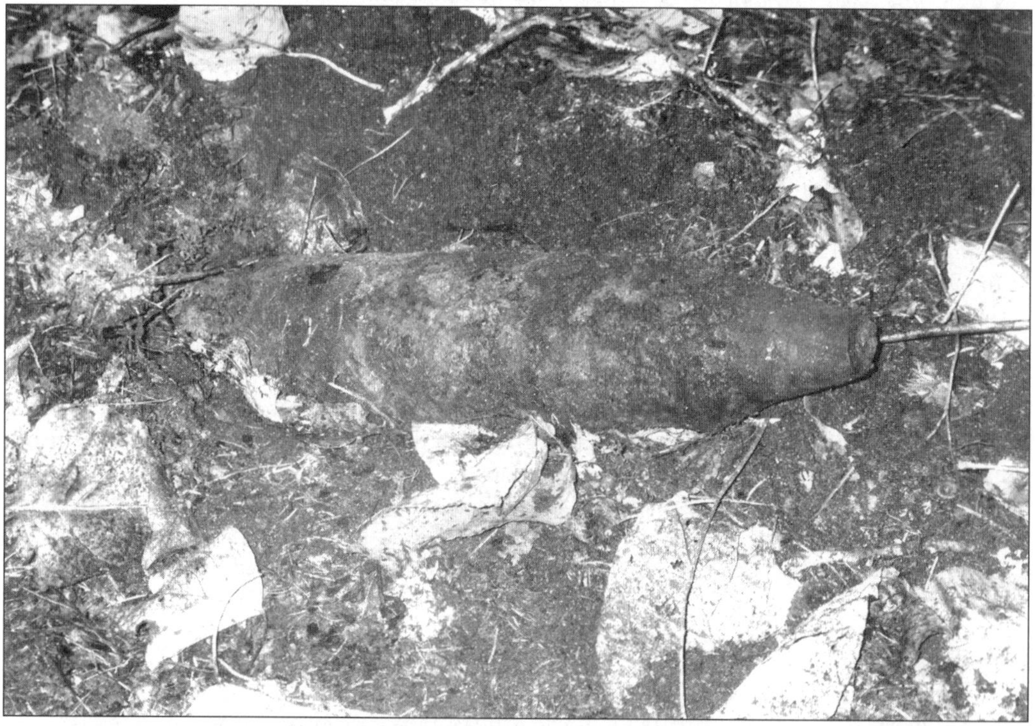

A Panzergranate 39, 75 mm APCBC shell uncovered by the author in 1994 in the wood by the Norfolks' start line. Its cintered iron driving band and ballistic cap were missing, but the soft cap remained. It weighed 6.8 kg, and unlike its British equivalent contained a small 18gr RDX/wax explosive filler, making it unsafe. It was afterwards reported and doubtless destroyed by the authorities.

The Kervenheim battlefield pictured from a light plane piloted by Piers Colvin in 1984 with Murmannshof in the foreground. Kervenheim is on the right.

> The advance across open country bereft of any cover, was swept with murderous fire, and casualties were heavy. Despite this, Lt Lewis led and cheered his men forward, moving quickly from section to section. While doing this he was severely wounded; this was no deterrent to his fine leadership. He continued to direct and encourage his men, and entirely due to his supreme example led them onto the objective; once there he collapsed through loss of blood.[59]

Private John Woods of A Company wrote an account of going over the top at 9.15 am armed with a Bren to assault Murmannshof which was 350 yards away across an open field. Little happened during the first 200 yards, but then 'all hell broke out' with small arms and mortar bombs. The farm was fortified with machine guns in the windows, certainly with snipers on the roof, and with trenches in the field in front, some occupied and some not. John reckoned that within a few minutes A Coy lost over one hundred dead and wounded. He spotted a couple of defenders in a trench only 15 yards from the farmhouse, and therefore about 135 yards ahead, and charged them, firing his Bren as he ran. One occupant climbed out and ran behind the farmhouse. John jumped into the vacated trench to change the magazine on the Bren, and discovered the other German who was dead. With a full magazine the Bren would fire only single shots, and John was unable to correct the fault. His trench became drenched with suppressive fire. He was joined by his friend Cpl Cubbit who was out of ammunition for his Sten. The two decided to wait until dusk and try to evade in the dark. The could hear the wounded crying out in the field behind them. As dusk approached a 'German with a very cultured English accent' shouted out for them to surrender.

59 Battalion, *The History*, p. 77.

Cpl Cubbit looked out to reply and was shot dead between the eyes. Grenades were then thrown and John was wounded in the back. He removed his battle-dress blouse containing his pay-book, and then passed out. On regaining consciousness he saw three Germans staring down at him, including him of the 'cultured' voice. John was taken to a barn, given medical treatment, and interrogated. The loss of his paybook opened him to the charge of being a franc-tireur, and his transparent lies about not having his paybook because he had only recently arrived nearly led to his death when a Paratrooper pulled back his rifle bolt as if to kill him, but was stopped by angry words from an officer. John spent the rest of the war in Stalag 12A, Wetzlar.[60]

Woods' memoir has harsh words about Maj Donald Smith, OC 'A' Coy, whose death in the attack so upset Humphrey Wilson, calling him a 'glory hunting major with few brains that he carefully kept concealed', and a 'psychopath' who preferred frontal attacks in daylight to infiltration at night. Woods says he argued with Smith who was 'out to get him', and claims his argument for a night attack was vindicated by its success when used against Haus Winkel a few days later. Woods ignored, or was ignorant of, the long argument between Barclay and Matthews about a night attack that was observed by Thompson and published for Woods to read. Smith could have had no part or influence in the rejection of Barclay's night attack, and Smith was loyally supporting the chain of command in his response to Woods. Woods' book abounds in factual errors and impossibly tall stories, such as his claim to have observed Germans crossing the Maas at Wanssum on a submerged bridge, when the Maas was 500 feet wide and in flood at that time. This author was advised to ignore Woods, but he was there, his account of the death of 5778948 Cpl Cubitt rings true, and he did become a POW. His anger is justified. There were only three known ways of avoiding the massacre; providing the promised tank support as Foucard was doing for the KSLI a few fields to the left, in which the infantry lay down and the tanks shot up the farms over their heads with Besa; masking the farm as promised with a heavy smoke screen; or surprising the defenders by attacking at night, which the powers-that-be rejected. In the absence of any one of these, Barclay should have refused to attack until the Warwicks had obeyed their orders and dealt with Murmannshof.

The commander of 16 Bty, 7 Fd Regt was Capt George Haigh. He was acting as an FOO during the advance when he found himself to be the senior surviving officer of A Coy. He took command of its remnants and sensibly dispensed tea to them:

> Most of the close quarter fighting I was not able to see in detail owing to the usual smoke and confusion. [One gun per bty was firing smoke – insufficient to provide the promised smoke screen. Both Thompson and Banks described Kervenheim as shrouded in blue smoke produced by burning buildings, and from British ammunition which was not smokeless.] My operator and I were watching the battle from a shell-hole about seventy-five yards away from the farm [Murmannshof]. We were neither of us in very good form, having had about an hour and a half's sleep the previous night.[Ironically, getting a good night's rest was one rationalisation for rejecting the night attack. Another was a planned barrage and yet many complained of lethal shells falling short, such as killed Lt Rourke.] Before long the Company Commander and two of his officers had been killed, and the remaining officer [Lt William Lewis] I last saw with a wound in his leg being carried away by two of his men. I could count only fifteen or twenty men remaining [the 103 ORs and 4 officers were reduced to one senior NCO and 34 ORs],[61] who with the loss of their leaders and so many wounded requiring attention were already coming away from the farm. I assumed command of the Company, and gave orders to

60 John Woods. *Peace in My Time! One Scouser's War* (Preston: Palatine, 1995), pp. 65-70.
61 John Lincoln. *Thank God and the Infantry* (Stroud: Alan Sutton, 1994), p. 156.

> the only remaining sergeant [CSM E. Carr] to prepare a defensive position. After my operator and I had helped some of the wounded I returned to the carrier and, after passing on what information I had, ordered the driver to 'brew up' straight away, and this being done, we took some tea round to the remaining men.[62]

Deutsch's StuGs, and probably an 88 which could even have been the one that did the damage at Winnekendonk the following night, were positioned on the western flank behind Müsershof. A detached battle group of Mk IV tank destroyers from 33 Tank Destroyer Unit [Panzerjäger Abteilung 33] of 15 PGD was also in Kervenheim. The gunner, Hans Kühn described how he dealt with the first Churchill to appear. However, since the only Churchill destroyed in Kervenheim was in the town centre, Kühn either exercised artistic license, or muddled up his memoirs. The account is included because Kühn was present in Merdian's Mk IV in Kervenheim, which was almost certainly attacked by the Bombphoons witnessed by Alexis Napier. The resulting hole in the factory was seen by John Lincoln. Kühn wrote:

> As already mentioned, the 15 Panzer Grenadier Division [Wolfgang Maucke] together with the remains of the 84 Infantry Division [Heinz Fiebig] and the Panzer Lehr Division [Horst Niemack] were withdrawn from the battlefield Southeast of Goch and on 25 February 1945 were switched to the area of Krefeld [against the Americans].
>
> A Kgr comprising 5 to 6 Mk IV Tank Destroyers (Jagdpanzer IV) and StuGs of the 2nd and 3rd Tank Destroyer Unit under the command of Lt Merdian (whose command tank carried the number 321) remained behind in the previous battle zone to support 7 and 8 Parachute Divisions. Their task was to keep the feared British Crocodile flame-throwers away from our infantry. It was known that the base of the British *Schwerpunkt* was the line Weeze – Kervenheim – Üdem and was directed on Sonsbeck – Bonninghardt – Alpen with Wesel as the ultimate objective.
>
> On 26 February the Battle Group took up position on the right flank of the frontal sector from Kervenheim to the Otterbeck shoe factory that is located on the road leading out of town towards the Gochfortzberg and Üdem. In terms of infantry, the defence was in the hands of about 200 Paras supported by a few StuGs on the left flank.
>
> The 11th Armoured Division attacked the Gochfortzberg and the 3rd British infantry Division assaulted Kervenheim with 185 Brigade: 1 Royal Norfolks and 2 KSLI. In support were the tanks of the Coldstream Guards of the 6th Guards Armoured Brigade. The weather was cloudy and rainy, but the cloud level was high enough to permit Jabos to operate.
>
> The 321 commanded by Lt. Merdian, who had only recently been named to command the whole Battle Group, and who had issued his orders without knowing the exact position of the other Tank Destroyers, was positioned at the eastern end of the shoe factory. 321 was camouflaged under planks and doors. The tank crew and a section of Paras, entrenched in the ditch in front of the SP Gun, kept watch on the field to the front. This was some 600 metres of pasture ending in a wood. On 27 February, [a mistake for 28 February as weather prevented ground attacks on 27 February according to the ORB of 84 Group] the usual massive artillery bombardment began with attacks by Jabos, although they never struck directly where our tank destroyers were positioned.
>
> It all started on 28 February [must be 1 March]. The artillery stonk began during the night and lasted hour after hour. In the morning the Norfolks advanced on Kervenheim behind a moving barrage. They had everything with them; tanks, AVREs that laid down fascines,

62 Scarfe, *Assault Division*, p. 216.

Crocodiles etc., as reported by the Recce Troop. The infantry pleaded; 'If nothing else, keep the Crocodiles away from us.' We naturally paid close attention to that request. The Paras decimated the attacking infantry with MGs and mortars in violent close-quarter fighting.

Suddenly the first British tanks emerged from the wood into the field. 'We must engage them', Lt. Merdian told his crew. 'Our friends can't see them because of the rise in the ground between them and the Churchills'. We arranged for a diversionary tactic by the other tank destroyers on the right flank, and then advanced. Two Churchills had emerged from the wood and were turning their turrets this way and that searching for targets. As agreed in advance, two of our tank destroyers lying concealed near the Üdem road fired a couple of shells in the direction of the Churchills. Immediately they turned their guns towards the firing. 'Advance', ordered Lt. Merdian. 'Tank leeeeeeft … gooood' (Liiiiiinks … Guuuut). [The StuG had no turret and was turned within 10° of the target in order for the gun to bear. The commander shouted into the intercom 'lefffffffft' until the tank faced in the general direction of the target. Then he began to shout 'goood'. As he spat out the 't' of 'Gut', the driver stopped turning. The gunner could then lay the gun on the target by turning the wheels on the captive screws controlling lateral and vertical gun travel. At 350 metres with the target advancing, the gun would be laid directly on the Churchill's turret with no significant correction necessary for wind or for trajectory drop.] The 321 rolled forward into the wet field to attack the Tommy who, thank God, was still looking the wrong way. The 321's crew at once felt the SP Gun sinking into the wet ground. The bottom plate was constantly scraping the ground. [The final drive housing of the front-sprocket drive protruded below the bottom plate and was the first part to hit the ground]. But repeated use of the steering brake, giving a 'Left – right – accelerate' movement, made it possible to advance. Reversing was out of the question. [Accelerating raised the front. Reversing would make the front dip and the drive housing dig in.] After advancing 150 metres into the field our StuG stopped.[The aerial photograph shows a hedge running out into the field where the Paras would have been dug in with a good view. When the Churchills appeared, 321 would have run to the end of the hedge and stopped. Merdian and Kühn would have a good view and be shielded from ground observation and even from the other Churchill but not, of course, from the air]. The crew had become nervous because the ground conditions presented a constant danger of bogging. Target acquisition was jerky. An AP shell had been loaded earlier. The first shot roared away at a distance of 350 metres followed by a series of shots. The first was a ranging shot observed by the crew. [The StuG had a scissors-type range-finder, whereas the Churchills had none. The shot had tracer and was visible provided there was not too much smoke from the barrel. German chemists produced the best smokeless powder. The first guess was then corrected.] The Churchill's turret was blown off to the side and soon the Tommy was enveloped in billowing clouds of smoke. Its companion had still not noticed 321. That was lucky. Lt. Merdian decided. 'Withdraw to the road'. We reversed with the same method of 'left – right – accelerate' and with difficulty got back. [This author suspects that Merdian was in this ambush position but when no Churchills appeared, reversed out and camouflaged the StuG].

However the biggest trial was still to come, because a track had been left in the field continuing onto the road which the Jabos could follow with their eyes straight to 321's position. It would have been far better if there had been no track for them to see. But in these muddy conditions it was usually a hopeless task trying to keep the tank camouflaged and making as light a track as possible, especially in the final few metres before taking up a position. Meanwhile the second Churchill had withdrawn. Lt. Merdian discussed the details of the engagement with the Paras. He received corroboration of the kill from the commander of the assault company of 7FJD. [German tank commanders, like fighter pilots, had to provide written corroboration of each kill from an independent observer. The unit was FJR7 and not

7FJD, a common confusion. Unfortunately this commander's name has never come to light]. It is included in the number of confirmed kills (109) achieved by PzJgAbt 33 in the period to 9 March 1945. [Sturmgeschützbrigade XII by comparison had 260 confirmed kills from D-Day to the end of the War, of which Deutsch scored 44.]

The defence held against the enemy infantry who attacked continuously until the evening, the Paras giving no ground in spite of heavy losses from artillery fire. [The Bombphoon attack that blew the hole in the shoe factory happened mid-morning rather than late afternoon, so again this account is compromised].On the Üdem road the other tank destroyers hadn't 'let in a single goal' either. Meanwhile the crews gathered round 321 to have something to eat. It was more than a slice of dry bread, but not much more, being only two months before the end of hostilities. The hatch cover was open. The background noise of small arms and artillery fire never stopped. Nevertheless the crew suddenly picked up the well-known drone – Jabos! There were twelve of them flying in an elegant curve around Kervenheim. The crew of 321 knew the British procedure: whenever strong resistance was met and German tanks put in an appearance the higher commanders at once despatched Jabos. And here were tracks in the field leading to the road and giving away their position! Lt. Merdian held the big hatch cover open with a gap of about 20 cm to see through. The gunner could also watch the flight pattern. The Jabos rounded Kervenheim church tower, gained a little height and peeled off, with the first diving straight for 321. Pray to God the hatch is solid! Each man sank down into his seat and soon aircraft bullets rattled against the armour. Then there was a brief hissing followed by an almighty explosion. Instantly the inside of the SP Gun filled up with mortar and brick dust. Everyone was coughing and gasping for air. It was a very dangerous moment. But the next bomb dropped further away. The hatch cover could not be opened. 321 was buried. As night fell, Lt. Merdian ordered the engine started. [It must have been only a little later the same morning. 321 was gone by 11.10 am when John Lincoln entered the factory through the gaping hole in the wall. Alexis Melikoff in his Churchill remembered watching the Typhoons dive-bombing near the factory that morning]. It actually fired up and the tank crawled out of the pile of rubble. The Paras greeted the crew with delight and described what had happened in the bombing attack. The first of the twelve Jabos had released two bombs which were overs and had hit the wall of the shoe factory, producing an enormous cloud of dust. This had made the Tank Destroyer invisible to the following planes and was the biggest stroke of luck for the 321's crew. They were Lt. Merdian, Commander; Sgt Kühn, Gunner; Sgt Voit, Driver; and Cpl Stürzbecher, Wireless Operator and Loader.

The next day [the same day], 1 March 1945 the British 2 KSLI succeeded in getting into the shoe factory [actually Norfolks and later the Lincolns]. On the German side there was an immediate German counter-attack that threw the British out of Kervenheim [no, the counter-attack failed]. The 321 fired HE with decisive effect in endless street fighting giving cover to the Paras in close-quarter fighting with the KSLI [Norfolks and Lincolns in the street-fighting]. By evening things quietened down as the British regrouped. The Kervenheim garrison had fulfilled its orders. The Paras withdrew to positions in the Winnekendonk area while the battle group of PzJgAbt 33 drew back towards Sonsbeck. Here 321 caught one of the dreaded Crocodiles. [Another questionable claim; 'I don't understand. We were not in action in this area – our contribution ended with the Carroll episode'].[63] At the first shot it flew up into the air. This was confirmed in the report made by Lt. Krippe of 10FJR23.

63 JG Smith in a letter on 18 April 2004 commenting on Kühn's story.

The enemy artillery hammered Kervenheim all night. In the morning their attack was against an empty town![64]

The above narrative does not correspond with the known dates and times, and is included as colour by one who was there. In correspondence with this author, Hans Kühn was at pains to explain how little he could see and know when in action and but later wrote this reconciliation with the events of 1 March.

321 was in Kervenheim the entire time from 26 February to the evening of 1 March, and mostly by the factory. The officer commanding in Kervenheim was from 7FJD [he must mean FJR7]. You could not call it a Pakfront; our battle group was on the right flank, and the paratroops had their anti-tank defence on the left flank. [A Pak Front required the two flanks to be coordinated; he said they were not]. The two Churchills appeared at 10 am on February 28. [A mystery]. About 10 am 321 drove past the factory and took the right fork towards the cemetery to fire high explosive, [obviously against B Company in the ditch]. We stayed there until evening, sometimes taking cover among the houses by the fork in the road. We could not see what was happening between the factory and the tower. We also knew nothing about what the other StuGs were doing near Boemshof. We were ordered to keep radio silence. In the evening the road going to the factory, the tower and the crossroads became clear, and we left for Sonsbeck past where Stokes had been at 12.45 hours. [Hans misremembered the geography of Kervenheim; the Sonsbeck road leaves from the south and not the north]. We had no problem with supplies of fuel and ammunition either in quantity or timeliness. Re-supply happened of course at night. We liked to engage the heavily armoured Churchill at 350 m range, and that was also true for the Sherman. With the JgPz [Mk IV chassis] the range increased to 1,000 m. I do not remember which type of ammunition we fired in Kervenheim. We did not get the JgPz IV L70 until the end of March. The crews preferred the JgPz IV because of its heavier armour, greater internal space and more powerful gun. The Stug III was a bit faster. Opinions about the L70 gun were mixed; the barrel was long which required great care among trees and houses. If you hit a tree, the sights were put out of alignment. Otherwise it was top-heavy and slower. You need to replace the command 'Links-rechts-Anziehen' with 'Sicht-fest-fahren'. [In other words, when you see a target and aim the StuG its only a matter of left, right, hold it, while with the JgPzIV it's a matter of look at the barrel, check it's not going to hit anything, and then go]. Sending Crocodiles against StuGs and JgPz was irresponsible as they did not have a chance. There is no photo of the crew. I made contact with Lt Merdian after the war in Karlsruhe, but he died young while having kidney dialysis; lucky in war and unlucky in peace![65]

On the left of A Coy, Maj Jack Dye's C Coy was ordered to attack the western edge of Kervenheim, which meant crossing right across the front of Murmannshof and Müsershof. His platoon commanders were Leon Sabel, Norman Rowe and Kenneth Wilson. Sabel and Rowe were both killed.

Withering fire from the front and flank halted this attack as it reached the open ground some three hundred yards short of the objective. With calm deliberation, Maj Dye – himself

64 Sent by Hans Kühn to this author. *KGR der PzJgAbt 33 in Kervenheim – Aus dem Alltag der Panzerjäger.* It is of unknown authorship, publication & date. Translated by this author.

65 Letter from Hans Kühn on 9 March 1997.

Maj Jack Dye, OC C Company 1 R Norfolks, who got into Kervenheim and was counter-attacked. (© John Lincoln)

pinned to the ground by accurately aimed spandau fire [when he had to pretend he was dead for a time while being covered by some stubborn enemy][66] – by means of his 18 set reported the situation accurately and clearly to his CO. Under cover of the smoke screen that was then put down [by the mortar pl] he led his company forward – still in the face of intense spandau and mortar fire – to the near edge of his objective. Heavy casualties were here incurred throughout his command, but with determined drive Maj Dye led his men on to the first block of houses. Realising the necessity for the exertion of his personal influence over his three platoons, whose casualties in officers and men were heavy, Maj Dye moved quickly from house to house, controlling and directing the clearing operations. Although regularly sniped at from point blank range, this officer moved from section to section throughout his company with complete fearlessness. Having gained his objective, he consolidated his position. Almost at once a strong German counter-attack was launched against the buildings in which his command was located. So thorough were his orders to meet this contingency, and so promptly was the offensive action that he had planned carried out, that the counter-attack was broken up with heavy loss to the enemy.[67]

Lt. George Dicks commanded a platoon in Denis Millar's B Coy, which was on the left of Dye's C Coy. He produced an account of his recent war experiences in 1945 while recovering from his wounds. It was written entirely from recent memory, uninfluenced by the writings of others or discussions with them. He wrote about Kervenheim, his last battle:

66 Wilson. *My Morning Time* Unpublished, p. 25.
67 Battalion, *History*, p. 75.

during periods at home on leave with my left arm completely paralysed and in a cock-up of a splint. I can distinctly remember after about a month or so of scribbling that I was getting fed up with the whole exercise. For that reason I do not think my account of Kervenheim is anything like so lucid or detailed as the earlier chapters.

On the 24th February the expected news arrived and we were to move off North immediately to the scene of the current fighting. Platoon commanders left the night before the men in order to be able to get a picture of what was happening although as it eventuated this was unnecessary. I wangled a seat in the CO's van, [a Humber 'Box' 4WD, with full-width rear doors, split horizontally and carrying the spare wheel and a tent extension; it had a folding map table between the front seats, roof lamps, parcel nets, folding seats and full blackout equipment] the CO being away – my companions were Terry Rourke and Lt (ex-Sgt) Smith [both killed at Kervenheim]. We soon lost the convoy by acquiring a puncture but we had a general idea of our destination so we were not unduly disturbed. We continued north into Holland, passed once more through Helmond and then crossed the Maas into the flat country between the Maas and the Rhine at Gennep. The dusty, disheveled nature of the ground, trees, houses and men indicated the proximity of battle, and the roads packed with transport indicated by ciphers on vehicles and roadside signs that nearly every formation in the Canadian and British armies were involved.

We entered Germany and found that all blank walls were covered with whitewashed slogans exhorting the German people to believe in the Fuhrer and all would be well, etc, etc. We found the advanced parties of the battalion installed in the village of Pfalzdorf; Denis [Millar] and Friar [Balsom] were out visiting Goch and Cleve having a look at the effect of allied bombing. Later that day the Battalion arrived and we settled down to wait for the order to move forward, spending our time in the interim checking all weapons, ammunition and the 101 other things that need to be considered.

The next day we moved off in single file and later in the afternoon stopped to bivouac in a wood which had been the scene of fighting the day before. The next morning we were given the details of the planned assault we were to undertake. In B Company Friar and I were forward platoons and the objectives which were to be our limit were pointed out to us both on maps and air photos and then digested by examination of a cloth model prepared by the Intelligence Section. (My dog-eared and defaced map of Kervenheim is still in my possession. Despite being under water in my pocket for some 2 to 3 hours, it still shows a faint pencil line down from the front edge of the wood across open country, right through the centre of Kervenheim and out the other side. In the event small arms fire from Murmannshof and Müsershof caused me to veer to the left to secure the cover of the hedge. Friar agrees that no exact objective was specified". This pencil line was without doubt the centre-line. The cloth model for me was a first. It may have been the idea of Peter Barclay; it was his first battle with us. It was set up by the Intelligence Section on 27 February while we were stationed in a wood. I cannot remember who briefed us).[68]

One hour later we moved off, fully expecting to be launched into action the same day. During the afternoon we contacted a squadron of Scots Guards (mea culpa – Coldstream Guards) who were to support us with their Churchill tanks; and having indulged in a field conference (Dicks commented; 'We merely stood around in a field by a Jeep (or perhaps a Bren carrier) and discussed ways and means. It was probably the afternoon of 28 February. I cannot remember what plans were made) on what each expected of the other we moved

68 The content in the round brackets was sent by George in a subsequent letter.

forward again only to be brought to a halt once more by the sporadic noise of a small battle going on ahead.

The battle occurring just ahead of us was affecting the Warwicks who had already put in an attack and had one company marooned out front [the only reference to a marooned company but would explain the War Diary's reference to Renningshof being occupied]. We prepared to get ready for one more night before we acted. At one time it looked as if we should attack the same night [From the same 1999 letter; I was told at a B Company O Group, probably during late afternoon or evening that a night attack was a possibility by my Company Commander – Denis Millar – who seemed doubtful whether it would happen. With hindsight it was a mistake not to carry out a night attack; Peter Barclay got his own way 3 days later when Hauswinkel was taken after a night attack with negligible casualties] but as time went by the chances grew dimmer and eventually I received orders for the attack to go in at 9 am the next morning. The KSLI, our partners in the attack, had already reached the assembly point but we were prevented by the Warwicks' trouble from reaching ours. So we moved off at 3.30 am [4.15 am] to make good the deficiency. The assembly point was the backward edge of a wood and I led the company down the path without interference. Here we dug in and waited for zero hour.

Friar and I agreed that it was doubtful whether we should even reach the objectives which had been optimistically allotted to us unless we met no opposition at all, and the truth is we both felt a little uneasy about the plan generally. It did not seem to us to ring true. (George later added; I don't think the Warwicks' problem had any relevance to my unease. I had no idea what trouble the Warwicks were in or where or what they were attacking. It was not until last year that I learned from John Lincoln that the Warwicks should have been in possession of Müsershof when our attack went in. I had realised for many years that the Muhlen Fleuth flowed between the two farms but had idly thought that A Company had been given both farms as objectives. I have a gut feeling that Friar's and my unease was that there was no definite objective – so different from Overloon and Venraij when we were given objectives and then advanced and reached them. I have spoken to Friar on the phone and he concurred with this assessment. It may also have been that before the attack we couldn't see how tanks could give B company any direct support since we had to walk through a thick wood which tanks could probably not barge through. But they should certainly have been in support of A company whose approach to Murmannshof was clear of the woods).

A heavy artillery barrage of the creeping type had been arranged and we were promised a smoke screen on our right where there was open country which might prove dangerous. (From the same 1999 letter; The only contact I had with the Battalion after I was wounded was a letter from my Company Commander – Denis Millar – in reply to mine telling him how I was getting on. In the letter Denis said; 'I'm afraid Kervenheim was a bloody 'do' for this Company. 50% of our strength gone – 11 dead and 30 odd wounded. A hell of a knock and nothing to show for it. You may well ask what happened to the smoke'. [At Company O Group prior to the battle, we had been assured that a smoke screen would be provided on our right. I had a feeling that Denis, sensing the danger when he was at the CO's O Group, had specifically asked for it. But not a puff appeared!] The barrage details show no provision was made for smoke other than the normal one gun per battery. It wasn't until 2002 that a post-battle analysis by 9 BIB came to light explaining that the RA had no stock of smoke shells, and that smoke could be provided only if ordered well in advance.)

The tank commanders were scared, quite rightly, of the possibility of anti-tank mines in the wood which we had to traverse, and very much more scared of odd Germans carrying Panzerfausts – anti-tank weapons.

The time passed slowly from 4 am to 9 am. We dozed, thought and dozed fitfully in a state almost of suspended animation. I sent one section through the wood to check for any stray Boche and to protect the pioneers who were laying a white tape as a path through the wood.

At 9 exactly the barrage started and I had just time to see A Company go into the attack on the right before I moved off forward through the trees. We emerged at the other side to see the roofs of the town of Kervenheim and the spire of the church about half-a-mile distant. (From the same 1999 letter; 'Nothing went through my mind about the tanks. I never saw a tank until I got off the battlefield. I was far too concerned about the predicament I was in and the fate of my men even to think of tanks. Nothing concentrates the mind more than a continuing fusillade of small-arms fire with its characteristic air-tearing crack as it passes nearby.') [The church steeple was his aiming point before heavy fire from the right drove him left towards the factory. Then he would have been heading directly towards Kühn's StuG, which might also have fired at him.]

At 9.15 with Friar left and me right, the two platoons moved out into the open. Our rate of advance, dependent upon the rate at which the artillery barrage would be lifted, was set at 100 yards in 4 minutes so we had to move very slowly. Evidently I was not moving slowly enough because Denis sent me a runner to tell me to slow down, so I told my lads to get down for a few seconds to allow the barrage to lift. I was unaware what luck had attended A Company's efforts; there was such a din going on that once more I experienced the sensation of hundreds of things occurring and being observed by me without any conscious effort of thought. I was therefore not surprised when my eyes, not my brain, told me that Gable and Capstick had obviously been wounded, Gable lying with his arm up in the air and Capstick stretching a leg out painfully. A split second afterwards my brain told me that bullets were coming from the right, and my natural impulses were therefore to remove myself from the position in open country which was jeopardizing the security of both myself and my platoon.

I therefore ran forward round the edge of the hedge on my left and observed another hedge about 150 yards ahead of me which looked as if it might afford some shelter for enough time for me to reorganize my platoon and continue the attack.

As I ran forwards I saw many tracer bullets pass from right to left in front of me, and suddenly I felt a sharp stinging sensation on the inside of my left thigh. I continued running, examining my trousers at the same time but could find no break in the cloth. I therefore decided that I could not have been hit – and then I realised that it was caused by blast from a shell which had fallen about 6 yards to my right. All these things happened within the space of a second, including the grim thought that it was probably one of our own shells – which had shown a tendency as usual to fall short.

I continued to run and eventually reached the shelter of the hedge in front of me. At least I thought it was shelter, but when I turned round to wave on and encourage those of my men who were following, I suddenly received a kick in the shoulder which threw up my left arm and rendered it completely numb and useless. I realised I had stopped a bullet and so dropped back into the ditch alongside the hedge. This was filled with green slimy, and stagnant water but I was very thankful to accept its cold embrace in comparison with what open country had to offer me.

Looking back I saw several of my platoon running across in my direction – Sgt Larkins, L/Sgt Smith, Cpl Mason, L/Cpl Hopkins and Pte Blood – but I was as yet unaware of the fate of the rest of the platoon. I had started the attack with 22 men, rather a small number owing to my having several men on home leave and courses – and in addition Pte X had deserted. (From the same 1999 letter; I have no objection to your mentioning that one man in my platoon deserted. He left while we were at Pfalzdorf. He had successfully evaded action in October at Overloon and Venraij by claiming illness viz, bleeding via the anus

– he bled as he shed! If I had been more experienced I might have taken stronger action. Despite this one defector, I must put on record my profound respect and admiration for the way in which the ordinary infantry squaddie stuck to his task. He deserves far greater recognition than he has ever received for his conduct in the Second World War.) [Dicks gave the deserter's name. It was said that in any section of ten men, two led, seven followed and one would do almost anything not to be there, including desertion.] As soon as the five soldiers reached me I heard the story – nearly all the others had been hit and Pte Cariello at least had been killed by a bullet in the brain. Sgt Larkins whipped out his jack-knife and sliced up my clothes, whilst I removed the cover from my field dressing with my teeth. The rest huddled in the security of the filthy water. We found my wound was a small hole just above the arm-pit and bleeding had already stopped. Larkins put on the field dressing and I told them to push on round to the left where there seemed to be more cover. By this time other remnants of the company had reached me – I remember seeing Friar and L/Sgt Moore from 11 Platoon and Sgt Smart and several of his men from 10 platoon. They all made their way up the ditch splashing the malodorous water as they went and responded to my orders to move over to the left for cover. Several of them grinned at me, knowing that I had got a 'Blighty', [from the Urdu 'Vilayati' or 'Bilati' meaning 'far removed', as the Victorian soldier was from Britain.] and I grinned back partly to cheer them up and partly because I knew too that I had got a 'Blighty'.

Soon they had all passed out of my limited range of vision with the exception of a private in 10 platoon who was wounded and stayed with me, and the mangled corpse of another soldier lying about 5 yards away where it had received a direct hit from a shell. All that was visible was a head and the bloody inside of his ribs.

Although the sound of men's voices had gone the sound of battle remained and the characteristic crack of small arms fire when it passes nearby was sufficiently frequent to cause me to stay low. In addition both our own and enemy artillery were firing and both, to my no doubt biased mind, seemed to be concentrating on the area between the town and the wood. Dirt and dust thrown up by near misses kept spattering over us and I had difficulty in restraining the soldier from jumping up and making a dash for the wood.

I was hit about 9.30 am and I had to stay lying in the ditch until about midday before there was a slackening in fire. Then I moved cautiously around to the left to find that D Company were in the process of putting in an attack. I stood up and saw a Churchill tank at the side of a house about 100 yards away. Calling the soldier, I made a dash for the house and ran into the arms of L/Sgt Smith who assisted me round to the back of the house where I saw the disconsolate seated figure of Denis Millar. He was very upset because he could not find out where the Company was and urged me on my way back to the RAP to see the CO and explain what had happened. But this I was unable to do because the Churchill which took me and several severely wounded back did not go to the Royal Norfolk's area. Instead it dropped me with some Canadian stretcher bearers who quite obviously already had their hands full. Seeing I could get no attention there I asked the way to the nearest RAP, and accompanied by McHugh, the soldier who had been in the ditch with me, I strode off down the road. The RAP was about half a mile away and no sooner had I arrived than a burst of artillery fire hit the road up which I had come.

I had a shell dressing for my wound applied by an MO attached to the 15/19 Hussars [11 BAD divisional troops] and then started a series of ambulance drives back to home, sanity and safety via ADS, CCS and General Hospital in Tilburg. My morale was excellent throughout; I had none of the depressing symptoms associated with shock.

Wounded on 1st March I was being flown home in a Dakota two days later having in the meantime had one operation and innumerable injections of penicillin.

> Although no doubt given the opportunity I should have avoided service in the infantry, in many ways I am glad of my experiences. They enabled me to see how man reacts to danger, to realise in my contacts with others that it is not necessarily the man who is a criminal at home who is the best soldier abroad; rather that it is the man who is scrupulously clean and correct in the barrack room who is often the best type of man to have at your side in the field.[69]

Lt Bryan Balsom, known as Friar after the famous medicament, was of that best type. George Dicks declined this author's request to provide thumbnail sketches of the battalion's officers but did in the case of Friar:

> I will make an exception in his case because I need to get it off my chest!! Friar's record is exceptional. He joined the battalion as a reinforcement on 9 July 1944 and served in a rifle company until cessation of hostilities, first in C Company and then, after Sourdevalle (Pavee) when C Company was almost annihilated, in B Company. He joined B Company at Tinchebray in August, advanced to Holland in September, was in command of a platoon in one of the assault companies at Overloon and Venraij on October 14 to 16, moved forward to Wanssum on the Maas in November, endured the exhausting and bitterly cold winter months actively patrolling the Maas from December to February, took part on the attack on Kervenheim on 1 March and after that was deeply involved in the battles of Lingen and Brinkum in April. Few can have lasted longer in command of a platoon in a rifle company. In my opinion he deserved an award higher than the one which he was given viz, a Divisional Commander's Certificate of Gallantry.[70]

Friar Balsom:

> We were soon moving north by truck and crossed the Maas to Gennep (just opposite our old OPs, the windmills of Oeffelt) and on into Germany to Pfalzdorf. Over the next two days we marched south first to one wood and then the next day to another some distance short of the Rhineland town called Kervenheim. There we waited expecting the attack that evening. An artillery barrage was considered necessary and, as it would take time to lay on, the attack was postponed until the next morning.[Confirmation that the Venus Barrage was planned that night]. We were to attack with A Company far off to the right, B Company in the centre and the other companies on the left. [Not true; C Coy was in the centre between A and B]. There was to be a full creeping barrage and we were to follow up close behind it. We also had tanks to come with us to capture the town.
>
> The night of the 28th we spent in that wood – another wet and dank one. [Friar is saying that his company slept in the wood at the start line. This is the only source, and it seems Friar misremembered]. We thought it only rained in England! We awoke and ate early and as light was breaking the barrage opened up. We began to advance according to our timetable through the wood. It wasn't very comfortable, as some of our shells seemed to be falling short and bursting in the trees above. We persevered and moved out of the wood on to the long expanse of newly ploughed heavy clay. I remember wondering where the tanks were as we crossed the startline. We moved out at a trot and the enemy small arms and machine gun fire was heavy. I could see our men being hit, as it was all so exposed. I cannot remember any German shelling, mortaring or nebelwerfers during the advance, but too many of our shells seemed to be falling short. We had to get across before we could attack the town. Half way over I heard a crack and

69 Letter from George Dicks on 29 November 1999 with later additions.
70 Ibid.

thought I felt a push. I threw myself down and asked George Hardy, who had thrown himself forward at the same time, 'Have I been hit? – he didn't think I had. (I found out much later that the crack of the round had been loud as it passed through the jacket on my left shoulder close to my ear). Much of the firing seemed to be coming from the right, though the round that removed my epaulette came from the front. We seemed to take many more casualties as we approached the town – perhaps we were entering an area of fixed-line enfilade fire. So on we pressed and many of us reached a ditch and hedge that surrounded the edge of the town.

We collected ourselves and moved across an open space to a high wall that curved round for some distance to the left. The space to the right of the wall was bare and open and appeared to be swept by heavy and accurate small arms fire. We paused behind the wall for a while to collect stragglers and to take stock of the situation. We could have done with the support of tanks at this stage. (It was so different when we had the close support of armour at Brinkum, near Bremen – we cleared it out with barely a casualty). I remember wondering if they were even now likely to appear behind us, and how we would know they were there.

There was no sign of our tanks nor any sound of them either to indicate that they had left the woods behind us. We did not have a radio to find out what was happening, as the company radio and company HQ did not appear to have got across. No platoon mortars appear to have got as far as us either to help us over the open ground with smoke.

As I appeared to be the only B Company officer left, I collected all the remaining B Company troops and with what covering fire we could provide for ourselves we moved into the open gap. The enemy response was prompt and accurate and we had serious casualties especially in Cpl Moore's section, including Cpl Moore himself. There was no way round that way as fire was coming at us from many directions, including from the far right.

We moved with survivors back under the cover of the wall and I went back to the gap to see if I could find another way round. All the firing I could see was from small arms. If the enemy had had tanks or heavier guns they would have used them on us. My judgment seemed to be confirmed a few minutes later when a Panzerfaust bounced at my feet and skidded on without exploding.

Without support we could not move to the right, but if we moved round to the left we might find a way of infiltrating behind the enemy firing positions. I began moving all of B Company who were with me to the left. Very soon we found other of our companies moving in front of us in the way we needed to go. We did not wish to interfere with their operations and fire at our own men, so I decided to ask for further orders. It was in fact this movement from the left that won Kervenheim.

At one stage – I cannot remember what time this would be – we were on the main road into Kervenheim – D Company must have passed through by this time. I do not recall seeing any KSLI.

It was a despondent evening as 11 Platoon and B Company had had many casualties [According to L/Cpl Seaman MM, only 26 members of B Company ate dinner in the wood that night instead of the usual 110], and although Kervenheim was won, we had not achieved what we had hoped for. Of the several casualties in 11 Platoon the partnership of Taffy Wheeler and Wally Sowle, two old soldiers who were always ready to raise the spirit with their buffoonery, was broken up as Wally had been killed. George Dicks who had led 12 Platoon for as long as I had led 11 Platoon had been hit as we reached the first hedge, but fortunately only wounded. We had become used to working together over a long period. So that night we all felt disappointed. It had not been the way to celebrate St David's Day.[71]

71 Memoir written by Friar Balsom for his family in 1984. It has been slightly edited and additions made in answer to written questions.

Humphrey Wilson, the Norfolks' 2ic, continued:

> The left was now the only possible approach to the town. With three coys committed, D Coy was now put in to work round to the left flank, close to the KSLI, there being a bit more cover that way. [There was no difference in cover, but it was safer as the KSLI had silenced Boemshof.] B Coy had not got on very far, but C Coy was now able to join up with D Coy, and a finger-hold on the eastern extremities of the town was made.
>
> At this point the Boche put in a counter-attack, but were unable to throw out C and D Coys. Unfortunately, Lt L. Dawson was killed by the enemy getting back into a house that had already been cleared. The Boche were also firing on wounded men who were trying to crawl to safety, and on several occasions the Red Cross was disregarded.
>
> Capt R.C. Wilson, MC, had been wounded just as his coy (D) was getting into the town. Our tank support had not been all that it might, and that intimate fire to help us on to the final objective was not forthcoming at the vital moment; it therefore became a purely infantry battle.
>
> By 1500 Hrs the enemy had had about enough and C Coy were able to back up D Coy, and the key to the town had been won. [Note that Humphrey ignores the support of the Lincolns.] Some house-to-house fighting still took place with a few suicide paratroops holding out – they would not give up or run away and became a menace by sniping. One tank managed to get forward to the central cross-roads of the town, but was bazookered from a doorway. [Possibly the Churchill gun-tank that preceded the Crocodile]. A factory which had by now fallen to D Coy became a bastion from which to operate.
>
> To review the picture at last light: A Coy were on the right flank, B Coy at the edge of the wood, and C and D Coys in the northern part of the town. By now there was no fight left in the enemy, and late that night he pulled out what he had left.
>
> Our losses in officers consisted of Maj D.W. Smith, MC, Lt G.A. Smith, MM, Lt N. Rowe, Lt. T.M. Rourke, MC, Lt L. Dawson, killed; Capt R.C. Wilson, MC, Lt L.N. Sabel, Lt R.J. Lincoln, Lt. G.D.H. Dicks, Lt W. Lewis, wounded. Our losses in other ranks were 36 killed and 115 wounded, 4 missing. Success had been achieved but at a heavy cost.[72]
>
> Having settled the battalion as best we could and tied up patrols, Peter Barclay and I found a nice cellar with a lovely heap of coke in a corner. On this we slept like babes till first light next day. Coke is very comfortable as it moves to the shape of your body and yet gives support.[73]

Humphrey Wilson, 2ic sorted out 'A' Company and continued the pressure on the right. He asked Robin Dunne, the BC, to use the gunner net to bring down fire. He knew very little about what the KSLI were doing on the left. He went on to say something quite surprising; that the tanks never arrived and that it was never a set piece battle but just a probing attack. More guns and Typhoons should have been used, he said, against the houses with open windows and with MG 42s placed well back in the rooms. He remembered in particular a row of four such houses and bringing down artillery fire onto them. Most of the killing took place in the first attack but the battle went on all day. It was Jack Dye (C Company) and Millar (B Company) between 11 am and 3 pm who won the fight. Humphrey finally went into Kervenheim at 5 pm and examined some spandaus in the rooms. He had a high opinion of Peter Barclay, and they were good friends for the rest of their lives.

72 Battalion, *History*, pp. 45-46.
73 Wilson, *Morning Time*, p. 26.

Capt Robin Wilson, 2ic D Company 1 R Norfolks. (© John Lincoln)

Capt Robin Wilson:

> I was commanding D Company, which was initially in reserve. When it became apparent that the other companies were unable to get nearer to their objectives, I received orders to try and find a way into the town taking a line further to the left. With the help of smoke from our mortars, and finding a modicum of cover here and there, we managed to advance without incurring many casualties on the approach. We got into the main street and occupied buildings on either side of it – a factory building on one side and houses on the other. To keep control of the company it was necessary on a number of occasions to sprint across the street and liaise with Leslie Dawson, my second in command, in the factory area. This was an unpleasant procedure as snipers were still active. I did it once too often and got a bullet in the thigh. I hung on for a while but once our carriers were able to enter the town allowed myself to be evacuated after putting Leslie as fully as I could into the picture. To this day I regret not having stayed put as, though immobilised, I was still able to function after a fashion, while poor Leslie was killed soon afterwards. No, Kervenheim is not a place of happy memories.[74]

Lt John Lincoln MC commanded 17 Platoon in D Company, and was the first into a building in Kervenheim. He recalled how the day after arriving in Pfalzdorf there was a memorable get-together of D Company's officers organised by CSM Wilkie. It was the last time they were together as John was wounded in Kervenheim:

> I don't remember what we talked about but I do remember the comforting feeling of being at ease with friends, of talking with fellow men who have faced and will face the same dangers, who are trusted and who trust you. All with the unspoken knowledge that death or injury could instantly claim any one of us.

74 Lincoln, *Thank God*, pp. 160-62.

There is a unique bond which exists in war between men who trust their lives to those fighting with them and accept the same trust from their companions. The giving and accepting of this trust is seldom, if ever, spoken of but is essential and absolute in any group of men facing extreme physical danger.

On the 27th we moved forward along rough tracks through wooded country under the artillery fire supporting the attacking troops. [In response to a phoned question, John said the shells were 'whiffling' overhead. 'You got used to them'.] Progress was slow on foot, at times even slower for vehicles as tracks were quickly churned to thick mud and road surfaces had to be improvised from tree trunks, brushwood, whatever came to hand. We were not troubled by enemy artillery but as the enemy had only very recently been cleared from the area mines were a danger.

That night we dug in wherever we could and the following day continued our slow advance behind the forward troops. Details of the next day's attack were given out and our slow progress was continued through the night which was far from quiet for heavy fighting was still continuing to our front.

1 March was an overcast, dull day with rain threatening. The battalion started moving into its assembly area shortly after 0400 hrs, along a single track and before dawn were formed up ready for the attack, A Company right, B centre and C left, D Company in reserve.[The narratives only make sense if it was A Coy right, C centre and B Coy left, with D in reserve]. The startline was the forward edge of a wood some 600 yds from Kervenheim. The trees in the wood were widely spaced and provided little actual cover.[The thinness of all the woods is visible in the aerial photographs and was due to heavy wartime cutting.] Kervenheim could be seen across fields in front which provided no cover at all.

The attack commenced at 0900 hrs under a heavy artillery barrage. The three companies were advancing almost due east, [B & C Coys south-east, and A Coy south] and immediately came under fire, not only from Kervenheim but also most heavily from two farms called Murmannshof and Müsershof. Heavy casualties were caused. A Company lost all its officers, the acting sergeant-major taking charge, B and C companies faring little better. Artillery fire was called down on Murmannshof, some shells falling short, but did not succeed in removing this serious threat to the attacking troops.

In D Company, in reserve, orders were received mid-morning [between 1000 and 1030 hrs] to enter the town from the left in order to relieve the pressure on the other companies. Robin (Wilson) was commanding D company, Philip (Searight) having been temporarily seconded to Bde to his chagrin. Robin gave out his orders to Eddie (Hastings), Jack (Laurie) and I (sic) in the wood to the constant accompaniment of shell-bursts, mortars, machine guns and 'Moaning Minnies'.

'The other companies are pinned down from the town and from Murmannshof and Müsershof'; Robin gave us all the information he could and we studied the maps we carried. 'We are to move into Kervenheim on the left, advancing along this track until it meets the road then along the road into town'. The map showed we had to advance 400 yards along the track to our left to meet the road where it curved left and continue in the same south-easterly direction for another 400 yards until the road curved right and entered the town. From the map we could see that there were isolated buildings along the first stretch of road and after the final bend, beyond other houses, a factory built at a right angle to the road. This was agreed as the first objective, further movement to be determined according to the resistance we met. 17 Platoon was nominated as the leading platoon.

I went back to my platoon, called the section leaders together and told them what we had to do. We would move along the verges of the road, using the ditches we assumed would be there as cover, the leading section on the right of the road, myself heading platoon HQ on the left, the other two sections right and left behind, everybody well spaced out to present the smallest target.

I gave the order to move and we left the relative shelter of the trees for the hazard of the open ground. We had no close support, no tanks, [John was unaware of Melikoff following behind alone], no rolling barrage to flatten the opposition ahead of us. Just the will to get up and move forward. Only a small proportion of Servicemen can apprehend the feeling of exposure, of vulnerability which is experienced when those first steps are taken into the unknown. However good his training, however wide his experience the infantryman cannot know what lies ahead.

The track was over flat ground, no ditches, no hedges, an occasional tree, nothing to prevent the enemy seeing us – luckily our advance did not seem to attract the enemy shell-fire immediately. This was not a set-piece attack, just a flanking movement of less than one hundred men attempting to ease pressure on the rest of the battalion probing forward to find an alternative way into the town. Not a death or glory charge but a slow advance against heavy fire, unable to see your enemy, not knowing what dangers you are up against.

We reached the road, which I crossed as quickly as I could to find a shallow ditch no more than two feet deep which gave an illusion of cover. We progressed slowly, carefully but without stopping, the leading section across the road from me, along the ditch on that side, I level with them in the ditch on the left of the road. The enemy must have seen us as I distinctly remember grit from the road surface being sprayed in my face as bursts of machine-gun fire hit the road. Mortar bombs [fired from Pastorat Straße in Kervenheim] fell too in fields close by yet we did not stop to take cover – it was a sub-conscious reaction to continue moving for as long as possible because, once you have taken cover from fire, it becomes progressively more difficult to get up and go on again.

We were now coming to the first houses of the town, to my right, and I must be prepared to take action if any of them were occupied. This was the first time, in my experience, that we would need to fight house-to-house and, although we had been trained in the techniques, alertness and skill were required against an enemy who had the advantages of cover, prepared positions and knowledge of the ground.

Those first houses were empty, yet I had a most uncomfortable feeling as we moved slowly past them knowing that the enemy could still be waiting in hiding. [On John's left was a water tower, which he never recalled seeing, and on his right a row of houses. In their cellars were over 60 civilians. The houses were occupied by the Germans soon after midday and re-taken in the VC-winning exploit of James Stokes, Z Company 2 KSLI.] Again that feeling between the shoulder-blades warning you cannot see, may never see until too late. The leading troops in such an attack as this do not have time to investigate all possible dangers. They must take certain risks in order to keep the impetus of the advance going.

We had covered almost half a mile and were now approaching the final bend of the road beyond which were houses on both sides, built on the edge of the road, without gardens at the front. Some casualties had been suffered in the platoon but we were still pressing on. At the bend we came under fire from a spandau located at the cross-roads ahead [a distance of 350 yards] and I knew that it would be suicidal to continue up the street. The ditches we were using ended at the houses and movement at the front of the houses would be in plain view of the enemy. The only way in was to the right using the factory building as cover from view from the town and from Murmannshof.

I shouted across to the section opposite, warning them I was coming over and that they should move to their right, then told my platoon HQ to prepare to cross the road under cover of smoke. I threw a smoke grenade ahead of me then ran crouching across the road. On again to the factory which was built end-on to the road with no entrance on our side although part

In 1994 John Lincoln and his party retraced the steps he took around the corner in 1945 from the transformer tower to the shoe factory on the right. Here he crossed the road from left to right under fire. On the left is the paddock and Vogelsangshof. At the end of the street are the houses from which the MG42 was firing straight up the road which earlier was a race-track for the defending StuGs.

way along the side wall a shell had made a large hole in the wall. [The hole is assumed to have been made by Bombphoons missing Kühn's StuG IV.] The leading section flushed two or three Germans from this hole and we could only gesture to them that they should make their way back to our lines and get out of our way. In an attack the assaulting troops seldom have time to deal with prisoners – that is left to those behind.

A quick look round the inside of the factory for other enemy then out again through the hole in the wall and to the end of the building leaving one of the sections in the factory. Look round the corner briefly then run forward to the next building, a private house, probably the manager's home. Here I established one of my sections and platoon HQ whilst the third section investigated the outbuildings.

We had achieved our first objective and were the first troops into the town. [True of this end, but it is possible that Jack Dye had got into buildings at the other end of town, but was counter-attacked and thrown out]. We had unfortunately received further casualties from 88's, mortar and machine-gun fire, and from the weight of opposition we encountered from the centre of the town I felt that my platoon could not progress without further support. I decided to leave the sections where they were, little more than 100 yards from the cross-roads, and report back to Robin so I made my way back the way I had come. Mortaring was heavy at the time and, rounding the corner of the factory, a closer than comfortable group of explosions to my left caused me to drop on one knee. I felt a hard blow on my left hip. Looking down I saw only a very small hole in my trousers. I got up and as I started to walk forward realised I had been hit, for although I felt no pain from the wound I could not walk properly.[75]

75 John Lincoln in a letter of 14 October 1996.

The paradox of the tiny hole and the incapacitating but not immediately painful wound was explained early in the Second World War by high-speed photography, and described in a government publication by F Green & G Covell in 1953. Small 0.1 inch steel balls were fired through blocks of gelatine and through rabbit legs. As the ball enters the gelatine a 'tail splash' develops on the entry side which increases in size as the ball traverses the block. The emerging ball pushes out a head cone of gelatine which it leaves behind. This is the only distortion during the first few microseconds taken by the ball to pass through the target. But immediately after the ball has gone the gelatine expands to three or four times its original volume and immediately returns to its original size and shape. The only visible effect is a small thread-sized hole like that caused by pushing a needle through the block. What happens is that a huge cavity 5 cm in diameter is caused in the block. The tissues are stretched around this cavity. The minute puncture holes are the only external sign of considerable internal injury. The skin holds it together. Comminuted fractures could occur in bones even when the projectile passed 1 cm away from them. But unlike bones, the arteries, veins and nerves can escape injury unless actually punctured. A rabbit's artery was not broken by a ball passing 0.5 cm away. But they had been stretched and transient paralysis and analgesia could result.

John Lincoln continued:

> Company HQ by this time was established in the factory through the hole in the wall and there I reported the situation to Robin [Wilson] also telling him that I had been hit. He told me to go back to the Regimental Aid Post but, for some reason, I determined that I should first go back to my platoon.
>
> I hopped and hobbled back, took off my pack, got out my field dressing and examined my hip. Very little blood, just a purplish puncture at the hip joint. Bound the field dressing over the wound, left the platoon in charge of Cpl Carter and made my way back to Company HQ where Robin asked me, on my way to the RAP, to report to the CO and give him the latest information.
>
> A member of my platoon, a ginger-haired lad about my height, had been wounded in the arm and together we returned along the road and ditches we had used earlier. It was now after midday and firing had not slackened at all, shelling and mortaring continuing incessantly from both sides. I hobbled along, the pain not at first excessive but soon found that I was grateful for the support of my companion for we had the best part of a mile to walk before we reached battalion HQ, where I made my report [witnessed by RW Thompson]. The CO was pleased to receive news of D Company's advance, asked about my wound and sent me off to the RAP which was further back in a farmhouse. There both Trevor, the adjutant, and Jimmy Green, the Padre, had a word with me and the MO after taking a look at my hip, gave me a shot of painkiller, [Morphine was normally used. To avoid the risk of a second and lethal dose being administered too soon John's forehead would have been date-marked] put me on a stretcher and sent me off on a jeep to the ADS.
>
> The first stage in the evacuation of casualties was by jeep, on a stretcher supported on a metal framework above the jeep-driver's head. Two stretchers were carried, side by side, and as I lay there, six feet above the ground, I felt terribly exposed, painfully unprotected from shell-bursts as enemy artillery was shelling the approach route. The road was rough, parts surfaced with logs to overcome mud and though the driver took the greatest care the ride seemed very bumpy, the pain in my hip increasing as I clung to the sides of the stretcher to prevent myself rolling about.
>
> I arrived in due course at the Advanced Dressing Station, situated in the gloom of a disused brick kiln – I had parted company with my trousers, underpants and boots at the RAP and as a result of the injection was in a somewhat stupid state so that when I heard two doctors talking about me say something about ATS my immediate thought was 'ATS girls so close to

the front' followed by 'but I haven't got my trousers on'. ATS, I found, was not a promise of caring feminine hands from the Auxiliary Territorial Service but turned out to be anti-tetanus serum, duly administered probably with more pain-killer for I remember very little of a long journey by ambulance to a hospital near Turnhout where I was operated on in the early hours of the next morning.

Kervenheim had been taken at a heavy cost. Shortly after I was wounded Robin had been hit, and Leslie [Dawson] taking over from Robin had been killed by enemy getting back into a house previously cleared. [Part of a general German infiltration to seal off and eliminate the incursion. The houses by the tower were by now occupied by enemy firing at Z Company, KSLI in the field in front of them.] My platoon suffered numerous casualties, including Cpl Carter, with whom I had left platoon HQ, wounded within minutes of my departure so badly that he remained paralysed from the waist down after a long, long stay in hospital.

I awoke from the operation on the morning of 2 March to be told that while the surgeons had located the piece of shrapnel within my hip joint, they had been unable to extract it. That afternoon I was loaded aboard a Dakota aircraft hoping that evacuation by air meant that I was going back to the British Isles; but not so, after a short flight to Belgium I arrived at 110 British General Hospital, what I believe had previously been a TB sanatorium near Bruges where, almost immediately, I had another operation, again without success. My worldly possessions consisted of a vest, a shirt, a pullover and a jacket, nothing else than the contents of my jacket pockets – but very soon, from the nursing staff and from the red cross, toilet gear, cigarettes, writing paper etc. appeared and I settled down to enjoy the ministrations of the sisters and staff. Life seemed so sublimely peaceful.[76]

John Lincoln was awarded the Periodical MC for five months of outstanding achievement. The citation was raised and signed by Barclay (25 June) and signed by Bray for 185BIB (26 June), Whistler for 3BID (15 July) and Kirkman for 1 Corps (31 July).

MC. 185BIB, 3BID, 1 R Norfolk, Lt 308407 John Robert LINCOLN

This officer joined the Battalion in August 1944. While the Battalion was in the REICHSWALD in October he commanded his platoon with marked efficiency and on one occasion by the skill with which he led a most successful patrol a number of Germans queuing up for their food were killed.

At the OVERLOON – VENRAIJ action he again led his platoon to their objective with the minimum of casualties and the maximum effect on the enemy. At this moment, when the Coy Comd and 2 IC were both casualties and when morale was at its lowest, he assumed command of the Coy. He showed himself to be the best subaltern in the Battalion.

During the very difficult winter months he divided his time between commanding his platoon and officiating as second in command of the Coy until he was wounded at KERVENHEIM when leading his platoon in the first wave of the assault into the town. It was entirely due to the successful capture of the first objective and penetration beyond effected by this officer that the subsequent capture of the town was possible.

Both as platoon commander and as 2 IC of the Coy his work was of the highest order at all times, especially in view of his youth and inexperience. As 2 IC of the Coy he worked wonders in maintaining the morale of the Coy at a very high pitch in spite of the greatest difficulties. The platoon which he commanded was by far the most efficient in the Coy and had the highest fighting morale – a direct result of his first class leadership. Lieut Lincoln is

76 Ibid.

> one of those officers who, by their quiet honesty and unostentatious efficiency, could lead their men anywhere. His influence in preparing his men for battle and his personal example and leadership have proved themselves battle winning factors.[77]

John returned to his unit and in 1994 wrote a 'straight ungarnished narrative' of his battalion: *Thank God and the Infantry*. After discussions with this author, he updated it in 1999 and added this epilogue:

> I knew that a VC had been awarded to a man in 2 KSLI for outstanding gallantry at Kervenheim, but I did not know the details until 1996 when I learned that the action which prompted that award took place in a spot I had passed on two occasions only shortly before, moving into Kervenheim and hobbling back. More than 50 years after the event I could not, at first, accept that the details were correct; I could not believe that, not more than 30 minutes before the KSLI attack, I had walked past the very spot where this action took place. The picture which commemorates the VC features a water-tower [actually a transformer tower], which I do not remember and which does not now exist. I checked independently and found that the facts were correct. I still could not believe that I had twice passed a position at which a bitter battle was fought after I passed it. If the enemy was there when I passed why didn't they fire at me? Did they stay concealed as we moved in, believing our strength was too great for them? If so, why didn't they fire on my return? If they moved into the houses after I had passed, where did they come from? Not from our right surely, they would have been visible to the other companies of the battalion. Only from our left, possibly along the line of a road shown on the map as 'under construction', detouring around D Company to get behind them. [Heinrich Kempkes in 2014 observed that the mounds of earth from the bypass construction were high enough to conceal crawling men]. I have asked myself so many questions. I can remember enemy fire as we walked into town but where did it come from? Why was D Company able to walk down the main road without massive opposition? [Because by then Boemshof had been neutralized or occupied by the KSLI and Stokes, which closed off all opposition from the left flank]. How did around 80 men get into Kervenheim along the road when the other 3 companies were so badly mauled? [For the same reason]. I can only believe that the enemy defence was based on strongpoint outposts at Murmannshof and Boemshof with a mobile reserve in town, part of which reserve was moved to support those strongpoints when the attack started, leaving a smaller force in the centre. As the British attack progressed and D Company entered the town the natural tendency for the enemy forces would be to draw in towards the centre, part of which was denied to them by D Company, or attempt to contain the British troops. I will never know. I have accepted the facts. I was very lucky. I do know that, as a result of learning more of the fateful day, I am now more conscious than ever before of my great good luck, that I survived to live a good life for more than 50 years when so many of my contemporaries did not. My life since those days has all been quality time, a bonus, an added extra'.[78]

In 2013 this author and John discussed the matter again, as the intervening eighteen years had not removed his bafflement. He would, he said, not be surprised if evidence yet appeared that the KSLI had mistaken the houses and tower for others 500 yards away.

Pte Gil Attwood was in 18 Pl commanded by Jack Laurie in D Coy, although he identified no officers. He remembered a sleepless night in a slit trench, the early start, and following behind the

77 TNA: WO 373/56: J Lincoln's citation.
78 Lincoln, *Thank God*, new edition, epilogue.

Some of 11 Troop, 3 Squadron, 4 Coldstream Guards. (L.-r.) Gdsmn Rice, Gdsmn Hunt, Lt Prince Alexis Melikoff aka Napier, Gdsmn Joyce, Gdsmn Lewis, Sgt Hodgson, and Gdsmn Hall. Alexis was sent into Kervenheim in support of D Coy 1 R Norfolks, but was wounded in the head by Panzerfaust splinters. He retired up the Udemer Straße and waited until he had recovered his sight and his senses. (© Alexis Napier)

other three companies to their startline while suffering in the wood from shells falling short. He witnessed the attack by A, B, and C Coys collapse and survivors crawling and running back into the wood, with German mortars hitting the trees overhead to rain shrapnel down on them. He said it was in order to avoid further casualties that his company was sent scampering through the trees to the road on the left and then slowly along the ditches into town under mortar fire. They fought their way into the first house: whether it was right or left of the road he does not say, but they cleared it room by room. They went into the next building, a barn, but the straw caught fire and they had to retreat back to the first one, which was then counter-attacked with bazookas with Germans gaining entry and killing the defenders in a fire fight. He says that most of the defenders, including LCpl Allan, were killed, and he was then joined by members of 17 Pl from across the road. They spent the night in the house and in the morning heard another battalion attacking across the rear of the enemy, who withdrew. Gil was asked to remove and bundle all personal items from Cpl Allan's body for sending to relatives. He did not attend the funerals before moving on. His story describes the fear and confusion of a young man's first battle, but no Cpl Allan is among the list of dead – perhaps Allan was a forename – and no further details are provided so that Gil's history can be fitted more completely into the narrative. Enquiries of the BBC received the reply that this project is now a closed, dead file.[79]

79 BBC-WW2 People's War. *Gil's war(3) Kervenheim recalled.* Article: 2069859, 22 November 2003http://www.bbc.co.uk/history/ww2peopleswar/categories/

Bandit, a Churchill IV belonging to the leader of 11 Troop 4CG, Alexis Melikoff, pictured in April 1945 in laager. The tank straddles the trench used for sleeping, with soil banked to prevent anyone from seeing underneath. Note the track plates on the turret that exploded the Panzerfaust when Alexis had his head out of the hatch, and the helmet that saved him hanging to hand. (© Alexis Napier)

Lt John Lincoln and Canloan 171 Lt Jack Laurie, 1 Royal Norfolks in the Netherlands in November 1944 while training to detect schu-mines using metal prods. (© John Lincoln)

Alexis Napier, then known as Lt Prince Alexis Melikoff of 3 Sqn CG, was sent by his Sqn Commander, Francis Holdsworth-Hunt, into Kervenheim in his tank *Bandit* to support D Coy, but without his troop, who stayed back with the remainder of 3 Sqn to provide supporting fire. Melikoff followed behind the infantry, although John Lincoln cannot remember seeing him at any stage. Melikoff met up with some Norfolks at the tower and then proceeded down the Üdemer Strasse at about 11.40 am. He fired one shot at a house at the end of the road using a delayed action fuse which blew the front off the house. Melikoff saw soldiers with helmets moving about and assumed they were Norfolks. As usual he had his head half out of the turret, accepting the risk of being sniped in order to see and sense dangers, but was wearing his helmet which most tank commanders refused to wear as it reduced their awareness of what was happening around them. A German stalked his tank with a bazooka, and hit the tank tracks festooning the side of the turret. The tank was not damaged but a piece of shrapnel went right through Alexis' helmet and the beret worn beneath it, into his head, but luckily without penetrating the skull. The blast blinded him, so it was the wireless operator who ordered the driver to reverse back up the street, and to park by the tower. Shortly afterwards a shell went through the tower, presumably from a StuG, and the hole can be seen in the photos. After about twenty minutes Melikoff could see again and reversed his tank a further 200 yards back up the road. There he was joined by the other two tanks of his troop. It was about midday.[80] During this time he observed British troops and Lt Alec Foucard walking among them at the tower in front of him.[81] The best estimate of when the KSLI and Stokes attacked the houses is 1300 hours.

After John Lincoln's departure, the fighting around the factory and in Vogelsangshof on the south side of the street opposite the factory became bitter as the Paras tried to turn the Norfolks out of Kervenheim. D Company came under command of the Canloan officer (171) Lt John (Jack) A. Laurie, who received an immediate MC and was killed on 16 April in Brinkum. The citation was raised by Barclay (8 March), signed by Matthews (9 March), by Whistler (10 March), by Horrocks (15 March), by Crerar (28 March) and Montgomery (undated).

> **MC. 185BIB, 3BID, 30 Corps, 1 R Norfolk, Lt CDN/171 John Alfred LAURIE.**
> On the capture of Kervenheim on 28 Feb [1 March] this offr was a pl comd. On his coy comd [Robin Wilson] becoming wounded and the 2IC [Leslie Dawson] being killed, he immediately assumed command of the coy. With great skill and under perpetual sniper fire, he organized his coy and was personally instrumental in beating back an enemy counter attack. Not content with defensive fighting from within, he led fighting patrols against the Bosche counter-attack force, and by his forceful leadership and skillful use of fire, wrought havoc amongst the opposition. During the whole of the operation his leadership and disregard of danger were most conspicuous, and the manner in which he accepted his new responsibilities and discharged his duties as coy comd were commendable beyond words.[82]

Private Ken Wilby was in Vogelsangshof and kept the paratroopers out. He was another who deserved better than a Divisional Commander's Certificate. In his words:

> We went in on the left hand side over wide open spaces and eventually, in Kervenheim, after we looked round the first house we entered, when I opened the back door I could see several good places in the next house for German machine gun posts, such as open windows, and I

80 Alexis Napier in conversation.
81 Letter from Alexis Napier on 4 December 1999.
82 TNA: WO 373/54: Laurie's citation; Smith, *Code Word*, p. 200.

> got my Bren gun and sprayed all these windows and firing points that were of advantage to the Germans. I found out later I had fired on the rectory.
>
> From that house we went out on to the main road into Kervenheim and came to this farmhouse, the whole platoon under Lt Laurie. We entered the farmhouse [Vogelsangshof] and then went on into the barn, a few yards further up. Opposite the farm was a big tall building. We didn't know at the time what it was but we found out later that it was an asylum which the Germans had taken over and they were firing at us. We opened fire back through the windows and doorways in the barn and after things quietened down a bit the rest of the platoon withdrew to the farmhouse and I was left in the barn with two friends of mine. One had been killed outright, the other badly wounded – I stayed with him; after five or ten minutes he died.
>
> After that I was still stuck fast in that barn. The Germans were still counter-attacking the barn with only me in it. There was hardly any roof to the barn, but the Germans must have seen me through some hole or something and they kept throwing grenades over into the barn – they knew exactly where I was so I thought rather than stand here I'll go to the other end of the barn. This carried on for five or ten minutes, me dodging from one end of the barn to the other – it wasn't funny at the time.
>
> When that finished I managed to get through into the farmhouse with the rest of the platoon – I got settled with them and put my Bren gun through the window. After about ten minutes the Germans with a Bazooka team came round the buildings and into the barn where I had been, they must have been looking for me. I saw this Bazooka team, switched from safety and lined up my Bren on the Bazooka man as silently as possible so that he couldn't hear me but he turned round and I fired straight away and killed him and wounded his No. 2.[83]

D Coy had centred its defence on Vogelsangshof. This was the home of the van Doornicks and had been in their family since 1386. In 1740 the family name changed when Theodora Vogelsang married Jan van Doornick and in 1947 it changed again when Maria van Doornick and Gottfried Hoogen were married. Warhorses have been bred on the farm since feudal times, and their Trakehner breed was registered in 1732. By then, following the war of succession between Jülich and Cleve (1608-1614), Kervenheim within the Dukedom of Cleve had become attached to the House of Brandenburg-Prussia and was its westernmost enclave. All the van Doornicks joined the colours of the Prussian Cavalry, either Guards in Berlin or Hussars in Wesel or Münster. Their records were lost during the Second World War, but it is almost certain that a van Doornick fought with von Blücher alongside 3 BID at Waterloo.

Maria Hoogen remembered being in the cellar while upstairs there was fighting:

> Every day as February 1945 drew to an end the front came closer to Kervenheim. We endured two days of heavy shelling (Trommelfeuer). A German tank [StuG IV] was stationed in Vogelsangshof in front of the stables and took part in the armoured assault on the Gochfortzberg [witnessed by Heinrich Kempkes]. The German Paras fired their machine guns from the balconies and from behind the broken windows. They fought like lions. In the afternoon two English tanks reached the Üdemerstrasse and captured several houses and the factory. However, when evening came they withdrew. [This is the second reference to British tanks being in Kervenheim on 28 February. They could have been a battle group of 2 KRRC and 44 RTR approaching from the Gochfortzberg on the Üdemer Straße and seeking to leave on the Sonsbecker Straße, to avoid strong opposition.[84] Hans Kühn called them Churchills, which limited them to 6 GAB

83 Lincoln, *Thank God*, pp. 165-66.
84 Delaforce, *Black Bull*, p. 198.

or to the Funnies of 79 BAD.] It was the calm before the storm which arrived the next day on 1 March. German soldiers took their badly wounded captain and comrades towards the rear in a cart pulled by our very pregnant mare. [This perhaps explains why the officer in command of Kervenheim on March 1 has never been identified]. Two women, Frau Umbach and Maria Schlotz, were killed in our neighbour's house behind the barn [the rectory], while Leni Schlotz had her leg amputated.

Our 85-year-old grandmother lived with us in the cellar and reacted very badly to the shell-fire. She died early on the morning of 1 March as the heavy shelling began. During a break in the shelling we carried her to a sheltered spot in the house. After much coming and going over many hours the climax of the battle was reached. That part lasted many hours. Once we heard an English machine gun nearby but then it moved away again [possibly Ken Wilby]. Above us in the kitchen German machine-guns were firing. At long last we heard the sounds of people being captured. Then at last there was peace!

Our old Dutch milkman said, 'Ek gon toerst herütt' (I'll go out first). But then a hand-grenade was thrown into the cellar. My arm began to bleed but it was only a small splinter. We were ordered out – father, mother, A de Vries, two Ukrainian girls [foreign slave workers of which there were millions in Germany, and well treated by these God-fearing farmers] some neighbours and me. We had to leave the house and the farm, which had been in the family sincc 1386, lcaving onc dcad grandmothcr and many livc animals.

We approached the firing line. The English soldiers were lying down in a long line with machine guns ready to attack. My father said we had to pass through the firing line, to hurry up and not to stop until we were past them.

The battle continued behind us and we were sent into the first houses on the Üdemer Strasse. Before the door of his house van Gemmeren lay dead with a white flag in his hand [shown in Cuneo's painting of the scene]. We were then sent further on to Üdem. It was a dangerous journey as shells were flying overhead the whole way there. In Üdem we were given hot tea and a little later were given the use of a warm room. We moved on to the Donkers [sic, Deckers] in Endtschenhof. The father Donkers (sic) told us to stay there because fighting was still going on in Kervenheim.

The next morning [2 March] there was peace. So mother, M. Gesthuisen and I went back home. That wasn't so easy. The first thing we saw as we approached Kervenheim was our horse which came whinnying up to me with a deep wound in its flank. We found our piano sitting outside on the pavement in front of the house. To this day I have no idea why I sat down at it and played the melody, 'Im schönsten Wiesengrunde ist meiner Heimat Haus, [My home is in the loveliest meadow. Words are by Wilhelm Ganzhorn (1818-1880), and music by Friedrich Silcher (1789-1860, who is better known for composing *Ich hatt' einen Kameraden*). A psychologist will find no difficulty in finding reasons why the young Maria would have thought the song appropriate in the circumstances on three levels: it was prescribed teaching in Prussian schools in the sixth grade where Maria would have learned it; Ganzhorn expressed her feelings on returning home to the lovely water meadows of Kervenheim; the tune, thirdly, had been adapted by Gustav Kneip (1905-1992) to become the popular marching song, *Drei Lilien, Drei Lilien* which Maria would have frequently heard sung by soldiers, and known the gist of its death-loving sentiments that were common in this period of Götterdämmerung. In the soldiers' version, a corpse asks a proud knight passing by not to pick the three lilies growing on his grave but to leave them so his sweetheart can look at them one last time. The knight replies that the grave and the sweetheart mean nothing to him, and he will pick the lilies because he is going to his death and on the morrow will himself be buried.]

We asked permission to go back and look after our dead grandmother. Then we were taken for our safety to the Catholic church. All the inhabitants of Kervenheim were to be evacuated to a camp in Bedburg-Hau. In the church were collected all the civilians who had been wandering about. The interpreter [Lt Harrie DeRooij, had been in the resistance in Helmond and joined the Norfolks as a sergeant but was later commissioned. 'He became more 'Norfolk' than anyone from our home county and insisted on wearing his Britannia badge', according to John Lincoln] told us that the commandant [2ic Humphrey Wilson] had lost his best friend [Maj Donald Smith] killed in the battle. We were sent into the church with all the others. The next morning the commandant went with us to Vogelsangshof. He wrapped grandmother up in an army blanket and placed her on a stretcher. [Buried wrapped in an army blanket tied up with string, like all dead British and Canadian soldiers.] English soldiers carried her and placed her in a grave which they had dug.

That was the beginning of a life-long friendship between the van Doornick-Hoogen family, the Kervenheim Historical Society and the Royal Norfolk Regiment. May our children and our children's children never ever get involved again in such a war.[85]

Vic Everitt was in Vogelsangshof during the battle and met Maria Hoogen in 1999:

I had a laugh with the German lady whose house I was in throughout the battle, that we had stolen her piano!! An infantryman has enough to carry without acquiring a piano. My greatest memory I suppose was of the German Paratroops crawling round the building and lobbing small grenades through the windows. We replied by rolling 36 grenades [aka Mills bombs] out for them to share.[86]

The IWM and RCAHMS, uniquely amongst government-owned collections, claim the copyright of all official wartime photographs and movies whose copyright in fact has expired, and sell expensive licences for their publication. Ownership of a series of stills and movies taken of L/Cpl Peter Gould and others of 17 Pl while 'clearing up' Kervenheim on 2 March is contestable for many reasons but also because a verbal contract was not fulfilled. Peter Gould:

Two War Photographers [Sgt Carpenter and Sgt Hutchinson] came up to me the next day and asked if I could get my section together and do a reconstruction. I told them I would have to get permission from my platoon commander (who was the platoon sergeant after John Lincoln was wounded) as I was only a full corporal at the time. He said that as far as he was concerned it was OK, so I got together the few of my section that were left and did the reconstruction of what we did the day before, but of course without the bangs and the bullets flying around. [Neither were they dressed in full battle kit]. Before we did it I made sure all our weapons were unloaded as we always had one up the breech ready for action and we did not want any accidents. After we had finished we were thanked by the correspondents. I held my hand out but all I got was a packet of cigarettes and the promise of more later. We never did and I never saw anything about it until I got into some of the history books and saw the photos of myself and the boys.[87]

The sergeants had no expense account with which to pay exhausted infantrymen to run around for them in their hard-earned moments of leisure, which could have been their last opportunity to relax and catch up with their mates and their correspondence. All concerned did it willingly for posterity which has abused their trust by commercializing them.

85 Letter from Maria Hoogen in 1997; author's translation.
86 Letter from Vic Everitt in February 2000.
87 Letter from Peter Gould in 1997.

2 March 1945 Picture K2 in Map 28 item 6. L/Cpl Peter Gould, Pte Freeman and Pte Duffill of 17 Platoon, D Coy, 1 R Norfolks performing a re-enactment for the movie and still cameras. They are crossing Schloß Straße from Pastorat Straße into a narrow lane that has since been built over. The soldiers are not in battle gear and their weapons are empty. They were promised remuneration which never materialized. (© Crown Copyright IWM, B 15047 by Sgt Carpenter)

The same scene in Pastorat Straße in 1994. This was the centre of the defence and where the mortars were set up. Consequently it was heavily shelled.

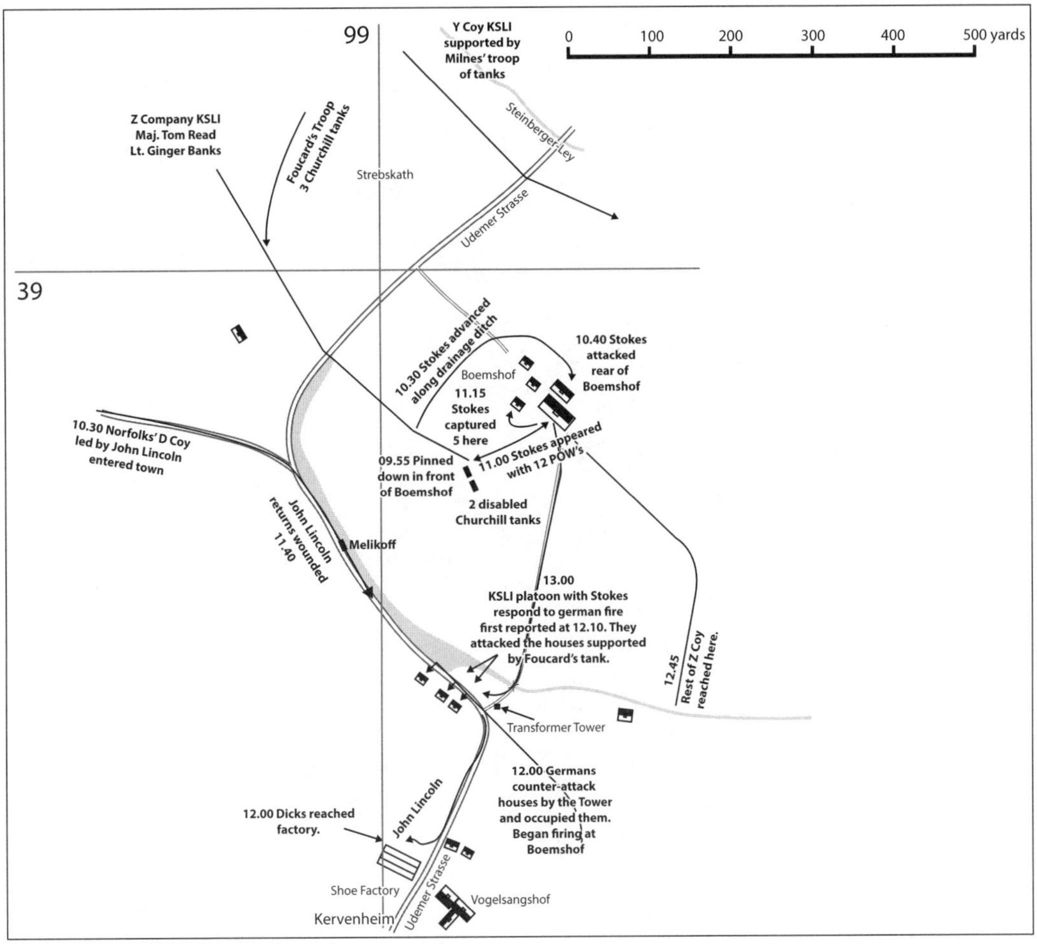

Map 27 Stokes's VC exploit.

2 KSLI attacked on the left flank at the same time as 1 Norfolks. They had been dug-in in the woods around 988395 with Tac HQ at 982395. Shortly before the barrage started at 9 am the enemy mortared the battalion and killed Lt Aldridge and Sgt Fisher of the pioneer platoon. The unit historian wrote of Aldridge:

> In battle his platoon was normally allotted out to the companies with a small reserve under his sergeant. He might well have moved at Tac HQ with the CO. But he seldom did; he would dodge about the battlefield in his Jeep or on foot, ignoring completely either shelling or mines when there was something which he thought needed doing. Helping to evacuate the wounded, carrying messages and reports of the situation, aiding his sections or the sappers, all the odd jobs of the battle he performed. He was quite the greatest character who served with us, and had a sure touch and knowledge of his job which can seldom have been equalled. He was equally useful out of battle, being able to make anything out of nothing. He was a very great loss.[88]

88 Radcliffe, *KSLI,* p. 72.

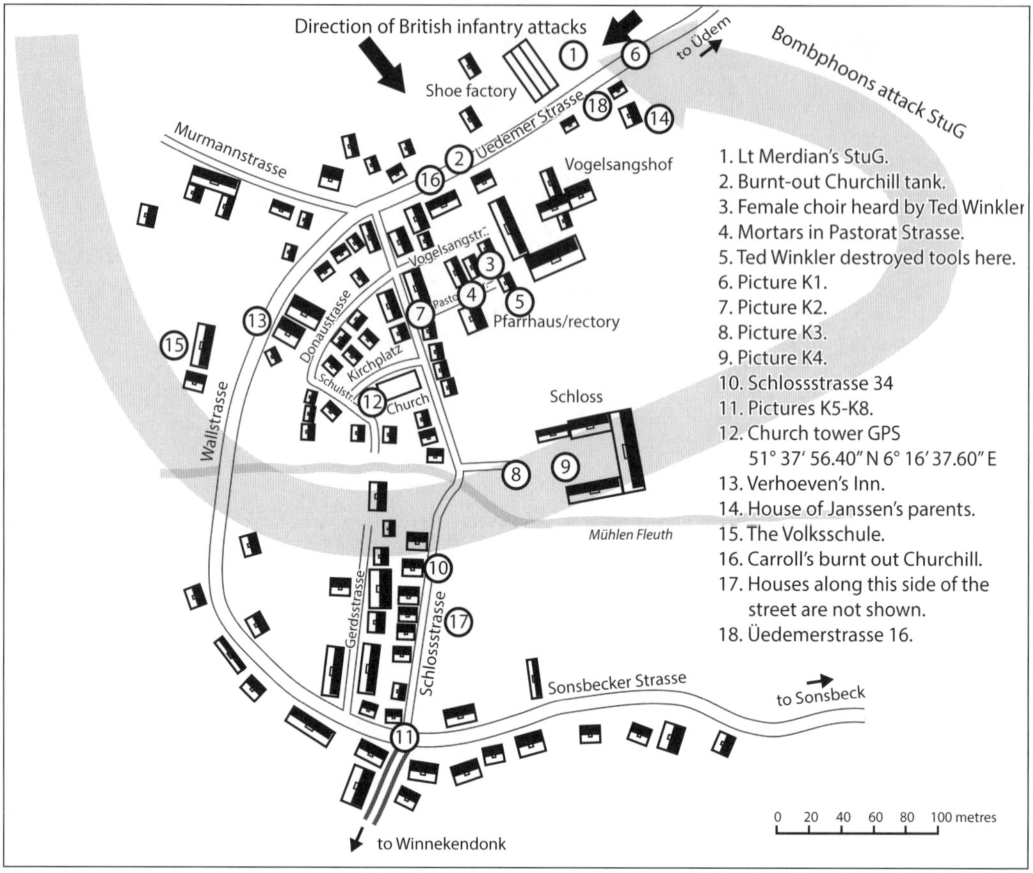

Map 28 Places mentioned in Kervenheim.

Bob Littlar knew Bert Aldridge as a very efficient Pioneer officer but a bit dour. He had won the MC at Periers Ridge and more renown later for finding a prototype German Riegel anti-tank mine. Tom Read remembers him as a 'first-class funny old boy' of 35 to 40 years of age who had been in the regiment a long time. Littlar said Aldridge came to him in the morning after sweeping for mines and said he had to go and see the CO and needed an escort. Littlar sent a L/Sgt who later returned and told him four men had been killed. Littlar asked if they had gone up the ride and when it was confirmed he called the Sergeant an idiot. The FOO had warned all of them that the rides and the leading and reverse edges of the woods were zeroed for German mortar fire and should be avoided.

At 9 am on 1 March, Y Coy on the left and Z on the right passed through the KSLI's reserve companies, which stayed put in their positions, and advanced across the startline at the edge of the woods into the open. There was no barrage since Venus stopped 150 feet to the right of the Űdem-Kervenheim road. The 120 or so men of the assaulting companies were in extended battle order. Major Tom Read led Z Company in the centre with Lt Ginger Banks's 17 Pl on his left and another platoon on his right and a third at the rear. With four yards between men and the section leaders shouting 'Don't bunch', each company's frontage easily filled the allotted area, which was half the width of 550 yards between the Steinberger Ley and the road. About 50 yards behind the infantry the three Churchill tanks of Alec Foucard's troop followed in arrowhead formation, having arrived from the north through 11 BAD's area. However, although the Steinberger Ley was both the divisional and corps boundary, there appears to have been no boundary specified between the KSLI and the Norfolks, who assumed that the road was that inter-battalion boundary. This lack of a clear boundary is an unusual feature of this battle, as boundaries were necessary to prevent friendly-fire incidents. The front narrowed to 400 yards at the Üdem road, and then increased to 700 yards as the Ley did a sharp left and right dog-leg turn.

Tom Read's ultimate objective, he told this author,[89] was the row of buildings on the outskirts of Kervenheim by the tower that John Lincoln always assumed were inside the Norfolks' boundary. It is therefore surprising that they did not go directly to secure them, as we shall see.

The first farm that was only 400 yards from the startline was unoccupied. There is no mention of an expendable enemy occupant with the duty of reporting the enemy's approach before surrendering. Poor going impeded the tanks throughout, and they would have been constantly stopping and reversing while searching for firm areas that could hold their weight. After a further 100 yards they had to cross over the Űdem-Kervenheim road which here is in the middle of a large S-bend. The attackers could now clearly observe Boemshof, from which machine gun fire was pouring into the Norfolks crossing the open fields on their right. Again they would have stopped while the tanks cleared the roadside bank and ditches, while keeping watch for StuGs at a distance to the front and right flank. The going became bad as they moved down a slight slope into a lower field and the tanks got further behind. Tanks and infantry were protecting each other, with the infantry eliminating all threat of Panzerfausts.

Foucard had his head out of the cupola watching the infantry. They approached Boemshof, whose defenders would have switched their fire from the Norfolks, pinning them down. The defenders would have been firing not only from slit trenches out in front, but also from the shadows at the back of upstairs rooms, from behind chimney-stacks, and from holes in the roof where slates had been removed. They could move between the buildings and the attackers had constantly to switch fire, never able to pin the defenders down. The infantry were now under fire from both flanks and went to ground to minimise casualties. The time was 9.55 am according to an entry in the War Diary recording Z Company at 992387 just beyond Boemshof, while Y Company was at 994390 clear of the small wood. Z Company closed to within effective range of the three tanks' six 7.92 mm Besas with their low (500 rpm) or high (800 rpm) rate of fire. The infantry lay down and the six Besas went to work, raking the buildings repeatedly. After a while, Foucard climbed down from his tank and asked Read if the 'suppressive fire' had done the trick. Read agreed, thanked Foucard, then ordered 17 Pl to get up and storm the place. Banks led the charge and set the tone, constantly exposing himself with complete disregard for his personal safety while encouraging his men. For this Banks was awarded the MC. Jimmy Stokes, responsible for Banks's safety, must have decided the best way to fulfill his task was to rush ahead on his own, which he did and returned with 12 prisoners. However he had been wounded in the neck. Banks told him to go back to the RAP and have the wound attended to. Stokes refused, so Banks appealed to Read who added his force to the command. The little Glaswegian again refused to leave his company, so the advance continued. The time was about 10.50 am.

At some point two of Foucard's three Churchills were incapacitated either by a StuG or by mines. Heinrich Kempkes saw two damaged Churchill tanks undergoing track repairs outside Boemshof,[90] which were perhaps the same ones Fendick noted on 2 March.

89 Tom Read in conversation on 10 May 2000.

90 H Kempkes. *Die Kampfhandlungen und das Ende des Zweiten Weltkriegs im Bereich von Kervenheim* (Geldrischen Heimatkalendar, 2001), p. 137.

Lt Alec Foucard, 4CG, with his dog, Astrid, in Monschau in July 1945. Foucard's tireless and skilful work in dismounting when necessary to keep his tank moving up in support of the KSLI and James Stokes achieved the breakthrough on the left flank that broke the German grip on Kervenheim. Cited for a DSO he received the MC, but surely deserved the VC together with Pte James Stokes. (© Dominic Norman-Rowsell)

Pte James (Stokie) Stokes VC, 2 KSLI. (© Shropshire Regimental Museum)

> At first light we were ordered up through Kervenheim, where things were badly knocked about. There were tanks bogged, and several with tracks blown off. The mines were thick in the ground, and we moved very carefully along taped lanes. We had plenty of unditching practice with the carriers. We passed the scene which was later recorded for posterity by Terence Cuneo, where Stokes won his VC… by this time the village was cleared.[91]

Therefore, of the three tanks in Foucard's troop, only Foucard's own tank was available to support Stokes's attack on the houses by the tower.

The result of eliminating the German occupation of Boemshof allowed John Lincoln to lead D Coy into Kervenheim.

At around 10 am, Jack Aitkin was called up by the CO and told Z Coy was meeting resistance. So he and Derek Clapham went forward to recce.[92] At 10.50 am, Z Coy was reported as still being no further forward than 992387,[93] while 'Y' had progressed to 998387. At 11.45 am Y Coy reported being on their objective at 000387. Then at about 12.10 am – and only minutes after John Lincoln hobbled past – Z Coy reported strong opposition from the buildings near the tower, and it was in the following half hour that Pte James Stokes won his posthumous VC.

At 12.45 pm, Z Coy was reported on the farm track 400 yards beyond Boemshof at 994385 while Y Coy was still at 000387. It must have been around this time that a decision was made to silence the opposition from the houses by the tower. Banks wrote to this author that to do it they made a 90-degree turn. He added that while forming up after taking Boemshof they were fired on from the houses by the tower. This would have been at 12.15 pm at the earliest, and the attack would have gone in around 12.30 pm. At 1.05 pm, X Company was sent forward to reinforce Z Company. They dug in in the field between Boemshof and the houses by the tower where they stayed for the rest of the day. By 2.05 pm the KSLI were reported to be down to the river and had cleared the wood at 000387. At 2.50 pm Z and X Coys reported still making very slow progress against strong opposition. At 3.15 pm W Coy moved up and established a firm base in farm buildings behind Y Coy's original objective. The Anti-tank platoon was put under the command of W Company as the battalion completed its dispositions to defend against the expected counter-attack.

There is confusion about which farmhouses were attacked by Stokes, especially as the citation for Banks's MC spoke of the first house being close to the SL. However, a map sent to Maj Tom Read in 2000 with a request to identify the houses, received the following reply:

> I cannot identify the two farmhouses on the map. All I can tell you is that about ¼ mile [400 metres] after crossing our start line, my Z Company came under intense fire from farm buildings on our left and so we attacked these and overcame them!!! [Strebskath is 320 metres from the SL but was not defended according to Kempkes]. This was where Private Stokes was first wounded and refused to be evacuated. We then continued our advance across open country to our Main Objective ie the Enemy Held Buildings on the outskirts of Kervenheim near the TOWER. That was when we were again fired on from more farm buildings on our left flank [Boemshof] and when Private Stokes took it upon himself to go off on his own (away from our main objective and line of attack) to deal with the enemy and rout him out – which he did on his own initiative and most successfully!!!! He then rejoined our Company before we went in with fixed bayonets to secure our original and final objective.[94]

91 Fendick, *Canloan Officer*, p. 174.
92 Bob Littlar in a transatlantic phone conversation in 2000.
93 TNA: WO 171/4130: 2 KSLI war diary.
94 Letter from Tom Read in 2000.

This is the site by the transformer tower where James Stokes won the VC on 1 March 1945, pictured on the following day. The three Churchill Mk VIs and right-hand Jeep were from HQ Troop of 3 Squadron 4CG, with that of the Squadron commander, Francis Holdsworth-Hunt second from the right. The scout car belonged to 3 Squadron's LO, Hans Veenbrink. The carrier and left-hand Jeep would have been KSLI. The infantry unit is unknown, but probably were from 9 BIB moving up to Winnekendonk. Up the path is the plant nursery where the German FOO was positioned, and beyond it is the van Dongen's farm in de Weyen. The high ground to the right of the transformer tower is the Gochfortzberg, and to its right in the far distance is the Hochwald. This is the picture seen by Terence Cuneo that got him into trouble with Col Musson. (© Crown Copyright IWM, B 15076 by Sgt Hutchinson)

2 March 1945. Hans Veenbrink had now climbed aboard his scout car. He was the interpreter and would have been telling the evacuees and refugees that trucks would be coming to take them to the Bedburg camp. The troops are KSLI. The hole in the transformer tower was made by a StuG, possibly a ranging shot to zero the sights. (© Crown Copyright IWM, B 15072 by Sgt Hutchinson)

2 March 1945. Troops from X Coy KSLI stand near to their carrier across from the houses by the tower. Note the un-military figure striding between the civilians and the soldiers – Sgt Carpenter? – and the standing water on the left. (© Crown Copyright IWM, B 15075 by Sgt Hutchinson)

Tom Read added a significant conclusion about the quality of the support received from Foucard, and which the Norfolks sadly lacked.

> My only wish is to emphasise my Complete and utter admiration for the Courageous and dedicated support FOUCARD and his troop of tanks gave us throughout this battle. If it hadn't been for the Continuous fire from his Tank Machine Guns over our heads when we came under enemy fire from all these enemy positions, we would have suffered many many more casualties, as we were advancing over open and unprotected ground the whole way. They were brilliant, so was Foucard!!!
>
> I think the detailed account of The Battle of Kervenheim [you sent me] quite brilliant!!! Very detailed and highly accurate. I can't fault it in any way and I must congratulate you on its exceptional quality!! Please excuse my near illegible scribble, but I suffer acute arthritis in my wounded leg and right (writing) hand!!!!. With my Kindest Regards & Best Wishes. Yours Aye, Tommy Read.[95]

Stokes' bravery stood out from a company of brave men.

> Stokes was born on 6th February 1915 in a slum tenement in Crown Street, Hutchesontown, in the St. Luke's district of the Gorbals, Glasgow. He was one of four children born into an environment of grinding poverty. When he lost both parents at an early age and the family was split up, Stokes spent some time in a Catholic children's home before becoming a labourer on his uncle's farm at the age of 14. He later travelled into England and worked for a time as a waiter in London before returning to Glasgow to work in the building trade. In 1939, he married a local girl, Janet Kennedy, and they set up home in a single-room apartment at 20, Clyde Street.
>
> On the outbreak of war, Stokes followed his elder brother George into the army, enlisting into the Royal Artillery on 20th July 1940. He seems to have had a varied service career: he spent some time in the Royal Army Service Corps (52 Drivers' Training Unit) before passing into the Gloster Regiment in October 1943. Though he stood only 5 feet 4 inches tall, Stokes was said to have 'a temper out of all proportion to his stature' and had learned street fighting the hard way. On leave in 1944, he became involved in a brawl in a Glasgow dance hall after a perceived insult to his wife. The fight left one man in a wheelchair and Stokes in prison. Sentenced to three years for grievous bodily harm, he was offered the chance of release into the infantry and then (according to the Transfer Books of the KSLI) went into the Royal Warwicks, from which he was posted to the 2nd KSLI in October 1944.[96]

Friar Balsom of 1 R Norfolks by coincidence knew Stokes:

> Pte Stokes was previously in the first reinforcement draft of the 4th Bn Welch Regt. I was a platoon commander in this battalion and was sent to 47 RHU to take charge of their Bn's first reinforcements. I began to get to know the group from about mid-May 1944. I took them across the Channel on about D+6, landing on Gold Beach in small LCAs. Stokes and I being short got very wet! We moved on to the 47 RHU camp in an orchard just outside Bayeux – a crazy existence of peace and leisure while the war was raging all around. I remember quite

95 Letter from Tom Read on 6 June 2000.

96 Shropshire Regimental Museum: http://www.shropshireregimentalmuseum.co.uk/regimental-history/shropshire-light-infantry/victoria-cross-regimental-awards-after-1914/

> a number of my group – particularly little Jimmy Stokes who was having marital problems. I put him in touch with a chaplain, but compassionate leave for someone who had just been put on foreign shore was very unlikely. In the meantime storms in the Channel intervened and 53rd Div arrived later than their reinforcements, so we were all sent to bolster up D-Day Divisions. ORs were drafted, officers were 'asked'. Early in July Stokes went to 2 KSLI and I went to 1 Norfolk. A few years ago I checked that Stokes VC was my Jimmy Stokes by visiting the KSLI museum at Shrewsbury castle (before the IRA burnt it) and there I saw his photo. I wonder if just before Kervenheim he had home leave. We both landed at the same time and I qualified for home leave at the end of Jan 45.[97]

Friar's question was referred to Bill Banks who said that Stokes had not had home leave.

Stokes was valued and had influence. Some weeks before he had refused an order from his pl sgt to go out on patrol in the middle of the night. The sgt had wanted to charge Stokes with disobeying a lawful command, which was a military offence with the sanction of hard labour. Banks, Read and the sgt agreed this was pointless so the offence was overlooked.[98]

They knew their man, and this event may well have influenced Stokes to see in the battalion a home where cultured, brave and decent men in authority accepted and valued him, treating him as family. Tom Read had been a rackets Blue at Brasenose College (BNC), Oxford in 1939-40, and Ginger Banks had been promoted from the ranks from sheer ability. Patrolling was necessary for the safety of the battalion and Stokes may have reflected that his refusal had caused someone who had not deserved it both danger and lost sleep. The officers had not only turned a blind eye to Stokes' offence but gone further by giving him new responsibility for looking after Ginger Banks, who had returned that morning from UK leave spent with his family. The battalion was now Stokes's home and received the fierce loyalty of the rough diamond. Within a couple of miles of Stokes' heroics another graduate of BNC, Lt Robert Runcie, was waiting by his tank to be called forward for his MC-winning attack on Winnekendonk the following day. In 2000, and three months before his death, Runcie was interviewed by Graham Turner and spoke about Glaswegians who he had got to know when 6 GTB was for a while in 15 Mixed BID with Glasgow Highlanders. Runcie said Church hadn't meant much to the Glaswegians with whom he slept under tanks during the war, yet they were some of the finest characters he had known, and often more worthwhile than some of his fellow-believers.[99]

The citation for James Stokes's VC is not in TNA, which is the only official repository. Published in the London Gazette, it began with a glaring mistake that put Kervenheim in Holland, and ended with a grammatically illiterate and defamatory paragraph claiming that Stokes's one objective was to kill the enemy, when his actions showed clearly that he was not a killer but intended rather to take the defenders' surrender. The slander and bad grammar showed that tampering had occurred with the citation after it had left Lt Col Daly of the KSLI in order, presumably, to make it useful as propaganda. Unfortunately, all attempts to find the original citation and identify whose hand perverted the award, failed with fruitless enquiries made of TNA, the VC Society, the MOD, the KSLI Museum, and the IWM. Finding the original citation would also identify who first stated that Kervenheim was in Holland, as no soldier in the field could have made that mistake. It appears to this author that what was published in The London Gazette six weeks later was a press release date-lined Cuijk in Holland, and reflecting input from many unknown people

97 Letter from Friar Balsom on 1 March 2000.
98 Fax from Tom Read on 8 May 2000.
99 The Electronic Telegraph, 20 April 2000.

with various motives. It is therefore scarcely surprising that the actions cannot be reconciled with the geography.

> **VC. 1592376 PRIVATE JAMES STOKES**
> In Holland, on 1st March, 1945, during the attack on Kervenheim, Private Stokes was a member of the leading section of a Platoon. During the advance the platoon came under intense rifle and medium Machine gun fire from a farm building and was pinned down. The Platoon Commander began to re-organize the platoon when Private Stokes, without waiting for any orders, got up and, firing from the hip, dashed through enemy fire and was seen to disappear inside the farm building. The enemy fire stopped and Private Stokes re-appeared with twelve prisoners. During this operation he was wounded in the neck.
>
> This action enabled the platoon to advance to the next objective and Private Stokes was ordered back to the Regimental Aid Post. He refused to go, and continued to advance with his Platoon.
>
> On approaching the second objective the Platoon came under heavy fire from a house on the left. Again, without waiting for orders, Private Stokes rushed the house by himself, firing from the hip. He was seen to drop his rifle and fall to the ground wounded. However, a moment later he got to his feet again, picked up his rifle and continued to advance, despite the most intense fire which covered not only himslef (sic) but the rest of the Platoon. He entered the house and all firing from it ceased. He subsequently rejoined his platoon – who, due to his gallantry, had been able to advance – bringing five more prisoners.
>
> At this stage the company was forming up for its final assault on the objective, which was a group of buildings, forming an enemy strong-point. Again, without waiting for orders Private Stokes, although now severely wounded and suffering from loss of blood, dashed on the remaining 60 yards to the objective, firing from the hip as he struggled through intense fire. He finally fell 20 yards from the enemy position, firing his rifle until the last, and as the company passed him in the final charge, he raised his hand and shouted goodbye. Private Stokes was found to have been wounded eight times in the upper part of the body.
>
> Private Stoke's (sic) one object throughout this action was to kill the enemy, at whatever personal risk. His magnificent courage, devotion to duty and splendid example, inspired all those round him and ensured the success of the attack at a critical moment, moreover, his self-sacrifice saved his platoon and company many serious casualties.[100]

Ginger Banks commanded Jimmy Stokes. Banks had landed with the battalion on D-Day as a sergeant and been commissioned in the field. He returned on the evening of 28 February from 10 days home leave [he had been lucky and his sailing code, which he was required to listen for on the radio, had been called late giving him a two-day extension with his wife and family] and went straight to see John Sale in A Echelon. Those back from leave were supposed to wait 24 hours before going to the front line, but Sale told him battle was imminent and drove Banks to the assembly area in his Jeep, arriving at 6 am and reporting to his company commander, Major Tom Read.

Banks described the events for a newspaper article.[101] He said that Stokes was assigned as his minder because the Germans were targeting officers. Stokes was recklessly aggressive and therefore a good person to have alongside in a fight. Banks saw some Germans disappearing into the smoke that was drifting across the battlefield from burning Kervenheim, and turned to follow them. But

100 KSLI Museum. *London Gazette*, 17 April 1945.
101 *The People*, 5 June 1994.

Stokes knocked him down just as a burst of machine gun fire came between them, and a bullet gashed Stokes's neck. Banks ordered Stokes to report to the RAP, but he refused to go. Instead he attacked a farmhouse through its front door on his own while dodging machine gun bullets, to reappear with twelve prisoners. Then he ran towards a barn while firing from the hip, but was hit in the chest, with bullets going right through him and his haversack. Even so he returned with five more prisoners, although now badly wounded and covered in blood. Banks remembered calling him a stupid young bugger because he had got himself hurt, but despite everything he was still with the platoon. As they attacked the objective Stokes fell, and some said that even on the ground he managed to wave an arm and call goodbye. Banks recommended Stokes for the VC, and himself received an MC for his bravery. He said the medal was for the men who stayed with him while he only did his job for as long as the Germans failed to kill him.

> **MC. 2/Lieut 329514 William Banks**
> On 1 Mar 45, 2/Lt Banks was commanding the leading Pl of Z Coy. Shortly after crossing the start line [untrue] his Pl came under heavy fire from an enemy strong point in some farm buldings. Without hesitation 2/Lt Banks led his Pl in a charge at the strong point and captured it and the enemy garrison. During the advance to the final objective 2/Lt Banks' Pl came under intense enemy shell, mortar and MG fire, and point-blank small arms fire from 60 yards away. Despite heavy casualties which his Pl had suffered 2/Lt Banks coolly remained in the open and reorganised the remainder of his Pl and led them in a charge on to the enemy position, killing or capturing the entire garrison of twenty. There is no doubt that the great gallantry shown by this Officer was the inspiration needed by his men to enable them to carry on in the most difficult circumstances.[102]

Tom Read clearly remembered the events by the tower. The company had gone to ground, presumably on the near side of the ditch, and Read was lying near Foucard's tank which was shooting up the houses with Besa. Germans kept popping up and throwing stick grenades. Read called to Banks to bring up the PIAT whose hollow-charged shell could blow holes in the brick walls and let the tank's bullets penetrate into the rooms. But the PIAT had been dropped earlier as the operator had been too worn out to carry the heavy weapon. So Read shouted up to Foucard in the turret to use armour-piercing shells to knock holes in the walls. But Foucard had exhausted his stock of AP firing at a StuG which had been bothering them, and said he was too close to fire high explosive rounds. Read then ordered the platoon to fix bayonets where they lay on the ground.

The officer commanding 2 Sqn 4CG was the efficient Maj Milbank, later Master of the Queen's Household. The other troop commanders were Barton, Carr Gomm and Milne whose troop was alongside Foucard but some way distant. Forbes wrote that the nearest 2 Sqn got to Kervenheim was when Milne, 'reached a large crossroads north of the town from which he was able to provide invaluable covering fire'. It must have been to Milne that Darby Hart of the Lincolns spoke.

Alec Foucard recalled that SPs [the Mk IV Tank Destroyers of Lt. Merdian's PzJgAbt 33] were the problem that day. There was one on the left flank and another behind the buildings next to the tower.[103] The Squadron's only runner, Foucard's tank, was alongside the hedge, and facing south to give the infantry protection. Foucard took his tank past the farm to the tower and was sniped at from the left. Foucard thought strongly that the infantry should keep up with the tank because separately both were vulnerable. He therefore dismounted and fought outside the tank in order to communicate with the infantry and to co-ordinate the attack, 'instead of everyone doing his own

102 TNA: WO 373/54/331: Ginger Banks's citation.
103 Alec Foucard in conversation.

Private James Stokes winning the VC at Kervenheim by Terence Cuneo. (© Shropshire Regimental Museum)

The scene of Stokes's VC in 2004. The trees facing the camera where the transformer tower once stood have since been removed.

thing'. He found the KSLI efficient but shell-shocked [the lieutenants were green because of their serious loss rate. 'You won't see this battle out, Sir', an NCO told Bob Littlar] except of course Stokes who, Foucard said, was a born rebel and visitor to the Glasshouse, which was the military prison for terms of hard labour. Stokes avoided prison by volunteering for the infantry. It is said that Stokie's full story remains to be told. He is believed to have received a Dear John letter just prior to the battle. The source is Bob Littlar, who believes there are other unexplained aspects to this battle. The wounded were evacuated on three Sherman tanks, and Bob asked in November 1996, 'Where did they come from?' The Coldstreamers had only Honeys and Churchills. The nearest unit operating Shermans, other than the RA, was 3/4 County of London Yeomanry of 11 BAD whose territory started 500 yds to the east. They were preparing to attack Dickmanns 009378 where 'the enemy are being a nuisance', according to 3 BID's Ops log at 2.05 pm. 11 BAD was trying to open the road to Sonsbeck. It was surely their tanks that evacuated the KSLI's wounded.

To return to Foucard; heavy shelling was being directed at the buildings by the tower and he saw a lot of Germans moving in and around the houses. The StuG moved off and Foucard believed that he put it out of action. He remembered moving with Stokes's platoon and Stokes (?) asking for shells to be fired into the houses. The range was too short for Foucard to fire without endangering his own troops from the instantaneous HE burst. 'I can't fire', Foucard told Stokes. 'OK', Stokes replied. 'Fuck it; let's go'. With Stokes dying and Read's company in the houses, Foucard took his tank to the corner and stood up on top to get a better view down Üdemer Strasse into the centre of Kervenheim. This corner is now unrecognisable – the water-tower has been demolished and its base is in the garden of a new house. A German sniped Foucard, the bullet making a hole in his tank 'pixie suit'. Rex Fendick described them as, 'a sort of cover-all of heavy, wind-proof material outside, lined with wool serge, and fitted with an amazing array of zippers so it could be put on and off easily, and could also be re-zipped to form a tight but comfortable sleeping bag. Everyone tried to scrounge them, but they were in short supply and needless to say, any Armoured type who had one wouldn't part with it.' Foucard jumped off the tank but landed on a shell case spraining his ankle. He was evacuated to Louvain. Foucard knew nothing about the VC application for Stokes, but said he knew that his own name was put forward by Milbank to Bill Smith for a VC but not passed on. Smith put him in for an immediate DSO on 6 March, which was changed by Greenacre to an MC on 7 April, signed by Crerar on 1 May and later counter-signed by Montgomery.

MC. WS/Lieut 326835 Alec George Foucard
On March 1st 1945 no. 2 Sqn Coldstream Guards was supporting 2nd Bn KSLI in the attack on Kervenheim (9938). The tanks were in difficulties owing to the bad going and were unable to keep up with the Infantry, who were halted by heavy Spandau fire from both flanks as well as from the objective. Lt Alec George FOUCARD, the Troop Commander, with complete disregard for the enemy fire, dismounted from his tank and led his troop forward on foot to ensure that they should not become bogged down, and guided them into fire positions from which they were able to subdue the enemy. As a result of this very gallant action the Infantry were able to advance and capture the objective.[104]

Read told Daly, the CO, about the exploits of Stokes and Foucard. Daly told Read to write a report about Stokes which was completed after a couple of days with Read checking the details with Banks.[105] VCs are awarded for conspicuous gallantry which has an impact on the result

104 TNA: WO 373/54/581: Alec Foucard's citation.
105 Information from Tom Read over the phone in May 2000.

of the battle. The action checkmated the Germans who had just cut off B and D Coys of the Norfolks in Kervenheim. The King presented the medal to Stokes's widow and young son, James, in a post-war investiture at Buckingham Palace. This author has asked and searched for a photo of this for thirty years; Tom Read had one but could not find it. Stokes's medals were bought at Sothebys for £18,000 in 1982 by a private collector. For some time they were on public display in a military museum at Strawberry Farm, Jersey, but the museum closed and their present location is unknown.

In 1963 Terence Cuneo was commissioned by the KSLI to paint the battle. Read flew out to Germany with Cuneo, and they visited the water tower with Banks and the CO of 1 KSLI stationed in Münster, who was the erstwhile 2ic of X Company but now Lt-Col Derek Clapham. Read wrote:

> The next morning after we landed I was asked by Lt Col Derek Clapham to carry out, for the benefit of Cuneo and officers & wives of the Regiment, a running commentary on the ground of the actual events of the battle; & they had British troops dressed in Battle kit and some dressed in German uniforms re-enacting the last charge on the defended houses as pictured in the final Assault. Cuneo painted sketches and took numerous photographs. Finally some months later Cuneo invited me over to his studio to see the finished painting and ensure its accuracy before presentation.[106]

Cuneo painted Jimmy Stokes going down for the last time supported by Cpl Coles, Lt Banks, Pte Field, Sgt Evans, and Pte Devonport. Ginger Banks is pictured wearing a para smock and firing a Schmeisser at a defender also armed with a Schmeisser over the dead body of Verhayen who had been carrying a white flag.

Alec Foucard was not invited to attend. His tank from 2 Sqn was originally included by Cuneo, but not placed where Tom Read said it should have been – just to the rear of Z Coy's forming up position about 70 yards from the enemy-held houses. Instead Cuneo placed it to one side as pictured in the IWM photograph B15076 taken the following day of Holdsworth-Hunt's 3 Sqn HQ Troop. The Colonel of the KSLI, General Sir Geoffrey Musson, was not therefore wrong to point out that its position was wrong and a "'military nonsense' which if left uncorrected could only cast doubt on Stokes's action".[107] The problem was due to the absence of Foucard, since Cuneo could not know where to place the tank, and therefore took it out altogether. The result upset both the CG and the KSLI, and especially Tom Read who had choice words for the colonel; 'Stupid bloody old fool. He wasn't there. Ginger Banks, Foucard & I should know. We were in the thick of it'.[108]

Read thought the KSLI's officers were a bit wet to accept Musson's edict. Foucard is said to have written a letter to The Times about it. Cuneo, however, said later that it was the right thing to do because the infantry charge was correct in every detail and it was their picture. In fact the details were not correct. Cuneo's footbridge is nonsensically placed alongside the tower where there was no stream. An aerial photograph shows the stream was thirty yards to the left of the tower. This author wrote to Banks, who provided more details, and said of the bridge:

> It covered a drainage ditch which my platoon had to dive into earlier to escape enemy fire. It then held about ¾ foot of water and meandered around the Tower [not true, it remained

106 Fax from Tom Read on 10 May 2000.
107 G Landy. *The Military Paintings of Terence Cuneo* (London: New Cavendish, 1993), p. 116.
108 Fax from Tom Read on 10 May 2000.

behind the Tower] and broadened out to about 10 to 12 ft wide and 12 to 18 in deep immediately in front of the houses [but still 30 yards distant]. The footbridge covered the point where it began to widen out. I crossed it many times that day, as did many of the KSLI members. You either went by the bridge or got wet up to your knees.

Initially we took four prisoners from those houses we entered but I noticed a further two were winkled out nearby a little later. One of the four was a member of the SS.

With regard to the numbers in the cellar, as I recall it was a fairly spacious cellar. We had to use candles to see and I went down with our interpreter [a Dutch volunteer who enlisted in the battalion for the duration. His name is not recorded]. It was exceptionally tidy and obviously used as a bunker by more than one family. It held between 30 and 40 women and 15 to 20 children, most of whom were in arms. They were quite tightly packed in without being too tight if you know what I mean, and I can vividly remember seeing their upturned faces when we stood at the top of the steps.

Two other main points I don't think I've touched on before. The first point is we wouldn't have attacked these houses in the first place if they hadn't fired upon us inflicting some casualties as we were forming up to move on after clearing the second farmhouse. [Banks here contradicts Read who said the houses by the tower were the company's objective]. We had to do a ninety-degree turn to take them on, but the Shropshires are a funny old lot. If somebody has a go at them, they have a go back. The second point is a theory I have that after we had taken our second farmhouse and were preparing to move on, the enemy HQ would have known we had taken two of their defences and sent troops into these houses between noon and 1 pm (if they weren't already there) to engage us, which of course they did.

From my own personal point of view I would only add that after almost seven years with my regiment from 1 October 1939 to August 1946, of all the many incidents that occurred, this is top of my list, and I have often failed to understand why these houses were not searched beforehand or even occupied, particularly as people seemed to be passing by so frequently.[109]

One unusual aspect of these events which surprised John Lincoln when he found out about them fifty years later, was how Z Coy, KSLI and 2 Sqn 4 CG attacked towards Kervenheim at right angles to the line of advance of Y Coy and crossed the road, which the Norfolks understood was the inter-unit boundary, without apparently knowing it. 'There was a potentially disastrous situation developing where Z Company would attack along the Üdemer Strasse with the Norfolks established about 200 m ahead of them.'[110]

Banks referred to the houses by the Tower as being their objective, although he also stated that they went there only because they were the source of enfilade fire. Read said the houses were his objective. It is impossible for the same objective to be assigned to two battalions. It was true that attacking companies set their own detailed objectives within the overall task, and Stokes proved he was in a mood to go after any Germans with the audacity to fire at his company. For good reason troops will not trespass into another battalion's area. If the boundary, however, were the road, then the houses were right on the boundary.

There are three possible explanations. Bill Smith, the CO of 4 CG, who was in touch on the battalion net with 2 & 3 squadron commanders, Milbank and Holdsworth-Hunt, (although Melikoff stationary within 100 yds of the houses and Foucard could not communicate because they were in different squadrons operating on individual nets) could have passed down an order

109 Letter from Ginger Banks on 12 November 1999.
110 Letter from John Lincoln on 14 October 1996.

for the latter to cut across and the former to support him with fire from the flank. If that were so, then the memory of the verbal order has been lost. Alternatively the KSLI might have been carrying out the original plan issued on 26 February, which assigned the capture of Kervenheim to the KSLI and the Warwicks with the Norfolks in reserve. But this is unlikely because the KSLI did not push on but stayed put. Humphrey Wilson, the Norfolk's 2ic, told this author that he had not been briefed about the KSLI. It is therefore quite possible that they in their turn did not know what the Norfolks were up to, and the fault in that case would have been Matthews's. Then again the reason could have been, as Bill Banks states above, that the Shropshires are a funny old lot and someone had a go at them, and this has the ring of testosterone-truth. If it meant crossing a boundary then the action possessed the Nelson touch, which rightfully brings honour and awards to successful local initiative.

Rex Fendick wrote about boundaries in general:

> Boundaries were essential, to define tasks and routes, help maintain direction, to avoid confusion, exposure to adjacent friendly fire, etc. But the enemy never knew what our boundaries were and their positions often straddled them. A unit and sub-unit advancing/attacking had to deal with opposition which interfered with its movement, so if fire came in from a flank which was in a neighbour's area, across a boundary, of course it would be dealt with. The other side of the coin would be that perhaps buildings/defence works were outside one's own boundary, so would NOT be investigated/searched/cleared, certainly if no immediate fire came from them. BUT, as the enemy re-grouped and took up alternate positions (which a good defence always provided for) places which had been passed could easily suddenly become thorns in one's flanks/rear. Similarly, changes in direction of an advance could be forced on a unit/sub-unit by ground features which had not been properly assessed/evaluated during planning, by unexpected enemy reaction from an unexpected direction, or by encountering enemy killing grounds. These diversions could result in the real objective (ie, the place where one killed enemy and took ground) ending up being different from the one originally planned and assigned. And, maintaining direction was always a major problem in the heat of battle. A marker or landmark could be very close and never register; one focused very narrowly on the important things, like where the shots aimed at you were coming from![111]

John Lincoln added that every participant in war has only limited knowledge of a battlefield that nearly always looked empty:

> I personally do not remember the tower although this is not surprising in the circumstances, but I am certain that no tanks were in support during D Company's advance nor have I any memory of British troops on my right as I returned to Bn HQ before 1200 hours.[112]

Ginger Banks would have been half a field away on John's right as he hobbled back, and John must have passed Melikoff's tank without seeing it either. It is clear that the Norfolks' D Coy did not search or occupy the houses because it would have diverted them from the objective of getting into the town.

We saw above how Heinrich Kempkes in 'In de Weyen' watched 11 BAD being attacked from Kervenheim. On 1 March he found himself in the line of fire.

111 E-mail from Rex Fendick.
112 John Lincoln by letter.

On 1 March the British began their assault on the area called 'In de Weyen'. The German signallers could no longer get messages through to the battery commanders, so one of them had to deliver the target information by bicycle. I stood in the hall with two paratroops and explained the geography to them. Then I took the soldiers' advice and went down into the cellar. The staircase was packed with soldiers. At that moment an AP shell came through the gable end of our house, knocking the cellar door into my back. A short while later heavy fire from the British tanks' machine guns swept through the entrance hall destroying the front door. The signaller in the cellar tried to get through to the regiment. Again and again you could hear him calling; "Saucer here. Saucer, I am receiving you faintly", but there was no reception. Then the medics were ordered to put out a white flag. The English stopped firing, and the paratroops went into captivity. The last order rang out; "Caps on, so your bald heads will be covered when you reach the PW camp." The English searched the German soldiers. Everything the British soldiers did not need was thrown away. The lieutenant had to surrender his anorak.

When I heard the first English soldiers come into the hall, I climbed the cellar steps. I was asked about weapons and handed over two assault rifles, two ordinary rifles and a pistol. The English left satisfied. A short while later our neighbour, Peters, noticed his farmhouse was on fire. I took two buckets of water and ran to put it out. Another Englishman appeared and asked if I was a soldier. I said I was not and ran on. The enquiring Englishman had a captured paratroop with him who was removing the covers from the slit trenches.[In order to ensure no defender was missed.] Everywhere as far as the road to Uedem there were clouds of smoke. From Kervenheim could be heard the firing of machine guns and tank guns. At Peters the rear of the farm house with the stables was beyond saving. Gerd Peters managed to get the horned cattle out of their stalls and also released the pigs and horses. His horse bolted and jumped the hedge to be shot dead by an Englishman.

Van Dongen's farm was completely burnt out, and all of the animal stalls and byres were consumed by fire. Three Englishmen were killed in the area of the farm. Everywhere lay discarded English weapons and equipment.

The paratroops surrendered once bullets were fired through the cellar windows. The members of the Peters and van Dongen families were sent towards Uedem. Around 4 pm German shelling started and the English soldiers took shelter in our cellar. When the shelling died down we also were told to leave the farm. We were allowed to take with us a horse and cart with necessities. The journey was towards Tofürtzhof, but was cut short because the horse's harness had been broken. Finally we found refuge in Peters' cellar.[113]

Heinrich Kempkes tells a very different story about how Stokes won his VC, and it has the ring of truth. Kempkes gave his story to this author when asked if Strebskath had been defended and whether it could have been the first farm that Stokes attacked. Kempkes replied that Strebskath was undefended, and he was in a position to know what his neighbours experienced. He wrote this:

According to what I know, the following happened. Z Coy's attack came to a standstill. Private Stokes went on without orders. After crossing the Uedemer Strasse he found himself in a low-lying meadow and out of sight of Boemshof. From the meadow a drainage ditch led to Boemshof, providing him with good cover. He therefore was able to infiltrate behind the paratroop defenders and take all fifteen of them prisoner. Z Coy then took up position in Boemshof. Around noon, the paras put in a counterattack with support from a StuG, and

113 Kempkes, *Die Kampfhandlungen*, pp. 135-36.

> occupied the row of houses by the Transformer Tower. The Norfolks in the Shoe Factory were then surrounded on three sides. Stokes saw the danger and formed up with his platoon to attack these defended houses by the Transformer Tower. The Germans were forced back to their original starting position. Stokes noticed that they were being fired on from the left. Already seriously wounded, he attacked these enemies. 10 metres in front of the German position, he collapsed and died. Another five Germans were taken prisoner. On the way into the Weyen was a market garden where the Germans had established a position. The KSLI needed a cemetery for the unit, so here in the Weyen they buried three members of Y Coy and Stokes from Z Coy.[114]

The reader will have to make up his/her own mind from the conflicting evidence.

The close co-operation between aggressive infantry and tanks had gained the second significant success of the day and re-opened the left flank. Brigadier Matthews now ordered his reserve battalion, 2 Lincolns, to take Kervenheim with the support of Crocodile flame-throwers of the Buffs under 4 CG command. Around 2 pm, RW Thompson saw Matthews, Barclay and Firbank of the Lincolns conferring in the wood by the original startline. The meeting must have decided against wholesale commitment of the Lincolns because only A Coy under Sam Larkin was sent in. The Lincolns' historian:

> Towards evening on 28th Feb they came under their (185 Brigade) command [actually at 0100 hrs on 1 March] with orders to be concentrated in an area astride the axis of advance, and about 4 km from the village itself by 0730 hrs next morning (9640). So at 0600 hrs on 1st March, the Lincolnshires set off [in the steps of the Norfolks] and were dug-in and ready for anything by the time ordered.
>
> In its early stages the attack by 185 Bde went well and by the middle of the morning all three bns were investing the village from the north. The Lincolnshires moved forward in open order and dug new positions behind the 2nd KSLI (at 9839, Bn HQ at 983394), who were on the left. The fighting now increased in intensity and conditions gradually became worse; it began to rain and movement off the roads across the soggy ground became a nightmare. Repeated attacks to gain a footing inside the village were all repulsed, and finally the Bde Cmdr called on the Bn to assist the Royal Norfolks with one coy. A Coy, under Maj S. J. Larkin, MC, was given the honour, and after a fierce struggle, in which Lt F.R. Seabrooke was killed and Lt J.C.T. Welch wounded, they cleared and consolidated the factory area at the north end of the village and secured a footing astride the main road from Üdem.[115]

Capt Darby Houlton Hart, MC was 2ic of A Coy.[116] The coy moved off down the road towards the houses just seized by Z Coy and travelled during the morning by the Norfolk's D Coy. The enfilade fire [from Murmannshof] was still heavy and the platoons advanced in rushes using the protection of the ditch as much as possible. They turned down the Üdemer Strasse and rushed the factory building captured during the morning by John Lincoln and presumably later abandoned. Lt Seabrooke then crossed the road and was killed as he returned to report. Hart needed to communicate with a Churchill tank standing battened down and stationary in the road outside the factory. It would have had a phone, but using it would have invited a sniper's bullet. In Italy the NIH had a drill for slewing the tank to the left and opening the co-driver's door to protect an

114 Letter from Heinrich Kempkes on 13 November 2014.
115 Gates, *The History*, p. 252.
116 Darby Hart in conversation.

infantryman wanting to pass a message to the tank commander. The Churchill Mk VII Crocodile was equipped with a 38 set for communication with the infantry but, although the Crocodiles were ready and trained to communicate, the infantry were not.[117]

The tank Hart tried to communicate with would have been in Milne's 2 Sqn which was supporting the KSLI. Norfolk veterans also remember seeing this tank in the afternoon but had no contact with it. Hart went back to the corner to speak to the troop commander – presumably Milne – and asked him to radio the tank and relay a message requesting it to stay in position to support the newly-arrived Lincolns. It was while on this errand that he found the wounded Colin Welch. That night Hart made a quick jotting in his little pocket diary; 'Thurs 1st March. Kervenheim. Moved up and advanced down road swept by Spandau tracers. Got through to village. Left Seabrooke and 10 casualties. Spent night in burning billet.'[118]

The twenty-year old Colin Welch would rather have joined the Gloucesters, the Coldstream Guards or the Warwicks, but it was to the Lincolns he was posted, arriving on D+12 in the brick-yard in Benouville, where everyone looked ill and the mosquitoes were as bad as the food. He remembers many things about Kervenheim where he received his second wound, the first one was between Vire and Tinchebray. In the woods in front of Kervenheim he entered the dim cellar of a woodcutter's house containing seven dead and swollen German civilians sitting around a table, their ring fingers severed. [John Keenan, D Coy, 2 Lincolns, told this author that he knew of a member of the battalion in Normandy cutting ring-fingers from German corpses to 'liberate' their gold rings.] He believed there were many Hitler Youth at Kervenheim, which must have been true as all young recruits to the Fallschirmjägers would have served in the Hitlerjugend. The Lincolns had received a large intake of reinforcements from the King's Liverpool Regt. These had been given only primary training and pushed straight through. It was very difficult in his experience to make such people attack. By the time of Kervenheim the idea was gradually dawning on him that survival of the war might yet be possible. Larkin's Company was ordered off, told that there would be smoke to mask their advance from the right, but no smoke appeared for reasons given above. They were sniped at from Kervenheim as they advanced, but all felt it was safer to keep going. Welch remembers using a Bren to stop something, at least other people have said so, and this would have been the second time he had killed an enemy; the first being again near Vire.[119]

George Wall also remembers the Lincolns' intervention in Kervenheim.

> We were on a road and as the Germans retreated they felled trees across the roadway hindering our movement. The RE were ahead of us with their bulldozers clearing the road. We could hear a ruckus in front of us. We were told it was 'A' Coy well into the industrial estate of Kervenheim. It was being held up by German snipers and two of our officers had been wounded – a Lt Seabrooke and another [Colin Welch]. I remember Maj Clarke taking Cpl Spye and myself forward to see if we could help. As you know we were equipped with binoculars and a telescope. We were unable to help. What I do remember, we saw the biggest buildings I'd ever seen [the Otterbeck shoe factory]. Today we would call them freight buildings. From there we went back into the wood with 'D' Coy and a lot of Churchill tanks which were making quite a commotion which attracted a lot of AP shell that screamed as they ricocheted off the trees. At the same time we were digging in and the water line was two feet. The water was cold. I can still hear the ricocheting running up and down my spine.[120]

117 JG Smith in a letter on 18 April 2004.
118 Darby Hart's diary.
119 Colin Welch was a political journalist, satirist, and the Daily Telegraph's first Peter Simple. He and Sybil entertained this author to a memorably hilarious lunch at their home in Froxfield in 1984.
120 George Wall in correspondence.

It was at this time that Sgt Frederick Boothman won the MM. Firbank & Renny signed 5 March, Whistler 10 April, Horrocks 21 April, Crerar 7 May, Montgomery undated.

> W/Sergeant 4348892 Boothman, Frederick.
> On March 1st 1945 this NCO, normally a Carrier Platoon NCO, was attached to 'A' Company 2 Lincolns as an additional Stretcher Bearer NCO for the operation connected with the capture of Kervenheim, in conjunction with 1 Royal Norfolks. During the advance to the village one platoon of the company suffered several casualties from German machine gun fire whilst crossing an exposed length of road. Sgt Boothman with his fellow Stretcher Bearers went to the aid of these casualties immediately, although the machine gun fire was extremely intense, and he had previously been told to wait until the firing thinned. At great risk to himself, and with complete disregard for his own personal safety, he succeeded in bringing in the wounded men by his bravery, coolness and fine example to his fellow Stretcher Bearers.[121]

3 BID's G Ops Log records the following message entered at 2.05 pm from 185 BIB, which optimistically implied it was time for mopping up. It explains both why RW Thompson concluded the battle was won and why the Crocodile commander ignored the soldier trying to warn of danger ahead, as we shall see below.

> Norfolk not up to river and fighting in main sq – Enemy still in RITTERGUT – KSLI down to river and cleared wood 000387 but enemy still in wood across the river – Enemy in MUSERSHOF 982382 and HATTERSHOF 976373 – MURMANNSHOF believed clear – Lincolns are now passing through Norfolks to clear up centre of town, cross stream and get coy across second stream on main rd – one coy to seize high ground 985378 – Warwicks to move SOUTH and clear MUSERSHOF [at last] and in conjunction with 53 Div clear HATTERSHOF – BGS asked to give ETA 53 Div at corner of wood 968384. Enemy being a nuisance at DICKMANNS 009377.

The participation of 2 Lincolns was limited to one company that got no further than the factory. A hint as to what might have been going on is contained in the notes of the 9 BIB conference held on 8 March. In that forum without Peter Barclay, who was in 185 BIB, Brigadier Renny was asked by Lt Col Firbank, CO 2 Lincolns, how it could be decided which CO was fighting the battle when two battalions were engaged in the same area on the same task. Renny replied that the CO of the senior battalion commanded in the absence of any other instruction, which gave command to the Norfolks (IX Foot) who were senior to the Lincolns (X Foot). This may not have been to Firbank's liking, and the reason he restricted his involvement to one company, but this is conjecture.

In the original orders, 185 BIB was to be given strong Crocodile support by the Buffs. According to its War Diary, 141 Regiment RAC (The Buffs) had a strength of 58 tanks and 664 men on 28 February. 'C' Sqn was allocated to 185 BIB, and should therefore have fielded at least 12 tanks in Kervenheim. In the event they fielded one Crocodile and one Churchill gun-tank. Trooper J.G. Smith authored a book, *In At The Finish*, and commented:

> Would it not be more apropos to give 'C' Squadron strength rather than that of the Regiment as we never worked as a regiment. 'C' Squadron strength was 4 gun tanks and 15 Crocodiles although it seems only 12 of the latter were available. As we hadn't lost any to enemy action since leaving Nijmegen the missing 3 must have been breakdowns. The War Diary speaks of a

121 TNA: WO 373/54: Fred Boothman's citation.

> composite troop under Lt Carroll. In fact 8 tanks was near enough a half-squadron which was quite a usual formation for us and should have been adequate for the reported situation. The error, with the wisdom of hindsight, was the failure to allow for the mechanical condition of the tanks after 3 weeks of hard slog and the resulting high rate of breakdowns.[122]

The Buffs' War Diary entries show long periods of waiting for action and the effect of the faulty assessment of the situation made by Matthews:

> 26 February. At 1700 hrs the Squadron moved to area SE of GOCH, now being attached to 3 Infantry Division under command of 6 Guards Armoured Brigade.
>
> 27 February. At 0700 hrs the Squadron moved EAST behind the advance, being on call. They were not required during the day and harboured area EAST of GOCH. 'B' Echelon moved to GOCH.
>
> 28 February. At 0900 hrs the Squadron moved to a wood NW of KERVENHEIM and waited at call all day, not being used.
>
> 1 March. Composite Troop under Lt Carroll moved to support the LINCOLNS of 185 Brigade with 4 Tank Coldstream Guards. On the approaches to KERVENHEIM the leading Croc was hit by a bazooka, which smashed the front hatches and wounded the crew. The Troop Leader pulled near and evacuated the crew into his own tank, but on withdrawing his tank was also hit by a bazooka and Lt Carroll was killed. It was able to withdraw with the third tank of the troop to the area NW of KERVENHEIM. The Forming Up Point had not been reached and it was clear thro false information that that sector of the town had been reported clear. Total casualties 1 officer killed, 1 officer and 5 ORs wounded.
>
> 2 March. The squadron moved to Goch.[123]

Tom Carroll was fed the same faulty and optimistic intelligence that Brig Matthews was feeding up to Division. Carroll got his orders from Lt-Col Bill Smith of 4 CG. Carroll was motoring to the FUP to meet the Lincolns when he passed an infantryman in a doorway signalling a warning. Carroll chose to ignore him because he had not reached the designated FUP. Again the lack of wireless contact between tanks and infantry and the confusion that often accompanied the concept of 'in support' led to a breakdown in the attack, produced another fatherless family this time in Southgate, inflicted yet more head wounds and what was new, dreadful recrimination. J.G. Smith strangely blamed the map overprints, implying that nobody in the know briefed Carroll who had only the map to go on:

> I think the map I have sent you offers some explanation here. Mr. Carroll would have had the same map showing very little in the way of defences in Kervenheim and this view would have been reinforced by the intelligence from 185 Brigade. Anyway, I remember him as being of a 'press-on temperament' so a decision to go on would come more naturally than to stop.[124] [The map Smith sent is overprinted with defences and dated 6 February 1945 – three weeks old. In any case, the positions of the aggressive paratroops and StuGs/ Mk IVs would never have been shown, so these overprints gave a false sense of security. The overprints appear to have been made available only to the tanks as Cathcart of 3 SG showed this author the same one, while the infantry and RA had the map without overprinting.]

122 Letter from J.G. Smith on 18 April 2004.
123 TNA: WO 171/4718: 141 RAC (The Buffs) war diary.
124 Letter from JG Smith on 18 April 2004.

Firbank, the Lincolns' CO, recalled nothing of Kervenheim except the Crocodiles being placed under open arrest by Bill Smith.[125] J.G. Smith believed that:

> Col Smith seems to have had a rush of blood to the head that day, putting all and sundry under arrest. Perhaps I was more percipient than I knew when I wrote 'the Guards were slinging mud at us in the hope that some would stick (*In At The Finish* p. 268)'.[126]

Trooper Geoffrey Kirk was in the Crocodile, and remembered being arrested:

> In the morning the RSM came up with the mail. I received a packet of 200 Churchman's No 1 which my mother always sent to me. When I first joined the army, knowing that my mother would always send me something, I made an allowance of a shilling per day to be deducted from my pay, as I felt that I should contribute toward the cigarettes that she would always send to me. The pay in those days was 3 shillings per day. I always asked my mother to try and arrange for the cigarettes to arrive on a Tuesday as we were getting desperate for a smoke, caused by lack of funds.
>
> I wrote a 'field postcard' – a postcard pre-printed with such items as *I am well, I am in hospital, I will write later* etc and you were only allowed to address it, cross out as appropriate and sign your name – to my mother and gave it to the RSM for posting.
>
> We were due to do an attack on Kervenheim but there were only two tanks going in, due I think to air leaks on the trailers of the other tanks. This was the most common fault as the flamethrower fuel was pressured to 3,000 lbs per square inch in the trailer but reduced to 350 lbs/in^2 from the trailer to the flame gun. Because the linkage from the trailer to the tank was both the method of carrying the fuel and towing the trailer, the twisting and turning could cause leaks, which also occurred in the fuel tanks and the compressed nitrogen lines and connections which were under pressure to the much higher level and therefore more susceptible to leaks.
>
> For some reason Capt HCD Barber our usual commander was not on the tank. I believe he had impetigo and Capt Carroll took over. Tom Carroll was due to go on leave the following day and put a doll and some other toys in the bin on the back of the turret and climbed aboard. Tom Carroll was an old soldier about 40 years old and had served both in Africa and Italy before joining us in Holland in November 1944. It is possible that he came home on one of the schemes that started either LIAP or PYTHON for soldiers who had been abroad for a long period of time. I have a feeling that he lived somewhere in the Southgate area of London.
>
> We started down the road that led into Kervenheim – there was a high wall on the left hand side and some terraced cottages on the right – then stopped. I can only surmise that the Guards Armoured Brigade, which I presume were supposed to be supporting us in were not ready, as Capt Carroll kept calling on the radio to ask if they were ready. But the only answer that he could get was 'Be with you in figures one'. This went on for some time when Capt Carroll said, 'What do you mean, figures one minute, one hour, one day or one week?'
>
> In the end he said we have got to go in, so we started down the street with Lt Bottomley's tank [a Churchill Mk VII Crocodile crewed by George Steel (wireless operator), Bob Taylor (gunner), Chris Bright (co-driver) and Ted Denham (driver), although J.G. Smith stated that Ted Denman (sic) was not driving the Crocodile but his (Smith's) tank] leading about ten

125 Cecil Firbank in conversation in 1985.
126 Letter from JG Smith on 18 April 2004.

Picture K1, which is item 6 in Map 28. 2 March. Civilians leaving Kervenheim along Udemer Strasse. The shoe factory is on the immediate right. The British ordered all civilians to the camp at Bedburg, whether they were homeless or not. (© Crown Copyright. IWM, B15045 by Sgt Carpenter.

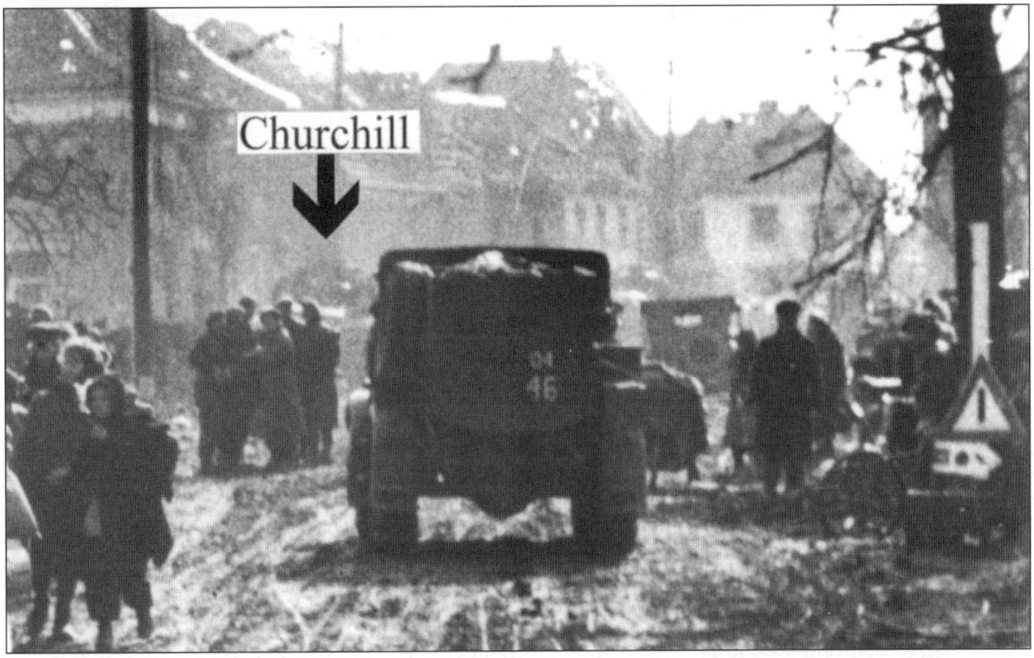

An enlarged part of the above photograph. A vehicle is visible beyond the water carrier with the tactical number 46 (20 Anti-tank Regt) and behind the group of soldiers. It was identified by J.G. Smith as a Churchill, and therefore could be the one abandoned on 1 March. It must have been recoverable because Kempkes saw none and there is no record in the audit performed by regional government in 1947. The picture is unusual and possibly unique in showing destroyed allied equipment yards in front of us [in Carroll's Mk VII gun tank crewed by Bob Cheney (driver), Jack Halliwell (co-driver), Jack Washington (wireless operator), and Geoff Kirk (gunner)].

I was Gunner on Capt Carroll's tank at this time. As I looked out of the telescope I observed what I presumed to be the leading infantryman laying down in the doorway. He was waving his arm up and down as if to say slow down. I said over the intercom, 'Leading infantryman signalling on the right'. Bob Cheney, our driver, started slewing the tank towards him. We had a telephone on the back and he could have given us 'the drill', but Capt Carroll told Bob to keep going. We had not gone far past the leading infantryman when the leading tank stopped about ten yards in front of us with a huge explosion. After what seemed like ages the crew got out and ran round to the rear of their tank. We pulled up near the men and Capt Carroll told the co-driver, Jack Halliwell, to get out and help the men into our tank.

I kept traversing left and right to see if I could see where the shot came from. In the meantime Jack Halliwell was pushing the crew from the knocked-out tank in through the pannier door. The Churchill tank was unique in that it had a door either side of the driving compartment. Before the Mk VII it was a square door as was the driver's vision window, but in the Mk VII all were circular, possibly for ease of manufacture [actually to reduce the chance of its jamming]. Lt Bottomley and another member of the knocked-out crew were on the toolbox situated behind the driver. I had to get down from my gunner's seat and bend down to drag George Steel through from the driving compartment into the turret compartment. It is impossible to come through from the other side of the gun as that area is closed off by the 'ready ammunition bin'. I put George under the gun near the feet of Jack (George) Washington, our Wireless Operator. I then had to get further down to enable me to reach into the driving compartment to drag Chris Bright into the turret. To reach him I had to put my feet under the commander's pedestal to get low enough to get under the gunner's seat to enable me to reach into the driving compartment. The problem was to squeeze between the tube of the gunner's seat on my left-hand side and on my right what I think was a metal box with ten Bren gun magazines strapped down to the centre point of the turret.

I had just managed to grab Chris Bright and started to pull him into the turret as Capt Carroll was saying over the radio, I presume to Capt Barber who was our rear link, 'It was definitely not a bazooka but a huge shell' [fired by Heinz Deutsch, probably], when we got hit.

I remember Capt Carroll falling on me and a packet of Churchman's No 1 floating about in the blood. They must have fallen out of my pocket as I was dragging George Steel into the turret. The next thing I can remember I was floating in the air above the turret looking down through the hatch at the chaos that was going on in the turret and all was quiet. In my mind's eye I could see a round hole in the turret wall and a shot was going to come in through that hole and straight into my back. I kept very still in anticipation but it did not happen and I couldn't understand why.

Bob Cheney shouted that he was not getting any orders, so I shouted through to him that Carroll was dead and he would not be getting any orders and that he should reverse until he could see to turn round and go back.

When we got back, I do not know how [they were towing a trailer], I could not get out. My feet were under the commanders' pedestal and Capt Carroll was lying on top of me. I could get no leverage to lift him as his body was jammed under the gunner's seat, and I couldn't move to the left because of the tube of the gunner's seat, nor to the right because of the fixed magazine box.

'Yossel' Franklin got into the turret and released the box of Bren gun magazines fixed in the centre of the turret so that I could get free. I then climbed on to 'Yossel's' tank as I felt I should warn someone that we had lost both tanks. I was not thinking or talking coherently and the only message I got over the radio was, 'Message not understood'. I remember throwing the headset at the radio and saying, 'The buggers don't want to understand'.

A Jeep ambulance arrived and took away some wounded but I do not know who they were. Some Moaning Minnies came raining down and I dived under the tank and I think if anyone had tried to stop me I would have killed them. I then climbed into another tank but do not remember whose and smoked two cigarettes in two minutes. I then climbed down and went over to the mortar battery that was dug in nearby and asked them if they knew where the HQ was, but they just stared at me, perhaps because I was covered in blood and going off my rocker.

I then went back to the tank and Bob Cheney and I fixed the harness on to Capt Carroll's headless body and tried to lift him out of the turret. But he was a very big man and we could not get him through the cupola. He used to squeeze himself in but we could not get him out. I had lost my pistol and when trying to get him we unbuckled his belt with the pistol and holster and I took it over. I can still remember it was a Smith & Wesson .38 no. 840481 and was stamped New York State Police. I presume he was issued with it in the Middle East and was part of the Lend Lease supplies.

While we were trying to lift Capt Carroll out a colonel in the Guards arrived in a Jeep and asked to speak to our 'Sunray'. I said he was in the turret and would not speak to him. The colonel said 'He will', and ordered me to tell him to come out. I said that he would not as he was dead. The colonel then said, 'You are all under open arrest for desertion at the front', and drove off in his Jeep.

'Dan Duffy', our Major, arrived and told us to go back to the fitter so that they could remove the cupola. We said we could not move as we were 'under open arrest' but Dan said that we were to ignore that order. We went back about half a mile to the fitters, one of whom, Jim Farrington, removed the cupola and helped us get Capt Carroll's body out. We put him on a stretcher, covered his body with a blanket and left it on the track guards.

I think it was Sgt Webb who gave me a drink of whiskey (sic). I then went back to see the MO because I had a head full of small splinters of steel shrapnel, only the size of a match head or a broken lead of pencil. The MO said to me that you don't need a doctor but a large magnet. He gave me some Vaseline and cotton wool to plug up my ears he said were damaged and gave me a 'chit' to put in my pay book which stated that I was to be kept away from all loud noises. The pain in my ears was so great it was like red-hot needles being pushed into them. That night I went to rear echelon who were in cellars in Goch and I remember Paddy Scallon going round and collecting some blankets for me. But I could not sleep as every time I seemed to close my eyes all I could see was three neck bones protruding from Capt Carroll's tank suit. In the morning I was given a new tank suit as mine was saturated with blood, both mine but mainly Capt Carroll's.

Capt Carroll's head had been blown to pieces by the blast of a German bazooka – either panzerfaust or panzerschreck. The blast was so great that it had blasted blood into the racks where the boxes of machine gun ammunition were stored. I heard that Jim Harding had the job of cleaning up the mess in the turret the following day and that when Capt Carroll's cap badge was found it had holes blasted through it.

I felt that I must have a guardian Angel looking after me, or the Good Lord was serving me for another purpose'.[127]

Geoff Kirk sent this memoir to his fellow veterans, probably in 1999. He said it was a 'clarified version' of a letter he wrote to Lt Ian Sutherland Sheriff in 1945 because in India Sheriff met Lt. Bottomley who told him he could remember nothing about the incident.

127 14414859 Tpr Geoffrey Robert Kirk. *1st March 1945. The events as I remember them* (Unpublished).

> I had three escapades in Normandy, one of which was with you [Sheriff] near Hill 112 or Estry when you came back with the recovery tank and a gun tank to pull Macfarlane's tank and trailer out.
>
> The other near miss that I know of was just before the end of the war near Cloppenburg. We were swanning along and as usual we had a couple of jerricans of water tied near the exhaust to heat up either a quick brew or to put the water in a biscuit tin to heat our Meat & Veg or whatever was in the tins for lunch. One of the jerricans got so hot that the can burst open. Capt Barber told me to get out and release the pressure on the other can as it was beginning to swell. We were still rolling along as I climbed over the turret to reach the can. I prised up the lid of the jerrican and the steam shot up my arm scalding it. I sat on the air louvre so that the air could cool my arm. I could not stand the pain any longer so I climbed back over the turret, dropped down into my seat and said to Bob Cheney the driver to pass me the first aid kit. At that moment there was a large explosion and the tank stopped. We had run over a double mine. It had blown off the air louvre I had been sitting on a few moments before. It also ruined the siamesed twin bogy (sic) and broke the track.
>
> Sorry to ramble on but it was when you mentioned that Lt Bottomley did not know what had happened to Capt Carroll when we were talking in Den Bosch that made me think about putting it down on paper.
>
> There are two times when I feel comfortable; one when I am with members of our Regiment or other soldiers, and when I can curl up in bed with my wife.
>
> You can throw this away anytime you like; perhaps it has helped to get it out of my system.[128]

Geoff left the army in 1947, and worked as a building site manager for Bovis. He had a stroke in 2004, and died in 2013 aged 89.

J.G. Smith commented on Geoffrey Kirk's memoir:

> When my book was published I sent Geoff a copy as Chairman of our Regimental Association. He rang me up to tell me I was wrong to give Jack Washington credit for turning the tank and getting it out of action – stated he was in a blue funk (which doesn't surprise me but I only reported what I was told). He did not challenge anything else in my account and as this was written within a year of the events I believe I can make some valid comments even though my part in them was so minor.
>
> Mr. Carroll had led the squadron on at least two previous occasions and if Capt. Barber was sick and Maj. Duffy was safely ensconced in his ACV he was probably the most senior lieutenant. According to me he commanded 2 gun tanks and 6 Crocodiles, but of the latter 2 had been sent back for repair (mine and Sgt Jackman's) and 3 left in the FUP with trailers u/s (a not uncommon fault as Geoff rightly says). So what went into Kervenheim was Mr. Bottomley's Crocodile followed by Mr. Carroll in a gun tank. Why Mr. Callingham in his gun tank isn't mentioned I don't know because according to what I was told he was following Mr. Carroll. In this it seems I was wrong so probably he was left as nursemaid to the cripples.
>
> It must have been while the Crocodile crew were being picked up that I heard Mr. Carroll talking to the ACV about the Guards' 'stoppage'. I never served on our gun tanks but I have a vague memory they were fitted with two 19 sets and this would have enabled Mr. Carroll to net to the Guards whereas I could not.
>
> Obviously I cannot comment on the scene in the turret described by Geoff but I find it difficult to reconcile some of what he says about the events subsequent to Mr. Carroll's death

128 Letter dated 15 June 2004 from Geoffrey Kirk.

with what I recorded. Geoff's tank must have got back to the FUP for Yossel Franklin to be able to release him and for Geoff to go to another tank. And I am surprised that even a Guards colonel protecting his back would be so callous as to put a crew with a dead commander in the turret under arrest without the minimum of enquiry. And where was Mr. Callingham when all this was going on? I have the most vivid recollection of the column of tanks coming down the road (IATF[129] p. 288) and of Mr. Callingham securing our change to open arrest so he must have been around. I am also surprised that, given our predicament, no mention was made of Mr. Carroll's crew being put under arrest as well, particularly as we were so exercised about it. Mr. Carroll's body must have been removed back at the harbour where we spent that night and here my account and Geoff's dovetail after a fashion'.[130]

This author sent J.G. Smith copies of the IWM photos of Kervenheim. He replied:

On the photo with Mr. Bottomley's (?) tank on it, it is definitely a Churchill with the nearside front wing missing (as most were by this time). With a glass the distinctive tracks show up quite clearly. The photo of the water (sic) tower is interesting. The Churchills are Mark VIs (cast turret and 75 mm gun) and I note they hadn't removed the centre section of track cover and still have the covers on their air louvres.[131]

Given the horror and fear Crocodiles provoked among the German defenders, it is not surprising that Lt Bottomley's tank was hit by a Panzerfaust or Panzerschreck. Carroll thought it was a StuG, but he could not be sure and he was certainly hit by a Panzerfaust. The missile could have been fired from a first floor window at the same level as Carroll's head and only yards from it. The infantry told the Buffs the next day that both Panzerfausts had been fired by Hitler Youth.[132]

J.G. Smith believed the Guards were out to get them because the Buffs had refused to take Crocodiles into the woods to support 4 GG, as described in the previous chapter. Later JG Smith refused to shoot the 14 year-old Hitler Youth who claimed to have killed Carroll. Smith's account of Kervenheim began on 28 February in Goch:

Steve woke me and it was still dark… We were on call to the Guards Tank Brigade so Steve said we had all better shave. There was a rumour that the Guards had it in for us. Capt Shearman was supposed to have refused a job in which they wanted us to go down a forest track and flame positions 50 yards from it. As for getting out afterwards, that was our worry. The Guards had had nine tanks bazookaed in the wood and our officer would have nothing to do with the job, on this occasion having the right to take that attitude. [Both sides were reputed to kill the crews of flame throwers, according to Brian Perrett. However, the only recorded instance was given by Andrew Wilson in his book *Flame Thrower*]. Word went round the Squadron that the Guards were really mad with us and would land us in a mess if they could – and they had a reputation for being good at this. However, no one was greatly worried…

129 JG Smith. *In At The Finish: NWE 1944-45* (London: Minerva Press, 1995), p. 288. Both page references given by its author differ by one digit – 288 for 268 – from the paperback edition of the same book owned by this author.
130 Letter from JG Smith on 18 April 2004.
131 E-mail from JG Smith on 3 March 2004 commenting on IWM photo B15076 of Churchillls at the tower and B15045 of Uedemer Straße.
132 Smith, *In At The Finish*, p. 290.

In the morning (1 March) came the awaited order to move. Having failed to hold Goch, the Germans were putting up strong resistance around Kervenheim, a small town a few miles to the south-east. Our task was to flame troops of the 3rd British Division into the town. Although reveille was put forward we did not move out as early as had been planned... The day was sunny and our route lay mainly through shaded woodland paths along the side of the scarp [north of Schloss Calbeck]. There were a number of civilians living in the woods besides carts piled with furniture, standing in groups to watch us go by, a dismal ragged collection. The men raised their hats, the women smiled nervously. They embarrassed me – it was not pleasant to watch them crawling even though they were Germans. Valentines of the 3rd British also stood under the trees. [Almost certainly Archer SP guns, a 17pdr on a Valentine chassis, waiting in case of a German armour attack]. We lost a tank at a very nasty right hand bend, where the road had been filled with loose bricks. ... We crossed the Goch-Üdem railway. The crossing-keeper's hut was pitted with bullets and a gap had been torn in the roof. A little further brought us to where an AVRE had ploughed its way through the forest, sinking deeper and deeper until well and truly bogged. It lay in the middle of the track, the muzzle of the petard lifted towards the sky. We squirmed past and onwards. Presently we were out of the woods and into a hedge along a beaten track. Across a ditch into a meadow. Then another ploughed field. We were half way across when there was the hiss of boiling water and the turret filled with steam. ... Mud had overflowed from the track, blocked the louvre, and caused the near side cooling bank to overheat. Nothing could be done save to scrape away as much mud as possible and wait for the temperature to return to normal. ... When we caught up our tanks were harboured in a space, part garden and part orchard, behind a burnt-out farmhouse [964404]. A dead horse lay by our off-side front wing, half buried in mud. Some infantry in a German dugout were trying to coax a few chickens within their reach. A thin misty drizzle was falling and some of the crews had spread sheets over their trailer links and huddled underneath... Ambulances and Jeeps moved sluggishly along the Üdem-Weeze road on our left. Towards Kervenheim a pall of smoke hung in the damp air. Shells whined overhead and all around the guns were banging away. Dinner was out of the question since the order to move might come at any moment. We sat and read ... and listened to the wireless. There was a lot of traffic between the Squadron and one of the scout cars, which appeared to be lost and a long way away.

At about midday we crossed the road and headed along a muddy track [Endtschen Strasse] towards Kervenheim. We were back in the woods again and sunk deep in the mud on a corner. A large Red Cross banner was displayed before a house half hidden among the trees. Then with a fork in the road and a cluster of buildings came the end of the woods and we were out in open country, driving along a narrow road with low hedges. The fields on either side were pockmarked with mortar craters and a thin haze of smoke drifted sluggishly down upon us. There were no more 'soft' vehicles to be seen and such infantry as were visible were well down in their holes. With the crump of bursting mortars we also judged it time to close down, as did Mr Carroll who was in command. He called up 11 Troop Officer, 'I wouldn't sit up there if I were you'. Mr Bottomley looked all around as if waking from a deep sleep and then sank into his turret. Ted reported that the temperature was rising, and then Jinx ... complained that the turret would not traverse. Peering cautiously over the side, Steve discovered that mud was again blocking the air louvre and had piled up on what remained of the track guards so as to jam the turret. Although Steve was prepared to take the tank into action with the turret jammed, provided we could still flame, the overheating of the engine was a serious defect that could leave us as a sitting duck if we had to stop to cool down. The FUP was a green and soggy field bordered on three sides by woods and on the fourth by a road. Directly we arrived we called the fitters over but they had hardly started their inspection when the mortar bombs began to fall. Steve leapt from the engine deck to the turret, tearing his trousers and barking his shin, while the fitters bolted for their Half-track. Chris Pye, the fitter sergeant, said he could not work under such conditions and secured an order for us to go back to the previous harbour in company with Sgt Jackman. Three other tanks were left behind in the FUP with trailers U/s, and the two HQ tanks, with Mr Bottomley's flame tank, moved out to attack Kervenheim. We had reached the fork and the comparative safety of the country behind when we were met by a scout car, coming up the road at a furious rate. It halted in the middle of the road and as we swerved into the field to pass the officer passenger jumped to the ground, shaking his fist and signalling us to stop. We complied, wondering at such vehemence. He was a perfect specimen, and I called Jinx to have a look at Colonel Blimp. Sergeant Jackman descended to meet the officer, who was standing by the car firing remarks into a microphone. We watched him shouting and gesticulating until Sgt Jackman, impassive as ever, returned to his tank and drew it off the road. Steve jumped down, waved Ted in behind him, and conferred with the sergeant. The scout car bounced away. Presently a sprucely attired officer came walking up the road and Steve and Sergeant Jackman went away with him. A quarter of an hour passed in speculation. The Colonel – from his complexion he could not be less than a colonel – was out of sight. Steve was the first of the two tank commanders to return. He looked concerned and our questions were anxious. He said that we were to stay put, as both tank crews were under close arrest for 'misbehaviour' – in other words, for desertion. We were first amused and then very angry. The whole charge was so ridiculous that it seemed impossible that even the Guards could have made such a mistake. We were out of action – as were most of our tanks by now – and had our orders to retire, so what was all the fuss about? Then someone mentioned the rumour that the Guards were gunning for us, and that while the charge was farcical no doubt the Guards were slinging mud in the hope that some of it would stick. I went back to the wireless in time to hear what might almost have been a sequel. Our flame tank had been knocked out. Mr Carroll had picked up the crew and was calling the ACV for instructions. A battalion of Guards tanks stood in a field outside Kervenheim, and their commander wanted our two HQ tanks to go in on their own. He had a 'stoppage'. What sort of stoppage? Mr Carroll was not informed but the Guards would follow as soon as this defect was rectified. Then I could no longer hear the ACV, but it appeared that Mr Carroll was going to attack without support. The wireless was silent for a bit. Unfortunately we were not on net to the Guards, for I would have liked to have known more about a stoppage that could immobilise a whole battalion. There were a few disconnected phrases from the tanks and then suddenly another voice, that of Jack Washington, Mr Carroll's operator, cried hysterically, 'My Sunray is hit – seriously wounded – dead – hit very bad!' Then silence again. I shouted to the other tank. Nothing more came from the wireless. Everyone got very indignant about the 'stoppage'. 'It's like misbehaviour', said Jinx. 'It's a polite name for desertion'. At this moment – and probably fortunately, for we were getting worked up – a Verey light shot up from a wood away on our left. There were explosions and the crackle of rifle fire, and smoke billowed into the still air. We all got into our tanks, reloaded the guns and traversed to cover the wood. I looked on the Defence Overprint and saw that the area was marked 'probably fortified'. [Hebbershof?] Presently we got news. Two members of the knocked out flame tank walked down the road and stopped to talk to us. They were in a bit of a state – pale and jumpy and spotted with blood. Mr Bottomley and his gunner, Bob Taylor, had been taken into a Field Dressing Station, but neither was seriously hurt. Their tank had been knocked out by a bazooka and they had all sheltered under the trailer until Mr. Carroll had picked them up. There had been ten men in the HQ tank when Mr Carroll was killed – they believed by the same bazooka. Jack Washington, it appeared, had done a very good job in turning the tank and getting out of further danger. However, they obviously wanted to get away and Len flagged a Jeep to give them a lift back to echelon. An hour later a column of tanks came down the road. First came a flame tank, then Mr Callingham's Mark V. Then its consort with the cupola blown off, Bob Cheney in the driving seat chain-smoking cigars and Geoff Kirk seated on the wing giving him directions. Two more flame tanks followed. They were all very surprised to see us. Sergeant Jackman told Mr Callingham the position and he went away to see the Guards adjutant [possibly Capt CCI Schofield MBE] and got our condition changed to one of open arrest. This allowed us to move. Everyone was furious with the Guards. There was a lot of wild talk about doing something – such as getting a courts martial which, with the evidence we could bring, would clear us triumphantly and ventilate the subject to the embarrassment of the Guards. Steve, however, counselled letting the matter drop if possible. The officers would stick together whatever the facts; the Guards Colonel was undoubtedly wrong and might have acted spitefully, but he need only say he was mistaken and we should be left with the reputation of trouble-makers. No good ever came of appealing to one officer against another. Steve had been in the army five years so his opinion carried weight. The affair blew over, and if we ever were officially released from open arrest no one bothered to tell us. It was dark before we could get back on the road and reach the Squadron, and the wind was getting up. An artillery barrage was going down to distract the attention of the Germans and my head ached dreadfully. I went back to the turret of my tank when the watch was over and I could hardly keep my eyes open. … Then Bob Cheney wanted help to lift Mr Carroll from the track guards to the ground. He sounded all in. 'It's all right', he said. 'I've got him out of the turret and his head is covered up. I just want a hand getting him to the ground, that's all'. I felt I had had enough already and pretended to be asleep. Steve and Ted went in the end, but not very willingly. In the morning everyone still felt bad. The dead man lay on a stretcher in front of his tank and although he was covered with a blanket his feet and one gloved hand were visible and it was nasty to see him there. Of the tanks only ours was fit for action. Of the men, not one was really fit… I was feeling the strain so people like Bob Cheney must have been very near the breaking point. … There was a lot of traffic on the road, particularly staff cars with stars all over them. The Guards were harboured on the opposite side of the field and had all got their best battledress with belts and gaiters. This only increased our contempt for them as being nothing but a bunch of bullshitters! Later in the morning, some infantry brought back a number of German children, boys of about fourteen and presumably members of the Hitler Youth. They pointed out one of them as having fired the bazooka which brewed up our flame tank and killed Mr Carroll, although how they knew this they did not say. The boys all seemed very pleased with themselves and the infantry called them cocky little buggers. They suggested we go into the woods and shoot them as they were escorted to Üdem. Mr Carroll had not been greatly liked but he was dead and there was a feeling that somebody ought to pay for it. None of us, however, would have been prepared to take up the infantry officer and soon the boys were marched away and we were glad to see them go.[133]

Andrew Wilson was wounded in the spine on the Meijel road and spent the winter in an English hospital. His replacement as OC 14 Troop was Tom Carroll, so when he returned to his unit, he wondered whether he would get his troop back. The difficulty was resolved by Carroll's death. Wilson described rejoining his troop, noticing that of the tanks:

133 Smith, *In At The Finish*, pp. 265-70.

> standing outside the troop billet, the old *Superb* and *Sublime* were battered and caked with mud, while the new *Supreme* smelled of grease and tarpaulins. Later he was taken to Carroll's grave near Kervenheim to pay his respects. Carroll's name and the names of some other tank soldiers were on a row of plain crosses, while nearby were crosses with flowers marked 'Unknown German Soldier'.[134]

Post-war, the body of 258165 Lt TA Carroll was re-buried in Plot 54 Row B Grave 4 in the Reichswald War Cemetery.

On the right flank, as we have seen, 1 Sqn CG and the Warwicks were stopped by StuGs, leaving that flank open with deadly consequences for the Norfolks. The Divisional G Ops Log for 1 March recalls where some of these SPs were located. One StuG and a spandau were logged at 10.05 am in a position 300 to 500 yards behind Müsershof between the Kevelaer road and the Vorselaerer Ley; 'Unlocated SP in sq 9737 shooting AP. Spandau at 982378 being dealt with'. At 10.50 am another record was made about the same area; 'SP guns at 972383, 974377.' At 2.05 pm, a message was logged from 185 BIB: 'Warwicks to move SOUTH and clear MÜSERSHOF and in conjunction with 53 Div clear HATERSHOF – BGS asked to give ETA 53 Div at corner of wood 968384.' At 5.50 pm Horrocks was logged sending a message to Whistler, asking him to get a bridgehead and route that night; and to ring back at 7 pm to Main Corps HQ; and to get the Warwicks forward that night and set for first light if possible. Also at 5.50 pm reference was made to an intercept of a wireless message from Battalion Grafing and Battalion Para Lehr asking for artillery support for a counter-attack at Kervenheim, and another request for artillery support on the road south from that place. These were taken seriously, but as always it could have been deception.

The vital tanks had performed patchily. 1 Sqn in support of the Warwicks was frustrated by StuGs in ambush behind Murmannshof, led probably by Deutsch, and by the conditions, but they and the Warwicks showed no drive to solve these problems and close the Norfolks' right flank. 2 Sqn in support of the KSLI meshed with the infantry and performed brilliantly. 3 Sqn committed only Melikoff, who was wounded, and no explanation has ever been offered for the lack of tank support for the Norfolks other than the conditions, which were the same for 2 Sqn. The outrageous behaviour of Lt Col Smith in arresting the Crocodile crews, together with the transparent excuse of a 'stoppage' affecting the whole of 4 CG so that no support was provided for Carroll, raises the question whether a mutiny existed in an exhausted 4 CG that Smith covered up when it was realised they had gone too far.

The woods where the tanks formed up and the fields leading directly into Kervenheim are the lowest land in the area at 19 metres elevation. It was raining and the tanks bogged. The only hard going was the road, and Humphrey Wilson explained why the route that later proved to be the only way in was at first rejected:

> We had a naked startline, open country entirely dominated by the village, and a long straight road, tree lined, leading from us to the village by way of an axis of advance. Right flanking looked the best bet.[135]

Around 11 am:

> Eventually, Lt Melikoff entered Kervenheim but was immediately bazookaed, slightly wounded in the face and forced to retire. The enemy defences guarding the town had been

134 Andrew Wilson. *Flame Thrower* (London: William Kimber, 1984), pp. 173 & 176.
135 Wilson, *My Morning Time*, p. 25.

> skilfully arranged and the weight of the machine-gun fire frustrated all the attempts made by the Infantry to penetrate it.[136]

Details are scarce, and the impression is one of confusion, lack of aggression and stalemate. The Lincolns complained at the Bde conference that Crocodiles were of no value in Kervenheim. Brig Renny explained that the commander had been killed and that Brig Matthews considered that a close understanding was essential between Crocodiles and infantry before the start of an operation. The Norfolks' History, as we have seen, complained that, 'the tank support was not all that it might have been, and that intimate fire to help us on to the final objective was not forthcoming at the vital moment,' and again when describing the exploits of Sgt J. Ming:

> During the battle of Kervenheim a volunteer was asked for to go back through murderous fire from machine-guns to bring up a troop of tanks to support the platoon. Sgt Ming volunteered and dashed back to the tanks. When he found he could not get the tanks to move forward he returned to find that his platoon commander had been killed.[137]

The frontal attack on Kervenheim was through some of the lowest ground against the strongest opposition. The map gives the elevation of the road where it leaves the wood past Nachtigallskath as 19.5 metres, which is 1 metre lower than the ground on either flank. RW Thompson describes tanks getting into difficulties behind Nachtigallskath even before H-Hour. Once the crust is disturbed and ground water mixes with it, the load-bearing capacity of the soil is destroyed. There was even a pond in the field forward of B Coy's section of the startline into which a wounded member of B Coy fell while staggering back, and was rescued by LCpl Dykes and Pte Bock of the Carrier Pl.[138] The infantry digging slit trenches described how they reached ground water 2 feet down. Rex Fendick described these conditions:

> There is mention of the high water table and tanks having trouble, but nothing can describe the truly impossible ground conditions in this area. Tracks became bottomless morasses with the mud a terrible glutinous consistency. And it was usually NOT possible to move aside onto unbroken ground adjacent to the tracks, because mines were thick everywhere. Tanks could not manoeuvre, as they must when fighting; they were fortunate if they could keep moving, with tracks churning and bellies scraping. My carriers repeatedly bogged and going half a mile could take hours.[139]

The infantry heroics took place in the presence of a discerning and appreciative eyewitness. RW Thompson was an established writer when appointed War Correspondent of *The Sunday Times* and War Feature Writer for Kemsley Newspapers in July 1944. He called his job, 'providing colour for Kemsley'. Thompson had joined the infantry in 1940 and 'volunteered for everything but done nothing'. He was commissioned in the Intelligence Corps and promoted Captain in May 1941. He had a brief interlude in the Caribbean, but in May 1944 was made Report Writer and Censor, and given responsibility for reporting on the mental and physical condition of the invasion army. He had a casebook with details on every Corps, Division, Brigade and special assault group, and even on many battalions, which gave him unique knowledge of the army. In May and June 1944 he

136 Forbes, *6th Guards*, p. 115.
137 Battalion, *History*, p. 82.
138 Op. Cit., p. 86.
139 E-mail from Rex Fendick in June 2002.

R.W. Thompson by Howard Coster undated. Thompson wrote a first-hand description of the battle quoted herein by courtesy of Mel and Reg Thompson. (Image x2194 © National Portrait Gallery, London).

had to brief the Commander, presumably Montgomery, sometimes twice in 24 hours, and report whether any units should not go on the great adventure. The casebook has never come to light. With this background and as a trained infantry officer and Brigade IO, he leaped at the chance of living with the army in action as a Correspondent. He said that he was determined to do the best by the common infantry soldier because 'I knew that he alone in the last resort won wars'.[140]

Thompson quickly lost respect for the majority of his fellow correspondents who never visited the battlefield. Some occasionally wrote as if they did by using a false dateline or, as it was termed, a 'magic carpet dateline'. Thompson explained that no correspondent working for a daily paper could go to war and send a daily message about it. Anyone getting involved in a battle would never knew when he would get out, with reliable communications available only far from the battlefield. Furthermore, while away the correspondent had no access to 'news' at the front, because 'news' was the 'stuff given out by Army or Army Group and passed by the censors'.[141] Thompson liked a cartoon in which the 'Conference boys' were shown sitting deep in their armchairs, doubles at their elbows, looking up at a grimy colleague fresh from the battle-field and remarking to him: 'You missed a magnificent hand-out, old boy'. Editors wanted the 'news' and reporters who had not been near the action 'date-lined' the report from Brussels, which became their effective front-line. What upset Malone were the 'think-artists' who retired to London or Paris and wrote imaginative stories based on their non-existent experience.

Thompson said that he had no need to cheat because working alone and with a weekly deadline he could range widely. He had witnessed the capture of Goch and visited Schloss Moyland. He returned to Brussels to file his report and on Wednesday, 28 February, travelling always by jeep, turned up at the HQ of 185 BIB in a farmhouse near Stein. He wasn't sure why.

140 Thompson, *Men*, p. VIII.
141 Op. Cit., p. IX.

> Over the weekend the pace quickened. Dusseldorf was closely threatened. While our troops were fighting hard for every yard, the Americans were racing to join us. It seemed almost a waste of time to return to the Reichswald, but I did, and straight into the battle of Kervenheim.[142]

He described the farm building holding HQ 185 BIB in a better-known book with the chapter titled 'All Quiet On the Northern Front'.

> On the morning of Wednesday, the 28th February, tactical headquarters of the 185th Infantry Brigade of the British 3rd Infantry Division, was established in an isolated farmhouse forward of the Üdem-Weeze road [incorrect; it was behind the road at 971414], and some 4,000 yards short of the village of Kervenheim [correct; 4,100 yards as the crow flew to the village centre]. The farmhouse lay sheltered under the lip of a shallow sandy bowl, and with thin rectangular belts of trees spacing the flat brown patches of arable land in the foreground. Probably because of its isolation and because at the last it had offered very little fight it had not suffered damage, except that it looked stripped and unlived in as a farm.[143]

This passage is part of a tidied-up version of an original diary of the battle of Kervenheim. We will use the earlier text[144] without the often inaccurate additions and glosses. When re-writing his diary several errors crept in showing that Thompson had only a vague idea of the details of the battle he had experienced at first hand. For example, he stated the Norfolks crossed the river when in fact only the Warwicks did this; and he said that 53 BID eventually took Müsershof when again it was the Warwicks. Otherwise his Diary accurately recorded what he saw, even his personal rebuff. Thompson referred to Humphrey Wilson as 'Charles' and to Cresswell as 'Spike', but there is no confirmation that these were real nicknames. This author's additions and comments are, as always, in square brackets.

Diary Of A Battle – Kervenheim,
by R.W. Thompson.
War Correspondent and War Feature Writer, 'Kemsley Newspapers'.

> *In the Battle of Kervenheim. Thursday, 1 March.*
> It's two in the afternoon. Masses of blue smoke veil the burning mass of Kervenheim from which the black silhouette of the church steeple stands out solid against the driving mist of rain. That steeple has been the cause of a good deal of our trouble. So has that house 500 yards away to the right flank. [Murmannshof]. It still is. All day the spandaus have crackled to strew the unavoidable piece of open ground with the bodies and blood of Englishmen. The Nazis are still there holding out fanatically and some of these heroes lying now on the fringe of the woodland belt will die before that house is in our hands. The Colonel has come up. He speaks to each man as he walks along the position: "Going better now, going along much better now. D Company are well in. You've done fine. Good boys. It's been tough".
>
> The faces look up at him from the wet earth of the woodland fringe, red boyish faces under the netted tin hats. The whites of their eyes are very white and their eyes shine. They smile up at the Colonel. They are glad of his words. They call him 'Two-gun Pete'. He may or may not

142 Thompson, *Men*, p. 72.
143 RW Thompson. *The Battle for the Rhineland* (London: Hutchinson, 1958), p. 212.
144 Thompson, *Men*, pp. 73-94.

know that. Peter Barclay is a man they have faith in. Some of them answer: "Thanks, thanks, sir", and say half to themselves, an echo of the Colonel's words – "Tough, yes sir".

They've been deep into the town and are glad to know D Coy are secure now – we hope. D Coy went in to relieve them.

High explosive is smashing into the woodland belt. "Get yourselves well down, boys", says the Colonel. The hot metal shrieking through the trees like hail is tearing men's flesh. The Red Cross private has rushed into the fringe across the road to get one man out. He's got him on a stretcher and now can't carry him. He calls to us: "Can you send a carrier, sir?"

It's an armoured tracked carrier he wants. Meanwhile someone helps him lift the wounded man out of the forest and carefully over the ditch.

"Easy now, easy".

Feet slip on the greasy banks out of the ditch water. The man's face twists with pain as the leading stretcher-bearer's water-bottle rasps his tin hat.

"All right, old chap, you'll be all right", and he tries to grin back…

How am I going to write this? How am I going to get back? We are being heavily shelled, and the track [Endtschenstrasse] leading back – the one we came over long before the dawn this morning – is now twisted to deep ruts of mud and great spouts of earth and smoke and flame explode all round it, around the jeeps skidding and twisting and bumping back over it with the wounded and the RAMC men standing shielding the men on the stretchers with their arms and bodies and trying to hold them steady while the air is thick with flying metal. It won't be news, anyway. The news will be going back now:

"British infantry have occupied Kervenheim against stiff enemy opposition. Our men are now clearing the town".[145]

Thompson used RAMC (commonly referred to as *Rob All My Comrades*) as shorthand for the stretcher bearers carrying the wounded from the field of battle to the RAP. These wore Norfolk badges, were part of Norfolk coy HQ, were often regimental bandsmen, and were trained to deal with casualties. The dreaded cry of 'stretcher bearer' meant someone was wounded, and they came running. The Germans left them alone since they never knew when they might be needing one themselves. German stretcher bearers wore a white poncho which was more visible than the British armband. The RAMC provided the RMO, who was on permanent attachment from division, and was assisted by the medical sgt who was a member of the battalion like the stretcher bearers. The RAMC provided the field ambulances which had units permanently attached to brigade as an ADS. These also had stretcher-bearer squads who would attend the RAPs, and provide the ambulances back to the ADS and field hospitals.

Thompson continued about what he guessed would be being reported in the press:

> Something like that, I suppose. I didn't know whether or what army headquarters knows about this battle, or what the 'censorship guidance' will be.[146]

The censorship guidance was actually more nuanced than Thompson would have expected. The Toronto *Globe & Mail* of 2 March 1945 published the following dispatch from Ross Monro dated 1 March and based on a handout:

145 Thompson, *Men*, p. 74.
146 Ibid.

> British troops fought into Kervenheim and battled to the outskirts of Weeze today as Canadians continued their bitter efforts to widen their corridor in the Hochwald against German counter-attacks. The Tommies were mopping up Kervenheim, 3½ miles south of Udem tonight after throwing back a counter-attack, and were fighting in the outskirts of Weeze, 4 miles west of Kervenheim. Canadian infantrymen and tanks are still held up in the eastern end of the corridor. Ontario troops fought through the Hochwald along the Goch-Xanten railway Tuesday now the end of the second day of General Crerar's offensive. The Germans are blocking the eastern exit and the road to Xanten.[147]

Monro made clear that the British were advancing while the Canadians were blocked. In the previous day's press briefing which is reported at the start of this chapter, the Germans were said to have thrown in 'plugs' where they thought the main threats were being made (the so-called *Schwerpunkten*), and 'if these plugs go, then the battle should open up again.' Monro would have been aware through background briefing that Crerar intended as usual to reinforce success and abandon failure, and these events on 1 March would naturally lead him to anticipate that if 3 BID knocked their plug out at Kervenheim and Winnekendonk and opened the battle up then the Canadians would be thrown in to reinforce the breakthrough. An unexplained mystery, discussed in Chapter 1, is why when this occurred the expected development never materialized and the Canadians continued to reinforce their failure.

Thompson continued:

> That's the last entry before an armoured scout car got me back to Tac Bde [which had moved in the meantime from Stein to the wood at 966403 close to the junction of the Üdem-Weeze and Kervenheim roads], and I walked three more miles over a piece of ground that to me is one of the richest experiences of my life, and finally hitch-hiked back to my communications over roads and tracks already churned once more to seas of mud since the morning rain. [It appears he had forgotten where his Jeep was at Stein, which was just over a mile from Tac Brigade. Instead of walking there he walked 2½ miles back to Division at Hebshausen and then got a lift to Stein]. Won't the weather ever be on our side? Won't the going ever be decent for these men of the infantry battalions who go on day after day, night after night, into battle to bring us victory? It's all happened in 24 hours, and every hour or so, sometimes sitting on top of an armoured car, sometimes in a tank, sometimes under a tank, sometimes crouching in a narrow slit cut into the sodden earth, I've jotted down the things happening. But it's enough for a full-length book, this 24 hours that has made me know a fact we all know – these men of the British infantry are heroes. They are the men, who in their flesh and blood, buy victory. You can smash from the air, pound to rubble with artillery, thrust through with armour, but always these men on foot, the men with the rifles and the bayonets and the steady slogging courage, must go on. Without them all else is vain.
>
> In the middle of the battle I jumped into a tank because there did not seem to be any other fairly sure way to go on living. The gunner said to me: "I wouldn't have their job for a pension. Compared with them it's a picnic for the rest of us. They're bloody heroes".
>
> *Brigade Tac Somewhere South of Stein.* [Wednesday 1359 Hours. 971414. 28 February].
>
> The Brigadier [Francis Raymond Gage Matthews] is leaning his left arm on the farmhouse table, with his eyes on his wrist-watch. He looks up: "One minute to go", he says.

147 Ross Munro dispatch dated 1 March 1945 published in the *Globe & Mail,* 2 March 1945.

> In one minute, two o'clock, an intense barrage is going to come down on a narrow front for 16 minutes. At this moment, two battalions of British infantry [Warwicks right and KSLI on the left] are crouching on the startlines two thousand yards ahead of us. They will go in leaning on the barrage as near as any man dare.
>
> The faces at the table are tense. The Brigadier glances at his map, at the red and blue lines and arrows and circles indicating our own and enemy positions, and at the objectives all named with code names, such as George – Albert – Crab. The Brigade Major sits facing the ten across the table. Both have similar maps in front of them. The Brigade Major is writing up the war diary – the 'ship's log' – of the operation.[148]

The Brigade Major was certainly not writing up the war diary that is lodged at The National Archives. War diaries are scanty and written up by the IO usually weeks and sometimes months later. They often contained purple passages to direct the chosen unit historian. 185 BIB War diary for the following momentous day, 1 March, reads as follows:

> Intensive patrolling during the night disclosed that there were very few enemy on the left of the bde front but that the right was still held. [This patrolling was not intense enough to reveal the Boemshof strongpoint on the left.] In the early hours of the morning 1 NORFOLK moved up into posn on the right of 2 KSLI. Bde Tac HQ moved into wood 966403. 1 NORFOLK on right and 2 KSLI on left crossed startline supported by arty barrage. After heavy fighting against tks and inf 1 NORFOLK succeeded in establishing one coy in the northern part of KERVENHEIM 9938 and on their left 2 KSLI also reached the village. 2 LINCOLNS who had been put under comd 185 Inf Bde moved up and cleared the village up to the line of the river. In the late afternoon 2 WARWICK advanced against negligible resistance to conform with advance of 53 Div on their right.[149]

These 143 words, some of which were inaccurate since the Lincolns did not achieve the objective of reaching the river line that day, are all that Matthews and the IO left to posterity to describe an extraordinary day. The Brigade Major observed by Thompson was, according to Rex Fendick, 'most probably working on notes for the Operations Log, which recorded minute-by-minute messages sent and received, orders received and issued, patrol reports and intelligence of all kinds received, SITREPS from forward units, and from which the Ops maps were kept up to date. The War diaries were supposedly condensations or paraphrases of the Ops Log, and units often attached copies or extracts of the actual Ops logs to the War Diaries as appendices.'

Thompson continued:

> The Intelligence Officer has his notebooks …
>
> There it goes!
>
> The most terrific deluge of screaming din is lashing over us. It makes us gasp. We are under the guns within 100 yards of the Bofors firing flat out and rending the air to tatters with the high-pitched vicious screaming. Behind them are the mediums and 25-pdrs crashing and booming. [3 BID's gun-lines were in the fields between Stein and Buchholt, 7 Fld Regt was at 9642; 33 Fld at 9543 and 76 Fld had just moved to 955430. The Bofors AA guns nearby were firing on enemy trenches to thicken the barrage in what was called a 'pepperpot']. Underneath this fury is the crackling uproar of the medium machine-guns all in the fire plan, weaving

148 Thompson, *Men*, pp. 74-75,

149 TNO: WO 171/4434: 185 BIB war diary.

the terrible pattern of din in the air, death and destruction on the ground ahead of us. [The Vickers machine-guns manned by 2 Middlesex were firing on fixed lines along the flank of the advance to interfere with German movement into the area being attacked. Rex Fendick wrote; 'The term 'fixed lines' is misleading. We were in fact firing on a series of selected targets, engaged by either Direct or Indirect fire, (depending on whether they were in view from the guns or not), their pre-selection based on Intelligence of enemy routes and positions, and between which fire was switched from time to time on a planned programme. Any other targets would be engaged whenever called for by the forward troops. We didn't use the term 'fixed lines' although it appears in various contexts as a loose generic term. We had a Zero Line, which was the basic datum line established for each position and from which directional switches could be calculated from one target to another'].

Not much can happen now for 15 minutes until this lifts. A Signals lance-corporal and a Signals private sit with head-phones and faces completely absorbed, listening. [They were on 'listening watch' of the wireless comms of the attacking units that demanded undivided attention. Germans would be listening to, or intercepting, the same messages]. The Brigade Major has a set of headphones and mouthpiece beside him. The Intelligence Officer has a field telephone. [Field telephones using signal wire were secure, and the IO would be in touch with Division].

The Brigadier begins to explain the plan. The Brigade object is to take the small German town of Kervenheim at an important road junction about five miles from Üdem. [Thompson was inaccurate. The distance between the centres of Kervenheim and Üdem is 4 kms or 2½ miles. Ross Munro above gave it as 3½ miles. Thompson may have mistaken the map's km squares for mile squares]. At the same time our right-flanking units are moving against Weeze, and the twin thrusts will threaten considerable bodies of enemy between us, and probe dangerously deep into the ever-thinning crust of enemy defences. This sector has seen the heaviest fighting of the week. Collecting all possible stragglers from Goch and other broken defence lines, the German commander of 7th Parachute Division has stiffened up his battle group, and is fighting furiously to hold in this area. [Thompson meant 7 Para Regt (FJR7) in 8 Para Div. 7 Para Div (7FJD) held Weeze].

"A lot depends on how the Warwicks hold on", says the Brigadier. "If they can get a bridgehead right off the mark the rest may be easy". [Getting the bridgehead turned out to be the 'easy' part. The severe reaction of the German counter-attacks showed how the Warwicks held the key but lacked the strength to take Müsershof].

On the small-scale map the thin blue line of the Muhlen Fluth runs through a cluster of farms and cottages. [Spelled Muhlen Fleuth on the map, German Mühlen Fleuth; Fleuth is cognate with the English 'fleet', meaning stream].It doesn't show at all on the big maps, but it's 24 feet wide and too deep for wading. Once this crossing is secured, the Warwicks will advance on the right flank, clearing the woodland belts and the KSLI will advance left. The moments the flanks are secure, the Norfolks will go through on the centre line and take the town of Kervenheim. [The plan was quite clear to everyone. It is unknown why Matthews allowed the Norfolks to attack before the Warwicks secured the lethal right flank, or why Matthews did not use his reserve bn, the Lincolns, to reinforce the Warwicks and secure that flank. Matthews was a pusher, careless of consequences, and climbed fast and far up the greasy pole as such people often do]. Each battalion has a squadron of tanks in support as well as the 'funnies', the extraordinary and monstrous armoured devices with animal names, Avres, Crocs, Crabs, and as for the artillery support, the gigantic pattern of sound blasting our ears shrieks for itself. The Brigadier is shouting on the field telephone. He is in touch with the Warwicks. They are leading 200 yards from the river on the right. The attack has gone in.

"Barrage lifts in one minute, sir", shouts an artillery officer above the inferno of sound, and suddenly there is almost peace as the deluge of din gives way to intermittent bursts of supporting fire. [The barrage rested for 15 minutes before lifting, which required a period of cease firing while the sights were adjusted. The RA officer, identity unknown, was from 7 Fld Regt RA.]. Two thousand yards ahead through the woodland, British infantry are fighting and dying. How are they getting on?

While the barrage was at its height officers were coming into the Brigade Command Post. One tall, well-built young major with a wide, smiling face and ginger hair, a large grin of a mouth.

"Good leave, Charles?" the Brigadier shouted. [Charles was Major Humphrey Wilson, MC, 2ic of 1 Norfolks. Many who had been out since Normandy got home leave during this period and some, like Wilson and Bill Banks of 2 KSLI, returned from leave straight into battle. Rex Fendick commented; 'Although the UK leave scheme started sometime during late Normandy, many men who had landed on D Day didn't get leave until very late, eg, March or April '45. It depended on numbers of vacancies allotted and numbers of men in a unit qualified by date of landing in NW Europe. Leaves were also granted for shorter periods, 48, 72 or 98 hr passes, usually to Brussels'].

"Grand, sir".

A burly Lieutenant-Colonel comes in.

"Hello, Peter", says the Brigadier. [Peter was Lt-Col Peter Barclay, DSO. He was 2ic of 1 Norfolks when in April 1944 he had been promoted CO of 4 Lincolns. He had just returned to 1 Norfolks as CO].

This is the CO of the Norfolks. They are going through to take Kervenheim when the Warwicks and KSLI have secured the river crossing and the startline. If all goes well, these will be secured within the next two hours. Then the Norfolks will dash through. [Already fatal confusion had set in, because securing the river crossing was not the same as securing the startline].

I grasp a chance to speak to the CO. He is drinking a mug of tea and munching a huge sandwich. "Can you take me with you, sir?"

"Sorry".

"If I can find a way, do you mind?"

"No. Glad to have you". [The number of vehicles in the front line was restricted because they were difficult to disperse; they damaged the roads; and were at risk of destruction. Those up front were there either for communications, for carrying weapons and ammunition or were medical. Barclay was in a Universal Carrier which would have been packed to the gunwales with a bulky wireless, a wireless operator, driver, personal weapons, spades, spare ammunition, spare medical supplies, camouflage net, and personal kit. Everything had its place and there was no room for an additional person. Thompson had his own Jeep that was essential to his work and could only with difficulty and delay be replaced, and which he intended to leave safely at Brigade Tac HQ. He never asked to take it forward, and would have been refused if he had. He now had a problem].

Outside in the farmhouse yard a young captain of the Guards is standing by his armoured scout car. [A small, two-seat Humber Mk II Scout Car].

"Are you going into battle?"

"Yes. I'm LO tanks". [The Liaison Officer was Capt E.R. Cresswell MC of HQ Squadron, 4 CG].

"Take me?"

"Welcome. Ride outside and dive in somehow if things get too hot". [There was no room inside. In the event of shelling he would more likely have dived under it].

"Thanks. Don't go without me".

Around the yard are three German tanks captured undamaged. [A troop of StuGs captured by Mike Carver's 4 BAB in 11 BAD early that morning in a now famous night attack]. The crews were surprised sleeping early this morning. It is impossible to assess how hard the enemy will fight. Sometimes he surrenders after a few shots. Sometimes he doesn't. A German officer has been found bound, gagged and shot by his own men in the wood this morning. [This information was in the Divisional Intelligence Summary in the possession of the IO. It is evidence that Thompson was allowed to read it but of course would not have been given a copy].

"It may be easy – it may be a walk-in", says the Guards officer. [Possibly more evidence that Kervenheim was never a set-piece battle].

But it has been mostly hard going on this front as the Nazis strove desperately to hold their escape route open across the Rhine at Wesel, and get out all the men they can. Meanwhile the Americans are racing northwards to meet us against a defence that seems to have disintegrated; the spearheads 'swanning' almost at will. [A common phrase of the time describing a semi-unauthorised journey, usually in search of pleasure. Rex Fendick commented that, "'swanning' did not imply a 'pleasure' jaunt. A patrol into enemy territory would "swan around" doing its recce job. I often went 'swanning', trying to find a unit HQ, or a recce party, or looking for an alternate platoon position, or…? In other words, it was a broad term to describe any un-planned, un-directed or un-coordinated movement, or movement NOT as part of an organized party or group. The trip might have an aim, but not a geographic objective." J.G. Smith wrote; "I still use 'swanning' frequently. We had another expression 'poodling' which corresponds to the current 'skiving-off', but this has not stood the test of time"].

1445 Hours.

One company of Warwicks over the river. One company at the bridge [Endtschenhof holding Pastor Coenders]. AVREs and tanks ordered up to river bridge. [Thompson is referring to the Churchill AVRE fascine layer or perhaps bridgelayer, which was not technically an AVRE. Thompson is silent about the troop of Churchills supporting the company of Warwicks and possibly already over the river to the west, but maybe not because the Mühlen Fleuth may have been too wide for the fascine. Rex Fendick commented: 'AVRE stands for Armoured Vehicle, Royal Engineers, and that in our jargon incorporated all Hobart's 'Funnies'. The bridgelayers were RE vehicles too, except for three on charge to 6 GAB. I never saw the fascines used to cross any significant water obstacle. Ditches and craters, but not streams. For one thing, they were brush and might float away! And an armoured bulldozer or a dozer tank could usually fill a crossing place better and quicker than the fascines, if it didn't actually need a 'scissors' or other bridge due to a flow of water'].

The thunder of the guns is rising again.

"You can hear the bursts", shouts the Brigadier.

The battle seems to be going well. They are seeking the soft spots. Asking for fire to be brought down on the enemy machine-gun nests. The guns are still striving to blast a path with masses of bursting metal, but the men on foot will have to do the job finally. An hour ago I was with the gunners 200 yards back having a last brew-up before zero. We were talking about leave … the one monumental grouse of the British soldier, the one subject he talks about even in his slit-trench ready to leap into action.

"Right! Off you go, Peter!" says the Brigadier. [If the Warwicks had been unable to cross the Mühlen Fleuth, then presumably Matthews and Barclay would have made another plan. As it was the 'release' of Barclay was premature because the Warwicks were unable to expand their bridgehead. So Barclay went back repeatedly for the rest of the day and night to confer with Matthews].

The CO of the Norfolks rushes out and his armoured carrier is away in seconds. I jump on behind the scout car as it lurches in pursuit. The Guards captain leans back, his body half out of the turret. [Believed to have been named 'Linnet', this was one of the superb armoured, two-seat, Humber Mk II Scout Cars, with 4-wheel drive and fitted with wireless, often called a Dingo. Cresswell had a rear-hinged hatch to stand up in. Thompson must have sat or lain and generally hung on to the tarped bed-rolls and camouflage net roped down to the flat engine cover at the rear].

"Call me Spike", he says. "Everyone does. I feel it's going to be good today" [This is evidence that Cresswell really was called 'Spike'].

We are bounding, lurching and twisting and skidding over the mud tracks rushing towards the battle. The Norfolks are forming up trailing through the woodland belts in single file either side of the track. We come to a clearing and halt for 15 minutes. That's where I'm writing this. (See map 21 and 22) [From Stein they would have gone north-west and then south-west over the farm-bridge and met the Norfolks around Babbe, the 'clearing' Thompson speaks of around 962407. The Norfolks would have occupied the same assembly area vacated an hour earlier by the KSLI. Turning left they were 500 yards from the Üdem-Weeze road which had been the startline for the Warwicks and KSLI].

It's 1515 hours. Spike shows me the layout on his map. In the woods ahead of us the battle is raging. Our men are kneeling in the ditches just in the shelter of the woods, and a line is strung out towards the battle. There is a kind of crimson mist over the woods. The flails are moving steadily over the flat open ground, a strip of arable between woodland belts, and the huge armoured vehicles looking like fabulous beasts with the rolls of fascine for bridging – all the amazing array of mechanical warfare moves slowly across us. Now the Churchills are coming in with the infantry. Red Cross men are close up. The shell bursts are sending the earth spouting in grey clouds. But this is not our battle. We are waiting our turn. Spike is making contact with his tanks over the radio:

"...This is Prince Charlie Six... Prince Charlie Six... Report my signals... Moving up to startline in five minutes".

Five hundred yards ahead are bursts of flame that seem to well up out of the earth like blood and hover there. The Typhoons swoop like wild birds making patterns in the sky with their rocket trails. [The ORB of 84 Group records the establishment of bridgeheads on this day at 003392, which was 11 BAD at Gochfortzhof northeast of Kervenheim, and 968393, which was the Warwicks crossing between Hoxhof and Wettermannshof with fascines. 'The FCP (Forward Control Post) worked continuously all day. The number of targets being put up warranted 100% of the R/P Sqns of 123 Wing reverting to FCP work. Weather conditions made air ops difficult at times and it was not possible to observe results of many of the close-support attacks which were made'. This was the penultimate day of all-out air support. The Typhoons seen by Thompson were directed by Division on 975376, 977375 and 979372, which were all on the high ground 2,000 yards south of the Warwicks on the Kevelaer road; entry in G Ops Log, 3 Division].

Spike reports his squadron ready. The CO gives the word. Out of the ditches the men of the Norfolks rise to go forward, half crouching along the rim of the woods. On our flanks the Warwicks and the KSLI are fighting hard. In the woods just off the road the bodies of 25 Nazi dead lie around one of our tanks. [Thompson was told of this gruesome scene. It was one of the GG tanks knocked out the previous day when it became separated from the S Lancs. It made a big impression, and was the probable cause of the friction between the Guards and the Buffs who had refused to provide Crocodile support in the woods]. There is no walk-in ahead of us. We know that. The colossal crash of fire and flame and spouting columns of earth is closing in on us as we advance.

Slowly the scout car moves forward over the arable.

"Always a good idea to keep in someone else's tracks", says Spike. "But I'm always lucky".

From this moment it seems impossible to refrain from saying "famous last words".

1600 hours. Wednesday.

Spike is leaning on the side of the scout car surveying the scene in front of us through his glasses. We have been here for about 15 minutes expecting the order to advance. [Probably at 969401, facing south. Thompson and Spike were watching the Warwicks attack from the Üdem-Weeze road towards Hoxhof and Endtschenhof to establish a bridgehead at Wettermannshof. They would see the Decker's farm burning, as described above by Pastor Coenders]. Straight ahead is arable land, a plain of about 100 acres, surrounded on three sides by woodland. In the centre of the plain is a farmhouse and outbuildings [966398 Volbrockshof containing Maria Raadts], beyond that woods, and to the right more woods, and woods again immediately behind us. Carriers are on the narrow road, and the carrier section are standing behind them. This road leads to a small village about 150 yards on our left [Aengen 973398]. This will be the axis of our advance. It leads to Kervenheim. The village is blazing furiously, having been shelled and taken by the left flank battalion to clear a way for us [C Coy, 2 Warwicks]. Spike has his squadron of tanks out in and around the village, and just to the left of the farmhouse on the plain, a tank of another squadron [3 Sqn] is covering the advance of infantry to the farm. A stream of red tracer from its Beeza (sic) pours lazily across in front of us. The red balls are twenty yards apart and are one in fifteen bullets, I think.

A terrific fight is going on in the woods across the plain. An SP has begun to shell us. It's firing south-east. [In the woods at 962396 firing north-east rather than south-east. They were being cleared by 1 Suffolk who completed the task by 2000 hr: Message 62 of 3 BID G Ops Log]. Spike is trying to spot it from the muzzle flash. We think we have it and give an approximate map reference to the artillery. We're getting the mediums down on to it. [StuGs were immune to HE from 25pdrs, but not from the medium 5.5 inch. Countering the StuGs was a task for towed 17pdrs or the 17pdr Archers, which Spike's 4 CG had under command. The 17pdrs could have dominated the plain and sniped the StuGs]. This is going to be a diary of a battle really and truly written in the battle. I'll try to keep it up… Ah – here comes a bombard, a vast creature of steel with its enormous mortar. [This was a Churchill AVRE of 284 Assault Sqn RE of 1 Assault Bde RE, 79 BAD. Thompson called it a Bombard since he personally recalled the first spigot mortars which were called the Blacker Bombard when produced for home defence in 1941. He probably trained on them. The AVRE fired a powerful hollow demolition charge nicknamed the 'flying dustbin", and was muzzle-loaded through the front hatch. The correct term was the 290 mm Petard Mortar. Fendick wrote; 'We called them 'Petards'. I don't remember ever hearing 'Bombard' used for them']. The whole village and the wood is crimson now and there is a slight gold rift in the dull grey of the sky. Birds fly madly as though caught in an invisible cage. A hare sits motionless…

One of the first of our wounded is coming out. He looks fairly comfortable. His face is grey, but there's plenty of life in him, I think. He's on the roof of a jeep, one of those double-decker jeeps of the RAMC.

Now here is a white goat running ahead of the section into the farmhouse. A great shell burst sends a dense white puff of smoke into the still air. The machine guns are crackling now like fire rushing wildly through dry bracken, and making an invisible but deadly barrier across a patch of ground. All the din and colour of the battle stays; it does not disappear.

The Typhoons are dive-bombing ahead of us… The tanks are moving across us in clouds of dense blue smoke from their exhausts. [The attack was coming from the Üdem-Weeze road to Volbrockshof and on to the Mühlen Fleuth. The action was at Volbrockshof]. The Typhoons are coming in again. You can see the bombs coming down in pairs. They're dive-bombing, not rocketing, and the whole front is a mass of smoke and flame. [A common mistake. The Typhoons were technically 'skip-bombing' at an angle of 30° to 45°. The RAF in NWE adamantly refused ever to operate dive-bombers, which delivered their bomb in a vertical

90° dive and were accurate. Skip-bombing was inaccurate, but the RAF referred to 'skip-bombing' as 'dive-bombing' to confuse the issue, and Thompson was taken in].The infantry are coming out of the farm. They've got seven Germans… [Message 43 of 3 BID G Ops Log was timed at 1500 hr; '2 Warwicks has tks over water obstacle 967394. They have missed some isolated pockets of resistance. 2 KSLI at 977399'. It is possible that Thompson witnessed a missed pocket at Vollbrockshof being cleared up].

"What the blazes are you doing, Tommy?" yells Spike. "Writing a book?"

"Trying to keep a diary", I yell back.

It's hotting up. The infantry aren't lolling around carelessly any more in the woodland fringe behind us. Two stretcher bearers are toiling slowly across the plain, the sticky brown soil is heavy on their boots, and after every few yards they halt and put down their burden. They must rest. They are surrounded by death, but they don't hurry.

The high fluffing of enemy shells is overhead.

"Get ready to move – we ought to move on now", says Spike. The infantry are crouching now in the ditch steady and ready. Any minute now our barrage should begin. We are all waiting keyed up for the deluge of sound, the appalling din against which we are going to lean. It will half-paralyse us, I think, but completely paralyse the enemy.

Now out of the crimson mist of smoke and flame and spouting earth the Germans come running… They're civilians from the farm… the old and the young… A man in the lead with a dog is stumbling, looking around him wildly. He doesn't know which way to go. He's looking back and coming half forward like a crab. The farmyard stock are coming too… goats and geese, bewildered… [Vollbrockshof? Endtschenhof?]

1700 hours.

Sid Bowman looks at his wrist-watch. "It's five o'clock", he says. "It's getting late". He's anxious. We're all anxious. We've been lying flat together in the ditch now for nearly half an hour. The earth is wet and cold and trembling to the shell-bursts and the thunder of the tank tracks. Suddenly we were in the ditch, as the enemy machine guns found us out and the bullets fled through the trees with a sound of heavy seas on iron decks. We are held up now by the spandaus. The bullets are clipping the trees above us. Our tanks are wheeling around into battle, churning up the soft sticky earth. Some of the boys are digging in fast in the wet clay. A barrage is coming down ahead of us in grey spurts. Something must be holding us up. Soon it will be dark, and the tanks will be unable to support us. [Thompson knew that British tanks moved only at night in very exceptional circumstances].

Every time it's eased up a bit, I've gone across the narrow road to 'get the form' from Spike in the scout car. He's amazingly calm all the time. He wears the ribbon of the MC and sucks his pipe as the muck comes over. He's pleased because the mediums are coming down on the SP. Our tanks are filling the sky with red and white tracer across us. Now it is just pandemonium in which men go quietly about their jobs. It's this waiting – this lying in a wet ditch that men hate. We do not talk much – you cannot probe men's minds at such a time. They will talk if they wish, or be silent. We've exchanged names, just this small group of us in the ditch on the fringe of the road.

Private Sid Brown of Tottenham, London, is on my left.

Gilbert Harrison of the Mermaid Inn, Hedenham, Suffolk.

Derek Jeeves of High Barnet. Then on my right within a yard Danny Freeman of Lowestoft is crouching, and beyond him a yard or so is Corporal Harry Morris of Manchester. Sid, I think, it is says: "You're lucky. Here's Tommy Atkins".

A young lance-corporal has come up crouching as he moves in the cover.

"You wouldn't fool me?" I say.

"Well the name's Leslie Atkins, but they call me Tommy", he answers. He's from Wallingford, Berkshire. So it is a fair representation of the men of England in this small group in the ditch beside me. I think they are heroes.

1730 hours.
Spike and I are leaning on the side of the scout car, and Collier the driver is 'brewing up' inside. He has to shut down the lid to get the pressure stove going decently. Spike doesn't think we will attack tonight. Obviously there's a devil of a battle on our right flank. [The Warwicks would have established their bridgehead by this time but were making slow progress against Hans Deutsch and the Paratroops]. The Squadron Commander won't want to go in without some light. It's no fun, blind in a tank, Spike says. I can imagine. Our CO is off somewhere having an 'O Group' with Brigade. An 'O Group' in case anyone doesn't know, is an orders group. Meanwhile a platoon are digging in about 50 yards out on the plain to cover us in case we get stuck, and everyone else is digging in in the wood. It's something to do anyway, to keep occupied. [A rare nonsensical statement revealing Thompson's infantry training was theoretical. Infantry dug in against mortaring and shelling to save their lives and never for recreation].

1745 hours.
The CO is back. He is standing in his slit trench that shields him just above the waist. His Company Commanders are sitting around him on the wet earth of the woodland, and I'm squatting with my back against a tree and a pad on my knees. The white [dangerous colour, and especially at night] roll collar of the CO's sweater and a red spotted scarf show above the Paratroop jacket he is wearing.

"We attack", he says. "The tanks will stay with us. Zero 1815. Right, I'll give you the word: Go or off, quite clear?"

The Company Commanders go off to their companies. I go back to Spike and the scout car. Spike is on the radio with his Squadron Commander [Maj Francis Holdsworth-Hunt] who thinks it's too late. He's coming back for a word with the CO.[150]

This was the reality behind having tanks 'in support'. If they had been 'under command', then Lt Col Barclay could have given Maj Holdsworth-Hunt a direct order to accompany him into Kervenheim. The ground was drier than it would be on the following morning when as forecast it was raining, so given the will to try they might have been able to cross the meadows into Kervenheim as Foucard succeeded in doing after the rain had fallen. Two nights later at the identical time of 5.45 pm, an attack with tanks at Winnekendonk succeeded. But Maj Holdsworth-Hunt was 'in support' and could appeal to his CO, Lt Col Bill Smith. He would have suggested to Lt Col Barclay that they meet with the Brigadier and discuss the matter, and by then it would be dark. The Coldstreamers seemed to have had their eyes on withdrawing to harbour, reflecting exhaustion and a traditional dislike of fighting at night without visibility.

Meanwhile we sit and wait in the din. The men are having 'brew-ups' in the shelter of the trees, and squatting down in the shallow slits they have dug, two men to a slit. Some are munching sandwiches from the 24 hour ration packs. Spike and I drink a brew-up and share a bar of chocolate. Spike curses some prisoners acting as stretcher bearers. [Displacement activity by Cresswell reflecting perhaps his upset with the instruction from the remote Holdsworth-Hunt that the tanks were withdrawing to harbour. Cresswell might have seen the benefit of

150 Thompson, *Men*, pp. 75-83.

> attacking at once but ran the risk of being accused of 'going native']. They keep putting the stretcher down every few yards. There's a dead Tommy on the stretcher. We hate them with a terrible livid hatred.[151]

Thompson was right that such a feeling was terrible. Hatred of the enemy is recognised today, and probably known instinctively then, as being paradoxically bad for morale. If Cresswell had really felt that way rather than just feeling uncomfortable by Holdsworth-Hunt's lack of cooperation with the infantry, then it could be more evidence of poor morale. According to a contemporary letter 4 CG knew it needed, and had been promised, a complete rest. But how would Thompson have known Cresswell's feelings? J.G. Smith wrote to this author; 'I agree we didn't hate them with a terrible livid hatred, and I suspect Capt Cresswell didn't either. He simply swore at the stretcher bearers which, given the circumstances, seems reasonable'. Attitudes towards Germans varied in these days before Belsen was uncovered and a universal wave of anger struck all Allied soldiers, leading this author's father to abuse an SS prisoner, but only the once before checking himself. This author has spoken to veterans of 3 BID, and especially his father, who have disagreed with these sentiments of hatred. They had a sneaking regard for the Germans and believed that in similar circumstances they would not have fought as well. The armoured corps may have had a different attitude. J.G. Smith stated that he cannot 'recollect feeling respect for the fighting quality of the Germans nor can I remember anyone expressing admiration for it. We would have preferred them to give in rather than fight'. Whistler wrote in his diary that 'The Boche is a swine in every way', which revealed contempt. There was a feeling held by civilians, and Thompson was a uniformed civilian, and certainly held by this author's mother, that Germans had brought the world to ruin twice in their lifetime through inate aggression, and that it was something in their blood and that given the opportunity they would do it again. Such feelings of distaste and fear could be misconstrued as hatred. Thompson, however, recognised the genuine voice of the 1945 soldier – stressed, wet, cold, lacking sleep and in constant danger of death or disfigurement, and never knowing if he was 'mark'd to die'. Thompson had overwhelming sympathy for him, but no word of sympathy for the civilians caught up in the disaster to their farms and livestock, which was caused it seems largely by their own side who were torching the farms to delay pursuit. Other formations, however, such as GAD did routinely set fire to farms to prevent being sniped from them, but those in tanks had the means to destroy a farm by simply aiming and pulling a trigger, while the infantry did not.

> *1815 hours.*
> The attack seems to be off for tonight. The old man is off again somewhere. It's growing dusk – what Henry (Williamson) calls dimmit light. Great spouts of flame leap out of the woodland belt as the barrage supporting our right flank comes down upon it. The spandaus are still crackling, but everyone is dug in now. The Spitfires flying the last sorties of the day hurl their bombs 400 yards ahead. [An attempt by this author to identify the Spitfire sqn by searching every 2TAF ORB in TNA failed. Some ORBs are missing. Hurling well describes the inaccurate bombing technique]. The great fascines, the huge rolls of mattress for bridging, are coming up on the armoured vehicles, looking like terrible, ungainly monsters. Fires are blazing all around the woods, and the light wind is fanning the flames in the village as we sit on the edge of the plain, waiting…
>
> It's too dark to write any more now. The barrage seems to be increasing. It reminds me of the jabberwock: "with eyes of flame came wiffling through the tulgy wood, and burbled as he came"…

151 Ibid.

Thursday, March 1st.

The next entry in my diary is 0500 hours on the morning of March 1st. I couldn't see to write during the night, and we weren't allowed a glimmer of light as we crouched in the slits in the woodland. I made some rough notes, rather scrawled across the paper, and simply headed "Things to remember". The first scrawl is: "O Gp under the tarpaulin".

The CO came back at about 1930 hours. By this time an angle slit had been dug big enough to accommodate six men huddled together. [The Norfolks remained in the woods 968402. Remains of slit trenches were visible in 1999. In 2014 most of the wood had been replaced by a lake.] A tarpaulin was flung over the top and supported on spades and boxes. Into this, ankle deep in mud, we all huddled. A hurricane lamp showed the map and the shadowed faces of the Company Commanders, the cheek bones high lighted, as they crowded round the CO, seeming a giant of a man amongst these youngsters. A decision had not been reached. He ordered another O Gp for 2300 hours, and a possibility of another night attack. [One can imagine the arguments raging at Brigade as Barclay and Matthews and possibly Whistler tried to persuade Bill Smith and Holdsworth-Hunt to make a night attack, while the Churchill crews slept in trenches dug under their tanks in harbour]. Meanwhile the cooks were ordered to bring up a hot meal in containers. Smoking above ground was forbidden. The rim of the small plain was now lit with the steady flames of many fires. Spike had 'whistled in' the tanks to harbour, [in the vicinity of Sophienhof] and was trying to have a flail tank towed out of a ditch. It was blocking the road.

At about 2030 hours the cooks arrived with a magnificent meal. It was piping hot. The CO and three or four of us ate ours standing around a Bren carrier. It was some kind of stew, and there was a mug of hot tea all round. It put warmth and heart into all of us. The men hadn't expected such a meal. [It is questionable whether the meal was unexpected. Battalions prided themselves on feeding the men cooked meals regardless of the circumstances. It was and remains the single most effective way of maintaining morale and making men comfortable in extreme conditions. British troops usually died with full stomachs. Thompson made much of these meals, but veterans have no memory of such routine events].

While we were eating, a staff sergeant came up to the Colonel with a batch of papers for signing. "They must go first thing in the morning, sir. The War Office insists". The Colonel swore and laughed and dived back under the tarpaulin. It struck us all as very funny: the War Office insisting on the returns in a wood at night under fire as a battalion awaits the order to attack. About an hour later a post corporal brought up a batch of letters and papers, and I crouched with two corporals in a slit trench sorting them by candlelight. No one would be able to read that night, and in the morning many would be dead. They would die, perhaps, with the unread letters in their pockets. [Unlikely; there was plenty of daylight in the morning before H-Hour].

At about ten o'clock Spike tucked himself into a woollen sleeping bag under the trees. The CO had gone off again and he didn't come back until after midnight. Meanwhile the most terrific barrage any of us had ever sat under screamed overhead against the town of Weeze about 2,000 yards or slightly more on our right flank. [The firing started at 10 pm, and is recorded in 3 BID's G Ops Log, message 65, at 2010 hrs from 53 Div. 'RADNOR at 2300 hrs. Div arty in sp from 2200 hrs.' The centre of Weeze was 4,400 yards distant, and the Norfolks were directly under the line of fire between 3 BID's artillery around Buchholt and the target of Weeze. At 9.35 am the next morning 4 RWF were at 934386, still 800 yards from the centre of Weeze]. It was the most fiendish din, and it went on all night. We didn't think any of Weeze could possibly exist.

When the CO came back just after midnight, we had another O Gp under the tarpaulin, and now things were cut and dried. We should move forward to the rim of the wood outside

Kervenheim at 0415 hours, dig in and attack under a barrage at 0900 hours. The cooks should be aroused at 0130 hours to prepare a hot breakfast, and this must be brought up in containers not later than 0330.

"Now get some sleep", said the CO. [This was the fatal compromise, and was no doubt based on the assumption that the Warwicks would be able to neutralise the Murmannshof/Müsershof position. Instead the Germans were at that moment preparing to counter-attack the Warwicks].

It was about 0100 hours on the morning of March 1st when I crawled under the tarpaulin covering a Bren carrier and found myself in amongst the other bodies. The din was ferocious, but I slept for about one and a half hours and awoke cramped and cold. The moon shone brilliantly out of a clear sky. I could see the dark outline of the men in the forward slits about 50 yards out on the plain. [This was the outpost line listening and watching for the enemy].

Out on the plain, around that farmhouse, there were night patrols, ours and the enemy. I walked in the woodland, looking down into the dark black slits. In each one two men lay huddled, facing each other, squatting with their backs to the ends of the slit, and their knees up together. They slept in their tin hats and wrapped in their greatcoats. One or two had got some straw from somewhere and made a bit of a roof over the slit, and they lay in some comfort. Last night, I knew, they had slept in much the same way, but not under fire. On the next night things might even be worse. So I stood a long time reflecting on all this while the sky filled again with cloud and hid the three quarter moon.

At 0315 the cooks arrived with the hot breakfast in containers. It was magnificent. A young officer beside me said: "Bet you never thought you'd really enjoy a bowl of porridge at 3.15 in the middle of the night".

Somebody suddenly said 'Rabbits' and we all said 'Rabbits', remembering it was March 1st; but it was too late. The porridge was thick and creamy and sweet, and there were sausages and potatoes and a mug of tea each. Someone said: "Well done, you cooks. First class". [A common way of expressing satisfaction was to say, 'Well done, that man!' This author's father, who was nearly killed that same day only yards away, used it to the end of his life].

Everyone had the good meal under his belt. Spike got himself out of his sleeping-bag, and we went over to the scout car while the men formed up along the edge of the wood. The barrage was still terrific, and the fires still blazed unabated, seeming to have closed in upon us. As soon as the scout car was ready and the engine running, warming up, I stood by the side of the 2ic, the Major with the large wide grin.

At this point I made an entry in my diary: "The silent procession of human pack animals. It is the infantry, the men who fight".

So they filed past, [they came out of the wood on to the road, turned left and headed straight towards Kervenheim, the centre of which was exactly 3,000 yards away], their faces framed in their scarves under tin hats, like visors. On their backs their packs and short spade or pick, their rifles slung. Steadily they trudged along in single file. As each platoon commander led his platoon the officer by my side would say: "Lo, Harry (or John or Norman). 'Morning". And the answer: "Lo Charles. 'Morning".

Then it was time for us to go ahead with the scout car through the burning village [Aengen 973398], the faces of the men dark and seeming deeply bronzed in the light of the flames. At the edge of the village an old man stood with his back to the road and his head bowed. By his side a woman of about 40 grasped the arm of an aged woman, a bundle of skirts with a small wrinkled face and taut grey hair above it. As we pass, these two women begin to stumble out over the fields, and about 20 yards in from the road a man is digging, probably burying the dead.

Suddenly as we emerge from the village to open country, a fight breaks out in the woodland belt about 300 yards on our right. The wood is lit with a mass of small arms and machine gun fire strong enough to silhouette a house deep in the woodland. The red tracer is hitting the roof of the building, ricocheting and soaring high. And return fire is pouring out of the house. It is faintly worrying. [The first wood is 500 yards to the right of their track about a mile beyond Aengen. Thompson appears to use the phrase 'woodland belt' of the trees lining the Mühlen Fleuth and amongst the farmhouses alongside the stream, such as Köttershof, Schneidershof, Weykermanshof and Renningshof. This was where the Germans were counter-attacking the Warwicks and sealing the Norfolks' fate. If Thompson saw this fight as he left Aengen, then he is referring to Köttershof and Schneidershof].

Spike says: "May be just two fighting patrols – the Warwicks have met something".

A hundred yards further on we are under fire ourselves, the red and white tracer winging across the road. Spike gets down into the hole, and I jump off to run crouching in the cover of the car. Everyone is doing the same, the dark figures crouching behind the Bren carriers as they move forward. Presently we pause by the burning shell of a farmhouse [Nachtigallskath, 984381]. Patrols have gone forward to make a recce. A company is strung out close in to the hedge ahead of us. Another company is behind us. I can make out the figures dimly along the line of the trees about 50 yards from the road. I walk along a line of men, and there is a kind of wonder in me, and a sense of despair to make you know about them. Here is one with the heavy cases of mortar bombs. Another with the heavy mortar tube over his shoulder. Another with a Bren over his shoulder. They pause and wait, and plod on, ready to fight, ready to charge with bayonets fixed, ready to die. I just want you to know about it. [This was unlikely but Z Coy, 2 KSLI fixed bayonets and charged the houses by the tower that day with Stokes winning the VC. Tom Read said it was probably the last bayonet charge in history. The spike bayonet carried in its frog on the belt was usually used only for spiking tins of stew before placing them in boiling water to warm].

0500 hours. Thursday. 1 March 1945.

I am writing now under artificial moonlight with my pad on the back of the scout car. The twin beams from the giant searchlight somewhere back on the Meuse I should think, form a gigantic V for victory in the sky, dense black between their incandescent white outlines, and the outer edges are fringed with purple light that merges with the lurid flames of the blazing buildings around the narrow horizons of the woodlands. [The searchlights weren't far away, although the location is unknown. The CRA on 28 February had ordered the AASL to recce a site near the crossroads at 984405, Tokatshof, and report back by 1400 hrs on 1 March]. A section of KSLI are sheltering in the roofless shell of a farmhouse, warming themselves in the last of the embers of the burning roof beams[Nachtigallskath]. The gaping roof frames the moon and the trees in a sky of scudding broken cloud, [the night before was clear, but now the clouds were building and by mid-morning it was raining], and the sky is filled with curious gentle noises, the noises of an unseen host shuffling, shuffling with the peculiar fluffle-fluffle sound, and moaning and whining in the many voices of many calibres as the procession of death flits ceaselessly overhead. We are going to dig in here and await the dawn. Beyond a strip of wood, beyond the wide arch of trees, is Kervenheim, straight down the road.

0710 hours. Thursday. 1st March.

We are under fire from small arms sniping us from the woods across the lane 20 yards on our right. Mortar bombs [being fired from Pastorat Strasse in Kervenheim] and shells are coming in all the time. We can sometimes spot the mortar bombs falling. We are having casualties, and the Red Cross men are running swiftly wherever the shells or bombs are bursting to bring in the wounded. We don't like the sniping. Every minute or two a bullet goes smack, sometimes only a foot or two away. You don't know whether the sniper is observing you or not, or whether it's just chance. No one likes it. It's a nasty feeling. [Some snipers would have been up in the trees tied to the trunk].

The sunrise is beautiful, the eastern sky full of feathery clouds stained scarlet, and now the heavier cloudy sky to the west behind us is the dusky colour of ripe peaches. A young officer has just come in from patrol. He's been right into Kervenheim. His face is broad with smiles and excitement. He is panting slightly, keyed up, keen. His report is clear and valuable. The CO stands with his head slightly lowered, listening intently. The young officer has located a platoon of enemy in a house, and several spandau nests. He has also chased some Boche. Suddenly the CO seems to wake up from his intense concentration on the story.

"Well done, Norman [Lt Norman Rowe]. Absolutely first-class. Grand work".

The boy is thrilled. He salutes and runs out of the shell of the building, in which we are standing.

"He's a good officer", says the Colonel. "He loves it. Always out on these patrols".

Note: I've had to cross his name out from this part of my diary because he was killed two hours afterwards [believed to have been a Pl Cmd in C Coy]. [The content of Rowe's report was not passed to the companies, according to Friar Balsom, George Dicks and John Lincoln, Pl Cmds in B Coy. They agree Rowe was an experienced patroller and of that rare breed who welcomed a task disliked by most but necessary in order to dominate no-man's land. Every battalion patrolled when in contact with the enemy].

A good deal has happened since my last real entry at 5 o'clock. We found a section of KSLI sheltering in this shell of a farm by the last embers of the burning roof beams. There were eleven of them huddled round the fire, some sitting against the wall in the rubble with their heads in the tin hats slumped forward, some standing. In the firelight the faces seemed like dark glowing masks of weariness. From them we located the KSLI right up against us only 50 yards across a kind of garden and small paddock in a woodland strip. Our left flank was secure. We began to dig in right away, and it was peaceful until the dawn. Spike got out a cleaning kit and polished up his cap badge and even had a shave while Collier cooked up a bit more breakfast of scrambled eggs and greasy bacon with a hunk of bread. Spike says he always wears his riding breeches when he thinks it will be a bloodless victory. He has put his riding breeches away, and is well zipped into his tank suit. I wish I had one. [Everyone wanted a zippered tank suit, and deserved one. Their provision should have been a priority. The German paratroop opponents enjoyed a superior uniform befitting their importance, but the cream of the British infantry was kitted out cheaply but with good quality like everyone else]. We feel uneasy about our right flank. There shouldn't be snipers in the woods right up against us.

At first light Spike whistled up the tanks, and they are churning up the small paddock behind us and on the left. It is very soft going. Two tanks nearly got stuck in a wide ditch with a tiny brook running through it 30 yards back. Spike is running out now into the paddock to give advice to a Tank Commander about how to come in best. His radio isn't working. A mortar burst looks to have missed Spike by about 5 yards, but he's still running. The shells and mortars are bursting all around us. The RAMC men are running to bring in the wounded.

Spike is OK. He's diverted the tank and is coming back.

Just before dawn we realised we should be under direct observation through the arch of trees at the edge of the wood. We've been working hard trying to make a screen and to tuck our vehicles round behind the farm shell out of sight. And everyone has been digging in furiously and fortifying their dugouts with earth clods. [Under trees the great danger was from mortar bombs bursting in the tree tops and raining down death, so slit trenches needed overhead protection]. The forward companies are lying out in the woods. The Signals are trying to lay lines. Spike is mending his radio. One tank has wheeled round into the small side garden in which we are sheltering. So now there is one armoured carrier, Spike's scout car, a tank and about 5 dugouts. It's as well to have these shelter spots in view.

0750 hours.

It's getting hot round here. This mortaring is getting casualties all the time, and every 15 minutes or so there are masses of bursts all round us – I mean within a few yards. The Red Cross men are magnificent. Wherever the bursts are thickest they run. A corporal rallies them and leads them getting the wounded out of the woods from the tree-bursts, and the jeeps rush back over the dangerous piece of road.

We are going to attack at 0900 right up against a barrage. One company goes in on the right [A Coy], another centre [C Coy], another left [B Coy], one company in reserve [D Coy]. The tanks will go along by the back gardens of the houses, and the troops clearing and winkling down the streets.[Interesting evidence that the tanks fully intended to be up with the infantry, but instead became bogged, or did not risk bogging in full view of the enemy and Merdian's Mk IV].

0825 hours.

Our guns are ranging, filling the air overhead with the whines, moans, whispers and gentle fluffle-fluffle-fluffle.

0840 hours.

The barrage is coming down ahead of us. Nothing like the racket under the guns, but an ominous noise as the hundreds of bursts begin to turn the township of Kervenheim into rubble.

"There won't be a decent billet in all Germany if we go on like this", says a Tommy by my side.

At 0900 hours the barrage will lift 200 yards and a further 200 yards every 8 minutes for 24 minutes (see Map 25). [Venus Barrage. It actually lasted 56 minutes as it advanced 1,400 yards in increments of 200 yards every 8 minutes]. The tanks are drawn up behind us. Everyone ready …

1100 hours.

Very hard going. Two tanks bogged down. Twenty men are struggling back, all that remains of the right flank company. [This was A Company which attacked Murmannshof. It suggests that Thompson was on the right of the wood at that time]. It's been hell, and it is hell. SPs and mortars are smashing down on us all the time. I'm writing now leaning on the front ledge of the reserve tank. The snipers are still sniping. A crash of tree bursts on the edge of the woodland has just shattered the whole rim of the forest. The Red Cross men are rushing across. A German has just run out of the wood slightly to the right. He falls with his hands up. A corporal is running to pick him up – our Red Cross corporal I mean. The shells and mortar bombs are bursting all around him. He drags the wounded German in … He's at my feet, blood welling up out of his chest over his shirt. He's cursing, but the blood is frothing in his mouth. He will die in a minute. One of his own men has shot him for trying to surrender. [Interesting, but Thompson gives no reason to conclude the man was shot by his own side].

Spike gives me the earphones. Two tanks are bogged down. They can't give the infantry proper support. They are 500 yards behind them. There's terrific spandau fire coming from a group of farms called Muserhof (sic) about 500 yards away on the right flank with a clear field of fire across the open ground in front of Kervenheim. [Müsershof lay behind Murmannshof on the other side of the Mühlen Fleuth]. I can hear the guns firing in the tanks.

"You're right flank's awfully bare..."

1200 hours.

So we lost our OP tank. [The one Melikoff saw go into Kervenheim where the commander was sniped through the head. The site of its destruction is unknown]. But the infantry of the Royal Norfolks have gone in again for about the third time and they are staying in. It's been inferno this last two hours. It has been impossible to write more than an odd note. I have never seen such heroism as that of the RAMC men. Every few minutes they came in slowly under terrific fire, sometimes with walking wounded, an RAMC man in the middle with the arms of two Tommies round his neck. Sometimes coming slowly and carefully with their stretchers, and then on the armoured carriers rushing back over a few hundred yards of heavily shelled road with their bodies protecting the wounded and their arms holding them steady.

It began to rain an hour ago. Another hour of this and tanks will be quite useless.

"A fearful stonking", says Spike.

I have found myself flat on the ground or crouching behind a tank, or a scout car, and twice right out in the open with the air full of vicious flying metal, and always looking into somebody's face. Curious. You don't believe in your own immunity any more. It just disappears in some conditions. Faces are always flaming red bronze, very dark, and the whites of the eyes shine. Perhaps that order about wait till you see the whites of their eyes was because of this. The signal wires have several times got caught in the tank tracks and the phones been pulled away. Rushing out to hold the wires and disentangle them is one of the ways you get caught in the open. [Telephone lines were necessary because wireless sets had restricted range and were insecure].

The faces of some of the boys coming in are indelible on my mind. A boy, red face wide eyed with a kind of wonder under his tin hat, a kind of reproach. Poor kid. His legs are all shot up, but he's dragging along with one of these RAMC heroes. The other boy on the other side is pale, white, ginger-haired. His arm is in a mess. A young officer comes in half-hopping. "It's going OK now".

"Are you hit?"

"Only a bit of stuff in the thigh".

He's going back to battle. [Unfortunately John Lincoln, the young officer, did not return for two months – see above].

From the forward edge of the wood I look over the smoke and the flame veiling Kervenheim. We've got two companies well in now, and have left the right flank for the moment. The buildings of Muserhof (sic) from which the deadly fire came are half-veiled in the driving mist of rain. The tower of Kervenheim church stands out from rich billowing clouds of blue smoke shot with flame.

A Tommy on a Bren says: "B Company lost all its officers... How many came back, d'you know?" [This rumour was untrue].

"I counted twenty", I said.

A Tommy is coming back with two prisoners with hands clasped behind their heads. We've had about thirty during the morning, some sullen, some talkative, all dangerous. It's been a terrible battle. It still is. Along the road the RAMC men are working with that steady, wonderful, unhurried calm that gives hope and confidence to smitten men. Here's a man face down on a stretcher. The corporal has cut his trousers away from his wounds.

The shell bursts are scattering the trees worse than ever. [The source of this shellfire was known, but 2 TAF was unable in the conditions, or because of inaccuracy, or unwilling because of losses, or because of lack of communication, to silence it]. There were six wounded in that last burst. Right in the midst of it the RAMC men working calmly, and the armoured carriers swoop and swerve back towards safety.

1300 hours.

I got inside a tank. The Tank Commander put his head out of the turret and said: "Come inside". So I went inside. There did not seem to be much future in being outside. But I'm outside again now to write the last bit. The battle is won, but we're under shell and mortar fire. [Around the time Thompson was writing this, Stokes was winning the VC. The battle was in fact far from having been won, but this was the optimistic conclusion at Brigade]. Guardsman Richard Clark is looking at me out of the narrow slot of his window in the tank driver's seat. By his side is Guardsman Norman Wright. We've just got rather intimate this morning. When things have been very rough and I've been keeping company with the underside of this tank we've shouted pleasantries at each other, such as: "If I have to go forward I'll think of you".

"Oh, thanks awfully. Drop a line to the wife and kids".

There he is now grinning out of his 'safe deposit' window, but the men inside this tank have left no doubt in my mind about the opinion of the infantry. These infantry are heroes. We all know that. They go in on their feet.

The CO is coming along. He looks tired. I'm going with him to look at things.

1430 hours.

The CO had a word for everyone.

"Well done ... well done", to a kid bringing back two prisoners. "First class" to the remnants of one company momentarily in reserve. "Thanks ... Thanks".

It's still damned dangerous here, but the Norfolks have won Kervenheim. "We'll sit on the river line all night", says the CO. "Another rotten night".

I say good-bye and shake hands. Spike is ordering up some SP guns. They are passing us now. Lovely craft, lovely-looking things. [M10 3 inch SP anti-tank guns of 198 Battery, 73 Anti-Tank Regiment RA, 2 Army attached to 3 BID].[152]

"Take care of yourself", says Spike.

The Brigadier is coming up, and the Colonel of the relieving battalion. [Cecil Firbank of 2 Lincolns, who were not relieving but reinforcing the Norfolks. Their task was to clear Kervenheim, and then take Winnekendonk. The CO of 2 KSLI was Daly]. The Colonel of the KSLI is here now, too. Another 'O Group', another battle, another night.

I know I've forgotten lots of important things. There were two more barrages after the first one. It's been inferno all the time, anyway, and men dying and facing death bravely all the time. Yet I believe it will all be in my mind forever, and slowly bits will come to the surface. I would like to give you a hundred pictures of heroes I've seen this morning. I'm going out in a minute lying on the back of an armoured car the way I came in. The RAMC men are doing it all the time with the shells bursting all around them... An officer, weary-eyed, shook hands just as I left. "We won", he said. "We always do".

To which I would like to say: "Amen. Thank God and the infantry".

152 http://www.ra39-45.pwp.blueyonder.co.uk/atk/page30.html.

Kervenheim was typical of the worst battles of the Reichswald forest. From the moment of crossing the Maas the infantry had a gruelling slog in appalling weather conditions. It was as hard as anything in the war. It was mostly underwritten because the 'big picture' showed a defeated enemy, disintegrating in places so that the Americans were 'swanning' in a spectacular manner. Battles like Kervenheim were not spectacular and they were not 'News'.

I had to trudge back to find 3rd British Division about 6 miles from Brigade Tac, which had moved up into the wood where we had spent the night. [Brigade Tac had moved, but his Jeep was where he had left it; 3.5 kms away in Stein. Thompson walked 6 kms (not miles) to 3 BID's Main HQ in Hebdhausen 944445 and presumably got a lift from there to Stein, a journey of 4 kms. Cuijk, where Thompson was lodging, was 40 kms away. Div Tac HQ had already moved to Stein at 8 am that day, according to the War Diary]. When I got back to my village in Cuick, just across the river in Holland, I wrote the first part and got it away that night with X,Y,Z for battalions. We weren't allowed to name battalions at that time until ages after the event. It was one of the things we Correspondents fought for, and was always a sore point with the men.

I thought it would be a waste of time to write the rest of the story, but I got down to it and typed from my grimy and very muddy notes. I got fed up with 'X,Y,Z' and left it to the censors. The next thing I knew was that the Chief Censor had passed the whole story and rushed it through without a cut. I think that was the first time that regiments were credited without delay.

It was worth doing. My editor liked it, and the troops appreciated it. But a Daily man might well have been sacked for incompetence had he lost himself for several days, and sent back this kind of stuff. From start to finish it was a week's work and not a line of 'News'. And the story itself illustrates the difficulty of getting to a battle even given the best will in the world. You have to arrive at the right Brigade at the right time, and there is no certain way of knowing. You might live with a Brigade for a whole week and nothing happen.

Brian (sic) de Grineau did one or two drawings from this script, and cabled his office to give me acknowledgement. They used the drawings.[153]

No drawing by Bryan de Grineau of this action was published in *The Illustrated London News*, and he was never, it seems, at Kervenheim. At this time he was illustrating the night attack of 11 BAD across the railway and along the Üdem-Kervenheim road at approximately 990413 when Stein was captured, and he had not been there. He dated it 2 March, but the action took place on the night of 26/27 February. The scene was close to Bde TacHQ where Thompson first joined Matthews. Thompson berated the correspondents for date-lining stories from battles they had not seen, but Bryan de Grineau was drawing battles he had not seen. He was not always accurate, annoying 6 GAB by drawing them in Sherman tanks during the attack on Appelhülsen near Münster that was published on 2 April. It shows dismounted figures labelled 'Scots Guards from Churchill tanks ready to advance'. The magazine misleadingly stated that their Special Artist accompanied the spearhead.

After surviving all day unscathed, and after Thompson had departed, Cresswell's Humber was hit at 6 pm by AP when parked outside the Norfolk's bn HQ at Nachtigallskath. StuGs were still operating freely from behind Müsershof. Cresswell was wounded in the foot but Collier, his driver, lost a foot.

At 5.45 pm as the light was going, Bob Littlar in 'W' Company was still entrenched in the field next to the Tower. He saw a medical half-track parked by the tower and then three Shermans

153 Thompson, *Men*, pp. 83-94.

arrived to evacuate the wounded. These must have been from the neighbouring 3/4 County of London Yeomanry in 11 BAD giving assistance.

At 4.15 pm, 53 BID was reported to be south of Kervenheim at 970374, and with the British now in Kervenheim in strength the Germans had to decide whether to withdraw or to counter-attack. At 6.40 pm a heavy British stonk was put down 500 yards south of the river in Kervenheim to dissuade the Germans.[154] During the night 3 CID and 53 BID were asked to agree to 3 Divisional artillery shoots on points southeast and southwest of Kervenheim at 998377, 976376 and 977374. So the eventful day wound down as the Norfolks collected their dead.

Sgt Joe Collinson of 2 Lincolns went into Kervenheim the next day, 2 March:

> The following day began with two companies of Lincolns being detailed to clear the village of Kervenheim. As we advanced we came to what appeared to be floodwater with barbed wire in front. Laid on the wire were three members of the Norfolk Regt. [evidence perhaps of the extent of B or C Coys' penetration into the centre before being counter-attacked].[155]

Maj Leslie Colvin, 2ic 2 Lincolns, also saw dead Norfolks and tried to hurry his battalion past. He was critical of the fact they were placed so untidily, with apparent disrespect and in overwhelming numbers, and worried about the effect on the morale of the Lincolns advancing to contact at Winnekendonk.[156] Two villagers spoke later of the same terrible sight.

> Two old townspeople told me at the Norfolks' Memorial in March, 1965 on the occasion of the 20th anniversary of the battle, that on 1 (or 2) March 1945 they had seen the bodies of 42 members of the Royal Norfolk Regiment placed together in rows on the edge of the Murmannstrasse cemetery, where they had been placed after being brought in from the battlefield. The two added emotionally that they had never before or since seen such a moving and saddening sight. One of them told me that he was present when the bodies were buried in the north-east section of the cemetery, and that years later he saw them exhumed for reburial in the Reichswald war cemetery.[157]

On 2 March the whole of 185 BIB congregated in and around Kervenheim, and Bolo Whistler moved Tac Div from Stein into Schloss Kervenheim.

Frau Käthe Schmitz described the events of 1 March on two separate occasions, and her accounts are here combined:

> I was 20 years old in March 1945. My parents decided to remain with their four daughters aged 11, 13, 18 and 20 (our brother had been called up in 1944 at the age of 17), in our home at 34 Schloßstraße south of the Fleuth in Kervenheim, and let the Front pass over us so to speak. My father rejected every call by the German soldiers to leave the area, and we feared for our lives when they said the English soldiers would shoot us all when they arrived. That was the reason why those who lived on Üdemer Straße left their homes on 1 March and were captured. [A surprising piece of information, and a local initiative. No one, even Goebbels, claimed the Anglo-Canadian soldiers were murdering civilians because they would not have been believed. All knew the Russians did so after the press published photographs taken of

154 Logged by G Ops at 1845 hours.
155 Letter from Joe Collinson.
156 Leslie Colvin reminiscing at Kervenheim during a visit in 1994.
157 Letter from Bernhard Meiners on 11 February 1997.

Picture K4 which is item 9 in Map 28. HQ vehicles of 1 Norfolks surrounding a horse-drawn seeder in the courtyard of the Kervenheimer Schloss on March 2. (© John Lincoln)

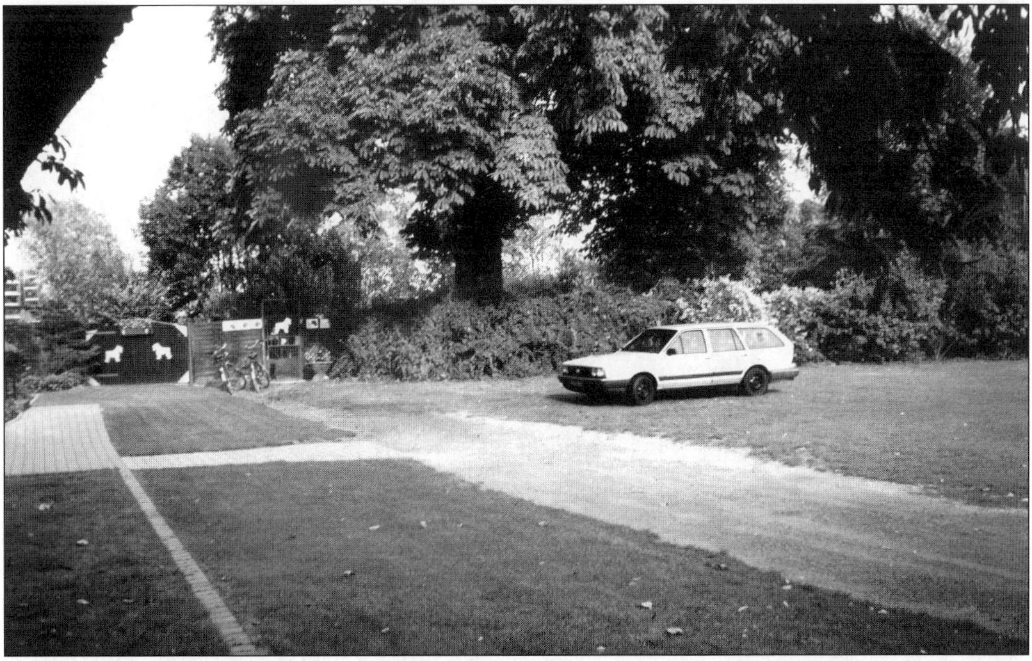

A white car is parked where the Jeep and the seed drill stood in 1945. All the buildings on the west and south of the courtyard were demolished.

Picture K3 which is item 8 in Map 28. Schloß Straße pictured from the entrance to the Kervenheimer Schloß alongside the Mühlen Fleuth. (© John Lincoln)

The same view in 2004.

Picture K5 which is part of item 11 in Map 28. Lt Jack Laurie leads Pte Scott and Cpl Lubbock of 18 Platoon 1 R Norfolks out of Wallstraße into Winnekendonkerstraße in Kervenheim on 2 March 1945. (© John Lincoln)

Picture K6 which is part of item 11 in Map 28. Ptes Peck, Young, Duffill, Rose, Dodd and Cassidy of 17 Platoon 1 R Norfolks make the same turn on 2 March 1945. (© John Lincoln)

The junction of Wallstraße and Winnekendonkerstraße in 20014.

Picture K7 which is part of item 11 in Map 28. Troops of 1 R Norfolks also left Kervenheim straight down Schloß Straße into Winnekendonkerstraße. The road to the left leads to Sonsbeck, and would have been used by Hans Kühn when he left Kervenheim on the previous day, March 1. (©.John Lincoln)

The junction has been modified into a true crossroads. The picture was taken in 2004.

murdered civilians in a recaptured village. In the case of Kervenheim, either it was a misunderstanding and the German soldiers were warning civilians of the risk from shelling, from grenades thrown into cellars or from crossfire, or the soldiers invented it]. Father decided to stay because he knew the house would be burnt down as soon as we left it. [Defending troops burnt the empty houses to preempt the attackers' doing so and thereby forcing the defenders into the open where they could be killed].

Up until the week preceding 1 March 1945, I had been cycling daily to work at the Savings & Loans Bank in Winnekendonk. Then the road became too dangerous because of low-flying aircraft, so I remained in Kervenheim. On one occasion I went to Kürvers bakery to buy bread with Trautchen Spittman and Frau Schwartges, who came from Winnekendonk. As we reached the centre of the bridge spanning the Fleuth a German soldier in a window up in the church steeple began to wave his arms and to shout; 'They're attacking'. We discovered years later the wireless set had just been set up in the rectory [the site of the German Bn HQ in Pastorat Straße] and this was the only way the soldier could communicate. Knowing no better we carried on but the shelling soon began. We fled into the next house (20 Schloßstraße, now the home of the Horlemann family), which stood open and empty at the time. Frau Schwartges received a head wound and was taken to an aid post in the Schloss where she died. Her husband was also killed in the war, so her sister in Winnekendonk brought up their two small children. After this incident, I stayed in our cellar until the morning of 2 March when English soldiers made us leave.

In addition to our own family (6 people) sheltering in our small cellar there were the married Spittman couple (70 years old), Gertrud Schmitz who was a widow from Gerdtsstraße (80 years), Frau Visser née Bär from Wallstraße (also 80 years), Frau Klara Schwartges, Frau Anna Laarmanns from Kevelaer and Frau Josef Schmitz with her three small children.

When the firing died down on 2 March, father decided to leave the cellar and visit the neighbours on our right (the siblings Fritz, Anna and Klara Janssen). We had heard that their house had been burnt down. The Janssens had been ordered by the German soldiers to leave their house and go to the Schloss, but even before they arrived there they could see their house burning. So father and the neighbour, Johann Brouwers, tried to save the house. While doing this he was taken prisoner by English soldiers. They took him by road to Üdem as far as the Hinkers farm in Steinbergen. An English officer then discovered he was a civilian and allowed him to stay at the Hinkers.

So father was no longer with us. Shortly afterwards English soldiers entered our house and ordered us to leave the cellar and the house itself. In the road outside there was an English tank. We were ordered to go to the Schloss, and from there to the shoe-factory (the Otterbeck factory on Üdemer Straße). During the course of the day every inhabitant of Kervenheim who hadn't fled arrived at the factory. There were a lot of people. On the way to the factory and full of anxiety amounting to panic, I spoke to an English soldier who certainly didn't understand what I was saying. He did however send me a medical orderly, who I remember carried a Flemish Red Cross bag, because no doubt he understood my sister was wounded. It was a humane thing for him to do during these ghastly events, and raised our hopes for a good outcome.

For some of the day we moved about freely, and we spent the rest of the time in the last houses on the Üdemer Straße (Tillmann Borghs and the Verhoeven's carpenters' shop).

Towards evening we were ordered to the church. An English officer stood at the church door and told us: 'This is for your and our safety'. But he gave me permission to go back to the house and fetch things to eat and some necessities.

During the night English lorries took us to Bedburg-Hau where we stayed about six weeks. Much has been written about this period in Bedburg-Hau. Then we were returned to Kervenheim. On returning there began for us a happy (actually inconceivable) time clearing the rubble and rebuilding our Heimat.[158]

Arnold van Elst wrote:

I still have vivid memories of 1 March, 1945. I was 14 years old. My parents and six siblings lived in Hatershof [977373], which is about 2 km west of Kervenheim… During the previous week a Paratroop unit had set up a wireless transmitter in our cellar.

In the middle of February 1945, long-range artillery began shelling. This lasted about a fortnight and marked the approach of fighting. On the day before 1 March, English troops had occupied the neighbouring farms to our west in Vorselaer and Weeze. On 27 February they took Wickermannshof [sic, Weykermannshof]. On the same day a Paratroop Recce unit brought a wounded English prisoner to our house. His wounds were immediately treated by a Paratroop medical orderly billeted there. The prisoner was then moved into the kitchen and some hours later into the cellar with the transmitter.

Early in the morning of 1 March, as on previous mornings, severe shelling began and through the explosions could be heard the chatter of machine-guns and rifles. For 14 days we had sheltered in a cellar under a building about 10 metres from the farmhouse. From there

158 The first letter from Käthe Schmitz was forwarded by Bernhard Meiners on 11 February 1997, and the second was sent directly on 27 January 2013; this author's translation.

it took only a few minutes to water the cattle and feed them their hay and beets. But it was dangerous. Müsershof was engulfed in flames. There were ten of us in the cellar, all family and relatives. During the night of 1-2 March the Paratroops left our farm in retreat. They left the wounded English soldier behind in the cellar with a stock of rations.

On 2 March English soldiers [Warwicks] came on our land. Daybreak brought extensive shelling which lasted for two hours. Then silence. About ten minutes after the shelling stopped, English soldiers appeared at our farmhouse. We hung a white flag on the gable end of the house to show the German troops were gone. The English soldiers stood with stens and rifles at the cellar entrance where we had our refuge and ordered us out. I have to emphasise that the English soldiers behaved very correctly. At once we stopped being frightened. My cousin who spoke some English told the soldiers that a wounded comrade of theirs was in the farmhouse cellar together with two unarmed Paratroops.

The wounded English prisoner had already been found and released from the farmhouse, and the two German soldiers captured. They had been left behind during the hasty evacuation and they surrendered without a struggle.

On 2 March the English soldiers took the civilian men away to Wickermannshof [sic, Wykermannshof], including my father and the Dutch herdsman who worked on our farm. Both were released and returned on 3 March.

Our farm bore the marks of battle. We counted 24 shell-holes in the walls and the roof, and about 2,000 shell-holes in the 20 hectares surrounding the farm. It was a moon landscape.

A few days later, near the Vorselaerer Ley, we saw two graves holding an English and a German soldier. They were later exhumed and re-buried in the military cemeteries – in the Reichswald and at Weeze.

We will never forget and always be thankful for that moment when the English soldiers appeared on our farm and freed us.

In reflection at the end of this memoir: I have visited the USA and Canada several times. I spent a year (1950-51) in the USA as an exchange student from the Agricultural College in Geldern. In 1993 I was in Canada and visited the Peace Tower on Parliament Hill in Ottawa. There I read the names of many Canadians who died on 1/2 March and are buried in the Niederrhein area. I prayed then and there that we'd never be at war again.[159]

Theo Stenmans wrote 'Memories of a Kervenheimer during the War: 1944/45'.

Living conditions deteriorated month after month. Even though we lived on the land, it wasn't simple for a family of six to get enough to eat. My father was in Russia and my mother was looking after five children on her own (the oldest 15 and the youngest 3 years old).

I got an opportunity to leave home and live on a farm [in de Weyen] as part of a family. From there I went to school in Kervenheim. The lessons were often interrupted at 9o'clock by the sirens. We took refuge in the school cellar or in the old castle whose vaults and thick walls offered more protection. Those children who lived near the school went home.

I used the opportunity to visit my family or I hurried there after school. Afterwards I went back to the farm which was my second home.

The Allied air forces enjoyed complete air superiority. We scarcely ever saw a German aircraft. The old Boxteler Railroad was a main supply line to the front and a frequent target. The roads and fields were also dangerous. Everything that moved was shot up.

159 Letter from Arnold van Elst written on 29 January 1997 for Bernhard Meiners at this author's request and forwarded on 11 February 1997; this author's translation.

Orders came down to extend the Siegfried Line which ran in our area. The 12 and 13 year olds were required to dig trenches. I remember this happening on September 19, 1944. We were digging firing positions and one-man slit trenches [funk-holes for travellers visible on the aerial photographs] along the Üdemerstraße at 9 o'clock when the sirens went. We soon saw our first dive bomber and then a deep growling and droning could be heard. There were vapour trails in the sky. Large aircraft formations passed overhead and we realised something special was happening. Several hours later we heard the news of a large airborne landing at Arnhem.

The Front came nearer. Then the soldiers stationed with us became engaged in the fighting. Staff officers were quartered on our farm. A Flak battery was emplaced close by on the Nienhuis farm, which had also been a guesthouse at one time. The next morning a recce plane saw the position and that afternoon it was shelled and destroyed. The shelling lasted for only a few minutes but we were terrified when a piece of shrapnel broke the window of the living room where we were about to sit down and eat. The light fell from the ceiling onto the table and was broken. Outside an officer was killed and a soldier seriously wounded.

The front now ran near Goch and the artillery built emplacements all around our neighbourhood. A howitzer battery was emplaced in our vegetable garden while another battery with large guns and Flak was positioned along the old Kuhstraße between Kervenheim and the van Dongens. There had been no schooling for some time. It was too dangerous to move between the farm and my parents' house. For that reason I decided to remain with my mother. The Allied forces had reached Goch, Kalbeck and Weeze. Kervenheim was being shelled. We became frightened and chaos threatened, so we decided to leave the area.

A lorry was in the process of removing the last piece of machinery from the Otterbeck shoe factory when we were offered the opportunity of being evacuated with it. We hurriedly packed up what we could take with us, and mother departed with her five children into the unknown. We had to leave the lorry in Homberg am Rhein. From there we went by tram to Walsum where we were taken in by an old lady.

A few days later on 24 March 1945 Montgomery's Army crossed the Rhine. After a few days the defending troops retreated to Dinslaken. They included many dead and wounded who had to be taken away in horse-drawn wagons. The little effect our troops had on the enemy made it a waste of time to carry on. In our row of houses there was a small section of soldiers. They had placed their MG on a pram to give themselves a little mobility.

I remember hearing a section leader address his men. He gave the order to fight to the last drop of blood. Half an hour later they had all disappeared. Was it a secret way of telling them to run?

The following morning the first Allied tank arrived. All houses were searched. We were amazed and astonished how peaceful and free everything then became. But what we saw next was too much to take in. So many Allied soldiers and so much war material! Columns of tanks, guns, half-tracks and lorries. That same day we evacuated the house and spent a couple of days in the cellar of a Protestant church. After another week we could go home.

At the end of April we heard a rumour that on 1 May 1945 a refugee convoy would be permitted to cross over the pontoon bridge at Orsoy. There was great joy at the news. We had no idea what to expect but we wanted to return home as quickly as possible. So we prepared to return. We acquired a small handcart and piled everything we had into it. On 30 April 1945 we started off.

First we came to a large collecting-point on the Rhine. We spent the night there. But who could sleep in this turmoil and amidst such excitement? In the early hours of 1 May, the great trek over the Rhine began. It wasn't easy to get over. Horse-drawn and hand-carts jostled together and people were pushed aside inconsiderately. The first day we reached

Bonninghardt. Then we brought all the handcarts together. It was late and impossible to think of going further that night. In a barn on an old farm we found shelter and slept a little. The next morning we pushed the wheels with more strength towards home.

On 2 May we reached our beloved Kervenheim.[160]

The priest-in-charge in Kervenheim, Father Franz Nellis, kept a diary:

The bullets whistled overhead, but you got used to it. The air-raid cellar in the rectory [Pastorat Strasse] was overcrowded. Since 15 February, more than twenty children with their mothers slept there. Grotendonk was now in the front line. On 20 February, Endtschenhof [a different one] was taken by the enemy. The Deckers family together with the priest, R. Coenders and a sister escaped from Kevelaer with their lives. On Sunday 25 February, Holy Mass was celebrated at 10 am and 11.30 am. But only the inhabitants and refugees in Kervenheim could participate. All roads into Kervenheim were under shell-fire, as well as being strafed by low-flying aircraft. Prof. Patureaux from Kevelaer, who for weeks had lived in Rouenhof with Pfarrer Mütter from Weeze, continued to attend church, but then was seen no more. [Pfarrer Wilhelm Mütter (1886-1968) was a leading light throughout the war years in Weeze, and after the war supervised the rebuilding of the parish church destroyed in February 1945. The council unanimously voted to name a street in the new suburbs after him]. Artillery shelling of Kervenheim got worse. On Monday three celebrants appeared for mass, but on Tuesday none. The situation became ever more dangerous. On Monday night new troops arrived. The unit of troops under punishment [nothing is known of them] left for Veen, and on 19 February was pulled back across the Rhine to Rheinberg. [This makes no obvious sense since both Veen and Rheinberg are south of the Rhine and the date is out of sequence]. New troops arrived from the Roermond front: paratroops, a hard lot. They installed a transmitter in the church tower and ignored all complaints. On Tuesday enemy artillery scored a direct hit on the tower under the clock. A second transmitter was set up in the rectory. The commanding officer [he has never been identified] wanted the cellar air-raid shelter emptied. That was out of the question because the one in the Schloss was already bursting at the seams. Soldiers arriving from the Üdem front were despondent, wanting to give up the useless resistance. A Nebelwerfer and a mortar were emplaced in front of the rectory, and right in front of the window of the cellar air-raid shelter. The Priest confronted the Lieutenant [the CO?], demanding he take proper care of the civilians. But the Nebelwerfer and mortar remained, and were in action for the first time on 27 February, 1945. At 5 pm the first shell [British counter-battery fire] hit the rectory in the upper North-West corner; at 7 pm the upper middle room on the west side was hit, and the window and side wall were blown out. About midnight the inn on Wallstraße caught fire (the Verhoeven Inn, used by the soldiers to store ammunition). The wind blew a heavy shower of sparks over the rectory. The civilians in the cellar air-raid shelter, especially the women and children, became restless. The priest went out with two men to establish if there was an immediate fire risk, warning the women and children not to leave the shelter of the cellar except in an emergency because the guns were aiming mainly at the rectory and the Schloß. But at the very moment the priest and Hermann Straaten with his brother-in-law from Üdem reached the entrance gate to Pastoratsstraße, a new artillery salvo hit. The first shell went through the open front door into the hallway, the second went to the right and the third hit above

160 Theo Stenmans' memoir published in *Unsere Heimat; Beilage zum Kevelaerer Blatt* (Blätter des Vereins für Heimatschutz und Museumsförderung e.V. Kevelaer. Nr. 2 – 1995). Sent by Bernhard Meiners on 11 February 1997; this author's translation.

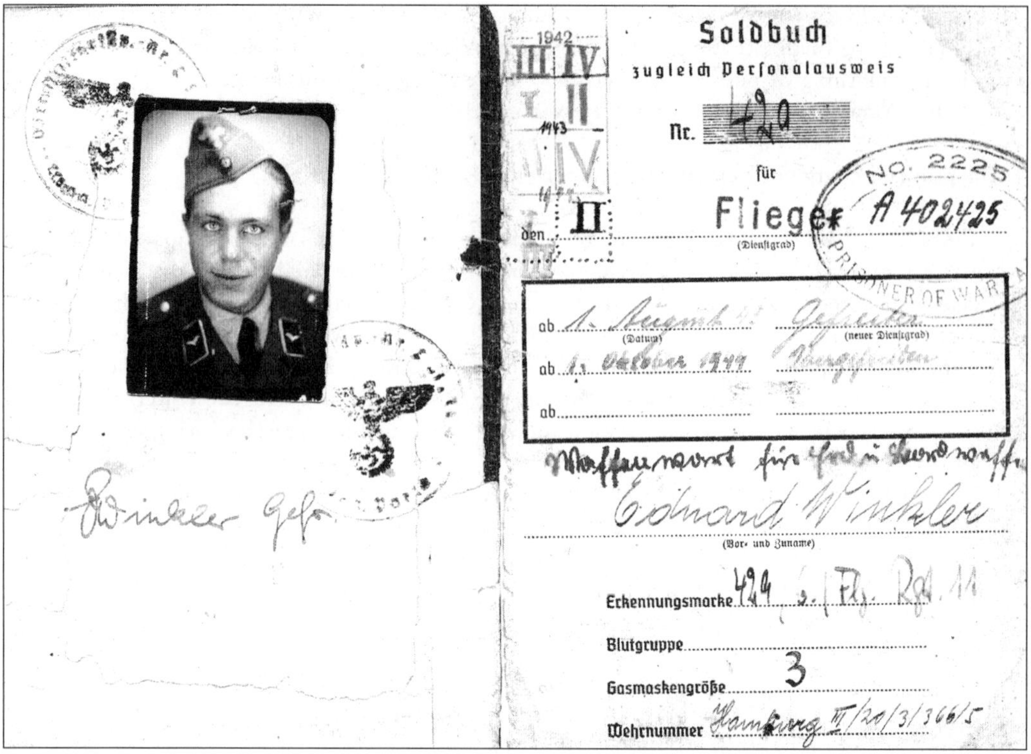

Ted Winkler's Paybook. Ted's identity disc was inscribed 429, 6./Fl.Regt11.Enlisted as an airman (Flieger) he was promoted L/Cpl (Gefreiter) in August 1943 and Cpl (Obergefreiter) in October 1944. He is pictured in the uniform of the Hermann Göring Regiment with its green tab with a white border (Grüner Spiegel mit weißen Rand) to deceive Allied intelligence in France, but soon exchanged it. (© Ted Winkler)

the front door. The men outside were uninjured, but in the hallway women and girls who had come up out of the cellar were severely injured. Frau Umbach was killed, Jean Schlootz and Maria Schlootz each lost a leg, Leni Schlootz lost an arm, Anneliese Schlootz had a leg injury, while Marlies Straaten and Maria Umbach were severely wounded in the thigh and stomach. Leni Schlootz died during the night. New calls were then made for the soldiers to give up the useless struggle, but they answered with threats to clear the cellar and expel the Priest because of his call to surrender. At dawn the third attack on Kervenheim came in. The study on the right of the front door got a direct hit. The attacking troops reached the first houses in the Üdemerstraße but were driven back by the Nebelwerfer and mortar emplaced in Pastoratsstraße. During the night the roofs of the houses in Kervenheim suffered badly, with most being destroyed, including that of the rectory. The situation became ever more threatening. The soldiers sought shelter in the cellar and pushed the civilians into the second cellar at the front of the building that was exposed to the shelling. Kervenheim was now the front line! Then during a lull in the firing, all of the civilians in the rectory cellar decided to get away from the danger in Kervenheim and seek shelter out of town. It was not long after they had left that resistance in the town collapsed. The roads leading to Winnekendonk, Sonsbeck and Kevelaer across the Schravelener Heide were under fire. Nevertheless all the refugees came through without injury from shellfire, but the last ones were caught in the air raid on Winnekendonk. Then things developed quickly. On Wednesday towards evening the shoe factory was in enemy hands, then retaken during the night [nothing is known about this], but on Thursday 1 March, 1945 it was lost for good. By 9 am on Friday the enemy had passed through Kervenheim and were in Gresumshof.[161]

FJR7's armourer, Ted Winkler, whose biography is in Chapter 6 was in Kervenheim maintaining weapons during the battle. He began his active service as a paratrooper in Wageningen in December 1944, when he joined Stabskompanie II/FJR7 (HQ Coy, 2 Bn, 7 Paratroop Regt) as regimental armourer. He was quartered in a ship research station containing a test-tank near the famous agricultural research centre. His workshop and store was in a large villa. All Dutch civilians had been evacuated from the area. To facilitate his work he converted a Dutch laundry van into a mobile armourer's workshop. II/FJR7 was entrenched 2 km south of the Niederrhein around Zetten, and on *The Island*, as the Anglo-Canadians called it, which lies between the Niederrhein (Arnhem) and the Waal (Nijmegen).

The Germans tried by all means to destroy Nijmegen Bridge, using frogmen, submarines, midget submarines, mines attached to logs and the Me 262. As a last resort they tried to make the bridge unusable by flooding The Island, and on 2 December 1944 blew holes in the Niederrhein dike just east of the rail bridge at Arnhem, and another hole in the railway embankment two miles south of the river towards Elst. Within three days Elst was underwater and FJR7 attacked 49 BID on the remaining dry ground but were driven back with heavy losses. The flooding, however, was the trigger that decided the Allies to direct their offensive through the Reichswald to Wesel instead of over the bridges at Nijmegen and Arnhem.

When Operation *Veritable* started on 8 February, it sucked in German troops, and led to the temporary splitting of 2FJD. Its FJR2 was sent across the Rhine on ferries to the east flank of the German defensive line on the Maas at Kasteel Bleijenbeek and placed under command of 7FJD. Ted's FJR7, under Oberst Riedel, followed over the Rhine to the area of Üdem where it assembled on 21 February under command of 8FJD. FJR23, together with 2FJD's HQ, went south along the East bank of the Rhine to cross the bridge at Ürdingen to reach Krefeld.[162]

Ted made the move in his armourer's van from Arnhem across the Ijssel to Zevenaar and on to Emmerich and Rees on the east bank of the Rhine. For fuel he used a mixture of engine oil and alcohol procured from the agricultural research station at Wageningen, starting the engine with petrol. The camouflaged paratroops transported their equipment in whatever they could steal, using bicycles without tyres, wheelbarrows, carts and prams, and their column was strung out over three or four miles. In Emmerich Ted slept peacefully in a hotel while the others bivvied in kilns in the brickworks. The following day they reached Rees on the Rhine under observed Canadian fire from artillery on the high ground near Calcar about 4 miles away. When shelling began, Ted and his companions took cover in an air-raid shelter whose entrance was below street level. They all piled in with the man behind Ted falling on top of him. Ted told him to get off him, but getting no answer, checked and found he was dead. Ted was ordered to abandon his armourer's van in the grounds of a public house. They crossed the Rhine from Rees in ferries under artillery fire which sank two of the ferries. This was reported in the Manchester Guardian of 1 March – see above. At the first building they reached, Reeserschanz, which was a public house with its own shooting range, all were ordered to leave their rucksacks, which implied that imminent action was expected. There was no action and Ted never saw his rucksack again. Their mission was to stem the Allied advance, which they called *verheizung*. [*Soldaten im Kriege verheizen* translates to send soldiers to the slaughter, or burn as fuel].

161 The article was sent by Frau Käthe Schmitz on 27 January 2013.
162 Busch, *Fallschirmjäger Chronik*, p. 88.

THE
YELLOW FLASH
Official Organ of 1st Bn. The Royal Norfolk Regt.

IX

No. 8 | $^1/_2$ RM | 8. March 1946

KERVENHEIM MEMORIAL

March 1st 1945. The Battle of KERVENHEIM

On March 1st this year the first anniversary of this battle, the Bn. gathered together to pay tribute to those men who gave their lives so gallantly in the capture of this vital village. Their splendid courage, their spirit of self sacrifice and their devotion to duty are perpetuated for all time in the memorial which was unveiled after the service. This consists of a large granite cross inscribed

"In undying memory of those who so gallantly gave their lives in the battle of KERVENHEIM – 1 March 45. Erected by their Comrades".

On it are engraved all the names of those who fell this day.

In the shell-scarred church at KERVENHEIM the Bn. assembled. It was an unforgettable occasion. As our Norfolk Padre the Rev J. L. G. Prior with our Brigadier and the C. O. entered the church, the wind rattled through shattered stained glass fragments that remained in the windows.

The C. O. opened the service by recalling to the audience of 200 men of the Bn. the history of the epic battle and the part played by those fine comrades whose memory we had come to honour. He told of the great defence put up by the German Paratroop Regt. whose task it was to defend this key position in the German defences. How, after repeated attempts, the crust of these defences was broken, the position finally penetrated and the stubborn enemy force routed, leaving behind its weapons and equipment. Many were the instances of heroic bravery during those few hours of gruelling fighting, none more magnificent than performed by those who gave their lives that KERVENHEIM might be ours.

The Padre then conducted with great depth of feeling a short memorial service. During this he read the roll of honour of the forty two Officers and men who gave their lives in the battle. On conclusion the Bn. bugler sounded the Last Post and Reveille.

The service was terminated by an address by Brigadier C. L.

Firbank D. S. O., who, while then commanding the 2nd Lincolns, had fought alongside us in the final stages. In his short most fitting address, he laid particular stress on the fine spirit of comradeship which had brought us through so many strenuous battles. This factor, bringing out as was invariably the case, the very best in every man, was responsible more than anything else for our final victory. May that same spirit, he concluded, remain with us to overcome also the difficulties which lie ahead.

Outside the ground was covered with snow. A steady wind blew falling flakes across the landscape. Clustered round the new memorial at the head of the neatly railed in cemetery those of us remaining to maintain the Bns fine traditions awaited the unveiling ceremony.

The Brigadier slipped the large Union Jack which covered this magnificent granite cross. "Tell England as you pass this monument we died' for her and here we rest content" Then once more the Last Post and Reveille.

Finally moving through the line of neatly kept graves, each with its spray of fir and budding willow, three representatives, Brigadier Firbank, Lt/Col. F. P. Barclay, and Pte. Barton who had fought through the battle laid wreaths on the memorial. To these was added a fourth sent by our Div. Comdr. Maj. Gen. F. R. G. Matthews, who was commanding our Brigade during this critical battle.

As we all silently moved through the line of graves, this tribute, this ceremony of homage to our gallant comrades ended. An indellible memory.

1 Royal Norfolk Regt's newspaper reported the return to Kervenheim of the battalion to dedicate a memorial to the fallen on the anniversary of the battle. Barclay was still CO, but Brig Matthews, who was widely blamed for the disaster and been promoted divisional commander, sent a wreath but did not attend. Cecil Firbank, promoted brigadier in 53 Welsh Division, gave the address.

Ted and his unit made their way to Kervenheim where there was a nunnery under shell-fire. He asked the nuns why they didn't go down into the wine cellar for protection, but they refused and stayed praying in the chapel. He heard later it had suffered a direct hit. Ted stayed in the rectory where the priest in charge and a family were praying in Latin. Not understanding, he asked a friend what they were praying and was told they needed water, but would not ask such a favour of protestants. So Ted went and fetched water in a couple of buckets from the pump, losing some when a couple of shells landed nearby. He knocked on the cellar door and gave them the buckets of water, but they said nothing. Ted described what happened on 2 March, 1945.

> I woke up at about 7o'clock, and made some breakfast in my billet, which was owned by the local priest, who spent the time with his family in the cellar. I was expecting a normal day. At 9 o'clock I had a visit by my commanding officer who ordered me to destroy all my armourer's equipment, and then rejoin the unit. I knew that Germany had lost the war, and realised the futility of carrying on, so I moved what I had, which was not very much, to a nearby farmer's yard, and set fire to it. After I had done that, I obeyed the instructions, which was to rejoin my unit on foot. [Ted departed an hour or two before 2 Lincolns declared Kervenheim clear of the enemy].[163]

Ted joined a different unit in Winnekendonk. His story will be resumed.

163 Letter from Ted Winkler on 7 December 2012.

4

The Battle of Winnekendonk

Friday, March 2, 1945. Weather: rain

> *It is suggested that this will surely rank as one of the finest small scale Tank/Infantry battles ever executed and well worthy of more close study.*
>
> War Diary: 3 Scots Guards

Summary

Objectives:

British 3 BID to clear Kervenheim, take Winnekendonk, and release GAD to take the Wesel bridges over the Rhine

German Hold road junction at Winnekendonk to keep open the Kevelaer – Wesel road permitting orderly retreat to the Rhine bridges

Troops:

British 9 BIB; 2 RUR secure SL; 2 Lincolns take Winnekendonk; 1 KOSB take Bruch
3 SG LF Sqn support RUR, 'S' Sqn support KOSB, RF Sqn support Lincolns
3 BID Artillery with 84 Medium Regt under command
609 Sqn, 84 Group, 2 TAF in support

German Gruppe Krahl of IIFJR7 and III FJR7 and about 200 men
IFJR22, aka Para Lehr about 150 men
Two Luftwaffe DP 88 mm guns
2 Troop XII FJ Assault Gun Brigade with 2 – 3 StuGs
3 Pln, Fortress Anti-Tank Coy 51(X) with six 50 mm Pak38s
Nachtschlachtgruppe 20 with FW 190s
Corps artillery
Total: 400 – 450 men, 2 AFVs and 8 anti-tank guns

British Intelligence Winnekendonk held by a weak battalion (PW interrogation)

Outcome:

3 BID's objectives achieved.
GAD delayed til 4 March, 185 BIB & 4 CG exploited to Kapellen

Casualties:

British About 120, of whom 96 were in 2 Lincolns, including 25 killed
German About 252, including 62 killed, 60 wounded & 130 P/W.[1]

1 Gates, *The History*, p. 254. Firbank's citation gives 200 prisoners, and Cathcart's 250.

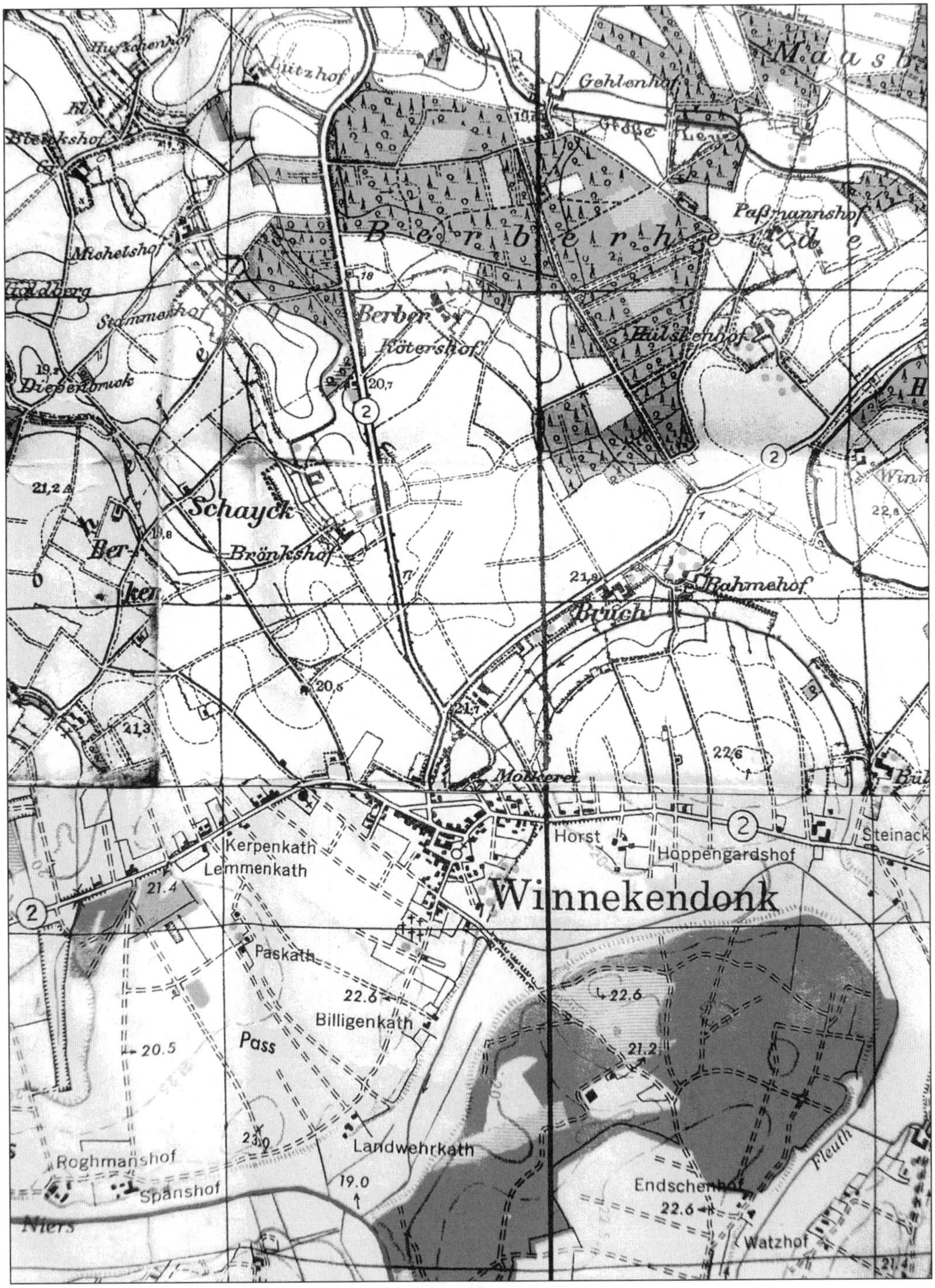

Map 29 The Winnekendonk battlefield, 1:25,000.

Map 30 Aerial photograph of the Winnekendonk battlefield on 16 February 1945. (NCAP/ncap.org.uk)

Map 31 Aerial photograph of the Winnekendonk battlefield on 12 October 1944 and used by 33 Field Regiment RA in the battle. Orientation is west-east.

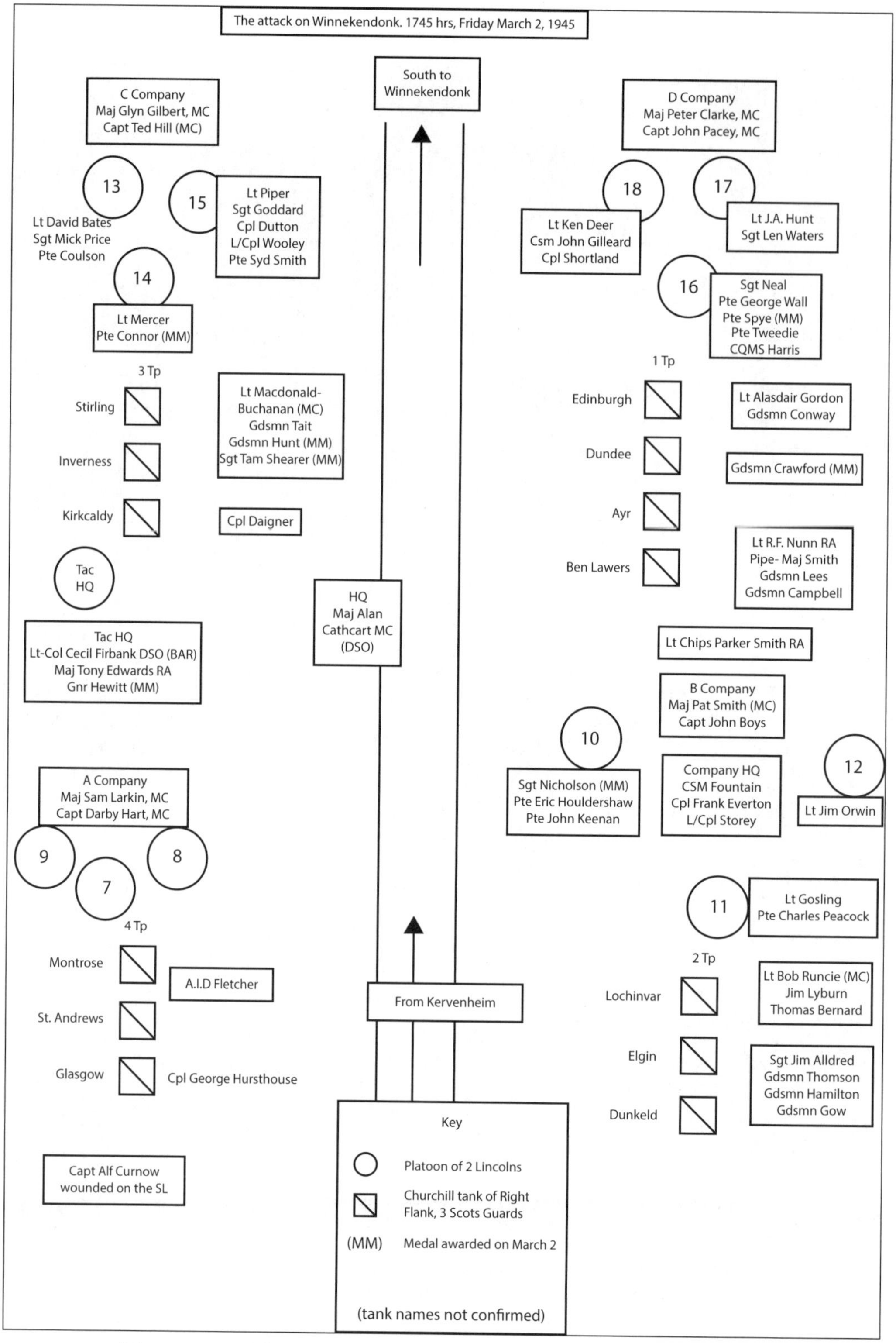

Map 32 British battle dispositions during the assault of Winnekendonk.

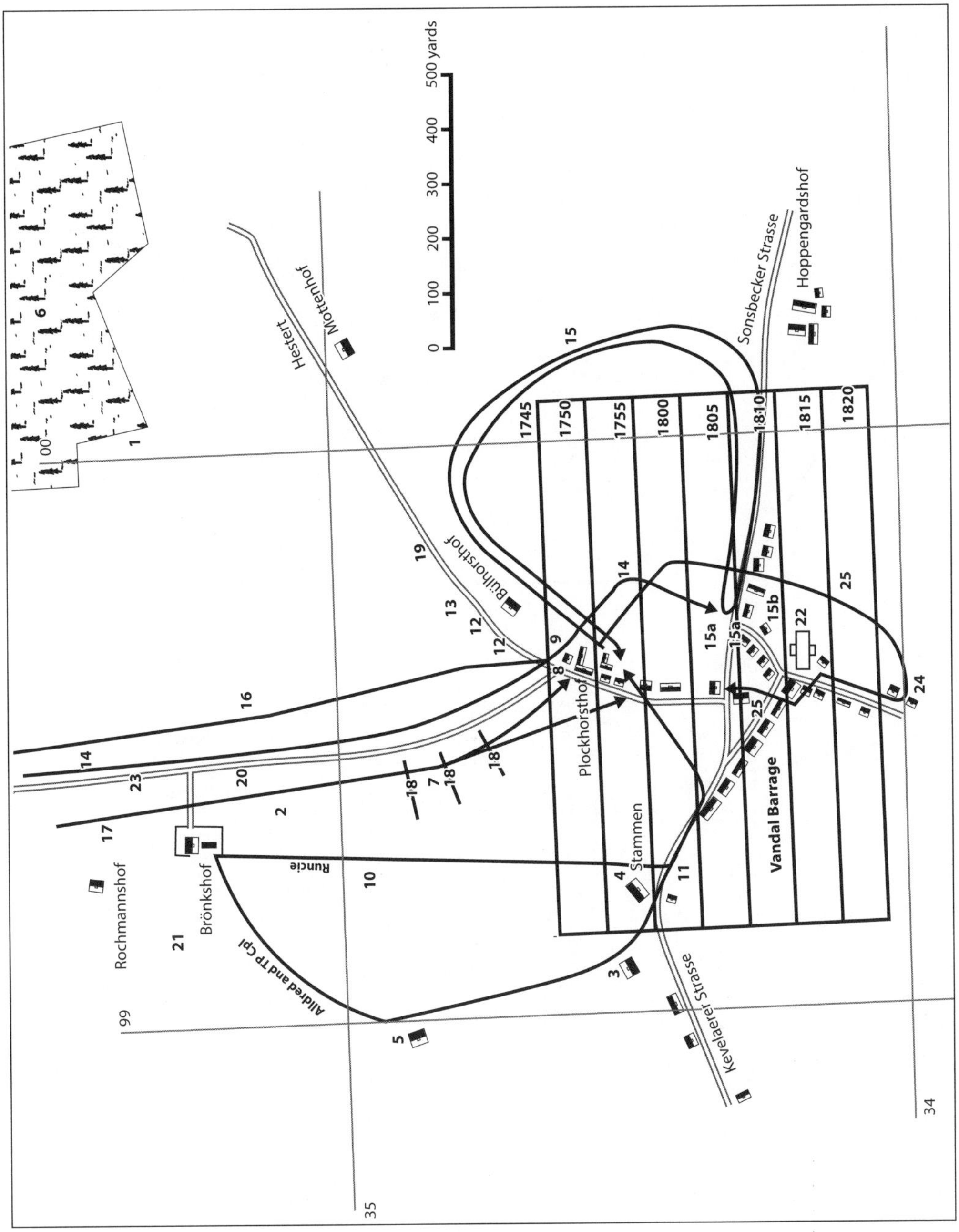

Map 33 Battle of Winnekendonk.

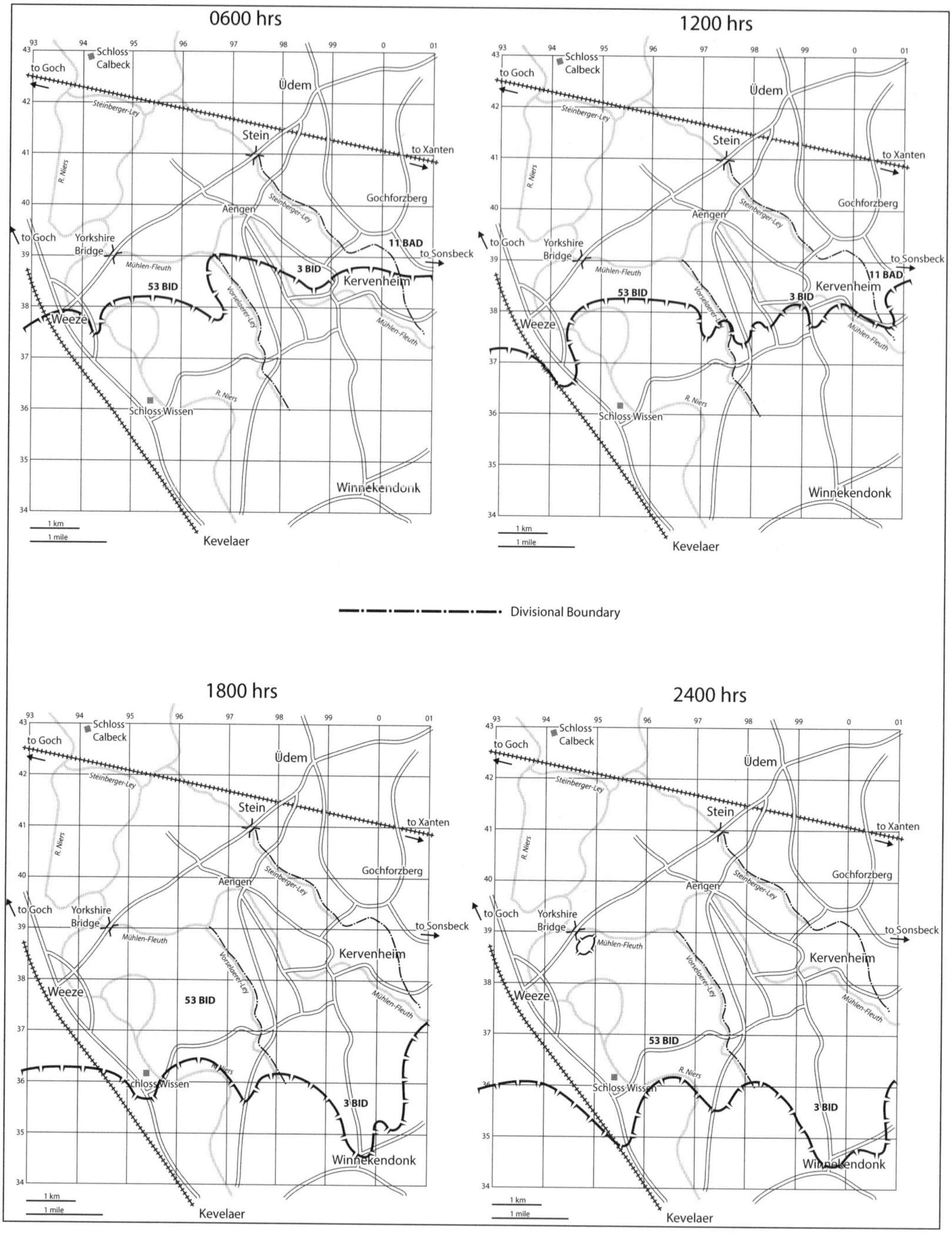

Map 34 The front line during 2 March 1945.

Maj Peter Clarke MC led D Company 2 Lincolns at the right front of the assault. This was the most dangerous part of the battlefield, and where he was killed.

Major Peter Clarke, MC died in his twenty fourth year at the head of D Coy, 2 Lincolns whilst leading the assault on Winnekendonk. Cecil Firbank called him, 'quite brilliant and would have gone straight to the top,'[2] and Jack Harrod wrote that Peter, 'was beloved by his fellow officers and almost worshipped by his men'.[3]

In a battalion of eight hundred men, where everyone knew of everyone else, deaths of popular men so late in the war such as Peter Clarke, Pipe Major Willie Smith (3 SG), and Lt Bert Aldridge (2 KSLI) were traumatic for their battalions. Other deaths could even shake the entire division, such as that of Maj-Gen Tom Rennie, GOC 51 BID, who had commanded 3 BID, and 'Banger' King (2 E Yorks) killed outside Bremen in the last battle. These, however, only represented the tip of the iceberg of human suffering, and the picture of F-M Montgomery, ashen-faced and weeping while saluting the grave of John Poston at Soltau, the unnamed Private in 2 Lincolns chasing a paratrooper around a farm in Winnekendonk shouting, 'He shot my mate', the devastation of Humphrey Wilson by Donald Smith's disfiguring death, show that few avoided personal loss.

The British infantryman generally respected his German 'oppo' as a fighter, who was suffering untold losses himself as he sang hauntingly, *Ich hatt' einen Kameraden, Einen bessern findst du nicht*,[4] a song owing nothing to the Nazi Party. People on both sides, with the exception of racists, agreed with Napoleon that, 'when we fight, no matter in what country, it is a civil war we wage' – pace George Carlin's quip, 'How is it possible to have a civil war?' A typical soldier's view was expressed by Bolo Whistler in his diary entry for 22 January 1945, before the discovery of Belsen; 'The hun must have nearly had it now. He has more honour as a fighter even though he is such a swine in every way'.

Winnekendonk had about 2,000 inhabitants in 1939, small compared with the garrison city of the attacking infantry battalion. Lincoln was home to 63,000 people, living in view of the Gothic cathedral on the ridge above. It houses the best extant copy of Magna Carta, which in 1215 institutionalised the concept of inalienable human charter rights that came to distinguish the thinking of the English-speaking peoples, which led eventually to 3 BID's mission to kill the beast in his Berlin lair, although another promptly took possession.

'Beastly Germans', 'les sâles Boches', and 'the Hun' were common epithets the barbarous Nazi state had worked hard to earn. The stated aim of the western armies who marched against them

2 Cecil Firbank in conversation in 1983.
3 J Harrod. *The History of 2 Lincolnshire Regt in North West Europe* (Germany: 2 Lincolns, 1945), p. 57.
4 Words by Ludwig Uhland in 1809 to music by Friedrich Silcher written in 1825.

was to restore the rule of law and decency to European affairs. The origin of this thinking can be dated to the ending of the Roman Empire, and was embedded deep in British culture.

Both Winnekendonk and Lincoln had been on the extremities of the Roman Empire, and have Roman graveyards.[5] Lindum, as the Romans called it, was a legionary fortress whose northern gate survives. Winnekendonk was an outpost of Colonia Ulpia Traiana or Xanten, birthplace of Siegfried. Their people would have understood 3 BID's rôle of *Restitutor Orbis*, loosely translated as 'Saviour of Civilisation from the Barbarians.' The ancestors of the British soldiery had first performed that rôle when the Romans departed in 410AD and told the British to look to their own defences. This led to the myth of King Arthur and 'The Matter of Britain' which, second only to the great religions, became the most enduring tale to capture men's hearts. Britain, unlike Gaul, achieved legal self-rule before the barbarians moved in, fighting on alone, surmounting disaster and laying the foundations of a heroic tradition. This Arthurian Fact became a source for British judgments about their obligations. Within his sphere Arthur was *Restitutor*, attracting poetry and rhetoric that could move mountains. Churchill spoke from the same tradition, and 3 BID fought in the conviction that there was a job to be done regardless of the cost: restitution, if not of innocence, then of legality, fairness and decency. They were chivalrous knights leaving the King's round table to battle men whose myths were the Germanic themes powerfully based on ideas of racial destiny, force and strength. These were embodied in the pure Siegfrieds and Sieglindes of the *Niebelungenlied*, with dark ambitions of power and domination which comprised 'The Matter of Germany'. Other mediaeval rivals were 'The Matter of France', martial, masculine and unsubtle in the *Song of Roland*, and 'The Matter of Rome' with its classical Greek and Roman legends going back to the siege of Troy.

Then there was Shakespeare's *Henry V*. If Arthur was in the British Army's set of unconscious values, Henry V was central in their mind with its Arthurian resonances and references. When Falstaff died the Hostess declared, 'He's in Arthur's bosom'. Most had seen, or knew of, Laurence Olivier on screen preparing his troops for battle against the French, and they had seen Exeter hanging Bardolph for looting. Olivier has been hailed by many as the greatest actor of the 20th century. He was 35 when he returned in 1942 after his second trip to Hollywood with his second wife Vivian Leigh. He wept on seeing Britain again, joined the Fleet Air Arm but was 'too old' for front line duty. He did his bit in public appearances and acted in *The Demi-Paradise* in 1943. He then directed, edited, produced, wrote and acted in *Henry V*. In his *Autobiography* he wrote; 'as you will deduce, I am somewhat proud of it and look back on it always with a happy glow'. It was filmed in Eire and at Denham Studios in 1943 and, when released in 1944, was a sensation. Henry V, 1387 – 1422, was a chaste, temperate and pious man 28 years old, fond of sport, cultured with a taste for literature, art and music, and with a strong sense of justice that impressed the French. He was merciless to disloyalty but scrupulous of the rights of others. A gentleman and a scholar, he was the embodiment of the British view of themselves. The effect of Olivier's film was profound, and inspired the infantry to persevere against a better-equipped enemy, an irony since the British longbow did to the French what the 88 mm and MG42 was doing to the British.

> That he which hath no stomach to this fight,
> Let him depart; his passport shall be made,
> And crowns for convoy put into his purse:
> We would not die in that man's company
> That fears his fellowship to die with us.

5 Heinrich Janssen. Karl Schumacher, Margrete & Theodor Gerrits. *700 Jahre Winnekendonk 1282-1982* (Geselligen Vereine: Franz Josef Drißen, 1982), p. 9.

> This day is called the feast of Crispian:
> He that outlives this day and comes safe home,
> Will stand a tip-toe when this day is nam'd,
> And rouse him at the name of Crispian.
> He that shall live this day, and see old age,
> Will yearly on this vigil feast his neighbours,
> And say, 'Tomorrow is Saint Crispian:'
> Then will he strip his sleeve and show his scars,
> And say, 'These wounds I had on Crispin's day.'
> Old men forget: yet all shall be forgot,
> But he'll remember with advantages
> What feats he did that day. Then shall our names,
> Familiar in his mouth as household words,
> Harry the King, Bedford and Exeter,
> Warwick and Talbot, Salisbury and Gloucester,
> Be in their flowing cups freshly remember'd.
> This story shall the good man teach his son:
> And Crispin Crispian shall ne'er go by,
> From this day to the ending of the world,
> But we in it shall be remembered:
> We few, we happy few, we band of brothers:
> For he that sheds his blood with me
> Shall be my brother; be he ne'er so vile
> This day shall gentle his condition:
> And gentlemen in England, now a-bed
> Shall think themselves accurs'd they were not here,
> And hold their manhoods cheap whiles any speaks
> That fought with us upon Saint Crispin's day.[6]

James Agee reviewed the film in *Time Magazine*, and described what the infantry felt at Yorkshire Bridge, Kervenheim and Winnekendonk.

> The most inspired part of Shakespeare's play deals with the night before the Battle of Agincourt. It is also the most inspired sequence in the film. Olivier opens it with a crepuscular shot of the doomed and exhausted English as they withdraw along a sunset stream to encamp for the night. This shot was made at dawn, at Denham against the shuddering objection of the Technicolor expert. It is one of many things that Olivier and Cameraman Robert Krasker did with color which Technicolor tradition says must not or cannot be done. And here poem and film link the great past to the great present. It is unlikely that anything on the subject has been written to excel Shakespeare's short study, in Henry V, of men stranded on the verge of death and disaster. The man who made this movie made it midway in England's most terrible war, within the shadows of Dunkirk. In appearance and in most of what they say, the three soldiers with whom Henry talks on the eve of Agincourt might just as well be soldiers of World War II. No film of that war has yet said what they say so honestly or so well. Here again Olivier helped out Shakespeare. Shakespeare gave to a cynical soldier the great speech: 'But if the cause be not good, etc.' Olivier puts it in the mouth of a slow-minded country boy (Brian

6 W Shakespeare. *The Chronicle; History of Henry the Fifth* (London: Thomas Crede, 1600), Act IV, Scene III.

> Nissen). The boy's complete lack of cynicism, his youth, his eyes bright with sleepless danger, the peasant patience of his delivery, and his Devon repetition of the tolled word die as doy, lift this wonderful expression of common humanity caught in human war level with the greatness of the King. Henry V is one of the great experiences in the history of motion pictures. Henry V is a major achievement – this perfect marriage of great dramatic poetry with the greatest contemporary medium for expressing it.[7]

As Americans might say; 'Goebbels, eat your heart out!' The film was released in November 1944 to be shown widely and repeatedly in the field; Hobart's diary entry for 6 March 1945 records he saw the film again at HQ for the third time. Some knew these lines by heart; Banger King declaiming them to A Coy, 2 E Yorks in the landing craft on D-Day before the film's release and recalling Wolfe's reading of Gray's *Elegy* at Québec, first among the battle honours of the East Yorks. To these soldiers, every day from 6 June to 8 May became the Feast of Crispian, and every battle an Agincourt. The exceptions were those so traumatised by the horrors that they never spoke of them, but which every night re-visited them in nightmares. The other exceptions were, of course, those who were buried in their thousands along the route to Bremen in the cemeteries of the CWGC.

The dialect spoken in Kervenheim and Winnekendonk has many words that are the same in English, such as: *Waterkötel*, which sounds and means the same as 'water kettle', *kookpott* as 'cook pot', *bötterkänn* as 'butter can', etc. Common phrases like, *Sent Petrus, Sent Paulus, makt oopen de Döör*, needs no translating for someone from the Fens but makes no sense to a Silesian. The name Winnekendonk, familiarised by the British soldier into 'Winnie can stonk,' is old German, meaning *die Donk des Winneke*,[8] there being over two hundred Donken in the area which runs into the Netherlands and Belgium. A Donk, or Dunk, was the underground dwelling of one of the natives, described by Tacitus; 'Germans in the winter live in dugouts roofed with dung,'[9] and by Pliny as a good place to weave linen.[10] There is a saying; 'Der Schmied bei den Funken, der Weber bei der Dunken', meaning the blacksmith at his forge and the weaver in his damp dunk.

While the battle raged in Kervenheim on 1 March, 9 BIB and Fendick were resting:

> Thursday 1 March 1945. Word comes in during the night – no rush for me in morning. 0900 hrs I leave for RUR HQ to get dope – just my carrier with O'Dowd and Whalley. Nothing doing until 1100 hrs when CO returns from Bde O Gp. Then nothing doing until 1445 hrs after a second Bde conference. The RUR CO is a new man – I hadn't met him before. [The RUR's CO was unchanged. Fendick met his 2ic.] Still plenty of familiar faces though. I'll stop here and brew up, until next O Gp. Raining. 1730 hrs. O Gp, but nothing new. Next news 2100 hrs – I get a chit saying no move before 0730 hrs. Have sent for Tony Hewett [OC A Coy 2 Middlesex] to tell him my plan for both platoons in position and self as FOO. He hasn't arrived yet. Sure am tired. Doing wireless watch for first 1/3 night, 3 hours.[11]

Late on Thursday afternoon, 1 March 1945, as the Norfolks, KSLI and Lincolns gradually asserted themselves in Kervenheim, Brig Douglas Renny of 9 BIB met with Brigade Maj Jessel to prepare for the expected German counter-attack and possible loss of Kervenheim that night, and to formulate plans for aggressive action on the morrow based on Whistler's orders. They were in the farm at Stein, 968417, recently vacated by 185 BIB and to which they had moved from Schloss

7 James Agee. *Henry V* (Time Magazine, 8 April 1946), http://www.murphsplace.com/olivier/henry5.html.
8 Janssen, *700 Jahre*, p. 111.
9 Tacitus, *Germania*. Ch. 16.
10 Pliny the Elder, *Natural History*. Ch. 19.2.
11 Rex Fendick's diary.

Calbeck. Jessel constructed a brief, and gave the document to the clerk for typing on a waxed stencil. He ordered nineteen copies to be cranked out on the Gestetner, subsequently increasing the run to 22 when he realised that 2 Lincolns could get a copy only through the Brig of 185 BIB. Each one the clerk numbered by hand, giving them to despatch riders at 7.25 pm for delivery to the units. The document required acknowledgement of receipt, presumably by telephone, wireless or despatch rider, and the sending of a representative to an O group scheduled for 9 pm.

9 BIB comprised; Brig Renny – GOC; Maj Jessel – Bde Maj; Maj Driver – DAA & QMO; Capt Quamby – GSO3; Capt Badham – BTO; Capt Duncanlea – EME; Capt Nettleton – BRASCO; Capt Quinn – BIO; Capt Griggs – LO; Capt Jones – Padre 2 Lincs; Capt Easton – Padre 1 KOSB; Capt O'Brian – Padre 2 RUR; Lt Scanlon – CAMP; Lt Barker – LO; Lt Verrall – LO.

9 BRIT INF BDE.

SECRET Copy No 1 Mar 1945

Tasks and Possible Roles as known at 1830 hrs 1 MAR

ENEMY

1. The enemy has already reinforced his KERVENHEIM posn and still further tps are being brought forward to reinforce it. [Not true]

2. It is possible he may intend to counter-attack across the river in order to drive back 185 Inf Bde.

3. There is still strong enemy resistance incl SP guns from 9737 SW of KERVENHEIM. [Operating against 53 BID and Warwicks – see 4(b)]

185 INF Bde

4 (a) 2 LINCOLNS has passed through 1 NORFOLK to clear KERVENHEIM, but exact posn not yet clear.

(b) 2 WARWICK had coy posns at 971397, HOXHOF 967391, WYKERSMANSHOF 933389 and RENNINGSHOF 978387 and was ordered this afternoon to press SOUTH on RIGHT of 1 NORFOLK to destroy enemy in that area. 53(W) Div are conforming on their right.

Tasks for 9 Brit Inf Bde night 1/2 Mar.

5. 9 Brit Inf Bde will be prepared to restore situation should enemy counter-attack NORTH of river during the night.

1 KOSB

6. 1 KOSB will be prepared:

(a) to lend depth from present area to existing 2 WARWICK posns.

(b) on orders from this HQ to take over posn at pesent held by 2 WARWICKS (as given in para 4(b) above) and hold it against enemy attack.

7. Recces will be carried out forthwith for task given in 6(b) above.

2 RUR

8. 2 RUR will be prepared:

(a) on orders from this HQ to move SOUTH to take over bn posn in woods 984390 – 988395 and hold it against enemy attack [bringing them up behind the Lincolns].

(b) to counter-attack from posn given in para 8(a) above to restore situation in KERVENHEIM.

9. Recces will be carried out forthwith, but there will be no move of tps unless ordered by this HQ.

Forecast for 2 MAR.

10. (a) wherever 185 Inf Bde firms up for the night, it will probably remain.

(b) 9 Brit Inf Bde will be ordered to pass through 185 Inf Bde and resume the adv SOUTH towards WINNEKENDONK as soon as possible after first lt.

(c) 2 LINCOLNS is to rejoin the bde when we pass through.
11. Nothing can be decided until it is known what progress 2 LINCOLNS and 2 WARWICK made today. A situation might arise in which the main thrust of the bde could best be delivered through 2 WARWICK rather than SOUTH of KERVENHEIM.
'O' Gp at 2100 hrs
11. Bn Comds need NOT attend in person but may send reps.
Ack. Jessel (Maj)
Time of signature 1925 hrs
Distribution and Copy No

1 KOSB	1	D Coy 2 MX	8	Camp	15
2 RUR	2	9 Fd Amb	9	A/CMO	16
3 SG	3	Comd	10	War Diary	17-18
33 Fd Regt	4	A/Q	11	File	19
45 Atk Bty	5	GSO 3	12	Tac 3 Div	20
253 Fd Coy	6	Bde 10	13	8 Brit Inf Bde	21
A Coy 2 MX	7	Sigs	14	185 inf Bde	22

PS. Bn 8 Brit Inf Bde is likely to relieve 1 KOSB on 2 Mar. MBJ

The distribution list identified the constituent parts of Renny's all-arms brigade-group: three battalions of infantry, 3 SGs' tanks with their own recce, 33 Field Regiment's 25pdrs, platoons of 2 Middlesex's 4.2-inch mortars and Vickers medium machine guns, a troop of 45 Anti-Tank Battery's 17pdr anti-tank guns of which half were SP M10 Achilles and half were towed, engineers, signals and field ambulance. Crucially absent, however, were any air assets; neither a spotter nor communication plane to allow Renny, Firbank or Cathcart to 'take a shufti', nor CAS dive-bombers or flying anti-tank guns to suppress the heavy enemy weapons being deployed in ambush. In the event significant air support was provided on March 2, but had no value because of the way it was applied. At the time in the late afternoon when it was needed, 609 Sqn was stood down, careless of impending battle of which it was in ignorance.

The British soldier could dig a slit trench with his mate in five minutes or so in these alluvial soils, lie in the bottom in his greatcoat and go to sleep even with the enemy close by and expected to counter-attack. His companion would stand in the trench on watch. In a wood, branches would be trimmed with a machete and placed over the slit trench. They would then be strengthened with soil against both airbursts and the weather. An enlightened soldier explained:

> Among the parachute containers I found [in Normandy] one with axes. It had two large axes and a series of small axes. I picked this axe up, a small one, and it was one of the most valuable bits of equipment I had. It was terribly valuable. I was able to do all sorts of things with it. One of the most important was that we realised that slit trenches as slit trenches didn't give us a lot of protection from mortar bombs and air bursts so we used to get wood and stick it over part of the slit trench and then mound earth on top. For getting the wood to do it an axe was very valuable.[12]

No noise would be heard at night in the scattered bivouac area of the disciplined, experienced, and dug-in units of the élite 3 BID. The soldier slept secure in the knowledge that only an improbable direct hit from a shell could harm him, and that sentries would be wide awake under threat of severe punishment if caught dozing or lacking in alertness. Extra security would come from

12 John Keenan's audio-taped memoir.

knowing that aggressive patrolling to maintain contact with the enemy removed his ability to surprise. At night in a wood little could be seen even when searchlights lit the sky with Monty's Moonlight. Trip wires, stretched in front of the most forward trench, were connected to a tin of pebbles or to a grenade to give warning.

The tank crews had a routine when harbouring, and no need of axes. Assigned a spot within a layout for all-round defence, they drove their tank over and beyond it, stopped and dug out a pit between the track marks, reversing the tank over the freshly dug pit to provide top cover. Tanks normally, and controversially when in action, laagered away from the front line at night, feeling sightless and vulnerable, and requiring replenishment and maintenance.

George Wall remembers being extremely uncomfortable that night of 1 March in the woods just to the north of Kervenheim. They were intermittently shelled. The water table was only two feet down so the choice was standing in the bitterly cold water or taking the chance of being hit by shrapnel. Lt. J. A. Hunt also remembers that night as being so exceptionally cold that few had any sleep.

> It was the coldest night I ever remember without greatcoats or blankets with most of the time spent stomping around trying to make the best of a gas cape and leather jerkin for some warmth. [Their greatcoats and blankets were in the lorries back at A Echelon and parked, presumably near the Udem-Weeze road.][13]

The next night in Winnekendonk many caught up on their sleep, like Jack Hunton and Ted Hill who slept 12 hours once the tension was released, remembering on waking being told by Leslie Colvin, the Lincolns' 2ic, that sleep wasn't a commodity that could be stored like a battery. Colvin spoke from experience of forcing himself to stay awake for three days after D-Day until told to get some sleep by his 2ic, John Boys. Colvin had been following the orders of his CO, Lt-Col Welby-Everard given in a pep-talk on the eve of D-Day and recorded in the war diary:

> The next point I want to talk on is the mental attitude to get into before you start. I did mention this to those of you to whom I spoke at Stobs [Camp near Hawick]. You must be ready and prepared for the first four or five days to be really tough – really tough. You will be lucky if you get any sleep at all. You may be able to snatch a few hours possibly – if you are lucky – but there will be very little time for rest, and it is up to everyone of you to get yourselves prepared in your own minds, because the first engagement – which always makes one more tired than anything else – will make us all really exhausted. But you have to get into that frame of mind where however tired you are, however exhausted you feel, you have just got to go on. Now that is a state of exhaustion that a great many of you, I am sure, have never experienced at all. I have only experienced it once, and that wasn't really bad, but we shall really be up against the problem and we have just got to pull ourselves together. If you realise it beforehand it will be very much easier to compete with when the moment actually comes.[14]

This bad advice with its lack of discipline over the need for sleep is surprising in an army led by Montgomery, who insisted on having his own six uninterrupted hours. Sleep-deprivation destroys judgment, degrades performance and leads to hallucination. Pilots also were suffering. A fortnight earlier, on 14 February 1945 R.K. Gibson, an Australian flight commander in 609 Sqn, asked to see the MO, Dr Bell:

13 Letters from George Wall and JA Hunt.
14 TNA: WO 171/5231: 2 Lincolns' war diary.

2 Lincolns at Lengerich on 15 May 1945. Most were at Winnekendonk. The CO, Douglas Wilson, had been wounded in Normandy, and returned when Firbank was promoted brigadier so was not at Winnekendonk. Note that the older members were distinguished by wearing a forage cap and filled the front and rear rows. (L.-r. back row:) Capt Hart RAMC, Lt Hamlet, Lt Robinson, Lt Gosling, Capt Paulet, Lt Deer, Lt Pinchin, Capt Parsons, Capt Jones RAChD; (middle row): Lt Sellars, Lt Hitchin, Lt Verrall, Lt Mercer, Capt Buckmaster, Maj Shaw, Capt Griffiths, Lt Stewart, Lt Bates; (seated): Capt Hargreaves, Capt Sanders, Capt Boys, Maj Gilbert, Maj Colvin, Lt Col Wilson, Capt Harrod, Maj Larkin, Maj Hart, Capt Hill, Capt Kidney.

Pte George Wall served in 16 Platoon, D Coy 2 Lincolns. At Winnekendonk he was immediately in front of Lt Gordon's troop of Churchills.

> It surprised me, as he was a fit, hard character, and to my astonishment he related the following story. He had awoken suddenly that morning to find his Australian fiancée sitting on the end of his bed. He insisted that he saw her in great detail, spoke to her and was absolutely certain he was not dreaming. When he reached out to touch her she disappeared. I tried to explain to him that the phenomenon was really a hallucination, but as frequently happens he insisted that she was really there.[15]

An hour or so later Gibson was killed when his aircraft was hit by *flak* with all rockets aboard and blew up in mid-air. The MO did not have the authority to take Gibson off ops and order a minimum 48-hour leave in Brussels when so many were suffering in the same way.

These symptoms cannot be relieved either by will power or training. Exhaustion was a serious matter at Kervenheim on the previous day, as we have seen. The GOC of the neighbouring 53 BID, Maj-Gen Ross, was away on sick leave due to insomnia. It appears this part of military training had been neglected. Young soldiers were notorious for falling asleep anywhere, and the wise officer, George Dicks, slept the afternoon away on 28 February waiting to attack Kervenheim. But many worried and few officers could relax without drinking, smoking, and playing cards, although Montgomery managed without them.

CSM Gilleard recalled everyone's exhaustion as they lined up to attack Winnekendonk.[16]

At Division a clerk was typing out the Intelligence Summary to be given to Bolo Whistler when he woke at 5 am.

3 Br Inf Div Int Summary No 230

SECRET (Based on infm received to 2359 hrs 1 Mar).

Part I

> Fwd of Bde HQ this summary will be destroyed by 2400 hrs 3 Mar.
>
> ENEMY SITUATION – OWN FRONT.
>
> 1. Att at Trace P is an estimate of the enemy order of battle as at 2200 hrs tonight. This will appear in the Int Summary daily during battle.
>
> 2. We renewed our adv towards KERVENHEIM at 0900 hrs this morning. Within 90 mins tks and inf were fighting in the outskirts of KERVENHEIM having disposed of light opposition of elts of III Bn 24 Para Regt on the left and III Bn 7 Para Regt on right. In the town itself resistance came to life and a counter thrust was quickly mounted against our hold on main rd at 986383. The main enemy force concerned was III Bn 7 Para Regt which has recently kidnapped a draft of Bn CRAHS [a reserve battalion which shifts its allegiance from 6 to 8 Para Divs as the situation warrants][17] sent from the area NORTH of CALCAR to join their parent unit. A tough fight then ensued for the village of KERVENHEIM. The garrison appears to have been made up of III Bn 24 Para Regt and III Bn 7 Para Regt but the enemy undoubtedly reinforced it in an effort to keep the town. Two SP guns and a strongly held post at 981383 [Müsershof] lent him assistance from our LEFT flank (sic). With some difficulty the town NORTH of the stream was cleared with the exception of an enemy posn, apparently encircled, in the cemetery 988383. On the far bank the German is strongly holding RITTERGUT 993382 [actually on the near bank] and the buildings at 981383 [Müsershof] are still in his hands.

15 Frank Ziegler. *The Story of 609 Squadron* (London: Macdonald, 1971), p. 312.
16 Undated letter from John Gilleard in the 1990's.
17 LAC: II Canadian Corps Intelligence Summary No 136.

3. The enemy has every reason to hold onto KERVENHEIM. He has not yet withdrawn all his guns and tps from the EAST of the MAAS and as he is still holding tightly to WEEZE he must retain WINNEKENDONK if he is to preserve order in his withdrawal.
4. It is anticipated therefore that the enemy will counter attack during the night by infiltration over the stream, probably with the sp of SP guns from SOUTH of the stream. [The Germans were expected to use their armour at night, but British tankmen insisted that for them it was impossible.] In any case resistance to a further advance tomorrow will be organised and tough.
5. The forces that the enemy has at his disposal for these efforts is estimated to be the equivalent of six paratp coys, with the possibility of one equivalent bn in reserve. There are several battered para units which have slipped from contact but it is difficult to see how he could produce more than one bn as a res force astride the rd KERVENHEIM-WINNEKENDONK where it can defend this vital axis against our brheads over the stream and by defence of the streams, woods and buildings that lie along the route. [The expectation was that the approaches to Winnekendonk would be defended, ignoring the existence of another lateral road further south through Wetten and the German predilection for villages].
6. On our RIGHT WEEZE has been firmly defended by 22 Para Regt and stiff fighting has taken place at 933390 [by the stream called the *Ottersgraben*]. EAST of the river NIERS our neighbours [53 BID] have cleared area as far EAST as 968380 [Schilbergshof] and as far SOUTH as 960374. Over 100 PW were taken during the day.
7. On our LEFT limited advances have been made to advance our line to the stream as far as 015373 [Bossenhof] and to main enemy def line at 027377. Further progress has been made in the NORTH and centre of the HOCHWALD.
8. Americans have reached VENLO and the RHINE.
9. Tac R has revealed that the process of evacuation between the MAAS and the RHINE is in full swing. Last night the harbour area of DUISBURG was lighted without regard to security and hy tks were seen crossing the RHINE to the EAST of 2726 [Orsoy]. Barges have been busy all day and the movement of tpt is continuous.
10. In view of the debacle in the SOUTH the paratps on our front can be expected to maintain an even stiffer resistance than before in order to preserve the RHINE crossings for the fugitives from the Americans.

Lt Col [Graham Peddie] GS 3 Br Inf Div

<u>Return of PW by units at 3 Br Inf Div Cage between 1800 hrs 28 Feb and 1800 hrs 1 Mar.</u>

Coy	Unit	Offrs	ORs
KAMPFZUG KAHLEN	7 Para Regt		7
EINHEIT KRAUS	"	1	15
7	"		2
HQ	"		1
14	"		1
15	"		46
16	"	1	5
9	Regt HÜBNER (24 pPara)		5
12	"		1
4	Bn CRAHS		14
		2	97

Total PW taken by the Div in the operation so far – 13 Offrs, 837 ORs incl 112 evac through med channels.

PART II

1. ENEMY ORGANISATION AND ORDER OF BATTLE.

a) EINHEIT KRAUS.

Was formed in Coy strength about eight days ago from coy and bn "B" Ech personnel of III/7 Para Regt and any other spare oddments of the bn who had not been in action before. They were held as an emergency reserve some 4 Km EAST of UDEM until 26 Feb when they were put into the line in the area of HOXHOF 9639. Original strength 100-120. The comd is O/LT KRAUS [defending against Harry Illing's A Coy 2 Warwicks].

b) EINHEIT RICHTER.

Is in fact 15 Coy/7 Para Regt. They were engr coy but have lost all their engr equipment and are fighting as inf under O/LT RICHTER with a present strength of 30-40. Night 28 Feb/1 Mar they were in the area KOTTERSHOF 9739 [Köttershof in the KSLI's area].

c) 16Coy/7Para.

It is called the Assault Coy and particulars of its origin are not quite certain. It appears to have been drawn from the whole regt as an emergency reserve and held in reserve EAST of UDEM with EINHEIT KRAUS. It was put into the line 26 Feb NE of KOTTERSHOF 9739. Org is said to be three pls of 30-35 strong, each armed with one Panzerschreck and three LMGs [A heavily-armed counter-attack force].

d) 14 Coy/7 Para Regt.

Stated to have lost one of its three pls. The remaining two have an LMG each, two or three Panzerschrecks and each man is armed with a Panzerfaust.

e) 401 Volks Arty Corps.

It is thought to have been organized as follows:
I Bty – (1), 2, 3 troops each with 6 × 7.5 LFH
II Bty – 4, 5, (6) troops each with 6 × 10.5 LFH 18
III Bty – 7, 8, 9 troops each with 6 × 10.5 LFH
IV Bty – 10, 11, 12 troops each with 6 × 12.2 (R) guns
V Bty – 13, 14, (15) troops each with 6 × 10.5 LFH 18 or heavier guns
According to PW 1 Trp had lost all its guns, 3 Trp had 5 guns left, and 8 Trp four left and 6 Trp had been broken up to supply refits. (source: First Cdn Army)

f) 3 Trp 7 Para Arty Regt.

(i) Org. Tp is equipped with 4 × 10.5 cm gun/hows LFH 18/40/M. Formed by RSOs. Other two tps in bn are similarly equipped and are thought to be up to strength.

(ii) History of Unit. Until 24 Feb guns of 3 trp were in posn 6 kms SOUTH of AFFERDEN, but activity was limited by amn shortage of 20 rpg per day. On 24 Feb guns moved into area REYSHOF and took up posn just EAST of track junc at 97753690.

(iii) Chain of Comd. As from 24 Feb bn has been in Sp Regt HUBNER. OP from 3 T sent fwd 25 Feb but failed to locate 1 Bn. On 26 Feb PW, however, contacted HQ 2 Coy HUBNER and est OP in BUISSENHOF [Büssenhof].

(iv) Task. 3 Tp had task of putting down DF on front edge of wood 944399 – 948402 [by Geurtshof to defend against 2 E Yorks] but owing to faulty comn brought no fire to bear before OP was overrun 27 Feb [Renison in his diary for Feb 27 reported finding an abandoned OP in Kampshof 500 yards from Büssenhof].

(v) Amn Supply. 1 Bn was allotted 800 rds on 24 Feb and these were delivered to two houses WEST of track 97703685 [south of Reyshof] whence they were to be collected by other two tps. In view of emergency situation FOOs were given unrestricted right to call for fire [the British system and unusual in German and US armies].

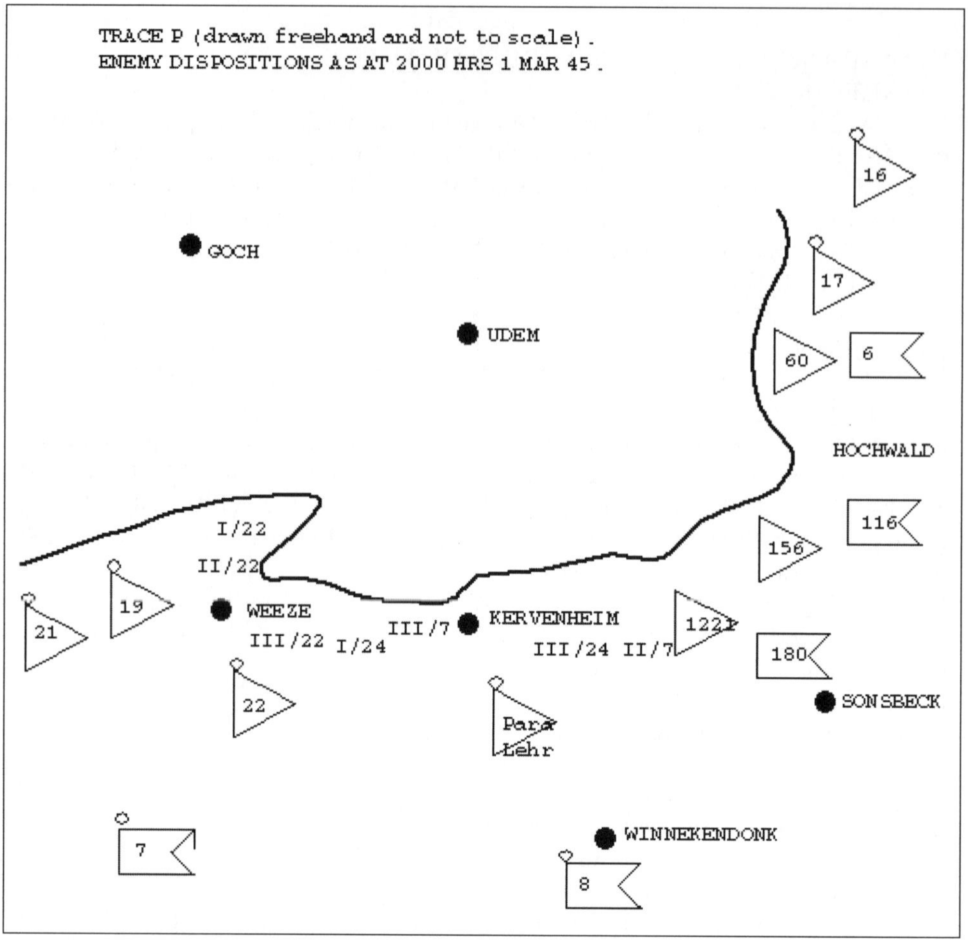

2. FPNS.

HQ II/7 Para	– 61201	3/741 Atk Bn	– 06612
HQ III/7 Para	– 62227A	I/24 Para	– 61771
14/7 Para EINHEIT		3/7 para Engr Pn	– 61845
RICHTER (15Coy)/7Para	– 63168	7 para Atk Bn	– 53143
16/7 para	– 63102C	III/7 para Arty Regt	– 63250

3. PERSONALITIES.

OC 6/7 Para Regt – Lt BERNDL
OC 7/7 Para Regt – O/Lt RITZ

OC 8/7 Para Regt – O/Lt KUPPE
OC 14/7 Para Regt – Hpt EMPSMANN
OC 15/7 Para Regt – O/Lt RICHTER
OC 1 Pl 15/7 Para Regt – Lt ENGELHART
OC 2 Pl 15/7 Para Regt – Lt KOMAREK – PW

OC EINHEIT KRAUS – O/Lt KRAUS
OC 1 Pl EINHEIT KRAUS-O/LT STREHLE-PW
OC 7 Para Engr Bn – O/Lt HÜHNING
OC I/24 Para – Ofw KLADDE – dead
OC 2/24 Para – O/Lt MÜLLER
OC 2 Pl 3/24 Para – Lt OHLAND
OC 1/7 Para Atk Bn – O/Lt HEMSIN

The Lincolns were still under command of 185 BIB during the night of 1-2 March. Brigadier Matthews had moved Tac HQ from Stein into the woods alongside the Üdem-Weeze Road (966403) and close to where Thompson, Cresswell and the Norfolks had waited for thirteen hours. The Norfolks, after their heavy losses, had been reorganised by Barclay into three composite companies, reinforced by 'A' Company of the Lincolns under Sam Larkin. These units were snatching sleep in the houses and the factory on the Üdemer Strasse in Kervenheim as far as the crossroads (990383 – 991385). The Norfolks' Diary reported the night as quiet.

The three other companies of the Lincolns were out of contact and, as we have seen, spending a cold and miserable night 700 yds to the north in the woods (987390, 988393, 984392). They were dug in alongside another composite company of the Norfolks to their immediate right (982385-984386). The Norfolks' anti-tank guns and the dismounted carrier platoon were ready with those of the Lincolns for the counter-attack expected from the enemy in Kervenheim. Whistler at 11 pm had ordered that in this event the road junction in front of the woods (989388) 'must be held at all costs'.

The men of 33 Fld Regt were collapsed in exhaustion another 2,000 metres to the north half way to Üdem (983406), having taken 5 hours to move up the 3 miles of mud tracks from Buchholt. The unwritten rule of the RA was that the infantry must never miss an H-hour due to unready artillery. They therefore had to move to be sure of being in range of Winnekendonk. Their twenty-four 25pdrs, with a maximum range of 12,200 m with supercharge, were now a comfortable 6,000 m from Winnekendonk and well within the 7,132 m range of Charge 2. It wasn't until 11.30 pm that they reported in their state of readiness to the CRA, Gerald Mears, who would have been relieved that his Divisional command of 72 guns would be ready at first light and even earlier against any German counterattack against Kervenheim.

In support of 3 BID were the sixteen 5.5 inch guns of 84 (Sussex) Medium Regt RA. They remained in place north-west of Buchholt (932444), a distance of 14,000 m from Winnekendonk and close to their effective maximum range of 16,000 yards with a 100-lb shell. Firing an 80-lb shell, however, extended the range to 18,500 yards. They were not to move up to Kervenheim until 3 March when they were transferred from 5 AGRA to under command of 3 BID.

The HQ RA of GAD was also in support of 3 BID and 6 GAB from 28 February, but out of range with its HQ at 908488 near Forst Cleve. They expected to move up into the areas vacated by 3 BID, but by noon on 2 March only 86 Fld Regt had moved within range of Kervenheim at 909456, but out of range of Winnekendonk. Their War Diary reported:

> CRA decided that as Regts now out of range, guns must be moved forward. The mud and lack of suitable deployment areas made this impossible, except by moving into Gun areas of 3 Br Div as they were vacated. This was a very slow and cumbersome process [although since they were SP far easier than for the towed arty of 3 BID] as the battle was not moving as fast as anticipated. Information received all day of slow but steady progress of 3 Br Div.[18]

Their absence might have had serious consequences, as explained below.

The KSLI were dug in on the Brigade's left flank just to the East of Kervenheim with coys at 994384, 991385, 992384, 998387, holding the site of Pte Stokes's VC-winning exploits. There was confusion about the location of the inter-corps' boundary; at 3.15 pm on 1 March, 3 BID's G Ops Log recorded 185 BIB asking their LO with 11 BAD to clarify where CLY were. In the remarks written alongside is the statement that, 'They thought the river was the boundary', which it generally was but not in the gap between the Mühlen Fleuth and the Vorselaerer Ley. The LO

18 TNA: WO 171/4104: War Diary of HQ GAD for 0900 hrs on 1 March 1945.

was then asked to find out the intentions of troops at 002383 and 000375. There seemed to be little co-ordination across the inter-corps boundary, and this was probably normal. The Warwicks were lying back in their bridgehead over the Mühlen Fleuth, 2,000 yards to the north-west with coys at 971386, 978387, 973391, and 972396. They were conforming with 53 BID, which was attacking Weeze on their right and advancing east from Yorkshire Bridge in Vorselaer.

At last light the Germans supported by 50 howitzers were holding Kervenheim strongly, especially Müsershof (981383), Rittergut (992382) and the cemetery (988383). Their departure as they slipped away during the night was not noticed by the extensive patrolling of the Warwicks, nor did a unit from 53 BID realise that Weeze was emptying. Two Warwick patrols, which must have gone out early in the evening before the Germans disengaged, reported that both Oberfeldshof (976376) and Müsershof (981382) were occupied by the enemy at 5.45 am. But one hour later, the G Ops log records that returning patrols had found the Germans gone from there and from Müsershof, which had been reduced to a burnt-out ruin containing the charred corpses of five defenders.[19] Oberfeldshof was also empty and the patrol heard motor transport in the area. The Germans had slipped away just before first light rather than earlier, ensuring that the British focused on their set-piece attack and several hours would elapse before their advance could be continued. Likewise Weeze was found to be very quiet with all its bridges blown.

While the Germans prepared to leave, at 2 am a German aircraft machine-gunned transport on Endtschenstrasse running from the Üdem-Weeze road towards Kervenheim, alongside the wood where Thompson and the Norfolks had spent their long wait. The aircraft was almost certainly from Nachtschlachtgruppe 20 operating out of Twente. The Duty Officer of 185 BIB was convinced it was a German aircraft and informed G Ops 3 BID who checked with Corps. They replied that it was definitely enemy action. A discussion then took place between Division and Brigade about dispersing vehicles when possible, but with unchallenged air superiority the allies had for some time ignored the Luftwaffe's pinpricks. Also ignoring the dangers of the night were civilian refugees, twenty of whom were found around 2 am on the same piece of road which had just been strafed near 185 BIB's Tac HQ. They were dispersed into nearby houses by the Military Police, and almost certainly directed next day to the holding camp at Üdem and thence to the vast tent city being set up at Bedburg. Here, by the time of the Rhine crossing, 24,000 women, children and old men were being looked after by the army under Military Government dispensing Military Law.

At 5 pm the previous evening, a conference was held at 9 BIB's HQ to hand out tasks to the brigadiers. Dunbar attended for 3 SG and the Diary reflected the expectation of having to fight fiercely for the objectives, and especially for Reyshof. The plan was to cross the Mühlen Fleuth into the bridgehead established that day by the Warwicks. Then 9 BIB would by-pass Kervenheim, which was to be cleared by 185 BIB, take the Berber woods in Berberheide and drive for Winnekendonk straight down the main road.

The plan was laid out in three phases. In Phase I, 1 KOSB with S Sqn 3 SG were to start from 2 Warwicks area (975388), on the west of the Mühlen Fleuth, and take the line Reyshof (979371) and the ring contour (985379). Simultaneously, 185 BIB was to attack Murmannshof (983383) to secure that flank at last. In Phase II, 2 RUR in Kangaroos with Left Flank Sqn of 3 SG, were to pass through and capture Berberheide with its woods on both sides of the main road (in 9936). Then in Phase III, 2 Lincolns were to revert to 9 BIB after Kervenheim was cleared, and with Right Flank Sqn 3 SG take Winnekendonk under an artillery barrage. This farsighted planning of the artillery was to become significant later in the day and would permit the last light gamble at Winnekendonk.

19 Bosch, *Der Zweite*, p. 239.

253 Field Coy RE placed one section with each battalion. They also made a platoon responsible for the routes in each Phase. Support for Phase I (973396 to 981382, Wettermannshof to Müsershof) was to be provided by 2 Pln, with 3 Pln for Phase II (987371 to 993363, Lützhof), and with 1 Pln held in reserve and earmarked for Winnekendonk. They were to have a busy day clearing roadblocks and repairing bridges and cratered roads.

'O Groups' were held at the various brigades. At 9 pm Firbank, Macdonald and Drummond were given their orders. The KOSB, exceptionally, sent their 2ic so that 'Wee Mac' could concentrate on his recce, having earlier arranged for Brigade HQ to give him the outline plan over the telephone. Soldiers live by the motto that 'time spent on reconnaissance is seldom wasted'. Sending the 2ic rather than attending in person was an innovation Macdonald recommended at the post battle conference, 'in the case of O groups called for the night before first light attacks'.[20] MacDonald would have had the fate of Barclay's Norfolks uppermost in his mind but, having absented himself from the O Group, he saw no inconsistency in complaining at the same conference that, 'Bde failed to let 1 KOSB know that 2 Lincolns were attacking Winnekendonk'.

> With all details tied down, the Artillery could now revise their fire plans to support each phase. Operation Order No 79, issued on 28 February was already out of date. We know of its replacement only through an entry at 1.30 am in the log of HQRA GAD; Fireplan received on telephone from 3 Br Div (tasks Vigilant, Vanguard).

The details have not survived. 86 Field Regt moved at first light and reported ready (909456) at noon, the only one of GAD's Artillery in range. It fired until 1.30 pm, but then the front line advanced and it was out of range for the assault on Winnekendonk.

The cold front which had crossed Europe the previous day, cleared the area by dusk on 1 March, bringing clearing skies.

> Cold front crossed all areas during the day; SE England between 1200 and 1500 hrs, and the continental areas between 1000 and dusk clearing the Eindhoven area by 1600 hrs and the Brussels area by 1700 and the Cologne area by dusk. Conditions ahead of the front: Variable low cloud at front mainly 7-10/10 above 3,000 ft with patches below and occasional breaks to less than 7/10 and visibility 3 plus miles. Cloud gradually lowered and became 10/10 between 1,000 and 2,000 ft with extensive patches 600 – 1,000 ft in slight rain which reached 51N Lat by 1000 hrs and 50N Lat by 1300 hrs persisting until passage of front. Visibility 2,000 to 4,000 yds in rain. Cloud became well broken behind front with a base 2,000 – 3,000 ft and decreased towards dusk inland. Visibility plus 3 miles.[21]

The temperature dropped and men in the open became very cold as we have seen. Snow showers were forecast for the following day, and some fell during the morning.[22] At 3 am the few Lincolns who had managed to sleep woke to a hot meal and a rum ration that 'warmed many a chilled body'. Rear HQ moved up the 500 yards to join Tac HQ at Nachtigallskath (984391), located in a clearing 200 yards behind the breakfasting troops.

Jack Hunton, a Troop Commander with 33 Fld Regt, was up with the Lincolns, and just after VE Day wrote a diary. He described how the small German rearguard held up the Lincolns:

---

20 Appendix No. 2: 9 BIB Post-battle Conference, 8 March 1945.
21 TNA: 2 TAF ORB for 1 March 1945.
22 Darby Hart's diary.

> 2nd March. We moved forward with C Coy at 0500 hours to attack Kervenheim. Actually 'A' Company had previously taken the first two or three houses the night before but with heavy casualties. Fortunately, we arrived safely, but only just in time as the enemy fired everything onto the road a few minutes later. House to house fighting began and eventually the place was cleared. We moved on with the forward coy and were first across the bridge south of the town.[23]

Darby Hart of 2 Lincolns' A Coy had spent the night in a burning billet by the factory. He recorded in his little pocket diary; 'Fri 2nd. Snow! Moved into village. Civvies in cellars. Prisoners – no opposition.'

At 5.45 am, Bolo Whistler in Stein (969415) was given a résumé of the night's activities, and a note in the G Op's Log told the Duty Officer, 'Don't be afraid to go and see him if necessary'.

When the Germans left Kervenheim at 6 am, they left behind as we have seen a small covering party to slow down the British and make them believe the town was still occupied in force. In this they were successful. The Norfolks were still reporting at 7.15 am that they could not 100% guarantee Müsershof empty, and the KSLI were sure that the 'position in the village is the same as yesterday'.

185 BIB was out of wireless touch with the Warwicks and Norfolks, which was a comment on the limitations of the 18 set, which was short wave, operating in the range of 6 mc/s to 9 mc/s. It performed badly in the woods where Battalion Tac HQs usually located themselves to escape observation; it suffered interference from tank wireless; and was usually useless at night. The ritual complaint about it was made later at the Brigade Conference on 8 March, but in this as in everything the army 'sucked the hind tit' in comparison with the RAF whose mastery of communications and radar was world-leading. The British had a crystal-controlled VHF No.13 set under development in the 1930's, but abandoned it in 1937 as an economy measure. The Americans designed and introduced the same thing as the SCR 300 'walkie-talkie' in 1940. They produced 50,000 unts during hostilities, but provided none to the British army. Eventually in 1947 the British put the SCR 300 into production as the Wireless Set No. 31.[24]

By 8.25 am, 2 Norfolks occupied Murmannshof (984383), and the mopping up of Kervenheim after that progressed quickly. A prisoner taken in the town confirmed that the defenders had withdrawn, but added that a stand would be made in the Berber Woods. Based on this false information, Division asked the Air Liaison Officer (ALO) to provide a Typhoon strike on the woods. The target was accepted at 9.30 am, and the strike scheduled for 9.55 am. It will be described shortly.

At 10 am the western of the two bridges in Kervenheim (990381) was captured intact, and at 10.30 am it was reported to brigade that the Rittergut bridge (991382) was standing although mined, and that Kervenheim was clear. The Norfolks reported at 10.45 am that the bridge (992375) south of Kervenheim on the road to Winnekendonk was Class 40 (rated to carry a 40-ton Churchill tank), and it was standing while 'Sappers were removing the mines'.

Meanwhile 9 BIB less the Lincolns was advancing quickly against negligible opposition. The KOSB under Macdonald, who had done a careful recce the previous evening, crossed the start line at Wettermannshof with S Sqn, 3 SG under Charles Farrell on time at 7.15 am, in spite of all the tanks having bogged before the stream was reached. The doubtful Coldstream bridge held up, and they were away without opposition, capturing ten prisoners on the way to taking Oberfeldshof (975377) and Müsershof (982383) by 7.50 am, and Reyshof (979371) at 8.40 am. The objective,

23 Pages from Capt Jack Hunton's diary provided by Capt Ivor Norton.

24 S Godfrey. *British Army Communications in WW2* (London, Bloomsbury, 2013), p. 231.

which was the crossroads at Reyshof, was secured by 9 am after an advance of 3 kms, the KOSB taking ten prisoners.

Renny ordered the RUR at 8.30 am to move up to the KOSB's position in Kangaroos and attack through it to take the Berber Woods (code-named Dover and Birmingham) on either side of the road. The Kangaroos were, however, delayed by the conditions around the bridge at Wettermannshof, according to the SG's war diary, and Erskine added that the RUR decided not to wait for them but to advance on foot.[25] The Battalion together with John Mann's LF Sqn, SG was ready on the Start Line on the forward edge of the KOSB's position at 10 am, when a one-hour delay was ordered so that a Victor artillery concentration of six field regiments could support the attack on the woods. At 11 am they advanced, although Fendick's diary records 10.30 am.

Rex Fendick had to rush to catch up with the RUR, and later experienced the section of Typhoons passing over him so low he imagined he could reach up and touch them.

Up at 0600 hrs. Conference. I'm to meet CO in Assy Area about 1000 hrs.

> Tony arrives and has breakfast with me. He is our Coy Comd now, and we're darned glad to have him. Pat has gone as 2 ic of 5 Manchesters in Eng. Tony OKs plan and I go forward, calling Mac to follow up. I leave this too late – Mac is late getting up but he gets the guns in OK. We have passed John [OC 3 Platoon] with KOSBs west of Kervenheim.
>
> I watch the RUR move off with Churchills at 1030 hrs [or 11 am].
>
> Later at 1200 hrs we move forward 2000 yds and set up Battalion HQ. The Typhoons supported the attack very closely.[26]

At 9.55 am Typhoons had attacked DOVER, code-name for the Berber Woods. They were from the famous 609 (West Riding) Sqn, part of 123 Wing commanded by Wing Co Johnny Baldwin. Their CO was Sqn Ldr E.R.A. Roberts and they were stationed in barracks at the old Luftwaffe airfield of Gilze Rijen in the Netherlands. The previous morning there had been no flying after the CO went up on a weather recce over Weeze, Goch and Cleve. But at 4.45 pm, as the cold front was clearing but still in foul weather, the wing attacked a group of houses southwest of Weeze (917362) with R/P, observing much smoke.

This morning nine Typhoons were up soon after breakfast at 9.35 am, led by the Wing Co Ops, Johnny C. 'Zip' Button. [OC 193 Sqn in Normandy, he took over 123 Wing on the death of Walter Dring]. He was accompanied by four Belgians, Mathys, De Bruyn, Jacquemin and Goblet, a New Zealander, Harkness and three from the British Isles, Cables, King and Mountjoy. Flying time was 20 minutes and the attack on the wood went in from west to east with 74 rockets and cannon fired. Much smoke was reported from the northern edge of the wood with a small explosion. One MET was reported damaged [belonging to the rearguard *Pionieren* as they laid aircraft bombs and mines to blow a 70 ft wide crater in the road]. Mathys[27] wrote in his log that he saw a big concentration of enemy troops and some MET, the defenders of Kervenheim retreating to new positions through the woods 1 km to the east of the Kervenheim-Winnekendonk road. [The woods rather than the open main road were chosen because they provided cover against air attack]. The section of Typhoons was back on the ground at 10.15 am having logged 40 minutes. The nearest British troops were the KOSB 1 km away, waiting for the RUR and Fendick to pass through and take over the advance.

25 Erskine, *Scots Guards*, p. 409.
26 Rex Fendick's diary.
27 Letter from retired Brig-Gen Mathys in 1983.

There then followed a series of events which could have had serious consequences, but resulted only in anguish and a great deal of ordnance wasted on an undefended wood. At 10.35 am Division asked Air for a repeat attack on the wood because the RUR had been unable to take advantage of the first Typhoon attack. The Air Liaison Officer (ALO) at Division said that another attack would not be possible because of heavy commitments elsewhere, so Brigade made plans for an artillery shoot. But 10 minutes later at 10.45 am, based presumably on the debriefing of the first flight, a report came in to Corps that 20 MET had been seen 500 yards north of Bruch (005355). Horrocks told Whistler to ask for Typhoons, which he did at 11.15 am. Meanwhile Brigade had directed a Victor artillery shoot by six field regiments on the woods for 11.40 am, ordering the RUR to attack the woods through the KOSB at 11.45 am. This had just been accomplished at 11.55 am, and the tanks and RUR were actually attacking when the ALO at Division said that the Typhoons would after all be attacking the Berber Woods at 12.05 pm. The makings of a disaster stared everyone in the face. Brigade told the ALO to divert the Typhoon strike to the woods south of Winnekendonk to which a recently captured PW had said that his unit had withdrawn. This PW was from an Ersatz Bn under command 8 FJD and he was found in a cellar at Bleickshof (986366).

It was too late to divert the planes that had taken off from Gilze Rijen at 11.40 am, this time led by the CO Roberts, with Mathys, Harkness, Mountjoy, King, De Bruyn and Jacquemin. In the 10 minutes left before the planes attacked, a frantic effort was made by the ALO to contact them and redirect the attack, and by 9 BIB to keep the RUR and tanks out of the wood. The LF Sqn tanks received the message and started streaming recognition smoke. The RUR stopped 600 yards from the Berber woods to the north of Lűtzhof while the Typhoons swept in towards them from the East. This time the planes saw no sign of the enemy but they all saw the SG's Churchills 500 yards away, and Mathys remembered them ever afterwards as 'belching coloured smoke for identification as friendly.'[28] A forward company of the RUR was machine gunned by the planes,[29] and several 'overs' fell amongst the leading tanks and infantry, luckily causing no serious damage.[30] 9 BIB thought it, 'a miracle no cas were inflicted'.[31] The risk, however was low as OR had earlier established that RP-3 60 lb rockets buried themselves in the ground before exploding with minimal damage to troops. The RUR's war diary recorded the events:

> During night 1 KOSB told to attack at first light followed by 2 RUR at 1000 hrs. SL a track at front edge of 1 KOSB posn. A Coy on left, B Coy on right each with one troop of SG. Recce of ground possible because no enemy. At 1000 hrs decided to put forward (sic) zero hour to 1100 hrs so an arty concentration of 6 Fd Regts could be fired in support of Bde. When advance began forward Coys had to be halted 600 yds from Dover and Birmingham while Typhoons dived to attack the woods. No opposition. B Coy patrolling from Sthn edge of Birmingham had skirmishes with enemy – 2 men wounded.[32]

Everyone on the ground had a fright. At the Brigade conference on 8 March, the notes record in three words the concern of 2 RUR; 'Attack by Typhoons'. Renny said the error was at Corps or Army, but the problem was systemic.

We can infer that since Corps told Division to request the air strike that the decentralised FCP system was in operation that day. The decision to use it was taken during the battle, and permitted Group Control to deal with demands in real time. We can assume there was a Contact Tank at

28 Letter from retired Brig-Gen Mathys in 1983.
29 TNA: 171/5279: 2 RUR's war diary.
30 Erskine, *Scots Guards*, p. 409.
31 TNA: WO 171/4330: 9 BIB's war diary.
32 TNA: WO 171/5279: 2 RUR's war diary.

Division in Stein with its ASSU tentacle in direct contact with Group Control at Goirle. The FCP would have been at Corps in Cleve with its ALO and RAF team. It intercepted all requests from the Contact Tanks and decided with Group which to accept. Once the request was accepted the Contact Tank was switched to direct R/T contact with Group through ASSU control, receiving verbally the details of smoke and arrival timing and then being cut off. This abrupt disruption of communication only became serious in unusual circumstances like the Berber Wood. Post-war analysis identified the problem as resulting from insufficient system capacity:

> For no longer than necessary was the demanding tentacle kept on R/T as in a moderately fast moving battle normal ASSU traffic accumulated during the time tentacles remained on R/T to the FCP.[33]

What was not explained was why the Contact Tank at division did not warn the aircraft by VHF wireless. Perhaps the Germans were jamming, or the operator was relieving himself.

These two air attacks were reported in some British newspapers, datelined 'Western Front, Wednesday', presumably 7 March by Ronald Walker under the headline:

> CALCAR HEAVILY BOMBED IN CLOSE-SUPPORT T.A.F. RAIDS.

The gist of the article was that 2 TAF had flown a thousand sorties, which is the measure of a busy day. The 84th Group was principally concerned with close Army support. Its fighters were asked by British troops, thrusting out of Goch to lay a carpet of rockets and cannon fire in a wood to the south-west. They laid a carpet, flew home, refuelled and rearmed, and put in the second attack inside one hour. The three key towns of Calcar, Udem and Weeze, to the east and south-east of Goch, received individual attention. Fighter-bombers of the 83rd Group attacked Calcar all the afternoon with high explosives, anti-personnel and incendiary bombs, while the Mitchells of the Second Group went to Udem and Weeze.[34]

The article is a collage. It covered five days from Monday 26 February, when Üdem was bombed[35] to Friday 2 March with the two attacks on the wood described here. This was reporting based on handouts. Walker, the Australian aviation correspondent for the Express group, or the RAF publicist who briefed him, used the familiar concept of strategic 'carpet-bombing' of German city centres. This was the spin put on 'de-housing' factory workers since the RAF never admitted targeting civilians, including women and children. Here the concept was applied tactically, conjuring up a picture of 2TAF thoughtfully laying a welcoming mat for the Army. Reality was different; frightening and dangerous on both sides. 'Bafflegab' was used extensively by the RAF to spin its expensive and counterproductive practices.

After the Typhoons had departed, the RUR advanced, and at 12.34 pm Division was informed that a sub-unit was in the wood. Brigade Diary noted that there was no organised opposition but some 'Volkssturm sniping etc'. By 1.30 pm Brigade estimated that the RUR would be on the objective and the Lincolns' Start Line had been secured.

Both the divisional field regiments and the medium regiment under command fired during the afternoon:

33 TNA: WO 233/61xC 7225: *Air Support & Air Recce Aspects of Combined Operations in NW Europe: June 1944 – May 1945.*

34 Summary of an undated *News Chronicle* cutting sent by Mathys to this author in 1983.

35 C Thomas & C Shores. *2nd Tactical Airforce, Vol 3* (Hersham: Ian Allan, 2006), p. 434.

> VICTOR target fired on WINNEKENDONK and on woods to S. Lincs require quick barrage and concentration for attack on objective. H Hr for barrage 1745 hrs. KOSB clear N side of stream to E of WINNEKENDONK supported by fire plan of Div Arty.[36]

Again the intelligence source for choosing the Victor targets was a PW; '1400, 1410, 1420 hrs shot on V target. These three targets were different parts of wood where PW reported that enemy had concentrated.'[37]

Meanwhile A and C Coys of the Lincolns under Sam Larkin and Glyn Gilbert, had moved through Kervenheim and cleared Potthaus. When during the morning information came through that the enemy had withdrawn to the Berber Woods, the Lincolns would have decided they would not be needed for some time while the RUR cleared the woods. At 2.45 pm they reverted to the command of 9 BIB and the whole Battalion consolidated at Potthaus (9992378). At the same time the Lincolns were ordered to move up ¾ mile and assemble at the bend in the road by the crater next to the Berber Woods (994366), to join up with Alan Cathcart's RF Sqn 3 SG, and assault Winnekendonk.

The FUP was close to the large roadblock of felled trees (993363) which had been discovered at midday.[38] Bulldozer equipment was ordered up and 17 Fld Coy cleared the block. Soon afterwards 1 Pln, which was responsible for the road, reported a crater on the Winnekendonk road opposite Brőnkshof (995353). This caused delay to 3 Recce Regt, which at 3.40 pm was still reporting to GAB that there was no movement past it. The Germans were cratering roads with 500 lb aircraft bombs buried in low ground and over a culvert. The explosion left a hole 12 feet deep and up to 75 feet wide which rapidly filled with water. It required bridging and the advance would be delayed until one could be brought up. At 3 pm, the RUR occupying the Berber Woods heard a loud explosion, which they correctly guessed was a crater being blown in the road junction at the entrance to Winnekendonk (998347), and into which a Churchill tank subsequently fell. The Fallschirmjägers had turned Winnekendonk into a fortress, confident of repeating the punishment they had inflicted on the Norfolks the previous day by channelling the attackers into a killing ground.

At the same time on 2 March 1945, 1 KOSB returned to the front line after two days of inaction:

> The Battalion remained in its positions astride the Üdem-Weeze road for two days, while the rest of the line was straightened out, and whilst another Brigade attacked Kervenheim where it encountered very determined resistance.
>
> It was therefore decided that we, with the support of a squadron of tanks, should by-pass the town and carry out an attack at dawn. So early on the 4th [(sic); 2nd is meant] March we started this attack, but found that the Germans had withdrawn and consequently we managed to take prisoner only a few stragglers.
>
> It was important that we should make contact with the retreating enemy, so fresh plans were made while we rested in the barns and outhouses of the ruined farms, where solid German peasants – with characteristic phlegm – were already beginning the hard task of restoring order out of the chaos of dead cattle and torn up fields.
>
> As the morning passed we found the farmyards and tracks filling up with Kangaroos, until a whole company of these troop-carrying tanks established in the Battalion area. At the same time the 2nd Battalion the Royal Ulster Rifles secured the western edges of the woods north of Winnekendonk.

36 TNA: WO 171/4816: War Diary 33 Field Regiment RA.
37 TNA: WO 171/5036: War Diary of 84 Medium Regt RA.
38 TNA: War Diary 253 Fld Coy RE.

Our next task was to secure Bruch, a small village on the outskirts of Winnekendonk. [The word, *Bruch*, meant swamp, misinterpreted by the British cartographers. The 'village' was a farm, Mottenhof, 300 yards from Rahmenhof].In the early afternoon we piled into the Kangaroos and set off across country. A most impressive column we were; a squadron of Churchills led the way, followed by some Self-Propelled guns, and we brought up the rear in our fifty Kangaroos.

That was a crazy afternoon. In the pale spring sunshine the tanks moved through the soft green fields, past farms and plantations while over to the left Kervenheim stood out clearly, with the Church spire and battered houses. Everybody had a curious feeling of exhilaration, as if the hunt was on – as indeed it was! Jeeps raced through the slowly advancing tanks, and the Brigadier leaned out of his scout car, to cheer us on.

Eventually we reached the line of the Kervenheim-Winnekendonk road and the edge of the woods. There we left the Kangaroos as the going was no longer suitable for them, and moved the Companies into the dank and chilly jungle of undergrowth, floored with mosses and bogs, which spread through the woods. The tanks were sent along a track in line with the reserve Companies ready for an attack on Bruch. Unfortunately there was a huge crater at the end of this track, as the Commanding Officer discovered on his reconnaissance, and it was realised that this would seriously hamper the tanks, which would therefore have to give the best support possible from the edge of the wood. The attack was planned, with 'C' and 'D' Companies forward, to start at 6 pm.

In the meantime the enemy had detected tanks, and had begun to shell the woods very heavily. Along the track his marksmanship was remarkably accurate, as those in Jeeps well knew. But he also bracketed the Company positions, and some feverish digging was done in the sodden ground. A few casualties were caused and came back on stretchers borne by prisoners, who were still being collected.

The attack was delayed, however, as at 6.15 pm all available artillery was required for an assault on Winnekendonk itself, carried out by the 2nd Bn The Lincolnshire Regiment. The attack by the famous English County Regiment will go down as one of the finest actions of the campaign in North-West Europe. It was fought with utter fury by both sides, and entailed most serious losses for the attackers, who were magnificently led and covered themselves with glory as they drove the Germans steadily out of the village until it was firmly held.

While this exploit was being carried out, we spent an exceedingly uncomfortable five hours in the woods, where a hail of shells came down upon us. Many consider this was the worst shelling that we ever experienced. At midnight our attack went forward as originally planned and was completely successful. The forward companies struggled through the dense undergrowth, negotiated two streams in the darkness, and then advanced across open country under spandau fire to the final objective.[39]

Charles Farrell commanded S Squadron and remembered the crater holding up the KOSB:

It was, for S Squadron, a frustrating attack on Winnekendonk. We were bottled up in a wood, which had been badly chosen as our line of advance with the infantry battalion, and a huge crater at the exit of the wood prevented us fulfilling our role. Our time in the wood was an unpleasant one for the infantry. However, we could find no way for our tanks to debouch from the wood with its old and densely planted trees.[40]

39 Wilson, *Short History*, p. 45.
40 Charles Farrell. *Reflections 1939-1945* (Bishop Auckland: Pentland Press, 2000), p. 126.

2 March 1945. 1 KOSB mounted in Kangaroos moving up to Lützhof, before entering Berber Wood for the assault on Bruch. The line of trees marked the Kervenheim to Winnekendonk road. The going in the plowed fields would have been the same for Sgt Alldred six hours later when attacking the 88 just 2 km to the south. (© Crown Copyright. IWM, B 14974, taken by Sgt Carpenter)

The Kangaroos were from A Squadron, 49 APC Regt, RAC.

> Mar 1. Fallsdorf (sic) A Sqdn moved to 922468 (from 918483) and planned with 9 Brit Inf Bde to lift 2 RUR on 2 March 1945 South of Kervenheim. A Sqdn at 974408 [Ratzenhof] under comd of 9 Inf Bde.
>
> Mar 2. A Sqdn plan was changed and they lifted 1 KOSB to wood 9936 – no opposition encountered. 618 men 136 vehicles.[41]

The distance to the Berber Wood was under a mile, but since the Kangaroos were present, it was felt that they they might as well be used to save the infantry from fatigue, a point made by the KOSB at the subsequent Brigade conference:

> Moving in Kangaroos didn't save much <u>time</u>, but saved the infantry much fatigue in marching through deep mud. Forming up by Kangaroos well organised by the Kangaroo officers.[42]

Details of the route taken by the KOSB and SG through the wood were recorded on a slip of paper found by Chips Parker Smith in his satchel in 1983, recording the target numbers and their headings.

M221 9959 3641 100°	M222 9979 3638 100°	M223 9998 3632 100°
M224 0015 3628 100°	M225 0033 3624 100°	M226 0052 3620 100°
M227 0039 3570 170°	M228 0029 3558 170°	M229 0035 3543 170°

German fire started around 5.15 pm, when the Brigade Diary recorded that Spandau fire was opened from 003350. Mortar fire then landed on the leading companies accompanied by the

41 TNA: WO 171/4722: 49 Armoured Personnel Carrier Regt war diary.
42 Appendix: 9 BIB post-battle conference.

CO with his R group when they reached the edge of the wood (004355). The large crater made it impossible for the tanks to reach the objective and they supported as best they could from the edge of the wood. Timed for 6 pm, the attack was postponed as we have seen. There is no report of tanks supporting the postponed attack in the dark, so they must have decided to return to harbour, pace the quotation in Farrell's book – 'Spens praised 6 GTB ... and said they would go anywhere with them, even through woods by moonlight.'[43]

In Tony Edwards' notebook there is a section dealing with the artillery support for the attack on Bruch. The map references of the target numbers are given below. The code is not in the notebook.

> Fire Plan from 15 [15 referred to the RA CO, Lt-Col Maurice Hope. LL was Gilkes, Cdr 109 Bty, 33 Fld Regt] relayed by LL. Fire plan H-15 to H. Tgt 6220 E100 1 Regt. Tgts 6216, 6217, 6223 each 1 Bty. Tgt 6222 1 Regt. All rate 1 1/2. Other Tgts required will be affected by safety restrictions. LL would like Counter Bty during programmes & subsequently. Considerable shelling from 150° from area Ramsgate. Time of shelling 1800-1830. Guns considerable distance away. H hour now MPKS (2).[44]

At 9 pm, with C and D coys forward, the KOSB occupied Mottenhof to Rahmehof (002349-006353) where 12 prisoners were taken. They had struggled through dense undergrowth, forded two ditches in darkness, and then advanced across open country to the sound of the bagpipes against heavy machine-gun fire. There is no mention of the pipes in the battalion history, but George Wall of the Lincolns heard them from across the fields in Winnekendonk. The night that followed was unpleasant. The Germans were sensitive to the advance of KOSB and 'S' Squadron on the eastern flank. They would remember their defeat from the same quarter in Kervenheim on the previous day by the KSLI and CG. Hugh Gunning believed that the Germans discounted a frontal assault on Winnekendonk:

> The Lincolns in a furious hand-to-hand battle took Winnekendonk by storm after advancing across open country to the 'front door' of the village, an approach so hazardous that the enemy considered that troops would not dare to make the attempt from that direction. The KOSB and RUR supported the Lincolns in this gallant action, but the main credit went to the English battalion whose men fought a series of back garden battles of a ferocious character with both sides hitting hard and angrily. The men of 9th Brigade, fresh from their well-earned rest, were in great form.[45]

If Gunning is correct, then the Germans interpreted the KOSB's attack as the *schwerpunkt*, and possibly believed that the KOSB intended to turn east to cut the Sonsbeck road. However, it was in Winnekendonk that the Pak-Front was set up, so the defenders covered all contingencies. Even so, the speed of the assault caught the defenders off-balance, since if the section with two MG42s ambushed by Glyn Gilbert's company at Plockhorsthof in Winnekendonk – see below – had been sent across the 600 yards from Mottenhof ten minutes earlier when the German commander realised the real threat was coming down the main road, they might just have slaughtered Gilbert's company before being destroyed by MacDonald-Buchanan's troop, and have possibly changed the course of the battle. In the event they were killed to a man before firing a shot.

43 Farrell, *Reflections*, p. 121.
44 Tony Edwards's notebook.
45 Hugh Gunning. *Borderers in Battle* (Berwick: Martin's Press, 1948), p. 180.

The Germans still possessed much artillery, and the allies estimated that over a thousand guns were in use against the Canadians in the Hochwald Gap. Some of the bigger pieces were emplaced on the east bank of the Rhine. When required, the full force of German DF could be overwhelming, as the Borderers discovered.

At a distance of 2 kms to the West of 3 BID's axis, a good road ran south from Reyshof (980372) to Kevelaer, conforming after 1 km with the East bank of the River Niers. 3 Recce had reached Reyshof at 11.25 am. Now they began to move down the road and at 3.07 pm reported meeting, and soon clearing away, another roadblock and mines (973353). At 3.29 pm, an SP gun (at 974346) stopped them. Nearby the enemy held a wood, so at 3.45 pm artillery support was obtained to assist the advance. Brigade interpreted Recce's problems in the light of a wireless intercept made at midday, which had stated that the enemy was holding a semicircle of battle outposts running about 1.5 miles from Kevelaer. 3 Recce were understood to have bumped against that semi-circle.

S and LF Sqns of 3 SG assembled in the Bleickshof – Lützhof area (9836 and 9936). The only opposition so far was from houses near Bleickshof which were shot up by LF to yield 15 prisoners. In the meantime around 3 pm, Capt Rawdon (Harry) Pember, who commanded the SGs' Recce Tp with two troops of Honey tanks, was told to patrol down both sides of the road and, 'find out what opposition there was in Winnekendonk'. The Honey was still the vehicle of choice of the Recce tps. It combined better cross-country performance than the Daimler Scout Car, with a good turn of speed at 35 mph (56 kph). What, however, was particularly prized, was the ability to rest up quietly on watch with main engines turned off and batteries kept charged by a single cylinder petrol engined generator.

Pember was highly regarded, although notorious for having cheated on Exercise *Blackcock* in Britain by bluffing the umpires and crossing a 'blown' bridge. Brig Verney was pleased. The War Diary noted the bluffing, revealing the connivance of the CO and probably of Verney in this jolly jape.[46] Pember was killed on 29 March 1945 outside Dorsten by a sniper according to the official history,[47] but actually by a volley of fire from an American paratrooper riding on 3 SG tanks behind Pember. The witness was Trooper J.E. Davies in Pember's tank.[48]

The right-hand recce troop bogged when trying to go round the large crater in the road (995353), blown where it runs in a shallow cutting opposite Brőnkshof. The left-hand troop followed the track past Kötershof (997359), which was occupied as Rex Fendick discovered the following day, but the occupants had not reacted against Pember; their task was to report events to the defence in Winnekendonk which ordered a StuG to destroy the Honey. Fendick later captured the occupants.

> On the next bound forward, on Saturday 3 March, we had a short holdup on the road as it was stonked. I sent a couple of the lads over to check a farmhouse which sat in the open a couple of hundred yards off the road. I saw them suddenly begin to make very war-like moves as they got near the house, and in a couple of minutes two Jerrys came out with their hands up, one a Captain. We went back to the RUR's Bn HQ in the Berber Wood, to turn him over to the Bn IO. A little later, I was standing near the CO's Command Post when we were stonked heavily and everyone went to ground. I glanced up and our German Captain was standing coolly and looking down at us disdainfully. Maybe he thought his own artillery and mortars couldn't harm him![49]

46 TH Place. *Military Training in the British Army* (London: Routledge, 2000), p. 24.
47 Erskine, *Scots Guards*, p. 425.
48 BBC. http://www.bbc.co.uk/history/ww2peopleswar/stories/21/a4538621.shtml
49 Rex Fendick's diary.

Sgt Brown's Honey knocked out on the approaches to Winnekendonk on 2 March 1945. Harry Pember, OC Recce Troop, was following behind and asked for smoke which was laid by Mark Fearfield, which allowed the crew to escape into the wood. The Honey did not burn and would have been recovered as it was not in the postwar list of wrecks. (© Cathcart family)

After passing Kötershof, the left-hand patrol under Pember himself reached the tip of the wood (001354), reporting the wood clear but Bruch held. At that moment the Honey, which was commanded by Sgt Brown was knocked out by an SP firing from the road junction (997347) on the outskirts of Winnekendonk, at the place where the road was cratered soon afterwards. The crew of the Honey baled out unhurt but were in an exposed position in the open. Pember in the other tank went into cover and called for smoke, 'which was beautifully placed by a troop of LF and HQ tanks, and behind it went out into the open and rescued them.'[50]

Pember's request went to Mark Fearfield, an LF trp cmd, who remembered it clearly:

> I was located at the forward edge of the Berber Wood (996362). I believe that Pember had broken from cover and had gone to ground after being fired on, maybe in Bruch. He now had the problem of getting back. I was sitting around, brewing up, when instructions came from LF Sqn Commander [John Mann], to be prepared to receive a message from Pember and to help him. Pember switched his net and asked for smoke, giving a map reference. But my Troop was not trained in firing as artillery at map references, so I told the gunner to load a smoke shell, point the gun in the general direction of Pember and fire. We couldn't see Pember since he was behind the woods. Pember said, "Very good", and gave directions, so the

50 TNA: WO 171/1258: 3 Scots Guards war diary.

> troop fired smoke until he had got back. After this we watched the attack on Winnekendonk and were ready to help if needed.[51]

At 3.15 pm, 2 Lincolns were ordered to take Winnekendonk, with H Hour set for 5.45 pm. At Battalion HQ the map was consulted, and the long stretch of open ground noted. At 4.40 pm, in full battle array, the Battalion moved down both sides of Winnekendonkerstraße, snaking towards the FUP, marching by section, a few paces between each man, under strict discipline with no smoking, their boots noisy on the road making the only sound, foot-slogging to war as soldiers had been doing on this very road for the previous eighteen hundred years.

This land between Rhine and Meuse had seen man coming and going for over 12,000 years, but the first soldiers were probably the Roman legionaries marching from their camp at Xanten in the second century AD. Frankish tribes moved in along the road in the sixth century and settled. A priest started using the road in 1080 and the Church here maintained its allegiance to Rome in spite of Luther's theses. In 1420 the landowner fortified his house. In 1448 knights and retainers passed by, burning Winnekendonk to the ground as part of the upheaval caused by Philip The Good, Duke of Burgundy, self-styled 'Grand Duke of the West', in building the foundation of a first experiment in European federalism. For a few years he organized a state that stretched from Amsterdam to Amiens and Mâcon. Spanish troops travelled the road in 1586 to raze Winnekendonk again. In 1689, a column of French soldiers plundered and destroyed it for a third time. Then for two hundred and fifty years the road knew only peaceful traffic, until 1939 when singing Todt Organization workers built the West Wall, aka the Siegfried Line, nearby.

Now the Second Battalion of the Lincolnshire Regiment, the Tenth of Foot raised on 20 June 1685 to fight under John Churchill to put down the Monmouth Rebellion, and which had travelled since then via all four of Marlborough's extraordinary victories at Blenheim, Ramillies, Oudenarde, and Malplaquet, to Concord where they ignited the American Revolution by seizing the colonists' arms, to the Peninsula under Wellington, to Sobraon in the first Sikh War and celebrated every 16 February, to Mooltan, Goojerat, Punjaub, Lucknow, Atbara, Khartoum, Paardeberg, Mons, The Marne, Messines, Ypres, Neuve Chapelle, Loos, The Somme, The Lys, The Hindenburg Line, Suvla, Dunkirk, Hérouville,[52] Troarn, and Venraij, was swinging down that same, worn road. This time Winnekendonk was already a ruin, destroyed by 2 TAF on 28 February. None, even those who had been through Caen and Goch, had seen worse destruction.

The sounds of war were all about the Lincolns as they moved up; the fluffing of shells overhead; the clank of the carriers lifting ammunition or 3 inch mortars or towing 6pdr anti-tank guns; the whine of the Jeeps with the stretchers, of the lorry with the RAP soon to be set up in Berber wood near the SL, and of the half-track with the communications. All direction was forward. The four rifle companies in full battle-order moved in single file along both edges of the road, in number 300 to 400 men. They were the tip of the allied war machine stretching back through half the world. The vehicles were from Willys Overland in Toledo, Ohio; White Motor in Cleveland, Ohio; Massey-Harris in Racine, Wisconsin; Studebaker in South Bend, Indiana; Ford and Chrysler in Windsor, Ontario; General Motors in Oshawa, Ontario; Humber Works in Coventry, Warwickshire; BSA Cycles in Birmingham, Warwickshire; Ford Motor in Dagenham, Essex; and Vauxhall and Bedford Motors in Luton, Bedfordshire. Everything the troops wore and carried was made in Britain, with the exception of: the officers' radioactively luminous watches imported from Switzerland in the bomb-bay of a Mosquito; the tobacco from Virginia which

51 Mark Fearfield in conversation in 1984.

52 Edward Dunstan. *The Forgotten Battle of Herouville, 2004* (http://richi.co.uk/charnwood)

they could smoke only after ordered to 'fall out'; their tins of bully beef from Argentina; and their pistols if made by Colt, Smith & Wesson – or Luger.

The road was lined with trees each painted with a white band that was thicker on the bends. Branches and debris covered the roads, which although metalled, are shown in photographs as covered in mud from shelling and tracked vehicles. Along the road at 80 yard intervals were zig-zag trenches or funk holes dug by local labour, including children, to provide shelter from *Jabos*. The troops moved carefully, watchfully and silently in line. The temporary and acting majors, who were substantive captains made up to replace the battle losses of Black Orchard, Pont de Vaudry, and Overloon, led their companies, and the subalterns their platoons. Officers wore cloth insignia but carried a .303 rifle to be indistinguishable from the men, doing nothing to attract the attention of German snipers. Each man's only protection was a mild steel helmet, some of the old World War I pattern or the newer, deeper drawn and less popular 'Canadian' D-Day style, some covered with a net holding scrim. Everyone carried a spade, and none a pick. Darby Hart carried the spade facing forward across his heart. Others preferred the metal to protect their back. Individually these troops were less well protected than the soldiers of 1486 and, compared with the power of modern munitions, completely and terrifyingly vulnerable in the days before Kevlar and laminated plastics. Within two hours the commander of D Coy was dead on the battlefield without a visible mark on his body. Their only protection was a well-developed sense of the battlefield around them, which allowed them to distinguish instinctively the potentially dangerous from the harmless, and the certain power of retaliation against aimed fire.

Horrocks, with the wisdom of experience was planning for the possibility of the Lincolns' failure, but with his characteristic lack of thought had chosen a course certain to produce complete disaster. At 4.30 pm he sent a message to Crerar, who was in the air within fifteen minutes of landing at Uden after visiting Horrocks and Simonds. The message came from Capt Moyle:

> The enemy is withdrawing along the whole Corps front and with few exceptions contact is lost with them.
> INTENTIONS. 3 Brit Inf Div: have been directed onto WINNEKENDONK. Gds Armd Div: will be passed through 53(W) Br Inf Div and depending on facilities will adv on axis:
> a) GOCH – WEEZE – XRds 950362 [Schloss Wissen] EAST along main rd to rd junc 992375 [Potthaus] – SOUTH to WINNEKENDONK – then onto KEPPELN and eventually ISSUM
> b) GOCH – WEEZE – KEVELAER – WINNEKENDONK – then to KEPPELN –ISSUM.
> It is NOT expected that Gds Armd will move before first lt 3 Mar.
> If 3 Brit Inf Div meet considerable opposition at WINNEKENDONK, they will be stopped and Gds Armd Div will attack WINNEKENDONK.[53]

This message revealed the cloud cuckoo land (*Wolkenkukucksheim* in German), that the Allied commanders inhabited. The Germans had re-equipped to counter the excellent Russian AFVs, and were contemptuous of Allied armour. The Allied infantry noticed the inexplicable inability of GAD to use holes that 3 BID punched in the German line ostensibly for them and with such loss, and there must have been chattering about GAD's role in the Arnhem fiasco. Rex Fendick commented:

> It is worth remembering that while 3 Div were carrying out these attacks on heavily defended sections of the Siegfried Line, we were following orders to open a hole for the Guards Armd

53 LAC: Canadian Army Ops Log.

> Div to break out. They were to exploit to the Rhine, hopefully cut off the Jerrys who hadn't yet made it across, and link up with the Yanks who were approaching slowly from the south. In fact, 3 Div opened a hole three times. The first two times, the GOC of the Guards Armd Div decided the hole wasn't big enough and delayed his advance. When on the third try by 3 Div, he was satisfied and went through us, 3 Div Recce Regt had already gone through, and it was they, not the Guards Armd, who made first contact with the Americans... Because of the delay in the Armour breakout, practically all German troops on our side of the Rhine were able to make a successful withdrawal across the river, avoiding the attempts to cut them off; the POW bag was quite small.[54]

In the event that 3 BID/6 GAB had failed at Winnekendonk and GAD had been sent in, the result would have been even worse than the contemporary Canadian fiasco in the Hochwald involving 11 BAD and 4 CAD. Shermans could not manoeuvre off-road, and on-road they would have been destroyed. The Sherman was vulnerable even to the six 50 mm anti-tank guns in fixed emplacements in Winnekendonk, which the Churchills swept aside. Because of equipment vulnerability, no Sherman commander could have conceived of what Cathcart and Firbank were about to pull off. After the breakthrough at Winnekendonk, GAD was camped only a dozen miles behind from the front with roads to travel on and without opposition, but nevertheless proved incapable of getting forward in a timely manner. For three weeks they had been at 4 hours' notice to move, but when ordered by Horrocks to do so at first light on 3 March – and no good reason existed why Horrocks failed to order them to move at midnight – GAD found the going so bad that as early as 7 am they were predicting their arrival in Kervenheim would be as late as 2 pm. They did not finally make contact with the enemy until 65½ hours after the breakthrough occurred at Winnekendonk, travelling the 15 miles (the front had moved three miles by then) at an average speed of 404 yds per hour, or the speed of a soldier with full equipment crawling on his belly.

In 1940 and before converting to armour, the men of GAD had been 7 GIB in 3 BID, and the finest infantry in the world. By 1944 they had not only ceased to perform a useful function but were degrading the performance of the entire 21 AG. When eventually they took the lead after Winnekendonk nearly three days late, they were stopped cold on the Bonninghardt Ridge by a hastily erected German defence that 3 BID and 6 GAB would have swept aside in a few hours. It was a repeat of their hesitant, even incompetent, performance at Arnhem, which should have resulted in their disbandment and re-employment as infantry reinforcements. Constantly ill, Horrocks, the self-styled 'subaltern-general', seemed unable to grasp the realities of his command and do something, anything, to break GAD's lethargy. Montgomery briefed Horrocks about Arnhem on 12 September 1944, but Horrocks failed to brief his senior officers until 16 September. The Garden advance by the Irish Guards Brigade Group – 2 Armd Bn and 3 Bn Irish Guards under Lt Col Vandeleur – did not begin until 2.35 pm on 17 September, which was two hours after the Market element of the first airborne troops had arrived on their landing areas. The delay was due to Vandeleur's command being unready. A unit with the necessary sense of urgency would have started at daybreak, and helped divert German attention from the airborne landings. Vandeleur's timetable required him to be in Eindhoven at 5 pm, but he was only half the distance there at Valkensward and four hours behind schedule when he unaccountably and irresponsibly stopped for the night. This made him 12 hours behind schedule when starting up again the next morning, having given the Germans all the time they needed to ensure *Market Garden* turned into a fiasco.[55]

54 Fendick, *A Canloan Officer*, p. 175.
55 WF Buckingham. *Arnhem 1944; A Reappraisal* (Stroud: Tempus, 2002), pp. 96-97.

At 4.45 pm an RUR patrol saw fourteen enemy troops in Schayck (988354) and was fired on from Brőnkshof (994353). In Tony Edwards' notebook there is a record of M Targets being fired at 4.53 pm and 4.58 pm. The targets were in Winnekendonk, which was still out of sight from the ground. The information came from an intercept of a message from HQ (QLC) to Gilkes, BC109 (22), indicating that the source was probably an AOP over Winnekendonk in an Auster. The entries in Edwards' notebook are: 'QLC/22 M Tgt. 6210 [0072 3586 Huelsenhof to the east of the Berber wood] Scale 3. Engage 1653 Enemy occupied houses. QLC/22 M Tgt 997344 [Plockhorsthof] Scale at (blank). Engage 1658 – Spandaus.' The next line in the notebook is an untimed entry: 'QLC/22 Spandaus firing from village 004349 [Bruch] Demolition.'

If an AOP Auster was over Winnekendonk, then it raises the unanswerable question whether the pilot could see the defences and have warned both the Lincolns and RF of the ambushing 88s and StuGs, and advised the Fld Regts to stock up on smoke shells. There is no record of such a report.

Tony Edwards remembered questioning the Lincolns CO, Cecil Firbank, about whether they should fire into Winnekendonk, 'because civilians are there'. Cecil told him to go ahead. Tony also remembered that there was no counter-mortar operation[56] presumably because of the haste. Mortars killed Peter Clarke for sure, and added to the mayhem.

For the civilians in Winnekendonk the end of a long ordeal by bombing and shelling was almost over. The following undated letter was sent from Winnekendonk in the days before the assault by an inhabitant of Kevelaer. The dotted parts refer to items about Kevelaer that have been left out.

> Dear Sister-in law and Brother.
> As you can see, we have had to leave home. It was high time. Kevelaer was bombed because troops were there. We've lost everything. At least until mid-week your house was undamaged, but I don't know what has happened to it since then. … Elly is here in Winnekendonk with Lissa Klümpen, and I am staying with the Hoppegard-Waden's, big farmers. … Winnekendonk has taken in about 3,000 from Kevelaer. The people here are generous. The smallest household has taken in 6 to 10 people.
>
> … In Winnekendonk you can't get bread or groceries. … On Friday 10 bombs fell on the town at the crossroads. This meant more people in Winnekendonk lost their roofs. The planes follow us everywhere, and are the same everywhere. There's no point in going further. I came here with the pram. My sister-in-law is staying on the other side of the road with the Stevens's brothers and sisters. Franz Vorfeld is with the Fishers and was earlier with the Rohrmeisters. I was just listening to the farmers below them talking about the front. The artillery bombardment is terrible. It went on all night and strongly from 1 until 6 in the morning. Entepuhl is the brother-in-law of Frau Waden, who dared to get out of Geldern. Well Geldern is completely flattened.
>
> Ziska and Fritz have gone to Bad Schwalbach. We have had news that they got there all right. Fritz has found work in a hospital. I've had no news of Ketty's husband. Ketty was hoping that Willy would get leave. Dean Holtmann did not dare to return to Kevelaer. He is staying with the Priest in Düsseldorf-Rattingen. Now I must give you Ziska-frit's address in Bad Schwalbach/Taunus/Badweg 2, Pension Herka. My address is Family Waden, Hoppegardshof/Winnekendonk, which is the first farmhouse on the way to Sonsbeck. Just as you leave Winnekendonk, it is the first farm on the right.
>
> Now dear Hanna and Jac, we cannot for the time being return to Kevelaer. If exceptionally your home is spared, then let us all get together there even if it means lying in the rabbit

56 Tony Edwards in conversation in 1985.

> hutch. For those who stay here the life will be terrible. No water and no light. The cellar is flooded. If we survive we will have to start again from scratch. I would like to live to see what happens. It's a pity we don't have a radio, and for 8 days we have had no light. Keep well if God wills, and a sad farewell. As soon as the danger is past we will go to Kevelaer. Everyone here sends his or her best wishes. Hanna[57]

Winnekendonk lay on the supply route to the Kervenheim-Uedem front. As such it would inevitably be targeted by 2 TAF which first bombed it on 16 February. The big raid was on 28 February when 80% of the town was destroyed. The Daily Telegraph in London reported that 'nine raids with bombs and rockets were made on Winnekendonk, where the Kevelaer-Sonsbeck road formed a junction with the road to Uedem through Kervenheim.' The aiming point was the housing on Sonsbecker Straße. Fires broke out in Marktstraße and Kevelaererstraße which were visible throughout the night from some distance away. The Gellings House in Kevelaererstraße was totally destroyed killing eight people. Fifty one houses were destroyed by about two hundred bombs. The streets were impassable and 80% of the town destroyed or severely damaged. The destruction stopped movement of supply trucks and, it was said, facilitated the taking of the town.[58]

Flt Lt Richard Hough was in 197 Sqn at Mill, flying Bombphoons. They were equipped for carrying two 500 lb incendiaries or two 1,000 lb HE bombs. He bombed Winnekendonk visually on 16 and 28 February, and blind bombed on 27 February, and apparently ineffectually since German accounts don't mention it:

> Feb 16th. Ramrod Duty. – 2 × 500 on WINNEKENDONK. 17 aircraft [two sqns] on the show and all bombs in the already flattened village. Very intense and accurate light flak.
>
> Feb 27th. Ramrod Duty. – 2 × 1000. Blind bombing by ground controlled Radar. WINNEKENDONK. Bombed straight and level – curious sensation – from 10,000 feet. No flak.
>
> Feb 28th. Ramrod Duty. – 2 × 1000. To WINNEKENDONK again, visual dive-bombing this time. Spectacular results. Village wiped out, though some light flak.[59]

Hough described the blind bombing on February 27:

> And then, by late February, thick cloud was no longer a deterrent to us dive bombers. Some scientist, who became very unpopular with us, had invented a form of blind bombing, straight and level, by radar. We felt very stupid flying in loose formation above 10/10th cloud and in blazing sun all pressing the bomb tit together when the distant voice over the R/T ordered us to do so. We were told the bombing was highly accurate. "If we're going to have a wizard prang, I like to see it", someone complained. We shrugged our veteran shoulders and talked gloomily of the imminent end of the pukka fighter pilot who judged by eye and instinct and flew by his ass.[60]

57 *Rheinische Post* (Saturday 6 February 1982); this author's translation.
58 August Wormland. *Als das Dorf in Trümmern lag* (Rheinische Post, 13 January 1979).
59 Richard Hough's logbook
60 Richard Hough. *One Boy's War* (London: Heinemann, 1975), p. 140.

The Typhoon bombing did have some effect. A German supply truck, identified by its double rear wheels, is shown overturned in a bomb crater in Winnekendonk at the junction of Kervenheimer Strasse and Sonsbecker Strasse. The truck was returning from Kevelaer, and may well have been supplying Deutsch's StuGs. (© IWM Film A70 257-1)

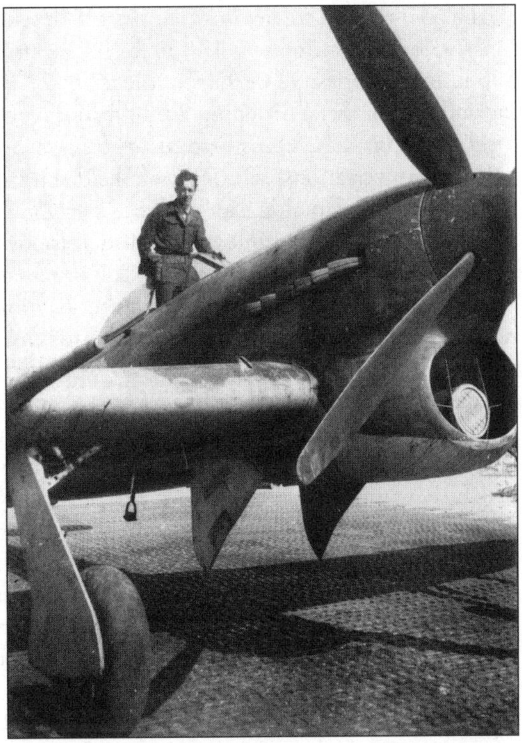

Richard Hough at forward airstrip, B.89 Mill, Holland. He bombed Winnekendonk on three separate occasions in this Bombphoon. (© IWM, HU 22324)

The bombing was intended, according to the RAF

> to prevent the enemy taking advantage of his effectively stabilised front by passing up reinforcements. The villages of Winnekendonk and Sonsbeck were strongly attacked; the first village by 64 Typhoons and Sonsbeck by 50 Spitfires. Winnekendonk was reported completely destroyed.[61]

This author visited Dick Hough to check his logbook against his book's narrative which was out of sequence. He described the routine at Mill:

> Word got around we were on ops. We climbed into Jeeps and went through the appalling mud to the briefing hut, which was on wheels, at Dispersal. The briefing took place with a brown job in attendance – target is so and so. But most of the briefing was technical – bombs being used, fusing (eg 0.25 seconds, or 5 seconds delay) according to the height of the raid. Then take-off in pairs and form up over Mill – usually 8 if there was one sqn and 17 if two sqns were on the op – and off to the target.[62]

61 TNA: 84 Group ORB.
62 Notes from a conversation with Dick Hough in April 1983.

The 64 Typhoon sorties flown against Winnekendonk dropped 111,000 lbs of bombs (50 metric tons), calculated as follows; 17,000 lbs in the 16 February raid by 17 Typhoons each carrying two 500 lb incendiaries; 94,000 lbs in the 27 & 28 February raids by 47 Typhoons (the 64 less the 17 incendiary bombers) dropping 2,000 lbs HE each.

At 4.45 pm 2 Lincolns arrived in the Assembly area at Lützhof (993366) where brief tank-infantry conversations with RF were held. From there the Lincolns moved through the wood to the FUP in the gap alongside the road at 993363. The War Diary records; 'The assault coys, 'D' and 'C' moved forward in extended order, followed by 'B' Coy on the right and 'A' Coy with Tac Bn HQ on the left.'[63] The 2ic Leslie Colvin remained here with the LOBs.

There has been controversy about the location of the SLs on either side of the road. On the right of the road the wood extends 500 yards further than it does on the left. So unless the SL was split, then either the right forward coy would have 500 yards of woodland to cross with the risk of getting behind, or the left hand forward coy would have to line up in the open invite shelling. George Wall, however, describes a different scenario, so unlikely that it could be true, of the whole Battalion lining up in the open opposite Roghmanshof, (Schayk on the map), waiting for the tanks which then appeared coming up the road and joining them at Roghmanshof. It seems that it was about there that the tanks did join them.

Forbes's diagram was drawn with the aid of participants and is one source for the location of the defenders' guns, and for the routes taken by the tanks. It shows the Churchills came round the wood on the right to avoid the Berber Wood crater and joined the road, and then fanned out to join the rifle coys extended in battle formation on either side of the road. We know from Pte Sid Smith and Maj Leslie Colvin that C Coy started at the edge of the wood on the left of the road. It was therefore not a split start line but a split FUP, which would explain why D Coy on the right saw no one on the left of the road, and why C Coy advanced for several minutes before the tanks fell in behind them on the SL.

Before describing the violent and bloody battle, it should be noted that the British had tried but discovered nothing during the day about the defensive preparations in Winnekendonk. Patrols by the RUR on foot, and the recce by Pember in tanks, had been beaten off before gaining information. There had been no night-time opportunity to send a patrol into Winnekendonk, and no time for Firbank to do an aerial recce. Pember had discovered only a StuG which knocked out his number two. Nothing had been revealed from prisoner interrogation or wireless intercepts, except the (dis)information that the Germans had fallen back to the woods south of Winnekendonk, where their mortars were set up. Nothing was known about minefields, which in the event were not a factor although the civilian diarist quoted below reported seeing them being sown everywhere, nor about the extensive trench system dug in the open fields and gardens in front of Winnekendonk and only partially manned in the German manner. The two or three 88 mms, the six 50 mm PAKs, and the troop of StuGs do not seem to have been located. The AOP in the Auster may have seen them but did not brief the COs. In short the attackers had no information and did not know that the Germans were present in considerable strength. Furthermore, the only known aerial photograph used on the battlefield was taken in the autumn with the trees in leaf. Why the artillery received this rather than one taken only two weeks before and showing the first dug defences is unknown. Renison said he never saw aerial photographs, but other infantry COs did. Cathcart and JG Smith, but not the infantry, had a map overprinted with information from this aerial photography. All speak of rush and last minute arrangements.

63 TNA: WO 171/5231: 2 Lincolns' war diary.

By 5.30 pm, with dusk only half an hour away, the Germans had probably decided from their knowledge of British drills and the known British disinclination to fight at night, and from their success in delaying the thrust on Bruch, that there would be no more fighting that day. Like the British tank crews they would already have begun preparing their evening meal. They would expect a British attack the next morning in strength, preceded by Typhoons and a heavy barrage in the set-piece Montgomery manner. There are many sources for this enemy view of the British, one example being Rudolf Langhauser's post-war debriefing by the Americans, countersigned by Plocher, who was facing the Canadians a few miles to the north-east at the time. *Blockbuster* took Simonds the predicted three days to implement:

> The enemy conduct of battle was highly schematic. Every assault could be recognised in good time (and) would be preceded by a long barrage, lasting up to 8 hours. After an attack had been repelled, a pause of 3 days usually followed, used by the enemy for the relief of the attack troops and for the new organisation of his next assault.[64]

There is an element of conceit in this view of a predictable enemy, and both sides shared it. It arose from familiarity with the other's methods. For example, Whitelaw said that if the Germans were mortaring one wood it would be safe to laager in another one nearby.[65]

However things were changing; Mike Carver had shown the benefit of night attacks when taking Stein during the night of 26/7 February and catching a troop of StuGs asleep, and again in the morning of 2 March only a few miles from Kervenheim at Neuenbauershof. He achieved this even with the unbattleworthy M4 Sherman. Brig Carver wrote of The Royal Scots Greys:

> These two night attacks, both originally planned to take place in daylight, were among the most difficult and yet the most successful that the Regiment had carried out. The enemy were in considerable strength, in well-prepared defences and supported by a heavy concentration of artillery, as well as by a high proportion of tanks and anti-tank guns. The ground was very wet and the weather equally so. The Regiment's success was due in large part to the fact that its morale was very high, everybody was fresh after a long period of rest, and the standard of training was as high as it had ever been. This was particularly the case as far as co-operation with the infantry was concerned. 4th King's Shropshire Light Infantry was a first-class battalion, and it had trained with the Regiment before the operation.[66]

It is clear that by contrast with the Scots Greys, 6 GAB were exhausted and did not know 3 BID sufficiently well. Nevertheless, Smith's refusal to support 1 Norfolks in their proposed night attack on Kervenheim on the night of 28 February/1 March was unconscionable, and the decision to optimize his command by suboptimising the whole operation should never have been his to make.

6 GAB did not make their first night advance until 28 March 1945. Then Brigadier Greenacre was ordered to take Münster at night with a task force comprising 4 CG, 3 SG, 515 Paratp Regt of 17 USAD, 3 Recce Regt, 6 Fld Regt and 61 Med Regt. It was a success.

Firbank's discomfiture due to the rush and absence of preparation, and his general lack of regard for Renny, were never concealed. 'Another Renny F***up,' he called Winnekendonk.[67] Miscalculation or chance could lead to a bn being destroyed in minutes and this fear haunted

64 USAHEC: Manuscript B-368.
65 Lord Whitelaw in conversation with the author.
66 M Carver. *Second to None; Royal Scots Greys* (Edinburgh: The Regiment, 1954), p. 165.
67 Cecil Firbank in conversation in 1985.

their commanders. Whitelaw and Cathcart had seen their sqn trashed at Caumont in minutes, and these memories never left them. Firbank told fellow officers that he regarded command of a bn in war as a privilege and fulfillment of his greatest desire in life.[68] He had seen what had happened to Barclay's Norfolks the previous morning and was doubtless determined to resist pressure from the Brigadier to do anything dangerous. The disastrous consequences of denying Barclay his night-attack on Kervenheim hung over them.

Renny was now ordered to gamble 2 Lincolns and RF 3 SG that evening, and it was subsequently rationalised as a fair risk of war and a point Firbank himself made at the subsequent Brigade Conference. Renny was being pushed by the hard-driving Whistler, who had no time for Renny and probably concluded that he had already been given enough time to get the job done, and had done little fighting so far in Op *Heather*. Whistler and 'Fish' Elrington (deputising for the sick Ross of neighbouring 53 BID) were under pressure from Horrocks to crack on and meet up with the Americans and cut off the German retreat. Horrocks had been visited by Crerar and by Simonds, who was bogged down in the Hochwald Gap, while Crerar had Montgomery breathing down his neck as the Americans 'swanned' against negligible opposition because the bulk of quality German forces were stuck to the Anglo-Canadian flypaper. Any German allowed to escape would be lined up on the east bank of the Rhine to resist the coming assault crossing.

The essential barrage was prepared, and the details were copied by the FOO, Chips Parker Smith into his notebook:

> **VANDAL BARRAGE**
> Opening line 500* [yards] to EAST and WEST of 6224 9973 3470, height 22 metres, [the cratered fork in the road in the approach to Winnekendonk]. Axis 180° [due South]. SEVEN lines at 100* every 5 mins. Rate 1 1/2. Third Regt superimposed + 200*[69]

There is a footnote in Tony Edwards' notebook. He was BC 101 Bty, twinned with 2 Lincolns: 'Barrage QWV first 5 open fire H to H + 100. 100 yds lift over 5 mins final lifting to long stonk 993339 170°' [just before the bridge on the Winnekendonk-Sonsbeck road]. This meant that the divisional artillery was to lay a line of shells, 1,000 yards wide, centred on the cratered fork at the entrance to Winnekendonk, lifting 100 yards every 5 minutes seven times. The barrage would start with 48 guns of two regiments for the first 10 minutes, and be thickened to all 72 guns of the three regiments for the remaining 25 minutes. Finally it would end in a stonk or concentration on the rear of the village to interdict enemy reinforcements (see Map 33).

The planned artillery barrage weighed 85,500 lbs or 38.8 metric tonnes, calculated as 48 guns firing for 35 minutes at a rate of 1½ rpm (2,520 shells), and 24 guns firing at the same rate for 25 minutes (900 shells), making 3,420 shells @ 25 lbs = 85,500 lbs This weight of ordnance was in addition to the 111,000 lbs or 50.4 metric tonnes of bombs dropped by 2 TAF's Typhoons. The combined tonnage was 89 metric tonnes dropped on, or fired into, an area of 700,000 yd^2 (1,000 yd × 700 yd), 145 acres or 59 hectares in two weeks, 16 February to 2 March. It comprised 3,420 shells, 34 (500 lb) US M.76 incendiaries, and 94 (1,000 lb) HE MC bombs. The average density of the ordnance was ¼ lb/yd^2 or 0.14 kg/m^2, or 1.6 tonnes per acre. In fact it was not distributed evenly, since Hough's raid on 28 February was aimed at the houses around the centre of the village, where little was left standing or not burnt out, and was spread over 14 days.

The dice were rolled. About 300 to 400 Lincolns, it being impossible to say exactly how many because the whole army was below establishment, on foot in four rifle companies led by Lt-Col

68 As recollected by Leslie Colvin from many conversations with Cecil Firbank.
69 Chips Parker-Smith's notebook in this author's possession.

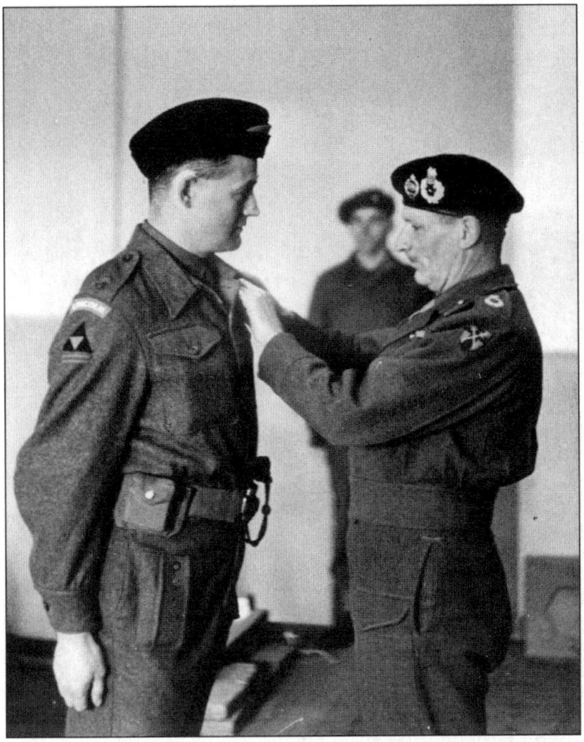

Lt Col Cecil Firbank received the DSO at Gimers Monastery on 11 December 1944. He was awarded a bar for his performance at Winnekendonk. (IWM B 12763, taken by Sgt Morris)

Maj Alan Earl Cathcart received the DSO for Winnekendonk in Plön on 12 June. (© Crown Copyright. IWM, BU 7824 by Sgt Morris)

Lt Alasdair Gordon led 1 Troop RF Squadron on the right at Winnekendonk. The photo was taken in 1944 during a DR's course in Britain on a BSA W-M20. (© Donald Gordon)

Cecil Firbank in person with his Tac HQ, supported by the direct fire of 15 Churchill tanks manned by 75 Scots Guardsmen under Major Alan Cathcart, and by the indirect fire of 72 guns of Brigadier Mears' 3 BID's artillery and a battery of mediums with their own FOO in a sixteenth Churchill, attacked the prepared and complete defences of a similar number of the élite of the finest and most professional army the world has ever seen, fighting for their homeland and with a grudge against the country remorselessly killing their women and children in the safety of their homes. The Germans were supported by six 50 mm and one, possibly three, 88 mm guns, by 3 StuGs, by divisional mortars and Nebelwerfers, and by the guns of 7 Fallschirmjägerdivision. The odds were stacked heavily against the British who, in conventional military wisdom as the attacking force, required not equality but a preponderance of three to one.

The unit ordered to lead the attack in the most exposed position on the right was Maj Peter Clarke's D Coy, supported by Lt Alasdair Gordon's troop. George Wall remembered a D Coy HQ meeting in the afternoon at the FUP near Lützhof with Peter Clarke and Alasdair Gordon's unidentified troop sergeant.

> Major Clarke told us we would be attacking Winnekendonk which was poorly defended, but on taking the village Guards Armoured would sweep down to the Rhine on the following day. The Guards Sergeant told us that the armour would be supporting us in the attack on Winnekendonk, and not to worry about the 88 mm German guns as the 88 would bounce off the tanks. They certainly didn't bounce off; they split them in two. We were told that once the Germans saw the infantry supported by tanks they would run. We were told we would come out of the woods and line up near the farmhouse [Roghmanshof]. It would be 1,250 yards to the target. There wasn't one obstruction in the way until we got near the field in front of the

houses. We came out of the woods to the farmhouse [Roghmanshof] and moved into the open and lined up facing Winnekendonk. We couldn't see the village from there. We were about 50 in D Company. I know we were nowhere near the strength we should have been. We had to wait a week for reinforcements. Anyway, we lined up; myself, Cpl Spuggie Spye, with CSM Gilleard next to Major Clarke. Major Clarke looked at me and said: 'You can fall out and join the reserve and follow at about 50 yds with the others'. The reserve consisted of CQMS Harris and George Tweedie who used to play goalie for Grimsby Town. We were told he had played for England. Among that lot was a fellow who helped with the cooking. I went back and joined them. We heard the occasional mortar drop in the woods which we had just left.[70]

Maj Pat Smith, MC commanded B Coy and remembered the haste and sketchy information:

Starting off in the battalion area south of Kervenheim in mid afternoon the battalion O Group was hastily summoned at which briefing we were informed that the enemy was on the run (that wasn't the first time we'd heard that to our cost) and we were to attack and occupy Winnekendonk. We were taken up to the assembly area and given the briefest of instructions – artillery cover would be provided (no details) and we would have tank support. The Start Line for 'D' & 'B' companies was the front edge of a small wood with a few straggly trees. I have a vague memory of the CO being most disturbed by the lack of information and the haste with which the whole operation was being carried out. There was no time to call company O Groups and as the company commanders were being briefed the whole battalion was already being brought up. I don't know if Peter Clarke had time to do any detailed briefing to his company, but I distinctly remember briefing John Boys (2ic) as we crossed the SL.[71]

Firbank also remembered the rush. First he was told by Renny to rest in Kervenheim, then late in the day told to take Winnekendonk as quickly as possible. The recce was done only by the SG and produced nothing of value. Firbank's following comment on the action included the brutal aside that marked the successful Lt Col on whose shoulder rested the success of the whole operation, given the vulnerability of the tanks to the 88 mm and the absence of accurate CAS. In the event Firbank could not even rely on his RSM to keep the men on their feet, since RSM Butters went to ground in a slit trench to be hauled out later by an irate Firbank.

Another Fuckup by Renny. It was a First War attack. The secret of success that day was to keep the men on their feet. Once men get down, they don't get up again.[72]

All that can be said is that out of a combination of not willing to let the side down and a collective feeling that someone had to do it, none of the officers gave in to their fears and most of the men also drove themselves to follow the officers through the hail of bullets and mortar bombs.

Jack Harrod, the Lincolns' Adjutant, recorded this exchange that took place on the SL.

Peter Clarke looked at his watch. It was 1745 hrs, but there were no tanks and no artillery. He looked over towards the CO. 'Shall I go, Sir? he asked. 'Wait', said the CO, and almost as he

70 Letter from George Wall to this author in 1994.
71 Letter from Pat Smith to this author in 1983.
72 Cecil Firbank in conversation in December 1982.

> said it the noise of the first salvo of shells was heard, and the first tanks appeared in sight. It had been a tense moment.[73]

Alan Cathcart was shown this passage and commented:

> I was of course very surprised to learn for the first time of the Lincolns' anxiety over our last minute arrival at H-hr. The infantry lie up, concealed, as close to the start line as they can before H-hr and hope that their presence and intentions have not been spotted by the enemy. Imagine what the effect would have been if a Squadron of Churchill tanks had joined them before H-hr behind the start-line, or even the two leading troops. All hell let loose, and how popular we would have been. Even if the tanks could have remained concealed, the noise of their engines would have destroyed surprise. Our normal "drill" was to have the tank FUP further back, say 500 yds from the SL. A tank can cover 500 yds very quickly, in a matter of 3 or 4 minutes [at 4½ to 6 mph]. We would time our arrival at the start line at H-hr and not a minute before. Furthermore a SL had much greater significance for the infantry than for the tanks since for infantry it was like "going over the top". For the tanks the action began the moment they break cover whether or not they have reached the SL. Often if an FUP was in dead ground behind a ridge (and not merely concealed by woods) the best fire positions for the tanks would be from the ridge firing to the flanks or over the heads of the infantry and before the tanks had even reached the SL. I believe the misunderstanding occurred because we were thrown together at short notice without ever having trained together at Inf/Tk co-operation. The Lincolns' history describes exactly the right procedure: 'It was not until the Battalion was actually moving forward that the Churchills came lumbering up the road'. That would have been the two leading troops moving to the SL. The supporting wave of tanks would without doubt already have been deployed in fire positions to support them and the Lincolns across the SL and forward.[74]

Cathcart is talking here of other engagements because the supporting wave at Winnekendonk did not stop to take up fire positions but all troops joined the infantry on the battlefield. Also the Lincolns' War Diary does not mention 'lumbering up the road', only 'appeared in sight', although Harrod believed they used the road: 'The tanks had been hampered in their progress to the start line by the trees felled to block the rd by the enemy and which had to be bulldozed out of their path'. The Churchills did not come up the road but avoided the roadblock and the crater by approaching through the fields to the right of the wood to take up position either side of the road. Cathcart was efficient and recced the route in advance, arriving as he said at exactly the right moment. But his split-second timing was also misinterpreted by 6 GABs' own War Diary which recorded that, 'RF had a very difficult route to the SL but got there with 30 seconds to spare, and all went forward behind the barrage'.

Other evidence that 3 SG and 2 Lincolns had never met before, which is not strictly true as they had cooperated as recently as four days earlier in the first engagement of the Operation, is in the War Diaries. The Guards' Diary refers to 2 Lincolns as '1 Lincolns', and the Lincolns' Diary believed that LF rather than RF Sqn supported them. After the battle, Firbank wrote to their CO, Dunbar, addressing him as 'Dear Drummond' – see below. This was at least more complimentary than the sobriquet of 'Clappie Claude' used by the irreverent subalterns. But if the battalions were relatively unacquainted with each other, each quickly recognised the quality and professionalism

73 TNA: WO 171/5231: 2 Lincolns' war diary.
74 Letter from Lord Cathcart in 1983.

of the other, showing total commitment to the task of turning the enemy out of Winnekendonk which in the end is the ultimate and most important task and one that can only be done by infantry.

Peter Clarke was uncharacteristically tense and unhappy, according to John Gilleard (see below), as he waited for H-hr at 5.45 pm, suffering a premonition that he would be killed. George Wall, the sniper who as Clarke's escort had also got to know him well over three months, says that all men had these thoughts, and that he himself used to brief the cook to write to his sister and tell her that he had met the fate he had expected ever since leaving England. He wrote:

> I can recall Major Clarke blowing his whistle for the off. There were a lot of men on the left [showing that Glyn Gilbert's C Coy had drawn level], but no tanks, then all of a sudden, there was a rushing of tanks to join us. As if they had been waiting for us, the Germans opened up. As we came out of the bend, the Germans hit the tanks with their anti-tank guns. There was one 88 mm over to the right, way over. I seem to think that gun accounted for two of the tanks. The tank nearest the road on the left was hit by, I can't imagine what, but its turret fell off, then it opened up as if it had been split in two. What amazed me, three fellows ran from it to the roadside and crouched down. What happened to them I couldn't say. I was told that the other tank that was behind us turned and disappeared into the woods. Later, I was told that this tank accounted for the SP gun near the house and also the anti-tank gun over to the far right. [This tank belonged to Sgt Jim Alldred or his Cpl, both of whom drove off to the west and destroyed the 88 and StuGs, as recounted below. This is evidence that the infantry knew about 2 Troop's destruction of the anti-tank guns which makes the mystery of why Jim Alldred's action went unrecognised even more unaccountable – but see below].[75]

All went well with the tanks for the first 400 yards but,

> immediately the leading troops came into the open south of Brőnkshof they were met by a hail of SP from the front and flanks, augmented by HE. All three of the leading tanks of the right forward troop and two of the left forward troop were hit by AP, one no less than five times, and the FOO tank which was close behind them blew up.[76] [This happened in the second field from the farm so it was not 'immediate'.]

Cathcart:

> At the start of an operation Sqn HQ tanks tended to stick to the centre line so as to be found and identified by infantry, and Bn HQ in particular, more easily. We advanced up the road in order to try and maintain communications with Cecil Firbank's Bn HQ until the tanks came under ATk fire. In open ground we would not have been too near them in order not to draw unwelcome fire. If cover from buildings or trees was available we would endeavour to join them. That was a standard drill. In the case of this battle, soon after we crossed the SL and as soon as the leading tanks broke cover we came under heavy fire from SP and 88s. My HQ tanks found some cover in the area of the farm on the right of the road [Brőnkshof] where I believe Cecil's HQ was also pinned down. It was here that my FOO's tank (my only link with the artillery) failed to remain under cover and got knocked out with all the crew killed. They were Pipe-Maj Smith, Gdsm J Campbell and Gdsm F. Lees. The remainder of my HQ tanks

75 Letter from George Wall in 1994.
76 TNA: WO 171/1258: 3 Scots Guards' war diary.

> engaged the SP and 88s in order to try and cover the leading tanks who at that stage were fully exposed to their fire.[77]

Lt Chips Parker Smith, aged 24, was doing FOO duty for Capt Jack Hunton, aged 28, who was standing in for the 25 year-old BC, Capt Ivor Norton, who was absent on leave. Chips had expected to be in the FOO tank, which was following so close to the leading troop that George Wall believed that four, not three, tanks were in support. Chips recalls that on the previous morning his BC, Tony Edwards, had told him to go as FOO in one of the tanks with Signaller McNight. This would have been a first for Chips. The task was actually given to Jack Hunton who said to Edwards, 'Why not give the job to Chips?' and Edwards had agreed. At the last minute there was another change, and Edwards had told him; 'Sorry, Chips, a senior officer has been given us – so you go on foot.' So Chips walked behind the tank with McNight and remembers it quickly turned a white orange colour as it was hit and brewed.[78] The FOO killed in the tank was Lt R.F. Nunn of 84 (Sussex) Med Regt RA, which had just come under command of 3 BID. Nunn's identity was unknown to the Fld Regt officers, and the whole thing was rather a mystery. 'Well, that's who it was. We always wondered', was Edward's comment when informed by this author. The commander of the tank was Pipe-Major Smith. The Churchill was one of four at Battalion HQ and normally commanded by Major Whitelaw, the Battalion 2ic. He loaned it for its good communications' capability, and lost with it his driver and co-driver, Campbell and Lees.[79]

Each BC had for his personal use a carrier, an M14 half-track, a Jeep and a Sherman tank, which Parker Smith could have used. However they were back at the gun-lines and unable to get through in the very heavy going. Edwards commented:

> I don't remember what Chips was supposed to do with the Guards' Tank. If he took a Sherman he would have been unnecessarily vulnerable among the Churchills. The turned-around Poles in 9 Canadian Bde used to call the Sherman 'Tommy Cookers'. If he or any of our officers was put into a Churchill he'd have been unfamiliar with their wireless bandsheet. Although it was open plain there was undoubtedly bad communication. I must have thought we'd be stretched, as I left Jack (Hunton) by the Start Line, to do relay. Chips couldn't get through. What set did he have? I suppose he felt that he'd never get fire orders through on the Guards' net and that's why he packed it in and joined Jack. Jack then took Leslie (Colvin) and Chips to the village.[80]

A diary was kept by a civilian, probably of the Opgenhoff family living in Roghmanshof, just north of Brönkshof on the road leading from Kervenheim at 993354. It is called Schayck on the military map, and was probably the SL where 3 SG and the Lincolns married up:

> 17 February. The road to Kervenheim is the most important supply route to the front. At night enemy planes drop bombs. On average there are 50 soldiers and 10 wagons at Roghmanshof. Each day they are a different lot.
>
> 18 February. Today a meeting of farmers was told to hand over 30% of their cattle. Mass is to be said only at 6 and 7 o'clock because of the danger from bombers. The detachment of

77 Letter from Lord Cathcart in 1983.
78 Chips Parker Smith in conversation in 1983.
79 Lord Whitelaw in conversation in 1983.
80 Letter from Tony Edwards in 1983. They went by carrier equipped with wireless; possibly an 11HP set.

artillery stationed at Lemnes [982357 Diepenbruck] has already fired many times. There are artillery emplacements throughout the Berberheide and Wettener Busch. Guns, trucks and Tiger tanks [actually StuGs] moved throughout the day up the road to Kervenheim.

21 February. A signals unit was set up in the house. Everywhere there are Flak units. In and around the Hof there are 4 large guns. Mines were laid. Enemy artillery fire was intensive during the night.

22 February. A wounded soldier who had lost a foot could not be evacuated to the main dressing station at Kapellen because of a shortage of petrol. Personnel from the rations' unit later drove him to the hospital. A soldier and his horse were killed on the road by shelling.

25 February. Sunday. From today Mass will no longer be celebrated. More animals were commandeered.

27 February. Heavy shelling throughout the day.

28 February. The staff pulled out with the Signals. Shelling continued throughout the day. Mines were laid everywhere. Fighter-bombers and spotter aircraft constantly crossed over the area. Now soldiers arrived with handcarts and even perambulators. Bursting shells could often be seen, and the chattering noise of machine guns could be heard.

1 March. Today the front approached to within 4 km. The soldiers say that the fighting in the East was child's play compared with the fighting here. A dressing station was set up at the Hof.

2 March. The last soldiers who came in no longer looked human. They were dirty, tired, hungry and unshaven. Their behaviour was similar. 40 men were to hold up the enemy from here. They hid themselves throughout the house and in the hedges. On the orders of the Fallschirmjägers we descended into the cellars. The road outside and near the Musers was cratered. The noise of machine gun fire and artillery shells reached us in the cellar. The company of Fallschirmjägers withdrew to Plockhorsthof. Around 1300 hrs the English soldiers reached the Schanz's. Two hours later the first tanks arrived [Recce Honeys that bogged]. Infantry came crouching between the tanks. Around 1800 hrs we heard machine-gun fire and voices in the Hof. Father and I came up during a period of silence and we saw a tank moving behind the garden hedge with infantry accompanying it on both sides [17 Pln and Gordon's tank]. After that we ran quickly back into the cellar and saw no more. When father went into the barn at about 2030 hrs two English soldiers confronted him, held a pistol to his chest and told him to take them through the house. At the entrance the English soldiers turned back, frightened of coming in. About midnight the English soldiers did enter. We were brought out of the cellar and locked in the living room. Bedclothes were thrown in for us. Whenever the door was opened a gun would be pointed at us. Most of the soldiers spent the rest of the night in the cellar. At 0630 hrs father was allowed out to feed the cows. All the rest had to remain in the room. Then an interpreter arrived [probably Daniëls, the Dutch LO], who explained that everyone had to leave the house. We would be loaded into a truck and transported away. That produced screams and entreaties. At father's request, mother, Maria and I were allowed to stay. We were told; 'You are German and you are our enemies'. The Hof was full of vehicles. During the night the English troops had built positions around the house. Doors, shutters, mattresses and beds had been used in their construction. In the pasture was

> a park for vehicles and tanks. The meadow next to Elders was being used as a temporary landing ground for three aircraft. Guns were being emplaced.[81]

The British troops the diarist had briefly seen were almost certainly D Coy of the Lincolns with Alasdair Gordon's tp. The following letter to his mother on Sunday 19 March 1945 by Alasdair is one of the earliest accounts of that day to reach the outside:

> My dearest Mum,
> I have three letters to thank you for, all of which arrived in the last week. In your letter of March 4th you asked two questions – do you remember them? The first I answered myself in my last letter. The answer to the second is yes.
>
> We are now sitting back on our bottoms waiting for the next stage of proceedings and spending most of our time getting the tanks in good order and resuscitating German cars for our own use. The junior officers of the squadron now have a resplendent Mercedes-Benz to go visiting in, such as would put Montgomery and his Rolls Bentley to shame!
>
> I hope the doodlebugs and various V weapons have eased off again by now.
>
> Yes, on the first occasion [the attack on the bridge at Endtschenhof on February 27] the tank I was in was bogged and hit and things were very hot, so I gave the order to bale out. They were even hotter outside as they were using what they call Nebelwerfer or we call Moaning Minnies on us; they are multiple rocket mortars which make a bloodcurdling moaning noise as they come at you. However, apart from a bit of a shaking we all got away allright.
>
> The second time – only two days later – I was leading troop in an attack on a small town (Winnekendonk); when I was crossing a wide open piece of ground a tp of SP antitank guns opened up on us. I was hit five times in quick succession, but luckily nothing came right through although the turret was unmovable and the engine was put out of action. The tank on my right was brewed up (caught fire) and the crew (including Pipe Major Smith also from Skye) were machine gunned as they tried to get out. I pressed my local smoke which for a short time gives a very thick smoke screen – waited for it to thicken up then gave the order to abandon tank again. By this time the [crew of the] third tank of the troop has thought discretion the better part of valour and had abandoned tank and gone for cover. I got out of the tank quicker than I thought humanly possible, took a nose dive out of the tank and lay down by the bogies while spandau bullets went overhead with a ping-ping-ping-ping noise. I crawled to the ditch beside the road much better than I ever thought possible at Sandhurst! The rest of the crew got into a slit trench, which I had overlooked. Later on when things had died down a bit we took the tp Cpl's tank and went on to the objective.
>
> Now that we are static again and some way behind the line looting has become a serious offense, so we now have to live on army rations again, although I must say that we do very well and now have a squadron mess.
>
> The weather has been superb, really hot and sunny, but today it is cold and raw.
>
> Much love from Alasdair.[82]

The tanks of Gordon's troop fared as follows: Gordon's tank was disabled and abandoned, but since it did not burn would have been recovered the next day and repaired; the troop sergeant's tank was damaged, abandoned and later re-occupied by the heroic Guardsman Crawford as described below;

81 Bosch, *Der Zweite Weltkrieg*, pp. 240-42; translated by this author.
82 © Donald Gordon from Dave Alldred's website: https://sites.google.com/site/6thguardstankbrigade/personal-accounts/personalaccounts

while the troop corporal's tank was abandoned undamaged and later occupied by Gordon and his crew who motored in it to the objective. This is confirmed in the Bürgermeister's list of wrecks in 1946 which lists only the one destroyed Churchill belonging to the Pipe Major was left behind at Brönkshof.

Alasdair Gordon emigrated to the West Coast of Canada and years later reflected on the Battle of Winnekendonk in the presence of his son, Donald, who wrote:

> Regarding Winnekendonk... (yes, I was there too with him in 1980, when I was 14). I was too young to ask him why he wanted to go back there. No question the events there had made a great impression on him, likely for two reasons: 1) he had great respect for the leadership they were operating under. However, he always referred to that assault as the textbook example of what NOT to do. I can hear his voice yet, as though quoting from a Sandhurst manual: 'Do not undertake a frontal attack on a prepared position across open ground ... especially in daylight!' I asked him if he felt responsible for the decision to attack and he laughed as he explained that he was just a very junior officer doing what he was told. The overly hasty attack and tactical error of a frontal assault resulted in the death of several of his troop, including his friend the regimental Pipe Major. 2) It was in this engagement that his friend, fellow Skyeman Pipe Major Smith was killed while bailing out of his tank. He wasn't trained in tank warfare or operation, and ended up in charge of a tank shortly before the battle as the next rank available. He didn't have a chance in the machine gun fire. The compounding errors of the assault and lack of training resulted in the waste of a fine piper who provided plenty of exuberant jigs and reels in the officers' mess, standing on the table piping, while the surrounding officers filled his boots with looted beer or spirits. I have several letters of Dad's that refer to him, and I've tried to find where in Skye PM Smith was from (Dad was from the north; Smith was from the south). I scanned various war memorials when I was last there, without luck. I'd love to find any members of his family to pass on copies of the letters to, to give them a picture of a long-lost uncle.[83]

Jim Alldred told his grandson that Pipe Major Smith used to play 'Highland Laddie' on his bagpipes over the [tank] radio which gave the men a surge of confidence,[84] while the effect it had on any Germans listening in can only be left to the imagination.

Sgt Len Walters was the outstanding Platoon Sergeant of Mike Hunt's 17 Pln:

> I had the privilege of knowing your father reasonably well because he was a good friend of Major Clarke under whom I was serving at that time. I will try and enlighten you about the battle, but you must be aware that on this occasion I was unable to reach the objective. A white flag was waved at the start line [presumably Roghmanshof and by a German officer who would have just fired a warning signal] which was normal for the start of this kind of set-piece attack. We cleared the houses satisfactorily [Roghmanshof and Brönkshof] and then tried to break out into the open ground with a troop of tanks operating in front of us. I saw two of them picked off by the 88 and some of the men made it to cover. Then the 88 started to concentrate on the tanks on the left which were more fortunate as they were in lower ground and, although I cannot confirm it, they seemed well on their way to the objective.
>
> Then the 88 seemed to switch to us and that's when I forgot to dodge and fell wounded [from an airburst]. I remember someone crawling to me for support and encouragement, but then Gerry opened up with small arms' fire. Whilst lying there time seemed to stop, but I was removed to a small ditch to my left. At this point it was becoming dark and unfortunately

83 E-mails from Donald Gordon on 15 September and 17 December 2014.
84 E-mail from Dave Alldred on 15 September 2014.

Sgt Len Walters received the MM at Gimers Monastery on 11 December 1944 for his bravery in Normandy. Len was 2ic 17 Pln under Mike Hunt. Both were wounded in the battle. (© Crown Copyright. IWM, B 12782 by Sgt Morris)

> several of my comrades trod on me. Later I was put on a stretcher on a tank and then of course was taken back through the normal channels. I was lucky to get away with only 20% disability so am still going strong. It is only in these last few months that I have taken any interest in my army life. I will be going to Lincoln on the 11th September and hope to have the privilege of meeting your father once again.[85]

The tank which took Len Walters and Mike Hunt out of any additional harm's way had been hit five times by a StuG and/or 50 mm Pak, and was driven by Gdsm Duncan Crawford in Alasdair Gordon's battered troop. Duncan Crawford received the MM with this citation:

> **MM. 2701039 Guardsman Duncan John Crawford**
> During the attack on WINNEKENDONK on 2 Mar 45 the tank in which Guardsman CRAWFORD was co-driver, was hit five times by 75 mm AP shot by an SP. In spite of this Guardsman CRAWFORD continued to fight his Besa before it became essential to bail out owing to fire. When out, though the shelling and mortaring was severe, he went round giving first aid to a number of wounded infantry until dark, when he returned to the tank and found that though much knocked about, the fire was out and it would still move, so he put some of the wounded infantry on it and drove them back to medical assistance. This Guardsman's cool courage undoubtedly saved a number of lives.[86]

85 Letter from Len Walters in 1994.
86 TNA: WO 373/54/935: Duncan Crawford's citation.

The Lincolns fortifying themselves in the garden and sleeping in the cellar of Roghmanshof would have been part of the anti-tank and mortar platoons building a defense line in case the rifle companies were counter-attacked and thrown out of the village. Waging war has always been a matter of endless adjustments of position, of digging in and fortification, of being prepared for any eventuality which in an instant could kill the unprepared or unprotected.

There is no evidence that the Lincolnshire soldier, many of whom would have come from farms themselves, treated the German civilians in his power with anything but correctness and a certain rough kindness. The soldiers were free to remove anything of military value, including doors and shutters, even wardrobes which they laid on their side and filled with soil to serve as as a parapet. They disobeyed orders by permitting the women to stay on the farm, knowing that cows required feeding and milking and feeling that they must also be considered.

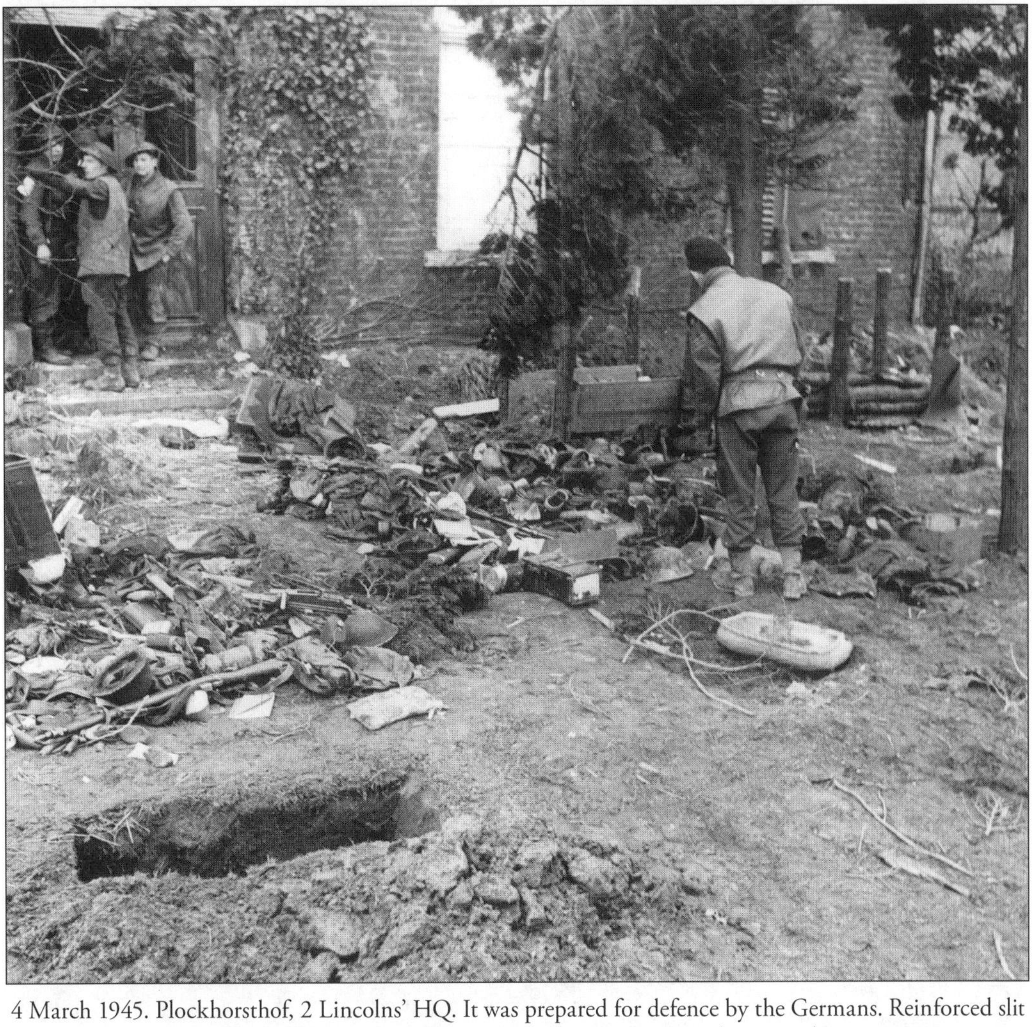

4 March 1945. Plockhorsthof, 2 Lincolns' HQ. It was prepared for defence by the Germans. Reinforced slit trenches were constructed in front of the cellar windows that were removed to provide intercommunication with the house. It was among the first buildings to be occupied in Winnekendonk. Equipment collected from the battlefield has been placed in two piles, and the sergeant is looking at the German pile on the right, with two helmets and two K98s recognisable. Photographers were told not to photograph anything British that was destroyed or abandoned, but the left-hand pile is British with two Para helmets, a coal scuttle helmet, a Bren and a .303. (© Crown Copyright. IWM, B 15143 by Sgt AH Jones)

Plockhorsthof in November 1982 when its barns were in the process of being demolished for a housing estate.

Lt John Pacey receiving the MC on 11 December 1944 for bravery in Normandy.
(© Crown Copyright. IWM, B12772)

Plockhorsthof, slightly left of centre, in 1984 without its barns. The road from Kervenheim comes in from the left beyond the houses, and was the axis of advance into Winekendonk. The line of houses and farms was the HKL. The photo was taken by Jonathan Colvin from a light aircraft of the RAF Laarbruch flying club piloted by Flt Lt Piers Colvin, cousin of this author. In 1945 the fields on the left were open. John MacDonald-Buchanan's tank went straight past Plockhorsthof to circle around its wall and head into the centre of Winnekendonk on the right. The road heading to the top of the photo is Hestert, where 2 Lincolns' cemetery was located, and leads to Bruch.

Capt John Pacey was 2ic D Coy:

> The intelligence report we received did not indicate the strength of the opposition. Indeed I remember being told that two tanks on the right of the village were 'knocked out' German ones, which came to life when the attack began. [This may be evidence that intelligence was received from an AOP which had no easy way of telling if a StuG was dead or alive unless it was burning]. As 2ic I was bringing up the rear of the Coy when the attack started. The enemy opened fire in earnest. There seemed to be bullets everywhere and men were falling like flies. I saw Peter Clarke go down and went up front to lead the attack. We obtained temporary cover in a ditch opposite the houses the Germans were firing from. We returned their fire and as darkness was falling managed to cross the road into the shell of some buildings, I only had three or four men with me. However we were lucky enough to join up with Glyn Gilbert, Ted Hill and some of their men. We had several exchanges with the enemy and then darkness fell. I remember going on patrol, rather tentatively, as I did not know the plan of the village, when we heard voices and crept up to where they were coming from, found one of our own tanks who was most surprised to learn he was in front of everyone else. On the way back a number

of Germans surrendered. I cannot remember much more, except that in Peter Clarke we lost a very good officer and friend. The mass burial of so many of one's comrades is something one never wants to experience again.[87]

Lt. J.A. Mike Hunt was a subaltern commanding 17 Pln in front and on the right in what was the most exposed and dangerous position on the field.

On passing through Kervenheim, 'D' Coy settled in the houses on the outskirts [Potthaus] attracting some fire, but mainly as interested spectators of the Typhoon rockets and the attack on the woods between Kervenheim and Winnekendonk by the KOSB or RUR. We then passed through these woods for the final push to get Winnekendonk. We were quite heavily shelled in the woods and as we moved at the outset we had to pause at a group of buildings [Roghmanshof] to await the Scots Guards' tanks. Fortunately they appeared just as we received the order to attack from the CO. We actually started with the Churchills just behind us but catching up rapidly. Obviously we had been seen as red Verey lights were fired from the next group of farm buildings just ahead [Brönkshof]. I think the one who fired the lights decided it would be better to give up as he came out and surrendered to us as we got into the farmyard. He was the first we captured that day. By that time the light was fading as we debouched into the open before the village and I distinctly remember the amount of tracer flickering across the whole front – so far as No 17 was concerned from our half right. Things were made worse when the tank with us was hit giving out a black pall of smoke and I seem to remember the second tank also being hit. As we neared the German positions – about half way across from the farmhouse where the Verey lights were fired to the forward edge of the village – at that stage the tracer became very heavy. We were vulnerable to their Spandau fire and my active part came to an end with a burst of Spandau which went clean through my right leg, chipping the bone and breaking the Achilles tendon. Others had fallen nearby and I have a vivid recollection of the 2ic John Pacey ducking from a burst of tracer which seemed to surround him, miraculously without hitting him. The assault passed through but that was not the end. It is quite an eerie sensation to be left on a battlefield all night and that night a fair amount of shelling continued for some time – mainly Nebelwerfer. I believe the moon came out quite early and this and the shell bursts lit the scene with a number of bodies lying there or crawling around – again most eerie. Platoon Sgt Walters, one of the best I ever knew, had been hit in the stomach and was lying nearby. I don't know how but somehow we pulled each other into a shell scrape for some protection and lay there joined by two or three others until we were found well after midnight by a patrol led by Jim Parsons of the Mortar Platoon and carried into the ditch by the side of the road for safety. The road had been cratered so the carriers sent to collect us could only come part way – probably fortunate as we were still fired on, and I felt very indignant about that! We were evacuated to the ADS in the woods where we started. However all went well and we were delivered into the hands of some very attractive and efficient Canadian nurses who made 3 hourly penicillin injections night and day almost bearable.

I was pleased to read you consider we were a formidable unit – we couldn't help being so with Cecil Firbank as CO and your father as 2ic. Certainly the Lincolns did not hesitate and as they had done on many occasions since the beachhead walked straight through the tracer. The Scots Guards tanks also pressed on in spite of the fire they attracted.[88]

87 Letter from John Pacey in 1983.
88 Letter from Mike Hunt in 1983.

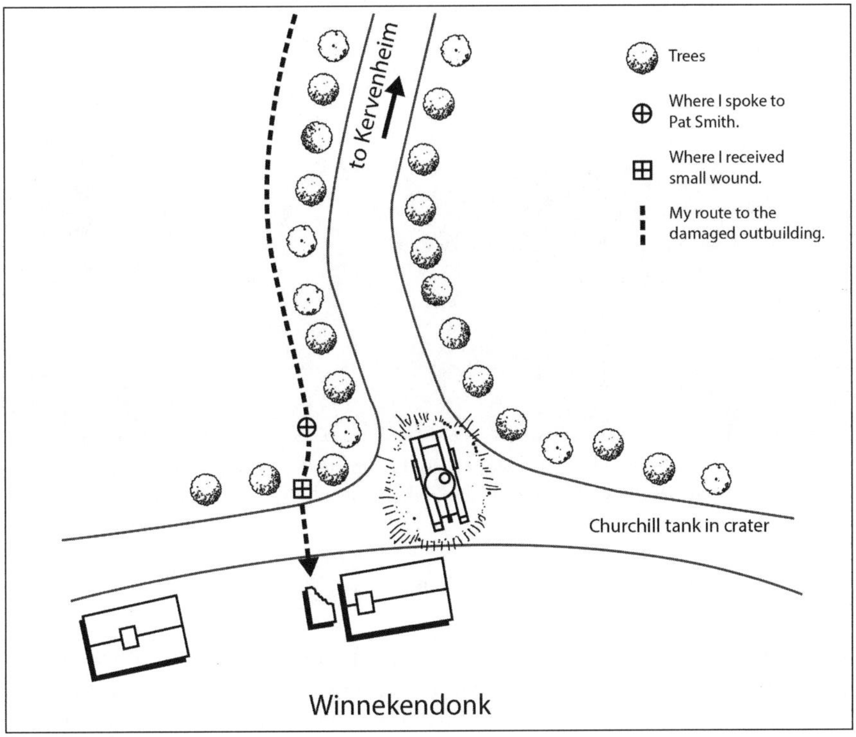

Map 35 Taken from Ken Deer's sketch of his entry into Winnekendonk.

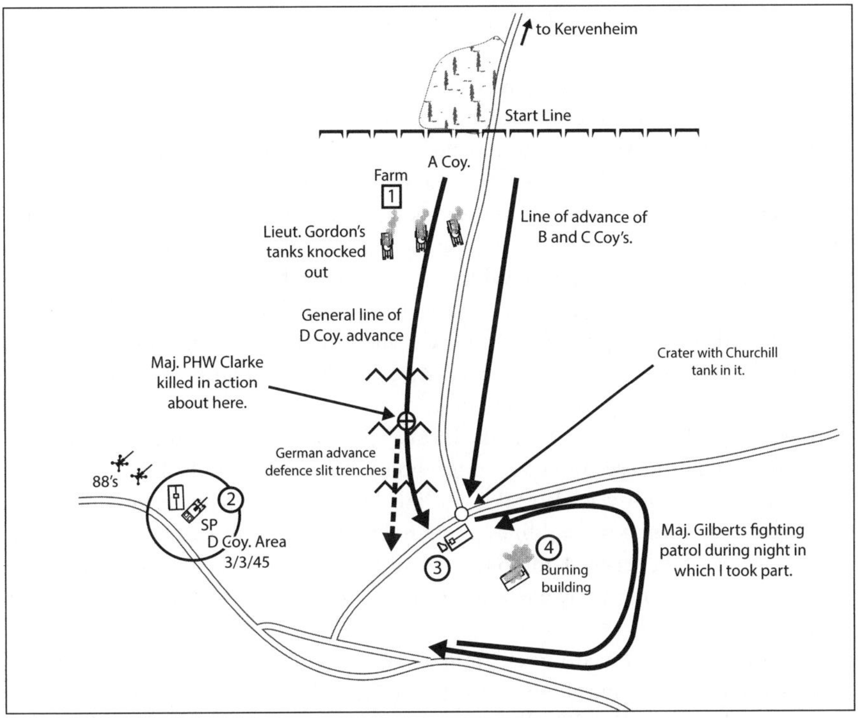

Map 36 Taken from Ken Deer's sketch of the Winnekendonk battlefield.
1. Brőnkshof 2. Stammen 3. Plockhorsthof 4. Milk factory.

The barn at Plockhorsthof in 1982. Lt Ken Deer entered from the fields opposite which in 1945 were open. The barn had just been demolished when this photo was taken in 1982.

Lt Ken Deer was a subaltern commanding 18 Pln in D Coy.

Before commencing, may I make two notes of caution. First, it is awfully difficult to remember [in 1983] after all this time and, second, I once remember talking to David Bates about the battle and you would have thought we had been in different battles on the same day, so different were our personal impressions. Anyway, here goes.

The tanks were nearly late, but they arrived with seconds to go. The artillery barrage came down and off we went. No sooner had we cleared the farm at Brőnkshof (figure 1 on my map) than the tanks under Lt Gordon came under accurate fire from the right front. All three of the forward tanks were knocked out and I can remember the crews dismounting as sharply as possible and diving for the lower ground near the edge of the road. It was eventually discovered that two 88-mm guns and a self-propelled 75-mm had done the damage.

At this time we came under accurate enfilade fire from the right and Major Clarke sent Lieut Hunt and his platoon to sweep over that side and deal with it. Lieut Hunt was wounded in the legs by machine gun fire. Left without tank support, we pressed on across the open ground between Brőnkshof (1) and the village. I took this to be about 800 – 1,000 yards with fire from small arms becoming more intense and mortar fire now included. We later learned that we had good reason to be thankful for the support troop of tanks on the right under Lieut Runcie because it was they who knocked out the SP gun and the 88s plus some spandaus. These are marked at figure 2 on my map.

The attack pressed on but I was horrified, this being only my second battle, to see Major Clarke fall from what appeared to be a mortar bomb. I have also marked the place he fell on the map. My own Platoon was also taking a 'fair knocking' from the enemy dug in in slit trenches before the village – several lines of them. I had started out with a sergeant, 3 corporals and 29 men and by the time I got to the area of the road junction (where a Churchill tank had fallen into a crater completely blocking the junction) I found that I had one corporal and about six men.

At this point I was wounded myself from a small piece of mortar bomb shrapnel. I can remember Corporal Shortland hauling me to my feet with the words, 'It's nothing – only a scratch – you'll be all right'. While getting to my feet and seeing if I was all right I can remember Capt Pat Smith appearing from my left shouting 'You're too far over (to the left) get further over to the right'. He was then evidently wounded and I didn't see him again until I met him at the Regimental Dinner some 30 years later. He was right, of course. You will see from the map that the road from Kervenheim bends a short way before the junction at the beginning of the village. I had hugged the line of the road too tightly and should have carried on where the dotted line is marked on my map. However I did what most people would have done – I dived across the road into the shelter of the first houses, marked figure 3 on my map. Here in a partly demolished outbuilding [Plockhorsthof had a range of barns since demolished] I found Major Glyn Gilbert. Having no idea where my own company headquarters had got to, I asked if I could stay under his command for a while. To this he agreed. It was while we were in this building – no roof and only the remnants of walls, that we became aware of two spandau machine gun crews making their way across the back of the buildings and into the same yard wherein our building stood. It was a matter of who fired first and we just managed it. Jack Harrod refers to this in page 56 of his wartime history of the second battalion – he refers to the eight men being a bazooka crew (or crews) – I won't argue – I thought they had spandaus. ['found a Boche bazooka team stalking through the back gardens towards them. They held their fire until the leading man was only five yards away and then let fly. Eight Germans met sudden death'.][89] What I would take issue with Jack about is that we didn't 'wait for them' as he says. We came face to face and it was who fired first. [The eight lay in a line where they had fallen, and were later shown to Bolo Whistler.] By now darkness had fallen, lit only by a blaze in a nearby building (marked 4) [*Mölkerei* or dairy], and Major Gilbert decided to take out a fighting patrol to see why the enemy had suddenly gone quiet. I accompanied him and have marked the approximate route on the map. On this patrol we encountered some tank officers who had been offered the surrender of a group of Germans in a chapel. The tank officers had evidently declined the embarrassment of 30 or 40 prisoners on a darkish night and had recommended that they leave it till morning. The morning came and things were straightened out. 'D' Company, now under the command of D.R.F. Hart, MC took over the area, marked 2 on my map, which is approximately where we should have been aiming for in the battle.

Some afterthoughts: 1) it was a good job the enemy caved in as darkness fell. 2) the real battle for Winnekendonk was won before the village itself was actually reached. 3) it certainly was an ideal situation for a tank/infantry battle. Open ground and a clear objective. 4) I wouldn't like to do it again'.[90]

John Gilleard was D Coy's CSM, but this evening he was with the platoons:

On reaching the Start Line I remember how exhausted we were and the Major [Clarke] was very perturbed about it, saying 'Hold the fort, Sergeant Major', and off he went to the platoons. I presume he gave them one of his 'pep' talks. This little incident seemed strange to me at the time because I usually went with him on all his excursions. Thinking back to this day, he was also perturbed about the action we were going to perform; i.e. no recce and under strength. Then to top it off the tank balls-up. Yes, Peter was a rather worried company commander that evening. On his return from the platoons he said to me; 'Sergeant Major; you may have to take up your old role as Platoon Sergeant in one of the platoons (forgotten which) [probably 18 Pln]. This was his last conversation with me. Whilst waiting for the tanks, as recorded in the battalion history, he asked the CO if we could go. After the Start (with no tanks) all hell

89 Gates, *The History*, p. 254.
90 Letter from Ken Deer in 1983.

CSM and Mrs John Gilleard having laid the Lincolnshire Regimental Association's wreath at the Scunthorpe cenotaph during the 1990s. John was Peter Clarke's CSM, and acted as 2ic 18 Pln under Ken Deer during the battle of Winnekendonk when he was seriously wounded.

was let loose and the company were dropping like flies. It was bloody horrible. Eventually I was one of the flies and spent the rest of my service in hospitals and convalescent homes, medically boarded out of service in November 1946. As a matter of interest my eight medals are on the top row: general service medal with Palestine clasp awarded in 1936 with my rank (lance corporal) and number inscribed; 1939-1945 star; France-Germany star; defence medal; victory medal; long service medal. On the bottom row: French medaille de la liberation sent to me in 1956 by the French government; Normandy campaign medal.[91]

Spuggie Spye was awarded the MM. His citation:

MM. L/Corporal 4541601 Ernest Spye

During the attack on Winnekendonk on the evening of March 2nd, 1945 Cpl Spye was leading his section in the right forward Company, 'D' Company, 2 Lincolns. This company was on the most exposed flank of the attack and soon came under very heavy fire from machine guns to the right. Casualties quickly occurred. Cpl Spye saw a Spandau post firing across the Company at the troops advancing on his left. This post was about 100 yards from his line of advance. He immediately left his section and rushed forward and shot the crew of two Germans who were firing the gun and regardless of the fact that he was himself a very prominent mark and was being fired at by other machine guns over to the right. By this prompt and very brave action, Cpl Spye saved numerous casualties to the platoon on his immediate left, which was being fired at by the gun in question and thereby enabled the advance to flow through by his initiative and complete disregard for his personal safety.[92]

91 Undated letter from John Gilleard in the 1990's
92 TNA: WO/373/54/409: Ernest Spye's citation.

4 March 1945. Some of the ruins of Winnekendonk. Heavy bombing by Dick Hough's Bombphoons of 197 Sqn destroyed Hauptstraße. The gap further away in the line of buildings was the home of the four members of the Gellings family, all of whom died. As usual, the church tower remained standing while the rest of the building was destroyed. (© Crown Copyright. IWM, B 15142 by Sgt AH Jones)

Hauptsraße in 1984. The white Audi Quattro belonged to Fl Lt Piers Colvin, who flew Tornados in 15 Squadron from RAF Laarbruch.

George Wall of D Coy continued:

> During my advance I had been joined by another soldier from where I don't know. Anyway, he stayed with me until I asked 'Mousy' from Bermuda if I could help him as he had been shot through the leg. I asked if he wanted my first aid. He replied: 'You had better get down or you'll be shot'. By then I had swapped my rifle for a Bren gun. It was whilst talking to 'Mousy' my Bermuda friend that I saw the KOSB putting in their attack with the bagpipes playing. [Only George heard bagpipes. The KOSB were entrenched 1,000 yards away on the left flank and enduring severe shelling. They did not attack until several hours later.] I made my way into the white house [probably the house on the crossroads where Kervenheimerstraße met Kevelaererstraße], to be confronted by an officer. Seeing I had a Bren gun, he shouted: 'Hey you, cover that window with your gun, there will be a counter-attack any minute'. I took up my position looking into the yard where three British soldiers lay dead. One was a blond youth of about 18 years old. I remember him well by his blond hair. He was always asking us when we would be having a go at the Germans – and there he was a few weeks later laying dead on German soil. Whilst all this was taking place I was peering out into the yard all night. I was told the Germans might send bombers over to bomb the village. I didn't believe that – not their own village. Just after midnight I heard the drone of a single engine plane go over the village. He made a pass then came back. I heard a plonk! never giving thought that it would be a delayed bomb. It dropped right on or near the crossroads about 50 to 100 yds from the white house. There was a terrific explosion. I should imagine the pilot intended to drop it in the field. We were told the next day, had it not been on clay soil it would have collapsed the house we were in. Come daylight we were stood down. There was still spasmodic firing – I handed over my Bren gun to a white house Sgt who pointed out there were only seven rounds in the three magazines. Terrible wasn't it? I forgot to mention that all through the night there were comings and goings in the white house. I was told there was a German doctor in the cellar attending the needs of the wounded of both sides. I ventured out into the open to look for my friends. From the next house I was seen and called. It was Spuggie Spye and another. He said he thought I was dead as they had found a sniper's rifle in the field. I explained where mine was. As we stood talking near the door a ricochet hit the wall making us dive for cover. Spuggie said not to worry as the RUR were in the village and the tanks were on their way to the Rhine. I remember meeting up with the chap who had my rifle. It must have been late in the morning as we were walking down the street to the lone house with the SP [Stammen]. I met a German civilian – an old boy. I remember asking him if he had any food and I can still remember what he said in German: 'Nix in de Winkel alles im de kelder.' [This phrase, meaning 'There's nothing in the shop; everything's in the cellar', became famous throughout the battalion]. In the cellar they had bottle after bottle of fruit and you name it. In the same house they had on the wall the battle insignia of several regiments and a sword and dagger. I took the sword and my colleague took the dagger. I hid the sword and was going to take it back to Bermuda as a souvenir but when I got to Dover there were signs warning us that if they caught us taking guns or swords etc into the country we would be sent back to our unit, so I immediately disposed of my sword by dumping it into the waste disposal. What a fool I was!
>
> From that house we met a number of our men who belonged to 'D' Coy. Among them was a Lieutenant whose name I do not know. I remember they had a Luger pistol and were trying to hit a bottle. The Lieutenant looked at me and said, 'You're a crack shot, you try to hit the bottle'. I did with the first shot. He wanted me to try again but as my luck had been with me since yesterday I declined and said I was on an errand. I went across the road to the house with the SP beside it. Inside the house was a Corporal and about six men as well as the German

family with a girl of sixteen. [The family was called Lemnes]. The Corporal had been told that should the men interfere with the girl they would be shot. I don't know who gave that order. It could have been Major Hart. I believe your father knows him. I would be interested to know if it was him. [Darby Hart was shown this and denied it was he but it was possibly Ken Deer]. There was still a dead German sitting in the driver's seat [of the StuG]. [Runcie told a biographer that he went up to the StuG, looked in, saw the corpses of four young men he had killed, and was sick. It was after this that he began to be called 'Killer Runcie' in the mess. Later, when he was Archbishop of Canterbury, *Private Eye* got hold of it and in the same spirit referred to him also as 'Killer Runcie.' Some took this nonsense seriously; a letter from Nigel Store in Grimsby accused the satirical magazine of implying the Archbishop had earned the sobriquet by shooting POWs, and demanded an apology. The letter was printed under the heading 'Runcie Balls'.] We knew that he would be sitting on a Luger pistol that was worth at least fr2,000 but again we knew they would have booby-trapped him, so we left him alone. Not so the RASC, they put a rope around the German and pulled him out. Yes, the pistol was there.

Later in the afternoon we went to visit our battalion HQ situated on the corner [at 997343] near the Church, of what would now be the road to Kevelaer. As we were standing on the road we noticed a dispatch rider pull up and go into the building. He was riding a German bicycle, but before we could go across the street to tell the regimental police the German came out with his hands up smiling. We all had a laugh. I would say that after the Battle of Winnekendonk the numbers remaining in the Company, including HQ staff, would have been about twenty or so. There was a Lt Deer and five men, a Cpl and six men in the house with the SP, four in HQ Company and a Sgt, but I don't know what happened to them. I don't remember any tanks escorting us into the village although I could hear them. I saw one flame-thrower firing its flame in the vicinity of the lone house which I have spoken of. He could have been aiming at the SP thinking it were still alive. It did have burn marks on it. [This is the only reference to flame throwers at Winnekendonk. There were no Crocodiles, and as far as is known the Lincolns at that time had no Wasp carrier flamethrowers.] In our earlier briefing we weren't told the truth about the German defenders. I can understand when we first came into sight he would have seen 'D' and 'B' Companies. He wasn't to know there were only 120 troops instead of 240 (I believe a full company is 120 troops). Had I been defending and seen all these troops with six or seven tanks, I would have been scared, but to see them all knocked out in minutes would have raised my morale to a high degree. Had I known what was in store, I would have been scared.[93]

The bomb dropped that night was from a FW 190:

> 40 Fw 190 (NSG 20). Attack on enemy concentration in Goch-Uedem area. On the target: 38 aircraft from 1845-0043 at 1800-700 m. Explosions and several fires observed. After discharging bombs, road traffic shot up without any special results being observed.[94]

Nachtschlachtgruppe 20 was commanded by Maj Kurt Dahlmann, who had received the Knights Cross as commander of I/Schnell-KG 10 on 27 June 1944, and Oak leaves on 24 January 1945. The aircraft were either based at Germersheim, where they had been since January 1945, or they had just moved to Twente or Zwolle in the Netherlands.

93 Letter from George Wall in 1994.
94 Luftwaffenkommando West War Diary.

Maj Glyn Gilbert received the MC at Gimers Monastery on 11 December 1944 for bravery at the crossing of the Escaut Canal. (© Crown Copyright. IWM, B 12765 by Sgt Morris)

Lt John MacDonald-Buchanan received the MC for aggressive action in Winnekendonk which led the garrison to surrender. (© Alastair MacDonald-Buchanan)

Sgt Tam Shearer received the MM in Plön on 12 June 1945 for his actions in Winnekendonk. (© Crown Copyright. IWM, BU 7841 by Sgt Morris)

German anti-tank position captured in the action during which Maj FA Tilston won the VC, Hochwald, Germany, 1 March 1945. There were six of these identical wheel-less 50 mm Pak 38 anti-tank guns mounted on concrete plinths with the shuttering boards still in place at Winnekendonk. They were manned by army and not Luftwaffe troops; Ted Winkler was directed to join them.The gun was effective against Shermans but not the Churchill, although it created spalling on the inside of MacDonald-Buchanan's tank. Note the 3 cm mortar designed to kill infantry following behind the tanks. (Ken Bell/Canada/Dept of National Defence/Library & Archives Canada/PA-113683)

Lt Mike Barnes of 3 SG models a German gas cape and helmet while on a Panzerfaust familiarization course. The Panzerfaust operated on the principle of the firework, and could penetrate a Churchill anywhere at up to 30 m. It was aimed by tucking it under the arm and aligning the top of the hollow charge with the range hole punched in the flip-up leaf sight. Firing was by squeezing down the piece of metal at the rear of the sight. The launcher was then discarded. Barnes holds a Panzerfaust 30 with improved head and on the ground is a missile with its spring fins extended. (© Cathcart family)

Leading on the left and roughly alongside Peter Clarke's D Coy and Alasdair Gordon's troop, and even probably ahead since they had no farms to clear, were Glyn Gilbert's C Coy and John MacDonald-Buchanan's troop. They were sheltered to an extent from the 88 and SPs on the right by the raised road and the line of trees. Their tanks did however receive the attention of at least two emplaced 50 mm PAK 38 L/60s and perhaps an 88 mm on the left of the road to the front. Considering, however, the damage an 88 could inflict, and the fact that 3 SG's history[95] shows it to have been a StuG, and the witness statement by Ted Winkler that he saw no 88, we should discount its presence. The 50 mm PAK was ineffective either against the 6 inch/150 mm frontal armour of a Churchill VII or the 4 inch/102 mm of the Churchill IV, which was what MacDonald-Buchanan was probably commanding. The 2 kg shell of the 50 mm Pak 38 could penetrate only 70 mm at 500 yds.

MacDonald-Buchanan remembers being muddled earlier in the day about which division he was supporting. The presence of the KOSB in 9 BIB, called the 'International Brigade' because it contained Scots, Irish and English battalions, made him think he was back with 15 BID. He remembered the afternoon being the usual thing of hanging around, and about 4 pm he was talking to Corporal Daigner, a pastry cook in civilian life, about cooking dinner because, 'they were not going to do much more today.' Then he was told, 'Come on; got to marry up with the infantry.' There was an immediate O Group at 4 pm, when he met Glyn Gilbert. Then there was a tremendous trouble to get the tanks over the SL at the right time, and a fearful rush (*pace* Alan Cathcart). The reception was awful and a lot of shot started coming. He could see the puffs from the enemy guns and he thinks the infantry got ahead [confirmed by Syd Smith, 15 Pln; 'At no time did the tanks get in front of 'C' Coy's advance into Winnekendonk'].[96] So he went flat out, realising he had been hit because he could see the armour coming away in flakes on the inside [called spalling], as the shot hammered the outside without penetrating. He found good ground against a wall or ditch but could not avoid a wounded German officer lying on the ground and motored over him. He drove into the centre of Winnekendonk and could find no one, although there was a lot of noise and he could hear two or three SPs moving around. He reported back that he couldn't find the infantry, so he dismounted to go and look for them. It was beginning to get dark when he met Ted Hill, 2ic 'C' Coy. He saw a German and shot at him four times without result, so threw the pistol at him.

It was twilight and very eerie as he pushed on ahead to near the church. He was respectful of the Germans and there were a lot of young fanatics around, wearing black [?] helmets and keeping together in groups. Ted Hill had a lot of prisoners. He remembers reporting back, "can't get any further" because of craters. Then the tank went into a crater and he said he would take the prisoners back. There were 20 prisoners and as he returned with them they passed a lot of buildings burning to the right. He reached the second tank which was badly hit and limping. [The Churchill could keep moving even without half its eleven road wheels on one side]. He made prisoners climb on the front and others on top of the tank. Then, still on foot, leading the tank carrying the prisoners, they went down the side road to the main road, where they turned left (west) heading for the rallying point that, he believed, was the central house on the corner [Plockhorsthof]. But he saw a lot of troops milling around in the road in front of burning houses, and realised they were Germans. He prodded a gun into the nearest German prisoner and indicated to him that he would be shot if he didn't tell the Germans up ahead to get back. The prisoner screamed to them to get away, which they did. But MacDonald-Buchanan took no chances and ordered the driver to reverse the way they had come and away from the enemy. Once clear, they turned north through the backs of the houses to Battalion HQ. After he had delivered the prisoners, MacDonald-Buchanan remembered

95 Erskine, *Scots Guards*, p. 408.
96 Letter from Syd Smith in October 1994.

he had left the slidex – the encoder/decoder typed on a small piece of paper, that changed daily – in the tank. So he and Guardsman Hunt returned to the tank to retrieve it. Hunt was cited for, and Shearer was awarded the MM based on evidence provided by Macdonald-Buchanan, while he received the MC based on 2 Lincolns' letter of commendation, and a rare survivor of the genre.

> 2nd Bn The Lincolnshire Regt, B.L.A. 4th March 1945
> Dear Drummond, (sic)
> I enclose the account sent into me by my Coy Comd [Glyn Gilbert; it has not survived] about the doings of Macdonald Buchanan in our attack on Winnekendonk. All my men were very impressed by his coolness and bravery at a time when rifles and bazooka parties were all over the place. The presence of his tank in the middle of the village did a great deal to cheer up the isolated Platoon who at that time were fighting a lonely battle.
>
> My men have nothing but praise for the very gallant and efficient way in which your Right Flank Squadron supported us throughout the battle.
>
> Will you please thank Alan Cathcart for all his help. Without him we could not jointly have taken the village. Yours ever, Cecil Firbank.[97]

The letter was unbound when this author read the file in the Public Record Office in 1983. The desk was asked to bind it in and send a copy to MacDonald-Buchanan, who acknowledged its receipt to this author. The letter failed to show up in the file in 2014 among mostly loose pages.

The citation for Sgt Shearer:

> **MM. 2696971 Sgt. Thomas Shearer**
> During the attack on WINNEKENDONK on 2 March 1945 Sgt Shearer was troop sergeant of the troop given the task of capturing with the Infantry the far end of the town. Despite very heavy opposition of all kinds both before, when his tank was twice struck by AP shot, and in the town, the troop reached its objective almost in the dark and there became engaged in close quarter fighting with large numbers of enemy paratroops armed with bazookas and grenades. Not only did Sgt Shearer fight the whole armament of his tank with outstanding effect, but he also killed a number of enemy with a Bren out of the top of his turret and then helped to round up a considerable number of prisoners. At one period during the battle his tank was isolated by houses for over an hour in the darkness, but he coolly maintained his position covering the Infantry and taking prisoners. On the way back to forward rally through the village he again became involved in very hard fighting including being attacked by a Bazooka team which he eliminated. Soon after this his tank was hit three times by a Bazooka and he himself temporarily blinded for nearly two hours. In spite of this he got it back to the rendezvous and continued to carry out his job as troop Sgt and to give great encouragement to everyone until the battle was fought to a successful conclusion. This Sergeant's courage, cheerfulness and offensive spirit were outstanding through this very difficult battle.[98]

A citation was written for Gdsm John Hunt but rejected by Brig Greenacre.

> **MM. 2700630 Guardsman John Hunt**
> Throughout the battle for WINNEKENDONK – 9934 – on 2 Mar 45 Guardsman HUNT fought in his tank with outstanding coolness. In the course of the action his tank and others

97 TNA: WO 171/5231: 2 Lincolns' war diary.
98 TNA: WO 373/54/627: Tam Shearer's citation.

in his squadron were responsible for the elimination of two 88 mm A tank guns, two SPs and at least six other A tank guns, besides over-running a strong enemy locality which was most stoutly defended by German paratroopers. In the late hours of the action, in the dark, one tank fell into a bomb crater near the troop objective at the far end of the town and had to be abandoned as its armament could not be used and the enemy were still in large numbers and fighting nearby. On reaching the 'forward rally' it was discovered that the secret codes, including the SLIDEX card, had been left in the tank. This Guardsman immediately volunteered to accompany his Officer [John MacDonald-Buchanan] back through the village, and into the enemy lines to recover them. This task they successfully accomplished though at times hand to hand fighting, with considerably stronger parties of Germans, occurred. Throughout the day Guardsman HUNT displayed outstanding coolness, utter disregard for danger and a very high sense of duty.[99]

A mistake in the records held at HQ Scots Guards resulted in John MacDonald-Buchanan's citation not being sent by the Archivist of 3 SG who believed it had been awarded for Uelzen.[100] This mistake was only corrected by chance in October 2014 when this author bought a copy of it from the National Archives. John MacDonald-Buchanan seemed vague about which action he had received it for.

MC. WS/Lt P/320186 John MacDonald-Buchanan
In the attack on Winnekendonk (9934) on 2 Mar 45 Lt MACDONALD-BUCHANAN was fighting his first battle as a tp ldr and was in comd of the tp of two tks detailed to sp the inf to the far end of the village. [Presumably because one of them fell into the crater by Plockhorsthof]. In spite of the very strong defences, narrow streets, many para tp Bazooka parties and snipers, he managed by dusk to fight his tp and the inf into his objective. Here, though he had only one tk left as his own had fallen into a large bomb crater, he maintained his posn and liaised with the inf, on foot, with outstanding coolness and courage, giving invaluable moral and physical sp to the inf coy who were, by now, isolated – greatly reduced in numbers, trying to look after a large number of prisoners and surrounded by the enemy.

When this situation cleared up he took the two crews and the remaining tk back to the fwd rally, but on the way the tk was attacked and hit three times by a Bazooka. He immediately led his unhorsed crew in a hand to hand fight which drove off the Germans and got back to fwd rally successfully. On arrival there he discovered that his Slidex Code had been left in the abandoned tk so with Gdsmn Hunt [and more crossed out that is indecipherable and replaced with 'a Gdsman'] returned through the enemy infested streets and brought the code safely back, though they were again involved in hand to hand fighting on the way back.

The inf he was supporting could not speak highly enough of this offr's coolness and courage and the assistance given them.[101]

Reflecting on these events after 40 years, John MacDonald-Buchanan believed that the ground was so bad, wet and flooded in parts, that the Germans believed that tanks couldn't come that way unless they stuck to the cratered road where they would have been knocked off easily and the advance stopped. He himself, and presumably his troop, avoided bogging by staying off the road but yet close to it where it was firmer. In the village he kept his tank close to walls for the same

99 Sent by Maj Clarke Brown of 3 SG's Archives on 22 November 1996.
100 Letter from Maj Clarke Brown on 29 November 1996.
101 TNA: WO 373/54/582: John MacDonald-Buchanan's citation.

reason, and why he drove over a wounded German officer. If the defenders' miscalculated, then the victory was due to the superior cross-country capability of the Churchill, which constantly surprised the Germans whose StuGs were confined to the roads.[102] There were, however, other and major contributory events on the right flank to be considered below.

Capt Darby Houlton-Hart, 2ic A Coy, described how C Coy, was arranged in front of him as it advanced ahead of the three tanks of MacDonald-Buchanan's troop. The Coy was in extended order with 5 yds between men. In the centre at the front was the Coy Commander, Maj Glyn Gilbert with his Coy Sgt Major and batman, and immediately behind him, and ready to take command, was his 2ic, Capt Ted Hill. With Hill was the Coy HQ consisting of signallers with the 18 set and the support weapons, the 2 inch mortar and the Piat. On left and right of Gilbert in the front row would be a section of 10 men in extended order, then the Pln Comdr, a subaltern, and then another section. On the left of Gilbert was 13 Pln, commanded by Lt David Bates and Sgt Mick Price, and on the right 15 Pln under Lt Pip Piper and Sgt Goddard. The front row contained about 50 men spread out on a frontage of about 250 yards or the length of two rugby fields. The third section of each Pln was extended behind the Pln Commander and alongside the 2ic. Behind was 14 Pl under Lt R.H. Mercer and an unknown sergeant.[103]

Pte Syd Smith was in 15 Pln, and met McDonald-Buchanan in the centre of Winnekendonk.

> In June '43 I volunteered for the Duke of Wellington's Regiment and joined the 10th Bn. I was serving in N Ireland on D-Day, but was drafted to join the 7th Bn which was serving with 49th Div in Normandy. But the 7th Bn was disbanded and so they asked for men to go into 2 Lincolns. I joined then at Château Beauregard where the dinner was held in June this year [1994]. I was eighteen and a half years old. That night (July 8th, 1944) we were marched into Hérouville and I found myself in action for the first time.
>
> The day (2nd March) began with two companies of the Lincolns, 'A' and 'C', being detailed to clear the village of Kervenheim. As we advanced we came to what appeared to be flood-water with barbed wire in front; laid on the wire were the bodies of three members of the Norfolk Regiment. We cleared the village without any further action and then dug in. As we dug the trenches were filling with water due to the ground being saturated and the rain that was falling. As the day went on we were moving forward and digging in and then we were told that we were to capture the village of Winnekendonk. We moved to the start line which was the edge of a wood and lay there viewing 1,200 yards of flat open ground which we knew we would have to cross, the road being on our right. I would like to point out 'C' Company did start from the front edge of the wood on the left side of the road which you have marked 'C'. I don't know the Start Line of 'B' and 'D' Companies and as George Wall said he did not see anyone advancing on the left of the road, neither do I remember seeing anyone advancing on the right of the road. I would say that the road was on a level with the land on the left hand side of the road that we were advancing on, but I have spoken to Joe and he confirmed that the land on the right of the road fell away and was much lower than the road. As regards training with tanks, I never did train with tanks. The only time I remember was later on in France when we spent a day with tanks which were demonstrating the effects of twisting around on a slit trench etc. We did manage to have a ride on top of a tank.[104]

102 McDonald-Buchanan in conversation in 1983.

103 Derby Hart in conversation.

104 This paragraph together with the first and last, are later additions from Syd Smith in October 1994 in answer to questions about the SL.

We got to our feet, having been given the order to move forward and almost at once we came under fire. After advancing for a few minutes we noticed the tanks travelling along the road on our right firing as they advanced and they immediately came under fire and one of them received a direct hit which blew off the turret and I was amazed to see members of the crew were able to jump out.

We were now approaching the village. During the advance I had been carrying, in addition to all my equipment, three Piat bombs and was feeling shattered. I asked if someone would give a hand but was told that as the Piat itself had gone missing I might as well dump the bombs and this I did with much relief. When we approached the centre of the village the German mortars were laying down a heavy barrage which we had to pass through and things were getting very bad as there was also lots of small arms fire coming from the houses just in front of us.

Major Gilbert was standing there waving us on and encouraging us to get into them. It was a miracle that he was never hit. We moved in and went from house to house clearing the Gerries out. As we came out of one we were met by an explosion which I assumed was an anti-tank shell and two of the section were badly hit. I went to give assistance but L/cpl Woolley MM, my section leader, told me to leave them, which I realised under the circumstances was the correct thing to do. As we made our way through the village we were picking up a few prisoners and two of the baled-out tank-crew tagged on. Eventually L/cpl Woolley sent the prisoners back in care of the tank boys.

When we had passed through the village there were six of our group and by now it was dark. As we were trying to find our way back someone said, "We have just passed a tank", which was standing near the church. Moments late it fired a round of H.E. which landed some distance in front of us, so we took cover in a crater before moving on. I can't remember making contact with any of my own company but I eventually found myself in a kitchen of a house [Plockhorsthof] with a member of 'B' Company, and there was quite a bit of mortaring in progress.

During the night a plane came over and dropped a bomb. We felt it hit the ground and then seconds later the explosion brought the ceiling down and blew the windows out. We made a strategic withdrawal under the table.

Early next morning I was sent with a party to bring up some vacuum containers of food and this was most welcome. I was then ordered to return to 'C' Company where we were ordered to prepare once again to clear the village. All went very well and there was no further action and quite a number (70 approximately) of Germans gave themselves up.

Later in the day Lt-Col Firbank came and spoke to us thanking us for a fine effort. We stayed about seven days in Winnekendonk before moving on.

I always understood our objective was the Dentist's House and that this was the house we finished up in. However 8 years ago (in 1986) I made a visit to Winnekendonk and went into a bar called the Golden Apple which is just opposite the Church. I was looking at the pictures on the walls around this bar when the old German lady behind the bar said they were all concerning the war. The man I was with told her that I was in Winnekendonk during the war. She started telling me about the panzer which got through to the Church and stayed at the Church (MacDonald-Buchanan's Churchill – see above). I told her I had been in the dentist's house, but she said there was no dentist's house in Winnekendonk and that it was a doctor's house. She took me to the back door of the bar and pointed to a house and said that was the doctor's house. Maybe I will go back some day and have a good look around.[105]

105 Letter from Syd Smith in 1994.

Ted Hill was 2ic C Coy.

We attacked astride the Winnekendonk road. I was roughly between and behind the two leading platoons, on the left of the road. Three Churchill tanks emerged from the SL at the same time, but unfortunately one or more 88s opened up on them, presumably over open sights, and knocked the turret off each one of them, which took the smiles right off our faces, and the hope from our heart that it would be an unopposed attack. We were fired on by desultory rifle and automatic fire from the farmhouse [Büllhorsthof]. Just before we reached the road in front of the farmhouse a lone white flag was waved and one German soldier surrendered, with suitcase already packed. The left-hand platoon reached the farmhouse. The right-hand platoon (Lt Piper's) sheltered in the lee of a brick wall. Several hand grenades were flung over the wall, which as far as I know did no damage. An NCO of Piper's platoon opened a door in the wall, dashed through and killed the grenade thrower, for which he was afterwards recommended for a medal. I, then, with Lt Piper (an ex-CSM of 2nd Bn who was killed in the last action outside Bremen) and his platoon advanced to the village by the back of the houses. We then took cover due to heavy shelling, which after a while we realised was our own barrage, which we waited a few minutes to lift.[Since the barrage was timed, this means it was 6.05 to 6.10 pm. They had advanced 1,600 yards in 25 minutes at a speed of 3.6 mph or 5.8 kph. This was brisk, and they caught up with the barrage, getting into the village before the defenders realised they were there]. While sheltering in the house, a Lt from the Scots Guards [MacDonald-Buchanan] ran into the house to find out what was happening. He was isolated in the centre of the town by the church and was under fire from small arms. He then accompanied us part way towards our objective. On our way we were fired at and one or two were wounded by grenades thrown from houses. We pushed on towards our objective. Noticing a lighted candle in a bottle in the cellar, an NCO fired a burst of Sten gun fire which resulted in a white flag and 3 prisoners. After a while I suggested to Pip that I would go back to the rest of the battalion and bring up the rest of the company, as nowhere could we see any of our own troops. He gave me a runner and off we went. When we reached the open ground (999345), we found CSM Smalley pushing forward, and he showed us where the company were and came back with us. We reported to Glyn Gilbert, and he immediately got the company ready, and we went back to our objective. On the way we talked to the tank commander [MacDonald-Buchanan] who was still in the centre of the village, and whom Glyn subsequently recommended for a decoration; he will no doubt remember his name.

Advancing to our objective, Glyn saw someone in a doorway of a house, and went to ask for information, but both were horrified to see that they were enemies, and a smart bit of legwork by both got them out of harm. We reached the objective after being away about an hour, to find that Piper and his platoon had retired, and subsequently he told us there was so much enemy activity around him, and no sign as yet of reinforcements, that he decided to pull out. Ultimately, after about a quarter of an hour, Capt Gilbert decided to pull his company back, which he did successfully. In summary I was surprised how everything got split up and lost contact with other people. I can only describe my state of mind as being in a bit of a twitter.[106]

106 Letter from Ted Hill in 1983.

Ted Hill's citation:

> **MC. T/Capt 129068 Edward Godwin Hill**
> During the battle for the capture of Winnekendonk on the evening of the 2nd of March 1945, Capt E G Hill, 2ic 'C' Company 2 Lincolns, was ordered to pass through the right assault company on the front edge of the village and take the rear edge of the village. In the confused fighting on the outskirts of the village two platoons of 'C' Company got held up by the same opposition that was already holding up 'D' Company, the right assault Company. Capt Hill with a third platoon by-passed the opposition and with great determination led his platoon right through the village to its final objective on the far side. During this action the platoon was constantly fighting, and suffered severe casualties, and arrived on its objective eleven strong. Capt Hill then organised the consolidation of the platoon on its objective, leaving the platoon under the command of the platoon commander, and then returned through the whole length of the village, which was then in enemy hands, to tell the Company Commander [Glyn Gilbert] that he had got to his objective. During this return journey Capt Hill was sniped at and in constant danger of being overcome by the very much larger force of Germans who were in the neighbourhood. Thanks to the information which he got back to his Company Commander, the Company Commander was able to take the rest of the Company to its objective and secure it. His bravery, leadership and clear-sighted initiative [the remainder recommends the award of the MC and was crossed out by Montgomery making it indecipherable].[107]

Pte Connor's citation:

> **MM. Pte 4343711 Robert Connor**
> During the attack on Winnekendonk on the evening of 2nd March 1945, Pte Connor was the bren gunner of a platoon of 'C' Company 2 Lincolns. This platoon in the advance by-passed the strong points on the outskirts of the village which held up the remainder of the Company and, led by the 2ic [Ted Hill] of the Company, fought its way through to the final objective. Very slow and bitter fighting took place during this phase of the battle. On one occasion Pte Connor noticed some enemy who were firing on the platoon from a nearby house upon whom he could get no fire to bear from his bren gun; handing over his gun he went forward on his feet and threw two grenades into the enemy post, killing the occupants, thereby allowing the platoon to continue its advance. For his bravery, initiative and very fine example to the remainder of his section [the rest was struck through by Montgomery].[108]

David Bates (inevitably called 'Master Bates' by Leslie Colvin, who called Glyn Gilbert 'The Bruin' for some reason, and Darby Hart 'McGraw' because in *Treasure Island* the ghost of Capt Flint called out, '*Darby McGraw*! Ho, Darby, *fetch aft the rum*') was a subaltern leading 13 Pln under Gilbert and Hill.

> Friday evening, 2nd March, was dull, cold and rather misty. Having only joined 2nd Lincolns in February 1945, Winnekendonk was my first major engagement. We formed up and at 1745 hrs we advanced over 1,000 yards of open country to the outskirts of the village. It was held by paratroops, and the fire was fierce, particularly if I remember correctly, from some farm

107 TNA: WO 373/53/389: Ted Hill's citation.
108 TNA: WO 373/54/952: Bob Connor's citation.

buildings, where enemy troops were firing at ground level [from basement windows]. Some fierce hand-to-hand fighting ensued within a farmyard [Plockhorsthof], and I remember one of my section leaders (Cpl Chambers, 6 feet tall and heavy with it) literally shoving equally large paratroops out of the way as the battle continued. Some half dozen of us pushed past the farm buildings towards a road. I cannot remember just who came with me, apart from my very loyal Batman, (Coulson), and Mick Price, the Pln Sgt. The noise, the fire, the smoke and the general chaos was unbelievable to a 19-year-old 2nd Lieutenant! Having got somewhat further than we were supposed to we heard the sound of tank tracks. I don't know to this day whether it was one of theirs or one of ours! Suffice to say that when its bulk appeared, spitting small arms fire, we decided that discretion was the better part of valour and withdrew back into the farm area. The first person I came across was our 2ic, Capt Ted Hill, brandishing his revolver, and complaining that he was out of breath. The understatement of the year! However, we started digging in and I remember the redoubtable Coulson urging me to dig both faster and deeper, if I wanted to see Saturday! Finally we regrouped, and my Pln (13) took up residence in an open barn. We placed timbers across the entrance (don't quite know what we expected them to stop!), had some food, and settled down for the night. I remember that I had a nightmare and in the early hours of Saturday morning thought we were being attacked. I cannot remember his name, unfortunately, but another section leader managed to quieten me down before the whole Company stood to! I remember joining a search party, retracing our steps, looking for the dead and wounded – Peter Clarke among them. The following morning an uncomfortably large number of enemy troops were flushed out of the buildings of Winnekendonk – perhaps as well that we didn't know of their presence before. We eventually took up residence in the local vicarage! I remember that the departed Parish priest left a note pinned to his front door, telling whoever turned up to treat the place with respect! My batman, Coulson, was something of a cook – a jolly good one too, and on the Sunday evening, using the remains of the Parish Priest's homemade wine (previously tested for poison), and a goose which seemed to have died of shock – we had a dinner party in the Vicarage kitchen. It was not until I met Glyn Gilbert at the Annual Dinner Club do at Armoury House in 1979, that I received my answer to my oft-repeated question 'Why didn't you eat the goose?' 'Because', said he, 'I saw where it had been feeding, you didn't!' Ah well! I'm still here to tell the tale. My observation of the battle can be summed up in three words – TOTALLY SCARED STIFF. I suppose that like most people, I just bashed on and, unlike some others, I was lucky and came through Winnekendonk without a scratch.[109]

Obergefreiter (LAC or L/Cpl) Ted (Eduard) Winkler of Stabskompanie II/FJR7 (HQ Coy, 2 Bn, 7 Paratrp Regt) was regimental armourer in Kervenheim until 2 March 1945 (see previous chapter), when he was ordered to join his unit in Winnekendonk.

I set off on my own and made my way to Winnekendonk which was very traumatic seeing German soldiers hanging from lamp-posts and trees who were supposed to be deserters. This made my situation as a single soldier dangerous. I asked directions from the MPs (*Kettenhunde*). First of all they wanted to know what I was doing on my own. I proved to them that I was the Regimental armourer making my way to my unit. I asked them the location of 7 Fallschirmjäger Regiment, but they did not know, and told me to carry on down this road to Winnekendonk. I was asking everyone I met where the 7th was, but nobody seemed to know. I arrived at the crossroads in Winnekendonk, where there was an army officer with a gun crew. [The only unit

109 Letter from the Revd David Bates in 1983.

Passierschein

(GÜLTIG FÜR EINEN ODER MEHRERE ÜBERBRINGER)

Der deutsche Soldat, der diesen Passierschein vorzeigt, benutzt ihn als Zeichen seines ehrlichen Willens, sich zu ergeben. Er ist zu entwaffnen. Er muß gut behandelt werden. Er hat Anspruch auf Verpflegung und, wenn nötig, ärztliche Behandlung. Er wird so bald wie möglich aus der Gefahrenzone entfernt.

DWIGHT D. EISENHOWER
Oberbefehlshaber
der Alliierten Streitkräfte

Englische Übersetzung nachstehend. Sie dient als Anweisung an die alliierten Vorposten.

SAFE CONDUCT

(VALID FOR ONE OR SEVERAL BEARERS)

The German soldier who carries this safe conduct is using it as a sign of his genuine wish to give himself up. He is to be disarmed, to be well looked after, to receive food and medical attention as required, and to be removed from the danger zone as soon as possible.

DWIGHT D. EISENHOWER
Supreme Commander,
Allied Expeditionary Force

Ted Winkler surrendered to Glyn Gilbert's C Company by holding up this Safe Conduct signed by Eisenhower that he had picked up in the south of France in 1944. It told him on the reverse to be unarmed, with his belt removed and holding up either this Safe Conduct or a white handkerchief.

of army troops, as opposed to Luftwaffe paratroopers, on the field that day was 3 Pln, Fortress Anti-Tank Coy 51(X), equipped with wheel-less 50-mm Pak 38 L/60s that were emplaced on concrete pedestals and camouflaged]. He ordered me to go to the right [now called Hestert, it runs eastward from the Kervenheimerstraße towards Mottenhof. Ted therefore turned left and not right, ending up on the right flank of the German defensive line] and join the soldiers who were there. I found some army soldiers who were going into a cellar which held about four more. We did not talk. I was in a situation where there was nobody in charge to tell me what to do. I was left on my own. Meanwhile the English attack had begun. There was a small brick building near the road, which I used as cover, to see what was happening. I got the biggest fright of my life when I saw the massive sight of tanks and massed soldiers in three lines coming towards our position. There was heavy shelling and I saw soldiers moving forward through the noise and explosions, but I saw no shrapnel so I assumed that the guns were firing blanks. ['Cardboard shells' is what Ted wrote, but the English term is 'blanks'. The charge was held in the cartridge case by a cardboard plug, which was blown out of the gun barrel harmlessly when the shell was fired. But these shells were not blanks.] I informed the Army soldiers of what was going on, and I observed that one of them was destroying an optical gun sight. I realised that these men were the gun crew and had no intention of firing. And I have to admit I never saw the gun. They refused to leave the cellar. Then I did the bravest thing I ever did in my life and decided to surrender, waving a Safe Conduct leaflet I had found in the south of France and kept in my pocket for more than six months. I knew that in surrendering I risked being shot in the back by the Germans and/or in the front by the enemy. When the enemy soldiers approached, I threw down my weapon, stepped forward from behind the brick building, and raised my arms holding the Safe Conduct up in my hand. The first English words I heard were; 'Shall I kill the fucking bastard?' I did not understand it all except 'Shall I kill'. Then they searched me and took some Dutch guilders I had in my pocket. They indicated to me to go back where they had come from. The next soldier I met was a medical orderly, who asked me the time. I looked at my watch, which he promptly removed from my wrist. I made my way forward towards a road where I saw a small gatehouse to a large house [not identified]. A soldier indicated I should go in there. An officer started questioning me about my unit etc., when suddenly a German Nebelwerfer started up. The impacts were very near but I heard the noise and took no notice, while the officer took shelter under the wooden table. Then I was taken to a farmyard where I heard a voice shouting 'I'm gonna heme'. I assumed it was a wounded Scottish soldier. Then I was introduced to 'bully beef and biscuits', and some tea, and realised I had not eaten since breakfast, and then I slept. I was still the only German soldier there. I think it was near Goch that I slept in the barn.

The next day I was with many Germans on a lorry, when I saw the interesting sight of a flail tank going about its business. We finished our trip in Tilburg in the cellar of a weaving plant, which was very noisy indeed, and British soldiers amused themselves intimidating us by putting some against a wall and firing their bren gun.

The next stop was a large POW camp in Brussels. There we observed an Me 262 shooting down two aircraft, and the camp went wild.[110]

Ted had a proprietary interest in this German jet fighter, having been seconded to convert the first production machines from bomber (see below) to fighter by fitting them with guns, after Hitler reversed himself about using them only as bombers. Ted surrendered to Glyn Gilbert's 'C' Coy. The soldier contemplating killing Ted would have been under command of David Bates and Mick Price.

110 Letter from Ted Winkler on 7 December 2012.

Drawing of Lt Col Cecil Firbank, DSO and Bar in 1945. (© Simon Firbank)

Maj Leslie Colvin as a captain in 1943. It was the author's mother's favourite picture of him.

Following behind C Coy on the left of the road was Tac HQ, comprising the BC, Tony Edwards, his wireless operator, Lance Bombardier Hewitt, his signaller, Bombardier Strutt, and the CO, Cecil Firbank with his wireless operator carrying the 18 set which failed. This was the link to Battalion Main HQ in the wood at the start line, where Colvin as 2ic was waiting for orders with the LOB and in the rôle he hated of 'waiting to fill a dead man's shoes'. Colvin commanded Maj Desmond Kidney's Support Company, comprising the Mortar Company, the anti-tank Platoon and the Carrier Company, while he could call for artillery support through Jack Hunton. L/Bdr Hewitt was wounded on the battlefield but continued to man the 18 set, calling to Fld Regt HQ to 'send another like me', which became a widely repeated saying in the unit. Hewitt received the MM. His citation is the most confused of all in this battle. Apparently Tony Edwards and Jim Hewitt lay out in the field on the left of the road as the battle raged so that Tony could act as FOO keeping the vital artillery informed, which role depended on his wireless once the FOO tank had been destroyed. Hewitt was a target and carrying the radio meant he could take no evasive action but wait for a fatal bullet. His plaintive call when he was injured – 'send another like me' – meant send another man with the intestinal fortitude that he had displayed. Of course it was deliberately misunderstood as men tried to control their own fears through joking. The signatures were Lt Col Hope (33 Fld Regt), Brig Mears (CRA), Maj Gen Whistler, Lt Gen Horrocks, Gen Crerar and Montgomery.

> **MM. Gunner (P/L/Bdr) 954767 James Hewitt RA**
> During the battle for WINNEKENDONK on 2 Mar 45, BN HQ 2 LINCOLNS advanced with the follow up Company. Before arriving at its objective the company crossed 1,000 yards of bullet swept ground which was also being shelled and mortared. L/Bdr HEWITT accompanied his BC [Tony Edwards] as his wireless operator through this fire and arrived on the objective with the company as they assaulted the farm [Brönkshof] which was held by a strong force of Germans [it was not]. There was considerable confusion and snipers and machine gunners kept up an incessant fire in addition to the heavy shelling and mortaring. Infantry signal communications failed and the only means of communication was by regt channels ['regt.' being shorthand for the Royal Regiment of Artillery]. Throughout the action L/Bdr HEWITT manned his set and maintained communications with great coolness despite the distraction of heavy fire and snipers. On one occasion two enemy were shot ten yards from his set as he sat in the open passing information. His bravery, dogged courage and devotion to duty were of great value at a critical time.[111]

Capt J.A. (Jack) Brymer the Adjutant of 33 Fld Regt at HQ, recorded:

> Progress slowed up in the afternoon, and 2 Lincolns, who had reverted to 9 Brigade once more, were ordered to attack Winnekendonk, which was softened up during the early afternoon by a Victor target. A quick barrage was fired by the Divisional Artillery which was worked out by command posts at very short notice. Enemy guns and mortars had now had time to re-organise and the attack on the village was met with mortar and artillery fire. Heavy fighting ensued, but by dusk Winnekendonk had been captured.[112]

For the artillery also, the last minutes before H-hr were a rush. The targets and the barrage had been worked out the previous night, but 33 Fld Regt had not expected to support an attack so late in the day. Jack Hunton had gone back 10 minutes before the attack to lay the barrage. He was hit

111 TNA: WO 373/54/378: James Hewitt's citation.
112 Statement by Jack Brymer provided by Maj Ivor Norton.

on his ammo pouch although there is no mention of this in his diary, which was last quoted from earlier in the morning in Kervenheim.

> We stayed with 'B' Coy HQ but later in the day the OP was hit; fortunately for us we had just left. We then had a real good meal, our first for 24 hours. Smith really excelled with his cooking. But about 1600 hours we left very hurriedly to go forward again. This time we dug in well behind a wood. I was then told to report FOO to the tanks who were supporting the next attack. Fortunately for me their FOO had just arrived and I returned back to find Chips and the BC [Edwards] setting off for the attack on Winnekendonk. I was told to stay and act as relay station. The attack went in and many casualties were suffered. Communications failed in this attack and Chips after being unable to get through on his wireless, having got half way there, had quite a bad time and returned to us. He was very concerned so we decided to get through with the carrier in the dark. All the crew came with me including the 2ic of the Lincs [Colvin] and Chips. We went up the road hoping we would not hit a mine and were the first to negotiate two large craters. It was quite a difficult and unhealthy job, but we got through eventually after being heavily shelled, and stayed the night in a large cellar with Bn HQ [Plockhorsthof]. It was now that I heard that the tank I should have gone with had been knocked out with only one survivor [none is known to have survived].[113]

All communications failed. Colvin went forward to satisfy himself that Firbank and the battalion were all right and to see if there was anything he and the rest of the battalion and the brigade could do, intending to return and see to it. When he arrived and found Peter Clarke was missing, Colvin disobeyed Firbank's order, and organized a search party to find Peter.

Sam Larkin's understrength A Coy followed up C Coy on the left of the road with Archie Fletcher's tp of three Churchill tanks. A Coy had been heavily engaged in Kervenheim over the previous 36 hours and was short two subalterns; Seabrooke killed in action and Colin Welch wounded. They occupied the farmhouse on the left, Büllhorsthof 998347, and acted as reserve Coy.

Alfie Curnow was an irrepressible, good-natured, courageous, and efficient Cockney ranker with a strong accent accent that he flaunted. He was 2ic A Coy, and wounded for the third time just before the start by the German DF registered on the wood.

> I joined 2 Lincolns from Sandhurst in October 1942 having been commissioned from a CQMS in the 1/6 Bn Queen's Royal Regt. It was with the Queens that I went to France in November 1939 as probably the youngest CQMS in the Army. Evacuated from Dunkirk on 4th June 1940. Went to Sandhurst in April 1942. Joined 2 Lincolns at Romsey and commanded 12 Platoon in 'B' Company under Bertie Dawson who was such a help to me in adjusting to 'officer' status. As a junior subaltern I was sent on any course that became available; ie street fighting course in the Gorbals of Glasgow; junior leaders' course at Moffatt; weapon training officers course at Hythe. Landed on D-Day at Lion-Sur-Mer. Wounded on night patrol at Galmanche – evacuated to rear dressing station; managed to rejoin the battalion. Wounded again at Black Orchard and again managed to rejoin the battalion. Promoted to Captain and given command of 'HQ' Company. This entailed becoming PMC and given 'dog's life' by Col Firbank, who insisted on having copies of 'The Field', 'Country Life' and 'Tatler' always available in the mess!!

113 Jack Hunton's Diary provided by Ivor Norton.

> Just before the Winnekendonk action I was posted to be 2ic to Sam Larkin in 'A' Company. I remember well sitting in a slit trench under a haystack doing the Times crossword with Sam. His wife regularly sent him the puzzle by post. It was just before the start when 'Moaning Minnies' opened up and I was wounded for a third time, and evacuated to the UK and finished up in Northfield Psychiatric Hospital in Birmingham. From there to the Holding battalion at Whatton-in-the-Vale, and to a Medical Board on September 6, 1945 when I was pronounced 'permanently unfit for any form of military service'. I would like to place on record how proud I was to serve in 2 Lincolns and how much I valued the friendship of your father, [Leslie Colvin], Sam Larkin, Bertie Dawson, Jack Ebbutt, John Boys, 'Twinkle' Pacey, Ted Hill, Ernie Mudge, Jim Bush, Paul Sutton, Mike Hunt, Jack Harrod, Peter Cliffe and many more 'Yellow Bellies'. [Yellow belly because of the yellow facings of the Lincolns' red pre-khaki uniforms].[114]

Capt Darby Houlton-Hart replaced Alf Curnow as 2ic of A Coy. Darby won the MC during the retreat to Dunkirk, but lost a finger on D-Day and was convalescent until September. During the advance into Winnekendonk, he remembers seeing two Churchills stationary on the left of the road with shot ricocheting over them. Darby was witnessing the consequence of the German gunners, both StuG and 88 mm on the right flank, firing eastwards in the fading light towards a sky darkening with nightfall, and failing to realise that the Churchills were hull-down behind the slightly embanked road. They could see the turrets, but in aiming down for the hull, which had much thinner side armour, were hitting the road surface and producing ricochets. Darby remembers a German tank destroyed on the left as they arrived at the farmhouse [Plockhorsthof], and Forbes's diagram shows a StuG in that position. It was not in the post-war list of battlefield wrecks implying that it was repaired or pulled away for some unknown purpose. After it became dark, Battalion Tac HQ arrived from Brönkshof and Darby was told to prepare the farm for defence. Firbank then sent him to locate Gilbert and Pacey and he found them in a cellar. After a night spent in a chicken house, he replaced the dead Peter Clarke as OC 'D' Coy. Years later, when visiting Winnekendonk, he found a British webbing pouch in use by the farmer as a mailbag on a blackthorn by the road.[115]

Maj Pat Smith, holder of an MC awarded after Overloon, was a Scot and commanded B Coy on the right of Larkin and Hart across the road:

> The Coy formation was the usual two platoons forward followed by Coy HQ with the third platoon following up. Having given John Boys the briefest of information and having crossed the SL I could point out our objective. I ordered John to get across and give what little information there was to the right forward platoon commander (who I think was Jim Orwin?). I myself contacted the left forward platoon under Sgt Nicholson and it was whilst doing this that I received a flesh wound on my right arm which bled quite copiously and I had to stop and get my field bandage tied around it. By the time the first aid had been applied the following platoon had overtaken me and I was able to give that platoon commander (Lt Gosling) what little information there was. I was with Peter Clarke on the SL just before H-hr and agonising on the lack of artillery and where the hell were the tanks. From memory only three Churchills came in support of 'D' Coy – they were late and 'D' Coy was well over the SL, and the tanks moved forward between 'D' & 'B' Coys. All hell had been let loose as soon as 'D' crossed the SL and one of the abiding memories I have of that day was one of the tanks just ahead of

114 Letter from Alf Curnow on 22 November 1998.
115 Darby Hart in conversation in 1983 and 1994.

us had been hit and the internal explosion blew off that heavy turret which lifted gently, as though in slow motion, overturned and fell to the ground – only the tank commander got out unharmed before it blew up. Another incident happened whilst with Sgt Nicholson – one of the sections had passed over a small slit trench situated in the middle of the field – why there only the Hun knew – when I noticed an arm come up lobbing a hand grenade. I drew his attention to this lone hero and without undue haste he himself walked over and emptied at least half a magazine into the trench. Nicholson had joined us from another Bn which had been broken up, an act which he resented very much. He was taciturn by nature – not easy to handle – but he was a first-class soldier and for ability I would have placed him high on any list. I was glad to hear later that he had been awarded the MM for this attack.

As I have mentioned earlier, all hell was let loose as the Lincolns debouched from the SL. I think the most frightening thing was hearing the 88's solid shell ripping through the air at the Churchills – that did at least cover up most of the small arms fire until the crack and thump of a bullet that was too near for comfort made you realise that the tanks were not their only targets. 'D' Coy ahead of us were beginning to suffer casualties as they came level with the first of the houses on their left leading into the village. 'B' Coy had about reached this point when I was hit for the second time. I was hit in the back and thrown on my face and landed face down on a tree branch which cracked my ribs and I couldn't even crawl. At that point my interest in the battle, NW Europe and the whole War ended. I wasn't in any pain. I had better hasten to add that it was a shell which landed behind me and not a 'bullet in the back' [alluding to the Lincolns' officer reputedly killed by his men in Normandy], and it wasn't until after dark that I was picked up and carried into a cellar which had quite a few wounded Lincolns including one lad whose leg was blown off below the knee sitting in the cellar working his own tourniquet – a brave Lincoln indeed. A Hun doctor was in the cellar and I remember being quite 'shirty' with John Boys when he asked my permission to allow the Hun to administer morphine to all the wounded. My feelings were that I was 'out of it', and he now commanded the Coy and felt he was wasting time by deferring to me. However I said by all means to go ahead and if there was any hesitancy on the part of any Lincoln wounded that I would volunteer for the first jab and they could see if I survived his administrations.

I was finally evacuated and made a good recovery. The good work of the RAMC plus liberal ingestions of Bell's whisky have worked wonders! From fairly early on only 'the Bruin' [Glyn Gilbert] and I were left in the Rifle Coys from those who had landed on D-Day. From that time on at any briefing for a move forward he and I used to bait each other by saying it's your turn to 'go'. I'm not sure but at that final briefing which I attended there was no time for such frivolities – it must have been fate and I was indeed glad to hear that he had survived it all ordering 'C' Coy in that 'clipped' tone which he used.[116]

Smith later mentioned that while lying injured in the cellar he was visited by Firbank, and asked him 'to do something for Nicholson'.[117] The result was the MM:

MM. W/Sergeant 4342240 William Nicholson

This NCO was commanding a platoon of 'B' Company during the attack on Winnekendonk on the evening of the 2nd March 1945. This platoon, just before it reached its final objective, was in a ditch some thirty yards from the defended houses which they had to take. Whilst in this ditch they were subjected to withering fire from the houses on their front and flanks

116 Letter from Pat Smith in 1983.
117 Phone conversation with Pat Smith in 1994.

10 Platoon 2 Lincolns at a reunion in Gosberton in Lincolnshire in 1992. (L.-r.:) Rifleman Houldershaw, Brengunner Herson MM, Piatman Hall, Rifleman Blood who was wounded at Winnekendonk, and section leader John Keenan. (© Keenan family)

> and suffered heavy casualties. Sgt Nicholson organised his platoon, moving from section to section while under very heavy fire, and led them in their final rush which carried the objective. But for his fine example of personal bravery and coolness under fire, which inspired all those under him, it is doubtful whether the objective would have been taken.[118]

John Boys was a dapper ex-Guardsman and took over B Coy when Smith fell. He was another survivor from D-Day when he was 2ic to Leslie Colvin in B Coy. Boys remembers Gilbert crossing his front, and wondering what the hell is Glyn doing? which remains an unanswered question and implies that Gilbert must have crossed the centre-line of the road. Boys said that with so many reinforcements and casualties he didn't know his men. Pat Smith strode out ahead like a piper, but then got hit as he was walking up and down across the front near the road. Then all the troops went to ground. Boys remembers dodging the tracer, and he commented that since he couldn't withdraw he had to go on regardless. He remembers a bullet which ran around the inside of his tin hat and down the back of his neck. Seeing an enemy in a slit trench, he bowled a smoke bomb into it followed by a grenade so that the cocky German wouldn't know what had hit him. He also remembers two men, RSM Butters and the battalion sniper, going to ground in a slit trench from which Firbank later hauled them unceremoniously before dressing them down. As he approached the farm by the road junction, Boys saw a lot of Germans firing from the top floor windows. He remembers seeing a soldier chasing a German around the house shouting 'He shot my mate!' Sgt Nicholson and Boys entered the house [Plockhorsthof] and Boys summoned the troops inside by beckoning them in with his finger. The troops were very young and Boys didn't know them all.

118 TNA: WO 373/54/408: Nicholson's citation.

Then they all stood around as if at a cocktail party wondering what to do next. Boys is quite sure that without the SG's tanks they would have lost the whole thing. He saw a duck eating from a German corpse in the farmyard. This might have been the goose which Bates later had cooked and Gilbert wouldn't eat.[119]

Eric Houldershaw was in 2 Section of 10 Pln commanded by Sgt Nicholson:

> After spending all night in slit trenches outside Kervenheim, we heard the noise of battle as 'A' Company helped the Royal Norfolks capture it. We did two hours on and four hours off throughout the night until stand-to in the morning. There had been very heavy dew and we were cold and wet. Everyone cheered up when breakfast came. Then later in the morning we had an O Group and set off in sections each side of the track for Winnekendonk. We reached the Start Line just before it became dark, lying behind a large hedge and peering through to see about half a mile of open fields into the village. Being eighteen years old at the time I thought we would be looked after by the tanks when they came. When it was becoming slightly dark we were given the signal to go. Pushing through the hedge with Cpl. Frank Everton to the left of the section and L. Cpl. Storey to the right we were spread out about four yards apart in extended order. The tanks had arrived and were to the right of us in formation [overtaking B Company to pull in front of them and behind D Coy in front]. Moving forward about ten yards we were now under fire with Spandau tracer criss crossing the field. The barrage from our guns was landing near the village, and mortars were landing around us. Then with a rush of air an 88 landed on the right hand side of the section. Looking straight into it I saw the middle was red fire with a perfect circle of black smoke around it. I was sent sideways by the blast and landed on the side of my head and neck next to Pte Chick Read. Lance Cpl. Storey was lying over to the right. After a minute or more, Pte Read started crawling away to the left. Feeling slightly dazed I followed him. He then lowered himself into a German slit trench. I followed him to ask if he was all right. He did not reply. By now blood was running under his helmet down his forehead above his right eye. At the same time Frank Everton's head appeared over the trench and he said come on let's go. I followed Frank Everton left towards the road where we went into a small ditch about fourteen inches deep. Crouching there still dazed I realised I was threatening a German with my rifle. Letting him pass to the rear we pushed forward again when we were held by Germans in a slit trench. We flushed them out with grenades and moved on again in the centre of the field. I saw a tank hit and go up in flames. Another one to the left of it did the same. Someone or something was blown into the air like a rag doll.
>
> By now it was nearly dark. The telephone wires were brought down into the ditch. I was running to get into the village and tripping every few yards trying to keep up with Frank. Down and take cover as the Moaning Minnies drop just in front of us. Run and get into the village and quickly dig in. Then down come the 88s. Someone is hit on the field and is calling out for help. We cannot get to them. Their cries get fainter and then fade out. The wounded are being treated in a cellar behind us by our MO and a German doctor.
>
> The 88s finally stop and all is quiet except for hearing the wounded in the cellar. Later, maybe midnight or after I watched AckAck fire a mile or more behind us slowly exploding in the sky. Then the sound of a plane above us followed by a terrific explosion. Pieces of earth and stones rained down onto my steel helmet like hail for a minute or so.
>
> When it was beginning to get light Frank Everton called across to me to go to the front of the house to see if breakfast was coming up. We had not eaten since breakfast the day before.

119 John Boys in conversation in 1983.

Going round the side of the house I saw someone near to the house in a crouching position although moving forward holding his rifle and looking straight ahead. Another member of 2 Lincolns was kneeling on one knee about ten yards away, still holding his rifle. There was not a mark on them or their equipment. Both were aged 19 or 20.

Going to the house and asking when breakfast was coming up I was told you are too late. It had all been eaten. Going back the same way and looking at the soldier near to the house the only part of him touching the house was his little finger. Getting back to the section and telling them there was no breakfast left and we had to wait until midday for some food and drink. Not speaking about what I had seen and trying to blank it out of my mind; only talking about it some forty years later. How did they die like this? What caused it? This has puzzled me over the years. Twelve or fourteen of the battalion that had been killed were laid out in front of the house by early morning. I noticed a German lady walking among them crying. Sometime later they were all buried in an orchard. I was not able to attend having to be on duty. We had to stop nine or ten days living in the cellar waiting for reinforcements. After a day or two someone decided to go and have a look in the attic. They came down with thirty-four German prisoners who had been hiding there.[120]

John Keenan advanced with B Coy's HQ.

We were digging in about 5 o'clock at night and it was already dark. I'd obtained some straw and got the slit trench worked out and we were thinking to ourselves to bed down for the night. Then we heard one of those calls that always tended to put the fear up us – O Group – there's an Orders Group. These came down from the CO; the CO had an O Group, the Company commanders had an O Group, then the Platoon commanders had an O Group. We were going to attack this place called Winnekendonk. Now Winnekendonk is quite a small village. It is basically in an L-shape formed upside down, on the right and in front of us. We had to follow a straight road and attack both sides of the road and across a field. I have no hesitation in telling you that we were walking into the jaws of cannons. It was a good job the Germans were more or less beat. The Reconnaissance Regiment had been into the woods on the left-hand side and alleged they had been into the village on the right-hand side. When we used to get the sort of information we got from the Recce Regiment to the effect that you needn't expect much opposition, most of the lads used to groan because they knew bloody fine there were. Right or wrong we had to go across these rather extended fields towards this village to this T Junction at the end of the road that was forming the direction of the attack. Well the attack went forward and we were supported by the Scots Guards out of one of the armoured brigades in Churchills. Well I was fortunate enough to be well back in Company HQ because at that time for my sins I was company clerk. At the T junction there was an 88, at least one 88, which was a damned effective German anti-tank gun. It was brewing up tanks like shelling peas. We had three tanks in our immediate place and I very clearly remember in the failing dusk – the light had probably gone anyway, I don't know – I saw the tank hit and the turret fly into the air in an arc. The turret must weigh 4 tons. It came down what in my mind looked slowly, and our lads were walking from underneath it. There are pictures in your mind and you never forget them.

I decided at this time that the sensible thing was to get into the ditch at the edge of the roadside, which I recall quite well was absolutely full of telephone wires and posts which had blown down. And I was joined by a lieutenant tank commander and his crew, [Alasdair

120 Eric Houldershaw in a letter in 1996.

> Gordon who had just had his troop destroyed] and the lieutenant tank commander said to me something to the effect, 'What shall I do now? Shall I go forward?' or whatever. And I recall sort of turning around to him and saying basically 'You've done what you're supposed to do. Beat it. Get back. Get out.'
>
> Anyway we carried on. We had one or two heroes in our company who managed to complete the blinking way of getting into the house directly opposite the crossroads, and we sort of captured the village. Mind you that was after crossing the fields with machine guns firing on us from three points of the compass. We lost an awful lot of chaps. Some of them, because it was night by now, quite a few of them were wounded and we couldn't find them in the dark. We could hear them calling but we couldn't find them.
>
> We got into this house, and when we got there the regiment was in a right mess with people all over the damned place – all mixed companies and platoons. I was in this house [Plockhorsthof] and reasonably happy there. One of the laddies who got mortally wounded on that occasion was an old soldier called [Frederick] Billings and they could hear him calling. One or two stouthearted blokes, I think George Harrison was one, went to try and find him. But they couldn't find him. The next day they found that Billings had actually got into a German slit trench, and the reason they couldn't find him was that he wasn't above ground. We set up our defences around this house and a pal of mine called Eric Houldershaw and another bloke called Sammy Hall, they were in slit trenches outside while I was inside. A little later in the night a German aircraft came over and dropped a bomb on us. The bomb was right next door to the house. How the hell he got the target or had any idea where it was, I have no idea. This bomb was a fairly heavy one and I know that Eric Houldershaw was more or less buried in his slit trench because the bomb covered him with earth. The basic situation was the Germans having been chucked out of the place they upped-sticks and went during the night.[121]

Charles Peacock was a twenty-year-old corporal from Hammersmith in Lt Gosling's 11 Pln. He had served in two units broken up for reinforcements – 10 DLI in 49 BID, dispersed on August 20, 1944, and 5 E Yorks in 50 BID – and joined 2 Lincolns at the beginning of December 1944 in Smakt on the Maas, witnessing Decima's birth in Battalion HQ.

> It was now February, and we moved into Germany through Goch. Our brigade moved towards a place called Kervenheim. We started in the morning helping 185 Brigade. The place was captured by dinnertime, and we then sorted ourselves out. Then we were told that we are not finished yet, and that we are going to capture a place called Winnekendonk. This was all in the same day. What we called our top knobs I can't print, having had no rest, no grub and getting tired as well. It was now the afternoon, and we are going to attack at 17.45 hours. We moved off, down through woods until we come to the edge of a wood, then we waited. We looked out to see our objective ahead, the town, and in front of that and us is 1,200 yards of open field, with a stream to cross. It was 17.45 hrs and time to attack. Two of our tanks came up to help. I did not make the jump across the stream. I got wet up to my waist, but had to carry on, for now I am a corporal with men under me. We get about 10 yards out, then hell opened up. A German 88-mm gun fired across our front blowing the turret off our tank, and to think I was going to go around the back of the tank for a bit of protection. There was this gun going off; then they threw mortars at us from the back of the town; and machine gun fire from the houses in front of us. All of this coming

121 John Keenan's tape-recorded memoirs.

> down on top of us was no picnic. We were getting to the other side of this field when I look round to my men to see them starting to get nearer to the ground. I shouted to them, 'Lads, for Christ sake, don't lay down, you won't get up again – keep going". They heard me and kept going until we got to the road. In the corner of the field where the road bends to the right were two slit trenches. In each of them were dead Germans with an MG. We advanced some more and crossed the road to a house with a lot of barns.[Plockhorsthof.] There were supposed to be German Paratroopers in the house. Everybody knew that. All of a sudden 2ic Capt Boys shouted that we all had to go to this house. Boys went up front, but all the other members were frozen to the ground. They saw Boys running to the house, he went into it by the backdoor. Came out through the front door (or it was vice versa), and ran back to his Company, telling his men that he had seen Jerry in the house. Whilst we were in a barn doorway, two Jerrys ran past the back where there was an open door. They fired at us. I did not know at the time that I had been shot in the finger. I only felt a sting. It was a long time after that I looked at my finger and found it was in a poor state, so our sergeant told me to go down to the cellar of Battalion HQ to get it seen to. Off I go, and down in the cellar I see our own and German wounded. To my surprise my finger is cleaned and dressed by a German doctor who spoke English. We talked, and he sees to my finger and said to open my mouth, which I did, and he started to feed me a couple of pears. They were from one of many bottles lining a shelf in the cellar. How strange are some things that happen. While the doctor was looking after the wounded, a British soldier was rifling the doctor's pack. Anyway, those Jerrys who fired at us were found next morning, but both of them were dead in the hedge at the back, killed by someone else in our lot who was around that way at the time. Things were starting to calm down now, and we take up positions in case of counter attack. One did not come, thank God, for we were really tired. We then learn that there will be no grub coming up to us, so we had to open our emergency rations, just a block of chocolate, a half inch thick and as hard as concrete. You could not bite it you had to grate it with your teeth. We got proper food the next day. It was a tough battle. Poor old Billings out there groaning, calling out for help and also some Germans as well. It was dark, so it was not possible to get to them. We were up against their "Paras". I have a knife as a souvenir from one of them. Luckily it stuck in a tree and not in me! The next day an old lady came past. One of the platoon pointed at his wrist. She thought he wanted to know the time, so came over and showed him her watch, which he promptly snatched from her.[122]

The day was saved and a massacre of 2 Lincolns averted, even though they lost 22 dead and 95 wounded, largely through the action of 2 Troop comprising Lt Robert Runcie, Sgt Jim Alldred and an unknown Troop Corporal. 2 Troop brought up the rear on the right behind the Lincolns' B Company, and their task was to cover Gordon's troop in front. As they entered the Brönkshof farmyard, Alldred saw the 88 firing from the right, and then saw Gordon's troop being hit, with the FOO's Churchill blowing up. Runcie stopped in the shelter of a barn with the other two in line close behind. They were faced with the question of what to do. Jim Alldred knew at once that they had to silence the 88, and told Runcie to get moving. But Runcie did not want his troop to be destroyed by going out into the open, and stayed put. So Alldred waved the Corporal to back up, turned to the right and the two left the farmyard, leaving Runcie behind the barn. Later, Runcie left the shelter of the barn and destroyed the StuG that was positioned beside the Stammen farmhouse.

---

122 Charles Peacock in a letter to this author of unknown date.

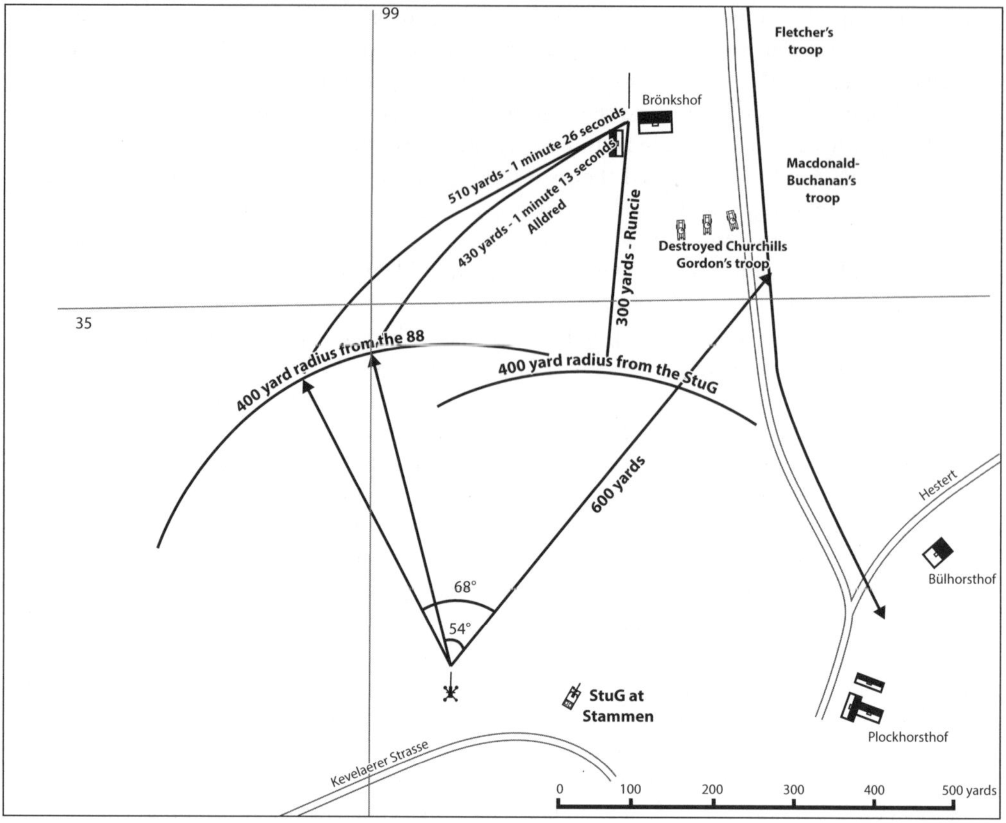

Map 37 Sgt Jim Alldred's exploits in leaving Brönkshof to the west and circling around the 88 to within the 400 yard killing distance, while Runcie went south for the StuG at Stammen.

Lt Bob Runcie, Gdsm Jim Lyburn, Cpl Thomas Moyes Bernard and two unidentified crew members in Holland in 1944. (© Alistair Pate)

Lt RAK Runcie receiving the MC for bravery at Winnekendonk. (© Crown Copyright IWM, BU 7831 by Sgt Morris)

Sgt Jim Alldred and his crew in the UK in 1944 before the adoption of the brigade shoulder flash. Gunner Hamilton is on the right. (© Dave Alldred)

14 of the 15 members of Lt Hector Laing's troop near Lütjenburg on 9 May 1945. (L.-r.back row:) Mick Murray and Sid Craik; (middle row:) L/S Thomson, Sgt Jim Alldred, Hursthouse and four unknowns; (front row:) Hamilton, Munn, Lt Laing, T.Smith and Forrest. Laing is wearing a U-boat commander's cap which he took from its owner when accepting his surrender after VE Day. Alldred was at all times, except at Winnekendonk, Laing's troop sergeant. (© Dave Alldred)

Lt Col CIH Dunbar, CO 3 Scots Guards received the DSO for the support given to 7 Canadian Infantry Brigade at Luisendorf on 15 February 1945 and not for Winnekendonk. (© Crown Copyright. IWM, BU 7822 by Sgt Morris)

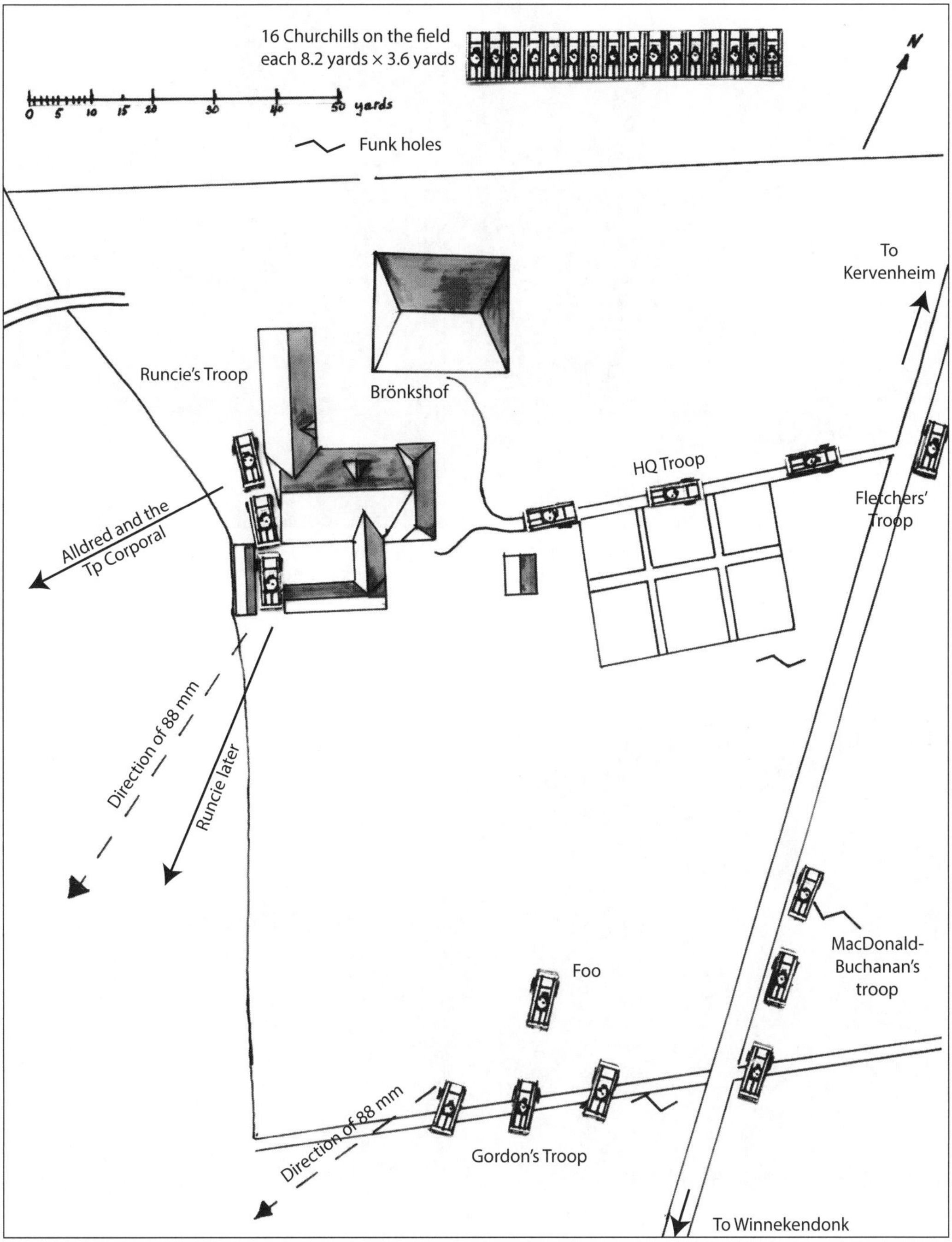

Map 38 When the 88 destroyed Gordon's troop and the FOO, MacDonald-Buchanan's troop continued along the lee side of the road, followed by Fletcher's troop. The HQ troop turned into Brönkshof to engage the 88 over the roof of the farmhouse. Runcie's troop stopped, and then split up, with Alldred and the Corproral heading for the 88 and Runcie accounting for the Stug.

Brönkshof in 1960. Gordon's troop and the Lincolns came through the orchard and gardens from right to left. Runcie's troop went behind the farmhouse – see Map 38. (© Josef Elders)

On the 70th anniversary of the battle Andrew, Steve and Dave Alldred marked the spots where the back end of each of the three Churchills in Runcie's troop stopped. Runcie had seen in horror Gordon's troop and the FOO being destroyed in the fields ahead. When Runcie would not move, Jim and the corporal immediately reversed, and headed out through the sunny gap to the left of the picture to hunt down the 88. Holding the framed 1960 photo reproduced above is Georg Elder, son of the owner. Hansgerd Kronenberg has his back turned while talking to this author; while Jenny Pearson stands where Runcie's troop roared into the farmyard. (© Rob Belk)

Sgt Jim Alldred's three sons, Steve, Dave and Andy, stand on the spot where Jim Alldred and the troop corporal exited the farmyard. The 88 was 800 yards away in the direction of the second house to the right of the thick tree trunk; there were no houses in 1945. Jim would have motored initially towards the barn that is visible over Andy's shoulder, but soon began to circle round left towards the 88, opening fire at 400 yards. (© Rob Belk)

The StuG III knocked out by Robert Runcie alongside Haus Stammen, photographed by Leslie Colvin in 1947. Runcie looked inside and was made sick by the sight of the four young crewmen he had killed. This earned him the sarcastic name of 'killer Runcie' in the mess.

Maria Meyer and Anna Gellings standing in front of Haus Stammen in the late 1930s. Note the lamp over the door is the same as in 1947. (© Anna Gellings)

The StuG by Haus Stammen was photographed from the front door in about 1947 looking back at Winnekendonk and its church. (© Georg Drißen)

Haus Stammen in 1984 after remodeling. It was externally rebuilt in 2014.

Alldred decided to hold his fire until he reached a firing position 400 yards from the 88 when destruction was guaranteed. They had a theoretical maximum speed of 14 mph or 411 yards per minute on good going, but in the prevailing wet conditions it was somewhat less. The gunners in the two tanks would at once have had the 88 pointed out to them by Alldred who had spotted its flash before stopping. From that moment until the end of the action Alldred's gunner Hamilton held his gun trained on the 88, probably firing the coaxial BESA periodically to shake up the German gunners when they started traversing. The Tp Cpl may have been ordered to fire speculatively at the 88 with HE while on the move for the same reason, but without hope of hitting it. We do not know.

For something like two minutes the two Churchills ploughed on against a darkening sky with no shots fired (see Map 37). They were driving an elliptical course towards the 88, gradually increasing their rate of turn. The commander of the 88 may have taken a while to notice them, and more time wondering what they were up to by driving across his flank and offering their thinner side plates. He cannot have been concerned to begin with for the 88 was concentrating on the threat to the German defenders in Kervenheim, and would have been targeting MacDonald-Buchanan's and Fletcher's troops at a range of 750 yards. He was probably puzzling why he was failing to stop them, not realising that the field beyond was lower. The 88 in aiming for the Churchill's hull was hitting the road surface, and the infantry observed the shells ricocheting off the metalled surface. At some point the German commander of the 88 decided to switch focus to Sgt Alldred and the Tp Cpl, or was ordered to do so by the Pak Front commander if such had been established.

By this time perhaps a minute or more had elapsed, and the 88's traversing angle had increased to 50°. Using high gear, the crew would take 5 seconds to swing through 50°, but high gear required a lot of physical strength. Alldred said he saw them hand cranking 'like mad' which indicates they

A DP 88 mm without shield on display in the Land Warfare Hall at IWM Duxford, photographed and uploaded by John at en.wikipeedia. Traverse and elevation were controlled manually with the wheels which had a choice of high or low gear selected by a gear lever; sighting was through a telescopic sight; and the gun was fired by a gunner standing on the left side of the gun. (CC-BY-3.0 Wicki Commons)

A DP 88 mm of the type believed to have been destroyed by Jim Alldred at Winnekendonk. This one was at Bir Hacheim in June 1942. (Bundesarchiv Bild 1011-443-1574-26)

Lt Alexis Melikoff of 4CG sitting on the barrel of an 88 Pak 43 on a cruciform mount in the Siegfried Line. It had been semi-entrenched to lower its silhouette by a further 2 feet. It is possible but unlikely, that this was the type of 88 at Winnekendonk. (© Alexis Napier)

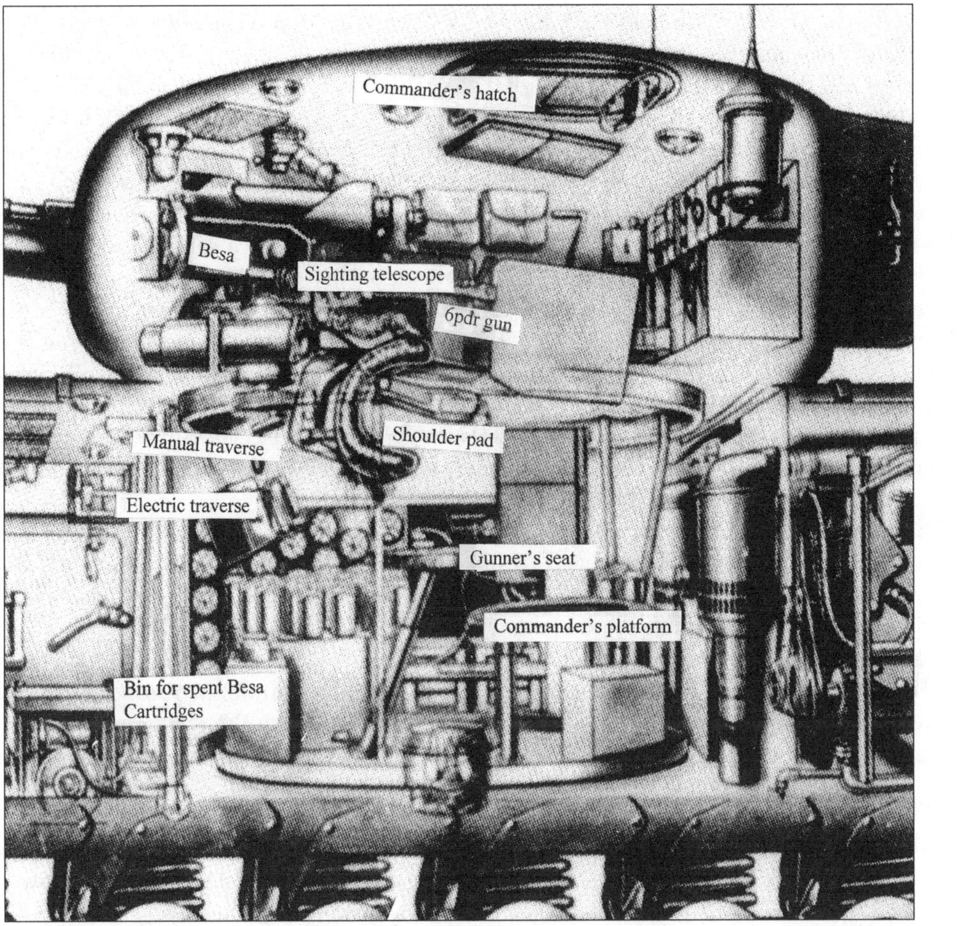

Inside Alldred's tank. Alldred stood on the platform with his head out of the open hatch, watching the 88. Hamilton sat on the gunner's seat with his right shoulder in the pad of the freely floating 6pdr gun, and with his hand on the coaxial BESA's trigger, which was close to the 6pdr's trigger. Hamilton's left hand was on the electrical traverse control. His eye was in the rubber cup of the sighting telescope while his forehead was pressed to the pad. His right foot was on the pedal that controlled the locking of the freely floating gun.

used the easier low gear requiring 10 seconds of cranking.[123] By this time the Churchills would have reduced the range to about 600 yards. It became a race for the Germans to line up the 88 and Alldred to reach the point where range was 400 yards and he could open fire with certainty that Hamilton would destroy the 88. The time-distance to run depended on whether Alldred told the driver to turn more steeply towards the 88, which would shorten the distance but give the 88 an easier shot as the rate of change of the angle would slow. Depending on the rate of turn the distance was 200 to 300 yards, taking 30 to 45 seconds to cover. Alldred always maintained it was a close-run thing.

123 USWD: TM E9-369A. German 88-MM Antiaircraft Gun Material, 29 June 1943.

No one, except Hamilton it seemed, fired on the move in 1944-5. In 1946, with the introduction of stabilisers for guns, gunners began again to fire on the move. A veteran who had crewed in Churchill Mk III and IV tanks in Italy wrote; 'We tried NOT to fire on the move as it was invariably a lost shot'.[124] The Americans forbade firing on the move even in training, but it was permitted in emergencies. The reason was that the big guns – 6pdr, 75 mm and 17pdr guns – weighed 1,200 to 1,500 lbs[125] (550 to 680 kg) and even when balanced the tank's violent movements in three dimensions created such high G-forces that they would injure the gunner. Therefore Germans, and later the Allies tethered the gun to an elevating screw device to keep it steady, and then of course they could install longer and longer guns that were not balanced.

Everyone, however, who had served in British tanks from 1939 until the arrival of the M4 Sherman in October 1942 had been instructed on firing the 2pdr on the move, which was safe as it weighed only 200 lb[126] (100 kg), and was balanced when loaded. The gunner controlled elevation by leaning on a shoulder pad with the first finger of his right hand on the trigger, while traversing it and himself with the left-hand on the hand-grip controlling the electric turret motor. Bringing a gun to bear was much quicker with free-float than with an elevating screw in a stopped tank, and in the hands of a good gunner could hit every time.

The 6-pdr was available with an elevating screw, but Hamilton continued to prefer the free-floating arrangement with which he was familiar. He had a foot-pedal for locking and unlocking the free-float, and for some of the time as they approached the 88 he would have locked the gun to save his strength to concentrate on the target.

An experienced veteran gunner and tank commander wrote that many gunners achieved top marks at range shooting, but the outstanding gunner, such as Hamilton, also performed well in the real battle when 'considering factors such as urgency, visibility, unknown ground, inconsistent movement by the enemy, weariness, delay in orders and wear and tear of equipment. It was the overcoming of these which made one gunner better than many others.'[127]

If firing on the move was generally a lost art in 1945, so driving the tank in the optimum way for firing on the move so it pitched but did not veer, became unnecessary. Alldred's crew, however, were experienced and the driver knew to keep the direction steady for Hamilton. Loading by the radio operator was virtually instantaneous, according to Ken Tout. In urgent firing the loader stood with a round held ready at gun height requiring a sweep of his arms of about 36 inches. The polished round slid into the smooth breach without need to push further, taking about one second as the breach slammed shut. The loader would be already lifting the next round from the bin on the floor as the gun fired.

Hamilton would have acquired the 88 as soon as Alldred pointed it out to him, and trained the gun on it as the Churchill picked up speed, never moving the gun and turret away from the target until it had been destroyed. The loader was told to load or re-load with APCBC and not HE or DSAP, because accuracy was more vital in this case than penetrative power. The accuracy of early DSAP was compromised by unpredictable separation of the segmented body from the round. Hamilton sat with his eye glued to the sight, left hand on the electric traverse switch and the first finger of his right hand on the firing trigger under the gun. His shoulder would be pressed into the horse-shoe shaped shoulder pad. His forehead would be pressed against the curved pad above the sight, and his right eye would be 'glued' to the eyepiece.[128] He held the 88 centrally in his sights with the electric traverse control, watching the image of the 88 rise and fall though the

124 T Canning; http://ww2talk.com/forums/topic/55353-coaxial-besa-use/#entry646078.
125 http://forum.worldoftanks.com/index.php?/topic/46164-tank-gun-weights/
126 http://www.quarryhs.co.uk/sgun.htm
127 Ken Tout in an e-mail on 28 October 2014.
128 N Montgomery. *Churchill Tank Owners' Manual* (Newbury Park: Haynes, 2013), p. 87.

cross-hairs in the sight once he had locked the elevation, or following it if elevation was unlocked. As the Churchill slowly straightened up from its circling right-around the gun and began to face it frontally, Hamilton had to traverse right had to keep the 88 central in the sight. After about two minutes of watching the image get larger and its crew scrambling to get a bead on them, Alldred ordered; "Range 400 yards. Fire at will". Hamilton set the sight to 400, ensured the elevator lock was off, aimed with his shoulder and fired. At that moment, the Churchill dipped and the shot fell 25 yards in front of the 88 and bounced over it. The gun was reloaded in two seconds, and Hamilton fired again after a lapse of about 4 seconds, hitting the 88 centrally, and no doubt in the trunnion.

Andrew Alldred, Jim's son, commented:

> As they approached the German guns which were now turning their attention towards them Dad gave the order to Hamilton "Range 400 yards, fire at will". They were moving fast across rough ground and as they fired the tank "jumped" and dad says he saw the shell fall 25 yards short of the SP gun [88] and bounce over the top of it. He was adamant that the first shot bounced over the German gun because the tank had 'pitched' as the shell left the gun. I assume the Besas opened fire as well on their approach to the guns but we have no idea when that would have started and what they hit. I am sure it would have put the fear of God into the defending Germans. He said to Hamilton, 'Reload and fire at will and don't f ...miss him this time.' He didn't. That is the only time I ever heard my dad use the F word – you may agree it has a ring of truth. His tank and the Corporal's then took out the other guns when they were joined by others from RF Squadron. As you record, the fighting in Winnekendonk went into the town and well into the night when to everyone's apparent surprise the Germans suddenly surrendered. I have read elsewhere that the German High Command were furious when they heard of the surrender. [The Whitakers mistakenly claimed this of Schlemm [129] – see above]. At the debriefing Dad recalled Col Dunbar saying "just like the set pieces we practised on Salisbury Plain..." etc. Dad's reply (again consistently to me) was "Yes sir, but the difference is we didn't lose 25 bloody good men on Salisbury Plain..." And he returned Col Dunbar's withering look.
>
> I should add that he certainly never wanted or expected a medal. We spoke about that many times and that was the least of his concerns. He knew in any event that he would certainly never have received a citation from Col Dunbar whatever he did – they had crossed swords before and would do so again later at Lubbecke [when the sergeants faced arrest for refusal to obey a valid order from Dunbar]. Nor was he even put out that Lt Runcie got the MC. He fully accepted that officers who directed or were i/c during a successful battle would be decorated. What upset him was when he read J Mantle's book and Lt Runcie said that his tank had taken part in the initial attack on the German guns when it hadn't. I was at home and remember he was clearly distressed when he came home and told me what he had read in the book. He read it in the bookshop – he didn't buy it – he wrote down the passage and showed it to me. So he didn't care about medals but he did expect Lt Runcie (or the Archbishop as he then was) to give a more accurate version of the action. All Dad wanted to do was to survive the war and get home to his family and he wanted to try and make sure that as many of his men and officers as possible did so too.
>
> His attitude to officers, with the exception of Kindersley and Dunbar, was not quite what you suggest. He was certainly outspoken but he knew his place. Whenever their names were mentioned, Whitelaw, Laing, Mann, Cathcart and even Runcie and others he would say,

129 Whitaker, *Rhineland*, p. 266.

> 'finest Officers in the British Army.' He did not just hold them in the highest regard but he revered them as I witnessed myself when I took him once to meet Laing.[130]

Lt Col Claude Dunbar wrote the citation for Robert Runcie's MC, and this became the official history after it was signed by Brig Douglas Greenacre, by Brig Church Mann for General Crerar, by Brig Bingham (BRAC) and by FM Montgomery. The absence of Whistler's, or even Horrocks's, signature had important consequences. *Heather* was a 3 BID Operation, and no one would have been more interested than Whistler in learning the lessons why Kervenheim was a disaster and Winnekendonk a success. Whistler's interest would have ensured that the approval of citations written by Dunbar would have been no formality. However, because 6 GAB were army troops operating in support of 3 BID and not under its command, the citation went for approval and signature to 1 Canadian Army, and only brigadiers Greenacre, Mann and Bingham saw the citation before it went to Montgomery as a formality. Therefore all of those who who had to be convinced to sign a citation written by a Lt Col held the same rank of Lt Col, since Brigadier was an appointment and not a rank. Mann was a highly regarded Canadian staff officer renowned for his sense of humour; in a planning meeting a few days later for Op *Plunder* he had the Americans guffawing and the British bemused when the Americans queried the unfamiliar, to them, 'Monty's moonlight'; 'Our American cousins are quite familiar with Kentucky moonshine', said Mann, 'This is another way of getting lit up.'[131] The Canadians at that time were preoccupied with their disaster in the Hochwald, and could have no interest in citations for Foucard and Runcie operating in support of XXX Corps. The degree of oversight for 6 GAB citations was therefore minimal to nonexistent in Op *Heather*. The citations for Uelzen on 14 April 1945, were treated very differently; Douglas Greenacre at Brigade, Maj Gen Evelyn 'Bubbles' Barker at VIII Corps, Lt Gen Miles 'Bimbo' Dempsey at Army and Montgomery at Army Group as a formality all signed. Runcie made an amusing suggestion that his MC was approved because Dunbar was very good at writing citations, but the facts show that Dunbar was unsupervised during this period by anybody above his substantive rank of Lt Col. In the cases of both Kervenheim and Winnekendonk, Lt Col Dunbar and Lt Col Smith sent citations to other ranking Lt Cols for signature. These appointees were too far down, and in the case of Mann and Bingham not even part of the operational chain of command. Both citations cried out for the input of Whistler, who had the big picture and the experience to perceive the crucial and exceptional nature of what Foucard had achieved at Kervenheim and Alldred at Winnekendonk. Whistler also enjoyed the standing required to ensure the reward was commensurate with their exceptional bravery and achievement, as he did in the case of the VC for Private Stokes. The result of this lack of oversight was injustice for exceptional men; Alldred for not receiving recognition and Runcie for being 'recognised' for actions that were largely due to Alldred. The result also deprived the Brigade of Guards of the honour of having two more VCs in the persons of Alldred and Foucard. Dunbar would not have appreciated the ultimate irony of his statement made in the War Diary that Winnekendonk was 'well worthy of further study'.

Runcie's citation:

> **Immediate MC. WS/Lt P/251985 Robert Alexander Kennedy Runcie**
> During the attack on WINNEKENDONK (9934) on 2 Mar 45 Lt RUNCIE'S tp was in sp of the leading wave of tks when they came under heavy and close fire of concealed 88 mm and SP's from the front and both flanks, all three tks being hit. ~~Though his own tk had been brewed up the previous day~~, (sic) Lt RUNCIE unhesitatingly took his tp out into the open

130 E-mail from Andrew Alldred on 1 October 2014.
131 Dickson, *A Thoroughly*, p. 407.

> which was the only place from which he could see the enemy weapons and engaged them so effectively that he knocked out two 75 mm SP's and one 88 mm, also causing the enemy to abandon a nest of 50 mm. During this time not only was he being shot at by AP from a range of not more than 500 yds, but also was being subjected to very heavy shell and mortar fire. A short time later whilst still being fired upon he personally successfully directed the fire of our arty onto an area from which fire was holding up the adv. There is no doubt that Lt RUNCIE'S courageous leadership and the magnificent marksmanship of his tp dealt so effectively with this strong enemy A tk screen that the tks and inf were able to get on, (sic) into the town. 5 Mar 45.[132]

It has taken this author from September 1983, when Robert Runcie was asked what happened, until October 2014 to establish a version of events consistent with all of the known facts, although unknown aspects persist. The delay was due to a combination of factors; a flawed process resulting in a citation containing four errors of fact; the lack of authoritative overview usually provided by the divisional commander; a regimental ethos of loyalty unable to countenance questioning a citation written by one of its senior officers and endorsed by Montgomery; the loss of Jim Alldred's testimony to Jonathan Mantle; and the caution due to the main protagonist being a revered Archbishop of Canterbury.

The rules about writing citations in the Second World War are unknown to this author, and enquiries made of the MOD have gone unanswered except to warn that there have likely been changes since 1945. The current rules are on the MOD website, but the MOD's institutional memory seems to have been the victim of budget cuts. This author believes, however, that it is likely that the unit's senior officer was required to speak to those present at an action in order to establish the facts. The family of Sgt Alldred find it improbable that given their mutually antagonistic relationship that Dunbar and Alldred would have spoken. Nevertheless, Dunbar's debriefing of RF showed that he clearly understood what had happened by reportedly stabbing the places on his map while commenting and claiming that it was his training of the unit that had produced the result. No one apparently disagreed with Dunbar's description of what happened, so Dunbar had his facts for the citations. Alldred, however, had implicitly disagreed with Dunbar's claim that it was his training that had produced the success by raising the matter of heavy infantry casualties. He had seen how Runcie, the product of Dunbar's training, had failed to act and he knew that the success was due to his own training that had pre-dated Dunbar's arrival and initiative. At this point Dunbar may have seen that his chance of getting a bar to his DSO had vanished, which would explain the depth of his dislike for Alldred and his determination that Alldred's action would not be recognized.

It would appear that neither Laing, who was Alldred's usual troop commander, nor Runcie made any attempt to influence Dunbar or to stick their necks out for him. There is no doubt about Dunbar's bullying nature: Dunbar had threatened Farrell with being sent home for making an innocent suggestion that Dunbar construed as insubordination.[133] But then Runcie confessed to his biographer that he was was one of Dunbar's favourites,[134] and favourites have influence.

Of course it is likely that Laing and Runcie never imagined that Dunbar would ignore Alldred's part in the action, and when they discovered after the war the depth of Dunbar's malice towards Alldred they would have decided there was nothing they could do. These subalterns were young and 'wet behind the ears', and far from even imagining being the Establishment Grandees that they became. Mantle reported that Runcie told Alldred at the debriefing that he would get a

132 TNA: WO 373/54/583: Bob Runcie's citation.
133 Farrell, *Reflections*, p. 104.
134 H Carpenter. *Runcie; the Reluctant Archbishop* (London: Hodder & Stoughton, 1996), p. 84.

medal, and that Alldred had replied that he would not but that Runcie would get one. Runcie knew of Mantle's book and never denied its truth. Earlier he had shown discomfiture on learning that Mantle had interviewed Alldred. From this it is reasonable to conclude that Runcie was conscious of having been credited with Alldred's bravery and successful initiative, while any explanation he could provide, namely that Dunbar was an unapproachable bully, who would have sent Runcie home for being insubordinate if he had pushed the matter of Alldred's receiving a medal, would have clashed with his reputation in 1983 as the Archbishop who stood up to Margaret Thatcher and the Queen. According to Charles Moore's biography of Thatcher, the Queen had said to Runcie after the Falkland's Thanksgiving service that you should never leave a Christian service feeling sad, and since she had felt sad the service was not well arranged. Runcie had had the temerity of praying for the dead of Argentina as well as Britain.

Brigadier Greenacre caught two of the errors in Dunbar's submission, crossing out the statement in the citation claiming Runcie's tank had brewed up the previous day, for Runcie never did experience a tank fire and it was not the previous day. The event referred to was Runcie's selfless rescue three days earlier of Philip from another tank in his troop that was burning. Runcie always claimed that this rescue played a part in his award of the MC, which is perhaps evidence that he conversed with Dunbar about it and therefore assumed it featured in the citation, which it originally did. The fact that it was later struck out still allowed Runcie truthfully to claim it was a factor, albeit one not recognised by Greenacre, in the award of his MC. It is perhaps indicative of the concern these citations caused Greenacre that he took a month from 7 March to 7 April, to approve five of the six citations after correcting Runcie's, and to reject that of the MM for Gdsm Hunt. The evidence shows that Dunbar was anything but adept at writing citations.

Two other significant errors remained, which had they become known would have been grounds for rescinding Runcie's MC. It was not true that 'Lt RUNCIE unhesitatingly took his tp out into the open.' What he did was stay in cover behind the farm while Tp Sergeant Jim Alldred and the Tp Corporal – whose name is unfortunately unknown – went out into the open without Runcie to knock out the 88 and, they believed, the two StuGs. After an unknown delay, Runcie followed after them and possibly destroyed one StuG. There are two sources for this interpretation of what happened. The first is Runcie himself who wrote: 'I can confirm that the M.C. was awarded largely for the action at Winnekendonk. There was an ancillary incident [rescuing Philip] but the primary award was for positioning myself to knock out the Stug III SP gun.'[135] The other source is the citation itself since it beggars belief that there was no factual backing to its claims. Jim Alldred, however, always maintained that Runcie "stayed behind the bloody barn" and that he and his Tp Cpl accounted for both StuGs and the 88. This may, however, be consistent with Runcie's claim, since the StuG in question may have been hit by both Runcie and the Tp Cpl. Andrew Alldred, Jim's son, believes that Jim could not have known what Runcie did, and that Runcie should have the benefit of the doubt. This author agrees, believing that while Jim and the Cpl were making their nerve-wracking wide circling move around the 88 and StuGs, that Runcie had time to come out from cover and to make directly for the nearest StuG, and to kill it with the first shot as he claimed. This StuG was behind Stammen and protected from the direction of approach by Jim and the Cpl, but vulnerable to Runcie's direct approach. In conclusion Runcie deserved his MC, but the Tp Cpl and Jim's gunner deserved the MM, while Jim deserved the VC for saving the day.

The final error in the citation was the claim that Runcie directed artillery fire onto the area holding up the advance. This is the most puzzling claim since Dunbar would have known that Runcie was not trained as an FOO to direct artillery fire from map references, and it is not something to be learned while doing it for the first time. Evidence that the subalterns could not direct artillery came

135 Letter from Robert Cantuar on 15 September 1983.

from Mark Fearfield's testimony about the event in mid-afternoon of that day when he was asked to help Pember, and did so by deliberately avoiding the use of map references, not having been trained in that skill he said. Runcie had not been in contact with the artillery to know their frequencies and operating procedures. All tanks had the 19 Set that combined the medium range shortwave A-Set (medium-range HF inter-tank and tank-to-HQ R/T and morse code communication over 10 miles on speech and 20 miles on Morse Code), and the B-Set (short distance VHF inter-troop tank communication over 1,000 yards in theory but in practice 300 yards). There was also an intercom facility for communication between the tank's crew, a factor that will shortly become important to understand. Fitted alongside the 19 Set was the 38 Set for infantry cooperation. Anything is possible, but what is stretching credulity too far is to imagine Runcie contacting or being contacted by the artillery and directing their fire. A few hundred yards away the Battery Commander, Tony Edwards and his radioman, Gunner Hewitt, were crouching on the open battlefield being shot at while doing just that, while the FOO of the powerful medium 5.5 inch gun battery had been vapourised in the explosion of the Pipe Major's tank. The regimental historian corrected the mistaken claim in the citation by stating that Runcie's troop used their own guns to get the advance going again, rather than directing the guns of the artillery: 'He [Runcie or his troop] also dealt with a number of Spandau posts which were holding up the infantry and enabled them to advance into the town.'[136]

This author required more detail about these extraordinary events, and wrote to Runcie in September 1983 enclosing amongst other material a picture of the knocked-out StuG alongside the Stammen farmhouse taken in 1947 by this author's father, and the nearest one for Runcie to have knocked out. Runcie replied at once that he and Hector Laing would shortly meet and be 'sure either to make suggestions or plot a meeting'. He specified why he had been awarded the MC, as we have seen, which amounted to an explicit disassociation from the exaggerated claims in the citation. In hindsight this turned out to have been the only information Runcie ever provided except to his authorised biographer, Humphrey Carpenter, which created more problems to be discussed below. Margaret Duggan[137] had sourced information from the citation and regimental history, and replied to this author's request for help; 'I do so sympathise. I found it impossible to get any further details about the Winnekendonk battle (from Runcie) other than those in the regimental history.'[138]

A week after promising that he and Laing would pore over the map, make suggestions and plot a meeting, Robert Cantuar wrote that he and Laing had "spent a little time poring over your map" but; "Frankly, we both agreed that there was nothing that we could challenge but neither of us could in the Winnekendonk action really remember much about it all".[139] At that time this author believed Laing had participated but later John MacDonald-Buchanan said he had replaced Laing, who obviously could not remember, writing; 'because quite honestly I have no idea where I was in that particular battle…'.[140] However, in July 1945 Whitelaw as CO of 3 SG, wrote a citation for Laing to be awarded the American Bronze Star, writing that 'Lieut Laing has commanded a troop in every action fought by the bn', which was clearly the communal, albeit faulty, memory. In his reply, Runcie wrote that the dispositions suggested by this author made sense, and suggested that Sgt Mildenhall and Sgt Mathieson could help, although it turned out that neither had been at Winnekendonk. Alldred's name was never mentioned, even by Laing in a reply to a separate request that again implied he had been at Winnekendonk. Alldred was Laing's usual troop sergeant and Laing wrote very highly of him; 'As my Troop Sgt I would have no other;

136 Erskine, *Scots Guards*, p. 411.
137 Duggan, *Runcie*.
138 Letter from Margaret Duggan on 7 February 1984.
139 Letter from Robert Cantuar on 21 September 1983.
140 Letter from Hector Laing on 4 August 1983.

he was totally brave and very conscientious.'[141] Alldred switched to Runcie's troop and only for Winnekendonk because Mathieson was still recovering from wounds received at Moyland. Laing himself was rested and replaced for Winnekendonk by MacDonald-Buchanan, who fought his first battle as troop commander with Sgt Tam Shearer.

On 1 October 1983, and therefore within weeks of this author's correspondence with Runcie, Margaret Duggan's book was published. It contained the (mis)information imparted from Runcie in their face-to-face conversations that his MC had been awarded partly for saving Philip from the burning tank. This was newsworthy and always referenced by Runcie, but not strictly true as Greenacre had struck it out of the citation, which Duggan knew as she published it. Runcie had pointedly failed to correct the two errors of fact described above which, had they become known, would have raised the possibility of Runcie's MC being rescinded. Instead of this, however, Duggan published Dunbar's exaggerated claims plus the added element of saving Philip which Greenacre had red-pencilled. Given the general view of Runcie in his obituaries, that 'he was a workaholic perfectionist, demanding impossibly high standards of himself and of his staff',[142] the good effect of Duggan's book on his reputation was likely to have been intentional.

Runcie's letter to this author stating categorically that he had been rewarded (only) for knocking out a single StuG can now be seen as putting the record straight should it become public. Runcie's position was in the final analysis impossible due to Dunbar's citation, and Runcie could only attempt damage control. He could not tell the truth publicly without blaming Dunbar for producing a fiction from which he and the battalion had benefited, and which had mocked the army's rules for the writing of citations. Even worse, the Scots Guards' officers had failed the ORs whose actions in delivering a memorable victory were deserving of recognition; the officers had blatantly and communally broken the code of *noblesse oblige*. Doing anything to let this cat out of the bag, however, would raise questions among Runcie's fellow officers who met together regularly, and make him appear an ingrate. Their next reunion would be embarrassing and perhaps Runcie would be unable to attend. The worldly Laing considering all of this would therefore have advised the other-worldly Runcie that the only policy was 'least said soonest mended', and from this decision followed Runcie's silence and feigned amnesia.

Donald Gordon commented on this matter having read a draft of this chapter:

> Runcie's MC. Very interesting. Dad was always, by nature, charitable. I asked him about Runcie's MC, and he said it was for 'pulling a man out of a burning tank, which made quite an impression on everyone.' When I said it was for his action at Winnekendonk, Dad was quite non-commital. Perhaps of 'least said, soonest mended?'[143]

During the following eight years nothing was published about Runcie's MC until in 1991, just as Runcie ended his term as archbishop, there appeared two unauthorised biographies; by Adrian Hastings and by Jonathan Mantle. Hastings' book added nothing to Duggan's Dunbar-plus narrative, even repeating Duggan's identification of the destroyed StuG as a Tiger Tank with a crew of four.[144] Mantle's book, however, sensationally re-wrote the history of the Battle of Winnekendonk by scooping an interview with Jim Alldred which placed Runcie's achievement in a very different light. The squared brackets as usual contain this author's comments.

141 Quotation supplied by David Alldred in an e-mail of 15 September 2014.
142 Margaret Duggan. *Robert Runcie: obituary* (The Guardian, 12 July 2000).
143 E-mail from Donald Gordon of 17 December 2014.
144 Adrian Hastings. *Robert Runcie* (London: Mowbray, 1991), p. 13.

> They were two squadrons of three troops, each troop of three tanks. [Actually there was one squadron comprising 5 troops of 3 tanks]. Before long, the squadron commander Lord Cathcart called an O Group. This was attended by the commander and sergeant of each troop. They were told that the plan was now to go straight into Winnekendonk. The troop commanders and sergeants synchronised watches and went through the plan of attack. Cathcart pointed to 2 Troop, represented by Lt Bob Runcie and Sgt Jim Alldred, a tough regular soldier who had been in the Scots Guards since 1930: 'Now', said Cathcart, 'order of march'. This was always a cause for trepidation at this point in the war, when the likelihood was that just around the next corner was a group of desperate Germans armed with an 88-mm anti-tank gun. Nobody ever wanted to lead. 2 Troop, said Cathcart, had led twice already. It was somebody else's turn. He told another young officer to lead. [He told two to lead; Alasdair Gordon to lead on the right of the road and John MacDonald-Buchanan on the left]. They moved off and formed up in readiness for the assault on Winnekendonk. This was to be a two-pronged attack by the usual combination of tanks and infantry. On the right, the lead troop moved out from behind the shelter of some buildings and almost immediately came under heavy fire. It was from an 88. The lead troop [and the fourth, FOO, tank] was destroyed within moments. It was Caumont all over again [the previous occasion in Normandy when 88-mm shells had exploded the ammunition and blown off the turret]. 2 troop, led by Lt Runcie, was next to advance. Alldred was behind him in the second tank: 'Go on!' he shouted over the radio. 'Go'. But still Runcie did not move. Alldred, however, could see the 88. Frantically he stood up in his turret and waved back the tank behind him [the Tp Cpl's tank] so that he had room for manoeuvre. Then they all [but not Runcie] moved. The radio frequencies were jammed with commands: '400 yards', screamed Alldred to Hollerton [Hamilton], his gunner, who fired and hit the [ground and ricocheted into the] barn. The Germans fired their 88 and missed [Not so; the Germans did not fire]. 'Up target!' he shouted, ["And don't fucking miss this time"] and Hollerton [Hamilton] fired again. Everybody [possibly including Runcie by this time] was firing at once. The 88 stopped firing [destroyed by Alldred], as did the two 75-mm self-propelled guns, [destroyed either by the Tp Cpl or by the Tp Cpl and Runcie who had followed out of cover] and 2 troop continued its advance…
>
> The next morning it was a beautiful day. The medical staff came and sewed up the dead in body bags [army blankets tied up with string]. Colonel Dunbar, the Battalion CO, told them with the help of the map: 'It was just like the set-piece we practised [in Britain]. We took Jerry on here 'STAB' and we came on here 'STAB' and we destroyed him'. 'Yes, sir', said Alldred boldly, 'but there's a difference, though'. 'What's that, Sergeant?' 'Last night we lost twenty-five good men' [22 Lincolns and 3 Scots Guardsmen, not counting the artillery FOO]. Dunbar looked at him as if, given the chance, he would have had him court-martialled and shot. Later, Robert said to his troop sergeant: 'You'll be decorated'. 'No, I won't', said Alldred. 'You might, but I won't'.[145]

There are two major problems with Mantle's account that contradict the collective memory of the Alldred family, who remember the late Jim's describing what happened many times using beer mats and glasses. They are adamant that Alldred did not tell Mantle that 'they all moved'. They remember how upset Jim was on reading these words in Mantle's book. Alldred always said, "Runcie never moved – he stayed behind the bloody barn".[146] In addition, Jim always referred to

145 Jonathan Mantle. *Archbishop* (London: Sinclair-Stevenson, 1991), pp. 14-16.
146 E-mail from Andrew Alldred on 9 October 2014.

his gunner as Hamilton not Hollerton. It is regrettable that the notes and tape of Mantle's meeting with Alldred are lost so the misunderstanding can not be corrected.

Jonathan Mantle noted that, 'Robert was very uncomfortable that I had talked to Alldred.'[147] In late 1983 Runcie had apologised to this author for not being able to remember these events, but Mantle dismissed the very possibility of such amnesia; "He (Runcie) would rarely talk about some of the events of that day; every moment of which he and others who survived would remember for as long as they lived".[148] Runcie became well-acquainted with Mantle's book, and never to this author's knowledge denied the accuracy of Alldred's recollections or contacted him to discuss them. Mantle wrote:

> My biography of Robert was unauthorised and his wife was very nervous of me in advance but we became friends and he always took it with him to give to people – in spite of various official biographies... We remained friends for the rest of his life.[149]

Runcie's memory returned for Humphrey Carpenter, his official biographer who published in 1996. Carpenter did not question Runcie about Alldred's recollections published five years earlier, which is the least problem with a biography that has been excoriated.[150] What Carpenter put into Robert's mouth was, however, extraordinary, and it is difficult to believe that ex Lt Runcie could have made such basic military howlers. Carpenter wrote:

> (W)e had to advance with three tanks going forward, and three tanks behind to cover them. We were in the second group, and in front of us several went into the open and were knocked out, and some people were killed. To everyone's astonishment the Pipe Major was killed. And a man called Thomson, who got the MM, the driver of another tank in my troop [Alldred's tank], located where the gun was that was firing on us, that was doing all the damage. So he manoeuvred his tank around, and said, "I canna see, sir, we'll have to go up into the open" [speaking as driver of one tank to his troop commander in another tank]. And I took my tank out on to open ground with his, and we had just one shot at this thing, and knocked it out immediately. "It was a mixture of tank and guncarrier. It had a big gun on it, and we knocked it out. It was critical, because it was surprising what this gun could do to anything we had. It was their last great resource. Of course there were other emplacements, but this was the troublesome one. [All nonsense, but see below]. And because we knocked that out, and things could move forward [very significant], that's the major reason why I got the MC. It's also mentioned that the previous day I'd rescued the character from the tank [mentioned by Runcie to Duggan and included in the citation as written by Dunbar but struck out by the Brigadier]. That didn't make any difference to the battle, but knocking out the gun actually moved things on [significant], and it came to the attention of my commanding officer, who subsequently had the reputation – because so many of us got decorated – of writing very good citations! [or enjoying a temporary lack of senior supervision]. So that's the story of that'. I remarked that most people remembered the rescue from the tank. That was the story that usually got attached to him. 'I'm glad in a way', he replied, 'because I feel that with the other one, actually we were in the wrong place [nonsense, but see below]! We shouldn't have been out there in view, and then the driver pointed out that that's where the gun was'. It was

147 Fax from Jonathan Mantle on 13 November 1996.
148 Mantle, *Archbishop*, p. 14.
149 Extracts from an E-mail from Jonathan Mantle on 5 February 2014.
150 http://anglicansonline.org/archive/news/articles/2000/000713a.html

his suggestion? 'Yes [a driver in one tank suggesting it to his troop commander in another tank]. Although he did, on my recommendation, get decorated [not for Winnekendonk but Thomson was decorated for Uelzen]'.[151]

There are so many and such overwhelming problems with this account that it is difficult, or rather impossible, to believe it represents in any respect but one what Runcie actually said. We are therefore left to conclude that it was intended not as a statement of fact that Alldred's interview had shown to be false but a cry for understanding from those knowing the military facts of life. This was Runcie's official biography, and he was responsible for clearing up misunderstandings or misrepresentations, and he did not do so in spite of being 'a workaholic perfectionist'.

The blatant untruths were as follows; John Thomson, probably Alldred's driver, may have received the MM on Runcie's recommendation, although we only have this report as evidence, but that is irrelevant since Thomson's citation was not for Winnekendonk on 2 March 1945 but for Uelzen on 14 April 1945.[152] Worse, Runcie had no physical means of communicating with Thomson, short of dismounting and walking over to him, except through Sgt Alldred, Thomson's tank commander. TCs had a control box in the turret that allowed them to switch mike and headphones discretely between the A-Set for talking to the troop commanders of other troops, the B-Set for talking to other tank commanders within his troop, and the Intercom for talking to crew members, so Runcie could not have talked to Thomson. Furthermore there is no room to doubt that Runcie claimed that Thomson, the driver, was addressing him directly since Thomson would only call a subaltern or above 'Sir' with everyone else in the troop called 'Sarge' or 'Corp' or addressed by name. Objectively the hero of the day was Runcie's anonymous marksman, but he is not mentioned, let alone identified and recommended for a medal. Furthermore Runcie was wrong to identify the StuG rather than the 88 as 'the last great resource' and that it was 'surprising what this thing could do to us'. The StuG could only damage and only rarely destroy a Churchill head-on, which is why only one wrecked Churchill was left on the battlefield by the 88 despite the attentions of three StuGs; and we saw above that Crawford's Churchill was hit five times by a StuG and still motored from the battlefield. Furthermore, the StuG was never 'emplaced' since it needed mobility at all times, and even to aim its gun. These statements that it was the last great resource and was emplaced were, however, true of the lethal 88 whose fate and even existence is ignored. Runcie consistently claimed one StuG destroyed and is given the benefit of the doubt here, but his claim that the StuG and not the 88 was the really 'troublesome emplacement' was wrong in fact, and he must have known it.

Finally, Runcie is quoted more than once as stating that "we shouldn't have been out there in view" although there was no other way of destroying the 88 and StuGs except in a stand-off dual that the 88 would usually win. Runcie's words resemble Cathcart's condemnation of the Pipe Major in a letter to this author; 'It was here that my FOO's tank (my only link with the artillery) failed to remain under cover and got knocked out with all the crew killed.'[153] Runcie's task, however, was different; not to avoid the 88, which was what the Pipe Major should have done, but to destroy it and all of the other anti-tank guns that threatened to destroy every Churchill on the field and expose the Lincolns to being massacred by the numerous machine guns and mortars. If Runcie did not immediately understand this, and it seems he never did as he was still repeating it to Carpenter 50 years later in 1995, then Alldred and his Tp Cpl certainly did. Without waiting to persuade Runcie of his responsibilities, or to ask his permission, they ignored him and got on with

151 Carpenter, *Runcie*, p. 81.
152 TNA: WO 373/54/936: John Thomson's citation.
153 Letter from Alan Cathcart on 29 September 1983.

doing their job of hunting the hunters, called 'providing cover'. With full throttle they charged out of the farmyard at their modest top speed and went for the 88 and StuGs.

It is also impossible to understand what Runcie could have understood from Thomson's observation of, 'I canna see, sir. We'll have to go out into the open.' The job of seeing from Thomson's tank was the responsibility of Alldred, who stood with his head out of the turret cupola at least 3½ feet above Thomson's periscope, and by turning his head had complete all-round vision. He had seen the 88. A tank is not a car where the driver has the best visibility; the tank driver has just enough visibility to fulfill the TC's commands. The job of driving a Churchill in wet conditions through its crash gearbox demanded high skill and concentration. The drag on the tracks meant the consequence of missing a gear was a full stop, giving the 88 the leisure to blow the sitting duck to smithereens. At all times it was the TC who commanded the driver where to go, and the driver of a Churchill in particular needed detailed instructions as his visibility through the periscope was restricted by the tracks on horns extending in front of him. Drivers never complained of not seeing, but only of not getting the TC's specific orders about where to steer. Runcie's conversation with Thomson as reported was in every respect bizarre; they did not have the means of communication, but if by a miracle Runcie and Thomson had enjoyed telepathy, the driver would not have been in a privileged position to see the 88 even out in the open. Runcie's memory, which had returned for his authorised biographer, was clearly trying to account for Alldred's revelations to Mantle, but served only to increase the tangled web of deceit.

Finally Runcie, as he always did, returns to the rescue of Philip from the burning tank as being part of the reason for the MC, which we have seen was not in the approved citation, and would have been unknown had Runcie not volunteered the information to Margaret Duggan for her to publicise.

Runcie's version as retailed by Carpenter does not attempt to explain the events for which the citation gave him credit and the MC – the destruction of the 88 and the StuGs. The only witnesses to what Runcie had done were his crew, and no one has found and talked to them. Alldred and the Tp Cpl were not witnesses; they were focussed on fighting for their lives as they headed south-west as fast as possible leaving Runcie to the north-east under a darkening evening sky.

Jim Alldred would not have been human had he failed to wonder why Sgt Tam Shearer, Gdsm Crawford, Lt Runcie, Lt MacDonald-Buchanan and Maj Cathcart received awards and he did not, but according to the Alldred family he accepted it. Andrew Alldred, Jim's son, wrote:

> Dad was never critical of Runcie – he just stated that he stayed behind the barn as a fact. He didn't know why he never moved out – he may have been unable to manoeuvre and Dad certainly never held it against him and I would say from the way he spoke of him and described him that he gave him the benefit of the doubt. As I said before what upset him was that in J Mantle's book Runcie said or at least implied that he had joined in the attack when Dad knew he hadn't and he had told J Mantle that in his interview. I am not surprised therefore that Runcie was "very uncomfortable" when he found out that J Mantle "had talked to Alldred". I was always the one who asked Dad "why didn't you get a medal?" That was even before I realised the significance of what he did that day which I did not appreciate until very recently. Apart from what he always said about his relationship with Dunbar etc he did say more than once "that's the way of the world Andrew" and dismissed it. He didn't need a medal to know what he had done but he'd have liked some recognition for it and expected it after JM's interview".[154]

154 E-mail from Andrew Alldred on 29 October 2014.

Jonathan Mantle agreed that Alldred,

> was more angry with the commanding officer [Dunbar] than he was with Robert. I remember my meeting with Jim and, although he had every opportunity, he did not single Robert out. If anything his tone suggested that Robert was a bit hapless but otherwise unremarkable, but the higher up the class scale we went in our conversation, the more withering Jim was about them in the best Scots fashion, especially Hugh Kindersley.[155]

Kindersley was the CO of 3SG from November 1941 to May 1943, driving them hard and even making them work on the tercentenary. Dunbar replaced Kindersley and was universally disliked. Andrew commented:

> I should also mention that Lt Col Dunbar was not just unpopular with my Dad (and vice versa) but also he was universally so with other NCO's, Guardsmen and many of the officers. I refer you to Charles Farrell's "Reflections" and his view of the CO. Also, the incident at Lubbecke at the end of the war when Dunbar ordered the Sergeants to drill the men and the Sgts refused. Major Whitelaw had to intercede to defuse a potential situation which could have seriously damaged the Brigade's [and the Bn's] reputation. Also, I met with Lt Tim Gilpin at his home in Somerset shortly before he died. He had a wonderful scrapbook of SG memorabilia but he confirmed to me the general view of Officers towards the CO.[156]

William Whitelaw did not agree with this view of Kindersley, who he said had had a great effect on the battalion. He assessed Dunbar as a good strategist but who flapped and routinely changed anything Whitelaw did. He added that there was a nucleus of police officers as sergeants, who were disciplined, still fairly young and completely reliable; and that the battalion had had a lot of trouble with Runcie to begin with.[157]

Mantle's account inexplicably refers to Alldred's gunner as Hollerton, when Alldred's family only ever heard him referred to as Hamilton. Mantle wrote, and without disclosing a source; 'Hollerton, Sergeant Alldred's gunner, was awarded the Military Medal.'[158] This author initially assumed the source must have been Alldred, which his family denies, so the source must have been Runcie. It could not have been Mantle doing his own research because no Hollerton got the MM, but Gdsmn (Unpaid Lcpl) 2700622 Thomas Ollerton did, and for action outside the tank at Uelzen and not for Winnekendonk.[159] The suggestion arises that Ollerton might have been the anonymous Troop Corporal who supported Alldred in his heroics, being rewarded by Dunbar for Winnekendonk on Runcie's recommendation. Enquiries made of the Scots Guards' archivist as to whether a Gdsmn Hamilton was on strength, and for anything pertaining to Greenacre's amendment of Dunbar's citation, have not been answered when this went to press. This account has the same problem of suggesting that Ollerton/Hollerton was given the MM for Winnekendonk when, like Thomsen, he got it for Uelzen. However all the other problems with Runcie's account are removed. Runcie's reluctance to move is explained by his continuing concern about leaving cover; 'I feel', he still said in 1996, 'that with the other one, actually we were in the wrong place! We shouldn't have been out there in view.'[160]

155 Jonathan Mantle in e-mails of 4 and 5 February 2014.
156 E-mail from Andrew Alldred on 8 October 2014.
157 Earl Whitelaw in conversation at the Home Office on 18 January 1985.
158 Mantle, *Archbishop*, p. 16.
159 TNA: WO 373/54/403: Thomas Ollerton's citation.
160 Carpenter, *Runcie*, p. 81.

From 1996 nothing new appeared about Runcie and Winnekendonk and that was the state of knowledge that would have appeared in this book had not this author in September 2014 found a website dedicated to 6 GTB,[161] run by David Alldred. Questions about Alldred's actions were referred by Dave to his uncle, Andrew, who by e-mail retailed Jim's account of 2 Troop's action. As usual square brackets denote this author's comments]:

> I am Sgt Jim Alldred's youngest son (youngest of ten) and I have three surviving older brothers (all retired ex Senior Police officers) and three older sisters. Dad was born 4.8.1910 and he was therefore 34 years old at the time of Winnekendonk [ten years older than Robert Runcie] and a father of six so he was considerably older than most of his troop and many of the officers. Contrary to what you say [Mantle said it] he was not a Scot. He was a Lancashire coal miner who joined the SG in 1930 for three years and then 9 years in the reserve. After his three years he joined Salford City Police until 1937 and then went back down the pit. Although coal mining was a reserved occupation he was called up again in 1939 as he was still in the [SG] reserve.
>
> I have read with interest your [draft] account of the battle of Winnekendonk and appreciate how difficult it must be to piece together a reconstruction of a battle in which so many took part and obviously Dad would have been another source for you, but at least you have Mr Mantle's interview with him.
>
> As the youngest and the last to leave home I was privileged and fortunate to be able to spend a lot of time alone with Dad and I spent many hours listening to his recollections of the war. Winnekendonk was one I heard many many times and I never tired of hearing it. Depending on where we were he would use salt cellars and plates and pepperpots to set the scene or beer mats and glasses and bottles. However, his version of events was always entirely consistent. It was either well rehearsed or well remembered and as you say it was something he would remember as long as he lived as "once engaged in events of life and death, memory rarely forsakes them [veterans]."
>
> First of all he was normally Lt Laing's Troop Sgt but he happened to be with Lt Runcie on this occasion. Dad never called Runcie "hapless". JM used the word. Dad thought he was a bit wet to be honest (eg the quivering top lip) but then they were from very different backgrounds. Dad was tough, disciplined and no-nonsense but as a senior and experienced NCO he cared very much about his men's safety. He found Runcie indecisive. Dunbar and others (Whitelaw) obviously found him good company. Lt Gilpin's scrapbook shows him as something of a joker or prankster even! As to Hector Laing I know he and Dad had considerable mutual regard and I cannot believe that Laing would have done or said anything to Runcie to influence him against you (or Dad) in the way you suggest. [This author had speculated that Runcie's initial welcoming turned to glacial non-cooperation only after he talked to Laing]. My eldest brother Eddie (also ex SG) met Laing at one of the SG reunions and Laing explained how Dad had "saved his life on numerous occasions"...Laing said he was a bit of a "gung ho young officer" keen to chase the Germans whenever possible...Dad pulled the reins in on him on many occasions and said "let's have a brew and find a billet sir and we can chase Germans again tomorrow" or words to that effect... Eddie [Alldred] also told me last night that Jimmy Gow was in Dad's tank but was not the driver. Interestingly, he said Dad's driver was called Thomson who Eddie took Dad to visit several times when Eddie first joined the police in Littleborough (Lancashire) in about 1960. Thomson had MS and was in a care home

161 Dave Alldred's website: https://sites.google.com/site/6thguardstankbrigade/

but he had made contact via the SG and asked for Dad to visit him which he did several times before he sadly died a few months later.

I have to say Dad's memory seems a lot better and more consistent than Lt Runcie's whose different versions to different people do appear to have elements of "elusiveness, if not evasiveness…" [remarked on by both Margaret Duggan and Humphrey Carpenter]. Dad told me that RF Squadron had five troops of three tanks each and on this day Lt Gordon was the lead tank/troop, then another three tanks, then Lt Runcie followed by dad and then the Troop Corporal. Two other troops followed [during the approach from the FUP, but drawing level on both sides of the road when they joined the infantry]. Dad had seen where the firing was coming from before he crossed the farmyard [Brönkshof]. They stopped when the first tanks of the first two troops [only one troop and the FOO tank] were knocked out. They were hidden from the 88 and the SP guns but they had worked out where they were. Lord Cathcart gave an order to attack them by driving across open fields between two farms. [Evidence for this has yet to be produced; it seems likely to this author that Jim Alldred acted by interpreting his existing orders to 'provide cover for the leading troop' and did not wait for new orders]. I have seen the plan in Patrick Forbes's book and visited the scene with my nephew Dave and my brothers. The plan and the visit gave me a much better idea of the scene especially the scale etc. The beer mats and salt cellars were still firmly in place! Dad was blocked in between Lt Runcie's tank and the Corporal's tank behind him. He shouted at Lt Runcie "Go!" but he did not move [because Runcie interpreted his orders as not risking his troop in the open] so Dad waved the Corporal behind back so he had room to manoeuvre. His tank and the Corporal's then moved into the open across the fields and between the two farms to attack the German guns in line ahead across the fields at top speed. According to Dad, Lt Runcie did not join them, but may have gone into the farmyard after Dad and the Tp Cpl left and engaged an SP from there. [Or after thinking about his orders to provide cover, he headed for the nearest StuG and did not follow in the tracks of the others]. He and his citation say he did…Dad said, "he stayed behind the bloody barn" but Dad would not have known or seen what Runcie did. However, I am convinced now that, contrary to what Dad always thought and said, (ie "he stayed behind the bloody barn") Runcie must have gone out into the open after Dad and the Tp Cpl had left the safety of the farmyard and fired at the guns from a static and exposed position. His citation cannot be a complete fabrication and of course if he did do that it gave Dunbar the opportunity to decorate Runcie both for his actions and for being the OIC of the Troop which knocked out the guns – and without having to decorate Dad, Hamilton or the Tp Cpl [unless his name was Ollerton]. I have just looked again at Runcie's version in Carpenter's book. If Thomson was Dad's driver (as Eddie Alldred has said) then it looks like an attempt by Runcie (years later) to recognise that another tank in his Troop (ie Dad's, driven by Thomson) went out into the open and knocked out an SP gun without revealing the full story or identities of the personnel involved thus giving himself sufficient credit (again years later) to warrant the citation and the MC. No wonder he felt uncomfortable when he heard that Jonathan Mantle had interviewed Alldred.

Looking at the range/distance on your picture then, for Dad to fire first from 400 yards and on the move means they would have travelled some distance from the farm before they opened fire. That again is consistent with what he always told me. I agree it would have taken about 2 minutes for Dad at that speed and distance to get into position to fire the first shot and he did so before the German guns could 'draw a bead on him' although they had clearly seen him coming and were frantically trying to turn their guns to meet him and the Tp Cpl. I also remember distinctly his physical description/imitation of the Germans hand cranking their guns round to face them. As I said before, Dad and the Tp Cpl outflanked, outpaced and outmanoeuvred the German guns but only just … and then, as you say, 'rolled them up'.

> I assumed that would have been the StuG but from what you say it could have been the 88 as well or instead if. Dad may well have gone for the 88 first and that makes sense because he definitely described the German gun crew hand cranking the gun towards them, and it was them and that gun they hit. [It was the 88 if they saw the crew hand cranking. StuGs without a turret used their engine to turn the vehicle on its tracks to within 10 degrees of the target, so Jim would have seen puffs of its exhaust smoke. When roughly facing the Churchill the StuG and its exhaust stopped, and the gunner with his eye to the eyepiece hand cranked the gun for traverse and elevation, but within the enclosed vehicle where Jim could not observe it. The 88's crew operated in the open, with their frantic actions clearly visible to the Churchill crew whose gunner, trained to fire on the move, kept the 88 in his sights and waited for Jim to shout the range and the order to fire]. Dad's gunner was not called Ollerton but I believe was Hamilton 'the finest gunner in the British Army.'[162]

The narrative requires background. Alldred is quoted as saying his tank had sabot, which means it was a Churchill III or IV with a 6-pdr gun that had HE, APCBC and DSAP or sabot, which was available only for 6-pdr and 17-pdr guns.[163] Each troop had two tanks with 75 mm guns firing good HE but poor AP, and the 6pdr Churchill with APCBC and the outstanding DSAP to provide over-watch against German armour, and especially the Panther. As an old soldier, Alldred might have acquired one of the two remaining Churchill Mk III 6-pdrs with their superior welded turret, which records show were on charge to 6 GAD on 21 January 1945 – see Chapter 7. Alldred told his son that he had a 'different' tank,[164] and a Mk III 6-pdr would certainly fit that description. Hamilton, however, would not have used sabot against the 88 because it optimised penetrative power at the expense of loss of accuracy since the discarding shoe unpredictably influenced the line-of-flight of the sub-calibre round at that stage in its technical development. Hamilton would have preferred the predictably accurate APCBC round. The 88 would be knocked out by any AP hit almost anywhere, so accuracy was more important in this case than penetrative power. Runcie and the Tp Cpl would have commanded the Churchills with 75 mm guns.

The Royal Armoured Corps under the influence of Hobart and other 'apostles of mobility' had concentrated from the 1920's onwards on firing on the move, and from 1936 had the excellent and well-balanced but small 2-pdr in their fast but lightly armoured tanks. These had been destroyed by heavier guns fired from better armoured, but still mobile, German tanks that always stopped to fire. The British followed suit in 1943, when Montgomery standardised on the M4 Sherman with 75 mm that always had to stop in order to fire accurately. Fortunately Montgomery was prevented from getting rid of the better armoured Churchills and turning 6 GTB/GAB into infantry.

Inevitably the offspring who were interested in their father's and grandfather's careers have tried to understand how medals were awarded. Nobody in the infantry saw what 2 Troop did out on the right flank, although they subsequently heard about it almost certainly from the guardsmen, and therefore Firbank could not have said anything more than he did about the value of 3 SG's support in the way he did for MacDonald-Buchanan and Cathcart by quoting infantry witnesses. The audit on what happened therefore became an internal 3SG and 6 GAB matter, where politics influenced perception. Dunbar is believed to have decided never to reward the recalcitrant Alldred with a medal, and therefore he ascribed the success to the way he had trained the unit in Britain, which begged the question why Runcie was convinced he should not have gone into the open and Alldred was convinced of the opposite. The cowed subalterns knew not to raise matters such as

162 E-mail fom Andrew Alldred on 1 October 2014.
163 BBC: http://www.bbc.co.uk/history/ww2peopleswar/stories/06/a2187506.shtml
164 E-mail from Andrew Alldred on 10 November 2014.

justice for Alldred. Dunbar's problem was therefore to recognise the battalion's success without mentioning Alldred. His solution was to heap all of the praise on Runcie but to recommend inconsistently not the proportionate recognition of the VC or DSO for Runcie, but only an immediate MC, which failed to be immediate when Greenacre sat on the citations for a month.

The choice of Runcie was, however, universally popular as Viscount Whitelaw later recalled in a brief encomium:

> I remember that he soon blossomed into a very efficient soldier, popular with everyone and always a most amusing companion. He also soon proved himself a brave leader of men in battle, and so it was no surprise when, as second in command of the battalion, I heard of his outstanding courage in the battle of Winnekendonk in early 1945. His award of the MC in this action was most popular with us all as we knew how richly deserved it was.[165]

'Everyone', even Alldred but not Runcie himself apparently, knew how richly deserved it was, and Dunbar must have seen his responsibility as putting down on the citation form what 'everyone' knew, and hence the four mistakes. Dunbar must have conversed with Runcie, MacDonald-Buchanan and Cathcart before writing six citations over the following two days and delivering them to Greenacre on 6 March 1945. Runcie did not expect a medal although he might have hoped for one, saying, "And when the CO brought the news of my decoration… I was totally surprised. You think, my hat! That's extraordinary! One of these moments'.[166] Andrew Alldred, who knows more about this matter than anyone, expressed this opinion:

> I suspect that Dunbar, especially after what Dad said to him at the debriefing (and the way he said it) would have shut up shop completely about Dad's role and imposed his ban on the junior officers there and then. They didn't dare gainsay him. Greenacre could therefore never find out and would never have known.[167]

The citations for Firbank and Cathcart were as follows:

> **Bar to D.S.O. 28072 Maj (T/LtCol) Cecil Llewellyn Firbank, D.S.O.**
> During the evening of 2 Mar, 2 Lincolns attacked the ruined town of Winnekendonk. It was held by about 200 men of the 7 Para Regt, 150 of the 22 para Regt and 4 SP A tk guns and two 88's. The enemy were in prepared positions, the Spandaus firing through loop holes knocked in brick walls at ground level and the snipers working from the windows of first floor buildings. The enemy were ordered to hold the town at all costs. There was no cover for the attacking troops. The town had to be captured at last light to let the armour break out. Lt Col Firbank carried out a quick reconnaissance under heavy fire from enemy 88's and 105 guns. The battalion was then quickly and calmly put into the attack, Lt Col Firbank moving behind the left forward company. The opposition was intense. Spandau fire lashed across the open ground and through the rolling smoke came the flashes and shot from the enemy SP guns. The battalion went on although many fell. It rushed into the town where bitter fighting ensued. Meanwhile Battalion HQ was fighting hard to take the enemy HQ. This was finally won by a fire and movement action carried out by Col Firbank and his batman. By this time

165 D Edwards. *Robert Runcie: A Portrait by His Friends* (London: Harper Collins, 1990), p. 6, in a contribution by Viscount Whitelaw. *A Soldier In The Pulpit.*
166 Carpenter, *Robert Runcie*, p. 81.
167 Slightly abbreviated E-mail from Andrew Alldred on 16 October 2014.

night had fallen and considerable confusion reigned in the burning town. It was known that many had fallen and that two companies had to be temporarily amalgamated. Strong enemy opposition came from the right flank. Col Firbank took hold of the situation. Under fire from snipers, with extreme coolness and great energy he selected 150 men and consolidated his gains, and in the morning cleared the town. In the morning a balance was struck. Lt Col Firbank's command had taken close on 200 prisoners and had killed at least 50 more Germans. 3 of the 4 SP guns had been knocked out and both the 88's were destroyed. The 2 Lincolns' losses were six officers and 54 men. The magnificent success was due to the courage, calmness and energy of Col Firbank. ~~He so inspired his men that in the words of the SCOTS GUARDS supporting them, "they fought like tigers" – how they got across that open ground we do not know". I strongly recommend that LtCol FIRBANK be given as an Immediate Award, a bar to his D.S.O.~~[168]

Immediate DSO. WS/Capt T/Maj P/106720 The Earl Cathcart, M.C.

At 1600 hours on 2 Mar 45 LORD CATHCART'S squadron was ordered to attack and capture WINNEKENDONK in co-operation with 2 LINCOLNS. The attack which went in at 1745 hrs had, by reason of various obstacles, to be frontal down the main road. This entailed an adv of 800 yds across flat open ground without cover and over heavy going. Stiff opposition was not expected, but immediately the squadron debouched into the open a concealed screen of at least 3-88 mm Anti tank guns, 4-75 mm SP's and numerous smaller Anti tank weapons opened up on them from the front and both flanks in addition to Spandaus and heavy shell and mortar fire. Five tanks were hit immediately though only one actually blew up at the time. In spite of the very serious and sudden opposition LORD CATHCART manoeuvred his squadron in support of the infantry straight across the open plain and stormed into the town itself where very fierce close quarter fighting took place. Whilst in the course of the adv, by his skilful positioning, his supporting tank troops knocked out two 88 mm and 2 SP's. The fighting in the village went on and the opposition was not defeated for at least three hrs after dark, during which time LORD CATHCART maintained his squadron fighting in close as possible co-operation with the inf, in spite of many bazooka and grenade attacks being made on the tanks in the various streets. There is no doubt that LORD CATHCART'S outstanding handling of his squadron and his magnificently courageous leadership and perseverance in the face of very considerable odds, combined with his determination to support the infantry at all costs, had a decisive influence on the final capture of this very strongly held town with a total of approximately 250 para troop prisoners and many dead besides.[169]

The two citations for the DSO in the same action in the same corps and army, in what became known as a model tank-infantry action, differ significantly in two respects; there was no agreement about the defenders' strength, and only Montgomery signed both citations. Brig Renny quoted two 88s with both knocked out and 4 SPs of which 3 were destroyed, with the opposition numbering 350 paras. Lt Col Dunbar referred to three 88s of which 2 were destroyed, 4 SPs with only two destroyed, and 250 enemy paras. Signing the infantryman's DSO were Brig Renny, Maj-Gen Whistler, Lt-Gen Horrocks, Gen Crerar and FM Montgomery. The tankman's DSO carried the signatures of Lt Col Dunbar, Brig Greenacre, Brig Mann, Brig Bingham (BRAC 1 Cdn Army), and FM Montgomery. In Cathcart's case the highest rank signing before the Field Marshal was a Lt Col, since brigadier was an appointment and not a rank. The conclusion must

168 TNA: WO 373/54/224: Firbank's citation. The crossing-out was by Montgomery.
169 TNA: WO 373/54/557: Alan Cathcart's citation.

be that if Firbank's citation was properly evaluated as to its importance and contribution to the success of Allied arms by every level short of Supreme Commander AEF, also an appointment and not a rank, then Cathcart's clearly was not. The true importance of RF's extraordinarily successful support of the infantry at every level down to Tp Cpl and Guardsman was not evaluated by those given the responsibility for doing so – Richardson and Hobart, who were Montgomery's two armoured advisers. Had Alldred acted like Runcie and stayed in cover, and the Lincolns were consequently massacred with the assault repulsed, Horrocks had arranged for GAD to take Winnekendonk. The fate of this formation would have been the same as that of 11 BAD and 4 CAD who at that time lay defeated in the Hochwald and unable to move against the same paratroop opposition. The Anglo-Canadian Army lacked the means of learning from its successes and failures and remained in the grip of the armoured mafia whose persistent intention was to rid the army of all of the Churchill tanks and of the units operating them.

On 4 March 1945, Churchill visited Crerar and argued publicly with Montgomery about the value of the Churchill tanks, but no one told him about Winnekendonk which had happened two days earlier. Instead of being acknowledged by the award of the VC, the extraordinary action of Sgt Alldred was covered up, and Runcie was given the MC 'because we knocked that (StuG) out, and things could move forward.'[170] Indeed; what Sgt Alldred and the Tp Cpl did led to the collapse of the morale of the defenders, to the winning of the day, and to the prevention of the alternative result – the death or capture of 2 Lincolns and of RF 3 SG.

There were three types of medal awarded for bravery in the face of the enemy. The VC was awarded for outstanding bravery that included independent action that materially affected the outcome of the battle. It is awarded only in exceptional circumstances: "for most conspicuous bravery, or some daring or pre-eminent act of valour or self-sacrifice, or extreme devotion to duty in the presence of the enemy." Thus Pte James Stokes engineered the significant crack in the defences of Kervenheim that had been re-established by the Germans through a successful counter-attack and, as followed Alldred's action at Winnekendonk, destroyed the belief among the defenders that they could win this engagement. Made from the Inkerman cannon and with a claret ribbon, the VC was awarded without distinction of rank and also posthumously. It carried a nominal pension. During 1939-45, 182 were awarded, of which 22 were in NW Europe.

For outstanding bravery in the face of the enemy there was a separate medal for ORs and for officers. The silver MM, with dark blue ribbon striped white and crimson was awarded to NCOs and ORs, with 15,225 being awarded between 1939 – 45. The silver MC, with a white ribbon striped with purple, went mostly to subalterns and captains who, after all, did the fighting and, disproportionately, the dying. From 1939 to 1945, 10,386 were awarded. Both the MM and MC were very highly prized.

The third decoration was for bravery usually at a senior level while performing a task that helped significantly to achieve the C-in-C's objectives. This was the silver gilt and gold DSO, with a blue-bordered white ribbon, of which 4,880 were awarded between 1939 and 1945. In Alec Foucard's citation submitted by Smith, an immediate DSO was recommended but changed to an MC by Greenacre. Alec told this author that the original recommendation was for the VC.

There was also the 'Divisional Commander's Recommendation' which, said Ted Hill, 'every officer received at one time or another and which your [this author's] father christened 'The Invitation to the Yacht Club Ball', which is what it did look like.'[171]

The Germans had two types of decoration awarded without distinction of rank; the Iron Cross dating from 1813 and awarded in seven cumulative grades for bravery with independent action,

170 Carpenter, *Runcie*, p. 81.
171 Ted Hill in a letter in 1983.

and the German Cross instituted by Hitler in 1941 in two divisions: gold for six acts of exceptional bravery or achievement in action, and silver for meritorious support action – the silver and gold were not worn together. There is no record of decorations being awarded for the three battles described here, with the exception of the StuG commander, Heinz Deutsch, whose kills during this period were still being accumulated. In 1939–1945, on all fronts 2.3 million Iron Cross 2nd Class were awarded; 300,000 Iron Cross Ist class; 5,070 Knight's Crosses; 569 Oak Leaves; 87 Swords; 13 Diamonds, and 1 Golden Oak Leaves. The German Cross in gold was awarded to 26,000 soldiers and the silver German Cross to 2,500.

Joe Collinson, the Intelligence Section Sergeant at HQ 2 Lincolns, described how Rear HQ moved up after the battle:

> I and my section moved forward with Rear Bn HQ, which I think would be under command of your father. As we were advancing there was quite a lot of 'stonking' going on and one of my lads got a piece of shrapnel in his back and had to be evacuated to the RAP. We eventually made a successful dash to the other side of the road and entered a house at the rear of the village [Plockhorsthof] which was occupied by the CO and Tac HQ. There had been a number of civilians in the cellar of the house but they had been moved to a room on the ground floor so that Tac HQ could use the cellar as a command post. During the move one of the male civilians had unfortunately been killed and his body placed on the sofa in the front room. Later in the day one of my section reported to me that the body was in danger of being roasted as the sofa was smouldering due to shrapnel which had entered through the window. So I along with another of the lads had the task of finding him a 'safer' place'. There was little of note for the Intelligence Section to do during the battle so there's little for me to tell you.[172]

Leslie Colvin had gone into Winnekendonk with Jack Hunton in a carrier equipped with wireless, as we have seen, to re-establish communications. Colvin heard that Peter Clarke had been seen to fall. He ignored the stated wishes of Firbank, who didn't want his 2ic killed by German mortars, and organised a search party to find and fetch Clarke and other wounded in from the fields. They found Peter's body already showing signs of rigor mortis. This sets in typically six hours after death, so would indicate that the search party found Peter at around midnight.

At 9 pm the defenders seem to have decided the day was lost because a message was intercepted and recorded in the Canadian Army Ops Log: 'Unidentified sta ordered 2110 hrs in area WINNEKENDONK E9934 blow up your atk guns.'[173]

The Lincolns War Diary described the assault on Winnekendonk:

> Resistance to the advance was strong and it soon became evident that the enemy held Winnekendonk in strength and intended to continue its occupation. Tanks and SP guns greatly added to the resistance, and throughout the advance the Bn was subjected to heavy artillery, mortar and MG fire, the latter coming especially from both flanks, and the Bn suffered a number of casualties. Coys however maintained a steady pace, neither halting nor deviating from their course. The assault coys fought their way against stubborn resistance into the Northern outskirts of the village, taking a large number of prisoners. 'D' Coy consolidated in the Northwest of the village and 'C' Coy pushed through to the centre where they consolidated. Meanwhile the reserve Coys and Tac Bn HQ moved into the North of the village, they too having to clear a number of houses before consolidating. The night passed without

172 Joe Collinson in a letter in 1994.
173 LAC: 1 Canadian Army log.

> incident except for the constant bombardment by enemy artillery. The support afforded by the Scots Guards and the 33 Fd Regt was excellent and contributed in large measure to what was a very noteworthy victory. The action was not carried out without loss, the Bn losing 3 officers and 77 men wounded, and 1 officer and 21 men killed. The officer killed was Maj P.H.W. Clarke, MC, who commanded 'D' Coy.[174]

In 3 BID's G Ops Log, which recorded Brigade intercepts, a message was noted at 6.25 pm from 2 Lincolns to 9 BIB; 'We have reached rd junc 997347 against fair opposition. 20 PW taken in last half hr.' Another message was logged at 8 pm from 3 SG to 6 GAB, 'Infantry in Winnekendonk in strength and tks now rallying back, plenty of prisoners taken.'

At 9.45 pm, again from 2 Lincolns to 9 BIB, 'Two coys Lincs at 997343. Two coys somewhere in action.'[175]

The evidence suggests that elements of 'C' Company crossed the centre-line of the road before the road junction was reached in order to occupy Plockhorsthof. Possibly they were diverted by an order given in person by Cecil Firbank since his citation refers to his using fire and movement to occupy Tac HQ. The barns and farmhouse were then fortified into a strong point. It was here that both Firbank and Cathcart set up their HQs alongside each other, and where the tanks rallied. In this confused situation, with a counter-attack expected and with heavy casualties, Firbank asked Cathcart to harbour his tanks with them for the night to strengthen the severely weakened and disorganised infantry. Cathcart agreed without hesitation, and this author doubts whether he even checked first with Dunbar or Whitelaw. All other tank units in the British Army save 3 SG and the NIH, even the sister-units in 6 GAB – 4 CG and 4 GG – categorically refused requests by the infantry to stay with them at night to resist counter-attacks, leading to rows as we have seen at Yorkshire Bridge.There the FOO's weakly armoured Sherman was driven unhesitatingly into the front line, while 4 GG's Churchills stayed back and refused to join them despite German armour attacking 2 E Yorks with impunity in the darkness. The same scene occurred the night after Winnekendonk when 4 CG rejected the entreaties of 2 KSLI and insisted on leaving them and withdrawing to laager. 4 CG's regimental history does not disguise this heated and angry scene on the road to Kapellen. The infantry were by now becoming outspoken in their demands and criticism, and not accepting excuses from anyone including Guards. It was no doubt by then widely known that infantry casualty rates were running at ten times the rate of the armour. If Churchill and Alanbrooke had been serious in wanting to know what ailed 21 AG even after six years of war, they should have appeared in Keilermannshof on the night of March 3 as their chickens loudly roosted. They might even have demanded an explanation from Montgomery, Richardson and Hobart as to why GAD had still to arrive to exploit the breakthrough achieved for them at Winnekendonk 24 hours earlier. They would have witnessed this scene:

> The infantry [2 KSLI], fearing a counter attack, were unwilling to let the squadron [2 Sqn 4 CG] return to harbour, but Maj Milbank was emphatic; tanks should not stay at night in a forward position; and at midnight, after repeated and expressive protests, the squadron was allowed to withdraw [rather it just motored away].[176]

The infantry had needed their own heavily armoured tank firing HE and with frontal immunity to the 88-mm, under their own command in their forward positions whenever they, the infantry,

174 TNA: WO 171/5231: 2 Lincolns' war diary.
175 TNA: WO 171/4130: 3 BID log.
176 Howard & Sparrow, *Coldstream Guards*, p. 328.

needed them. This was their arrangement in 1918 when, together with their own RFC air support also under command, they overwhelmed the entire German field army that was no longer fighting on two fronts. Postwar the tanks and aircraft were removed from infantry control by Churchill and others with the results only too visible in 21 AG.

Heavy German tanks were believed to be in the neighbourhood of Winnekendonk. Darby Hart had reported seeing a Tiger in the buildings on the other side of the main road in Winnekendonk, and John Boys recalls seeing a yellow tank or SP that might have been the same tank. No unit operating Tigers was in fact even close to the area, but their existence would not have been discounted that evening. Gates stated that two Mk IVs were knocked out, but he meant StuGs.[177]

That same evening while the infantry and the tanks battled it out in Winnekendonk, the Typhoon pilots of 609 Squadron were holding a party with Dutch civilians:

> This night was the night of the squadron party at Tilburg and it was unfortunate that the ground crews were so late in arriving. However when they did the first impression was that the place was full of girls waiting for them. Beer was free and everybody enjoyed themselves.[178]

The Anglo-Canadian forces owed Dutch and Belgian civilians an incalculable debt of gratitude for their wholehearted welcome. There were exceptions; John Keenan described one in Horst where the Priest forbade his parishioners from attending a dance put on by the Lincolns, who had gone to great trouble preparing food for the entire village; the only woman to turn up was the village prostitute. In those emotional and stressful days, many young men who had scarcely reached adulthood and did not survive, went to their graves with their brief lives enriched from receiving the milk of human kindness from families on whom they were billeted; such as the touching experience of Colin Welch in 2 Lincolns in Helmond.[179] Many formed enduring friendships, like Robert Runcie, Hector Laing, Archie Fletcher and Tony Stevenson in 3 SG with the daughters of a Dutch family in a country house near Valkenburg – indeed one of the daughters, Trees, was 'the one he [Robert] most probably would have married, if marrying had been thinkable at the time',[180] and like Leslie Colvin with Dr Wiegersma and his family in Deurne, and like RW Thompson with Mel in Eindhoven who he eventually married, and those who didn't survive such as Terry Rourke, whose memory is kept alive today by the Coenen family he was billeted on in Helmond. All found these friendships helped them survive the difficult days we have been describing without succumbing to what is now called Post Traumatic Stress Disorder. The Dutch experienced not only outrage that their neutrality had been violated by the nation whose kaiser had been given refuge there, but that the German occupation led to serious privations. Consequently the large number of Jeep-loads of victuals unofficially transferred from the cellars of Niederrhenish farms to Holland were treated as insignificant recompense.

Objects taken from Winnekendonk can still be traced. Firbank 'liberated' a finely chased Mannlicher shotgun from Battalion HQ, which Glyn Gilbert badly wanted, and bequeathed it to the Small Arms Museum of the School of Infantry in Warminster when pressure from police in the UK meant many wartime trophies were turned in. It was there in 1983, although not on show. Guns of all kinds were forbidden to Germans, so Firbank saved it from going under the tracks of a Churchill tank. In the same house, and now in the Museum of Lincolnshire Life along with the Lincolns' Regimental silver, were found two pennants from the staff car of Maj-Gen

177 Gates, *History*, p. 253.
178 TNA: 609 Sqn ORB.
179 Colin Welch. *The Odd Thing About the Colonel* (London: Bellew, 1997), p. 61.
180 Duggan, *Runcie*, p. 79.

Klosterkemper, GOC 180 GID, who held the Knight's Cross of the Iron Cross. Also taken was a drawing of a horse's head, inscribed as being presented to the Divisional Commander by Grenadier Regiment 1222, and a Nazi battle flag. Charles Peacock owns a dagger that was thrown at him in Winnekendonk.

Looting was forbidden, and on March 22 a stern rocket was sent from Eisenhower to every allied soldier. 1 Canadian Army issued it as 120/POLICY DISC/1/2, and distributed it to the Commanders of I British Corps, I and II Canadian Corps, who ordered it read to soldiers. Amongst other things it stressed:

> Behaviour in Germany
> 5. Wanton and unnecessary damage and stealing from unoccupied buildings is as much an offence in GERMANY as in allied countries. Captured military property which is required for the purposes of the army can be taken and civilian property required for military purposes can be requisitioned in the authorised manner, but the taking of any property for personal use or gain, and wanton damage, are serious offences for which stern disciplinary action will be taken.
> 6. Commanders at all levels will ensure that the Supreme Commander's policy in this regard and the reasons for it are well known to all ranks participating in ops in GERMANY.
> (J.F.A.Lister) Brig DA & QMS for Chief of Staff[181]

The order would have had little effect since looting in the Netherlands had been largely unconstrained. It was wishful thinking to believe troops would behave better in Germany.

Strict non-fraternisation rules were in force in Germany:

> Discipline – Fraternisation. [Readers of the War Diaries in TNA undertake to keep secret the names of all who are charged and convicted of crimes, even victimless crimes like fraternisation that Bob Runcie openly ignored to his credit]. Trooper X and Trooper Y were found guilty of fraternising with civilians in Germany on 6 Mar 45 and were awarded 21 days Field Punishment by the CO. All ranks are once again warned of the serious nature of the crime and reminded that all civilians regardless of nationality will be treated as enemy. [Given the large numbers of foreign slave labour in Germany, this was a convenient interpretation for the military if hard on the freed slaves. It probably explains the strange goings-on in Endtschenhof described below.[182]

Non-fraternisation was clearly defined in a policy paper issued in September 1944, which again was read to all ranks. Non-fraternisation was defined as:

> the avoidance of mingling with Germans upon terms of friendliness, familiarity or intimacy, whether individually or in groups, in official or unofficial dealings. However it does not require rough, undignified or aggressive conduct nor the insolent overbearance which has characterised Nazi leadership.[183]

The same document went into detail, stating that non-fraternisation entailed segregation in quarters, which is why the German civilians described in these pages were always put in one room

181 LAC: Crerar Papers.
182 TNA: WO 171/21769: 3 Recce War Diary, 6 March 1945.
183 LAC. Crerar Papers, and repeated in Howard & Sparrow, *The CG*, p. 328.

under guard; it prohibited marriage; required separate seating in churches and the restriction of contact. Completely prohibited were visiting German homes, drinking with Germans, shaking their hands, playing games and sports with Germans, giving or accepting gifts, attending dances or social events with Germans, accompanying them on the street, in theatres, taverns, hotels etc. and having discussions and arguments with Germans on the subject of politics or the future of Germany.

XXX Corps for a while believed that 1 KOSB had taken Winnekendonk, reporting to 1 Canadian Army at 8.25 pm; '9 Br Inf Bde. 1 KOSB well into Winnekendonk. Town not completely cleared as yet'. And again four hours later, at 1.02 am; '1 KOSB in Winnekendonk 9934 against fairly hy opposition. Still some fighting in town'.[184] The source of this confusion has not come to light, but is probably due to misinterpretation of a map reference and the later attack of the KOSB against Bruch.

At 9 pm, 9 BIB War Diary recorded that the enemy were at 997342 just beyond the church, and that the Lincolns were disposed as follows: (Main) HQ in Berber Wood at 995367, with companies at 998347, 997346, 996343 and 993352, next to the knocked-out SP. The SG Diary recorded that RF Squadron had concentrated at the Lincoln's Tac HQ at 997347 in Plockhorsthof at the road junction. Later at 3 am on 3 March the Lincolns' companies were recorded as being at 997347, 997342, 999343 and 004343.

At 11 pm, an entry was made in the 9 BIB War Diary that a spy had been identified amongst those captured earlier in REYSHOF, 979371 when one of three civilians who had crossed the Maas in January in the KOSB's area at Grubbenhorst was recognised. Neither the sex nor fate of the spy was recorded.[185]

The last entry in Edwards' notebook for 2 March is: '006 344 bg 180° H to H+15. 1 Regt. Rate 1.' Its significance is unknown, but the map reference refers to a point 1 km along the road to Kapellen, and probably referred to a German rearguard. Edwards did not record that at 1 am on 3 March a counter battery programme was fired on the wood (0033) to neutralise the artillery and mortar fire still falling on the Lincolns and SG in Winnekendonk. Edwards' notebook does record some messages in the early morning as the Lincolns extended their perimeter and then handed over the pursuit to others. The German rearguards were still at work blowing craters in the roads to slow down the British. '15/23 (Regt CO to Nicholson, BC113/114). 1 sub unit on final objective. P mines on track at 009344. Double crater on main rd 009342. 23/35 My friends now established on objective 1950. 15/32 Clear to PWXFCH'.

XXX Corps knew that they were now beyond all of the prepared German defences since Horrocks had ordered GAD to take the lead at first light to head for Bonninghardt and Wesel. However, the Schlieffen Stellung, which ran from Rees to Geldern and parallelled the Kervenheim-Winnekendonk road, was still about two miles in front of them. Whistler, who had commanded a brigade in an armoured division in the desert, wisely refused to hold back 3 BID on a promise. He sent 8 BIB in hot pursuit of the retreating enemy. At Division the clerk was typing a new intelligence summary for Whistler to read with his char at 5 am.

3 Br Inf Div Int Summary No 231

SECRET

(Based on infm received to 0100 hrs 3 mar 45).

Part I.

Fwd of Bde HQ this summary will be destroyed by 2400 hrs 4 Mar 45.

184 TNA: WO 171/4130: 3 BID G Ops Log.
185 TNA: WO 171/4330: 9 BIB war diary.

ENEMY SITUATION – OWN FRONT

1. This morning on our RIGHT flank WEEZE was found clear and it was therefore not surprising that we met no resistance in KERVENHEIM. Patrol reports show that the final withdrawal from the village did not take place until 0600 hrs. Shortly afterwards we adv from the NW and from the NORTH through the town itself. The enemy withdrew in one bound to WINNEKENDONK and anticipation of resistance in the woods of BERBER HEIDE 9936 proved groundless. The only opposition reported was that of snipers, doubtfully identified as 'VOLKSSTURM'. Since the beginning of Op VERITABLE only one 'VOLKSSTURMMAN' has been captured whilst fulfilling his duty and therefore specimens of the breed are eagerly required in the PW cage. Rd blocks and cratering hindered our progress more than the sniping and it was not possible to mount an attack on WINNEKENDONK until dusk.

2. Meanwhile on the RIGHT recce elts had cleared to 973350 where opposition from inf and SP guns was reported. It was then clear we had reached the battle outposts of the enemy's rearguard and that both WINNEKENDONK and KEVELAER were occupied. Under cover of a barrage an adv was made on WINNEKENDONK and the town secured after considerable fighting. Our hold was also extended to rd junc 009342.

3. There is no doubt that we have jostled the enemy out of WINNEKENDONK before he wished to leave. He could not willingly lose the 80 or so PW that have been captured and hoped to retain the pivot posn for many hours more while he evacuated KEVELAER.

4. It is unlikely the enemy will counterattack in view of his hy losses in the town. His most likely reaction is to speed up withdrawal from KEVELAER on the rd to KAPELLEN 049312 and if this op is completed tonight there will be no need for them to hold the woods SOUTH of WINNEKENDONK.

5. The majority of PW has proved to be from I Bn 22 para Regt which withdrew yesterday from WEEZE where it had suffered hy cas. This identification is a clue to the enemy's intentions for it shows he is withdrawing his tps in an Easterly direction using as a hinge the tough resistance displayed on our LEFT in the area 0437. It can be assumed that the bulk of 7 Para Div has slipped from its posns SW of WEEZE and is now largely back in the area of SONSBECK. Some rearguards of 190 Div may be sacrificed to secure the safety of the paratps. Another identification, by a single PW, is of battle Gp KRAHL which it is stated was formed of the remnants of II and III Bns 7 Para Regt yesterday for the def of WINNEKENDONK. [In Appendix A to II Canadian Corps Intelligence Summary No. 136, probably issued on 3 March 1945 Krahl is given as Kroll; 'Of 199 PW taken at WINNEKENDONK 9934 tonight, the majority were from 7 Para Regt. PW said that remnants of all three bns had been combined as Battle Group KROLL. KROLL was adjt of II Bn which came yesterday from SONSBECK 1535 to join the Battle Group. Many of them were very ready to give up. Present Battle Group str is estimated at 200'.] Some more prisoners from this Battle Gp which is estimated to be about 200 strong can be expected in the systematic search of the area, but the bulk of it seems to have got away. A new identification of 12 Para Asslt Gun Bde which is equipped with both fd and Atk guns on Mk III chassis. PW states that at least two eqpts have been knocked out by our arty.

6. There are many signs that the enemy is making his best speed to hold a shallow brhead around WESEL, incorporating the HOCHWALD and the features to the SOUTH of it, the

BONNINGHARDT ridge. In front of this posn runs the SCHLIEFFEN line [The Schlieffen Line was unoccupied, and the Germans stood on the Bonninghardt Ridge], which has not yet been penetrated SOUTH of the 40 Grid Line. The gap between the features is controlled by the town of SONSBECK 0535 and within the perimeter lies the forest of XANTEN 1038 in which intense activity has been seen today.

7. In the process of building up this brhead the enemy has allowed the neighbouring formn on our RIGHT [53 BID] to approach to the outskirts of KEVELAER at 960342 whilst on our LEFT he has savagely counterattacked the deep penetration through the HOCHWALD posns which had reached 063405. 16 Pz Div, aided by 17 Para Regt and 112 GR on the RIGHT and LEFT flanks respectively. Our tps were pushed back over a mile.

8. No doubt the enemy when he first set in motion this withdrawal intended to res an extensive brhead WEST of the RHINE from the HOCHWALD in the NORTH to KREFELD in the SOUTH. This hope has been smashed by the capture by the Americans of most of KREFELD which is the largest German city yet to fall into Allied hands. It is reported that 15 PG Div is fighting in the Northern outskirts of the town and this identification of a div that a day or two ago was on our front tends to confirm the worth of an enemy map captured by the Americans. This document showed 84 Div, 15 PG and 2 Para Div defending a line from KEMPEN 0808 and the RHINE. All these divs are from our front and one of them has been identified. 2 Para Div has only been represented on our front by two of its component regts – 2 and 7 Para Regts – both of which are still in the line against us. However PW stated that 2 Para Div was recently near SONSBECK and it may be that the HQ with or without its remaining regt is now controlling assorted battle gps near KREFELD.

9. Our Allies are on the bank of the RHINE NORTH and SOUTH of NEUSS 2689 and they report that the two brs between NEUSSS and DUSSELDORF are still in enemy hands. To the NE unimpeded progress continues. STRAELEN 9717 and WACHTENDONK 0212 have been taken and fwd tps are reported at 0317. Morning should see the Americans in GELDERN and a linking of the fronts may take place today.

10. Pontoons and barges are doing great trade across the RHINE and there is much activity on either bank. The enemy knows full well that the continuance of the war depends on his ability to man the EAST bank of the river within the next few days. The rate of wastage among his forces this side of the river raises considerable doubt as to his chances of success.

Lt Col GS3 Br Inf Div.

Return of PW Captured at 3 Br Inf Cage between 1800 hrs 1 Mar and 1800 hrs 2 Mar 45.

Coy	Unit	Offrs	ORs
1	7 Para Regt		2
8	"		4
16	"		4
March Bn	"		1
2	20 Para Regt		1
–	III/24 Para Regt		2
2	12 Para Asslt Gun Bde		1
	KG HUTZ		1
			16

Total PW taken by 3 BID in Op VERITABLE so far 13 Offrs 853 ORs

ENEMY DISPOSITIONS AS ESTIMATED 2300 HRS 2 MAR 45.

PART II

1. (a) Kp KRAUS
The following document addressed to the coys of III/7 Para Regt dated 21 Feb and signed by the Bn Comd – Hptmn Lisowsky – sheds further light on the above unit referred to in previous summaries:
"As the formation of Coy KRAUS has now taken place it is necessary to add the following detailed instrs:
(i) Coy KRAUS is tactically under regtl comd.
(ii) Disciplinary powers
The Bn Cmd retains disciplinary powers over the coy. Lt KRAUS will have disciplinary powers over the NCOs and men placed under his comnd. Offrs in Coy KRAUS will be disciplined by the Coy Comnd.
(iii) Str, weapons, amn and sup returns will be sent to bn. All other reports (ops, int) will go to the regt with copies for bn,
(iv) members of the coy will get their canteen rations etc from their original coys. Half the coy food will be drawn from 9 Coy cookhouse and the other half from 12 Coy. RQMS BERK is responsible for seeing that these orders are carried out.

2. PERSONALITIES

Sigs offr/7 Para Regt	O/Lt HAUSERMANN
OC 2 Pl 2/7 Para Regt	Lt NEUMANN
OC 4 Pl 4/7 Para Regt	Lt SCHWARTZ
Adjt II/7Para Regt	Lt LISSKE
OC 1 Pl Coy KRAUS	Lt NUBER
OC III /7 Para Arty	Maj MEISTERL
Adjt/7 Para Arty	O/Lt SAMBIKO
OC 12/26 Para Regt	Lt FENGLER

3. DEPARTMENT OF CORRECTION.
The Comd of 7 para Regt has been Obst RIEDEL since 16 Feb – documentary source. LISOWSKY and NAHM are the correct spellings of the names of III/7 Para Regt and Adjt respectively.

4. ENEMY METHODS.
The following rocket is from O/Lt NAHM – Adjt III/7 Para to the Coys and is dated 19 Feb: [At that time, III/FJR7 was fighting 15 BID which had just captured Goch and was thrusting forward past Schloss Calbeck].
'The Coys received written orders 18 Feb to maintain constant recce patrols in our front line and to get infm about the enemy. The results of the patrols should be sent in daily with the daily report. It is true that the coys have carried out the patrols and sent in the results but in such a scanty form that any sort of reasonable evaluation is totally impossible. In the reports of the individual patrols farms and places are mentioned which do not appear in the 1:50,000 map eg MOORSHOF or in the case of more than one place of the same name, more accurate designations are not forthcoming or else they are spelt incorrectly. In one report we have 'KASTELL KOHLBECK. In point of fact there are only two 'KASTEEL KALBEEK' one spelt with a 'C' and one with a 'K'.
There are sufficient maps in the coys so that there should be no need to have to mention that

recce patrols should be given 1:50,000 fd sketches on which rds and places which have to be recced are put in. Apart from that it is quite obvious and universally known that patrol reports are always accompanied by a sketch. Despite the numerous patrols since 17 Feb we have been unable to identify the various units on our front. The reason is that the patrol leaders are not properly briefed. If a patrol identifies a coy or unit the report must not only include places and time of identification but the patrol leader must find out all he can about the unit and put it in the sketch. If the patrols are carried out systematically thus, from left to right or the reverse, it will be possible in one day to obtain complete identification of the enemy on our front'.

5. ENEMY ADM.

The following order of 23 Feb by LISOWSKY to his bn – III/7 Para Regt – is a further indication that the 'last round, last man' principle of def is now only a polite fiction – even in paratp units:

DIRECTIVE

1. Recent ops of I/7 para Regt necessitates the constant reiteration of "Defence to the Last Man" by means of instr to every single man.
2. Whenever the order is to defend, no soldier is, under any circumstances, permitted to withdraw from his posn without a direct order.
3. If a soldier or a unit withdraws, it must be quite clear which individual gave the order to retire and in such a case the exact place must be given to which the man or unit should withdraw.
4. The experience of other bns makes it necessary for me to point out that it is the bounden duty of all coy comds to see that their men get sufficient good food. If they have any difficulties in this direction they are to report them to Bn HQ at once.
5. Junior leaders in coys are to be told once again that any changes in personnel in secs or plns are to be reported to the coy comd at once. It is an impossible state of affairs when coy comds hear first from higher authority that arrivals or departures have taken place in their coys.
6. If these various points are not observed I shall feel compelled to make examples. I order that written reports be submitted by 1200 hrs tomorrow saying that instr along these lines has taken place.
7. For the last time when I order a Coy Comds conference I expect extreme punctuality. Otherwise I shall in future take disciplinary action against the offender.

6. TAILPIECE.

Among the documents captured yesterday was a test paper set by the Adjt II/7 Para Regt for the potential offrs in his bn. Here is question 1: Lt MULLER is invited out for the evening to the house of a Frau von Waldorff. At 11 pm the party breaks up. Frau von W says to Lt MULLER: 'Herr Muller. Would you be so good as to see home Miss Risse, her sister and Miss Roth. The parents of the two sisters meant to fetch them but so far they haven't turned up'. On the way to the home of the two sisters the Lt and the two ladies are stopped by a certain Herr Griesinger, a civilian, who is mildly drunk. Herr G says; 'This is a jolly good show meeting you like this. My flat is only a few minutes from here. I've still got a few bottles left; let's carry on with the party there'. Miss Roth evinces some interest in the proposition. The problem is, 'What should Lt MULLER do?'
Steady, Lieutenant!

Part II. No 232. 4 March 45

Order of Battle.

1. a) 12 Para Aslt Gun Bde.
PW from the above unit (2 Tp) say that it is under direct comd of 2 Para Corps and that it has been in the general area VENLO-LOWER RHINE since Sept 44. Org as follows:

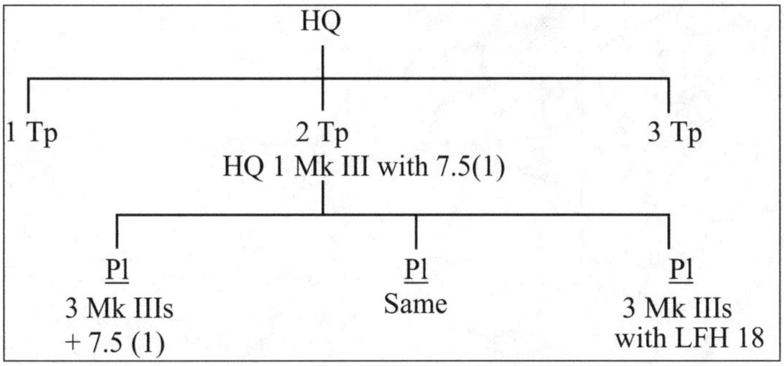

All three tps are said to have similar org. 2 Tp was the only one known to be in our sector and that was in sp of 7 Para Regt. It had lost two of its LFH 18. The other tps are thought to be in the sector. Amn scale is mixed AP and HE, 80rds per 7.5 and 60 per 10.5 cm.

b) Notes

(i) 8 Coy/7Para Regt is reported to have had orders to withdraw through WINNEKENDONK 28 Feb. At the time they are reported to have been well over 100 strong and to have 5 × 8 cm mortars and 6 HMG.

(ii) As a further indication of the manpower state two German meteorological offrs arrived in the cage today. One had been an experimental meteorologist and they were both put at the disposal of 7 Para Regt. One was used as a Pl Comd and the other was considered unfit to lead a Pl and he gave daily weather forecasts to III bn. The rank they held is 'Wetterdienstreferendar' which is equivalent to a rank between a 2 Lt and a Lt. They are 'Beamter' (officials) and not offrs.

c) Fortress Atk Coy 51 (X).

Coy was formed in Germany in December 44 and since then has been waiting for its guns in the area of KREFELD. The org is four pls each said to have four or five 'wheelless' 5 cm Atk guns. When the posn has to be changed the guns have to be moved by B ech tpt. 1 and 2 Plns were said to have been in KEVELAER and MARIENBAUM, while 3 Pl was in Winnekendonk and the B ech tpt was said to be in LABBECK. Two days ago 3 Pl received 300 rds of HE and 75 AP. Shortly after receiving the amn the pl was called together and the coy comd made them swear to fight to the death.

Personalities

C/O I/7 Para	Hptm WALTER – dead
OC 51 (X) Fortress Atk Coy	Hptm APPEL
Adjt II/7 Para	Lt KROLL – PW
FOO 8/86 WERFER REGT	Lt KÖRNER – PW
Attd I/7 Para	Wett Ref WALLEWTA – PW
	Wett Ref STEFFAN – PW
	O/Fhrh KAHL – PW
OC I/22 Para	O/Lt SCHEIDT
OC 4/22	O/Lt REISER

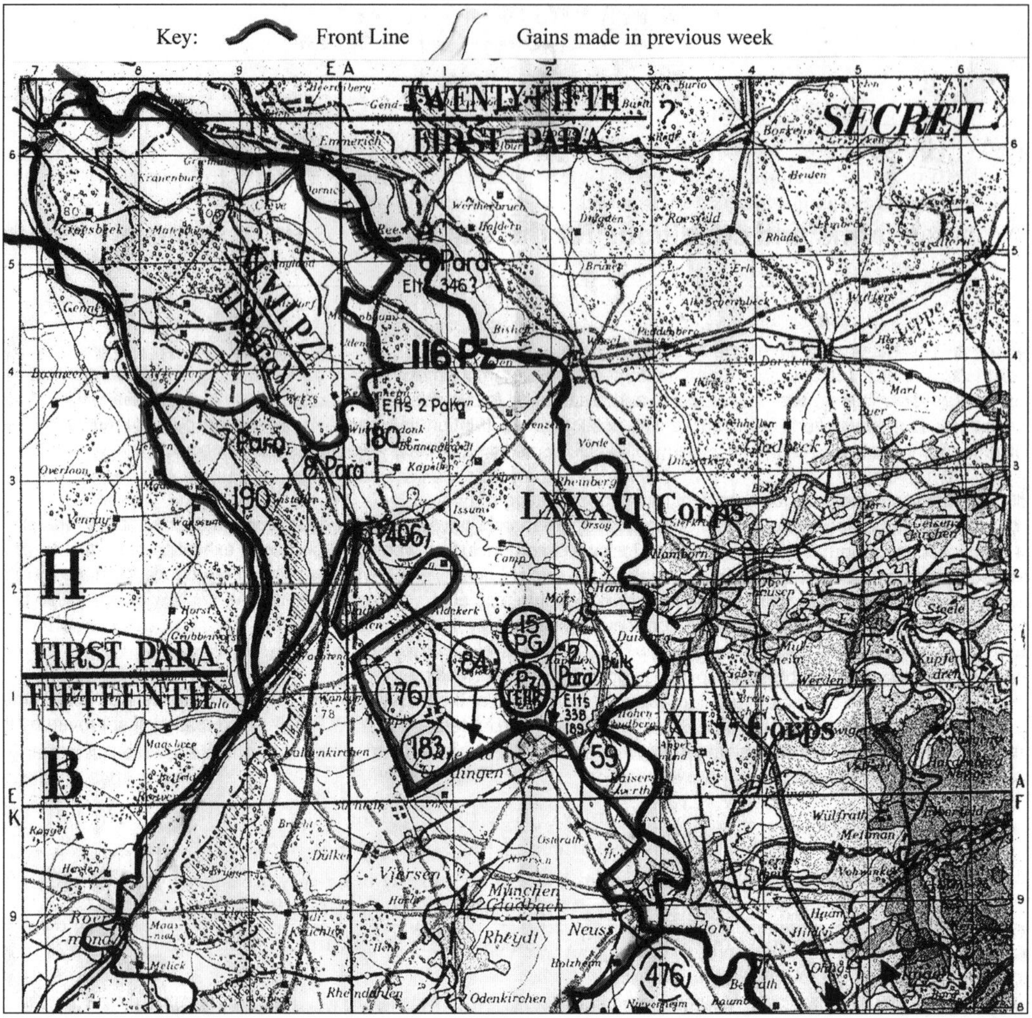

Map 39 Part of SHAEF's war diary situation map for 0900 hrs on 3 March 1945, having been updated with the capture of Winnekendonk only hours earlier. SHAEF and Montgomery now knew that 3 BID had broken through 8 Para Div and had turned east for Bonninghardt and Wesel ahead of the Americans and behind the backs of the German 180, 2 Para and 116 Pz Divisions who were holding Canadian II Corps to the north of Kervenheim in the Hochwald. The Canadians had earlier been ordered to reinforce any success gained by 3 BID, but instead stayed put and continued to batter away in the Hochwald. (TNA WO 171/26)

OC 12 PARA ASLT GUN BDE	Hptm GERTAUER
OC 2/12 PARA ASLT GUN BDE	O/Lt SCHUTZ
OFFR 12 PARA ASLT GUN BDE	Lt SALUTZ – wounded
OC III/22 Para Regt	Hptm WITTSTOCK
OC 9/22 Para Regt	Lt SCHREIBER – PW
OC 10/22 Para Regt	O/Lt BRUCKMULLER – wounded
OC 11/22 Para Regt	O/Lt BEHAGE
2ic 11/22 Para Regt	O/Lt STIELER
OC 12/22 Para Regt	O/Lt KRÖGER
MO	Oberarzt GENHARDT

C Sqn, 3 Recce, had provided flank protection to the Lincolns on 2 March, reaching the crossroads at 974354 where they made contact with the enemy. Two Daimler heavy armoured cars were blown up on the crossroads by 'R' mines buried deep in the road surface. They had not been the first cars over the crossroads. Later two more mines were found and empty holes.[186]

The RUR consolidated on the line of the road running east from Winnekendonk. The Lincolns remained in Winnekendonk from 3 to 12 March. On 3 March they cleared the village in the morning, keeping all traffic from the road junction while the Churchill tank of MacDonald-Buchanan's troop was hauled out of the crater at 995353 and an 80 ft bridge was laid, and completed at 11.40 am. The other two craters towards Kervenheim were filled with fascines and rubble using AVREs and Tippers. By 12.30 pm the route was opened for GAD, which in the event did not arrive for another two days, as the historian of 2 SG in GAD explained.

> On the 28th … the fog of war immediately descended: in four days the Second Battalion was under four different notices to move, ranging from 48 hours to one hour, and an advance party went to reconnoitre a reputedly vacant area south of Goch only to find it impossibly crowded with troops. But as the breakthrough south of Goch proceeded and the head of the column reached Kapellen the fog thinned, and by the evening of 5th March, creeping nose to tail in a solid mass of traffic, the Battalion had passed Goch and Weeze and reached Kevelaer. There, at 2100 hours, orders were received to attack and occupy the eastern end of the Bonninghardt woods next day in conjunction with 1st Welsh Guards and, of course, X Company. An Order Group was hurriedly assembled and Lt Col Dunbar and a party of officers from the Third battalion, fresh from their brilliant crowning action at Winnekendonk, were hurriedly ushered away from dinner. There was no time to spare; the Battalion was going into its first attack in Germany, and X Company into their last.[187]

Whistler acted as soon as the delay to GAD became known, and created another traffic jam on 3 March:

> As soon as news of the Scots Guards' success (at Winnekendonk) reached the Divisional Commander, he ordered the Coldstream to move into Kervenheim immediately so that one squadron could support one battalion of the 185th Brigade in a thrust east from Winnekendonk. It was obvious that the Germans were on the run, and the Divisional Commander wanted the success to be exploited with all possible speed. Although caught literally with their trousers down (for they had been promised twenty-four hours rest) the Coldstream packed up very quickly and moved to Kervenheim where orders were given out by the Brigadier of 185th Brigade. At midday No 2 Squadron with 2nd KSLI in Kangaroos started off for Kapellen, a town about seven miles from Winnekendonk. Just south of Kervenheim, however, traffic was in a state of chaos. Vehicles of all descriptions were jammed head to tail in all directions, and it was impossible to get past them as the tanks and Kangaroos immediately became bogged in the soft mud. The Commanding Officer worked furiously for two hours and by 2 o'clock had cleared a narrow passage through which the advance guard passed. Once through they pushed on rapidly.[188]

186 TNA: WO 171/21769: 3 Recce Regt war diary.
187 Erskine, *Scots Guards*, p. 415.
188 Forbes, *6th Guards*, p. 118-19.

HQRA 3 BID moved to Kervenheim into the Schloss. The Lincolns received prisoners all day captured by 3 Recce and by 185 BIB in their pursuit towards Kapellen. The Norfolks moved into the village with the Lincolns, all getting into buildings of a sort. John Keenan described his billet:

> We were left in this house. It was quite a large house, the sort of house you might expect the village doctor or the village priest to live in. It had a substantial cellar and obviously the bloke had been an officer or something in the German Army in France. The whole platoon was sleeping down there. A third of the cellar was occupied by loot. There was silk stockings and underwear, dinner services, tea services, candelabra, anything mundane that might have been regarded as of value. There were stacks of the stuff. The fellows were able once a month to send a large cardboard envelope that was not opened by the customs home to their parents. Tons of them sent French knickers and things like that and stockings home to their people.
>
> There was a safe in one of the rooms, and some bright spark decided to use a 75 Grenade, which was an anti-tank grenade that we used to carry. It was a hollow-charge which intensified the explosive value of the grenade which wouldn't have the area of a milk bottle. He blew this safe and found an awful lot of German Marks in it. We were reliably informed by our officers that German Marks would be no good because we would be using occupation money. Consequently there was one room in this house which was knee-deep in German Mark notes, at least a million, each one theoretically worth thrupence. So they were left. It was in a comparatively short period of time that we were using these German mark notes, so no doubt someone, who followed us up, probably in the RASC, would have a very profitable find.
>
> Another thing that happened in this house was that we had been there about two days, and nothing had happened, when someone happened to go into the loft where, lo and behold, there were 45 Germans, fully armed, who decided it would be as well to give up and they filed down into the house much to our, I might say, surprise.
>
> We had had a good beat up with a hell of a lot of blokes killed and wounded, and we got some reinforcements. About 20 blokes joined our company from the Royal Fusiliers who had not actually been into action, just young blokes. I was 19 and they were 18, and I was supposed to be a veteran – they were just arriving. One of the fellows was 'Dull' Walker and when we got to know each other we were more or less inseparable. They were Londoners and took the view that they had been sent to a regiment of yokels which to a degree offended us although we all came to some sort of agreement in the end.
>
> I can well remember in this house. I have always been a bit theatrical. I used to wear a leather jerkin. I got The Saint written on the back, the stick man with the halo. [The character of Simon Templar, aka The Saint, was created by Leslie Charteris in 1928 in his third novel, *Meet The Tiger*]. I had a captured German pistol in my web belt over the leather jerkin, and of course I was walking down the staircase doing my normal thing and although I didn't know it at the time, but one of these laddies, a fellow called Day, told me some months afterwards that when he saw me coming down these stairs he thought he had finally arrived and this was the epitome of soldiering etc., etc. that was walking down the stairs. He was a long way from the actual truth.
>
> This time I got to be a fairly proficient pistol shot actually. We had got quite a lot of German ammunition and German pistols, and when we couldn't think of anything else to do we would shoot tins and things like that to keep ourselves entertained.[189]

189 John Keenan's tape-recorded memoirs.

On 4 March the Lincolns reorganised and cleared up, checking up on all the civilians who were treated as enemy according to the rules of non-fraternisation. Bolo Whistler visited the Lincolns and was shown the line of German corpses outside Gilbert's house. 33 Fld Regt moved its batteries into Winnekendonk to 997345. At 1 pm GAD passed through on their way to Bonninghardt, where they were stopped by German rearguards.

On March 4 Bolo made the first note in his diary since returning from leave on Feb 24:

> It seems the hell of a long time since February 24th. I would say we have had our most successful battle. Damn difficult country – centre-line non-existent or on a mud track – yet we have done everything asked. We have captured 1,200 prisoners, nearly all paratroopers. We must have killed and wounded many more. The scenes of devastation in Germany are quite remarkable. There is nothing that has not been damaged or destroyed. The civilians are mostly old and have genuinely had enough. They are responsible after all and I do not think they will want another war. We have captured Kervenheim, Winnekendonk and Kapellen of the larger places. I would say that 9 Brigade under Renny have done best; 185 next under Mark Matthews. 8 Brigade have not had so much luck though E Yorks had a terrific night holding a bridgehead against repeated counter-attacks. The 7.2" Howitzer Mark VI, which was only fifty feet from my caravan, fired all night and the harrassing (sic) fire of the field guns firing just over my Tactical HQ was really a bit much.
>
> Where all have done well it is difficult to single out any, but the Gunners have been first-class as usual under Gerald [Mears] – the Sappers ditto under Tom Evill. The RASC, under the most trying conditions have kept us topped up with ammunition (and we have certainly shot off a bit!). The staff have been fine, Freddie Mellor at the top of his form. The Lincolns under Cecil Firbank are probably the best battalion in the division. They have had as hard fighting as any and have been most successful. The capture of both towns was largely due to them.[190] The Suffolks, who I think highly of, have had less to do but have done it efficiently. The whole standard is very, very high.
>
> Am getting on well with Jorrocks. He is a fine leader and well liked, quite ruthless but one has to be. Our casualties have not been light – but it has been so successful that it was worth it. In fact pretty well everything went right although it was a trifle difficult now and then and the bowling was faster than I am accustomed to. With Jorrocks you do at least know what is required. Gave Mark Matthews and Douglas Renny each a bottle of champagne for their work today.
>
> The latest news (March 4) is terribly good. The Boche are beaten pretty badly here. We are through the Siegfried line and very near the Rhine. The Russians are going flat out on the other side and I cannot see it going on very much longer, though it is easy to be too optimistic. I would not have missed this battle for anything – unpleasant and frightening though it has been. To fight on German soil after all this time is more than I ever expected. Now for the Rhine – which won't be too funny I expect. I now have my HQ in Kervenheim – too close to the enemy and far too dangerous really.[191]

This invaluable insight into the mind and attitude of a first-class British fighting general when savouring complete victory leaves a not entirely pleasant taste in the mouth. It is injudicious for any commander to think, let alone write down, that the death of any man resulting from his orders was 'worth it'. Commanders can never agonise over the deaths of their soldiers and remain sane and effective, but what jars is the complacency that his orders were optimal,

190 This author cannot agree with Bolo's opinion that the capture of Kervenheim was largely due to 2 Lincolns, considering the extraordinary efforts and heroism of Norfolks & KSLI.

191 Sussex Record Office: Whistler Diary.

German prisoners digging graves for Canadian dead. Hochwald Forest, 3 March 1945. The procedure for handling the dead was the same throughout 21 AG, and was described by Medical Sgt Doug Knight of the Hasty Ps serving in Italy. The man was buried in his uniform and boots after removing battle gear and the personal belongings in his pockets, which were sent to the next of kin.The ankles were tied together and the arms tied to the waist with signal wire. The corpse was laid face down on an army blanket, which was wrapped around and secured with string. Here a Para POW is measuring the depth of the grave with an entrenching spade which was 37 inches long, supervised by the guard who is out of sight on the right except for his gaitered leg. According to Doug, the man's estate was billed for the army blanket acting as his shroud, but nowhere has this author found confirmation of this shocking information. (Capt JH Smith/Canada. Dept. of National Defence/Library & Archives Canada/PA-153188)

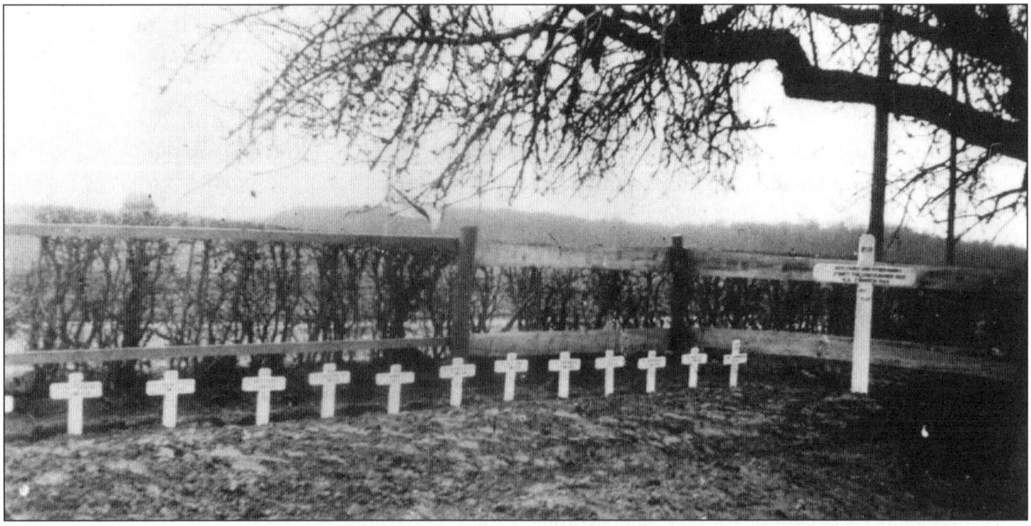

2 Lincoln's cemetery on Hestert in Winnekendonk about 6 March 1945. (© Simon Firbank)

Leslie Colvin returned on the first anniversary of the battle to attend mass in a house as the Church was still a ruin. His Frontier Inspection VW is parked on Hestert in 1947 when the family, including this author, visited the cemetery for the second anniversary.

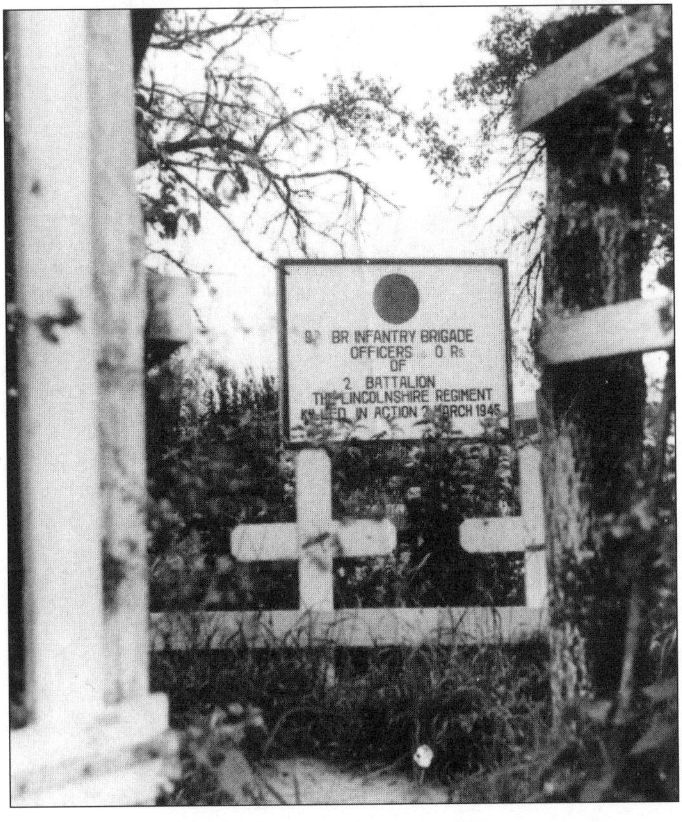

The sign at the entrance to the cemetery.

The grave of Peter Clarke between Frederick Billings and Frankie Monkman on the right. All graves were moved later to the CWGC cemetery in the Reichswald.

Peter Clarke's grave in the Reichswald War Cemetery on the 70th anniversary of his death. The ceramic poppy which was left there was from the 2014 Tower of London display.

Peter Clarke as a First Lieutenant on leaving Sandhurst in 1941.

which considering the chaos surrounding the planning for the assault on Kervenheim and the heavy losses resulting from the failure of the Warwicks and 4 CG to take, or at least neutralise, Müsershof and Murmannshof, reveals a lack of grip by Whistler which he could have mentioned to himself and done something to correct. It is probable that Whistler washed his hands of 6 GAB, who were really only nominally under his command; he knew that Horrocks was besotted with Guards in general, and that Montgomery wore with sincerity and not irony the black beret and badge of the RAC.

On 5 March 1945, 2 Lincolns buried their twenty-two dead in the orchard on Hestert, called in German the *Heldenfriedhof Wiese van de Flierdt, W'donk*. The names of those buried, with the sole exception of Cpl E.W. Monkman of the Bermuda Volunteer Rifle Corps, are written in the Roll of Honour in Lincoln Cathedral lying open below the fading colours. A page is turned every day. Written on the title page are these words:

> *They whom this roll commemorates were numbered among those who at the call of King and country left all that was dear to them endured hardness faced danger and finally passed out of the sight of men by the path of duty and self sacrifice giving up their own lives that others might live in freedom. Let those who come after see to it that their name be not forgotten.*

Pte John Stanley Bertenshawe
Pte Frederick Billings
Pte Reginald Bluett
Pte Leslie Richard Boam
Pte Arthur Brittain
Pte Harry Brown
Pte William Chatwood
Maj Peter Henry Woodthorpe Clarke, MC
Pte Bernard Coggins
Pte Eric Hartley
Pte Donald Jack James Hewitt
Pte Henry John Jarvis
Pte Sylvester Kennedy
Pte Edward Ronald Maiden
Pte Frank Mettam
Cpl E.W. Monkman
Pte John Morris
Pte Henry Maurice Needham
Cpl Wilfred Clement Purcell
Pte Richard Alfred Terry
Pte Stanley Walter Thorneycroft
Pte Edward Victor Waters

Frankie Monkman's name is recorded on the BVRC Memorial in Victoria Park, Bermuda and probably in Hamilton Cathedral.

In addition, the wounded numbered sixty-five including three officers, while six were reported missing. The total casualties were an appalling 93, or one quarter to a third of the 300 to 400 in the rifle companies. A wooden Cross of Remembrance was set up and a large painted signboard erected facing the entrance from the Bruch road, now called Hestert:

> 9th BR INFANTRY BRIGADE. OFFICERS & ORs OF 2 BATTALION THE LINCOLNSHIRE REGIMENT KILLED IN ACTION 2 MARCH 1945

Each grave was marked with its own cross. A photograph taken in 1947 shows flowers placed on Peter Clarke's grave by the author's parents. All the Lincolns killed since 27 February were collected at Winnekendonk, including two who died of wounds after the battle (Boam on 4 March and Chatwood on 3 March). From the dates of their deaths recorded in the Roll of Honour, it appears that two were killed on the attack on the Üdem-Weeze Road on 27 February (Kennedy and Waters) and the rest on 1 and 2 March. By 1947 the photographs show the graveyard a mass of bloom with the small crosses replaced with larger ones, and a low fence erected.

Pipe-Maj W. Smith, Gdsm J. Campbell, Gdsm F Lees and Lt R. F. Nunn, RA were buried, according to German records, on the left of the road to Kervenheim near Brönkshof (Links der Straße Kervenheim in d. Nähe von Brönkshof) where they were killed. Today all lie in the large Reichswald War Cemetery.

The mass burial and the large number of wounded who had been repatriated, decimated the rifle companies. The burial was an event no one, including this author's father, could ever speak about. The battalion, unfortunately, had time to brood about their loss and they took it hard. Their grief, however, was not tinged with the bitterness felt by the Norfolks, whose losses at Kervenheim were greater and the circumstance in which they occurred more controversial. Firbank, with a bar to his DSO and imminent promotion to Brigadier, was always satisfied with his performance and ready to criticize Renny. Leslie Colvin was distraught by the death of Peter Clarke. His diary reveals that on the first anniversary of the battle he returned to Winnekendonk to hear mass in an attic since the Pfarrkirche was in ruins. When on leave in Lincoln, Colvin drove over to Binbrook to give his condolences to Brigadier Clarke, and was shocked to find the old soldier – who as a youth had arrested de Valera in the Dublin Post Office in 1916 – showed little interest in Peter's death and could talk only about his new wife and expected baby. Later in 1946 when Colvin's last child was born he was named Peter, as was Jack Harrod's son, and Glyn Gilbert's son Graham remembers him as the godfather he never knew.

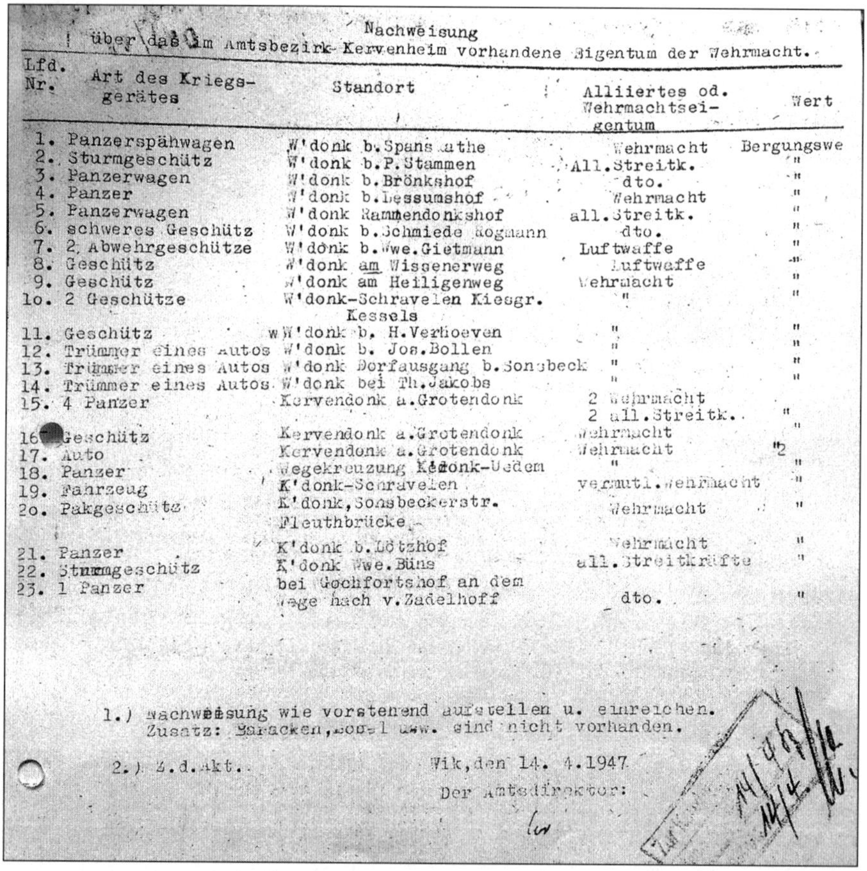

Nachweisung
über das im Amtsbezirk Kervenheim vorhandene Eigentum der Wehrmacht.

Lfd. Nr.	Art des Kriegsgerätes	Standort	Alliiertes od. Wehrmachtseigentum	Wert
1.	Panzerspähwagen	W'donk b. Spans [illegible]the	Wehrmacht	Bergungswe
2.	Sturmgeschütz	W'donk b. P. Stammen	All. Streitk.	"
3.	Panzerwagen	W'donk b. Brönkshof	dto.	"
4.	Panzer	W'donk b. Lessumshof	Wehrmacht	"
5.	Panzerwagen	W'donk Rammendonkshof	all. Streitk.	"
6.	schweres Geschütz	W'donk b. Schmiede Rogmann	dto.	"
7.	2 Abwehrgeschütze	W'donk b. Wwe. Gietmann	Luftwaffe	"
8.	Geschütz	W'donk am Wissenerweg	Luftwaffe	"
9.	Geschütz	W'donk am Heiligenweg	Wehrmacht	"
10.	2 Geschütze	W'donk-Schravelen Kiesgr. Kessels	"	"
11.	Geschütz	W'donk b. H. Verhoeven	"	"
12.	Trümmer eines Autos	W'donk b. Jos. Bollen	"	"
13.	Trümmer eines Autos	W'donk Dorfausgang b. Sonsbeck	"	"
14.	Trümmer eines Autos	W'donk bei Th. Jakobs	"	"
15.	4 Panzer	Kervendonk a. Grotendonk	2 Wehrmacht 2 all. Streitk.	"
16.	Geschütz	Kervendonk a. Grotendonk	Wehrmacht	"
17.	Auto	Kervendonk a. Grotendonk	Wehrmacht	"2
18.	Panzer	Wegekreuzung K'donk-Uedem	"	"
19.	Fahrzeug	K'donk-Schravelen	vermutl. Wehrmacht	"
20.	Pakgeschütz	K'donk, Sonsbeckerstr. Fleuthbrücke	Wehrmacht	"
21.	Panzer	K'donk b. Lötzhof	Wehrmacht	"
22.	Sturmgeschütz	K'donk Wwe. Büns	all. Streitkräfte	"
23.	1 Panzer	bei Gochfortshof an dem Wege nach v. Zadelhoff	dto.	"

1.) Nachweisung wie vorstehend aufstellen u. einreichen.
Zusatz: Baracken, [illegible] usw. sind nicht vorhanden.

2.) Z.d.Akt.

Wik, den 14. 4.1947
Der Amtsdirektor:

List of wrecked equipment available for scrap (Bergungswert) in the Kervenheim/Winnekendonk district compiled by the Bűrgermeister in 1947. Item 2 is the Stug destroyed by Runcie which is falsely described as being Allied, while Item 3 is the Pipe Major's Churchill. Item 8 is believed to have been the 88 destroyed by Alldred.

Lfd. Nr.	Name, Vorname	Dienst-grad	Erkennungsmarke	gefallen. verstorben am	Raum f. weitere Angaben (z.B. Lage des Grabes)	Nationalität	Zivilist od. Militär-
1.	4 unbekannte alliierte Soldaten	-	-	10.2.45	kath-Friednof Winnekendonk		
2.	8 xx " "	-	-	7.2.45	dto.		
3.	B. Billinger	-	R.C.	Killed in Action 2. Marz.1945	Heldenfriednof Wiese van de Flierdt, W'donk	Engländer	X 2 nd. Lincol
4.	P.H.W.Clarke	Maj.	C of E	dto.	dto.	"	dto.
5.	E.W. Monkmann	-	C of E	dto.	dto.	"	dto. C.[illegible]
6.	W.C.Purkell	-	-	dto.	dto.	"	dto. C.[illegible]
7.	Pte. Terrye	-	4341834 C of E	dto.	dto.	"	dto.
8.	Pte. Bertenschaw	-	I.L.5962244 C of E.	dto.	dto.	"	dto.
9.	Pte. Ewitt	-	D.J.168 78 80.C of E	dto.	dto.	"	dto.
10.	Pte. Brittain	-	A 14664300 R.C.	dto.	dto.	"	dto.
11.	Pte. Caussiers	-	R.C.of E.	dto.	dto.	"	dto.
12.	C.Hennessy	-	18005026 R.C.	dto.	dto.	"	dto.
13.	Pte.Thornycroft	-	14655446 C of E	dto.	dto.	"	dto.
14.	Pte. Nettmann	-	F 4804428 C of E.	dto.	dto.	"	dto.
15.	Pte. Brown	-	H 9191188 C of E	dto.	dto.	"	dto.
16.	Pte. Jarvis	-	H.I.147442 96 E of E	dto.	dto.	"	dto.
17.	Pte. Needham	-	H.4801876 C of E	dto.	dto.	"	dto.
18.	Pte. Haptley	-	E 46157772 C of E.	dto.	dto.	"	dto.
19.	W.Connor	Rfn.	14746215 R.C. R.U.P.	dto.	dto.	"	dto.

Local government return in 1947 listing war graves in the district: page 1.

CE. BASKE[illegible]. R.F.
AL NORFOLK REGT.
AL NORFOLK REGT.
AL NORFOLK REGT.
AL NORFOLK REGT.
AL NORFOLK REGT.
TE. DURLING. S- RIP
AL NORFOLK REGT.
AL NORFOLK REGT.
AL NORFOLK REGT.
AL NORFOLK REGT.
AL NORFOLK REGT.
AL NORFOLK REGT.

Bürgermeister

Kervenheim, den 26. März

An den
Herrn Amtsdirektor
in Winnekendonk

Zur Ergänzung der Kriegsgräberliste vom 5. Januar 194
noch folgendes gemeldet:

1. Deckers Heinrich, Kervendonk 21 1 unbek
2. Im Park an der Schuhfabrik Kervenheim 3 engli
Aufschriften auf den Kreuzen
1) PTE. BLUITT.R. 14746780 -2.3.1945- 2ND LINCOLNS (
2) PTE. MAIDEN 14376753 -2.3.1945- 2ND LINCOLNS (
3) K/A 1.3.1945 CE

Auf dem englischen Ehrenfriedhof sind 47 Grabstätten d
Regiments.

Theodor van Dornick, Kervendonk 11 1 unbeka Soldat

Pfarrhaus, Kervenheim, Pastoratstr. 1 unbeka Soldat

Am Friedhof, Kervenheim 4 deutsc
Aufschriften auf den Kreuzen
1) K/A FLAK. ERS. AB H 62
2) K/A 505 ALW. B.K.P. 9 XII.
3) unbekannt 3.3.1945
4) FL. Ers. Batt. III.

insgesamt 57 Gräber

Der Bürgermeister

Local government return: page 2.

Later the Bürgermeister counted 57 military graves in Winnekendonk and Kervenheim of which 47 were in British war cemeteries (Norfolks, Lincolns and Scots Guards), one unknown at the Deckers, two British (Bluitt and Maiden of 2 Lincolns, not buried with the Norfolks) in the grounds of the shoe factory in Kervenheim with one unknown, another unknown at van Doornicks, one more in the vicarage garden in Kervenheim, and four German soldiers in the cemetery in Kervenheim.

The war memorial in Kervenheim records 5 civilian deaths, and the Memorial in Winnekendonk the large number of 22 due to 2 TAF's heavy bombing. The farms in Kervendonk recorded 3 civilians killed.

The remainder of 5 March after the burial was spent resting. On 6 March Horrocks made a visit and congratulated all companies. Renny wrote to his command noting they had succeeded in breaking through whilst those on the flanks were held. Renny ignored Kervenheim, of course, and strangely mentioned the Scots Guards before the RA, who were always the right of the line.

Message from Brig G.D. Renny, Commander 9 Brit Inf Bde

> I congratulate the 2nd Battalion The Lincolnshire Regiment, the 1st Battalion The Kings Own Scottish Borderers, and the 2nd Battalion The Royal Ulster Rifles, on their fine successes in the action of the UDEM-WEEZE road and the Winnekendonk position.
>
> Our opponents were parachutists, the finest infantry in the German Army. They held prepared positions, the approaches into which were deep in mud, cut by water lines, and in some places barred against tanks by woods. On the flanks their fanatical resistance was holding up other troops.
>
> We attacked twice. In the first attack, we broke deep into the enemy's position. In the second, we broke through, thus allowing armoured troops to flood through the gap. We took about 500 prisoners, besides many killed and wounded. We destroyed four 88 mm guns, six SP guns and great numbers of machine guns.
>
> Our success was swift and complete. It was won by the bravery and resource of the three regiments and by the magnificent support provided by the 3rd Bn the Scots Guards, by the Royal Artillery (especially the 33rd Regiment), by 45 A Tk Battery, 253 Field Company, 'A' and 'D' Coys of the 2nd Bn the Middlesex Regt, by the 9th Field Ambulance and by affiliated members of the Royal Corps of Signals.
>
> 6 Mar 45.[192]

On 7 March the War Diary records only that Colvin visited enemy defences on the east bank of the Maas opposite Lottum. This would have been cover for a swan to Deurne with a Jeep-full of food and drink 'liberated' from German farms for the Wiegersmas. There must have been a grand party.

On 8 March there was a conference at 9 BIB, which offers an insight into what was on the minds of those involved, and the lessons learned. This business-like searching out of the bad with the good reveals the degree of professionalism at the unit level. They had little chance, however, of effecting real change in the vital areas of communications, inter-arms cooperation, and tank armour immunity. Whistler, Horrocks, Crerar, Coningham, Hobart, Richards, Montgomery and even Eisenhower should have attended this conference in the ruins of Germany, together with the boffins from the armaments ministry, including the aircraft and telecommunications' industries, and with those non-existent people responsible for ensuring that military equipment and

192 TNA: WO 171/5231: 2 Lincolns' war diary.

operational methodology were constantly improved to solve battlefield problems. As discussed elsewhere, the minds of the senior brass needed to start focusing on the next conflict which most knew would involve Marshal Georgi Zhukov's hordes. Montgomery, however, would never attend such a conference except to give out orders, and this attitude permeated the senior ranks of the army. Relations between many of them were such that it would have been impossible to get Montgomery and Mary Coningham into the same room. Cathcart did not attend so it seems likely that only COs were invited.

On 9 March 1 KOSB held a battalion conference, obviously inspired, or even ordered, by Renny who was a Borderer. Its conclusions were distributed to the participating companies and to 2 Lincolns, but not to 2 RUR for some reason. Renny then combined the two sets of conclusions into a paper titled Tactical Points from the Fighting in Operation *Heather*. It well summed up the state of the thinking in 3 BID, and was probably representative of 21 AG. These papers are in the Appendix.

The end of the War was only two months away. 3 BID did not take part in the Rhine assault. They had two more fierce fights, at Lingen on the Ems and at Bremen on the Weser. 6 GAB was formed into a quasi-armoured division with 6 British and 17 US Airborne Divisions, taking Münster in the van of the allied advance. They ended up around Lübeck in Schleswig Holstein where they were converted into infantry and disbanded. 3 BID went to Palestine and continues in the line to this day.

In Chapter 3, Pastor Coenders' story was suspended when Endtschenhof was occupied. He continued:

> On 1 March, Thursday, we had to stay in the cellar the entire day. The next morning an interpreter arrived. He could speak perfect German and said he was a Frenchman who had spent a long time in POW camps. Father Deckers asked him many questions and he answered most of them. Before leaving he warned us to be peaceful and to follow to the letter all the instructions given by the English. Towards evening refugees from Kervenheim arrived, including the district Burgermeister van Dornick and two Ukrainian girls [forced labour]. During Thursday night I kept watch for five hours until morning. That morning, 2 March, an old and needy woman, called Tante Kober, arrived. I did not know her, and took little notice of her. Later I discovered that this Tante Kober owned a large farm in Kervenheim that she ran together with her brother. The brother was killed during a raid on Kervenheim, and their Hof completely destroyed. Tante Kober was, I am told, always very charitable to the poor, and gave generously to good causes. A few days later she was reduced to poverty, and subsequently died in a strange house.
>
> At midday around 2 o'clock we received a terrible order. In half an hour the cellar must, the commander said, be emptied for 'strategic' reasons. One can imagine the turmoil this caused. Everything had to be laid out on the barn floor, and I had to keep watch to make sure nothing was stolen. But then we had to address the question of where to put all the people and their possessions. The answer was the stable, but it lacked windows, door and even a sound roof. The horses were led out and stabled in the barn, while we had to live in the stable; cook, rest and sleep there. Then to complete our misery, evacuees arrived from Kervenheim, including those from places such as Kranenburg who had found refuge in Kervenheim, and all had to be catered for by the Deckers family. Everyone had to be content, day and night, with living in the stables, where the kitchen was also set up. The first time we all slept in the stables was the night of 2-3 March. During the day we were allowed into the barn but not to leave it. The soldiers reserved the cellar and the whole area under the barn for their own use. The men obeyed the order to bury the dead animals; horses, bullocks etc. I was excused this work. There was a constant coming and going of soldiers.

On Sunday, 4 March, in the early morning while I was still in bed, I was awakened and told that Englishmen had come to collect me. I was to officiate at the funeral of those killed in the shelling. Two Englishmen led me through the meadows to a farm about fifteen minutes away. Here were three corpses. The Englishmen had dug a grave and wrapped the corpses in quilts. While I recited a psalm the Englishmen were quiet and thoughtful, and when I finished the prayers they laid the three bodies in a single grave and asked me the names of the deceased [for the marker cross]. In French I made it clear that Herr Deckers would provide the names. When the soldiers brought me back, I asked father Deckers for the names of the dead. He said they could only be Theodor Kühnen, Frau Theodor Kühnen and Wilhelm Kühnen. I wrote down these names for the soldiers.

It was impossible to celebrate Mass that Sunday, so I organised a Messfeier [a shortened form of the mass without the sacrament] in the stable with the devout participation of all of those present in the Hof, including those of other denominations. The immediate repair of the roof and the burial of dead animals were necessary. In the afternoon we were visited by Heerohm [Plattdeutsch, or Low German, for Pastor] E Mott from Asperden who had also ended up in Kervenheim. In the evening a large number of English tanks went by [GAD moving up from Pfalzdorf to Bonninghardt].

Monday, 5 March, was a fairly peaceful day, with the main task of making our living quarters habitable. After a quiet day, that evening there occurred a very dramatic scene. Most people were already in bed, when suddenly an English officer came in, looking for a girl who was supposed to have insulted an English soldier. The English officer searched all the bedrooms, or rather stalls, and threatened to shoot. Father Deckers managed to calm the officer down so the matter passed without any further disturbance.

The next day, 6 March, the tidying up operation resumed. Doors which had been taken away were brought back from shell holes and slit-trenches [where they provided top-cover] and re-hung. Cattle that were roaming about were caught and returned to their stalls. These tasks continued on Wednesday, 7 March. On this day a *Schlachtfest* [festival] took place when a large pig was slaughtered, and everything was done in an orderly fashion despite the primitive conditions. In the evening there was a repeat of the scene which had played out a couple of days earlier. This time a Ukrainian girl was accused of having insulted a soldier; a search was made for the girl amid threats of shooting etc. The disturbance was no less than that on Monday, but this time father Deckers knew how to calm the situation so nobody was singled out. The old story of the Garden of Eden constantly repeats itself: "And when the woman saw, that the tree was good for food, and that it was pleasant to the eyes … she tooke of the fruit thereof, and did eate" [Authorised Version]. Despite rebukes and warnings to keep away from enemy soldiers, and to dress as unattractively as possible to avoid unnecessary provocation, nevertheless …

On Thursday, 8 March, repair work was carried out. That evening we were visited by Fraulein Thassen and my old pupil from Bienen [between Emmerich and Rees], Johanna Hogenkamp, who were all helping on the Moll farm. They were happy to eat their fill with us again and to sleep in the 'first-class compartment', that is the stable.

On Friday and Saturday, 9 and 10 March, nothing out of the ordinary happened. Damage was repaired, more damage was identified, and slit trenches and shell holes filled in.

On Sunday, 11 March, the day of our return home arrived. It was not possible to celebrate Mass, so as on the previous Sunday I held a Messfeier attended by everyone present in the Hof. After the devotions I went for a bit of a walk, and on the way met a girl going towards Kevelaer. In the course of conversation it emerged she was called Jahnsen, lived on the marketplace, and had been evacuated to our neighbourhood. Now she wanted to go to Kevelaer to see how things were. She would certainly be back in Kervendonk around 12 to 1 o'clock. I asked her to make enquiries of Fraulein Beykirch in Kevelaer whether we could now return. When the girl returned at midday, we were delighted to hear Fraulein Beykirch had told her we could go back to Kevelaer, which is what we did.

We then quickly packed our things, said goodbye to the Deckers family and all our other acquaintances, and then were on our way. Angela and the two helps employed by the Deckers family, Sonnja and Luttka [obviously Ukrainians], accompanied us as far as the town gate. Half an hour later we were back home.

I must not forget here and now to thank all the members of the Deckers family from the bottom of my heart for all the goodness they showed myself and Sister from the moment we were expelled. I had to politely refuse their offer of an allowance of money. May the Almighty God amply reward the Deckers family, with whom we bore five weeks of the sufferings of war and the fear of death, for all the good things they did for us in our time of trouble! Help us, God, to find our way home from this earthly misery (Erdenelend). Pray for the poor writer, and with this request I will end.[193]

193 Sent by Käthe Schmitz on 5 March 2013. Translation by this author, Jenny Pearson & Jens Graul

Part II

Those Involved

5

3 British Infantry Division

We relied on ourselves, then, and we could be relied on to co-operate. I cannot think of any two qualities that better become men, whether their business is war or peace.
Norman Scarfe. *Assault Division.* 1947

Auf engl. Seite waren nur beste Truppen mit vorzüglicher Bewaffnung eingesetzt.[1]
Heimatkalender 1950 für den Landkreis Geldern

When Churchill spoke to a private soldier in the presence of Bolo Whistler, the three of them stood at the top, the bottom and the exact middle of the hierarchy of command. The top echelon was responsible for strategy and equipment, and for organising and supplying the bottom echelon, which was the 'commodity' on which the whole structure rested. The dividing or fault line midway between these echelons was the divisional commander.

The division was the currency in which nations calculated their military wealth, and with which they settled their differences on the battlefield. The Anglo-Canadians had 14 divisions in NW Europe in February 1945, representing only 18% of SHAEF's 76 divisions, which comprised 52 US, 11 British, 9 French, 3 Canadian, and 1 Polish division.

Every soldier belonged either to a regiment, a staff or a specialist corps, to be distinguished from army corps which were divisional groupings. All regiments and specialist corps had depots. The soldier carried the metal badge of his regiment or corps on his cap and a flash spelling it out on his shoulder. Soldiers were instructed in the Regimental and corps histories and achievements over nearly 300 years, annually celebrating a famous victory in the case of the infantry regiments.

Soldiers wore the signs of three entities on their uniform arm. At the top a curved shoulder flash carried either the regimental name in capitals (LINCOLN, SCOTS GUARDS, ARTILLERY), or the name of a specialist corps (REME, RAMC), or nothing in the case of staffs. Below the curved flash was a formation sign – the divisional badge or, in the case of 6 GAB, a brigade badge; otherwise, in the case of the higher staffs, they had a corps or army badge. Those serving in infantry brigades wore red bars below the divisional badge to identify the brigade; in 3 BID, 8 BIB had one bar, 9 BIB two, and 185 three.

Canloan provided 30% of 3 BIB's platoon commanders, 49 out of 162. They carried an additional CANADA flash sewn between the unit and divisional signs. There were so many of them in command of the fighting men, and their name CANADA so unmistakable compared with something outwardly meaningless such as, KSLI or RUR being worn by the same person that German memoirs referred to 3 BID troops in the battle of Yorkshire Bridge and on other occasions as Canadians.

Other ranks wore their rank stripes on their sleeves together with any qualification badges they had earned, such as signaller, sniper, driver, etc. In the same place, both officers and men wore their wound stripes. Officers wore cloth rank badges on the epaulettes. Medal ribbons were placed above the left breast pocket, with those awarded for bravery taking precedence.

1 The English side fielded only their best troops with excellent weapons.

The number of the soldier's section, platoon, company or even battalion was not signified, being unit housekeeping matters that were not recorded and provide ongoing difficulty for historians. The organisations above the division were also not shown. Corps, armies and army groups had no fixed composition, with divisions transferring between corps and corps between armies, remaining sometimes for only a day. 3 BID switched corps twenty-one times between September 1939 and August 1945. Some commanders, such as Horrocks, tried to give their corps an identity for reasons that look like self-promotion, and even published a history of 30 Corps called *Club Route* but few British troops identified with them even though they were very familiar with the corps sign used as a route marker.

The following diagram shows the relationship between a private soldier of the Lincolns to Churchill at the time of Operation *Veritable*. There were 13 titular appointments, with the divisional GOC half way at number 7. It should be noted that although Brigadier is shown as a rank it was an appointment, like Premier, CIGS and Theatre Commander, but not President.

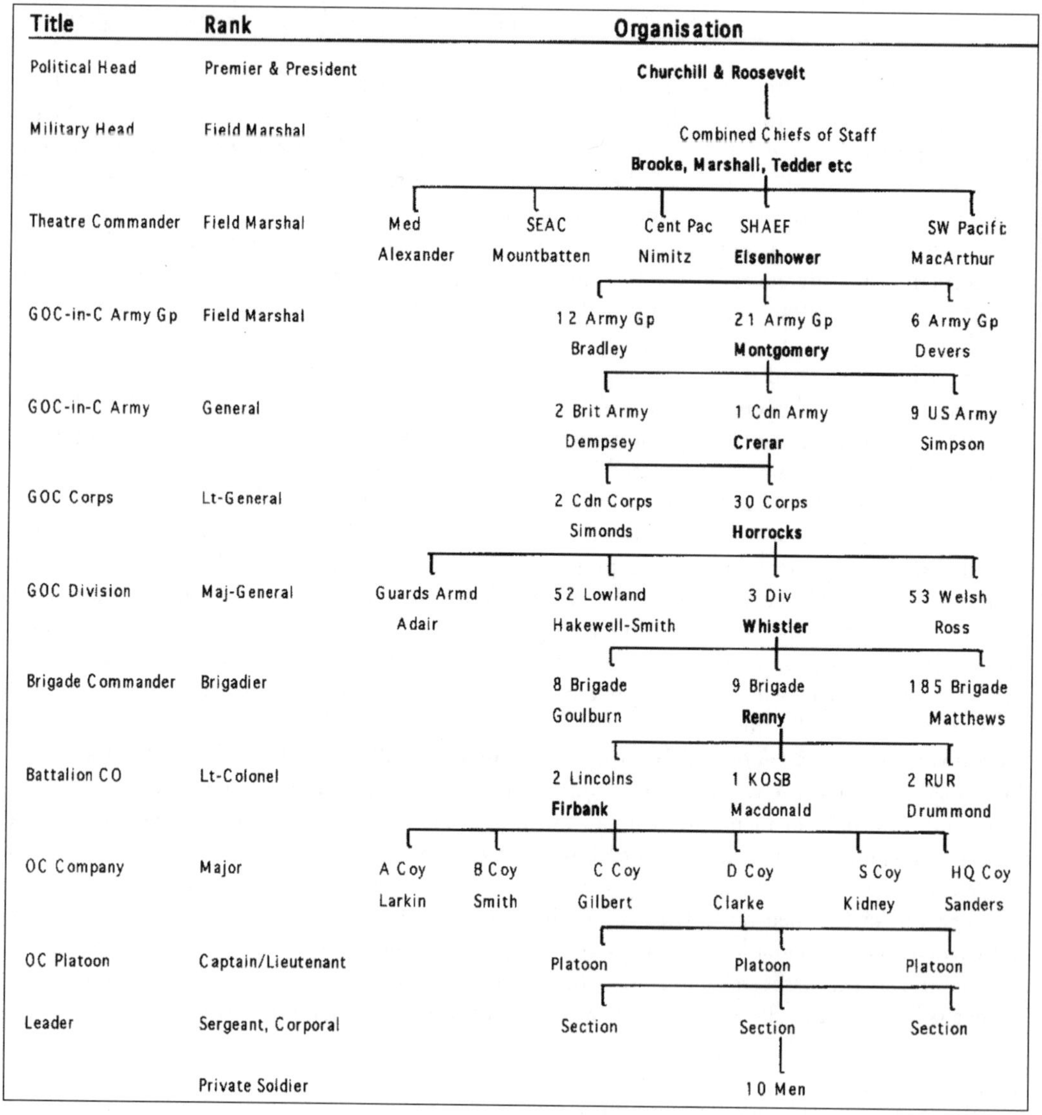

The number of service personnel was almost equal to those fighting. Total manpower was roughly 600,000 in 21 AG, with another 50,000 in 2 TAF. Note that there were more RASC than infantry.

Fighting Troops		*Service Troops*	
Royal Artillery	18%	RASC	15%
Infantry	14%	Pioneer Corps	10%
Royal Engineers	13%	REME	5%
Royal Armoured Corps	6%	Medical etc.	4%
Royal Corps of Signals	5%	Ordnance, Pay etc.	10%
Total Fighting	56%	Total Service	44%
Total	100%[2]		

The First and Second battalions of infantry regiments served regularly even in peacetime, and its members were called 'regular soldiers'. They were incorporated into the first six British regular Divisions, although in wartime their ranks were reinforced with territorials, volunteers and conscripts. In addition eleven first-line and sixteen second-line territorial divisions were formed, many disappearing after 1941.

Battalions of the same regiment had little to do with one another, with officers of one usually knowing those in the others only by name, if at all. Battalions of the same regiment rarely served together, but shared the unit name, barracks, history and regimental march which, for both British and German soldiers, held deep meaning and value. Band instruments were not taken on campaign and bandsmen often acted as stretcher-bearers, but some bands were sent over to play in the rear areas and at special events.

British regiments were numbered according to their seniority, (the Royal Norfolks raised on 19 June 1685 were IXth of Foot, the Lincolns on 20 June 1685 were Xth, and the East Yorkshires even later that same month were XVth of Foot). They were affiliated with a county in 1870 whose name the regiment bore and which contained its depot where in peacetime, if not in war, most of its recruits were raised. They were therefore called 'County Regiments'. On 4 March 1945 reinforcements destined for the Royal Fusiliers (VIIth of Foot raised on 11 June 1685) arrived to replace the Lincolns' losses at Winnekendonk:

> These Royal Fusiliers were Londoners and took the view that they had been sent to a regiment of yokels, which to a degree offended us. We all came to some sort of agreement in the end.[3]

The Guards' regiments of the Household Brigade were senior to the county regiments; the Coldstream were raised in 1650, Grenadiers in 1656, and Scots in 1660, and had barracks in London and Caterham in Surrey.

Most infantrymen regarded the battalion as their family whose ties during 'the duration' were often as strong as, and sometimes more reliable and meaningful than those of their families. Many soldiers heard disquieting rumours from home about wives and fiancées, or got 'Dear John' letters. One CO in 3 BID received news in the middle of the bloodletting in Normandy that his wife had left him for a woman. This author's mother, Edna Mary Colvin, was told by her gynaecologist in the Bromhead Nursing Home, Dr Hadley that she was the only wife in Lincoln loyal to her serving husband. Anthony Powell wrote of that time that he read in the newspapers of the splendid

2 Unrecorded source.
3 John Keenan's tape-recorded memoirs.

women's war effort, which seemed to consist of sleeping with as many men as possible while their husbands were away.[4] Some found out by letter in the field; Tom Dyson, serving with his twin in Churchills in 107 Regt RAC, received a letter from his wife with the news that she was expecting. His joy turned to anger when he calculated it could not be his. After speaking to his welfare officer and subsequently author of *Mailed Fist*, Lt John Foley who is quoted elsewhere, he divorced 'the bloody cow'.[5] These common stresses and ever-present danger meant that the soldiers became dependent on each other, developing true fellowship in their mutual dealing and usually treating each other with kindness and consideration.

Each rifle battalion was grouped together permanently in a brigade with two others, and commanded by a brigadier with a small staff. The brigadier in the Second World War was an appointment and not a rank. Three brigades were grouped permanently with supporting arms, but not tanks or aircraft, into an infantry division. Rex Fendick described the arrangement:

> The infantry battalions were permanently grouped in Brigades, but the 'supporting arms', that is Engineers, Signals, Div Support battalion, and artillery, were NOT permanently grouped to Brigades. They were Div troops, and could be re-grouped, or allotted in support or under command as each battle demanded. They were very flexible in their support of whoever needed it most, and as ordered by the GOC. However, there was always an attempt to establish and maintain a normal *affiliation*. Thus our A Coy, 2 Middlesex landed on D Day with 8 Brigade, but by the time I joined they were supporting 9 Brigade, and for most of Normandy 9 Brigade was 'our' Brigade. But later we were placed in support or under command of all the other brigades from time to time. Similarly with the RE Field Squadrons and the Artillery Regiments.[6]

Several divisions were grouped in a corps, but only corps' troops carried the corps' sign. For XXX Corps it was a black Wild Boar rampant on a white field, affectionately known as 'The Old Pig'. The route marker was the Ace of Clubs and all recognised 'Club Route'.

Brought up to full strength during January 1945, 3 BID numbered 18,347[7] including 870 officers holding the King's Commission. This was literally the case; each officer receiving a piece of paper signed by the King addressed to his trusty servant. The burden of the stress and fear of fighting fell on the 4,500 men of the Rifle Companies, who suffered with their replacements the majority of the 11,084 Divisional casualties suffered between D-Day and April 30, 1945.[8]

June 44	3,508	Oct 44	1,301	Feb 45	471
July 44	2,504	Nov 44	411	Mar 45	515
Aug 44	1,088	Dec 44	85	Apr 45	687
Sep 44	357	Jan 45	157	Total	11,084

This loss rate of 250% is the shocking statistic behind the battles described in this book and quite as ruinous as the infantry's experience in any 11-month period in the First World War.

A division is the largest formation with a semi-permanent composition. 3 BID underwent radical change during 1941-43. Both 8 and 9 BIBs were permanent fixtures, but 7 Guards Brigade

4 Anthony Powell. *Faces in my Time. Vol III* (London: William Heinemann, 1980).
5 Stephen Dyson. *Tank Twins* (London: Leo Cooper & IWM, 1994), p. 93.
6 Rex Fendick in an e-mail in June 2002.
7 LF Ellis, *Victory in the West: Volume II* (London: HMSO, 1962), p. 535.
8 Scarfe, *Assault Division*, p. 270.

(1 & 2 GG and 1 CG) left the Division in September 1941 to form GAD, and was replaced by 37 Independent BIB, renamed 7 BIB in December 1941. Between June 1942 and April 1943, however, 3 BID like many infantry divisions became a 'Mixed Division' with tanks, losing 7 BIB and gaining 33 BTB (43 RTR, 144 RAC and 148 Regiments RAC). On April 10, 1943 it reverted to an Infantry Division, losing its tanks and gaining 185 BIB for the duration. They had been part of 79 BAD, raised under Hobart in October 1942, but in April 1943 79 BAD had become the specialised armoured assault division and lost its infantry.

A Divisional GOC is a Major General, which is short for 'Sergeant-Major' General and therefore one rank below a 'Lieutenant' General. 3 BID had six commanders during the war; Bernard Montgomery until July 1940, James Gammell to November 1941, Eric Hayes to December 1942, and William Ramsden to December 1943. According to Leslie Colvin, when Ramsden, who had been sacked by Montgomery as 30 Corps commander in 1942, heard that Montgomery was the new GOC of 21 AG, he came round to say farewell and left. Ramsden knew Montgomery's first action would be to scan the list of officers and sack his rejects, giving no one a second chance. Tom Rennie became GOC until he was wounded in Normandy on 13 June 1944, to be followed by Bolo Whistler until the German surrender. Montgomery, Rennie and Whistler were exceptional commanders and held in some awe according to Anthony Powell who wrote that at battalion level, even brigadiers seemed infinitely illustrious, while the the divisional commander was a remote, god-like figure. Powell also described the different atmospheres at their HQs: companionable at battalion level, snugly compact at brigade, interesting with much variety at corps and army with their closeness to high command, while divisional HQ's atmosphere was somewhere in between them all.[9] Powell visited 21 Army Group HQ in November 1944, and had the feeling he was entering a minor public school which had just defeated its rival at football, with the young, aggressive and self-satisfied young men sometimes forgetting normal army courtesies.[10] The thin memoirs of Johnny Henderson and Carol Mather support this judgment.

Forty percent of the division – 7,389 of the total 18,347 – were in the nine battalions of the three infantry brigades. Of these, 4,572 or 62% were in the rifle companies and marked for death. It was extraordinary that those who performed the really dangerous task of advancing on foot comprised only 3.5% of 21 AG's total manpower (25% of 14%). In common justice these men should have been paid excessive danger money and a pension, as well as a special distinction.

Each unit in the division had both the divisional badge and a unique tac sign of a white number on a square coloured background. The exception was 6 GAB with its brigade badge:

Formation	**Ground**	**HQ**		**Units**	
6 GAB	Green	151	4 Grenadier – 152	4 Coldstream – 153	3 Scots – 154
3 Div – 8 BID	Red	81	1 Suffolks – 55	2 E Yorks – 56	1 S Lancs – 57
3 Div – 9 BID	Green	87	2 Lincolns – 60	1 KOSB – 61	2 RUR – 62
3 Div – 185BID	Brown	94	2 R Warwicks – 67	1 R Norfolks – 68	2 KSLI – 69
3 Div troops	Black	40	2 Middlesex – 64	– 65	– 66
	Black		Provost – 79	Postal – 80	Battle School – 81
	Green/Blue	41	3 Recce		

9 Powell, *Faces*, p. 106.
10 Op. cit., p. 170.

Red and blue horizontal stripes

RA Unit	No	RA Unit	No	RA Unit	No
HQ RA	40	33 Field Regt	43	20 Anti-Tank Regt	46
7 Field Regt	42	76 Field Regt	44	92 LAA Regt	47

Sky blue ground

RE Unit	No	RE Unit	No	RE Unit	No	RE Unit	No	RE Unit	No
17	48	246	49	253	50	15	51	2 Brdg Pl	52

8 Brigade was commanded by the Grenadier Guardsman, E H (Eddy or Eddie) Goulburn, DSO. He had distinguished himself as CO 1 GG in taking Nijmegen Bridge on 20 September 1944, although that distinction has not survived the test of time.

1 Suffolk, XII Foot from Bury St Edmunds, under Lt-Col R.E. (Dick) Goodwin, DSO, an able officer who after the war commanded the School of Infantry and was knighted as a Lt General.

2 East Yorkshire, XV Foot from Beverly, under Lt-Col J.D.W. (Bill) Renison, DSO. He was a rare TA officer commanding a regular battalion. He kept an unpublished diary of the whole campaign, which he lent for inclusion here, and which is now in the IWM (PPIMCR/248). His 2ic was Major C.K. 'Banger' King, DSO and Bar, killed by a mine while delivering rations to the forward companies in Mackenstadt on 18 April 1945. He had become a legend in 3 BID when reciting Shakespeare on the run-in to the invasion beach. As described, in the action at Yorkshire Bridge he won a bar to his DSO, adding to his legend. He was universally loved, respected and considered invulnerable. The divisional biographer wrote; 'The whole Division was proud of Major King and saw him as a representative of all that was best in themselves'.[11] Reg Rutherford said about Banger on film in the 1980s:

> I could go on and say much more, I think, about our Battalion's 2ic. He obviously relieved the whole situation by his daring and obvious gallantry in bringing that carrier load of ammunition through despite the fact he was passing through completely held enemy territory to the bridge. I remember Banger King coming to the battalion when I was a young second lieutenant. He was always an example to me and I remember just after D-Day when I was possibly a little bit nervous of one particular battle, and we were looking over where we were going to go in our next set-piece battle, and I was stood with Banger King. And I was surprised that he got up on a mound to expose himself to the enemy at that particular time, and he sort of bidden me up and with great shall I say reluctance I stood up alongside him. And he told me at that particular time, he said; 'They're just as frightened as you are, Reg, over there", he said, "and they're just as bloody bad as shots as you are.' That to me was my first real lesson in leadership by example and from that day onwards I tried to practice leadership by example. To give you some idea of what leadership by example meant to me at that particular time, and I saw it in action on a number of occasions that if the leader got down the rest of them got down and not until the leader got up did the rest of them get up. And for that I've got Banger King more than anyone else to thank for that I'm here today. In talking of Banger King he was one of the few professional soldiers that I spent a lot of time with. Most of the

11 Scarfe, *Assault Division*, p. 253.

> others I served with were what was known then as temporary gentlemen and officers, were either conscripted or volunteers'.[12]

Renison told this author that Banger's great strengths did not include those needed to command a Battalion.

1 South Lancashire, XL Foot from Warrington, commanded by the outstandingly brave Lt-Col W.A. 'Swazi' Waller, MC. He received his name in India. 'In the mess they used to sing, 'Hold him down you Swazi wallah, hold him down you Swazi King'. A fellow officer said, 'You're a Wallah', and the name stuck. 'Wallah' is believed to have been an Indian Army corruption of 'warrior'. The son of a regular officer killed at Gallipoli when Swazi was six, he went to a military boarding school aged 11 and at 17 joined the Worcestershire Regiment and served in Germany. At 22 he went to Sandhurst and served in India until 1939. He won the MC outside Dunkirk in command of C Coy, 1 Duke of Wellingtons, and was severely wounded. He married in 1940 while recuperating. On D-Day he landed as a Brigade Major. He was the fifth CO of the South Lancs since D-Day, with two killed in action, one wounded and one replaced. In the last days of the war Swazi was wounded again when his Jeep blew up on a mine outside Bremen.

9 Brigade was known as the 'International Brigade' – a famous Republican formation in the Spanish Civil War – because it contained English, Scots and Irish regiments. Colin Welch of the Lincolns, who was for a time LO at Brigade, recalled the fine work of the prim but admirable Brigade Major Toby Jessel, who worked for *The Times* after the war. Jessel had endured criticism from the Brigade Captain, Howarth, 'a raging and unpleasant queer' who created a bad atmosphere. When Howarth was transferred, Jessel said; "Go Howarth, and never darken the steps of my caravan again". 9 BIB was commanded by Brig G. Douglas Renny MC, a Montgomery protégé, of whom more below.

2 Lincolnshire, X Foot from Lincoln. Its CO was Lt-Col Cecil L. Firbank, DSO. He was a Somerset Light Infantryman, and related to the notorious gay novelist, Ronald Firbank. He was highly regarded by the Divisional GOC, Bolo Whistler and by most officers serving under him. Whistler got Firbank a brigade. On 4 March, after Winnekendonk, Whistler listed Firbank as one of the four outstanding characters in the Division, adding:

> The Lincolns under Cecil Firbank are probably the best battalion in the division. 30th March. Cecil Firbank's Bn in it of course as we were trying to save it up a bit. I hope he gets his Bde soon. 24th April. Cecil Firbank a Brig. A good show but replaces 'Fish' Elrington who was killed on a mine yesterday. Those devilish boche.[13]

Some held a different view of Firbank:

> Whilst he was with us he won two DSOs. It has been suggested he tried too hard. I knew a fellow who worked down the [Grimsby] dock who was his runner, I think, and he lost a leg and I'm afraid he was quite bitter against Firbank. He felt that Firbank had led him into a situation where he had no chance but to lose his leg.[14]

12 Transcribed from a draft by Athos Films sent by Jim Fetterley.
13 Whistler Papers (Chichester: West Sussex Record Office).
14 John Keenan's tape-recorded memoir.

By 1952 Firbank was a Major General and commanded the School of Infantry. In 1957 he served on the Whistler Committee on the Reorganisation of the British Infantry, which spelled the end of the Royal Lincolnshire Regt inside the Royal Anglian Regt. The Lincolns became the *Royal* Lincolnshire Regt after the Second World War. Most of the officers wanted to reject this 'common' title carried by the RASC, but found no way without offending the Sovereign.

1 King's Own Scottish Borderers, XXV Foot from Berwick-on-Tweed, commanded by Lt-Col R.C. Macdonald, DSO, called 'Wee Mac'. On March 5, he replaced Gibbs in command of 2 R Warwicks. He knew Montgomery, writing as a Major General:

> I can remember Monty coming to the battalion in 1925 and spending about a year with us at Shorncliffe. Even in those days everybody recognized the fact that he would probably go to the top of his profession – a rare bird in that he was a chap who was not only very astute of himself – but he'd really studied the business of soldiering, which not many people did in those days – not in the dedicated sense.[15]

Douglas Renny had commanded this battalion from June to July 1944, being replaced by Lt-Col J.F.M. Macdonald to November 1944, when Wee Mac took over.

2 Royal Ulster Rifles, LXXXIII Foot from Ballymena, under Lt-Col J. Drummond. He was adjutant at Dunkirk, and became GSO3 at X Corps in 1940-41. In 1943 he was 2ic of 1 RUR in the Airlanding Brigade of 6 AD, taking part in Overlord and the Ardennes Offensive. In early 1945 he took command of 2 RUR, later winning the DSO outside Bremen.

185 Brigade was commanded by F.R.G. (Mark) Matthews, DSO (see below).

2 Royal Warwickshire, VI Foot from Warwick, whose CO was Lt-Col D.L.A. Gibbs, DSO and Bar, won at Venraij, of the Queen's Regiment. He took command on 11 June 1944 and ensured that two companies and 14 officers of 1/7th R Warwicks joined him on the breakup of 59 Division at the end of August. He moved on to command an OCTU on about 10 March 1945.

1 Royal Norfolks, IX Foot from Norwich under Lt-Col F. Peter Barclay DSO MC, recently appointed after his predecessor, Lt-Col Hugh Bellamy, was promoted to command 6 Air Landing Bde under Maj-Gen Bols. Barclay was experienced and also independent, famously having a brush with Montgomery prior to D-Day when as CO 4 Lincolns he refused to break ranks and cluster round the General's jeep, on the grounds that it was against Lincolnshire tradition for men to face one another. Montgomery called him, 'a very obstinate young man'. He subsequently refused Montgomery's request to write a pamphlet on morale.[16] He had commanded 4 Lincolns in 49 BID for seven months. Landing in Normandy on 10 June, Barclay won the DSO at Fontenay in his first battle on 24 June when the battalion lost 11 dead and 64 wounded. After employment at Harfleur, 4 Lincolns came under Canadian command, but on 23 October, both 6 and 27 CABs were placed under Barclay's command in Impforce for the attack on Breda. The Canadians were impressed and requested permanent brigading with 4 Lincolns, which was denied. On 20 October, Montgomery said to Barclay while pinning on the DSO that, 'I am always hearing of the fine achievements of your battalion'. On 4 January 1945 Barclay became acting commander of 185

15 Macdonald's Memoir (Warwick: Royal Regt of Fusiliers, Royal Warks Museum).
16 Humphrey Wilson in conversation in 1985.

BIB until 20 January when he went to 1 Royal Norfolks. His 2ic, Humphrey Wilson, called him 'very intelligent and dogmatic'.

2 King's Shropshire Light Infantry, LIII Foot from Shrewsbury, commanded by Lt-Col Pat D. Daly, DSO. He had been Bde Maj on D-Day and was promoted after the battalion had lost two COs. Major Tom Read, MC & Bar called him 'absolutely marvellous'.

Divisional troops:

2 Middlesex, Duke of Cambridge's Own (DCO), was the LXXVIIth of Foot (The Pothooks) from Mill Hill. It was the Division's Support Battalion, armed with 36 medium machine-guns and 16 4.2 inch mortars. The CO was Lt-Col G.P.L. (Pat) Weston, DSO, who was appointed on 27 June 1943 and served until the end of hostilities. Rex Fendick wrote that his CO was; 'slightly reserved, not outgoing, somewhat inarticulate, very thoughtful and considerate of his men, highly efficient and professional, firm, fair, respected and admired by all ranks. Trained by the RAF pre-war, he wore pilot's wings. Later he became the Brigadier of a British/ Dutch/Indian brigade in the FE, and post war commanded the Land/AirWarfare School at Old Sarum. He retired as Maj Gen, Director of Land Air Warfare in the War Office'. Fendick wrote:

> As I mentioned, I am learning (from reading draft chapters of this book) a great deal which I never knew from my worm's eye view with a platoon, although my function did frequently get me into the Battalion CO's level and occasionally Brigade, and my Coy commander was always at Brigade level and our CO with the GOC, and as they visited frequently, we probably had a better overview than many in the Rifle battalions. When we were Under Command of a battalion, we could be considered as in the same position as a platoon of that battalion's Support Company. Indeed, frequently the CO would place us under command of his Support Company OC, rather than have another support arm to bother with directly. During OP GOODWOOD, I was placed under the wing of one of the forward rifle companies of the Ulsters. Those grouping and command decisions depended to a great extent on the training, experience and personality of the individual CO. Some used us very effectively, and some didn't appear to know how. I suspect the same applied at times and in varying degrees, to their use of armour and artillery and even at times their own Support Company weapons.[17]

3 Reconnaissance Regiment, RAC, was formed from 8 Royal Northumberland Fusiliers, which had been the Motor Cycle battalion of V Foot – The Fighting Fifth after Wellington had called them 'the ever fighting, often tried, but never failing Fifth' – from Newcastle-on-Tyne. It was commanded by Lt-Col H.H. Merriman DSO, MC.

CRA (Commander Royal Artillery) was Brigadier Gerald G. Mears, CBE, DSO, MC, who was highly regarded by Whistler. In 1961 he became Admiral of the Royal Artillery Yacht Club in BAOR. He commanded 72 units of 25pdr gun-howitzers in three regiments.

7 Field Regiment RA, comprising 9/17, 16 and 43 Batteries under Lt-Col H.C. Bazely, DSO, was in support of 185 Bde. Bazely was appointed on New Year's Day, 1945 and came from the division's 92 LAA Regiment, RA.

17 Rex Fendick in an e-mail.

33 Field Regiment RA, made up of 101, 109 and 113/114 Batteries, supported 9 Bde and was commanded by Lt-Col M.W. Hope DSO.

76 Highland Field Regiment RA from Dundee, made up of 302, 303 and 454 Batteries, was in support of 8 Brigade. The CO was Lt-Col Mervyn Foster.

20 Anti-Tank Regiment RA under Lt-Col G.B. Thatcher, DSO.

92 Light Anti-Aircraft Regiment RA, which originated from 7 Battalion The Loyal Regiment, XLVII and LXXXI Foot from Preston, under Lt Col Peter R. Henderson RA. He was appointed on New Year's Day, 1945 from 97 Anti-Tank Regiment.

CRE (Commander Royal Engineers) was Lt-Col T. (Tom) H. Evill, DSO, commanding 17 Fld Coy (supporting 8 BIB), 246 Fld Coy (185 BIB) 253 Fld Coy (9 BIB), 15 Fld Park Coy, and 2 Bridging Pln.

CRS (Commander Royal Signals) was Lt-Col G.D.T. Harris. The HQ's tac sign was a red 40 on a white over blue ground. All others adopted the serial number of the unit to which they were attached, painting it in red over the signals' colours. There were also brigade Signals' Companies with the Brigade tac sign in Signals colours.

CRASC (Commander Royal Army Service Corps) was Lt-Col A.K.Yapp. There were three brigade companies and one divisional company. Their tac signs had a diagonal red over green ground, with HQ numbered 40 and the companies numbered 70, 71, 73, and 72 respectively.

CRAMC (Commander Royal Army Medical Corps) was Lt-Col Hugh O. Hinton, OBE. They were divided into three field ambulances, two field-dressing stations and a hygiene section. Their tac signs had a black ground, and the units were numbered 75, 76, 77, 82, 83, and 78 respectively. There were in addition 24 medics in each battalion headed by the battalion doctor, who was on the staff of brigade. The doctor had a medical sergeant, Jack Linley MM in the case of 2 Lincolns who had 2 Corporal stretcher bearers. Each of the five companies had a team of 4 private stretcher bearers who collected the wounded and took them to the doctor's team at the RAP, which was always in a building as tents were a nuisance and unsafe during shelling. The stretcher bearers could administer a quarter grain of morphine to take away the pain and to counter shock, writing on the forehead of the wounded man in indelible pencil 'M' with the time and the date. Neglecting to do that would risk the man getting a lethal second dose, which killed Capt Tony Mander. The job of the RAP was to stop the bleeding and dress the wound so the man could be carried back on a Jeep fitted with stretchers on a rack to the ADS run by the Field Ambulance where surgery was performed if necessary. Medical sergeants indented for supplies from the ADS.[18] In Winnekendonk a German doctor was pressed into service at the RAP in the cellar of Plockhorsthof because of the overwhelming number of wounded.

CREME (Commander Royal Electrical & Mechanical Engineers) was Lt-Col EHW Biggs, whose tac sign was a white 40 on a blue over yellow over red ground. They were organised into three infantry brigade workshops, whose tac signs were numbered 88, 89 and 90 on their colours. In addition, the HQs of division and brigades, as well as the field regiments, the anti-tank regiment,

18 Medical Sgt Doug Knight of the Hastings & Prince Edward Regt in conversation in 1994.

the LAA regiment, the divisional signals and the machine gun battalion, all had light aid detachments displaying the unit's number on the REME colours.

CRAOC (Commander Royal Army Ordnance Corps) was Col W. Hamilton, OBE, whose tac sign was a white 40 on a vertical blue/red/blue ground. There was one ordnance field park, whose tac sign was a white 92. In addition, RAOC stores carrying sections were attached to the infantry battalion workshops, and known as 'Spare Parts Stores Sections'. Their tac sign was the same as the unit number over the RAOC colours. The RAOC also provided a Mobile Laundry and Bath Unit, whose tac sign was the number 52 on the RAOC colours.

Specialist troops played an important role in this story. They were mostly Army Troops assigned to corps and to division as needed. In support of 3 BID for Operation *Heather* were: A Troop 356 AA SL Battery RA, responsible for providing Monty's Moonlight; a Detachment from 4 Survey Regiment RA; and a Section from B Flight, 662 Squadron, 83 Group RAF as an Air Observation Post. Other units are referred to in the tables operating equipment such as Kangaroo Armoured Personal Carriers (APCs) and Crocodile flame-throwers in 79 BAD. Also supplied by Army were 6 Independent Guards Armoured Brigade with Churchill Infantry Tanks, the Army Groups Royal Artillery (AGRAs) with medium and heavy guns, and Typhoon and Spitfire support tasked by Army.

It was the task of the division to do the dangerous work. This required the appropriate equipment and skill in its use. But success depended also on the establishment and maintenance of a social organisation that could command men's obedience, and this is the subject covered here. It needed personal leadership by officers and NCOs, which was reinforced by the motive of helping your mates. Backing this up was the sanction of military law and, whenever necessary, the exercise of brute force to rally the wavering.

The thirty-six rifle companies of the nine infantry battalions supplied the cutting edge equipped with rifles, Brens, mortars and PIATs – Table 1. In addition, each battalion had its own support company with larger mortars, 6pdr anti-tank guns and carriers. The carrier platoon was a sub-unit of the battalion's support company armed with Bren LMGs, for reconnaissance, and for holding and protecting flanks. Division provided additional support with artillery, heavy mortars, medium machine guns, large anti-tank guns, and anti-aircraft guns – Table 2. Additional support came from corps and army as required; a brigade of Churchill Infantry tanks, Funnies from 79 BAD including APCs, flamethrowers, bridgelayers, fascine and flail tanks, a battery of M10 3-inch anti-tank guns, artillery of three additional divisions, two medium regiments, an AGRA, a battery of searchlights for Monty's Moonlight and an Auster artillery spotting aircraft– Table 2.

Table 1 3 BID's Organic Weapons

Bn Rifle Coys	Offrs	Men	All Ranks	Rifles	Bren	2-in mortar	PIAT
Section		10	10	9	1		
Platoon	1	36	37	32	3	1	
Company	5	122	127	107	9	3	3
Battalion	20	488	508	428	36	12	12
3 BID	180	4,392	4,572	3,852	324	108	108

Battalion Support Companies	3-in mortars	6pdr anti-tank guns	Carriers
Battalion	6	6	13
3 BID	54	54	117

3 BID – Under command	Rifle Coys	Others	Total 3 BID
Men – all ranks	4,572	13,775	18,347
Rifles & pistols	4,572	7,693	12,265
Bren Light MGs	324	938	1,262
Mortars, 2 &3 & 4.2 inch	162	197	359
Vickers Medium MGs		36	36
PIATS	108	328	436
25pdr Gun-Hows		72	72
6 & 17pdrs Atk	54	32	86
20 & 40 mm AA		125	125
Archer & M10 17pdr SPs		24	24
M4 Sherman tank FOO		9	9
Carriers	130	465	595
Armoured cars		63	63
Trucks & lorries	Na		1,937

Table 2 Additional Weapons in Support of 3 BID

In support of 3 BID	All ranks	Equipment type	Number
6 Guards Armoured Brigade	3,400	Churchill Infantry tanks	147
		Stuart Recce tanks	18
'B' Sqn 1 Lothian &Border Horse	210	Sherman 'Crabs'	17
'C' Sqn 141 Regiment RAC	210	Churchill Crocodiles	13
'A' Sqn 49 APC Regiment	210	Ram Kangaroo APCs	53
284 Assault Sqn RE, less 1 troop	140	Churchill AVRE fascine	12
82 Assault Sqn RE – part	30	Churchill bridgelayer	3
198 Anti-Tank SP Battery	176	M10 SP 3-inch guns	12
A Troop 356 AA Searchlight Bty	70	Searchlights	3
Section, 'B' Flight, 662 Sqn RAF	10	Auster aircraft	1
RA Guards Armoured Division	1,187	25pdrs	48
RA 15 BID	1,780	25pdrs	72
RA 53 BID	1,780	25pdrs	72
72 Medium Regiment RA	586	5.5 inch howitzers	16
79 Medium Regiment RA	586	5.5 inch howitzers	16
5 AGRA	4,400	5.5 inch howitzers	32
		7.2 inch howitzers	8
		155 mm howitzers	8
Total	14,775		551

Altogether, 3 BID's establishment of 18,347 men was supported by 14,775 others for a combined total of 33,122 men committed to *Heather*. It was a powerful force.

3 BID was formed on 18 June 1809 in Portugal when Wellington grouped brigades following French practice and Cathcart's experience in Denmark in 1807. The benefit of the divisional structure was a reduction of Wellington's 'span of command' – allowing him effective control of a greater number of troops – while giving brigades permanent supporting services and staff, who could train together into a self-contained divisional team.

On 22 February 1810, after being commanded by Mackenzie who was killed within a month, and by 'Black Bob' Crawfurd who was transferred to the Light Division, 3 BID received its first commander of renown in Lt-Gen (later Sir) Thomas Picton. He had joined the XII Foot, subsequently the Suffolks, at the age of 13, and was 51 years old when he took command until the end of the war in 1814. 3 BID earned its title of 'The Fighting Division' under Picton in three great Peninsular battles. Bussaco showed steadiness and initiative; Badajoz, bravery and determination; while at Salamanca, swiftness and flexibility gained the victory. All three victories were due to the courage, skill and energy of Picton. In the three engagements within a great battle examined in this book, the same attributes recur; steadiness and initiative at Yorkshire Bridge when it held against heavy German attack as it had withstood Heudelet, Merle and Foy under Massena; bravery and determination at the storming of Kervenheim when it was ambushed but doggedly recovered, winning a VC with as much determination as it had shown performing the impossible with great loss to take the Moorish Castle in Badajoz; and swiftness with flexibility at Winnekendonk when, with the support of RF Scots Guards in their Churchills, the overwhelming German defensive advantage was flung back in the enemy's face with almost the same contemptuous ease as that with which Wallace's, Campbell's and Champalimaud's brigades had deployed into line on the move at Salamanca and scattered Thomiere's division, killing half the Frenchmen and capturing all their guns. Bolo Whistler was a worthy successor to Thomas Picton in courage, skill and energy. At Waterloo, 3 BID was commanded by Sir Charles Alten and held the Sunken Road and the farm of La Haye Sainte in the centre of the line.

During lengthy periods in the 19th century 3 BID stood down, but on being reformed the same character reappeared. The name 'The Fighting Division' mutated during the First World War into 'The Iron Division' under Aylmer Haldane, whose tirelessness and resolution in providing for the troops were combined with tactical skill to produce a formation that was regarded as the ultimate in reliability. The Germans knew it too, and Haldane recounts that on more than one occasion were heard shouting: 'When the 3rd Division leave we will retake the trenches.[19]

The Division showed its skill by turning the Germans out of their defences on the Somme between Longueval and Bazentin Le Grand at first light on 14 July 1916 in a spectacularly successful exploit involving the move of 22,000 troops at night through Caterpillar Wood to within 250 yards of the enemy. It was achieved over the objections of Haig himself. After only a brief bombardment lasting five minutes, 3 BID broke through the German defences. but were forbidden from following through to High Wood by Rawlinson, who told them exploitation was the job of the Deccan Horse. The cavalry failed to arrive until the evening, by which time the Germans had organised a second line of defence. We will see below that 3 BID knew not to repeat that same mistake on 3 March 1945. In 1917, 3 BID took part in the First battle of the Scarpe outside Arras and defended the same area in 1918 when Ludendorff's offensive was stopped by 3, 4, 15 and 56 BIDs, leaving the way open for Monash and Currie to finalise their war-winning innovations with all arms including tanks.

19 Robin McNish. *Iron Division* (Shepperton: Ian Allan, 1978), p. 57.

In 1937 Brigadier B. L. Montgomery commanded 9 BIB in 3 BID at Portsmouth and trained it hard for real war including a landing from the sea. Soon after taking command his beloved wife died from an insect bite and he found his loss impossible to accept. He left for Palestine but returned in 1939 to command the Division in an army that had forgotten most of what it had taught the world in 1918 under Monash. McNish recounts how 2 Lincolns of 9 BIB laid on with great effort an isolated demonstration of tank-infantry co-operation at Bovington in early 1939 to the surprise and incredulity of spectators. Montgomery commented in his memoirs that in 1939, 'the British Army was totally unfit to fight a first class war on the continent of Europe'.

During the Phoney War in France around Lille, Montgomery trained the Division in the difficult exercise of a fighting withdrawal and how to dominate the battlefield. The Division returned through Dunkirk in good heart and confident in its professionalism. Only Montgomery's Wattrelos 'raid' on 24 May 1940 struck a discordant note and provided a worrying omen for the future.

Those who had done well in the retreat to Dunkirk received promotion: Horrocks, CO of 2 Middlesex, got 9 BIB; Montgomery himself was soon appointed to 5 Corps; and Alan Brooke, GOC 2 Corps began his meteoric rise to CIGS. Others were earmarked for later promotion, including Renny of the KOSB and Whistler.

3 BIB continued to pride itself on reliability and steadiness in battle.[20] On 10 June the Division was re-equipped and ordered back to France, but after the French capitulation it dug in on the Sussex coast and awaited the Germans. On 22 July Montgomery departed and under Maj-Gen J.A.H. Gammell 3 BID was relieved on the coast by a TA Division and moved back to Gloucestershire. There it became the army's mobile reserve. In the autumn it moved to the southwest where it remained until early summer 1941 when it switched to Buckinghamshire. In September 1940, 7 GIB was removed to form GAD to be replaced briefly by 37 BIB and from December 1941 to June 1942 by 7 BIB. In June 1942, 3 BID was converted to a mixed division, exchanging 33 BTB for 7 BIB. Gammell was replaced on 15 December 1942 by Maj-Gen W.H.C. Ramsden CBE, DSO, MC who until July 1942 had commanded 50 BID with distinction in the desert. In April 1943, 3 BID converted back to its traditional role as an infantry division, receiving 185 BIB and losing its tanks.

The Division had been selected for the July 1943 landings in Sicily, but at the last minute 1 CID was substituted. Ramsden used the disappointment to get a promise from the CIGS that 3 BID would be the Assault Division for Normandy. From that point on the division's training was focused on Exercise Overlord. At the Divisional Battle School at Moffatt in the Lowther Hills and at the Combined Training Centre at Inverary on the west coast of Scotland, the Division trained in extreme weather conditions and in the large Atlantic swell, becoming extremely fit. Others said, unkindly, that they also became over trained and stale, pointing to an inability to take Caen on D-Day.

27 BAB (13/18 Hussars with DD Shermans, 1 East Riding Yeomanry and the Staffordshire Yeomanry) became associated with 3 BID on 20 October 1943. In December Montgomery was recalled to command 21 AG, and Maj-General Tom Rennie, DSO, MBE was appointed GOC. He had been captured with 51 BID at St Valéry en Caux in June 1940 but escaped within ten days. He won the DSO commanding a battalion of the Black Watch at El Alamein, and in December 1942 was promoted Brigadier of 154 BIB in 51 BID. He was wounded on 7 January 1943, returned to service on 13 May 1943 and came straight to 3 BID.

The criticism of the performance of 3 BID made by Chester Wilmot and David Belchem that the leadership of Rennie and the brigadiers was too conservative, and that having disembarked the Division failed to show any drive, have been answered in detail by Carlo D'Este in *Decision in Normandy*. The problem, as ever in the Second World War, was poor tank-infantry co-operation and indeed the absence of the armoured brigades at the crucial time. Without them it would have

20 Scarfe, *Assault Division*, p. 17.

been folly to advance into Caen, even had it not been occupied by 21 PD. The 27 BAB played no major role in the attempt to capture Caen, and then spent weeks holding ground.

3 BID attacked Troarn on the left flank during Operation *Goodwood*, and then switched to the extreme right flank alongside the Americans during the attacks on Vire in August when the breakout occurred.

In September 1944, 3 BID cleared the right flank of the corridor, formed by 82 and 101 US Airborne Divisions, up which XXX Corps was attempting to reach Arnhem. It was briefly earmarked for the prospective Reichswald attack in Operation *Gatwick*. It was next involved in heavy fighting for Venraij as the west bank of the Maas was cleared. In this battle it was supported by 6 GTB and together they succeeded where 7 USAD had failed. The rest of the winter was spent on the Maas. February 1945 found it in good heart, very experienced, up to strength and still led by Whistler, who was held in awe.

Maj-Gen Whistler, Lashmer to his wife but 'Bolo' to everyone else after his experience with Bolsheviks or Bolos in Russia, was described by Montgomery with his usual brutal frankness and inconsistency as

> the very finest type of British soldier, but he always gave me the impression that he lacked a strategic sense. Strategy is the art of the conduct of war; tactics are the art of fighting in battle, and here Bolo was superb up to and including a divisional command. If the war had continued longer he might well have become a corps commander.[21]

Montgomery referred to Whistler's ability to fight the Division as an integrated whole instead of treating it as a collection of brigades each to be engaged separately. This is also the point emphasised by Norman Scarfe:

> Bolo Whistler had been commander of the Infantry Brigade of 7 Armoured Division in the desert, and Monty knew he wouldn't hang about. Monty set store by *Divisional* battles. My feeling now, looking back to 3 Div on D Day, is that we still on D Day tended to think and fight as part infantry brigade or brigade group, more than anything bigger. I think Bolo did much to alter that… Bolo wasn't at all an intellectual soldier but very strong on leadership and human relations.[22]

He was in fact another Horrocks, which Montgomery obviously recognised. Smyth in his biography praises Bolo for his warm humanity, humility, gaiety of spirit, charm and boundless courage, which added up to being a great leader. He was also a strict disciplinarian.

Reaching the military age of 18 in 1917, Whistler was captured very soon after reaching the front and spent the remainder of the war in a German PW camp. He joined the Archangel expedition of 1919. On his return he received the name Bolo because he talked incessantly about Bolsheviks or 'Bolos'. He served in the Royal Sussex (XXXV Foot) and in 1940 commanded its 4 TA Battalion in France in 44 TA Division, winning the DSO. In 1942 the Bn went to North Africa where he was promoted Brig first of 132 BIB and then of 13 BIB in 7 BAD under John Harding and Bobbie Erskine. Here he came to the attention of Leese and Montgomery, who thought him, probably the finest fighting Brigadier in the British Army at the time. Bolo adopted Montgomery's habit of housing his personal HQ in a caravan. He stayed with Montgomery during the preparation for the Gabes Gap battle and was in Horrocks' XXX Corps until the Germans capitulated in North

21 John Smyth. *Bolo Whistler* (London: Frederick Muller, 1967), Montgomery's foreword.
22 Letter from Norman Scarfe in 1984.

Africa. His commanding officer, Bobbie Erskine, gave Whistler a glowing confidential report in 29 May 1943, although training was never Whistler's strength:

> This officer has great personality and drive which is combined with a very sound professional military knowledge. He has proved himself on the battlefield a cool and courageous leader. Always in the right places, always ready to take responsibility and give a decision. A capable organiser and trainer. He immediately secures the respect and co-operation of other arms working with him. Has the temperament and ability to command a division.[23]

In June 1943, Whistler recorded in his diary; 'Have been recommended for command of a division but think personally a brigade is about my ceiling.'[24]

Bolo always regretted failing to qualify for Staff College. He fought at Salerno and on the Volturno and was transferred back to the UK with two bars to his DSO in November 1943. He went temporarily to the inexperienced 160 BIB in 53 BID under Ross to pass on his knowledge after Montgomery had announced publicly that he would get a division. His chance came on 12 June 1944 when Rennie was blown up in his Jeep on a British mine near Cambes. Since it was first thought that the wounds were not severe, Brigadier Cass of 8 BIB took over the Division, but on 23 June Rennie was evacuated to hospital in England, and Whistler took command. He was forty-five years old and thirty-fourth in command of 3 BID since Mackenzie first commanded in 1809, and as great in his way as Mackenzie at getting his command to perform.

In the last two months of 1944 all three brigade commanders changed amid some friction. The change in command of 8 BIB went smoothly on 27 October 1944 from Copper Cass to Eddie Goulburn for the duration. In 9 BIB the changes occurred amid a minor earthquake at the end of the year when Douglas Renny replaced Dominic Browne on New Years Day, while at 185 BIB the changes took over a month to be implemented after Eric Bols was promoted GOC 6 Airborne on 8 December 1944. The replacement was E.H.G. Grant until 15 January when there was a hiatus filled by Gibbs and Barclay until Mark Matthews took over on 20 January 1945.

Eddie Goulburn of 8 BIB was a 'courteous, laid-back guardsman", according to Eddie Jones of the South Lancs.[25] Norman Scarfe wrote:

> The only Brigadier I, a subaltern, got to know at all (as distinct from listening to them at O groups) was Eddie Goulburn, who took over 8 Brigade when Copper Cass was injured on a mine out pheasant shooting! Eddie had done very well as a Grenadier CO (1 Grenadier Guards), arranging a brilliant attack that secured Nijmegen Bridge intact. Like Bolo he had a good sense of humour and of human relations – though I'm not sure how far his being a Grenadier put off some of the County Regiment chaps. He was very brave, and a lot friendlier than Copper Cass, who seemed bad tempered. Eddie advanced on Bremen with a 12-bore![26]

Both Cass and Goulburn were well regarded by those they commanded, but Whistler's good opinion of Goulburn deteriorated with knowledge, and on 17 April 1945 wrote in his Diary:

23 Whistler Papers (Chichester West Sussex Record Office).
24 Ibid.
25 Letter from Eddie Jones in 2000.
26 Letter from Norman Scarfe in 1984.

> SL [South Lancashire] who are a bit down were put in by Eddy [sic], who must have been quite mad to do so. However it worked out & I relieved them as soon as possible. I think Eddy is pretty stupid one way and another.[27]

9 BIB had been commanded by Montgomery in 1937 and by Horrocks in 1940. Both retained a personal interest in it which, in Montgomery's case, later turned to interference. On D-Day it was commanded by Jim Cunningham, who was injured on the beach within minutes of landing, ending the confusion to all including the Germans of both a Canadian and a British 9 Brigade in a 3 Division commanded by a Cunningham. A.D.G. Orr, who had been Brigade 2ic, took command until he was sacked in tears, it is said, for refusing to carry out Whistler's orders in Normandy after judging them too risky. On 6 August, Dominic Browne was sent from Division and by 17 August Whistler declared him a success. At the end of the year Browne was promoted and left on 1 January 1945. Montgomery told Whistler that G. Douglas Renny would replace him. Whistler refused to take him, and on 8 January 1945 wrote these words in his diary. This author's comments as always are in square brackets.

> Got myself into quite serious trouble the other day by refusing a Brig. The Great Little Man's [Montgomery's] own selection but I knew him and did not approve. Lost heavily for the moment & was told to accept him or go. Rather fancy should have gone but that would have left the Div with the chap on their hands and no prospect of clearing him. Anyway here I am with that trouble ahead & I must do the right thing by him & the Div. Lost Browne into the bargain who, if not brilliant, was at least adequate & a man. This chap is neither – or at least that is how I feel at the moment. It will be very difficult to be fair to him at the Div & I expect I will get chucked out for it in the end. By being chucked out one has a black on the Div which I don't want to happen. Anyway I feel that Brigs should not be sent if Div comdr definitely does not want them & I have said no. Not with much success but a registration of my opinion. Always prepared to take a Brig if nothing known of him naturally. The other one in replacement of Eric Bols is a dismal Scot who is slightly deaf, stutters but is really quite a good chap [E.H.G. Grant]. Adequate? He [Renny] is a personal selection of Army Commander which makes things as awkward as possible too! Yes I feel the bowler dangling near. A pity as I would like to remain a Maj Gen and get E her K! ['E' was Whistler's wife, Esmé. The 'K' was the KBE, Knighthood of the British Empire.] Always said I would but never believed it nor do I now. What a start to a New Year! I am now a real Lt Col [promoted from substantive Major] anyway – they cannot take that from me. I am very well – very cheerful & very obstinate. Stubborn is a nice word I think. Snow covers the ground & the roads are iced over. Damn cold too.[28]

The cause of this outburst was Douglas Renny, a 35 year old regular KOSB officer and the son of Lt-Col S.G. Renny. He attended Sandhurst and spent some time in India. On 14 July 1937 when serving in 1 KOSB in this same 9 BIB and stationed in Portsmouth, he married the debutante Margot Wortham. His Brigadier was Montgomery who was obviously impressed with the young officer. Margot remembers 1937 as having been a wonderful time in Portsmouth. Her brother-in-law was serving in the battleship HMS *Nelson*, and the young marrieds had the pick of naval and army entertaining.[29] Late in 1937, Renny sat the Staff College examination and received high placing,

27 Whistler Papers (Chichester: West Sussex Record Office).
28 Whistler Papers (Chichester: West Sussex Record Office).
29 Letter from Margot Renny on 15 January 1995.

passing tenth in a group that included Capt Belchem, RTR. He attended Staff College, Camberley in 1938 and after receiving his *p.s.c.* was promoted Lt-Col and commanded the 5/7 Gordons in 153 BIB, 51 BID. He succeeded in getting his people away to England when the rest went into Rommel's bag at St Valéry. He was appointed GSO 2 in XI Corps and subsequently commanded 1 KOSB, being wounded in the arm by shrapnel at Troarn. When sufficiently recovered he again commanded 5/7 Gordons in 153 BIB and in late October 1944 was engaged in heavy fighting at Wybosch. From there he moved to command 9 BIB. It would be difficult to find a better combination of intellectual attainment and practical fighting experience. Whistler never explained his reasons for rejecting Renny, and it is almost certain that the CO of 2 Lincolns, Cecil Firbank, was behind it. Even in 1983, Cecil spoke disparagingly of him as someone who had, 'shone in front of Monty at a map table but didn't know how to fight a battle.'[30] The charge was preposterous, but Firbank believed it and claimed that he had also worked to get Renny removed. Francis Plaistowe served at Brigade under Renny's predecessor, Dominick Browne, and said that Firbank's dislike of Renny was common knowledge, and that Firbank, 'hated people in the rear areas, even as close as Bde HQ!!!'[31] Dislike of staff officers was a commonplace in both world wars amongst fighting officers, who referred to them as 'the gabardine swine', or worse; in Egypt those living 'up the blue' would refer to those in Cairo as 'Groppi's Light Horse, and 'The Short-Range Shepheard's Group', named for Cairo's world-famous restaurant and hotel. Firbank virtually admitted the fact in writing:

> General Bolo had some very good Brigadiers and some not so good. He also knew his Battalion commanders well and took their advice on some matters of detail when necessary. He was a very human man and had the 'feel' of his command and was very sympathetic to atmosphere.[32]

It would therefore appear that Bolo in making his stand against Renny was supporting Firbank. Bolo would have seen it, and correctly so, as his duty to support Firbank who personally faced the dangers of the battlefield and was an effective battalion commander who could deliver success. Subsequently, and this was forty years after the event, Firbank seemed to re-evaluate his attitude by advising himself, perhaps since he had become one and later a major-general, against being too hard on Brigadiers. Brigadiers, said Cecil, 'tried very hard, but it wasn't always easy.'[33]

After Renny's great success at Winnekendonk, Whistler, if not Firbank, had the grace to upgrade his opinion of Renny to 'outstanding':

> I would say that 9 Bde has done best under Renny who I did not like. 185 next under Mark Matthews & 8 who used to be the best have not had so much luck though E Yorks had one terrific night holding a bridgehead against repeated counter-attacks. John Mc still trying to do everything with less success than usual. Thus outstanding characters Quacky (Mears?) – Freddie (Mellor) – Cecil (Firbank) – Douglas Renny. Gave Mark Matthews and Douglas Renny each a bottle of champagne for their work today.[34]

It is not recorded whether Whistler ever mentioned his new opinion of Renny to Montgomery. The widowed Margot Renny[35] believed the trouble was due to the perception that Douglas was

30 Cecil Firbank in conversation in 1983.
31 Francis Plaistowe in conversation.
32 Letter from Cecil Firbank in 1984.
33 Ibid.
34 Whistler Diary, West Sussex Record Office, entry for 4 March 1945.
35 Margot Renny in conversation in 1994.

'too clever by half'. Leslie Colvin, Firbank's fiercely loyal 2ic, when asked what was wrong with Douglas Renny replied that he was disliked for being churlish.[36] Firbank's intransigence towards Renny was no doubt fuelled both by knowledge that he was better qualified than Renny for appointment to brigadier, which was proved later when Cecil reached Maj Gen, and by his wife's leaving him, eventually divorcing in 1952.[37]

This episode demonstrated three things; the close-knit tribal relationships and rivalry within 3 BID that provided the primary source of its cohesion and fighting-power, but could always slip into parochialism; the individual influence of successful battalion COs who carried the burden; and the small-mindedness and waning influence of the eccentric Montgomery in pushing his protégés. What, after all, was a Field Marshal doing arguing with a divisional commander, and threatening him with the sack about who should be one of his brigadiers, especially as Montgomery was notorious for surrounding himself with people he felt comfortable with and yet objected to Whistler doing the same. Montgomery's attitude was never better revealed, showing he could not let go of minor detail nor resist interfering. There were great tensions, especially between the infantry and the armour that Montgomery did nothing about, and would not solve by wearing an RTR black beret – a subject examined in Chapter 10. Margot Renny knew little of what her husband did, but will always remember Douglas hated the tanks.[38]

Renny was never promoted beyond brigadier, which ceased to be an appointment and became a substantive rank in 1946, although still only of field officer rank when other armies ranked it as a general officer. Post-war he remained in Germany as Col Hamburg District and then took various commands in Britain and at the War Office from 1956-59, when he retired.

Mark Matthews was appointed to command 185 BIB on January 20, 1945. Why Whistler called him 'Mark' when he was christened Francis Raymond Gage is unknown. Aged 42, he was a South Wales Borderer and staff officer who became Director of Military Training for the Middle East in 1943. In May 1944 he was appointed Brigadier of 168 BIB in 56 BID briefly under Gerald Templer and then John Whitfield until October 1944 when he moved to command 13 BIB in Palestine, but for only a month. His expertise was troop training, and this might be the reason Montgomery agreed to his appointment. He did not impress the COs. His predecessor, Eric Bols, had gone to command 6 Airborne Division on 8 December and for six weeks there had been no permanent replacement. In wartime that must have been unusual. Both Gibbs of 2 Warwicks and Barclay of 1 Norfolks had been acting Brigadier, and probably felt better qualified than the new arrival, as no doubt Firbank did with regard to Renny. Humphrey Wilson, 2ic 1 R Norfolks, stated that none of the COs took much notice of Matthews; 'If at an O gp they were unhappy with Matthews' plan, they would meet outside and simply agree on another one more to their liking.'[39]

Peter Barclay gave an example of why Brig Matthews was disliked:

> A series of sticky and not so sticky battles followed until Kervenheim which was a sod. The tenacious defence, because it was a German pivot position held by grounded parachutists, took us a whole day to overcome. The following day my Brigadier, regrettably another futile operator, sent for me to go back to his HQ. My remonstration that I could not leave my forward position was dismissed. 'I want you to capture the next village (Kapellen) tomorrow morning. After breakfast will do.' I explained that were he to come forward and look for himself he would see that it was as flat as a pancake and bare as a baby's bottom, but that

36 Leslie Colvin in conversation in 1994.
37 http://www.thepeerage.com/p44894.htm
38 Margot Renny in conversation in 1994.
39 Humphrey Wilson in conversation in 1984.

> instead I would get round it and cut it off that night. In my hearing he then got onto the Divisional Commander. 'I've got a marvellous idea, General, I'm sending Peter Barclay round to our next objective to cut it off tonight'.[40]

Matthews contravened Montgomery's rule, insisted on even with Ike, that the senior commander goes forward rather than the junior one going back. However Eddie Jones stated that Copper Cass called his COs back for orders, so the rule was not hard and fast in 3 BID.

Barclay now took a firm line with Matthews about a night attack after being denied one at Kervenheim. Matthews saw the way the wind was blowing and let it fill his sails with Bolo, who didn't always see through this and blew hot and cold about Matthews. On 17 April 1945 he wrote in his diary that, 'Mark Matthews may be tiresome but he is good,'[41] but was soon recording on 4 June that:

> Mark Matthews is going soon. I am not sorry. I have a new car & so am happy.
>
> 28 June 1945: Mark M has gone and a good thing too. Mark is making his name & is full out for promotion which I think he will get before long. Hope I don't serve near him then![42]

Bolo did not serve near him and Mattthews was soon a Maj General. In 1946 he was Commandant of the RMA, Sandhurst, in 1948 GOC British Forces, Hong Kong, in 1950 GOC 1 BID, and in 1952 Director of Infantry before retiring.

Senior commanders in 21AG appeared to have been promoted either for their fighting qualities or because they were Montgomery's protégés, rather than for their intellectual attainment. It was observed that a fighting man cannot make a good general:

> We British persist in making Generals out of the wrong kind of man. Our idea of the kind of man who makes a good General is a brave, bull-necked, red-faced roarer, who will stand no damned nonsense from anybody and who may be relied upon to see that discipline is rigorously maintained. That type makes the ideal battalion commander: a man who can show his men how to fight and who will *make* them fight. Such men make perfect Colonels, and it is the Colonels who win battles. We waste our valuable Colonels. When they win their fights we turn them into Generals. We think that because they can fight a battle they can plan a battle, whereas the natural-born fighter never was a thinker and never will be. When the fighter begins to think, he ruins himself as a fighter.
>
> It became clear to me that the one thing a General must not be is a fighter. A General must be a thinker with an artistic temperament and a sensitive imagination, which makes him shudder at the thought of personal combat. A good General is the kind of man who makes the worst kind of Colonel. This is not to say he must be a coward; but physical bravery is not important if one possesses spiritual courage and daring of mind.
>
> Our nation is prolific in Colonels. They naturally despise the artist-thinker type, and savage that sort of man to death, professionally, at sight. Hence the lack of genius in our High Command.[43]

40 Unpublished memoirs of Lt-Col S.P. Barclay DSO, MC, provided by John Lincoln.
41 Whistler Diary, West Sussex Record Office.
42 Ibid.
43 Weston Martyr. *The Wandering Years* (Edinburgh: Blackwood, 1940), p. 194.

In all human endeavour there is a conflicting choice between the leader who is followed out of respect for a powerful and charming personality, and the man of intelligence who can assimilate knowledge and reason to a right answer, even if he is not persuasive when explaining it. Montgomery had no time for the latter according to Nigel Hamilton, holding that, 'character is more important than knowledge. Eisenhower lacks character. He, and the American nation, do not understand that character is more important than knowledge'. The result was that 'fighting men' were in all the important positions. Both Horrocks and Whistler were intellectually limited and knew it, while Montgomery was but didn't know it – see Chapter 10.

On 7 April 1945 Whistler noted in his diary that he had fallen out with 'Jorrocks', 'Jock' or 'J' as Horrocks was called:

> Bellyaching from my boss (J). 1. That a certain bridge that we held was not held. 2. That the bridge Recce got they hadn't really got. Expressed my displeasure at the 'belly aching'. Moving to Neil Ritchie [GOC XII Corps] immediately. I am not sorry. J has little ideas really on managing a battle – what can and cannot be done etc. Very brilliant when things go well but depressing to all when not so well.[44]

3 BID remained, however, in XXX Corps. On 17 April Whistler reverted to the subject of Horrocks with yet another example of Montgomery's interfering, this time countermanding Horrocks's orders although apparently retaining confidence in him:

> Well having been left to J I was given the job of capturing a place called DELMENHORST – just in front of BREMEN all by myself with both flanks quite open – 30,000* (yd) front and about 100,000 sq. yds. of ground to clear. I presumed to say it was a bit much. I was told to get on with it. So I did so. Slowly J came round to my way of thinking aided by a slight lecture from Monty I fancy. Monty had been to see me & I had explained my task to which he had said "Nonsense". Now the job is perfectly possible.[45]

Horrocks gave his side of the story, in ignorance of Montgomery's previous discussion with Whistler:

> Bremen was on my plate. The more I studied the problem the less I liked it; without going into technical details, we were not properly balanced [classic Montgomery-speak] for this task. While I was thinking it over, the telephone rang and a Staff Officer from Twenty-First Army Group said that the Field-Marshal was on his way down to see me. A few minutes later he entered my caravan and said, 'Jorrocks, I am not happy about Bremen'. 'Nor am I, Sir', I replied. 'Tell me about it', he said. So, sitting in the map lorry I described the problem to him and made certain suggestions. He said not a word until I had finished. After a short pause, while he considered the problem on the map, he said, 'We will do A,B,C and D.' These four decisions were vital – and Bremen was finished'. I have deliberately mentioned this because it was typical. Montgomery was not my immediate Commander, but he always kept in such close touch with the battle that he knew when and where 'the shoe pinched'. He then went down to see the Commander on the spot – in this case, me – and listened to what he had to say. He then made up his mind immediately.[46]

44 Whistler Diary, West Sussex Record Office.
45 Ibid.
46 Brian Horrocks. *Corps Commander* (New York: Scribners, 1977), p. 216.

Horrocks may have been the nominal 'Commander on the spot', but these extracts show it was not he commanding but Whistler, and with less information. Montgomery would already have made up his mind before marching alone into Horrocks' caravan without Dempsey, Horrocks' commander, and pretending to think about the problem. Both accounts agree, and show objectively that Horrocks was out of his depth whenever it came to analysis. There was a postscript to the Battle of Bremen showing that Horrocks actually knew full well that it was Whistler's plan when he ascribed it to Montgomery. On 27 April 1945, Horrocks wrote to 'Dear Bolo' and signed himself 'yours sincerely' rather than 'My dear Bolo' and 'yours ever' as used by Dempsey in his letter of farewell to Whistler on 24 June 1945:

> Dear Bolo, I am writing to congratulate you on the very fine performance put up by your Division during the recent fighting. While fighting for the Bremen approaches you met some very stiff opposition, notably in Brinkum and Leeste, but this was overcome thanks to the fine fighting qualities of your troops. **Your plan for the capture of Bremen, south of the River Weser, was extremely well conceived and it was brilliantly carried out by the whole Division** [this author's emphasis]
> yours sincerely,[47]

Horrocks and Whistler cut each other after the War, and the reader will search Horrocks's book *Corps Commander* in vain for any mention of Whistler, even over the matter of Bremen. Whistler's biographer naively dismisses the break as unremarkable, writing that,

> It was unfortunate that during the closing stages of the war in Europe Horrocks and Bolo 'parted brass rags' so to speak and never patched it up. This was really due to a clash of temperaments between two very brilliant and colourful personalities, which is apt to occur in a period of great strain and tension. It was 'just one of those things'.[48]

It was no clash of temperaments, and obvious from his Diary that Whistler judged Horrocks as dangerously inadequate, and Whistler was in a good position to judge. With first-rate men available of the quality of Douglas Wimberley, sidelined in a staff job at Camberley because Montgomery had judged him 'tired' in Sicily, it is necessary to understand the charge against Horrocks who clearly misunderstood the task of the corps commander when he could write that the Corps is the largest formation which fights the tactical battle,[49] and then spend his time 'smelling the battlefield' rather than making plans to outfox the enemy.

Many held a higher opinion of Horrocks than Horrocks had of himself. His biographer, Philip Warner, quotes Horrocks calling himself a subaltern-general, who saw Montgomery as the architect of success and himself as a mere assistant; 'God never meant me to be an army commander'. It can be argued a man not capable of being an army commander should not have been given a corps. Furthermore, Warner continued, Horrocks never liked problems of politics or logistics, being unable to achieve intellectual detachment. He felt he had limited aims in accordance with limited ability, and had reached the highest point at which that ability could be used successfully. His great strength was in clarity of exposition of other people's work.

Horrocks was not a well man when he replaced Bucknall in command of 30 Corps on 4 August 1944, but it never seemed to have occurred to him that concealment of his ill-being was either

47 McNish, *Iron Division*, p. 134.
48 Smyth, *Bolo Whistler*, p. 159.
49 Horrocks, *Corps Commander*, pp. xiv & 31

dishonest or irresponsible. He suffered recurring bouts of fever as the result of severe bullet wounds received at the Battle of Armentières in October 1914 and from a German fighter aircraft in Bizerta in 1943. He nearly died of typhus in Krasnoyarsk in 1920, and had a bad case of 'gyppie tummy' when he reached the desert in 1942. He was to have several more operations after the Second World War when pieces of khaki drill shirt were fished from his intestines, and he was invalided out of the service in 1949 because he could no longer concentrate on desk-work.

The suspicion always exists with Horrocks that he was hiding his illness, although in 1924 he represented Britain in the Olympics and into old age could eat anything he wished without ill effect. Montgomery knew of Horrocks' deceit and tried to keep a close eye on his health, giving him home leave in January 1945 to rest before *Veritable*. But Horrocks was incorrigible, remembering that during *Veritable*:

> I grew to like him (Crerar) very much, though I am afraid I must have been a terrible pain in the neck, for during part of this long drawn-out battle I was feeling very unwell (a recurrence of the attack I had developed before crossing the Seine), though this time I managed to conceal it from everyone other than my A.D.C.s and senior members of my staff. The outward and visible sign was that I became extremely irritable and bad-tempered, yet Crerar bore with me patiently.[50]

Horrocks was ill when he released 43 BID in *Veritable*, creating in the approaches to Cleve one of the most notorious traffic jams of the entire war.

Horrocks qualified for Staff College in 1931 after five years of trying. Nevertheless, in 1938 Wavell selected him as DS. He had an ear for languages, speaking French, German and Russian which he learned in a POW camp, 'in order', as he explained many years after the war to Khrushchev in the House of Commons, 'to stop your officers spitting on the floor'. Prematurely grey, rather untidy looking, he was renowned for an obsession with punctuality and efficiency, a liking for fast driving – only Oliver Leese drove faster and more dangerously – and a gift for giving firm and decisive advice in a positive yet modest manner which left the recipient wanting to do better. He had a natural generosity that Montgomery lacked, and he could hold an audience while explaining the basics of an operation, never getting bogged down in detail, later using this talent as a TV presenter. He was liked and respected by the troops who saw in him a general who led from the front and showed a belief that in most circumstances there was more to be gained by cheerfulness and resourcefulness than by authoritarianism.

Horrocks commanded 2 Middlesex for 17 days during the retreat to Dunkirk. These were corps troops allocated to the divisions as required; the 1939 infantry division having no MG battalion until the reorganisation of 1941. Horrocks was noticed by Brooke and Montgomery who promoted him to command 9 BIB from 17 June 1940 to 4 February 1941. He was then promoted to command 44 BID from 25 June 1941 to 14 March 1942, the Division being disbanded in the Middle East on 31 January 1943. He then became the first infantryman to command an armoured division, 9 BAD, from 20 March to 12 August 1942. It never left the UK and was disbanded on 31 July 31, 1944. When Montgomery went to the desert he arranged for Horrocks to follow him out to command XIII Corps. He and Montgomery understood each other and he contributed to Montgomery's success.

Churchill disliked him initially, according to Warner: 'That chap Horrocks is no good. Get rid of him.' Horrocks fought Alam Halfa successfully even though he was not fit in de Butts' opinion. He successfully commanded Freyberg and Tuker at Mareth, but was less successful at the

50 Horrocks, *Corps Commander*, p. 183.

Gabes Gap where an opportunity was lost to destroy the German army. Warner believed that, 'if Horrocks had been a Rommel or a Guderian he would have smashed through or around obstacles and annihilated the rest of the German opposition.' Such squandering of hard-earned major opportunities should have stopped Horrocks' career. Things continued to deteriorate and at the end of April 1943, Horrocks, 'had the worst few days of my life', in Warner's words. It happened when Montgomery went to Cairo for a conference about the invasion of Sicily, and left Horrocks in command. Horrocks could not decide what to do. He agreed with Freyberg and Tuker that the attack along the coast decided by Montgomery would be costly, but failed to come up with an alternative. Montgomery returned to find Horrocks still dithering. A year later the pattern repeated itself at Antwerp where Horrocks believed he had again dithered and taken the wrong decision, while failing to push 30 Corps hard enough at Arnhem. Again, Montgomery had left Horrocks to make his own decisions.

Montgomery only once asked his junior for strategic advice. It concerned Operation *Gatwick* to attack through the Reichswald after the Battle of Arnhem. Montgomery was on his way to a conference with Eisenhower and called in to ask Horrocks how many divisions he would need. Horrocks said six. The biographers of 30 Corps, writing for Horrocks, supplied the background:

> Two days later (Oct 8?) all the troops on the "Island" came under the command of 12 Corps and 30 Corps HQ turned its attention to planning for an attack Eastwards through the Reichswald Forest, in which it was intended that 43rd Division should play the major part. This attack, as it was planned, never took place, but the work done was to prove very useful some three months later when the Corps started planning for the famous Operation 'Veritable'.[51]

Both passages are disingenuous. Horrocks went ahead with only three divisions until stopped.

> Operation *Gatwick* was then contemplated, in which 3 Div was to clear the Reichswald with the 15 Div on its right and 43rd Div on its left. General Bolo told the Corps Commander [Horrocks] that he thought this operation was more difficult and would require more troops than had been envisaged. Nevertheless the full programme of complicated reliefs was ordered and 185 Bde relieved the American glider troops, though not without some German opposition. However, on October 7th, the Army Commander (Montgomery) decided that the operation would absorb too many troops in view of the current operations further west to clear the Antwerp approaches. Operation *Gatwick* was therefore postponed and 3 Div ordered to re-cross the Maas to take part in the elimination of the enemy pocket west of the river.[52]

Montgomery agreed:

> At the end of the first week in October I had to inform the Supreme Commander (Eisenhower) that it was necessary to postpone the projected Rhineland attack, because my resources were not sufficient to continue with this plan because of other more immediate commitments. I therefore ordered that the offensive between the Rhine and the Meuse would be postponed and that the immediate objects would be to open Antwerp and to clear the enemy bridgehead west of the Meuse by Second Army.[53]

51 Gill & Groves, *Club Route*, p. 92.
52 Smyth, *Bolo*, p. 131.
53 Montgomery, *Normandy*, p. 158-9.

There was wrangling at the top as Bradley and Patton fought with Montgomery for resources from Eisenhower. Patton wasted his army fruitlessly around Metz, losing more troops than the British at Arnhem. On 5 October, at a meeting of commanders with Eisenhower and Brooke at Versailles, Montgomery had to endure the public criticism of Ramsey and the loss of Brooke's support for failing to open Antwerp. Then on 10 October, as everything fell apart, Montgomery sent his critical observations on Ike's command to SHAEF which would have got him fired had he not backed down on 14 October. According to Belfield it was only on 16 October that Montgomery issued unqualified orders to open Antwerp.

Many points emerge here. Horrocks does not inform his readers that he was responsible for planning Operation *Gatwick* and would have gone ahead with only three divisions. Instead, Horrocks takes credit for telling Montgomery that more than three divisions were needed for an attack through the Reichswald, implying that Montgomery was uncertain and that Horrocks had corrected him. We have seen that this opinion actually came from Whistler. Indeed it is possible that Montgomery and Whistler had already talked about it and Montgomery was just checking with Horrocks to see if he agreed. Horrocks would never give credit to Whistler. The pattern was repeated at Bremen, and the result is that nothing Horrocks wrote can be accepted at face value.

When caught out by his seniors, Horrocks accepted responsibility for failing to clear the Scheldt Estuary, and by so doing disarmed his critics. The consequences of his mistake were far-reaching and widely felt. Instead of the attack on 10-12 October 1944 in good going against weak opposition, the Reichswald Battle was fought between 8 February and 11 March 1945 in mud by a sick Horrocks against an opponent with time to bring up reserves. The operation bogged down, and casualties mounted as divisions became worn out. 3 BID, which was training for the assault crossing of the Rhine and an advance on Berlin, was instead sucked into an operation that had gone badly wrong. Whistler, who had been involved from the beginning, could not have failed to blame Horrocks.

Conservatism dominated practice within 30 Corps. Horrocks considered ten minutes a day sufficient for attending to staff matters before leaving to 'smell the battlefield', rationalising his dislike of thinking and analysis. He met Simpson's highly regarded 9 US Army in November 1944 in the Geilenkirchen Salient during Operation *Blackcock*, but did not like what he saw and criticised American methods of careful thought and analysis as 'a complete waste of time'. The hands-on and interfering Montgomery had no complaints. No one made more of a fetish of being seen up front than Horrocks who lectured the Americans on their need to be recognised by their troops and to avoid living in comfort in grand houses behind the lines with big staffs. One cannot help concluding that for the troops battling on the Űdem-Weeze road in the February mud, the size of the building where the plans were hatched was less important than the quality of those plans and of the equipment.

A Second World War Canloan veteran and career soldier commented on Horrocks's statement:

> Horrocks was quite right, and his statement of needing only a few minutes each morning with his C of S reflected the quality of staffs in the British Army, and the trust and confidence in them by Commanders. His statement, as written is an over-simplification, but valid. It must be remembered that the Corps Comd and staff's real task was *before* the battle started. Once battle was joined, the Corps Comd's main function was to observe, analyze progress, encourage or drive as required.
>
> Similarly, Monty, having given his direction for *this battle,* well before it commenced, would have been giving his attention to the next but one, having selected another Corps to start planning while Battle 1 was just being teed up.
>
> The Americans were slow to learn this, indeed perhaps never have. I saw a little of them first hand in Korea and have studied their operational methods and command philosophy at Staff

> College and elsewhere, and am NOT impressed. They are big and powerful, but abuse their troops and achieve any successes by hard-nosed driving and not by good planning, organization or staff work.[54]

This is powerful testimony, but does not contradict the charge that Horrocks was too lightweight for the task of corps commander since his input into the plans Rex was talking about was minimal, and he relied on the ideas of Whistler and others. To revert to the Bremen example; what Montgomery decided outside Bremen was based on Whistler's thinking and was to feint with 51 BID and provide 3 BID with Buffaloes to get behind the German defenders. The German defending General Becker complained of this unfairness:

> When he [Becker] was captured a little later, he confirmed the success of our plan by saying that the main attack came in on the right. This was of course the feint attack. He said: "Then you put your soldiers into the Verdammte Schwimmpanzer, and you came up behind us. It was unfair".[55]

Such creativity even using available equipment was beyond Horrocks's abilities. Instead of spending his days smelling the battlefield, the corps commander could have been demanding better infantry radios and, as an absolute priority, a Churchill tank with frontal immunity to the 88 mm and better flotation.

Crerar and Horrocks believed that provided they gained surprise in Operations *Blockbuster*, *Heather* and *Leek*, and had a sufficient number of divisions, they would be able to break the German defensive line and unleash Guards Armoured on its 'sweep down' to the Rhine, pushing through to Wesel in a matter of days. But the Germans had learned from Kursk and in a thousand other engagements across Europe to extend their defences in depth. Crerar failed to notice from his flights over the area that the defended locality stretched all the way to the Rhine. Trenches had been dug in front of every town and could within minutes be dug around every farmhouse as needed. Cleve and Goch had been turned into fortresses.

Horrocks should have known this, and the charge against him of being over-optimistic and facile is again validated. In 1970 Horrocks was unapologetic about his plans for *Veritable* and blamed the weather, stating that: 'What was so maddening was that the whole thing could have been so easy if only frost had continued.'[56] The Canadian official historian, Stacey, put it rather differently in a biting aside; 'Operations actually developed rather differently and less rapidly due to interference by the enemy.'

The sad fact is that most of the Allied commanders, with the exception of Simonds perhaps and certainly Slim, saw themselves as managers of battle and had neither been trained, nor had the intellectual powers, to initiate a wide-ranging review of what could be done to master the German techniques which they all knew about intimately and which were killing their troops in large and intolerable numbers.

Horrocks described how he managed the Reichswald battle almost as an onlooker, leaving his HQ at 8 am and having nothing to do except visit the troops and smell the battlefield, while the same anecdote in identical language is repeated about Montgomery's practice as GOC 3 BID during the retreat to Dunkirk. Brig Essame appreciated Horrocks and his methods that resulted,

54 Rex Fendick in an E-mail in June 2002.
55 Gill & Groves, *Club Route*, p. 183.
56 Elstob, *Battle*, p. 7.

he said, in increasing morale, although Essame was talking of 43 BID in *Blockbuster* in II Canadian Corps:

Others such as Peter Elston disagreed, writing that the battle had led to, recriminations and accusations between units at all levels up to divisions. Montgomery's set-piece attack promised an almost mechanical advance, which when it failed resulted in disappointment which was bad for morale. When the original schedule became impossible to fulfill, the rigidity imposed by the tight interlocking of forces removed flexibility and it took two to three days to implement a new plan.

Whistler would have agreed, telling his diary on 7 April 1945: 'J [Montgomery's name for Horrocks] has little ideas (sic) really on managing a battle – what can & cannot be done etc.'[57] Horrocks recognised that the outcome was beyond his control and he lacked the generalship to adapt. The battle became a slogging match in the mud – a battalion CO's battle.

That might describe what actually happened, but the story of Barclay's inability to persuade Brigadier Mark Matthews and presumably Bolo Whistler that a night-attack was preferable shows that it happened in the context of inexcusably inadequate generalship. However, it was in the end up to the Lt-Cols commanding the infantry battalions to lead their rifle companies against the German defences and drive the defenders out. The following piece was written from experience in First World War but was just as true of the Second:

> A Colonel's main work, aim, and object must be to make his men fight when he wants them to. That, to cast cant and humbug aside, was what all Colonels had to do and what all Colonels did do. To *make* men fight. That is the task. To *make* men kill men; to *force* men to risk their lives to kill. There was the horror. Let no one sneer at the men who undertook that task and carried it through. The way the Colonels went about their awful work varied, of course, according to their characters and temperaments. I have heard of only one Colonel who disdained all subtleties and obtained the effect he desired by a show of naked brutality. Before an attack he would walk along the assembly trench of the battalion, with a revolver in each hand, and warn the men that he would shoot with his own hand anyone who hesitated, wavered, or retreated. The attacks by the man's battalion were invariably successful and the percentage of its casualties was abnormally low. I doubt if his men hated him; for he would not have lived long if they had. He survived the war, became an active pacifist and died in his bed.
>
> The average Colonel preferred to obtain results without an open display of ferocity. He did not threaten to shoot you if you did not obey his command to kill, but the success of his battalion in attack corresponded to his success in instilling into the minds of his men the conviction that they must kill *or be killed.*
>
> There were a few Colonels who found it impossible to stifle or conceal their naturally humane feelings. The battalions commanded by such men were usually happy when out at rest, stubborn in defence, but unreliable in attack.
>
> Other things being equal, the ferocious brute will always defeat the decent, humane man. It is, therefore, a vital necessity, if the decency is to survive, temporarily and at the critical moment to transform the decent man into the most ferocious brute possible by making him desperate through fear. That is the lesser evil. A ferocious attack made by desperate men will succeed with comparatively few casualties, certainly with fewer casualties than results from a half-hearted attack, which consequently, fails.[58]

57 Whistler Diary, West Sussex Record Office.
58 Martyr, *Wandering Years*, pp. 210-13.

In a battalion attack the COs usually, with the exception of Kervenheim, advanced in the midst of their men and shared the same risk of wounding or death. Personal safety was never a concern and all of the COs were brave and exceptional men, suppressing their fear and taking pains to set an example in all ways, and even to the enemy. One was 'Swazi' Waller of 1 South Lancs, described by Eddie Jones:

> He was gifted with extreme personal bravery, which proved a great inspiration to all the battalion. To see him walking about, as he frequently did, amongst the leading troops and forward positions, completely indifferent to the heaviest enemy fire, was a great morale-boost to all. In addition, whatever the circumstances and however great the demands of the situation, he was always carefully shaved and immaculately turned out. During the attack on the Udem-Weeze road a group of about 10 German prisoners were being escorted past us from the wood. 'Swazi' started to question them. At this moment, a heavy salvo of German shells came over and landed close by. All the British officers and men instinctively ducked, except 'Swazi'. The Germans didn't duck either. As 'Swazi' said to me later, 'That was a tricky situation. I didn't want the Germans to think that we were scared of their shelling.[59]

The COs could handle physical fear. The cause of their enervating stress was fear of unnecessary losses resulting from failure to stand up to the brigadier and divisional GOC. Kervenheim was an example of this as we have seen, but it was a common and often tragic situation with both COs and generals claiming to be in the right. Eddie Jones witnessed the firing of two COs in two days:

> At some stage, about midway through the operation on October 14, 1944 during Aintree, the capture of Overloon and Venraij, Brigadier Cass came up and took Lt-Col Orgill [1 S Lancs] to one side for consultation. I was not privileged to hear what was said, but when the Brigadier had left the CO intimated to me that he would be 'piping down in the future and leaving things to Major Waller', and he left for England the same evening, Major Waller taking command of the battalion. I can only assume that the battalion's rate of progress had not been to the satisfaction of the Brigadier and he had made the change of command. We were sorry to see Lt-Col Orgill go. He was a gentleman and had concern for his men.
>
> I accompanied the CO to a Bde 'O' Group after dark on the 16th October, presided over by Brigadier Cass. It was a strange 'O' Group, and the Brigadier gave out his orders in very peremptory manner. Briefly our Bn was to be in reserve, whilst the other two Bns of the Brigade advanced, with the E. Yorks left and the Suffolks right, crossing the start line of the Molen Beek at first light. In response to the Brigadier's final question, 'Any questions', instead of the normal reply of 'No', or the checking of the odd detail or two, the CO of E Yorks, Jimmy Dickson, who had just returned to the Bn after a wound received earlier in the campaign, said to the Brigadier, 'Do you mean that I am to be across the Molen Beek with my Bn at first light tomorrow, when the leading troops of 9 Bde are still some four hundred yards short of it? (It was already late in the evening when these orders were given out). The Brigadier replied to the effect that it was not for him to instruct a Bn commander how to move his Bn forward, and when the CO of E. Yorks persisted in his questions, he remarked that he was obviously tired, not yet fully recovered from his wound, and had better send for his Second-in-Command, Major Renison, who duly took over and received the orders for the Bn's advance. As we left

59 Unpublished memoir of Eddie Jones.

> the 'O' Group, the CO (now Swazi since 14 October), remarked to me in a low voice that he thought we were best out of it (i.e. in reserve for this Bde operation).[60]

The three battles described in this book were fought primarily by three battalion COs in three brigades; Bill Renison of 2 East Yorks (8 BIB), Peter Barclay of 1 Royal Norfolks (185 BIB) and Cecil Firbank of 2 Lincolns (9 BIB). They were all intelligent, ruthless, experienced, successful and demanding men.

Firbank was a notorious martinet. His arrival in the battalion after Douglas Wilson had been injured at Pont de Vaudry near Vire in Normandy, galvanised the Lincolns who were worn down by casualties and endless fighting. The 2ic, Leslie Colvin had taken over the battalion temporarily and been called to Brigade for orders, returning with Firbank who had been GSO.1 (L) at Div HQ.

> It was a strange – almost historic – meeting that took place in a filthy old stone farmhouse that morning of 7th August: weary and unshaven Company Commanders, the Second in Command, and the Adjutant, the Battery Commander, Major A.B. Edwards, RA and Colonel Firbank himself, just a little bewildered at his sudden translation in the very middle of the battle, but at the same time giving off his orders clearly and firmly.[61]

For Colin Welch, who was wounded in Kervenheim, it was clear that fame and fortune were dispensed randomly by Firbank who was not always governed by reason. A Coy was undergoing a Firbank blitz when Welch joined it, but when Welch was declared a good officer by Firbank, A Coy's stock went up. On the Maas two young soldiers who had come from the King's Liverpool Regt as reinforcements were up in front of Firbank on a charge of being asleep on duty. Welch expected Firbank to give them a headmasterly dressing down, but Firbank said to them, 'How old are you?' '18' and '19' were the replies. 'Case dismissed', said Firbank to Welch's amazement. 'Mr Welch', said Firbank. 'Never put two young men on guard together'. The fact that many of the men were young was not something Welch could point out to his CO.

Firbank was often didactic, according to Welch, who recounted the following story. Once at dinner Sam Larkin served up a pig he had had trouble shooting with a sten gun because the bullets had flown off it. Firbank was laying down the law that every British redcoat was worth at least two Krauts, four Frogs and 10 Wops, when the mess waiter, Private Homer, arrived with the food. Homer was mess waiter because he would have been a danger to himself and his colleagues in a rifle platoon. He was uncoordinated, looked like Leon Brittan, and everything about him from his tie to his steel-rimmed glasses was askew. Larkin took one look at Homer and asked Firbank innocently how many SS *Obersturmbannführers* Private Homer was worth once he had put on his redcoat. The answer was not recorded.[62]

There is a case of a private soldier answering Firbank back. George Wall, whose outstanding memory held details of his second birthday, wrote:

> I used to think Lt Col Firbank a great officer. Our first meeting was around the beginning of December 1944, near Swolgen in Holland. He wanted Major Clarke to be his beater and I was asked along as his escort as he was going duck shooting. I saw him shoot a duck. He yelled at me. 'Fetch!' I yelled back, 'I'm not your bloody dog', and ran off in search of his duck! I was to meet Major Clarke who was also sniffing out the duck and told him

60 Unpublished memoir of Eddie Jones.
61 Gates, *The History*, p. 234.
62 Colin Welch in conversation in 1984 and 1994.

> what I'd said. I was concerned. He thought it funny. The next day, still full of fright I asked what the Colonel had said. He casually said the Colonel thought it took a lot of guts for a Private to tell a Colonel he wasn't a dog! That's when I thought he was a great officer. Our next meeting was on the River Rhine in late March 1945. He had come to visit us for the first time since the battle of Winnekendonk. With him he had a Collie dog. I had entrapped an Alsatian dog in a house and befriended him by feeding him. He became quite a pal. I was always fond of dogs. I always had one when a child. It growled at him, which is only natural. He looked at the dog and said: 'Shoot it'. I said I wouldn't and that it was a friend. As a fellow dog lover, I hoped he would understand. He didn't. Spuggie Spye stepped forward and said he would shoot it, and that's what he did. My opinion of the Colonel changed after that.[63]

Problems with Firbank over animals happened on other occasions. Tony Edwards, the BC permanently attached to the Lincolns, wanted to kill a cow that was making a terrible noise and upsetting everyone, but Firbank absolutely forbade it. John Boys, 2ic of B Coy, who was an ex-Guardsman and far from being a hit with Firbank but refused to allow it to worry him, failed to improve matters between them by ordering a bull killed which was menacing his troops. After the deed was done he was resting in a house with his feet up on the window-less window sill, reading Punch – 'which we didn't see very often' – when Firbank rode up on a horse he had acquired from somewhere, and, looking down on Boys, demanded to know about a bull which he heard had been killed. Boys said that it had been a danger to his troops so he had ordered it killed, 'Sah!' Firbank got very angry and said that it should have been bled properly since it was now unfit for human consumption and a perfectly good carcass had been ruined, etc, etc. Boys replied that he was trained as a soldier and not as a butcher, Sah'.[64]

COs were masters in their own house and did not brook interference. Eddie Jones recalled a breakfast with 'Swazi' Waller of 1 South Lancs:

> I am reminded of an amusing incident in which he was involved. He and I had been out all night with forward battalion HQ established in the CO's carrier to conduct our part of the operation against an enemy pocket at Wanssum early in January 1945. We had returned, rather battle-weary after our all-night operation, shortly after dawn and were sitting down to breakfast together, which, I remember, consisted of compo-sausage. Communication by radio was always tricky and I had decided to run out for our operation of the previous night a signal-cable with a field-telephone as a reserve link to rear Bn HQ, and, in fact, this had turned out to be the only reliable contact we had throughout the operation. We were about halfway through our breakfast, when a young, dapper, beautifully turned out Royal Signals Captain came in, saluted smartly and introduced himself as the Brigade Signals Officer. 'I have been sent', he announced importantly, 'by the Brigadier [Eddie Goulburn], to investigate the failure of your communications during last night's operation'. I felt Colonel Waller begin to bristle, but he said nothing, and went on methodically chopping his sausages into neat, regular lengths and popping them into his mouth. The Signals Officer, perhaps a little disconcerted by the failure on the Colonel's part to reply, went on and on about the importance of communications in battle, how best to achieve them, etc, etc. Colonel Waller finished his final sausage, carefully placed his knife and fork beside each other on the plate, fixed the Signals Captain with a gimlet eye and said quietly, 'Young man. You speak more balls to the

63 Letter from George Wall in 1994.
64 John Boys in conversation in 1984.

> square inch than anyone I have met for a long time. Go back and tell the Brigadier that if I want to conduct an enquiry into my signals set-up I will do it. Good morning!' The officer left without a word.[65]

An officer, even a martinet was respected, if he was respectful:

> Proctor was detailed to do guard in front of the company office. Leslie Colvin, who was a major and a bit of a martinet and was hot stuff on saluting and 2ic of the battalion, jumped out of his Jeep and dashed into the company office. Proctor presented arms, which is the proper salute from a sentry to a field officer, which is a major and above, and Leslie Colvin didn't respond. When Leslie Colvin came out again, Proctor turned round to him and said, 'Isn't it correct that a field officer should respond to a sentry when he gives him a present arms?' Leslie Colvin, to his eternal credit, said 'Yes, you're quite right', stood in front of him and gave him a bloody smashing salute and got back in his Jeep again. He was that type of bloke. Bloody good leader of men.[66]

Leslie Colvin visited his batman, Harry Hatfield, in Grimsby in 1983. Hatfield was reminded of a daily ritual.

> I would be leaning against the wall outside Battalion HQ, having parked the Jeep, waiting for your father and chatting away to someone or other, when your father would come out and, without even looking around, would always yell; 'Where's that fucking batman?' 'Here I am', I would reply, getting into the Jeep and starting it up.'[67]

George Wall reminded Leslie Colvin of their first meeting:

> The morning after that dreadful October 14th, in the wood to the right of Overloon, I was sent to find our QMS Harris who was on the right flank. We were on the extreme left. When making my way to find him, I heard a flurry of mortar about to land in the immediate vicinity. Like a shot, I jumped into a nearby dugout, colliding with another body. His first remarks were: 'By the sound of your voice you must be a Bermudan'. The conversation continued with him asking my view of Barbadians. I replied that I only knew of those working in the Dockyard in Bermuda, and I gathered they were none too impressive. By the time of my departure from the dugout I could see and recognise again the face of the person to whom I was speaking. A few days later, I was out with Peter Clarke and from a distance he and the fellow I had been talking to acknowledged each other. I asked who it was, and Peter replied: 'That's Major Colvin, Second in Command of the Battalion'. I said, 'Oh, my God', and told of my meeting with you. He said, 'Don't worry. He's one of the nicest people you could meet'. He went on to say that you had come from Barbados to join the Lincolns in 1939.[68]

65 Unpublished memoirs of Eddie Jones.
66 John Keenan's tape-recorded memoirs.
67 Harry Hatfield in conversation in 1983.
68 Letter from George Wall to Leslie Colvin.

David Bates recalled Leslie Colvin stopping the battalion on the way into Goch.

> We were in convoy with your father leading in a Jeep. Suddenly he stood up and stopped the 3-tonners. He ordered everybody to de-bus and line up against the hedge. He ordered them to unbutton their flies. 'Now urinate. We are at last in Germany'.[69]

Officers set the example and attacked literally at the head of their men. The result was a high attrition rate and they were all wounded, some many times, or killed with only the rarest exception. The problem in the British Army was that when the officers were shot the men lost heart and there was no one left to persuade them to advance. Shelford Bidwell explained that all he could do with his men was to persuade them to get out of their slit-trenches, march up to the objective, dig a slit-trench there, and get into it.' It was very different in defence. The British soldier was personally offended when attacked and refused to give ground on principle. Thus the most effective British infantry tactic was to seize ground wanted by the Germans and to resist their counter-attacks. This, however, led to slow progress.

The major responsibility for leadership fell to the commanders of the four rifle coys.

> The requirements of a Company Commander are simple in the sense that (with the exception of creative imagination in the arts) they demand almost every good quality a man can possess: energy; initiative; conscientiousness about detail; capacity to delegate authority; instinct for retaining the liking and confidence of subordinates, while at the same time making them work hard, and never develop the least doubt as to who is in command; all these combined with a sound grasp of handling weapons, and practical application of the theory of small scale tactics. Off duty the Company Commander must spend most of his spare time coping with the personal problems of his men, such as having got a girl with child, or receiving news that a wife is being unfaithful at home; not to mention minor matters like being reduced to one pair of socks too shrunk to wear.[70]

The relationship between the coy commanders, the coy 2ics and the men was sometimes avuncular, even fatherly. The ex-guardsman, John Boys, was 2ic of B Coy, 2 Lincolns.

> I remember Capt. Boys, who when in England was always exquisitely dressed, coming charging over the area where we had our trench saying, 'Keenan, Keenan. I've got some *camembert*'. Well what with the period of the war and my age I had no idea what a *camembert* was. Anyway he was carrying in one hand a box of *camembert* and in the other hand a spoon, and anybody who was willing to try it he was dishing out a spoonful of *camembert*. Well this *camembert*, I might say, which was the first time I'd ever tried it, was absolutely delicious, really very similar to cream in consistency. Not really very much related to the kind of thing you get in the supermarket today.[71]

This was not the experience of Lt John Foley, none of whose troop liked 'the peculiar tang of the fluid Camembert cheese',[72] resulting in more for him.

---

69 Revd David Bates in conversation.
70 Powell, *Faces*, p. 103.
71 John Keenan's tape-recorded memoirs.
72 John Foley. *Mailed Fist* (St Albans: Mayflower, 1975), p. 49.

It was held as a truth that there were no bad troops; only bad officers. The gap between officers and men was wide in disciplined British units, with unquestioning obedience reinforced by the class division of civilian life, made more evident through differences in accent. All was more than leavened, however, by a type of *noblesse oblige*. Officers were responsible for the mens' welfare. Although they messed separately, officers never ate until after the men had received their meal, and distributing a hot meal was a matter of the highest priority. In the battles described there was usually a hot breakfast served with rum before battle. Officers like Banger King of the East Yorks, who won a bar to his DSO at Yorkshire Bridge, were not uncommon. Tearing around in their open-topped carriers regardless of the shelling and of their personal safety, their fanaticism for the men's welfare revealed a kind of love, which of course begat respect and the willingness to follow. Sometimes, as at Winnekendonk, the men did not receive a hot meal for 36 hours, and had to forage in farmhouse cellars, but all reasonable men realized this was due to force majeure.

Being in a regular battalion, some of the officers, such as Peter Clarke and Glyn Gilbert, had graduated from Sandhurst, which was the college for regular infantry officers. During the war all went to the OCTU, after passing the WOSB. There were many stories about the questions asked by the Board and its resident 'trick cyclist', appointed after it was learned that the Wehrmacht used psychological assessment in officer selection. 'Which pack do you hunt with?' was felt to be a typical question of someone who never hunted. Once selected, officers were instructed not to drink in the same pubs as the men and to keep their distance. The German paratroop officer, Herr Volberg, who served in FJR6 at Monte Cassino and in Normandy, expressed surprise[73] when in 1966 at a Desert Rat reunion the sergeant he was talking to moved away to eat elsewhere. Volberg told him to sit down and eat with him, being used to no such class distinction in the Wehrmacht. It was the same injunction Maj Peter Clarke gave to Pte George Wall.

> It was whilst around Venraij that the Germans kidnapped some of our officers. An instruction came out that all officers leaving their unit should take an escort with them. It was decided in our company that it would be the two snipers. That was myself and Cpl Spye who was my immediate superior. He was a regular soldier. I imagine he did not hit it off too well with Peter Clarke, because every time Peter was leaving the position he would yell: "Wall, you are my escort", and away I would have to gallop to catch him up. He seemed to know a great deal about me. It wasn't until after he was killed that I found out why. He used to censor my mail. I only used to write to my mother. Peter was a tall man – probably about 6 feet 4 inches. I went out with him to see a German patrol change over. He wanted to check that they did not add to their numbers. From there we went back to the Battalion HQ. He asked if I were hungry and ordered bacon and eggs. I hadn't had them since joining the army, other than when I had been home on leave. I was sitting eating with him at a trestle table and along came another officer and said; "Other ranks are not allowed to eat with officers". Peter Clarke replied: 'Why don't you eat somewhere else?' With that the other chap walked away. I asked if I should move on but he said: 'No, sit down and finish your breakfast'. I did and had all the more respect for him. He asked if I had ever thought of promotion or a commission. I said that I had but was quite content with what I was doing until I returned to Bermuda.
>
> 2nd Lincolns was stationed in Bermuda at the outbreak of the First World War. On leaving in 1915, they took with them 139 Volunteers from the BVRC. More were to follow. At the request of the Bermuda Government, the Lincolns used to send a sergeant major and an adjutant to train the BVRC. At the outbreak of WWII, Bermuda sent a token force of forty to join the 8 Bn Lincolns. In 1943 the 8th was disbanded and the men were posted to a

73 Herr Volberg in conversation in 1983.

> regiment of their names i.e. Aitchison to the Black Watch, Felix Mullin to an anti-tank unit of the Argyll and Sutherland Highlanders. In the four battalions there were about 110 spread around. There were 50 odd in the 2nd Bn. When we joined we had to surrender our stripes. I remember one chap who fought in WWI with the Lincolns as a Sgt Maj and had to surrender one of his stripes to come abroad with us. His name was Sgt E. Ward, a most likeable chap.[74]

Not all of the Bermudans arrived by that route; Maj Glyn Gilbert, a regular and OC C Coy from D-Day to Bremen, and the only officer in 3 BID to survive unwounded, was from Bermuda and chose the Lincolns when graduating from Sandhurst because of the historical connection.

The officer as leader was always on show. No officer, according to Leslie Colvin, could show the fear he felt, and attempts to lessen one's personal danger ran the risk of ridicule. Officers who allowed their fear to overcome them, like one Lincolns' officer who would not come out of a slit trench during the DF mortaring of Black Orchard at Troarn during *Goodwood*, just vanished to end the war, it was said, manning an AA battery in the Orkneys. The Germans and Russians sent such people to punishment battalions where they were given high-risk tasks, which in a sense was just, if inhumane. George Wall and others believed that British officers shot cowards:

> What makes the UK soldier so full of vigour? I think it's the fear of being shot by your own officer, and your family having to live with it for a lifetime. They say the shame goes on after your death. I'll tell you a story – no, a couple – of desertion. It was whilst making our way towards Sint Anthonis for the battle of Overloon. The soldier behind me said if anything happened to him, all I'd have to say was that he had fallen down. Whilst I looked at him he fell with his arm across a branch of a tree deliberately breaking his forearm and yelling: 'Stretcher Bearer'. They did ask me what happened. I told them he had fallen down. The date of that 'accident' was 12 October 1944. On another occasion, in November of that same year, we were making our way down to Overbroek in our preparation to push Jerry back across the River Maas. It must have been about the 18th November of the same year. The Regimental police brought back a deserter from the Battle of Overloon. I was in the cellar when the Police were dismissed. Major Clarke looked at the deserter and drew his pistol. I made excuses to leave but I was told to stay where I was. Major Clarke said to the deserter that the next time he went into battle he was to walk beside him, and if he attempted to desert he personally would shoot him. 'Is that understood?' The answer was, 'Yes, Sir'. Asked why he deserted, he said he was scared. The major said what would happen if we were all scared and ran away? With that he was dismissed and sent back to his platoon: 'And if you have any trouble, come back and see me'. I remember the next battle, but I do not remember seeing that soldier again.[75]

A platoon commander was a lieutenant, often young and inexperienced. Promotion from 2nd Lieutenant to Lieutenant was automatic and happened after 6 months, and was quicker if promotion had been from NCO.[76] Their generic name was subaltern. The wise among them relied on the Platoon Sergeant, and the order, 'Carry on, Sergeant' was the acknowledged form whereby the officer asked for tuition by demonstration. Those promoted from the ranks of course already knew their stuff. Sometimes the subaltern with nowhere else to turn in the stress of battle took advice from a younger private soldier.

74 Letter from George Wall in 1994.
75 Letter from George Wall in 1994.
76 Letter from John Lincoln.

> A new lieutenant, a chap called Canna from Lincoln, joined us as our lieutenant. And of course I was his batman which meant I was his runner, which was no easy job because when everybody else was sat down doing nothing you were toddling about the countryside looking at this and going to see the CO or whatever. It wasn't the best job in the Platoon by a long way. By this time I was a veteran of seven or eight days and in our area we were still only five miles into Normandy. Lt. Canna used to defer to my opinion on what he ought to do or not ought to do to an extent that was a little bit ridiculous considering the relationship of our ranks. But always having been fairly intelligent and somewhat cautious, possibly my advice might have helped the Platoon more than somewhat – modesty being my middle name.[77]

The platoon commander had the most dangerous task, with death decimating their ranks every month. On rare occasions a subaltern was disliked, even hated.

> Lt. Brown, it was alleged, had been shot by his own people in C Coy. This particular officer was very unpopular. I'd had some experience of him when we were doing a detachment as the enemy in Scotland. His general attitude towards the men was that they were a combination of the beasts of the field and performing animals. As to whether it was true, it was certainly true that one or two people in C Coy had been heard to say that they would do such a thing once they'd got in action.[78]

Lt. D.T. Brown was killed in action at Cambes at the end of June. The regimental history states; 'A comparative newcomer to the Battalion, he had earned the reputation of a first-class leader of men,'[79] which does not mean that the IO, Capt Jack Harrod, who would have written that believed it was true.

The hallmarks of the good battalion were respect, good manners and a sense of humour by all ranks even in trying circumstances. John Keenan spent many hours in advanced and isolated positions on the banks of the Maas at Smakt in the dead of winter.

> It never ceased to amaze me that although that place was exposed and you might have thought that you'd been deserted by everybody, the sense of humour and comradeship used to carry you through. People still used to laugh, joke and what have you.[80]

Sometimes joking and the inevitable punishment of cookhouse duties were part of a ritual. A squad of the Lincolns was standing to attention when someone farted: 'Stop that', said the officer. 'I can't, Sir', replied Tommy Atkins; 'I don't know where it's gone'.[81] The story went round the battalion, bringing great kudos from all ranks to the joker.

If the officers set the example, the NCOs ensured that a consensus existed that the job had to be done, and that there was no easy way of avoiding it. NCOs were the unsung heroes of the British Army, and it fell to them to insist orders were carried out – even in the not necessarily rare cases when the officer hesitated, as in the drama involving Sgt Alldred and Lt Runcie at Winnekendonk.

> There was Jewish fellow called Goldsmith who had just joined us and was obviously very nervous. And there was a Sergeant in 12 Platoon and it was alleged that this chap wouldn't

77 John Keenan's tape-recorded memoirs.
78 John Keenan's tape-recorded memoirs.
79 Gates, *The History*, p. 226.
80 John Keenan's tape-recorded memoirs.
81 Leslie Colvin in conversation.

go forward, and it was alleged that this sergeant in 12 Platoon shot him dead like. Whether he really did I don't know.[82] [There is no Goldsmith in the list of 2 Lincolns' recorded dead].

The section leader, usually a Corporal, often had to put up with the arguments of the conscripted men, although the regulars knew better. Two were observed by John Keenan:

> Soldier Robinson was a jolly good soldier. He had been a Sergeant in India but had been reduced because of bad behaviour. So although these two chaps knew more about soldiering than I'd ever encountered, if you gave them any sort of legitimate order they never argued. Not like their fellow citizen soldiers who were inclined to argue with the bloke who gave them an order.[83]

3 BID was fresh and up to strength when committed, although no replacements arrived during the battles described herein. Some, such as Whistler and Firbank, went home before *Heather*. Leave entitlement was decided by balloting amongst those who had been out the longest. Many were away during these battles, either on leave or on a variety of courses. Others went on 48-hour passes to Brussels:

> It was a bit of a disaster. We were supposed to have a 48-hour leave in Brussels. Like all leave it was looked forward to, and eventually my name came up to go to Brussels. We went, and the roads were broken up by frost and snow and what have you. I think at the end of the day I spent 18 hours in Brussels. It was a nice change. Brussels was full of American and British soldiers and really I would rather have been back at the battalion.[84]

Officers and NCOs were supported by social pressure, tradition and military law. Crerar, the Army Commander, issued a memorandum on this subject to Simonds on 2 September 1944. It would have applied to Horrocks' XXX Corps and to 3 BID when they came under his command.

> <u>Discipline</u>
>
> 1. It is essential to battle discipline and fighting efficiency that the appropriate disciplinary action is taken in all cases of absence, cowardice and desertion. It is quite improper and bad for the general morale of the troops to place a soldier, who is regarded as not being dependable as a result of previous experience, in a rearward echelon and thus keep him out of battle. I emphasise that if improper conduct in action is permitted to go unpunished, or to be condoned, morale will be seriously affected. Prompt discipline is essential. The following will guide commanders:
>   a) Unauthorised absence for the purpose of avoiding action constitutes desertion under sec 12(1)(a) of the Army Act. In such cases a charge of desertion should be laid and not a charge of cowardice. Upon such charge it is necessary to prove (i) that accused knew with reasonable certainty that he was required for some particular service or duty and (ii) that he absented himself and thereby avoided or attempted to avoid such service or duty.
>   b) Cowardice is an offence under Sec 5(7) if it consists of misbehaviour before the enemy in such manner as to show cowardice or inducing other soldiers to misbehave

82 John Keenan's tape-recorded memoirs.
83 Ibid.
84 Ibid.

in such manner. It must be shown that the accused, from an unsoldierlike regard for his personal safety in the presence of the enemy, failed in respect of some distinct and feasible duty imposed on him by the well-understood action of the service, or by the requirements of the case, as applicable to the position he was placed in at the time.

c) There are other secs in the Army Act which deal with improper conduct in relation to the enemy. Commanders may obtain legal advice.

2. For the offences of desertion and cowardice penal servitude may be awarded. The minimum period of penal servitude is 3 years and maximum is life. Experience indicates that punishment of 3 years penal servitude has been awarded for the offences of cowardice or desertion in face of the enemy.

H.D.G. Crerar GOC in C First Cdn Army[85]

In Crerar's briefing notes, the Army Act was divided into morale offences, civil offences and military offences. Morale Offences comprised offences in relation to the enemy, both those that were and were not punishable by death, offences punishable more severely on active service than in peacetime, mutiny and sedition, desertion, fraudulent enrolment, assistance or connivance with desertion, AWOL, permitting escape from custody, enlistment of someone discharged with ignominy or disgrace, traitorous words and injurious disclosure. Civil Offences comprised scandalous conduct of an officer, fraud, disgraceful conduct, irregular arrest, corrupt dealings with a supplier, falsifying official documents, neglect to report, false accusation, offences relating to billeting and the impressment of carriages, duelling and attempted suicide and offences punishable under English law. Military offences were striking or threatening an officer, disobedience to a superior, insubordination, neglect to obey orders, drunkenness, deficiency or injury to equipment, offence in relation to a court martial, general offences in relation to enlistment and conduct prejudicial to military discipline.

When Crerar started commanding British troops the question of his disciplinary powers over them was spelled out. He could court martial, defined as dealing summarily with any officer below the rank of Lt-Col or a Warrant Officer. He had, however, to reserve to the CinC, Montgomery, all sentences of death and, in the cases of officers, all sentences of penal servitude, imprisonment, cashiering and dismissal the service. But he could himself confirm all sentences on other ranks other than death, and in the case of officers all sentences of forfeiture of rank, severe reprimand, reprimand or stoppage.

Even keeping silent when ordered to speak was classified as the military offence of insubordination or 'dumb insolence'. Officers believed that training in instant obedience was the only way that they or their men could face the daily horrors. There had to be a suspension of doubt and questioning if they hoped to have the authority to insist that men advance steadily into mortar and small arms fire.

From 29 October to 5 February, the Lincolns patrolled along the Maas. The Regimental History reported:

> At Swolgen an event almost unique in the annals of war took place; a girl child was born at Battalion Headquarters on the night of 17th/18th January, 1945. To mark her connection with the Regiment the name Decima was added to those chosen for her by her parents, and a Regimental badge and a bar of soap were given to her mother – all the Battalion had to offer.[86]

85 LAC: Crerar Papers: Adm HQ First Cdn Army, 120/POLICY DISC/1/2.
86 Gates, *History*, p. 249.

Enquiries in 1995 about the lady named by Leslie Colvin after the Tenth of Foot, identified her as Johanna Lambertina Maria Decima Keursten, born 27 January 1945, and living in Geleen. Her story either showed the inaccuracy of the War Diary or a breakdown in the timely registration of births in wartime Netherlands.

It was reported in the Lincolns' Diary that February opened very quietly, with patrolling the only activity until 5 February 1945 when the advance party left for the area around Louvain. On 6 February the Battalion was relieved and on 7 February the Lincolns motored through rainstorms over roads that were breaking up in the Peel Marshes to Wilsele, a small village three miles from Louvain, well known to Darby Hart and others who had been there five years earlier. On 8 February Renny visited the Battalion, and would have been received by Leslie Colvin in the absence of Firbank. On 11 February Firbank returned from leave and Maj Gen A. Galloway, who was commanding in Whistler's absence on leave until 25 February, visited on 19 February probably to warn Firbank. It was Galloway who had done the initial planning for Operation *Heather*. It wasn't until 22 February that the advance parties began to leave for Germany to relieve 15 BID in Goch.

On 23 February at 6 pm, the COs received their orders, and Operation *Heather* was on. The name never became widely known and for most troops it was Operation *Veritable*, of which it was a part.

While Whistler took leave, Maj Gen Galloway commanded 3 BID and planned Operation *Heather*. He briefed Cecil Firbank on 19 February and discovered him out shooting near the Maas. (© IWM B14182)

3 BID which moved up from around Louvain into Germany was among the best in the British Army. It had modernised and learned its profession since leaving Louvain in May 1940, when Montgomery had declared the British Army unfit to meet the Germans. It was called forward to Goch in one lift, climbing aboard the 3,347 vehicles bearing the attractively simple Divisional sign chosen by Montgomery when GOC in 1940 as a symphony of threes: three black triangles surrounding an upended red triangle, representing perhaps the three brigades each with three battalions. Some said red represented the blood of the brigades, others called it red tape.

> It should be remembered that the concept of threes in field formations was fairly new at the outbreak of WWII. Until shortly before the war, the principle of fours, eg "form fours", four battalions to a Brigade, etc had been standard from WW I. So Monty's choice of the triangle was a further recognition and reinforcement of this concept of threes in organization and tactics. As usual, he was in the forefront of operational thinking.[87]

With each vehicle taking 30 feet of road, the divisional column would have stretched for 17 miles, and taken three hours to pass an amazed onlooker if it had moved as one. But everyone made his best speed, with 8 and 9 BIBs going first on 24 February followed by 185 BIB a day later. The traffic movement included 595 tracked carriers, 63 armoured cars and 1,937 jeeps and lorries. Although classed as mechanised, the Division needed an additional 270 3-ton lorries fitted with benches, and called TCVs, sent from Corps to make the move in a single lift.

A large contingent of 49 Canloans served in 3 BID at one time or another. One of them, Capt Rex Fendick, CDN/453, has contributed greatly to this book. Canloans (motto *Transiens in Britanniam*) were Canadian officer volunteers accepted in the ratio of one captain to seven subalterns. In all respects they served in the British army except for drawing Canadian rates of pay and wearing an additional Canada shoulder flash on a battle dress of superior quality. Their fixed term was 90 days, when they had the option of RTU or staying for the duration.

The author had an illuminating conversation with two of them who served in 2 E Yorks, Jim Fetterley, CDN/267 and Robbie Robertson, CDN/193, at a Canloan reunion in the Royal Connaught Hotel in Hamilton, Ontario on 10 June 1989. Robbie explained:

> It was said that one British brass said to a Canadian brass that they were short of officers in Britain to which the Canadian replied they had buckets of them in Canada sitting and doing nothing and were grinding out more.

Robbie said that he was warned in Canada by his colonel not to be a damned fool and volunteer because the British would use him as cannon fodder. In the event he was LOB only once which implied the advice was not incorrect. They both said that an MC was more difficult to win with the British because they felt British officers had priority. Fetterley went first to 7 Royal Hampshires (130 BIB, 43 BID) where he was told by the worst type of British officer that 'I'll have you know you are dirt under our feet' and his life made miserable, while neither could have been happier than they were with 2 E Yorks. Canloan officers could choose their units, but if they wanted to serve together then the British chose for them. Robbie and four other Canloans arrived at 3 BID camped at Cowplain near Portsmouth at the end of April 1944 and were taken to the E Yorks. The Colonel, Hutchinson, was called and the four Canloan officers came to a smart salute. The colonel was without a hat and casually 'threw us a salute and this shook us'. The colonel then said; 'I didn't ask for any bloody colonials, but I said I'd take you if you're here by Friday at 5 o'clock.

87 Rex Fendick in an e-mail in June 2002.

It's just a quarter to five – welcome aboard'. 'We got treated famously from then on' although they had to learn about the British army's class distinctions. At first they would pitch pennies with the men and walk into town with the lance-corporal until the battalion 2ic had a little chat telling them 'not to do those things'. They both found the Yorkshire accents impossible to understand at first. Within a week the Colonel had thoughtfully written to the mothers, or wives if they were married, of each of the Canloans telling them that their son or husband 'has arrived in our battalion, and I want to leave you well assured that it is a well-trained battalion in the best trained army in the world'. The colonel used to drive up in his big Daimler and take the Canloans for trips to Winchester Cathedral, to HMS *Victory* and to other spots. The Canadians never disguised their origins. Jim Fetterley took to wearing German jackboots, carrying a Luger because it fired Sten ammunition and a German rifle. Robbie told him at the time he was crazy because the Germans would shoot him if he were captured, but Jim did not desist and said he never felt the Germans would retaliate. In Normandy when Panzer Meyer's SS started killing Canadian prisoners his CO asked him to remove his CANADA shoulder flash worn below the EAST YORKSHIRE, but he wouldn't. The British 'called me a total nut, but I got letters from kids wanting to come and serve in my platoon from other platoons. They thought we were more down to basics.'

> Once we had the pick of two reinforcements, one British and one Canadian and I said to the men, what do you want? Bring us the goddamn Canadian. That was the answer. It was Hebb, a good choice. Most Canadian officers came up through the ranks (as they both had). That was the main thing. We didn't find it inhibiting to go and talk to our lance-corporals.[88]

They were both wounded and RTU'd which was unusual for Canloans. Both still own their battle dress blouses; 'you couldn't let these things go,' although in the author's experience few British soldiers have theirs. The Canloans are proud and contented men with a superb record. They numbered 673 of whom 128 (19%) lost their lives and 75% were casualties. 3 BID received 50 Canloans of whom 11 (22%) were killed in action. They were distributed as follows: 8 BIB had 24 (1 Suffolks 5, 2 E Yorks 12 and 1 S Lancs 7) with 6 KIA; 9 BIB had 14 (2 Lincolns 2, 1 KOSB 11, and 2 RUR 1) with 3 KIA; while 185 BIB had only 9 (2 Warwicks 3, 1 Norfolks 4 and 2 KSLI 2) with 2 KIA. One served in HQ 3 BID and two in 2 Middlesex. The Canloan scroll shows the 6 GAB as a recipient, but an examination of each Canloan's service record as given by Smith shows none served in any of its constituent units, which is puzzling. Some served in 1 GG in GAD, which might explain the confusion. The reaction of their fellow British officers to the Canloans is universal admiration. Thus the Norfolks' subaltern, George Dicks, MC, who features in the Kervenheim battle narrative, wrote to this author in 1999: 'The Canloan exercise was one of the most gallant and romantic stories of the Second World War'. George sent a photograph of himself with CDN/171 Lt. John Alfred Laurie, MC (awarded at Kervenheim), killed in action near Bremen on 16 April 1945, for inclusion in an exhibit in 1999 of 'Flags Held High' at the Chatham-Kent Museum in Ontario. Fred Laurie grew up in Chatham, graduating from Chatham Vocational School before enlisting in the Canadian Army in July 1940. Having had the added experience of serving in the Kent Regiment as a member of the militia prior to the war, Laurie became a Sergeant after his enlistment and was subsequently attached to Platoon Weapons Training in Nanaimo, BC as an Assistant Instructor. Later, after completing additional courses in small arms, Laurie received his commission as a Lieutenant and in 1944, after four years' service in Canada, sailed for England. 'With the help of Lt. Laurie's family, the Chatham-Kent Museum has been fortunate to be able to borrow a wonderful selection of the officer's personal effects including

88 Jim Fetterley in conversation.

his commission, memorial plaque, training certificates, photographs, and medals including the Memorial Cross given to the next of kin of deceased soldiers'.

There were Canloans from Quebec in 3 BID. One was CDN/320, Lt Georges Bellavance in 2 KSLI, who won the MC at Venraij. His English was excellent. Littlar, a fellow officer in X Coy, remembers being told by Bellavance that he was francophone and thinks he was from Quebec. *Code Word Canloan* does not identify the number of francophone Canloans. Of one million Canadian men and women who wore uniform in the Second World War, 20 percent of them were French-speaking, while the country's francophone population was approximately 30 percent. Of the 200,000 serving, 150,000 were volunteers. Certainly not all of them went to the front, but the Régiment de Maisonneuve was one of the first to fill its ranks and, after being decimated at Dieppe in August 1942, the Fusiliers de Mont-Royal rose from the ashes to play a key role in Normandy. There was, however, no structure to channel francophone efforts and over 3,000 Francophones – the equivalent of an infantry brigade – were incorporated into Anglophone combat units. They had a difficult time during and after the war. Canadian propaganda glorified them but the armed forces remained very British both in the language they used and in the way they functioned. Furthermore, a large segment of Quebec's francophone élite, such as Pierre Elliott Trudeau, did not participate in the war and fought for the 'no' side during the referendum. They closed their eyes to the nature of the Vichy régime and after the war kept silent about the veterans from Quebec, undoubtedly in order to forget their own error of judgment. Upon returning to their country, this wartime generation of soldiers saw their children embrace the grumbling nationalism of the sixties and excoriate the federal state. Many therefore resolved to keep silent themselves, and the rare memorial ceremonies held on 11 November and on other occasions, were degraded to the point where they lost all real meaning in the collective life of Quebec. To a certain extent, the people who had fought for liberty at the age of 20 made the decision, once they had reached 40, to hush up their glorious past. This silence of the élites and to some degree of the veterans themselves meant Quebec's history texts are silent on the subject of its participation in the 1939-45 war. The above is a précis of a speech by Serge Bernier, Acting Director of the History Department of DND, in Quebec City on 15 October 1994 on the occasion of the Jubilee of the Second Allied Conference at Quebec. Francophone Quebec remains ambivalent about the war. US participation made the Allied cause respectable so no one says a word against it, but for Quebecois, as to a certain extent for the Irish but not the Scots, emotional antagonism to 'Les Anglais' is too powerful to be put aside.

On 3 June 1961, the Governor-General, Maj Gen Georges Vanier, the British High Commissioner, and Canadian and British government and veterans' representatives, unveiled a memorial in Ottawa recording the names of the 128 fatal Canloan casualties. The inscription reads in part: "Their Fallen are honoured in this quiet place in gratitude and remembrance of the cost of liberty."

Germany was severely destroyed by British forces, especially the RAF which convinced Churchill of the proposition that destroying 100 German cities would terrify the population into surrender. The British Army from the beginning rejected this scenario but was overruled, while Bomber Command was kept beyond the jurisdiction of the CCS and reported directly to Churchill. The Army upheld the traditional rules of civilised conflict and the Geneva Convention that forbade the deliberate killing of non-combatants and POWs. The battlefield of Operation *Heather* was dotted with farm houses undamaged by the RAF, but were nevertheless universally burnt and many levelled. The question is who was responsible. Both RW Thompson and Decker agree that all the farms were in Grotendonk were ablaze. One suggestion was that because it was February there would have been fires in the hearths and cooking stoves easily dispersed by shelling, and the target lists show that most farms were subject to artillery concentrations. Pastor Coenders said the fire in Endtschenhof started 30 minutes after the farm was occupied and the farmers were initially forbidden by the Warwickshire soldiery to put it out, which was suspicious. However, this may have been due to their failure to understand German and fear of a trap, and the fire having had time to take hold. Coenders then asked the question; 'But who had set fire to the house? We suspected that German soldiers, who until the last minute were dug-in in slit trenches and shell holes, had torched the house as they retreated.' As nerves calmed, Franz was allowed to save the barn although the British troops offered no assistance. The author finds no evidence for a British scorched earth policy, especially as these farms were regarded as potential billets, although many attest to the thoughtless destructiveness of the Anglo-Canadian army. There was certainly no British policy to minimise damage, although again there were exceptions. Horrocks was appalled by the destruction of Cleve and later Edwards did not want to shell Winnekendonk because of the presence of civilians. Churchill had set the tone in 1942 when he said in the House that the damage inflicted by the British should be used by the Germans for reflecting on the harm they had brought the world, and in great part this was how it was understood in post-war Germany. Looked at in this light it could be said that the more the damage to Germany, the greater the German soul-searching and repentance. However, there was a military reason to destroy a farm to make it more defensible and remove the risk of its burning when occupied by German defenders. Erich Freund records that German Paratroops blew up some of the farms he visited as a runner because the ruins were easier to defend and more difficult to hit with observed artillery fire. Shelling, bombing by BC and 2TAF, and deliberate destruction by German defenders caused the damage. Nowhere to this author's knowledge has there been any charge of malicious destruction to buildings by Allied forces. J.G. Smith agreed with this assessment; 'You are correct in thinking there was no 'scorched earth' policy and I never knew of anyone destroying anything just for the hell of it. We did bag a lot of poultry and after our first foray into Germany we took a lot of furniture back for our Dutch hosts. The feeling in my crew was that the Germans had started it and if Germany was knocked about it might teach them not to start another war, so we didn't feel sorry for the Germans but on the other hand didn't go out of our way to trash them'. J.G. Smith added; 'Everybody looted, including officers. Mostly it was to fill an immediate need and I give plenty of examples of this in my book. After the shortages we had endured for so long in England we were amazed at how well off the Germans appeared to be and taking their possessions, especially food, didn't weigh on our consciences.[89]

The fate of most of the County Regiments mentioned in these pages was amalgamation in the 1960s on the recommendation of Whistler's 1957 Committee on the Reorganisation of British Infantry, one exception of course being Montgomery's Regiment, the Royal Warwicks. A faint memory of these old county regiments is invoked by the names of the companies in the Royal Anglian Regiment headquartered in Bury St Edmunds since 1964. Its 1st Bn, called 'The Vikings', with HQ in Bulford, comprises: 'A' (Royal Norfolk) Coy; 'B' (Suffolk) Coy; 'C' (Essex) Coy; 'D' (Cambridgeshire) Coy. 2nd Bn, 'The Poachers', with HQ in Cottesmore: 'A' (Lincolnshire) Coy; 'B' (Royal Leicestershire) Coy; 'C' (Northamptonshire) Coy; 'D' (Bedfordshire & Hertfordshire) Coy. 3rd Bn, 'The Steelbacks', with HQ in Bury St Edmunds: 'A' (Norfolk) Coy; 'B' (Lincolnshire) Coy; 'C' (Leicestershire & Northamptonshire) Coy; 'D' (Essex & Hertfordshire) Coy; 'HQ' (Suffolk & Cambridgeshire) Coy. The Royal Anglian Regiment is called 'light rôle' infantry, meaning it has minimal armour and is lightly armed to be 'fast moving to seize ground in lightning strikes'.[90] Readers of this book may react to such language with disbelief, having seen how infantry without its own armour and the means of providing overwhelming retaliation will suffer numerous and avoidable casualties.

89 JG Smith in a letter.
90 https://uk.answers.yahoo.com/question/index?qid=20080615124758AA7CqPr

GOCs of 3 British Infantry Division

3 September 1939	Maj-Gen B.L. Montgomery
30 May 1940 (acting)	Brig K.A.N. Anderson
3 June 1940	Maj-Gen B.L. Montgomery
22 July 1940 (acting)	Brig J.A.C. Whitaker
25 July 1940	Maj-Gen J.A.H. Gammell
20 November 1940	Maj-Gen E.C. Hayes
15 December 1940	Maj-Gen W.H.C. Ramsden
12 December 1943	Maj-Gen T.G. Rennie
13 June 1944	Brig E.E.E. Cass (acting)
23 June 1944	Maj-Gen L.G. Whistler
22 January 1945	Maj-Gen A. Galloway
25 February 1945	Maj-Gen L.G. Whistler

Brigades in 3 Division

7 Inf Bde (Guards)	3.9.39 – 15.9.41
8 Inf Bde	3.9.39 – 31.8.45
9 Inf Bde	3.9.39 – 31.8.45
37 Indep Inf Bde	27.11.41 – 7.12.41
7 Inf Bde	8.12.41 – 4.6.42
33 Tk Bde	22.6.42 – 28.4.43
185 Inf Bde	10.4.43 – 31.8.45

Commanders of 8 British Infantry Brigade

3 September 1939	Brig F.H. Witts
21 February 1940	Brig C.G. Woolner
3 November 1940 (acting)	Lt-Col T.F. Given
27 November 1940	Brig G. Syme
26 June 1941	Brig Hon W. Fraser
3 March 1942	Brig B.W.S. Cripps
7 October 1943	Brig E.E.E. Cass
13 June 1944 (acting)	Lt-Col M.A. Foster
23 June 1944	Brig E.E.E. Cass
27 October 1944	Brig E.H. Goulburn
11 July 1945	Brig J.N.R. Moore

Commanders of 9 British Infantry Brigade

3 September 1939	Brig W. Robb
17 June 1940	Brig B.G. Horrocks
4 February 1941	Brig J.F. Hare
10 March 1942	Brig T.N.F. Wilson
4 July 1942 (acting)	Lt-Col P. Reid
18 July 1942	Brig J.C. Cunningham
7 June 1944	Brig A.D.G. Orr

9 August 1944	Brig G.D. Browne
1 January 1945	Brig G.D. Renny
1 April 1945	Brig W.F.H. Kempster

Commanders of 185 British Infantry Brigade

1 September 1942	Brig G. Mc I.S. Bruce
4 June 1943(acting)	Lt-Col N.C.S. Young
17 June 1943	Brig K.P. Smith
2 July 1944	Brig E.L. Bols
8 December 1944	Brig E.H. Grant
15 December 1944 (acting)	Lt-Col D.L.A. Gibbs
4 January 1945 (acting)	Lt-Col F.P. Barclay
20 January 1945	Brig F.R.G. Matthews
7 June 1945	Brig R.N.H.C. Bray.

HF Joslen: *Orders of Battle Vol 1.* London: HMSO 1960

6

8 Fallschirmjägerdivision (8 FJD) and Civilians

The parachute is a means of delivery, not a way of fighting.

Anon

The paratroops are so valuable to me that I'm only going to use them if it's worthwhile. The Army managed Poland without them. I'm not going to reveal the secret of the new weapon prematurely.

Hitler to Student 1939

The day of the parachutist is over. The Parachute arm is a surprise weapon and without the element of surprise there can be no future for airborne forces.

Hitler to Student, July 1941

I have a reactionary army, a National Socialist air force, and a Christian navy.

Hitler

This cult of special forces is as sensible as to form a Royal Corps of Tree Climbers and say that no soldier, who does not wear its green hat with a bunch of oak leaves stuck in it, should be expected to climb a tree.

FM Sir William Slim

The idea of vertical envelopment attracted those who had fought in the trenches of the First World War and sought answers to the reinforced concrete of the Maginot Line and West Wall. VVF Marshal Schtscherbakov commented to Marshal Petain during a tour of the Maginot Line that enemy paratroops made such fortifications superfluous by jumping over them.[1]

Airborne offered a choice of ground and surprise but at the expense of being fraught with problems of operation, intelligence, organisation, communications, weapons, timeliness and relief. The first German airborne operations were successful and had low losses in Denmark, Norway and at Eben Emael in April-May 1940, but already in that same month losses climbed in the Netherlands, with 186 of the 400 transports destroyed and many paratroops captured. The next airborne operation, in April 1941 at the Corinth Canal, was a failure when 2FJR arrived too late to take the bridge which had been used to block the canal; and the attack on Crete was a Pyrrhic victory, with 271 of the 500 transports lost and half the troops. Hitler concluded that the necessary element of surprise had been irrevocably lost, and stood the paratroopers down.

At first sight it is mysterious why in the light of Hitler's decree that paratroop formations including 8 FJD should have been raised in 1943 – 1945 when there was no means, or intention,

1 Bruce Quarrie. *German Airborne Troops 1939-1945* (London: Osprey, 1983), p. 4.

of delivering them by air to battle. The answer is to be found in the surprising result of three years of trial and error in the unforgiving laboratory of the Eastern Front, and in the existence of a 'paratrooper's spirit' that owed a lot to the Luftwaffe's aura, selection privileges and Nazi enthusiasm.

The Soviet Union pioneered the development of paratroops during a period of social and military experimentation based on Marxist insight that since economic laws governed society, there were military laws to be discovered. In a spirit of discovery, during manoeuvres in 1930 a small unit of NKVD *spetsnaz* paratroops was dropped to neutralise the enemy's HQ, reflecting also a British obsession in Plan 1919 with using fast tanks to destroy corps and army HQs. By 1933 the Russians had formed a brigade comprising a battalion each of paratroops, mechanised infantry, and artillery with three squadrons of aircraft. Following debate, the army assumed command of this and several other such brigades.

In 1935 General Köstring, the German Military Attaché in Moscow, watched and reported on a drop of 1,188 paratroops followed by an airlanding of 1,765 troops supported by armour. Göring saw the report and issued instructions for a parachute battalion to be created within *Regiment General Göring*. This was a militarized police force he established as Prussian Minister of the Interior to terrorize communists and other resistance. On 1 September 1935 Major Bruno Bräuer started work on creating the battalion from scratch at Stendhal. He asked for volunteers and in one day recruited 24 officers and 800 men.[2] Within three weeks *Regiment General Göring* was absorbed into the LW under the same name,[3] and on 29 January 1936 the Fallschirmtruppen were officially inaugurated.[4] Hitler recognised that he had a psychological tool for cowing his enemies, and an attractive weapon of surprise. For Göring paratroops expressed moral and racial superiority, since he believed the fallacy demonstrated by the fate of Zulus and Maoris who threw themselves at Gatling guns, that; 'Personal heroism must always count for more than technical novelties.' Baron von der Heydte recalled the feeling of physical and moral superiority that came with jumping into battle:

> Being dropped in battle is always a wonderful experience. You are, of course anxious but feel you dominate the enemy – as if you're descending from heaven. The enemy is earth-bound and this gives you a feeling of strength. This feeling however disappears the moment you are on the ground when you feel very weak because you have to free yourself from the parachute, you have to look for your weapons, and you are shot or, at least, you are in the line of fire.[5]

Hitler personally wrote ten commandments for the new force, calling them the chosen fighting men of the Wehrmacht of the master race, the cream of the élite.

The Heer formed its own paratroop battalion in 1936 under Major Richard Heidrich, which performed in the 1937 manoeuvres. In July 1938 Göring detached Bräuer's regiment and placed it in the newly established 7 Flieger-Division under Kurt Student. In January 1939 Heidrich's unit was transferred to the LW, and he was instructed to raise FJ Regiment 2 (FJR2). It was organized in the standard infantry manner with three battalions of four companies and with three support companies.

The Russians continued their airborne development. In 1936 Maj-Gen Wavell and the tank expert Lt-Col Martel watched 1,800 paratroops jump from 2,000 feet en masse, sliding off the wings and bumping into each other in the air. Martel observed they were scattered over a wide

2 Charles Whiting. *Hunters From The Sky* (London: Purnell, 1975), p. 20.
3 http://www.skalman.nu/third-reich/polis-reg-goering.htm
4 Quarrie, *German Airborne*, p. 5.
5 C Hadjipateras & M Fafalios. *Crete 1941 Eyewitnessed* (Anixi Attikis: Efstathiadis Group, 1989), pp. 75-77.

area; were without heavy weapons; landed with limited amounts of small arms ammunition; and took over an hour to assemble into units. There followed an air landing of 5,700 men with heavy weapons. By 1938 the Soviets fielded 6 airborne brigades comprising 18,000 men. Parachute training was widespread in civilian clubs, called *Osoviakhim* and a million or more had received parachute training by 1941. After the Molotov-Ribbentrop Pact the airborne was expanded to five corps, with two facing Romania and threatening Germany's oil supplies. When Germany invaded Russia the force was being expanded to ten corps. Those raised were used as infantry.

The Russians dropped paratroops unsuccessfully in the counter-attack at Vyazma in January 1942, supposedly securing strong points for advancing Soviet troops, and possibly even earlier, but they certainly suffered a disaster after dark on 24 September 1943 in the Dnieper Loop north of Kanev, or the Bukrin Bridgehead as they called it. Three guards paratroop brigades numbering 7,000 men were dropped straight onto assembling German troops and destroyed with only 2,300 surviving to join the partisans. Further landings planned as a follow-up after two days by freight-carrying gliders and tanks were cancelled, and the Russians abandoned airborne operations for the duration except for small-scale partisan support. A Russian paratroop colonel explained to James Gavin in 1945 at Tempelhof that; 'we just couldn't make sense out of all those men and aeroplanes.'

Airborne is a method of delivery and not a way of fighting. The difference was understood but often ignored, just as 'fighting terror' makes as little sense as 'declaring war on Blitzkrieg', since terror, like Blitzkrieg, is only a way of killing people and destroying morale. This category error, however, survives even Zbigniew Brzezinski's condemnation.[6] Parachute troops are light infantry that are equipped and trained for skirmishing, and when employed as regular infantry risk defeat from second-class troops equipped with standard infantry weapons. To overcome their vulnerability, Student combined paratroops with glider-borne infantry on a divisional scale. The drill, which the Russians sensibly could never be bothered to make sense of, was first to clear the landing grounds by strafing with ground-attack aircraft; then to send in gliders with infantry and light field and anti-tank guns to secure the landing grounds; followed by paratroops; the whole lot to be relieved as soon as possible by real troops before the massacre.

Such a force required special training and aptitude, and the support of a technologically advanced industrial base. It took 53 Ju52 aircraft to lift a battalion of 600 men. In technology Germany led the world in the 1930s and possessed a comparative advantage in producing the necessities for an airborne force that was represented as a German way of warfare. Even so, the burden on German industry was considerable, and between 1939 and 1945 amongst all of its other commitments only 3,000 Ju52 were produced, of which only 150 survived at War's end.

Airborne was as controversial in Germany as it had been in Russia. The Luftwaffe favoured a limited rôle in 'special purpose' and sabotage actions ahead of the main army, while the Army promoted its use *en masse*. Both concepts were implemented, but large-scale deployment of airborne was due almost entirely to the single-mindedness of the ex-infantryman and fighter pilot Kurt Student, supported by Göring and Hitler. On 4 July 1938 Student became Commander of the parachute and air landing troops, and in September GOC Fliegerdivision 7 and Inspector of airborne troops. He set about raising the airborne.

Heinz Trettner[7] described his commander, Student as unimposing, with a high voice and a hesitant manner that worsened after a bullet was removed from his skull by Dutch surgeons in 1940. He was industrious but worked slowly and precisely, writing out his appreciations in detail before handing them to his staff.

6 Zbigniew Brzezinski. *International Herald Tribune*, 15 November 2003.
7 Corelli Barnett. *Hitler's Generals* (London: Weidenfeld & Nicolson, 1990).

> And here faced with an unknown and almost nebulous task, the General who until then was known mostly for meticulous precision and military competence, developed himself abruptly into a visionary designer of a new branch of the service complete with instructions and tactics, organization and weapons, and above all an unsurpassable spirit. All were entirely due to his unexcelled mind.[8]

In 1944 Hitler decided Student's slowness revealed lack of intelligence and sacked him. But Student had a good memory and could learn maps by heart, and was also calm, patient, fearless, warm towards his troops, generous, modest and created the 'Paratroopers' Spirit' that partly explained their effectiveness. Completely honest, he scorned personal favour and advancement and was severe on himself. He was wounded in the First World War commanding a fighter squadron, Jasta 9. He worked post war with the *Fliegerzentrale* of the General Staff and planned an air force based on manpower recruitment from the gliding clubs. There followed a term of five years in the infantry, when he was appointed Director of Technical Training Schools for the LW and then commanded the LW Test Centre at Rechlin. He was director of flying schools.

Student's success with the paratroops came from combining the skills of army and air force. From the Heer came Heidrich's trained infantry battalion that transferred into the LW on 1 September 1939 as IIFJR1 (2 Battalion of 1 Paratroop Regiment). The Heer also provided Meindl's Mountain Artillery Regiment together with knowledge of army signals. From the LW Student acquired: skills in mass transportation, with the Ju 52 using ex-Lufthansa pilots and maintenance personnel; the Ju 87 in both ground attack role clearing the landing fields, and as a glider tug; and the air-superiority fighter Bf 109 to protect the slower Junkers aircraft and gliders including the later *Me Gigant*. From his own resources at Stendhal Student developed parachuting equipment and tactics with ways of transporting paratroops *en masse* in the Ju 52 and supplying weapons by canister and glider.

Jäger Erich Freund, whose experiences in FJR7 are described below, saw Student three times:

> First in Gardelegen, when in batches of a few hundred we had to enter the dining hall where he asked us the question; "Why do you think we want so many paratroopers". Half the men answered they were needed to jump into Russia and the other half into England.
>
> The next time was somewhere near Arnhem. It was cold, frosty and deep snow. I wore a dirty white smock for camouflage, and was leading a makeshift cart with two horses in makeshift harnesses and without horseshoes, carrying food up to the battle groups. Both the horses had fallen and were lying on the ground. The staff-car with General Student couldn't get by. The rule was that you saluted a superior, especially one with a Ritterkreuz, and told him who you were and what you were doing. I forgot all that in my concern for the horses. Our company commander (Otto Einert) was in the back of the car and told me to report who I was and what I was doing. I was in a flap, but saluted, pointed to the horses and said; 'Horses fallen to the ground'. Back came the high-pitched voice; 'Carry on!' Well we got the horses up and he was off.
>
> The last time was in a place called Randwijk between the Lower Rhine and Waal. Student had come over the Rhine in a rubber dinghy. I couldn't see him but could hear him shouting his head off because the village of Zetten had been lost to the Canadians and we were ordered there to stabilise the situation.[9]

8 Heinz Trettner in memoriam Generaloberst Karl Student. *Deutsches Soldatenjahrbuch 1980* (Munich: Schild-Verlag, 1980), p. 59. This author's translation.

9 Letter in English from Erich Freund in February 1997.

The FJ divisions – 2, 6, 7 and 8 FJD – that resisted Operation *Veritable* were the last scrapings of the German manpower barrel. Formed or re-formed within the previous three months, there was virtually nothing behind them except garrisons in Denmark and Norway, and no reinforcements. Their capitulation in northern Germany in early May marked the end of the Third Reich in its Flensburg outpost.

It is impossible to know when Churchill abandoned his conviction that bombing would force the Germans to capitulate, or even if he ever did do so. In the real world, however, where bombing made civilians angry rather than submissive, and soldiers knew that peace would come only after the German army was defeated, the Allies had reason on two occasions to expect an easy and early end to hostilities. The breakout from Normandy and capture of Antwerp convinced SHAEF that they were repeating the endgame of one hundred days after Amiens in 1918, as Simonds claimed on the Falaise Road on 8 August 1944. It would be easier this time, they thought because unlike 1918, when the entire Wehrmacht faced them in the west, in 1944/45 two-thirds were in the east and Germany was 'devastated' by bombing. The second occasion was in February 1945 when SHAEF interpreted German recovery at Arnhem and in the Ardennes as a last gasp, with nothing left to prevent 21 AG from seizing Wesel within a week, and driving on to Berlin. As in 1918 Canadians were in the van, but this time under command of a Canadian army. Every hope, however, was dashed, and instead of Eisenhower being in Berlin in November 1944 as predicted in August, or in March 1945 at the latest as the thinking was in early February, Montgomery was not on the Elbe until May with the Russians already in Berlin.

It is not fanciful to identify SHAEF's nemesis as being the three fifty year-olds who raised a paratroop army to block the route to Berlin. All holders of the Knight's Cross, they were Generaloberst Kurt Student (1890-1978), C-in-C Paratroops; General der Fallschirmtruppe Alfred Schlemm (1894-1986), commanding 1 Fallschirm-Armee; and General der Fallschirmtruppe Eugen Meindl (1892-1951), commanding II Fallschirmkorps. Schlemm and Meindl's feats of organization, leadership and tactical brilliance in the face of great odds have been underappreciated.

Schlemm and Meindl both served as junior officers in the field artillery throughout the First World War, and stayed on postwar in the Reichswehr. In 1925 both took staff positions and afterwards returned to the artillery. Schlemm went to the Reich Defence Ministry in Berlin until 1930, and Meindl to 5 GID and then into the Reich Defence Ministry until 1927. Meindl rose through various artillery appointments to command Mountain Artillery Regiment 112 in 3 GMD in 1940. Schlemm rose further. He was an artillery battery commander from 1930 to 1932, when he was back in the Reich Ministry until 1934, followed by appointment as 1a (head of manpower) in two Wehrkreisen. He attended the Wehrmacht Academy in Berlin in 1937, followed by another year's detachment to the Reich Air Ministry. In 1938 he transferred into the LW as an Oberst in the LW General Staff, becoming Chief of Staff of Air Defence Zone West. In 1939 he was Chief of Staff of Luftgau XI at Hanover, and then in Hamburg.

They both joined the Fallschirmtruppen in 1940. Schlemm was appointed Chief of Staff of XI Fliegerkorps in December at Jeschonnek's suggestion as Student prepared to return after his head wound had healed, and he remained in that post until February 1942. Meindl's artillery unit supported the airborne in Norway where he jumped without training. He went into Führer Reserve, and was detached in August for jump training, transferring into the LW in November as commander of Parachute Air Landing Assault Regiment 1 (Assault Regiment Meindl).

The team of Student, Schlemm, and Meindl assembled for the first time in April 1941 for the invasion of Crete. They respectively commanded, planned and led the assaulting Battle Group West. After the catastrophic loss of 6,000 dead, during which Meindl was wounded and replaced by Ramcke, Student and Schlemm made plans to rebuild the airborne, but Hitler declared the day of the paratrooper was over. Jeschonnek then dispersed the airborne to Russia in September, with Lt-Gen Petersen commanding 7 Flieger Division.

Schlemm was detached in February 1942 to General Command of VIII Fliegerkorps under von Richthofen, and became commander of Luftwaffen-Gefechtsverbande (Battle Group) Schlemm one week later. Hermann Plocher, who was C-of-S of V Air Corps in IV Air Fleet, described one element of what became the LWFDs (Luftwaffe Field Divisions):

> In 1941-42 the Luftwaffe used its own personnel to defend its airfields and signal & command installations. At first these units only defended LW facilities, and the LW High Command did not envisage a broadening of their involvement. These units were organized on the spot in the various areas and initially differed greatly from one another with respect to organization, strength, command, equipment and even employment. Everything was improvised, their equipment was faulty, and their training wholly inadequate.
>
> The usual policy was to organize all available air signal and flak troops as quickly as possible into companies or battalions for immediate combat commitment. Ground service personnel, second reserve guard units, and so-called general office personnel from staff and supply units were also included in the manpower pool from which these combat units were formed. Most of these units were named after their commanders and displayed excellent morale and combat behaviour.
>
> The first instance of committing such troops in battalion strength was at Rzhev in January 1942 whwre airfields within the sector were defended by LW field units. In March the same units were transported to Krassilina airfield, south of Spas Demyansk, endangered by a major Soviet penetration at Sukhinichi. There the units were consolidated under Generalmajor Alfred Schlemm. Reinforced by flak battalions, LW Brigade Schlemm's mission was to assault the enemy around the airfield and to clear the enemy beyond the range of small arms. LW Brigade Schlemm was supported by aircraft of VIII Air Corps of LW Command East, and was completely successful. [The Kriegsgliederung (Orbat) dated 22 April 1942 showed 'Gruppe Schlemm (Luftwaffen-Verbande)' assigned to the XXXX Panzer Corps. The Kriegsgliederung of 11 May and 24 June 1942 listed 'Gruppe Schlemm (Luftwaffen-Verbande)' as serving with the LVI Panzer Corps. Both were part of General der Infanterie Gotthard Heinrici's 4th Army in Army Group Centre].
>
> A ground combat organization was established by LW Command Moscow at Smolensk to protect its ground service installations. Established in regimental strength, it was employed with success primarily along the Smolensk-Roslavl rail and road routes. The partisans had destroyed telephone wires and railway tracks over which LW fuel needed to move to the two airfields at Shatalovka and other bases in the rear of Army Group Centre. The regiment was therefore employed specifically in a LW mission.
>
> The LW field units were courageous, with good morale, and fulfilled their missions. After the activation of the Luftwaffe Feld Divisions, a highly controversial problem outside the scope of this study, all LW ground combat units were integrated into divisional size units, which were only under the tactical control of local Army HQs. By end 1942 in Combat Zone Centre, II LW Feld Korps consisting of 3, 4 and 6 LWFDs was engaged in a successful defensive battle in the Vitebsk-Neval sector.[10]

With the coming of spring, Schlemm handed command to the new organization at Smolensk, and from June to September 1942 led 1 Flieger-Division at Dugino that controlled various air and ground support units under von Greim's Luftwaffe Command East. He returned to command a corps of LWFDs being raised by Meindl.

---

10 Hermann Plocher. *The German Air Force Versus Russia 1942* (N Stratford: Ayer, 1968).

Meindl arrived in Russia in December 1941, accompanied by HQ Company of his Assault Regiment, to command a battle group of SS, Flak and ground personnel that successfully defended the airfield of Mölder's JG 51 at Juchnow. A few months earlier in October 1941, seven Luftwaffe field regiments had been formed and hurriedly trained in East Prussia from volunteers, and attached as independent battalions to various divisions under heavy attack in and near the Cholm and Demyansk pockets. By February 1942 the regimental staffs had control. In March 1942 Meindl took control of four of the field regiments to form Division Meindl in Staraya Russa. It was well led and uniquely strong, according to Ruffner, producing plaudits from OKH for bravery and effectiveness in a despatch dated 23 June 1942. It trained and hunted for partisans. In October under its new commander, Odebrecht, it was involved in Operation Winkelried to expand the corridor into the Demyansk Pocket. In December the division received an artillery regiment and was designated 21 Luftwaffenfelddivision (LWFD).

The success of Division Meindl led Göring to believe the LW could raise effective ground forces, and he issued a call for volunteers on 17 September 1942. At the same time OKH was asking for 10 to 20,000 replacements from the Kriegsmarine and 50,000 from the Luftwaffe. Hitler at first agreed, but changed his mind when Göring argued that the reactionary army was no place for his Nazi boys and that Nazis should stick together. The Army replied that only they had the ability to arm and train the men effectively. Göring then offered to expand his field force to 100,000 men in 10 LW Field Divisions armed by the Army and under its tactical control, but remaining in the loyal LW. Hitler issued orders to that effect on 15 October 15 1942, according to Ruffner and Muñoz.

Schlemm and Meindl became corps commanders in October 1942 with the task of raising and training 200,000 men in 22 divisions. Schlemm established a new II LW Feldkorps near Vitebsk to command 2, 3, 4 and 6 LWFDs in Army Group Centre, while Meindl was told to establish I LW Feldkorps which in the event was never actuated,[11] and to take over XIII Flieger Korps at Grossborn in Pomerania. There he organised the raising of the divisions and their basic training. On 21 July 1943, Meindl became Inspector of Luftwaffe Field Formations.

Göring's Basic Order Number 13 specified the employment of LWFDs in 'only defensive missions on quiet fronts', and Göring called on the Army to provide ongoing training in the field. Training was sketchy given the urgency to get men into the field before the winter offensive. Some of the new divisions were inevitably attacked by forces which they were not trained, manned or equipped to withstand. This was the fate of 2 LWFD near Byeloy in the Rzhev Salient. Together with its neighbouring 246 Infantry Division, it was attacked on 25 November 1942 by ten Soviet rifle and five tank divisions. 2 LWFD broke and ran in the first few hours while 246 ID held on for over two weeks. On the same day, 8 LWFD marched across the steppe to relieve Stalingrad and straight into a superior Russian force that destroyed the van and scattered the remainder after only a few hours.

Their weakness was ascribed to lack of training, inexperienced leadership, poor equipment, and an establishment of four battalions instead of the nine in an infantry division – 6,500 officers and men (compared with 12,500 in the 1944 type infantry division), although a USWD source disagreed; 'It is believed that the basic pattern was originally a two-regiment, three battalion division with normal supporting units and an additional anti-aircraft battalion', but then a different TOE of 3 regiments of 2 battalions with an establishment of 12,500.[12] The LWFDs benefited from a powerful Flak battalion comprising four 88 mm and twenty-seven 20 mm guns that were not in the TOE (Table of Establishment) of an infantry division and were effective in the ground role, and a Pak battalion with 9 units of 50 mm Pak 38 and 9 units of captured Russian 7.62 cm guns. Their artillery, however, was nominal. Both 2 and 8 LWFD had two batteries of four 75 mm

11 http://www.ww2.dk/

12 USWD. *Handbook On German Military Forces, 1945*: TM-E 30-451, Sect II-29 & II-8.

Geb K15 mountain weapons of Czech origin that could be carried on horseback, five StuGs and six 105 mm Nebelwerfer 40 mortars that were not army divisional issue. They were also better motorized according to the TOE than any German infantry division except the FJDs. The best of the LWFDs, Feld-Division 12 (L), remained motorized until March 1945, reaching Danzig from Courland with 443 motor vehicles and 4,571 men. At 10 men per vehicle it surpassed its TOE.

TOE of Mechanized Infantry Divisions

Type of Infantry Division	Men	Vehicles	Men per vehicle
Heer Old type	17,000	942	18
Heer 1944 type	12,500	616	20
LW Feld	6,500	616	11
LW Fallschirmjäger	16,000	2,141	7
British	18,347	3,347	5

Maj-Gen F.W. von Mellenthin had first-hand experience of LWFDs during the attempted relief of Stalingrad. He made no mention of their small establishment, but was scathing about their lack of training and experience, classing them as excellent material but commanded by LW men who knew nothing about ground fighting.

Most commentators agreed the LWFDs reflected Göring's madness, and none found method in it. Göring, it was said, aspired to command ground troops (von Mellenthin); he raised them out of vanity and in a power struggle to protect his turf (Muñoz and Ruffner), and to safeguard his right to mount large future operations (Mahncke quoted in Muñoz); while Hitler is said to have acquiesced in order to divide the Wehrmacht and reward LW loyalty to the NSDAP (Ruffner). All agreed that they were 'a recipe for disaster' (Muñoz).

It was, however, a considered response to German weakness. In 1941 the LW could claim expertise in providing support to the army both through close air support and on the ground. It had provided the indispensable solution to the army's nightmare of having its tanks and anti-tank guns outclassed. LW flak battalions with dual-purpose 88 mms operated in the van of advancing armoured columns. Beginning at Arras, and indeed earlier in Spain, the army relied on their 88 mm to restore the situation when the Allies' Matilda, T-34 and KV-1 rolled over the 37 mm 'door-knocker' Paks and passed by the Mk III, which was the army's most heavily armoured tank. Plocher, who was a Flak General, recorded how infantry divisional commanders shouted 'Flak nach vorn' when attacked, and the boys in blue took the lead.

It was a small step, taken also by the RAF, to move from claiming indispensability to claiming mastery of the rules of land warfare. Kesselring claimed as much in a 1941 edition of the *Essener National Zeitung* quoted by Plocher:

> During the recent campaign of the 'war of movement', the LW could never have fulfilled the tasks of its leaders had it not continually kept in mind the importance of training their personnel to become an integral part of the German armed forces. The men were trained to study thoroughly the rules of land-fighting and to submit themselves unreservedly to its laws.

The LW knew intimately how the army fought its battles of encirclement in Russia, and was unimpressed with their combination of fast, motorised and armoured forces of *Schnelltruppen* supported by Stukas as 'flying artillery', with slow infantry forces that marched on their feet with horse drawn supply wagons and artillery. Many in the army knew the resulting delay, which allowed thousands of Russian troops to escape encirclement, threatened victory, but the OKH had designed and trained their forces in that way and had no short-term alternative. The LW, however, knew their volunteers had the intelligence, education, physical fitness and aptitude to handle higher speeds. Proof that a small and completely mechanized force could destroy a much larger unmechanized army was provided by O'Connor's handling of 'Butcher' Graziani at Beda Fomm in February 1941, which got Germany's full attention and resulted in Rommel's immediate despatch to Tripoli. Germans were not blind to parallels, however misleading, with their own situation, and Kinzel, who headed the General Staff Intelligence Department, provided then with one. He stated that the Russians had followed the advice of the British and changed their infantry over to a brigade system in order to create formations that were smaller, more manoeuvrable and easier to control. These attributes would have been music to the ears of the LW who already used Kampfgruppe for groups of three or four bomber squadrons. These same principles would explain the success of the LW *Alarmeinheiten* and *Kampfgruppen* that were cobbled together during the winter of 1941-42. They would have been tempted by the British thinking behind Jock Columns and Brigade Boxes, that small numbers of LW volunteer Jägers made mobile and equipped with motor-drawn 88 mm and Nebelwerfers would be able to produce the same amount of work as larger numbers of enlisted footslogging Landsers with their horse-drawn transport and artillery. The LWFDs were given an establishment of 615 motor vehicles representing 11 men per vehicle that compared with 18 to 20 men per vehicle in the infantry divisions. Mechanization was considered the key to productivity, especially when they could count on help from LW aircraft.

Finally, the attribute of being easier to control meant that a division the size of a brigade would have minimised the impact of a lack of senior LW officers trained and experienced in the land battle. The LW would have believed that they had found the free lunch of mobility preached by Liddell Hart and Fuller, and could have sold it to a Hitler receptive to trying new ideas put forward by the most nazified branch of his armed services, since the old ideas were inadequate in the face of superior Russian tanks and an unexpected fierceness of Russian will. The shortage of petroleum that would eventually ground the LW was not considered a problem in 1941 as plans were finalized to cross both the Caucasus and Egypt to seize Baku, Kirkuk and Abadan.

Meindl wrote a report in May 1943 explaining that the difficulties experienced by the small mobile LWFDs were due to their being employed as permanent replacements for full-size infantry divisions, with only half the men and resources. This role differed, he wrote, from their original purpose of temporarily relieving infantry divisions so they could obtain rest and recuperation out of the line. Meindl then proposed that LWFDs be formed into two air-landing Sturm divisions in the ratio of five to two. Their new role would be one of surprising and neutralising the Russian defences for the period needed by the armoured divisions to break out. This was a topical subject as the Germans planned how to employ their new heavy armour to encircle and destroy the Russian forces in the Kursk salient. At the same time as Meindl wrote his paper, the Russians were fortifying the salient to great and impenetrable depth. Jeschonnek supported Meindl's proposal and forwarded it to Göring who promised to speak to Hitler about it. In September 1943 Milch, who succeeded Jeschonnek, proposed to regroup the LWFDs into half the number of Luftlande-Divisions (airborne divisions) with 12,000 men, but Hitler had already decided to transfer the LWFDs into the army.

Two events are consistent with the hypothesis that the LWFDs had raised Hitler's hopes and he was reluctant to end the experiment. He permitted Schlemm and Meindl to raise a paratroop army in France, and to remove 10,000 men from the LWFDs in order to continue a related non-army infantry initiative. Hitler did not blame Schlemm and Meindl for the LWFD failure, and intervened in the fate of 20 LWFD. The Heer intended to dissolve 20 FD (L) as it became known, for use as reinforcements. Hitler ordered instead their re-equipment as a 'fast brigade' with the full TOE of motorised vehicles. One historian, Muñoz has said Hitler acted for 'some reason which has now been lost to history', but it was possible that all he was doing was continuing the experiment.

The Heer kept 20 FD (L) as a cavalry division with one regiment on bicycles since motor vehicles were unobtainable.

Schlemm transferred to the Fallschirmtruppen, taking his HQ to Italy where it became IFJKorps in January 1944. He commanded it until October 1944 when he handed over to Richard Heidrich. From November 1944 to March 1945, Schlemm commanded 1 Fallschirm-Armee. He was wounded on 20 March 1945 and spent the rest of the war in hospital, handing over to Günther Blumentritt who described Meindl as a particularly energetic and able officer whom he had met at an instructor course for generals.

Meindl commanded XIII Flieger-Korps and 1 LW Feld Corps from October 1942 to August 1943, and was Inspector of LW Feld formations. When the LWFDs were transferred to the Heer in November 1943, Meindl, like Schlemm, returned to the western front where he commanded IIFJKorps from February 1944 to the end of hostilities. Blumentritt described Meindl as a stern and tough former inhabitant of Wurtemberg, experienced as a fighter and leader of troops, always frank in his judgement, and held in high esteem by his troops.

The British in 1940 accepted Hitler's military challenge head-on, but being overawed by German military prestige decided to imitate and outperform Germany in every respect including airborne and storm-troops, which they called commandos. On 18 June 1940 Churchill lectured General Ismay on the concept of Storm Troops, saying the Germans had benefited from them in the First World War and that in this war they were a leading cause of their victory. He said he now wanted 20,000 Storm troops or 'Leopards' withdrawn from existing units, ready to battle with small landings or paratroop descents.[13] Churchill never seems to have understood the damage he thus caused to the infantry divisions by removing their best.

The British made their first demonstration jump of 50 paratroops in November 1940 and, in the same month, General 'Boy' Browning was appointed GOC Airborne Troops. By the end of December 1940 everything was in place to create 1 Airborne Division. In the USA, an airborne brigade was discussed by the Chief of Infantry in 1939. The following year a parachute (sic) test platoon was formed under infantry command, and expanded to a battalion in the autumn, with a parachute school founded at Fort Benning.

The German High Command never established commandos and special forces along British lines. The Brandenburg battalion was a department of the Abwehr and used for special tasks such as border infiltration and seizure of bridges in advance of the main force, often wearing the enemy's uniform. They were more like SOE than commandos. Hitler however was insistent, so a special forces commando unit, SS-Sonderverband z.b.v. Friedenthal, renamed 502 SS Jäger Battalion, was established under Otto Skorzeny which undertook three major operations; the Gran Sasso raid to free Mussolini, Operation Rosselsprung to eliminate Tito, and dressed as GIs to cause chaos during the Ardennes Offensive. There were also minor operations such as kidnapping Horthy's son, and perhaps a plan to assassinate the Big Three at the Tehran Conference.

Imitating Germans was the only rationale given in the Official History of the British airborne for Churchill's instruction of 22 June 1940 to his Chief of Staff:

> to have a corps (*sic*) of at least five thousand parachute troops.
>
> The possibilities of this new form of warfare were obviously very great, and it was therefore high time to plan ahead, so that when the moment came and the tables were turned, the British Army should have at its disposal a force capable of achieving all that the enemy had achieved and much more.[14]

13 WS Churchill. *The Second World War, Vol II: Their Finest Hour* (London: Cassell, 1949), p. 147.
14 Anonymous. *By Air To Battle* (London: Ministry of Information, 1945).

The number was subsequently reduced to 500. Churchill in his dilettante way misunderstood the lessons of Crete on 27 May 1941. Instead of congratulating himself on his foresight in cutting his airborne losses, he reverted to his earlier instruction and reminded Ismay that he wanted 5,000 para-stormtroops and an airborne division on the German model.[15]

While Hitler concluded that Crete showed that the day of the paratroop was over, Churchill was impressed by their victory and persevered with a flawed system that could never deliver its promise despite major British improvements on German techniques of weapon delivery, parachutes and aircraft. The British paratrooper landed with 100 lb of arms and ammunition on the end of a 70 ft rope attached to his waist. This system was developed in 1942 and had the advantages of speeding the descent until the bag had landed when the paratrooper was unweighted and his descent slowed, and permitting the paratrooper to arm himself instantly with SMG, rifle or Bren. By contrast the German had to search for the canister that landed separately, during which time he was armed only with a 9 mm machine-pistol and hand grenades. The British parachute and harness were superior, attached at the shoulder rather than the waist so that it was possible to steer by reaching up and pulling selected shroud lines which the German couldn't reach. The British parachute was released by punching a quick-release box rather than by undoing four buckles. Exiting the aircraft required no German swallow dive, and landing did not require the German forward roll onto heavily padded knees, which limited the load that could be carried.

By optimising the airborne sub-system, which was never a war-winner, Churchill and his staff unintentionally sub-optimised the all-arms infantry in two respects; the vital infantry were significantly weakened by the loss of outstanding men of action like Lord Lovat, Peter Kemp, Martin Lindsay, Freddy Chapman, David Stirling, John Frost, and hundreds of others; while the need to find employment for the airborne distorted post-invasion campaigning, and specifically contributed to the disastrous delay in opening Antwerp and to the fiasco of Arnhem.

The War Office sent letters to officers requesting volunteers for 'special air service battalions'. ORs were provided by the COs of line battalions, who were told to send only volunteers of A.1 physical fitness and good character. The consequences were known at the time as Churchill admitted, writing that he had to press hard in 1940 against the grievances of colonels of infantry regiments who asked what could commandos and airborne do that his battalion could not? They complained that the plan robbed the whole Army of its prestige and of its finest men. Answer came there none. Sydney Jary felt that the traditional skirmishing skills of his Regiment, the Somerset Light Infantry, should have been upgraded to airborne instead of removing its best men into new airborne units. Bill Slim in Burma agreed, and trained ordinary infantry brigades to move routinely by air, saying there was as much need for a parachute regiment and other special forces as for a Royal Corps of Treeclimbers. Slim practised his conviction that airborne was a means of delivery and not a way of fighting.

Churchill suffered from the illusion propagated by the prophets of mobility like Liddell Hart and the RAF, that 'danger came from parachute descents or, even worse, the landing of comparatively small but highly mobile German tank forces which would rip up and disorganise our defence, as they had done when they got loose in France.'

Unlike the British case, the later expansion of the Fallschirmarmee into eleven divisions was an elegant solution to the problem of using surplus Luftwaffe volunteers as élite infantry to optimise the Wehrmacht. Men like Erich Freund remained in the Luftwaffe when underemployed due to petrol shortages that reduced flying, and were trained in 1944 as paratroops without jump training from aircraft. They could then fight alongside Army units in the same corps and armies.

15 WS Churchill. *The Second World War, Vol III: The Grand Alliance* (London: Cassell, 1950), p. 683.

The Germans retained flexibility in the employment of the three arms, eventually using even the Kriegsmarine in the land battle.

The British never developed the same level of inter-service co-operation. Churchill permitted the RAF to retain its excessive establishment. Portal as head of the RAF was nominally one of the Chiefs of Staff, but he reported in effect directly to Churchill and could ignore the needs of the other services, and with Bomber Harris try and win the war on their own. A manpower crisis erupted in the Army, which was forced to disband two divisions in 1944 to provide reinforcements, even when some 2,000 aircrew were idle and the RAF's deferred lists were large enough to man two entire infantry divisions. Eventually 17,000 men were transferred from the RAF into the Army, but it was a token gesture and too late. The RAF peaked at 1,185,833 in 1944 compared with a Luftwaffe peak of 1,700,000 in 1943, but the LW was also responsible for Flak and had LWFDs. In May 1944, only 2,191 British airmen were transferred to the army, of whom 1,500 came from the RAF Regiment and 691 volunteered. In July, 5,000 ground staff were transferred mostly to the Army and in December 20,000 more, but of these latter only 10,000 had arrived by June 1945.

Churchill sowed the seeds of military inferiority in 1940. He told Hopkins that he 'looked forward with our (US) help to mastery in the air and then Germany with all her armies will be finished. This war will never see great forces massed against one another.'

In the field the Allied airborne were inflexible, under-armed and of restricted value. They were not integrated into the day-to-day management and planning of the land battle and were unavailable at short notice. When Col Hinds of 2 USAD found the Adolph Hitler Bridge at Krefeld-Uerdingen blown on 3 March 1945, he asked his Army commander, Simpson for a company of DUKWs with which to sneak over the Rhine. When this request was denied he suggested a swift parachute assault on the opposite bank, forgetting that the Allies' airborne possessed high mobility only with a relatively long lead time.[16] Airborne operations were difficult and complicated to mount, and the airborne lobbied constantly to be employed. Operations such as *Market Garden* and Varsity/*Plunder* were tailored to their requirements. The tail wagged the dog, making airborne another fissiparous element in an already divided Anglo-Canadian Army that never mastered all-arms. Overall progress in the end depended on the infantry, who were sent into battle against strong opposition under-strength and under-equipped, because resources were diverted to special forces and to the strategic bombing campaign. Infantry officers cynically described their function as being reduced to providing an escort for the artillery FOO on his walk through Europe.

After initial small-scale German successes in 1940, the day of reckoning for the airborne concept was postponed from 1940 by the cancellation of Operation Sealion when RAF Fighter Command with its Chain Home radar would have destroyed the JU52s. The Germans planned to use their airborne in the same way as 6 Airborne was used on D Day. They planned to seize a bridge over the Military Canal in the Romney Marsh and to hold off attacks just as 6 Airborne seized the Orne Bridges and held off 21 Panzer. Student tried to interest Hitler in dropping the paratroop force into Ulster as a diversion for Sea Lion. In the event of its failure, Student told Hitler, the parachutists would cross into Eire and be interned. Hitler listened politely and left it to Göring to tell Student that Sea Lion was cancelled and that the airborne would instead be used to take Gibraltar. So the day when reality destroyed the dream duly arrived for the Germans in 1941 on Crete, for the Russians in 1943 in the Dnieper Loop, and in 1944 for the Allies at Arnhem. The heroic stories of Crete and Arnhem are interchangeable; crack troops armed with grenades and small arms being attacked by tanks.

16 Weigley, *Eisenhower's*, p. 615.

Student stated that the first employment of airborne was literally a leap in the dark and every operation was close to disaster. The vital intelligence service did not serve him well and in all the operations, except Eben Emael, the enemy situation was unclear.[17] The same complaints were made at Arnhem, and no doubt at Vyasma and in the Dnieper Bend.

FJR1 under Student and later Bräuer, was formed in 1936 from elements of the General Göring Regiment, and in 1938 came under command of Luftwaffe General Kurt Student's new 7 Flieger-Division. In 1939 the Division acquired FJR2 and was in truth only two thirds complete when employed in Norway, Denmark, Belgium and Holland. It operated in association with 22 Air Landing Division under Graf von Sponeck, which comprised IR16, IR47 and IR65 that were trained for glider-borne operations.

Such was the tiny airborne force that shook the world in 1940, and led to an airborne invasion panic in Britain after Dunkirk that spread irrationally as far as Maritime Canada. The British feared the Germans had five airborne divisions in 1941 when they had only one.

FJR3 was formed in 1940 and it was the complete 7 Air Division that suffered 30 percent casualties – losing 3,250 dead and missing and 3,400 wounded out of 22,000 – while taking Crete in 1941. It was next employed as infantry in the Siege of Leningrad and at Rzhev and on the Mius where the Russian winter offensive of 1941 was held. In late 1942 the name was changed to 1FJD under Heidrich. In March 1943 it transferred to France to recover and regroup.

The XI Air Corps under Student commanded 7 Air and 22 Air-Landing Divisions, together with Meindl's Sturmregiment (FJStR). It planned the Crete operation in 1941 under command of Löhr's 4 Air Fleet, and during 1942 continued to plan airborne operations such as Malta and Gibraltar. Hitler vetoed these from fear of another disaster like Crete, and hoped Rommel's success would remove their need. However Skorzeny's adventure on 12 September 1943 in freeing Mussolini with ninety men drawn from Paratroop Lehr Battalion and with 50 special SS troops, which was organised by Student from Rome, changed Hitler's mind about paratroops. Göring had been pressing Hitler to expand the paratroop force, and now got approval for eleven paratroop divisions. Student at once started raising and training new divisions in France, and in November Meindl and Schlemm were each given command of a paratroop corps.

In 1943 Student raised 2FJD in February under Ramcke and later Lackner, 3FJD in October under Schimpf, and 4FJD in November under Trettner. There followed in 1944 5FJD in March under Heilmann, 6FJD in June under Plocher and 7FJD in November under Erdmann. 8FJD and 9FJD were founded in October 1944 but cancelled and re-founded in January 1945, with 8FJD under Wadehn and 9FJD under Wilke. The last one, 10FJD was founded in March under von Hoffmann because 11FJD under Gericke never amounted to more than a battle group. From 8FJD onwards the FJDs lacked integral artillery. The Hermann Göring Paratroop Armoured Corps was established in October 1944 and employed in the east, but in practice had little to do with the paratroop forces although it remained part of Student's plan to provide paratroops with heavy weapons delivered by *Me Gigant* gliders. The paratroop divisions received armoured support from the StuG IIIs of Paratroop Assault Gun Brigades XI and XII raised in early 1944.

Hitler ascribed Skorzeny's success to the paratroop spirit and training. The task of duplicating eleven quality paratroop divisions rather than more of the pedestrian LWFDs was given to Göring, then at the lowest point of his relationship with Hitler who screamed at him ceaselessly, according to David Irving. His success was exceptional. The paratroop force of nearly 11 divisions raised in 1943/45 became almost as large as the British Army in NWE of 12 divisions, after the dispersal of 49 and 59 BIDs. Man-for-man it was more effective. Göring called an air staff conference

17 Rudolf Böhmler & Werner Haupt. *Fallschirmjäger: Bildband und Chronik* (Dorheim: Hans-Henning Podzun, 1971), p. 8.

at Karinhall to plan the command structure and to identify those able to form units with the required characteristics.

Göring appointed Meindl in late 1943 to command II Paratroop Corps at Melun with 3FJD and 5FJD, while Schlemm was appointed to I Paratroop Corps in Central Italy in January 1944 with 1FJD and 4FJD. With the great expansion underway, XI Air Corps was upgraded and its name changed to 1 Paratroop Army under Student. It formed at Nancy in April 1944 and was made responsible for training, which was the key to performance. When Student moved up to command Army Group H, Schlemm replaced him at 1 Paratroop Army on November 20, 1944. It was units under Schlemm, Meindl and Blaskowitz, who replaced Student in January 1945, which provided the backbone of the defence against Operations *Veritable*, *Heather*, *Leek* and *Blockbuster* in February 1945.

Alfred Schlemm was born in 1894, and served in the First World War in the field artillery. He received general staff training in 1925 and had staff appointments in the Reich Ministry before returning to be a battery commander when the Nazis took power. More staff appointments in Berlin were followed by attendance at the Wehrmacht staff academy in 1937, afterwards transferring to the Luftwaffe in 1938 and joining its general staff as a colonel. He commanded the Hanover and later Hamburg Luftgaus. When Student was recovering from his head wound, he discussed the need with Jeschonnek for a chief of staff of XI Fliegerkorps as the Paratroop were called, who recommended Schlemm. Student had never met him before, but was impressed by Schlemm's creative, strong and energetic personality combined with good military judgment and logic. He planned the Cretan landings. He left the Paras in 1942 to command his own battle group, which was renamed 1 Flieger Division in June 1942. In October he was promoted to command II LW Feldkorps in Russia and later Italy. In January 1944 Schlemm was sent to Italy to command 1 FJKorps comprising 4FJD and 3 PGD. It was employed in containing the allied landings at Anzio-Nettuno. On 20 November 1944 he was promoted to command 1 FJArmee in the Rhineland where he remained until wounded in March 1945. He died in 1986.

What Schlemm had learnt about defence in depth in Russia and Italy he applied in the Reichswald, where he always had the measure of the Anglo-Canadian offensive and never lost the overall initiative. He claimed to have predicted the direction of *Veritable*'s *Schwerpunkt* eastward through the Reichswald, rather than northward from Geilenkirchen as predicted by Blaskowitz. The area between Groesbeek and Wesel was turned by Schlemm into one continuously defended locality in which the Anglo-Canadian forces could advance only by taking each farmhouse and village one at a time. After a month of slow retreat during which the Americans arrived at his back, Schlemm eventually withdrew his battered but intact forces into the Wesel perimeter and then transported them over the Rhine in his own time, blowing the bridges behind him on 10 March 1945. Schlemm was a man of exceptional ability and intelligence, small, dark-skinned with a broad face and a large nose, and as little resembling the Aryan paragon as Hitler himself.

Under Schlemm, and directly responsible for the German conduct of the defence of the Reichswald, was the 53 year old gunner Eugen Meindl commanding II FJKorps His association with the airborne dated back to 1940 when he dropped with his mountain artillery regiment at Narvik without prior jump training. Soon afterwards he transferred to the airborne and commanded 1 Assault Regiment in the invasion of Crete where he was wounded while landing with his men in 80 gliders exactly 15 minutes before the paratroops descended on Máleme. He fought in Russia in January 1942 in command of Battle Group Meindl at Juchnow and then with Division Meindl at Staraya Russa from March to November 1942. This led to his appointment as commander of Fliegerkorps XIII at Grossborn from October 1942 to August 1943 when he raised Luftwaffe field divisions.

The staff of XIII Air Corps transferred to France in late 1943 with the name changed to II FJKorps. Its task was again raising divisions. It created 3FJD and 5FJD from Luftwaffe personnel and a nucleus of paratroops in the Rheims area. They were committed to the Normandy beachhead in June 1944 at St. Lô. The Corps was destroyed in the Falaise pocket but Meindl escaped, sliding past a blocking force of the South Alberta Regiment on foot in the dark, the most important escapee through 'Patton's Gap'. At Cologne-Wahn he set about rebuilding with young Luftwaffe volunteers. The new 3FJD was still incomplete when it was rushed with II FJKorps' troops to contain Operation *Market Garden* on 18 September 1944. On 20 September, Meindl took over responsibility for the Reichswald sector between Rhine and Maas.

At the beginning of September 1944 Meindl supervised the establishment of 7FJD. The core was a scratch Division put together in the Bitsch area of Alsace by Erdmann who had been Student's Chief of Staff. The units were; FJR Menzel made up of soldiers from 1 Para Army weapons school; FJR Grassmel comprising two battalions from the destroyed 6FJD; FJR Loytweg-Hardegg made up of another two battalions from 6FJD and a third battalion from 1 Para School; and a training unit under Grünwald. It was committed on 20 September against *Market Garden* and in early October withdrew to the Venlo area. There in the second half of October it changed its name from Division Erdmann to 7FJD with Erdmann as GOC and Maj Ferdinand Foltin, who had been seriously wounded on Crete and had commanded IIFJR3 at Cassino, as 1a.

On 3 January 1945 it moved by train to Alsace against 7 US Army, and returned at the end of January into 1 Para Army reserve together with XII Assault Gun Brigade. On 10 February the Division took up positions outside the Reichswald to the east and south. From there FJR19 and 20 fell back either side of Goch. FJR21 became separated as it moved east to the Cleve-Calcar road under 6FJD. It returned to support FJR20 north of Weeze on 20 February. The Division held the front line from west of the Goch-Weeze road to Keppeln, where FJR19 fought 3 CID as *Blockbuster* started on 26 February. Its losses numbered 270, and more than a company. In general 7FJD was engaged on either side of 3 BID's axis.

The divisions were formed in one of two ways. In some cases, battalions were transferred from established divisions and their cadres used to build new battalions. For example, 7 Flieger Division became 1 FJD and in the process spun off cadres for 2, 3 and 4 FJD. 10 FJD received a battalion from each of the Jäger and Artillerie regiments in 1 and 3FJD that arrived in nine trainloads from Italy on 8 April 1945. One week later the division had recruited its establishment of 10,700 men, and set about training. The other means was used by 8FJD, whose cadres came from the weapons school, from what was left of the FJ Lehr battalion, and from the corps storm and recce battalions. Such units carried their leader's name while they trained, and were then numbered and placed in divisions. The cadres of all of the divisions were composed of paratroop veterans, or from units whose original cadres were paratroop veterans. It was difficult to maintain quality, and by December 1944 Heilman of 5FJD was negative about his officers. This cloning, non-sequential regimental numbering, incomplete TOEs, and battalion name changes made it frustrating to Allied intelligence and to historians. It is noteworthy that modern historians, Busch and Simpel, do not credit 8FJD with three regiments. FJR7 should have been in 3 FJD but was under command of 8FJD at Kervenheim and Winnekendonk.

Allied intelligence issued the following summary on 4 March 1945; this author's comments are in square brackets as usual.

> <u>Sorting Out The Paratroops.</u>
> Amongst the parachute formations in the WEST the Order of Battle problem has been consistently complicated by the inconsistent numbering of regiments within divisions, and worse still, the tendency to form ad hoc battle groups with an operational role before they are absorbed into normal divisional formations. Since early in September 44 when the High Command desperately flung hastily-assembled units on to the MAAS to stop the Allied advance there has been constant reference to personalities with the most frequently heard

names being men like ERDMANN, MENZEL, GRASMEHL, HARDEGG, MULLER, HERMANN, HUBNER, JUNGWIRT, GRAMSE, CRAHS, HUTZ, LECOUTRE, WIEGAND and ADLER. These men have largely been associated with the labour pains involved in the formation of the 7 and 8 Para Divs, as well as the ambitious programme of the Para AOK for the organization of 9, 10, 11, and 12 Para Divs. The drive in the East as well as the current Western offensive so dampened this ambitious programme that to date only 7 and 8 Para Divs have emerged after 2, 3, 4, 5 and 6 Para Divs had been reinforced and reformed.

The bulk of the paratroops in the WEST have variously made their way into the present paratroop divisions through the remnants of the Luftwaffe Field Divisions, conversion of aircrews and ground crews of the Luftwaffe to an infantry role, and finally the parachutists who were originally designed to carry out parachute jumps. Personnel of the GAF, training for either an air or ground role, carried out their training in Flieger Ausbildungs Regiments. Of these a number seem to have been converted wholesale to provide manpower for the new paratroop divisions. 51 Flieger Aus Regt at TILBURG, 53 Flieger Aus Regt at GRONINGEN and 92 Flieger Aus Regt at WINTERSWIJK seem to have provided the bulk of the personnel first met when the Allies invaded HOLLAND. It is probable that their proximity to the actual fighting determined their conversion, and while 51 Fl Aus Regt may no longer exist, both 53 and 93 still seem to provide personnel for the Fallschirmjäger AOK.

On the other hand the regiments used for training paratroops proper did NOT seem to be numbered, but rather carried the name of their regimental commander. Thus there was Fallschirmjäger Ers and Aus Regt HARDEGG being formed at BITSCH, France late in Aug 44, and Fallschirmjäger Ersatz and Ausbildungs Regiment GRASMEHL stationed at WAHN, near COLOGNE. These units carried on their training as complete regiments, and when needed for an operational role they were merely upgraded and given a number and made part of a parachute division. This policy of training complete regiments independent of divisions, and then combining regiments into a parachute division, may explain the reason for the piecemeal manner in which the parachute divisions made their way to the front. The regiments seemed to come independently, take up a part of the line, and when two or three regiments had arrived, they were provided with an official divisional number, Using these rather sweeping generalizations as a basis, it is hoped in this article to clarify some of the problems arising from the welter of unclassified personalities now facing First Cdn Army.

1. ERDMANN – MENZEL – GRASMEHL – HARDEGG [7 FJD so irrelevant.]

2. HUBNER – MULLER – HERMANN

These three personalities are now finally associated with 8 Para Div. These regimental groups having existed under 606 zbv Div were finally given respectable numbers. Fallschirmjäger Ers and Aus Regt 'HUBNER', formerly at ELSENBORN/EIFEL, is now 24 Para Regt, while MULLER, a Para Ers Regt at GROENLO A28, became 22 Para Regt. It is reported that MULLER has been replaced by SCHELMAN. The third regiment is the Para LEHR Regt HERMANN, which was originally formed for CRETE as an experimental battalion. This battalion fought in CYRENAICA in 1941 and 1942, took part in the rescue of MUSSOLINI and was subsequently enlarged to a regiment in ITALY in 44. With this distinguished record it is probable that the regiment will retain the designation LEHR in preference to a number, [it actually became FJR32] although its relationship to 8 Para Div seems definite. HERMANN has apparently left to take on jumping duties [to command 10FJD] and has been replaced by Oberst KRAHL [probably commanded at Winnekendonk]. The regiment has under command Bns ULBRICHT and GRAFING [probably commanded at Kervenheim], the former officer now reclining in an Allied PW cage.

> JUNGWIRT – GRAMSE – CRAHS – MULLER
> Maj JUNGWIRT first came into prominence early in Oct as the commander of a regimental battle group in the area of TILBURG. Following the retreat across the MAAS, JUNGWIRT was given a Fallschirmjäger Ersatz Regiment to form. This unit was located at WINTERSWIJK A3075 and its personnel came largely from 93 Flieger Regiment. In Dec the regiment consisted of three battalions, CRAHS, GRAMSE and MULLER as well as 13, 14 and 15 Coys. It seemed at this time that the regiment would follow the path of other similar parachute training units and form part of a parachute division. Late in Dec something seems to have gone wrong. Either enough regiments were already formed for the available divisions, or JUNGWIRT fell into some disfavour. In any event JUNGWIRT was deprived of a regimental command, and was sent to take over 12 Para Recce Bn, the recce unit of 2 Para Corps. The elements of the regiment were then split up and scattered to the four corners of the para empire. Bn MULLER became III Bn of Regt MULLER, now known as 22 Para Regt of 8 Para Div. The remaining two battalions seem to have become Para Army reserves. Bn CRAHS first appeared in mid-January 45 in the abortive attack against ZETTEN E6272. After a severe pummeling it reorganized and came into the line again in the REICHSWALD battle, apparently as a reserve battalion which shifts its allegiance from 6 to 8 Para Divs as the situation warrants. Bn GRAMSE is now believed to be SOUTH of ARNHEM, holding the island formerly held by 23 Para Regt of 2 Para Div.
>
> This cannibalization left only 13, 14, 15 Coys of the former Regt JUNGWIRT. To prove the thriftiness of the Para AOK even those remnants were used to form a battle group ERDMANN, which was sent to the commander of GOCH to form part of the defence garrison. Its name indicates that it was probably destined for a part in 7 Para Div, but it apparently never achieved this goal.[18]

This information was painstakingly compiled in real time by Army intelligence from intercepts and prisoner interrogation. Martin Pöppel, who served in 8FJD's Sturmbataillon and kept an excellent diary that unfortunately stopped in 1945, found British intelligence accurate in his own case. After being captured in Rees-am-Rhein on March 26, he was taken to a bus filled with files where a British captain in good German told him that they could now account for all his unit's officers except Hauptmann Hűber. The captain took a file and read out current and accurate details of positions occupied by his unit, their casualties and even his own career. Unfortunately none of these records except the summaries survived.

It was 8FJD with FJR7 under command that defended against 3 BID. 8FJD was ordered into existence by the Luftwaffe Supreme Command on 24 September 1944 when the staff of 606 GID, which was not even Luftwaffe, was told to move to an area between Venlo and Roermond under command of 1 Para Army.

Sources disagree about the composition of 8FJD. Contemporary Anglo-Canadian military intelligence, whose sources were prisoner interrogations, captured documents and radio intercepts, concluded that 8FJD had three regiments: Para Lehr, 22 Para Regiment, and 24 Para Regiment. The Sturmbataillon was placed under command of Para Lehr, which lacked the 13, 14 and 15 weapons companies.

Captured code-lists of 8 Para Div provide the following information: On 21 Dec 44 the Div was known as 606 ID (z.b.V). On 8 Feb 45 the Div was known as Para Battle Group WADEHN. On 19 Feb 45 the Div was known as 8 Para Div.

18 LAC: Appendix A to 2 Cdn Corps Intelligence Summary No 136.

The Order of Battle (ORB) of the Div on 19 Feb 45 was as follows:

1 8 Para Div HQ and Staff (including "Verm Brautschule") [Brautschule=finishing school].
2 Para Lehr Regt
Assault Bn HUBNER
13,14,15/Para Lehr Regt
41 Fortress MG Bn
12 Para Art Regt
3 22 Para Regt
I, II, III, 13, 14, 15/24 Para Regt
Battle Gp LUCAE
4 24 Para Regt
I, II, III, 13, 14, 15/24 Para Regt.

FJR22	Major Müller
I/22	Major Wiedemann
II/22	Hauptmann Adrian
III/22	Hauptmann Wittstock
FJR24	Oberst-Lt Friedrich Hübner
I/24	Hauptmann Uferkamp
II/24	Hauptmann Strohlke
III/24	Hauptmann Fischer
FJR32 (Lehr)	Oberst Krahl
I/32	Hauptmann Gräfing
II/32	Hauptmann Crass
Sturmbataillon	Hauptmann Hübner
1 Kompanie	OberLt Joswig
2 Kompanie	OberLt Stephan
3 Kompanie	OberLt Pöppel
4 Kompanie	OberLt Sönke
FJR7 under command and transferred from 2FJD	
OC	Oberst Riedel
I/7	Hauptmann Walter
II/7	Hauptmann Kahlen
III/7	Hauptmann Lisowski
LW Festungsbataillon XXVII	
Pionieren	Hauptmann Matern
Artillery	None raised

Personalities:

7 Para Regt	Col Riedel	GOC 8 Para Div	?Gen Meindl?
1/7 Para Regt	Capt Walther	III/24 Para Regt	Capt Fischer (OC)
1/7 Para Regt	Lt Sommer		Lt Schönfeld (Adjt)
2/7 Para Regt	Lt Einert	9/24 Para Regt	2/Lt Rief
3/7 Para Regt	Lt Keller	0/24 Para Regt	Lt Schares
4/7 Para Regt	Lt Kellermann	11/24 Para Regt	Capt Dochow (PW)
III/7 Para Regt	Capt Lisowski	12/24 Para Regt	Capt Fengler
15 Engr Coy, 7 Para Regt	Lt Richter	7/Para Lehr Regt	Lt Wester
		8/Para Lehr Regt	Lt Schmidt[19]

19 LAC: 2 Canadian Corps Intelligence Summary No 138.

Sources agree on the presence of FJR 22, formed in January 1945 at Köln-Wahn from FJRSchellmann, and of FJR 24, formed in February 1945 also in Köln-Wahn from FJRHübner. The composition of Para Lehr/FJR32 is less sure. All agree that it contained the Para Army Sturmbataillon, but German sources do not call it Para Lehr. Bliss & Bosshammer stated that Para Lehr, or Fallschirmjäger-Lehr-Regiment, ended its days as FJR21 in 6FJD when it was captured at Mons in August 1944. Its commander, Harry Hermann and a few others escaped to form Battle Group Hermann that fought in September near Mook, and in January near Roermond. In February 1945, according to Bliss & Bosshammer, Battle Group Hermann was disbanded and its remaining personnel scattered, with Hermann himself appointed to command 10FJD that was soon defending Berlin. The remainder transferred to II/FJR25 in Skau, to Kampfgruppe v.d. Heydte, to FJR32, and to FJBataillon Balzereit/Crass/Gräfing. The last two are associated with 8FJD.

Erich Busch stated that in February 1945, FJR32 comprised only II Battalion under Crahs, while I Battalion was raised later after the retreat across the Rhine. A website[20] agrees that FJR32 consisted only of IIFJR32 under Crahs and gives L62497 as its FPN. But this site mistakenly identified Major Hans Jungwirth as commander when the British and Busch agreed that Jungwirth commanded 12 Para Recce (Fallschirm-Aufklärungs-Abteilung 12), which were corps troops. Busch doesn't identify the commander of FJR32, which British Intelligence claimed was Oberst Krahl, and who was probably responsible for the defence of Winnekendonk.

Another reason for equating FJR32 with Para Lehr was the Storm Battalion's origin (Armee-Sturm-Btl.) as the Fallschirmarmee-Waffenschule in Aalton near Arnhem. These were Lehrtruppe. OberLt Pöppel was recovering from his wounds in September 1944 when his old commander, von der Heydte, wrote to tell him he would be returning to command 12FJR6. But still not fully fit, he was ordered to report to the Para School under Hauptmann von Hütz as an instructor in heavy weapons. They were training the newly established Para Army Storm Battalion. However, v.d. Heydte removed the best officers for the Ardennes Offensive, where they were dropped and wiped out. The training school was disbanded, and re-formed under Hauptmann Edouard Hübner as the Paratroop Army Storm battalion, with Pöppel commanding its 4 company.

> In the autumn of 1944, the Battle and Weapon Schools (Kampf-und Waffen-Schulen) moved to Aalten in Holland. They were taken over by Lt-Col v.d. Heydte and placed under command of the of 1 Parachute-Army's Weapon School (Waffenschule 1. Fallschirm-Armee). But not long afterwards they were organised into fighting formations and committed to the Western Front. In February/March 1945 various units were withdrawn from the centralised Army Weapons School under Major v. Hütz and committed to the Reichswald Battle, particularly near Wesel.[21]

This author believes that the presence of one of these units in the defence of Winnekendonk would explain the repeated reference to Para Lehr and the unusual quantity of weapons. Other groups directed into 8 FJD were Luftwaffe No. 6 Unteroffizier-Schule that became I/FJR22, FJR Müller, which became II/FJR22, and FJR Wittstock that became III/FJR22. Luftwaffe-Festungsbataillon XXVII became III/FJR24.

A POW told his captors that the personnel of FJR22, 'are mainly young and of the parachute arm, though not necessarily jumpers'. One of them was Willi Thielecke of III/FJR22. He was a mechanic on a Freya radar in Evreuse after joining the Luftwaffe in 1942. When the Allies got

20 www.lexikon-der-wehrmacht.de

21 Busch, *Die Fallschirmjäger Chronik*, p. 279, translated by this author.

near in August 1944, the crew destroyed the Freya, withdrew into Germany and volunteered for the Fallschirmtruppe. They were sent to Gardelegen where they were trained and indoctrinated by Paras, although they received no jump training. In November 1944 they moved by train to Winterswijk for basic infantry training, and took up defensive positions at Roermond in December. In the middle of February they were marched north to Weeze to attack 2 East Yorks defending Yorkshire Bridge on 27 February, as described in Chapter 2. On March 1 a group of forty from II and III/FJR22 surrendered, probably to 53 BID.[22]

In the middle of February, FJR7 moved from the Island to south of the Goch – Üdem railway. The British noted its arrival on 22 February, and that it had left Arnhem on 17 February. It joined FJR22, which moved up in lorries on 16 February from its position on the Maas near Roermond, to the area of Weeze – Kervenheim – Üdem. FJR7 came under command of 8FJD. British Intelligence Summary No 228 is categorical on this point although Busch is silent on the matter and Stacey states that the commander of FJR7, was 'directly responsible to General von Lüttwitz', whose 47 Panzer Corps comprised 6FJD, 116 PD and FJR7.[23] There was obviously some connection between FJR7 and von Lüttwitz at least for a period, because we will see below the testimony of Hans Kühn that tank destroyers of 15 PGD supported FJR7 at Kervenheim, afterwards going their separate ways to Sonsbeck.

FJR7 formed in February 1943 in the Vannes area of Britanny, with II/FJR7 being raised from the Lehr-Battalion of XI Fliegerkorps, and later renamed FJR21. A new FJR7 was formed from 1/FJR6, but it surrendered in Brest in September 1944. A completely new FJR7 was reformed in Amersfoort in November 1944 under Col Eggersh. He was replaced by Graf Kerssenbrock in December 1944 until February 1945, when Lt.Col Gerd Riedel took command in the Udem area.

On 15 January 1945 Maj-Gen Wadehn assumed command of 8FJD and transferred into Meindl's II Para Corps. The evidence points to their knowing each other well. Only sketchy details of Wadehn's career are available, and no record has survived about his personality or even what he looked like. He was born in 1896, and was therefore old enough to have served in the First World War. He must have made his career in the Luftwaffe because in October 1939 he was sufficiently senior to get command of III Gruppe of Kampfgeschwader 77 flying Do 17Z aircraft at Koniggrätz, and later at Düsseldorf. From March to August 1942 he commanded Flieger-Ausbildungs-Regiment 72 (Pilot-Training Regiment) in the east, when he must have met Meindl and become his protégé. He was almost certainly involved with Meindl in raising the new Luftwaffe-Feld-Divisions (LWFD), and in September 1942 was given command of 10 LWFD, where he remained until November 1943. This was in Lindemann's 18 Army in von Küchler's Herresgruppe Nord. 10 LWFD suffered heavy losses in the Oranienbaum bridgehead west of Leningrad and at Narva, being disbanded in February 1944 under his successor. Wadehn's performance must have impressed Meindl, who selected him in August 1944 to command 3 FJD when Schimpf was wounded, in spite of Wadehn's lack of Para background. Wadehn withdrew 3FJD from France to Aachen in September, and had rebuilt it in Oldenzaal by early October. During this period it saw some action in Arnhem as Kampfgruppe Becker, and later took part in the Ardennes Offensive. When Schimpf recovered from his wounds, Wadehn handed back command of 3FJD to him on 5 January 1945. The next day Wadehn began raising 8FJD at Köln-Wahn from various ad-hoc units, assuming command on 6 January 1945. He led it throughout its epic battles against 3BID as recounted in this book, withdrawing it across the Rhine battered but intact. He then managed a fighting retreat into northern Germany until his death, which may have been

22 Letters from Willi Thielecke on 10 October 2002 and to Greg Way on 21 January, 21 February and 4 March 2000.

23 Stacey, *Victory*. His source was MS B-215 and MS B-601.

suicide, on 1 May, only four days before 8FJD's surrender. Wadehn had spent his last three years leading three divisions in catastrophic retreat, and with his country prostrate before the enemy he may have decided enough was enough.

8FJD lacked its own artillery. It relied on 7 Para Artillery Regiment, whose guns were set up in 8FJD's area at Reyshof on 24 February[24] and by other units such as the 401 Volks Artillery Corps, the Artillery Regiment 12 which were Corps' troops, and by the 86 Werfer Regiment. There was, however, no shortage of artillery during this period, and the Canadians estimated that 1 Para Army disposed of 717 mortars and 1,054 guns not including StuGs.

It was clear to British Intelligence that FJR24 and Para Lehr were engaged when 3 BID took prisoners from both units and made positive identifications of III/FJR24 on 27 February.

The British stated, and the veteran Thielecke confirmed, that the counter-attack on Yorkshire Bridge was initiated by I/24 and carried on by III/22. But a large question was raised in the Intelligence Summary No 228 on 27 February:

> Largest query is whereabouts of 24 Para Regt. I Bn which was yesterday at 953395 [near Yorkshire Bridge] and this morning at 973398 [Wettermannshof] has not been found in the fighting. Our neighbours [11BAD] report that II Bn has been met at 003393 [Gochfortzhof] and III Bn to the NE of this point. I Bn is therefore probably in Kervenheim. Now that we are wholly concerned with 8 Para Div, with 7 Para Regt under command, the only Regt of the Div out of contact, and therefore available as reinforcements, is Para LEHR Regiment. This formation was the first of the Regiments from 8 Para Div to appear in this sector and has suffered considerably in the battle. But it has now been out of the line for a few days, and must be reckoned an effective reserve.[25]

In fact British Intelligence was wrong. It is known through Stacey[26] that a fresh battalion of FJR24 counter-attacked the A&SD of Canada on 28 February in the Hochwald Gap, 'The opponents included a fresh battalion of the 24th Paratroop Regiment which von Lüttwitz …had brought in from the 8th Paratroop Division', and was confirmed in Busch[27] and Guderian.[28] The Storm-Battalion, aka the Paratroop Army Assault Battalion that was part of Para Lehr/FJR32, was ordered up to Xanten from the Maas on 26 February and supported FJR24 in the Hochwald Gap on 2 March. Stacey wrote:

> Once again an attempt to break through to the east had failed. … Since the morning of the 2nd the Algonquins had had 87 casualties…; the Lake Superior Regiment had lost 53… The credit for stopping the Canadian attack seems to belong to the 24th Parachute Regiment and the Parachute Army Assault battalion, supported by tanks and artillery of the 116th Panzer Division.[29]

Examination of the British Intelligence Summaries show that Para Lehr and FJR24 were thought to be opposite 3 BID throughout the period from 26 February to 2 March, although a question

24 TNA: WO 171/4130, 3 BID Intelligence Summary No. 230.
25 TNA: WO 171/4130, 3 BID Intelligence Summary No 228.
26 Stacey, *The Victory*, p. 507.
27 Busch, *Die Fallschirmjäger Chronik*, p. 161.
28 Heinz Günther Guderian. *From Normandy To The Ruhr With The 116th Panzer Division in WWII* (Bedford: Aberjona, 2001).
29 Stacey, *The Victory*.

mark was often attached to its whereabouts. Erskine called Para Lehr, 'a unit of some distinction, composed in the main of young nazi fanatics whose ages ranged from 16 to 20'.[30]

The day after Winnekendonk was taken, the Scots Guards counted 43 German dead and 250 PWs, two 88 mm, 2 StuGs with the track marks indicating the presence of a third, six 50 mm PAK38s, and a large number of Spandaus and infantry weapons of all kinds. 3BID Intelligence Summaries, written on 3 and 4 March, identify the units involved as being from I/FJR22, and II/FJR7, merged to form Battle Group Krahl in battalion strength under a Lt-Colonel. Also identified as present were 2 Troop, XII Para Assault Gun Brigade with 9 StuGs, and 3 Platoon Fortress Anti-tank Coy 51(X) with five 50 mm wheel-less anti-tank guns. The whole was backed by the support of 7 Para Artillery and the 86 Werfer Regiment. FJR7 was normally part of 2FJD which at that time had been moved to the Krefeld area against 9 USArmy. The Fallschirmjäger considered themselves part of one large Regiment of ten divisions, and could serve in any part of it. This flexibility within a common allegiance was one element making the German forces effective.

The Wehrkreis X Anti-tank units emplaced their guns in fixed positions. No lorries or horse-drawn vehicles were available should a change of position be required. When it became necessary to withdraw, the gun crews were given orders to destroy their guns. However, instead of carrying out orders, the Intelligence Summary reported that they merely threw away the bolts, and Ted Winkler witnessed them doing that.

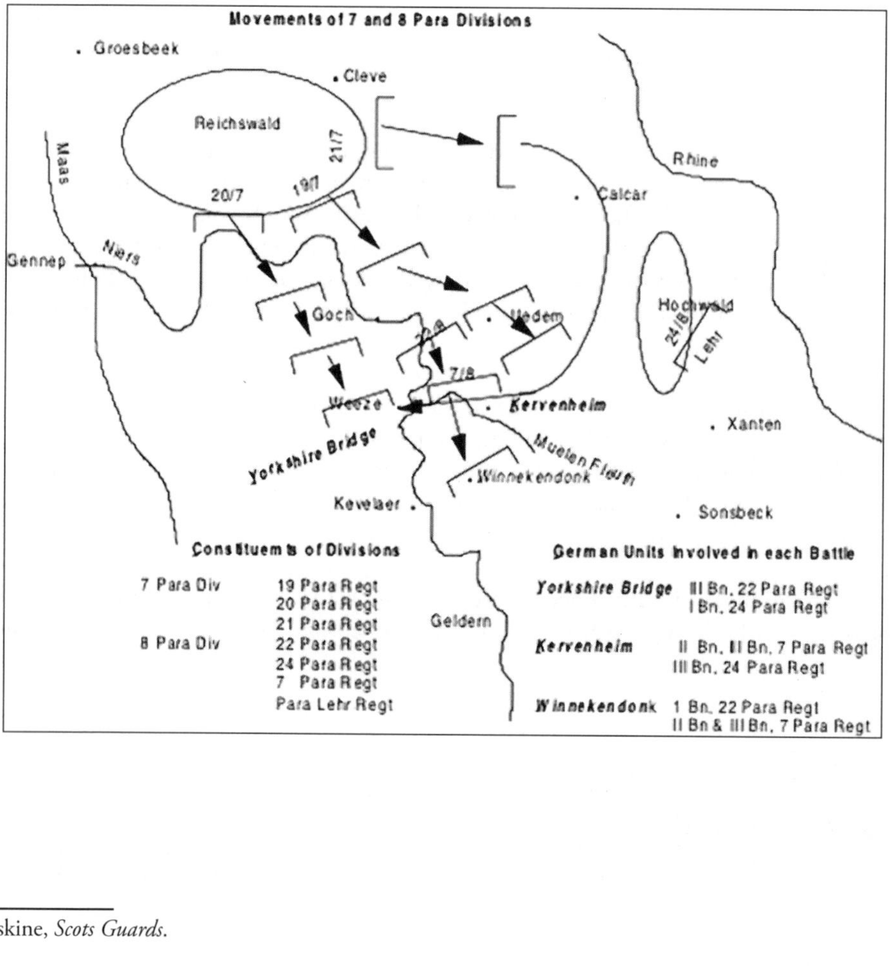

30 Erskine, *Scots Guards*.

In December Meindl's corps was ordered south from the Reichswald to St. Hubert/Kempen, and was replaced by LXXXVI Corps, soon to be commanded by the ambitious Straube. Meindl's Corps comprised 7FJD (Erdmann), the 180 GID (Klosterkämpfer) and some combat groups that Wadehn formed into 8FJD in the Roermond area. Also in December, 7FJD was moved into Army Reserve for training where it remained until called forward against Operation *Veritable.* Corps' reserve was 12 Recce Bn. On 23 February, 7FJD returned to Meindl from Army Reserve and on 28 February and after Operation *Heather* had started, Meindl received 190 GID (Hammer) and FJR2. Paratroop Assault Gun Brigade XII was also under command. FJLehr supporting 24FJR arrived from Xanten on the evening of 27 February.

The paratroop forces had a reputation as crack troops able to use surprise. Their expansion to eleven divisions in three paratroop corps reflected Hitler's suspicions about the loyalty of the army and its General Staff – confirmed by his attempted assassination on 20 July 1944. From then on he would trust only the Luftwaffe, the SS and the Navy as fitting places for the drafts of young men who had all served in the HitlerJugend and believed its promise that the world was theirs for the taking. Twenty Waffen SS Armoured and Motorised Divisions and a similar number of Luftwaffe field formations were raised.

Symptomatic of the increasing Nazification of the forces was the absence of the traditional *Gott Mit Uns* from the paratroopers' belt buckle. Blumentritt when interviewed after the war said that the

> New 'Armies' came into existence mostly for political reasons. They received the best replacements and the best arms. After being in action they were generally given a period of rest. This took more and more strength from the Army proper, and in particular from the Infantry divisions, whose fighting power grew weaker and weaker.[31]

The paratroop force created its own traditions largely but not entirely untainted in the West by the licensed murderous habits of the Waffen SS. The attempt by the Waffen SS through HIAG to distance itself from the licensed murderers of the concentration camps, and furthermore to besmirch the name of the German Army and paratroop forces by claiming to be *Soldaten wie Andere Auch* (soldiers like any others), was systematically answered, at least for SS Totenkopf by Charles Sydnor.[32] SSTK was recruited from the camp guards by the organiser of the terror system, Theodor Eicke, who trained them to hate the enemy behind the wire and to believe themselves élite. This made them reckless in the assault, suicidal in defence and capable of atrocities when frustrated. As early as 27 May 1940 1SSTKRI casually murdered 100 members of 2 Norfolks at Le Paradis. Wehrmacht General Hoepner received evidence against SSTK but did nothing beyond reminding all troops that murder and looting were court martial offence. His inactivity showed the SS had de facto exemption from military discipline, and were therefore unlike other German troops in the West. In the East the Wehrmacht was involved in a criminal *Vernichtungskrieg* (War of Extermination).[33]The SS Paratroop Battalion 500/600, raised in 1943 from convicts, had no connection with the Luftwaffe.

In 1936 Hitler gave the paratroop volunteers 'Ten Commandments', one of which read; 'Against an open foe, fight with chivalry, but extend no quarter to a guerrilla'.

Student himself set the honourable tone in 1940 when he was severely wounded by a stray bullet fired by the SS Leibstandarte Adolf Hitler as he stepped between them and a group of surrendering

31 Manuscript B-283. Library of US Army War College, Carlisle, PA.
32 Charles Sydnor. *Soldiers of Destruction* (Princeton: University Press, 1977).
33 Hannes Heer and Klaus Naumann. *War of Extermination* (Herndon: Berghahn, 2000).

Dutch. Others say a sniper hit him. For his part in killing British POWs and 200 Cretan hostages, Student was convicted and sentenced to 5 years imprisonment on 10 May 1946 at Luneberg but the sentence was never confirmed due to ardent advocacy in court by the New Zealand Brigadier Inglis who had fought against him in Crete. The Germans said they fought cleanly but complained that the British never restrained the murderous Cretan guerrillas.[34] There are many examples of honourable behaviour by German Paratroops who were generally respected by the Allies who fought them. General Ramcke, who managed the classic withdrawal and defence of Brest, had the distinction of receiving the approval of both Hitler and US General Troy Middleton who rated him as 'outstanding' among the 12 German generals he captured. The paratroop force made much of one of its recruits, the former World Heavyweight boxing champion and convinced Nazi, Max Schmeling (I/FJR3) who fought by the Queensbury Rules and was wounded on Crete. Gerhard Schacht (XI Air Corps' staff) countermanded Hitler's *Führerbefehl* to murder Commandos, saving Lt Hughes from the firing squad outside Anzio. Major Koch of FJR5 is rumoured to have been killed by the Gestapo in a mysterious traffic accident in Germany in 1944 as revenge for intervening to save the wounded of 2 Para from being murdered at Depienne in Tunisia in November 1942. The hard, politically reliable Paratroops could have been custom designed to fight the 'racially equal' (in German eyes) Western Allies on their own terms. Their civilised behaviour was known to the German Nazi bosses. Bernadotte recounted that Himmler spoke approvingly in February 1945 of the gentlemanly methods of warfare in Normandy, citing an example when action was interrupted so that both sides could collect their casualties. This was unthinkable on the Eastern Front where the SS led the Wehrmacht in a crusade to destroy Communism in an orgy of beastliness and uncivilised savagery which was returned with interest by the Red Army. The nearest to such savagery that developed in the West was the contact between the Canadians and the SS Hitler Jugend in Normandy.[35] Landsers referred to Canadians as 'Tommy SS'.

The German forces blocking Operations *Heather* and *Blockbuster* at the end of February 1945 aligned west to east as follows;:

> Erdmann's 7FJD held the line from the River Maas to the River Niers at Weeze against 1 Commando Brigade on the Maas, against Hakewell-Smith's 52 Lowland BID and against Elrington's 53 Welsh BID. All three units were in Horrocks's XXX Corps. Wadehn's 8FJD with 7FJR under command[36] opposed Whistler's 3 BID (XXX Corps) and Roberts' 11 BAD (II Canadian Corps) in the line from the River Niers to Uedem. On its right Klosterkämpfer's 180 GID, von Waldenburg's 116 PD and to the north Plocher's 6FJD held the line from north of Uedem to the Rhine. Against them were Simonds II Canadian Corps, comprising Roberts's 11 BAD, Spry's 3 CID, Vokes's 4 CAD, Matthews's 2 CID and Thomas's 43 Wessex BID. Adair's GAD was in reserve. This Sitrep is derived from several sources.[37] Some of the evidence conflicts and the truth may never be known.

34 Hadjipateras, *Crete.*

35 Tony Foster. *Meeting of Generals* (London: Methuen, 1986).

36 TNA: WO 171/4130. 3 BID Intelligence Summary No 228 of 27 February 1945.

37 Busch, *Die Fallschirmjäger Chronik.* Edwards, *German Airborne.* Böhmler & Haupt, *Fallschirmjäger*; MOD's Tactical Doctrine Retrieval Cell; TNA: WO 171/4130, 3 BID's War Diaries' Intelligence Summaries.

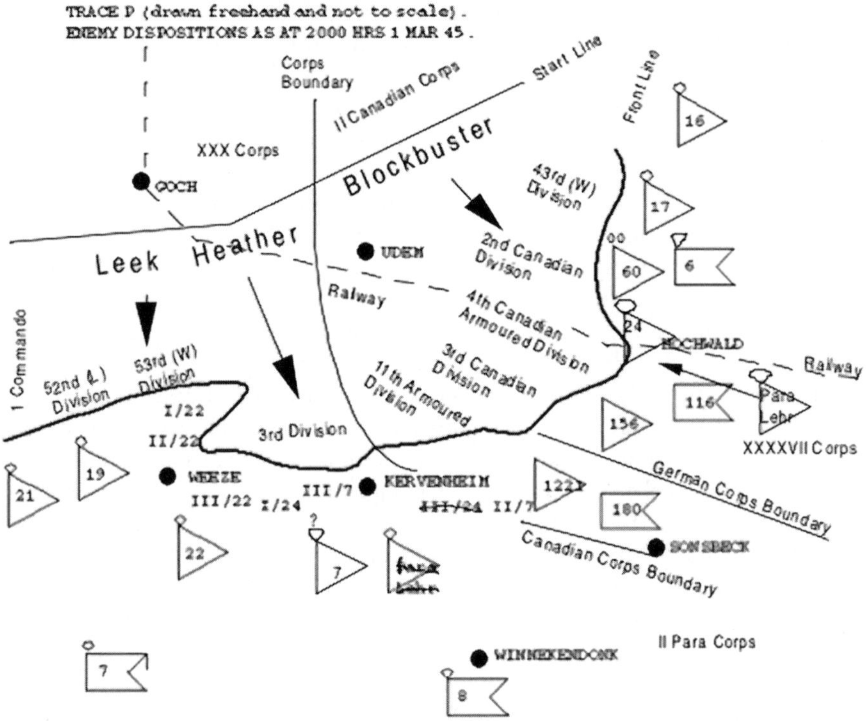

Schlemm was interviewed by the Americans in March 1946.[38] He estimated the strength of Anglo-Canadian forces in *Veritable* as being six or seven full corps. In reality only XXX British Corps (Horrocks) was employed initially, and was joined by II Canadian Corps (Simonds) for Operation *Blockbuster*. At this point the Germans were also fielding two corps; II Para Corps (Meindl) and XXXXVII Panzer Corps (von Lüttwitz). There were 8 Anglo-Canadian divisions attacking 5 German divisions. Meindl stated that his regiments were reduced to battalion size by 24 February due to allied artillery expenditure of 80,000 to 100,000 rounds per day while he could manage only 10,000 rounds. 500 allied tanks, he said, dominated his 50 AFVs. He pointed out with evident satisfaction that the enemy managed an advance of only 20 km in 16 days and that all crises had been managed. German morale, he said, remained high and troop performance excellent. In his opinion the overwhelming allied air supremacy had little effect on the fighting at the outset due to unfavourable weather. He was proud that most of the Rhine bridges escaped unscathed from allied attempts to bring them down.

Meindl was interviewed in June 1946.[39] He stated that he guessed the Reichswald would be attacked and was surprised how quickly the forest and Cleve were lost by Straube in spite of Meindl having sent over the 655 Heavy Anti-tank Hetzer Battalion. Jagdpanzer 38(t) Hetzer, was a small, mass-produced, Czech-built tank destroyer weighing 15.8 tons mounting the 7.5 cm Pak 39 L/48 in a sloped armoured glacis of 60 mm thickness. Its small silhouette made it easy to conceal. It was considered one of the best S.P mountings for its size of the Second World War, and it was adopted by Switzerland post war. In a conference on 18 February 1945 with Blaskowitz

38 Manuscript B-084. Library of US Army War College, Carlisle, PA.
39 Manuscripts B-051 and B-093. Library of US Army War College, Carlisle, PA.

and Schlemm, Meindl was given responsibility for the Goch sector. He thought it was a bit late since the damage had already been done. He moved his HQ up to Sonsbeck and was therefore Horrocks's opposite number when Operation *Heather* kicked off from Goch one week later.

Meindl's defence against the Anglo-Canadians was to use heavy calibre artillery weapons to break up the attacks, including the difficult trick of placing an advancing barrage in lock step behind the British barrage, and to establish an echelonned defence in great depth making the Allies fight for every inch. It soon produced results by significantly slowing the rate of allied advance. He viewed the Anglo-Canadian attacks as following the same formula as used in Normandy, of heavy artillery preparation in the morning followed by an armoured assault in the afternoon. The antidote was to forecast the point of attack and cover it with his Corps artillery, since the Germans lacked air support. Meindl prided himself on his accurate prediction of the place and the timing of the Anglo-Canadian attacks. He saw it as a simple mathematical problem based on the factors of road junctions, the nature of the terrain, the overall thrust line, the tactical direction and the time. We know, however, that he was exaggerating his powers of prediction and was not always right, being surprised by the developments around Uedem. Meindl almost certainly underestimated the cross-country capability of the Churchill tank, having had little or possibly no previous exposure to it. But he was right about the village road junctions of Kervenheim and Winnekendonk, which were subject to direct attacks and which he defended fiercely.

German performance was not without its faults although Meindl admitted to none on his own part. Meindl explained that he handed over 12 Paratroop Reconnaissance Battalion under Major Hans Jungwirth, which was his Corps reserve, to von Lüttwitz at the beginning of Operation *Blockbuster* on 26 February to stop 8 CIB of 3 CID from breaking through at Keppeln.[40] Meindl observed that 12 Paratroop Reconnaissance Regiment had difficulty in co-operating with the tanks of 116 PD, which was evidence of declining German skills. It, repulsed the attack…but was then encircled and suffered heavy casualties. It did not receive the support it deserved from its own tanks. During the night the remnants managed to escape. They pleaded not to be committed again alongside tanks. This was a repeat of what had happened in Normandy.[41]

This battle was at Hollen against the Canadian Régt de la Chaudière, who called the fighting 'as hard as any it had met to date' and at Keppeln against the North Shore Regt. The Chaudières took 224 prisoners from the Recce Regt[42] in a well coordinated all-arms attack with tanks and artillery, and the North Shore stormed Keppeln with 81 casualties and 9 tanks destroyed. Hollen and Kappeln were captured, and yet that night von Lüttwitz credited 116 PD and 12 Recce with having prevented a break-through towards Uedem, and Meindl repeated the claim. However, both von Lüttwitz and Meindl failed to mention a well-executed Canadian encircling move during the night through Todtenhügel to the Katzen Berg north west of Uedem. The troops were Tiger Group under Brigadier Moncel and Smith Force of 4 CAD. It was executed on schedule and with few casualties and surprised the defenders including Erich Freund, whose account is below. This force cut off 12 Recce Regt and by the next night Uedem had fallen. 116 PD was out-manoeuvred and outfought with the defenders encircled and losing over 700 men.

The impression the Anglo-Canadian forces made on Schlemm, he said in his interview, was that they had suffered severe losses in earlier fighting and were proceeding only slowly. Schlemm therefore concluded that he could hold the Reichswald front without reinforcement, keep ground from

40 Stacey, *The Victory*, Map 10, makes an uncharacteristic error in writing Kappelen for Keppeln, the two towns being 10 miles apart.

41 Manuscript Meindl B-051. Library of US Army War College, Carlisle, PA.

42 Stacey, *The Victory*, states they were from 6FJD's Recce Regiment, but Meindl identified them as Corps troops, 12 Recce Regt.

being lost, and prevent a breakthrough. His defence, he concluded, depended on von Zangen's 15 Army to the south holding the Americans. He noted that on 2 and 3 March heavy fighting developed in what he called the first bridgehead (the Winnekendonk-Hochwald line) resulting in several deep enemy penetrations. The penetrations during this period were the captures of Weeze and Winnekendonk on 2 March, which has been described in Chapter 4. Schlemm added that he withdrew to Bonninghardt and echelonned his Flak units in depth to defend against enemy armour since he lacked tanks. His PAKfront indeed stopped GAD and 11 BAD.

With the breakthrough at Winnekendonk and the advance of the 9 US Army from the south, Schlemm decided he had to plan withdrawal across the Rhine. He believed that his ten divisions, which had been reduced to regimental size, and his 20 tanks were opposed by ten corps with 3,000 AFVs. On the other hand, in Schlemm's opinion, the defenders had sufficient artillery. They had lost few guns and managed to withdraw 40 batteries from the West Wall, transferring them to the east bank of the Rhine where they were joined by two artillery corps with five battalions each. By 9 March he had moved 70 batteries across the river by night to the east bank with little loss.

No *Kriegstagesbucher* survived. Stacey[43] states that virtually no German records are available for this phase, subsequently confirmed by the German Military Archives. The central archive at Zossen was destroyed during the last months of the war. Enquiries in Germany and a search at the IWM produced contact with six veteran Fallschirmjägers; three had been in 7FJD in the vicinity of 3 BID and three in 8FJD who had fought against it:

> 7FJD: **Willi Lennartz** was a divisional sapper in 7 Pionier Bn; **Heinrich Schlömer** and **Heinrich Nattkamp** served in FJR19:
> 8FJD: **Erich Freund** was a company runner and **Otto Einert** his company commander in I/FJR7; **Ted Winkler** was the armourer of II/FJR7.

Their testimonies form the basis of the rest of this chapter.

Willi Lennartz was a sapper in 2 Company commanded by Lt Rahn Hubers of 7 Engineer (Pionier) Bn under Capt Manfred Hünichen in Erdmann's 7FJD. He built the defences of Müsershof outside Kervenheim that were later occupied by 8FJD. In the opinion of Lennartz[44] it was not a difficult battle for the German defenders. He remembers being always very tired and overworked, constantly carrying mines, bridging materials, and wire here and there, summoned by field telephone. The British he found were cautious, *langsam aber sicher* (slow but sure). His Bn had 3 coys of 3 plns, each with 3 sections of 12 men, adding up to 324 men to supply the engineering needs of the entire Division. He described how he built the defences around the many farms. They were built in depth with lines of slit trenches dug in front of the farms, many of them empty one-man slits designed to confuse. In centre front, at a distance of 20 metres from the farm, a three-man slit trench was dug for a rifleman and an MG42 crew of two; the rifleman's job was to prevent the machine gunners from being surprised at close quarters while they concentrated on the attacking infantrymen. The farm contained a 12-man reserve section firing through the upstairs windows over the heads of those out in the fields in front. With the men dispersed and dugin they were relatively immune from shellfire. Each farm was therefore defended by 15 men, which is the number of POWs Stokes took at Boemshof.

43 Stacey, *The Victory*, p. 507.
44 Willi Lennartz in five letters, July 1984 to 16 August 1985, and in conversation. He visited England and visited the Tiger and Churchill tanks at Bovington.

Another paratrooper who passed close to Winnekendonk was Heinrich Schlömer,[45] of 13 Coy, FJR19 in 7FJD. Schlömer's was the last company to leave Weeze. He headed for Bonninghardt where he was wounded and captured. He remembers crossing the River Niers on a floating bridge of rafts, and fighting from one farmhouse to another, almost certainly against 3 BID. He must have passed through Winnekendonk as he headed east. He says the British usually came on slowly with a spotter plane overhead. An attack was always preceded by smoke, which the spotter plane used for registering the artillery. Schlömer was running across the fields when a smoke shell actually went between his legs. The Panzerfaust was a dangerous weapon, according to Schlömer, because its smoke brought swift retribution. All he can remember was fighting, sleeping and eating. The cookhouse was always 2 km away, so he and his comrades had to forage. Once when the QMS wouldn't issue food to them because the warehouse was scheduled for demolition, they shot their way in and took what they needed. When they made a stand they dug one-man slit trenches with only the mg teams in two-men slits. They all became exhausted by the never-ending struggle. There was some discussion amongst the troops about how it would end, but the subject was forbidden and punishment for talking about defeat was believed to be transfer to a *Straf-Bataillon* (punishment bn) on the Eastern Front.

Schlömer remembers no threat from allied fighter-bombers around Weeze, and doesn't know why they were spared. He does remember the British artillery as strong and powerful, spreading or 'steering' their shells over a wide area. (His word for this was *Steuerungsfeuer*.) Schlömer said the Fallschirmjäger saw themselves as the fire-brigade unit, being despatched to put the fires out. This rôle, in his opinion, was possible only with specially trained troops and those who were highly motivated. He remained proud of his training and had the badge awarded for 6 jumps. He said that young replacements often arrived without weapons. When frightened, many ran into the bullets and were killed.

Schlömer's story represents the experience of many of the young German paratroops. He graduated from the *Hitler Jugend* in March 1943 aged sixteen and a half and volunteered for the Luftwaffe. As a *Freiwillig* (volunteer) he could choose his unit. He trained as a *Funker*, or signaller on the two-man *Dora* set. It required one man for the transmitter and one for the receiver which weighed 30 kg and had a range of 40 km. Schlömer said it was not liked by the troops who thought the British were able to locate and shell it. This fear appears to have been unfounded. Schlömer transmitted only by key and always in a code that changed daily. His personal arms were the MP40 Schmeisser and an 08 pistol using the same 9 mm ammunition.

He did his equipment training in Augsburg, probably at a central Luftwaffe school, and field training with the Paratroops near Nancy in France where 1 Paratroop Army was formed in April 1944 and made responsible for training. There they mounted operations against partisans, or *Terroristen* as the Germans called them. 7FJD was formed in Holland in the autumn of 1944. He fought on the Wilhemina Canal and near Neerdeweert, and was resting near Sonsbeck when around Christmas they were sent to Strasbourg to stop the American offensive. He faulted the Americans for putting too much faith in *materiel*, and for believing that planes, artillery and tanks would save the infantry from fighting. He faulted all the Allies for lack of experience! 7FJD returned to the Niederrhein at the end of February, and fought most of the time between the road and the railway in Weeze. He was captured on 3 March 1945 on an emergency airfield near Bonninghardt, where all his comrades were killed, he believed unnecessarily. Schlömer was wounded and evacuated by ambulance to s'Hertogenbosch, then by train to Ostend, reaching Tilbury by boat on 1 April 1945. He went via Hampden Park to a two-part camp holding 5,000 P/W in Northwich, Cheshire where he spent nearly a year. He worked with British troops unloading ships in Liverpool

45 Heinrich Schlömer in phone conversation in August 1984.

during the dock strike, and could never understand why the dockers wouldn't unload food for their own people. Strikers attacked the buses in which they were taken to the docks so they were sent after that in army lorries. In 1946 the barbed wire was removed from the camp and they were free to travel within 5 miles and sleep on farms. One of their number was the famous goalkeeper Trautmann, who married an English woman and stayed in England. Schlömer was repatriated in March 1946.

Heinrich Nattkamp served in 11FJR19 in 7FJD. He was injured early on 28 February by a British artillery concentration 800 metres south of Yorkshire Bridge fired by 3 BID. He was born in 1921 into a religious and anti-Nazi family, joining the Hitlerjugend in order to graduate. He joined the Luftwaffe in February 1941 becoming *Rechnungsführer* of *1 Batterie Flakersatzabteilung 16* in Greifswald on the Baltic. In July 1942 his unit was part of 7 Flak Division in Cologne. He was promoted to command a unit of 1 Battery, 130 Searchlight Regiment operating on various sites in the Cologne – Bonn area. In October 1944 he was transferred to the paratroop barracks in Wittstock where he was trained with recruits from all trades and ranks. With 250 others he was sent as reinforcements in the middle of February 1945. They were transported to Dülken, 40 km south of Kevelaer, and from there marched to Weeze and into action. For four days his group of 25 Paras fought between the Niers and the Mühlen Fleuth, alongside 8FJD and against 3 BID. He was wounded but patched up at the hospital in Kapellen. He was returned unfit to his unit, and consigned to the baggage train. On 4 March near Sonsbeck while retreating to Wesel, he was bombed by a Spitfire and received a severe wound in his right calf. He was treated at a field dressing station and taken by ambulance across the Rhine at Walsum. He was held convalescent in a PW cage at Sennelager and released on 24 July 1945, returning to his home in Duisburg. After recovering he became a salesman and then trained as a teacher. He lived near the battlefield in Kevelaer.[46]

Erich Freund served as a runner in 2 Coy in 1/FJR7, under command of 8FJD. He carried messages between Company HQ in Hovesaat and later in Geurtshof and Bodenhof opposite 8 BIB in 3 BID. Battalion HQ was in Fasanenkath and later in Rahmenhof, with regimental HQ in Uedem and the field kitchen in Kervenheim. In the event, when 4 CAD attacked north of Kervenheim, 1/FJR7 was sent to stop them. It was overrun and wiped from the order of battle with Erich being captured. He wrote in English, having met and married an English woman as a POW in England, where he lived for many years before moving to Cleves:

> Again many thanks for your letter with request for some information about the battle area of the lower 'Niederrhein'. I will have to start some years earlier to make you understand how it all was. There was a festival of harvest thanksgiving together with country-dances and folk-singing in Bückeberg. [The famous *Reichserntedankfest* on the Bückeberg near Hameln in Niedersachsen attracted up to one million attendants. It was one of the largest annual mass events of the Nazi regime, comparable only to the Nuremberg rallies and the Mayday celebrations in Berlin].[47] But also in the show was parachute jumping. That was in the autumn of 1938. I was fascinated and could see myself jumping out of a plane in the company of a few daredevils, and me being one of them. I wrote to ask if I could join? The answer was yes, but!! Being under 21 years of age I had to have father's permission, then a medical in Greifswald, a four day's aptitude test in Stettin and then wait for papers to come with instructions about where to report. I must have had about four in 1939 after the war had started, the new one always replacing the previous one. Then one day the real ones arrived with instructions to report to

46 Letters from Heinrich Nattkamp on 8 December 1996 and 19 January 1997.
47 K Magry. *After The Battle Issue No. 160* (Harlow: Battle of Britain Intnl, 2013), pp. 2-16.

Fliegerausbildung Regt 11 [aircrew-training] in Berlin-Schönwalde. When I asked about my parachute jumping they told me you don't want to go there; you'll be shot dead. From then on I worked at several bases, learning more and more about aeroplanes. When I dared again to volunteer for paratrooper training they said forget it, we need aeroplane mechanics. After completion of initial training in Schönwalde, some of us were sent to Jüterborg. During the day we learned everything about planes. I even had my first flight there in a Heinkel 45 with a trainee pilot, one of those *doppeldeckers* used in the Spanish Civil War. But I could see I was making progress. We served in Warsaw, Magdeburg, Speierdorf, Eschborn and Schleißheim. By this time it was 1943 and I was fully qualified as a Mechanical Under-Officer. The next move was to Mannheim-Sondhofen which occurred at the time of the Italian collapse, which brought with it bombing and a general petrol shortage. A paratroop-recruiting commando came to show us how nice their life was. Well, with no flying and no petrol what could I do but volunteer. I had to see the Squadron Leader who tore up my application and told me I was staying put. Joining the Paras would only end in my getting shot. But things got worse for us with nothing to do and still no petrol, so they let me go. I had to go to Gardelegen. What I saw there shook me a little. I had never seen so many ruffians in one spot. Never mind, now I was one of them. I managed to get to Kraljewo, 160 km south of Belgrade, arriving sometime in December 1943. There was an SS unit there, all big strong men who had broken the SS rules and were training to redeem themselves by jumping into Tito's HQ with free-fall chutes. We made two jumps out of JU 52s and four from HE 111s. On May 3 we went via Belgrade, Hungary, Austria, Germany to Metz. May came with the nicest weather you could imagine and clear skies. The twin-engined Lightnings flew overhead and not a German plane was in sight. Again and again you heard the word, invasion. Then it arrived. Enemy forces had landed. After only a few days we lined up. Everyone with good shoes and uniform had to step forward. The next thing they knew they were on the way to Normandy. No wonder I was not included. I usually looked like a scarecrow, tatty and worn out. Our turn came just the same. We went by train as far as Amiens. From there I was guided through fields and woods and landed up near Abbeville, hiding during the day and moving at night. The twin-engined Marauders were coming in very low, trying to spot anything hidden away in the orchards, which of course included us.

I haven't said yet what unit I was in. They told us we belonged to the 6th Parachute Division and you, pointing at where I was standing, are in Battalion *Schmitt*. We criss-crossed the countryside along the coast. Going west we could hear the heavy guns of the warships. Back again to an area outside Abbeville where we heard the uproar of the 20 July attempt on Hitler's life. We didn't want to obey the order to use the Hitler salute, but in the end we did obey but not voluntarily, that is for sure. There we were, sorting out our Hitler salute or the military salute. Then another twist most of us didn't like. Himmler was made our senior commander. The next order was to get ready for 2200 hours to go to Paris by train. At 2100 hours a squadron of fighters completely destroyed our train. Our commander said: 'We march'. It was about 40 km to Amiens and when I got there early in the morning I had blisters under my feet the size of pigeon eggs and couldn't walk any more. I was carried away to some first-aid post and later my friend got a car from somewhere and drove me to Paris. On the evening of the 15th we were still in St Denis when the French and Americans entered Paris on the other side. From there it was more like a rout. We crossed the Oise to Mons on the Belgian border, slipping through during the night. On September 2 to 3, we went on to Hasselt, followed by a week on the Albert Canal in contact with the Canadians coming from the direction of Bavay. The Canadians crossed the Albert Canal in front while behind us were British forces. Suddenly someone said that anyone who could get away could make his way out as best as he could. I went along the banks of the Maas and at a point crossed over and saw a signpost to Heinsberg. So we were in Germany somewhat north of Aachen. We had a week's rest and then I and my comrade Otto made our way to our reserve unit in Aschersleben. They directed us on to Nürnberg, where we rested for another week or two with heavy bombing nearly every night. They then gave me charge of 15 fully-fledged paratroopers and off we went to Brandenburg to prepare for the arrival of the whole company. It must be about 50 km from Berlin to Brandenburg. The Company travelled in from all over Germany. None of them had jump training, but we were called 2 Company, 1 Battalion, 7 Para Regiment under command of 2 Parachute Division.

I was jack-of-all-trades, keeping the company in as good order as possible. We moved to Arnhem. Christmas came with hard frost and snow. We changed our positions several times and every day we had to make sure we knew where to find Company HQ. When we moved into the area between the Niederrhein and the Waal we were flooded out. Someone on the German side blew up a dike and we had to scramble to find the banks of the Rhine. I got out at midnight with a horse which I called Paula. I was trying to ride Paula but I didn't know how to get up onto her. I was up to my armpits in water and everything was pitch black. Oh well – we made it in the end but don't think I wasn't afraid. There was a sea of water and we still had the river to cross. We made it though. The village was Renkum. We looked back in the direction we had come and it was frightening – just water. Our clothes and books hadn't dried when we had to move on. Some lorries turned up and took us through Wesel to Marienbaum. The drivers wouldn't go any further because the rumble of battle was loud and clear. We marched in the direction of Uedem to the roar of the heavy guns. The company HQ was in the cellar of the saw-mill at the end of Uedem on the road leading to Weeze. The field kitchen was in the middle of Uedem. Some units had to take up position on the railway line, the rest in reserve in Kervenheim. We got plastered every day by dive-bombers. The kitchen was hit and moved 7 km into Kervenheim because it was thought to be safer there. The next morning was February 19. I got the order from the sergeant major to go to the right bank of the Rhine and find our mortars, the company office and the paymaster. I didn't find them that day. There was another attack on the Rhine bridges and the road bridge was brought down. Through sheer luck I found our office staff and mortars in a village called Hafen-Mehr near Rees. We had to wait until dark and then we made our way to Uedem. I went to the saw-mill and directed the others to Kervenheim. In the cellar of the saw-mill there was only one other man from our company and he had been wounded near Arnhem. His rank then had been Aspirantoffizier, but now he was a Lieutenant. He told me to stay there and that our CO, Oberstleutnant [Lt Col] Einert would be sending another runner to take me to the new location of Company HQ. The one who came for me was Lance Corporal Waldemar Böhmer, about 21 years old and a youngster compared with my 25 years. When we had nearly reached HQ we had a stretch of perhaps 200 metres of open ground to cross. Above us was a plane like a Tiger Moth flying from left to right and back again. I told Waldemar I would sprint about 20 metres and then we would both shoot at him with cross-fire from our rifles. Since he was only 50 metres up we had a chance of hitting him or even of shooting him down. You may not believe it but suddenly he flapped his wings up and down and went away. But it wasn't long before a barrage of mortar bombs hit the open space we had just crossed. We passed Battalion HQ in Fasanenkath and saw some of our StuGs nearby. At the spot where the road turned left in the direction of Company HQ in Hovesaat, we saw some of our men trying to mend a broken telephone line. They weren't having much luck because one moment they were giving the OK sign and the next it was no go. One of them was Gerd Kersten who later lived not far from us but died a few years ago. I said that I was everywhere. I heard all the news. But no sooner had I arrived than I was ordered to return to Kervenheim to drum up at least 30 men if possible, even if they had to be from 3 Company.

Early next morning we were back in Hovesaat. We were fired on from the Kaken Bruch and when we approached our machine gun post someone shouted half the password, which was *Kraft* and I answered *Freude*. Everyone was getting ready to attack at 0600 hours. At the last minute Oblt. Einert asked to see me. 'Go to the StuGs', he said 'and tell them when they see a red flare they should fire more to the east'. I had nearly reached the StuG when it fired and for the next few hours I could hear nothing. I delivered the message and returned to Einert.[48]

Otto Einert, who is named above in 3 BID's intel summaries, survived the war and wrote:

At the end of February 1945 my company was organised as three platoons with about 30 men. They were equipped with SG44, MP40, Panzerfaust, Panzerschreck (Ofenrohr), and MG42 – whether 3 or 6 I can no longer say. I originally enlisted in the Flak. I served in France, Greece and Russia. That's where we developed the strategy of emplacing the MG42 to fire indirectly and diagonally across the front. 2-cm Flak was added alongside. In the spring of 1944 when retreating from Stalingrad I developed a very high fever of 40 to 41.5°C. After recovery I was sent to France to join the Paras. I became adjutant in Col. Eggersh's Kampfgruppe. After its dissolution I commanded 2 Company in FJR7. At the end of April 1945 I walked and cycled from the Ruhrgebiet to my home in the Erzgebirge. I was never in a P/W camp. I reached home on May 9, 1945. I had to report to the Russian army every month later every three months – until 1950. In 1958 I took my family to the west.[49]

Erich Freund continued:

We captured 12 prisoners but I could see it wasn't going well. It was still dark at 0600 hours and opposite me was a British Brengunner no more than 15 metres away. His burst of bullets shot away the metal loop which held the strap on my rifle. The bullets grazed the fingers of both my hands and the marks remain visible to this day. They also ripped the straps under my right arm. At that moment I told myself I must be a little more careful. The stretcher bearer who came running up from behind thought it was me shouting for help, but I could hear someone asking to be left where he was and that was Feldwebel X – I have forgotten his name. He had been shot in the groin but there was someone else wounded in the stomach. Just then there was another burst of fire and the stretcher-bearer fell face downwards in about 15 cm of water next to me. [Stretcher-bearers had immunity from both sides on the Western Front, for the obvious reason that you never knew when you might need one. But accidents happened and each side usually gave the other the benefit of the doubt, as Erich does here]. Getting down I turned him over and pulled him away from the water, but there was nothing anybody could do for him. Later during my first trip to Germany in 1949 this man's father came to see me from Cologne and wanted to know about his son and how he had died. But reverting to the Karken Bruch, I think we lost that battle, but my *Husarenstück* [daring escapade] was still to come. We could see a British tank at Hovesaat firing shells into the farm building while in the meadow there was a section digging themselves in. [If this was 24/25 February, then the tank was from 3 Sgn of 4 GG in 6 GAB supporting the KOSBs of 15 BID while waiting relief from 8 BIB in 3 BID]. At about 2100 hours our Company Commander visited me in the chicken house. He indicated the forester's house and said that in it were Feldwebel Witwer and Oberjäger Becke. Nothing had been heard from them or their unit throughout the day,

48 Two letters in English from Erich Freund dated January 11 and 18, 1997.
49 Letter from Otto Einert on 24 April 1997 from Stuttgart.

he said, so he told me to go and get them out. I pointed to the tank and the British digging into the meadow and told him that I had never been there before and didn't know the layout of the buildings. "I don't care how you do it", he said. " but I know you can". Well, it was no good arguing so off I went. To the right of me was a burning barn, in front were the British troops, to the right the tank and to the left the River Niers running high in its banks. So I climbed over the fence and headed towards the Niers. I turned right behind the hedge where the British were digging. The Steinberger-Ley was now to my left also very full. I moved away from the British who were on my right and towards the tank. One of the crew was in the turret speaking to his colleague on the ground. I wasn't very far from them when I turned left to cross a bridge over the Steinberger-Ley. The bridge was shielded by some large trees and the forester's house [probably Hovesaat] had an archway. Coming towards me through the arch was, and he remains, my best friend. One eye was nearly closed and he presented a sorry sight. He was waving a towel, and I can't remember whether it was white or just dirty. He said, "Erich. We saw you coming. How did you make it?" I replied I had come to get him and the others out of there and asked how many were with him. He said they were twelve with one who had to be left behind because he was so badly wounded. He added that there were civilians including the 80 year old forester with a long beard, together with women and children who were staying behind. I explained how I had got through and told him I had to return and would be awaiting them. I reported back to the Company Commander and then we waited. Nobody came and the CO must have begun to wonder whether I had made the whole thing up. Then a sentry ran up asking whether he should shoot at some approaching figures, but I said it had to be Erwin Becke, and so it was. The CO asked why only four had come out, and the sergeant explained that they had not dared follow Freund because of the danger and so they had got into the water-course and walked with water up to their shoulders. When the CO saw Becke's eye he told him to stay put while he sent FW. Witwer and Freund. I didn't want to push my luck again so went like them through the water. I forgot all about my cigarettes. We got another eight men out. The wounded man did recover and I saw him in November last year together with another comrade who was badly wounded on February 27. It was after 2200 hours when the CO told me to take the twelve men to Uedem to dry out. We also had to find a duty officer near Saarbrockshof and tell him that around 2300 hours a StuG would be coming in with all the wounded both inside and on top, and that he was to hold his fire. We carried on to Uedem and to the same sawmill cellar. Next day I went to Kervenheim to scrounge a sack full of things to eat plus cigarettes, and then went via Uedem to Geurtshof. On arriving the CO wanted to know if I had been fired on. I replied I hadn't and when I asked why he should ask, he told me to look over at the wood. Well, I have never seen so many tanks in broad daylight. They were stretched right along the edge of the wood. I was then ordered back to Kervenheim to inform the cook that a good soup would be welcome. The CO said they would withdraw across the road to Bodenhof, while the rest of the battalion was ordered to Rosenhof down the Uedem-Weeze road on the right hand side, whatever for I don't know. The move cost them a man and then they returned to Rahmanhof, which was the farm beyond Bodenhof. The soup never reached my unit. I explained to the sergeant major and the staff sergeant where they should leave the soup. I stayed behind in Kervenheim to catch up on some sleep. When they returned they woke me up to say that my unit no longer existed. That really woke me up.

I ran off at once, as always taking the safest route via Uedem [sic]. I ran in the direction of Weeze as far as Kampshof, turning left to Bodenhof. The building stood empty. I went on to Rahmenhof and found the rest of the battalion. Oberleutnent Einert, Captain Walter and the MO Bonhard. He was washing himself thoroughly in a bowl of water to be clean in case he got work to do. He asked after the soup. We counted everyone and they numbered a proud 71 men. I left at once for the field kitchens which meant a dangerous trip through the artillery positions. One had to be a good runner when the shells came in our direction. It was decided the cook should prepare enough food for 75 men, and that they should come to Kervenheim and eat it nice and hot. There would be a little over for the really hungry. Then heavy artillery began to bombard Kervenheim. The following day after I had been captured I saw them hard at it. It was now February 26. [The Whitakers[50] called that Thursday, February 26, 'The Grisliest Day', with 214 Canadians killed. On only three other days in Normandy were losses higher. The attack went in at 4.30 am. 'From February 26 until March 10, there was never a moment when they were not rain-soaked, cold and afraid, or when the threat of defeat did not hover over them…Only the first day, February 26, lived up to expectations… In demonstrations of personal courage, few days in World War II can match it']. The hungry l Company were still eating and discussing events. Then the armourer was called – his name escapes me[51] – and Oberjäger Freund. We were then ordered to look at the map and find three farms where the men could be dispersed so they wouldn't be lost all at once if caught in an artillery bombardment. The farms were in Uedemer Feld just east of Uedem. The men found the barns. One farm was called Reindershof. Everyone was satisfied with the soup in their belly and ready for a rest. Even I needed a little kip. I told several people where I would be in case I was needed. I was in a little white house on the other side of the road snoring with my steel helmet as a pillow. It wasn't long before someone called out and woke me and I saw everyone was preparing to leave. It wasn't far to the top of the ridge. Slowly it got dark and looking through the binoculars you could see the Canadians approaching. Christmas trees [flares] were hanging in the air, while behind us a machine gun was barking and to the right there was a cutting being used by the men for shelter. I suggested to the CO that we get into the cellar of the farm behind us. That way we could make out our exact position. I took water and milk out to the boys. Then the CO despatched me to our right flank where there was supposed to be an infantry unit. When I arrived they were packing to leave. I asked for the officer and found him in a house along the road. He said they were going, and so what? I told our CO that our flank was in the air and he told me to report this to Captain Walter who was in Beerenhof to the west of our farm. By now there was pandemonium. I went out again to see how the boys were doing. The first group in the cutting said they were out of ammunition, so I went to battalion HQ to beg for some. They answered there was no ammunition and no vehicles to fetch any. What had happened to our armoured vehicles? I realised then that the vehicles which had been there during my last run had departed. There was another runner who worked the other direction from me. The noise of battle grew louder and more of our men fell back on the farmhouses. My last run had not been far and, yes, we were told ammunition was now on the way. Oberleutnant Einert told me to report to Battalion HQ that if no ammunition arrived soon we would have to withdraw because our men now only had stones to throw. So off I went. Captain Walter was in a barn behind Beerenhof. I repeated the message and asked for something in writing. He said we could withdraw but no further back than the spot on the map which he pointed to with his finger. I got my piece of paper and off I went. When I got to the road I couldn't believe my eyes. A tank stood facing the farm with a crowd of Canadians behind the bank. Then the tank began firing into the farmhouse. I ran back to Capt. Walter to inform him about the tank and to say I would make a detour around the back. A private gave me a front-line parcel which I had never seen before. It was 4-inch cube and I put it in my pouch. I decided to run through the wet meadow about 50 to

50 Whitaker, *Rhineland.*

51 Ted Winkler was shown this on 8 March 2014 and confirmed it was him.

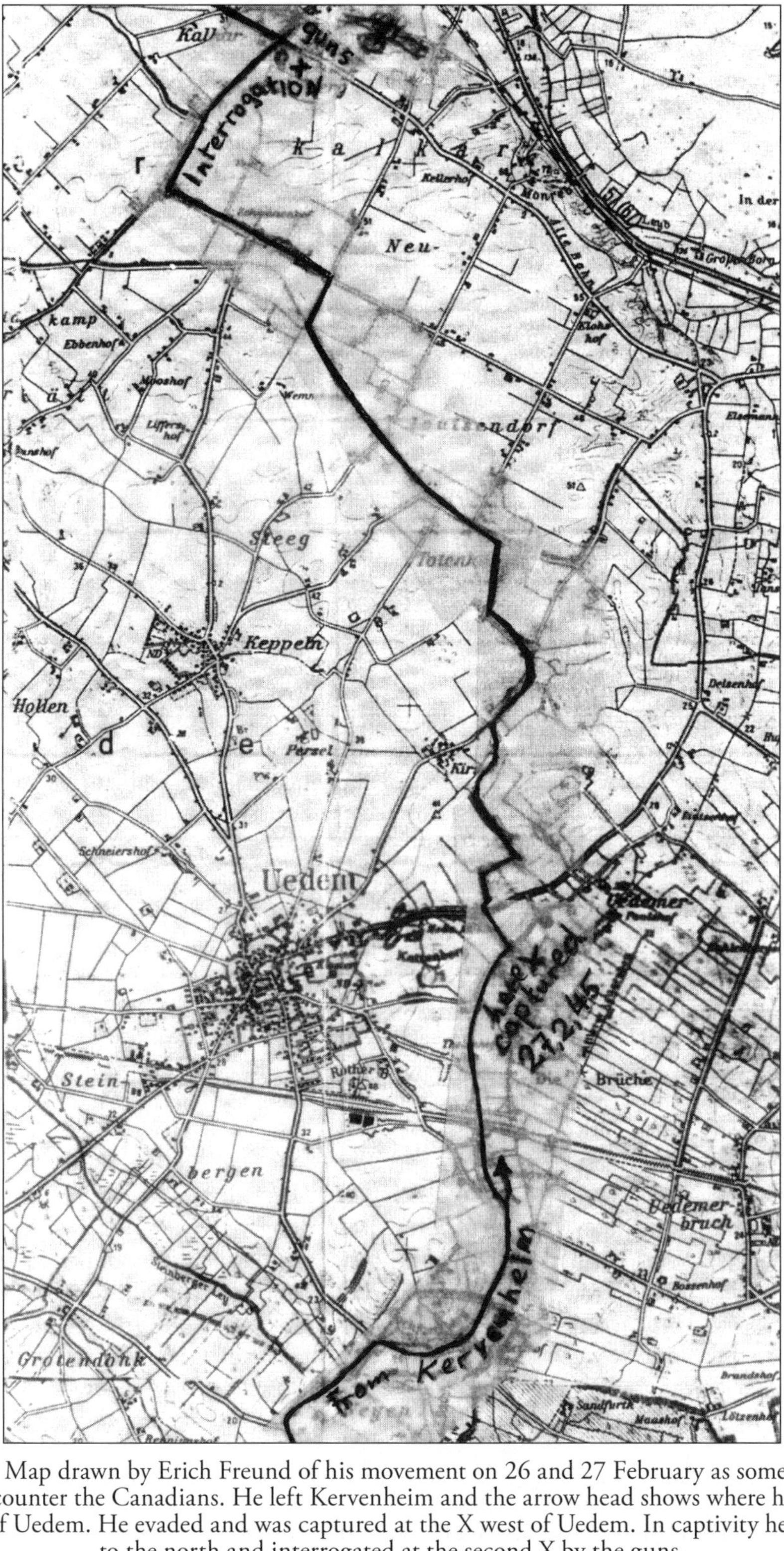

Map 40 Map drawn by Erich Freund of his movement on 26 and 27 February as some of 7FJR moved to counter the Canadians. He left Kervenheim and the arrow head shows where he met Lion Force SE of Uedem. He evaded and was captured at the X west of Uedem. In captivity he was taken to the north and interrogated at the second X by the guns.

> 60 metres in from the road. I reached a fence, lifted my rifle over followed by one leg, but the other leg caught. I remember it was quite dark. While I was trying to keep my trousers in one piece I heard someone talking. I answered back telling them to stay out of my way as I was in a hurry. Then this fellow knocked me on my steel helmet with his Sten. I had to part with my hat, put my hands up and off I went. I was on this narrow lane and 30 Canadians came towards me. They were not as soft-hearted as the first. My left arm took the brunt of it and the parcel in my pouch was reduced to crumbs. When I reached the road I could see the tank was still there shooting into the farm. I had to duck down. It was 100 metres below the ridge.[52]

Erich was in the middle of the attack by Lion Force commanded by Brigadier Jefferson of Chris Vokes' 4 CAD. It was directed on Point 73, code name 'Albatross', in the Hochwald Gap. Erich met them at the stage when things were going reasonably well for them. The infantry were the Algonquin Regiment supported by tanks of the 29 Armd Recce Regt of the SAR. This group was commanded by the Algonquin's CO, Lt-Col Bradburn. The infantry unit that gratuitously beat up Erich in contravention of the Geneva Convention after he had surrendered, was probably part of the company which had been riding on tanks that had bogged down. They had dismounted and were now hurrying to catch up. The entire Force had been floundering over the ruined roads and muddy fields since soon after midnight, and by 4.30 am had formed up outside Kirsel. At 5.15 am, Bradburn gave the order to advance. Stacey[53] records; 'The Germans manning the outpost area were completely surprised,' which is borne out by Erich's story. The Canadians continued to meet little resistance as they moved down the slopes of the Uedem ridge. By daylight they were across the railway line at Üdemerbruch and faced the last German prepared positions before the Rhine. They immediately became the target of every German gun in range including heavy artillery firing from the other side of the Rhine. This was 'The Valley of Death' and the target of an estimated 1,000 German guns. A diversionary unit of the Algonquins going south to Üdemerbruch was destroyed, and suddenly the Germans had regained the initiative. Erich continued:

> I came to realise that my involvement in the war was over. I came to a steep bit of the ridge which I couldn't see over, but at my feet there was a hole in the ground and inside a soldier with a machine gun. He made an excuse that his gunner had left him. I told him to come out and we would go on together. Then I remembered the front-parcel. I opened my pouch and retrieved a few biscuits. I gave him one and said that when it got light in a few minutes we would be able to see where all the others had got to. When he had calmed down I suggested that we go on and meet our fate with the Canadians. It was February 27. We climbed up the steep incline and then saw a fantastic sight. Row upon row of tanks and other vehicles stretching away to left and right. The nearest tank was about 15 metres away. One of the crew had his back to us and was doing something to the tank with a big spanner. He looked round once then carried on for a few seconds. Then as if he hadn't believed his eyes he turned round and shook himself. The only sound he made was something like 'Wow'. With his big spanner he knocked on the tank. All the hatches opened and everyone pointed a gun at us. They had a confab about us and then gave signs for us to turn around and in the distance we saw a Canadian with a bandaged head leading 5 German prisoners. We were told to move with the tank behind us until we caught up with the wounded Canadian. He then had 7 charges. I took a good look around going through Kirsel. The guard suddenly dived for shelter as about six heavy shells burst all around us seven prisoners who remained standing on the road. When

52 Two letters in English from Erich Freund on 11 and 18 January 1997.
53 Stacey, *The Victory*.

the guard came out from his shelter there were no more incidents and he smiled at us as we all moved on [happy that he knew they would not escape and get him into trouble].

The guard delivered us to a sort of interrogation post at a cross-roads on the Kalker Berg overlooking Kalkar. In a barn behind us there were civilians and on the other side some of the heavy guns shooting intermittently at Kervenheim. I had to enter a tent and stand in front of a table with a map pinned on it. A two-foot square was marked on the floor. The Captain wanted to know who I was, the name of the Company's CO and the location of our field kitchen. I made evasive statements. Asked again I repeated that I didn't know but he then asked what it was that I didn't know. I stepped forward one pace out of the square and said I could pinpoint it on the map. Wow. He grabbed his revolver and shouted at me to get back into the square or else. That was it and he must have seen I wasn't co-operating. Late afternoon we were taken by lorry through the Reichswald into Holland. It was getting dark so I hung about near the spot where the barbed wire could be opened. I was lucky [that they chose me for a task that would mean different and better treatment] and they loaded a few lorries, each carrying 50 prisoners and two guards. We didn't know where we were going but next day we arrived at a factory in Tilburg. The following day we moved into a clean cellar. There I met someone I knew, Karl Fink from Amberg. We were both with the Luftwaffe and he joined the Paras, I think, in March 1943. Towards evening a few more arrived from our company including Captain Walter, the battalion's CO and his adjutant. They were kept a little separate from us. Later at least two more from our company arrived and after that at least six more. There was Hans Müller and Erwin Becke with his swollen eye who had escaped from the forester's hut. Both are still in England. We went to one of the big PW camps near Zeebrügge, numbered 2226, 2227 and 2228. Each had three cages holding 6,000 men. I arrived by train at 2226 on March 2, 1945. On April 26 I spent a night in a brickworks. Then on April 27 we went by boat from Ostend to Tilbury arriving on the 28th. We moved to a transit camp at Camden Park until April 29 when we were transferred to Otley in Yorkshire. We left Otley on July 24 and arrived the same day in Fareham in Hampshire. I was then an inmate of POW Camp 25 where 1 remained until May 13 1948. Christmas came 1946, and English people invited German prisoners for a Christmas dinner. Helmut Arnds from Hannover and I were chosen. First I didn't want to go because my English was limited to yes and no. But all afternoon and evening we had a jolly good time. The master of the house was responsible for returning us to camp. It must have been after a mile or maybe a little more during our return to camp when I said to Helmut that this Irene will be my wife, I think. Well, after another two years it happened. After that I did various jobs to try and earn a living, mostly as a cowman because it paid a little better and had a decent cottage. In 1961 I was offered a job without a tied cottage. We moved to Fareham between Southampton and Portsmouth. I worked there in a factory for over 8 years and earned good money. Things looked a bit bleak and with a job waiting for me we went to Germany in the autumn of 1968. However not everything went easily but I worked until I was 65 years old and could even have gone on a bit longer.[54]

The ace, Second Lieutenant Heinz Deutsch,[55] was commanding a troop of StuGs in support of 7FJD and 8FJD. In 1940, straight from school, he joined a heavy flak unit but finding it too sedentary for his taste volunteered for paratroop training. He was commissioned and directed to the new XII Assault Gun (StuG) Brigade, which after extensive training was formed in March 1944 in Fontainebleu. The GOC was Captain Gersteuer and troop commanders were Capt. Heinrichs

54 Two letters in English from Erich Freund on 11 and 18 January 1997.
55 Alman, *Sprung*.

(1 Troop), Lt. Behne (2 Troop) and Capt. Krall (3 Troop). Deutsch became a platoon leader commanding three StuGs in 3 Troop. The 3 Divisional Intelligence Summary No. 231 stated that 2 troop was in support of 7 Para Regiment and was the 'only one known to have been in our sector'.

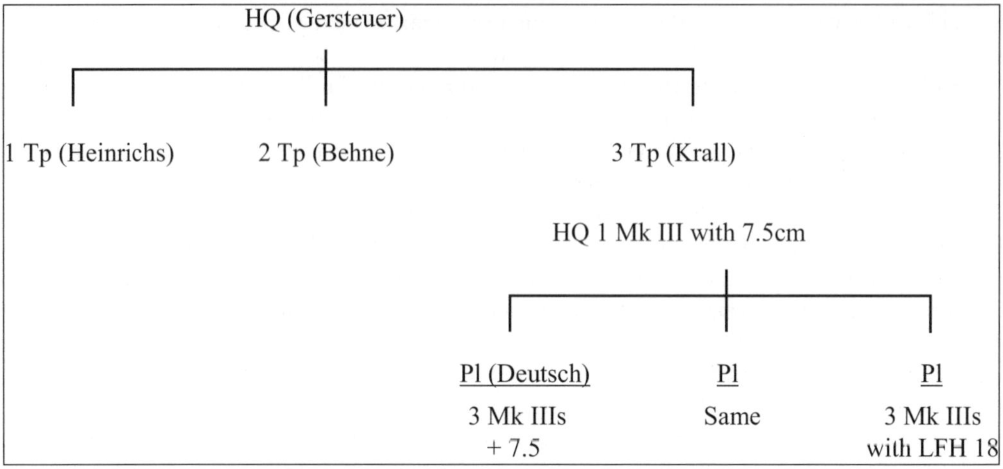

Each Platoon had 6 StuG IIIs with 75 mm and 3 with a modified version of the 10.5 cm LFH 18, the standard German light field howitzer, and were designated 'Sturmhaubitze 42' (StuH 42).

The XII StuG Brigade with 30 StuGs was smaller than 6 GAB with 45 Churchills. The German Platoon was equivalent to the British Troop, both with 3 AFVs, the German Troop of 10 StuGs with a British Squadron or battalion of 15 Churchills.

Deutsch destroyed his first Sherman outside St Lô on 13 July in support of 3FJD. He fought at Vire and Tinchebray and escaped the Falaise pocket. The Brigade rallied at Cologne-Wahn and was soon directed to Wyler and thrown against the Nijmegen bridgehead on 18 September during Op *Market Garden*. They stayed there until January 1945 when new StuGs were issued in Amersfoort and the Brigade of 30 StuGs moved south to the Roermond-Venlo area with 7FJD.

Sturmgeschütz translates literally as 'Assault Gun', and was abbreviated to StuG. It was the only tracked German weapon system serving throughout the war in the same basic format. The chassis was the same as the MkIII tank, and hence the name StuG III. It had no turret, and to lay the gun it was turned towards the enemy. The backbone of German defence against *Veritable*, and indeed everywhere on both fronts, it was a relatively inexpensive, sophisticated, handy and effective weapon. The Russians copied it with their SUs, and the Anglo-Americans did not.

The need for an assault gun was detected as early as the Polish campaign when the Staff, according to Blumentritt, noticed the inadequacies of the infantry who:

> never reached the high standards of 1914 – no comparison. Tank and assault guns became an indispensable help to the infantry. Without them we would never have won the great victories of 1941/42.[56]

56 Library of US Army War College, Carlisle, Manuscript B-283.

The first StuG was used in France in 1940 with a 75 mm L/24 short howitzer with a barrel length of 1.8 m. When it proved ineffective in 1942 against the T34 in Russia, Hitler demanded the fitment of the L/43 with a barrel length of 3.2 m, which was called the StuG III *Ausführung F.* Finally in 1943 the *Ausführung* G received the L/48 KwK40 gun with a length of 3.6 m. This was the unit operated by Deutsch. The gun could not penetrate the front of the Churchill IV at battlefield ranges but could go through its sides when achieving an enfilade position. Its dimensions of 7 ft in height and 10 ft in width meant ambush concealment was relatively easy. It was fast, moving at 50 kph (31 mph) on good going, making it difficult to pin down as it could change position quickly. Its frontal armour was only 80 mm (3.2 inches) thick, and its ditch-crossing performance and flotation were poor compared with the Churchill and it bogged more easily in soft ground.

Both StuG and Churchill had a similar 75 mm gun but the turreted Churchill could lay its gun far more quickly than the StuG could be swung round. The Churchill was a bigger target and more likely to be hit, and it motored at half the speed of the StuG. The Churchill could move through woods because its gun did not project beyond the front of the chassis, and it was forgiving in soft going. The StuG, with its long over-hanging gun, had to keep out of woods and avoid soft ground and obstacles that the Churchill could manage. The StuG used the roads, travelling at speed, knowing the location of mines and craters, and often taking cover beside or in buildings, trying to set an ambush. The Churchills preferred the open country, moving with an infantry escort and rarely bypassing the ambushing StuG which was looking for a flanking shot through the Churchill's weak side armour. The two came face to face when the Churchills crossed the roads or attacked a defended village on a crossroads such as Kervenheim and Winnekendonk.

On the afternoon of 8 February as *Veritable* started, the 'Green Devils' (*Grüne Teufel*), as they were called, were ordered forward with 7FJD and took up positions to the southwest of the Reichswald between Goch and Gennep. When 8FJD arrived, XII Brigade supported them as well. On 25 February, Deutsch moved from Weeze and attacked the flank of the advance at Todtenhügel and Keppeln (2, 3 and 4 CIDs), destroying two Shermans and a Cromwell. This placed him west of Uedem fighting against 11 BAD which was the only formation in the area operating Cromwells.

From Weeze to Uedem, Deutsch used the road which 3 BID reached on 27 February to seize Yorkshire Bridge. Deutsch recorded that during the next few days he operated out of Kevelaer to counter attack the Allies. The nearest enemy was 3 BID. Early on 1 March, Deutsch destroyed two Churchills at Kloppermannshof, identified for the reasons given in Chapter 3 as Wettermannshof, and the other StuGs in his Troop claimed kills. These must have been the StuGs seen south west of Kervenheim on the high ground which gave the Norfolks and CGs a difficult time. Two StuGs belonging to the XII Brigade were destroyed the next day at Winnekendonk in exchange for three Churchills and a Stuart, but from the PW returns it is believed that 2 Troop rather than Deutsch's 3 Troop was responsible for the defence of Winnekendonk. That day Deutsch destroyed 2 Shermans and a Churchill while rescuing Battle Groups which were in difficulties. He withdrew to Kapellen through Wetten.

> Slowly the enemy came on. They had learned respect for the fast-moving StuGs with their long effective gun. Again and again, Lt Deutsch ambushed the cautiously advancing allied tanks as a predator stalks its prey. Again and again the guns boom, the flames leap and the shells explode. Under the protection of the StuG's machine-gun, the Paratroopers decimate the attackers. The fight continued around Kapellen until March 4th.[57] [The troops outside Kapellen were GAD who were held for two days 'by strong infantry rearguards well supported by SP A-tk guns', according to Stacey].

57 Alman, *Sprung*, p. 236.

Deutsch had been awarded the EKI (Iron Cross 1st Class) on 25 February for destroying 13 enemy tanks. On 5 March he received the German Cross in Gold, followed on 15 April by the *Ritterkreuz*, one of only 5,070 awarded. His eventual score was 44 tanks, making him the top scorer in the west. The Brigade as a whole was credited with 260 tanks. He survived the war with all his crew except one killed by shellfire when outside the vehicle relieving himself.

Schlemm, the commander of 1 Para Army, Meindl of II Para Corps, and Lackner of 2 Para Division, all gave written commentaries to their American captors in 1946. Unfortunately there was nothing by Erdmann of 7FJD or Wadehn of 8FJD.

Schlemm was interviewed in PW Camp no. 11 at Bridgend, Glamorgan on 18 March 1946. He complained of lack of reference material and spoke from memory. He said he held the Uedem-Weeze area with II FS Corps comprising: '7FJD, Genlt Erdmann (brought up from Lorraine by OB West, 7 Feb. 45), 8FJD, Genlt Wadehn (brought up on my orders from the Roermond area, 16 Feb. 45), 84 ID, Gen Fiebig (elements only)'.[58] When the American forces threatened from the south, Schlemm, 'announced to Army Group my intention to establish a bridgehead on the general line Marienbaum – Kevelaer – Geldern – Kempen – Krefeld and to reduce its size as the situation might require'.

Meindl was interviewed on March 18, 1946. He said that; 'Owing to the rapid development of events in 1945, my recollections of events which took place in that year are even more vague than those of 1944'.[59] He was, however, interesting, opinionated and experienced, receiving one of only 569 Knight's Cross with Oak Leaves. In Sept 1944 he was ordered to Groesbeek with his 'untrained children' formed into Combat Groups. He expressed himself forcefully on the subject of Combat groups, which is probably a translation of *Gefechtsgruppen*. He wrote, 'Personally I hate the expression 'Combat Groups', for it is a colourless term which means anything. It is a propaganda term, coined during this war, designed to conceal the true facts'.

Meindl in his Welsh prison camp foresaw a bleak future. The following is from the US Army translation, the original being unavailable.

> The large scale attack was in full swing. It was now a matter to wage the battle in the first place with weapons of heavy calibre and to make the Jaeger and infantry personnel experienced to deeply echelonned and prolonged combat. Fortunately the troop commanders and I knew each other and the reorientation occurred rapidly. We very soon had achieved some very nice defence successes, especially during the period that we were sufficiently supplied with artillery munition; unfortunately this became more scarce every day. [The Anglo-Canadians did not agree. 'Attacks by 3rd and 4th (Canadian) Divisions on 1st and 2nd March were halted by enemy artillery fire that could not be neutralised'. And again on 6 March, Nicholson recorded that 2 Canadian AGRA harrassed enemy columns crossing the Rhine in the vicinity of Wesel. 'Every battery on the far bank retaliated vigorously, and Canadian regimental areas experienced some of the heaviest shelling of the Rhineland battle'].[60] The Jaegers alone could not prevent a breakthrough. Even heavier than the battle against the unheard of enemy material, was the inner battle against the impossible commands of our superiors who continually ordered us to 'halt' the front. I always tried to keep my conscience clean in regard to my leadership in battles. I often visited my troops and I gradually developed quite a good sense which allowed me to predict the main points of impending operations, which I almost always guessed rightly as far as time, as well as location was concerned. It was a simple

58 Library of US Army War College, Carlisle, Manuscript B-084.
59 Library of US Army War College, Carlisle, Manuscript Meindl B-051.
60 Gerald Nicholson. *The Gunners of Canada* (Toronto: McClelland & Stewart, 1967).

mathematical problem which was based on the following factors: road junctions, nature of terrain, the purpose, the tactically planned direction of the forward thrust, and the scheduled time. Accordingly I established my defence lines and directed my concentrated fire of heavy weapons.

The following facts had a demoralising influence upon the troops, to some extent already then, but even more so during the following period:

1. The serious lack of ammunition which was almost catastrophic
2. The feeling of impotence in face of enemy air superiority, including the air raids against the home country (particularly the latter)
3. The serious situation in which we found ourselves on all fronts
4. The feebleness of our highest commanders in regard to many ridiculous things. Many a misfortune could have been prevented if one was seriously prepared to bear the consequences
5. The untrue and disagreeable propaganda of our superior military and political leadership
6. The failure and rapid disappearance of the uniformed Nazi people from the present combat zones who, up to a short time ago, had made life almost intolerable for us
7. The unauthorised and also dishonest privileges which were granted to them in all things
8. The employment of under-age people for the combat forces, despite the fact that they were still children
9. The misery of the millions of refugees from the East. The fact that the German as a human being was without protection
10. We were opposed by the entire world, filled with a merciless spirit of annihilation. On our own side, there was a dictatorship, out of whose chains a liberation was only possible from the outside. A contradiction in itself. Either alternative was equally slim [surely a mistranslation of *schlimm*, meaning 'seriously bad']. We were doomed in either case. It would be wrong to believe that the ordinary soldier did not realise this and that he did not ponder over these problems. This was certainly often the cause of the seemingly contradictory attitude of our soldiers on the front, in combat, and in captivity, dependent on what particular aspect temporarily dominated their soul and conscience. The great military and political intoxication was followed by a terrible sobering. We soldiers were the victims of the black day of the political scene. We could not be fooled any longer. Thus, today, the German people, after the capitulation, if they emerge alive, will do so sober and naked, susceptible to any kind of national disease.[61]

A few of the defenders would have been wearing the standard army rimmed helmet, but most wore the rimless, padded, blue-grey paratroop helmet, with twin forked chinstraps passing either side of the ear, with the Luftwaffe eagle painted on its side. Some helmets would have the 'splinter' pattern cloth covers, with bands in a 'hot cross bun' pattern to hold foliage, while others would have netting or even chicken wire to retain camouflage. Some who had been in Normandy would have jump smocks, a baggy garment of strong cotton drill cloth with four large zippered pockets, manufactured in several versions and designed to prevent ballooning out during a parachute descent. The first pattern with short legs had been replaced in 1943 with skirts that could be fixed between the legs with press studs to give the same effect. Later in the war the conventional infantry three-quarter length camouflaged jacket in splinter pattern with Luftwaffe eagle sewn on the right side was issued to the newly raised divisions, and it is probable that many at Kervenheim and Winnekendonk were wearing these over their Luftwaffe blue greatcoats against the cold weather.

61 Library of US Army War College, Carlisle, Manuscript Meindl B-051.

Similarly, some would have on the early jump trousers, but most would be wearing the usual blue-grey service trousers. Conventional front-laced boots would be almost universally worn, with gaiters. Many would have brown leather straps, but some would be wearing the black army issue type. Toques and gloves would be worn to keep out the cold and, like all German troops, they would not be wearing socks in their boots but *Fusslappen*, a cloth square folded over the foot.

Fallschirmjäger were always heavily armed, but all the British accounts mention the extraordinary number of infantry weapons of all kinds taken at Winnekendonk. This fact is surely the mark of the *Fallschirmarmeewaffenschule* or Para Lehr with its stock of weapons normally used for demonstration. After the battle the weapons not retained by the British as souvenirs, [Colvin took a Schmeisser which was kept at home in Germany] were laid on the road and destroyed under the tracks of a Churchill as a precaution against their being recaptured. Large numbers of MG34s and 42s (Spandaus), FG42s (Fallschirmgewehr 42), MP43s and 44s (the pressed steel assault rifle that the Russians developed into the AK47), MP40s (Schmeisser), Beretta MP 739s, (the best of the lot according to Sydney Jary), Kar 98k (Mauser) and the shorter, lightened Gewehr 33/40 were destroyed in this way. The fate of the resulting scrap is unknown.

Ammunition would be carried both round the neck in bandoliers made of cloth with six pockets sewn on each end, and in the normal pouches attached to the belt. The defenders would have the two-man, 3.5 inch rocket propelled Panzerschreck, known to the troops as the *Ofenrohr* (stovepipe) and a good copy of the American bazooka. It could penetrate 8 inches of armour from 165 yards, making any part of the Churchill tank vulnerable. Also available would be the Panzerfaust 60 or 100, an ingenious recoilless gun working on the principle of a firework rather than a rocket, with a projector that was discarded after use. The 100 referred to the sighted range in metres. It could penetrate 200 mm of armour, or nearly 8 inches, easily defeating even the 6-inch frontal armour of the Churchill MkVII.

Of most danger to the attacking infantry were the German mortars. As the war progressed, German defence came to rely increasingly on mortars rather than the artillery. They were more flexible and easier to hide and the Germans were expert in their use. The British were trying to develop counter-measures based on radar at the end of the war. The paratroops used the 8 cm Short Mortar Model 42, or *Stummelwerfer*, as well as the 10 cm *Nebelwerfer* 35, and the 120 mm *Granatwerfer*. The latter was a copy of a Russian design and regarded as the best mortar of the war. In support was the 15 cm *Nebelwerfer* of the 8/86 Werfer Regt whose FOO, 2nd Lt Körner was taken prisoner on 1 March.

What almost certainly killed Peter Clarke of 2 Lincolns in front of Winnekendonk was the unique German 'bouncing bomb' designed for the *Stummelwerfer*, whose strange fin was found by his body by Leslie Colvin. This resembled a conventional bomb in appearance, but the rounded nose had a blunt head and a short pyrotechnic delay fuse. On landing, the bomb's impact fuse immediately ignited the propellant powder which exploded, shearing the pins holding nose and body together and blowing the bomb's body back into the air and igniting the pyrotechnic delay as it did so. After the bomb had 'bounced' to a height of anywhere between 20 and 50 feet depending on the softness of the ground, it exploded giving a First World War type of lethal airburst.

The paratroop defenders of Kervenheim and Winnekendonk were mostly skilled and experienced. The Allies were aware of the German methods and what is known about the defence of Kervenheim and Winnekendonk reflects standard German practice. Towns and villages were turned into strong points, and villages consolidated as single defended localities. Advanced positions were manned 5,000 to 7,000 yards out, which meant that Kervenheim became in effect an outpost of Winnekendonk. Outpost positions were occupied by a platoon 2,000 to 5,000 yards in advance of the defended locality and when abandoned the defenders would slip away unseen while their vacated positions were shelled and mortared. Machine-guns opened fire on the enemy from 1,300 yards and riflemen at 850 yards. Einert talked of using the MG42 in enfilade fire positions firing diagonally across the battlefield. Numerous dummy positions were constructed so the enemy could not guess which ones were occupied. Anti-tank guns were grouped in pairs when available with up to 10 under unified command and sited to fire in enfilade, as at Kervenheim and Winnekendonk, or on reverse slopes. Anti-tank guns opened fire at ranges up to 1,000 yards but sometimes as close as 150 to 300 yards. At Winnekendonk the 88s began firing at 750 yards.

The Germans relied on heavy concentrations of fire and powerful, coordinated counter-attacks. A Canadian officer described the German reception of the *Blockbuster* attack in the Hochwald after Erich Freund was captured. Ben Dunkelman thought the German tactics brilliantly conceived and excellently implemented with tenacity by some of the best soldiers in Europe. There was no rigid defence, and when attacked the Germans held on for as long as possible in their excellently concealed slit-trenches and then withdrew to a position further back. There was then an instant pounding of the vacated positions by mortars and artillery, co-ordinated with an infantry counter-attack to retake the lost ground.[62] The point of main enemy effort, the *Schwerpunkt*, was identified or guessed at, and the main defending force placed to block it. The defence line was centred on any available buildings, from individual farms to a village or built-up area. Kervenheim and Winnekendonk, being built around road junctions, were naturally selected. Unoccupied buildings were booby-trapped and, when time was available, the entrances blocked up. All windows would be opened so as not to disclose which particular rooms were occupied. Weapons were fired from the middle of the room and well back from the window in the shadows so they couldn't be seen. Riflemen fired aimed shots from the upper storeys while machine-guns were sited low, usually in basements to provide grazing fire. Some men would climb on the roofs and station themselves behind chimneys and cornices. Others removed tiles to provide loopholes. All these techniques were noted at Kervenheim and Winnekendonk. A special battle commander (*Kampfkommandant)*, Gräfing at Kervenheim and Krahl at Winnekendonk, would plan and co-ordinate the defence and establish the PAKfront.

We have seen how two of Alasdair Gordon's troop of 3 SGs and the FOO's tank were destroyed at 750 yards as soon as they came into the open past Brönkshof at the beginning of the long approach to Winnekendonk. One Churchill was split in half and the turret blown into the air. Such damage could only be inflicted by the 88 mm, L/71 Dual Purpose gun at a range of 700 m. The flight time of its AP shell would be seven tenths of a second, and the projectile's solid 20.7 lb bulk would hit the tank at a velocity of 1,000 m/sec (3,280 ft/sec or 2,236 mph), which is about Mach 3.

The 88 mm of legendary effectiveness was designed as an AA gun firing HE to a predicted height of 35,000 feet, and the Flak version was always under Luftwaffe control. In the Spanish Civil War it was used experimentally in a ground rôle against armour and bunkers, and its abilities noted. An AP solid shot with a small charge was developed at that time and added to its stores together with a sighting telescope, and the gun was towed by a soft-skinned Büssing or Krauss-Maffei half-tracked prime mover carrying crew and shells. It became dual-purpose, and in the anti-tank or *Panzerabwehrkanone* (PAK) rôle, the scourge of all armour. The first time the British felt it was when Rommel destroyed the RTR Matildas in the 1940 Arras counter-attack. Subsequently it ruled the desert, often being emplaced so that its shell would clip the top of one hill and destroy British tanks clearing the crest of the one beyond. Its great bulk would then remain hidden to view.

The AP projectile called a *Panzergranate*, was 14.5 inches long and held a small 0.37 lb bursting charge of TNT and a tracer. The whole was painted black for ready discrimination from yellow HE shells. Aerodynamics were improved by welding a steel cap over the forward end which was already capped to stop the shell disintegrating on impact. The designation of this round was APCBC or Armour-Piercing Capped Ballistic Capped. A practised 6-man crew could get off 15

62 Ben Dunkelman. *Dual Allegiance* (Toronto: Macmillan, 1976).

rounds in a minute, fired electrically, and could bring the gun into operation from the travelling position in just two and a half minutes. It is believed that the Pzgr. Patr. 40/43 with a tungsten core (*Wulframkern*) was not employed in the second half of the war because of a tungsten shortage. This round weighed only 16 lb but the muzzle velocity was increased from 3,280 to 3,710 ft/sec, which likewise increased penetration at 1,000 yards from 6½ to 7¾ inch of homogeneous steel plate. Either round could therefore penetrate the 6 inch armour thickness of the hull and turret fronts of the Churchill MkVII, which was almost certainly not fielded at Kervenheim or Winnekendonk, and of course the more numerous Mk IV with 4 inch frontal armour which were used there. The Churchill presented a target measuring 8.2 ft high, 10.7 ft wide and 25.2 ft long.

In 1943 two Pak or anti-tank versions of the 88 mm gun were introduced. One used a form of the original cruciform platform and could be fired with or without the wheels removed. The other version had a split-trail and was fired from its permanently attached pair of wheels. The type employed at Winnekendonk was the dual-purpose version identified from Alldred's observation of the traverse wheel being turned by the crew. The advantage of the PAK's cruciform platform was its low overall height of only 4 ft 6 in, compared with the 6 ft 3 in of the split trail version and the 6 ft 11 in of the original Flak version, whose other drawback was the lack of a protective shield.

Also at Winnekendonk was a Fortress Brigade equipped with 5 cm Pak 38 anti-tank guns mounted without wheels. Their 5 lb APHE (Armour Piercing High Explosive) shell could penetrate only 2-inches of plate which was good enough to destroy carriers, half tracks and the Honey reconnaissance tank but only bounced off Churchills. The gun crews were made to swear to fight to the finish since they could expect to be run over by the Churchill or hit by its HE shell. The crews of the Churchill tanks remembered feeling the thump of the impacts and seeing metal spalling from the inside of the armour plate as a result of the hammer blows of the little shells which lacked the power to penetrate. Ted Winkler was sent to join one of their gun crews when he finally arrived in Winnekendonk after a fruitless search for his unit. He saw them taking apart the breech blocks of their guns and going down into a root cellar to hide. These were German Army troops and not Paras.

British and German forces were similarly organised. As an example, the chains of command as existed for the Battle of Winnekendonk are shown in the following table, which is set out with the hierarchical top at the bottom.

German	**Anglo-Canadian**
StuG Platoon commanded by Lt Salutz of 2 Troop under Lt Schutz of XII Assault Gun Brigade under Maj Gersteuer	Right Flank Squadron 3 SG under Major Alan Cathcart
Fortress Anti-tank Coy 51(X) under Capt Appel	No equivalent
Battle-Gp of II & III Bns & Para Lehr under Lt-Col Krahl	2 Lincolns under Lt-Col Cecil Firbank
7 Para Regt. under Colonel Riedel	9 BIB under Brig Douglas Renny
8 Para Division under Maj-Gen Wadehn	3 BID under Maj-Gen Bolo Whistler
II Para Corps under Lt-Gen Meindl	XXX Corps under Lt-Gen Horrocks
1 Para Army under Col-Gen Schlemm	1 Cdn Army under General Crerar
Army Group H under Col-Gen Blaskowitz	21 AG under FM Montgomery
C-in-C West under FM von Rundstedt	SHAEF under Gen Eisenhower
OKW under Hitler	CCS
Hitler	Churchill & Roosevelt

The opposing armour and artillery were organised in a similar way. 6 GAB with Churchills were army troops, and were opposed by XII Para Assault Brigade with StuGs who were corps troops. 3 BID's three Field Regiments of Royal Artillery with 72 Gun-Howitzer 25pdrs were not matched by 8FJD, which had no heavy weapons of its own but relied on the guns of 7FJD – mortars, 24 howitzers of 105 mm calibre and 12 howitzers of 150 mm.

Each Para regiment, (brigade in English) of 3,206 men consisted of 3 battalions (I, II and III), each with 4 companies (1-4, 5-8, 9-12). In addition there was a 13th Anti-tank Company, and a 14th Mortar company. From June 1944 a 15th Pioneer company was added.

Each battalion of 853 all ranks comprised 4 rifle companies of 3 platoons numbered 7-9, 10-12, 13-15, 16-18 and 1 machine-gun company with 4, 8 and 12 platoons. The rifle company had 170 all ranks armed with 72 rifles, 43 machine pistols and 20 light MGs, while the MG-company had 205 all ranks, with 2 light MGs, 8 heavy MGs, 4 units of 81-mm mortars and 2 of 75-mm recoilless guns. The total battalion had 66 light MGs, 8 heavy MGs, 13 units of 81-mm mortars and 2 units of 75-mm recoilless guns.

13 company had 186 men, with 3 units of 75 mm AT guns (towed) and many infantry AT weapons.14 company comprised 163 men, with 9 or 12 units of 120-mm mortars.15 company had about 100 men.

Comparison of the Tables of Establishment (TOE) of 3 BID and 8FJD

3 British Infantry Division		**8 Fallschirmjägerdivision**	
Div HQ	144	Div HQ	194
Recce Regiment	793	Recce Company	200
Divisional Signals	(est) 500	Signal Battalion	379
Infantry Brigade	2,944	Paratroop Regiment	3,206
Infantry Brigade	2,944	Paratroop Regiment	3,206
Infantry Brigade	2,944	Paratroop Regiment	3,206
3 Field Regiments	2,016	Artillery Regiment	none
LAA Regiment	850	AA Battalion	824
Support Battalion	740	120 mm Mortar Battalion	594
Anti-tank Regiment	850	Anti-tank Battalion	484
Engineers	917	Engineer Battalion	620
Divisional services	2,705	Divisional services	1,492
Total	18,347		14,405

It is now almost impossible for anyone, and especially a German, to understand the psychology of the first and only generation of Hitlerjugend that fought in 1944-45. They had grown to manhood with Hitler's teaching that destiny decreed the world belonged to them, the master race. Hitler handed them the keys of the universe at stirring torch-lit rallies. To claim their inheritance they had to prove true to Hitler, to be hard, loyal and worthy of his trust in them; *Der deutsche Junge der Zukunft muß schlank und rank sein, flink wie Windhunde, zäh wie Leder und hart wie Kruppstahl* (The German boy of the future must be slim and slender, as fast as a greyhound, tough as leather and hard as Krupp steel). The fittest survived, they were told, and they would be proved in hard conflict, *im harten Kampf.* They had to reject all thoughts of pity. The only test of morality was Germany's self-interest. To enjoy their future as masters they had to seize it through fighting those who would deny them.

A dead German officer found by 3BID bound and gagged 2 km east of Schloss Calbeck on 26 February 1945[63] was judged by the British commentator to be a victim of his less than enthusiastic colleagues. The better explanation was that he was judged to have broken trust with the *Volksgemeinschaft*.

Ideology can be understood on a number of different levels, and the average Landser and Jäger exhibited and embraced various forms of ideological commitment to Naziism. The very emphasis the Nazis put on comradeship and community was an aspect of ideology, since in many respects the close-knit infantry company was the model for the larger Volksgemeinschaft envisaged by Hitler. Camaraderie was seen as a vital component of the Wehrmacht not only in order to enhance fighting efficiency but also to break down the economic and social barriers hindering the establishment of a genuine national community. In practice, the NSDAP leadership began from the moment it seized power to establish the preconditions for a new community.

Hitler intended to create a new man and a new society through intense efforts at socializing the young and eliminating what he regarded as ruinous vestiges of class conflict. These he believed had brought Germany to a state of weakness and degradation. The ideals pressed into the minds and souls of German youth were service to the Volksgemeinschaft, a life of camaraderie, and belief in the German people and Hitler as Führer. Every HJ song celebrated death in the service of the community or Volksgemeinschaft. 'Laugh, comrades, our death will be a celebration. Germany must live, even if we must die'.[64]

The Labour Service (Reichsarbeitsdienst) appeared to the HJ as the embodiment and the realisation of the Volksgemeinschaft. Everyone worked with the spade on German earth and belonged to the great national community over and above rank, status and class – the living comradeship of the Volksgemeinschaft. Their values were camaraderie, sacrifice, loyalty, duty, honour, endurance, courage, obedience and contempt for those outside the Volksgemeinschaft.

Nazi ideological practice reinforced the Wehrmacht's goals, contributing to the creation of those tight groups of men who would fight, suffer and die together. They were the Kameradschaft, which was the original Prussian term for a small unit. 'My Kamaradschaft was my home, my family, which I had to protect'.

The Second World War Volksgemeinschaft grew out of the First World War Frontgemeinschaft. With the so-called Burgfrieden (domestic truce) of 1914, Germany seemed to have overcome class division and internal disunity as people from every segment of society came together in a profound wave of national enthusiasm. Thomas Mann wrote:

> Why did Germany recognise and welcome the war when it broke upon us? Because she recognised in it the herald of her Third Reich. What is her Third Reich then? It is the synthesis of might and mind, of might and spirit; it is her dream and her demand, her highest war aim.[65]

Stefan Zweig wrote of the war; 'Thousands and thousands felt what they should have felt in peacetime, that they belonged together'. Hitler felt it. He had been an outsider but later claimed that the First World War made, 'the greatest of all impressions by demonstrating that individual interest could be subordinated to the common interest'. The trenches of the First World War bred this new idea of national unity and it remained the potent political force until after 1945. Hugo von Hofmannsthal claimed in 1927; 'It is not freedom Germans are out to find, but communal

63 TNA: WO 171/4130: 3 BID Intelligence Summary No 228.

64 Stephen Fritz. *Frontsoldaten: The German Soldier in WWII* (Lexington: University Press of Kentucky, 1997), p. 161.

65 Letter by Thomas Mann to the *Svenska Dagbladet* in May 1915.

bonds'. The secret of Nazi popularity lay in understanding this truth and reviving the passions of 1914. Hitler called it 'trench socialism'. Walter von Brauchitsch noted in 1938; 'Hitler simply recast the great lessons of the front-line soldier in the form of National Socialist philosophy. Above and beyond all classes, a new unique fellowship of the nation has been created'. The Nazis promised a new beginning, a national community that would restore the lost sense of belonging and camaraderie. In this respect it was idealistic, even if it was based on a sense of crisis. It was a call to the national spirit, a promise of salvation at all levels.

The basis of this myth of renewal was the community of comrades forged at the front. The purpose, belonging, sacrifice and meaning found in the war would be restored to a life based on values. Hitler thus proposed to transform the German Volk into a group of comrades, equal in status if not in function, under the strong leadership of the new man just back from the front. Once in power Hitler promoted both the symbol and the substance of Volksgemeinschaft. Debate rages about how far he succeeded in reshaping German civil society, but there is no doubt that his ideas won universal acceptance in the Wehrmacht. Even before 1933 the Wehrmacht was intrigued by the notion of Volksgemeinschaft, seeing it as a way to promote a more cohesive and effective military force. Since total war required the complete mobilisation of German society, so military leaders pursued the Volksgemeinschaft idea as a means of creating effective national unity. Hitler said in September 1942; 'An old world is truly being brought to a collapse. Out of this war will emerge a Volksgemeinschaft established through blood, much stronger than we National Socialists through our faith could convey to the nation after the World War'. The twin pillars of this new Volksgemeinschaft would be the party and the army, assisted by the HJ, Labour Service and Wehrmacht.

What gripped the imagination of Landsers was Hitler's apparent ability to fulfill the promise of Volksgemeinschaft that was aborted in the defeat of 1918. In spite of being chauvinistic and totalitarian, the Nazi Volksgemeinschaft had explosive appeal, and the entire Wehrmacht with insignificant exceptions bought into it. This included principled opponents of the regime such as the rebel Pastor Leutnant Dietrich Karsten, a student of Karl Barth, whose granddaughter living in London asked in rhetorical incomprehension, 'Where were the Christians in the Third Reich?' and wondering how a Christian minister with strong anti-Nazi convictions could willingly take part in the invasion of foreign countries wearing the swastika on his chest.[66]

The Volksgemeinschaft balanced individual achievement with group solidarity, competition with cooperation, as the individual fulfilled and developed his potential within the framework of community. The allure of Naziism lay in its creation of the belief that everyone was in service to an ideal community that promoted both social commitment and integration. The Volksgemeinschaft was worth dying for. Even after the war half of the German POWs could find nothing wrong with National Socialism, believing Hitler's only mistake was to lose the war. Volksgemeinschaft was the leitmotif for most soldiers; 'I would gladly die for my people and for my German Fatherland. Germany was always my primary earthly thought'.[67]

Even so some did not confuse Naziism with Volksgemeinschaft. One was Erich Freund, who refused to join the HJ in Hamborn, even when it incorporated through *Gleichschaltung* the group he had joined as a ten-year old in 1930 – the *Deutsch Nationale Partei*. Instead Erich joined the SPD's *Arbeiter Sport* with a flag bearing the German colours of black, red and yellow. It wasn't until 1934 that the first Nazis marched through Hamborn where he lived, and on Mayday in 1935 there was still one lonely red flag flying in his street.

66 Lena Karsten. *Confessions of a German Soldier*: History Today, Vol 57, No. 12, December 2007. Tony Wilson produced a film of the same name for www.flotsamfilms.com.

67 Hermann Witzemann in June 1941, quoted in S Fritz, *Frontsoldaten*, p. 211.

> In the end the Nazis got so strong that everyone thought it better to shut up. In the Luftwaffe and the Paras the feeling for Hitler was not very great. It depended on the officers. There were some for and against him but nobody spoke out either way.[68]

However, being for or against Hitler made no difference to the performance of the soldier who was motivated to serve the non-controversial and 'right' Volksgemeinschaft. This motivation survived the death, defeat and vilification of Hitler. People hung on to its inspiration. Volksgemeinschaft along with the countrywide apprenticeship scheme were the drivers of post-war reconstruction, and their absence led to Britain's relative decline from internal bickering and disunity.

It is said that one paratroop division outside Berlin in April 1945 did break and run from the Russians, but in March 1945, the Para arm could generally look back on a fairly fought war without the murder of prisoners and civilians, at least in the West. An exception was the massacre at Kondomori on Crete on 20 May 1941 by III/Luftlande-Sturm-Regt. 1 under Oberleutnant Horst Trebes and filmed by Horst-Peter Weixler.[69] German paratroops did not fear capture by the British who were offering terms in the Safe Conduct (*Paßierschein*) leaflets. An honourable surrender, however, could happen only after exhausting all the alternatives. Sometimes, according to veterans of 6 GAB, who suffered from it, this meant the young and still naive German soldier fired a Panzerfaust at a tank killing the driver and co-driver. He then stood up with arms held high in surrender waving his leaflet. The answer was usually a bullet in the head from the outraged tank commander who had just lost half his crew.

Letters from home taken from PWs were analysed by the British, such as the following to an unknown member of FJR7 printed in 3 BID's Intelligence Summary. Sent from Jena meant the recipient was probably recruited from the areas of Dresden and Halberstadt by FJR2, which was FJR7's sister unit in 2FJD.[70] FJR7 itself was raised in Brandenburg/Havel.

> My Dear Beloved Darling.
> Jena. 14. 2. 45
> Today once again I waited in vain for mail from you. None arrived at all because the train was cancelled owing to the fact that there were two terror attacks on Dresden last night. I need hardly tell you how we cried, 5 hours in the shelter in the dark. It was so cold. A number of planes circled round incessantly dropping flares. I wasn't scared at first but during the night I really thought our last hour had come. The AA fired away like mad and the whole ground shook – it was really terrible. This time they didn't drop any bombs on us. Heaven knows what they are trying to do driving people crazy hour after hour. At this rate they will soon succeed. [This would have been music to Bomber Harris's ears, as his and Churchill's intention was to terrorise the German people into demanding capitulation]. I would just like to know why we are on this earth at all, our whole lives are nothing but care and sorrow. I have lost my faith in a better future. How can people believe in anything with the Russians so far into our country – we need a miracle to save us anyway. So far, in German history, no Russian has ever set foot in Berlin [untrue, they entered Berlin on 4 March 1814 to liberate Prussia from the French], and now it looks as if he is going to. It's unthinkable. Only today they were saying in the paper what will happen to us if we are the losers. I hope it doesn't get that far; there must be something we can do to defend ourselves. But for the terror the war would be bearable. It is that that breaks

---

68 Letter from Erich Freund in 1997.

69 http://en.wikipedia.org/wiki/Massacre_of_Kondomari

70 Busch, *Fallschirmjäger Chronik*. 'Die Masse der Soldaten stammt aus Ersatz-Einheiten der Standorte Dresden und Halberstadt'

people up and disheartens them so. There is no longer any fun or joy in existence and it is only because of the children that we pull ourselves together. It is nearly a year now since you were home. How much we have to do without. If only all goes well and you can come home safely we shall be content. Now my sweet you are going to worry about us. If the bombs don't smash us and the Russians don't come, you needn't worry about a thing.

Today I must see to the washing or as much of it as is dry. It's rather windy outside. Already the planes are buzzing around up there. It's bound to be more intruders. Norbert says they are German planes. He is such a funny little chap. He has to see and put up with so much. It's a good thing that he doesn't understand much of it. He is saying that they dropped bombs on Jena too. Thank God they were only 500 pounders. Still they cause enough suffering and destruction. 85 dead so far apart from those they have been unable to identify. [Thuringian targets such as Dresden, Jena and Nordhausen had been spared because of their distance, but with the absence of air defences BC and the USAAF destroyed them in February 1945. There were 709 killed and 2,000 injured in Jena].

Now I am off to grandma's and see how our meal is getting on. Good-bye my darling, and write again soon.

A thousand greetings and loving kisses from your
Annie and little Norbert.[71]

If Annie and Norbert stayed on in Jena they would have been liberated by Grow's 6 USAD on 11 April 1945. She would therefore have avoided the fate of the 1.3 million women in Berlin when the Russians arrived, of whom tens of thousands were raped. That is the best estimate of the number, which can never be accurately known. Zhukov was embarrassed by his army and managed to establish control at the end of May only by calling in a new division from Moscow that had not experienced any fighting. Many Germans believed that the Russian Jew, Ilya Ehrenburg, incited the peasant soldiers to rape and pillage, but this theory ignores the fact that rape was a Russian military offence and that strong edicts were put out by the Army command, while Ehrenburg had by then been rejected by Stalin, who permitted the rape of Germans. 'Can't he' (Djilas, who had complained) 'understand it if a soldier who has crossed thousands of kilometers through blood and fire and death has fun with a woman or takes some trifle'? The soldiers had sex on their minds and witnesses were amazed at the speed with which the deed was done, and that it happened at any time of day or night even in full view of others. Some German men successfully protected their women while others were shot. Some women were driven insane by the gang rapes while others fell in love with their rapist. This author has little knowledge of German attempts to quantify the serious emotional harm that befell women in the East Zone of Germany, but knows firsthand of the terror of Russians spoken daily to him by their housemaid, Fräulein Rasmussen, in Flensburg in 1949. Being only ten he realises now she could not tell him what had happened. Women who sought refuge at the top of multi-storey blocks of flats seemed to have escaped because Russians feared long flights of stairs, while one woman with great presence of mind got out a train-set and diverted 6 Russians into playing with it on the floor. Many women sought protection by associating with officers who were known to summarily execute rapists caught in the act. There were Russian court-martials for rape but the numbers are unknown. The subject was covered up, and never recurred. All pregnancies seem to have been aborted with the German police and judiciary turning a blind eye. Even though abortion on any grounds was illegal there were no prosecutions from May to December 1945. Today in Germany there are the offspring of the troops of all of the allied nations except, apparently, Russia.

71 TNA: WO 171/4130: 3 BID Intelligence Summary end February 1945.

The Nazis practised *Sippenhaft*, or kin liability, arguing that the act of desertion proved bad blood flowed in the family's veins and implicated them all. Himmler told Gauleiters that the practice dated from the ancient Teutons. In effect, as the following directive from the Divisional Intelligence Summary showed, its implementation in 8 FJD was relatively mild, requiring only that relatives disown the deserters who were condemned to death.

> 8 Para Div HQ National Socialist Educational Branch 15 Feb 45
> *Div Information Bulletin No 10 (To be made known to all judiciary officials immediately)*
> The foundation of all being is loyalty. Loyalty to the Supreme Commander, thereby loyalty to the state and nation.
>
> There are mistakes that are human, that can be forgiven and are being forgiven. Of the few mistakes that can never be forgiven, is above all disloyalty. Disloyalty disrupts the organisation of a state and paralyses its armies. Disloyalty is the downfall of a nation.
> It is an ancient German custom that the family and relatives answer for every member of the family. If one has proved disloyal and the relatives cannot prove that they have disowned him, they too will be called to account. Everyone is aware of this. On the night of 8 February 1945, the following blackguards deserted, under the command of, and led by CSM LŰTTICH,
>
> L/Cpl DOERING — L/Cpl EUCHLER
> L/Cpl KANTE — L/Cpl HACKL
> L/Cpl MONATSBERGER — L/Cpl JAKOB
> L/Cpl ZIMMERMANN — Pte HAGEMEISTER
> all belonging to 10 Coy 22 Para Regt.
>
> It is ordered that the serious dishonour thus brought upon the para troops shall be paid for by the next-of-kin.
> Wife Marianne LUTTICH with son — Mother Luise DOERING
> Father Johannes MONATSBERGER — Mother Hedwig EUCHLER
> Father Jakob ZIMMERMANN — Mother Pauline HACKL
> Father Friedrich JAKOB — Mother Elli HAGEMEISTER
> if they do not solemnly and forever disown their husbands or their sons, who have brought unspeakable disgrace upon their families. The expected death sentence of the Field Court Martial on the deserters will be published at home.
>
> For the Div Comd, The Nat Soc Educational Officer, Signed KAMMER 2/Lt.[72]

This immunity to punishment was a weakness rectified by Hitler in a *Führerbefehl* of 5 March 1945 that cancelled payments of allowances or assistance to relatives of those who had dishonourably failed to fight to the utmost.[73] In specifying financial consequences for deserters and cowards, Hitler was imitating the Stavka's notorious anti-cowardice Order No. 270 of 16 August 1941, which he would have known about. Stopping allowances was Stalin's attempt to stop the string of mass surrenders at Smolensk, Belostok-Minsk and Uman, although it possibly precipitated the worst mass surrender of all at Lokhvitsa on 20 September 1941 when General Kirponos refused to

72 TNA: WO 171/4130: 3 BID Intelligence Summary.
73 Robert Loeffel. *Family Punishment in Nazi Germany: Sippenhaft, Terror and Myth* (Basingstoke: Palgrave Macmillan, 2012).

act on Marshal Timoshenko's verbal permission to break out until he received it in writing. It was perhaps too late in any case.

Hitler by February 1945 had ceased to hope for another *Miracle of the House of Brandenburg,* and accepted the war was lost. He gave up on the German people and prepared to commit suicide because they had failed him and deserved the consequences.

> Everyone has lied to me, everyone has deceived me, no one has told me the truth. The armed forces have lied to me and now the SS have left me in the lurch. The German people has not fought heroically, it deserves to perish. It is not I who have lost the war, but the German people.[74]

In practical terms there was nothing Hitler could do to the German people that could match their terror of the Russians. Hitler took terrible revenge on the families of the plotters of 20 July 1944, but the families of those executed for allowing Remagen Bridge to fall into American hands on 8 March 1945 would have been punished only by loss of allowances.

In 1945 the morale of the *Landser* was cracking, although that of the SS and Fallschirmjägers never did. Maj-Gen Pfuhlstein was secretly recorded by his captors in Trent Park POW Cage on 20 April 1945 describing to Generalleutnant Ferdinand Heim what he had seen in the Battle of Wertheim am Main on 1 April against 42 USID, with regimental courts martial everywhere shooting anyone found in the rear. Orders always had an addendum that if the order was unsuccessful that person given it would be shot. Therefore those in the front line stayed where they were and only pretended to fight, hoping for a slight wound.[75]

Heinrich Schlömer of FJR19 in 7FJD said the troops sometimes discussed how it would end, but the subject was forbidden and punishment for defeatist talk was thought to be transfer to a *Straf-Bataillon* (punishment battalion) on the Eastern Front.[76]

Convinced or 'fanatical' Nazis as the Allies called them, believed honour required them to behave heroically even unto death. Sensible men, however, valued themselves above being expendable cannon fodder, knowing that their leaders took the same attitude towards them that was expressed by Falstaff to Henry V; 'Tut, tut, good enough to toss; food for powder, food for powder; they'll fill a pit as well as better [men]'.[77] Sensible men had three options when faced with overwhelming might; retreat, resist and die fighting, or surrender. To be ethical any order requiring a soldier to die fighting must have some point or justification. In their absence such an order is a death warrant and therefore criminal in European, but not Japanese, eyes. Generals, and especially German generals, knew this. Britain debated surrender in 1940, when FM Sir John Dill agreed with Churchill that the British could fight on after Dunkirk only because there was a realistic chance the USA would join in. FDR had given his word to King George VI in 1939 at Hyde Park on the Hudson that the USA would fight on Britain's side should any bombs ever fall on Britain. Hitler's public ridicule of such a possibility was realistic since the USA never did declare war on Germany, and almost certainly never would.

By July 1944 the German General Staff knew that all chance of winning had gone and the only choice was surrender. Von Rundstedt told Keitel, and therefore Hitler, on 1 July 1944 that they should, 'make peace you fools; what else can you do?' He was sacked the next day, which presented

74 From an appreciation by the British JIC contained in a diary kept by Guy Liddell, Deputy Director General of the Security Service; Daily Mail, 26 October 2012.

75 Sönke Neitzel. *Tapping Hitler's Generals. Transcripts of Secret Conversations 1942-45* (Barnsley: Frontline, 2007).

76 Heinrich Schlömer in conversation.

77 Shakespeare Henry IV, Part 1, Act 4, Scene 2.

the Party with the fear that the army was considering the teachings of Clausewitz condemning hopeless resistance:

> However highly we may esteem bravery and steadfastness in war, there is however a point beyond which holding-out in warfare can only be described as the madness of despair, and can therefore never be approved.[78]

There is evidence the Nazi Party did issue guidance on the subject in the form of a document addressed to officers. However, this might have been a British Secret Service black art since Sgt Trevor Greenwood received a circular from HQ 34 Tank Brigade on 14 October of such a translated German Party document.[79] It directly addressed the argument about the necessity of surrendering in hopeless conditions, and indeed the obligation to do so in order to save one's life for future service to the Fatherland rather than die a needless death. This was said to have been taught by Ludendorff, who never identified who had the responsibility to surrender; it was always, the document asserted, a decision in fact reserved to the higher command. The individual soldier or junior officer must therefore always fight on and never consider surrender unless authorised to do so. Officers were reminded of their importance and the need to abandon their men if capture was inevitable. The war-aim was asserted to be global domination, and because the possibility of failure was foreseen, officers were told they had a duty to survive as a cadre for victory in a future world war. By ticking all of these boxes, real doubt arises about the document being genuine. It was circulated on 14 October 1944, ten days after William Douglas-Home of 141 Regt RAC had been court martialled for refusing a legal order to attack Le Havre with his flamethrowing Crocodile. Douglas Home argued that the German request to evacuate French civilians had been refused by the Allies who had thereby committed a war crime. The high Allied command might well have decided a forged document was needed to put the blame for the war's continuation on to the soldiers facing the Crocodile crews in order to make the Allied soldiers feel better about using flame throwers and to strengthen their backbone. Enquiries made to IWM-Duxford in December 2012 failed to turn up the document. Greenwood himself had doubts about its validity, and believed Mr Eden had recently referred to it in the Commons. Whether this document was genuine or not, however, the Trent Park recordings showed the German generals abandoned their Prussian military heritage of avoiding pointless death, and sacrificed their men from fear of summary conviction in front of a flying court martial.[80]

The German lower ranks were trained as a group to obey and to support their comrades, and few surrendered before being overwhelmed. Those who followed Clausewitz's advice and surrendered usually did so when isolated from their fellows and in the face of overwhelming might and certainty of death. The Lincolns attacking Winnekendonk saw a Fallschirmjäger in an outlying farm fire the alarm rocket, lock the door and surrender holding his luggage. Another Fallschirmjäger alone in a forward trench was observed throwing a hand grenade in the direction of Major Smith and Sergeant Nicholson, who walked over and executed the 'lone hero', who might have survived had he stayed hidden and overlooked. Obergefreiter Ted Winkler, the armourer of II/FJR7, was isolated from his unit on the battlefield with no rôle, no orders, and an unsuitable 9 mm pistol. Faced with certain death if he resisted, he walked towards the attacking Lincolns holding aloft Eisenhower's leaflet hoping they would accept his surrender.

78 Carl von Clausewitz. *Vom Kriege*. (Berlin: Ferdinand Dümmler, 1832), quoted in Neitzel, *Tapping Hitler's Generals*, p. 50.

79 Trevor Greenwood. *D-Day to Victory: the Diaries of a British Tank Commander; edited by S.V. Partington* (London: Simon & Schuster UK, 2012).

80 Neitzel, *Tapping Hitler's Generals*, p. 50.

Ted was born in 1920 in Barmbek-Süd and brought up at 55 Eilbeker Weg in Hamburg-Eilbek. This was an area that was subsequently obliterated by bombing and only 600 m from the firestorm of Operation Gomorrah. Hamburg had close historical connections with London dating back to London's mediaeval Hanseatic Steelyard, and until German unification Hamburg was an independent and sovereign state within the Confederation. It had an anti-Nazi majority of socialists and communists, which gave its inhabitants false hope of lenient treatment by Britain.

Ted's father, Robert, won the Iron Cross at St Quentin in March 1918 and the First Class on the Hindenburg Line (Siegfried Stellung) in June, when he lost his right hand. Gas gangrene set in and the arm was amputated and replaced with a wooden arm without, unfortunately, eliminating the gangrene. For the rest of his short life the gangrene was slowed through surgical debridement until, in 1937, it fatally reached the shoulder. The effect on Ted was traumatic, hearing his father crying that he did not want to die.

In 1927 Robert had joined the NSDAP, almost certainly after attending an inspiring mass meeting in Altona addressed by Goebbels to mark the founding of the SA. The Nazi strategy was to move into the working class strongholds (Hochburgen) to contest the streets with the Social Democrats, who refrained from street fighting, and with the RFB, who excelled in it.[81] On direction from Moscow, communists lumped together all of the opposition as 'social-fascists', until Stalin eventually woke up to the threat of Hitler in 1935 and formed the Popular Front against fascism together with the socialists. These socialists claimed in 1933 that Stalin created Hitler's opportunity by fragmenting the left, and without Stalin there would have been no Hitler.[82]

Robert was active in street fighting where his wooden arm doubled as a weapon, and Ted remembers him returning at night with head wounds. Robert was brave and effective and became an *SA Scharführer* or NCO and the Party's representative in Eilbek, nicknamed *Das beamten Viertel* or the quarter inhabited by civil servants. The KPD district organiser was a neighbour, and the two rivals ignored one another. The street struggle was aimed at taking over taverns, and although Nazis controlled fewer taverns than the SPD and KPD, theirs were in key positions. In Ted's view his father was more a nationalist than a socialist and therefore would have been attracted by Nazi condemnation of the SPD and KPD, the 'Weimar Marxists' with their international Marxist and Jewish connections, who had engineered the 1918 'stab-in-the-back' and Versailles Treaty, and indulged in criminality and violence. SA members appeared in uniform, in small disciplined groups, presenting a picture of positive, military order. However, everything for Robert changed with the Nazi *Machtergreifung* (seizure of power) in 1933 when he was banned from the victorious Nuremberg Rally because of his crippled arm. He never got over that rejection. The communist neighbour disappeared into a concentration camp and returned a chastened, and even broken, man. Robert saw the rise of turncoat communists in the Nazi ranks, and became ever more cynical about the Party. One of Ted's uncles remained a closet communist, keeping his membership card in his copy of *Mein Kampf*, which was presented by the State to all married couples, and provided a large royalty for the author.

Ted, like his mother, had little interest in politics, but became hooked on gliding. His introduction was on Sylt in 1930 where he went for his health to a sanitorium, and the following year he visited the renowned gliding and aeronautical research centre at Wasserkuppe in the Hohe Rhön mountains of Hessen. Gliding was encouraged by the Weimar government as a means of mitigating the Versailles restrictions on military expenditure. In 1932 Ted joined the junior section of the *Deutscher Luftsport Verband (DLV)* to build model gliders. After 300 hours he was allowed to sit in a glider, and in 1935 began to glide. The DLV was nazified in 1933 by Hermann Göring

81 http://www.libcom.org/history/street-politics-hamburg-1932-3

82 PMH Bell. *The Origins of the Second World War* (London: Longman, 1997).

under the principle of *Gleichschaltung*, or 'forcible co-ordination', which automatically signed Ted into the *Hitler Jugend*. Meanwhile in 1934 he had left school to become an errand boy for a Jewish shipping firm.

In 1935 Ted started work as an apprentice at *Menibum* (Metalwerk Niedersachsen Brinkmann und Mergell) in Hamburg-Harburg, becoming part of an extraordinary exercise by the Nazis in social engineering that bore dramatic fruit postwar. Hitler promised full employment and implemented two off-the-shelf programmes that had been devised by the Weimar government; Autobahn construction, which had no military significance and was opposed by the General Staff, but more importantly a joint campaign of the trades unions and industrial associations for reform of vocational training. In November 1936 all metalworking and construction companies with more than ten employees were obliged to create apprenticeships and to organise appropriate training programmes. Between 1937 and 1945 almost all males and an increasing number of females who left elementary school completed three-year apprenticeships. This produced unintended consequences that Hitler came to regret but felt powerless to reverse. A shortage of untrained and unskilled workers was soon apparent, and efforts to reduce substantially the number of apprenticeships in 1942 and 1943 to provide recruits for the armed forces failed because the Nazis were prisoners of their 'skilled worker ideology'. At war's end there were 480,000 apprenticeships in metalworking, 19,000 training as butchers and bakers, 59,000 as secretaries and even 5,000 as hairdressers, but with very few in the strategically important but unpopular mining sector.[83] Ted spent five years learning his trade and in 1936 qualified as a *Flugzeugbauer* (aircraft constructor), building sub-assemblies for the Ju 34 and Do 17. He registered for military service with the Hamburg police on 31 May 1939, when *Menibum* was building the BV 138 *Seedrache* (Sea Dragon) aka the *Fliegende Holzschuh* (Flying Clog) for Blohm+Voss.

Ted became keen on American and British jazz and dance music, frequenting jam sessions at the US Consulate in Hamburg where he was presented with a collection of twenty jazz records on its closure in 1941. He was denounced and questioned about this interest in 'degenerate music', being accused of trading Blohm+Voss secrets in exchange for the record collection, which the Gestapo confiscated. Later, when on sea defence duty in Dunkirk, he heard his own Harry Roy record being played on *Germany Calling,* recognising the scratch where he had accidentally dropped the needle. He had a Jewish girlfriend for a while, Ingrid Kohn, who vanished without warning with her entire family. All this was recorded by the police.

In 1941 Ted was directed to *Flugzeugwerk Graudenz GMBH* in Graudenz on the Vistula in the Danzig Corridor as a quality inspector. He was one of very few Germans in this ex-Polish factory and in effect was responsible for preventing sabotage. The company repaired and refurbished the FW 58 *Weihe* (Harrier), a multi-rôle trainer, transport and air ambulance, the STOL Fi 156 *Storch* (Stork) used for reconnaissance and communications, the FW 189 *Uhu* or *fliegende Auge* (Eagle Owl or Flying Eye) used for tactical reconnaissance and army cooperation, and the air-superiority fighter Me 109E (Emil).

In August 1942 Ted was called up, reporting to 6 /FL.Rgt. 11 (6 Battalion, Luftwaffe Flieger Regiment 11)[84] in Fliegerhorst Schönwalde, [now an abandoned ruin called Schönwalde-Glien] in Brandenburg. Ted was not there long before being sent in a draft to Cambrai and Douai in France for basic training. There his technical knowledge and proficiency marked him out, and he was sent for specialist armourer training in Dresden, almost certainly to the Flieger-Waffentechnische

83 Article by Werner Abelshauser in Stephen Broadberry & Mark Harrison. *The Economics of World War Two* (Cambridge: CUP, 2009).

84 www2.dk/ground/infanterie/flausb11 & http://www.axishistory.com/index.php?id=10370. In November 1941 the Flieger-Ausbildungs-Regimenter were renamed Flieger-Regimenter.

Schule 4 in Dresden-Nickern[85] where he received excellent training in the disassembly and repair of weapons, including aircraft cannon. He passed out top of the class, but was uniquely passed over for a commission because, as he subsequently discovered, his police record marked him as politically unreliable. He was posted as a Flieger Waffenschmied (Airman Armourer), to the well-equipped airfield at Berlin-Döberitz, [now Dallgow-Döberitz] where he serviced infantry small arms. This involved such tasks as straightening barrels and such work.

On 29 December 1942 Ted went with an officer to Salies de Béarn in the Basque Pyrenees, halfway between Pau and Biarritz, as advance party for 18 Luftwaffe Feld Division (previously Flieger-Ausbildungs Regiment 52) newly-formed under command of Oberst Ferdinand-Wilhelm Freiherr von Stein-Liebenstein zu Barchfeld. Ted spent much of his time playing golf and stayed in the Hôtel de France et d'Angleterre (with a rickety electric lift) until 7 January 1943. Ted's unit has not been recorded but was probably (III/LJR35) (3 Battalion, Luftwaffe Jäger Regiment 35).[86] Between 18 and 21 February 1943 the division moved by train to Libourne and into a large training camp at Souge, 16 km west of Bordeaux, with a brothel outside the gates where Ted saw long queues of airmen. The division's time was spent on 'futile' basic training comprising mostly drill. The division moved again between 6 and 11 April 1943 to Grand-Millebrugghe in the Nord-Pas de Calais, about 8 km south of Dunkirk,[87] under its new commander, Maj-Gen Dr. Wolfgang Erdmann (later GOC 7 Fallschirmjäger Division). They formed part of LXXXII Corps, 15 Army. Their task was coastal defence around Dunkirk-Bray-Dunes, with their area of responsibility extending eventually to Calais. Ted was part of the garrison of Stützpunkt (Strongpoint) Adolph in Bray-Dunes. Ted serviced the Belgian field guns in the fort and performed trial shoots, and he also patrolled with dogs and radio along the coast to Stützpunkt Berta and back. He remembered trying to receive Harry Roy and Nat Gonella on *Germany Calling*, and firing a Boys .55-inch anti-tank rifle that he dug out of a dune where it had been abandoned by the British in 1940, and experiencing its notoriously fierce recoil-kick. Ted engineered a system of trip wires connected to incendiaries attached to flattened-out oil drums painted white and nailed to posts to warn of enemy landing of saboteurs. He was walking along the beach once, carrying a machine-gun and rifles over his shoulder, when a Spitfire dived to take pot shots at him.

On 24 May 1943 Ted failed a routine test for colour-blindness, having passed on all previous occasions by memorising the Ishihara tests. He was now categorised as unfit for paratroops (*untauglich als Fallschirmschützen*) but fit for air-gunner duties (*fliegerschützen tauglich*). Ted was informed that his home in Hamburg had been bombed and his family was missing, so on 8 August 1943 he took a week's home leave. Ted's mother had survived the bombing by taking shelter in the Hochbunker at the junction of Wielandstrasse and Schellingstrasse. She was evacuated to Poland, living in straitened circumstances with nothing except the family's documents and the clothes on her back, the only things she had taken into the Hochbunker. Ted spent his leave helping survivors of the bombing which ten days previously had destroyed whole districts including his home and those of 250,000 others, killing at least 44,000 civilians, mostly women and children, wounding 37,000 more and causing a million to flee. His home district of Eilbek had uniquely been bombed twice; on 28 July, the day when everything in neigbouring Borgfelde, Hamm and Hammerbrook exploded in a firestorm that failed to reach Eilbek only because the railway that ran between the two areas formed a firebreak; and on 29/30 July when the neighbouring district of Barmbek suffered the major disaster of the Karstadt department store where 370 perished in the basement shelter. Hitler may have said that 'further raids of similar weight would force Germany

85 http://www.ww2.dk/ground/schule/flwtech.htm
86 III/LJR36, redesignated LJR48 in February 1944, and in May 1944 was Ted's unit.
87 http://www.ww2.dk/ground/infanterie/lfd18.htm

out of the war',[88] but certainly the effort by Churchill and Harris to repeat it in other cities, notably Berlin, in order to bring about capitulation without a D-Day invasion, proved an unsuccessful gamble. Ted's application for leave extension was granted by the military Kommandant when the police discovered from his paybook that he was a qualified armourer, and found he could handle dynamite. So Ted equipped himself with a hand cart loaded with boxes of dynamite and fuses, and proceeded to blow in the facades of rows of burnt-out houses to make those using the roads of Eilbek safe from falling masonry. When the demolition charges had been prepared by him, the police cordoned off the area.

In February 1944 Ted's unit was re-designated II/LJR48, Feldpostnummer 06 358 D according to a letter dated 29 May 1944 from Obgefr. A. Schönstetter to Ted. In June he was posted away from 18 LWFD. After Ted had left it remained in place to resist the fictitious FUSAG (Operation Fortitude South) until the Allied breakout in August 1944, when it was sent to an area south of Mantes to delay the Americans. It suffered major losses, withdrew northwards, and surrendered in the pocket south of Mons on 4 September 1944. Ted went to Fliegerhorst Istres-le-Tubé in Provence near Arles as ground crew for a squadron of anti-shipping Ju 88 torpedo bombers. It was there that he collected the Safe Conduct *Paßierschein* used later at Winnekendonk. In less than a month, however, on 4 July 1944 he was relieved from military duty and ordered by the Air Ministry HQ in Leipzig to report to Messerschmitt in Augsburg on secondment to a programme of air rearmament (Ausrüstungluft), on which he remained until the end of the year. His transfer was repeatedly questioned by the Feldpolizei acting on an order forbidding all movement from France to Germany after D-Day. To overcome this interference he was given permission to travel by air in the Ju 52 belonging to FM Albert Kesselring. Ted did not know it, but his removal to Germany was a consequence of the Luftwaffe generals' decision to arm the jet-powered Me 262 as a fighter in contravention of Hitler's decision to restrict its role to that of Blitz-bomber.

Speer recalled the background. Hitler had halted large-scale production of the Me-262 in September 1943, but Speer and Milch continued to prepare for it at a much-reduced tempo. In January 1944 Hitler changed his mind after reading British reports of working on jet engines, and he now wanted them produced in volume as soon as possible. The best Speer and Milch could promise was 40/month in April/May, 60 in July, when Ted started to fit cannon, 50 from August to October, increasing to 210 in January 1945, 440 in April, 670 in July and 800/month from October 1945. Hitler ordered that there would be no Me-262 fighters but only unarmed bombers flying straight at great height and throttled back to spare the engines. Everyone criticized the decision because the bomb load was an insignificant 1,000 lbs while as a fighter it could play havoc with the US day-bombing fleet and stop them destroying Germany. At the end of June, Göring and Speer approached Hitler again, but he was adamant and conceding only that eventually some Me-262s could be used as fighters. His generals continued to argue about it so in the autumn of 1944 Hitler banned all discussion.[89]

Ted's work at Messerschmitt in July went ahead despite Hitler's ban. He installed the Rhein-Metall Borsig Mk 108 30 mm cannon into the Me 262 and trained eight employees to do the work. Ted provided method sheets, advice and training until satisfied the trainees could do the job, when he reported to management that his task was completed. He was sent to Erla Maschinenwerk in Leipzig-Heiterblick which was building Me 262, and repeated the assignment. After that he was sent to Dresden-Klotzsche, now Dresden International, which had been built in 1935 in two parts, civil and military. Ted went presumably to the abandoned civil part where hangars contained twenty Me 262s of the same mark that had been damaged in air raids. His task was to audit each

88 http://en.wikipedia.org/wiki/Bombing_of_Hamburg_in_World_War_II
89 Albert Speer. *Inside the Third Reich* (London: Macmillan, 1970), pp. 362-64.

aircraft to establish what was needed to make it airworthy, and he advised cannibalisation of some to provide parts. On completion of that task he was sent back to Graudenz which was repairing Me 109 Mks E, F, and G. After flight test he rolled them under their own power to the butts, tethered and levelled them by jacking up the tail, and adjusted the guns by test firing and zeroing the guns with the engine running. He was helped with the menial work by two Hiwis. At this time Ted was still fairly confident Germany would win the war.

At the beginning of November 1944 Ted was recalled to the colours at the large Bergen-Belsen Barracks of the Panzer Training School on the edge of Lüneburger Heide near Celle. It was later transferred to the SS in April 1945 to become Camp 2 of KZ Bergen-Belsen for 15,000 slave labourers from Dora-Mittelbau who had built V weapons underground. There were thousands of soldiers, mostly army, being formed into units, most destined for the Eastern Front. Ted was initially assigned to one of these, but an officer called for an armourer able to adjust heavy machine guns with optical sights, required by 2 FJD that was being re-formed by Lt-Gen Walter Lackner in Amersfoort since the FJR2 and FJR7 of 2FJD had surrendered to the Americans on 20 September 1944. The order for divisional re-formation was given on 24 September and re-formation of FJR2, FJR7 and FJR23 was completed in December 1944.[90] Ted volunteered, his colour-blindness was ignored, and he was assigned to a small group destined for Holland, being kitted out with paratrooper's uniform. He was relieved to be going west as he had heard first hand from soldiers serving on the Russian front how brutal it was. He was given physically hard training until 19 November 1944 when he was posted to Arnhem as armourer. While they were training in a field near Arnhem a rogue low-flying V1 hit a tree and headed straight for Ted's group who ran towards it, but it hit another tree and luckily belly landed without exploding. They had to put a guard on it until it was collected. A more serious incident occurred when Ted was billeted with others near a bridge in a square block of flats that was hit centrally by a V1 that killed about 16 men.

The events that followed at this point up to Ted's arrival as a POW in Tilburg are described in Chapters 3 and 4 dealing with the Battles of Kervenheim and Winnekendonk.

After Tilburg, Ted was moved to a POW camp in Brussels, almost certainly Camp No. 2226 at Zedelgem, where conditions were reasonable. Next he moved to Camp No. 2225 at Caen, where he is recorded as working in November 1945 collecting scrap for shipment to England. Later in Auchineux and Bayeux they worked disinterring Allied and German bodies for re-burial in the war cemeteries. Treatment of POWs was good until the German surrender, and Ted received goods which could be traded with the French, including tins of 50 cigarettes, razor blades and soap. At Ranville Ted traded soap for lighter flints with which he manufactured a crude lighter for sale or exchange. After the German surrender conditions deteriorated, and there were no more cigarettes, blades and soap. In the winter of 1945/6 Ted was interned for over a month in life-threatening conditions in POW Camp No. 2224 at Jabbeke near Ostend in Belgium where, it was said, a Jewish commandant made the POWs live on concentration camp rations. Ted lost a third of his weight, and weighed only 7 stones when he was transported from Antwerp to Tilbury on the ferry Princess Astrid, arriving on 19 May 1946, and by train to Scraptoft Camp at Thurnby near Leicester, where he was on 19 June 1946. The locals were unfriendly but later at a camp at East Wilton near Leyburn in the North Riding of Yorkshire he found only friendliness. It was here Ted repaired a grandfather clock for a farmer in Caperby, which led to repairing watches, a skill he mastered and still practises. Ted's English improved in Gilling Camp at Hartforth Grange, Gilling near Scotch Corner, then in Thirkleby Camp at Sandhill, Little Thirkleby near Thirsk where he arrived on 19 March 1947, in a camp at Roos near Withernsea, and in others at Reyhill and Kilnsea near Hull, a camp at Middleton-on-the-Wolds on 15 November 1947, at Thomas

90 Busch, *Die Fallschirmjäger Chronik*, p. 87.

Street Camp in Selby on 25 November 1947, in Overdale Camp in Skipton on 22 January 1948, in Longbridge Camp at Hampton Lovett, near Droitwich on 27 January 1948, Teddesley Hall Camp at Penkridge in Staffordshire on 1 April 1948, Rugely on 2 April 1948, and finally Little Haywood Navigation Farm on 2 October 1948 where he was released on the last day of 1948. The British kept as many of the hard men of the SS and Fallschirmjägers as possible out of circulation in the British Zone at a time of strikes and civil unrest caused by the unpopular Allied policy of industrial dismantlement in Germany.

Ted discovered there had been a quota for ex-POWs wishing to remain in Britain, but although the quota was full he bribed an officer with a gold watch to include his name. He was entitled to a month's home leave in Germany from 1 January 1949 when he stayed with his bombed-out mother living in a single room in 121 Weidestrasse in Barmbek-Süd, Hamburg. Conditions were far more difficult in Germany than in the UK, where there was a large and growing aircraft industry: this was banned in Germany, where ex-aircraft companies built bubble cars; Heinkel *Kabine*, BMW *Isetta* and Messerschmitt *Kabinenroller.* Ted returned to Holderness and resumed working on farms near Withernsea in Yorkshire, at Halsham and Holmpton. He began to practise his tool-making skills unofficially at Seathorne Steel Constructors at Withernsea, an engineering shop that in order to employ him had to persuade the local MP, Sir Richard Wood, to have Parliament reverse a ban it had imposed on the employment of ex-POWs in industry. He became a naturalised British citizen on 14 July 1954 when living at 59B, Bannister Street, Withernsea, giving his profession as tool fitter. Ted made tools for Blackburn Aircraft, but later moved to Priestman Brothers, a manufacturer of cranes and excavators in Marfleet, where he worked for 13 years. By this time he was married, but his English wife spent his savings on a boyfriend so he divorced her. He later worked for Shiphams and Imperial Typewriters. He was offered a job by Blohm+Voss, who withdrew the offer when they found out he was over fifty. He moved to Hedon near Hull, re-married to Thelma, and became a partner in Modern Metal Finishers until retiring in 1979.

In retirement Ted became well-known locally as a expert in local history and numismatics, serving as president of the local, and later the Yorkshire, Branch of the British Numismatic Society. He is knowledgeable about aircraft of the 1930s and 40s and has authored several books and many articles. He has established an important collection of local photographs. He and Thelma were active in the Red Cross and the Handicapped Club of Hedon. When Thelma died of cancer, Ted established a charity in her memory to fund a bus for the handicapped and other local groups. He has left his extensive collection of documents and badges to the IWM. Ted found contentment in England. He liked the Yorkshire people, made good friends and a living, and had no complaints. He has found little unpleasantness in England, only once being cursed as a 'Nazi bastard', but this inspired an ex-soldier left for dead by the British Army at Dunkirk and nursed back to life by the Wehrmacht, to cross the street to thank him and tell the other man that Germans like Englishmen are a mixture of good and bad.

Asked in the interview he gave to the IWM how he felt about the war, Ted replied he resented it for depriving him of his best years. He enjoyed a good conscience about his involvement, knowing nothing of extermination camps or deliberate starvation of millions of Russian POWs but seeing first-hand the pitiless result for civilians of British area bombing. The appalling scenes he saw in Hamburg where the ruins were still hot and being cleared of bodies, changed him. Like all Germans, he knew of the concentration camps but believed they existed to punish anti-social elements. He believed the war, like the First World War, was the result not of German aggression but of self-defence, believing it could have been avoided if Germany had regained her colonies and their Lebensraum. In Graudenz he heard first-hand from Volksdeutschen of their persecution by Poles, and Ted believed one of Germany's war aims was to build an Autobahn across Poland to East Prussia for the benefit of all. In fact, building a German-controlled road and rail link to East Prussia in a corridor across the Corridor, together with the annexation of Danzig by Germany, were part of the bullying pressure applied by Ribbentrop and Hitler in late 1938 in an attempt to get Warsaw to join the Anti-Comintern Pact signed by Germany and Japan in 1936. Beck saw acceptance would mean an end to Poland's balanced position and signify its subordination to Germany, so rejected the offer on 19 November 1938. Beck was admired for refusing to be bullied, but Poland's reputation had been sullied by their illegal seizure of Teschen from Czechoslovakia in October 1938 in order to prevent the Germans from controlling the important railway junction in Bogumin.

Ted was, like many, impressed by the improvements in working conditions following the *Machtergreifung*, and rightly so. The Cambridge Keynsian economist, Joan Robinson, stated that Hitler had already found how to cure unemployment before Keynes had finished explaining why it occurred. In this regard Hitler demonstrated expert competence and political effectiveness, predicting already in 1933 that the NSDAP would gain unrivalled authority by solving unemployment. This made his social-revolutionary pretensions credible, and permitted him to lay the foundations for the complete mobilisation of resources for the coming war.[91] In consequence Ted never felt moral or aesthetic repugnance towards the NSDAP, even though he had no particular interest in politics and did not volunteer for the Hitler Jugend. His origins in Hamburg, the most international of all German cities, his English and American acquaintances and his love of their popular music and jazz, gave him immunity from the ignorance and fear of the democracies that affected most Germans. Ted was lucky in that during much of the war he was able to practise his trade and develop his skills as Flugzeugbauer and Waffenschmied. He lacked emotional investment in the Nazi narrative, with the result that defeat never meant the end of the world for him as it did for the generation of Hitler Jugend who had believed in Hitler's promises.[92]

91 Mark Harrison. *The Economics of World War Two* (Cambridge: CUP, 2009), article by Werner Abelshauser.

92 There are three sources for Ted Winkler's biography; a meeting and correspondence with Ted in December 2012 and January 2013; an IWM sound interview, SRD 18523 recorded on 10 June 1998 by Conrad Wood; and an article by Bill Jardine in *The Gazette* of 31 July 2003.

7

The Tanks

> I always choose my officers from the nobility, for nobility nearly always has a sense of honour. It can be found among bourgeois of merit but it is rarer. If a noble loses his honour he is ostracised by his family; whereas a commoner who has committed fraud can continue to run his father's business.
>
> Frederick the Great. 1712-1786

> The true role of the infantry was not to expend itself upon heroic physical effort ... but, on the contrary, to advance under the maximum possible protection of the maximum possible array of mechanical resources, in the form of guns, machine guns, tanks, mortars and aeroplanes; to advance with as little impediment as possible; to be relieved as far as possible of the obligation to fight their way forward.
>
> General John Monash. 1918

6 GUARDS ARMOURED BRIGADE AKA 6 GUARDS TANK BRIGADE

Wearing his black tank beret, heavy with symbolism, Montgomery addressed the ranks of 6 GAB in June 1945 at a Farewell To Armour parade in the German town of Rotenburg near Bremen. As he announced their new status as the 6 Guards (Infantry) Brigade, he said:

> I want to say, here and now, that in the sphere of armoured warfare the Guards have set a standard that it will be difficult for those that come after to reach. In modern war it is the co-operation of all arms, armoured and unarmoured, that wins the battle, and in this respect you have achieved great results.[1]

No one asked why Montgomery disbanded his best tank unit. No one knew until Charles Farrell[2] read his papers in the IWM that Montgomery had acted out of irritated pique in holding them back from Normandy until mid July 1944, and by so doing carelessly degraded the performance of 21 AG and cost lives.

6 GAB changed its name during the war according to military fashion. It was founded as 30 Infantry Brigade that was captured in Calais and re-formed as 30 Guards Infantry Brigade. The reaction to blitzkrieg was to greatly expand the number of armoured divisions which Martel insisted were manned by elite personnel such as the guards so it became 30 Guards Armoured Brigade in Guards Armoured Division. In 1943 divisions were reformed. The armoured divisions swapped an armoured for an infantry brigade which freed 6 GAB to convert to infantry tanks and join 15 Mixed Division as a tank brigade. The distinction was institutionalised between armoured

1 Erskine, *Scots Guards*.
2 Farrell, *Reflections*.

brigades equipped with cruiser tanks and tank brigades with infantry tanks. In February 1945 Montgomery had got his way to phase out the infantry tank in favour of his universal tank, so all became armoured brigades once more pending re-equipment so it was as 6 GAB that the brigade fought in Operation *Heather*. By June 1945 it had become recognized that more infantry were needed and the brigade reverted to infantry without ever having re-equipped with the latest Centurion Universal tank. To summarise 6GAB's history:

24 April 1940	30th Infantry Brigade
17 October 1940	30th Guards Infantry Brigade
15 September 1941	6th Guards Armoured Brigade
15 January 1943	6th Guards Tank Brigade
2 February 1945	6th Guards Armoured Brigade
17 June 1945	6th Guards Infantry Brigade

Guards have a long history. The Scottish Guard was the first, being formed between 1400 and 1415 by the French King Charles VII to protect his person and to serve the Auld Alliance.[3] From then until the Restoration of the English Crown in 1660, Scots as well as Swiss and French guarded the French kings. Indeed, Henry II was accidentally killed when jousting in a tournament with the Captain of his Scottish Coy, Jacques de Montgomery in 1559.

In 1444, King James II of Scotland had a guard, and Henry VII established a permanent Yeomanry of the Guard in 1485. They wore white and green before adopting red in 1520. By 1530 it was the fashion for all European sovereigns to maintain a guard.

In 1563 the French king started a new fashion by raising an infantry regiment of *Gardes Françaises*. Louis XIII was the first monarchs to take pleasure in drilling, manoeuvring, reorganising, and fiddling with the uniforms of his guards, and to fight alongside them. This led to the concept of a *Corps séparé* from other troops by the personal connections they maintained with the monarchs they guarded, as well as by their duties, privileges and appearance. The guards, who since 1400 had been present in increasing numbers within the palaces, were now also in barracks at their gates, keeping order in the capital cities, and leading the army in battle.

The Scots Guards claim that they were raised in 1640 by Archibald, Marquis of Argyll, who received letters patent two years later on 18 March 1641, old calendar, or 1642 on the new calendar. Their tercentenary was celebrated with scarcely a break from training under their hard-driving CO, Hugh Kindersley.

The English court had few guards. Charles II always thought his father might have kept his head had he employed more than a few gentlemen Lifeguard of Horse, and a Lifeguard of Foot recruited from Derbyshire miners. These disappeared when Cromwell employed a standing army. Charles II in exile organised a guard in 1659, which became established in London as three troops of gentlemen Life Guards, joining forces with the Gentlemen Pensioners and Yeomen of the Guard. The guards became ever more closely involved with the King and in 1685 the Captain of the Guard, Gold Stick in Waiting, stood directly behind the King at the coronation.

In 1660 a Regiment of Foot Guards was raised, not yet Grenadiers as that title was not adopted until they destroyed the French Grenadiers at Waterloo 155 years later. In 1661 General Monck's Regiment was reconstituted as the Lord General's Regiment of Foot Guards, the 2nd Guards, also called The Coldstream Guards. The next year a Scottish Troop of Life Guards was formed in Edinburgh under Lord Newburgh, and marched to London in 1686. Given English hatred of a

3 Philip Mansel. *Pillars of Monarchy* (London: Quartet, 1984).

standing army, the King was permitted to raise troops only for his personal protection. The consequence was a rapid expansion of the guards.

The French continued to lead the fashion in guards when Louis XIV in 1676 raised the *Grenadiers à Cheval de la maison du Roi*. The King of England formed a similar troop of horsed Grenadier Guards two years later, not to be confused with the First Foot Guards, later the Grenadier Guards. The next innovation came from Charles XII of Sweden when in 1701 he used the guard as a training school for officers and a model for the rest of his army.

After the Union of 1707, the Scottish Foot Guard moved to London. It was called at first the 3rd Guards, then from 1831 to 1877 the Scots Fusilier Guards, and then the Scots Guards.

The French guards disgraced themselves against Marlborough, and were christened the 'Ducks of the Main' after their headlong retreat through that river at Dettingen. Their performance at Malplaquet was no better. Their decline was hastened by the rise of Prussia. Frederick William I discounted the concept of a *Corps séparé*, and placed his Guards in the line. From that point on, large, independent and expensive royal guards fell out of favour. Privilege in all its forms was questioned in the age of reason. In 1756, for example, the Guards in St James's Park were being drilled like Prussians. In 1787 the Life Guards and Horse Grenadiers were amalgamated and questions were raised about their fitness to fight. The disloyalty of the *Gardes Françaises* in the Revolution raised further questions about their general usefulness. However, in 1799 they were transformed into Napoleon's Garde Impériale, and quickly became a model for the wildly popular Revolutionary Army that swept through Europe.

The social composition of the British guards was not always aristocratic. In the 1660s many robbers and hackney coachmen served in their ranks, which until 1699 contained only 40 peers or their sons. Between 1700 and 1800 the number of those with landed and moneyed interests in the guards grew rapidly as the guards became bait to attract nobility into the army. This did not save the disillusioned James II, who left London under an escort of William's Dutch guard in 1688. He had alienated the aristocracy with the result that Churchill, Grafton and Ormonde deserted him. The Coldstreamers were the least disloyal, but all were rapidly despatched to the provinces by William, who changed most of their officers.

In all times and nations guards have lived an extreme form of army life. Being particularly close to the monarch and living in the capital gave them unlimited opportunities for an existence based, it has been said, on 'drill, drink and sex'. A private income was and is indispensable in peacetime, and from John Churchill onwards many found advancement through the bedchambers of the influential, particularly those of royal mistresses. The life appealed to men of boundless energy and an uncomplicated view of life's obligations and pleasures. It also involved them in Royal scandal and division. In September 1737 the commanders of the three regiments of foot guards received instructions that by command of His Majesty no notice should be taken of the Prince and Princess of Wales or any of their family.[4] These were Frederick Prince of Wales and his wife Princess Augusta of Saxe-Gotha, who were both loathed by his parents, George II and Queen Caroline, and content to pursue their quarrels over Wales's allowance in public.

In 1900 the Irish Guards, and in 1915 the Welsh Guards, were formed, although a Welsh influence had existed as far back as the Tudor Yeomen of the Guard. In the Great War all the guards fought in separate divisions or, in Russia's case, separate corps. No monarch kept the guards at home, and only one battalion stayed on in London for 'public duties'. In July 1915 the Prussian and Russian Guards clashed at Krasnostav, and the Russian Guard was worsted. The Prussian Guard was disbanded in Berlin and Potsdam in December 1918, being resurrected a decade later

---

4 Ibid.

as a criminal organisation, the SS Leibstandarte. On 22 March 1919 the British Guards returned to London in a spectacular parade.

The Household Division's duties are now military and ceremonial. The task of guarding the monarch's person has been given to special security forces, although the guards have 'gone tactical' and patrol the palace grounds with loaded guns at night. There is a G Squadron of Guards in the SAS, which was itself founded by two guardsmen, David Stirling (SG) and Jock Lewes (WG). For the rest the guards remain a distinguished part of the British Army, although officers who have not been to public schools, like Robert Runcie, are still regarded as generally a mistake.

British guards' officers from Waterloo onwards were influenced by the aristocratic tendency towards unintellectual high-spirited barbarity of the Bullingdon variety, but it was usually controlled by a strong sense of duty, fierce discipline and good manners. These were exactly the attributes of perhaps the most famous guardsman of the Second World War, the extraordinary Irish Guardsman, Harold Alexander. In 1923, and while still unknown, Rudyard Kipling, whose own son was killed at Loos while serving in the Irish Guards, wrote of Alexander:

> It is undeniable that Col Alexander had the gift of handling the men on the lines to which they most readily responded, as many tales in this connection testify. At the worst crisis he was both inventive and cordial and, on such occasions as they all strove together in the Gates of Death, would somehow contrive to dress the affair in high comedy. Moreover when the blame for some incident of battle or fatigue was his, he confessed and took it upon his own shoulders in the presence of all. Consequently, his subordinates loved him, even when he fell upon them blisteringly for their shortcomings; and his men were all his own... The discipline of the Guards, demanding the utmost that can be exacted of the man, requires of the officer unresting care of his men under all conditions.[5]

The Household Division fought bravely from Namur in 1695, through Dettingen, Waterloo, Inkerman, Omdurman, Modder River and the battles of the First War to the ones examined here. But although the guards were brave, expensively dressed, and with a strong sense of duty and fierce discipline, they were not different in kind from the County regiments. Their uniqueness was a consequence of their officers' personal wealth, which meant at that time being part of an 'old boy' network of public school, university and clubs.

They had a special salute, which was, 'a kind of aloof camaraderie poised on a knife-edge between Grand Seigneur and back-slapping.[6] When Farrell received a 'full regimented salute' outside Munster instead of the usual casual wave from Brigadier Greenacre, he was gratified but immediately suspicious about what it betokened. Also it was the regimental custom in the Scots Guards to refer to senior officers only by their Christian name, so Lt Col Claude Dunbar was Colonel Claude.[7]

The Guards shared all officers' avoidance of much 'wrong' behaviour, such as eating before or with the other ranks or in any way socializing with them, pushing a pram, carrying a parcel, unfurling an umbrella even in the rain unless it was to hold over a woman. In addition to these marks of an officer and a gentleman, they dressed more expensively and smartly than other officers, and practised a language code known only to themselves. They used a vocabulary distinguished by the number of common phrases that were taboo, and in which they needed to be schooled. They never 'went up to town', but 'visited London', used the Underground and never the Tube, asked for

---

5 R Kipling. *The Irish Guards in the Great War* (Garden City: Doubleday, 1923), p. xiv.
6 TES Turner. *Gallant Gentlemen* (London: Michael Joseph, 1956).
7 WA Elliott. *Esprit de Corps* (Wilby: Michael Russell, 1996) p. 18.

a 'glass of whisky' and never simply for a whisky, and so on. Newly arrived officers attended lessons in which they were taught phrases to avoid and the ones to use. Charles Farrell's book[8] is full of such phrasing like 'visiting' London. Robert Runcie fifty years later still complied: 'all of which, I have to say, I assiduously keep to today, and I can't stop myself wincing when people reveal themselves in these ways. (But don't take me too seriously!)'[9]

Britain was inordinately class conscious, which meant everyone knew his position. The middle and upper classes avoided the speech, dress or deed of the common man, and it was easy to equate lower orders with 'lowlifes', for the guiding principle of such things was succinctly put by Gore Vidal: 'It is not enough to succeed. Others must fail'.[10]

Common was what no one admitted to being. It was not good enough to live in Mayfair in London or 'Uphill' in Lincoln by the Cathedral, but others had to live in *common* Pinner or 'Downhill'. Snobbery was a ranking and positional device, and sometimes used in the strangest contexts; for example Edward Windsor complained to his brother about the latter's *common* wife, Elizabeth Bowes-Lyon. She disapproved of giving up the throne for a *nobody* like Wallis Simpson, and for a *common* reason like falling in love, when for people of quality duty came first. In *The Gondoliers*, the Grand Inquisitor on finding that the Republican gondoliers had promoted everyone to the nobility, explained that there must be a distinction because, 'when *everyone* is somebody, then no-one's *anybody*.'[11] Being *common* was revealed by your accent, by your language, where you lived, your school or university, your attitudes, clothes, food, pastimes, friends, your regiment and even the source of your income. 'Polite society' did not go yachting with its 'grocer', as Sir Thomas Lipton knew despite owning the grandest yacht, and even a successful woman like Mrs Thatcher several generations later would sometimes be called 'a grocer's daughter'. Trade and commerce were vulgar and *common*, and not the pastime of polite society who owned land, went into the Church, the forces or the professions, and in general exercised power and influence – and maintained the status quo.

Guards regiments were at the social apex of a stratified society. Their senior officers knew, or had connections with, the monarch, being able to have words in the King's ear to prevent Montgomery from turning them out of their Churchill tanks. The officers of the County Regiments could claim the status of gentlemen, as Elizabeth Bennett said when castigating the aristocratic D'Arcy for showing ungentlemanly bad manners,[12] and although the regiments were graded into good and ordinary, they considered themselves every bit as good as the foppish Guards where, they said, intellectually-challenged chinless-wonders were carried by magnificent NCOs. Viscount Whitelaw told this author something similar, that 3 Scots Guards had magnificent sergeants. Guards' officers hearing the chinless wonder jibe returned the compliment by calling the County Regiments *common*.

The subject of Guards' behaviour and attitudes has to be addressed, as these represented another fissiparous element in a fragmented 21 Army Group where armour, air and infantry-artillery usually fought separately, resulting in battlefield performance that was often pedestrian at best. A vicious circle developed after Churchill separated air from the infantry in 1918, and after armour went its own way, with both armour and air concentrating on winning the war on their own through bombing in the one case, and planning to disrupt enemy command and control with cruiser tanks in the other. Nevertheless, Montgomery preached that the various arms should take the field at the

8 Farrell, *Reflections*. p. 21
9 Carpenter, *Robert Runcie*. p. 64.
10 George Plimpton. *Writers At Work: The 'Paris Review' Interviews, 5th series* (London: Penguin, 1981), concerning Gerald Clarke.
11 Arthur Sullivan and WS Gilbert. *Libretti of Operas* (London: Chappell, 1884).
12 Jane Austen. *Pride and Prejudice* (London: Egerton, 1813).

same time, and later in the war self-preservation led the armour, at least, to seek infantry defence against the Panzerfaust. The general perception among the rest of the army remained, however, that the Guards were arrogant, obsessed with spit and polish and acting in the belief that an ounce of image with the top brass and monarch was worth a pound of performance. The battles narrated here reveal a patchy performance; from the outstanding – Alec Foucard of 4 CG at Kervenheim and Jim Alldred of 3 SG at Winnekendonk; through the bizarre – Lt Col Smith's placing the Buffs under arrest at Kervenheim; to the disappearing trick – the Grenadier Guards' absence from the East Yorks bridgehead and the Coldstream Guards' disappearance behind the bridge at Aengen to leave the Norfolks with an open right flank from which they were decimated at Kervenheim.

On 17 October 1940, the 30th Independent Guards Infantry Brigade was formed in the UK under Brigadier A.H.S. Adair, comprising 4 GG, 3 SG and 2 WG. On 15 September 1941 the Brigade was mechanised as 6 GAB in the GAD under the guardsman, Oliver Leese. At the same time 3 BID lost the 7 Guards Infantry Brigade (1 GG, 2GG and 1 CG), which became 5 GAB in the same GAD, and received 185 BIB as a replacement. The decision to put the Guards into armour was due to Martel, who believed that trained soldiery was the most important element in creating military success, while good equipment 'would follow along,' with quality of staff work mot meriting a mention. Martel reversed the priorities established by Monash, and which was instrumental in gaining the victories of 1918, that staff work, equipment and trained soldiery were important in that order of priority. JFC Fuller believed that correct equipment was 99% of success, while Charles Farrell of 3 SG gave the guardsman's view of quality as being 'based on first-rate discipline, a high standard of training and first-class weapons, which will be reflected in high morale and performance'.[13] Farrell likewise made no mention of staff work, nor of how his first-class weapons were to be specified, designed or procured in its absence.

In 1942 the infantry – and of course the entire British armed forces – was fatally weakened by four factors; the removal of the Guards; the wholesale poaching of volunteers for Special Forces such as airborne and commandos; the failure to give the Churchill Infantry Tank frontal armour resistant to the common anti-tank weapons; and the failure of the CIGS to establish army aviation. These matters are discussed in Chapter 10.

In November 1942 GAD was reorganised, and 6 GAB was removed and replaced by lorried infantry as the over-emphasis on armour began to be corrected. 2 Armoured Welsh Guards left 6 GAB to be replaced by 4 CG. At the same time 6 GAB lost its inadequate Valentine I-tank (which had replaced the Covenanter cruiser tanks) and was re-equipped with Churchill I-tanks. This warranted a change of name on 15 January 1943 to 6 GTB to signify Infantry tanks. On 4 January 1943 the Brigade was transferred into Bullen-Smith's 15 Mixed Division of two infantry brigades and an armoured brigade. Six months elapsed before the units met up. Adair had left on 21 September 1942 to command GAD. His replacement, G L Verney, took them to war.

Establishment was at first 174 Churchill and 18 Honey tanks, also called Stuarts. In each of the three bns there were 58 Churchills and 6 Honeys, manned by 38 officers and 632 men. A bn was organised as three Squadrons with 18 tanks each, called Right Flank, Left Flank and 'S' Sqn in the Scots Guards and 1, 2 & 3 Squadrons in GG; Farrell[14] stated that 'S' Sqn did not signify 'Support'. A squadron comprised five troops and a Squadron HQ troop of three tanks each, with four tanks at Battalion HQ. In August 1944 the shortage of replacements led to a reduction in the establishment of all tank brigades to four troops and an HQ troop, bringing their number into line with the infantry organisation of four rifle companies and an HQ company. The number of Churchills in the Brigade was thereby reduced from 174 to 147, and in the battalion from 58 to 49.

13 Farrell, *Reflections*, p. 100.
14 Op. Cit., Frontispiece.

The Churchill had a crew of five; commander, gunner and wireless operator/loader in the turret, with driver and co-driver/machine-gunner in the hull.

The persistent rumours of disbandment of 6 GTB were the result of a belated general realisation in 1943 that infantry and not the support arms was the key to victory. Montgomery wanted to disband all I-tank units as infantry reinforcements. In Chapter 10 the argument is presented that it was the armoured divisions that were redundant in 21 AG, and the I-tank regiments needed increasing in number and re-equipping with tanks immune to the common anti-tank weapons, including the 88. Churchill's campaign in favour of his eponymous tank in February 1943, and its success on the Tunisian djebels in April 1943, led to the design of the Churchill VII with 6 inch instead of 4 inch frontal armour. This did not satisfy Martel on his return from Russia in September 1943. Having seen the impact of Panther and Tiger at Kursk, Martel started pushing strongly for a Churchill immune to the new anti-tank guns. The cumulative effect of all these factors, together with Hobart's advocacy of heavy specialised armour based on the Churchill, thwarted Montgomery's campaign to abolish the Churchill and its tank brigades. The Guards finally saw off Montgomery by having a quiet word with the King at Thoresby Park in March 1944, although Montgomery exacted his revenge by holding 6 GTB back from D-Day, one of his most fateful decisions. A surprising discovery during research for this book was that the introduction of the better armoured Churchill VII was not noticed by the Tank Brigades because Hobart took most of them for conversion to Crocodile flame-throwers in 79 BAD. Only unrecognised dribs and drabs went to the Tank brigades.

Guards were insubordinate when it suited them, and being caught cheating would not have endeared them to senior officers or anyone else playing by the rules in a competitive environment. In Exercise *Blackcock*, on 2 October 1943, Lt Pember (who performed the recce at Winnekendonk and was a famous character in 6 GTB) managed to bluff an umpire and cross the River Derwent at 8.30 am in his troop of armoured cars by the 'blown' regular bridge, rather than wait for the sappers to construct a Bailey Bridge. Once across by this prank, Pember radioed the Brigade GOC, Verney, who personally congratulated him. It was never clear whether Verney knew of the cheating, for an account of the exercise by Brigade HQ that is appended to the war Diary of 3 SG stated Pember crossed legitimately. The War Diary, however, mentions the 'bluffing' of the umpire, showing that 3 SG's CO, Dunbar, was complicit.[15]

Success in operating equipment vulnerable to anti-tank guns demanded compensating excellence in the areas under their control, and good luck. In the provision of these items the Brigade had good days and some that were not so good. Their reputation is inconsistent within 3 BID; Norfolks and Warwicks are jaundiced about them; East Yorks, Suffolks, RUR and KOSB are neutral; while South Lancs, Lincolns and KSLI are fans. Greenacre, Brigade Commander, had his own view about the capabilities of individual tank battalions, regarding the Scots Guards as the best, whilst battalion COs would have reached conclusions about the abilities of individual squadron commanders.

The key point in the Battle of Caumont on 30 July 1944 was reached when the tanks proceeded without 15 BID, who were unable to keep up. At La Mougeraye at 11.05 am, Dunbar of the Scots Guards told the tanks to press on and keep up with the barrage. At 12.15 pm the tanks stopped for an hour to wait for the infantry to catch up, but the infantry did not pass La Mougeraye until 1 pm. Dunbar received permission from Verney to take the Les Loges' ridge without infantry. The Battalion consolidated on Point 236 on the ridge at 2.30 pm and two companies of infantry reached them at 4.15 pm but without anti-tank guns. With the flanking 43 BID far behind, the Scots Guards' left flank was up in the air. It was from this direction at 6 pm that they were

15 Place, *Military Training*, p. 24.

attacked by Jagdpanthers that destroyed 11 Churchills. The two Jagdpanthers which had attacked, and a third which had provided covering fire, were all found abandoned in the woods the next day without fuel or ammunition. British losses were 2 officers and 21 other ranks killed, with one officer and 18 other ranks wounded. This represented one third of all its casualties in the whole campaign from Normandy to the Baltic. There was alarm that the Churchills had caught fire and blown up with such ease, but these events rarely recurred except at Winnekendonk, and appeared to be the result of 88 mm shot fired at point blank range with such impact that the shock-wave set off the ammunition in the racks. The risk of death or maiming for tank crews throughout the campaign remained much lower than for infantry.

The battalion especially mourned Major Sydney Cuthbert's loss. He had long been 2ic and one of the chief innovators in developing tank-infantry co-operation. The day's success owed much to his energy and detailed preparation in training. He met his death facing the enemy head-on with shot holes right through the heaviest frontal armour and the turret blown off by an ammunition explosion. William Whitelaw became 2ic, and Farrell took over S Squadron.[16]

The Coldstreamers were told to take Point 309 to the south. It was decided by Verney and Macmillan (GOC 15 BID) to push the tanks again without infantry up the hill from La Morichesse les Mares. The summit was seized at 4 pm, and all through the night the infantry laboured to bring up the anti-tank guns to secure and fortify the hill.

The Guards were surprised how easily the day had gone. The serious losses to 3 SG were ascribed to chance. The victory electrified a British Army grown used to the ineffectiveness of tanks. Messages reached Verney from all over the world, and the GOC VIII Corps, O'Connor, wrote; 'No tank unit has ever been handled with greater dash and determination'.[17]

A year later Dempsey told the Brigadier that he considered the Battle of Caumont one of the most important battles of the war. But no one drew the conclusion that since Churchills could exploit their own breakthroughs, the Cruiser tank was redundant, and the armoured divisions should be broken up.

Verney was rewarded with promotion on 3 August 1944 to command 7 BAD. There he made little impact and was absorbed without trace by the culture derived from Hobart and sanctioned by Montgomery, that the task of armoured divisions was to go through the Gee in Gap created by the PBI and the tank brigades. His replacement was Sir W. de S. Barttelot, Bt, CO 4 CG, who was replaced by his 2ic, Bill Smith. At Estry in the first week of August on the left flank of VIII Corps, the Brigade and 15 BID were fought to a standstill by 9 SS PD. Meanwhile 8 miles to their west on the other flank of VIII Corps, 3 BID had taken Montisanger and La Houdenguerie across the River Allière from 3FJD and elements of 10 SS PD, and was in touch with the Americans who entered Vire on 6 August 1944. The Germans then started their suicidal counter-attack around Mortain.

In the second week of August the first contact between 3 BID and 6 GTB occurred. 4 CG supported 8 and 185 BIBs on the Vire-Tinchebray axis. 3 SG were detached to support GAD in the assault on Chênedollé on 10 August 1944 with 2 Lincolns of 9 BIB in support. 6 GTB then came into support of 3 BID on 10 August for the first time, but the battle was winding down as the Germans failed at Mortain and began their dash to escape the Falaise Pocket. On 18 August 1944, Barttelot was killed when his scout car ran over two Tellermines on the way to a Divisional conference. His replacement was Douglas Greenacre from the Welsh Guards in GAD who arrived on 20 August 1944. Forbes's biography of 6 GTB has high praise for Barttelot but silence for Greenacre.

16 William Whitelaw. *The Whitelaw Memoirs* (London: Aurum, 1989).

17 Forbes, *6th Guards*.

Brigade and Division parted company on 14 September 1944 when 3 BID left to expand the flanks of *Market Garden* under XXX Corps. The Brigade did not follow until 27 September 1944 when it moved to Geldrop under VIII Corps. They met up again on 1 October 1944 to plan Operation *Gatwick*, and were moving up on 6 October 1944 when the operation was cancelled, only to reappear four months later on 8 February 1945 as Operation *Veritable*. Instead 3 BID and 6 GTB moved to the attack on Overloon and Venraij, involving heavy fighting until 18 October 1944. 3 SG did not engage the enemy but guarded the flank between Geldrop and Eindhoven.

6 GTB as XII Corps' troops was sent with 15 BID to take Tilburg on 20 October 1944 and back across the salient on 29 October to Meijel. 3 BID meanwhile began its three month long watch on the Maas until it was called forward for Operation *Heather* in February. 6 GTB were in Helmond on 7 November 1944, with all three battalions billeted together in the same place for the first time since landing in Normandy. They fought eastwards to the Maas. On 20 November 1944 the Coldstreamers supported 8 BIB in the destruction of the Kasteel at Geysteren on the Maas, then back to Helmond where on 31 November 1944 Eisenhower inspected them. He showed interest in the Churchill tank, still the heaviest in service with the Western Allies and with a good reputation. The American Army was preparing at that time to ship to Europe for troop acceptance trials the M26 Pershing with a 90-mm gun, which was first used in Operation *Grenade* in February.

The Brigade remained in Helmond until the Ardennes Offensive. Between 18 and 28 December 1944 they spent time in three different armies, spending Christmas at Maastricht in support of 51 BID in 9 USArmy in 21AG. 3 BID was also on the Maas but further north, not far from Kervenheim. On 12 January, 6 GTB moved to clear the Maastricht Appendix with 43 BID in Operation *Blackcock*. By 25 January no German forces remained south of the River Roer, and it was from this area, taken over by 9 US Army, that Operation *Grenade* launched on 23 February.

The Brigade moved through Maastricht back to Tilburg at the end of the month where many received 10-days home leave. On 2 February the tanks moved to Nijmegen for Operation *Veritable* and reverted back to their designation of 6 GAB, serving again with 15 BID.

The contrast between the Brigade with its large proportion of the people who had come out with it and the infantry was stark. An officer of 3 SG wrote:

> Every time that I see an infantry battalion that I know well, I am appalled at the number of new faces, but we have remained substantially unchanged from the beginning. There is no doubt that it is much safer in a tank, even though at times you think that everything in the world is firing at you.[18]

A comparison of survivors in 3 SG and 2 Lincolns proves the point. Both units landed in Normandy with 42 officers. 3 SG, however, arrived over six weeks later than the Lincolns and after the worst bloodletting was over, so the comparison is not exact. In 3 SG, 20 or just under half the originals were on parade on VE Day compared with only 12 or about a quarter from 2 Lincolns, all but one of whom had been wounded and many had been in hospital in England. The following originals were present on VE Day: 3 SG – Bankes, Bruce, Bull, Cameron, Cathcart, Duffin, Dunbar, Farrell, Fletcher, Laing, Llewellyn Smith, Maclean, Mann, McNight, Reid, Runcie, Scott-Barrett, Seymour, Stevenson, and Whitelaw; 2 Lincolns – Boys, Colvin, Gilbert, Hamlet, Harrod, Hart, Hill, Kidney, Larkin, Pacey, Pawlett and Wilson. Of these survivors Boys, Hart, Hill, Kidney, Larkin, Pacey and Wilson had all been in hospital with wounds, while Colvin was wounded but stayed in action. Only Glyn Gilbert survived without a scratch, and in this he was unique as an officer in 3 BID.

18 Erskine, *Scots Guards*.

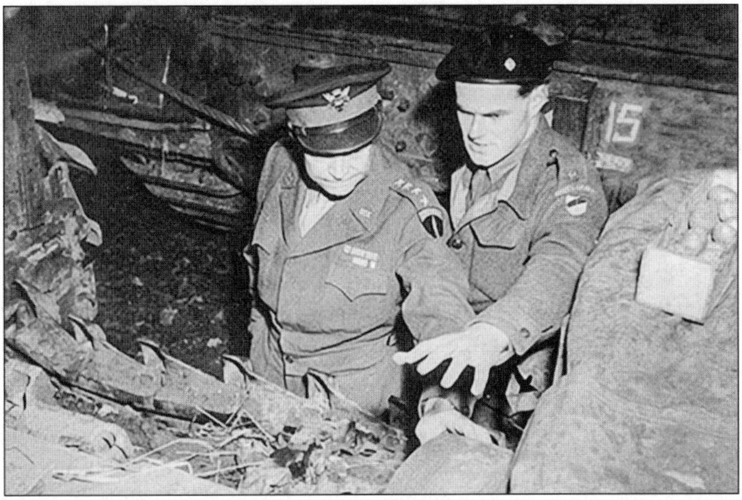

31 November 1944 in Helmond. Gen Eisenhower was commenting to Maj Charles Farrell on the thickness of the Churchill's frontal armour. Farrell agreed, but pointed to the failure to slope the armour which largely negated its thickness avantage and left it vulnerable to the 88. Farrell pointed to the field fix of welding track plates on the front of the tank to give extra protection. The visit was arranged by Lt Col Jimmy Gault, Scots Guards, who was Eisenhower's British Military Assistant from 1942-45 and again from 1951-53. (© D.Farrell)

In 6 GTB's biography, Greenacre reached a conclusion which would have transformed the performance of 21 AG had it been enacted in 1943 with infantry-tank troops incorporated gradually into the infantry divisions:

> Finally 6th Guards Tank Brigade proved two things: Firstly, that there is no mystery about armoured fighting. It is more technical, it is far more exhausting than most Infantrymen believe, and, with its good wireless communications, the average member of a crew has to react more quickly than is normally demanded of an Infantryman. But any good Infantry unit, well officered and well disciplined, can quickly be trained as an armoured unit. With plenty of training, equipment, and good instructors, it can be done in a year. Secondly, the value of Infantry training in a tank unit. Most of the senior subalterns and all above them in the 6th Guards Tank Brigade had had experience in Infantry problems. Thus their co-operation with the Infantry they supported was more sympathetic, as they had a shrewd idea of what their problems were and how to help them solve them. The mutual respect and understanding that this developed reached a very high standard, never more successful than with the 15th (Scottish) Division.[19]

1943 was the year when the army as a whole could have developed its operational methodology for defeating the German army. At the minimum, drills and equipment for defeating StuGs, Panthers and Tigers, and for locating and destroying mortars and MG42s could have been developed. More technical research could have been initiated; armouring the Churchill to be frontally immune to all anti-tank weapons; radar location of mortars; armoured aircraft equipped with

19 Forbes, *6th Guards*, p. 194.

accurate anti-tank guns instead of inaccurate rockets; and accurate vertical dive bombers instead of inaccurate skip bombing. Also, the infantry divisions could have been maintained as Mixed Divisions with Churchill Tank units and even dive-bomber squadrons being integrated with the infantry battalions as closely as the artillery always were.

6 GTB showed it could equally well co-operate with 3 BID and 15 BID as with 6 and 17 US Airborne Divisions. On 9 February 1946 as the three battalions of the Brigade were dispersed and sent as reinforcements to the regular battalions, 3 SG was addressed by Maj-Gen Sir John Marriott, Deputy Director of Infantry at the War Office:

> As to your conduct in battle, your Brigade Commander, Douglas Greenacre knows far more than I do, but I believe he looked upon you as the best battalion in his brigade – a Brigade which never failed the infantry to whom it was allotted, and especially the 15th Scottish.[20]

Bolo Whistler considered 2 Lincolns the best battalion in 3BID, so its performance when combined with the highly rated 3 SG at Winnekendonk should not have been unexpected.

3 SG believed their success in tanks stemmed directly from their beginnings as infantry. They were re-raised in October 1940 – colours existed in Buckingham Palace that had been carried from 1899 to 1906, and 1914 to 1919 – and joined 30 GIB. On 18 March 1942 they celebrated their tercentenary by being worked hard by Hugh Kindersley – who left in May 1943 to command 6 ALB. His place was taken by the 2ic, Dunbar, who continued as CO until after war's end. He was a good strategist, in Whitelaw's opinion[21] but with a tendency to flap. Whitelaw had to endure Dunbar's changing whatever he did. Farrell recounted how Dunbar praised him for success against German armour at Le Bas Perrier, saying; 'Charles has shown us how to do it'. Shortly afterwards Farrell got a rocket from a furious Dunbar who threatened to send Farrell back to England immediately if he ever again questioned any of his orders, even those of a minor administrative nature that Farrell had mildly raised with the Adjutant. Dunbar had overcome real physical difficulties. After losing his right eye he taught himself to fire from the left shoulder, according to Darby Hart who served with him in Berlin.[22]

It was counter-intuitive that guardsmen with a minimum height of 5 ft 10 in were chosen by Martel for tanks designed for men with an average height of 5 ft 7 in. Tanks could have been made lower and easier to conceal, and able to carry thicker armour, if they had been designed instead for short men with a maximum height perhaps of 5 ft. The SG rationalised being made into "rude mechanicals' by pointing to their connections with Scotland, the home of the most mechanically minded race in history, but this could have been allied with recruiting the small and stunted men of Glasgow instead of tall guardsmen. 6 GTB's infantry training gave them an understanding of the needs of those they supported, and also the insight to know when not to accept any nonsense. The story is told of Robert Runcie[23] turning his main gun onto a 'sticky' unit of Glasgow Highlanders to 'persuade' them to advance, although this sounds more like the action of a troop sergeant than of Runcie who always behaved, according to Jim Alldred, like Sgt Wilson of Dad's Army.

Whitelaw believed that the battalion gained benefit from a nucleus of NCO tank commanders who had served as police sergeants and learned discipline. As we have seen, such NCOs could be towers of strength to a young subaltern, although Mark Fearfield[24] believed that some of the experienced sergeants held back probably from worry about their subaltern's youthful impetuosity,

20 Erskine, *Scots Guards*, p. 466.
21 Viscount Whitelaw in conversation at the Home Office on 18 January 1985.
22 Darby Houlton-Hart in conversation.
23 The name of the informant is in this author's notes of the conversation.
24 Mark Fearfield in conversation.

and from the older family man's natural feeling of responsibility for wife and children. Death would leave the family with little from a 'grateful nation', and more worrying than death was, of course, disfiguring and disabling wounding. The presence of these remarkable NCOs reinforced the stereotype held by many in the infantry that thick Guards officers were carried by NCOs, although it was untrue of 3 SG.

3 SG contained many officers who later became eminent. They included six generals, an Archbishop of Canterbury, a Home Secretary, a Moderator of the Church of Scotland, a headmaster of a public school, a Lord Chamberlain, two Lords Lieutenant, a Senior Steward of the Jockey Club, eight High Sheriffs, a Director of the Board of Trade, two chairmen of merchant banks, two chairmen of large businesses, six Deputy Lords Lieutenants, and a best selling author.[25]

Some of the SG officers in this narrative are men born into wealth and position: John Macdonald-Buchanan of Cottesbrooke Hall, acquired by his father in 1937 and the centre of the Pytchley Hunt whose kennels are situated on the estate; Alan Earl Cathcart, Viscount Cathcart and Baron Greenock in the United Kingdom, Baron Cathcart in Scotland, who succeeded his father as 6th earl in 1927 and whose ancestor implemented the divisional structure; Hector Laing, Baron Dunphail, of the McVitie and Price biscuit company; William Whitelaw, whose grandfather was Chairman of the LNER and whose father died of war wounds in 1919; Charles Farrell, whose father took over Beaverbrook's interests in Canada and also died in 1919. Both Whitelaw and Farrell were friendly with Ludovic Kennedy, related to the Marquis of Ailsa and who declined a commission in the SG, preferring the RN. Others in this narrative had middle class backgrounds, such as Robert Runcie, a BNC scholar, who asked for a commission in the KOSB but was offered one in the SG. They had decided that, to maintain numbers, they would recruit selectively from the grammar schools and from Oxbridge men that were *common* by every yardstick of dress and accent, but outstanding. He could not, however, have expected the penurious, but even that was no more a stumbling block than Runcie's hairdresser mother's Gracie Fields accent, or his background and attitudes. The Guards officers, who had moved en masse from Winchester and Eton, looked at Runcie askance, and decided SG was scraping the bottom of the barrel. Few spoke to Runcie for weeks, and Whitelaw said they had a lot of trouble with him.[26] He won acceptance because of his intelligence, and talent for mimicry. He was also a good man, and soon looked the part of a charming guards officer. A guardsman who served with him wrote:

> I was happy to be attached to Right Flank as apart from our highly efficient Troop Leader Captain Pember, we came under the command of competent officers one had trust in such as Lieutenants Laing, Scott-Barrett and Runcie. The latter an earthy humorous man who really surprised me by becoming the spiritual leader of the Anglican Church.[27]

There was more to this group of men than accident of birth and inherited fortune. Some were men of the first water, who held to noblesse oblige with high-minded principles and noble actions. Farrell provided a small example when he wrote that he had not applied for an Oxford scholarship because his mother held that those who could afford it should pay and leave the bursaries to the needy. But often, and perhaps usually, principle deferred to class solidarity. The matter of Runcie's MC was dealt with above, where Dunbar untruthfully identified Runcie as having performed Sgt Alldred's actions so the recalcitrant Alldred could be denied recognition and kept in his OR box. It might be tempting to dismiss Dunbar as an extreme example, but the 2 ic of

25 List provided by John MacDonald-Buchanan, Senior Steward of the Jockey Club.
26 Viscount Whitelaw in conversation.
27 JE Davies. http://www.bbc.co.uk/history/ww2peopleswar/stories/21/a4538621.shtml

3 SG, William Whitelaw himself acted in a similar way when as Home Secretary he refused to right a wrong done to a member of hoi polloi by distinguished members of Whitelaw's own class. Ludovic Kennedy, friendly with Whitelaw since childhood, criticised the Home Secretary for protecting judges of his own class at the expense of granting a free pardon for *common* Cooper and McMahon, who were convicted in 1970 of the 1969 murder of Reginald Stevens. Five times in the 1970s successive home secretaries referred the case, only for senior judges to dismiss the appeals. Ludovic Kennedy published his damning exposé,[28] and three weeks later Whitelaw issued a special order for the release of the two men. Whitelaw did not, however, quash their convictions, which was not done until 2003 when the men were dead and the judges had retired or died. Whitelaw's record as Home Secretary made headlines again in 2014 claiming that he had ordered police to scrap an enquiry into a VIP child sex abuse ring.[29]

An interpretation of what Whitelaw had meant by saying that 'they' had had problems with Runcie at the beginning, was that Runcie had taken a while to 'go native' and abandon the Christian principle of treating everyone in the way he would like himself to be treated. As Archbishop he had of course re-espoused the principle, and the discomfiture he displayed to Mantle on hearing that Alldred had been interviewed was that he could be revealed as having run with the fox and hunted with the hounds.

No survey of the attitudes and behaviour of guards' officers in the Second World War is known to this author, but there are anecdotes of ordinary soldiers using the expression, 'fucking guards officers', and others knowing what was meant by it. The Buffs when arrested by Lt Col Bill Smith of 4 CG on a trumped up charge outside Kervenheim used the phrase, as surely did the driver in September 1945 when Stephen Spender visited a Transport Officer to get a reliable car:

> I left my driver in a waiting room while I talked with the officer. He was sympathetic and asked many questions about the Humber. I said: "My driver is in the next room, perhaps you would like to speak with him?" Quite a new expression came on the Transport Officer's face, and he said "yes," tersely. The driver came in and the officer addressed him abruptly: "Are you this officer's driver?" "Yes, sir". "Well, if we're going to do anything about it, for a start it might be helpful if you stood to attention in my office". "Yes, sir." The officer got very little information out of my driver who suddenly seemed quite stupid, and who, while standing all the while at attention, nevertheless kept looking sideways past me out of the window, and blowing slightly out of the corner of his mouth, with a longing expression in his eyes as though he wanted to fly out of the window. Finally the officer rang up a Colonel to whom he spoke in quite a new voice, different from the one he used with me, and different from that he used with the driver. He suggested to the Colonel that he should ring up the garage and ask them to get a move on. When we left the office, my driver exploded: "A Guards' Officer! A Guards' Officer! The bloody Guards. If you hadn't been there, I'd have told him what I thought of him, sir." I said I was glad he had said nothing, as it would have been awkward for me to have to take sides against him. "It isn't that," he said. "It is that if I'd been alone with him, there wouldn't have been a witness. I could have said exactly what I liked, and he'd never have been able to prove it. The [fucking] Guards' Officers!"[30]

28 L Kennedy. *Wicked Beyond Belief: The Luton Murder Case* (London: Granada, 1980).
29 Paul Calahan and Peter Henn. *Mail on Sunday*, 7 December 2014.
30 Stephen Spender. *European Witness* (London: Hamish Hamilton, 1946), p. 170.

Frankie Chamberlain, the elegant wife of the 2ic the Royal Lincolnshire Regiment, expressed a view of the Guards that would have been held in the county regiments, and recalls Elizabeth Bennett's condemnation of D'Arcy in *Pride and Prejudice*:

> I didn't meet up with the Guards until after the War in Berlin [where Dunbar was later GOC]. Certainly they considered themselves superior beings. As I was brought up to believe that had one any standing in life one should never be condescending or patronizing, my thoughts were that it was a pity the Guards did not know how to behave and what a bad advertisement they were for GB. So perhaps it was the Guards who were the peasants and not the Lincolns.[31]

It has often been said that the morals of the aristocracy and the working class were similarly unconstrained in comparison with the strait-laced middle class who upheld the conventions and 'knew how to behave'. However, many Guards' officers held to a view that social and military order and effectiveness relied on the maintenance of an unbridgeable distance between leaders and led, which would be undermined by any form of familiarity. This was the polar opposite of the highly effective Anzacs and Canadians, and of the Fallschirmjäger with their belief in the Volksgemeinschaft that grew out of Hitler's experience of the First World War Frontgemeinschaft. This demanded that civilian class distinctions be left at the barrack gate, and that every man in the Wehrmacht was a Kamerad of equal value and equally obliged to achieve victory for the German race. Fallschirmjäger POWs in Britain could not believe that British automotive workers were on strike over pay during Operation *Market Garden*, and that dockers struck after the war, requiring these same POWs to be used to unload food from strike-bound ships. "These dockers were striking against their own people", one ex-POW explained in disbelief to this author.

Each Battalion had a complement of 49 Churchill tanks, of which four were at Battalion HQ and 15 in each of the three squadrons. Two Churchills per Squadron in HQ Troop were the Mk V with a 95 mm howitzer for blowing holes in bunkers, demolishing houses and strong points and firing on 88s from behind farm buildings, as at Winnekendonk. Most Churchills, 64% of them in 6 GAB – see the following table – were the Mk IV with a cast turret with either a 6-pdr firing AP including DSAP, or a 75-mm firing HE with such a sensitive fuse that even brushing a twig would explode it, and a few mediocre AP rounds for knocking holes in buildings to allow the HE to penetrate inside. If you saw a Panther, according to Mark Fearfield, you didn't fire your 75 mm in case you drew its attention to yourself. A couple of Churchill Mk IIIs could still be found with the superior turret made of steel plate and the 6pdr gun firing APCBC and DSAP, which was good enough to destroy a Panther. It was one of these two tanks that Sgt Alldred had probably acquired and referred to when telling his family that his tank was different from the others. Technically and confusingly, but to be accurate, the MK IX is included in the listing; this was the MK VI, while others say it was the MkIII/IV, fitted with additional hull armour to bring it up to MK VII standard. There is apparently no evidence that any were built.[32]

31 Frankie Chamberlain in a letter in May 1997.
32 http://en.wikipedia.org/wiki/Churchill_tank

Inventory of Churchills in 6 Guards Tank Brigade on January 21, 1945[33]

Mk	Frontal armour inch	Turret	Armament		Produced	On charge 21/1/45
			Turret	Hull		
I	4	Cast	2pdr. Besa	3 in how	1941	0
II	4	Cast	2pdr. Besa	Besa	1942	0
IICS	4	Cast	3 inch how. Besa	2pdr	1942	0
III	4	Welded	6pdr. Besa	Besa	1942-3	2
III	4	Welded	75 mm. Besa	Besa	1943	1
IV	4	Cast	6pdr. Besa	Besa	1942-3	51
IV	4	Cast	75 mm. Besa	Besa	1943	71
V	4	Cast	95 mm how. Besa	Besa	1943	22
VI	4	Cast	6pdr. Besa	Besa	1943	1
VI	4	Cast	75 mm. Besa	Besa	1943	30
VII	6	Cast/steel top	75 mm. Besa	Besa	1943-5	13
VIII	6	Cast/steel top	95 mm how. Besa	Besa	1943-5	0
IX	6	Cast/steel top	75 mm.Besa	Besa	1944	0
Total						191

The Churchill brigades were Army troops allocated to the corps commander for supporting the infantry divisional spearheads. Their job was to breach the German lines so an armoured division could exploit. In the case of *Heather* that task fell to GAD. A tank brigade normally supported an infantry division, with a battalion allocated to an infantry brigade, a squadron to an infantry battalion and a troop to an infantry company. If enemy armour intervened, then the tanks would fight together as conventional squadrons.[34]

At Winnekendonk RF Sqn, 3 SG supported 2 Lincolns. RF Squadron comprised HQ and four troops. The Squadron was commanded by Major Alan Cathcart who was respected but not, it was said, particularly loved. Troops were led by subalterns and the 3 Churchills were commanded by the Troop Leader, the Troop Sergeant and the Troop Corporal. Troops were commanded by Alasdair Gordon (1Tp), Robert Runcie (2 Tp), John MacDonald-Buchanan (3 Tp), and Archie Fletcher (4 Tp).

The drill, practised in the UK and refined in France and the Low Countries, was to advance with each troop behind an infantry rifle company with HQ Troop in the middle. Because of losses, some troop commanders were recent replacements such as Mark Fearfield of LF Sqn, who had never trained formally in tank-infantry co-operation.[35]

Communication between tanks within the troop was good up to 300 metres by means of the 19 Set. The wild card for the tanks was always the choice of infantry. The Guards felt they experienced difficulty working properly with those with whom they had only a passing acquaintance. Strangely they never once supported guardsmen. Some divisions were not impressive, including the 51 BID, the 43 BID and their old friends the 15 BID itself which was mediocre towards the end, in the opinion of one troop commander, having taken dreadful losses.[36] Others they met were impressive,

33 TNA: 21 Army Group return.
34 Bryan Perrett. *The Churchill Tank* (London: Osprey, 1980).
35 Mark Fearfield in conversation.
36 The identity of the informant is in this author's notes.

such as 3 BID, 6 Airborne Division and 17 US Airborne Division, whose relaxed air of effortless superiority appealed especially to guardsmen.

Like the Typhoons of 2 TAF, RF's Churchills were technically 'in support' of the Lincolns. Fearfield's opinion:

> An awful lot of heat was generated about the command of tank-infantry battles. The heat was generally at the senior and bn commander level and was never a problem at the junior level. The inf often thought and spoke of tanks being under command but tanks would never accept that status since only they knew what a tank could or could not do.[37]

Many sources disagreed with Fearfield. One example will suffice; 'The tanks would remain under infantry control for the duration of the operation'.[38] Fearfield's opinion, however did reflect 6 GAB's practice as proved by the refusal of 4 CG to fight at night at Kervenheim. The decision seems to have been made by the Squadron Commander who had carte blanche. Holdsworth-Hunt refused Berkeley's wish to attack at night on 28 February, but Cathcart willingly stayed with Firbank in Winnekendonk overnight on 2 March, while Milbank refused to stay the night of 3 March with the KSLI. Very different was the view in Italy in 25 ATB, who were trained, 'to put the infantry on to the objective with the minimum of [infantry] casualties and to remain there until they [the infantry] feel safe to release you'.[39]

Communication between tanks and infantry was limited. The telephone on the back of the tank hardly ever worked, and Fearfield remembered many occasions when an infantryman would be trying to work it at the back whilst the tank commander stared fixedly ahead until the infantryman climbed up and spoke to him, exposing himself to sniper fire. At the Brigade conference on 8 March 1945, 3 SG made the comment that, 'No really good way exists by which inf can indicate targets to tks, and Brigadier Renny 'recognised' this.[40] No one was, it appears, responsible for finding a solution to this grave operational weakness that, for example obliged Darby Hart to leave his position in Kervenheim and pass a tank he could not communicate with, to go down the dangerous Üdemer Strasse to tell a tank commander on the corner to send a message to the first tank. Of course had Darby possessed a 38 set he could have communicated with the TC in safety.

At Winnekendonk a Squadron of tanks commanded by a Major operated 'in support' of an infantry Battalion commanded by a Lt-Colonel, with each obeying the same orders issued by two Brigadiers: Renny of 9 BIB and Greenacre of 6 GAB. As Montgomery had decreed back in 1942, command on the battlefield was being jointly exercised, and where command is joint there is no responsibility. In the event of disagreement, Maj Cathcart, although junior to Lt Col Firbank, could refuse what Firbank wanted and vice versa. The procedure for resolving a theoretical dispute entailed an appeal up the chain of command to the GOC 3 BID, Whistler, theoretically commanding everybody on the battlefield that evening. It was theoretical because it was never tested, and theoretical because Whistler was not part of the system for approving citations for 6 GAB's medals and therefore not part of 6 GAB's hierarchy of command. As far as this author knows, Whistler was never asked to rule on anything, even the traumatic dispute in front of Kervenheim on 28 February over a night attack, when 4 CG declared they were off to laager until the next morning, and Matthews stalled Berkeley who accepted the Guards' fait accompli.

37 In conversation with this author.
38 Bryan Perrett, *The Churchill.*
39 Montgomery, *Churchill Tank,* p. 145.
40 The notes of this conference are appended.

At Winnekendonk, Cathcart kept his HQ Troop close to Firbank's Tac HQ. When the 88s and StuGs disrupted the attack both went into the shelter of Brönkshof and conferred. With the infantry pressing on disastrously without tanks on the right, and leading the tanks under heavy pressure on the left, the job of looking after the defenders' guns could only be Cathcart's responsibility given that artillery links were destroyed and there were no Typhoons. Without hesitation Cathcart ordered his 95 mm Churchills to shell the 88s and ordered Runcie to destroy the StuGs. That was what Cathcart told this author, but Charles Farrell disputed whether the 95 mms were ever fired under any circumstances. Sgt Jim Alldred told his family that he acted instinctively and without his troop leader and went 88 hunting with the Tp Cpl, obviously believing he already had his orders from Cathcart to act as cover for the troop that had been destroyed.

The gap between officers and men, which is large in any disciplined army, was increased in the British case by the social gap between the classes, and to exaggerated lengths in the case of the Guards. The give-away was the accent. Nowhere was this difference greater than in Britain and particularly in the Guards, although it was leavened sometimes by *noblesse oblige* and good manners when the cost was reasonable. Mark Fearfield denied class was ever a problem:

> Before the war a guardsman who was asked if he didn't feel resentment that officers went shooting on grouse moors [during the weekend] whilst he stayed cleaning up the barracks, said that in the war to come the officers would be killed first so they deserved every pleasure they could get.[41]

This 'contract' came back to haunt the guards' officers who could not renege or revoke it, but always led their troops – as it did the infantry officers, but they had never left their men at weekends. Those such as Runcie, who had never lived a life that included fun weekends on grouse moors, failed to understand the contract, as he demonstrated by refusing to leave cover at Winnekendonk, but Sgt Alldred understood and acted without Runcie, perhaps instinctively understanding the reasons for Runcie's hesitation. It was obvious to everyone, and in Italy became the practice because there were no Guards in Churchill tanks there, that in the interests of effectiveness the Troop Corporal, who was the junior tank commander and by implication the most expendable in a Mk IV-75 mm, should lead the troop into action so that when the troop was fired on he would take the hit and give the Tp Cdr time to observe and respond, and the Tp Sergeant with the potent 6pdr gun firing sabot in the cover/oversight role time to find and fix the problem. However, troops in 3 SG were always led by the subalterns, in this author's assessment.

Leading was doubly dangerous because not only was the lead tank inevitably the first hit by concealed StuG or 88, but the German infantry always picked off the officers because of a well-known weakness of the British Army that when the officer was killed his troops became defensive. By leading, the TC was offering his head on a platter and facilitating the defenders' job. Michael Harrison led 1 Sqn, 4 CG across the Mühlen Fleuth at Endtschenhof on 28 February 1945. He was sniped through the head and his tank hit by AP. His death stopped the advance on that flank for the entire day with dire consequences to the Norfolks, as recounted in Chapter 3.

It is possible that the Scots Guards' custom of the subaltern always leading was peculiar to them. A Troop Commander in 4 CG denied that in his unit the Troop Leader always led:

> As for the Troop Leader always being the leading tank, in our battalion we were encouraged to rotate troop leadership between the Troop Leader and the Troop Corporal, which was a fairer distribution of risk. Inevitably however the Troop Leader spent more time in the lead.

41 Mark Fearfield in conversation.

> The Troop Sergeant's tank was always slightly to the rear in an anti-tank rôle. His tank was usually a Mk IV with a 6 pounder gun firing special SABO [sic] armour piercing shells.[42]

There is a documented case in a contemporary letter sent home by a Guards officer,[43] of a subaltern reporting his troop sergeant and troop corporal in *Heather* to his Squadron Commander for their repeated hanging back due to 'mechanical difficulties'. In both German and Russian armies the offenders would have been court-martialled and shot or placed in a penal battalion to lead the next assault. The British Army lacked the stomach for that, although had it become known the CO might have been replaced. Bill Smith's extreme reaction in failing to get the facts and acting immediately to put the Crocodile crew under arrest for 'motoring out of battle' at Kervenheim on 1 March, showed not only prejudice but also how close his command was to getting out of hand at Kervenheim. Smith's behaviour was treated with contempt by the Buffs, who saw it as confirmation of general attitudes about the Guards, and contempt is destructive of morale. The sergeants were older and had families when war, as everyone throughout the ages has known, was a young man's occupation paid for disproportionately by the subalterns. However, hotheaded subalterns could get everyone killed, and Sgt Jim Alldred had to rein in Lt Hector Laing on occasion, advising him to stop and rest, and leave chasing Germans to the morrow. Laing would accept this advice knowing that the older man talked sense.[44] Every officer knew that when NCOs hung back the battalion was finished as a fighting unit since vital trust was destroyed when people only went through the motions. This was one more piece of evidence that parts of 6 GAB were teetering on the edge in these battles. The signs were everywhere that they required a rest, and the letter home mentioned above said this had been promised and was long overdue. Luckily for the Brigade, RF 3 SG was supporting the outstanding 2 Lincolns on 2 March to produce the breakthrough at Winnekendonk. Their snatching victory from the jaws of defeat gave the whole Brigade a new lease on life and uplifted morale, which they displayed six weeks later at Uelzen after a long rest.

6 GAB had been almost continuously in the line for nearly three weeks before supporting *Heather*. Their stress was visible to the fresh infantry. One Norfolk officer outside Kervenheim recalled being briefed by a Coldstreamer with an uncontrollable twitch who appeared to be having a nervous breakdown.[45] Few tanks crossed the Start Line, and two that did bogged in the wet fields and not far from a StuG bogged near Murmannshof. There was little tank support for the initial assault by the Norfolks on that day, and on the previous afternoon the Coldstream Guards had vetoed the suggested night attack. The Warwicks were not impressed by the support they received from 4 CG on the right flank after Harrison was killed, and that flank remained open all day. On the other hand, Coldstreamer support for the KSLI was magnificent and saved the day by eliminating Boemshof and securing the left flank. Tom Read for the KSLI had nothing but praise for Alec Foucard and his troop, while Alexis Melikoff was sent alone with the Norfolks into the built-up area where he was wounded in the head but stayed in action. The Grenadiers at Yorkshire Bridge appeared cautious and the FOO, John Ford, never understood why his relatively unprotected Sherman should have been the only tank in the bridgehead. However, the Grenadiers supporting S Lancs in the woods on 27 February paid heavily for their activism and were admired by the infantry. LF 3 SG at Winnekendonk were impressive beyond praise and had been thrustingly active three days earlier when Runcie's troop tried to seize the bridge at Endtschenhof, in spite of Dunbar's assessment of Renny's orders as foolhardy. What all this showed was that the

42 Alexis Napier (né Prince Melikoff) by e-mail on 29 September 2013.
43 This author was denied permission by the writer of the letters to quote them.
44 Retailed by Andrew Alldred.
45 Permission to quote was denied.

magnificent 6 GAB was being taxed to the limit in these battles, being called on to dredge up its last ounces of finite strength and courage. They found enough collectively to win through in conditions where other units had given up the unequal struggle, as the Canadian infantry on their left flank were discovering to their cost from lack of tank support in the Hochwald.

The Churchill was a fine tank yet scarcely adequate for its breakthrough rôle. Its 4 in frontal armour was less than that of the Tiger at 4.7 in. It could resist the 50 mm Pak but was easily penetrated by the 88. What was needed to provide frontal immunity from this frightening weapon, which had destroyed its first tank in Spain in 1936, was an additional thickness of 6 inches of preferably angled plate for a total of 10 in. The Churchill VII had 6 in, still not enough and no one knows whether or how many Mk VIIs were in use by 3 SG, who did not appreciate its extra armour thickness. MkVIIs were issued only as replacements for worn-out or destroyed tanks.

Operating any tank was a team skill acquired only through long experience:

> The skill of the driver, and indeed of all those men in the crew, was remarkable: the operator struggling to keep the wireless on net and the guns loaded: the gunner with eyes always at the telescope however much the turret revolved and crashed around him; the hot stoppages in the machine guns; the commander with his head only above his hatches, not quite standing, not quite sitting; always the wireless pounding at his ear drums.[46]

There is no description of fighting one of the Scots Guards' Churchills in the sodden landscape between the Rivers Maas and Rhine, where driving any vehicle, and especially a tank, in deep mud requires expertise. A novice driver in very muddy conditions can start a tank in first gear, but as soon as he depresses the clutch to change up and match the walking speed of the infantry, the mud-drag on the tracks will stop the vehicle dead. The Churchill's engine produced only 350 hp when at least 600 hp was required for its 40 tons. With such power that even Russian tanks of similar weight enjoyed, it could have been started in really heavy going from second gear as an agricultural tractor is designed to do. At its rated engine speed of 2,200 rpm, first gear in the Churchill gave a top speed of 1½ mph and was too slow to keep up with infantry moving between 2 and 3 mph when crossing dangerous ground. Second gear with a top speed of 4½ mph was needed. The Churchill lacked synchromesh and to change up in thick mud required a racing gear-change instantly matching engine and gearbox shaft speeds. If speeds were not identical the gears would crash and even chip and refuse to engage. In any case the tank would stop. The German StuG had a higher power to weight ratio and a pre-selector gearbox that did the driver's work for him. In all modern vehicles and even between first and second gears on a Second World War Jeep, synchromesh cones are fitted to guide the gears into mesh and make adjustment for any differences in speed. The problems of driving a 41-ton tank through a 4-speed crash gearbox with a nominal 350-BHP engine are described optimistically, in the handbook:

> Start off in second gear. First gear should be used only for obstacle crossing, freak hills, towing or where an extremely low speed or small turning circle is required. The first gear reduction is more than one hundred to one, giving a maximum speed of under 2 mph. Third gear can be used for starting on a down grade on a road, or in similar favourable conditions. As the vehicle is fitted with a crash gearbox, a certain amount of skill is necessary to achieve quiet changes, but this will be acquired fairly easily after a little practice. A quick change is essential, due to the high rolling resistance of the vehicle. If the operation is not carried out quickly, particularly on grass or heavy going, the vehicle may have time to rest while the change is being

46 Erskine, *Scots Guards*.

> made. It is therefore necessary to learn to use the clutch stop correctly when changing up. The gear ratio steps are such that it is unwise to change up until road conditions have eased sufficiently for the engine to pull in the higher gear. If you can, choose a moment when the ground conditions are favourable. Keep the engine revolutions well up before changing, and never steer while making the change, or immediately after making it. Always wait until the engine revolutions have risen again. A very rapid change of the racing type can be made once the driver has mastered the amount of travel and pressure necessary on the clutch pedal to ensure the correct amount of clutch stop. The actions of moving the lever out of gear and depressing the clutch pedal should be synchronised as nearly as possible. If the clutch is depressed fully before the gear is disengaged, the gear will be nipped. The top gear performance is exceptionally good for this type of vehicle, but top gear should not be used for heavy going or for turns on grass. With the double declutching method it is possible to effect a very rapid and silent change down, and the intermediate gears give more power for turning on heavy ground.[47]

The 'going' between Goch and Winnekendonk was appalling. The enemy anti-tank gunfire at Kervenheim and Winnekendonk was damaging. Anxiety reached fever pitch in the tanks. Cathcart complained that the Pipe-Major's tank containing the Forward Observation Officer (FOO) failed to keep in cover and was knocked out. It can be speculated that driving in such conditions was so difficult that the driver of the FOO tank, who was usually Whitelaw's driver and may have had limited experience of extreme conditions, did not want to stop and lose his second gear advantage which he had achieved by starting on hard going in a farmyard. He therefore may have driven on with the troop ahead. We will never know, but those who have been in battle say that often just such a factor could explain otherwise incomprehensible behaviour.

After welding track plates to hull and turret and learning to remove their steel helmets to give themselves better hearing and an extra millisecond of reaction time, the TCs overcame their fear of explosive tank fires after Caumont and gained confidence in the Churchill. The crews came to like and respect their vehicle. The hard suspension had built-in redundancy so that many of the 11 wheels on either side could be shot off without stopping the tank, although it then banged, lurched and dragged to one side, described as 'limping'.

The author John Foley in another unit described how the Churchill often surprised them, and similar episodes must have occurred with 6 GTB:

> But the most gratifying episode to happen during the first few days of the advance was just outside the village of Nieuwmoer. We heard a sudden fusillade of AP shells from the centre of the village and heard Ian on the air saying he was being fired on by an SP gun sitting on the usual cross-roads. He fired back and took some evasive action…And that night in harbour we gathered round Ian's tank and pointed in awe to seven dents in the front of his Churchill, where the enemy shots had failed to penetrate. "See?" I said to McGinty. "We can keep them out too". Until that moment I don't think he had really believed my profound statement that some British tanks were better in some respects than some German tanks…But he gingerly fingered the gashes on the front of Ian's tank, and went away to polish his telescope.[48]

Foley described a typical attack with Scottish infantry that all Guards TCs would recognise:

47 Tank Museum. *Churchill Tank: Vehicle History & Specification* (London: HMSO, 1983).
48 Foley, *Mailed Fist*, p. 120.

> I remember we left the shelter of some buildings, firing our little smoke mortar and thickening it up with smoke grenades hurled from the turret. From time to time I kept an eye on the infantry, but they were plugging doggedly forward like plough-horses homeward plodding their weary way. The enemy reacted with some heavy mortaring. Craters appeared as if by magic, and the din of exploding mortars drowned the noise of our own 25-pdr creeping barrage. Here and there infantrymen were folding up like puppets suddenly released from their strings, while others took cover in ditches and shell-holes. These things were bursting quite close to us as we motored slowly along behind the infantry, but it somehow never occurred to me that one of them could land on us. But it could, and did. Quite suddenly there came a brief flash of orange flame from the front plate of the tank, and a tremendous explosion almost split my eardrums. I ducked down in the turret to find the *Avenger* a thick cloud of dust and smoke. "Everyone all right?" I said over the IC. "What was it, sir?" said Pickford. "Mortar bomb", I replied briefly. "And it's blown every bit of dust out of every crack in the tank". But apart from the thick dust which now coated everything inside the tank, we seemed all right. I gave the Infantry Company Commander a thumbs up sign, and he nodded.[49]

Brigade History.[50] 6 GAB contained about 3,400 men of all ranks.

30 BIB
24 April 1940. Formed in UK under Brig C. Nicholson with 2 KRRC, 1 RB
22 May 1940. Landed in Calais with 3 R Tks under command
25 May 1940. Captured in Calais

30 Independent Infantry (Guards) Brigade
17 October 1940. Reformed under Brig A.H.S. Adair with 4 GG, 4 CG, 3 SG
15 September 1941. Redesignated 6 GAB

6 GAB
21 September 1942. Brig G.L. Verney took command
15 January 1943. Redesignated 6 GTB

6 GTB
3 August 1944. Brig Sir W. Barttelot took command and was killed on 18 August 1944
18 August 1944. Brig W.D.C. Greenacre, DSO, MVO took command
2 February 1945. Redesignated 6 GAB

6 GAB
17 June 1945. Redesignated 6 Guards Brigade

6 GB
31 August 1945. Dissolved

49 Op. Cit., p.127
50 HF Joslen. *Orders of Battle: Volume 1* (London: HMSO, 1960).

Commanders during Operation *Heather*

	4 Grenadier Guards	4 Coldstream Guards	3 Scots Guards	No. Churchills
CO	The Lord Tryon	AWA Smith	CIH Dunbar	4
2ic	CMF Deakin	AC Pilkington	WSI Whitelaw	
1 Sqn/ RF	RH Heywood-Lonsdale	JH Hamilton-Stubber	Earl Cathcart	15
2 Sqn/ LF	GE Pike	MV Milbank	JP Mann	15
3 Sqn/ S Sqn	IG Crosthwaite	F Holdsworth-Hunt	C O'M Farrell	15
Total Bn				49
Total Bde				147

Battalions and Squadrons were paired with the Infantry

4 Grenadier Guards	8 BIB	4 Coldstream Guards	185 BIB	3 Scots Guards	9 BIB
1 Sqn	2 E. Yorks	1 Sqn	2 Warwicks	Right Flank	2 Lincolns
2 Sqn	1 Suffolks	2 Sqn	2 KSLI	Left Flank	1 KOSB
3 Sqn	1 S. Lancs	3 Sqn	1 R Norfolks	S Sqn	2 RUR

In *Heather*, Churchills fought against StuG IIIs and IVs. The StuG III was adapted in 1936 by Daimler-Benz from its own Mk III tank designed in 1935 to the Lutz/Guderian cruiser rôle of breakthrough and exploitation. The turret with its 50 mm gun was removed and replaced with a fixed weapon. In the Ausführung G of 1945, this was the 75 mm L48 high velocity gun. Glacis thickness was increased from 50 mm to 80 mm (3¼ inch). The positions of loader and radio operator were combined, reducing the crew to 4. The others were commander, gunner and driver. The StuG was well designed and built. It had an excellent power to weight ratio with good acceleration, which is more valuable in war than speed. It possessed an agile and sophisticated preselector 10-speed gearbox, and the vehicle was front sprocket drive. But the flotation of the StuG, but not that of the MkIV Jg Pz, was inferior to those of the Churchill. Employed in the marshy woods there would have been a risk of bogging and in retreat no possibility of its retrieval. In addition, the limited-traverse gun was a liability in such terrain. To bring its gun to bear a StuG had to swing round quickly and accurately to face within 10 degrees of the enemy. When in ambush this was rarely a problem, but in difficult going in deep muddy ruts with tree stumps and logs, aligning the gun quickly was difficult and even impossible without manoeuvring. The long, overhanging gun protruded well forward of the vehicle where it caught in trees and undergrowth with serious risk of damage to its trunnions, as the StuG lurched among the trees. StuGs therefore stuck to the roads, and both avoided the woods, being surprised when Churchills appeared from them.

The 88 mm PAK L 71 had a muzzle velocity of 3,340 ft/sec. At 500 yards it could penetrate 187 mm of armour sloped at 30° and could easily overpower the Churchill. The IS-2 of 1944 with 120 mm sloped at 60° was the first tank that could hope to resist the 88 mm at battlefield ranges. All tanks however, including the IS-2, were vulnerable to the Panzerfaust that could penetrate 200 mm but only at a maximum of 100 yards. Against the Churchill, and especially against the flame-throwing version called Crocodile, the Germans were beginning to field at this time the Jagdpanzer IV with the extra long 75 mm as fitted in the Panther. These did not reach PzJgAbt 33 until it had retreated over the Rhine.

The Main AFVs used in Operation *Heather* and *Blockbuster*, with IS-2 for Comparison

(p) = petrol (d) = diesel	StuG III ausf G Sd.Kfz.142/2	Jagdpanzer IV Sd.Kfz.162/1	Churchill IV/VII	Sherman M4A4 Firefly	IS-2
Crew	4	4	5	5	4
Engine (petrol) (diesel)	300 hp(p)	300(p)	350 hp(p)	425 hp(p)	550 hp(d)
Speed mph/kph	25/40	25/40	14.0/22	20/32	22/35
Weight tons	24	26	38.5/40	31	47
Ground clearance	1 ft 3 in (39 cm)	1 ft 4 in (40 cm)	1 ft 8 in	1 ft 5 in	1 ft 6 in
Height	6 ft 4 in (215 cm)	6 ft 1 in (185 cm)	8 ft 2 in	8 ft 7 in	8 ft 11 in
Width	9 ft 8 in (296 cm)	10 ft 5 in (318 cm)	9 ft 2 in	8 ft 7 in	10 ft 6 in
Track width	16 in (40 cm)	16 in (40 cm)	22 in	16.5 in	27.6 in
Ground Pressure on road at bogging point lb./in^2 (kg/cm^2)	14.8/1.04 9.7/0.68	12.8/0.90 9.1/0.64	13.9/0.98 8.6 /0.60	13.2/0.93 9.4/0.66	10.3/0.72 7.5/0.53
Track area % of hull area	26%		41%	31%	
Step	24 in	23 in	43 in	31 in	31 in
Trench crossing	7 ft 6 in	8 ft 6 in	10 ft	7 ft 6 in	9 ft 10 in
Length less gun with gun	18 ft 0 in 21 ft 9 in	19 ft 9 in 28 ft 3 in	25 ft 2 in 25 ft 2 in	20 ft 6 in 24 ft 7 in	 32 ft 6 in
Gun standard high velocity option	75 mm L48 K40	75 mm L48 K40	75 mm L40 6pdr	75 mm L40 17pdr	122 mm L43
Muzzle velocity std ft/sec high velocity/APDS	2,460	2,460	2,050 3,550/4,000	2,050 2,900/3,950	2,562
Armour with 30° slope penetrated @ 500 yds	96 mm	96 mm	68 mm	68 mm	200 mm +
Armour side	30 mm	30 mm	95 mm	51 mm	90 mm
Armour frontal mm/slope	80/45°	80/45°	102/152/0°	76/47°	120 /60°

A tank bogs when its belly contacts the ground, unweighting the tracks, which then spin without purchase. Once this happens, great force is required to break the suction between the wet ground and the bottom plate. The tank sinks when its ground pressure exceeds the load capacity of the soil, which in turn depends on soil type but, more importantly, on the amount of moisture it contains. The ground water in the area between the Rhine and Maas was often only inches below the surface, and in these conditions the countryside turned into a bog as soon as shelling disturbed the dryer topsoil crust with its plant life. Today, with the great rivers back between their banks, the water level of the flooded gravel quarries in Gravendonk indicate the height of the ground water, which in 1945 was significantly higher.

Tank flotation is a matter of ground pressure and can be improved only by lightening the tank or increasing its track area. Shermans achieved this in the field by adding track-extenders called grousers or 'duckbills', which were not practicable on Churchills and unavailable on StuGs.

The reasons why Shermans bogged down all over the Hochwald battlefield leaving the infantry unsupported, and why the StuGs kept to the roads while the Churchills got through with the infantry, were to be found in the differing combinations of armour, flotation and cross-country agility. The lightly armoured and tall Shermans were vulnerable to most German anti-tank guns and the crews rushed from cover to cover to avoid being hit. They therefore ran quickly into soft ground and bogged before the driver had time to react. The Churchills, on the other hand, lumbered along protected by their thick armour from anything except the bigger guns. When entering a soft spot and feeling the tank sinking, they had time to stop, reverse and try another route. In Weyen, Foucard dismounted and led his troop, testing the ground to avoid soft areas. Provided the ground held them, they could cross ditches up to 10 feet wide compared with 7 feet 6 inches for StuG and Sherman, and they could crawl out of deep holes and over steep banks. They made haste slowly.

The historian of 11 BAD summed up its cruiser tanks; 'Except as morale-stiffeners for the infantry, the tanks had proved practically useless, although they had struggled on most determinedly.'[51] The Canadian Armoured Divisions and Armoured Brigades in the Hochwald used the M4A4 Sherman. It was designed for the fast cruiser rôle of exploitation, and employed *infra dignitatem* to support the infantry.

6 GAB fought in the Churchill tank which, it was said, because of its wide tracks, was the only armoured vehicle capable of movement in the Reichswald fighting.[52] This is a misunderstanding. The ground pressure of the heavily armoured Churchill was 14 lb per square inch and higher than the 13.2 lb/in^2 of the lighter Sherman. Even when the tank had sunk into the ground and was at the point of getting bogged, the ground pressure of the Churchill at 8.6 lb/in^2 was only marginally better than that of the Sherman at 9.4 lb/in^2.

A Sherman had similar flotation to a Churchill, but all the records refer to Shermans becoming bogged in the Hochwald. On 28 February 1945 Lt-Col Rowan Coleman of the Lincoln and Welland Regiment in the Hochwald Gap, remembered about the Shermans:

> every tank was stuck. You couldn't even dig them out. The only tracked vehicle which could run properly was the old (Bren) gun carrier which the pioneer platoon had resurrected and put together again. It was light.[53]

The Churchill bogged less frequently than the Sherman, although bog it did in these conditions, simply because of the way it was operated by crews who felt more secure behind its thicker armour and were more committed to infantry support. The Churchill was more forgiving and gave the crew greater and more advanced warning of its intentions. The Churchill's bottom plate stood 1 ft 8 inches above the ground, which was higher than the Sherman's 1 ft 5 in. Like all tanks when it sank the Churchill's ground pressure decreased as more track came into contact with the ground. Churchill track length in contact with the ground increased from 12'3" to 19'4" when bottoming, reducing the ground pressure by a significant 38%, from 14 lb/in^2 down to 8.6 lb/in^2. The crew felt the tank sinking and could judge whether they could pass through the soft spot without bottoming, or whether they had to stop and reverse out before it bottomed. The Sherman's ground pressure also decreased but by the lesser amount of 29%. However it had only 1 ft 5 in to sink before it bogged. With more power at 425-hp than the Churchill's 350-hp, and being 9 tons lighter, the temptation of the more vulnerable and worried crews was to move the Sherman quickly and to keep moving in search of cover. It often bogged before the crew realised the danger and could prevent it.

In nearly all respects the Churchill was the better tank than the Sherman for the important task of protecting the advancing infantry and its own crew. It was able to limp along when over half of its eleven bogies had been shot off on one side, while the loss of any of the three bogies on one side of a Sherman was immobilising. It was able to cross trenches 10 ft wide while the Sherman could manage only 7 ft 6 in, and climb out of bigger holes and mount a higher step. This was because the

51 Anon, *Taurus Pursuant.*
52 Whitaker, *Rhineland.*
53 Hayes, *The Lincs.*

Churchill's front idler was mounted high on horns while the Sherman's driven front wheels were much lower down. It followed, however, that the driver of the Sherman had a better forward view than the Churchill's driver who looked out between the two horns.

The Churchill was better armoured than the Sherman with 102 mm on the MkIV and 152 mm of frontal armour on the the MKVII with 50 to 75-mm on the Sherman, which was however sloped. The Churchill could resist bigger shot than the Sherman, and was less likely to burn and explode when penetrated. The Sherman had a dreadful reputation, and its crews were 'very concerned with self-preservation'.[54]

There is no doubt that this concern and the doctrine of 'in support' affected the tactical deployment of Shermans in the Hochwald Gap. 'The tanks got up and quickly moved away', is the title of a cartoon by Private McKay of the Lincoln and Welland Regiment drawn in March 1945 in the Hochwald when he was left, as always, to fend for himself. It typified the uneasy relationship between infantry and armour and vitiated their joint effectiveness, and was very different with 6 GAB.

The Churchill, however, was inadequate to the tasks it was given and required major upgrading. It needed face-hardened, sloped frontal armour, since by the cosine law a 100 mm plate angled at 60° gives the same protection as a vertical 200 mm plate – a trick known to Christie in the 1930's and adopted by the Russians and later by the Germans with Panther. It also needed an engine of 600 hp at least, like the Meteor aero engine installed in the Cromwell and Comet; reduced ground pressure of 10 lb/in^2 by increasing track width from 1 ft 10 in to 2 ft 4 in as used on the IS-2. A bigger gun, 76.2 mm or even 105 mm, with stabilisation would have been an advantage, but armour upgrade was infinitely more important than the gun. It also required better communications with the infantry so that the crew could be in continuous contact with platoon commanders, and better night-fighting capability based either on the German infra-red technology, known since 1934, or through image intensification by advancing the key discovery made in 1956 of bialkali antimonide photocathodes. These would have been invented and developed if a fraction of the money spent on the RAF had been devoted to improving the infantry's capabilities, and it was, after all, infantry-based all-arms that won wars.

54 Whitaker, *Rhineland.*

79 BRITISH ARMOURED DIVISION (79 BAD)

79 BAD on 1 March 1945[55]

	1 Assault Brigade RE	**30 BAB**	**31 BAB**	**33 BAB**	**HQ, RASC, RAMC, RAOC, REME**	**79 BAD**
OCs	P. Sydenham	N.W. Duncan	G.S. Knight	H.B. Scott		P. Hobart
Units	5 Assault Regt RE	22 Dragoons	***141 RAC (The Buffs)***	1 Northants Yeomanry		
	6 Assault Regiment RE	Westminster Dragoons	1 Fife & Forfar Yeomanry	144 Regt RAC		
	42 Assault Regiment RE	***1 Lothians & Border Horse***	7 RTR	1 E Riding Yeomanry		
			49 APC Regiment	4 RTR		
			1 Cdn AC Regt	11 RTR		
				5 Armd Engr Regt RE		
				77 Armd Engr Sqn RE		
Crab Flails		180				180
Crocodiles			183 (2,303)			183
Kangaroos			275 (1,178)			275
CDL			36 (193) 'B' Sqn 49 APC Regt			36
Buffaloes				415		415
AVRE	179					179
Total Funnies	179	180	494	415		1,268
Other AFVs	114	39	73	72	166	464
Total AFVs	293	219	567	487	166	1,732
Total Men; all ranks	3,652	1,990	3,674	3,344	6,135	18,795

Units taking part in Operation *Heather* are written in ***bold italic***.
For comparison, an armoured division contained 14,400 men and 350 AFVs.

79 BAD were GHQ troops under army group command. Montgomery wrote that, 'its employment was always a matter of personal interest and concern to me.'[56] It was large, and the only all-

55 Anon, *The Story*.
56 Ibid.

armour formation in the British Army. In mid-March 1945 it was further swollen in preparation for the Rhine crossing with a brigade of DD units, which are excluded from the table.

79 BAD was raised in September 1942 as a conventional armoured division, and was the last British division of any type formed in the Second World War. It comprised 27 BAB and 185 BIB. Major General Sir Percy Cleghorn Stanley Hobart referred to as 'Hobo',was transferred from 11 BAD to 79 BAD, being its first and only GOC. His chequered history with the irrelevant whiff of sexual scandal for having married the wife of one his students is important in any analysis of the performance of 21 AG. He was one of the original apostles of mobility and therefore guilty with the other apostles of destroying the integrity of the Army in pursuing the chimaera of the all-armoured force without all-arms. Jumbo Wilson sacked him as GOC 7 BAD for being unsound with regard to all-arms, but his connections with Liddell Hart and his brother-in-law, Montgomery, were sufficient to give him a second chance when an article by Liddell Hart was brought to Churchill's attention. His stock had risen with the reputation of 7 BAD, the Desert Rats, in 8 Army. When 7 BAD destroyed its reputation in Normandy, Hobart's cult leadership position with powerful protectors made him immune from either criticism or any requirement to explain why his creation had been unable to cope in the new environment.

The disastrous Dieppe raid of 19 August 1942 had just occurred when Hobart took over 79 BAD, and Alan Brooke, CIGS, was focussed on its lessons. Churchill tanks had not landed with the infantry, and not all had been able to climb the gravel beaches and surmount the concrete sea wall. A feeling of inferiority to the Wehrmacht dating from Dunkirk had been reinforced by the fall of Tobruk on 17 June. In November came the turn of the tide at Alamein and Operation Torch, bringing renewed pressure from both FDR and Stalin to return to the Continent in 1943. Churchill and to a lesser extent Brooke, had been under the illusion that the war could be won indirectly by area bombing which precluded direct contact with the Wehrmacht. Brooke at last realised this was fanciful and that one day soon they would have to face the full German army. He had the idea that the equipments and tactics for a successful landing on a hostile shore could be developed by an armoured division. Therefore he approached Hobart, and on 10 March 1943 got his agreement to convert 79 BAD to the task of developing and operating tanks that were amphibious, could sweep mines, cross obstacles and fight at night. The invention of these special equipments happened elsewhere and in the case of the AVRE dated back to the First World War. The logic of combining these special equipments in one enormous division was never formally justified, and the logic seemed to be that, 'since Hobart knows how to train armoured divisions, let's put him in charge of one containing all of the special armour.' There was never a mention of flamethrowing tanks, which in the event were placed at the very last minute into 79 BAD with no rationale or consistency since Wasp flamethrowing universal carriers were not placed there but issued to the infantry divisions.

Before accepting the offer, Hobart consulted his fellow apostles, Pile and Liddell Hart, since the task could have looked like providing infantry with the support which the apostles still railed against as old-fashioned. Hobart also extracted a promise from Brooke that he, Hobart, would remain as GOC when the division was committed in action.

Many of the problems that later afflicted 21 AG were the unintended consequences of Brooke's decision to select and protect Hobart, who was antithetical to all-arms and had the temperament of a cult leader. He was given *carte blanche* and appointed judge and jury of the outcome when Brooke refused to appoint a CRAC to keep Hobart in check, or at least find out what he was doing and why. Hobart therefore dug in for the duration to exercise his influence behind the scenes. Brooke, however, was more than satisfied with Hobart's performance, writing on 2 January 1944; 'Hobart has been doing wonders in his present job and I am delighted that we put him into it.'[57]

57 Alan Brooke. *War Diaries 1939-1945* (London: Weidenfeld & Nicholson, 2001), p. 517.

Lt Gen Giffard Le Q Martel was an apostle of mobility who had seen the light. He was also the only British soldier who managed to rattle the Germans in 1940, commanding the Arras counter-attack which allowed the army to escape from Dunkirk. He was also the only British soldier to get close to, and be welcomed by, the Russians. He returned from Russia and in effect asked Brooke for the job of CRAC on 23 March 1944, telling him the Russian experience was more relevant to Normandy than that of 8 Army, and asserting that no account was being taken of the new German tanks and tactics of defense in depth which he had witnessed in Russia – and which were of course to be met in Operation *Heather*. He argued for an I-tank that could withstand all anti-tank guns. Brooke, Hobart and Montgomery all disagreed on the grounds that a large gun and high mobility checkmated armour thickness, and installing the 17-pdr in some M4 Shermans was all that was required; even the Churchills could now finally be scrapped, according to Montgomery, since the Sherman fulfilled his idea of a Universal tank. Such was the depth of feeling against Martel's apostasy, that nothing was done to employ him when his retirement age came round in June, and he vanished from the scene.[58] With Martel went the last chance of the RAC reforming itself and belatedly adopting all-arms. It paralleled the consequences for the RAF when Churchill allowed the Air Ministry to sack Dowding.

Hobart first developed the First World War designs of Armoured Vehicle Royal Engineers (AVREs), manned by Sappers with an RAC driver. Nearly 200 units were available by D-Day, and about 600 were subsequently converted. The AVRE was a Churchill tank with the gun replaced by a 290 mm spigot mortar or petard. This fired a dustbin-sized container of explosive in a shaped charge weighing 40 lbs a distance of 80 yards to crack open concrete bunkers and buildings. The choice of Churchill for this role has not been explained, but it must have been for practical reasons like having a flat deck, and its cross-country capability. Its lack of mobility must have pained Hobart, but his attitude to its 4 inch armour cannot even be guessed at. He was certainly blind to its lack of armour when he chose the M4 Sherman for the rôle of Crab Flail tank, condemning the crews to brief lives of terror. As a child being driven across the battlefield of Operation Clipper near Geilenkirchen in 1946, this author was struck by the number of burnt-out Sherman 'Crab' flail tanks.

The AVRE had mounting lugs to carry a variety of stores. One was a great fascine of brushwood twice as high as the tank itself and held across the horns by wire ropes. It was dropped into streams or anti-tank ditches to make a crossing, or on the far side of walls to break the tank's fall when surmounting a sea wall. Alternatively the AVRE could carry a small box girder (SBG) bridge of 30-ft in length, used in Operation *Heather* to bridge a crater in the road or at least provide firm going near its rim. For soft going on the beach or in a swamp it could carry a large bobbin reel from which a carpet made of canvas and wood was laid down under the advancing tracks. Other equipment carried were: lengths of explosive called snakes; shaped General Wade charges for blowing up reinforced concrete, which were placed by the dismounted crew; a plough for turning up mines on the beach; and another dangerous device called a Conger consisting of a hose filled with explosives for gapping minefields. This was used successfully in the assault on the batteries at Cap Gris Nez, according to the biographer of 79 BAD,[59] although J.G. Smith[60] who was there said it didn't work and that was the only time it was tried. It was finally abandoned after a disaster, and the 100 units sent to the US Army were abandoned without being used. Today all armies use an updated version such as the US mine-clearing line charge – MCLC.

58 Op. Cit., pp. 534 & 560.
59 Anonymous, *The Story*. p. 136.
60 Smith, *In At The Finish*.

> But they were dangerous weapons. I have visited a spot in Holland where British tanks – equipped with a more sophisticated flame weapon-called Conger – ignited in a massive fireball when preparing to attack the Germans. The unit lost over 50 men – we stopped using nitroglycerine after that episode. The men were Canadian truck drivers who were delivering the nitro and the tank crews were sappers from Wales![61]

Hobart developed the Duplex Drive tank based on Nicholas Straussler's invention. The engine drove a propeller as well as the tracks, and the tank floated within collapsible canvas sides that rose as the tank went into the water. None, of course, was used in *Heather*. The Sherman was naturally chosen for this role since it was a cruiser that could immediately after landing start deep penetrations. It is, on reflection, doubtful that a Churchill could have been converted into a DD because the high top run meant there was nowhere fore and aft to affix the rails holding the canvas sides.

The division adopted a flail tank called a Crab that had been developed in North Africa. These were Shermans mounting a frontal frame holding a revolving drum with chains and a wire-cutting device. They led the attack, flailing the ground and raising a column of dust that restricted vision, while exploding mines. The armour and infantry followed in the pathways of 'our flogging friends' as they were affectionately called. Early versions were driven by an auxiliary engine, but on the Sherman there was power enough from the tank's engine. They suffered a loss of over 50% (see following table) with 13 units lost on the beaches and the remainder spread from month to month, while most AVRE losses were concentrated on D-Day (35) or when clearing the Channel ports in September (25). Hobart's decision to base the Crab on the Sherman was criticised at the time:

> The Sherman retained its armament so it could also act as a normal gun tank. Successful as the device was, it seemed a thoughtless act on the part of some military genius to attach it to the relatively thin-skinned Sherman whose crews had to operate in close and slow-moving order, often at point-blank range.[62]

Destruction Of Selected Equipment in 79 BAD[63]

Equipment type	Establishment	Losses	Percentage lost
Crab flails	180	98	54%
AVREs	179	82	46%
Crocodiles	183	53	29%
Kangaroos	275	30	11%

For the last part of his remit, which was to provide night fighting capability, Hobart adopted the *Canal Defence Light* (CDL), or *T10 Shop Tractor* in US Service. This was a 13 million candle-power searchlight emerging from a vertical slit 2 inch by 24 inch fitted into the turret of an M3 Grant tank. It had cost £20 million to develop and to convert 1,850 tanks, an extraordinary sum of money considering that HMS *Vanguard* cost £11½ million and that a fraction of that sum could have equipped the infantry with tanks immune to the 88. The development was concentrated at Lowther Castle, and 6,000 British and 8,000 American troops were schooled in its use. For D-Day

61 Graham Watson. *A Brief History of 141st (Regt) Royal Armored Corps:* http://orbat.com/site/history/open1/uk_141rac.html
62 Smith, *In At The Finish.*
63 Anon, *The Story.*

Hobart had a brigade of CDL (3 battalions) and Bradley had six battalions, four of which could have been available in Normandy with a combined punch of 72 gun-armed Shermans, 216 CDL's and the attached 526 Armored Infantry Battalion, all trained to work together in night operations.[64] By March 1945 all CDL troops and gun-tanks were dispersed, although 79 BAD retained 36 CDLs in the inventory of 31 BAB with 'B' Sqn 49 APC Regt trained in their use. These could have been used at Kervenheim and in the Hochwald.

The extraordinary explanation why the potentially effective CDL was not used was that no one planning Operation *Heather* or Operation *Blockbuster* knew of its existence and therefore could not request it – Catch-22. Hobart neither volunteered the equipment, which was his obligation if conditions were favourable, nor revealed its existence to those responsible for sending men over the top.

CDL was first demonstrated on the night of 5 May 1942 to Brooke, who called it 'a very interesting and promising demonstration' in his Diary.

> At another demonstration, American troops were placed on a hill and warned they would be attacked from a hill 1½ miles away. At the start of the attack, two CDLs came round each side of the hill on 'scatter' [meaning an armour-plated shutter covered and revealed the light at 6 times per second. Later blue and yellow glass screens to cover the slot were available. Their use was intended to enhance the difficulty of estimating the range of the CDL tank from an enemy position, and particularly whether it was closing the range or stationary.] This manoeuvre broke up the hill's outline and enabled three others to move on to the crest. When on top, they opened their shutters to display a 'steady' beam which was the signal for the two 'scatter' CDLs to change to 'Steady'. The tanks moved down the hill in line abreast, with troops and and tanks hidden in the 'cloaks' of darkness (outside the beams). At the bottom lay the River Lowther with a small bridge that had to be crossed. This was achieved by the outside CDLs closing their shutters and moving across the bridge where they again opened their shutters when spaced thirty yards apart. This enabled the other CDLs and supporting vehicles to move across unseen before opening up as well. The first thing the American officers and troops knew was when the lights were extinguished revealing British troops holding fixed bayonets at their chests. General Eisenhower was so impressed when he saw the CDL that he ordered that they were not to be used before American units had them. It was also laid down that this device would not be used by either British or Americans without prior approval of the British Chiefs-of-Staff. In this connection it was considered to be inadvisable to use it in small numbers as an experiment but in large quantities in a worth-while operation.
>
> As more experience was gained with the device, it became clear that some of the earlier claims were exaggerated. The schemes for using the triangles of darkness to cover the approach of assault troops necessitated using CDLs for flank protection. It was found, too, that the blinding effect was not as great as originally thought. Moreover the whole device depended on the maintenance of secrecy until it was first used as it was realised that antidotes could be rapidly improvised and the value of CDL correspondingly reduced. An even more serious setback was the discovery that the German 88 mm anti-aircraft gun fitted with a green sunfilter enabled its gun-layer to see clearly the actual slot through which the light passed.[65]

64 E-mail from Richard C. Anderson Jr of the Dupuy Inst. in December 2003.
65 Winston G. Ramsay. *After The Battle No. 16* (Stratford: Battle of Britain Pubs, 1977), p. 52.

CDL was used just twice, in March and April 1945 to illuminate the Rhine and Elbe crossings. This constituted misuse as a searchlight. Indeed the biographer of 79 BAD, Hobart's amanuensis, deceptively called it such; 'CDL: a form of searchlight, mounted on a gun-tank (Churchill or Grant).'[66]

Martel and Fuller charged that a culture of extreme secrecy in 21 AG prevented the revolutionary CDL weapon from being used in battle. Its history revealed surely that centralization dominated by advocates of the failed all-tank operational methodology had become a dead hand stifling experimentation and innovation. It was also another case of history biting Hobart in the backside, because he had been one of the self-appointed experts criticising the First World War field commanders for introducing tanks in penny packets on the Somme rather than accumulating them for use *en masse* in a decisive area like Cambrai. The 'experts' waited for a decisive moment in a tomorrow that never came, and not only controlled the weapon's use but kept it secret from those on their own side who were dying on the battlefield without it.

The early employment of tanks in small numbers on the Somme actually worked advantageously. It ironed out problems in their use; it made the tanks familiar to the infantry; it gave the Germans a false sense of security; and it gave the designers and users time to introduce the MKV, which in Monash's opinion was as great an advance over the original MkIV as the Lee Enfield was over the Brown Bess. Hobart therefore failed his remit to introduce night-fighting techniques. Furthermore, the very knowledge of CDL's existence among the top brass almost certainly inhibited any need to develop infra-red night vision, which was the better technology for night-fighting. The Germans introduced this successful technology in early March 1945 in the Hochwald, in the form of the Sperber FG 1250 (Sparrow Hawk) Nacht Jäger with a range of 600 m. This comprised a 30 cm infrared searchlight and image converter operated by the tank commander.

Flame throwing was an established technique dating back to the First World War and updated with the anti-invasion devices of 1940. The man-carried Lifebuoy or Ack-Pack flamethrower was introduced but disliked because of its short range of 30 to 40 yards and resultant risk to the operator. In May 1941 Andrew McNaughton was impressed by a demonstration of a flamethrower developed by the Petroleum Warfare Dept (PWD). On 5 August 1941 an order was placed for 17 prototype flamethrowers for the Canadian forces installed in Canadian-built carriers called Ronsons. In July 1942 1,300 Ronsons were ordered in Canada with 818 delivered to the Canadian forces in Britain by end July 1943. The units proved difficult to maintain. Meanwhile the Wasp was designed and in June 1942 a prototype ordered, followed by an order for 30 on July 22, 1942. The Canadians still preferred the Ronsons although 1,000 Wasp Mk Is were ordered and delivered by late 1943. A smaller and lighter Wasp Mk 2 was then designed using new fuel designed by the Canadian Petroleum Experimental Unit in conjunction with the British Petroleum Warfare Department, and this was the unit finally adopted. Wasp carriers were first used in action in Operation *Tractable* by 3 CID at Montboint on the Laison near Falaise.

The policy in 21 Army Group was for the Wasps to be available for use by infantry carrier platoons as an occasional weapon, with stocks held in advanced ordnance depots made available on 7 days' notice. Training was given at the Canadian Training School on the British Wasp 2. The first Wasp 2C (for Canadian production) was ready about 1 June 1944. On the scale of 8 equipments for each infantry divisional reconnaissance regiment, motor battalion and infantry battalion, I Canadian Army had a requirement of 192 with wastage estimated at 29 per month. Up to the latter part of November 1944, I Canadian Army had received 134 Wasp 2 and 73 Wasp 2C,

66 Anon, *The Story*, p. 15.

but many of these had gone to equip 49 and 51 BIDs. Efforts were being made to have I Canadian Army equipped entirely with the Canadian model.[67]

Wasp carriers were vulnerable to all anti-tank weapons and mines, but flaming became safer for crews by fitting the Wasp into an AFV, and especially the Churchill VII its main gun and coaxial BESA. This configuration required a trailer to carry the flame fuel, which in its turn required the design and manufacture of a tank-trailer link. This Churchill Crocodile flame-thrower was developed in 1943 with the assistance of the Petroleum Warfare Department and Lagonda Cars, which built the trailer holding 400 gallons. Range was about 100 yards and the flame lasted for 80 seconds, although it was usually fired in short bursts. A demonstration in late 1942 received Hobart's support, and another one of the finished product on March 23, 1943 produced a decision to give control of the design to the MoS. An order for 250 Crocodile conversion kits was placed in August 1943. The first 60 kits reached 141 Regiment RAC at the end of March 1944, and were ready for D-Day.

Flamethrowers were not part of Hobart's remit for 79 BAD in March 1943. Soon afterwards, however, Hobart was impressed by a demonstration of the Churchill Crocodile and he began to pressure the Ministry of Supply for a development plan, and then got Brooke's agreement to add them to 79 BAD. The plan was to issue one per troop in each Churchill regiment, but due to short supply an interim decision was made to equip 141 Regiment RAC in time for Overlord. At that time the plan was to adapt the Wasp for fitment also into the US Army's Sherman I and the Canadian Sherman III and V. At the end of August the Canadians cancelled their requirement on learning that the US Army was not continuing with the project. The Canadians instead asked for units of Wasp II for fitting into the Ram APC. Called a Cougar and later a Badger, with the nozzle of the Wasp fitted upside down in the bow machine-gun slot, it was issued for trial purposes in December 1944 on the scale of 6 to each armoured regiment in 2 CAB and 6 to the Lake Superior Regiment, which was the motor battalion of 4 CAD. The Badger first saw action with them in February 1945. A second batch was ordered, known as Badger MkII, in which an armoured roof was added to the turret ring opening. When 5 CAD relocated to NW Europe, they modified several Ram tanks, complete with turret, into Badger configuration

Early plans to produce Wasp kits for Crocodiles for retrofitment of Churchill Mk IV and VIIs in the field were abandoned due to their impracticability. Instead it was decided to produce all of the new Churchill MKVIIs with lugs for fitment of the Wasp in the field, and this became the Churchill Crocodile. In all about 800 Crocodiles were converted from the Churchill MkVII, which came prepared off the production line with Wasp mounting lugs. It was also decided that the Buffs, 141 Regiment RAC, should be the specialist Crocodile unit and by D+8 they were in operation in Normandy. 141 RAC came under command of 31 BAB in 79 BAD on June 21, 1944, and the arrangement was formalised in August 1944.[68] In October 1944 a second Crocodile unit, 1 Fife & Forfar Yeomanry, was formed and in February 1945 a third, 7 RTR.

The Crocodiles were used for set-piece attacks while the Wasp MKIIC Carriers were employed on a more immediate and flexible basis. Any unit could apparently order Wasp carriers from the advanced ordnance depot on 7 days notice, and get crews trained at the Canadian Training School. However, no complete list exists of participating units. The following are known to have operated them; QPR of Canada in 3 CID; 8 Royal Scots in 15 BID; 9 Flanders Rifle Battalion; 4 CAD; 8 R Scots; 2 Wilts; 4 Wilts; 10 HLI.[69] Alternatively, or in addition, an application could be made for the support of a Churchill Crocodile. In Operation *Heather*, there was no call for

67 Canadian Mil HQ Report #141. http://www.dnd.ca/hr/dhh/history_ar…mhq_e.asp?cat=1
68 David Fletcher. *Churchill Crocodile Flamethrower* (Botley: Osprey, 2007).
69 http://ww2talk.com/forums/topic/52049-wasp-carrier-units/

using Wasp carriers but there was one call for a Churchill Crocodile in support of 2 Lincolns at Kervenheim, and it was put in under command of 6 GAB. Unfortunately no explanation exists why 3 BID neglected Wasp Carriers, although 1 Royal Norfolks in 185 BIB are said to have used them later at Lingen. The Canadian developments appear to have passed 3 BID by during the winter when they were stationed on the Maas, and focussed on crossing the Rhine where Wasps would not be needed. When they were called forward for Operation *Heather* in *Veritable*, it is easy to surmise that Horrocks discussed his needs with Hobart and Brigadier Knight of 31 BAB, and made arrangements for Knight to visit HQ 3 BID with a fait accompli. It seems unlikely that 1 Norfolks and 4 CG contemplated flaming Müsershof on the troublesome right wing at Kervenheim on 1 March in combination with smoke, or 2 Lincolns and 3 SG at Winnekendonk on 2 March, but had they been Canadian units it is likely Wasp Carriers would have been used or at least contemplated. This remains an unresearched matter.

As we have seen, the decision to include 31 BTB on D-Day was made after Montgomery excluded 6 GTB. Two troops of Crocodiles only could be landed on D-Day because of a shipping shortage. 13 Troop landed at Ver-Sur-Mer and 15 Troop at Le Hamel. The first reference to Crocodiles in 79 BAD's history is their successful cooperation with Crabs at Crepon on D + 2 or 3, and it may or may not be true that it was then that Hobart decided he wanted them in 79 BAD. This matter was discussed with a veteran of 141 RAC, who said that the only person with the answers would be the late Lt-Col Waddell.[70]

After much testing and evaluation, 79 AD chose five equipments for use on the continent: CDL, DD, Crab, AVRE (with Fascine, SBG Bridge, Petard, Bobbin, Snake, Conger and Plough) and armoured bulldozer. Later it took on charge Crocodile flamethrowers, Buffaloes developed for the Pacific theatre, Kangaroos that had originated within 1 Canadian Army in Normandy, and a second regiment to provide a regiment for each army in 21 AG, although in fact each largely followed its nationals; *Heather* was a Canadian operation, but 49 APC Regiment and not 1 CACR carried 3 BID into battle.

The RAC mustered its personnel from many different sources. All were represented in 79 BAD.

There were the regular cavalry regiments, such as 22 Dragoon Guards formed in 1940 for the duration from cadres supplied by the 4/7th and 5/6th Dragoon Guards. These dated to 1685 and were mechanised in 1938 with Light Tanks. They considered themselves élite, and with needs that often had priority over those of other troops, so orders could be regarded as mere suggestions. Relationship with the infantry which suffered the consequences of this type of insubordination could be poor. None of these units supported *Heather*.

There were the TA yeomanry cavalry formed in 1761 as a volunteer cavalry force. An example in 79 BAD was The Lothians and Border Horse Yeomanry. It had been formed in 1892 by an amalgamation of three regiments raised in the Napoleonic Wars – the East Lothian Regiment of Yeomanry Cavalry, the Royal Midlothian Regiment of Yeomanry Cavalry and the Linlithgow Yeomanry Cavalry. In 1920 it was mustered into the Territorial Army and had its HQ in Edinburgh. In the same year it joined the Tank Corps as an armoured car company, and automatically became part of the Royal Armoured Corps in 1939. The officers and senior NCOs were schooled at RTR Training Centres, and in 1939 it was common practice to transfer in a few key men from earlier mechanised units.[71] 1 Lothians and Border Horse supported Operation *Heather* with Crab flails clearing mines for 6 GAB.

Thirdly there were the Royal Tank regiments that had long since shed their animus towards the infantry. They could look back to a successful rapport established originally with Monash's

70 Phone conversation with Geoffrey Kirk on 2 January 2004.
71 E-mail from Gerry Chester in December 2003.

Australian Corps at Hamel and Amiens in 1918. Success at Arras in 1940 and Beda Fomm in 1941 was due both to the Matilda II and its aggressive use.

Another source of troops for conversion to armour were the infantry battalions transferred when Martel built up the armoured force in 1941. Such units treated the infantry with consideration as equal partners. An example in 79 BAD was 141 Regiment RAC, which was formed as 7 Royal East Kent Regiment, The Buffs. It dated back to 1572 when Thomas Morgan formed it for service in Holland. Refusing the oath of allegiance to the Estates General in 1665, they returned to re-form in England as The Holland Regiment. Every British infantryman knew the phrase 'Steady the Buffs'. 7 Battalion was a TA unit formed for the duration in July 1940 for home defence duties. Together with thirty-three other such TA units they converted to tanks in 1941. 141 RAC retained the Buffs' cap badge but made it out of white metal to conform with the style of the RTR badge.

Finally there were two types of ad hoc unit. Sappers with RAC drivers manned the AVREs, while the men operating the Kangaroo APCs, 1 APC Regiment and 1 CACR, appear to have been raised by the old method of getting volunteers, "You, You and You". They came from RAC replacement depots, delivery squadrons, the infantry and even from the artillery, according to a veteran.

Crocodiles became available to any unit in 21 Army Group at the request of the corps commander. There was logic to this arrangement. Flamethrowers required specialized training for both the operating crew and supporting fitters. The equipment required a lot of maintenance, and loading the viscous fuel from drums was arduous and time-consuming. Flame was used only occasionally in any one division, and its need was usually identified at the last moment. It was therefore efficient to send the trained teams from division to division as required. The drawback was lack of familiarity between the supporting flamethrower and the infantry.

All suitable Funnies were used in Operation *Heather*, with the exception of the CDLs, Congers, Buffaloes and DDs. If, then, Crocodiles, Kangaroos, AVREs, Crabs and armoured bulldozers were used as routinely as I-tanks in support of operations, two obvious questions arise. Firstly, why were the Funnies placed within a division rather than in independent brigades, which was how they were organised in every other army group? In Italy in December 1944 locally manufactured ARKs, which were turretless Churchills fitted with ramps front and rear and deployed by being driven into a ditch or stream to carry the advancing tanks, and AVRE fascines, were all placed under command of 51 RTR, which became the Funny regiment within 21 Tank Brigade. There was never a suggestion of creating a Funny division or even brigade in Italy. It was unlikely, therefore, that everyone but Montgomery was out of step. Secondly it needs to be questioned whether the status of Funnies as 79 BAD troops commanded by Hobart resulted in their underuse, or even in their misuse, since the CDL was not used until the end of hostilities and then only as a searchlight. Furthermore, as we have seen above, the specialised Wasp Carriers in 21 AG were not under command of 79 BAD, and neither were all of the Churchill bridgelayers. Every armoured brigade and tank brigade in 21 AG was allocated three Churchill Bridgelayers, which was developed in 1944 in time for Overlord, and of which 99 units were eventually constructed. It was different from an AVRE equipped with an SBG, and it was not an ARK. A Bridgelayer was a turretless Churchill carrying a 30-ft bridge rated Class 60 for tanks and Class 40 for wheeled vehicles. The space vacated by the turret basket contained a hydraulic drive that operated a pivoted launch arm fitted with rollers for positioning. It had a crew of two men; a driver who operated the laying mechanism under directions from the commander. Three bridgelayers were issued initially to each tank brigade in 21 AG, and then to other units as additional numbers became available.

In Italy there was no Funny division. A veteran explained:

> Towards the end of 1944 ARKs and Fascine Carriers were added to inventory. Tank States for November show NIH had 3 ARKs and 6 Fascines. 51 RTR had 3 ARKs, and 4 Fascines, while 142 RAC had 6 Fascines. I do not know how the latter two handled them. After initial

> training – almost everyone was made familiar with the vehicles – each NIH Squadron added a Troop of one ARK and two Fascines. There was no reduction in the number of gun-tank Troops. During December, the structure of the Brigades changed. NIH became the senior regiment of 21 Tank Brigade. 51 RTR became a Funnies equipped unit. I do not know complete details of the inventory, but know they had Crocodiles, various AVREs, ARKs and Fascines. The reason for the changes was due to the fighting having moved out of the hills into the Po Valley.[72]

Montgomery's justification for the 79 Armoured Division was tendentious:

> In modern war we have learnt that much highly specialised equipment is necessary in order to compete with the varying conditions of summer and winter, water obstacles, mud, snow, and so on: the great essential being to maintain the tempo of the operations, without pauses in which the enemy could recover his balance. All this equipment was centralised in the 79 Armoured Division; there it was maintained and kept in good order; and there the technique of its use in the tactical battle was studied and developed.[73]

The development of a technique for the use of Kangaroos was not due to 79 BAD but to the Kangaroo Squadron that in August 1944 was placed under 25 Canadian Armoured Regiment (The Elgin Regiment) for administrative purposes by Crerar. The installation of the first sixty Crocodile kits was done by 141 RAC's LAD and not by 79 BAD, while the development of its tactical use was also done outside 79 BAD. Furthermore, laying fascines and bridges, and firing petards required familiarity and training with the units involved in which lever to pull, or which page in the instruction booklet to read, but did not require a 79 BAD. Any member of the Royal Engineers trained in the use of explosives could handle a General Wade charge carried in an AVRE, while any REME detachment in a tank brigade could ensure that Churchill AVREs and Crocodiles were 'maintained and kept in good order'. Indeed, the fitters of GAD once repaired the Crocodiles of 141 Regt RAC, according to J.G. Smith,[74] and GAD, it should be noted, lacked knowledge and experience of Churchills.

Soon after D-Day, 79 BAD began to blame the infantry for the heavy equipment losses rather than take stock of its own many shortcomings in AFV specification.

> It was already evident that Crabs and AVREs placed under command of infantry would be mishandled and suffer heavy casualties. Particularly did they not allow for the short range of the Petard and consequent vulnerability of AVREs.[75]

The statement is unfair. The petard had a range of 100 yards and its job was to destroy bunkers containing 75 mm and 88 mm anti-tank guns. Hobart should therefore have increased the AVRE's frontal armour to make it immune to the defences. In the attack on Trout on D-Day, two Commandos took three AVREs under command, but before the AVREs could get within range of Trout to fire their petards, all three were knocked out and the troop commander, Captain McLellan killed.[76]

---

72 Gerry Chester in an e-mail in December 2003.
73 Anon, *The Story*, Montgomery's foreword.
74 Smith, *In At The Finish*.
75 Anon, *The Story*.
76 M Reynolds. *Eagles and Bulldogs in Normandy 1944* (Havertown: History Press, 2003).

Insufficient armour thickness was the cause of the losses. On 9 June, 2 RUR in 9 BIB of 3 BID attacked Panzer Meyer's 25 SS PG Regiment in Cambes, and were decimated. Shermans of the East Riding Yeomanry stayed back to shoot them in, while three AVREs accompanied the infantry to deal with pillboxes that were believed to exist.

> This was not so but instead they took on a German Mk IV and knocked it out with their bombards. They behaved with the utmost gallantry and advanced beyond the village where they were all destroyed by 88-mm guns.[77]

Destroying the Mk IVs and the 88 mm was the task of the Shermans of the E Riding Yeomanry, who were following Montgomery's doctrine and were not up with the infantry. The specification of the Sherman and its tactical use were the responsibility of Montgomery and Hobart, who naturally preferred that the finger of blame pointed at the infantry rather than at themselves.

No AVREs supported the crucial D-Day assault on Hillman. Examination of aerial-photographs had failed to identify seven machine guns in steel cupolas and two infantry guns in 3.5 m thick concrete emplacements. Six USAAF B-17s failed to appear, and the Suffolks tried to take Hillman with mortars and PIATs, and with the support of 76 Field Regiment's SP 105 mm gun-howitzers and the Shermans of C Squadron, 13/18 Hussars with 75 mms and 17pdrs. Nothing succeeded. Had 13/18 Hussars possessed AVREs, and had they been equipped with Churchills and the 95 mm Close Support version, the cupolas and emplacements could have been destroyed. Instead two hours passed before a second attack could be mounted.

Few AVREs were made available to the infantry, even after most of the Assault Squadrons were released into reserve on the evening of D-Day.[78] Hobart saw himself as the arbiter of their use to prevent abuse by the infantry. This was a throwback to the struggle between Fuller and the obstructionist 'Uncle' Harper of 51 HD during Cambrai in 1917 when the infantry became the enemy of the tanks. 3 BID was left to struggle on without adequate armour support.

J.G. Smith argued that 79 BAD contributed nothing to the Buffs who had no need even of their own regimental HQ. Only once for a few weeks in July was a Tactical HQ established when the Buffs' Crocodile squadrons were concentrated.

> I was reminded that when we were in action, most of the time RHQ did not know where we were and when they did they held no communication with us. We drew our own rations, fuel and ammunition direct, and since both Recce and Ack-Ack troops had been broken up long before there seemed no reason for RHQ to exist.[79]

Smith's book showed how the units in 79 BAD provided support on their own terms. His Crocodile bogged down at Buchholz during *Veritable* in February 1945. The crew took refuge with a platoon of 15 BID, which Smith called a 'bullshit division', while awaiting the arrival of an armoured recovery vehicle. The infantry were severely weakened by heavy losses and at their wits' end. They saw the arrival of an I-tank as a means of strengthening their position. The tank commander, who was a sergeant, disobeyed a direct order from the infantry field officer, and simply motored away as soon as he could in pursuit of what turned out to be an uninterrupted night's sleep and an opportunity for looting. Smith explained:

77 McNish, *Iron Division*, p. 107.
78 Anon, *The Story*.
79 Smith, *In At The Finish*.

> There had been a quarrel between the infantry major and Sergeant Jackman. The major had said that since we were staying in the house we must help with its defence. Sergeant Jackman had said that while we were quite willing to do so at night, in the daytime our first duty was to our tank, and as soon as we got it clear we should be off. The major then ordered us to remain at the farm until he gave us permission to leave. Sergeant Jackman retorted that he already had his orders [from 79 BAD] – to rejoin the squadron as soon as possible. So no wonder the major was upset – the free and easy atmosphere of the tank corps never went down well with officers of other arms.[80]

On another occasion the infantry were found to too much trouble for Smith's unit:

> The Essex have crossed the Rhine at Renkum as planned … and we are to ferry the troops into Wageningen. We are tired and dirty and do not relish the idea of acting as troop transports. Nor do our officers and the plan is abandoned as suddenly as it is proposed. The infantrymen are used to being mucked about and make no objection when we leave them sitting on the bank at the roadside.[81]

The reason for not maintaining and not dissolving 79 BAD was to be found in the characters of Montgomery and Hobart. Montgomery enjoyed micro-managing operations down to the level of corps and sometimes division, and his insistence that personnel from 79 BAD be involved in the planning of every operation in which they were used was a proxy for his own control. He also had an aversion to allowing anyone to learn by his mistakes. 79 BAD was the perfect tool through which to exercise this control. Montgomery mandated its involvement in every aspect of planning and execution of operations. Hobart liked wielding power and influence, so 79 BAD served both their needs.

When he arrived in Britain to command Overlord, Montgomery made Hobart his Special Adviser On Armour. From then onwards Hobart had power and influence, and stopped overtly criticising Montgomery. Montgomery ordered that the Americans should get their fair share of all of the Funnies, but apart from the DD and CDL that Eisenhower himself insisted be adopted by the US forces, the decision about the others was left to Bradley who passed it onto his staff. The Americans tried to develop a super-petard rocket of their own, but nothing came of it. Their disappointment seems to have soured them towards specialised armour. They rejected Montgomery's offer, citing as the reason training difficulties with Churchills, even though the Crab flail was mounted on a Sherman. The Americans paid for their decision on Omaha Beach, when they came to experience the problems of Dieppe for themselves.

Guy Simonds created Kangaroo APCs from a suggestion by Lt-Gen Richard O'Connor in July 1944. Initially 72 Priest SP 105 mm guns, which had been turned in by 3 CID, were converted to carry troops. All the assault divisions, including 3 CID, were issued with 105-mm Priests for use in the initial bombardment, requiring firing from the deck of the landing craft during the run-in. The SP guns were also faster to disembark and to move up. They were always anomalies, so once the lodgement was secure and more Anglo-Canadian divisions were ashore with their towed 25-pdrs, the Anglo-Canadian supply chain insisted they were exchanged for 25-pdrs. A shortage of US 105-mm ammunition reinforced the decision.

First used in Operation *Totalise* on 7 August, the Priest APCs were manned by a single driver from the delivery squadrons. Having been proved useful, they were established on 28 August as a

80 Ibid.
81 Ibid.

separate unit, called 1 Canadian Armoured Carrier Squadron, under Captain Corbeau.[82] It was upgraded to a regiment on October 19 under Lt-Col Churchill of the Elgins, and re-equipped with converted turretless Ram tanks. Steel rungs were welded to the sides so that a section of 10 men could mount. The TOE of a regiment was 106 carriers, organised in two squadrons each comprising an HQ with 5 Kangaroos, and 4 troops with 12 Kangaroos. Each squadron had the capacity to lift one infantry battalion at a time to the Start Line for an unfatigued start. In October a sister unit was founded, the 49 APC Regiment, and the two were placed under command of 31 BAB in 79 BAD. It was 'A' Squadron, 49 APC Regt that supported 3 BID in Operation *Heather*. They were disbanded on 20 June 1945.

79 BAD reported directly to 21 AG. Units were allocated according to need, and in Operation *Heather* they were placed under the command of 6 GAB. The senior officer representing Hobart was Lt-Col J.K. Shepherd, who was CRE of 6 Assault Regiment RE. On February 28 he found himself swamped with requests and sent the following to 30 BAB:

> Could not earmark one Tp from 30 Corps to 2 Cdn Corps on 2 Mar. 81 Sqn in support both 11 Armd Div and 4 Cdn Armd Div are overstretched and request the Sqn be in support of only one Div as soon as possible.

The following units were allocated to support 3 BID:

- 'B' Squadron, 1 Lothians & Border Horse in 30 BAB, operating Crab flails. On 27 February they supported the advance by 2 Lincolns and RF SG by flailing 200 yards east and west of MR957424. This point is in the woods approaching the railway embankment before Krüsbeckshof.
- 'C' Squadron, 141 Regiment (The Buffs) RAC in 31 BAB, operating Crocodile flamethrowers. They were supporting an attack on Höst on the west bank of the Niers on 24 February, and on the next day moved back towards Goch. On the following day they were attached to 3 BID under command of 6 GAB. On 27 February they followed behind the advance on call but were not required. Smith believes that they were asked by 4 GG to flame German positions in the woods where the Guards were being attacked and their tanks destroyed. Smith believes that in refusing the request Carroll angered the Guards. On the 28 February they went to a wood northwest of Kervenheim and waited throughout the day without being used. On the afternoon of 1 March 1945 a composite troop combining 12 and 14 Troop under Lt. Carroll was called to support the Lincolns and 4 CG. The Guards refused to participate, leaving a Crocodile and an HQ gun tank to go in alone. Carroll was killed, and the Coldstreamer CO placed the survivors under open arrest for motoring out of battle with the decapitated body of Carroll stuck in the turret. On 2 March 1945 the squadron moved to Goch and did not support the Lincolns in their attack on Winnekendonk.
- 284 Assault Sqn RE less one troop provided AVREs. It was part of 6 Assault Regiment in 1 Assault Brigade. They were attached to 3 BID on 26 February when 2 and 3 Troops moved to Square 9343 northwest of Schloss Calbeck. On 27 February, 3 Troop dropped two fascines to get 9 BIB forward and 2 Troop dropped one fascine into a 30 ft crater. As the second AVRE approached the crater it went up on a mine taking off three bogies. The track was repaired but when the tank moved the other track was mined injuring Capt Green and forcing them to abandon the AVRE. Two bridges were laid. A composite troop was then formed with four fascines and a bridgelayer and put in to support 185 BIB on 28 February when two bridges were laid, including one at Aengen or Endtschenhof. Fascines were not required. It is unclear whether any of these bridges was an SBG laid by an AVRE or whether both were laid by the Brigade's own bridgelayers.

82 http://www.1cacr.org/hist.html

The procedure was for the Funnies to lead the attack. First went the Flail with an infantry company following in the cleared path and protecting the flail from Panzerfausts. If Crocodiles were required they followed next behind the leading infantry, led by a Churchill gun-tank with a hull Besa. Then came the fascines and the bridgelayers followed by the Churchills of the supporting armoured brigade and the rest of the infantry.

Two books described life in 'C' Squadron, 141 Regiment RAC from 1943 to 1945. Andrew Wilson passed out from Sandhurst in February 1943 and joined The Buffs. He was given command of a troop in 'A' Squadron but his frequent absence on courses led to his removal. He went to the Reserve Squadron a disappointed man early in 1944 just as 'C' Squadron was introduced to the top-secret Crocodile flamethrower. New Churchill Mk VIIs arrived with their much thicker armour. Then amid great security in March 1944, 60 Crocodile kits were received, and for two months the Squadron worked hard to get all the equipment installed and tested. The King paid them a visit. They concentrated at Farnborough prior to D-Day and waterproofed the tanks. Being in reserve, Wilson did not take part on D-Day but waited in Eastbourne as the V1 bombardment started. The Reserve Squadron took replacement Crocodiles over to France through Southampton and made a wet landing at Courseulles. They joined the regiment and Wilson was given command again of a troop in 'A' Squadron. He was soon on operations in the Tilly area, on Noyers Ridge and was in Villers Bocage at the end of July. He described the fighting in Normandy as an endless repetition of the same limited actions, varied only by the number of casualties'.

Wilson took part in closing the Falaise gap and was then hospitalised with dysentery. There was a German officer in the same ward who presence upset a wounded Canadian boasting of killing prisoners. Wilson was discharged but had to wait in the Delivery Squadron. After ten days he made his way back to the Regiment near Boulogne, being given command of 14 Troop in 'C' Squadron. He took part in the attack on Cap Gris Nez. The squadron moved up on tank transporters to Winssen west of Nijmegen and took part in the attack on Rosmalen. Here he took his first close look at the burnt corpses of the German defenders, writing of himself in the third person.

> He walked down the front of the trees, where here and there the brushwood still smouldered among the blackened trunks. The burning away of the undergrowth had completely uncovered some trenches. He looked in the first and for the moment saw only a mass of charred fluff. He wondered what it was, until he remembered the Germans were always lining their sleeping-places with looted bedding.
>
> Then, as he turned to go, he saw the arm. At first he thought it was the charred and shrivelled crook of a tree root; but when he looked closer, he made out the hump of the body attached to it. A little way away was the shrivelled remains of a boot.
>
> He went on to the next trench, and in that there was no concealing fluff. There were bodies which seemed to have been blown back by the force of the flame and lay in naked, blackened heaps. Others were caught in twisted poses, as if the flame had frozen them. Their clothes had burned away. Only their helmets and boots remained, ridiculous and horrible.
>
> He wanted to vomit. He'd vomited before at some sights. But now he couldn't.
>
> 'Come and see what's by the gun', said Randall. They went. The gun itself was crushed. One of the Cromwells or one of the Crocodiles had run over it. A little to the side were the bodies of the crew. One of them had been caught by the flames as he ran away, splashed with the liquid which couldn't be shaken off. His helmet had fallen off and now he lay with black eyeballs, naked and charred and obscene.

> There came out of it all an enormous disgust, which couldn't be expressed, yet somehow one had to say something. 'We certainly did a proper job of it', said Randall.[83]

The battalion was convulsed when Hobart relieved Lt-Col Waddell, the CO and famous rugby player. He had delayed by two days a report that William Douglas Home, the adjutant, had refused to obey a legal order in protest against the way the war was being prosecuted, and in particular the demands for unconditional surrender. No doubt Home had also looked at the 'proper job' his unit was making of the War. He went to prison and later became a successful playwright.

They attacked in s'Hertogenbosch and defended on the Meijel road. Wilson was sent forward with a sergeant from the flails and AVREs to recce a canal crossing. They were ambushed and Wilson seriously wounded. He convalesced at Tattenham Corner in England from October until February 1945. At the beginning of March he was back with the regiment near Cleve to find that Lt. Carroll had taken over command of his troop.

> Then, as emotions came crowding in on him, he wondered if somehow his absence had made a difference. Later, and distressingly, he remembered that the troop was now Carroll's. Would he get it back again?
>
> Someone sat on a doorstep smoking a pipe. He looked up, shielding his eyes against the sun. It was Dunkley. While they walked to the cellar which was Duffy's HQ, Dunkley gave him a quick account of all that had happened in the past few weeks. The question whether Wilson would take over his troop again was answered without being asked. Carroll was dead. He'd been killed at Weeze (sic), a few miles down the road. While they drank he told Wilson how Carroll had been standing up in the turret, trying to back down a narrow street, when a bazooka took the flaps off. 'You'd better go and see your troop.
>
> The first afternoon Dunkley took Wilson over some fields to show him where Carroll was buried. There was a row of plain crosses, with Carroll's name and the name of some other tank soldiers. [Almost certainly the dead of 6 GAB]. A little beyond were crosses garlanded with flowers, marked 'Unknown German Soldier'. That evening, as they ate their meal, Wilson remarked to Grundy, who sat next to him, about the flowers on the German graves. 'Yes', said Grundy. 'It's a mystery how they get there. No one ever sees a German civilian about'.[84]

Carroll was killed not in Weeze but in Kervenheim and the events are described in Chapter 3.

Items of interest in Wilson's narrative include information that the Germans successfully jammed the tank radio frequencies; that it was always the gunner who got out last when the tank brewed up; that the pattern of support was always the same – a call to pressure up, a quick conference with the infantry, a run across the fields to flame an enemy you never saw; that pressuring up meant Wilson and the co-driver dismounting and opening the valves on the trailer to release the nitrogen; that wet-flaming meant dousing the target in fuel and adding the flame at the end; that the troop commander had to keep checking the pressure which slowly diminished, meaning that if the attack was delayed for more than a few hours the Crocodiles had to break off to change the nitrogen bottle and pressure up again; that the Crocodile crews feared the German anti-tank guns and imagined them behind every leafy branch and in every farmyard.

J.G. Smith was at Kervenheim, and his insights into those events belong in that chapter. He wrote that he had heard little good of 6 GAB, calling them 'a bunch of show-offs', ready to take all the praise that was going, and interested, like 15 BID, in bullshit. He added that 51 BID had

83 Wilson, *Flame Thrower*, pp. 122-24.
84 Op. Cit., pp. 171-77.

a reputation for not liking tanks. He was cynical about planning and observed that events never worked out, while he was given an appreciation of the military situation only once. He stated that his tank had a 38 set for communication with the infantry but it was never used, and neither was the telephone on the rear of the tank provided for that purpose. Relations between the Crocodiles and the infantry appear to have been non-existent, and supposedly mediated between 6 GAB. In these circumstances 3 BID would have done better to have taken Wasp Mk IICs on charge and provided their own flame.

8

The Royal Regiment of Artillery

The infantry do not understand their orders; the cavalry ignore them, and the gunners make their own arrangements.

Anon

And as their firing dies away the husky whisper runs
From lips that haven't drunk all day: "The Guns! Thank God, the Guns!"

Rudyard Kipling. *Ubique*

Just send in your chief an' surrender – it's worse if you fights or you runs:
You can go where you please, you can skid up the trees,
But you don't get away from the guns!

Rudyard Kipling. *Screw-Guns.* Unofficial Royal Regimental song

In the nation of many tribes constituting the British Army, the gunners and the sappers were in most respects the antithesis of the Guards. Instead of privilege there was merit. No gunner or sapper had to purchase a commission since knowledge of arithmetic was never considered a defining characteristic of a gentleman. As a result, gunners never suffered from the system in which old and grey headed lieutenants carried ignorant majors and colonels on their backs.[1] Promotion was, however, by seniority, while in the infantry it was by merit, purchase and exchange. In the small artillery corps a subaltern could therefore easily serve for 25 years before becoming a captain. In two cases during the American revolutionary war, brilliant gunners were promoted by making them captains in line regiments on merit.[2]

The Royal Regiment of Artillery was founded in 1716 out of the Train of Artillery, and dressed not in scarlet but in the blue of the Master General of the Ordnance. The tactical fire-unit soon became a battery of six guns commanded by a Major. The Battery was the equivalent of an infantry coy or tank sqn, while command of a gun was the equivalent of commanding an infantry platoon or troop of tanks. Gunners have forever associated themselves with their Battery and the Regiment, there being many regiments in the army, but only one Regiment. The gleaming, pampered guns became their totems, and to lose a gun was as disgraceful as the infantry's loss of their colours.

The artillery offered a career open to talent, and lack of money was no bar to promotion. 'The Shop' was founded in 1741 for the professional education of Artillery, and later Engineer, cadets. The Royal Military Academy was called the 'workshop' with the implication that its cadets were a bunch of tinkers. Discipline was severe, and the curriculum a mixture of drill, applied mathematics, riding and military engineering. It bred generations of warlike and competent officers who had the advantage of knowing what they were doing.

1 Shelford Bidwell. *Gunners at War* (London: Arms & Armour Press, 1970).
2 Turner, *Gallant Gentlemen*, p. 229.

In 1838 a group of officers founded the Royal Artillery Institution in Woolwich to study the science of artillery. The School of Artillery at Larkhill superseded it in 1920. There then existed all the elements of a private army and corps d'élite with its own system for cadet selection and training and with its own professional head and research facilities. The gunners were conscious of their ability, their indispensability and their superiority, and they had done it all by themselves.

Although most officers came from public school, that school's identity was of no consequence since graduation from 'The Shop' was the only qualification needed for acceptance. There was no vetting by regimental colonels, and no enquiries about private means, about family background or about regimental connections.

The attractions of the Artillery were cheap living, and crucially the availability of horses. Most could not afford to idle, to become playboys or to miss promotion through lack of application, so they continued the study of their profession. Most were men of the field with a passion for hunting, pig sticking and polo closely followed by shooting and fishing. The infantry lacked horses and expense ruled out the cavalry for all except the wealthy. But a young gunner officer posted to the field branch found himself in the enviable position of owning two chargers complete with grooms, and with twenty-six horses of the gun teams under his immediate care. He was encouraged to use as many of them as he could for recognised sports. Being therefore mobile, and living within his small battery where he could understudy and practice the responsibilities of his immediate superior, gunner officers matured quickly in developing a sense of responsibility and independent judgment much earlier than in the other arms.

The 1938 army reorganisation, in which Liddell Hart notoriously had a hand, produced confusion and resentment. The 72 field guns of the infantry division had been previously organised into three brigades of four batteries each containing six guns, a survey section and a signals section. There were thus 12 batteries of 6 guns per division, reflecting the pre-1918 divisional organisation of 12 battalions. Under Liddell Hart's reorganisation, the seventy-two guns were divided into three regiments of two batteries containing 12 guns, with each battery made up of three troops with 4 guns each. This halved the number of batteries with significant reductions in manpower and opportunity for promotion, which was indeed one of the objectives of the reform. The survey sections were abolished.

The result, which Liddell Hart wanted, was the destruction of co-operation between artillery and infantry, and was therefore dangerous. It will by now be apparent that Liddell Hart and his theories were antagonistic to all-arms, and therefore responsible for ensuring that the tank-infantry co-operation that Monash established at Hamel and Amiens was forgotten; and through this Artillery reform he nearly did the same for Infantry-Artillery co-operation. The 12-gun battery was too large for good control by the battery commander, and six batteries failed to relate to the nine battalions of the division. The reorganisation thus failed to promote the objectives of the artillery, which were to support infantry and armour intimately and to produce concentrations of fire within minutes. The campaigns of 1940 and in the desert showed up these and other deficiencies. So in 1941 the divisional artillery was reorganised into 9 batteries of 8 guns, reflecting the number of battalions in the division. It allowed permanent pairing of a battery with an infantry battalion, and an artillery regiment with an infantry brigade.

The Organisation of Divisional Artillery

Troop		Number of			
		Troop	Regt	Survey	OP
1716-1937	12 batteries of 6 guns = 72 guns	na	na	3	12
1938-1941	6 batteries of 12 guns = 72 guns	12	3	0	12
1941-1945	9 batteries of 8 guns = 72 guns	18	3	3	36

NB. Each bty comd and 2ic, and each Tp comd were equipped to form an OP.

The design of the standard 25pdr gun-howitzer was the result of experience in France during the First World War, when the field artillery was equipped with two pieces; the 18pdr gun with a calibre of 3.3 inch (83.8 mm), designed to fire shrapnel over open sights; and the 4.5 inch (114 mm) howitzer. Both, however, had a range limited to 6,500 yards, but for different reasons. In the case of the 18pdr, its pole trail limited elevation to 16°. Greater ranges could be achieved by digging the trails down a foot for each additional 1,000 yards range desired, and laying the gun by a field clinometer, but even after irksome and time-consuming digging, the maximum practicable range was still only 9,500 yards. In the case of the 4.5 inch howitzer, its carriage permitted an elevation of 45°, but range was limited to 6,500 yards by its short barrel, and even this combination of elevation and range sometimes proved insufficient to clear the crests of hills. There were occasions in France, and especially during the Hundred Days, when attacking infantry went out of range of their supporting artillery, which could not move forward because of the state of the ground in which guns and horses bogged.

In 1919, the RA Committee recommended combining the 18pdr gun and 4.5 inch howitzer in a new design of gun-howitzer with a range of 15,000 yards, firing HE and AP, that could be manhandled, that could tackle moving targets and would weigh no more than 30 cwt, which was the maximum that a standard team of six horses could easily pull. By 1933 various combinations of shell weight and calibre had been tried, with the choice falling on a shell weight of 25 lb and a calibre of 3.7 inches (94 mm). This was quickly rejected because the Treasury insisted that existing 18pdr carriages be used, and they could not absorb the force from 3.7 inch calibre. Thus the compromise was reached; of a 25 lb shell with a calibre of 3.45 inch (87.6 mm). The old demand for 15,000 yards was unobtainable and dropped in favour of 13,500 yards. That, however, still required a new carriage, which was eventually designed, and even then the maximum range with supercharge was 13,400 yards. A split trail carriage would have weighed 41 cwt and been less handy to traverse quickly. The weight of the new box carriage at 3,908 lb (34.9 cwt) was also more than the 3,360 lb (30 cwt) of the original specification, but because of motorisation was found to be acceptable, and with its firing platform, easy to handle. Elevation ranged from –5° to +40°.

Thus was born the legendary 25pdr Mk 2 that first saw action in Norway in 1940, and of which 12,000 were eventually built in Australia, Britain, and Canada. Few modifications were required to an excellent design; the most important being a muzzle break, and radiusing of the corners of the breech ring to prevent cracking.

It had three serious shortcomings. Firstly an inability to reach out to 15,000 yards, which translated into a significant reduction of coverage requiring more frequent movement. This mattered in Operation *Heather*, when exceptionally bad ground conditions made movement difficult and exhausting. The Battle of Kervenheim, for example, was planned on the assumption that GAD's field artillery would participate, but they remained out of range. It was not, however, uncompetitive in this regard. The range of the German 105 mm at 13,479 yards was no greater than the

13,400 of the 25pdr, while the range of the US 105 mm was only 12,325 yards. Secondly, 25 lb was light for a field gun in the Second World War, when the standard 105 mm howitzer fired a 33 lb shell. Thirdly, the British decided to manufacture the 25pdr shell out of standard engineering steel of 19-ton yield strength, when the USA used 23-ton steel. The result was that the walls of the 25pdr shell had to be thicker to withstand the tube pressures, which again reduced the weight of HE shell filling. In consequence the 25 lb shell had only 7% fill compared with 15% for the US 105 mm shell made. HE weight in the 25 lb was 1.75 lb, while the Germans achieved 3.07 lb (+75%), and the Americans 4.9 lb or 180%.[3]

It was calculated that the relative effectiveness of the standard field guns was 1.0 for the 25pdr, 1.3 for the German, and 1.7 for the US 105 mm HE M1.[4]

The 25pdr was a superb piece of engineering. It showed that the British Army could design excellent weapons when given the means, and when clear about the way the weapon was to be used. In the case of tanks, as we shall see, neither condition was met. The 25pdr gained its effect by rapid firing of its light but effective shell at a rate of up to 12 rounds per minute, although at Winnekendonk they fired at the slower than slow rate of 1½ rpm. OR studies showed that a greater number of smaller bangs was more effective than fewer bigger bangs. Germans and Americans fired the heavier 33 lb shell at a maximum rate of 10 rounds per minute to a shorter maximum range of 12,205 yards.

A US infantry division had 36 units of 105 mm and 12 of 155 mm in 4 battalions. In addition the US Army had a total of 2,832 non-divisional pieces for roughly 54 divisions, or 52 additional pieces per division. By comparison, the Commonwealth AGRAs had a total of 672 pieces for roughly 15 divisions, or about 45 additional pieces per division. In addition, each US infantry division had an additional 18 units of 105 mm howitzers in the regimental cannon companies. The result was that the average British infantry division was supported by 117 howitzers, and the average US infantry division by 120. In Operation *Heather* only 88 howitzers supported 3 BID. Their weight of fire was inadequate and did not produce the required suppressive effect.

3 BID artillery during *Heather* commanded 168 guns and howitzers of all kinds. At Kervenheim and Winnekendonk, these artillery pieces supported an attack by an infantry battalion of 200 to 300 riflemen, which meant that there was one artillery piece indirectly supporting every 1¼ to 1¾ infantrymen on the battlefield. In addition, there was a squadron of 15 Churchill tanks providing direct fire support:

25pdr howitzer	72, in 7, 33 and 76 Field Regiments
5.5 inch howitzer	16, in 84 Sussex Medium Regiment; attached
17pdrs towed	20, in 20 Anti-Tank Regiment
SP 17pdr Archer	12, in the same 20 AntiTank Regiment
SP 3 inch M10	12, in 198 battery RA; attached
40 mm Bofors	36, in 92 Light Anti-Aircraft (LAA) Regiment
Total	168
of which howitzers	88

This artillery was organised in six regiments, a regiment being the gunner's name for a battalion. One regiment, 84 Sussex Medium, and 198 Anti-Tank Battery were assigned by XXX Corps for the Operation and placed under 3 BID's CRA, Brigadier Gerald Mears, just as the Buffs' Crocodiles were placed under 6 GAB.

3 http://nigelef.tripod.com/wt_of_fire.htm
4 Ibid.

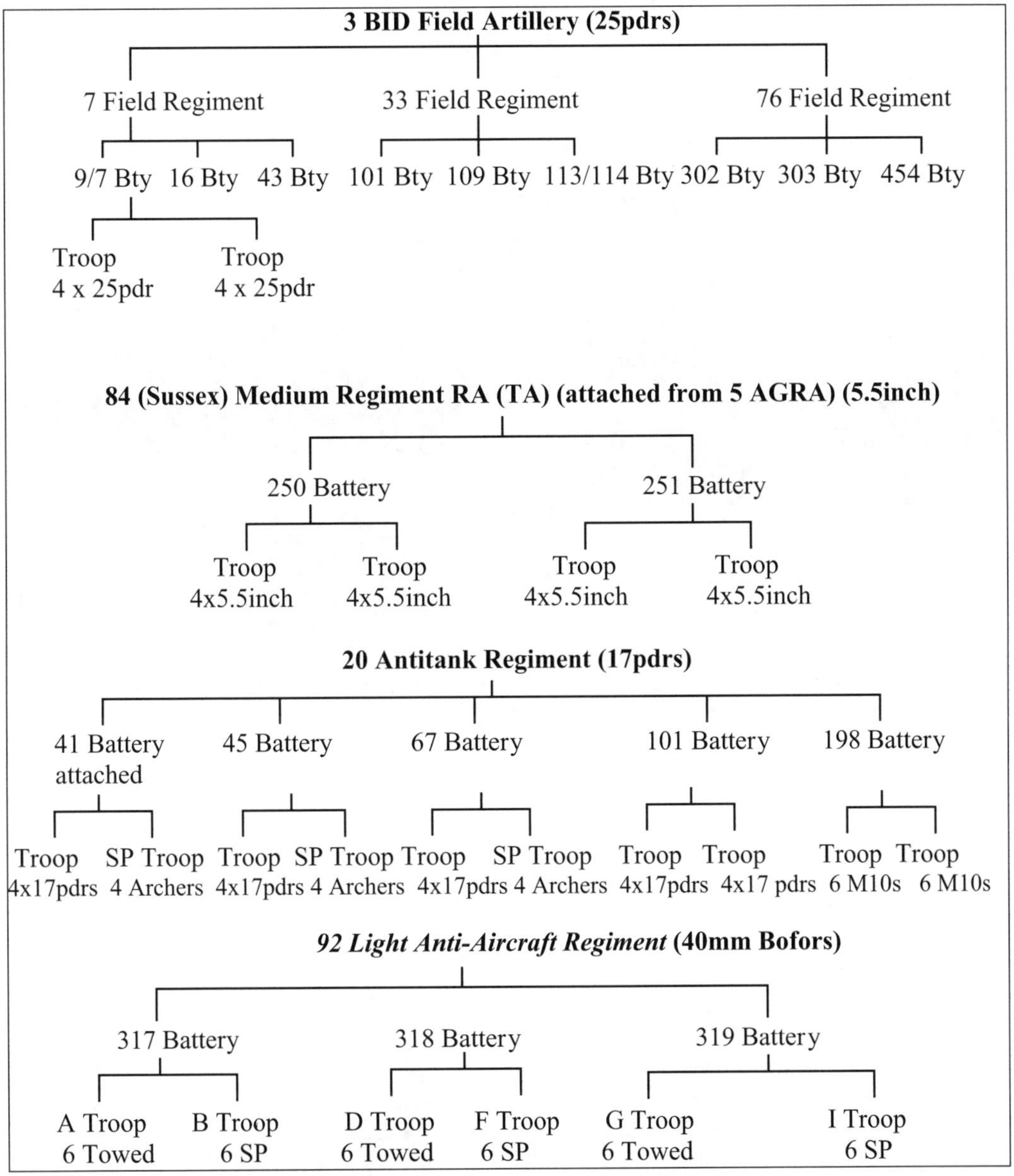

For D-Day the 25pdrs were replaced by M7 SP 105 mm Priests which, being self-propelled, could fire from the deck of the landing craft during the run-in and be ready for almost instant action on landing. These guns were popular with the crews but for a variety of reasons, including weak recuperators, shortage of US-made ammunition and the need for standardised ammunition supply, they equipped only the three Assault Divisions until July 1944, when they were turned in for towed 25pdrs. Some were later converted into Priest Kangaroo APCs. The Division might then have received the SP 25pdr Sexton, but these seem to have been reserved for the armoured divisions whose raison d'être was mobility.

Heavy bombardment was provided by 84 Medium Regiment, which was transferred to 3 BID on 28 February from 5 AGRA. The CO, Lt-Col Fitzgerald, commanded 27 officers and 567 men. They served sixteen 5.5 inch howitzers in two batteries of two troops each. Its shell at 100 lb was

28 February 1945. A 25 pounder in action on the outskirts of Goch. This would have been one of 3 BID's Fld Regts supporting the attack on Kervenheim. (© Crown Copyright IWM, B 14956 by Sgt Hutchinson)

1st March 1945. 'F' Troop 318 Bty 92nd Light AA Regt fire their Bofors into a wood in support of advancing infantry. This scene at Stein was described by RW Thompson. This weapon was a 40 mm Bofors mounted on a Morris Commercial C9/B chassis. (© Crown Copyright IWM, B 14965 by Sgt Carpenter)

four times the weight of a 25pdr, since shell weight increases according to the cube of the calibre. A hit by a 5.5 inch weighing 100 lb caused certain destruction to a weapon like the StuG, which could shrug off a 25pdr HE shell.

	25pdr	5.5 inch	Total
Calibre: mm	88	140	
Calibre: inch	3.5	5.5	
Weight of shell: lb	25	100	
Number engaged	72	16	86
Weight of shell per salvo: lb	1,800	1,600	3,400

20 Anti-Tank Regiment had four batteries and eight troops. Three of the four batteries had one troop of four SP Archers and one troop of four towed 17pdrs. The Regiment had in total 20 towed 17pdrs and 12 Archers. In addition, 198 Battery was attached to the division from Corps, bringing 12 M10 3 inch self-propelled guns operated by 169 other ranks and 12 officers. In total the Division therefore had 44 antitank guns under centralised RA command, although there is a slight discrepancy with the War Diary, which lists 45 antitank guns.

The Archer had replaced the divisional M10s that landed in Normandy. With its low profile, it was easy to camouflage and made a fine over-watch weapon or backstop. It could not advance, however, while in action because it faced backwards and the driver had to leave his seat to avoid the recoil. This left a role, therefore, for the M10, whose 3-inch gun was almost as powerful as the 17pdr, and could act as a kind of assault gun or mobile backup to the Churchills if required. The infantry simply called it another tank,[5] and the M10s were placed under command of 6 GAB.

92 Light AntiAircraft Regt RA had started life as 7 Bn The Loyal Regt. It had 36 units of 40 mm Bofors guns, half of which were towed and half self-propelled. They were organised in 3 batteries of 2 troops. The Bofors was often used in a ground role – the first time on D-Day:

> That evening, finally reaching the outskirts of Benouville, the Bofors crews found buildings still occupied by snipers. One German was targeting the troop from the belfry of a church tower and was rooted out with a blast of 40 mm. The guns were also fired at short range directly into windows and doorways and the troop took 12 prisoners.
>
> Because the 40 mm shells self-destructed after a few thousand feet, they could be used in open country for low-level airbursts against enemy positions – sending out a fierce hail of shrapnel. Fired into buildings or wooded areas, the shells would explode against walls or trees, with similar devastating anti-personnel effects.
>
> 'By the time we left the Caen sector we were confident that we could shoot along the ground and shoot with success,' wrote Captain Almond. 'A salvaged steel pipe sawn into cross-sections, tinned and engraved by REME personnel, provided our sight drums, and officers and NCOs trained hard in the new method of firing whilst keeping watch on the skies.'
>
> The first major indirect fire shoot took place in support of Operation *Wallup*, a divisional artillery barrage, on August 11. Some 1,200 rounds were fired at a crossroads, but the Germans had pulled out of the target area.[6]

5 Rex Fendick in correspondence.
6 http://www.geocities.com/lightackack/loyals26.html

In *Heather*, Bofors were used extensively in the ground role at Kervenheim.

> Two days later, at 2.30 am on Tuesday February 27, it (92 LAA Regt) crossed the German frontier at Hekkens and deployed around Goch, setting up headquarters in cellars on the south side of the town.
>
> Shoots were carried out on enemy-held woods south of Udem and there was a major indirect fire operation to support 185 Brigade's attack on Kervenheim. In 20 minutes, 318 Battery poured 2,400 rounds on enemy trenches. Later, infantry observers reported `considerable execution.'[7]

Each battery contained a mobile counter-mortar observation team consisting of a sergeant, a bombardier and four gunners, equipped with wireless, Jeep and a 15cwt truck. The plotting centre for the Bofors and an armoured observation post were furnished by 20 Anti-tank Regt.

92 LAA Regiment had only half the guns and troops with which it landed in Normandy, reflecting the diminished threat from enemy aircraft. Until 8 August 1944, it had been equipped with 54 Bofors and 24 units of 20 mm Oerlikon-Polsten guns. The redundant crews were transferred into the infantry.

The methods used by the artillery were developed during the Second World War into a refined and effective system that when used in support of infantry was in some ways better than in the First World War. The key was identity of interest. For much of the First World War there was an entrenched stalemate, almost a siege, and it was thought that artillery employed en masse could be used to produce a breakthrough. Haig, the cavalryman, was thus persuaded by Noel Birch, and while it seems obviously fallacious today, the same thinking re-surfaced in Normandy with the belief that heavy bombers would be able to create a gap for tanks to pass through unsupported by infantry in Operation *Goodwood.*

The ingredients of good infantry/artillery co-operation were the same as for effective tank/infantry co-operation. Both could be achieved only when the equipment was to the right specification and the two arms had identity of interest and their officers comingled and co-planned. Chapter 10 explores the reasons why this never happened with tanks/infantry, while it magnificently occurred between the artillery and the infantry. They were so integrated on a day-to-day basis, that the bty comd who was acting as FOO took over the decimated infantry coy outside Murmannshof during the Battle of Kervenheim and as Maclean did at Yorkshire Bridge.

Under the 1938 reforms the British artillery in France and North Africa were split up and dispersed amongst brigade groups and Jock Columns, while the integrated artillery command system of the First World War was destroyed. In the desert, the 25pdrs in the absence of anything more powerful were employed as a forward anti-tank screen and destroyed from afar by the bigger 105 mm German towed field guns, and by 88s. The benefits of large intense artillery concentrations were unappreciated and actually unobtainable with the dispersed artillery command fashionable after Dunkirk.

It was not until Montgomery took control of the army at Alam Halfa in 1942, and brought in Sidney Kirkman,[8] that the lessons of the First World War began to be relearned and re-implemented. According to Bidwell, Montgomery supported the unknown Kirkman during an indoor exercise in 1941, saying; 'The business of Gunner COs was first to train their regiments, and then to train the infantry brigadiers to use them properly'. From this time on artillery was concentrated instead of being decentralised and dissipated amongst the brigades. Apart from defensive fire

7 Ibid.
8 Bidwell, *Gunners at War.*

intended to stop damaging German fire, the British doctrine was that artillery should provide fire to cover movement, going so far as to insist that there should be no movement without fire, and no fire without movement, defined as a waste of resources. The objective of the artillery was to neutralise the defenders' fire with what was called 'suppressive fire', and to keep the infantry alive for the succeeding phase of the infantry 'dog-fight'. Under Montgomery and Kirkman brigades once again fought in divisions instead of Jock Columns, and artillery was concentrated to provide the division with effective barrages and concentrations.

Covering fire was provided by a 'barrage' line, which was advanced on a pre-determined bearing in increments of a hundred yards. The curtain of shells moved forward in bounds at an average speed agreed with the infantry for their rate of advance. The infantry 'leaned' on the barrage by getting close to the line of bursting shells just before firing stopped and the range lifted. Ideally the infantry maintained a steady pace. As they closed with the line of bursting shells these would jump ahead a hundred yards, pausing on the new line while the infantry caught up again. It was rather like a frog out walking with a mouse.

Artillery fire was said to be 'concentrated' in 'stonks' when it was focused on specific targets. These were selected in collaboration with the infantry, numbered and entered on a 'trace' with all the details of range, elevation, heading and charge worked out in advance from the map. Few 'traces' for Operation *Heather* survived, being battlefield ephemera, but those that have are discussed in the relevant battle chapters. The numbered targets also acted as useful reference points for a secure shorthand between the FOO and his battery which could be broadcast en clair. For example the FOO could wireless in to the battery: 'Mike Target. 6221. Go SE 500.' By this order all 24 guns of the Regiment were directed to concentrate on a point 500 yards south-east of the map reference decided in advance as number 6221 and known only to these particular Gunners. This saved the time, on both ends of the wireless, required for calculating a 6-figure map reference, encoding it, communicating, decoding, and drawing it on the talc, before working out range, heading, elevation and charge. This methodology saved vital moments in an emergency. Lists of such targets for Operation *Heather* have survived, and they usually refer to farmhouses or road junctions. The concentration of so many shells in one area all at once caused tremendous damage to those German troops caught in the open. In these battles artillery caused most of the German casualties.

'Barrages' and 'concentrations' were put together in great programmes that took hours to prepare. The aim was to get the infantry unscathed to the objective and to protect them against an immediate German counter-attack by his best troops reserved for just such an emergency. At this stage the barrage became inappropriate and a different method of flexible response was required. Targets had to be acquired quickly according to fast-changing and unpredictable circumstances. A suitable method for fire control was worked out by Parham, another artillery innovator.

Parham based Anglo-Canadian fire control on three unique propositions and demonstrated them at Larkhill in 1941 to a group of generals who were nearly killed in the stands during it.[9] A single wireless net connected FOOs, CP and BCs. Secondly, everyone was trained to spot a target by eye to within 100 to 200 yards, which was considered the normal spread of a single gun firing without correction. And thirdly, the man in front was always in charge. The FOO advancing with the infantry and sharing their fate literally had control of the guns whenever he and he alone decided he needed it. No American, German, Russian or the First World War British CRA equivalent would accept this last proposition, except in the brief period of Monash's war-winning innovations of 1918.

9 Ibid.

The British method sometimes rubbed off. Carlo D'Este reported that Col Gregson of 7 BAD was receiving support from American artillery that was also supporting 1 USID at Caumont on 15 June 1944, The American LO, Capt Chuck Babcock, called for a Serenade, the US equivalent of a Victor shoot, which arrived quickly and accurately. Gregson remembered Babcock said; 'If we get out of this I'll be court-martialled – only Commanding Generals can order a 'Serenade'.

In every other army it was axiomatic that the CRA reserved the right to double-guess or pass judgment on the FOO. After all, it was argued, the task of the commander was to command and give orders. The result of Parham's innovation was that any FOO could shout 'MIKE TARGET' and gain control of the 24 guns of the Regiment, or 'UNCLE TARGET' for the Division's 72 guns, or even 'VICTOR TARGET' if the emergency were grave enough, for up to 400 to 500 guns or however many were within range. Gunners would drop whatever tasks they were doing and switch immediately to the threat, coming to the infantry's assistance without question and with immense goodwill. A vivid example of the working of the system occurred during the Battle of Yorkshire Bridge, when the FOO John Ford in the bridgehead directed the artillery right up to corps in successful SOS and DF shoots that saved C Coy 2 East Yorks from being overrun. As we saw above, at one point Ford brought the massed artillery down on the farmhouse they were in after ensuring everyone had taken cover.

Since the BC and FOO lived with their infantry, and each battery was permanently affiliated with its battalion, and each field regiment with its brigade, they became personally well acquainted. In his diary Capt Darby Hart of 2 Lincolns records dining with Jack Hunton, the 33rd Regt's FOO, on 20 February outside Louvain; 'CO [Cecil Firbank], Leslie [Colvin] and [Jack] Hunton came to dinner. 6 courses! & v well done', and on 5 March in Winnekendonk; 'Had party in evening. Parsons & Dick Griffiths came & Jack Hunton. Good evening'. This familiarity was so accepted that in an emergency a gunner officer automatically assumed command of an inf coy, as Haigh commanded the rump of 'A' Company of the Norfolks at Kervenheim and Maclean at Yorkshire Bridge. The degree of intimate trust and goodwill established between the two arms shines through in the great majority of statements made by infantrymen about the gunners in the Second World War, and often conclude with an expression of eternal gratitude. The exception is 1 Royal Norfolks who appear to have suffered exceptionally from shells falling short. Perhaps this statement should be rephrased to say that the Norfolks were more aware than the other battalions that casualties were caused by shorts, and they were traumatised by Kervenheim.

This trust was rarely true of the relationship with tanks of any unit, with the exception of parts of 6 GAB, the SAR and NIH, and was not always true even with regard to these units. Maj Harry Illing, who commanded a company of 2 Warwicks during this period when supported by 4 CG, said he would always trade a tank for another gun.[10] Neither was it true of 2 TAF's Typhoons. The complaint, however, ignores a fundamental reality. When an infantryman called for an emergency shoot through the FOO – who shared the same risk as the infantry – he did not usually risk gun or gunner. By contrast the crew of both tank and Typhoon put themselves directly at risk when supporting the infantry. Being close-quarter weapons, they had to close within range of *Pak* or *Flak*, which in the case of the 88 was the same gun. Gunners normally ran no such risk, having mastered the art of indirect fire and being under no threat from Luftwaffe gunnery reconnaissance. There was no case during Operation *Heather* known to this author of any field gun being destroyed by German artillery. In the First World War, by contrast, entire batteries of 18pdrs were destroyed. William Carr, a BC in the First World War described what happened when visibility improved one morning after a series of misty days. An enemy balloon rose beyond Hangard Wood, and Carr could see two figures in the basket through his binoculars. His blood froze as he realized

10 Harry Illing in conversation.

one of them was an artillery observation officer, who would immediately see the flashes from Carr's brigade and direct the heavies onto his position. His battery would not survive. Carr's request to Corps for permission to move his battery was refused, although a French 75 mm battery alongside departed quickly.[11] During *Heather*, guns and crews were imperilled only by unobserved CB fire. If there had been more danger, the infantryman might have received from the RA the same questioning and possible refusal or prevarication that he received from operators of tanks and aircraft. These possessed, in their own estimation, expertise carrying its own imperatives that the PBI could not, they insisted, understand.

The infantryman, however, could not appreciate the difference. Ordered to risk his own life and having to lead by example, the infantry officer demanded every support and was entitled to receive it. He needed control over his own armour and air as he had effectively over his own artillery, becoming often angry and uncomprehending when it was denied. The Battles of Yorkshire Bridge and Kervenheim provided examples of the infantry being left without the armour they demanded, doubtless on professional grounds with words such as these spoken with the tone of a tired master addressing an ignorant schoolboy; 'Can't fight at night, old boy. It would be a disaster. Can't see a bloody thing, you know, and we have to do maintenance. If we don't the tanks won't run for long, and then where would you be?' The unspoken answer would have occurred to many; 'Give us the tanks then, and you Foxtrot Oscar and get your beauty sleep – schedule the maintenance for the morning.' Gunners never talked like the 'mobile arms'of tanks and aircraft. They prided themselves on always being available to 'their' unit when required at any time of day or night. They did maintenance, re-supplied themselves and moved position at times guaranteed not to inconvenience the infantry. Often this happened at night and gunners suffered from sleeplessness and exhaustion every bit as severely as the infantry, and would be found asleep by their guns in slack periods. The exception to the rule in these battles was GAD's artillery, which failed repeatedly to keep in range. However, in this regard not only did 6 GAB have no artillery, it had absolutely nothing to do with GAD, was not regarded even remotely as one of 'their' units, and GAD was itself fragmented at that time; its armoured brigade was sitting around doing nothing while its infantry brigade was fighting and dying in support of an infantry division elsewhere and required artillery support. Even the RA could not be in two places at once, although being tracked SP they could move far more easily than the wheeled Quad tractors that had to pull the 25pdrs out of the morass whenever ordered to move.

In the final analysis it was the presence of the FOO and his power to call down almost instant retribution that did more than anything else to keep the infantry semi sane. It was said by infantry officers that their role was to provide a guard for the FOO as he walked from La Brèche to Bremen.

The guns, however, were not effective during the assault, and the breakthrough at Winnekendonk could not have been achieved without armoured support, and not just because all communication with the guns broke down when the Pipe Major's Churchill containing the FOO was destroyed. The tanks provided the essential directly aimed mobile gun and machine-gun needed to overcome resistance in real time that the artillery could not see to hit. And they were vital for morale. Therefore the terms of their use in support had to be negotiated on behalf of the infantry CO who was on the battlefield. This required a strong and persuasive infantry Brigadier acting as an advocate with the Divisional GOC and with the Brigadier who controlled the armour. It was at this stage in the process that any lack of effectiveness at Brigadier level weakened the division.

The KSLI at Kervenheim and the Lincolns at Winnekendonk were the exceptions that tested the validity of all these generalisations. As we have seen, communication with the artillery broke down completely at Winnekendonk, but the infantry never flinched and Sgt Alldred and the Tp

11 William Carr. *A Time To Leave The Ploughshares* (London: Robert Hale, 1985).

Landing field used by artillery observation planes, about three miles from Udem, Germany, 27 February 1945. Such an airfield was established at Brönkshof soon after its capture. The system whereby 2TAF supplied, serviced, maintained and repaired these Austers flown by artillery officers under army command could have been extended to the entire 2 TAF's Close Air Support. By so doing, a most significant step towards combined all arms would have been taken, and the performance of 21 AG immeasurably improved. (Donald I Grant/Canada. Dept.of National Defence/Library & Archives Canada/PA-153189)

Cpl without hesitation risked all to destroy the StuGs, 88s and MG42s to let the infantry into the village. Without 3 SG, according to John Boys of the Lincolns,[12] the battle would surely have been lost. But without the infantry's pressing on and not waiting for the tanks when they were busy on the right flank, the Germans would have held.

Shelford Bidwell compares the interdependence of infantry, artillery and tanks with the finger game of paper, stone and scissors. The comparison is inexact because each arm of the military plays a multitude of rôles; for example an infantryman with a PIAT or a Panzerfaust could destroy a tank. But generally the infantry (paper) could be cut down by tanks (scissors), which themselves were destroyed by anti-tank guns (stone), which could be enveloped by the infantry (paper).

The RA's tactics and gunnery methods, including the technique of surveying in the guns, are explained in a website,[13] and will not be further discussed here. There is also detailed coverage in a recent book by Ben Kite published by Helion.[14]

Parham was also responsible for introducing AOPs. Their establishment had involved a knock-down argument with the RAF and the intervention of Alan Brooke. After the order was given, opposition quickly died and the concept proved in Tunisia. The RAF then displayed energy and understanding in training the pilots, producing the ground crews and generally making the scheme work. On 2 March 1945, B Flight of 662 (AOP) Sqn, RAF, operating Taylorcraft Auster Mk IIIs out of a field near Cleves (907522), came under command of 3 BID. Nominally within

12 John Boys in conversation.
13 http://membership/~nigelef/index.htm (2002)
14 Ben Kite. *Stout Hearts* (Solihull: Helion, 2014), p. 152-80.

83 Gp, the 20 officers and 83 ORs were all from the Royal Artillery. Even the ORBs are filed with the military rather than with the air. In the War Diary an entry recorded that the planes were, 'At call from 0800 hrs. On CRA's net: flick to 84 Med Regt.'

The squadron ORB gives no details of their tasks. The squadron was concerned on 27 February with the disappearance of Lt Laffey over Üdem. This concern turned to 'grave alarm' on the 28th when still nothing had been heard from him. In general losses were rare and therefore remarkable. The Germans had learned in Tunisia that high performance fighters could not shoot down Austers as they danced and weaved between the hills. In Europe they would simply disappear behind a stand of trees.

Not all of the small planes over the battlefield were manned by AOPs. On 2 March 1945 Crerar's War Diary records:

> Left at 1045 hrs for an aerial reconnaissance of the battle area. Returned to my Tac HQ at 1210 hrs. Left at 1530 hrs by air for my daily conference with the Corps Commanders. Returned to my Tac HQ at 1645 hrs.[15]

Crerar piloted himself in an Auster or L-5. His diary does not record what he learned that day. It was only 30 miles from Crerar's HQ at Uden in the Netherlands via Boxmeer across the Maas to Kervenheim, the nearest part of the line to his Tac HQ, so it is possible that he was over Kervenheim just after 11 am as the Auster cruised at 80 mph.

To place shells consistently on target, the Gunners had to keep constant tabs on all of the variables. They had to know the state of barrel wear by periodically checking the muzzle velocity of *every* gun, a difficult chore avoided by the wealthier Americans who simply replaced worn barrels. Barrel wear reduced barrel pressure, leading to lower muzzle velocity and reduced range. To compensate for wear either elevation had to be increased or a greater charge of gunpowder employed. The Norfolks claimed that many guns fired short at Overloon and Kervenheim. This implied that the regiments were not keeping tabs on barrel wear. They received no feedback because the FOO could not identify the particular gun or guns falling short. Another possibility exists that some of the complaints were ill founded. The Germans practised the difficult art of placing a moving barrage in lock step behind the allied barrage and on top of the attacking infantry. However, experienced infantry believed they could distinguish British from German shelling, and their claims merited serious treatment, although it is not obvious they received it. This is the only criticism that could be levelled against the CRA Gerald Mears.

Meteorological conditions affected the flight of shells. Every 3 to 4 hours a weather telegram called a 'Meteor', was circulated to the guns from 2 TAF giving wind speeds, barometric pressures and temperatures at various altitudes. The gunners worked on a trace showing the guns' position and that of the targets, with the height above sea level given for both. This was called 'surveying' and, when completed, the range, bearing and elevation of each target could be calculated and the required charge of powder and flight time determined by checking the height reached by the shell's parabola.

> Periodically the actual performance of the guns was checked in order to identify the size of the difference or error between predicted and actual performance. This was known as 'registration' of the guns. The War Diary of 33 Fld Regt on 28 February recorded; 'Capt Palmer tests out Div Arty on one target in view of no opportunity for registration prior to barrage.[16]

15 LAC: Crerar Papers,
16 TNA: WO 171/4816: War Diary of 33 Field Regiment RA.

The results of the registration were not recorded but would probably have been consistent with the findings of No. 2 OR Section in October 1944 (Report No. 16) and again on 8 February 1945 (Report No. 31) that not more than 5.1% of rounds fired in a counter-battery programme fell within an area of 100 yards by 100 yards around the target while the 100% area was a square kilometre.[17] Plots of impacts taken from aerial photographs showed them dispersed across 400 to 500 yards with the MPI displaced 200 to 300 yards to the west of the targeted German batteries. Not one shell landed on target. The main cause of the inaccuracy was wrong weather forecasting by 84 Gp 2 TAF. For instance the forecast for the hours from 5 am to 10 am on 8 February was for an upper air wind speed of 47 mph on a bearing of 286 degrees, while the actual wind at 8 am was blowing at 30 mph from 258 degrees. The temperature was forecast at 44° when it was actually 41°. These errors accounted for misses of up to 700 yards. But errors and mistakes were also found in the gun lines accounting for discrepancies of 75 yards, from guns being laid parallel when they should have been distributed around Number 3 gun, from surveying errors with the guns not in their calculated positions, from the German targets placed 13.7 metres on average from their actual positions, and from errors in recording, calculation and interpolation from tables. These were the types of error that would have accounted for the concentration fired on Murmannshof falling short amongst A Company of the Norfolks and doing severe damage to them. The audit suggests that the RA was not immune from sometimes resting on its laurels.

The OR Section also examined the dispersion of shells around the opening line of the *Veritable* barrage. They found 74 craters in an area of 100 yards by 100 yards at a distance of 500 to 450 yards in front of the opening line. These shells would have fallen on top of the attacking troops and confirmed the view of the Norfolks that shorts were common rather than exceptional. The OR Section also examined the results of post-shoot calibration, finding that the predicted muzzle velocity varied from the actual by as much as 9%; for example report number 24 for liner number L1371 of a 5.5-inch gun produced a muzzle velocity of 820 feet/second compared with an estimated 892 f/s. This type of error would have explained the observation of the Norfolks that one gun in particular always fired short, and that the RA had failed to find and fix the problem.

Dealing with such matters comprised the intellectual aspect of gunnery. The part requiring brute strength was hauling ammunition over mud tracks and advancing the gun lines to keep them in range. Both presented severe problems during Operation *Heather*. Today heavy lift helicopters can guarantee guns will be moved and supplied in an emergency, but in 1944-45 it required human and mechanical brawn. The night of 27/28 February during the Yorkshire Bridge DF task was the only time in the entire campaign from Normandy to Bremen that 33 Fld Regt feared it was running out of ammunition.

The artillery of several other formations within range was available as needed. 53 BID and 51 BID both fielded another seventy-two 25pdrs each before 51 BID was withdrawn on 28 February. The guns of 5 AGRA of XXX Corps comprising 7, 64 and 121 Medium Regiments with a total of forty-eight 5.5 inch howitzers were within range. 9 AGRA of II Cdn Corps with two medium and one heavy regiment comprising thirty-two 5.5 inch, and a regiment of US 155 mm and 7.2 inch howitzers was also well within range since their normal task was counter-battery work at distances of up to 20 km away. There is no evidence any of the big guns fired in direct support of Operation *Heather*, but 3 BID had access to all of these 511 guns of all calibres in an emergency. This was, however, only half the estimated 1,000 guns the Germans had assembled to keep 1 Cdn Army west of the Rhine.

In 1983, Chips Parker Smith found his carbon copy of a pencilled list of 30 targets 'at call' for the attack on Winnekendonk. It was a copy of target List Number 2, included in Operations

17 Terry Copp. *Montgomery's Scientists* (Waterloo: Laurier Centre for Military etc. Studies, 2000), pp. 295-330.

Order Number 19, and issued by Mears on 28 February 1945. Written on the bottom are the details of the barrage for the attack on Winnekendonk. No other mention of this barrage has survived in the War Diaries or elsewhere as far as is known. It must have been created at Division and at a date subsequent to 28 February, or it would have been included in the Operation Order. It probably dates from 1 March 1945.

All barrages for Phase III of *Heather* were given names beginning with 'V'; VINEGAR, VACUUM, VENUS, VIGILANT, VANGUARD and now VANDAL. For Venus see Map 26 and for Vandal see Map 33.

> VANDAL BARRAGE. Opening line 500* [*=yds] to EAST and WEST of 6224. Axis 180°. SEVEN lines at 100* every 5 mins. Rate 1 ½. Third Regt superimposed + 200*

Tony Edwards was Bty Comdr of 101 Bty, 33 Fld Regt and alongside Firbank in Tac HQ on the battlefield. In his notebook there is a footnote to this barrage:

> Barrage QWV first 5 open fire H to H + 100. 100 yds lift over 5 mins final lifting to long stonk 993339 170°.

This map reference identifies a point in the fields to the south of Winnekendonk and presumably the direction from which a counter-attack could have been expected. These two notes mean in layman's terms that a line of shells would fall 500 yards either side of the road junction, referred to as target number 6224 (99733470) over a period of 5 minutes. The line would then be advanced 100 yards in the direction of almost due south, repeating the movement seven times, and then finally lifting to cover the approach from the south. The guns would fire 3 shells every 2 minutes at Rate 1½, which was slower than slow – Very slow-1 rpm; Slow 2 rpm; Normal-3 rpm; Rapid-4 rpm; Intense-5 rpm – starting with two regiments and increasing to three after 10 minutes.

The distance from the Start Line to the road junction at the entrance to the village is about 1,000 yards. The rate of advance possible in these conditions was given by the KOSB at the Brigade Conference on 8 March as 100 yards across country every 2½ minutes – the equivalent of 1.4 mph. At this rate the Lincolns, starting at 5.45 pm, would have expected to reach the road junction after 25 minutes at 6.10 pm. At 5.55 pm the barrage would have lifted twice and be landing on the StuGs and 88s, while at 6.05 pm it would have advanced another 200 yards and be falling on the church.

Seventy-two 25pdrs firing at a rate of 1½ shells per minute on a 1,000 yard front to a depth of 100 yards, would drop 540 shells in an area of 100,000sq yards during the 5 minute period. A few shells would be smoke, fired typically by one gun per regiment. In total the barrage landed one shell per 185 square yards. Not included in the barrage were the sixteen medium 5.5 inch howitzers firing a 100 lb shell. Their FOO was killed in the battle, and they could have contributed some extra punch at a rate ⅔ per minute. However, according to a brief entry in Tony Edwards' notebook, the mediums were conducting a counter-battery shoot against guns located 7 kms to the east of Kevelaer: 'Regt Med Tgt during barrage. M5000 901 335, M5001 899335, M5002 905331.'

The density of the Winnekendonk barrage was 2,400 shells or 60 tons per hour per square kilometre. It is possible to assess its effectiveness by comparing it with the results published on 5 March 1945 by Lt-Col P. Johnson of Main HQ, 21 AG.[18] Johnson commanded No 2 OR Section, and his conclusions were based on interviewing 76 German POWs. His conclusions were that all line communications to the forward defences were cut, and defenders kept in their shelters, at any density exceeding 650 to 1,300 shells per square km. A density of 2,600 shells per hour per map

18 LAC: Crerar Papers.

square, which was slightly more than at Winnekendonk, was enough to neutralise the quality of defending troops. The number of own casualties did not fall much with weights of fire of over 100 tons per map square. At that level it was found that returns diminished rapidly.

This research leads to the conclusion that British casualties at Winnekendonk would have been lower had the barrage been increased in weight to 100 tons from its actual 60 tons per hour. GAD's two Field Regiments with 48 units of 25pdrs provided the planned means of doing this, but as we have seen, the mud prevented them from moving within range.

Johnson also concluded in his report that:

> there are indications that numbers of shells are more important than sheer weight of shells and that pepperpots are therefore a most valuable way of increasing fire effect without much increase in weight of ammunition.

A pepperpot was the employment of guns of all calibres to thicken the barrage. It included the Division's Bofors and 17pdr anti-tank guns, together with the main guns of any tanks or SP guns in the area. He warned, however, that pepperpots must not be used in planning barrages, but only to thicken them after the required minimum has been provided. No evidence has appeared that a pepperpot was fired at Winnekendonk although one was fired on 28 February and was witnessed by RW Thompson.

The modest weight of the barrage at Kervenheim and Winnekendonk raised again the question about the capacity of the 25pdr gun-howitzers in the howitzer rôle to produce the weight of shell that the Germans, Russians and Americans were getting from their 105 mm howitzers.

The aim of the barrage was to suppress or neutralise the defenders' fire, to drive the defenders to ground and to 'soften up the objective'. This reflected the doctrine of no movement without fire. From all the accounts of continuous and heavy defensive fire emanating continuously from Winnekendonk and Kervenheim, the barrages were not successful in achieving their aim. Nothing was done to neutralise fire coming from either the trenches dug forward in the open fields, which appeared to have been undetected when battle was joined, and were not covered by the planned barrage nor from the mortars firing from the woods behind Winnekendonk. Neither the 50 mm nor the 88s were suppressed and the StuGs were immune to 25pdr artillery.

The thinness of the barrages in Operation *Heather* was questioned by 33 Fld Regt at the 8 March Brigade Conference; 'Is a barrage on a front of 2000 yds from one div arty possible?' Renny replied that, 'It might be required when opposition is slight and an adv on a broad front possible. Usually, however, other types of fire sp will be used.' Renny elaborated in a second document; 'For attacks against villages, the fire of heavier weapons is needed to supplement the field artillery. A useful sequence is:

i) Typhoon attack.
ii) Medium guns and 4.2 in mortars.
iii) Field artillery (3 in mortars are better employed on the flanks).'

His reply cannot have satisfied Firbank, but the question should have been put to Whistler and Mears, the CRA, whose responsibility it was to arrange for a substitute if GAD's artillery could not get to the party. The artillery of 53 BID was available but not included in the Winnekendonk barrage although it was included on 27 February. Mears's reply would probably have been that the system allowed any Battalion CO through the FOO to declare a VICTOR target and gain the attention of every XXX Corps gun within range. Horrocks in *Corps Commander* stated that 400 guns were available for *Veritable*. This figure was made up of 216 field guns from three divisions, 128 medium and heavy guns from two AGRAs (each AGRA having four regiments of 16 guns), and 48 guns from two AA regiments of 3.7-inch firing HE in a ground role. The potential on the evening of 2 March was never more than 328 howitzers without GAD, but even this very useful three-fold increase could not be tapped because, as we have seen, the FOO was killed and all communication with the artillery broke down.

At Kervenheim and Winnekendonk, 3 BID lacked a means of delivering overwhelming suppressive fire in the moments before the infantry closed on the objective, of the sort that the Red Army pioneered in 1941 with the free flight Katyusha rocket barrage, and which the Germans implemented with their Nebelwerfer. The British Army had a Land Mattress which was not employed.

The complete target list for Winnekendonk comprised:

6200	9865 3676 18 m	6201	9913 3667 18 m	6202	9967 3663 19 m 190°
6203	0037 3695 20 m 150°	6204	0006 3665 19 m	6205	9910 3637 20 m
6206	9886 3617 19 m	6207	9915 3615 18 m 155°	6208	0033 3635 20 m 215°
6209	0077 3615 20 m	6210	0072 3586 20 m	6211	0112 3589 20 m 150°
6212	9970 3596 19 m	6213	9856 3513 20 m	6214	9932 3541 19 m
6215	0006 3586 20 m	6216	0105 3547 21 m	6217	0117 3527 22 m
6218	9917 3470 20 m 150°	6219	9961 3505 18 m 150°	6220	0005 3494 20 m 215°
6221	0043 3455 21 m 215°	6222	0035 3505 21 m	6223	0100 3448 20 m
6224	9973 3470 21 m	6225	9810 3570 19 m	6226	6205 EAST 500
6227	6205 EAST 1000	6228	6207 EAST 500	6229	6207 EAST 1000

3 BID's artillery was permanently allocated to the infantry:

7 Field Regt under Lt-Col H.C. Bazeley	– 185 Brigade – Brig. F.R.G. Matthews
9/7 Bty – Hendrie Bruce	– 2 Warwicks – Lt-Col D.L.A. Gibbs
16 Bty – Robin Dunn	– 1 Norfolks – Lt-Col P. Barclay
43 Bty – Ian Rae	– 2 KSLI – Lt-Col P. D. Daly
33 Field Regt under Lt-Col M.W. Hope	– 9 Brigade – Brig G.D. Renny
101 Bty – Tony Edwards	– 2 Lincolns – Lt-Col C. Firbank
109 Bty – M.G. Gillies	– 1 KOSB – Lt-Col R.C. Macdonald
113/114 Bty – Roger Nicholson	– 2 RUR – Lt-Col J. Drummond
76 Field Regt under Lt-Col Foster	– 8 Brigade – Brig E.H. Goulburn
302 Bty – Hamish Lindsey	– 1 Suffolks – Lt-Col R.E. Goodwin
303 Bty – Burton Pirie	– 2 E Yorks – Lt-Col J.D.W. Renison
454 Bty – John Waring	– 1 S Lancs – Lt-Col W.A. Waller

Tony Edwards's 101 Battery, like most of them, can be traced back to the Train of Artillery.

1705	Train of Artillery
1757	became 3 Coy, 1 Bn RA
1859	became 7 Bty, 2 Bde RA
1877	became 6 Bty, 7 Bde RA
1882	became 1 Mountain Bty, RGA
1920	became 1 Pack Bty, RGA
1927	became 1 Light Bty, RA
1935	became 101 Field Bty, RA

Its war service was similar to that of the infantry battalions it supported:

1760	Warburg	1855	Sebastopol
1779	St Lucia, Island of Granada	1888	Black mountain expedition
1793-5	Low Countries	1891	Hazara Field force
1797-1801	Bomb vessels	1897-8	Malakand Field Force
1801	Madeira	1899	Khyber Field Force
1808	St Domingo	1914-9	India, Afghanistan

20 Anti-Tank Regiment was loosely assigned to support a particular brigade.
41 Battery supported 185 Brigade
45 Battery supported 9 Brigade
67 Battery supported 8 Brigade

92 LAA Regiment, under Lt-Col Peter Henderson attached its batteries to brigade HQs.
317 Battery under Maj. N.H. Joynson supported 185 Brigade
318 Battery under Maj. M.S. Gonall supported 8 Brigade
319 Battery under Maj. P. Crane supported 9 Brigade.

9

2nd Tactical Air Force

Alas, all the castles I have, are built with air, thou know'st.

Ben Jonson: *Eastward Hoe*[1]

... small part specially trained for work with the army, becoming an arm of the older service.

Trenchard White Paper, 1919

No battle on the ground should be fought without the Air Service making its honourable contribution.

The motto of the IGAF & LW, 1916–1945

The aircraft is not a battlefield weapon. Specialised aircraft in such a rôle are uneconomic.

Wing Co Slessor; 1934

I instructed my air force and flak generals to consider the wishes of the Army as my orders.

FM Albert Kesselring, 1942

Tanks in the lead, artillery in the rear and aircraft overhead – only then will the infantry advance to the attack.

Lt-Gen Hermann Plocher, 1942

It is considered that the employment of the dive-bomber of the Vengeance type would be most uneconomical if used against targets in Europe.

Air Ministry, 1943

2 TAF was designed to accompany the Army into the field while accomplishing a multitude of rôles indispensable to its success, which is defined as being able to turn the enemy out of his defences at will without serious loss. 2 TAF's rôles, about which there was no disagreement, were the following: maintenance of air superiority; conduct of armed, photographic and tactical recce sorties; provision and maintenance of spotting aircraft for the artillery; and provision of close and direct air support. The clarity of the aims was not matched in their implementation. Whatever aspect of 2 TAF is examined, with one exception – command, organization, resources, manning, equipment, weapons and even 2 TAF's own success criteria – serious questions arise and anomalies, inconsistencies, inefficiencies and confusions appear. Indeed, the very effectiveness of the vast resource dedicated to British airpower was not apparent on the sanguinary battlefields examined herein, with the single exception of the Auster spotter aircraft operated by the RA and provided by 2 TAF.

The RAF dominated access to the UK's manufacturing resources and diverted them to the unfettered pursuit of their strategic bombing offensive. This was said to benefit the army by tying up a million Germans in defending against Bomber Command and so reducing German battlefield numbers, and by starving the dimished number of defenders who reached the battlefield of

1 G Chapman, B Jonson & J Marston. *Eastward Hoe* (London: William Aspley, 1605).

their fuel and supplies. Nevertheless, 3 BID encountered at Yorkshire Bridge, and in Kervenheim and Winnekendonk no lack of StuGs, and were on the receiving end of German artillery bombardments judged the heaviest encountered in the campaign. The defenders were supplied across Rhine bridges which the RAF were unable to destroy, and along roads at night by convoys of trucks that were never significantly interrupted. 2 TAF maintained air superiority by day, but not by night, and Allied fighter-bombers and bombers were frequently in attendance on the infantry, but destroyed few StuGs and guns. Whenever this was pointed out to them the RAF recounted the mantra first heard at Dunkirk: that armed recce was the most effective form of air support, and was performed out of sight of Pongos, whose progress, however excruciatingly slow, was entirely due to the hard work of the RAF who received no thanks or recognition for it.

Evidence of the RAF's ability to inflict localized damage was visible everywhere with Goch, Cleves and even Winnekendonk almost totally destroyed. 2 TAF also suffered, and their Typhoon pilots suffered such crippling losses that rationing of fighter-bomber sorties was implemented on 2 March 1945. By this time Horrocks had banned 2 TAF's medium bombers from XXX Corps' area of operations because of their repeated bombing of Allied troops, and from resentment that BC had deceived him about its plan to destroy Cleves. The four-engined heavy bombers of BC that a fortnight before the events described herein had burned out an undamaged Dresden, continued to churn over the ruins of apparently dead cities such as Cologne. Very late in the day Churchill distanced himself from BC which received no campaign medal. 2 TAF had no official history.

On 7 October 1942, a quarter century of wrangling between the Army and the RAF over the provision of military aviation was 'settled' by Churchill. This was ironic as it had been his decision twenty-four years earlier to form the RAF and to give it a monopoly of all aircraft that had caused the dispute. Churchill was a member of the Trenchard bombing cult, but his irritation with the inability of the RAF and Army to get along together, for which he was responsible and concerning which he felt vulnerable, resulted in the negligent carelessness of his way of settling it.

Churchill treated Bomber Command as his personal fief. It reported directly to him outside the decision making hierarchy of the COS and beyond the control of the Ministry of Supply, whose civil servants decided what the country could afford to give the army after BC had taken all it wanted. The Churchill settlement placed army aviation under the control of the RAF, which remained free to act in its own self-interest. For example, the RAF was able to get rid of its failed air-superiority Typhoon fighter by bolting on exterior R/P rails and bomb racks and declaring the result a superbly stable ground attack platform that would fulfill every need of the Army for close and direct air support. The RAF denied the army the accuracy of a true dive-bomber in a battle of wills that Churchill allowed them to win. But even worse was Churchill's permitting the RAF to control the air side of all army operations, including airborne. The major reason the Arnhem operation failed was the great distance between the landing grounds and the bridge. An historian explained the reason for this was the power of the Air Ministry to minimise the risk of aircraft losses. Churchill gave the RAF control of all of the air aspects of airborne in 1940 as the price for their reluctant agreement to cooperate.

> The result was an airborne planning machine totally controlled by the RAF, in which the planners formulated their schemes absolutely divorced from any operational considerations but their own, and with no requirement to act upon, or even acknowledge, those of the airborne soldiers tasked to carry them out'.[2]

The result of RAF obstinacy over the landing fields and their refusal to accept a night landing by the bridge was the destruction of 1 British Airborne Division.

---

2 Buckingham, *Arnhem 1944*, p. 9.

The RAF retained veto powers over army complaints in 1944-45 about the quality of RAF support. They succeeded in this partially by arranging the two hierarchies to be buttoned together with a spare RAF button at the top and an empty army buttonhole at the bottom. According to German practice and to common sense, 21 AG should have been supported not by a Tactical Air Force, which was the equivalent of a LW Fliegerkorps, but by its superior formation, an RAF command, perhaps called the Allied Expeditionary Air Force (AEAF) and the equivalent of a LW Luftflotte. This AEAF would have had 8 TAFs, the equivalent of Fliegerkorps, under its command, one TAF for each of the eight armies in NWE in March 1945 as follows: 1 TAF – Dempsey's 2 British Army; 2 TAF – Crerar's 1 Canadian Army; 3 TAF – Simpson's 9 US Army; 4 TAF – Hodges's 1 US Army; 5 TAF – Patton's 3 US Army; 6 TAF – Gerow's 15 US Army; 7 TAF – Patch's 7 US Army; and 8 TAF – de Lattre de Tassigny's 1 French Army. Such an organisation would have followed the logical and clear German practice, which the British were no doubt trying to emulate in 1942. For example, in September 1939, General der Flieger Kesselring's Luftflotte 1 supported Generaloberst von Bock's Army Group North. Kesselring wrote that he was independent of von Bock, 'but voluntarily felt myself to be under his orders in all questions of ground tactics'.[3] This subordination was anathema to the RAF, who insisted on never being in a position where they would be obliged to subordinate themselves to any soldier and especially to Montgomery, who was the man the RAF claimed to have made and whom they later loved to hate.

The first two columns in the following table are the actual Ground/Air Anglo-Canadian organisation with affiliation non-existent below the Crerar/Hudleston level. Column 3 is a British version of the LW organization in Column 5.

Anglo-Canadian and German Army and Air Forces' Organisation in March 1945 with a Preferred Alternative in Column 3 to replicate German practice and common sense

Anglo-Canadian			German	
Column 1 Army Actual	Column 2 2 TAF Actual	Column 3 2 TAF Preferred	Column 4 Heer Actual	Column 5 Luftwaffe Actual
MOD – Churchill			Hitler	
COS – Marshall/Brooke/Portal			OKW	
SHAEF – Eisenhower/Tedder			C-in-C – Rundstedt	
21 Army Group Montgomery	2 TAF Coningham	AEAF Robb	Army Group H Blaskowitz	Luftflotte
1 Canadian Army Crerar	84 Group Hudleston	2 TAF Coningham	1 FJ Armee Schlemm	Fliegerkorps
XXX Corps Horrocks	123 Wing Baldwin	84 Group Hudleston	II FJ Korps Meindl	Fliegerdivision
3 BID Whistler	609 Squadron Button	123 Wing Baldwin	8 FJDivision Wadehn	Geschwader
9 BIB Renny	Section Roberts	609 Squadron Button	FJR7 Riedel	Gruppe
2 Lincolns Firbank	Flight Mathys	Section Roberts	Kampfgruppe Krahl	Staffel
D Company Clarke	Pair King	Flight Mathys	Kompanie	Schwarm
17 Platoon Hunt		Pair King	Zug	Rotte

NB: In the Second World War the Anglo-Canadian forces called a Group a USAAF Wing and vice versa.

3 Albert Kesselring. *The Memoirs of FM Kesselring* (London: William Kimber, 1953).

This mistake in placing Coningham too high up the reporting ladder was not the worst. All-arms required intimate planning at all levels, and in its heyday subordinate LW HQs reported directly to the Heer in the interest of unity of command. The British, although at all times claiming to believe in all-arms, established joint responsibility so that the RAF could participate only on its own terms. The RAF refused to subordinate itself to the army under any condition or at any level. A British Kesselring would never have been permitted by Trenchard and his clique to say what Kesselring said above, although Broadhurst saw the need for it and was almost dismissed for insubordination, while 'Bingo' Brown, GOC 83 Group, was actually dismissed for that very reason. Any chance of the British developing an all-arms capability along the lines of Monash during the 100 Days was therefore impossible.

Effective all-arms required the joint planning and implementation of operations, with army units operating together with designated 2 TAF units, since effectiveness could only have been developed by personal contact and combined training as demonstrated with the way artillery was seamlessly coordinated with the infantry. Divisions would have been paired with Wings, Brigades with Squadrons, and Battalions with Sections.

The worst mistake of all, however, was to locate army-air control at the level of 1 Canadian Army, which was too remote from the users. The correct level was where the Germans and Wann-Woodall placed it – at corps (Korps) and airforce group (Fliegerdivision) – and not at the level of Army (Armee) and airforce group (Fliegerdivision). Montgomery and Coningham initially placed it the level of 8 Army during a crisis and in disobedience of the Wann-Woodall Report, which they had been instructed to implement. The result of these two gross mistakes and of other factors was an adequate quantity of air support for most of the time, but a serious deficiency in quality and control.

In 1945 the pairings of army group and tactical air force commanders were Bradley with Vandenberg, Devers with Webster, and Montgomery with Air Marshal Sir Arthur 'Mary' Coningham. Mary was a corruption of 'Maori' as Coningham was from New Zealand. His score was fourteen. His rank was the equivalent of a three star Lt General, and two ranks below F-M Montgomery. Even so Coningham did not report to Montgomery, his rival in unpleasantness, but to a vacuum nominally filled by Eisenhower's deputy, the four star general, Air Chief Marshal Sir Arthur Tedder. Until 15 October 1944, an Allied Expeditionary Air Force (AEAF) under Air Chief Marshal Sir Trafford Leigh-Mallory had theoretically exercised command over all of the Allied tactical air forces. But the AEAF as constituted and manned was redundant, and was eliminated along with Leigh Mallory. He had irritated the Americans who refused to work with him. Tedder declined to act as Leigh Mallory's replacement, although reserving the right to meddle in air matters. For example, in the debate over Montgomery's request to have the Rhine bridges destroyed, Coningham declined the request, citing flak, and Tedder supported him. With Leigh Mallory gone, Tedder delegated the now empty task to a new Chief of Staff (Air), Air Marshal James Robb, who was ignored by everybody.

In reality 2 TAF assigned a Composite Group, or the equivalent of a Fliegerdivision, to each army: 83 Group supported 2 British Army, and 84 Group 1 Canadian Army. No RAF formation below Group was associated even semi-permanently with any formation or unit, preventing the development of army-air familiarity or coordination of plans on which all-arms effectiveness depended. By doing this the RAF avoided both subordination and, what they must have equally feared, insistence on target destruction. The VVS (Soviet Air Force) was under command of the army, and had to persist until the target was destroyed or losses became unacceptable. This philosophy resulted in the development of armoured aircraft necessary to increase the chances of survival, and of dive-bombers that were indispensable for accuracy, neither of which the RAF would acquire or operate in NWE if acquired for them – as in the case of the very good Vengeance dive bomber bought by Beaverbrook and placed by the RAF on target-tug duties. Except on rare

2nd March 1945. The PM being introduced to an Air Commodore probably at B56 Evere ALG by an obsequious AM Sir Arthur Coningham, prior to leaving for lunch in Brussels. Note the press on the right. Churchill, Clementine, Alan Brooke and others had disembarked from Churchill's personal Douglas C54B Skymaster, which ten days earlier had taken him to the Yalta Conference. Churchill was on his way to visit 1 Canadian Army at Materborn in the Reichswald. (© Crown Copyright, IWM B 14995 by Sgt Midgley)

occasions when the specific objective was the destruction of a structure such as the Möhne Dam with specially designed and developed bouncing bombs, the RAF couched its success criteria in terms of delivering ordnance to an area or map reference, arguing that any bomb dropped on Germany or the enemy army represented an allied benefit. This refusal to link themselves in any way to target destruction, led them to ignore the high percentage of dud bombs they dropped – between 15 and 25% – having no interest in reducing their number despite their cost. And it even led them to ignore the need to keep bombing the Möhne Dam to prevent its repair.

The RAF used metaphors, obfuscation and untruths in self-promotion. We have seen how the nearly disastrous attack on the Berber Woods between Kervenheim and Winnekendonk was presented as 'laying out a welcome carpet' for the Army. A similar metaphor described the RAF's area bombing as 'carpet bombing'. They also told lies. For example, on the night of 11/12 February 1943 they attacked submarines on the stocks in the Bauhafen in Wilhelmshaven. A strong NE gale was blowing, and although the skymarkers were perhaps placed over the submarines, by the time the bombers arrived they were 4 km down wind and over the naval ammunition depot at Mariensiel. Thus occurred by chance the biggest explosion of BC's war on Germany. The before and after photographs were spectacular, and were placed in Harris's three Blue Books chronicling his 'successes'; one was on Harris's desk, one on Churchill's desk and one in the Moscow Embassy for showing to Stalin. The caption masterfully misrepresented the truth that the naval dockyard and the targeted submarines were untouched 3.8 kms away from the chance destyruction of the redundant shells and mines stockpiled for Germany's surface fleet which by then had been sunk or neutralised by the RN. The valuable stock of AA ammunition was off-site in Aurich. The BC caption to the photographs read; "Wilhelmshaven. This was an interesting and important raid by 177 aircraft – 129 Lancasters, 40 Halifaxes and 8 Stirlings. The Pathfinders found that the Wilhelmshaven area was completely covered by cloud and they had to employ their least reliable marking method, skymarking by parachute flares using H2S. The marking was carried out with great accuracy and the Main Force bombing was very effective. Crews saw through the clouds a huge explosion on the ground, the glow of which lingered for nearly 10 minutes. This was caused by bombs blowing up the naval ammunition depot at Mariensiel to the south [actually 251° or west] of Wilhelmshaven. The resulting explosion devastated an area of nearly 120 acres and caused widespread damage in the naval dockyard and in the town [untrue as they were 3.8 kms away]. Much damage was also caused by other bombs."

BC's effectiveness was unchallenged until the Butt Report in 1941 proved bombing was inaccurate. At that point Churchill should have closed down BC as a failure, but chose to accept assurances that technical advances and a redefinition of success as 'carting' bombs to the centre of German cities, would give BC the ability to destroy civilian morale and make Germany surrender. This they attempted at vast expense, but since the connection between destroyed morale and surrender was negative in both Britain and Germany, the policy if anything prolonged the war and was without mitigation an expensive and immoral failure.

84 Group ORB on 1 March 1945 (based on a Squadron establishment of 18 A/c)

Airfield	Wing	Squadron	Number of A/c	Aircraft Type
Gilze Rijen	35 (Recce)	2, 4, 268	54	Spitfire XIV, XI, Mustang II
Gilze Rijen	123	164, 183, 198, 609	72	Typhoon IB (R/P)
Gilze Rijen	135	33, 222	36	Tempest V
Grimbergen	131 (Polish)	302, 308, 317	54	Spitfire XVI
Woensdrecht	132 (Norwegian)	66, 127, 322, 331, 332	90	Spitfire XVI
Schijndel	145 (French)	74, 329, 340, 345	72	Spitfire XVI
Mill	146	193, 197, 257, 263, 266	90	Typhoon IB (Bombs)
Melsbroek	Detachment	616	18	Meteor III
Open Fields	A.O.P.	652, 660, 661	54	Auster IV
Total			540	
Of which CAS	123, 135, 131, 132, 145, 146 = 6 Wings	21 CAS squadrons	378	Typhoon 1B, Spitfire XVI

Group affiliations with the Army were changed to meet 2 TAF priorities, but the army was indifferent to such changes given the absence of personal contacts and joint training. During *Veritable*, when nearly all British divisions were under command of 1 Canadian Army, and 2 British Army was engaged in holding, training and planning for the Rhine crossing, 2 TAF ceased to allocate 83 Group to either Army and switched it instead to operating east of the Rhine, leaving 84 Group to operate west of the Rhine.

All-arms could only be realised through intimate cooperation of infantry, tanks, artillery and air at the unit level. In the Hitler Line battle in Italy, NIH tanks and infantry rehearsed their moves together in order to become familiar with each other's strengths and weaknesses, and each rifle company was assigned a troop of three tanks and a troop of two guns, but without air support. At Winnekendonk cooperation between artillery and infantry was intimate between people who had fought together since Normandy, and although cooperation with RF 3 SG was not at the level that the Canadians had enjoyed with NIH, Cathcart placed himself alongside Firbank on the field and the SG subalterns and NCOs were experienced and knew what to do. Always absent from unit planning was the RAF, because they insisted on it.

Effectiveness also required unified command. For Winnekendonk, Lt Col Cecil Firbank (infantry) in theory commanded Maj Alan Cathcart (tanks), in fact commanded Maj Tony Edwards (artillery) and neither commanded nor knew Sqn Leader (Major) Eric Roberts (609 Sqn). The four men should of course have been together in the afternoon at Lutzhof to discuss the recce results and to create a joint plan. All should then have gone onto the battlefield, with Roberts in direct contact with his aircraft overhead and the gunners with their artillery. All were present except Roberts whose Squadron had knocked off for the night and was at a party. Roberts had twice been over 9 BIB that morning, judging his visits a success even though they had resulted in not one enemy soldier killed. He would have had no idea of the identity of the Pongos below him, their problems or whether he could help them. The organisation was set up to preclude his knowing or even caring. This made the presence of his section during the morning over the Berber woods a formality, a charade carrying some danger to his aircraft if the enemy had ambushed him with Flak, and certain danger to 9 BIB and LF 3 SG tanks in the line of fire of his rockets that he released against no specific target but just a map reference. Of course 2 TAF labelled it a complete success, when in reality it was a futile and scandalous waste of energy and resources.

Ground and air forces were two solitudes, and the result was degraded Allied effectiveness. No one at 2 TAF knew of the assault on Winnekendonk, unless they picked it up while gossiping over a drink with the army LO, nor were they invested in its outcome. Infantry and RAF had learned to expect nothing of the other. Infantry battalions in the battles analysed here never requested close air support (CAS), or planned on its availability. No soldier fighting on the ground ever spoke to an airman overhead before, during, or after the battle. Aircraft were not a resource available to the battalion CO when planning his battle, and were therefore completely ignored. Aircraft were thrown in by 1 Canadian Army after discussion with corps commanders going through the motions on the sketchiest of knowledge about what was happening on the battlefield gleaned by wireless intercepts and haphazard reporting.

84 Group had 21 CAS squadrons of Spitfire XVI and Hawker Typhoon 1B on 1 March 1945 when it officially supported the 24 brigades of 1 Canadian Army, of which 10 brigades were Canadian in II Canadian Corps and 14 were British in XXX Corps. The following table summarises the above conclusions as to how infantry, artillery, tanks and aircraft were and should have been operating jointly on the Winnekendonk battlefield to implement all-arms.

The obvious consequence of supporting 21 AG with a single TAF of two CAS groups can be seen in the table (overleaf); 3 BID in Operation *Heather* was supported by a single squadron of 18 aircraft when the LW in its heyday would have put in a Geschwader of 120 to 150 a/c, and the Russians a Division of 96 a/c. At Winnekendonk 2 TAF should have fielded 10 CAS aircraft alongside the 15 tanks and 72 artillery pieces.

The question of the relative sizes of strategic versus tactical air forces in the Russian and British armed forces was discussed by Solly Zuckerman, the RAF's OR pioneer, and Tedder in January 1945 in the train from the Crimea to Moscow. Zuckerman wrote that Tedder was impressed by the enormous strength of the VVS which was mainly a CAS force but considered that the Russians had no understanding 'of the proper use of an air force. To them it had been perfected as another form of artillery. In the note that I made of this conversation, I asked myself who was right – the Russians or us.'[4] The answer by now should be clear; the Russians were right in nearly everything

4 Solly Zuckerman. *From Apes to Warlords* (London: Hamish Hamilton, 1978), p. 320.

Infantry support from artillery, tanks and aircraft, actual and ideal, compared with LW and VVS

Infantry unit/ formation	Company	Battalion	Brigade	Division	Corps / 3 divisions	Army	Army Group
No of men in assault	100	420	1,250	3,750			
Rank of commander	Major	Lt-Colonel	Brigadier	Maj-General	Lt-General	General	FM
Artillery – actual No of organic guns	2	8	24	72			
Unit/formation	Troop	Battery	Regiment	Div Artillery			
Rank of commander	Lt	Major	Lt-Colonel	Brigadier			
Tanks – actual No of tanks	3	15	45	147			
Unit/formation	Troop	Squadron	Regiment	Brigade			
Rank of commander	Lt	Major	Lt-Colonel	Brigadier			
2 TAF – actual No of aircraft			9	18	54-90	540	1,650
Unit/formation			Section	Squadron	Wing	Group	TAF
Rank of commander			Squadron Leader	Wing Commander	Group Captain	Air Vice Marshal	Air Marshal
2 TAF – ideal No of aircraft	2	10	18	54	162		
Unit/formation	Flight/Vic	Section	Squadron	Wing	Group	Tactical Air Force	Command/ AEAF
Rank of commander	Pilot Officer	Flight Lieutenant	Squadron Leader	Wing Commander	Air Vice Marshal	Air Marshal	Air Chief Marshal
Luftwaffe No of aircraft	4 **	12	30-48	120-150			
Unit/formation	Schwarm	Staffel	Gruppe	Geschwader	Flieger-division	Fliegerkorps	Luftflotte
Rank of commander	Ober-Leutnant	Hauptmann	Major	Oberst-leutnant	General-Leutnant	General der Flieger	General Oberst
VVS No of aircraft	4	9	32	96			
Unit/formation	Zveno	Eskadrilya	Polk	Division	Front	Corps	Air Army
Rank of commander	Starshiy Leytenant	Kapitan	Podpol-kovnik	Polkovnik	General-Mayor	General-Polkovnik	General-Armii

to do with defeating Germany on the battlefield, while Britain's rightful place was alongside them rather than investing in Trenchard's delusion of bombing a country into surrender.

Many historians equate the British sqn of 18 aircraft with the German staffel of 12, and Russian eskadrilya of 9, planes. In British terms these, however, were sections or half sqns, while a British sqn was the equivalent of half a German gruppe of 40 aircraft or Russian polk of 32 planes. The British wing of 54-90 aircraft was then the rough equivalent of the German geschwader of 150, or Russian division of about 100 planes.

On average, four squadrons each containing 18 aircraft and 28 pilots and commanded by a Wing Commander (equivalent to a Lt-Col) made up a Wing of 72 aircraft commanded by a Group Captain (Brigadier). 6 Wings made up a Group commanded by an Air Vice Marshal (Maj-General) with 432 aircraft. Air Marshal (Lt-General) Coningham commanded 2 TAF of 5 groups with an actual 92 squadrons with about 1,650 aircraft. Tedder was an Air Chief Marshal and equivalent to a full general such as Bradley, but a step below Montgomery. As a Field Marshal Montgomery was the equivalent in rank to Eisenhower who was appointed Supreme Commander.

Organisation of 2 TAF on 1 March 1945

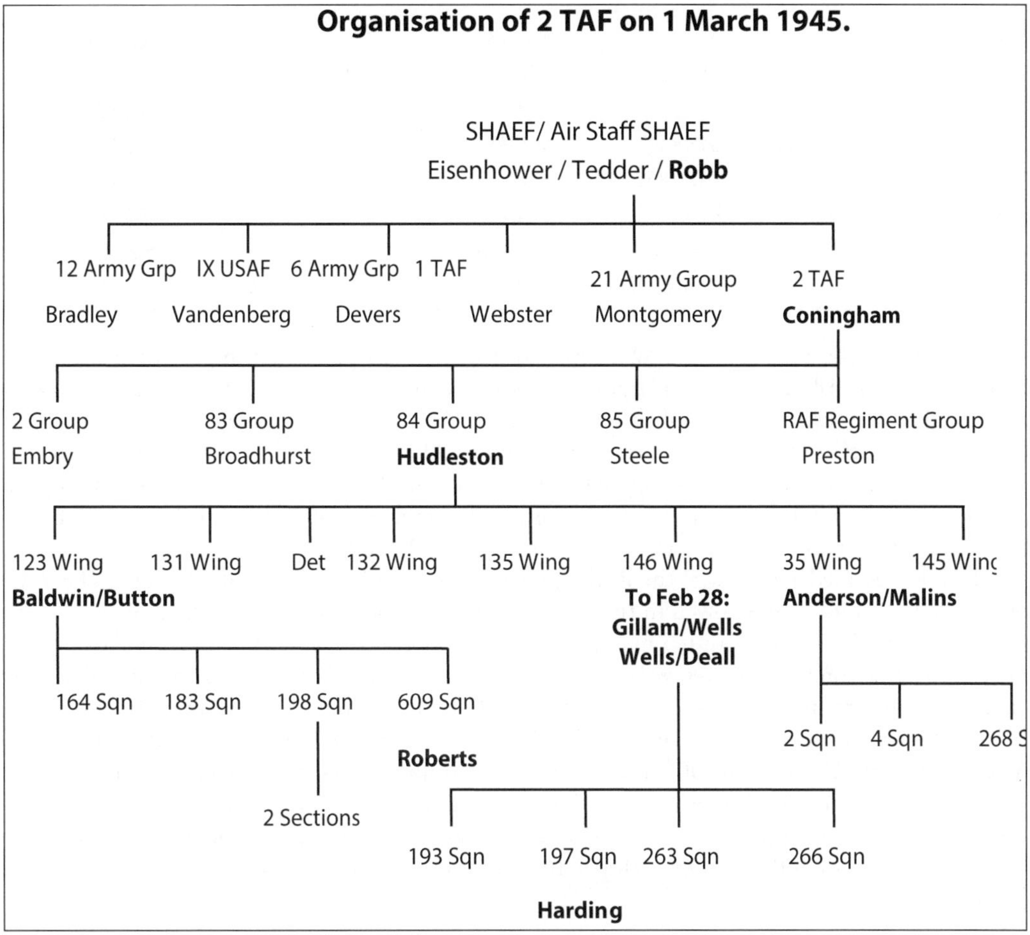

The 2 TAF hierarchy known to have been involved in *Heather* are shown in bold. The identities of two squadrons operating at Winnekendonk are known. 15 aircraft from 609 Sqn, under Sqn Leader Eric Roberts, supported the advance south of Kervenheim on two occasions. 609 Sqn was in 123 Wing, and had two masters. The Airfield Commander at Gilze Rijen, Group Captain Johnny Baldwin (who replaced the original commander, Desmond Scott, on 22 February 1945) was responsible for everything on the ground, while the Wing Commander Flying, J.C. 'Zip' Button (who replaced Walter Dring killed in a flying accident in January 1945), commanded

operations in the air.[5] On 28 February 1945 Winnekendonk was destroyed by the bombs of 197 Sqn commanded by Sqn Ldr K.J. Harding.[6] The biography of 2 TAF identified the CO as Sq-Ldr R.C. Curwen, DFC, but the book[7] states confusingly on the same page that Sqdn Ldr H.M. Mason was promoted to lead 123 Wing, while earlier on page 76, Zip Button had already been correctly identified in the post after Dring was killed. The commanders of 146 Wing changed on 28 February; Gp Capt Denys Gillam, whose contribution will be described below, was replaced by his Wing Co Flying, Johnny Wells. Sqn Ldr J.H. Deall filled the resulting vacancy.

Personnel Strength in NW Europe on 30 April 1945[8]

'000	Army (%)	Airforce (%)	Navy (%)	Total (%)
British	835 (65)	460 (35)	16 (0)	1,311 (100)
Canadian	183 (85)	34 (15)		217 (100)
Anzac		13 (100)		13 (100)
Subtotal Anglo-Canadian	1,018 (67)	507 (33)	16 (0)	1,541 (100)
US	2,618 (85)	448 (15)	7 (0)	3,073 (100)
French	413 (95)	24 (5)		437 (100)
Others	34 (68)	15 (36)		50 (100)
Total	4,084 (81)	994 (19)	23 (0)	5,101 (100)

Both sides in the Second World War invested heavily in air power, but none in relative terms more than the British. 2 TAF was a large organisation with, it is said, 100,000 men but only 1,800 aircraft[9] out of an establishment of about 2,500 to 2,750 aircraft. The more efficient FAA fielded double the aircraft with three quarters of the men (3,700 aircraft and 72,000 men).[10] This was roughly the size required by a military RFC, and its establishment in lieu of 2 TAF would have released enough men to form an infantry division. The table includes all the RAF in NWE and not just 2 TAF; the RAF grand total in all theatres being 970,000.

2 TAF represented a quarter of the RAF's global inventory of 7,500 to 9,000 aircraft. The RAF overall had 507,000 men involved in the NWE campaign, comprising over a third of the Anglo-Canadian forces' entire committed manpower. This proportion was twice the average for the US forces. Given a comparable average, an additional 260,000 men or thirteen infantry divisions could have been transferred to the British army, representing a doubling of its front-line strength. In global terms one out of every five (21.3%) British uniforms (970,000 out of 4,553,000 – the others being the RN with 781,000 and the army 2.8 million)[11] was light blue, of which 193,313 were aircrew. In May 1945 there were 105 men per aircraft (970,000 men and 9,200 aircraft) compared with 13 men per aircraft in 1918 (22,000 aircraft and 291,000 men) and 88 men per front-line aircraft (3,300 plus 103 airships). In 1945 each aircraft had on average 21 aircrew, and many of them were idle.

5 Desmond Scott. *Typhoon Pilot* (London: Leo Cooper, 1982).
6 Richard Hough in conversation.
7 Christopher Shores. *2nd TAF* (Stroud: Osprey, 1970).
8 Ellis, *Victory: Vol II*, p. 406.
9 Terraine, *The Right*.
10 http://www.fleetairarmarchive.net/History/Index.htm.
11 CSO. *Fighting with Figures* (London: HMSO, 1995, Table 3.4), p, 39.

The RAF absorbed a third of the productive capacity of the entire nation. BC in March 1945 had 1,880 aircraft of which 1,591 were heavy bombers. The Secretary of State for War, James Grigg, commented on this matter in 1944:

> We have reached the extraordinary situation in which the labour devoted to the production of heavy bombers is believed to be equal to that allotted to the production of the whole equipment for the Army.[12]

2 TAF was organised with an HQ, an RAF Regiment and 5 Groups containing 92 squadrons, disposed as follows in March 1945:

HQ was in Brussels with its own 34 (PR) Wing of 3 squadrons stationed at Melsbroek operating about 100 Spitfires, Wellingtons and Mosquitos.

2 Group was under AVM Basil Embry. He had been shot down in his Fairey Battle in 1940 and escaped. He was SASO to Tedder in the Desert Airforce and had 19 operations to his credit as an AVM. He provided tactical bombing support with 14 squadrons in 5 wings containing about 250 mediums (Bostons, Mitchells and Mosquitos). Airfields were at Coxyde, Vitry, Epinoy, Melsbroek and Rosieres.

83 Composite Group was under AVM Harry Broadhurst, who had been a fighter pilot in the Battle of Britain. He became Group Captain Operations in Fighter Command in 1941 when he wanted to make the Typhoon into a night fighter. He was probably involved in rejecting the P39 Aircobra that was valued by the VVS. He went as SASO to Coningham in the Desert Air Force which he then commanded. He returned from Italy with his personal Storch to command 83 Group. He was cooperative with Montgomery. 83 Gp operated 37 squadrons organised into 8 wings. Strength was nominally about 1,110 air superiority day fighters, fighter-bombers, recce and AOP squadrons – Tempests, Mustangs, Typhoons, Spitfires and Austers. They occupied 5 airfields at Eindhoven, Volkel, Helmond, Heesch and Evere.

84 Composite Group was under Air Vice Marshal E. (Teddy) C. Hudleston, with Main HQ at Goirle and Rear HQ at Breda. It operated 30 squadrons organised into 7 wings. They controlled 6 airfields: Gilze Rijen, Grimbergen, Woensdrecht, Schijndel, and Mill with a detachment of Meteors at Melsbroek and operated nominally 900 examples of the same equipment as 83 Group but with Meteors instead of Tempests. With the exception of the jets, all the Group's aircraft were located in the Netherlands.

85 Group under C.R. Steele had 6 squadrons in 2 wings with about 180 Mosquito night fighters. They were stationed at Amiens-Glissy and Lille-Vendeville. Their task was to ensure Base Defence for all the Groups at night and to this end flew intruder missions over selected enemy airfields. They also flew balloons and operated Air-Sea Rescue Beach Squadrons with Walrus amphibians, and managed an Airfield Construction Wing. It is doubtful that they, or anyone, was responsible for defending the Army at night from the attentions of Nachtschlachtgruppe 20.

12 David Divine. *The Broken Wing* (London: Hutchinson, 1966).

The RAF Regiment under R.L. Preston protected the airfields from ground-based attack. This was a task that could have been handed over to the Dutch in the Netherlands and to the civil police in the UK, and thereby freed up a majority of the RAF Regiment of 80,000 men, who could then have been mustered as infantry reinforcements. Alternatively, and following LW precedent, they could have been kept together with the thousands of surplus RAF personnel and formed into RAF divisions to join the order of battle under Montgomery's command, or turned into RAF paratroopers like the FJDs.

The RAF divided Army Cooperation into tactical recce including artillery spotting, air transport, and air attack. Air attack was either 'direct' support by attacking lines of communication and enemy troops outside the battle zone, or 'close' support in the battle area.

Hudleston was a regular and struck Desmond Scott[13] as both 'shy and retiring', and the over-cautious type who would 'guard their cigarettes in musical boxes'. The lack of rapport between them was put down to the generation gap, but it was more likely due to Hudleston's personality. Scott was the youngest group captain in the RAF. He had previously commanded 486 (RNZAF) Sqn, and RAF Station Hawkinge. He led 123 Wing in 84 Group during Operation *Heather*. His wingco flying before Zip Button had been Walter Dring, a Lincolnshire farmer who became as close as a brother, and whose death in a landing accident at Gilze Rijen in January 1945 devastated Scott. Scott had greatly enjoyed the company of Hudleston's predecessor, the rotund and jovial South African AVM Leslie O 'Bingo' Brown, who flew himself around in a white-nosed Auster. Brown had served in the desert under Longmore and Tedder, and was not a Coningham man. Coningham had tried to sack Brown in the autumn of 1944 for 'subservience to the Army' and rejoiced to see him go in January 1945 because he had 'never convinced the Canadians that aircraft were a support, not a substitute, for ground action.'

Teddy Hudleston was one of Coningham's favourites from North Africa and Italy. If Coningham could have had his way he would also have sacked the best of them all, AVM Harry Broadhurst of 83 Group, for getting on too well with Montgomery, the man Coningham loved to hate.

Without aircraft, infantry could advance against prepared defences usually only with great loss. The danger was from mines, mortars, machine guns and artillery. Where conditions permitted, tanks suppressed machine guns and cleared mines, but the German goal was always to separate the infantry from the tanks and destroy each individually. Paks, German AFVs and the ubiquitous 88 destroyed the tanks leaving mortars and MG 42 to destroy the infantry. The Allies relied on indirect artillery fire to suppress enemy fire, but the 25pdr lacked the necessary weight of shell, and it could never attain the accuracy of direct fire. In the battles described in this book the infantry and tanks repeatedly attacked into the cannon's mouth because the fighter-bomber, even when present, lacked the accuracy necessary to destroy small targets. The answer to all these weapons was accurate aircraft: a dive-bomber and an aircraft firing armour-piercing ammunition.

The fighter-bomber as developed by the Germans was an oxymoron. The design criteria of a fighter conflicted with those of a bomber, which was its prey. Second World War fighters optimised speed, acceleration, manoeuvrability and firepower. They were small, flimsy, light-weight, streamlined, single-seat cramped airframes attached to the most powerful and fuel-inefficient engine available, with additional boost available on demand that shortened engine life, and able to climb and dive quickly. Their only intelligence was provided by or through the pilot's brain. The bombers were the opposite in every respect, being optimised for load carrying, survivability, range, and navigational capability. They were bulky, expensive, slow, multi-engined, fuel-efficient, and multi-crewed, clawing extra feet of altitude by 'climbing the stairs' through periodic dropping of

13 Scott, *Typhoon Pilot*.

the landing flaps. Devices with rudimentary artificial intelligence such as the autopilot, X-Gerät, Gee, H2S, the Norden bombsight and the BZA-1 gyroscopic bombsight with computer, reduced the overload on pilot and navigator.

Bomber and fighter pilots were trained for different aptitudes. The fighter pilot was a hunter (Jäger) with fast reactions travelling in a pack (Schwarm) under the directions of ground control broadcast en clair, chattering on the radio, making short sorties to defend his territory and to kill people like himself wearing a different shade of blue in the pursuit of medals, and expecting dinner with a respectful enemy if captured. The bomber-pilot, by contrast, was responsible for the lives of his crew, travelling usually at night to avoid fighters and alone because even in the centre of a bomber stream he might never see another aircraft, on long trips, far from ground control and in strict radio silence, controlling the latest gadgetry, invading enemy territory to destroy lives and property, avoiding heroics, fearful of being hunted and of being lynched if captured.

Turmoil was therefore the outcome of a decree from the OKL on 2 September 1940 ordering a third of the fighter sections (Jagdstaffels) facing Britain to fit racks to their Me 109E,[14] and start a bombing campaign against Britain. Disbelief and insubordination resulted. There was a precedent; Baron Manfred von Richthofen had refused to let his pilots strafe the trenches in 1917; 'The duty of the Jäger is to patrol his area of the sky, and to shoot down any enemy fighters in that area. Anything else is nonsense.'[15] The fighter ace, Adolf Galland, was apoplectic over the degradation of his aircraft's performance, and relations with Göring were irreparably damaged. Galland wrote that 'the fighter was made into a fighter-bomber as a stopgap and a scapegoat.'[16] Galland's analysis was half-right. The failure to achieve tactical air superiority was collective and not just the fault of the fighter scapegoats. The LW did not attempt the daylight aerial domination of Britain that the Allies achieved in 1944/45 over Germany with the long-range P47 and P51, but they did realise the need to destroy the infrastructure of RAF airfields and Chain Home radar, and to reduce British fighter production. This was, however, beyond their capability after Udet and Göring had reconfigured the LW following Wever's death on Hitler's assurances of continuing peace with Britain, and had postponed the four-engined heavy bomber.[17] Medium day-bomber losses were unacceptable, and the fighter-bomber was no answer. Its 550 lb load was insignificant compared with the 4,400 lb of the He 111, let alone the 11,000 lb of the He 177, large-scale production of which was planned at 140 per month from mid 1940.[18] The British ignored the fighter-bomber's pinprick, and relished the opportunity of an easy kill as they dominated a fighter force weakened by the introduction of the fighter-bomber.

> Instead of being strengthened, the fighter arm whose task it had once been to wear down the English fighter defense was now so weakened that from this point on it was clearly at a numerical disadvantage.[19]

The OKW realised that the overall configuration of their armed forces left them powerless against Britain.[20] Hitler contemplated switching resources massively into strategic bombing to

14 Chris Goss. *Luftwaffe Fighter-Bombers over Britain* (Manchester: Goodall, 2003).
15 http://www.skygod.com/
16 Goss, *Luftwaffe Fighter-Bombers.*
17 William Murray. *La Luftwaffe: une Stratégie d'Échec* (Aéro Journal No. 33).
18 Ernst Heinkel. *Stormy Life* (Oberhaching: Aviatic, 1991.
19 Jochen Prien & Gerhard Stemmer. *Jagdgeschwader 3 'Udet'* (Atglen: Schiffer, 2003).
20 HR Allen. *Who Won The Battle Of Britain?* (London: Arthur Barker, 1974).

destroy Britain,[21] but concentrated instead on building a fleet of U-boats to starve Britain out, and on invading Russia where he got his brains beaten out.

Galland was, however, wrong to believe that the fighter-bomber was a stopgap weapon. It was a permanent addition to the armoury, and one that could have arisen only in Germany. An historian of the LW has stated that while the British and French also considered the 'fighter-bomber a viable proposition', being in extremis they had to ensure that 'the deployment of fighter aircraft would be to defensive interceptor duties, notwithstanding the allocation of a certain number of Spitfires to the PR rôle'.[22] No evidence was provided for this opinion which in any case misrepresents the development of the PR Spitfire, which was resisted by the Air Ministry that then sacked the inventor. It was strange both that the British would copy an *ersatz* weapon when they had access to American industry, and even stranger that enthusiasm for it persists.

CAS was the fighter-bomber's later *raison d'être*, and its employment as a bomber substitute an aberration. CAS originated in the First World War when the RFC and IGAF were part of the army. A German maxim from 1916 remained valid for the LW through 1945, and abhorrent to the RAF; 'No battle on the ground should be fought without the LW making its honourable contribution.'[23]

Trenchard[24] ordered his pilots to strafe German trenches at Messiness in June 1917. At Third Ypres he armed Sopwith Camels with four 20 lb bombs to increase their destructive power. At the same time the Germans introduced the Halberstadt CLII and organized them into ground attack sections (Schlachtstaffeln). In November 1917, 320 British tanks and 300 CAS aircraft supported the infantry in the momentous breakthrough at Cambrai. Two squadrons, 8 and 73, were tasked with attacking German anti-tank guns and developed unique expertise. Major Trafford Leigh Mallory commanded 8 Sqn, writing; 'It is difficult to estimate the very effective work they did in harassing the German gunners and thus assisting the progress of the tanks.'[25]

Losses to ground fire on both sides, however, were crippling, with entire squadrons destroyed. Both sides therefore introduced armoured CAS aircraft, and by mid 1918 the Germans employed more than 38 Staffeln containing 230 two-seat, all-metal and armoured Junkers J1 aircraft[26] for trench fighting, and the armoured Albatros for contact patrol. The British followed suit with the single-seat Sopwith Salamander trench fighter, whose entire forward fuselage containing engine, pilot and fuel tanks was constructed of armour-plate, and the two-seat armoured Sopwith Buffalo for contact patrol. All were designed to fly at 500 feet with immunity from rifle and machine-gun fire. It is possible that the Armistice came before the RAF had experience of the Salamander's survivability and remembered only the Camels' destruction, while Germans retained better memories of the Ju 1.

The knowledge did not exist during the First World War to optimise the performance of fighter aircraft. Aerodynamics was in its infancy and there was no science for comparing the efficiency of different wing forms or even to decide on the number of wings. The science was still incomplete when the Me 109 and Spitfire were designed in the mid 1930s, with Laminar flow wing form making its appearance on the P51 Mustang in 1940. Streamlining was scarcely a factor with low-powered engines and drag from struts and wire bracing of non-cantilevered wings. Design oddities and dead-ends, such as the rotary engine and triple wings, persisted almost as fashion statements. Since all designs were inefficient, a bomb rack inflicted no detectable penalty. Indeed Manfred von

21 Paul Deichmann. *Spearhead for Blitzkrieg* (Barnsley: Greenhill, 1996).
22 John Vasco. *Bombsights Over England* (Drayton: Jac, 1990).
23 Paul Deichmann. *Spearhead for Blitzkrieg* (Barnsley: Greenhill, 1996).
24 http://www.firstworldwar.com/airwar/groundattack.htm.
25 B. Greenhuis. *The Counter Anti-Tank Role* (Aerospace Historian, Bolling, June 1974).
26 www.constable.ca/JunkersJ1.htm.

Richthofen's Fokker Dreidecker was not even the fastest aircraft. The fighter-bomber did not exist, even when fighter pilots sometimes dropped bombs.

In 1918 the British and German staffs were in agreement about the use of airpower, fielding almost identical aircraft, but postwar they diverged. The RAF adopted the motto of 'victory through airpower alone'. They rejected CAS as 'uneconomical' but insisted on controlling all aircraft, which resulted in force dissipation. The Germans by contrast built onto their First World War experience. Analysis of the reasons for their defeat confirmed the principle that war was decided on the ground through concentration of force and all-arms cooperation. This insight inspired Air Field Manual No 16 in 1935, (Die Luftkriegsführung) listing the following missions: establishment of tactical air superiority in the area of military operations; action in support of ground forces and the Navy; interdiction of enemy lines of communication; implementation of strategic operations against sources of hostile military power; destruction of enemy centres of government; and in certain circumstances retaliation against civilians. Crucially the LW agreed to attack ground targets both near and far identified by the Army and to place its fighters under army command in certain circumstances. This principle of concentration at the Schwerpunkt was popularly known as *klotzen, nicht kleckern*, meaning 'Drown it, don't just splash water on it', and was the proximate cause of the LW's invention of the fighter-bomber.[27]

OKL used the same principle of concentration of air power but at a higher command level than an army, in order to resist the soldiers' demand that all fighter aircraft operating in that army's area of operations should always be under command of the land forces. They committed, however, to bringing in aircraft from other areas in an emergency, and agreed to place those LW headquarters assigned to armies under the tactical control of the land forces. Kesselring commanded Air Fleet 1 in 1939 in support of von Bock's army group and voluntarily applied the rule to himself.

This unique LW focus on the support of land forces was explained as unreformed thinking by army staff officers recently transferred into the LW,[28] but it also came from detailed analysis of the First World War and of the Spanish Civil War. The LW learned from its strategic campaign with Zeppelins and Gothas in the First World War that bombing civilians did not end the war. The bombing of Guernica on 26 April 1937 was declared a failure because 24 bombers aiming for the Renteria Bridge over the Mundaca River could not score a hit. The LW focussed on testing the effectiveness of weapons and technique, and the staff evolved a theory and practice of combined operations grounded in real combat. This was in sharp contrast to British memories of being under the bombs in the First World War while unable to catch the raiders, reinforced by the untested theorising of Douhet and Liddell Hart promoting the strategic decisiveness of mobile bombers and cruiser tanks, and it was a world away from the insistence by the RAF and the French Air Force on their independence, tinged with an undisguised contempt for the land forces.

In Spain the He 51 biplane was outperformed by the Rata monoplane and replaced by the Me 109. But instead of relegating the He 51 to training units, the Legion fitted them with fragmentation bombs, and tested them in March 1937 against battlefield targets that horizontal bombers were unable to destroy. Some have claimed that this represented the first use of a fighter-bomber since the First World War,[29] but the He 51 was no longer a viable fighter aircraft, and the resulting weapon was if anything a trainer-bomber. The transfer of the obsolete HE 51 to fighter-bombing rather than scrapping it was a precursor of the RAF's 'saving' of the failed air-superiority Typhoon by fitting it with bomb racks and rocket rails and claiming it was an outstandingly stable platform.

27 Deichmann, *Spearhead.*
28 Ibid.
29 Goss, *Luftwaffe Fighter-Bombers.*

There was no move in Spain or at first in Poland to hang bombs under the Me 109 and Me 110 to create a fighter-bomber.

Three Ju 87A-1s were sent to Spain in September 1936 for evaluation, and the lessons learned were incorporated in the Ju 87 B-1 which arrived there in October 1938. The Stuka was a vertical dive-bomber, and accurate against pinpoint targets. The LW, and especially the previously sceptical Wolfram von Richthofen, whose inaccurate bombing of Guernica was a fiasco that gave the LW a temporary aversion to causing civilian casualties, adopted this potent weapon, and set about establishing a force of 340 Stukas for the invasion of Poland as flying artillery. Experience with the He 51 showed that bombing in a shallow skip-dive was inaccurate, and the weapon was rejected.

The immediate cause of the decision to fit bombs to the Me 109 and Me 110 was the Polish counterattack on the Bzura River that was defeated only through prompt concentration of all available force according to the German doctrine of all hands to the pump. Kesselring explained that the horizontal bombers such as the He 111 contributed little, and after the experience of Guernica that should have been anticipated.

> The Polish forces had enormous fighting spirit and in spite of the disorganization of control and communications were able to strike effectively at our points of main effort. Crises on the German side, as on the Tucheler Heath, in the Polish breakthrough battle on the Bzura and in the area covering Warsaw, were overcome by exemplary co-operation with the ground forces, and by throwing in every close support aircraft and bomber in a recklessly concentrated attack.[30]

Heinrich Koppenberg was recruited from the Flick Company, and as general director of Junkers was responsible for the Ju 87. He then built the Ju 88 medium dive-bomber that was presented by Jeschonnek as the solution to the LW's problems because its increased accuracy as a dive-bomber permitted replacement of large numbers of level bombers. In 1940 Koppenberg drunkenly shouted, "I have already killed the Do 217; now I have killed the He 177 too". Heinkel stated that Koppenberg should have realised the He 177 was the only four-engine heavy bomber under development, and needed to defeat Britain.[31]

After withdrawing across the Bzura on the night of 12/13 September 1939, the Poles were subjected to low-level attacks by hundreds of aircraft for several days. Amongst them was Major Grabmann's Sqn of the long-range tactical experimental (Lehr) fighter wing I/LG1 flying Me 110C from East Prussia on 16 and 17 September. The fighter pilots were unhappy with being assigned to CAS with orders to fire their entire ammunition load of mg and cannon in ten minutes over the target at anything they could find.[32]

The Bzura counterattack was the 'exceptional circumstance' foreseen in the Air Manual. Kesselring's action pre-empted any request from Von Bock to exercise his right of command over the fighters. It was clear in practice that Grabmann's fighters would have done more damage with high explosive and fragmentation bombs, and this was probably confirmed in post war analysis. Therefore in the spring of 1940 a request went to the Research Department (Forschungsamt) to design streamlined and ventrally mounted bomb racks, called ETC,[33] for the Me 109E to carry one 250 kg or two 100 kg bombs, and two 250 kg bombs under the Me 110C, subsequently increased by four 100 kg bombs outboard of the engines. All racks could be retrofitted in the

30 Kesselring, *The Memoirs.*
31 Heinkel, *Stormy Life.*
32 Cajus Bekker. *The Luftwaffe War Diaries* (New York: Ballantine, 1969).
33 Goss, *Luftwaffe Fighter-Bombers.*

field or installed on the production lines. Existing factory orders were changed to the B(omben) sub-variant.

This was the second time that extra weight had been added to fighters. In early 1940, the Me 109E-3 added 82 lb of cockpit armour for pilot protection, and the Spitfire followed suit. The first Me 109E, Me 110C and Me 110D equipped to carry bombs were delivered to Erprobungsgruppe 210 that had been formed on 1 July 1940 under Hauptmann Walter Rubensdörffer. He was transferred from the Rechlin LW Test Centre to develop CAS equipment and technique for the Me 210. The Sqn existed for less than ten months, but during that period tested methods of dropping bombs, evaluated a 3 cm cannon on the Me 110, and a *Seilbomben* line for cutting high-tension cables.[34]

A suggestion has been made that the fighter-bomber's introduction was a means not of providing the army with extra support in an emergency, but as a form of insurance against what actually occurred over Britain when the Ju 87 was withdrawn as a consequence of the LW's failure to achieve air superiority. The Me 210 with dive brakes was the planned replacement for the Ju 87, but never became airworthy. One author claimed without providing evidence that the Jabo was, 'a tactical support arm to the land forces which could also be competent enough in combat to look after itself'.[35] The argument is *post hoc ergo propter hoc*. It is possible that the name Erpr.Gr 210 was cognate with the planned replacement for the Me 110.

At Denain near Lille in northern France Erpr.Gr 210 finalised a technique of diving from 3,000 metres at an angle of 45° at 600kph. The pilot obtained the angle by aligning a black line painted on the windshield with the horizon, controlling speed through pitch selection since the Germans had not fitted automatic pitch. The target was centred in the standard Revi sight, and wind drift was avoided by bombing upwind. Pullout began at 1,000 metres at a rate that made the target move half way down the vertical line of the sight over a two-second period, when the pilot released the bomb in a lobbing motion. Diving from the higher altitude of 5,000 m required a speed of 650kph, but the reason for the change is not given.[36] The angle of dive could not exceed 45° on the Me 109 for two reasons; there was no cradle-crutch to swing the bomb or bombs outside the propeller arc, and without air brakes there was nothing to restrict speed. This would build up quickly and risk the propeller and reduction gear separating from the engine, and the elevator tearing off. This was also a problem with the early Merlins, according to Duane Freeman, Chief Engineer at the Warplane Heritage Museum in Hamilton, Ontario. It was also how Udet destroyed the He 118 Stuka prototype, and nearly killed himself. Heinkel had told him to be careful with the propeller pitch control, but Udet dived without checking the adjustment.[37]

It was inevitable that Göring would order his new and reluctant fighter-bombers to replace the daylight bombers which were suffering unacceptable losses over Britain. Galland knew the effect it would have on the morale and effectiveness of his hunters (Freiejägern).

> Their element is to attack, to track, to hunt, and to destroy the enemy. Only in this way can the eager and skilful fighter pilot display his ability. Tie him to a narrow and confined task, rob him of his initiative, and you take away from him the best and most valuable qualities he possesses: aggressive spirit, joy of action, and the passion of the hunter.[38]

34 Vasco, *Bombsights.*
35 Ibid.
36 Goss, *Luftwaffe Fighter-Bombers.*
37 Heinkel, *Stormy Life.*
38 www.skygod.com.

Galland criticized Göring's blatant attempt to disguise his failure to establish air superiority by imposing face-saving and self-defeating tactics.

> During the Battle of Britain the question: fighter or fighter-bomber? had been decided once and for all: The fighter can only be used as a bomb carrier with lasting effect when sufficient air superiority has been won. To use a fighter as a fighter-bomber when the strength of the fighter arm is inadequate to achieve air superiority is putting the cart before the horse.[39]

Relations between fighter pilots and Göring deteriorated into mutual recrimination, with Göring threatening to disband the Jagdwaffe. Osterkamp called fighter-bombing 'senseless operations', and Galland famously asked Göring for Spitfires, whose lower wing loading gave them better manoeuvrability than the Me 109 at slow escort speed. Winter weather shut the campaign down, and the LW was slowly re-directed against Russia with the morale of the fighter arm dented. A screen of fighters was left in the west to keep the RAF in check. A few fighter-bombers continued operating, but with the improvement in British defences, the Germans flew low to keep under the radar. Sometimes they had no specific target in what they called 'nuisance raids' (*Störangriff*), and the British called 'tip-and-run'.

There then appeared a man of the hour. During 1941 Oberleutnant Frank Liesendahl returned to JG2, and the fighter-bomber found its first true believer and promoter, to be imitated, of course, by an underemployed Fighter Command. A man of mystery, Liesendahl had been a tank gunner before transferring into the LW in 1936. He probably[40] piloted an Me 110 of II/ZG1 during the Polish campaign, and no doubt took part in the destruction of the Polish army on the Bzura River through Tiefangriff. He liked the experience, and graduated to shooting up British and French soldiers at Dunkirk on 26 May in an Me 109 of II/JG2, but was shot down by a Spitfire and captured by British troops, who treated him kindly. He was liberated and went to hospital, but on return to his unit was shot down again by a Spitfire on 10 July 1941. This second occasion must have completed his aversion therapy to fighting on an equal basis with enemy air superiority fighters, for he then revealed a vocation for ground attack, and committed his thoughts to paper. Back with JG2 in September, he showed the paper to his Wing Commander (Geschwader Kommodore) the ex-gunner and fighter ace Lt-Col Walter Oesau (127 victories). Oesau almost certainly saw this as a heaven-sent opportunity of ridding himself of his misfits and fighter-bombers, and he shunted them off into a new and specialist ground attack section, 13/JG6 under Captain Bolz's II/JG 2. This unit he placed under Liesendahl, probably suggesting to him that in the absence of British troops he should target their shipping.

Liesendahl went to work with a will, developing anti-shipping tactics, and training his section until February 1942 in an eponymous procedure – Liesendahl Verfahren. This involved crossing the water at an altitude of 5 metres at 450 kph until arriving to within 1,800 metres of the target ship. The pilot then popped up to 500 metres, levelled off, and at once entered a shallow dive at an angle of 3° while increasing speed to 550 kph. Having closed the target the pilot pulled up and lobbed the bomb. On 10 February 1942 Liesendahl gained his first success by damaging a 3,000-ton ship off Cornwall. On 18 February his section was declared operational, and Jagdfliegerführer 3, Major Carl Hentschel, ordered JG 26 to form a second fighter-bomber section to be effective on 10 March. Again unsuitable fighter pilots such as the undisciplined and insubordinate were dumped into a new 10/JG 26 under Erwin Busch from the original Jabo section, and Liesendahl's section

39 Adolf Galland. *The First and the Last* (London: Methuen, 1955).
40 Goss, *Luftwaffe Fighter-Bombers*.

was renumbered 10 (Jabo) JG 2 at the same time.[41] The two sections had a combined strength of 28 aircraft. In May 1942 they were brought together and placed directly under command of F-M Hugo Sperrle's Luftflotte 3's fighter HQ in Paris. The German commitment was modest given the size of the target and the opportunities it contained, but was inhibited by the strength of the defences. These ensured that only low-level surprise tip-and-run attacks could be contemplated with any expectation of keeping losses in check.

An analysis of this tip-and-run campaign over fifteen months from March 1942 to June 1943 by up to 118 fighter-bombers revealed 68 were lost. The assessment was that the 'raids met with considerable success, especially for much of 1943, by normally hitting the designated target whilst keeping fighter-bomber losses to a minimum.'[42] The success criteria had little or any military value, as Galland had said in 1940. Raids were said to have worked well if the pilot found his target, dropped or jettisoned his bombs roughly near to it, and got home. Targets were chosen not because of their importance but because they permitted achievement of the success criteria. A militarily valuable target of three RN destroyers was attacked without damage by six aircraft of 10/ JG 2 in Plymouth Sound on 16 May 1942. HMS *Wolverine*, a W Class Destroyer of 1,100 tons, shot down an Me 109 killing the pilot, and damaged another, while HMS *Brocklesby* and HMS *Cleveland*, both Hunt Class destroyers of 1,000 tons, fired their AA guns. One rating was killed on the *Wolverine* and three injured on the Brocklesby. Lt Hans-Joachim Schulz was buried with military honours in Plymouth. The consequence was that, 'Plymouth and similarly well defended naval targets were very rarely attacked again.'[43] Instead a soft civilian target such as Torquay was attacked on eight occasions, two of which resulted in heavy loss of life. The attack of 30 May was characterized by the author of the analysis as successful; `from a German viewpoint, it had been both a successful and costly attack'[44], which was self-contradictory, as Liesendahl's remit was to inflict damage with low losses. Leutnant Leopold Wenger was on that raid, and also agreed that it went well. 'As usual in every large-scale effort, it worked well.'[45]

It is impossible to identify one German benefit other than personal satisfaction at killing English civilians. The raid was in Sqn strength, with 22 to 26 Fw 190s dropping 21 bombs weighing nine tons on St Marychurch near Torquay. They killed 45, including 21 Sunday school children, and injured 157, mostly civilians. RAF casualties were 5 killed, 11 wounded and no aircraft. At least 50 buildings were destroyed and 3,250 damaged. The Germans lost 5 aircraft, with 4 pilots killed and 1 POW, for a crippling sortie loss rate of 23%.

It has been argued that the Germans achieved a positive balance sheet from the tip-and-run campaign. In addition to the mainly civilian deaths and injuries that drove incensed citizens to petition the House of Commons demanding that something be done, and damage to buildings, the raids are said to have destroyed or damaged an indeterminate number of small ships, landing craft, gasometers and barrage balloons, and forced the deployment of light anti-aircraft (LAA) regiments and fighters that 'could have been better used',[46] presumably elsewhere.

The last-mentioned factor is in conflict with a contemporary account. In the autumn of 1941, I Canadian Corps took over 85 miles of Sussex coastline centred on the towns of Hastings, Brighton and Eastbourne. They installed three LAA regiments equipped with 40 mm Bofors. Canadian HQ later issued a report that summarised their experience of tip-and runs; 'Such raids have little

41 Ibid.
42 Ibid.
43 Ibid.
44 Ibid.
45 Ibid.
46 Ibid.

military significance, but occasionally Canadian military personnel become casualties.'[47] The Canadians claimed to have destroyed or damaged 5 Fw 190s – at Eastbourne on 23 January, 3 April, and 6 June 1943, which were confirmed in Goss, and two damaged at Lewes on 10 May, which were not mentioned in Goss). The Canadians' own biggest loss occurred at Hastings on 23 May 1943 when a raid by 20 Fw 190s killed 10 soldiers and wounded 31. The report does not mention it, but the German raids gave to Canadian soldiers and LAA regiments in training for Dieppe, the invasion of Sicily and D-Day, valuable practice in shooting to kill under hostile fire. Drills were developed, critiqued and refined covering all aspects of defense against low flying aircraft including shelter construction, the layout of gun emplacements and radar. The enemy action provided training in watch-keeping, communications and constant preparedness. The LW flew in under the radar, giving the radar operators invaluable practice in optimal set location and calibration, and in quick response to enemy pop-up. The same benefits accrued to the RN, to other army units on the south coast, and to the RAF and Observer Corps who benefited from the experience when the serious V1 campaign began in 1944.

Senior LW officers had been reluctant to authorize Liesendahl's campaign, rightly dismissing him as a busy fool. Liesendahl himself of 10/JG 2 was shot down and killed during an attack by four Fw 190s on a tanker and two motor launches near Brixham off Berry Head on 17 July 1942. His decomposing body was recovered in the area on 6 September 1942 and buried at sea. The LW command was rightly suspicious of his claims[48] for the same reason that Göring had permanently lost confidence in the Jagdwaffe during the Battle of Britain.[49] Damage was almost entirely civilian, and that to housing was insignificant when compared with the almost nightly destruction of German cities. The resultant uproar in Britain was enough, however, for supporters of area bombing to claim moral equivalency with the tip-and-run-campaign, and to muffle unease felt by many about the disproportionate bombing aimed at burning out the 120 largest German cities. LW staff would have been even further discomfited had they known that they were providing target practice for eager and otherwise bored soldiers suffering from inadequate and unrealistic British training facilities.

As with the LW, the RAF's inability to hit specific targets is well attested. Objective studies of damage caused by fighter-bombers were recorded in several reports by No. 2 Operational Research (2AOR) Section with 21 Army Group.[50] Report No. 4, for example, compared the physical evidence on the ground in the Mortain area of Normandy with the claims made by pilots of R/P Typhoons and Thunderbolt fighter-bombers of 2 TAF and IX USAAF in the period 6 to 11August 1944. The results were separately investigated and confirmed by another OR team from 2 TAF. The two OR teams visited the site between 12 and 20 August. The results were disappointing. The pilots claimed to have destroyed 301 armoured and motorized vehicles, but the teams found on the ground only 33 due to the air forces and 36 to US ground troops. Conditions for the fighter-bombers were variable, but there was no shortage of rabbits for a toothless dog.

The RAF feigned surprise at the Mortain findings, but their own evaluation had revealed the limitations of fighter-bombing in 1943, when the effect of rockets and bombs on a mock-up of a German artillery position was examined. The damage done was negligible.[51] To war's end, however,

---

47 DND: www.dnd.ca/hr/dhh/history_archives/engraph/cmhq_e.asp?cat=1: Report Number 106: *Enemy Air Action and the Canadian Army in the United Kingdom, 1939 to 1943.*

48 Goss, *Luftwaffe Fighter-Bombers.*

49 R Michulec & D Caldwell. *Adolf Galland* (Sandomierz: MMP, 2003), p. 57.

50 Copp, *Montgomery's Scientists*, pp. 173-80.

51 Terry Copp and Robert Vogel. *Anglo-Canadian Tactical Air Power in Normandy: A Reassessment* (Virginia: American Military Institute, 1987).

the RAF refused to adopt either dive-bombers or aircraft armed with armour-piercing cannon that were accurate, or armoured aircraft with improved survivability from flak.

The Condor Legion in Spain had discovered the difficulty of hitting a target with a bomb dropped in a 45° dive, and chose instead the dive-bomber. The fighter-bomber had no predictor and used rudimentary sights. Total reliance was placed on pilot judgment which could be distracted by incoming flak. The pilot could never quantify all the factors that decided where the bomb would hit, and he couldn't have computed them even if he had known them: the altitude he chose for beginning his pullout, the speed of his pullout, the straightness of his aircraft which always wanted to crab or slide, the speed and direction of the wind, and the exact moment he chose to press the bomb-release button that sent the bomb on a ballistic curve all affected where the bomb struck.

The rocket projectile (R/P) was even more inaccurate. Every pilot who had fired one knew that they roared off the rails and promptly dropped several feet under the influence of gravity before lurching onto an approximately parallel course. Joint Report No. 3 of No. 2 OR Section found that the chance of hitting a Panther tank, which was a sizable target, having a horizontal projected area of 50 square yards, in a 45° dive was an insignificant 0.2% requiring a whole Sqn of 18 Typhoons firing 140 R/Ps to give a 50% chance of a hit. Expert practitioners such as S/Ldr Cheval Lallemant, who commanded 609 Sqn, used vertical diving for accuracy when firing rockets because it eliminated gravity drop, although, he said, not all pilots could put their aircraft into such a position.[52]

Thus the story came full circle. It raised the question as to why the RAF insisted on operating inaccurate and vulnerable fighter-bombers to the exclusion of accurate dive-bombers, less vulnerable armoured aircraft, and accurate aircraft armed with a high velocity gun firing AP. The RAF owned the finest dive bomber in the world, but used it to tow targets in Cornwall. It is possible to imagine Cheval Lallemant in such a Vultee Vengeance MkIV dropping one ton[53] (four 500 lb bombs) of high explosive bombs in a vertical dive, followed by the fifteen other aircraft in his Sqn. Destruction of any tank or defensive position would have been virtually guaranteed, and would have made progress by the army faster and with far fewer losses.

Many possible reasons for the RAF's refusal to operate the Avenger have been suggested; unreliability of the Wright Cyclone 14 GR-2600, with Ferry Command refusing to handle the aircraft because of excessive oil consumption, but over 50,000 of the engines were built and fitted in four other types of aircraft; a psychological aversion to operating slow aircraft when air superiority was not guaranteed, requiring escorts; a dislike of diverting resources from the RAF's main task of winning the war with BC; or a preference for the fighter-bomber which could be stripped and used as a fighter in a showdown with a desperate LW.

The real reason was prosaic. The use of effective CAS aircraft was taboo to the high priests of the Trenchard cult, and Churchill was a cult fellow-traveller. They held that air power was decisive, that it must be concentrated, that it must be applied at the decisive place, and its flexibility never abused against targets that may appear to be favourable but which were not vital to the battle. The cult got widespread acceptance of these mantras, which appealed to the powerful who defined 'decisive' and who controlled the show.

> Not surprisingly, given RAF attitudes, air support doctrine in 1944, such as it was, stressed the importance of central and independent control of air power, so as to be able to strike at the decisive points.[54]

---

52 C Shores. *Ground Attack Aircraft of WWII* (London: MacDonald & Jane's, 1977).

53 Peter C Smith. *Vengeance!* (Washington: Smithsonian, 1987), p. 153.

54 *www.collectionscanada.gc.ca/obj/s4/f2/dsk2/ftp03/MQ50093.pdf* Paul Johnston: *2nd TAF & the Normandy*

The decisive point was held to be the 100 – 120 major German cities, whose complete destruction was the obsession of the RAF. Any other target was dismissed as one that only appeared to be favourable – what Arthur Harris called a 'panacea' target – but was not vital to the battle. The cult had held this view about every aspect of the war, including the Dowding System of air defence, which appeared to be favourable but was not vital and had been forced onto the RAF by Inskip and politicians who, according to the cult, pandered to the public's fears. The worst threat to the cult had come from Dowding himself who was being proposed by Churchill as the next Chief of the Air Staff. By the most disgraceful skulduggery the cult had engineered Dowding's dismissal with Churchill's concurrence.[55] The cult therefore saw it as a satisfactory solution to convert Fighter Command into 2 TAF and send it on campaign while the RAF concentrated on winning the war through bombing. Every now and then the Army impinged on them, demanding through Eisenhower the use of the Lancasters to bomb the French rail network prior to D-Day, or Caen, or the V-Weapons; and these had been reluctantly conceded. But when they asked for armoured ground attack or dive-bombers, the answer was adamantly negative.

One of the consequences of the French defeat in 1940 was the disappearance of a dive-bombing constituency that had paid attention to the lessons of the Spanish Civil War and was working up a capability. French naval dive-bombing units supported land forces in May/June 1940. AB-4 operated the new gull-wing Loire-Nieuport LN 401 dive-bomber armed with a small 150 kg anti-submarine bomb. AB-1 and AB-2 operated the Vought V156F, and the French specified the superb Vultee Vengeance for delivery in 1942. The USAAF established a large number of dive-bomber squadrons to counter German success, using the A-24, A-25, and A-36. They continued to operate them extensively through 1943, but by 1944 had lost interest, due to perceived operational limitations, and used fighter-bombers for CAS. The influence of other jurisdictions such as the VVS with its renowned Pe-2, the USMC, and the USN, were distant enough to be at best ignored and at worst misrepresented by the RAF, as happened with the Vultee Vengeance when it finally showed its paces in Burma against an enemy without air cover and with inadequate flak. But that was the situation also in NWE when the infantry went over the top under artillery bombardment. They desperately needed flying artillery.

In Britain the FAA on its independence in 1937 took over the few Blackburn Skua dive-bombers ordered by the RAF, but the promising Hawker Henley dive-bomber ordered by the RAF for the Army was diverted into target towing. On 10 May 1940 fifteen Skuas sank the cruiser *Königsberg*, tied up in Bergen the day following a failed raid by twice as many Wellingtons and Hampdens; these had shown the same inability to hit a target as the He 111s at Guernica. Skuas then sank the supply ship *Barenfels* in Bergen the next day, proving that the weapon was repetitively accurate. In late May, French LN and Vought dive-bombers desperately attacked the German armoured columns and were joined on 31 May by ten FAA Albacores and nine Skuas. These dive-bombed German pontoon bridges over the Nieuport Canal near Dunkirk, and drove off a German attack. The RAF provided little CAS to the British Army either during the Arras counterattack or in its hour of extreme need at Dunkirk. Dive-bombers stood out as being the only effective offensive weapon in the entire disastrous RAF and French Air Force campaign of 1939-1940, when a wide variety of horizontal bombers – Battle, Blenheim, Hampden, Wellington, Whitley, LO 451, Amiot 354 and Bloch 174 – could neither hit a target nor defend themselves. The lesson the RAF drew was that only fighters and not bombers could survive in daylight, and therefore the army would have to accept support from fighter-bombers that gave the pilot a chance of escape. The RAF said they needed 3,000 heavy bombers to end the war through night-bombing and these would take all

Campaign (Kingston, 1999).

55 Jack Dixon. *Dowding & Churchill* (Barnsley: Pen & Sword, 2008).

the available aircraft manufacturing capacity. Post Dunkirk and given US isolationism, the RAF had Churchill's ear. On 9 December 1940 the Vice Chief of the Air Staff wrote to the Minister of Aircraft Production:

> If the close support question is raised by the Army, I think we must go straight to the Prime Minister on the question of the fundamental strategical principle.[56]

The RAF's belief in the 1920s that the bomber would always get through, and that fighters were a concession to the public's weakness, had by 1940 given way to the cold reality of losing their star strategic bombers – Wellingtons, Hampdens, Blenheims and Battles. Only Spitfire and Hurricane fighters succeeded and propelled them into the public eye. The RAF saw how these could destroy Ju-87 Stukas, and concluded that Army support was 'uneconomical' in all circumstances below 6,000 feet. Only speed or extreme height permitted survival in daylight, they said, ignorant of the fact that the Ju 87 continued in front-line service in the East until 1945, where the LW could establish local air superiority until quite late in the war. The RAF would not, however, give up control of any land-based aircraft, and vetoed the Army's insistence on support from dive-bombers. When the RAF spoke of concentration of force, they referred not to the land battle but to their Douhet-inspired knockout blow with RAF and USAAF heavy bombers bombing around the clock.

The Army knew they had been abandoned by the RAF at Dunkirk. There was a story of soldiers preventing a shot-down pilot from boarding a ship at Dunkirk on the grounds that since he wouldn't fight he could just as well spend the war in a POW camp and reduce the number of useless mouths to feed in Britain. Alan Brooke, soon to be Chief of the General Staff, bitterly demanded an army aviation and began a two-year long campaign for one. The RAF played the strategic card, and argued persuasively that without plans to return to the continent, the army had no need of a separate aviation. Churchill refused to intervene but, becoming upset with the RAF's obduracy, asked Beaverbrook to place orders for 1,300 Vultee Vengeance dive-bombers in the USA. The RAF also tried to argue that the army had no business asking for air support. Slessor went as far as to say that the army was trying to make the RAF do its work, and that calling on aircraft became a drug.

> The Air could not, and must not, be turned on glibly and vaguely in support of the Army, which would never move unless prepared to fight its way with its own weapons.[57]

This should be compared with German recognition that an army would not proceed without all arms pulling their weight; 'Tanks in the lead, artillery in the rear, and aircraft overhead; only then will the infantry advance to the attack'.[58]

When the LW left for Russia, Fighter Command had little to do since Churchill refused to send them to Malaya where they had been promised and were desperately needed to save the British Empire. The devil makes work for idle hands, and these went looking for German shipping with their Hurricane IICs armed with 20 mm cannon. The British first test-fitted a pair of 250 lb bombs to a Hurricane IIA in early 1941 after they had been identified on the Me 109E/4B and the captured pilots interviewed, but it was not until the end of 1941 that Hurricane IIB and IIC were outfitted with bomb racks. Two squadrons then started low-level 'rhubarb' intruder missions into a relatively quiet France defended by 2 and 26 Geschwader. Whirlwinds, Kittyhawks

56 P Smith. *Close Air Support (*London: Orion, 1990), ref PRO Air 14/181/IIH/241/3/406.

57 Terraine, *The Right*, ref Tedder.

58 H. Plocher. *Unterstützung des Heeres* (Karlsruhe Document Collection, G VI 3a).

and Mustangs were similarly used. At the same time Coningham in North Africa introduced Hurricane Is carrying eight wing-mounted 40 lb bombs. In May 1942 the first Kittybomber units, and Hurricane IIDs with Vickers 40 mm 'S' guns arrived. RAF communication teams were placed at army level in what came to be called the 'Libyan Model' of army-air cooperation. But Coningham continued the tactic of bombing from 10-15,000 feet with fighter escort in spite of air superiority, and nothing changed until Harry Broadhurst took command of the Desert Air Force. On 25 March 1943 and despite Coningham's objections, Broadhurst implemented Montgomery's suggestion of hanging bombs onto Spitfires and Hurricanes, and persuaded the pilots to accept the task of CAS at El Hamma during the Mareth battle. At the briefing, the pilots called Broadhurst a 'murderer' of pilots. For the first time air-superiority fighters strafed the German Army with the addition of bombs as the RAF imitated LW fighter-bombing.

> Much of the Battle of Britain élite had been posted to the Desert Air Force and in general did not respond to Monty's ideas... [Broadhurst's] position with the fighter boys was unique, for he had been one of them as a most gallant and active wing leader... He very soon altered the attitudes of those who held that a Spitfire wasn't meant to be a fighter-bomber, and sacked anyone who didn't hold with the new rôle.[59]

A year earlier on 3 January 1942, Sholto Douglas, the head of Fighter Command, shocked the Air Chiefs by expressing a heretical interest in providing air support for the Army in Britain that was more than dropping bombs from Blenheims at 10-15,000 ft. On 30 March 1942, Paul Richey, who was Sqn Leader Tactics at Fighter Command, selected 609 Sqn for conversion to Typhoons. The Typhoon had first flown in February 1940 but the need for Hurricanes during the Battle of Britain delayed further work for eight months. It was twice as heavy and powerful as a Spitfire, but its thick (18%) Hurricane wing-form ruined the potential of the new 2,100 hp Napier Sabre engine, and it could not compete with the FW190 at altitude. It was therefore redesigned with a thinner (14½%) wing as the Typhoon II, and renamed the Tempest. The Typhoon was to be scrapped, but work was found for it while the Tempest was in development.

A Wing comprising 56, 266 and 609 Squadrons was formed at Duxford in September 1941 under the command of Denys Gillam to counter the Fw 190. He was said to be the most experienced ground-attack exponent in the RAF, where there was no competition for a career-ending specialisation. Gillam had fought in the Battle of Britain in 616 Sqn and then commanded 615 Sqn, attacking enemy shipping with cannon-armed Hurricanes. For two months 609 Sqn was virtually non-operational. The Typhoon was too unreliable to be committed. Dieppe was its debut when the RAF was defeated, and it was then, according to Gillam, that it dawned on many that the Typhoon was good for ground attack and army support because its high lift wing and speed at low altitudes made it a good gun-platform. On 18 September 1942 the three Sqn commanders gave up on the Typhoon, and disbanded the Duxford Wing. The squadrons dispersed to practise the role of defending against the 'tip-and-run' raiders while awaiting the Tempest. 609 Sqn under the young Langley test pilot, Roland Beamont, squared off against Liesendahl's two half squadrons, and inevitably studied his enemy's equipment and tactics. For many months at Biggin Hill and Manston they tried without success to intercept the tip-and-runners. From boredom Beamont started flying across to France at night, intercepting trains using a timetable he had acquired, and shooting up the locomotives with cannon. These lone sorties became popular with pilots, comprising a British *Störangriff*, taking the battle to the enemy through night bombing of enemy airfields, and early morning attacks on shipping. Their 'success' could never be quantified, but led to the formation of

59 Hamilton, *Monty: Master*, p. 201, ref Gp Capt F.H.L. Searl.

an ad hoc wing. Fitting drop tanks, they attacked airfields deep in enemy territory, and with 198 Sqn became the official long-range striking force. In January 1944 the Wing claimed 43 aircraft, representing three quarters of 11 Group's total achievement. They were congratulated by Leigh-Mallory, and told they had 'immortalised the Typhoon'. At the end of February 1944 they transferred from Air Defence of Great Britain (ADGB) into 2 TAF as the top-scoring RAF fighter Sqn in Europe. In 1945, 123 Wing comprised 164, 183, 198 and 609 Squadrons.

None of the squadrons had the experience, training, aptitude, equipment or weapons for their new rôle of army support. The Typhoon was optimised for air superiority, requiring long hardened runways with a sophisticated maintenance and repair organisation for the Sabre engine which was a fitter's nightmare. The airframe was flimsy and almost devoid of armour, which a two-cent bullet from the ground could and did bring crashing down by puncturing the lubrication or cooling lines and radiators. Rockets and bombs released in a shallow dive were inaccurate, and because of their vulnerability pilots were ordered never to go round again to make sure they had destroyed the target, thus institutionalising inaccuracy. Lallemant objected to being ordered by Dring never to make a proper recce of the target or return to an undamaged target, and continued to make a pass at low level before firing in order to pick out the tanks from the soft-skinned vehicles. Dring argued that this gave the accurate Flak a double chance to shoot the aircraft down and was therefore undesirable, while Lallement insisted it was essential.[60] The conflict was between the pilot's requirement to avoid rash and unnecessary exposure to danger and the need to destroy threats to the infantry, with Dring and Lallemant taking opposite positions. The Wann-Woodall system eliminated any contact by the pilot with the infantry, either in advance or in real time, and the lack of a spare seat in the Typhoon precluded a soldier from the unit being taken along to advise the pilot while in the air. The result was institutionalised pilot ignorance about the target's priority in CAS, or direct air support as it was then called.

Instead of a fighter-bomber, two specialised aircraft were needed to meet the requirements. The first was a two-seat, vertical dive-bomber able to drop a ton of bombs accurately. The degree to which the Vengeance could survive in the Flak environment of NWE is unknown because it was never tried, but it performed well in the Far East. The signs were good, and it should have been straightforward to armour the vital oil cooler and oil-lines as in the Hurricane IV. The engine was air-cooled without the vulnerable coolant system. The aircraft had a unique wing design, avoiding a main beam running through the fuselage and permitting a bomb-bay with an associated stance lower to the ground than the Ju 87 with its external bomb, with good rough terrain taxiing capability and a strong undercarriage. It was 'soldier-proof', almost indestructible and the RAF had them on charge.

Rather than being one of the Few, the pilot should, however, have been a soldier working to the same success criterion of target destruction as the men he supported, and able to contribute to the plan of attack together with infantryman, gunner and tank commander. A system was in place for the RAF to train soldiers as pilots of Austers and gliders, and there were hundreds of surplus RAF pilots produced by the BCATP who could have been enrolled into the infantry to fly dive-bombers. An infantryman from the unit being supported, or a gunner, should have been in the rear seat to observe and help with target acquisition while in constant communication with the ground forces. An open map marked with the artillery's target numbers would have provided the accurate reference points to enable real time participation. Over-flying and observing the threat to the infantry as it developed would have provided vital feedback to those on the ground, and led to target identification. When the dive-bomber had exhausted its stores, the observer would have briefed the relief aircraft flying alongside. The dive-bomber should have been able to operate off

60 Shores, *Ground Attack*, p. 156.

grass strips close behind the lines with minimal maintenance facilities. It should have been easy to bomb up, and have bad weather capability. The task required operating the Vengeance and using the experience to further refine it. It could never bear any resemblance to a fighter.

The second aircraft type required was the equivalent of a combined Ju 87G two-seat tank-destroyer with two high velocity 37 mm guns firing AP and the IL-2 armoured ground-attack aircraft. This could have been built under licence and re-engined with the RR Merlin while being fitted with all other stores such as anti-personnel and HE bombs. The RAF had gained some experience with this concept with the single-seat Hurricane IV armed with two 40 mm cannon and 350 lb of additional armour. Unfortunately, although Hawker carried on the Sopwith line with its armoured aircraft, Harry Hawker died in a car crash in 1920, leaving the company to its designer, Sidney Camm, who had been with Martin Handasyde in the First World War and was ignorant of Sopwith's experience with armoured aircraft. In the USA, the single-seat Bell Kingcobra RP63 aircraft with a 37 mm low velocity cannon and a ton of duralumin-alloy armour was another relevant design concept. But the right aircraft was never specified or built.

The genesis of 2 TAF occurred in October 1942 when Churchill determined to settle what he had at long last come to see as a 'hard and unhelpful' Air Staff attitude towards the Army. Churchill decreed Coningham's 'Libyan Model' be adopted as a working compromise. The Army C-in-C was to specify the targets and tasks to be performed by the Air Officer C-in-C, and the latter was 'to use his maximum force for those objectives in the manner most effective.' That left the RAF with its independence and was close to the Air Staff's traditional offer of sending all of their unsuitable aircraft to bail out the army in an emergency. It was light years away from Brooke's demand for a large and independent army air force equipped with suitable aircraft. Brooke, however, was determined to continue to maintain pressure on Churchill until he got his way.

At this time many with influence in the Army, such as Paget and Kennedy, said they were prepared to settle for what they could get in terms of air support from the RAF. Other influential military voices spoke in the same vein: Col Oxborrow, who was BGS Air at Army Group HQ; Brig Woodall, SASO Army Group Command; Lt-Col Carrington, ALO at Bomber Command; and Lt-Col Stockley, who was ALO at Fighter Command.

Brooke tried to rescue something. His experience during the retreat from Brussels to Dunkirk had illustrated very clearly the evils of the highly centralised system practised by the RAF. He had never seen a single aircraft throughout the retreat. Brooke presented Fighter Command with three conditions which he was sure they would be both unable and unwilling to meet; they must become capable of handling different types of operation; they must train continuously with the Army; and they must become fully mobile and accompany the Army in the field. Unfortunately he failed to include in his list of 'musts' the one real sticking point which would even then have ruled out the use of Fighter Command: the necessity of their providing specialised CAS aircraft (dive bomber, armoured bomber and armoured anti-tank gun) without which CAS could never be effective. This was a surprising omission for a man famous for his incisive intelligence and reveals failure to understand the minutiae of CAS, for even Churchill supported the army's need for dive-bombers and was fully aware that the RAF's opposition to them was motivated entirely by self-interest.

> I have always had grave doubts whether the Air Ministry were right in banning dive bombers. ... There is a widespread belief that we have not developed dive-bombers because of the fear of the Air Ministry that a weapon of this kind specially associated with the Army might lead to the formation of a separate Army wing.[61]

61 WA Jacobs. *Air Support for the British Army* (Military Affairs, Vol 46, No.4, 1982).

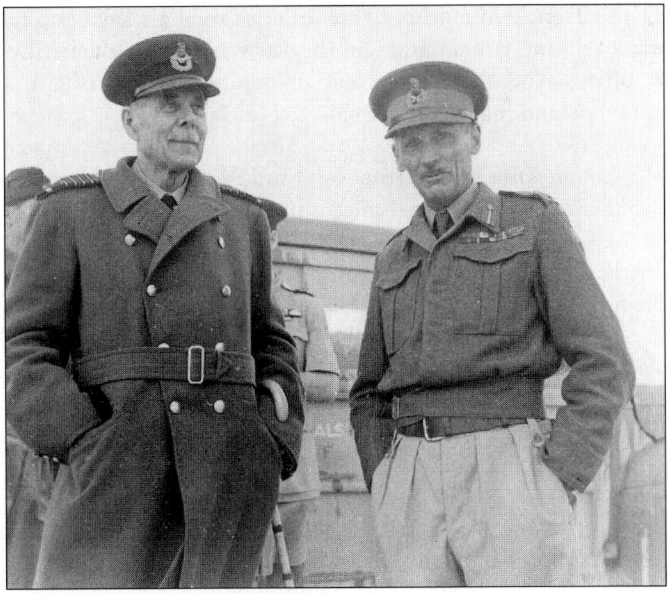

How the RAF stitched up the Army. Marshal of the RAF, Lord Trenchard with Lt Gen Montgomery on a visit to the Western Desert, 20 October 1942. What Trenchard and Montgomery decided, or even why Trenchard went to see him, was not recorded, but the following events revealed their private agreement. In London Brooke was close to persuading Churchill to re-establish an army aviation, which Trenchard saw as a threat to the RAF's control of more than half the productive resources of the UK, and to their totem Bomber Command. Following this Trenchard/Montgomery meeting, Leigh Mallory was promoted from AOC 11 Group to C-in-C Fighter Command, replacing Sholto Douglas because Montgomery had said he could do business with Leigh Mallory who was sympathetic to the army's needs. Douglas replaced Tedder as AOC-in-C Middle East, while Tedder became Air C-in-C Mediterranean Command, as Trenchard placed his men in all the influential positions. The RAF now promised that the Libyan Model, which Montgomery owned, would be extended everywhere by the new team. Trenchard had thus fulfilled his side of the bargain made with Montgomery by shuffling a few chairs and giving nothing away. Brooke was not to be fobbed off, and continued to insist with Churchill on full independence for a reconstituted RFC. It was then that Trenchard yanked Montgomery's chain, and Montgomery made an insubordinate statement without warning Brooke. Montgomery declared that "The soldier must not expect, or wish, to exercise direct command over air striking forces". Tedder gleefully reported this to Portal in February 1943, adding; "I suggest that CIGS is now in a cleft stick. He cannot disown Monty, but he must either choose to repudiate Monty's views, which are founded on battle, or be himself a minority voice". Brooke had no choice and accepted the inevitable. The RAF thus continued to 'service' the army with the wrong type of aircraft and on their own unsatisfactorily independent terms through 2 TAF, denying the army any chance of creating integrated all-arms. Trenchard had won his greatest victory, and Montgomery had stupidly, arrogantly but fatally condemned the army to ineffectiveness. (© Crown Copyright IWM, E 108087 by Sgt Gladstone)

Brooke underestimated, or maybe never fully understood, the devious cult-like character of his opponents, who were chosen by Trenchard, were beholden to Trenchard, and had stopped thinking any thoughts but those of Trenchard, if they could understand them. The reader may reject this as insultingly extreme language, but it reflects the truth as expressed by an RAF apologist who used cultic religious language to describe Bomber Command:

> And so we come to Bomber Command, the RAF's *Holy of Holies.* Since its very earliest days the belief in the offensive rôle of the Service had possessed *religious force*, with Bomber Command as the *priesthood*.[62]

62 Terraine, *The Right*, p. 77.

To the Trenchard cultists fighter aircraft were always a sop to the weak-willed and minded. The way to defend Britain and win the war was not with defensive fighters or with an army, but with an offensive bomber force able to obliterate the hundred largest German cities to cause a collapse of morale and make the Germans cry uncle.

> Counter-attack [of Germany by strategic bombers] remains the chief deterrent and defence (Swinton). The bomber force is fundamentally the basis of all air strategy (Air Staff).[63]

The RAF accepted Brooke's three conditions, making the bombing cultists happy by transferring the non-decisive sideshow of Fighter Command into 2 TAF, while Fighter Command was happy to oblige as it had already voluntarily converted its fighters into fighter-bombers and sent them over enemy-occupied France on Rhubarbs and Circuses at great loss. Every part of the RAF was content, having conceded not even their comfort, since come the winter they left their tents to take up residence in abandoned LW barracks, while Coningham lived in splendour in Brussels. The Army accepted Churchill's edict and made it work after a fashion. The soldiers died in their thousands lacking two essentials: support from a tank immune to the 88, and from accurate CAS. The exception was in Burma where the Vengeance dive bomber for a while provided the needed quality support until the Air Ministry caught wind of the plaudits it had gained and summarily scrapped it to avoid embarrassing questions.

In NWE the soldiers naively climbed out of their slit trenches and cheered as Bomber Command destroyed Caen without killing one German soldier. They cheered when Typhoons loosed salvos of R/Ps at the enemy over their heads, knowing the R/Ps terrified the German defenders, with the glaring exception of the Flak gunners who enjoyed shooting down Typhoons. The soldiers never knew that the Typhoons rarely hit anything. 2 TAF pilots 'loved' their enormously powerful steeds, but their days were ruined by the hated Flak that decimated them and made gibbering wrecks of some of them.

The 'Libyan Model' originated in the arrival in that place of No 2 AASC in December 1941 under Major McNeill. AASC was a system designed jointly by AM Sir Arthur 'Ugly' Barrett, Brigadier Woodall and Group Captain Wann in Army Co-operation Command. The system had four elements: dedicated (but not specialised) aircraft; trained soldiers to act as ALOs; a joint AACC staffed by both arms; and a dedicated communication network staffed with its own people. Tentacles were established at division, brigade and in the front line, linked on a common frequency with the AACC. It was intended that each corps have its own AACC, but unfortunately, in the confusion of Rommel's advance into Egypt, the AACC began working with 8 Army. This was too high in the hierarchy for effectiveness as it was the Corps commander who was responsible for operations. But AACC and Army became the accepted norm when the front stabilised at Alam Halfa. McNeill got Coningham and Montgomery together and the system went fully operational. Montgomery would never afterwards relinquish it, and as C-in-C 21 AG in effect ran the system together with Broadhurst, ignoring Coningham in his Brussels palace.

Irretrievably lost in this bureaucratic centralisation were the elements needed for effective air support as part of all-arms – appropriate specialised equipment and decisions taken at the level of those needing them. Artillery FOOs moved with the troops on the ground and commanded the artillery in each of the three battles described, a uniquely British contribution to all-arms. These FOOs could have been provided with the VHF radios needed to command the aircraft overhead and the ASSU tentacle radios needed for contact with the GCC to 'whistle' up aircraft. These, however, were the steps that kept the RAF awake at night because it would mean subordinating

63 Montgomery Hyde. *British Air Policy Between The Wars* (London: Heinemann, 1976).

themselves to the Pongos for whom they never disguised their contempt. Faced with this threat, the Trenchard cultists yanked the chain with which they controlled their fellow-traveller, Churchill, who magisterially laid down the bureaucratic system, institutionalising the RAF's power to supply support entirely on its own terms and even requiring the army to plan the required support in advance and to specify the targets. This Churchill-mandated system of Army-Air collaboration was inevitably at all times wasteful, unresponsive, inefficient, inaccurate and ineffective, condemning 21 AG to ineffectiveness. Nothing, though, could prevent Churchill from pontificating from the depths of his technical ignorance about aircraft while wearing pilot wings on his RAF uniform:

> Nevermore must the Army rely solely on aircraft for its protection against attack from the air. Above all, the idea of keeping standing patrols of aircraft over moving columns should be abandoned. It is unsound to 'distribute' aircraft in this way, and no air superiority will stand any large application of such a mischievous practice. Upon the Military CinC in the ME announcing that a battle is in prospect, the Air Officer CinC will give him all possible aid irrespective of other targets, however attractive. [This should have led to the suspension of strategic bombing of Germany and the transfer of Bomber Command to the ME for First Alamein, but Churchill carefully, and surely at Trenchard's prompting, restricted his edict to the air force *available in theatre*, ensuring Bomber Command never went to North Africa]. Victory in the battle makes amends for all, and creates new favourable situations of a decisive character. The Army CinC will specify to the Air Officer CinC the targets and tasks which he requires to be performed, both in the preparatory attack on the rearward installations of the enemy and for air action during the progress of the battle. It will be for the Air Officer CinC to use his maximum force for those objects in the manner most effective. This applies not only to any squadrons assigned to Army Cooperation permanently, but also to the whole air force available in the theatre.[64]

With this edict, Churchill ruled out the possibility for the duration that army-air, and therefore all-arms effectiveness, could ever be developed.

Allowing decisions about air support to be made at army rather than at corps level, which was Montgomery's interpretation of the edict, prevented the detailed needs of the troops and their task requirement from being addressed. These considerations were replaced with a far too elevated interpretation of what was 'decisive', and of course left the RAF with the power to decide what was and was not decisive. For the RAF, Alamein was not a decisive battle, but destroying the centre of Berlin or Dresden was decisive because it could lead, in the RAF's cultic opinion, and against all common sense, to German collapse. Making decisions about air support for the army at such elevated altitudes precluded the development of unit affiliation between air and front-line units in which airmen might have learned of the needs of the soldiers and how they were not being met. Centralisation prevented feedback, and precluded the application of pressure by the army to ensure targets were destroyed rather than just bombed or rocketed inaccurately and always 'successfully' in RAF-speak. Within 21 AG criticism was 'bellyaching' and punishable. 2 TAF attended conferences only at army level, and did not always remember to send someone of sufficient rank to issue instructions to Group. These conferences were held every other night to decide where aircraft should operate on the following days – to deliver ordnance to certain map references, to conduct armed recce in a certain geographical area, or establish a cab rank under RAF control.

Useful results could only have been obtained by joint planning at battalion or in the extreme at brigade level, but the RAF would never attend any such meeting. Their contact cars/FCP/VCP

64 Churchill, *History: Vol III*, p. 443.

were located at corps/divisional/brigade HQ, but only to ensure the RAF got the information necessary to fulfil previously agreed tasks unless the aircraft were part of a cabrank. The soldiers fighting and dying on the battlefield had no input into any planning decision, and they were never asked for feedback. The whole system was organized and controlled above the front-line soldiers' heads by Montgomery and Coningham supposedly in their interest, but Montgomery in effect used it to dispense largesse. He arranged for rockets or bombs to be delivered on the enemy in the same spirit that he handed out cartons of cigarettes to the troops. Montgomery was informed through his OR teams of the inaccuracy of air support, but never raised it or insisted that 2 TAF equip themselves with accurate aircraft such as dive-bombers or aircraft with large cannon. Montgomery the bully had learned early on that Trenchardism was a superior force that had captured Churchill, and he went along with it except at the inter-personal level with Tedder and Coningham. Montgomery in any case did not know one aircraft from another, and probably had persuaded himself that the inaccurate and vulnerable Typhoon was a 'capital' aircraft just as the ineffective and vulnerable Sherman was a 'capital' tank.

Until March 1943 at Mareth, air support consisted of inaccurate bombing by both twin-engined and fighter-bombers from altitude beyond the reach of light flak. Then occurred the full flowering of the 'Libyan Model' into a standard procedure. Freddie de Guingand, Montgomery's Chief of Staff, and Harry Broadhurst finalised the system, which Francis Tuker, GOC 4 Indian Div, planned with Broadhurst as a 'Blitz' attack by the whole Desert Air Force concentrating on the army's front and at low level.

> Broadhurst listened to the arguments, and after a long discussion said, 'I will do it. You will have the whole boiling match – bombs and cannon. It will be a real low-flying blitz, and I will talk to all the pilots myself.'[65]

This early success was, however, due to the element of surprise that was always short-lived with the Germans. There was plenty of evidence to Tuker throughout the 900 mile advance from Alamein to Benghazi, that the RAF lacked the right equipment or methods for long-term effectiveness. He concluded, 'That the RAF demoralized, there is ample evidence; that they destroyed there is little.[66] The RAF's apologist was reduced to suggesting that the Germans had deceived Tuker by taking their scrap metal away with them:

> Allowing for the fact that the enemy salvaged every available vehicle capable of being put in tow, inspection of the roads between Agedabia and Marble Arch led to the conclusion that, on the whole, the fighter-bombing had had disappointing results.[67]

The British knew the vulnerability of unarmoured aircraft to flak, and especially Stukas in their dive.[68] The Hurricane IID, which appeared in 1943, had the Merlin XX of 1,185 hp and metal wings holding two 40 mm Vickers 'S' cannon and two 0.303 machine guns, protected only by a small amount of armour. They were decimated by flak like any other unarmoured aircraft threatening valuable assets.

65 Francis Tuker. *Approach to Battle* (London: Cassell, 1963).
66 Ibid.
67 Terraine, *The Right*, p. 388, ref AHB/II/116/22 p. 76.
68 Tuker, *Approach*.

> With the intensive AA fire employed by the enemy in support of his armoured forces, attacks on tank targets in the battle area generally imposed too high a wastage of aircraft and could not be justified. Ideal targets were small groups of tanks away from the main armoured battle, and (6) Sqn's activities were generally limited by the availability of such targets.[69]

In March 1943, the Hurricane IID was withdrawn after sixteen were lost to Flak in five days, but in the same month the first flight occurred of the Hurricane IIE, which was then designated the Hurricane IV. This unique aircraft that surely was Broadhurst's brainchild, had 350 lb of additional armour protection around the engine, radiator and cockpit, an up-rated engine, and a 'universal' or HE wing carrying two 0.303 in machine guns and wiring for either two 40 mm Vickers S cannon or eight 60 lb rocket projectiles. It entered service in May equipping seven squadrons in the UK (137, 164, 184, 186, 438, 439, and 440 Sqns), two in Italy (6 and 351 sqns) and two in Burma (20 and 42 Sqns) with a total production run of 580. 2 TAF unaccountably but unsurprisingly rejected them, and instead converted 137 and 164 Sqns to Typhoons.

The RAF's dislike of armoured aircraft and dive-bombers was due to an insistence that day-bombers must be able to meet German fighters on favourable terms in the absence of air superiority. Their view was incoherent since 2 TAF operated vulnerable day-bombers (Marauders and Bostons) but continued to shun dive-bombers even after achieving air superiority.

An RAF apologist presented a rational argument for public consumption that concealed the RAF's refusal to operate dive-bombers under any circumstance in NWE even when they possessed the Vultee Vengeance but were using it as a target tug.

> There has been fairly general acceptance of the view that the initial German successes with dive bombers were due to the absence of effective fighter opposition, and that there was little justification for the development of the single purpose Stuka or dive-bombing aeroplane. For this reason Allied production has been concentrated on the fighter-bomber, capable of supporting ground operations by low level bombing and machine-gunning, yet possessing sufficient speed, manoeuvrability and armament to meet a fighter on favourable terms. When air superiority has been attained in a particular zone, dive bombers, provided with fighter escort, can be used with great effect against special targets, but adequate fighter cover is essential.[70]

Speed reduced the vulnerable period of exposure to Flak, and shortened it further if surprise were obtained, but degraded the accuracy of an intrinsically inaccurate weapon. Another RAF apologist[71] criticised the armoured Russian IL-2m3 Sturmovik for its slow speed of 231 mph, but praised it for being the first to carry rockets and cluster bombs. He argued that the 412 mph of the Typhoon corrected the 'weakness' of the Sturmovik, and with 60 lb rockets the Typhoon 'made its name in the skies of northwestern Europe in 1943'. He overlooked the Sturmovik's relative immunity to light flak that gave the pilot time to aim and a greater chance of hitting the target, and he failed to mention that the armoured aircraft concept was pioneered with the Ju-1, Sopwith Salamander and Sopwith Buffalo of 1918.

After extensive trials in 1942, the Germans rejected rockets because of their inherent inaccuracy. Instead they chose the gun pioneered by the Hurricane IID but fitted into a specialised two-seat aircraft. Two BK 3.7 cm guns were installed in the armoured Ju 87G, the preferred mount of

69 TNA: AHB/II/117/8(C), p. 217.
70 RA Saville-Sneath. *Aircraft of the United States* (Harmondsworth: Penguin, 1945).
71 Terraine, *The Right.*

Hans-Ulrich Rudel. The heavily armoured Henschel HS 129B received a 30 mm MK101 with 30 rounds, and later a BK 7.5 cm with 12 rounds. Such guns were accurate and devastating to armour

The Germans and Russians saw the benefit of armour, which reduced speed. Any low-flying plane had to fly through a curtain of steel. The Germans admired and greatly feared the Sturmovik for its resistance to both Flak and fighters.

> All German commanders describe the IL-2 as a highly useful airplane for ground-attack missions. Owing to its good armour plating, the plane could only be brought down by very well directed ground fire. It had a speed of 210 mph. General der Flakartillerie a.D Wolfgang Pickert adds that the IL-2 was impervious to light 20-mm armour-piercing or 37-mm shells. The same views are expressed by General der Infanterie von der Groben, who emphasises the nose armour and remarks that direct hits with 20-mm shells frequently had no effects on the plane. The experience of the 54th Fighter Wing also shows it was hardly possible to shoot down the IL-2 aircraft in an attack from the rear, because of its excellent armour protection.[72]

The forward fuselage of the IL-2m3 from spinner to behind the gunner was pressed as a one-piece armoured container from rolled 6 mm armour plate with integrally pressed engine bearers and cooler nest with 13 mm end-plates. The top of the cockpit and the ventral oil cooler were covered with 8 mm armour plate while the windshield and rear screen were made from 55 mm armoured glass. Its immunity from ground fire from infantry weapons was notorious. It could be brought down by fighters armed with machine guns only by shredding the tail and control surfaces, or sniping the pilot through his unarmoured sliding side window. There was also a small piece above the engine not covered by armour plate, and some ME 109 pilots aimed for that in a vertical dive, and Finnish pilots talked of destroying the forward wing roots. The installation of a rear gunner in 1943 prevented these antics, so the ME 109 Gustav was introduced with hub-firing 30 mm cannon to penetrate the armour. By this time competent Russian air superiority fighters were protecting the IL-2s.

The British knew about the Sturmovik. The head of the British Military Mission, Gifford Martel, discussed it with the Russians and became interested.

> First of all, it was clear that the Russians set great store by the Sturmovik aeroplane. No other nation had developed an aircraft which was armoured in this way. Were they all wrong and the Russians right?[73]

Martel's departure from Russia ended the debate whose results in any event would have been ignored by the RAF. None on the British side was informed about the heavily armoured Henschel HS129B, and lightly armoured Ju 87 G-1 and Fw 190F. Martel speculated that Flak was less intense on the Russian Front but had it been the case then there would have been more not less reason for the British to armour their CAS aircraft. Germans who overflew London and Moscow claimed Moscow was better protected by Flak. Thousands of Sturmoviks were brought down by heavy German Flak. British Flak by comparison was ill-disciplined and despised by RAF pilots like Pierre Clostermann, who wrote that he lowered the wheels of his Tempest to taunt the gunners.

Improved survivability, ease of service, and ability to operate from grass were the design requirements in any CAS aircraft, and the Typhoon was deficient in all of them. The one flown at Winnekendonk by the Leader of 609 Sqn, Roberts, was destroyed a few days later by a bullet from

72 W Schwabedissen. *The Russian Air Force in the Eyes of German Commanders* (New York: Arno Press, 1968).
73 Gifford LeQ Martel. *The Russian Outlook* (London: Michael Joseph, 1947).

an MG 42 penetrating the cooling jacket of the engine. By comparison with Russian and German ground-attack aircraft, the Typhoon had a similar all-up weight but differed significantly in four main areas. It had more power, smaller wings and fuselage, no armour to speak of and no armour-piercing gun. Small wings meant it needed a lengthened and hardened runway of 1,600 feet. Load carrying was better than the armoured Sturmovik but only a third of the armoured Stuka.

The appointment of Leigh-Mallory to Fighter Command in November 1942 put in place an officer sympathetic to the Army's needs. Brooke would not concede the principle that the TAF must be under Army command, until Montgomery inexplicably pulled the rug from under his feet, by declaring; 'The soldier must not expect, or wish, to exercise direct command over air striking forces'.[74] Tedder reported this to Portal in February 1943, adding:

> I am not adept at such matters but I suggest that CIGS is now caught in a cleft stick. He cannot disown Monty, but he must choose either to repudiate Monty's views, which are founded on battle, or be himself a minority voice.[75]

Brooke accepted the inevitable, and the RAF conceded his three conditions listed earlier – joint training, dedicated squadrons and being mobile. As a result on D-Day the Allies fielded 3,200 RAF and USAAF tactical aircraft and 1,100 transports.

On 1 June 1943, 2 Group Bomber Command was transferred to Fighter Command, followed a fortnight later by Army Co-operation Command. 83 Group (Bingo Brown) and 84 Group (Harry Broadhurst) were established by allocating airfields to them for assembling a wing of three squadrons. Ground crews and staff were removed from the unhappy squadrons and pooled at wing level. The wing acquired two commanders: one responsible for making the airfield mobile to fulfill Brooke's condition, and another to control flying duties.

The formation of 123 Wing[76] was described by its first ground commander, Group Captain Desmond Scott.[77] He was briefed by Bingo Brown at 84 Group's HQ at Oxford, and from there went to Manston, to form his Wing initially from 198 Sqn under Baldwin and 609 under Wells. Wing Co Brooker commanded the flying duties. Scott's job was to strip the squadrons of their non-flying personnel and produce a centralised organisation to service the planes as well as provide an Ops Room, medical services, kitchens, maintenance & repair, armoury, signals, and defence. 609 Sqn was reduced from 150 to 35 men, comprising two dozen pilots, an MO, and a handful of dependent erks in an Orderly Room. The Wing went tactical, which meant moving at a moment's notice. Scott was helped by veterans of the desert air force to make sense of a large convoy of vehicles that arrived at Manston, and into which he fitted the new Wing. After a few days shakedown they put everything to the test, packed up and moved to Thorney Island. The Wing was split into two parties; the 'A' party left for the new airfield while the 'B' party remained to service the squadrons. When the 'A' party was established, the squadrons landed at the new base and the 'B' party motored to join them.

609 Sqn was part of the AAF, and the top-scoring Sqn in Europe. Both its name and identification letters 'PR' were famous. It was formed in 1936 as the West Riding Sqn at Yeadon under Harald Peake. Its motto was Tally-Ho. By 1945 it could list a host of luminaries, and in that sense is reminiscent of 3 SG. From 1936 to 1945, it consumed 16 Leaders and 256 pilots or 10 times establishment, of whom 145 were British, 56 were Belgians, 15 Canadians, 13 Australians, 10 New

74 BL Montgomery. *Some Notes on High Command in War* (Tripoli: 1943).
75 TNA: AIR 29/2490: Tedder to CAS 17 February 1943.
76 Shores, *2nd TAF*. Events are timed a month earlier than Scott.
77 Scott, *Typhoon Pilot*.

Zealanders, 7 Poles, 5 Americans, and 2 French, with 6 other countries represented. Of this total, 74 were killed while serving with the Sqn and 30 subsequently. Only 8 were taken prisoner, while 3 evaded capture. Its pilots earned 3 DSOs, 41 DFCs, 4 DFMs, an AFC, MBE and BEM and uncounted Belgian Croix de Guerre.[78] They claimed 232 enemy destroyed in the air and 9 on the ground and countless tanks, MET and locomotives.

609 started in 1936 as a bomber Sqn with Tutors and Harts, but in 1938 joined Fighter Command and received Hinds. In 1939 they were taken under the wing of 72 Sqn at Church Fenton where they had their last Summer Camp and received their first Spitfire. They were at Catterick on the outbreak of war, converting on Harvards and having to wait for a gap in the traffic before taking off uphill over the Great North Road. They moved to Acklington in their Spitfires with only 12 pilots when establishment was 26, practising the scramble. They protected the RN operating from Kinloss and Drem where they stayed until May 1940. On 28 October 1939 with 602 Sqn they brought down the first German bomber on British soil near Drem; a Heinkel 111 whose crew were disgusted at being vanquished by 'Auxiliary amateurs'.

On 18 May 1940 they went south to Northolt in Park's 11 Group, but were not involved with the BEF prior to Dunkirk. On 27 May they received the controversial armour plate behind the pilot's back and neck. On 30 May at noon 12 of them flew to Biggin Hill to refuel and then, quite unrehearsed, flew their first patrol of the war. By the end of the evacuation on 4 June, four of the eleven Auxiliary pilots of August 1939 were dead and morale had plummeted. They escorted Churchill to France twice on 11 and 13 June, and were the only Spitfires to land voluntarily in France before 1944. On the first occasion Churchill returned without the escort, which couldn't find 100 octane petrol or starter batteries. On the second occasion a Hudson accompanied them with starter batteries, and they made do with *Essence B*.

On 5 June they received constant speed propellers which raised the performance of the Spitfire I to equality with the ME109E. On 28 June they received a Regular CO, George Darley, sent to restore morale by training them to Regular standards. They started by hating Darley and came to realise that they had needed him desperately. They moved to a newly built Middle Wallop on 5 July 1940 with still inadequate equipment and methods: their radios were HF; they lacked oxygen, rear-view mirrors and inflatable dinghies; exhaust flare made the Spitfire useless at night; and pilots failed to appreciate the advantage of height. Losses mounted to 9 by the end of July with reinforcements arriving from the OTUs. Two were Poles who had a positive effect.

On 13 August they shot down 5 Stukas and an ME109 into Lyme Bay in one of the most celebrated engagements of the war. Their four minutes of glory were in full view of Churchill, Brooke, Auchinleck, Montgomery and others standing on the cliffs above Portland. In four days 609 was credited with 30 without loss to themselves. During the big attacks 609 defended the west, and again it was responsible for a spectacular event over London on 15 September when they brought down a Dornier onto Victoria Station in full view of Queen Wilhelmina and thousands. There were big days on 25 and 27 September 1940 defending Filton, but the LW was already switching to fighter-bombers. On 7 October they downed 5 ME110s in another celebrated action. On 21 October 1940, 609 became the first Spitfire Sqn to reach a total of 100 confirmed kills. On 28 November, John Dundas, with a score of 13, shot down the ace Maj Helmut Wick, leading scorer with 56 and commander of JG2 (Richthofen) Geschwader. But Dundas disappeared with Baillon, his wingman. Dundas and Wick personified their two countries; the one an amusing gentleman and founder member of Hillary's decadent, effete 'long-haired boys', while the other was a humourless, rigid, militaristic Nazi who, however, was willing to answer Sperrle back when criticised for a sloppily turned-out ground crew. The next day the Sqn moved to Warmwell.

78 Ziegler, *The Story*.

On 4 October 1940 Michael Lister Robinson, who was a brilliant flyer and a showman, replaced Darley. At the end of February 1941 they moved to Biggin Hill, commanded by 'Sailor' Malan and re-equipped with Spitfire IIs. Immediately they were on operations flying top cover to the Biggin Wing bombing Calais. The new policy of 'leaning into' France had been set by Sholto Douglas as C-in-C Fighter Command, and by Leigh-Mallory as 11 Group's AOC. Fighter command was already searching for the new rôle that led to 2 TAF.

In April the first Belgian pilots arrived at Robinson's request and added a new dimension to what was now recognized as an extraordinary squadron. On 8 May 1941 the Battle of the Dinghy occurred in mid-Channel, when 609 claimed 6 ME109s for 2 Spitfires damaged. At the end of May they received Spitfire Vbs with two 20 mm cannon and 4 mgs to try and match the ME109F. They also got inflatable dinghies. Operations were now 'Circuses' of several wings escorting bombers to entice the GAF to come up and fight; Roadsteads against shipping; or Rhubarbs in which a pair sought targets of opportunity over France. In July the modest Scot, Sheep Gilroy became Leader. They moved to Gravesend, operating in a Circus that dropped a tin leg for Douglas Bader.

On 17 August 1941 the FW 190 was encountered for the first time. Experienced pilots now began to be shot down. On 14 November, Harald Peake presented the squadron with its crest and dined them at the Savoy with Leigh-Mallory and Willoughby de Broke as guests. Toasts, as always, were drunk to the King and to the King of the Belgians. The squadron took the hotel's prized ebony cat, but later returned it. At Biggin Hill they had been credited with 51 GAF planes destroyed and 41 damaged for a loss of 15 pilots. It was an exceptional gain-loss ratio and due to Darley's training. The squadron benefited from having Belgian pilots who stayed while the experienced British pilots were posted away to N Africa and the Far East.

On 17 November 1941 609 transferred to 12 Group at Digby in Lincolnshire. They were adopted by Marigold, Countess of Londesborough. The Digby Ops Room moved into her residence, Blankney Hall. Sheep Gilroy rode with the Blankney Hunt with his No. 2, Christian Ortmans, by his side. The station mess moved into Ashby Hall in Ashby de la Launde as 609 was received into Lincolnshire society. They lived among the families of those serving in the Lincolnshire Regiment, who they were to support without meeting on the morning of Winnekendonk. If only these first-rate units – 609 Squadron and 2 Lincolns – had been formally linked and given the resources as a Lehrgeschwader to experiment with equipment, such as the Vultee Vengeance, Hurricane IID, Pe-2 and Il-2 with communications to optimise all-arms and weapon accuracy, great and innovative things would have been discovered and perfected to improve 21 AG's later dismal performance. On 30 March 1942 they moved to Duxford and began conversion to Typhoons and later transferred into 2 TAF as we have seen.

609 trained in rocket firing at Llanbedr in April 1944 and it was clear what was in store; 'We will probably come in for a lot of casualties from Flak and personally I don't think much damage will be done by the rockets because of the many factors governing their accuracy when there's ten-tenths Flak around.'[79]

In May they lost 5 pilots to Flak while shooting up radar stations and trucks. This was stark warning of what was soon to become their biggest and most lethal problem, ignored by an RAF hierarchy in hock to the cult of bombing and happy that Fighter Command had been used to solve their problem with Army 'cooperation'.

They were at Hurn for D-Day, but only 83 Group moved to France. On 30 June, Manu Geerts replaced Johnny Wells as Leader. 123 Wing began to move to B-10 Plumetot, but that field became waterlogged and was shelled, so they moved back to Hurn where the pilots did nothing

79 Ziegler, *The Story*, ref Roberts's Diary.

for an entire week. On 8 July the squadrons moved to B-5 La Fresnoy Camilly which was an 83 Group field, leaving the Wing at Hurn. On 20 July, as 6 Guards Tank Brigade made its journey to Normandy, the complete Wing crossed to B-7 Martragny where Walter Dring replaced Brooker. 123 Wing absorbed 136 Wing, and took under command 164 and 183 Squadrons. This led to Scott's promotion at 25 to being the youngest Group Captain in the RAF. He soon afterwards injured his leg under a horse and was in a tented hospital for three weeks.

On 27 July 1944 609 Sqn operated under Visual Control Point (VCP) for the first time. An RAF controller with a VHF wireless set travelled with the army to improve communication but also to ensure that no soldier ever directly commanded a pilot. On 14 August Lallemant took over from Geerts on the day after the spectacular destruction of a German petrol dump.

The GAF struck back at the Typhoons on 17 August. 183 Sqn lost four aircraft and a fifth badly damaged out of eight patrolling Evreux. Three other squadrons also lost planes. Scott stated the losses were unexpected because Spitfires, Mustangs and Thunderbolts normally smacked the ME 109s down over their bases. Both RAF myths had now been destroyed; speed did not protect against Flak, and the fighter-bomber could not look after itself. The Wing claimed 42 tanks destroyed in the breakout and in the Falaise Pocket, which subsequent OR investigation could not substantiate, thus destroying the final myth of the fighter-bomber's accuracy. The Vultee Vengeance was by then freely available, but 2 TAF stuck with denial rather than submit its cherished prejudices to examination. 609 lost 5 pilots in August, and in September Lallemant was shot down by Flak and badly burned. Bob Wallace took his place. The wing moved to B23 Morainville, then to B35 Baromesnil, and against orders to B53 Merville near Lille. Scott hi-jacked one of 83 Group's supply convoys. They were a law unto themselves.

The Belgian contingent in 609 Sqn increased from 7 to 14, and now had the opportunity of entertaining their British friends at home. On 29 October, the Wing moved to B-67 Ursel and the airfield had to be extended to 1,600 yards for Typhoons, another of its many faults. Wallace, the 609's Leader, was shot down and killed over Dunkirk by Flak, Charles de Moulin coming from 164 Sqn to take over. He lasted three weeks, the shortest time yet, when he was shot down by Flak and captured. On 26 November the Wing established itself at B-77 Gilze Rijen, where it remained until after the Rhine crossing. It was there Eisenhower visited and praised them, fingering their aircraft with the same inquisitiveness as he fingered the frontal armour of Farrell's Churchill tank at about the same time in Helmond in December 1944. They were in 'Antwerp Alley', and in one 24-hour period counted 148 V1s. It was a comment on the limitations of air power that 2 TAF could not stop them.

Scott contracted with the Dutch to build permanent winter quarters, and a large building was put up in 5 days, as 2 TAF slipped back into the 'permanent base' mentality that Brooke had predicted in 1942 that they could never give up. On 6 December Eric Roberts became Leader of 609 Sqn. Described by Scott as a quiet, pleasant Englishman, he was experienced, having been with the Wing in Normandy although forced off operations by a road accident in September. He flew at the time of Winnekendonk.

During December 1944 it was decided the Typhoon pilot's tour should be set at 80 sorties or 80 hours compared with 200 operational hours for a Spitfire pilot, and 30 trips amounting to 150 to 200 hours in Bomber Command. Scott would have preferred 40 sorties because of the high risk of death from Flak, and because of the 'vile and pitiful trembling' of the pilots prior to ops. The RAF's prejudice against armour was now consuming its own children. If the aircraft was hit in the unarmoured vitals, the pilot was usually too low to bale out – there being no ejector seat – and was killed. Had the army been in control of its aviation, pilots would have served for the duration like all infantry officers, but have flown aircraft less vulnerable to light flak and machine guns, and flown them far more over the Anglo-Canadian lines, where there was no Flak, to concentrate on CAS, rather than the 'armed recce, which consumed at least half of 2 TAF's time and more than half the losses; 'Discounting the defensive fighter sorties, ... the figures become roughly 60% armed recce, 25% pre-arranged and 15% impromptu.'[80]

In response to the Ardennes Offensive, the Wing was ordered to A-84 Chievres on 31 December. Scott protested but Montgomery insisted, angering Scott, who revealed a reversion to a fixed-base mentality. Being absent, they avoided destruction in Operation Bodenplatte on New Year's Day. They were snowed in for most of the time, and Dring was killed in a landing accident when he hit a mound of snow. His replacement was Zip Button, who flew at Winnekendonk. Scott left for England on 22 February 1945 and was replaced by Johnny Baldwin, and on 28 February, Johnny Wells, who had risen from LAC to Group Captain, replaced Gillam. Deall took over 146 Wing.

The RAF believed that the Army lacked moral fibre and that its victories were due to the RAF. Starting from the time they entered Italy, there had been, it was claimed

> a growing reluctance of British infantry to accept casualties, a circumstance which was shortly to be noted again in disagreeable fashion in Normandy. This was not, let it be noted, a matter relating only to soldiers in the line; it affected their commanders also.[81]

Communication between Montgomery and both Tedder and Coningham broke down. Scott expressed a commonly held RAF view that: Montgomery accepted the accolade for what the RAF had achieved at Alamein; Tedder and Coningham were seldom mentioned, while Montgomery was presented as the god of war; the army treated aircraft and pilots as expendable weapons of convenience while quoting Montgomery as saying that he would rather use a thousand shells than lose one single life, meaning a soldier's and not an airman's life; 2 TAF's Typhoons and Bombphoons interdicted the Normandy battlefield and destroyed the German armour to ensure victory in the land battle; the RAF's role was consistently understated.[82] Every statement made by Scott, except perhaps the one about the 'god of war', was untrue; the Alamein victory was not due to the RAF; the shocking loss rate of pilots was due to the RAF's insistence on equipping 2 TAF with vulnerable aircraft and not to army target selection; and 2 TAF had failed to interdict the German Army, as they admitted at the Allied Air Commanders' Conference on 8 June 1944:

> the Air CinC ... admitted that the plan to hinder initial moves of enemy reserve divisions by the creation of choke points had failed owing to bad weather. The move of [German] immediate reserves into the tactical area was almost complete.[83]

That Scott and his colleagues should have believed such untruths reflected badly on the RAF leaders; on Portal, who infamously claimed that a long-range fighter was a contradiction in terms, and Tedder, who had the gall to write an autobiography in 1966 entitled *With Prejudice.* Tedder had skeletons in his cupboard just like his hated Montgomery's Wattrelos and Dieppe, being responsible for unilaterally littering Malaya with unused aerodromes for the army to be compromised in trying to defend in case the RAF decided to send out squadrons to use them.[84]

Reality convicted 2 TAF of incompetence, a lack of cooperation, ineffectualness and waste, being unfit for service. As we have seen, an average of 140 rockets fired by 18 sorties, or a complete squadron, were needed to destroy one Panther.[85] If the target was defended, several Typhoons

80 Paul Johnston. *2nd TAF and the Normandy Campaign* (Kingston, 1999, Jstor), p. 108.
81 Terraine, *The Right.*
82 Scott, *Typhoon Pilot*, pp. 112-13
83 Johnston, *2nd TAF*, p. 80.
84 Brian Farrell. *The Defence and Fall of Singapore* (Stroud: Tempus, 2005), p.p. 51-54.
85 Copp & Vogel, *Anglo-Canadian.*

could be lost. The RAF proved once more to itself that close air support by unarmoured aircraft was 'unprofitable and unacceptably dangerous'. Failed efforts to improve accuracy and availability as a result of the OR study[86] were window dressing. Typhoon pilots, however, denied these facts: Charles Demoulin of 609 Sqn believed, like Scott, 'the role played by 2 TAF in general and by the Typhoons in particular were the determining factor of Allied victory in Normandy.'[87]

Coningham promoted this myth, and blamed Montgomery for the stalemate in Normandy. Montgomery's reaction to this sniping was simply to bypass Coningham and deal with Harry Broadhurst of 83 Group on tactical, and with Leigh-Mallory on strategic, air support. The long-suffering Broadhurst told Carlo D'Este that he found the whole business of being in the middle of a personal squabble very unpleasant, and that Coningham's attitude was affecting operations. Broadhurst understood that 2 TAF was subordinate, and 21 AG could go on without 2TAF. Coningham's job, said Broadhurst to Carlo D'Este, was to support the Army plan while influencing it so that 2 TAF could be as effective as possible. Broadhuurst, however, showed no understanding of their equipment's inadequacy.

Montgomery, however, deservedly had to lie on the bed he had made for himself by torpedoing Brooke's effort to establish an army aviation at a time when Churchill was close to agreement. His later appeal to everyone just to get along with 2 TAF had a pathetic ring. As usual he interpreted matters from his self-absorbed viewpoint, imagining that the matter of all-arms was about him and Coningham and not about equipment and cooperation at the unit level. He was deluded in his adamant instruction to Dempsey that only by setting down the two HQs side by side and working together as one team would the army and TAF together achieve real success, rather than just pay lip service.[88]

The serious charge against the RAF top brass is that they were ambitious, ruthless and incompetent men who stabbed Dowding in the back and were in thrall to Trenchard and his cult of strategic bombing with a belief that any diversion from it was a waste of time and resources. To further their own ambitions they ensured the army never controlled one of only two available weapons capable of directly neutralising the German guns which destroyed armour and infantry, and which the army had invented in the form of the RFC. They are also convicted of using deceit to maintain their untenable position, and with abusing their pilots by requiring them to fly vulnerable unarmoured aircraft.

Things were different in Russia, but by no means perfect. The main task of the VVS, although a separate combat arm, was to provide assistance to the ground forces during military operations. A Sturmovik pilot described how the commander of his air-division, Polkovnik Getman, controlled the flight in real time when supporting an infantry attack on the Blue Line at Gorno-Vesely in July 1943, in order to ensure the pilots did not break off the attack until the target was destroyed:

> We dropped bombs, and dived firing at the target. I heard the command from the ground; 'One more attempt'. The division commander wanted us to press the enemy as long as we could. Colonel Getman … now spent almost all his time at the front line directing the Shturmoviks (sic) from the ground.[89]

At first the VVS believed that the lesson from the Spanish Civil war was that,

86 Ibid.

87 Charles Demoulin. *Firebirds! Flying the Typhoon in Action* (Shrewsbury: Airlife, 1987).

88 LHCMA: GB0099 KCLMA Dempsey Papers: Montgomery to Dempsey, 4 May, 1944.

89 Vasily Emelianenko. *Red Star Against the Swastika* (London: Greenhill, 2005), p. 225.

> there was no need for special ground-attack aircraft because their functions could be performed by multi-purpose planes, such as the short-range Sukhoi Su-2 and fighters with air-cooled engines.[90]

The VVS therefore developed with Polikarpov an unarmoured Sturmovik version of the variants of the R-5 biplane used in the battles of Khalkin Gol and, on Stalin's instruction, the new unarmoured Sukhoi Su-2 multipurpose combat aircraft equipped with a bomb-bay. There was therefore no single-purpose CAS aircraft prior to the Second World War although Grigorovich, Kochergin, Polikarpov and Tupolev studied the matter. In 1937 military engineers from the Air Force Research Institute [TsAGI; Tsentralniy Aerogidrodinamicheskiy Institut, the Central Aerohydrodynamic Institute] demanded urgent construction of a single-purpose ground-attack aircraft, which could 'operate at a low altitude, had the highest-powered engine and was equipped with powerful offensive and defensive weapons'.[91] Sergey Ilyushin, chief of the TsKB, volunteered in 1938 to construct a 'flying tank' IL-2 that in the event took him until 1944 to perfect with the IL-10.

The only precedent for the IL-2 was the Junkers J.1 of 1917, which had a chassis-less construction of an armoured steel 'bathtub' running from behind the propeller to behind the rear crew position, into which the engine and crew positions were bolted. The first prototype IL-2s were underpowered and overweight, requiring the special design of a more powerful engine and the elimination of the rear-gunner/navigator position before the design was accepted in March 1941. This uncharacteristic complaisance of the authorities is proof Ilyushin had friends in high places.

According to Vershinin, there was nothing special about the IL-2 except its armour, which was minimal and could not resist shells or even large-calibre machine gun bullets, while the rear fuselage was made of wood and canvas which could be shredded by MG bullets to make the aircraft unflyable. Experience, Vershinin said, showed that the IL-2's speed and manoevrability were more important than its armour. Emelianenko admired the accuracy of the Ju-87 Stuka diving at 90°, while the Il-2's angle of dive could not exceed 30° and then it was 'shaking like mad'. For Vershinin, the mediocre Il-2 succeeded only because of the quality of the pilots. The experienced Walter Schwabedissen certainly held them in high regard:

> The Soviet ground-attack crews were aggressive, courageous and stubborn. Their attacks were amazingly cool-headed. An average Shturmovik (sic) pilot was a fearless opponent. The weak side of the Russian character was less evident in the Shturmovik pilots than in the fighter pilots. The CAS squadrons were the best organised units among the VVS ... and their role constantly expanded until they became the backbone of the VVS.[92]

The Il-2s required fighter escorts, especially when German fighter-pilots found their quickest route to Oakleaves was by bringing them down. In the end, losses due to ground fire equalled those due to fighters. In 1943 a gunner-observer was introduced, and the power-weight ratio degraded. In Vernishin's opinion, the second crew-member was made unnecessary by routine fighter escorts, although he was always valuable as a navigator and second pair of eyes.

The Il-2, like the Typhoon, suffered from inaccuracy. The only suitable weapon against tanks was the PTAB shaped-charge AP bomb, not used by the RAF. The bomb bay of the Il-2 held 192 of them, although Emilianenko claimed he carried 400,[93] and when dropped simultaneously

90 Op. Cit.,Vershinin's introduction.
91 Ibid.
92 Ibid.
93 Op.Cit., p. 229.

produced a swept zone of 70 m by 15 m giving a high chance of a kill. The Il-2's normal attacking and defending, height was 50 m. Hits from 75 mm and 88 mm were rare because of the Il-2's speed, but the 40 mm Flak was devastating, and a single hit was usually enough. The 20 mm FLAK was marginally effective, while the Il-2 was immune from the 7.92 mm MG42 and K98 which could, and did, bring down Typhoons.

By 1943 nearly half of all Russian aircraft were armoured Sturmoviks and PE-2 dive-bombers of the type rejected in the West. They were used in conjunction with emplaced artillery since although the Il-2 was at risk from their shells, loss rates were reduced when artillery neutralised the Flak. The CAS Pe-2 by contrast aimed a small shell or bomb directly at the target from close up, usually at artillery and mortar emplacements. Both types operated often from adjacent fields, and were on call by the infantry and under unified command. By 1945 most Russian aircraft had radio receivers with transceivers in the leader's machine for control by liaison units assigned to corps and divisional HQs.[94] In the attack on Berlin, Zhukov directly subordinated the air force to the infantry as Monash had innovated in 1918.

Kurt 'Panzer' Meyer described the difference between Anglo-Canadian and Russian methods during his debriefing in 1945. Commenting on the drive on Falaise when Simonds had tried to neutralize opposition by bombing the flanks with heavy bombers operating blindly at height, Meyer said the Russians would have used tactical aircraft under the unified command of a fanatical young Communist who would have stopped at nothing. 'In a matter of hours instead of days Falaise would have fallen, for Russian leadership knows the value of time', and unity of command.[95]

After Stalingrad, a report was submitted to Stalin on 3 February 1943 by General Zhuravlev after a briefing by Novikov. The main recommendation was that close support units should be attached to the mechanised forces along with LOs and Signals to call in the aircraft and guide them to the target that was holding up the advance. This had long been the German practice, and was now adopted by the Russians.[96] The British never did so because of Churchill. The consequences were writ large at Kervenheim, where a British Pe-2 would have destroyed the StuGs and the Murmannshof strongpoint, and at Winnekendonk where the 88s and StuGs would have been knocked out with a great saving of life.

In conclusion, the Il-2 was a better CAS aircraft than the Typhoon, but suffered the same inaccuracy as all level or shallow-dive bombers that were not adequately armoured. The Ju-87 and Pe2 were accurate and valuable assets but the most important factors were unified command under the infantry, and skilful pilots committed to target destruction.

2 TAF did not perceive its task as one of destroying enemy weapons threatening advancing infantry and tanks. Instead they 'carted' ordnance to a map reference provided by the army, as Bomber Command 'carted' bombs to Germany. The emphasis was on delivery to an address with almost complete neglect of any other result, intended or unintended. Effectiveness was to be taken on trust. The real need that was never addressed was for tactical air to take responsibility for suppressing Paks, Flaks, mortars, artillery and machine guns in conjunction with the artillery. Instead, pilots shot their ordnance into the specified area and flew home to announce a 'great success'. If they had been told the gun was still firing and that they had to return through wakened Flak as many times as it took to silence it, the pilots would have turned in their ineffective Typhoons and demanded Sturmoviks possibly, but certainly PE2s or Vengeances.

94 Christopher Chant. *Ground Attack* (London: Almark, 1976).

95 Foster, *Meeting of Generals*.

96 Peter C Smith. *Petlyakov Pe-2 Peschka* (Ramsbury: Crowood, 2003), p. 77.

Neither Montgomery nor 2 TAF had any interest in revealing the damning OR analysis, so infantry and pilots believed what they wanted to believe, and generalities persist to this day. Thus a Canadian historian can imply that greater availability of 'cab rank' would have helped; 'This system worked well, but it was not much in evidence on the Canadian front even by the winter of 1944/45.'[97] 'Working well' in this context meant that ordnance was dropped quickly as directed by an inaccurate weapon system by pilots with no commitment to the desired outcome of a destroyed MG, mortar or PAK. It meant that all went through the motions in a practised manner.

The overall air plan for the following day was decided at a large Army/Air Force conference held supposedly daily but usually on alternate nights at 6 pm in the Joint Battle Room at First Canadian Army. The Army COS presided and twenty people attended, including the ALO for the GCC, and both the Group Captain and Wing Commander Operations. This conference would have decided to support 9 BIB at first light on 2 March if requested.

There was a staff officer, G(Ops)Air, responsible for air support at each HQ of Army Group, Army and Corps, where he was called GSO2(Air). No one was assigned to divisions or below. Both centralised and decentralised methods of control were in use. Under centralised control the requests came into Army and were vetted by the watch keepers of G(Ops) Air. Under the decentralised method of operation, the VCP or Contact Car passed requests straight to the FCP and to the GCC, where decisions were made jointly. This was the system in use at XXX Corps during Operation *Heather*.

We can assume that Horrocks called Whistler and told him that air support had been arranged. A VCP or Contact Car would have arrived and parked in the grounds of Whistler's HQ at Stein 969 415, which was close to Tac HQ 185 BIB. It contained an ALO, and an RAF controller and wireless mechanic. The ALO maintained touch with the Brigadiers, and the RAF controller with the FCP at XXX Corps, either by secure land-line or encoded wireless. They followed the Canadian version of the system.

> Great care was taken to ensure the 30th Corps effective impromptu air support once the battle was begun. Since No. 84 Group was operating with General Horrocks for the first time staffs of ground formations were briefed in the procedure for submitting targets by the wireless and line communications of the 1st Canadian Air Support Signal Unit. At Corps Headquarters a Forward Control Post would operate a 'cab rank' of fighter-bombers overhead, sending these in succession to accepted targets. It would be supplemented by a Mobile Radar Control Post, to be used for directing aircraft in bad weather. Arrangements were made for contact cars to be deployed to headquarters of divisions. These mobile wireless links would serve as visual control posts and might be allotted aircraft by the FCP against specific targets, and in special circumstances be given a small cab rank of their own.[98]

Stacey here clearly states that the visual control posts at divisional HQs in 1 Canadian Army, which would include Whistler's at Stein, were called 'contact cars', and so they have been in this history. However, Stacey may be mistaken, according to an MA thesis:

> Contact cars were initiated to improve contact between leading Army elements and the RAF, primarily for the purposes of improving the understanding of where friendly troops were on the ground, and secondarily to improve Army appreciation of what reconnnaissance information RAF aircraft could provide. As Air Vice Marshal Broadhurst recalled; "The reason why I

97 David Bercuson. *Maple Leaf Against the Axis* (Markham: Red Deer, 2004).

98 Stacey, *The Victory*.

> instituted them was … to report the position of our own army at any moment and to control the tactical reconnaissance aircraft'.[99]

On 28 February, and again on 1 March 1945 at Kervenheim, a cab rank was probably in operation under control of the FCP at Corps and accepting requests from 3 BID and 53 BID outside Weeze. No cab rank was operating on 2 March, but 84 Group was briefed during the previous night and warned to expect requests made directly by the ALO.

3 BID's War Diary described the working of the system on 2 March 1945. The defenders of Kervenheim were thought to have fallen back to the Berber Woods, codenamed DOVER. At 9.30 am Air Support at Army confirmed that the target was accepted with an ETA of 9.55 am (message 21). The infantry were unable to take advantage of the first strike, so a repeat was requested. 84 Group refused the request, and so informed the ALO in the Contact Car (if that is what it was) who passed it on at 10.35 am (message 27). Information was then received from the debriefed Typhoon pilots that twenty lorries, guns and many troops were seen on the Winnekendonk-Bruch road, no doubt retreating from Kervenheim. This information was passed by the ALO (message 31) straight to Whistler, who called up Horrocks to discuss the news. The Corps Commander suggested the Typhoons be recalled, and it is noteworthy that Horrocks was then able to get the priorities changed. Meanwhile the RA was softening up Winnekendonk (message 36), and the KOSB and the RA had planned to take the wood without air support. At 11.50 am the ALO informed 9 BIB that the Typhoons were in the air and would be arriving in 10 minutes at 12.05 pm (message 37), which they did, causing great alarm.

Extracts from 3 Division War Diary for 2 March 1945[100]

Sequence	Time	From/To	Message	Action or Remarks
21	0930	Air sp	Wood 995366 accepted as a target for TYPHOONS will be dealt with at 0955 hrs	GOC infm
27	1035	ALO	Owing to hy commitments TYPHOONS not available for a repeat attack on wood DOVER	G2 infm 9 Bde infm
31	1115	ALO	20 MT seen at 005355 at 1045 hrs. Corps Comd infm and told us to ask for TYPHOONS	G1 infm & asked to contact Corps
36	1150	RA	RA putting down VICTOR target on centre of WINNEKENDONK	
37	1155	9 Bde & ALO	1. ALO says TYPHOON attack on DOVER wood would be on at 1205 2. 9 Bde would like it on wood SOUTH of WINNEKENDONK instead 3. ALO trying to divert attack and 9 Bde trying to keep tps out of wood	

Requests from the ALO's Contact Car (?) at division passed through the FCP to 84 Group's Control Centre at Goirle. This was contained in 5 lorries with a large Operations' Room under canvas slung between three of them. Communication with the FCP came through the 1st Canadian

99 Johnston, *2nd TAF*, pp. 34 & 48.
100 TNA: WO 171/4130. 3 BID's war diary.

ASSU to the ALO (Mil) in the Ops Room. He and the Wing Commander Plans together vetted the requests. The result was a call put out to 123 Wing at Gilze Rijen.

At Wing the duty ALO was the Master of Ceremonies for the day. He supervised the manning of the phones, the maintenance of the battle boards and the handling of all traffic in and out. He watched the timings in close contact with the WingCo Flying, standing together with him on the platform before the vertical plotting screen and the state board. He ensured the details of the ETA, smoke and counter-flak were passed on to the Contact Car (?) and the RA. He did not leave the room to take part in briefing the pilots, which was done by the Number 2 ALO.

The formation leader was briefed about the accepted target. Briefing was always done centrally and never at dispersal, so that WingCo Flying, the Ops Officer and the IO could be available if required. It was said that detailed briefings were often completed in less than five minutes from initial warning. While the ALO was taking down the details by R/T from the FCP, the Number 2 ALO was shouting out the pinpoint for the Duty Clerk standing at the files to pull out the aerial photos and maps, and for the IO to prepare course and Flak details.

The Contact Cars (?) provided 8-figure map references supplemented by as much information as possible that would orient the pilot, such as; 'Strongpoint surrounded by wire at 12345678. One pillbox near centre with entrance WEST side, 3 machine gun positions in action in SE corner of position.'

While the Number 2 ALO briefed the pilots, the ALO gave the Contact Car (?) the details of smoke and timings and discussed all aspects of the operation with him. When this was completed the line was disconnected. At this point on 2 March the situation changed but contact could not be re-established since the ALO at Wing would have been tied up with the next request. Briefing of the pilots began immediately on the 1:100,000 Situation Map supplemented by a 1:25,000 map, and by aerial photos after being checked by the ALO. His responsibility was to ensure no pilot left the briefing without the bomb line clearly marked on his map, and with full knowledge of the location of the nearest friendly troops.

Each pilot carried up to six 1:100,000 maps numbered serially. Each map was divided into four quadrants with pencil lines. The pilot stuffed the maps into his map pocket located on his right thigh where he could flick through them while flying and select the one he wanted. The target was described to the pilots in terms of a) sheet number, b) 4-figure map reference and, c) the map quarter. For example; 'Sheet 5, 5326, North West Quarter.'

The simplicity of the system meant targets could be allocated or changed when the pilots were airborne. It permitted cab rank operations with the section circling pending target acceptance. Sometimes the pilots carried a 1:25,000 map, but those of any larger scale, such as town plans, were found to be useless.

The ALOs were soldiers from an organisational culture different in many ways from that of the RAF. Airmen were individualists going their separate ways:

> In an RAF station of 100 officers it sometimes happened that the station commander was the only officer watching the Saturday afternoon games, whereas on a nearby Army field every officer would be shouting for his team, if not playing.[101]

In the infantry men were trained, moved and commanded in the mass, but in the RAF, and the armoured corps, each man was required to develop a specialist skill from which he derived strength and status within the group. In the RN, RAF, RAC and RA the men manned the equipment, while in the infantry the equipment equipped the men. Furthermore:

101 Ronald Sherbrooke-Walker. *Khaki and Blue* (London: Saint Catherine, 1952).

> The essential difference is that an Army officer exists for one purpose only, to get his men to the battle, while the airmen in the RAF exist for one purpose only, to get their officer to the battle.[102]

Both Typhoons and Tanks lived their own demand for independent and unfettered action. Their conceit was to recognise élitism in the other. Desmond Scott recalled joining in February 1944 the temporary HQ of 84 Group at Oxford which housed also the HQ of the British Second Army. He was, he said, now introduced to the future interdependence of the tank and the aircraft. From then on, he said, the mingling of blue and khaki was to be the essence of combined operations, an example of the RAF's habit of making the world fit their theories.[103]

Typhoon and Tank were both mobile weapons differing in the dimension in which they operated, the amount of armour protection, and their accuracy. Both were mobile guns with an attitude that sub-optimised the whole by refusing subordination to 'immobile' infantry.

It is ironic that the two episodes that particularly riled Coningham and Tedder in Normandy – the retreats of 7 BAD from Villers Bocage on 14 June and of 11 BAD from Hill 112 on 29 June 1944 – were examples of the armoured élite in pursuit of their own mythical mission of independent exploitation, without thought of the need for co-operation with the infantry. This was the same imperative that Tedder, Coningham, Harris and Spaatz insisted was categorical in their case also. There were, in the language of the time, too many 'Popski's private armies', and no system for reflecting on operational methodology.

The armoured divisions believed their job was to 'exploit' through the hole in the German line punched for them by the infantry. But apart from the fast move up to Brussels after the German collapse in Normandy, 'exploitation' remained a dream. The Typhoons of 83 Group, however, actually lived Fuller's dream rôle of exploitation, being able to hop over the front line and fly at will beyond the Rhine into the back areas of Germany, shooting up anything that moved, rocketing German Tac HQs whose location was revealed by ULTRA, and generally doing random damage when not paralyzing the enemy 'nerve centres'. But just like the Germans in their bombed out towns who went on producing armaments in increasing numbers almost to the end of the war, including superb jet aircraft assembled in the open fields and woods, the German field army learned to live without air superiority and discovered moreover how to conceal themselves from the Typhoon, and also how to shoot it down in numbers which finally became unacceptable to 2 TAF by the end of February 1945.

It could be asked whether the Typhoon was at least better than nothing. We have seen that when dealing with the attacks by armour at Mortain and in the Falaise Pocket the destructiveness of the Typhoon was consistently and wildly overstated. The pilots reported the sorties on 2 March 1945 as 'extremely successful' when nothing at all was achieved beyond the pilots having a nice flight, and being busy fools. The Typhoon's usefulness for interdiction and destruction of enemy communications, transport, HQs and stores in their favourite mission of uncontrolled 'armed recce' beyond the battlefield was overstated, although much random damage was achieved, such as the wounding of Rommel and the threatening of countless soldiers.

It is clear that the British infantry welcomed the Typhoons out of ignorance. In Operation Switchback to eliminate the Breskens Pocket and clear the south bank of the River Scheldt, 3 CID spoke highly of the support they received from 84 Group. A later assessment denied that air power was decisive, and damned it with faint praise. The conclusion was that it made the soldiers' task somewhat easier, and reduced the number of lives lost and the length of time needed to clear

102 C Carrington. *Soldier at Bomber Command* (London: Leo Cooper, 1987), p. 4.
103 Scott, *Typhoon Pilot*, p. 93.

the Breskens Pocket and open the Scheldt to shipping.[104] However, this claim must be seen in the context of an operation, which although planned to last one week, took nearly a month. 3 BID also welcomed the Typhoons at Venraij, and it was said there was a feeling of dissatisfaction when requests for Typhoons were turned down that had an impact on infantry morale. A typical infantryman's unrealistic belief in their effectiveness was this:

> I realised just how terrible an attack by rocket firing Typhoons was. They were very effective in dealing with tanks. The Germans opposite and quite close to us were subject to one of these attacks. I know it terrified me so what it did to the Germans I really don't know.[105]

OR investigated the effect of the Typhoon on enemy morale. Normal infantry became anxious in the presence of Typhoons because the rockets were an unknown quantity and the subject of rumour. The noise of the plane was frightening in itself, but most terrifying of all was the noise of the rockets leaving the rails at a distance of 300 to 500 yards. Infantry responded by taking cover and remaining there for an average of 10 minutes. Some German tanks were abandoned by their crews under the threat of rockets, but then often reoccupied when the rockets invariably missed. Exceptions, however, were the LW Flak gunners, who were proficient and hated by the Typhoon pilots. Elite infantry such as the SS and many Paratroops were also able to recognise the Typhoon's bark was worse than its toothless bite and to keep firing at a Typhoon. The effect was somewhat similar to the Stuka fright in 1940, except the Stuka was immeasurably more accurate and the fright justified if one was the target. Few on either side knew that rockets were harmless because they buried themselves in the ground before exploding, while the chance of a small gun position being hit was a miniscule 0.2% requiring 350 rockets fired by 44 aircraft sorties to ensure its destruction. The infantryman could realistically thumb his nose at the Typhoon, if he could first overcome his angst.

Generally in the close, hedged and wooded countryside of Normandy and the Low Countries, the Typhoon could do little against ambushing StuGs, mortars and fixed defences concealed under camouflage or in buildings. At these times the Allied infantry would have been better served by improved tanks with frontal immunity to the 88 mm, by improved small arms, night-fighting aids, larger and more mobile artillery, better battlefield communications and of course a dive-bomber under their own control. To the extent that the RAF retained nearly a half of the productive capacity of the UK and employed 35% of all the troops in theatre compared with only 15% for the USAAF and RCAF, then the conclusion is that 2 TAF like the armoured divisions represented a misuse of scarce resources.

The 400 mph Typhoon was vulnerable to the 452 mph ME 109K, to the 472 mph long-nose FW Ta 152C and to the 474 mph Arado 335. It stood absolutely no chance against the lethal 541 mph jet ME 262. Pierre Clostermann of 122 Wing was flying in 440 mph Tempests in February 1945, and claimed that on these alone the entire offensive and tactical system on the British front depended. He described how tough it was for the Typhoon formations that 'frequently lost six or seven machines out of twelve in encounters with FW 190's and ME 109's. The Spitfire was powerless.'[106]

The rationale for using the vulnerable and inaccurate Typhoon was that it could look after itself when attacked by German fighters. The fact it could not revealed that the Air Ministry would use

104 Mike Bechthold. *Air Support in the Breskens Pocket* (*Canadian Military History, Autumn 1994*, Vol 3, No 2), pp. 53-62.
105 John Keenan's audio-taped memoir.
106 Pierre Clostermann. *The Big Show* (London: Chatto & Windus, 1951).

any excuse to maintain its monopoly on all aircraft, and was permitted to do so by Churchill who of course supported their true vocation for area bombing.

Punishment of Typhoons was swift. Fuel shortages limited the risk from the well equipped Luftwaffe, which right to the end was never short of aircraft or operational airfields, but was short of skilled pilots. The main problem, however, for the Typhoons was German 20 mm and 37 mm Flak and machine guns. All targets of value outside artillery range were protected, and the pilots had to 'go over the top' on almost every sortie. Losses of men and aircraft became so severe from Flak that by 1 March 1945 aircraft use had to be curtailed because the Germans would put up a 'carpet of 20 and 40 mm stuff. Little white puffs you could get out and walk on. Round about 3 – 4,000 feet this was and one had to dive through it. ... I personally felt very much afraid of flak on a low level op.'[107]

***Fliegerabschosskanonen* or Flak**

Flak	No. of Barrels	Ceiling (ft)	Rounds/min	Shell Weight
2 cm Flakvierling 38	4	3,500	700 to 800	4.2 oz
3.7 cm Flak 43	1	5,000	150	1.5 lbs
3.7 cm Flakzwilling 43	2	5,000	300	1.5 lbs
5 cm Flak 41	1	10,000	130	4.8 lbs
8.8 cm Flak 41	1	32,500	20	20.7 lbs

To protect the Flak gunners from strafing aircraft and to allow them to operate within artillery range of the enemy, the Germans mounted anti-aircraft guns on tank chassis from which the turret had been removed. At first the gun was surrounded by 30 mm armoured shields that folded down to form a platform around the gun. This was called the Möbelwagen (furniture van). The Wirbelwind (Whirlwind) and Ostwind (Eastwind) protected the gunners in a box of angled 16 mm armour. The Kügelblitz (Ball Lightning) was a new high performance 3 cm automatic cannon developed for U-Boats and installed in a fully enclosed ball turret. It was the forerunner of all modern Flak tanks, but only prototypes had been produced by war's end. The Germans had the answer to jet ground-attack aircraft before the Allies had them in operation. Against Typhoons they would have been devastating, and if supplied in numbers would have cleared the skies of all Allied CAS aircraft.

FlakPanzer

Gun	Chassis and Name	Production	Period
2 cm Flak 38	Flakpanzer 38(t)	140	Nov 43 – Feb 44
2 cm Flakvierling 38	Mk IV Wirbelwind	86	Jul – Nov 44
3.7 cm Flak 43	Mk IV Möbelwagen	240	Mar 44 – Mar 45
3.7 cm Flak 43	Mk IV Ostwind	43	Dec 44 – Mar 45
3.0 cm MK103 Doppelflak	Mk IV Kügelblitz	2	Mar 45

It was estimated that there were over 12,000 Flak mountings in Normandy. By February 1945, their numbers in Germany were overwhelming to Clostermann who said that 'Germany seemed

107 N Franks. *Typhoon Attack* (London: W Kimber, 1984), ref FO JG Simpson, 193Sqn.

lousy with flak. It was everywhere, even in the most unexpected places...and made any attack extremely dangerous.'[108]

The stress of attacking through these defences turned many pilots into nervous wrecks right up the last day of the war. Mention of flak was prohibited in the mess on pain of a £1 fine. Clostermann didn't mind aerial combat, but flak made him physically sick. His section attacked Schwerin airfield defended by 40 Flak. His stomach contracted and a wave of nausea swept over him as the airfield seemed to light up end to end with flashes from 20 mm and 37 mm guns. 'Physical fear is the most terrible thing man can suffer – my heart leaped to my mouth, I was covered with sweat, with sticky, clammy sweat. My clenched toes swam in my boots.'[109]

Six out of the eight Tempests and their pilots were lost over Schwerin in exchange for two ME 109s and five Arados destroyed, and another ME 109 damaged. Twenty-eight ME 109's escaped. Clostermann's conclusion was that the flak held too many trumps, and he said as much in his monthly operational report. Group took note and cancelled that type of show.

There is an extensive literature covering the Typhoons. In late 1944, 2 TAF had 21 ground attack squadrons and 2 fighter reconnaissance squadrons equipped with the type. In March 1945 two squadrons had been disbanded, and by September 1945 the aircraft had vanished. Only one complete Typhoon survived; it can be seen in the IWM at Hendon.

Typhoons are best remembered for rockets, although there was a substantial bombing element as well. The rocket was introduced in 1943 and was a crude weapon. It consisted of a 3 inch diameter cast iron pipe fitted with lugs to connect it to a launching rail, and a set of small cruciform fins for in-flight stability. The solid propellant charge was ignited and burnt from the front end, the gases being exhausted through a central orifice. Since the 60 lb HE warhead made the rocket front heavy, the system moved the centre of gravity rearward as the propellant was consumed. The ballistic characteristics left much to be desired. The rocket suffered badly from initial trajectory drop due to gravity, making accurate aiming difficult except in a vertical dive. Launching rails could not be jettisoned and inflicted a fairly substantial performance loss on the aircraft.

Results were almost impossible for the pilot to assess, as he was past and gone before the dust and smoke of the explosions had subsided. The cine film seldom helped, being activated by pressure on the gun-firing button. When the pilot switched his thumb from the cannon to the rocket-launching button the camera stopped and provided no evidence of where the rocket went. RAF refusal to correct this is suspicious. New pilots had a definite tendency to undershoot, and wrongly estimated both range and trajectory. The average error was reported to be 50 yards at a range of 1,200 yards. To make matters worse, some 20 to 30% of the rockets failed to explode. Pilots' claims were grossly exaggerated.

2 TAF knew the limitations of ground support from as early as 1943, when it examined the effect of rockets and bombs on a mock-up of a German artillery position. The damage achieved was negligible.[110] Nothing changed between then and the end of hostilities in spite of pressing need. For example on 1 and 2 March 1945, attacks by 2 and 4 CIDs were halted in the Hochwald Gap by enemy artillery fire which nothing in the Allied arsenal, including Typhoons, could neutralise.[111]

Brigadier General J.A. Mathys of the Belgian armed forces was a Flight Sergeant in 609 Sqn during Operation *Heather* on 2 March in his Typhoon IB.

108 Clostermann, *The Big Show*.
109 Ibid.
110 Copp and Vogel, *Anglo-Canadian*.
111 Nicholson, *The Gunners*.

The particular operation you are interested in, I can only describe in very general terms. My logbook confirms indeed the two sorties I flew on the dates stated. The short comments I noted in the margin state that the weather was foul, visibility not so good, but that nevertheless we located the target and that the attack was very successful [!]. What I do remember very well and I also noted this down, is the fact that whilst we were attacking we saw our own tanks coming out of the woods [they were heading towards the woods] belching coloured smoke for identification as friendly. It was very close, as I remember well only about two football fields away from them. This seems to be confirmed by the regimental history you enclosed with your letter. [David Erskine. *The Scots Guards*].

About the period 20 Feb. – 6 March 45 I do remember that we flew numerous sorties for army support on all sorts of targets going from observation posts to troop concentrations in woods and hidden armour in a group of houses, also on call VCP missions on mortar positions. For that whole period the weather was nothing to write home about, mostly low ceiling which is not ideal for successful rocket attacks.

How I joined the RAF and 609 Sqdn is quite a long story. In 1940 I was living in the Belgian Congo where my father worked for the railways. I was only 17 years old and there was nothing for me to do than to go to school. By the end of 1941 came my great moment, when I could join the Belgian section that had been formed in the South African Air Force. I did my pilot training in South Africa and was awarded my wings in December 1942. The idea was that we would serve with the SAAF in North Africa. For various reasons this did not happen (the South Africans had already too many pilots of their own). I was offered a job with the SAAF Coastal Command to fly Hudsons out of Durban. I refused and started looking around for better.

In May 1943 I could join the RAF and was promised that I would be sent to England immediately. With 10 other Belgian pilots we embarked in Cape Town on 22 July and we thought to be in England in 3 weeks. Actually it took us nearly 3 months. Our ship went from Cape Town to Montevideo, where we were put ashore for 2 weeks whilst our ship went to Argentina to pick up some frozen meat. We embarked again after this vacation and reckoned we would be in England in a matter of 10 to 12 days. Our next port of call was Freetown in Nigeria [sic]; by then we got quite desperate. We could not disembark because there was yellow fever in Freetown. We lay at anchor for 8 days in sweltering heat. After 8 days our spirits rose again as we set out by nightfall with a small convoy of 7 ships. England here we come! Wrong. We stopped at Gibraltar, 7 days in port, no disembarkation because the Rock was crowded. By then I was ready to shoot my best friend. Speculations, rumours, where do we go? Some had it first hand that we were going to Italy or to Alexandria. So when we put to sea again around nightfall we were having bets whether we would turn into the Med or go for the Atlantic. Before we were locked in for blackout we could see that we were heading due east, the Med.

Early in the morning, before breakfast we would usually gather on the front deck for a breath of fresh air and a chat about the turn of events. Even if I live to be a hundred years I will never forget the impressive sight I had coming on deck. There were ships everywhere, big P&O Liners, liberty ships and other huge cargo vessels topped by an armada of warships consisting of 2 cruisers and numerous destroyers (61 ships in total) going full speed and definitely in the Atlantic and heading north. What had happened was we had gone a short way into the Med to deceive the German observers in Algeciras, crossed the strait of Gibraltar at night and picked up the big convoy in the Atlantic. After a couple of U-boat alerts with no effect we reached Cardiff on November 3rd, 1943.

We were sent to Harrogate, where all the pilots trained under the Empire Training scheme were pooled. There coming from Canada I met for the first time my old friend Laforce. We have been inseparable since then. After some retraining, we went to an Operational Training Unit on Spitfires, and according to final results there (had to get above average), we could go on Typhoons and got to 609 Sqn by the end of August 1944.

609 Sqn is a story in itself. Activated on the beginning of the war from an Auxiliary Sqn (Yorkshire), it became one of the most famous squadrons of the RAF. You should try to read 'The Story of 609. Sqn of the Rose', by Frank Ziegler. The Sqn was a really close-knit family. The feeling to belong was very strong and we were very proud of our unit. There still exists an association of 609 pilots who meets every year somewhere in England. About seven years ago we met in Belgium with members from Australia and Canada attending. The Sqn itself was deactivated in July 45 at Wunsdorf in Germany. We stayed until the last and Laforce and I did the last flight with the CO as a farewell on 22 July. We really turned a page in our lives. It was a splendid unit with a fabulous history in the early days of the war. During its turbulent history it brought together people from all parts of the globe. At a certain moment we had more than ten nationalities. We even had an original Yorkshireman, from the Sqn's own shire. We also had a pilot who was an unnaturalised German Jew. His name was Claus Adams. We called him 'Heinnie'. How he got into the RAF as a pilot I don't know, but he was a very fine chap. He is now a British subject, Ken Adam, the man responsible for all the special effects (air) in the James Bond films.

The Belgians were always quite well represented from the beginning. They first got there somewhat by accident. The story goes that the CO in 1940 was shot down in Belgium and helped on his way by a farmer. Some months later in a train the CO meets 2 Belgian pilots on their way to God knows where. They start talking. He asks if they want to join his Sqn. The story goes that he had a weak spot in his heart for my country since his escape. They of course gladly accepted and we have since always been present, providing 3 Sqn commanders over the years.

Rocket firing needed a bit of practice but it was quite rewarding as expertise was fairly soon attained. The sight was an inverted gun-sight, crude but fairly accurate. It was the standard reflector sight used on all RAF fighters. A square box in front above the dashboard with a convex lens on top which reflected an orange ring and two adjustable horizontal bars on the front cockpit windscreen. On the box was a knob with graduations which could make the horizontal sliding bars move in and out towards the centre of the ring. Each graduation corresponded to the wingspan of an enemy fighter. Once this was set, when the wingspan of this particular fighter filled the space between the two bars, if my memory is correct I think it was 250 yards, the four guns or cannon were harmonised to converge in the centre of the target. On the Typhoon for rocket firing it was the same sight but the bars stood vertical and it was the top of the bottom bar that was the aiming point. On the knob the graduations had been replaced by degrees of angle of dive, 30-45-60°. I joined a small diagram which will better illustrate this.

Precision depended on many factors, a combination of angle of attack, speed and height of release. Ideal was a dive from about 6,000 ft at 45° angle to approximately 1,800feet release height. This was naturally not always possible due to the fact that the target had to be found, that it did not always present itself in the best position, and making another round for better positioning was always risky because of alerted flak gunners who were really proficient. A really good leader managed most of the time an approach that put the formation in such a position that one peel-off was sufficient to deliver an attack. Whether a second attack with guns or remaining rockets was carried out depended on the results of the first attack and the opposition encountered (flak). If it was really important or necessary, a second attack was made regardless of what flak there was. This was also true about the weather conditions. Low ceiling, say 1,000feet or less was really difficult for us as then the angle of dive was 15° or less and what mostly happened was that the aircraft flew through their own debris and were damaged by bits of their own rockets. This situation occurred during the crossing of the Schelde and the invasion of Walcheren. The ceiling was less than 1,000feet, but we were told to press on regardless. The Canadian brigade was very hard pressed and got in difficulty half way across the water, by fire from the pillboxes on Flushing Harbour. We went in at 600feet and took the pillboxes out, although there was quite some flak flying about we did not have any losses, but on returning to base 4 aircraft out of 8 were unserviceable through numerous holes in the underside of the wings. This was clearly a case of flying through our own debris.

Bombs were never popular due to inaccuracy. [This statement about bombs reflects the views of the R/P squadrons and conflicts with other evidence. Communication between squadrons within 2 TAF appears to have been non-existent]. During my time with the Sqn, the last 10 months of the war, we never used them. There was one Sqn in our wing who did the jobs that were thought suitable for bombs (very few). They were always delivered at very low level with a delay fuse [untrue]. Earlier in the war before rockets made their appearance there may have been dive-bombing deliveries but I have no knowledge of this.

Rockets came in all shapes and sizes. They had one thing in common, their weight, a 60 pound head. Therefore there was no difference in aiming for various types which could also be combined. High explosive GP, armour piercing and phosphor. The normal load was four under each wing. At the end of the war the two inside rails under each wing were fitted with double rockets mounted one above another and fired as one. Firing could be done in salvo (the whole lot together) or four times a pair.

As an aeroplane the Typhoon was quite remarkable. It was fast and very strong. It was also very stable in any position which made it an outstanding weapon platform. From what I know its debuts were not so promising and the first series that were manufactured were not all that safe. The engine was unreliable and the tail structure caused also problems, but this was remedied as G/C Beamont relates and from then it was a fine aircraft. The end products we got in 1944 were still more improved with the introduction of a blister type hood and a four bladed prop which made the engine run very smooth. I flew over 200 hours on the Typhoon and never had any mechanical trouble. [This statement would have been rejected by Richard Hough. One of his complaints about the Napier Sabre engine was oil leaks, a characteristic of British engines until the 1980s].

The question of identifying the target is quite a tricky one. For finding the target in difficult weather, it was a question of accurate navigation and map reading which required lots of practice and experience. Nearly all fighter-bomber pilots were expert map readers by the time they were eligible to lead a section of four aeroplanes in combat. Nevertheless it happened that we got lost or could not locate the target (in very few instances). It happened also that we got into the area but that we aborted the mission due to the fact that the ceiling was really too low for a rocket attack or that the target was obscured by rain or low cloud. An alternative was then to go in only with cannon if the target was suitable for that or in some cases we had been given an alternative (secondary) target some distance away where the weather was more suitable.

For very close support we were always talked down by the forward air controller who had the target well in view and with references to landmarks and grid references pointed out the target to the section standing by above our own lines. It worked very well. Another method used in close support was that the friendly troops laid out a line of smoke (called Winkle). Coming from behind our own troops we had then to attack just over the line of smoke. For the rest it was a keen eye and good map reading that did the trick. Some leaders were better in finding the target than others. What most pilots in a formation did not like was milling around above the target area. This was showing the enemy clearly our intentions and giving him all the time in the world to get ready and take aim. I can also assure you they were quite good at it and had plenty of guns and no seeming shortage of AA ammunition.

You ask also about life at Gilze-Rijen. It was our first real quarters. All through France we had lived under canvas and mostly flown from airstrips made out of PSP mesh. After France we spent a short three weeks on an airfield in Belgium (Ursel). There we were quartered with the local population, which was very pleasant, especially as four of my friends and I were billeted in the village pub. The front door gave access to a short corridor, a door left was our bedroom, a door right was the pub. What could we wish more! When we moved to Gilze-Rijen, it was a really big airfield built by the Germans with full-length runways. Billets were a very good barracks about three miles from the airfield where all modern conveniences such as flushing toilets and bathrooms were available. There was even central heating in the rooms. This was real winter quarters.

As we were self-sufficient in Gilze, we had less contact with the locals than we did in Belgium and France where if you wanted a decent bath you had to go into town to the public baths (which we did once a week). For the rest it was cold water in our safari-style bath and washbasin graciously provided by the RAF when joining 2nd TAF.

Before closing I want to tell you that after all these years it gives a great feeling to know that one has belonged to the greatest Air Force in the world in times that were difficult but still remarkable.

Please do give my kindest regards to your father from one old soldier to another, and tell him that if our rockets fell sometimes a bit close, it was really unintentional and for the best of causes.[112]

Desmond Scott disagreed with Mathys about Bombphooning:

As far as I am aware, all Typhoon pilots preferred bombs to rockets, due mainly to the trajectory of the attacks. In other words, dive bombing was much safer than the shallow rocket approach. It was unfortunate that the Germans referred to all Typhoons as *Jabos* (Fighter Bombers). I spoke to many Germans of all ranks and it was the Rocket Firing Typhoons they feared above all else.[113]

Brigadier-General A. Laforce left Belgium with his family in 1940, joined the Belgian Army and transferred to the RAF. He was trained in Canada in the BCATP and also flew with 609 Sqn. He had no problem with the Typhoon's gun-sight:

Contrary to what you mention, from the end of 43 the gunsight on Rocket Typhoons was excellent and enabled us to be very accurate indeed. Most pilots were well within 5-15 yards. We once destroyed a Gestapo HQ in the middle of a Dutch city. Our attack was so precise that we were able to destroy completely the two selected houses in one street...without damaging any of the other houses.[114]

Sqn Leader Raymond A. (Cheval) Lallemant, DFC and Bar and famous 'tank-buster', commanded 609 Sqn and was a good friend of Mathys then and in 1983. He summed up the subject of rockets, of which 222,515 were fired by 2 TAF in the Second World War; 'Most of the

112 Brig-Gen J. Mathys, retired, in letters in October and December 1983.
113 Desmond Scott in a letter in 1983.
114 Brigade-Generaal Vl A. Laforce in a letter in 1983.

rockets did end up short due to pilot inexperience, and because of flak.' He modified his aircraft in an attempt to increase accuracy, marking his artificial horizon to show the angle of dive, and making his radio produce a buzzer noise at a pre-selected height. He also fitted a special gyro-compass to his aircraft. Concerning 609 Sqn, Cheval said 84 Group was nominated as best group by Maori Coningham, and within 84 Group Bingo Brown nominated 123 Wing as best wing, and within 123 Wing Desmond Scott nominated 609 Sqn. as best sqn.[115]

W/O G.M. Reynolds also flew with 609 Sqn.

> Of the period in Europe between D-Day and VE Day, I think the time the Wing was at Gilze-Rijen was the hardest. This in terms of the weather, the operational difficulties and the social side. I mean by the last, that the off-duty times during our run through France and Belgium seemed considerably more sparkling than they did in Holland! Operationally speaking, life was more difficult, as the war had become static, and therefore the targets much better defended. Every flight at this time was carried out through heavy concentrations of flak, and the casualty rate was severe. However, had it not been for the extremely robust qualities of the Typhoon, things would have been much worse.[116]

Before considering the activities of the 'Bombphoons', the subject of blind bombing and radar control will be touched on since it was in use in Operation *Heather*. The Second World War was a time of rapid development in radar, of which there were two types: the light 20 cm target-acquisition airborne radars, which proved to be one of the main contributors to the defeat of the U-boats and were used to find night-time intruders; and the large, early warning and air-control radars, which at first were fixed but were later made mobile.

Nos. 83 and 84 Groups were sent to the continent equipped with four AMES Type 25 convoys. These were similar to those of the Base Defence Group and were to protect the airfields, unnecessarily as it turned out, against enemy aircraft. The Americans were also provided with a number of Type 25 convoys on reverse lease-lend in order to standardise radar equipment in the bridgehead. Special training was given to the American crews by the staff of the Telecommunications Research Establishment.[117] They had three purposes; to direct fighter interceptions; to present a general and continuous air situation picture; and to assist aircraft in navigation to ground targets where a cab rank would be set up under a forward controller using another frequency. This rarely occurred because the radar equipment lacked the range to control aircraft over enemy lines.

Full operational value was not extracted from these Type 25 Convoys. Instead there was a requirement for blind bombing in cloudy weather with an accuracy comparable to that of visual bombing. This was to be provided in a later stage of the campaign in the form of the mobile radar control post (MRCP).[118]

In July 1944 the RAF had formed and begun training the first MRCP, which was a Modified SCR.584. It was shipped to Erp in Holland in October and used for the first time to direct Typhoons on 11 November in the attack on Venraij when the MRCP put 6 aircraft of 247 Sqn on the target which, however, they missed. But on the same day 5 aircraft of 137 Sqn were directed to a battery 5 miles SE of Goch and claimed the destruction of 2 guns. The month's trial with 83 Group had shown that the MRCP had some small benefit in directing pilots in conditions of poor

115 Shores, *Ground Attack*.
116 Flt Lt G. M. Reynolds in a letter on 15 September 1983.
117 Documents sumitted by E.A. Munday in 1983.
118 Monograph supplied by EA Munday of the Air Historical Branch in July 1983.

visibility, but was limited by short range. The MRCP was then transferred to 84 Group for experiments in blind bombing, and used in the destruction of Winnekendonk.

> Its mean error of 350 yards indicated that its best application with Tactical Air Force Fighter Bomber groups was the blind level bombing of targets such as villages containing concentrations of enemy troops in forward areas behind the enemy lines, under conditions when visual attack by fighter-bombers was impossible. Although bombs dropped with this accuracy were of some effect, it in no way replaced the value of bombing by fighter-bombers under good visual conditions, when an accuracy possibly as good as 20 yards was obtained. Since the bombs dropped by fighter-bombers were of relatively small size, the value of their bombing depended to a great extent on the high degree of accuracy which was achieved when the bombing was visual.[119]

The effective range of the Type 25 Convoy was increased with the introduction of the American Microwave Early Warning Set (AMES) Type 70 Radar to 83 Group at Erp in Holland in early February 1945. A second Type 70 was built for 84 Group but was not operational at the end of hostilities. These developments were the beginnings of the modern worldwide Air Traffic Control systems. The work of the Telecommunications Research Establishment was commercialised after the Second World War by such firms as Decca.

> The Telecommunications Research Establishment produced the Type 70 set in thirteen weeks. The Type 70 was the most complex mobile ground radar developed during the war and comprised a technical convoy of 30 vehicles. The plan position aerials were of new design, consisting of a centimetre reflector of tubular shape, specially devised to minimise weight and wind pressure without reducing the range of the equipment. One plan position aerial was used to provide cover at low heights and a second to provide the high cover. Accurate height finding information was produced by two mobile and improved AMES Type 13 cheese aerials. The operations room was the main characteristic of this station. Inside a tent were housed four vehicles with prospect windows which allowed the occupants to view the information carried by plotting screens and 'tote' boards also standing in the tent. Greatly increased range, especially at low altitude, was provided. Five controlling PPI tubes were available, facilitating the close control of eight missions simultaneously by four deputy controllers, the fifth tube being normally reserved for the chief controller and emergency situations. In addition to the technical advantages of the Type 70, the identifying of the radar station with the group control centre overcame the difficulties in mobile warfare of transferring the air picture seen by several dispersed radars to the operational HQ. This information, together with that from Army Liaison, Intelligence, intercepts, Sqn availability states and latest reports from air crew, enabled the group control centre to plan and conduct day to day operations with the greatest efficiency.[120]

84 Group provided Photo Reconnaissance (PR) with 35 Wing commanding 2, 268 and 4 Sqns, which was responsible for the aerial photographs taken on 16 February 1945. At 2.40 pm on that day, Warrant Officer V.C. Ellis (1390548) took off from Gilze Rijen in his sky-blue Spitfire PRXI, serial number PM132, on High Level Photo Reconnaissance Duty (HLPR), and landed back at 4.10 pm.

119 Ibid.
120 Ibid.

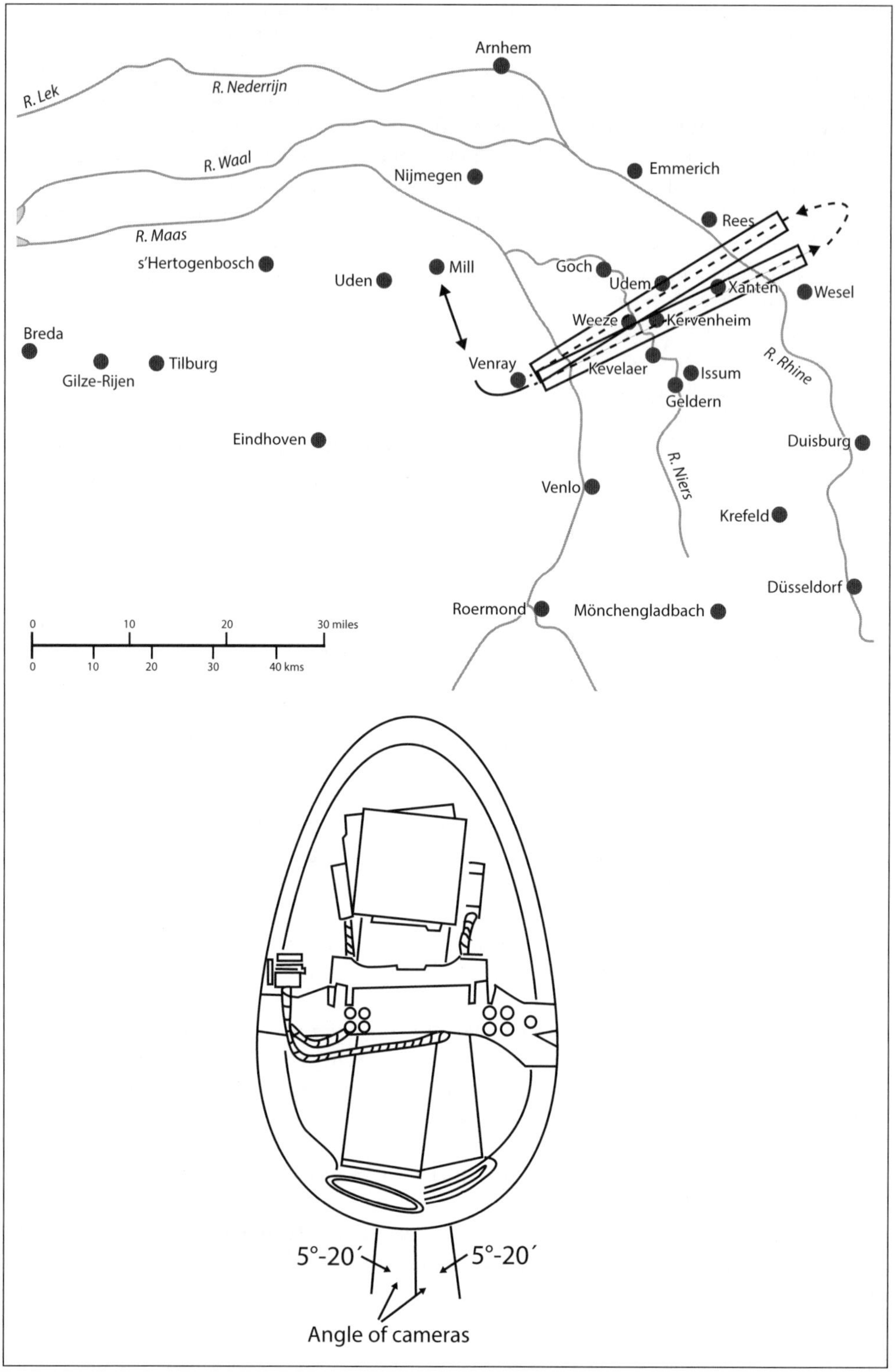

Map 41 Sortie R 4/1765 over Kervenheim and Winnekendonk flown on 16 February 1945 from Gilze Rijen. The split photography was achieved by the camera configuration shown in the diagram.

> Weather. After a morning of fairly thick fog which disappeared during the lunch period, the afternoon promised well for high level photography, fine weather with some patches of cloud prevailing for the remainder of the day.
>
> Operations. A late start owing to the morning fog enabled the Sqn to complete only nine high level sorties. These covered the battle areas of Reichswald – Goch – Milligen – NE Emmerich – Bierloo and Weeze.[121]

The sortie concerning us was R 4/1765, and was performed for 1 Cdn A.P.I.S. The task was CA630, and was presumably the 630th done for the Canadians. The mean time of photography was 3.10 pm. Ellis crossed from the Maas to the Rhine on the southern leg and back again on paths that were not quite parallel. Each pass photographed a strip of country 3.3 km (2.1 miles) wide, and 40 km (25 miles) long. The cameras in split configuration took a picture every 4.3 seconds as the Spitfire, travelling at 350 mph, advanced 720 m (800 yards) over the ground. Since a photograph covered a strip with a length of 1,350 m (1,500 yards), every spot of ground was in fact photographed twice from a different point. The resulting stereoscopic pair could be examined through a stereoscopic viewer that made objects appear three dimensional and aided photo interpretation.

The 40 km (25 mile) path was covered by about 56 shots on each camera for a total of 112 on both. Ellis would have returned with 224 exposures for the two legs having photographed an area of 264 sq kms (103 sq miles). He flew at 23,000 ft using a 3 ft F36 lens giving a scale of approximately 1/76,000 as estimated by the RAF. This author's calculation from a comparison of the photographs with the map is a scale of 1/81,500, a difference of about 7%. The contact prints of the split shots combine to a height of 40.5 mm, covering an area measuring 3.3 kms on the map. The quality was 'A + B' and the results over Winnekendonk-Kervenheim were very good. The sortie description also includes an item 'GSGS 4416 P1 + Q1', which has not been deciphered.

The pilot of a recce aircraft was often older than average because he had to be both a skilful flyer and an experienced navigator to avoid the many things which could go wrong and spoil the photographs. By this stage of the war the RAF was achieving outstanding results with an infinitesimal failure rate of 0.1%.[122] At 23,000feet on that cloudless mid-February day, Ellis could see both the Maas and the Rhine that were his start and finishing points. He had, however, to find the right line of approach, flying straight and level at constant speed on a compass bearing from a known point. We do not know which point he chose, but he did fly directly overhead Xanten on the way out and Kervenheim on the return. It is easy to speculate that he got either the initial bearing or start point wrong, because he made a correction to port north of Kevelaer, probably when he noticed he was heading south of Xanten.

As he circled for 20 minutes to gain height over Holland, Ellis passed through the level at which water vapour from his engine condensed. From then on he would have been looking out for any contrails to his front giving warning of a German plane rising to intercept him, possibly an ME 262 capable of 525 mph at his altitude of 23,000 feet. Just before crossing the Maas he flicked a switch to start the twin cameras, switching them off as he crossed the Rhine. He then made a steep turn to port, found his new reference point, lined up on the right bearing, checked his height and engine revolutions and switched his cameras back on at the right distance west of the Rhine. Between four and five minutes later he was over the Maas, switching off the cameras and turning slightly to starboard to drop down into Gilze-Rijen.

121 TNA: 4 Sqn ORB.
122 Roy M Stanley. *World War II Photo Intelligence* (London: Sidgwick & Jackson, 1982).

In the fuselage behind the cockpit was the split vertical installation for two F.52 cameras with 36 inch lenses. Of British design, built by Williamson Manufacturing Co. in Willesden and introduced in 1942, this was a reliable and small camera, light at 50-lbs, and ideal for high-performance aircraft. Drive was by an externally mounted motor connected by a flexible shaft, controlled by an intervalometer set by switches in the cockpit. The installation of the two cameras was fanned with a 5°20' inclination to the vertical giving a 10 percent lateral overlap. The two cameras working together covered in a single pass nearly twice the area possible with a single vertical. Heating was ducted to the camera as well as to the pilot's cabin to prevent freezing at high altitudes.

The Spitfire PRXI was unarmed and pressurised. Its Rolls Royce Merlin 61 produced take-off power of 1,290 hp at 3,000 rpm, or nearly four times the output of the 350 hp Churchill's tank engine. It could lift the Spitfire to a ceiling of 44,000 ft, with a maximum speed at operational height of 422 mph and a range exceeding 1,200 miles.[123] This was good performance for a piston-engined aircraft, but made obsolete by the arrival of the jets. However, for strategic purposes, the best all-round PR aircraft of the war was certainly the British built Mosquito. It was as fast as the Spitfire with more than double the range to cover all of Germany and northern Italy. It was able to climb out of trouble and was regularly forced to altitudes of 40,000 ft and more in early 1944 over Berlin, remaining the fastest thing in the air above 20,000 ft before the arrival of jets. The Americans demanded 200 of the planes but were supplied an inferior Canadian-built version. US industry was asked to create an American version of the Mosquito. All of the companies approached called the Mosquito an inefficient design. One wrote; 'This aircraft has sacrificed serviceability, structural strength, ease of construction and flying characteristics to use a construction material which is not suitable for the manufacture of efficient airplanes'. But although they all tried, none succeeded in producing an aircraft with the performance of 'The Wooden Wonder'. The Germans also produced aircraft that could not be caught. In mid-war the very high altitude Junkers Ju 86P flew above the RAF's ceiling at 45,000 feet with a range of 1,600 miles at 300 mph, with pilots and cameras carried in a pressurised bubble. It was brought down prior to the Invasion leaving the Germans blinded during that vital period. The jet Arado 234 later regained PR invincibility for Germany.

The film exposed by Ellis was processed at Gilze in completely dark rooms. The technicians unloaded the spools and placed them in developer by feel. Film was developed in open tanks or trays in mobile trailers, again built by Williamson, as well as in fixed installations. The prints were hand-lettered. It is not recorded whether Gilze had the big, high-speed Williamson device that combined photo printing, processing, drying and print cutting all in one machine called the 'Multiprinter'.[124]

There is no evidence that the results of Ellis's sortie were ever shared with the attacking infantry and tanks except in the form of overprints of the fixed defences on the 1/25,000 maps provided to the tanks only. 33 Fld Regt RA did have an aerial photograph of Winnekendonk giving the map reference of the church steeple, but it was taken on 12 October 1944 with the trees in leaf and before the defences were dug.

Mill, which was used by the Typhoons, was the last of seven airfields constructed or reconstructed by the Allies in the wake of the Arnhem Operation. Apart from local brick and concrete, the materials used were PSP, PBS and SMT. Initially Eindhoven and Volkel, which had been used by the Germans, were repaired as soon as the Germans left, but at Volkel reconstruction with PSP was delayed when the Germans returned. Eindhoven was re-laid with brick but broke up in the February thaw and became a continuous headache. Repaving was required also at Volkel that was close to Crerar's HQ at Uden, and contemporary pictures show aircraft taxiing through floods. The field at Grave was built close to the Maas but, after disappearing under water several times in

123 Leonard Bridgman. *Jane's All The World's Aircraft 1945-46* (London: Jane's, 1946).
124 Stanley, *World War II Photo.*

October and November, it was abandoned. De Rips also flooded, being like Volkel built too close to the Peel marshes.

Faced with all these problems and a serious shortage of PSP due to the delay from stranding of a shipful of that material, a decision was made in October to build away from the marshes. The first of these airfields was at Heesch. It was made of PSP and completed by end November and occupied by one wing. Helmond was built closer to the marsh from 8 million bricks and PSP. Finished for the start of *Veritable*, it survived the thaw. Petit Brogel in northern Belgium was in excellent terrain and completed on 2 March, and abandoned in 1946.

Finally B-89 Mill, to the north of the marsh, was built on heathland. Surveyed on 10 December 1944, plans were completed by 19 December and the first sod turned on 1 January 1945. Two feet of peat was scraped off to expose an excellent base of sandy gravel on which PSP was laid. The peat was mounded around dispersals to provide blast protection for the aircraft. A new airfield layout was adopted which found great favour with the RAF on account of its operational simplicity. There was a central flying strip with a wing located on each side. Taxi-tracks ran parallel to the strip and from these the aircraft standings of two for each Sqn, led off at right angles. There was a perimeter road for motor transport.

The construction in January was undertaken in bad weather with continuous snow, sleet and frost, and the strip became a frozen mass of sand and snow. Consolidation and grading became impossible but the deadline was insisted on and in desperation the PSP was laid on top of frozen sand and snow during January 1945. On 30 January the thaw came and the engineers were diverted with all their materials to emergency repair of the roads for *Veritable*. The landing strip and one half of the field were completed with civilian labour by the evening of 7 February. The following day after their first sortie over the Reichswald, 146 Wing flew in and took up residence. The other side of the airfield was completed by 7 March 1945 and occupied by 35 Army Cooperation and PR Wing, including 4 Sqn mentioned above, that moved in from Gilze Rijen.

> The end of the airfield came soon after the crossing of the Rhine, for we moved on to fields elsewhere and the RAF wings went too. I do not think it was ever used again. It was a good field and it is interesting to note that, in spite of laying the PSP on the frozen sand, the track bedded down beautifully and gave no trouble at all.[125]

The field is now obliterated by flooded gravel excavations.

Flight-Lieutenant Richard Hough was one of those who flew his Bombphoon into Mill on 7 February with 197 Sqn of 146 Wing. He had tried rockets in 1943, but preferred bombs because the rails reduced the speed and affected the handling. It was difficult to get the right angle in the dive and he kept missing because there was an immediate gravity drop. The only way to overcome that was by approaching the target vertically, and from a suicidally low altitude.[126]

Hough described the Typhoon as power and weight. Compared with the Hurricane it represented a new dimension in flying. The Hurricane IIC generated 1,185 hp and weighed 7,670 lb while the Typhoon produced 2,200 hp and weighed 11,500 lb. Each hp on the Hurricane moved 6.5 lb compared with only 5.2 lb of the far heavier Typhoon for a gain of 20% in power to weight ratio.

Hough described blind bombing of Winnekendonk by radar.

> Some scientist, who became very unpopular with us, had invented a form of blind bombing, straight and level, by radar. We felt very foolish flying in loose formation above 10/10th

125 After The Battle, Vol 20, ref Lt-Col Clark, CO 25 Airfield Construction Group, RE.

126 Richard Hough. *One Boy's War*. (London: Heinemann, 1975), p. 132

> cloud and in blazing sun all pressing the bomb tit together when a distant voice over the R/T ordered us to do so. We were told the bombing was highly accurate. 'If we're going to have a wizard prang, I like to see it,' someone complained.[127]

Hough described what it was like to go on an 'op'. Word would get around the mess that there would be flying. The pilots were collected in Jeeps or a 15cwt truck, to be carried to the briefing caravan near dispersal. There in the presence of a 'brown job' they would receive details of the target, its map reference and type, the height to be flown and the fuse details of the bombs. They could be set for either a 0.25 second delay, which was in effect instantaneous, or a 5 second delay. The setting depended on the height being flown and could not be changed in flight. Low flying required the 5 second delay to prevent damage to the aircraft. Then pilots would be assigned to serviceable aircraft, because only the CO and Flight Commanders in 197 Sqn had their own regular planes. They would climb into the aircraft, take off in pairs, and form up over Mill. Typically there would be seven or eight from one Sqn, and perhaps seventeen from two squadrons, and they would be off to the target.[128]

Hough bombed Winnekendonk on three separate occasions, recording in his log:

> Feb 16th. Ramrod Duty – 2 × 500 [lb bomb] (incendiaries) on WINNEKENDONK. 17 aircraft on the show and all bombs in the already flattened village. Very intense and accurate light flak.
>
> Feb 27th. Ramrod Duty – 2 × 1000. Blind bombing by ground controlled Radar. WINNEKENDONK. Bombed straight and level – curious sensation – from 10,000 feet. No flak.
>
> Feb 28th. Ramrod Duty – 2 × 1000. To WINNEKENDONK again, visual dive-bombing this time. Spectacular results. Village wiped out, though some light flak.[129]

In Winnekendonk, 28 February is still remembered as the black day when eighty five percent of the village was destroyed. '28. Februar 1945. Winnekendonk wird zu 85% zerstört'.[130] The bombing was intended

> to prevent the enemy taking advantage of his effectively stabilised front by passing up reinforcements. The villages of Winnekendonk and Sonsbeck were strongly attacked; the first village by 64 Typhoons and Sonsbeck by 50 Spitfires. Winnekendonk was reported completely destroyed.[131]

It is difficult to believe that Horrocks asked for the destruction of Winnekendonk. The degree of effectiveness was not analysed, even though it later caused SG to abandon several of their Churchills that fell into craters, and could have led to difficulties in a German counter-attack. German reinforcements could have been delayed by no more than an hour while a by-pass was established. The conclusion is inescapable that 2 TAF destroyed Winnekendonk because its weapons lacked the accuracy to hit anything much smaller, and because restraint had been abandoned by the RAF in the nighttime bombing campaign. The reason given was a rationalisation.

127 Op. Cit., pp. 139-40.
128 Richard Hough in conversation.
129 Copy of Richard Hough's Pilot's Log Book.
130 H Janssen. *700 Jahre Winnekendonk 1282-1982* (Winnekendonk: Vereine,1982).
131 TNA: 84 Group ORB.

At this time stresses long in the building came to a head. Their genesis can be traced to events earlier in the month. Horrocks was never happy with his decision to use heavies to 'take out Cleves', as Crerar described it. Horrocks wrote[132] that he felt almost physically sick when he saw the bombers do another Caen. His rationalisation was that he was in a race to the Nutterden feature, and destroying Cleves might give him an advantage by slowing up the German reserves. This was the same argument used for the destruction of Caen and Winnekendonk. His overriding objective was to save British lives. He added that he was blessed with too much imagination and that it was fortunate for the British Army that he never rose above the level of Corps Commander. For years after the war Horrocks had nightmares about Cleves, and the destruction turned out to have been far worse than he had imagined because the RAF used HE instead of the incendiaries he had specifically requested. Even worse, the craters held up his advance and cost British as well as many German civilian lives.

The destruction of Cleves was on 8 February 1945. A fortnight later on 21 February, 2 Group despatched a box of mediums comprising 35 Mitchells and Bostons to attack Weeze. Due to a mistake in navigation, thirty aircraft dropped 96 bombs on British troops in Goch and Üdem. Horrocks exploded, having

> a sudden revulsion to all types of air support and requested the removal of all 84 Group assistance from his Corps front. This outburst of indignation upset the planning and consequently aircraft of 131, which were to have attacked strongly defended positions and troop concentration areas on the front of 51(H) Div, were diverted to alternative targets at Weeze and Sonsbeck.[133]

Both Horrocks and Shores were silent about this in their books, but in 2006 Shores re-issued his history of 2 TAF in a multi-volume and magisterial re-write to include this and other information covering the Typhoon's gross inaccuracy.[134]

2 TAF was overstretched and its commanders were worried about losses. On 1 March 1945, 84 Group's Ops' Log reported a conference during that night during the routine meeting with the Army, leading to a decision to impose a severe restriction on the

> liberal use of aircraft in support rôles owing to the shortage of both Typhoon and Spitfire aircraft and the weariness of the pilots. The automatic use of aircraft in the counter-battery rôle, for instance, would be discontinued during static or semi-static periods, and indeed only accepted in special cases in an advance when our artillery could not take on the rôle, or if the menace of enemy guns was having a really serious effect. Moreover, the prolific use of Rocket Typhoons in cab rank under FCP control would have to be reduced and the scope of the FCP limited to a definite sector of front; for example a Div or Bde front rather than as at present on an entire Corps front. A further check was to be kept on the acceptance by GCC of targets so that effort would not be wasted.[135]

Ironies abound in this assessment of chickens roosting noisily. The high speed of unarmoured Typhoons and Spitfires was now recognised as providing no defence against the powerful Flak defending German gun batteries, so 2 TAF simply abandoned that most important target without

132 Horrocks, *Corps Commander.*
133 TNA: 84 Group ORB
134 C Shores & C Thomas. *2nd TAF. Vol 3* (Hersham: Ian Allan, 2006).
135 TNA: 84 Group ORB.

mentioning their previous adamant refusal to consider aircraft armour. It was back to 1917. Furthermore, 2 TAF now mentioned the idea of supporting specific divisions or brigades when previously they would recognise no formation smaller than a corps or army. 2 TAF had been defeated and forced to withdraw as surely as the U-Boats and Flying Fortresses had been defeated and forced to do likewise in 1943. It is in this context that it becomes clear why once the war was over the entire Typhoon fleet was immediately scrapped, and of course without any admission that the decision to build it had been a catastrophic mistake.

Group had a point, however. Their concern about wasting strength on low-quality targets was justified based on the events of Operation *Heather*. Fourteen wasted sorties were flown against the Berber Woods on 2 March based on nothing better than the speculations of POWs, whose interest was to embellish and invent in order to improve their treatment and, at the same time, do their duty to deceive and delay the enemy. The alternative target was another wood south of Winnekendonk, and this again was identified from a POWs debriefing. 2 TAF, through the RAF controller at Division, would know of these tainted intelligence sources.

2 TAF was not understating the problem of losses. Their ORBs show 78 aircrew were killed or missing in 83 Group in February, of which 27 were Typhoon pilots. Aircraft losses numbered 87 of which 30 were Typhoons. For 84 Group the losses were 38 pilots and 47 aircraft.

Roberts was shot down a week later on 9 March while shooting up barges off the north coast of the appropriately named Dutch island of Over Flakkee. Gp Capt Johnny Baldwin, who had just succeeded Desmond Scott, was on the trip. No flak was expected, but a machine gun (!) on the targeted barge shot down Roberts. He pulled up to 1,500 feet when the engine stopped, landing in a field full of anti-glider posts which were snapped off by the Typhoon. Dutch people swarming out of a farmhouse refused to help because of the presence of two Germans on bicycles who immediately captured him. Flt. Lt G.J. King, known as Kingy and who had flown on both the Winnekendonk ops, orbited overhead and saw the capture. King was a rarity with a score of six against the Japanese. He and Harkness were awarded the DFC after the war. The loss of the third CO in four months affected morale badly, according to the Sqn's MO. Roberts met his predecessor, Sqn Leader Charles Demoulin, DFC in the Stalagluft at Barth that also held Lt-Col Gabreski, the USAAF's top scoring Mustang ace.[136]

Since joining 2 TAF in May 1944, 609 Sqn had lost 30 pilots; 20 were killed, 6 became PW, 2 evaded capture in enemy territory and the fate of 2 is not recorded. C.H.D. Cables and R.D. Harkness, both of whom were at Winnekendonk, were the only two pilots on the squadron strength on D-Day who flew each month and survived until VE-Day. From 1936 to 1945, 74 pilots were killed out of a total of 256 who served at least one month with the Squadron. 8 were taken prisoner and 3 evaded capture.[137]

Two army officers, who were present when the Typhoons struck at the Berber Woods, have expressed views on the value of CAS. Mark Fearfield was a troop commander in LF Sqn, 3 SG. His view was that 2 TAF wasn't integrated with ground operations, and he quoted an occasion when he was rocketed with an FAC aboard, who became very angry in his indignation. The rockets missed as they always did. Harry Illing was an A Coy commander in 2 Warwicks. He couldn't call on Typhoons, so they formed no part of his battle, although he speculated that a Bn CO could possibly request their services. In Illing's view the main trouble was poor visibility. In the close, north European countryside dotted with woods and hedgerows and with a lack of sunlight in February, pilots could not see a camouflaged tank or infantry position, even with an FAC present. Therefore they could not strike effectively, but were themselves at considerable risk from invisible

136 Demoulin, *Firebirds!*
137 Ziegler, *The Story*.

ground fire. In open places such as desert or steppe, the tank's shadow made it visible at a distance, and aircraft could be used effectively. The problem of finding targets in 1945, even when the pilot knew one was below him, was compounded by the inadequate performance of the No 18 set which was too poor for ground-to-air communication. Illing was once attacked by a Typhoon without damage, although he found the experience frightening.

The impossibility of a Typhoon pilot finding a target even when told where it was, was known to 2 TAF who, of course, ignored it. During the 1943 OR ground attack evaluations, pilots were unable to spot well camouflaged guns even when the guns were firing.[138]

In 1945 at RAF Tangmere, Hans-Ulrich Rudel met several RAF pilots including Douglas Bader, Bob Tuck, Frank Carey and Razz Berry, but also Roland Beamont and Hawk Wells who had flown Typhoons with 609 Sqn. Rudel was credited with over 500 tanks and a battleship. Some of his success had come while flying the armoured Ju 87G fitted with a 3.7 cm Flak cannon under each wing firing tungsten cored (*Wulframkern*) ammunition. He claimed accuracy of 20 to 30 cm, and aimed for the tank's vulnerable parts such as fuel tanks and engine covers. He described his conversation with the RAF pilots.

> I soon perceive we have contrary ideas. … They boast of their rockets which I already know about and which can be fired from the fastest aircraft; they do not like to be told that their accuracy is small in comparison with my cannon. I do not particularly mind these interrogations; my successes have not been gained by any technical secrets.[139]

His hosts felt uncomfortable, climbed on their high horses, and threatened to turn him over to the Russians. Rudel, an unrepentant Nazi, enjoyed rubbing salt in their wounds and replied that the Russians would be interested in learning from his experience if they wanted to train up a force of tank destroying pilots.[140]

609 Sqn. ORB Extracts

Gilze Rijen

1 March.

The month does not open well. Weather does not look operational so at 0915 the C/O does a weather recce over WEEZE, GOCH and CLEVE. He reports non-operational weather. Squadrons are grounded until 1645 when W/Cmdr Button led Mathys, Cables, King, De Bruyn, Jacquemin, Harkness, Mountjoy and Goblet on D914/CXS 1,2, & 3 on houses at 915363, 917362 and 917360 West of WEEZE. CXS1 was attacked by the first section who fired 27 R/Ps at the houses. 2 salvoes were near misses and a cannon attack caused much smoke. The second section completely destroyed one house and had near misses on the other. One salvo caused much creamy black smoke. The third section took CSX3 and all R/Ps were in the target area. Mountjoy obtained one direct hit and much smoke was seen. There was some light Flak in the target area. After landing Mathys had a slight accident and ran into a pot hole but no real damage was done.

2 March.

The Sqn was up soon after breakfast when W/Cdr Button led Mathys, Cables, King, De Bruyn, Jacquemin, Harkness, Mountjoy and Goblet at 0935 hours on D923/OJN1 Kervendonk area. 74

138 Copp and Vogel, *Anglo-Canadian*.

139 Hans Ulrich Rudel. *Stuka Pilot.* (Dublin: Euphorian, 1952).

140 Ibid.

R/P and cannon were all in the target area. Much black smoke came up from the northern edge of the wood with a small explosion. 1 MET was damaged. Otherwise no movement was seen.
At 1140 the C/O took off. Mathys, Harkness, Mountjoy, King, De Bruyn and Jacquemin went with him on D931/0JN1 to the same area and the same target. Rockets and cannon were all in the target area and no enemy movement was seen. Our own tanks were seen approaching the wood from the North West.
At 1433 W/Cdr Button and 8 to Hochwald.
The C/O led the fourth show at 1700 with De Bueger, Laforce, Morgan, Inches, Deschamps, Crekillie and Reynolds on D958/XBQ10. Artillery billets at A012315 South of Winnekendonk. [3 kms SE of Winnekendonk, 1 km East of Wetten]. R/Ps were fired at a group of buildings and at least four salvoes were direct hits with the remainder in the target area. Much smoke and flames were seen and it is considered that most of the houses were destroyed.

This night was the night of the Sqn party at Tilburg and it was unfortunate that the ground crews were so late in arriving. However when they did the first impression was that the place was full of girls waiting for them. Beer was free and everybody enjoyed themselves.

Typhoon	Pilot	Duty	Up	Down
RB 431	W/Cdr J.C. Button DFC	D923/OJNS	0935	1015
MN 907	F/Sgt Mathys J.A. (Bel)			
MN 323	P/O C.H.D. Cables			
RB 489	F/Lt G.J. King			
SW 469	F/O J. De Bruyn (Bel)			
PD 449	P/O E.L.R.G. Jacquemin (Bel)			
RB 498	P/O R.D. Harkness (NZ)			
JR 294	F/Lt L.J. Mountjoy			
PD 519	F/O H.F.R. Goblet (Bel)			
SW 447	S/Ldr E.R.A. Roberts, DFC	D931/0JN1	1140	1230
MN 907	F/Sgt Mathys J.A. (Bel)			
R 8826	P/O R.D. Harkness (NZ)			
MN 701	F/Lt L.J. Mountjoy			
RB 489	F/Lt G.J. King			
PD 519	F/O J. De Bruyn (Bel)			
PD 449	P/O E.L.R.G. Jacquemin (Bel)			
SW 447	S/Ldr E.R.A. Roberts, DFC	D958/XBQ	1700	1740
JP 907	F/O G.F.G.H.A. De Bueger (Bel)			
JR 440	F/Sgt Laforce A.G. (Bel)			
JP 974	F/O J. Morgan			
RB 489	F/Lt J.D. Inches (Can)			
JR 294	Sgt Deschamps A.R.A. (Bel)			
PD 449	F/O A.F. Crekillie (Bel)			
JP 858	W/O Reynolds G.H.[1]			

Note:
1. TNA: 609 Sqn ORB.

Part III

Why? An Explanation

10

Why? An Explanation

Nothing is easier to demonstrate [than] that whatever happened had to happen. It is also a very satisfying exercise because it seems to confirm that all is always for the best, which cheers the common man and suits his betters. However, the trouble with historical inevitability is that it works only retrospectively, i.e. for the writers of history, not for its makers.

Prof Richard Pipes, *Russia Under The Old Regime*

The belief that what happened was bound to happen does not satisfy.

Dominick Graham. *Against Odds*

I keep six honest serving men
(They taught me all I knew).
Their names are What and Why and When
And How and Where and Who.
Rudyard Kipling. *The Elephant's Child*

FM Montgomery told the PM in a jocular vein: 'I still don't like the Churchill tank'.

Ned Nordness, AP Correspondent, March 1945

Summary

This chapter explains why British infantry suffered heavy losses during Operation *Heather*, which is taken as representative of the way 21 AG fought its battles in 1945. Death and wounding was caused by the same weapons used in 1918 – machine guns, mortars, and artillery – and with one new weapon – the mine.

According to the RAF's Trenchardian prospectus, which was endorsed and supported by Churchill against military advice that it was snake-oil and could never work, the battles fought in 1944-45 would never happen. Bombers would destroy German cities and with them the will and means of Germany to resist. The only task remaining for the army would be to occupy the ruins, and for that they would require only lorries and rifles. Churchill gave the RAF carte blanche to spend what amounted to £2.8 billion on its bombing fleet, thereby starving the army of equipment and men, bankrupting Britain and permitting Stalin to erect an iron curtain to divide Europe.

The Army did not help its case by peddling its own snake-oil nostrums. According to the Royal Armoured Corps, a fleet of cruiser tanks could act as an expanding torrent to pour through holes punched in the German lines. Once behind the lines, the cruisers would knock about and destroy German command and control centres, paralysing their ability to resist and obsoleting trench warfare with its high cost in human lives.

Tens of thousands of cruiser tanks were therefore bought, ending up across Europe as burnt-out hulks among the shot-down remains of the RAF's bombing fleet. Such a way of waging war was costly, careless of lives and ineffective.

Sir John Monash by Bassano Ltd in 1918. As commander of the Australian Corps, Monash invented modern all-arms operational methodology which destroyed the German field army in 1918. (Image x85341, bromide print, © National Portrait Gallery, London)

During the Hundred Days of 1918, the Commonwealth infantry under Monash together with its Allies defeated the German field army. To achieve this, Monash invented all-arms consisting of tanks, aircraft, and artillery under unified infantry command. In the Second World War it was possible to replicate such all-arms methodology only in Burma under Slim, who was in effect unsupervised, because the power of the cults of bombing and cruiser tanks did not stretch to Asia. In Europe the British army was commanded by cult followers – Churchill, Alanbrooke and Montgomery. The cults claimed the infantry were wedded to a costly war of attrition and therefore should not command mobile forces.

The cults of the mobile arms proclaimed the myth that their way of gaining success with minimal loss of life was to avoid the main German strength of its field army and secure victory through indirect approaches. Churchill, the instigator of the Dardanelles, Norwegian and Greek campaigns, and responsible for denying the necessary support to the defenders of Malaya and Singapore, used his position as Minister of Defence and Prime Minister to protect the cults from informed opposition.

Postwar, Churchill was in a privileged position to write the history of the Second World War and make himself wealthy. He created such an impenetrable smoke-screen that commentators in 2015 were still maintaining, at an official remembrance of his funeral, that although he was a peacetime disaster he was a wartime success. Attempts by RW Thompson in the 1960s and David Irving in the 80s to disperse the smokescreen were unsuccessful.

The Reichswald contains the largest British war cemetery. Its very size and the dates on the gravestones of February and March 1945 raise questions that demand answers. This chapter describes the people and circumstances that filled it with among others the corpses of the casualties of *Heather*. The first nine chapters dealt with the what, when, how, where and who of *Heather*. What remains to explain is the why: why more than 1,579 soldiers and civilians were killed and wounded in *Heather*, of which more than 855 (54%) were German but 724 (46%) were Bermudan, British and Canadian casualties including 161 dead, comprising 2% of the Reichswald Cemetery's total of 7,594 graves. All died at a time when the Allies ruled the skies and the oceans and were within five months of dropping nuclear bombs; they died in what was a marsh; they died fighting in a way guaranteed to produce great loss of life whilst the leadership claimed, and according to some claimed successfully,[1] that their priority was to minimise casualties.

1 John Buckley. *Monty's Men* (New Haven: Yale University Press, 2013).

The Casualties of Operation *Heather*

Battle of:	British				German					
	Killed	Wounded	Total	POW	Killed		Wounded		Total	POW
					Military	Civ.	Military	Civ.		
Yorkshire Bridge	72	262	334	c.0	c.150	3	c.300	NA	c.453	c.547
Kervenheim	64	206	270	c.3	c.95	5	c.180	NA	c.280	c.338
Winnekendonk	25	95	120	c.0	c.40	22	c.60	NA	c.122	c.130
Total	161	563	724	c.3	c.285	30	c.540	NA	c.855	c.1,015

NA = not available; c. = estimated

A caveat must be filed against this chapter. The Duke of Wellington claimed that the reasons for the outcome of any battle are essentially unknowable.

> The history of a battle, is not unlike the history of a ball. Some individuals may recollect all the little events of which the great result is the battle won or lost, but no individual can recollect the order in which, or the exact moment at which, they occurred, which makes all the difference as to their value or importance.[2]

Marshal Saxe would have condemned the exercise as a category error because social science is not a science at all.

> All sciences have principles and rules; war has none. The great captains who have written of it give us none. It requires much knowledge even to understand what they say. And it is impossible to base any judgment on the writings of historians, for they only speak of war as they imagined it.[3]

Professor Terry Copp agrees that battles can be analysed, and correctly warns against choosing facts to fit a preconceived theory or formula. He seems to leave open the question of whether generalisations are either possible or desirable.

> My own view of military history is that like all other history argument should be developed from the evidence not from Marxist, Feminist or Clausewitzian theory. During the Second World War various armies performed effectively in some circumstances and less effectively in others due to a complex set of variables of which doctrine, never mind tank-infantry cooperation, were sometimes significant and sometimes not.
>
> It seems to me that a number of successful and unsuccessful battles were fought in NWE and relative failure or success in each can only be understood if we are willing to examine what happened without fitting it into a pre-determined formula. I do not of course argue that it is impossible to discover the reasons for the outcome of any military operation. I argue that each military operation can be understood by examining the evidence of that military operation.[4]

2 Letter to J. Croker in H.T. Siborne. *The Waterloo Letters* (London: Cassell, 1891).

3 Maurice de Saxe. *Mes Rêveries. Ouvrage Posthume* (Amsterdam, 1757), quoted in FM Carver. *The Apostles of Mobility* (London: Weidenfeld & Nicolson, 1979), p. 101.

4 Professor Emeritus Terry Copp in two letters in 2000 and 2014.

By contrast with Copp, Saxe and Wellington, what is attempted here is the application of Popper's scientific method of examining what happened in *Heather*, creating a hypothesis to explain the outcomes, and testing that hypothesis more widely. One contrary example will destroy the hypothesis, while positive examples will not prove it but rather increase its likelihood of being correct.

By chance there occurred four battles in which every element except one – the type of tank employed – was the same, so that on the principle of ceteris paribus the differences in the result can be logically ascribed to the differences in that one variable. There are grounds for hope that the insight gained will satisfy Richard Pipes's incontrovertible statement that 'The purpose of true history is not only to learn what happened but also to understand why.'[5]

The mind achieves understanding, it seems, through knowing the context, and acquiring evidence-based generalisations and a simple set of rules that explain through data compression.[6] Such rules can be used to frame a testable hypothesis that is falsifiable, which is Popper's definition of scientific method.[7]

The first hypothesis is that there was a way in both world wars of consistently operating with untainted success. Untainted success is defined as having few casualties in contrast with a Pyrrhic victory marred by many casualties. The way was the infantry-based operational methodology engineered in 1918 by Lt Gen Sir John Monash, who claimed to have invented it – a claim that cannot be verified because other people unknown to Monash were involved. The biographer of Monash described it in these terms:

> A war-winning combination had been found: a corps commander of genius, the Australian infantry, the Tank Corps, the Royal Artillery and the RAF.[8]

The methodology was updated in 1939 by the Germans, and again in 1944 by Lt Gen William Slim.

This is a testable theory. The 'commander of genius' is defined as gaining an untainted victory with all-arms in the same environment in which defeat resulted from its absence. To test the hypothesis events need to be found where the presence and absence of all-arms is the only difference, everything else being identical.

'Social science' is an oxymoron. People are complex, and with motivations that are rarely fully understood. Therefore it is difficult to devise experiments where all of the variables are taken into account, and there are additional difficulties in data collection. Nevertheless, in the cases of Operations *Heather*, *Blockbuster* and *Chesterfield* in the Hitler Line, such objections may fortuitously have been absent, but the reader will judge.

The second hypothesis is that untainted success – with minimal casualties – required an efficient army. In the words of Monash:

> The essential components of such an army are a qualified staff, and adequate equipment and a trained soldiery. I state them in what I believe to be their order of importance, and my belief is based upon the lessons which this war has taught us.[9]

5 R. Pipes *Russia Under The Old Regime* (London: Weidenfeld & Nicolson, 1976).
6 G. Chaitin. *Conversations with a Mathematician.* (London: Springer, 2002).
7 Karl Popper. *The Logic of Scientific Discovery* (London: Hutchinson, 1959).
8 G Serle. *John Monash: a Biography* (Carlton: Melbourne University Press, 1982), p. 335, ref Maj Gen Hubert Essame.
9 John Monash. *The Australian Victories in France in 1918* (Sydney: Angus & Robertson, 1936), p. 270.

In 1918 the British Commonwealth army implementing Monash's methodology had all of these components and achieved untainted victory. By contrast, in NWE in 1944-45, the British suffered from poor staff-work, inadequate equipment, and trained soldiers in inadequate numbers. Their victory was predictably tainted by excessive casualties.

Monash's achievement was exceptional because his military victory was achieved uniquely with low casualties, which is the highest possible accolade for a general. Between 8 August and 5 October 1918, which was six days after Hindenburg and Ludendorff had decided they must stop the fighting, the AIF lost only 5,000 dead.

> In that war of 'bloodbaths', of 'murderous offensives', … this figure of 5,000 dead in sixty days of incessant attack seems all wrong, misplaced, incongruous. Yet there it stands, a reminder for ever that even on the bloodiest fields good training, high morale and sound leadership can procure victory at a price that does not make a mockery of the word.[10]

Good equipment is omitted from this list but is necessary, according to the hypothesis, not for victory per se, but to ensure it is achieved with low casualties. The Western Allies in 1944-45 lacked good equipment and suffered horrendous casualties as a result.

The armistice of 1918 created a hiatus in a struggle from 1914 to 1945 between Germany and Britain, France & Russia. The USA participated actively in only five of these 31 years, being neutral for the remainder. The USA received most of the benefits of victory in 1918 while bearing little of the cost in lives and even less in treasure. In 1942-1945 it deliberately repeated the formula but with greater losses of men, to end up in 1945 owning the bulk of the world's gold reserves.

The British, amongst others, never understood that victory in 1918 was due to the all-arms operational methodology of Monash in defeating the German army on the battlefield, believing instead that it was due to the destruction of German morale resulting from naval blockade. Armour and air turned this false conclusion into a rationale for their indirect approach of waging war by avoiding the enemy's main force to achieve victory with few lives lost. Their promise was to destroy the enemy's command and control systems on the ground with armoured forces, and by bombing civilians end the war by destroying the will to fight. This became the strategy of the Churchill administration, which treated the infantry as irrelevant until 1941, except for defence of the base, calculating that starving it of men and resources was risk-free. Furthermore, the strategic ambitions of the independent arms of tanks and bombers precluded cooperation with immobile infantry, with the result that the integrated all-arms methodology of Monash vanished even from discourse to be replaced by occasional talk of 'army co-operation'.

Armour and air were a cult supported by Churchill and based around gurus; Trenchard, Fuller, Liddell Hart, Hobart and their associates. These preached the innate superiority of mobility as war-winning methodology when used in the right way, and that way was revealed only to the mobility-minded or, as the RAF claimed, the air-minded. A popular magazine opined:

> Speed in mobile warfare being the essential to success in this present war of rapid movement, tanks and armoured vehicles are not only rapidly increasing their speed capacity, but every movement is anticipated to save time.[11]

10 J. Terraine. *To Win A War* (London: Sidgwick & Jackson, 1978), p. 187.
11 *The Illustrated London News*, 28 June 1941.

Bob Hope summed up the competing claims of these newly fashionable arms:

> Let's face it, the infantry is really getting old-fashioned. There's practically nothing left for them to do. After the planes get through their job, and the tanks get through their job, and the artillery has done its job, about the only thing left for the infantry is to step in and do all the fighting.[12]

The search by this author for an explanation began in 1947 when his father took the eight year-old to Winnekendonk on the second anniversary of the battle to honour the graves of the dead Lincolns. To a child they seemed a great number, which could easily have included his own father, and incongruous considering Britain's position in a destroyed Germany. His father explained that the British Army was ill-equipped and too small to succeed without great loss because prewar politicians had neglected it. He recited with bitterness a favourite poem:

> But it's Tommy this, an' Tommy that, an' "Chuck him out, the brute!" But he's a "Hero of 'is country" when the guns begin to shoot;[13]

His mother offered a different reason: the Germans hated Britain and were determined to destroy us. They had tried it twice in her lifetime, ruining her life, and were working to do it again as the British were too stupid to stop them. These explanations struck the eight year-old as childish and incomplete, and inconsistent with the friendly neighbouring children in Ratheim, whose family had just been reduced to the depths of despair by news that their man had died of blood-poisoning while clearing wreckage from Memel harbor for the Russians. It has taken the intervening sixty-six years and at least the requisite 10,000 hours[14] to find answers to this complex subject that are convincing to him and hopefully his readers.

6 GTB's biographer made an extravagant claim about Winnekendonk:

> It was the speed with which the attack was launched, the pre-arranged barrage and the magnificent courage and determination of both tanks and infantry that had undoubtedly brought about the success of this remarkable operation, *which will surely rank as one of the finest small scale Tank/Infantry battles ever executed.*[15] [this author's emphasis].

3 SG's war diary added that the battle was 'well worthy of further study'.

On that same day, 2 March 1945, and five miles to the north in the Hochwald, 4 CAD withdrew two battered units as Lt Gen Guy Simonds' confident '24-hour zip' to Wesel ended in bitter and costly failure. The biographer of one of the Canadian armoured units fought to a standstill by German paratroops wrote:

> For shelling and misery the battle had been unparalleled, because once the first thrust failed to breakout, the game was up and the succeeding days of ceaseless battering were agonies of hopelessness.[16]

---

12 PJ Grigg. *Prejudice and Judgment* (London: Jonathan Cape, 1945), p. 366.
13 Rudyard Kipling. *Barrack-Room Ballads* (London: Methuen, 1892).
14 M Gladwell. *Complexity & the 10,000-Hour Rule* (New Yorker, 21 August 2013).
15 Forbes, *6th Guards.*
16 Donald Graves. *South Albertas* (Toronto: Robin Brass, 1998).

We saw in Chapter 1 how Crerar warned both Simonds and Horrocks on 24 February that XXX Corps in supporting the right flank of II Canadian Corps,

> will, itself, however exploit to South East and South, should any favourable opportunities present themselves providing its primary responsibility is not compromised ... 30 Corps will develop a thrust South East, with Guards Armd Div, to cut and hold the Geldern-Wesel road in the vicinity of road and railway junctions in map square 2430,1431 and 1633. 3 Brit Inf Div keeping East of the Weeze-Geldern road, will be directed South, securing Winnekendonk and then Geldern. 53 (W) Inf Div will secure Kevelaer and make contact with 3 Brit Inf Div.[17]

The following day, 25 February, Crerar reverted to the same matter because 53 BID was being held outside Weeze, resulting in construction of the essential Wanssum-Well bridge being stalled. Crerar continued:

> If possible, 2 Canadian Corps will complete *Blockbuster*... If by D plus 1 [27 February] it is obvious that to complete *Blockbuster* a considerable regrouping, and a further deliberate attack is required, then a 'partial' *Blockbuster* will terminate the operation – i.e. the completion of Phase III and the securing of the high ground East of the Calcar-Udem road ... In either of the alternative results given ... above, the weight of the Canadian Army effort will then be transferred to 30 Corps – which, as a Canadian Army first priority will then proceed to acquire the Well-Weeze road, and eliminate the enemy to the North of it.

Crerar was stating the military principle of reinforcing success and abandoning failure.

> The rule of attack is, Never reinforce failure. In plain English that means: if you see some silly asses getting into a mess, don't get mixed up with 'em'.[18]

28 February saw no movement in the Hochwald Gap, but the attack was still not called off and the main effort was not switched to XXX Corps. On 4 March, Crerar and his visitors, Churchill, Brooke and Montgomery, watched Simonds sending more 'silly asses' into the Hochwald. Crerar had changed his mind on 28 February as 3 BID fought for Kervenheim and 53 BID was crossing Yorkshire Bridge and moving south past Weeze:

> Army Comd indicated that he would keep the main weight behind the 2 Cdn Corps thrust which now to be directed at RHEINBURG, with 30 Corps supporting the thrust.[19]

The rare breakthrough achieved at Winnekendonk on 2 March, and Crerar's failure to reinforce it was unremarked at the time and unrecognized in Canada until John English raised it. Dominick Graham,[20] a gunner in GAD, wondered why Crerar did not simply move the inter-corps boundary to the River Niers to give 11 BAD a wider front and take command of 3 BID. An answer was given by Ted Deeming of 15/19 Kings Royal Hussars in 11 BAD, who wrote his diary in his tank stuck belly deep in mud in a field in Sandforth, one mile east of Kervenheim during the night of

17 LAC: Crerar Papers: 958c.009(D93) file 1-0-4/1, Operational Directives Memo Crerar to Simonds & Horrocks, 24 February 1945.
18 Evelyn Waugh. *Men at Arms* (London: Chapman & Hall, 1952).
19 LAC: HQ II Canadian Corps' war diary.
20 Graham, *The Price*.

2 March, trying to rest while being persistently shelled and mortared from the high ground in the Hochwald.[21]

The hypothesis is that the necessary conditions for success, albeit with heavy casualties, were the Churchill tank and the use of infantry-based operational methodology. The way to reduce the casualties and increase the speed of advance was firstly to re-equip with a Churchill tank with 10-plus inches of frontal armour resistant to all anti-tank weapons. The second requirement was effective CAS which could only come from re-equipment with dive bombers and armoured aircraft equipped with artillery under army command.

Ted Deeming's distress was understandable and predictable, for he had the wrong type of tank for these, and in fact all battle conditions in North West Europe, and he was operating the wrong tank-based operational methods. His Challenger A30 Cruiser tank was designed for fighting enemy tanks, and for exploiting a breakthrough by attacking enemy command and control functions. It had a 17pdr gun firing AP to destroy any German tank, a 0.3-inch Browning MG against infantry, and a 32 mph top speed obtainable on good going because of its light weight armour of 2½ inches on the turret and 4 inches on the hull front.

The CO of 144 RAC who postwar became a general described the conventional view that there were two fundamental tasks for armour and each required its own type of tank.

> The first of these is to provide direct fire support for infantry as opposed to the indirect fire of artillery. Artillery provides a greater weight of fire but can only deal with an area target and must therefore cease during the last 150 yards of the infantry's advance to their objectives. This is where they usually suffer the bulk of their casualties from small arms fire, and it is here that the tank must fill in the gap by shooting with weapons of pin point accuracy up to the moment that the infantry close with their enemy.
>
> The second basic purpose for which the tank exists is to provide the hard core of the mobile portion of an army. This faster portion which provides the decisive action in battle is composed of armoured divisions, the tanks of which provide a concentration of mobile fire power which can disrupt, disorganise and pursue an enemy whose front has been broken or cracked by the slower infantry divisions and their supporting armour and artillery.[22]

The clarity of the first purpose contrasts with the obscurity of the second which assumed that the army was and should be divided into 'mobile' and 'slow' elements. Instead the army turned out to be divided into a slow mobile element and a fast immobile element. *Heather's* objective was to break through the German defences to release GAD, the 'hard core of the mobile portion', which would seize the Wesel crossing point and open the road to Berlin. But when the breakthrough came at Winnekendonk, nothing happened for days beyond what 3 BID and 6 GAB could provide from their own degraded resources. GAD turned out to be, and not for the first time, not the hard core of the mobile element, but the soft core of an immobile element. On 28 February Crerar had decided against reinforcing success with Canadian forces, so nothing was expected from that quarter, but GAD did not move for two days while 3 BID kept moving. The record is silent about the reason why 3 BID kept moving, but atavistic memories would have stirred among the historically-minded within 3 BID, and especially within its 9 BIB which had just broken through at Winnekendonk. On 14 July 1916, in the battle of the Somme, 3 BID similarly broke through the German line at Bazentin Le Grand at 1 pm, and Brigadier Potter commanding 9 BIB walked towards High Wood to confirm the absence of the enemy.

21 Delaforce, *The Black Bull*, p. 199.
22 Alan Jolly, *Blue Flash* (London: Alan Jolly, 1952), Epilogue.

> Haldane [GOC 3 BID] sought permission to launch 76 Brigade, fresh and ready, towards the wood, but his request was turned down; 76 Brigade was to be held back to deal with counter-attacks, and anyway, he was told, 2nd Indian Cavalry Division was moving up to exploit. However, the cavalry were still far away, having 12 miles to cover from their assembly area over rough slippery ground, and the leading brigade did not pass through 3 Div until 7 pm. At 9.30 pm, when it was too dark, the cavalry consolidated between Longueval and High Wood… That night the Germans established a defence line… and by the following day it was clear that a further costly break-in battle would be necessary.[23]

Twenty-nine years later in 1945 the rôle and indeed function of 2 Indian Cavalry Div was taken by GAD. They camped in a field in Pfalzdorf on 23 February, 9 miles from Winnekendonk, ready at the slightest opportunity to seize the Wesel bridges by *coup de main*. On 2 March at midnight the road to Wesel was opened by 3 BID's 9 BIB, but GAD took two days to move and nearly three days in total to reach the front. This compared with the 6 hours that 2 Indian Cavalry Division had taken to cover a greater distance. One of the guards of GAD – the IO of 5 CG in 32 BIB – wrote:

> We were just east of Goch at a place called Schule because Battalion HQ was in a school… Then on the night of the 4th we drove [two days after the breakthrough] into the ruins of Goch and joined up with the 1st Battalion tanks at midnight. The whole division was now going into battle. At Kappeln the Grenadiers were already in action, and during the night we went down the well-known route via Goch, Weeze, Kevelier (sic) and Wettin (sic) to join them. We were launched into an attack at about 5.30(pm) [three days after the breakthrough] and had as our objective a cluster of farms … called Metzekath.[24]

Metzekath is 15 miles from GAD's encampment in Pfalzdorf, so it had taken GAD 65½ hours to get into battle. During that time 3BID and 6GTB had 'exploited' for six miles towards Wesel. Whistler, Haldane's successor, knew not to wait for GAD but to bash on with infantry and tanks, and with Horrocks's agreement. GAD in the event was 88% less efficient than the heavily criticised Indian cavalry of 1916, managing but an average of ¼ mph compared with 2 mph in 1916. (2 Indian Cavalry moved 12 miles in 6 hours or 2 mph. GAD moved 15 miles in 65½ hours, or ¼ mph.)

Veterans of GAD seemed never to question either their equipment or their mission. On 28 February 1945 another GAD guardsman wrote in his diary:

> 28 February. There is excitement in the air. The attack on our front is going well. … Restless that we are not yet called upon…[25]

On 3 March his unit was put at two hour's notice to move.

> 4 March. …Warning came to move at 1 am, so early to bed…

> 5 March. At 1 am moved south through Goch and Weeze, not too bad a night's drive… Arrived just short of Kapellen village at dawn, cooked breakfast at the side of the road, and expected to have a battle later in the day. The General [Adair] drove past and took up his Tac HQ in a farmhouse just ahead of my troop… Beyond Kapellen 5th Brigade were having trouble in some

23 McNish, *Iron Division*, p. 60.
24 J. Pereira. *A Distant Drum* (Aldershot: Gale & Polden, 1948).
25 Robert Boscawen. *Armoured Guardsmen* (Barnsley: Leo Cooper, 2001), p. 188.

> woods [Metzekath], held up by SPs and an SS Para battalion [not possible], and the gunners solemnly stonked these woods. We were going to attack, Jimmy gave out preliminary orders and we stood to, but the plan failed to come off; other objectives had not yet been reached… We remained in the field with morale steadily shrinking. During the morning, General Jorrocks [Horrocks] arrived in a scout car to visit our General… All was a bustle… and he was there some while before he left. Shortly afterwards Div HQ upped stakes and moved off too.[26]

Boscawen later added an explanatory comment:

> The constrictions of the Reichswald, the extensive flooding and these small towns meant that the opportunity for an armoured breakthrough never came. Thus the Armoured Divisions, as we found, had a severely limited part. Casualties suffered by the Canadian and British (infantry) divisions were tragically high…It appeared there was no other way at this stage of the war, if we were to succeed in forcing the Rhine and beating the Germans quickly.[27]

Boscawen did not acknowledge that at midnight on 2 March 1945 GAD had the breakthrough handed to them. The road to Wesel was open. GAD's inability to move quickly over 9 miles of unopposed road revealed their existence was fundamentally pointless. Furthermore, when they reached the front and found a determined enemy with anti-tank guns, the task again became again unsuitable for an armoured division and required an infantry division with I-tanks. The conclusion is that Armoured Divisions had no raison d'être *and* should have been disbanded even before D-Day as an unaffordable luxury. Their armoured brigades should have been re-equipped with Churchill I-tanks before D-Day, preferably a new Mark with 10 inch frontal armour, and retrained as Tank Brigades. The armoured infantry brigades of the armoured divisions should then have been broken up as reinforcements for the infantry divisions. Through such actions would the fighting power of 21AG have been immeasurably improved and losses significantly reduced.

This conclusion was never drawn due to the power of another illusion held by all from Boscawen up to Montgomery. British armoured doctrine saw the cruiser as forming an 'expanding torrent' in Liddell Hart's phrase, of armour flowing through a hole in the enemy's defences punched by all-arms assault. The task of the cruiser tank was to put a bullet into the enemy's brain by 'cracking about', as Montgomery expressed it, behind his HKL front line, and destroying the enemy's control and communications. Montgomery and Brooke acquired this vision from Liddell Hart and consequently always prioritised mobility and a big gun over armour thickness. Montgomery came to believe in November 1942 that the Sherman was vital for exploitation but could also double up for the break-in battle. He initially took only Shermans to Sicily and Italy, claiming it was a Universal Tank, and he demanded the same uniformity in Normandy in order to simplify the mixing and matching of his forces. The biographer of the Churchill tank explained:

> This is not to suggest that a truly universal tank could not have been designed to fill all major rôles, but it does seem to show that that tank was not the Sherman, no matter what General Montgomery might have believed. Undoubtedly, in the end, the Sherman could have fought its way from one end of Italy to the other, without the help from Churchills – the Americans proved that – but it seems fair to assume that it would have taken longer about it and, what is worse, would have cost the lives of many more crews [and infantry] than was otherwise the case.[28]

26 Op. Cit., p. 189.
27 Op. Cit., p. 190.
28 David Fletcher. *The Universal Tank* (London: HMSO, 1993), p. 28.

The Americans were even more confused about the rôle of the tank than were the British. They did nothing after the First World War until they observed the British experiments with a mobile force in 1928, which prodded them to establish an experimental force and establish a board to consider the results. Work began on tank designs, but it was low priority during the social revolution of FDR's New Deal of 1933 in the administration of Rexford Tugwell, Prof Ray Moley, Hugh Johnson, Harold Ickes, Thomas Corcoran, Ben Cohen, Jim Farley, Cordell Hull, and Louie Howe. This administration failed to bring the USA out of recession, and in 1939 FDR saw the opportunity of ending the slump in time for the elections in 1940 by turning the neutral USA into the 'arsenal of democracy' at British and French expense, as had begun to happen in 1917. So began New Deal II under a radically different administration that abandoned social engineering in favour of arms dealing and manufacture. It comprised Harry Hopkins, Mrs Roosevelt, William C. Bullitt, General George Marshall, Lowell Mellett and Winston Churchill who formed FDR's new administration.[29]

American thinking followed Liddell Hart, Fuller and Plan 1919 in believing that decisive results could be achieved by releasing highly mobile tanks into the enemy's rear areas. One month after selecting the M4 Sherman to equip their new armoured divisions, the US Army defined the doctrine of its employment:

> The armored division is organized primarily to perform missions that require great mobility and firepower. It is given decisive missions. It is capable of engaging in all forms of combat, but its primary role is in offensive operations against hostile rear areas.[30]

It then defined what the M4 was not. It was not intended as an infantry support tank, being placed in the "striking echelon" of the armoured division with infantry relegated to the "support echelon", whose job was to punch a hole in the enemy line through which the Sherman would reach the vulnerable rear areas. The M4 was not intended to fight tanks, which was the rôle of the Corps of Tank Destroyers. The Sherman's field manual devoted just one page out of 142 to tanks fighting tanks.[31]

The joy expressed by Montgomery in getting the first Shermans, together with the thousands of orders sent by the British to the new Chrysler Tank Arsenal, led the inexperienced US Army to believe it had a good tank when in fact it was soon outclassed in every way except automotive durability and reliability.

Nevertheless, there was and remains a mistaken belief that even if the cruiser tanks were 'bloody useless'[32] in the set-piece battle, there was one rôle that only they could fulfill. They would come into their own in conditions where mobility was at a premium and victory went to the swiftest; when the enemy was 'back on its heels and has no time or opportunity to respond.'[33]

The armoured divisional construct was an inverted pyramid balancing on this one justification. The examples generally quoted of when cruiser tanks came into their own are the huge German advances of 1940-41 across France and Russia, the Allied advance from Normandy to the Scheldt and into Lorraine in 1944, and from the Vistula to the Oder in 1945. The incorrigible Montgomery stated that had the Germans possessed Shermans their Ardennes Offensive would have reached Antwerp. The conclusion, however, that such advances were due to the high speed of Cruiser tanks confuses maximum speed with average speed, and the reason why the hare was sure he would beat the tortoise. Instead, history revealed that 15 mph Churchills beat 28 mph Shermans, 40 mph Cromwells, and 32 mph Comets whenever they competed.

29 J Pritchard. *The Ring Around Roosevelt* (Chicago: Coronet, Vol 10, No.3, 1941).
30 USWD: *Operations.* Army doctrine FM 100-5, May 1941.
31 USWD: *The Tank Battalion.* Army doctrine FM 17-33, September 1942.
32 A phrase used by Dominick Graham in a letter in 1995.
33 Carlo D'Este in a letter in May 2000.

An earnest of the Churchill's high mobility occurred during the night of 26/27 February 1943 when the NIH in bad weather covered 90 miles in 8½ hours at an average speed of 11 mph from Le Kef in Tunisia, to go into immediate action at Hunt's Gap. Posters publicising this feat were put up in all RAC establishments in the UK showing a Churchill with the caption, 'We call this maintenance!' and with a description of the event.[34] Another such feat happened during the Breakout from Normandy on 7 September 1944 when 6 GTB grew tired of waiting for tank transporters, all of which were being used to ferry artillery ammunition to the front, and moved in a leisurely way on their own wheels over 100 miles from Flers to the Seine. This was a third of the way to Antwerp and a quarter of the way to Wesel. It was said of this move that,

> the overall speed of the move equalled that of the Guards Armoured Division in their Shermans, and yet the number of vehicles, both tanks and MT, which fell out on the way was infinitesimal.[35]

Final proof of the superior mobility of the Churchill occurred in April 1945 during the advance across Westphalia from the Rhine to the Osnabrück Canal. A battalion of Churchills covered a greater distance in a shorter period of time, and arrived ahead of, a larger number of the ultimate 32 mph Comet which incorporated every item of specification wish-list demanded by Montgomery, Hobart and Richards, with the exception of sloped armour. The Churchills,

> had come forty-two miles in five-and-a-half hours – the swiftest opposed advance ever made by a Churchill Squadron. The 'experts' who had claimed that Churchills could never compete with an Armoured Division had been proved manifestly wrong.[36]

There were no tricks involved. The Churchills of 4 GG carrying troops of 6 British Airborne Div 'Russian-style', beat 11 BAD, who called the result an impudence, in a fair race. The biographer of 11 BAD explained:

> Osnabrück, not our objective now, but that of 6th Airborne, who were keeping manfully abreast of us, impudently as it seemed to ourselves, for apart from their own reconnaissance regiment they had only one battalion of tanks under their command and these were Churchills from the 6th Guards Tank Brigade, excellent machines, but not designed to keep pace with Comets in pursuit. Yet every day they kept up on our right and even now as we were moving to cut off Osnabrück from the north their leading troops were within a few miles of its southern perimeter.[37]

Simultaneously on the Wesel-Munster axis, 3 SG and 4 CG were operating with 513 Regt of 17 US Airborne Div as 6 GAB Group under Brigadier Greenacre. 4 GG collected the British 6 Airborne on 28 March and raced north. No one, not even Alan Moorehead, was taking note according to Patrick Forbes:

> Alan Moorehead in his excellent book *Eclipse* writes: 'Nobody has yet succeeded in explaining satisfactorily how the 6th Airborne projected themselves for 300 miles across Germany to

34 Gerry Chester by e-mail on 9 December 2003.
35 Forbes, *6th Guards*.
36 Ibid.
37 Anon, *Taurus Pursuant*.

> arrive on the Baltic ahead of everyone else'. It is hoped that this chapter will provide a partial explanation.[38]

Moorehead created a fanciful myth that 6 Airborne, seemingly by steam roller osmosis,

> arrived on the Baltic ahead of the tanks and the armour – indeed ahead of everyone else. I only saw glimpses of the Sixth… Having no vehicles at the outset, they simply seized anything they could get hold of from the Germans – bakers' and butchers' vans, post-office trucks. They did not bother to repaint them. I even saw one man in a steam roller. Anything to get forward.[39]

The Churchill's faster average speed was due to its superiority in rough and opposed going, especially on the bad roads which held up the Cruiser tanks, and in the tank-infantry cooperation they had perfected, allowing quick and efficient defeat of death-defying Fallschirmjägers armed with Panzerfausts, StuGs and anti-tank guns defending towns and villages. The Comets could do neither, because

> Their progress though unimpeded by the enemy, was sadly delayed by the imperfect state of the roads. This was to prove a bugbear throughout the advance. 7th Armoured had even more trouble with roads than ourselves, and at one point did not move for over two days.[40]

The armoured divisions therefore avoided the towns and made huge detours around them, causing even more delay. They complained they could find:

> No road that doesn't lead from one town to another. So either the armoured division must take the town or bring up an infantry division to do it. The first is undesirable while the second involves much long and complicated manoeuvring.[41]

Bewitched by dreams and meeting circumstances that their cult leaders, Hobart and Liddell Hart, had never theorised about, the armoured divisions could never deal with the here and now because they had failed to master the basic task of turning the enemy out of his defences. It was not their bloody rôle. The would-be hare hankered instead after an idealized geography suitable for 'exploitation', which was neither the desert with its areas of poor going that were either too soft or too rocky; nor the road to Arnhem approached along the top of a dike and laid out as a German shooting-range; nor the bocage with its hedged banks; nor the North German Plain with its built-up areas and poor roads; nor anywhere else on this imperfect earth where a kind of a motoring club could 'split-arse'[42] in their sporty Cromwells and Comets to exploit into the sunset. Instead they had to go cap in hand to the foot-slogging infantry with their 'slow' Churchill tanks and ask them to prepare and make safe the way for them, as here with 3 BID:

> Bremen proved too well defended to be taken by an armoured division, so once again it was by-passed and left for the infantry; this time, 3rd Division.[43]

38 Forbes, *6th Guards*, p. 152.
39 Alan Moorehead. *Eclipse* (London: Hamish Hamilton, 1945), p. 208.
40 Anon, *Taurus Pursuant.*
41 Ibid.
42 'Split-arse' was a contemporary expression that the infantry imagined would result from fast horse-riding, and extended to mean any fast driving.
43 John Sandars. *British 7th Armoured Division* (London: Osprey, 1977), p. 32.

Consequently the armoured divisions were as redundant as First World War cavalry divisions, and their pretensions just as offensive. It was no wonder they were so often hated.

Having shown that the speed of the cruiser tank lacked any real-world advantage, the hypothesis is formulated that the Churchill tank, when operated by infantry-focused units such as 25 BATB in Italy and 6 GAB in NWE, was the necessary, although not sufficient, condition for battlefield success in 1944/5. This hypothesis will be the independent, or explanatory, variable in 'laboratory tests' forming a quasi-scientific experiment. Any proof is provisional and can be disproved by a contrary observation per Popper's scientific method. In non-technical language, the hypothesis states that for infantry to succeed they needed support from tanks that were immune to anti-tank weapons and whose crews were trained in infantry support. Furthermore there will be presented real world examples to prove (in the sense of test) that this was the case.

There is a caveat. The method of operating the Churchill cannot be separated from the tank itself; the two being a system. The crews of I-tanks were trained differently from those of cruiser tanks, who despised I-tanks and their crews as lackeys of the infantry. In the successful Hitler Line battle, 25 BATB fielded a temporary mixture of Churchills and Shermans. The Shermans had replaced Churchills while their 6pdr guns were being replaced with American 75 mm guns, but all were manned by Churchill crews. It cannot logically be ruled out, therefore, that, if trained Churchill crews had manned the Shermans of 4 CAD in Operation *Blockbuster*, the battle would have turned out differently. Vice versa, the Hitler Line and Winnekendonk battles might logically have failed had the Churchill crews been from the armoured corps. Therefore the hypothesis depends on crews and tanks forming an infantry-focused system. Differences in I-tank training in NWE and Italy were insignificant, although as we shall see the Churchill brigades fighting in Italy were *sans pareil*.

'Laboratory Testing' of the hypothesis that the use of the Churchill tank with an infantry-based method of tank-infantry cooperation was a necessary although insufficient condition for success. Events 1-4 are identical, i.e. ceteris paribus, except for the type of tank employed; Events 5-6 are identical except for the task and tank employed, i.e. ceteris imparibus and included by way of illustrating a line of further research into the other factors.

Event	Date	Units	Nationality of Army	Operation/ Location	Tank	Method	Div GOC	Result
Ceteris Paribus								
1	19.5.44	36 BIB & 1 CAB	Britain/ Canada	*Unknown* /Hitler Line	Sherman	Tank-based	Keightley	Failure
2	23.5.44	25 ATB & 1 CID	Britain/ Canada	*Chesterfield* / Hitler Line	Churchill/ Sherman *	Infantry-based	Vokes	Success
3	2.3.45	4 CAD & 2 CID & 3 CID & 11 BAD	Canada/ Britain	*Blockbuster*/ Schlieffen Line	Sherman	Tank-based	Vokes	Failure
4	2.3.45	3 BID & 6 GAB	Britain	*Heather*/ Schlieffen Line	Churchill	Infantry-based	Whistler	Success

Event	Date	Units	Nationality of Army	Operation/ Location	Tank	Method	Div GOC	Result
Ceteris Imparibus								
5	30.9.44	7 USAD	USA	*Pollux*/ Overloon	Sherman	Tank-based	Silvester	Failure
6	9.10.44	3 BID & 6 GAB	Britain	*Castor*/ Overloon	Churchill	Infantry-based	Whistler	Success

* 25 ATB's establishment was 153 tanks comprising 123 Churchills and 30 Stuarts. For this battle 54 Shermans had to replace 54 Churchills which were in base workshop having their 6pdrs exchanged for 75 mm guns from scrapped Shermans to create the Churchill Na75.

Four operations are examined in which all elements bearing on success or failure were the same, i.e. ceteris paribus, except for the type of tank and its concomitant method of tank-infantry cooperation. Events 5-6 are unique in that US 7 Armoured Division (7 USAD) under Lindsay Silvester was tasked with taking Overloon by Charles Corlett, GOC XIX Corps, IX US Army but failed and the task given to 3BID/6GTB which succeeded. However, although the difference in method was obviously part of the explanation for the different outcomes, there were too many other variables involved, and not least the ability of the American GOC, Silvester who was sacked on 31 October 1944 and replaced by Robert Hasbrouck, one of his brigadiers.[44]

Events 1-2 were attacks on the Hitler Line in May 1944, and 3-4 were attacks on the Schlieffen Line in March 1945. Two of the divisional commanders, Chris Vokes and Whistler, commanded in both sets. The interesting one is Vokes who commanded in both but with different outcomes, which eliminates the factor of generalship as an independent variable in the four events, and downplays the replacement of Silvester by Hasbrouck. Furthermore, none of the formations was in the same corps, leaving the intrinsic problem of a corps boundary affecting all four events. This was a significant factor in the Hitler Line battles in the Liri Valley which was known to be too small for two corps but still nothing was done to stop continuous enfilading of 1 CID in Burns's 1 Canadian Corps from the Germans to the front of 78 BID in Kirkman's British XIII Corps.

The Hitler Line was stronger and better prepared than the Schlieffen Line, being also better designed, and better constructed over a longer period of six months. It was also invested by Hitler with his name and his demand that it stop the Allies long enough to buy time for Vergeltungswaffen to work and for the Alliance to dissolve under its own tensions, especially those created by Katyn and the Warsaw Uprising. The Line was well-armed with emplaced Panther turrets and anti-tank guns formed as a Pakfront with 75 mm Pak40 and 88 mm DP guns, and was overseen by Panthers and StuGs. New Zealanders described the Hitler Line:

> From the hill town of Piedimonte San Germano the Hitler Line ran southwards across the Liri Valley to the vicinity of Pontecorvo and, after crossing the river, swung south-westwards over the mountains to Terracina on the coast. Although far from complete, its defences were even more elaborate than those of the Gustav Line; they included armoured pillboxes, reinforced concrete gun emplacements and weapon pits, underground shelters, and minefields and wire to obstruct tanks and infantry. The line's great weakness, however, was that there were too few troops to man it adequately. The 90th Panzer Grenadier Division, which held the sector in front of the Canadian Corps, had been reduced to little more than a motley collection of units

44 A Altes & N in't Veld. *The Forgotten Battle* (New York: Sarpedon, 1995), p. 56.

> in which men of every arm were intermingled. On its left, opposite 13 Corps, was 1 Parachute Division, and on the right in the Pontecorvo-Pico sector was 26 Panzer Division.[45]

Canadians also described the Line:

> The Hitler Line had no continuous natural obstacle...Hence it was built behind a continuous line of barbed wire...The defences were sited in depth... having no natural anti-tank obstacles, the emphasis was more on anti-tank defence. Anti-tank ditches blocked the best approaches and there were large numbers of anti-tank guns both in emplacement and otherwise.[46]

The Pantherturms were difficult to see, with a low profile and heavy camouflage. The attacking tanks were channelled into killing grounds by obstacles on the flanks and by minefields and wire in the centre. Lanes of fire had been cut in the scrubland and woods. The outpost line included snipers in trees who also acted as FOOs for artillery and mortars. The line was backed up by artillery and thirty tanks and SP guns.

Event 1 of 4 from the 'Lab Testing' in the previous table

Maj Gen Charles Keightley was an experienced tank man, who had been trained by Hobart and had commanded 30 BAB, 11 BAD and 6 BAD before commanding 78 BID. He was well regarded, and in August 1944 became the youngest British officer to command a corps (V Corps) in action. His 78 BID came into the line on 15 May 1944 and on 18 May isolated Monte Cassino from the Liri Valley, forcing the defenders to withdraw to the Hitler Line. This presented the classic opportunity that Liddell Hart, Fuller and Hobart had taught their pupils to recognise, of using mobile forces to bounce defenders out of their defences before they could become established. On 19 May, Keightley tried to bounce 3 and 4 Para Regts of 1 FJD out of Aquino. The Paras, however, destroyed the recce Shermans on 18 May, making the ensuing tragedy on 19 May inevitable.

36 BIB, part of 78 BID was supported by the Shermans of 11 Armoured (Ontario) Regt, which used tank-based tank-infantry cooperation. They arrived in echelon at the Hitler Line as the morning fog cleared on 19 May 1944, revealing its two leading squadrons to emplaced anti-tank guns. Every Sherman was hit and 13 knocked out. The infantry were then shot down by machine guns and the survivors withdrew. An attempt in the afternoon by 11 BIB supported by 6 Shermans was similarly mauled with 4 destroyed, forcing the unsupported infantry to withdraw. 78 BID did not try again after this complete repulse, and their regimental history was subsequently economical with the truth; 'Although the attack had failed, the Hitler Line was already beaten.'[47] Worse, 78 BID failed to interrupt 1 FJD's subsequent enfilading of 1 CID across the inter-corps boundary. The damage thus caused to the Canadians did not prevent Keightley from subsequent promotion to command of V Corps.

Event 2 of 4

Chris Vokes was a sapper and infantryman. His task was to break through the Hitler Line on 25 May 1944 in a set-piece attack by 1 CID after the repulse of 78 BID's attempted bounce. 1 CID

45 Robin Kay. *The Official History of New Zealand; Vol II* (Wellington: DIA, 1967). http://nzetc.victoria.ac.nz/tm/scholarly/tei-WH2-2Ita-c1-5.html

46 Report No. 158: http://www.cmp-cpm.forces.gc.ca/dhh-dhp/his/rep-rap/cmhqrd-drqgmc-eng.asp?txtType=2&RfId=158

47 Ken Ford. *Battleaxe Division* (Stroud: History Press, 1999).

was supported by 25 BATB with a mixture of Churchill and Sherman tanks, but all crews were trained in the infantry-based tank-infantry cooperation of the Dawnay Doctrine.

This Doctrine had been conceived by the CO of the North Irish Horse, Lt Col David Dawnay when the unit was part of 43 Mixed Division in the UK, and been updated from battle experience in Tunisia. The Doctrine was one of two initiatives taken by battalion commanders in tank brigades that are known to this author – Dawnay's NIH in 25 ATB and Dunbar's 3 SG in 6 GTB. Vokes recognised and acknowledged the effectiveness of the Dawnay Doctrine implemented by NIH, but failed to replicate it when given command of 4 CAD in NWE. Its main points were these commands:

> Never forget the Regiment's rôle is to assist ground troops in every way possible. Unless circumstances dictate otherwise, never go into action without first conducting joint field training. Explain straightforwardly to infantry commanders what Churchills can do or not do in a given situation. All ranks, prior to and during training, to establish a rapport with their infantry counterparts. Never leave an infantry unit hanging out to dry. Should the circumstances be such that 'A' Echelons are unable to reach tanks, then tanks may move back one (or in small groups) at a time, and when replenished return to enable the next tank/s to do the same.
>
> If, for exigency reasons, the ground troops are to be left alone, their commanders must be fully appraised as to the reasons why.[48]

The Doctrine also covered tank deployment:

> Whenever possible, attack the enemy in a location where it is least expected. Every endeavour must be made to engage enemy tanks within the 'killing' range of available weaponry. In order to use the Regiment's firepower effectively, the mark (Mk) of Churchill to lead will depend on the presence of APW (Armour Protected Weaponry):
>
> if APW is known to be present, then 6pdr gunned Mks to lead
> if APW is suspected to be present, then a mix of 6pdr, 75 mm, & 95 mm will lead
> if APW is definitely absent, then Mark Na75 [with 6pdr replaced by 75 mm] V and VII will lead.
>
> Given Allied air superiority, recce flights remove much of the guesswork about the deployment of enemy forces. Armed with such knowledge, best deployment is determined in advance for dealing with enemy APW, which consist of permanently dug-in tanks (Eingebaute Panzern), detached tank turrets (Pz Kw-Türmen), and SP guns (StuGs). If conditions change, then preloading of guns will be altered by wireless command to Troop commanders using the Slidex code of the day:
>
> if APW present – Code 1, all guns load AP
> if APW possibly present – Code 2, two guns load AP, one HE
> if APW unlikely to be present – Code 3, one gun load AP, two guns HE
> if APW known to be absent – Code 4, all guns load HE.[49]

48 http://northirishhorse.net/
49 http://northirishhorse.net/

25 ATB, comprising NIH, 142 RAC and 51 RTR, moved from Tunisia and concentrated at Lucera in Italy near Foggia by the end of April 1944. 25 ATB then trained 1 CID for a week (5 – 12 May) in the Dawnay Doctrine. Each unit in 25 ATB paired off with a brigade of 1 CID; NIH and 2 CIB, 51 RTR and 3 CIB, and 142 RAC and 1 CIB. The infantry also trained the tankers in infantry procedures, such as routine digging of slit trenches, which the tank men had never done before. The Seaforths' biographer:

> For the next few days the Seaforths and Irish were busily engaged in infantry-cum-tank exercises, thus beginning a brief but very close association with a unit with which it would share one of its hardest won battle honours. The North Irish Horse was equipped primarily with Churchill tanks, and although the Seaforths on more than one occasion had gone into action with the armour both on a regimental and squadron level, there were numerous reinforcements of all ranks who had no experience of this nature. The training took the form of lectures by the North Irish Horse officers to the Seaforths, demonstrations of the capabilities and limitations of a tank, rides on the tanks by platoons of the Seaforths, practising communications between the infantry and tanks while on the move and so forth. By and large the Seaforths had great respect for the huge monsters and their fire power... The infantry-cum-tank training went well, and one of the features of it was that the officers and men of both units could get together after the various exercises and got to know each other personally.[50]

The result was an unprecedented standard of tank-infantry teamwork that was soon to be tested in the attack on the Hitler Line. The Dawnay Doctrine systematised the best practice pioneered by Monash and Courage, while no units in NWE did so. For example, 3 SG, which was renowned for its tank-infantry expertise, never trained or formed a personal rapport with 2 Lincolns before Winnekendonk.

The intensive training of the tanks and infantry in the Dawnay Doctrine at Lucera meant that lack of time for detailed planning for Operation *Chesterfield* at troop level due to exhaustion after the long move up had no ill consequences.

> Thus the action was entirely of follow your leader. The infantry set off with an objective in mind, followed by the Churchills which in turn were followed by the Sherman troop. Starting out in darkness and thick mist, under a perpetual barrage from both sides, the tanks simply followed the troops and reacted to each problem as it occurred.[51]

The Seaforth Highlanders were the only battalion to reach the intermediate objective and hang on to it all day. Their success and that of the Carleton and Yorks on their left, led in turn to the further success of the Royal 22nd Regt and the West Nova Scotia Regt when they, as part of 3 CIB, further widened the initial opening to permit 5 CAD to motor beyond the Hitler line.

Success for 1 CID came at the cost of about 1,000 casualties, with the Seaforths accounting for about a fifth of them. NIH had 23 tanks knocked out and 18 damaged out of 58 tanks engaged from an establishment of 77 tanks.

> Writing later about this battle the Commanding Officer stated: "As it developed, in this battle, there was only one possibility of succeeding and that was for each individual to fight forward until he dropped or obtained the objective. Each man did just this and the line

50 Reginald Roy. *The Seaforth Highlanders of Canada* (Vancouver: Evergreen, 1969).
51 David Fletcher. *Mr. Churchill's Tank* (Atglen: Schiffer, 1999), p. 160.

> was broken. Certainly it was a battalion success, not one gained by overwhelming artillery support silencing enemy for this did not happen, nor by brilliant infantry-cum-tank tactics for the infantry had to go on and break the line without the tanks. But success was gained by the bravery and sheer guts of men in pride of regiment. I must repeat this was an other ranks battle, 'their finest hour'." *The Seaforths would be the first to express their gratitude to the North Irish Horse squadrons which gave them such tremendous support in the opening phase of the battle and which tried valiantly to help them in the afternoon* [this author's emphasis]. Mine fields combined with deadly concealed enemy anti-tank guns made the area between the belt of barbed wire and the intermediate objective a killing ground which the enemy had cleverly established when preparing his defences. The location of many of these guns was unknown prior to the attack and their location discovered only in battle. The broken ground and limited visibility added to the great difficulty of the tanks, and as their losses mounted squadrons were reduced to troops, and these shifted from one side of the brigade front to the other to help fill the demands on either flank as the infantry asked for armoured support. During the day the North Irish Horse, which now wears a maple leaf in memory of this battle with the 1st Canadian Division, lost 41 of its tanks, of which 25 were completely destroyed, which represented approximately half of its strength.[52]

Nicholson's Official History failed to connect the unprecedented drive of the Seaforths to succeed with the willingness of the NIH to support them regardless of heavy loss, so that both could gain the victory. The Churchill's armour gave the NIH a faint hope of survival, while the Shermans were too vulnerable to provide any hope for their armoured corps' crews. The Official Report of the battle quoted in the Official New Zealand History (given below) does conclude that the Seaforths and NIH inspired each other, which is the crux of tank-Infantry cooperation. Had the Churchill been immune to anti-tank guns, this effect would have been general.

> For the Seaforths the breaking of the Hitler Line was a never to be forgotten experience. Their losses were heavy. Forty-nine other ranks and three officers were killed, seven officers and 99 other ranks were wounded and two officers and 50 other ranks were taken prisoners of war. These 210 casualties were the heaviest in one day that the battalion ever suffered throughout the entire war. There were numerous bitter battles yet to be fought, but the Hitler Line victory was to be the hardest won battle honour awarded the unit during the Second World War.[53]

The conclusions to be drawn were: the Dawnay Doctrine inspired the infantry to extreme human bravery; the weakness of the Churchill to anti-tank fire resulted in the infantry losing their tank support and as a result suffering heavy losses; and the availability of Churchills immune to anti-tank guns would have helped the infantry succeed with far fewer losses.

The following day, 25 May, the battle-hardened New Zealanders drove up Route 6, and in awe,

> wondered at the evidence of the recent fighting. 'For miles the ground was all torn up by shells.' The Hitler Line 'looked really wicked… The boys had never seen anything quite like it, except photos of the Maginot Line away back in the very early days of the war. Even now that those large, cunningly hidden anti-tank guns were tame, the thought of advancing into their muzzles made you feel sick inside.[54]

---

52 GW Nicholson. *The Canadians in Italy, 1943 – 45* (Ottawa: Cloutier, 1958).
53 Roy, *The Seaforth.*
54 Kay, *The Official History.*

The report on the battle concluded:

> Summing up the day's fighting it may be said that at considerable cost the 1st Canadian Infantry Division had broken through the much-vaunted Adolf Hitler Line and completely routed the enemy troops in that sector. The Commander of the Division attributed its success to four reasons: a) the physical and mental fitness of the Infantry b) the superlative artillery support c) the Infantry-Tank cooperation which reached a perfection never hitherto enjoyed d) the success of the French Corps in gaining the high ground M Morrone and M Leucio on the left flank; the speed with which they passed Artillery and air targets to the Canadians and their eagerness to engage targets on the Canadian front.[55]

Vokes was impressed by the performance of 25 ATB. Brig Tetley, GOC 25 ATB, issued the following order of the day:

> General G.C. Vokes, DSO, Commanding 1 Cdn Inf Div, has intimated that he would be pleased if all ranks of 25 Tk Bde would wear a Maple Leaf emblem in token of the part played by the Bde in assisting 1 Cdn Inf Div to breach the ADOLF HITLER LINE. Commander, 25 Tank Brigade, has accepted the offer with thanks.[56]

Lt Gen Sir Oliver Leese told Tetley:

> The co-operation you established with the Canadians was admirable and *without it the operation could not have succeeded* [this Author's emphasis].[57]

As a consequence, personnel of 145 RAC in 25 ATB were told in June 1944 when back in Lucera that the capabilities of the Churchills were now recognised:

> Following the recent operations in which Churchill tanks have taken part, and the success gained, it is clear that the Churchill has made its name, and higher authority are now fully in favour of the tank and its capabilities.[58]

A first-hand report revealed that Canada's forces in Italy felt the same way.

> 5th Canadian Tank Brigade, after the Dieppe raid, had many of its Churchill Mark IIIs replaced by Mark IVs. The story, for which there is some significant evidence, is that Montgomery would not allow it to join 8th Army unless it was re-equipped with Shermans. After the breaking of the Hitler Line the North Irish Horse met up with the Canadians near Valmontone – while there we heard much anger from (Sherman) crews who suffered so badly during the advance up Italy's east coast, especially at Ortona. The Canadians wore 21st TB insignia on their vehicles.[59]

55 CMHQ: Historical Offr: Report No. 121 re Canadian Ops in the Liri Valley.
56 http://northirishhorse.net/
57 Ibid.
58 Fletcher, *Mr Churchill's Tank*, p. 161.
59 E-mail from Gerry Chester on 10 October 2013.

Canadians had good memories of the Churchill I-tank. They persevered with its early mechanical malfunctions during the period before the Churchills were rebuilt. Brig F.F. Worthington, who raised and trained 1 CTB in February 1941, championed them:

> The Brigade was originally to be organized with two battalions of Matildas and one battalion of Churchill tanks. While British officers did not like the Churchill, Brigadier Worthington, commanding the 1st Canadian Army Tank Brigade, requested that all three of his battalions be issued with the Churchill. By February 1942, this was nearly achieved, with four early Covenanter type Cruiser tanks in the brigade headquarters squadron, and 160 Churchills of an establishment of 174 on strength.[60]

The Churchill performed well at Dieppe with 15 of the 27 that landed climbing the sea wall onto the promenade, and ten of these returning to the beach to cover the withdrawing infantry.[61] The GOC Canadian Forces, McNaughton, however, did not think much of the Churchill,[62] committing himself to the Canadian-built Ram II Cruiser tanks that were issued to the Brigade in March 1943. At Montgomery's insistence, the Rams were changed to the similar Sherman Vs in May 1943 for Operation Husky. Many, according to Chester, would have preferred Churchills.

Vokes's enthusiasm for 25 ATB and the Churchill tank did not survive transfer to his new command even though he called the set-piece assault on the Hitler Line, 'the best battle I ever fought, or organized, even though we suffered so heavily.'[63]

Vokes is silent about 25 ATB's extraordinary support of his division, ascribing the success of 2 CIB (his previous command) to his having 'nursed them like babies, and trained them to the last inch'.

Event 3 of 4

On December 1, 1944 Chris Vokes swapped commands with Harry Foster of 4 CAD. Vokes had not been comfortable with his new corps commander, Charles Foulkes, who had replaced Eedson Burns. Vokes's attitude to Foulkes may have resulted from an inkling that the intention had been to give him the Corps, but his name was confused with that of Foulkes and the wrong man preferred.

Vokes now had the opportunity, and indeed obligation, to apply the lessons of his Hitler Line success to his new command in NWE. He could have argued for re-equipping 4 CAD with Churchills, including the Mk VIIs rejected in Italy because only 75 mm guns were available.

> Perhaps the most stupid decision was to replace 6 pdr guns with 75 mm ones on Marks that saw service in NWE. The delivery of Mark VIIs to units in Italy to replace Mark IIIs and IVs quickly came to an end.[64]

60 http://www.canadiansoldiers.com/vehicles/tanks/mainbattletanks.htm.
61 Fletcher, *Mr Churchill's Tank*, p. 79.
62 John Swettenham. *McNaughton, Vol 2.* (Toronto: Ryerson, 1969), p. 258.
63 Vokes, *My Story*.
64 Information from Gerry Chester on www.ww2talk.com

Vokes could have followed the advice which he gave 4 CAD on his arrival:

> I'm keen on the initiative of junior commanders. I include Lance Corporals. Any time you have to ask what to do, you lack initiative. Get on with it. There's no set solution to any tactical problem. Reason it out.[65]

Vokes could have reasoned out that the tactical problem that defeated him in the Hochwald could have been overcome by replicating this success in the Hitler Line with the Churchill tank, especially as he would have known of the dissatisfaction in Canadian ranks in Italy referred to by Gerry Chester.[66]

But despite being an engineer and infantryman with the same access to insights that inspired Monash, Vokes went along with the prevailing view that Italy could teach NWE nothing. He therefore kept the Shermans and tank-based Hobartian/RAC doctrine, while almost certainly agreeing with Montgomery and everyone else that the Sherman was superior in pursuit to the Churchill. He maintained that,

> a division of armour is slightly different (from an armoured brigade supporting and under command of infantry) in that its prime rôle is Breakout and second, Pursuit to Destroy.[67]

He was distinguishing between break through and break out, but found that when he was ordered to do both in the Hochwald, failure was inevitable. Such was the situation on 2 March 1945, the day of the Battle of Winnekendonk:

> It was growing light when two platoons of the Algonquins 'D' Company reached this position. All efforts to get forward to the Hohe Ley stream failed, and they were fain (sic) to dig in some 300 yards in front of the Lake Superiors and in plain sight of their objective. The deadly anti-tank fire forced the Canadian tanks (3 remained of 8 that had started) to withdraw from their exposed position shortly before 8 am. Left without armoured support, the Algonquins became the targets of counter-attacks by infantry and tanks ... and (were) overrun. The Lake Superior Regiment's 'C' Company suffered a like fate.[68]

They suffered the same fate as had befallen 78 BID at Aquino (Event 1) when the Shermans quit the field, as they now did in the Hochwald after digging themselves out. The South Albertas had a good reputation for infantry support, learned when they had been equipped with Churchills. They tried to help the infantry but found movement difficult in the mud.

By 1 March 1945 Simonds and Vokes had produced nothing but chaos:

> The combination of mud, rain, deteriorating communications, unexpectedly ferocious enemy fire – and the unrealistic decision-making from high command – had by now produced chaos. The tactical deployment of Canadian tanks in such conditions was a travesty. In postwar analysis, both Canadian and German commanders were sharply critical... Lt Col Rowan Coleman, commander of the Lincoln & Welland Regiment, and fresh from the 'straightforward' battlefields of Africa and Italy, was 'halfway up the wall'... General Plocher, the GOC

65 Vokes, *My Story*, p. 189.
66 Information from Gerry Chester on www.ww2talk.com
67 Vokes, *My Story*.
68 Stacey, *The Victory*, p. 512.

> of 6th Parachute Division, … wonders why – instead of the costly and slow forest slogging – the Canadians didn't concentrate all of their tanks and artillery at either end of the Hochwald and simply go round it.[69]

Event 4 of 4

Lashmer Whistler (known as Bolo) was a protégé of Montgomery, and made his name in command of 131 BIB in 7 BAD. He had almost everything – intelligence, modesty, instinctive leadership, height, a loving wife, high standards, physical and exceptional moral courage, straightforwardness, and sympathy for his men, but he was a great worrier, no trainer of troops, and had an abiding belief in the ability of Montgomery, who wrote this in May 1951:

> I write to congratulate you on your promotion to Lt-General. … As you know, I have always been very interested in your career since we first met, and I have taken you along with me on the upward path. You have always paid a good dividend and have never failed to carry out very well any jobs given to you. That is greatly to your credit.[70]

The admiration was mutual. Whistler wrote the following, presumably without irony, in September 1944 at the time of Operation *Market Garden*:

> This Army under Monty and Dempsey is a pretty remarkable show. There is no doubt about it. Their plans and conceptions are quite staggering.[71]

Satisfaction with the senior leadership of 21AG arose from shared experience of the chaos of 1940 in France, compared with which every subsequent laboured and costly operation with slow progress looked like an improvement and the best available. Returning to Britain on 1 January 1944, Whistler wrote in his diary:

> A bit nervous of the great offensive but do not wish to miss it – wish I could go with this outfit (7 BAD) but have been too long with it. Am not fit for an Armoured Division and do not want a Bum Inf Div.[72]

Whistler had never commanded a division when Montgomery announced publicly in January 1944 that he was the best and most experienced brigadier in the British Army and would get 160 BIB in 53 BID until a division became available for him. Erskine, OC 7 BAD, told Whistler his brigade had been the making of 7 BAD, and no one can disagree. Whistler got command of 3 BID on 20 June 1944 to replace the wounded Tom Rennie.

II Canadian Corps that was stopped in front of the Schlieffen Line in Event 3, and XXX British Corps that broke through it in Event 4, comprised almost identical troops, operating in almost identical conditions, at the same time, against almost identical opponents, but with two very different types of armour support in terms of equipment and operating methodology. The two corps produced different results, which points to type of armour support as having been the deciding factor.

69 Whitaker, *Rhineland*, p. 227-229.
70 Smyth, *Bolo Whistler*, diary entry for 20/9/44.
71 Ibid.
72 Ibid.

The two events occurred on 1 and 2 March 1945 in the same 1 Canadian Army commanded by Harry Crerar. Both the corps commanders were 'Montgomery men': Guy Simonds, commanding II Canadian Corps, was his favourite Canadian and at the peak of his powers, while his ailing protégé, Brian Horrocks, was once described as stupid but whose surplus of personality and earnestness disarmed criticism of his performance in *Market Garden* and *Veritable*.[73] Horrocks commanded XXX Corps 'in a battle he recollected with loathing'.[74] The advantage in quality of corps commander therefore went to the Canadians.

Both events took place in the same sodden geography 3 to 6 miles apart. The approach to the Hochwald at 34 m above sea level was still in places as low as at Winnekendonk, 21 m, so the Canadians had a small advantage.

The German defenders in both locations were under command of Schlemm's I Fallschirm-Armee. Von Lüttwitz's XLVII Panzer Korps, comprising 116 Pz Div & FJR7 from 2FJD, faced Simonds, while Meindl's II Fallschirmjägerkorps, comprising 8FJD, 7FJD and remnants of 15 PGD & 84 ID, opposed 3 BID and 53 BID. Elements of FJR7 faced both corps. The 116 Panzer Division facing the Canadians, called the Windhund, commanded three para units; 12 Para Recce Battalion under Maj Hans Jungwirth, who were II Para Corps troops – subsequently on 15 March re-designated FJR32[75] within 8 FJD; FJR 24 under Lt-Col Friederich Hübner, and the Para Assault Battalion under Capt Eduard Hübner. All came from 8 FJD, and both Capt Hübner and Maj Jungwirth were holders of the Knight's Cross. The Windhund's OC, Heinz Günther Guderian explained that the Paras latterly did most of the fighting; 'They fought within the framework of the Division and at times replaced its depleted Panzer-Grenadier units almost completely.'[76] The German defenders were therefore almost identical.

StuG IIIs of 12 Para Assault Gun Brigade supported 8 FJD, with assistance from Mk IV tank destroyers of 15 Panzer Grenadier Division. In the Hochwald, 116 Panzer Division provided 'the few tanks and (Mk IV) tank destroyers'.[77] A heavy concentration of German artillery covered the entire front without interference from 2 TAF. Some of the guns were on the East bank of the Rhine, and just about receiving their ammunition through the factory doors. German strength was evenly distributed between British and Canadian opposition, so *Blockbuster* and *Heather* faced equal opposition.

The German Army was confident, experienced and integrated, and von Rundstedt informed Hitler on 25 February that there was no immediate danger of an Allied breakthrough between the Rhine and the Maas. Stacey thought 8FJD comprised mostly green troops,[78] but provided no evidence and the masterly defence of Kervenheim does not support that judgment.

The attacking British and Canadian infantry battalions were similarly trained and equipped, with the same artillery and air support. The Canadian all-volunteer force had, in general, better motivation and morale, battledress of superior material and cut, and twice as much pay. A British private received 14s/week, increasing to 21s after six months service, the equivalent of £4.10s/month. A Canadian got twice the British rate – $1.30/day, which was $39 or £8.15s per month. The American received three times the British rate – $50 or £12.10s per month. (£1 = 20s. = Can$4.45 = US$4).

73 Buckley, *Monty's Men*.
74 Robert Boscawen in a phone conversation about his late neighbour in December 2003.
75 Michael Holm's website.
76 Guderian, *From Normandy*.
77 Ibid.
78 Stacey, *The Victory*, p. 495.

3 BID was a regular division of volunteers, although its decimated ranks by then contained numbers of TA, wartime volunteers, Canloans, conscripts and unhappy men transferred from broken up divisions. Reinforcements were a major headache for both Canadians and British, with the Canadians perhaps more degraded and worn out through having had to fight in tougher conditions for longer than the British, although they took perverse pride in reliably doing the dirty work. Canadian and British battalions enjoyed social and historical connections. The Lincoln & Welland Regiment from the Niagara Peninsula, where Lincolnshire place names proliferate, sent one battalion abroad. It had close links with the Lincolnshire Regiment with four battalions at the front. At the end of May 1945, 2 Lincolns concentrated at Oudenarde in Belgium in preparation for shipping to Baltimore to be equipped by the Americans to invade Japan. Douglas Wilson and 11 officers visited the Lincoln & Welland Regiment at Nijverdal to be 'entertained to a magnificent dinner', proving that in alcohol consumption also, Canadian & British units were indistinguishable. Both armoured battalions, 3 SG and the SAR, were experienced and infantry-minded with solid reputations for providing effective infantry support, although the advantage must go to the British as 3 SG, unlike the SAR, had never been trained to act independently. Corps staff work, which Monash rated as more important than quality of equipment or soldiery, was on a par in both Allied armies in 1945. Army staff work was identical as it was a Canadian army battle. The quality of Canadian regimental officers was outstanding, but numbers of the impressive Canloans in British service generalised that factor also.

The only significant difference lay in the type of tanks and the method of fighting them. XXX Corps maintained the distinction between Infantry and Cruiser tanks, with 6 GTB's Churchills making the breakthrough, and GAD's Shermans supposedly exploiting it. As we have seen, that did not work. Montgomery, and his protégé Simonds and everyone else in 21 AG who did not want to be sacked, believed the Sherman could perform both rôles, and so avoid the traditional hiatus between break through and breakout. Traditionally the cruiser moved up for exploitation once the German front was broken. Denis Whitaker suggested that Simonds's orders were known to be impossible to carry out.

> The next plan for an assault down the Hochwald Gap was even more stunning in its obliviousness to the reality of the situation. Notwithstanding the disastrous outcome of the day's attack by the Algonquins and the South Alberta Regiment, who had been driven back even before they reached the mouth of the gap, and by the Argylls and the Lincs, who had been pinned down, the Canadian Grenadier Guards were coolly directed to lay on a fresh assault… (aimed) at Xanten. It might as well have been the moon. As even securing the gap seemed a near-impossible challenge at this point, the prospect of achieving this and then advancing another eight miles to the Rhine at Xanten seemed totally unrealistic.[79]

Vokes ordered the Canadian Grenadier Guards to use the railway embankment, and when they refused, is said to have threatened to put the entire regiment under arrest.

There was a breakdown of discipline observed by Maj Leonard Parry of the A&SH of Canada who witnessed a troop of tanks abandoned by the Grenadier Guards of Canada on 28 February 1945 after shots were fired at them They had appeared over the hill but then appeared to vanish. He could hear their engines running so ran up to one and yelled his head off into the telephone at the back. There was no answer so he climbed onto the tank and, finding the hatch open, went inside. 'It was bare and empty, not a soul on board. I know it was one of the Guards' tanks'.[80]

79 Whitaker, *Rhineland*, p. 226-7.
80 Robert Fraser. *Black Yesterdays. The Argylls' War* (Hamilton: A&SH, 1996), p. 384.

The bankruptcy of Royal Armoured Corps theory and groupthink had been brutally exposed, and only the moral courage of Ned Amy, CO of the Canadian GG, prevented another massacre. Vokes, who had commanded the breaking of the Hitler Line with NIH's Churchills and the Dawnay Doctrine, lacked the moral courage to insist on emulating the successful method in 4 CAD. He cooled off and later sent a congratulatory letter to the Canadian GGs for their 'terrific efforts' in attempting to surmount 'this difficult obstacle'. Vokes is silent about all of this in his ghosted autobiography.

There were two flaws in RAC theory and practice; Cruiser tanks lacked the armour to break through a Pakfront, and their inferior cross-country capability in poor conditions restricted movement. In both rôles the Churchill was better. The Sherman V operated by 4 CAD and the Cromwells of 11 BAD had 3 inch frontal armour, while 6 GTB operated a mix of Churchill Mk IV, V and VI with 4 inch frontal armour, and a few Mk VII with 6 inch. In some respects Churchill and Sherman were similar; both had a crew of five, the same 13-14psi ground pressure, and a 75 mm gun of different manufacture but firing the same US ammunition. Cromwell's ground pressure was worse at 14.9psi. Both formations had tanks with high velocity anti-tank guns; some Churchill Mk IVs had a 6pdr firing sabot, some of the Shermans were the Mk V Firefly with the 17pdr, and some of the Cromwells were the Challenger version with the 17pdr. All were backed up with poorly armoured but powerfully gunned 17pdr M10/Achilles and Archer tank destroyers.

The differences between Churchill and Sherman were, however, significant and reflected their origins as Infantry and Cruiser tanks. In speed and acceleration the Sherman was greatly superior to the Churchill with a 50% superiority in power-to-weight ratio; Sherman V: 13 hp/ton; Churchill VII: 8.6 hp/ton.[81] In cross-country capability the Churchill was superior with both the bottom plate and front sprockets higher off the ground; ground clearance, vertical obstacle that could be mounted, and width of trench crossed for the Churchill was 0.5 m, 1.13 m, and 2.8 m, and for the Sherman, 0.4 m, 0.61 m, and 2.3 m.[82] But given the task of penetrating a Pakfront defended by Paratroops in the Hochwald, thickness of frontal armour assumed overwhelming tactical importance, and in this the Sherman and Cromwell were both unbattleworthy, with the Churchill marginal at best.

The Sherman V and Cromwell were vulnerable to every anti-tank weapon deployed in the Hochwald, and to fully three quarters of all such weapons in the German park, including the ubiquitous 50 mm Pak 38 (see the following tables). All Churchills were immune to the Pak 38 provided it fired normal and not the tungsten-cored APCR ammunition, which had ceased to be available, but only the Mk VII was immune to the even older dual purpose 88 mm L56 Flak 18, 36 and 37 and to the 75 mm Pak 40. Churchill Mk VIIs, however, still succumbed to the 88 mm L71 in Pak or DP Flak form, and to the long 75 mm gun fitted to Panthers, Jagdpanthers and JagdPanzer IVs, as well as the 88 mm and 128 mm fitted to Jagdpanthers, Tigers, Royal Tigers, and JagdTigers. The hand-held hollow-charge Panzerfaust and Panzerschreck could also destroy all Allied tanks.

Tiger I with frontal armour thickness of 120 mm was immune to the Sherman's 75 mm gun at 500 m but vulnerable to the Churchill's 6pdr firing APDS.

81 www.onwar.com.
82 Ibid.

NIH Churchill crews in Italy were unhappy crewing Shermans. They treasured the remaining Churchill Mk IIIs for their 6pdrs installed in a welded turret, and rejected the Mk VII because of its 75 mm gun and despite its 6 inch frontal armour. Gerry Chester wrote:

> After the slaughter in the Hitler Line, those crewing Shermans were not at all happy. Although some Churchill Mk IIIs were put out of action in the Hitler Line by hits on bogeys, none was penetrated. The only concern we had when crewing Churchill Mk IVs was coming up against a Panzer IV whose gun could penetrate the cast turrets but not the hulls – as happened to *Ballyrashane*. That is the reason we kept Mark IIIs in action until war's end. [Ballyrashane was the mount of Maj Gordon Russell, in which Gerry Chester crewed. It was knocked out 10 m from a Panzerturm. Churchill Mks I, II and IV had a cast turret].[83] Perhaps the most stupid decision was to replace 6 pdr guns with 75 mm ones on Marks that saw service in NWE. The delivery of Mark VIIs to units in Italy to replace Mark IIIs and IVs quickly came to an end. For some inexplicable reason, the lessons learned by the two Churchill Tank Brigades that fought in the Mediterranean Theatre were ignored by the powers that be in the UK, the foolishness of welding track plates on to turrets being one of them. When two tanks are within killing rage of each other the advantage lay with the one which could both lay on the opponent and get off shots the faster – hence the reason why the Churchill invariably got the better of both the Tiger and Panther. Following the order/suggestion to weld track plates on to Churchills, while OK to do so on hulls, tests showed when affixed to turrets the speed of traverse was slowed significantly. A joint report from both Brigade Commanders advised London of the results, coupled with the statement that their Churchill units had been forbidden to weld anything on to turret walls.[84]

Armour thickness at 30° penetrated at 500 yards by Churchill Mk IV & Sherman I; source: 25 BTB Technical Intelligence Summary No. 1

Nationality	Gun	Shell	Armour thickness penetrated	
British	6pdr Mk II & III	HVAP	82 mm	3.2 inch
	6pdr Mk III	APDS	118 mm	4.6 inch
	6pdr Mk IV	APDS	127 mm	5.0 inch
US	75 mm Gun M2	HVAP	60 mm	2.4 inch
	75 mm Gun M3	HVAP	66 mm	2.6 inch

83 E-mail from Gerry Chester on 27 October 2013.

84 Gerry Chester's post in www.ww2talk.

The Origin of the Infantry Tank and the Fallacy of the *Guerre de Course*

Sir Hugh Jamieson Elles by Bassano Ltd, undated. Lt Gen Hugh Elles specified the Matilda II tank with armour thick enough to resist all anti-tank guns, which saved the BEF and later defeated Mussolini in Libya. Unfortunately he was retired in 1938.(Image x84133 © National Portrait Gallery, London)

Sir JFC Fuller by Elliott & Fry, 1945. He was the original Apostle of Mobility. (Image x92542 © National Portrait Gallery, London)

Hugh Montague Trenchard, 1st Viscount Trenchard by Walter Stoneman, undated. Trenchard was the guru of the area bombing cult. (Image x31071 © National Portrait Gallery, London)

Sir Basil Henry Liddell Hart by Howard Coster, 1939. Liddell Hart was a facilitator of the cults of the mobile arms of bombing aircraft and cruiser tanks. (Image x25407 © National Portrait Gallery, London)

Sir Percy Cleghorn Stanley Hobart by Bassano Ltd, undated. Hobart was the guru of the mobile cruiser tank cult during the Second World War. (Image x184128 © National Portrait Gallery, London)

The attributes of a cult are: ability to influence and control events; enjoyment of the zealous commitment of influential people; promotion of a belief system, ideology and practice regarded as The Truth; discouragment of questioning, doubt and dissent; being élitist, and claiming a special and exalted status for itself, its leaders and members; being on a mission to save humanity; having a polarized us-versus-them mentality; its leader being unaccountable to any authorities; and holding that their exalted ends justify any means deemed necessary. Fuller, Trenchard, Liddell Hart and Hobart were cult leaders exhibiting some or all of these attributes.The first Infantry Tank was specified by Lt-Gen Hugh Elles, Master General of the Ordnance. Elles commanded the Tank Corps in 1918. Post war he commanded Bovington, became Inspector of the Tank Corps, and commanded 9 BIB before retiring. Elles had held discussions with the CIGS, Gen Sir Archibald Montgomery-Massingberd, but his identity is not revealed in either David Fletcher's or JP Harris's books. Montgomery-Massingberd had been Deputy Commander of Rawlinson's Fourth Army, and therefore involved with Monash's all-arms operational methodology. As CIGS he was the force driving the creation of the Mobile Division, but was dismissed and ridiculed by the Apostles as a Col Blimp. Montgomery-Massingberd and Elles were concerned about the continual denigration by the fashionable Apostles of the successful all-arms operational methodology. The following was typical of the Apostolic Fuller:

> Up to the present the theory of the tactical employment of tanks has been based on trying to harmonise their powers with existing methods of fighting, that is, with infantry and artillery tactics. In fact, the tank idea, which carries with it a revolution in the methods of waging war, has been grafted on to a system it is destined to destroy, in place of being given free scope

> to develop on its own lines... that is, the possibility of moving rapidly in all directions with comparative immunity to *small-arm fire* [this author's emphasis]. From this we can deduce the all-important fact that infantry, as at present equipped, will become first a subsidiary and later on a useless arm on all ground over which tanks can move. This fact alone revolutionises our present conception of war, and introduces a new epoch in tactics.[85]

Nevertheless, and despite the controversy, the General Staff in 1933 under Montgomery-Massingberd called for a, 'specialist Infantry tank that would be more suitable than existing lightly armoured tanks for supporting unmechanised infantry assaults'.

Fuller had devised Plan 1919 to begin the assault on the Germans with medium tanks and aircraft attacking German HQs to paralyse their capacity to command and control. How this would be achieved without first penetrating the German defensive lines, which were constructed in depth and width so that they could not be turned, and which were defended by anti-tank guns, was not explained. Next, heavy tanks, infantry and artillery would break through the German defensive lines that had been paralysed by the medium tanks, allowing cavalry, light tanks and truck-mounted infantry to exploit and harry the retreating Germans to prevent them from reforming and counterattacking. Nothing was said of the potential of German anti-tank guns to destroy the light tanks in their unsupported exploitation, nor was it hinted that a breakthrough operation in order to succeed required some form of all-arms operational methodology à la Monash.

The 'Apostles of Mobility' together with commentators as diverse as Hitler and Churchill started from the assumption that originated with Ludendorff, that the German Army had been undefeated in the field, and was on the point of prevailing when Jewish Bolshevik civilians stabbed it in the back. Bernard Baruch, for example, described this prevailing view:

> Sapping of economic strength will, in future wars, be the determining cause of defeat. As Ludendorff has so bitterly complained, his military front remained impregnable long after what he called 'the home front' had crumbled. Destruction of civilian morale defeated Germany.[86]

The Apostles believed that The Hundred Days of relentless victory starting with the Battle of Amiens and ending with the Armistice had been unnecessary. The naval blockade, they said, had made German defeat inevitable and the Allied Army, they implied, could have spent its time sunbathing. This myth, also believed by Montgomery,[87] gave traction to Trenchard's promise that RAF bombing would replicate the effect of the naval blockade by destroying civilian morale and the German will to continue any future war. Conveniently both lives and money would be saved, which made it irresistible.

Fuller's pen added to the death of common sense by claiming that Monash's all-arms operational methodology was not just made redundant by the blockade that had actually ended the war, but was simply another form of old-fashioned attritional 'body-warfare' which could be transformed by those who grasped the opportunity of mobility. Fuller wrote that attrition could be avoided by using mobility to render it inoperative, which meant finding the brains and blowing it out, or sending a tank to destroy the HQ.[88] The conclusion was thus clear to the Apostles of Mobility that a future war would be determined by 'the 'power of aircraft to strike at the civil will, the power of

85 JFC Fuller. *Memoirs of An Unconventional Soldier* (London: Nicholson & Watson, 1936).
86 Bernard Baruch. *American Industry In The War* (New York: Prentice Hall, 1941).
87 Hamilton, *Monty Making of a General*, p. 439.
88 JFC Fuller. *Military History of the Western World* (New York: Funk &Wagnalls, 1954).

mechanised forces to strike at the military will, and the power of motorised guerillas to broadcast dismay and confusion.'[89]

Such was the credo adopted by Winston Churchill as his Second World War strategy, although he added to the list the assistance of the USA that he bought with Britain's remaining wealth and the ending of Imperial Preferential tariffs. Churchill saw no need for infantry and their contemptible generals who had refused to welcome him to their ranks; Kitchener had tried to keep him out of the Sudan, and Haig had refused his request to be promoted brigadier general. An insightful historian wrote of Churchill; 'I believe he would have exchanged all else to have been, simply, General Sir Winston Churchill VC, GCB.'[90] Instead of promoting the army, Churchill placed his faith in a three-pronged offensive against Germany; Trenchard and his Bomber Command would 'destroy the civil will'; massed armoured divisions with 10,000 Cruiser tanks would 'strike at the military will'; and large special forces of motorised commandos, paratroops and SOE would 'set Europe ablaze' and 'broadcast dismay and confusion'. Having seduced with his vision, Fuller then carefully added a caveat that was ignored by the Apostles of Mobility; he began to express doubt that tanks after all could break through a well-organised anti-tank defence, and by extension that bombers could get through a well-organised fighter defence of the type that by this time was being planned by Dowding. Fuller then hedged his bets, arguing that the consequences of a successful anti-tank defence would lead to reliance on Bomber Command's ability to bomb Germany into submission. For he 'was willing to concede that if both sides constructed such defences complete stalemate on land might result…leading to but one end – attack on the civil will.[91] Fuller imagined the civil will being broken by bombing, but could not imagine breaking through a Pakfront with a heavily armoured tank.

Fuller's argument relied on the beguiling fallacy of *guerre de course* that was first exposed as error by A.T. Mahan.[92] *Guerre de course* is commerce raiding or, in German, *Handelskrieg*. The phrase is used here as shorthand for waging war through the 'indirect approach', of beating a superior enemy by tackling his Achilles heel, which was assumed for centuries in Britain's case to have been its merchant fleet. The fallacy reached its full flowering in Liddell Hart's *The Strategy of the Indirect Approach,* or *The British Way of Warfare*. *Guerre de course* first beguiled the Dutch in 1652, followed by the French in 1693 & 1710, into believing that although they could not directly defeat the Royal Navy, they could still indirectly defeat England by sinking its merchant fleet. The RN retaliated by blockading its commerce-raiding enemies, and reduced them to penury and starvation so that, it was said, grass grew in the streets of Amsterdam. The official historians of the RAF argued that Churchill fell for the same promise of a cheap victory through *guerre de course* and thereby inflicted on Britain the same disastrous and bankrupting consequences that always visit a weaker power that cannot, or will not, engage with the enemy's main force.[93] Trenchard's BC promised to win the war by overflying the Wehrmacht to destroy the homes and the morale and the civil will of the workers who produced the armaments and the war supplies. Failure was inevitable.

The same law ensured the failure of the *guerre de course* attempted by the Kriegsmarine's U-Boats. Kapitän Werner Furburger predicted that it would take Britain two years to build the anti-submarine assets required to force the German Type VII submersibles – they were not true submarines – to stay submerged and thereby reduce their effective surfaced speed of 17 knots to

89 JP Harris. Men, Ideas and Tanks (Manchester: University Press, 1995), p. 226, ref J.F.C. Fuller. *Armoured Warfare* London: Eyre & Spottiswoode, 1943.

90 RW Thompson. *The Yankee Marlborough* (London: Allen & Unwin, 1963).

91 Harris, *Men, Ideas*, p. 227.

92 AT Mahan. *The Influence of Sea Power Upon History* (Boston: Little Brown, 1894).

93 C Webster & N Frankland. *Strategic Air Offensive Against Germany, 1939-45* (London: HMSO, 1961). N. Frankland. *History At War* (London: Giles de la Mare, 1998).

3 knots and turn them into sitting ducks for destruction. It was only due to the fragmentation of Churchill's administration that it took more than Furburger's two years. Had Churchill in 1942 ensured that the new B24 Liberators and Lancasters were configured for VLR operation rather than area bombing, the Atlantic air gap would have been closed and the U-boats neutered a year earlier than May 1943, when VLR aircraft, escort carriers, hunter-killer groups and Huff Duff finally massacred them.

The Germans took only three months to massacre BC's daylight operations over the Heligoland Bight and force them to operate ineffectually at night. Dowding's system did the same to the Luftwaffe in the Battle of Britain, although their beam navigation system took a year to master.

It was perhaps no coincidence that the *guerres de course* of U-boats and heavy bombers were roughly equivalent in so many ways; both fleets lost roughly two thirds of their number (783 U-boats out of 1,168 commissioned, and 10,949 heavy bombers out of 16,266 built) and crews (28,000 submariners out of 40,000 and 79,172 aircrew out of 125,000). The weights of the hardware built by both sides were roughly equivalent; 1,170 U-boats weighed roughly 1 million tons, and the 41,00 twin-engined bombers and 47,200 four-engined bombers about 1.2 million tons. The costs of the German submarine campaign and of BC are calculable but so far remain uncalculated, although John Fahey has made an important start with BC that is enough to show how the bombing cult bankrupted Britain.[94]

The application of the *guerre de course* fallacy to the rôle of armour has been termed the 'Liddell Hart paradigm', and defined as a 'distinctive theory of armoured warfare whereby armoured forces would not do battle with the enemy's main forces but instead destroy his command and communication facilities, thus paralysing the fighting components.'[95]

Hugh Elles instinctively rejected the fallacy of *guerre de course* and put in place plans to provide the means of doing battle with the main force of the Wehrmacht. In 1934 he followed General Staff instructions to specify a tank immune to a well-organised anti-tank defence. For this he was vilified by the apostles of mobility as being at once orthodox, confused and unreliable, and 'quite unreceptive of Hobart's concept of tank versus tank combat and deep penetration' and 'no help to Martel or Hobart or to the consolidation of a progressive armoured policy,'[96] in fact a Colonel Blimp. It was this concept that gave Trenchard and Hobart their power and influence as self-proclaimed forward thinkers battling Colonel Blimps. Churchill was so terrified of being called a Col Blimp that he tried to stop Powell and Pressburger making their film 'The Life and Death of Colonel Blimp", and did prevent Laurence Olivier from playing the star role which went to Roger Livesey.[97]

Elles was not part of the cult of mobility, nor of course its Trenchardian offshoot. He was part of a late common sense counter-attack that crucially prevailed also against Trenchard. In 1937 Thomas Inskip became Minister for the Coordination of Defence, and dismissed the Trenchardian view that only bombers were needed to defend Britain in the air. Private enterprise had reached the same conclusion and funded designs by R.J. Mitchell and Sydney Camm for the Spitfire and Hurricane which along with Dowding's air defence system defeated the main German air force. Elles likewise ignored those obsessed with mobility and

---

94 John T Fahey. *Britain 1939-1945: The economic cost of strategic bombing* (University of Sydney, 2004. http://hdl.handle.net/2123/664).

95 Place, *Military Training*, p. 95.

96 Kenneth Macksey. *Armoured Crusader* (London: Hutchinson, 1967), p. 125.

97 http://www.telegraph.co.uk/culture/film/classic-movies/9334436/The-Life-and-Times-of-Colonel-Blimp-why-Churchill-wanted-it-banned.html

> asked Vickers ... to design a tank for close cooperation with the infantry, capable of *withstanding any existing anti-tank weapon* (author's emphasis) and cheap enough to produce in substantial numbers even in peacetime.[98]

A civil war was fought in the British military throughout the Second World War and even beyond the end of the shooting war with Germany when the Centurion tank perpetuated the cruiser tank/ *guerre de course* fallacy. For unlike the Russian and American armies in the Second World War and the British Army of 1918, the Anglo-Canadian Army never defeated the main German Army in the Second World War. A part of the British Army, however, ridiculed as reactionary, remembered how the 'invincible' German army was defeated in the Hundred Days, and wanted to update Monash's all-arms operational methodology so it could be done again. They gave the so-called revolutionary Apostles of Mobility short shrift, and when possible sacked them. Lt Gen Henry Maitland (Jumbo) Wilson, GOC Egypt, sacked the Apostle Percy Hobart in 1940 for training 7 BAD as an unbalanced 'mobile Farce' without infantry and artillery cooperation, and for having 'tactical ideas (that) are based on the invincibility and invulnerability of the tank to the exclusion of the employment of other arms in correct proportion.'[99]

Hobart had implemented the ideas of the Apostles of Mobility when training 7 BAD to operate without infantry, and so institutionalised those ideas within the RAC. His contempt for tank-infantry co-operation in the Second World War was pervasive. Liddell Hart was only a journalist who famously kept changing his mind, and what did he know of real soldiering? But Hobart put his indelible mark on the Army by training the mobile division as a kind of motoring club. He wrote: 'I decided to concentrate on dispersion, flexibility and mobility to try to get the Division and formations well extended, really handy and under quick control.'[100] Jumbo Wilson saw the extent of the damage and sacked Hobart because his 'tactical ideas are based on the invincibility of the tank to the exclusion of other arms.'[101]

The consequences of Hobart's training and belief in the mobile but lightly armoured cruiser tank were revealed in disaster after disaster from France in 1940 to Operation *Goodwood* in 1944. It began on 20 May 1940 when the vaunted 1 BAD under Roger Evans disembarked at Cherbourg. It was 'an event eagerly awaited by Lord Gort',[102] who sent Lt-Col Raymond Briggs, a member of the mobility cult, to order an immediate attack on the Abbeville bridgehead under French command. Evans complained that he was ordered to force a crossing over a defended, unfordable river and afterwards to advance some sixty miles, through four enemy armoured divisions to the help of the British Expeditionary Force.

In discussion with the French, he politely but without avail explained that a BAD was not equipped or trained for assault but only to exploit. The French thereupon ordered the British to make an 'independent exploit' or whatever the British chose to (mis)understand by this bizarre concept. Illusion met reality when McCreery's 2 BAB and Crocker's 3 BAB approached the Somme on 27 May 1940 and set the pattern for the next four years of sending tanks unsupported by infantry against anti-tank guns. On 28 May French tank units under the command of Charles De Gaulle relieved Evans's battered force and took over the responsibility for an assault over the Somme. De Gaulle succeeded with good quality French I-tanks and with infantry support where the British Hobartian methods had failed and managed to make a number of bridgeheads across the Somme, although the Germans contained them.

98 B Liddell Hart. *The Tanks, Vol I* (London: Cassell, 1959), p. 372.
99 John Keegan. *Churchill's Generals* (London: Weidenfeld & Nicolson, 1991).
100 Macksey, *Armoured Crusader*.
101 Norman Shannon. *Esprit de Corps. Canadian Military Then and Now*.
102 Gregory Blaxland. *Destination Dunkirk* (London: Harper Collins, 1973).

It is noteworthy that the Mobility Apostles produced disaster after disaster while those responsible – Hobart, Briggs, McCreery, Crocker, Trenchard, Tedder, Slessor, Harris – continued to be revered, promoted and supported by Churchill who preferred to sack the successful commanders – Dowding, Park and Wavell – and pay homage to illusion.

Liddell Hart described archly how Hobart had trained his tank regiments over the years in a kind of ballroom performance that could be called The Mobility Dance. The following occurred on Salisbury Plain in 1932 when Hobart's 2 RTC took the floor with Tilly's 5 RTC.

> Running on parallel courses they opened fire at 1,500 yards range. The 5th gained an initial advantage, but the 2nd retorted with a clever move – dropping out of sight by a somersault-wheel down a slope to westward, they came back and 'peeped' their guns over the crest, thereby profiting from well-aimed stationary fire. The scales changed again when, as the battle moved on, Tilly cornered a company of the 2nd between two of his own. But Hobart brought a still intact company round on their tail, with a decisive bite – showing that in tank battle the value of the 'last reserve' was likely to be even greater than it had been in the Napoleonic Battle.[103]

The only description of 1 BAD in action in France known to this author was provided by Brig Stewart of 152 BIB in 51 BID. He watched in disbelief as British tanks attempted to run around the Germans, dashing from cover to cover as they had been trained to do with fire and movement, searching for a gap to exploit or a flank to turn in order to gain access to the enemy's nerve centre and put a bullet into its brain.

> The tanks moving hither and thither, jerkily, with sudden rushes, were strangely reminiscent of insects darting across the surface of a pond. War, which had once been a solid thing, had become almost entirely fluid.[104]

Pierre Bosquet's famous words were more descriptive of this dance in front of the Germans than that of the charge of the Light Brigade in front of the Russians; *C'est magnifique, mais ce n'est pas la guerre: c'est de la folie.*

The pheasant has faith in his mobility as he soars and side-slips, looking down on the farmer below plodding through his fields. Throughout the close season of manoeuvres the illusion is maintained for the pheasant, until one autumn day the close season ends and the farmer shoulders his 12-bore. That day arrived for Evans and the RAC in May 1940 when German guns destroyed 65 tanks, and a further 55 suffered mechanical breakdown and capture. 1 BAD ceased in a moment to exist while thousands of Leicas snapped knocked-out British tanks and dejected prisoners who had no idea what had hit them.

Montgomery, always an Apostle but without experience of tanks, asked the Germans to dance The Mobility at Wattrelos on 24 May 1940 in the Gort Line in order, it was said by those involved, to 'raise morale'. He instructed 8 BIB in 3 BID to advance 3,000 yards without a barrage and in daylight to seize prisoners and afterwards to withdraw.

> Battalions were ordered to lead with their carriers, as if they were tanks; evidently the success of these vehicles in counter-penetration and withdrawal operations had resulted in an exaggerated idea of their capabilities. … They were excellent for providing mobile fire support and

103 Hart, *The Tanks Vol I.*
104 Eric Linklater. *The Highland Division* (London: HMSO, 1942).

> covering a withdrawal and the Germans had considerable respect for them, but to use them in a head-on assault was nonsense, and illustrates how much ignorance there was at the time concerning the characteristics of carriers, and their misuse as tanks… Casualties in 1 Suffolks were three officers killed, three wounded, two warrant officer platoon commanders killed and 67 soldiers killed and wounded. Four carriers were lost. There was a very strong feeling, which lasts to this day, about the entirely unnecessary nature of the affair. The Divisional commander (Montgomery) evidently decided that it was time to raise the morale of his troops by giving them a taste of the offensive, the chance to go forward rather than back…
>
> It has since been described variously as a 'counter-attack', 'reconnaissance in force', or 'raid', but its sole aim was to raise morale: prisoners and information could have been obtained more easily by patrol action… How Montgomery, invariably so thorough and sound in the planning and preparation, could have countenanced let alone approved this operation, is difficult, with hindsight, to understand.[105]

McNish implied falsely that the outcome would have been different had cruiser tanks been employed. Had they been Matilda IIs, however, which were frontally immune to all common anti-tank weapons, and been under infantry command, the attack would almost certainly have succeeded even though it was essentially a pointless vanity project.

The Official History states; 'It is not clear that any good purpose was served by this somewhat expensive sortie'.[106] The War Diary of 3 BID does not mention the event. Montgomery's biographer obfuscated the purpose of the operation and failed to mention the deaths of over 20 men, using the lucky capture of Kinzel's briefcase with the German ORB and plans as post hoc justification for destroying the effectiveness of a third of the command.

> Bernard had laid down a policy of offensive patrolling on his front which, although it resulted in a nasty encounter on 24 May when nine officers and almost a hundred men in the 8th Infantry Brigade were wounded (a 'raid' severely criticised in the British Official History), paid off suddenly in the most spectacular way.[107]

Another apologist for Montgomery opined that his rationale remains a mystery, but,

> one cannot be overly critical of Montgomery's decision to commit his troops to the ill-fated offensive.[108]

He added that the action reflected the classic opinion of Sun Tzu that a maximum gain justifies expenditure of a minimum amount of risk, and absolved Montgomery of blame because 'his intentions were highly commendable'.

The real reason for Wattrelos, however, will most likely be found in Montgomery's ignorance of armour – his recce commander, Clifton, had thrown away the 15/19 Hussars only a week earlier – and his relationship with the armour cult's guru, Liddell Hart.

105 McNish, *Iron Division*, p. 83.

106 LF Ellis. *The War In France And Flanders 1939-1940* (London: HMSO, 1953).

107 Hamilton, *Monty: General*, p.375.

108 Robert Hodgins-Vermaas. *A Bit of Binge: Montgomery's Command of the 3rd Division* (University of Calgary: http://hdl.handle.net/1880/26650, 1997).

> Bernard saw in Liddell Hart the sort of thinking, critical officer he had missed at Camberley, and commanding the ear of generals. Thus began their uneasy association, with its tones of subdued envy: both ambitious, vain and opinionated men.[109]

Wattrelos makes sense only in terms of two distinctive theories held in those days. The first, expounded by Liddell Hart and his friend Fuller, was that armoured forces should not do battle with the enemy's main force but instead destroy his command and communication facilities and thus paralyse the fighting components. The second was preached particularly by Alan Brooke and Vyvyan Pope, respectively Montgomery's corps commander and Tank Adviser, holding that tanks must be used *en masse* and not frittered away in small numbers or 'penny packets'. This became the catch-all excuse for the failures in France and North Africa, until Operation *Crusader* which failed to use the overwhelming British tank predominance to crush Rommel. Montgomery threw the armoured bren-gun carriers, which to him were indistinguishable from tanks, at an enemy infantry division in the expectation of causing a breakdown in its command and control nerve centre through the shock use of massed armour, and thus buy time and raise morale in 3 BID. No doubt the ambitious Montgomery also foresaw that its success would impress Liddell Hart and result in favourable press comment to further Montgomery's career.

No attempt was made by the British to study the tank disaster on the Somme, or even the success at Arras, and it was not only because the evidence was left in German hands and the survivors traumatized. Rather, the illusion of mobility was institutionalised and its practitioners placed beyond questioning by those said to be uninitiated in its art. The cult leaders pointed at the success of the German *schnelltruppen* and said the British needed more practice to become proficient. Alan Brooke had commanded 1 BAD in 1937 and bore responsibility for its disastrous performance. Learning nothing, he supported the raising of new armoured divisions rather than closing them down. He agreed with Martel and Pope in the autumn of 1940 to

> retain the two types of armoured forces, i.e. the armoured division for the more mobile work and the Army Tank Brigades for the heavier fighting in cooperation with the infantry.[110]

The rôle of the armoured division was never examined, and its failure ascribed to poor implementation. Instead of being abolished as its performance warranted, Martel was appointed to expand their number from two to ten, although five were subsequently disbanded before 1945. The following BADs were raised; 1, 2, 6, 7, 8, 9, 10, 11, 42 and 79. Disbandment was the fate of 2 BAD in 1941, 8 BAD in 1942, 9 BAD in 1944, 10 BAD in 1944 and 42 BAD in 1943. Their composition was altered to increase the proportion of infantry following changes in German practice.

The disbandment of the armoured divisions was foreseen by Hobart, no less, in the 1920s when he envisaged that the day of universal mechanisation would cause the RAC to wither away. But Hobart reacted furiously in 1936 when the new CIGS, Deverell, received a draft report from Maj Gen Squires, who was Hobart's boss and Director of Staff Duties, suggesting that the RAC could now be disbanded altogether because, opined Squires:

> the increased power of anti-tank weapons was all the time whittling away the power of tank formations; the chances of the Tank Brigade prosecuting its rôle successfully are getting more remote with the passage of time.[111]

---

109 Hamilton, *Monty: General*, p. 166.
110 Gifford LeQ Martel. *Our Armoured Forces* (London: Faber, 1945).
111 Kenneth Macksey. *The Tank Pioneers* (London: Jane's, 1981), p. 139.

Wavell upheld Hobart's dismissal by Jumbo Wilson, but Hobart was one of Churchill's friends and Montgomery's brother-in-law, as well as a protégé of Liddell Hart, and was re-employed at Churchill's insistence. This was even though Hobart circulated a paper showing he was incorrigible and of doubtful mental balance:

> His aim was to create wholly armoured Battle Formations which were aggressive 'and not tied to or clogged by infantry formations'. He wanted ten armoured divisions and 10,000 tanks, a huge training programme under a GOC Armoured Army [himself] who would have the full support of the Army Council and be a member of it himself.[112]

Churchill, even, found this excessive, probably knowing through Enigma that the ORB of each of the twenty German armoured divisions assembled for the invasion of Russia numbered fewer than 200 tanks for a grand total of 4,000 which, as part of all-arms, would have destroyed Hobart's armoured divisions of cruiser tanks even faster than they despatched the fast but lightly armoured Russian BT26s that had so impressed Martel when watching the Russian manoeuvres. Nevertheless Churchill ordered Dill, the CIGS, to give Hobart an armoured division to raise and train. This was 11 BAD, whose cruiser tanks we have seen bogged down in front of the Schlieffen Stellung on 2 March 1945. This, however, was not the end of Hobart's fateful influence. He became GOC 79 (Experimental) Armoured Division Royal Engineers. Here he applied his considerable dynamism to the circumscribed task of updating and expanding work done in 1918-1919 when a specialist 'RE Tank' was designed by Martel for laying bridges, clearing mines and wire and burying cables.[113] Hobart appropriated the latest Churchill tanks to update specialist armour for the assault on Europe. This was the only all-armoured division in the world, later containing 7,000 armoured vehicles, including floating tanks, flame throwers, APCs and the Canal Defence Light. Hobart, however, did not invent the Kangaroo APC or anything else, but simply managed the fleet and used his position to interfere in every operation. Montgomery appointed Hobart his Specialised Armour Adviser with Maj Gen George Richards as his Armour Adviser in 21 AG, a job Martel desperately wanted and for which he was better qualified. Nothing concerning the advice given by Hobart and Richards to Montgomery was put in writing, and Hobart is not mentioned in Montgomery's memoirs.

Churchill, Brooke and Montgomery failed to implement all-arms in the British forces, although paying it lip-service and holding to convenient myths to justify the status quo. All-arms to them meant having all of the arms showing up on the day and not that all of the arms should be integrated under unified command that trained together and developed appropriately effective equipment. The battle-lines of force fragmentation that destroyed the effectiveness of the British armed forces were drawn up in 1929 after the armoured force trials of 1927-28, when those surrounding the leaders of the armour and air cults insisted on the truth of their wrong-headed nostrum of all-tank or all-air rather than all-arms formations. Liddell Hart in the RUSI Journal stated against the evidence that an all-tank force could avoid the obstacles, such as anti-tank guns, without infantry co-operation, because he had hung his hat on the exclusion of 'old-fashioned' infantry.[114]

This hardening stance against reality adopted by the Apostles was in frustrated reaction to Montgomery Massingberd's decision to close down the Armoured Force. He did this to protect all-arms, as he explained in an unpublished memoir:

112 Martel, *Our Armoured Forces*.

113 Gifford LeQ Martel. *In the Wake of the Tank* (London: Sifton Praed, 1931), p. 123.

114 Harris, *Men, Ideas*, p. 220.

> After watching it (the Armoured Force) at training ... against... the other arms I came to the conclusion that, although invaluable for experimental purposes, it was definitely affecting adversely the Cavalry and the Infantry. What should have been done was to gradually mechanise the Cavalry Division and Infantry Division and not to introduce an entirely new formation based on the medium Tank. Nor was it sound to pit the new formation, with its modern armament, against the older formations, in order to prove its superiority. What was wanted was to use the newest weapons to improve the mobility and firepower of the old formations... What I wanted in brief was evolution and not revolution.[115]

He was not to get it. Based on his experience of directing the experimental mobile force, Maj Gen John Burnett-Stuart, GOC 3 BID, had in 1927 recommended creating an armoured force supported by the other arms rather than one integrated under infantry command. Burnett-Stuart had been on Haig's staff during the Hundred Days and seen Monash operate at first hand so should have known better, but military politics and cult adherence proved too strong for him.

It was to be another sixteen years in 1943 before all-arms operational methodology was re-introduced by Lt Gen William Slim in command of the XIV Army in Burma, and despite his never having seen Monash in action. Slim's success was possible only because the Apostles held no sway in Burma, and Churchill and Brooke had no detailed interest in it. Indeed, Churchill despised Indian Army officers and expected nothing of interest from the 'Forgotten Army'. The RAF, however, saw the risk to themselves from increasing publicity about the success of all-arms and their own contribution to it in the shape of the highly effective Vultee Vengeance dive bomber. They had the power to intervene and, almost certainly due to an edict from Trenchard, withdrew the Vengeance and dissembled about the reason.

Cost of Tanks[116]

Year	Type	Weight (tons)	Cost (£)
1937	Inf Mk I Matilda I	11	6,000
1937	Cruiser Mk I	13	12,710
1938	Matilda II	25¾	18,000
1938	Cruiser Mk II	14	12,950
1938	Cruiser MK III	14¼	12,000
1939	Cruiser MK IV	14¾	13,800
1939	Covenanter	15¾	12,000
1939	Crusader	17½	13,700
1939	Valentine	15½	14,900
1940	Churchill	38½	11,150
1942	Cromwell	28	10,000

NB the relative cheapness of the Churchill, made by Vauxhall Motors at Luton. This suggests the army could have been equipped with Churchills only at a considerable cost saving, which would have been compounded by their greater survivability.

115 LHCMA: GB0099 KCLMA Montgomery-Massingberd Papers.
116 Postan, Hay & Scott. *Design & Development of Weapons* (London: HMSO, 1964), p. 360.

The first I-Tank was the Mk I, a tiny, relatively cheap 11 ton Matilda I costing £6,000 and designed by Vickers. It had a crew of two, a radio on the floor that could be used only by the commander when prostrate, a machine gun and an unreliable Ford petrol engine. It appeared in 1936 with 2½ inch frontal armour giving immunity to all known anti-tank guns. It was followed by the outstanding 25¾-ton I-tank Mk II, Matilda II with a crew of four, and again fulfilled Elles's specification of a tank immune to all anti-tank guns. Matilda II was designed by The Royal Arsenal and appeared in 1938 with 3 inch frontal armour. Its diesel engine provided the excellent torque backup required by tanks (and today standard in agricultural tractors and heavy trucks). The French produced the excellent 28 ton B1 Bis, an I-Tank combined with a 75 mm SP gun with 2½ inch frontal armour giving immunity to the common tank and anti-tank guns. In a famous engagement on 16 May 1940 at Stonne by the 3 Div Cuirassée de Réserve, a single B1, *Eure*, commanded by Captain Pierre Billotte, destroyed 13 Panzer III and IVs before retiring. It was hit 140 times without being penetrated. Defeat came through overwhelming German numbers with excellent radio control in cooperation with air strikes and indirect fire by heavy artillery. Its design must later have influenced that of the Churchill. The KV1 with 3 inches of frontal armour appeared in 1940, but that was the end of trying to produce a tank with frontal immunity from all anti-tank guns. They were all in fact obsolete, because in 1937 in Spain the Germans began to use the LW's 88 mm Flak in a Dual Purpose (Flak and Pak) rôle as a long-stop against any tank that got through the Army's screen of anti-tank guns.

The option existed to update Elles's definition of an I-tank and specify it with 6-inch frontal armour to withstand the 88 mm DP gun. It is said, however, that no one appreciated the consequences of this powerful gun, although how British ignorance was possible is unexplained and a subject for research. The Spanish Republican army with its British volunteers must have known. A large amount of secret information came to the British from traitors such as Canaris, who would have supplied the information if asked, but the mechanism whereby this intelligence was requested or distributed depended on those in the know being interested and knowledgeable about what was really killing British soldiers. Macksey maintained that the British withdrew via Dunkirk in ignorance of the damage to the Matilda IIs and other tanks caused by the 88.

> It would be nearly a year before the 88 mm gun became identified as the weapon which could easily overcome even the latest Matilda II tank with its 80 mm armour.[117]

Kesselring of the Luftwaffe was the driving force behind the original use of the 88 in support of the army in Spain and its wide adoption.[118]

The British Army was responsible for AA and was equipped with the excellent 3.7 inch DP gun. This was not used in the anti-tank role in April 1941 when the 88 mm began its career of tank destruction in North Africa for a multitude of reasons. All-arms was alien to British military thinking, and AA troops being trained to defend Naval ports and RAF bases were not keen to join the front line and leave the bases undefended. The Germans, on the contrary, placed their resources wherever they were needed, with the LW and Heer working as one. Kesselring recalled the following; 'I instructed my air force and flak generals to consider the wishes of the Army as my orders.'[119]

Macksey, in his biography of Hobart, failed to mention how the British Army would have reacted had the 88 mm been identified earlier than 1941 in North Africa, and the answer undoubtedly was

---

117 Macksey, *The Tank Pioneers*, p. 162.

118 Kesselring, *The Memoirs*.

119 Ibid.

that they would have changed nothing. Doctrine was that Cruiser tanks avoided anti-tank guns and fought only other tanks or defenceless infantry. German tanks, however, frustratingly retreated through their anti-tank screens when the 88 mms without always being identified knocked out the British tanks. The Germans also had accurate Stukas that the RAF refused to emulate because they were easy for fighters to shoot down and therefore required escorting. Stukas could destroy 3.7 inch guns caught in the open, which was another incentive for keeping the guns away from the front line. The British lacked any aircraft accurate enough to destroy an 88. The British were checkmated. They lacked the all-arms system of thinking and were reduced to placing the 25pdr gun-hows in the frontline as anti-tank guns.

In 1939 Elles's concept of an invulnerable I-tank was further watered down when the army accepted the 15½ ton Valentine which they had rejected in 1938. Valentine had 2½ inch frontal armour, which was less than Matilda's 3 inches, and a three-man crew, which was the maximum weight the running gear of the Vickers' A10 cruiser tank could support. Later marks had a four man crew and a diesel engine but the design was obsolete from its first appearance in 1941 and a caricature of an I-tank as it could not even withstand the 50 mm Pak 38. Russians were sent volumes of them which they used for driver training. Finally in 1939 the worst decision ever to affect the Army was made when The Ministry of Supply took responsibility for tank design away from the Royal Arsenal in order, it was said, 'to co-ordinate the supply of equipment to all three British armed forces' although the RN and RAF were outside it. The MOS was interested in production quantity, and did not take kindly to demands for quality. They refused in 1940 to introduce the 6pdr, continuing to produce the 2pdr into 1942 on the argument, supported by Churchill, that any gun was better than no gun. The MOS contracted with automotive companies to produce tanks, Austin being the worst of a mediocre bunch in which Vauxhall Motors shone.

Matilda II, however, was triumphantly successful on 21 May 1940 in the Arras counterattack in creating panic among the SS Totenkopf. This was only a week after the exploits of Pierre Billotte's B1 bis at Stonne. These two attacks by 'unstoppable' tanks induced caution in Hitler who made the fateful decision to stop his tanks outside Dunkirk.

Matildas were instrumental in the defeat of the Italians in North Africa at the end of 1940. They were used without infantry in the shock rôle, smashing into the enemy position at 3½ mph, and subduing resistance before the infantry arrived to clean out the area. This could only be done because the Matilda had frontal immunity from all Italian anti-tank guns, with the exception of their few dual-purpose 90 mm/L50 gun which could penetrate 4.7 in or 120 mm at 1,000 m. During the entire campaign, 7 RTR lost only one tank, *Gitana*, which had a track shot away and, when all her ammunition had been shot off, was destroyed by her own crew in the face of the enemy. In the attack on 2 January 1941 on Bardia with 6 Australian Division the Matildas fought their way through the Italian positions, shooting up everything while being battered by the enemy's artillery and anti-tank guns.

> No other vehicle then in service, save possibly the Russian KV 1, could have absorbed such punishment.[120]

This extraordinary success of the heavily-armoured and 'slow' Matilda IIs led the GOC 7 BAD, O'Moore Creagh, to approach Col Jerram on the way west from Sidi Barrani about using cruiser tanks as I-tanks, but had quickly abandoned the idea on inspecting the dents and gouges made in the Matilda's armour

120 Perrett, *The Matilda.*

Matilda was designed before the success in Spain in 1937/8 of the 88 mm L56 became known, or Elles would surely have insisted on an upgraded Matilda with 6-inches of frontal armour. Unfortunately, by the time Valentine and Churchill were being designed, Elles had retired and the requirement that an I-tank be able to withstand 'any existing anti-tank weapon' had been forgotten or ignored. The Director of Staff Duties on 1 September 1939 specified the A20, which became the Churchill, with 60 mm/2½ inch armour sufficient only to resist the 2pdr[121] and by implication German 37 mm firing solid shot.The Churchill I-tank appeared in 1942 with an unprecedented 4 inch frontal armour but still vulnerable to the old 88 mm Flak 36, as well as to the 88 mm Flak 71, the common 76.2 mm Pak 36 (r) (using captured Russian barrels), and 75 mm L46 Pak 40 which could penetrate over 5-inches at 500 yards. Even worse, the Churchill was still equipped with the 2pdr anti-tank gun firing a tiny HE shell, when an I-tank should have had a 76 mm dual purpose gun firing HE and AP like Russian tanks.

The German generals were said by Liddell Hart to have liked tanks with speed, a characteristic that varied inversely with weight of armour. Manteuffel told his prison visitor, Liddell Hart, that 'Tanks must be fast. That, I would say, is the most important lesson of the war in regard to tank design. Fire-power, armor protection, speed and cross-country performance are the essentials.'[122] The fact that he immediately contradicted himself showed how desperate the generals were to please Liddell Hart who wanted them to say that their successes owed much to L-H's theories (and their failures to Hitler's interference). The *Schnelltruppen* were the Stormtroopers of 1918 re-equipped with tanks and Stukas, and they owed nothing to Liddell Hart.

The ordinary slow infantry divisions, which marched with horse-drawn supplies and artillery, were supported by the Mk IV with a low velocity 75 mm gun firing high explosive, and with 1¾ inch frontal armour. When the Mk III, which was designed to fight other tanks, was made obsolete by the T34-76, an up-gunned Mk IV took over that task. Infantry support then devolved onto the StuG III, an SP gun on a MkIII chassis with 1¾-inch armour. Tank destruction was the task of cruiser tanks, the Mk III, Mk IV, Mk V Panther and Mk VI Tiger, which was built in small numbers and with a limited field of operation due to its size and weight. The Russians copied the Germans, producing the Joseph Stalin in answer to the Tiger, the T34-85 against the Panther and T34-76 against the Mk III and Mk IV, with various SP guns using the same tank chassis in the German manner.

It was instructive that when testing Churchills captured at Dieppe, the Germans concluded that they had no need of such a concept, and surmised it was a failed and abandoned design that was deliberately sacrificed in the raid. This report, when captured, had the effect of reinforcing British prejudice against the Churchill.

In order to fulfill Elles' design requirements to be invulnerable, and by limiting invulnerability to frontal armour, which Elles never did, the Churchill I-tank required frontal armour in 1939-1941 of 6 inches, in 1942 of 8 inches, in 1944 of 9 inches, and in 1945 of 10-11 inches. The increase reflected the increasing effectiveness of German anti-tank guns per the following table.

121 Fletcher, *Mr Churchill's*, p. 13.
122 Liddell Hart. *The Other Side Of The Hill* (London: Cassell, 1948).

Thickness (inches/mm) of armour plate at 30° penetrated at 500 yd/m by German anti-tank guns, and by British versions for comparison

	1939	1940	1941	1942	1943	1944	1945	Prod'n Volume
German								
37 mm L45 Pak35	2/50	2/50	2/50	2/50				20,000
50 mm L60 Pak38			3.1/80	3.1/80	3.1/80			9,600
88 mm L56 Flak36	5.1/131	5.1/131	5.1/131	5.1/131	5.1/131	5.1/131	5.1/131	17,100
88 mm L71 Flak41				7.2/183	7.2/183	7.2/183	7.2/183	included
88 mm KwK36L56 Tiger I					4.8/122	4.8/122	4.8/122	1,347
76.2 mm Pak36(r)				4.8/120	4.8/120	4.8/120	4.8/120	560
75 mm L46 Pak40				5.3/135	5.3/135	5.3/135	5.3/135	32,000
75 mm KwK/StuK40 L48 StuG III & IV					5.3/135	5.3/135	5.3/135	11,300
75 mm KwK42 L70 Panther & JagdpzIV					5.5/141	5.5/141	5.5/141	8,000
88 mm L71 Pak43					8.3/210	8.3/210	8.3/210	3,500
88 mm L71 Pak43 Hornisse/ Nashorn/ Elefant					8.3/210	8.3/210	8.3/210	563
88 mm KwK43 L71 Tiger II, Jagdpanther						8.3/210	8.3/210	907
128 mm L55 Pak44 & Jagdpanther							10/250	466
British								
2pdr/40 mm	2.1/53	2.1/53	2.1/53					12,000
25pdr/88 mm	2.5/62	2.5/62	2.5/62	2.5/62	2.5/62	2.5/62	2.5/62	21,481
6pdr/57 mm APCR				3.0/75	3.0/75			36,605
6pdr/57 mm APDS						5.1/131	5.1/131	included
3.7 inch/93 mm L50	5/124	5/124	5/124	5/124	5/124	5/124	5/124	6,374
17pdr/76.2 mm APCBC					5.5/140	5.5/140	5.5/140	5,898
17pdr/76.2 mm APDS					8.2/209	8.2/209	8.2/209	included

For comparison, the post-war Chieftain's 120 mm L11 gun when firing L15 APDS could penetrate 14 inch/355 mm at 1,100 yards.[123]

Gun performance varied with type of shell. The Germans upgraded their smaller Paks with tungsten-cored ammunition surrounded by a lighter sleeve, called the Panzergranate 40 (PzGr 40). The British copied with APCR (Armour Piercing Composite Rigid) and the Americans with HVAP (High Velocity AP). The lighter weight of shell increased muzzle velocity and penetrating power by 25% in close quarter engagements of up to 500 yards. However at longer distances of a mile or greater, their lower kinetic energy made them more susceptible to wind resistance, and they lost accuracy. The Germans made 1.4 million PzGr40 rounds for the 37 mm Pak35, and 1.3 million for the 50 mm Pak38, but fewer than 50,000 for the 75 mm Pak40 and 6,000 for the 88 mm Pak43. The bigger guns had satisfactory performance at long range, and re-equipment of the infantry with the effective

123 http://en.wikipedia.org/wiki/Armour-piercing_discarding_sabot

short-range Panzerfaust and Panzerschreck lessened dependence on smaller anti-tank guns. The Germans nevertheless increased long-range performance of the smaller Paks by fitting the Gerlich barrel with a tapered bore to increase muzzle pressure and to reduce the shell's profile and wind resistance. The British copied this with the Littlejohn Adaptor using APSV (AP Super Velocity) ammunition. The next German development was the unsuccessful Pzgr Pak Patrone TS 42 for the 75 mm Pak 40. The successful equivalent British development was APDS (Armour Piercing Discarding Sabot). This did away with the light-weight sleeve, squeezed or not, leaving the tungsten core with high kinetic energy and low wind resistance. By 1942, however, the Germans felt the effect of the Allied blockade on tungsten availability, indispensable for cutting tools, and ended production of tungsten ammunition. This Allied success was due to the RN blockade rather than to RAF bombing.

All-or-nothing armouring (defined below) in inches required to provide the Churchill I-tank with frontal invulnerability to all anti-tank guns, compared with the armour of actual Churchills,[124] Panther, Tigers[125] and Centurion

Tank	Mk	Weight in tons	Turret Front	Hull Front	Turret Side	Slope	Toe	Hull Side	Hull Rear
These numbers refer to those in the diagram			1	2	3	4	5	6	7
			Inches of armour thickness @ degrees from horizontal						
Churchill	I, II	38.5	4.0@90°	4.0@90°	3.5@90°	2.0@40°	3.5@30°	2.3@90°	2.5@90°
Churchill	III	38.5	4.7@90°	4.3@90°	3.7@90°	2.0@40°	3.8@40°	2.3@ 90°	2.5@90°
Churchill	IV – VI	38.5	3.5@90°	4.0@90°	3.0@90°	2.0@40°	3.5@40°	2.3@ 90°	2.5@90°
Churchill	VII, VIII	39.5	6.0@90°	6.0@90°	3.7@90°	2.3@40°	5.5@40°	2.3@ 90°	2.0@90°
Churchill with all-or-nothing frontal invulnerability		45	10@90°	10@90°	10@90°	6.0@40°	6@40°	1.0@90°	1.0@90°
Panther	Ausf G	49	4.3@10°	na	1.8@25°	3.1@55°	3.1@35°	1.8@25°	1.5@87°
Tiger	I	57	4.0@80°	4.0@81°	3.1@90°	2.4@10°	4.0@65°	3.1@90°	3.1@82°
Tiger	II	69	7.1@80°	n.a	3.1@70°	5.9@40°	3.9@40°	3.1@65°	3.1@85°
Centurion	II	43	5.0@57°	1.2@10°	3.0@10°	3.0@10°	3.0@46°	2.0@78°	1.5@83°

na = not applicable

Churchill VII had 50% thicker armour than Tiger I while being 30% lighter, but was vulnerable to the 75 mm and 88 mm of Tiger and Panther. The requirement was for Churchill to have frontal immunity from Tiger II and Panther and all the SP and towed derivatives of the same guns, while still weighing 30% less than Tiger II and being the same weight as Panther. The table shows how that could have been achieved by applying the all-or-nothing principle of armour distribution. The hull front

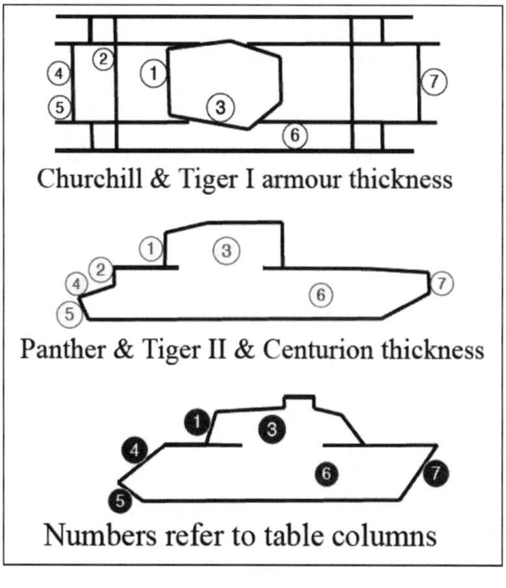

Churchill & Tiger I armour thickness

Panther & Tiger II & Centurion thickness

Numbers refer to table columns

124 Fletcher, *Mr. Churchill's.*
125 www.fprado.com/armorsite/tiger1.htm

would have 10 inches of armour, but the sides and rear only 1 inch. The turret, however, would have 10 inch armour all round to ensure that the turret could be reversed without affecting the tank's invulnerability, so long as it still approached the enemy gun front-on.

The Churchill Mk VII resulted from a Joint Memorandum sent from the Secretary of State for War and the Ministry Of Supply to the Defence Committee on 6 April 1943 offering unspecified reliability improvements and thicker armour to create a 'Heavy Churchill' with a weight increase of one ton. The Defence Committee on 20 April 1943 endorsed additional armour even if speed were halved to 6 mph. Winston Churchill on 14 May 1943 welcomed increased armour and asked for fitment of a High Velocity (HV) 75 mm gun which was not available. His sources were unofficial and included his son, Randolph, who served for a while in the NIH. So it was decided to fit extra armour, equip all turrets with a mounting that could take either the 6pdr or 75 mm gun, replace riveting with welding to save weight, and rectangular hatches with round ones to increase strength and eliminate the possibility of jamming, and fit every hull with mounting points for flame throwers. Speed was reduced from 18 to 13 mph. The result was the Churchill A22F Mk VII of which 200 were initially programmed and 1,600 eventually built. This number included the Mk VIII with the 95 mm howitzer which saw, however, little service.

Ideal armour thickness varied throughout the tank depending on the vulnerability of that part to enemy action. Vulnerability in turn depended on how the tank was used and how well it was defended, which in turn depended on how closely the other arms cooperated in its defence. I-tanks supported, and in turn were supported by, infantry. Tanks moved through lanes swept of anti-tank mines by Sherman Crab flail tanks, and at the speed of infantry providing protection from hand-held Panzerfausts and sniper fire aimed at the tank commander's head. Active air defence prevented enemy aircraft from aiming AP into the top plates and engine covers, and suppressed enemy artillery. Counter-battery fire suppressed heavy enemy plunging artillery fire, while enfilading fire from enemy anti-tank and tank guns was prevented as far as possible by choosing dead ground, or by masking the area with smoke screens, or by attacking along mutually supporting parallel routes, and by using aircraft and artillery to suppress enemy fire. Given efficient all-arms support, the I-tank's vulnerability could be limited to three factors: frontal fire from anti-tank guns; direct hits from the plunging fire of unsuppressed heavy artillery and mortars including ground-fired rockets (Nebelwerfer); and uncleared anti-tank mines. The threat of a direct hit from unsuppressed howitzers and mortars was remote and had to be accepted, and nothing could be done by definition to avoid an uncleared mine. The requirement that was never fulfilled or even specified after Elles's retirement, was for heavy frontal armour to withstand all anti-tank weapons, with minimal top, bottom and side armour to withstand only shrapnel and bullets on the assumption that the infantry would eliminate all threats from the flank and rear.

Had it been understood, the opportunity existed of applying to I-tanks the benefit of naval experience with regard to armouring battleships on the all-or-nothing principle. The Revenge Class launched in 1914-16 was the last to be designed for engagement at close to medium ranges where the objective was to shoot away the topsides containing the command and control systems. Battleships in those days were disabled by gunfire but rarely sunk. Advances in gunnery, however, lengthened the ranges at which battleships engaged, and they tried in consequence to sink each other by landing plunging fire through the decks into the magazines and other vitals in order to blow up the ship. Alternatively torpedoes blew in the sides. Experience showed that ships could survive any damage except these two forms. Logically therefore, armour could be concentrated to protect against these two forms of failure, leaving the rest of the ship unarmoured.

The concept of all-or-nothing armour originated in the USA pre-First World War, and first appeared in Britain in the design of the N3 Class of 48,000 tons battleships in 1918-20. Air blisters and compartments were designed to absorb torpedo hits, while an internal, inclined 14-inch thick armour belt, sloped at 72 degrees to the vertical, covered over the main magazines and control positions, with 13 inch armour protecting the machinery and magazines for the secondary armament. The rest of the ship was unarmoured. The Washington Treaty prohibited the building of N3 Class battleships and the battlecruiser versions, which meant that HMS *Hood* could not be scrapped. HMS *Nelson*, with a displacement of 35,000 tons to meet the Treaty restrictions, became the first ship built in Europe with all-or-nothing amour, and was launched in 1925.

All-or-nothing armour was not seriously considered for tanks, as far as is known, but there were two occasions when it was mooted. In April 1941 a study was ordered into ways of reducing the weight of the new Churchill Mk III which was approaching an unacceptable 40 tons. Pending the result of this study Col Bouchier was asked to approach the War Office and see what sort of reductions in armour they would consider. Mr. Little of Vickers suggested reducing armour thickness around the engine compartment but this was rejected because the General Staff had always insisted on all-round protection which, it was believed, the Germans did not have.[126] Secondly, in a report of September 1943 about how tank battle damage was distributed, the idea was floated by the School of Tank Technology. It concluded that since the sides of the Churchill were vulnerable and received one third of the shots, it would make little difference to the outcome if they were thinner and the weight saved was applied as extra frontal armour.[127]

Such an idea was anathema to the experts in the armoured corps and Ministry of Defence who controlled tank design after it was moved from the Ministry of Supply. Their priority was to increase effectiveness in tank versus tank combat, and this required modest but all-round armour, high speed and a big gun. I-tanks were never excluded from having to deal with AFVs, but knowledge of how an I-tank could be employed and protected so that it never presented its side, rear, top and belly to enemy threats was not part of RAC thinking, and the RAC 'owned' tanks as the RAF 'owned' aircraft.

Therefore the 1,415 crew of HMS *Hood* at the bottom of the Denmark Strait shared not just a death from explosion with the 1,020 crewmen of the tanks incinerated in Operation *Goodwood*, but for the same reason, namely an AP shell penetrating a magazine. The same plume of oily black and yellow smoke from burning TNT was pictured rising from the aft magazine explosion of HMS *Hood* in the Denmark Strait and from a Sherman tank on the *Goodwood* battlefield after its shells exploded.

Cruiser tanks were designed to fight enemy tanks in the absence of supporting infantry. Cruiser tanks could therefore be stalked and shot from any direction by anti-tank weapons either hand-held, towed, or mounted in SP, tanks or aircraft. The Cruiser's defence against this was four-fold; high mobility with good acceleration and top speed to shift quickly from an exposed to a protected position hull-down or out of sight; a powerful gun to keep the enemy AFVs at a distance with machine guns to kill infantry; armour to protect against anti-tank weapons; and AA tanks to provide protection against aircraft. Every Cruiser was therefore a compromise of incompatible requirements, since thicker armour and bigger guns were incompatible with manoeuvrability. Hitler and Krupp toyed with the idea of squaring the circle and designing an impregnable cruiser tank with a large gun – a 1,000-ton Landkreuzer P.1000 Ratte carrying both two 280 mm (11 inch) guns from the Scharnhorst Class battleship and a 128 mm L/55, armoured with 14 inch plate, and powered by two submarine diesel engines producing 17,000 hp. A smaller version that was actually prototyped was the 188 ton Maus with 8 inch frontal armour, 7½ inch side and rear armour, a 128 mm L55 gun and a 1,200 hp engine. As a cheaper alternative to either, Hitler tried blocking the road to Rome by filling the Liri Valley with emplaced Panzerturms, as we have seen. These had the benefit of infinitely thick "hull" armour but with poor turret protection and zero

126 Fletcher, *Mr Churchill's*, p. 60.
127 Op. Cit., p. 115.

Operation *Goodwood*; a Sherman burning from an ammunition explosion and fire caused by penetration of the magazine which has cracked the turret and blown off the cupola and its ring. (© Daglish family)

24 May 1941. Operation *Rheinübung*. The smoke clouds on the horizon were from the explosion on board HMS *Hood* in its battle with *Bismarck* and *Prinz Eugen* caused by penetration of the magazine. (Bundesarchiv Bild 146-1998-035095 by Lagemann)

mobility, which did not matter because the Allies had to come to them if they wanted to reach Rome. Had the Panzerturms been successful in the Liri Valley, there can be no doubt more would have been seen across Europe.

In hindsight the answer in 1944 to these sophisticated German defensive arrangements would have been a large number of mixed divisions equipped with Churchill tanks with 10 to 11 inch frontal armour, negligible side and rear armour and a mix of 6pdr or 17pdr guns firing AP, and 75 mm to 85 mm guns firing HE. The lightly armoured Shermans of the armoured divisions should have been de-turreted and used as APCs. This author has calculated that instead of building and maintaining BC's fleet of Lancasters, the army could have bought 40,000 Churchills with frontal immunity to all anti-tank guns, and been provided with the crews to man them.

The Cruiser tank was a solution looking for a problem found not on battlefields but in the mind of the mobility-minded exercising on their training grounds around Tidworth and Bovington, where RAC umpires and not AP shells made the decisions. The cruiser tank was an oxymoron; a throwback to the days when it was said that being tank-minded separated the quick-thinking and fast-moving from the slow-moving and slow-witted infantry. The sacrificial altar of Mobility was Operation *Goodwood* when 314 Cruisers out of 1,300 were destroyed by AP with 3,474 casualties (the equivalent of an infantry division's worth of rifle companies) including 1,024 deaths.

Americans in the powerful and influential persons of Lesley McNair and George Patton were also captivated by the benefits of mobility. They postponed the introduction of the M26 Pershing by a year from November 1943 in conformity with the British apostles and out of regard for logistical convenience. McNair's memo to Devers dismissed the need for the M26 Pershing to counter Panthers and Tigers on the basis that tank destruction was the task of the anti-tank gun; 'Both British and American battle experience has demonstrated that the antitank gun in suitable number and disposed properly is the master of the tank'. He then rejected the very possibility of armouring a tank to provide frontal immunity to anti-tank weapons with these words; *'Any attempt to armor and gun tanks so as to outmatch antitank guns is foredoomed to failure'* [this author's emphasis].[128]

The cult defence of the cruiser tank persisted unchecked post war with the introduction of the Centurion until a senior engineer assigned to 3 USAD published his wartime experiences.[129] He sensationally revealed that Eisenhower had called a meeting in January 1944 on Tidworth Downs to demonstrate the latest equipment to senior Allied commanders. A film was shown of the M26 Pershing which was about to enter full-scale production in time for D-Day or soon afterwards on receipt of a go-ahead from SHAEF. Patton attended as the highest-ranking armoured commander in NWE, but adamantly dismissed the need for the Pershing in the armoured divisions on the grounds that it was the task of the tank destroyers and not the tanks to fight tanks, and that the M4 Sherman was faster, more agile and better equipped for the mission of exploitation. Maurice Rose and other field commanders contradicted Patton, but were outranked. SHAEF then notified Washington to stick with the M4, although George Marshall kept the project alive with an order for 250 tanks. The meeting at Tidworth and its momentous result was unknown until Cooper's book appeared and obsoleted the work of apologists for the Sherman.

Any analysis of tank effectiveness can become mired in confusion, complication and uncertainty. For instance, sloping a tank's armoured glacis plate in the manner pioneered by Christie increased the thickness of armour plate to be penetrated by shot travelling parallel to the ground, but at the same time increased the weight of armour for a given increase in height which increased front sprocket wear. Sloping, however, had the happy result of inducing the shot to ricochet without causing damage, as was often observed with the Panther. However a poor design could deflect the shot into the driver's compartment with fatal results, as happened with the Churchill Na75. Sloped armour increased vehicle length and even width if the side armour was also sloped as on Russian tanks and the Tiger II, which increased target size. The Churchill always appeared to be more compact than Sherman or Panther.

Further complication arose from user confusion about what was available, which can be laid at Hobart's door. In January 1945, 21 Army Group disposed of 1,011 Churchills against an establishment of 496, representing a margin of over 100%, and with enough in store to equip a Canadian armoured brigade (174 Churchills) or two if Chris Vokes had said he required them for Operation

128 Steven Zaloga. *Armored Thunderbolt* (Mechanicsburg: Stackpole, 2008), p. 123,
129 Belton Cooper. *Death Traps* (Novato: Presidio, 2008).

Blockbuster after his good experience with them in the Hitler Line battle. There would have been no lack of experienced Churchill fitters in the Canadian forces, since they had persevered with them during the 'great re-build' in 1942.

About one quarter of all Churchills, or 245 units, were Mk VIIs, but only a negligible 4% or 18 units had been issued by that date to the gun-tank battalions; 5 were with the Czech Brigade and 13 with 6 Guards Tank Brigade. The other six battalions were said to have had none (which is known to be false), although there were 110 surplus Mk VIIs even after 7 RTR had been newly equipped with Crocodiles. J.G. Smith of 141 Regt RAC provided a reason why Mk VIIs were distributed to the gun-tank units only as replacements:

> At this stage all Mk VIIs on the Continent were sent to us. The reason lay in its armour being about twice as thick [actually 50% thicker] as that of the earlier marks. This was necessary as our work entailed very close support of the infantry and reduction in manoeuvrability due to the trailer.[130]

This was tendentious, as gun-tanks worked in even closer support with the infantry than Crocodiles, while the trailer significantly impeded manoeuvrability only when reversing. What Smith meant was that because crews of Crocodiles were summarily executed by the Germans, they therefore insisted on maximum armour protection which their GOC had the power to provide by appropriating them. Hobart did not advertise the advantages of the Mk VII in order to head off demands that he did not necessarily want to fulfill. Smith's contemporary observation would reflect Hobart's rationalization of his unconscionable handling of Mk VIIs.

Churchill availability, establishment and numbers issued to units in 21AG

	Mk VII gun-tanks	Other gun-tanks	Total gun-tanks	Crocodiles	Total Churchills
Available per 21 AG return on January 21, 1945	127	766	893	118	1,011
Establishment January 1945 8* battalions of gun-tanks 2 battalions of Crocodiles	406		406	90	496
Establishment February 1945 7* battalions of gun-tanks 3 battalions of crocodiles	364		364	135	499
Issued to the battalions on January 21, 1945	18	460	478	92	570

*The 8 battalions were 4 GG, 4 CG, and 3 SG in 6 GTB; 7 RTR and 9 RTR in 31 BATB; 107 RAC, 147 RAC and 153 RAC in 34 BATB. 153 RAC was disbanded in January 1945 leaving 7 battalions. In March 1945, 31 and 34 BATB were given other work leaving only 6 GAB/GTB equipped with Churchills. Each battalion had 50 Churchill gun tanks.

Fewer than 10% of Churchills in 6 GTB were Mk VII, which meant that only one or two were on average available in each squadron of 15 tanks. Compounding this problem of scarcity was an inability or unwillingness to take advantage of the Mk VII's superiority. They arrived in

130 Smith, *In At The Finish.*

the squadrons as replacements for worn-out tanks or those damaged beyond repair.[131] They were therefore used interchangeably with the Mk III and Mk IV, and given no special assignment. All Churchills were allocated to crews in the Guards by 'the luck of the draw',[132] and it is now impossible to know where the Mk VIIs went and how they were used. Some users, such as Charles Farrell and John MacDonald-Buchanan of 3 SG, seem to have been unaware either of the scarcity of Mk VIIs or even of their existence. With the exception of 203 Mk IIIs, IVs and VIs with 6pdrs firing the exceptional armour-piercing sabot, all marks were retrofitted with a 75 mm gun and appliqué side armour and became difficult to distinguish apart from the shape of the escape doors and front hatches in the hull. The cast turret of the Mk VII was like that of the Mk IV and a give-away, condemning the tank in the eyes of the NIH, who appeared always to be more technically savvy than 6 GTB. Frontal armour of non-Mk VIIs was not improved,[133] and this was the vulnerable part of any tank.

Sgt Gerry Chester served with the NIH in 21 ATB and 25 ATB in North Africa and Italy where things were done differently. In his unit every crew-member was given a lecture about Churchill upgrades and their tactical significance.[134] 6 GTB, however, seems to have ignored the upgrade and thus avoided the implications for discipline and morale of favouring certain crews with superior armour. In the name of efficiency and protection with 6 inch frontal armour, the Mk VIIs should have gone to the crew leading the advance. However, for various reasons this appears nowhere to have been the case. The NIH, whose troop leaders did not lead the advance, refused to accept the Mk VII at all because its 75 mm gun had poor AP capability; they insisted on the 6pdr, preferably in the Mk III turret made from rolled steel plate, and not the inferior cast Mk IV turret fitted also to the Mk VII.

Penetration Tests in Italy in 1943 on Armour Sloped at 30° (mm/inch)[135]

Range	US 75 mm		6pdr, APDS shot Mk I	
	M2	M3	Mk III	Mk V
500	60/2.4	66/2.6	118/4.6	127/5.0
1,000	53/2.1	60/2.4	104/4.1	110/4.4
1,500	46/1.8	55/2.1	92/3.6	95/3.7
2,000	38/1.5	50/2.0	87/3.4	83/3.2

In 6 GTB the officers led, but no guards' officer would accept the advantage of extra armour, even had he never heard of 'Red' John Campbell, 2nd Duke of Argyll who was struck three times at Malplaquet in 1709 by spent musket balls without ill effect. This led to murmurings among the troops that their officer was wearing a breastplate under his tunic. Discarding coat and waistcoat:

> The Duke of Argyll went open-breasted amongst the men to encourage them to behave as became Englishmen; you see brothers, said he, I have no concealed armour, I am equally exposed with you.[136]

131 Alexis Melikoff (now Napier) in an e-mail of 29 September 2013.
132 Charles Farrell in conversation.
133 E-mail from David Fletcher, Librarian at Bovington in 2001.
134 http://web.archive.org/web/20090829165501/http://northirishhorse.net/
135 www.northirishhorse.net
136 James Falkner. *Great and Glorious Days* (Staplehurst: Spellmount, 2002), p. 186.

Such ethical and practical considerations have led a historian to conclude that the only way of deriving benefit from the Mk VII would have been fully to equip every tank unit with it in a mixture of 6pdrs and 75 mms, and to train the users in its tactical use:

> Consequently, I suggest, that if the Mk VII had been available in quantities significantly greater than a few percent for most of the NW E campaign, it would have proven itself nearly as unstoppable an infantry tank as its ancestor the Matilda II.[137]

This author agrees with the only proviso that the MK VII should have had 10 to 11 inches of frontal armour to justify its place alongside the unstoppable Matilda given the improvement in PAK penetration.

Mk VII production began at the end of 1944, but Hobart diverted most of them, as we have seen, to equip his Crocodile units. In the event, Crocodiles played a negligible part in Operation *Heather*, and the shocking event in Kervenheim did nothing for the reputation of the Guards with *hoi polloi*. The predictable but unintended consequence of optimising the Crocodile part of 21 AG was sub-optimisation of the whole, resulting in overall higher casualties and slower progress.

The subject of the Mk VII became an issue when discussing it with veterans of 6 GTB. Few of them were aware of its increased armour thickness. One veteran, who had discussed the subject with Eisenhower, was convinced that all of 3 SG's Churchills in 1945 were Mk VII.[138] Ignorance and confusion were understandable. Many Churchills were upgrades; 401 were converted from 2pdr to 6pdr guns, and 257 subsequently had these 6pdrs replaced with 75 mms. Crews customised their armour by welding track links to turret and hull, without any apparent means of calculating the value of the extra protection. The practice was officially frowned upon and not only because it affected durability and speed. Pictures show the practice was common in NWE but never in Italy. Gerry Chester stated that it was forbidden to weld track links to turrets because it slowed the speed at which the turret could be turned, and this was the crucial factor in outperforming the slower Tiger and Panther turrets and getting the first shot away. It is therefore surprising that this factor was not mentioned in NWE, but goes along seemingly with the differing attitudes in Italy and NWE towards the 6pdr. The 6pdr's discarding sabot was apparently far more highly prized in Italy than in NWE, with crews using it against anti-tank guns and perhaps machine gun nests as well as enemy tanks and Panzerturms. In NWE they preferred a mixture of 6pdr AP and 75 mm HE. Likewise it is surprising that the NIH did not apparently prize the 6 inch armour of the Mk VII at least enough to overcome their dislike of its gun and cast turret. Gerry Chester made the surprising statement that in the Hitler Line battle none of the hulls of the Churchills was penetrated – even though none was a MK VII – but destruction occurred through penetration of the turret. In Winnekendonk, the Scots Guards' Churchills were likewise probably destroyed by hits on the turret, but it is not known which mark of tank these turrets belonged to. And finally, there was no acceptable way of deciding who should benefit from the Mk VII in NWE. Rationally, officers who led their troops into battle in the most vulnerable position should have operated Mk VIIs, and there is evidence this was the case in 9RTR. Peter Beale published an illustrated book.[139] This contains photographs showing a Mk VII was the Troop Commander's tank of 9 Troop in April 1945 (p.85), of 8 Troop in October 1944 (p.135), and of 14 Troop in February 1945 (p.191). The anecdote on p.145 reveals that the same was true for 11 Troop in October 1944. However, in January 1945, 13 Troop was commanded from a Mk IV (p.163), and the Sergeant's tank in 8

137 Colin Williams in a web discussion in 2000.

138 Charles Farrell in conversation.

139 Peter Beale. *Tank Tracks* (Stroud: Alan Sutton, 1995).

Troop in February 1945 was also a Mk IV. The tentative conclusion is that Mk VIIs were issued only to Troop Commanders, but not to all. This raises the question of how the Mk VIIs were allocated if not as replacement for worn out or damaged vehicles. We do not know, and cannot even be sure if these non-Guards units did act differently.

Lt Alexis Melikoff of 4 CG explained how the Mk VII meant nothing to his troop, and how the Troop Sergeant could never use a Mk VII because he needed a 6pdr firing sabot:

> To answer your question: ' on what principle, if any, were the superior Mk VII Churchills distributed within the tank battalion?' My answer is that nobody in the Battalion was given preference. The new Mk VII were distributed to replace tanks which had been 'knocked out' or were beyond repair. They certainly were not specifically allocated to Troop Leaders or Senior officers. Actually we did not consider the Mk VII to be all that special. It had this thicker armour, but only in a small area in the front. I think it had a more powerful engine [not in fact]. There certainly was not any clamour to have one in one's troop. As for the Troop Leader always being the leading tank, in our battalion we were encouraged to rotate troop leadership between the Troop Leader and the Troop Corporal, which was a fairer distribution of risk. Inevitably however the Troop Leader spent more time in the lead. The Troop Sergeant's tank was always slightly to the rear in an anti-tank rôle. His tank was usually a Mk IV with a 6 pounder gun firing special SABO (sic) armour piercing shells.[140]

In NIH they preferred the Mk III's welded turret to the cast Mk IV turret for 6pdrs because the welded turret had better armour resistance. Confusion about armour thickness appears to have been widespread. Lt Peter Beale commanded a troop of Churchills in 9 RTR, and in his book includes a description by a wireless operator, Bill Thompson, of an event on 29 October 1944 at Vinkenbroek. His tank was in 11 Troop and commanded by Cpl Freddie Horner, who saw through the periscope a flash from a mile away that he was sure was an 88 mm. When a second shot hit the ground next to his tank he quickly reversed out of sight. The Troop commander, Lt Eb Wood, moved into the vacated position and was promptly hit on the turret by a shot that, Thompson said:

> penetrated 7½ inches into the armour as though it had been a huge drill… At the point of impact the thickness of the turret armour was 9 inches, Mr Wood's tank being a new Mk VII. Ours was a Mk IV, and the thickness of our turret was only 6 inches.[141]

Thompson was mistaken; turret thickness on the Mk VII was 6 inches while the Mk IV was 4 inches. Beale states that the C Sqn newsletter quoted the crew as saying there was a hole 6 inches deep in their turret, and the driver, Taffy Leyshon, as saying the 88 mm shot had penetrated 8 inches. Beale summed it up:

> Whether it was 6, 7½ or 8 inches, it certainly made an impression! But the Churchill could take a lot of punishment. The 34 Armoured Brigade History recorded: 'One notable tank casualty was a Mk VII of 9 RTR which sustained nine direct hits in front from 75 mm AP shot at short range without being completely penetrated by any!'[142]

140 Alexis Napier (né Melikoff) by e-mail on 29 September 2013.
141 Beale, *Tank Tracks.*
142 Ibid.

This is consistent with the information given herein; the shots referred to from the 75 mm L46 Pak 40 would have penetrated 5.3 inches into the 6 inch front armour. The anecdote was used as a source for a statement on armour protection and the failings of Allied armour; 'Even the Churchill, despite its 150 mm-plus frontal armour, was still vulnerable to the latest versions of the 75 mm and 88 mm gun.'[143]

What the crews needed in order to advance aggressively and end the war was a tank they knew and had proven to themselves was immune to every enemy anti-tank weapon firing from their front. There were many reasons, none good, why they were denied such a tank. One was Montgomery's bewilderment, reinforced by Wattrelos, about the different types of armoured tracked vehicles. He believed that the best features of the various designs could be combined into one – his Universal tank.[144]

His belief was incoherent because armour and mobility varied inversely, or in other words were incompatible. Montgomery refused to accept this fact, in spite of Hobart's insisting it was true, and incoherence in tank employment became just another unintended consequence of appointing and maintaining Montgomery in command. The postwar claim of universality for the Centurion cruiser tank did not stop the search for impenetrable armour, leading amongst other developments to composite Chobham and reactive armour.

To maintain frontal immunity against the ever more powerful German guns such as the 88 mm L71, the high velocity 75 mm, and the 128 mm, the British needed to scrap or upgrade the 4 inch 39 ton Churchills III-VI, and upgrade the 6 inch 41 ton Churchill VII to a 9 inch 44½ ton Super Churchill followed by a 10 inch-thick 46 ton Heavy Super Churchill, or possibly an 11 inch-thick 48-ton Churchill. The calculation is based on the Churchill's frontal plate weighing 1,600 lbs (726 Kgs) per inch (25 mm) of thickness. Steel weighs 40.8 lb per inch thickness per ft^2, so 4 inches of thickness weighs 163.2 lb/ft^2. The Churchill's frontal area, including two-thirds of the turret sides, was 76.5/ft^2. The incremental weight of a Super Churchill with an extra 4 inch frontal armour thickness was therefore 6.3 tons (76.5 × 163.2 = 12,485 lbs = 6.3 tons). This tank had no reduction in side/bottom/top armour thickness to reflect all-or-nothing armour, which would have saved 2 to 3 tons – the exact amount has not been calculated. However, enough is known to show that the Churchill meeting Elles I-tank design with frontal immunity to all guns was technically feasible.

Actual frontal armour thickness (inches/mm) by tank compared with the vertical thickness required year by year by a Churchill with all-or-nothing frontal immunity to all anti-tank guns

UK	1939	1940	1941	1942	1943	1944	1945	Built
Light VIC	½/14	½/14						1,682
Matilda I	2½/65							139
Cruiser A9-13	½/14	1¼/30						1,030
Covenanter		1¾/40						1,771
Matilda II		3/78	3/78					2,987
Valentine		2½/65	2½/65	2½/65	2½/65	2½/65		8,275
Crusader		1¾/40	1¾/40	2/49	2/49			5,300
Cavalier, Cromwell, Centaur, Challenger					3/76	3/76	4/101	5,216

143 J Buckley, *British Armour In The Normandy Campaign.* (London: Routledge, 2004), p. 125.
144 Fletcher, *Mr Churchill's*, p. 182.

UK	1939	1940	1941	1942	1943	1944	1945	Built
Churchill I-VI				4/105	4/105	4/105	4/105	5,768
Churchill VII						6/152	6/152	1,600
Comet							4/101	1,186
Centurion							6/150	6
Churchill with all-or-nothing frontal invulnerability	6/150	6/150	6/150	7/178	9/229	9/229	10/250 or 11/280	
GERMANY								
Mk III	1¼/30	1¼/30	1¾/50	2¼/60	2¼/60			5,774
MkIV	1¼/30	1¾/50	1¾/50	3¼/80	3¼/80	3¼/80		9,870
StuG III & IV	1¾/50	1¾/50	1¾/50	1¾/50	3¼/80	3¼/80	3¼/80	12,439
MkV Panther					3¼/80	3¼/80	3¼/80	6,000
Tiger I					4/100	4/100		1,354
Royal Tiger II*							6/150	489
Other AFVs**					1¼/30	3¼/80	3¼/80	3,470
USSR								
T34-76			2/47	2½/65	2¾/70			35,119
T34-85						3½/90	3½/90	29,430
KV1, KV2, KV85		3/75	3/75	3/75	3/75			3,730
IS-1, IS-2, IS-3*						4¾/120	4¾/120	6,928
USA								
M2A1	½/16							na
M2A4		1/25						na
M3 Stuart			1¾/44					4,526
M3 Grant/Lee				2/51	2/51			6,258
M4A4 Sherman V				3/76	3/76	3/76	3/76	49,234
M4A3E2/WHVSS						5½/140	5½/140	4,796

*Glacis angle: Tiger II 40°; Panther 55°; IS-1 30°; IS-2 60°; and IS-3 72°.
NB; horizontal thickness of Tiger II's 6 inch/80 mm plate angled at 40° was 8.5 inches/215 mm.

In 1949 a Mk VII was up-armoured with appliqué armour to 9¼ inches or 235 mm, and tested three times against a 128 mm gun firing AP at a range of 100 yards. It was not penetrated, although the turret was dislodged.[145] Rabbits caged inside the hull suffered no discernible physical harm, which showed the crew would have survived, provided the shock had not exploded the ammunition.

In the event the actual incremental weight of the thicker frontal armour, calculated to weigh 3,200 lbs (1.6 tons) per inch of thickness, would have been reduced by up to a ton once crews stopped adding track links to hull and turret in a do-it-yourself effort to protect themselves. Satisfactory ground pressure and mechanical reliability would have been maintained by replacing the Churchill's running gear and other weight-related improvements, such as a more powerful turret rotating motor, with that designed for the 50-ton Black Prince, which had the same Churchill engine and clutch but a new 5-speed gearbox. Ideally, of course, the heavier tank would have been fitted with a diesel engine to Russian design to take advantage of its better torque backup, and one

145 Fletcher, *Mr. Churchill's*, p. 196.

A. The tank was rebuilt as a pilot for the T26E4 and was armed with the high-velocity T15E1 90mm cannon. Third Armored Division maintenance personnel, lead by Belton Cooper, author of "Death Traps" decided to increase the armor protection of the tank. An 80mm armor plate, cut from a Panther, was attached to the mantlet.
A
B
C
D
B. It was envisioned that the "Super Pershing" would engage in various tank duals with German Tigers, but this never came to pass.
C. The additional five tons of steel added to the tank no doubt handicapped the tanks automotive performance, which was underpowered when it left this US.
D. Two layers of spaced armor, made from boiler plate, were added to the front of the hull.

The 'Super Pershing', a T26E1 mounted with the L73 90 mm gun after field modification by maintenance units of 3 USAD. Additional frontal armour weighing 5 tons comprising a gun mantle removed from a Tiger, with a glacis and lower front plate cut from a Panther would have achieved frontal immunity. Such field modification could have been done for the Churchills to achieve immunity from the 88 mm. (US Army)

of the many ways in which Russian tanks led the world in the Second World War. Torque backup is the percent of RPM drop before reaching peak torque .

Opposition by Montgomery and diffidence by Brooke towards all Infantry tanks explain many things: the overall shortage of Mk VIIs in the gun-tank battalions, the priority given to their conversion into Crocodiles, the absence of a Churchill with frontal immunity to all anti-tank weapons, and the persistent belief in the efficacy of cruiser tanks in the face of overwhelming evidence to the contrary, and backed by complaints in Parliament. The importance of the Brooke/Montgomery opposition in any comprehensive explanation of the failure of 21 AG to reach maximum effectiveness cannot be overstated.

At various times six reasons were advanced for neglecting heavy armour:

i) It was said pre-war that there were insufficient trained crews for both cruiser and infantry tanks, and only cruisers suited the rôle of exploitation. Like so many assumptions this one was never evaluated and turned out in practice to be untrue. The two types of tank were designed to operate sequentially in breakthrough and exploitation, so theoretically one set of trained crews could have jumped from one type into the other.
ii) An improved cruiser, called the Cromwell, was planned for 1943 with armour increased from 76 mm/3 inch to 101 mm/4 inch to be on a par with the 105 mm of Churchill Mks I to VI. Of course by this time the Churchill needed 229 mm/9 inch, and shortly 250 mm/10 inch. Winston Churchill was falsely told that Cromwell was a Universal Tank.
iii) Heavy armour was associated with a large gun resulting in an I-tank outside the railway gauge, and thus requiring road transportation and ships with reinforced holds, and replacement of Class 40 bridges. None of these factors prevented 60 ton Tigers from being shipped to Tunisia from Kassel and being in action within two months. An I-tank required impenetrable armour, but only a 75 mm gun with good HE and AP provided there existed 17pdr Archers, M10s and towed anti-tank guns. Alternatively, one third could have had the 6pdr
iv) A large and slow-moving infantry tank lacking acceleration and with thinly armoured sides, roof and belly would be more vulnerable to Panzerfausts, anti-tank guns, aircraft, tanks and mines than a mobile cruiser tank with fast acceleration. In practice the absence of the GAF, the provision of specialised mine-clearing flail tanks, oversight by 17pdr tank destroyers and by 5.5 inch

medium artillery, the 6pdr APDS, and close protection from infantry advancing on a divisional front with two brigades and battalions up, neutralised all these factors.

v) Brooke argued the anti-tank gun could be increased in penetrating power more cheaply than tank armour could be increased in thickness, and he declined to sanction a race that the I-tank in his opinion could never win. Brooke failed to appreciate the material shortages preventing German industry from replacing its inventory of Pak 38 and 40s with bigger and more costly weapons, and overlooked the difficulty of moving and concealing 88 and 128 mm guns, let alone larger calibres.

vi) Analysis of Sherman tanks knocked out in June-July in Normandy showed that only 15% of penetration by AP was through the frontal armour.[146] The conclusion was drawn that because increasing frontal armour would do nothing to prevent the 85% of penetrations through the flank and rear armour, and because increasing armour all round would add too much weight, then the answer was to leave the armour unchanged and to install the 17pdr, to increase the enemy's vulnerability and keep him at a safe distance. This argument reflected a perennial belief in the effectiveness of speed, acceleration, and mobility. The correct conclusions were never drawn that the preponderance of penetrations to flank and rear argued instead for all-or-nothing amour and for flank protection by other means, and an end to Montgomery's faulty tactics of advancing cruiser tanks without infantry support in order to 'crack about' through 'deep penetrations'. The complete answer to the Pakfront was close infantry protection of the sides and rear of frontally invulnerable infantry tanks, and the provision of accurate air support to provide aimed fire. Enemy anti-tank guns that were missed or survived such protective and suppressive fire, such as the unarmoured 88s at Winnekendonk, would then claim only one victim before being faced with invulnerable frontal armour and destroyed.

Tank-Infantry Cooperation in the Armoured Divisions

The doctrine and training of the armoured divisions from 1940 until the Battle of Caumont in July 1944 have been described by Timothy Harrison Place.[147] Until the Battle of France in 1940, they trained without infantry to destroy enemy tanks, infantry and systems of command and control. In July 1940, in MTP No. 41, they were directed to keep away from all static enemy positions that included anti-tank guns, but training continued unchanged. In May 1941, in ATI No. 3, nine tasks suitable for an armoured division were defined. In hindsight there was no task for which the armoured divisions were uniquely suitable, and so they should have been disbanded as expensive luxuries. Eight of the nine tasks were either irrelevant, or could be done better by other means. Task 2, attacking enemy infantry caught without anti-tank guns, never existed except in North Africa against the ill-equipped Italians. Task 3, outflanking the enemy to attack his Lines of Communication was possible only in the desert and better done by the LRDG. Task 4, exploitation, was better done by I-tanks as we have seen above, although this fact was counter-intuitive and it remained for tank-men their imagined *raison d'être*. Task 5, Pursuit, ditto. Task 6, Recce in force, was the responsibility of the light tanks of the Recce Corps. Task 7, counterattack in defence, as was shown by Briggs in the following example, assumed tanks could suppress anti-tank guns. However, because they lacked HE, anti-tank gun suppression was beyond their capabilities, and forced them to charge the guns suicidally in frustration. Task 8, denial of ground during a retreat, was theoretical and never tested to this author's knowledge. And Task 9, action against airborne was irrelevant. The Germans gave up airborne after their Pyrrhic victory in Crete, and while they invested heavily in paratroops these were delivered by land to battle complete with

146 Copp, *Montgomery's*, pp. 395-98.
147 Place, *Military Training*.

Maj Gen Raymond Briggs by Eric Manning, painted in 1941. A career tank man dating from 1920, Briggs was on the WO AFV staff in 1936 and with GHQ BEF in 1939. GOC 2 BAB 1941-42, GOC 1 BAD 1942-43, 1943-45 Director of the RAC at the WO. (© Tank Museum Bovington)

Maj Gen George Warren Richards by Walter Stoneman in May 1944. Founder member of the RAC and intimate of Fuller, Lindsay, Hobart and Liddell Hart, Richards was OC 4 BAB 1941-43 and adviser to Wavell. From 1943-45 he was adviser on armour to Montgomery. (Image x169642 © National Portrait Gallery, London).

their heavy equipment including anti-tank guns. Therefore all that remained of the nine tasks was Task 1, engaging enemy tanks. Specialist tank destroyers, the half-tracked 75 mm M3 and full tracked 3 inch M10, were designed for this task as US Army doctrine held that tanks did not fight other tanks but supported infantry, with Tank Destroyer battalions fighting enemy tanks. Tank destroyers were liberally issued to both the US and British armies which called the M10 the Archer and had their own 17pdr Achilles. The advent of the Pershing tank signalled the end of the TD in US service.

Engaging enemy tanks was the unrealistic task Hobart concentrated upon to the exclusion of all other when training 7 BAD and 11 BAD, and which generated the adulation showered upon him.

The tactics of the armoured divisions were unclear to commanders who were outfought by the Germans and had no confidence in themselves. The infantry were ordered to cooperate with them but knew they would be abandoned at the first hint of trouble. The problem was rooted in the attitudes of the armoured divisions, described by Maj Moore of 11 BAD in December 1941 to a visiting portraitist as originating with Hobart.[148]

> The RAC trooper was the British public in a uniform dress… in a few weeks they suddenly acquire, in some mysterious manner, the tradition of the young corps … they feel something

148 E. Kennington & Maj Moore. *Tanks and Tank Folk* (London: Country Life, 1942).

Lt Gen Herbert Lumsden in 1943 by Walter Stoneman. A gunner turned cavalryman, he became GOC 6 BAD in 1941, and almost immediately GOC 1 BAD. (Image x165489 © National Portrait Gallery, London)

Maj Gen Howard Kippenberger in London in 1946. His brigade was abandoned by Briggs, Richards and Lumsden on 15 July 1942 with heavy loss. (© Alexander Turnbull Library, ref:1\4-017467-F. Permission must be obtained before any reuse of this image)

> special and selected with no doubts they are the cream of the Army, and they behave accordingly.[149]

The result was that Anglo-Canadian armour was 'very poor'[150] throughout the war. Brigadier Kippenberger described how the Commonwealth forces in the desert were outfought even when significantly outnumbering the Germans, and at times with armoured equipment parity.

The problem with armour was a witches' brew of personalities, attitudes, class, delusion, faulty operational methods, poor equipment, but also of command, as Kippenberger perceived in describing the planning for the attack on Ruweisat Ridge on 14 July 1942. Brackets identify information withheld in the original.

> We had a conference about the projected attack and heard with some scepticism that when we had taken the ridge our tanks would go through and exploit. I do not think anyone then

149 Jonathan Black. *The Face of Courage. Eric Kennington, Portraiture and the 2nd World War* (London: Philip Wilson, 2011), p. 78.
150 Dominick Graham in a letter in 1995.

> realised how much training and care and forethought are required to get good co-operation between infantry and tanks. We merely cursed one another when it was not achieved. Nor was the problem of command dealt with: the tank brigadiers [Raymond Briggs and George Richards] naturally and emphatically intended to keep their regiments under their own command and to act merely 'in support'. In the absence of any clear direction from Army they had to be left with their way.[151]

The tanks' orders were twofold; to 'exploit' the success of Kippenberger's 5 NZIB to the NW of Point 64, and to counter Axis counter-attacks (identified as Task 7 in ATI No. 3). The New Zealanders began their advance at 11 pm on 14 July and over-ran two German tanks on the way. But at first light 10 tanks of 8 PzReg saw 22 NZ Battalion, (who mistook them for British tanks carrying out their orders to provide protection), and immediately attacked, destroying the portee anti-tank guns and taking prisoner 350 NZ infantry before withdrawing with them. Briggs's vast fleet of 116 tanks allowed 10 German tanks to escape unharmed. The single word 'exploit' seems to have caused more trouble to the Allies than any other. The French *exploiter* means nothing more than 'to work at' something; *exploiter une entreprise* means 'to run a business', and *un exploitant* is a farmer. But 'to exploit' in English means to turn something to one's advantage, while an 'exploit' is a 'brilliant or daring achievement', destroying discipline and co-operation in a *look-at-me!* moment that would earn a medal. It was reinforced by the belief that the very act of getting behind the enemy's front line would bring about its collapse. Kippenberger continued:

> Twenty-second Battalion accordingly suffered the consequences. The unit did not suffer humiliation and captivity gladly, and the bitterness of the Ruweisat men against their senior officers and the Army in general lives on still today. As it was, the captives who trudged off into long, bleak years of hardship and captivity would be denied even the cold comfort that their fate had served as a warning to other New Zealanders. Later that very day 19 and 20 Battalions (and a week later 24 and 25 Battalions) shared the same grim fate in the Division's darkest hour.[152]

Kippenberger went searching for the missing tanks whose task was to protect his infantry from German tanks (Task 1 in Ati No.3).

> After ages, perhaps twenty minutes, we reached a mass of tanks (2 BAB under Brig Raymond Briggs). In every turret someone was gazing through glasses at the smoke rising from Ruweisat Ridge four miles and more away. I found and spoke to a regimental commander, who referred me to his Brigadier. The Brigadier [Briggs] received me coolly. I did my best not to appear agitated, said that I was Commander of 5 New Zealand Infantry Brigade, that we were on Ruweisat Ridge and were being attacked in rear by tanks when I left an hour before. Would he move up and help? He said he would send a reconnaissance tank. I said there was no time. Would he move his whole brigade? While he was patiently explaining some difficulty, General Lumsden (GOC 1 BAD) drove up. I gave him exactly the same information. Without answering he walked round to the back of his car, unfastened a shovel and with it killed a scorpion with several blows. Then he climbed up beside the Brigadier, who was sitting on the turret of his tank. I climbed up beside them and McPhail stood within hearing. The General asked where we were and the Brigadier pointed out the place on the map. 'But I told you to be

151 Howard Kippenberger. *Infantry Brigadier* (Oxford: OUP, 1951), p. 159.
152 http://nzetc.victoria.ac.nz/tm/scholarly/tei-WH2-22Ba-c6.html#name-001291-mention.

> there at first light', General Lumsden then said, placing his finger on Point 63. I jumped down and did not hear the rest of the conversation but in a few minutes the General got down and in a soothing manner which I resented, said that the Brigade would move as soon as possible. I asked for urgency, which both he and the Brigadier promised, and drove off.[153]

Briggs with his 116 tanks was sitting on Dei el Hima checking to see if the coast was clear before moving. There were 46 Grants, 11 Stuarts and 59 Crusaders belonging to 6 RTR, 3/5 RTR and 9 Lancers. The American Grant with its 75 mm gun was able to fire HE and was the equal of anything the Germans possessed at that time. Therefore the usual excuses of unreliability and equipment inadequacy could not excuse Briggs' insubordinate inactivity. The reason for his caution was fear of anti-tank guns. The Official History states laconically:

> Brigadier Kippenberger had gone to report presumably to General Inglis and was sent on by him to contact the British armour. He saw Brigadier Briggs and General Lumsden, and by 7 am the 2nd Armoured Brigade had moved off in a NW direction.[154]

By then the NZ prisoners were marching to the south-east in the boiling sun without water. Kippenberger did well to keep Briggs' name out of his account, because there were New Zealanders who would have settled a score with Briggs and Richards postwar given knowledge and the opportunity. Hatred can become all-consuming and the RAC had worked hard to foment and attract it.

At El Mreir less than a week later on 21 July, and on the eve of Montgomery's arrival, 23 BAB [Brig George Richards] was in support. Richards refused to move at night, arrived late and Kippenberger's brigade was destroyed. Kippenberger continued:

> I was very unhappy at the divisional conference. Again there was no Corps [XIII Corps under Strafer Gott, who was Winston Churchill's choice to replace Auchinleck] conference although this was a Corps battle, and we only knew at second-hand what the other formations concerned were to do. But the principal worry, of course, was whether the armour would really be up in time to support 5 Brigade. The armour Brigadier [Richards] was present and swore that he would be up, but though George [Clifton] pressed him hard he declined to consider moving at night. We knew the German tanks moved at night and, in fact, George's patrols had several times bumped into them; but the Brigadier insisted that tanks could not move at night. This meant that with the best intentions and no mishaps or mistakes in map-reading or over routes or minefields, and no enemy opposition, there must still be an appreciable interval after daylight before the armour could arrive on the infantry objectives. If the infantry had three hours of daylight unmolested, they could get their anti-tank guns sited and dug-in, even in this hard ground, and once that was done they were always happy to look after themselves. But during these three hours they were vulnerable, in fact helpless [in the face of HE fired by the German MkIV tanks]. I went back feeling profoundly uneasy. On return to my truck I said to Montgomery: 'Take this down: the Brigadier [Kippenberger, himself] has returned from the divisional conference and says there will be another bloody disaster.[155]

The official NZ history described the resulting NZ 'mutiny':

153 Kippenberger, *Infantry Brig*, p. 169.
154 ISO Playfair. *Mediterranean and the Middle East* (London: HMSO, 1960)
155 Kippenberger, *Infantry Brig*, pp. 183-184.

> Two infantry and two armoured brigades were employed. They had made three unrelated attacks from different directions at different times. A single small Panzer division of some 20 or 30 tanks and a fifth-rate Italian infantry division easily dealt with all three attacks in succession and inflicted crippling losses. The El Mreir disaster was 13 Corps' last attempt to smash its head through the brick wall in the Alamein central sector. The New Zealand Maj-Gen Inglis, furious at being let down again by the armour, outspokenly declined to consider any other operation of the same kind, and with this refusal every Kiwi agreed. The loss of so many good men in such a fiasco so soon after Ruweisat, plus all the discomforts of the desert summer, had 2 NZID in a sour, discontented mood, not so much against Jerry as against the Eighth Army's methods, and particularly against the British armour. The demand on all sides was: 'Why can't we have our own armour?' It was a question that was to completely change the life of 18 Battalion before many months had passed.[156]

The result of their mutinous anger and power as an independent Dominion force that could pack up and go home if the abuse continued, was their immediate conversion to a Mixed Division. 4 NZIB (18, 19 and 20 Infantry Battalions) drew 150 tanks from UK depots and 22 Motor Battalion took half-tracks. Unfortunately they chose Sherman tanks instead of Churchills. There was discussion about sending out the NZ Army Tank Brigade formed in 1941, but:

> Since then the Division had had a lot of experience, both good [with the Matilda brigades] and bad, with armour, and the GOC (Freyberg) now had his own ideas about what was wanted.[157]

Richards's refusal to move at night under Auchinleck at El Mreir foreshadowed a similar refusal by Greenacre at Kervenheim. Richards became Montgomery's armour adviser in 21AG, the job that Martel so desperately wanted. The choice of Richards, and the presence of tank men such as Harold Pyman and Hobart at senior level in 21 AG, revealed a reluctance by Montgomery to question the tank-cult. Richards may not have known, but Martel knew that British armour had had once been familiar with fighting at night. At Bucquoy on 22 June 1918, 5 female tanks of 10 Bn were employed with 5 plns of infantry. The infantry were held up but the tanks pushed on to the objective, immune in the darkness from artillery.

> It was a significant demonstration of the potentialities of tanks for night attack and deserved more attention than it received.[158]

In 1934 Hobart exercised the Tank Brigade at night, moving from Cranborne Chase soon after midnight and hiding up by 7 am between Salisbury and Andover. The next night the Brigade moved again to Tilshead between 9 pm and 1.30 am.

> The development of tank movement at night was one of the principal features and the progress made was remarkable.[159]

156 http://nzetc.victoria.ac.nz/tm/scholarly/tei-WH2-18Ba-c21.html
157 http://nzetc.victoria.ac.nz/tm/scholarly/tei-WH2Prob-c4.html
158 Hart, *The Tanks.*
159 Ibid.

Big operations were mounted at night, such as *Totalise* and *Tractable* in Normandy and *Blockbuster* during *Veritable*, and 'whenever bloody well ordered to do so' according to Dominick Graham from his experience in GAD, showing irritation with this author's suggestion that refusal to fight at night might have had a psychological cause.[160] The NIH attacked several times at night, including 18 April 1945 when A Sqn crossed 6,000 yards of difficult country using their own bridging devices. But there is also no question that normally tanks resisted night fighting. The usual excuse was the need for maintenance, but Brig Radley Walters, who came to the armoured Canadian Sherbrooke Fusiliers from the infantry, told the Whitakers that this was nonsense.[161] The real reason was lack of sleep leading to exhaustion. Tanks were in the line longer than infantry, and operating at night had to be exceptional or crews would crack up. This reason is significant, and inconsistent with the reason given for abolishing the Mixed Divisions – that since tanks could fight for longer than infantry, they would be underutilised in the Mixed Division. More realistically, ground conditions at Kervenheim were so bad that off-road movement even in daylight was difficult. Nevertheless, it was the lives of infantrymen that were at stake and if they wanted to attack at night then the armour should have obliged them or been ordered to do so.

The infantry expected intolerable behaviour by the RAC, whose units gave the impression of being a self-regulating and deluded élite beholden to no one. Instead of being court martialled for insubordination causing the loss of 350 infantry from 22 New Zealand Battalion, Raymond Briggs, who we previously met on the Somme in May 1940, was promoted by Montgomery to replace Lumsden on 19 August 1942 as GOC 1 BAD in the experimental *Corps de Chasse.* Later as Montgomery's tank guru in 21 AG he loyally supported his boss by producing excuses for the failures of the armoured divisions.

Montgomery's lessons from the success of Eighth Army at Alam Halfa were issued in MTP No. 41 in February 1943. No longer were armoured commanders to dart around the battlefield in pursuit of enemy tanks, but also they were not disbanded. Instead new and contradictory instructions were issued.

> The new teaching advised the armoured commander to arrange his troops in well-concealed hull-down positions in some locality that the enemy would wish to control. When the enemy ventured to do so, he could be attacked with stationary and obscure fire.[162]

This was equally unrealistic since Montgomery lacked the means of seizing a locality that the enemy would wish to control. The only means of doing this was the I-tank under command of infantry, but that meant retiring the Royal Armoured Corps, abolishing the armoured divisions and their cruiser tanks, and reorganising into mixed divisions equipped with I-tanks frontally immune to all anti-tank guns.

Instead, endless compromises were attempted. The 1941 doctrine that tanks required little support because their armour limited their vulnerability was rejected in 1943,[163] when tanks were declared in need of concurrent infantry support. Infantry now cleared minefields and other obstacles and accompanied the tanks to the objective if required. But the problem of infantry cooperation with cruiser tanks was not solved or even improved until after *Goodwood*. The unreformed 7 BAD, Montgomery's Desert Rats, was sent to 'crack about' at Villers Bocage on 11 June 1944, under the watchful eye of Brigadier Hargest.

160 Dominick Graham in a letter in January 1995.

161 Whitaker, *Rhineland.*

162 Place, *Military Training*, p. 109.

163 Army Trg Instruction No. 3. *Handling of an Armoured Division*, 19 May, 1941. Army Trg Instruction No. 2. *The Co-operation of Infantry and Tanks*, 2 May 1943.

> On the way back I met the Divisional Commander, General Erskine, and respectfully suggested that infantry were necessary to consolidate immediately and to mop up. They could prevent lateral movement by the enemy, and if they entered a position with the tanks they could take it with little loss. As it was the enemy lay down and peppered the rear after the tanks had passed. The GOC replied that he preferred to go on alone. The pace was too hot for the infantry. I suggested that they could be lorried up to the front by shuttle service. He said they would suffer casualties. At any rate he had advanced 6 miles – if he could maintain that for 30 days that would be 180 miles. The answer came the next day. The 7th Armoured Division advanced about a mile. On the 3rd it withdrew nearly the whole of that mile and then it disengaged.[164]

The infantry had been valued for a while after the disasters of Alam Halfa, but were once again marginalised with the arrival of the Grant and Sherman tanks whose DP 75 mm guns could provide indirect fire support. The tanks were back to thinking they could do everything themselves and did not want infantry to slow down their 'hot pace'. The armoured brigade was divided so it could use fire-and-movement, with part using their tanks as artillery to pin down the enemy while the other half manoeuvred towards the enemy in a set-piece attack.

The tactics of the armoured divisions until Operation *Goodwood* reflected these unmodified Hobartian pre war training programmes, implementing none of the later MTPs and ATIs except for those using the Sherman's own 75 mm gun as artillery. Roberts wanted to use APCs to keep infantry up with the tanks at *Goodwood* and to go after the anti-tank guns but was refused by Dempsey who would have discussed it with Montgomery and Hobart. Roberts was threatened by O'Connor, and showed no moral courage in agreeing when he knew better, probably having heard also through the grapevine of the advances being made by the American combined-arms teams.

Goodwood on 18 July 1944 was the Waterloo of Hobartian tank tactics, and the last throw of the cultic dice. The real scandal was that such methods were still being peddled so late in the war and after their conspicuous failures, but 2 Fife & Forfar Yeomanry of 11 BAD attacked Bourguébus Ridge on 18 July 1944 in the way Hobart had taught the RAC on Salisbury Plain. *Goodwood* was the last attempt by Montgomery and Hobart to rescue their credibility by choosing optimum conditions – Cambrai rather than the Somme – using vast numbers of reliable and fast Sherman cruiser tanks that had poured forth from the Chrysler Tank Arsenal in Detroit in the manner envisaged in Plan 1919 and would form an expanding torrent to pour through the German lines on exceptionally good going. Dempsey even said afterwards that he did not mind losing large numbers of tanks in this way because, he failed to add, the goal was so bewitching. The support of their RAF mobility blood cousins was called on to bomb the flanks of the expanding torrent to destroy the anti-tank guns and daze the survivors long enough to let the British tank hordes penetrate behind them. Nothing could go wrong, Montgomery must have told himself as he built up hopes with Eisenhower and the press of a massive breakthrough while pulling the Hobartian rabbit out of his hat. Montgomery's disasters from Wattrelos 1940, through *Corps de Chasse* 1942, to Villers Bocage 1944 would all be forgotten by a resounding victory by all those wearing the black beret (including himself), and it would be a victory won by them alone without infantry participation or losses. Montgomery and Hobart would show them!

Hobart's and Richards's finger prints are all over *Goodwood*. The absence of records of Hobart's daily chats with Montgomery show *Goodwood* was hatched in secret and the evidence afterwards destroyed so that Dempsey could be presented as its author. Hobart is a blank in Montgomery's

164 TNA: CAB 106/1060.

memoirs, and neither Hobart nor Richards appears in the index of Volume IV of Nigel Hamilton's official biography.

The opportunity presented by perfect tank country and massive tank forces was just too great. The late Ian Daglish was told this by his sources.

> One of the great attractions of open [*Goodwood*] country for the British tank squadrons was the possibility of employing the fire and movement tactics in which they had practised so extensively in England. The principle involved troops of tanks moving alternately: some using speed and manoeuvre to make themselves difficult targets while others behind gave covering fire. The moving elements would seek protection, ideally hull-down behind cover or simply using the folds of the ground, stop, and in turn open fire to cover the advance of the rear units. Unfortunately the ground over which the regiment now advanced was very open indeed. Opportunities for the leading tanks to 'go to ground' were few. Even the crops hereabouts in the triangle of fields between Grentheville, Soliers and Fours would steadily becoming (sic) flattened.[165]

2 Fife & Forfar Yeomanry advanced along a hedgerow using fire and movement while searching to break through to the Bourguébus Ridge and release the expanding torrent forming behind them. They reached the killing field selected by the German defenders. According to MTP 41, of course, they should not have been there at all as this was not the task of an armoured division, but Hobart had arranged things on manoeuvres on Salisbury Plain that fast tanks could find a way of avoiding the enemy anti-tank guns, and the umpires had agreed with him. The resulting funeral pyres signalled the absence of accommodating umpires and the final end of an illusion that Fuller, no less, had predicted would result from anti-tank guns, and the same prediction that had led Elles to specify the answer of the impenetrable Matilda II.

The RAC now reached the same point as the RAF during the night of 30 March 1944, a mere three months earlier, when the pyres of 96 Lancasters marked the route to and from Nuremberg and destroyed the first Trenchardian principle that 'the bomber will always get through' which was, of course, obsoleted by the Dowding System.

In both the cases of cruiser tanks and bombing aircraft, salvation from a strategic dead-end came from the Americans. It was they who devised the successful tactics of joint tank-infantry command, and they who introduced long-range fighters to destroy the German fighter force over their home airfields in complete violation of Portal's ex cathedra statement that a long-range fighter aircraft was an oxymoron.[166]

By destroying the Hobartian cult theory, the *Goodwood* disaster forced Montgomery to accept the innovative US combined arms battle groups. Again there are no records of the discussions, but the upshot were the orders given to GAD and 11 BAD to form battle groups on 25 July in time for *Bluecoat* on 30 July.

The American developments had been devised and implemented at divisional level, and are well documented.[167] The British adopted the American Tactics, just as they adopted the American long-range fighters. The British armed forces had ceased to innovate or apparently even to think.

The reason for the conservatism of the RTC in failing to adopt fully the May 1941 doctrine of all-arms was psychological, and paralelled the RAF's persistence in area bombing. Both RTC and

165 Ian Daglish. *Operation Goodwood* (Barnsley: Pen & Sword, 2005), p. 149. Discussion with Ian about his conclusions was cut short by Ian's death in a plane crash.
166 Webster & Frankland, *The Strategic*, p. 77.
167 Michael Doubler. *Busting the Bocage* (Leavenworth: US Staff College, 1988).

RAF were cults relying on the patronage of the Minister of Defence and Prime Minister, who was notorious for his anti-intellectual approach to warfare. RTC officers defended the primacy of the tank and protected their rôle, having internalised the teachings of the cult founders. Pretentiousness was often overlaid by social exclusiveness, and the two were immune to training, exhortation or even demonstration of the effectiveness of all-arms. Shock action by the army commander was needed, but to this author's knowledge only Bill Slim imposed it to reap the reward of effectiveness. Montgomery continued to wear the black beret of the RAC cult, and never seems to have recognised the systemic problem with armour.

In Burma Slim took the same material available to Montgomery and transformed it. He broke the socially exclusive pretensions of the Hussars on 18 April 1942 by placing Brig Anstice's 7 BAB under command of Lt-Gen Sun Li Jen of 38 Chinese Infantry Division. Clear thinking earned Slim the reputation of being, 'probably the finest British soldier to emerge from the second War.'[168] It was also the saving of the reputation of 7 BAB which became recognised by infantry survivors of the campaign as the solid core of its defence, while in NWE, by contrast, armour was generally disliked. Slim described Anstice as throwing him the 'look of a wounded sambhur'[169] when he received the order. It is difficult for a modern to understand the meaning of putting a socially élite British unit under the command of 'coolies'. 7 BAB had been trained by Hobart to feel superior, and was transferred from the Western Desert. It comprised 7 Hussars, 2 RTR, 414 Battery RHA, 1 West Yorkshire and A Bty 95 Anti-tank Regt. The Hussars had an incorrigible belief in the rightness of their own independent judgment, and in the superiority of their social origins. They had previously insisted, when they could get away with it, which was most of the time, on supporting British infantry and artillery only as and when they saw fit.

The success of Operation *Compass* against the Italians in 1940/1 was due to the Matilda tanks, and this tempted the War Office to emphasise the opportunity for unsupported action by tanks in the attack. ATI No.2 (1941) taught that tanks should precede infantry by 1 km and brought nothing but failure when Rommel arrived with his anti-tank guns including the 88 mm and a disciplined force trained in all-arms. The ATI was discredited but no replacement doctrine was published until May 1943, leaving infantry and tanks in the new Mixed divisions to make their own arrangements, usually some variation of the sandwich pattern (tanks sandwiched between infantry). The correct method presumably seen in the Hitler Line and certainly at Winnekendonk was for one tank troop of three tanks to be assigned to each of the five companies of the battalion (four rifle companies plus Tac HQ Company) which attacked in two columns. At Winnekendonk C Coy led on the left and D Company on the right, each followed by its tank troop, followed on the left by Battalion Tac HQ with the Tanks of HQ Troop alongside, followed on the left by A Coy and alongside on the right B Coy, each followed by a troop of tanks bringing up the rear. There was therefore one concentrated combined arms attacking echelon effectively under infantry command. At long last the British Army had got back to what Monash had invented in 1918, although lacking CAS made it still incomplete.

In February 1944, 3 SG practised assault-echelon work, but in that same month Montgomery issued a new pamphlet[170] insisting tanks should lead and the infantry should follow in two attacking echelons, reverting to ATI No.2 (1941). Everyone except Montgomery knew this was a retrograde step and would have deleterious results.

168 Nigel Nicolson. *Alex* (London: Weidenfeld & Nicolson, 1973).
169 William Slim. *Defeat Into Victory* (London: Cassell, 1956), p. 65.
170 *Notes on the Employment of Tanks in Support of Infantry in Battle.*

> Thus within the space of two months 21 Army Group published two quite different and mutually contradictory sets of doctrine for tank-infantry cooperation.[171]

Before Montgomery took command of 8 Army, its armoured divisional formations fought as units, with the infantry 'Support Group' maintaining a base for the fast cruiser tanks. Montgomery made them fight as a division, so they formed themselves into echelons with either the armour or the lorried infantry leading. Through minefields, or when attacking dug-in defenders, the infantry led. This was what Montgomery meant by all-arms co-operation, and it was how his armoured divisions fought every battle from Alamein to *Goodwood.*

In Normandy throughout June and into July 1944 there was stalemate both in the Plains of Caen, and in the bocage. The Americans also lacked both a methodology for the conditions and suitable equipment, but in the US Army, the corps commanders abdicated to divisional commanders all responsibility for engineering tactical solutions. The corps commanders did not see it as their responsibility to co-ordinate all of this activity. However, once he had been asked for help in managing the manufacture and fitment of the Culin hedgerow cutter designed within 2 USAD, the V Corps commander, Gerow organised a demonstration for Bradley on 14 July. Bradley then gave the order to First Army's Ordnance Section to fabricate and fit the device to Shermans for the *Cobra* breakout.

According to Patton, the responsibility for tactics lay even lower down at the battalion level. He saw no distinction between tactics and operations. Patton said:

> I am also nauseated by the fact that Hodges and Bradley state that all human virtue depends on knowing infantry tactics. I know that no general officer and practically no colonel needs to know any tactics. The tactics belong to battalion commanders. If Generals knew less tactics, they would interfere less.[172]

This was an unattractive aspect of the US Army. Generals, and especially Bradley, were far too ready to sack Divisional commanders for failure, when the Generals could do no better themselves. When *Cobra* was successful because of the inventiveness of Divisional and Assistant Divisional commanders, Bradley was quick to take the credit and claim success was due to his employment of Quesada's air power. Patton's own break-out proposal of 'placing one or two armoured divisions abreast and going straight down the road covering the leading elements with air bursts' showed inexperience. He tried it later in the year outside Metz and got nowhere with heavy loss.

Luckily the solution of the problem of the bocage required no advanced engineering or resort to the factories of Detroit or Toledo, and could be done with materials available in the bridgehead. Had that been impossible, there was no system whereby a divisional or even a corps commander could have called on the resources of Chrysler, Ford, Vickers or North American Aircraft to solve his problem. When soldiers at the front complained about their equipment, Montgomery refused to listen, labeling it bellyaching.

The American armoured divisions from 1943 were organised as combined arms units with equal numbers of armour, infantry and artillery. Their primary rôle was the usual pipe-dream of offensive operations against hostile rear areas à la cavalry of J.E.B. Stuart. The triangular infantry divisions lacked tanks, but independent tank battalions, called GHQ tank units, were available for attachment to the infantry as required by operations and legislated by the Army Commander.

171 Place, *Military Training*, p. 149.

172 Carlo D'Este. *Patton: A Genius For War* (New York: Harper Collins, 1995).

The weaknesses in the US forces were endemic and the German defences in the bocage revealed them starkly. The US soldier lacked aggression and had learned to stop when close to the enemy and call for help from his artillery. Tanks and infantry moved in separate echelons not always on the same axis, the one or the other leading depending on the nature of the terrain and the opposition. So although the manuals, like their British equivalents, insisted on the need for co-operation between all arms, in reality the man with the armoured shield and the firepower moved behind, in front or to the flank of the infantry, expecting the artillery to suppress the enemy and provide safe passage.

The fields in the bocage were typically 200 to 400 yards square surrounded by thick hedges and trees growing atop earthen banks. The defenders were dug into the banks with MG42s laid to fire diagonally across the fields that were targeted also by mortars. Sometimes anti-tank guns and tanks were dug into the banks and camouflaged to be invisible. Snipers were strapped into the trees, and there was a plentiful supply of Panzerfausts.

American infantry made no progress because the artillery could find no targets. Any tanks or infantry entering the fields were instantly destroyed. The Sherman tanks were unable to climb over the banks and were restricted to the gates. These unforeseen problems became immediately apparent, and as early as June 9 Bradley was asking whether a tank could blow a hole through the banks with its main gun.

Each division then worked out an appropriate operational method for itself through trial and error. Every technical innovation was rehearsed; in communications, using field telephones or having the infantry leader present in the tank with an infantry radio; in tank mobility, using explosives with pipe devices or Culin cutters welded to the glacis plate; in artillery, spotting fall of shell with aircraft; in the use of direct, observed fire from the Sherman's main 75 mm gun, firing HE at the corners of the field and using its machine-guns to rake the hedge-lines. But as 29 USID discovered on 20 June, the technical innovations still resulted in failure when tanks and infantry operated in echelon and not under unified command. The tank echelon could now burst through the banked hedge satisfactorily, but at once fell prey to Panzerfausts.

It was then that Maj-Gen Gerhardt, commanding 29 USID, directed the assistant Divisional commander, Brig-Gen Norman D. Cota to develop the tactics necessary to pull together the technical advances. Cota abandoned normal army doctrine of leading with either tanks or infantry, and formed them both into small and integrated teams. He rehearsed them on 24 June, making additional improvements and rehearsed them again until satisfied. The drills were written up and disseminated throughout the division.

They were first used in action on 11 July 1944. The integrated teams led 2 Bn of 16 USID in a successful offensive east of St-Lô. Each team consisted of a single tank fitted with a pipe device, an engineer team, a squad of infantry with BARs and a 60 mm mortar team occupying the hedge-line. The attack began when the Sherman nosed into the bank sinking the pipes into the soil. The turret crew dismounted to cut away the foliage to clear a view of the opposite hedge-line. The mortar observer climbed up onto the rear deck of the tank sheltering behind the turret. The Sherman then fired a white phosphorous round from its main gun into each opposite corner of the next field to destroy any MG42 nests. The mortar lobbed bombs behind the hedgerow to prevent movement and reinforcement. The tank then began to spray machine-gun fire along the entire base of the opposite hedgerow, which was the sign for the infantry to move through the hedge and advance in line until they masked the tank. The mortar then switched to firing smoke bombs to obscure the defenders' view. The Sherman reversed to uncover the holes made by the pipe device. The engineers placed explosive charges in the holes and blew a passage through the bank for the Sherman which accelerated to catch up with the infantry. Together they cleared the hedgerow while the mortar team advanced. All were quickly re-supplied as necessary with ammunition from half-tracks and the casualties evacuated. The process was then repeated.

The attack began at dawn on 11 July and by 11 am the Americans were through the German defences and moving on Martinville and St-Lô. Infantry casualties were light and not one Sherman was lost. Other divisions using similar methods were also successful. The 2, 29 and 83 USIDs, 2 and 3 USAD all developed different variations on the same theme of complete armour-infantry integration. Sgt Culin of 2 USAD invented the famous hedge-cutting plough device that bore his name and made engineers and explosives redundant. Bradley saw a demonstration of the cutter on 14 July and ordered its immediate adoption. Between then and 25 July, 500 Shermans were equipped with the device and were used, among others, by Brig-Gen Maurice Rose's CCA of 2 USAD and 22 USID as they trained from 19 to 25 July for Operation *Cobra.* Camouflaged infantry were now riding 'Russian style' on the second and third waves of tanks, with artillery FOOs in the first wave and infantry battalion commanders in command tanks with infantry radios. The meaning and benefits of 'under command and on the same axis' was now clear to the US Army.

News of these successful innovations must have filtered back to Montgomery, through his LOs or/and possibly directly from Bradley to Montgomery, his commanding officer. Around 16 July, the REME were ordered to make up 24 Prongs, as the British called the Culin Cutter, or Rhinoceros. They were fabricated from German beach defences and were ready by 20 July.[173] However, the next 600 were ordered from T.C. Jones in Shepherds Bush, London and arrived only at the end of August and too late for the bocage. This is the sole example known to this author of a corps commander using home industry to satisfy operational needs.

One way or another, the significant change in US practice was noticed by the British because suddenly around July 25 the VIII Corps Commander, Lt-Gen Sir Richard O'Connor ordered 11 BAD[174] and GAD[175] to form all-arms battle groups. They were formed around Caen, and were done in a rushed and *ad hoc* manner. Those who happened to be parked in neighbouring fields were told to get together and without training, rehearsal or the Culin Prong, GAD became involved in two weeks of fierce and disjointed action in Operation *Bluecoat.*

There is no mention of 7 BAD being ordered to form such battle groups in either unit history.[176] During the period 24 to 27 July they were in action supporting 2 CID and 3 CID in Operation *Spring* near Verrieres. On 28 July, 7 BAD lost 4 CLY and gained 5 RIDG from 9 BAD in the UK. The formation was then split up and while the infantry rested, the armour supported 43 BID. It seems that there was no reason to order 7 BAD to form battle groups as the senior commanders were all sacked and Verney was promoted from 6 GTB to command 7 BAD under new management on 4 August. Verney knew what to do.

A connection between the sudden regrouping of the British armoured divisions into all-arms battle groups on 25 July and the earlier demonstration by the Americans of their effectiveness has not previously been made. It got the attention of Ian Daglish when I contacted him about it shortly before his death. Historians had theorized about the reason: one wrote that *Goodwood* revealed that, 'the danger of having tanks on their own, where their infantry could not get up to them, was never forgotten within the Division', and that the regrouping into battle-groups was made, 'as a result of *Goodwood,* where the rigid separation of infantry and armoured brigades had proved unsatisfactory.'[177] Another historian acknowledged that Maurice Rose's 'CCA's recent days of armoured training with the attached 22nd Infantry Regiment paid off richly,'[178] but failed to connect that success with the new all-arms battle groups. Instead he ascribed the breakout to

173 Fletcher, *The Universal Tank.*
174 Anonymous, *Taurus Pursuant,* p. 30.
175 Sandars, *Guards Armoured.*
176 GL Verney. *The Desert Rats* (Germany: BAOR, 1945), and Sandars, *British 7th.*
177 Sandars, *Guards Armoured.*
178 Weigley, *Eisenhower's Lieutenants.*

concentration, and to air power. A GAD veteran and noted military historian stated in answer to a question that:

> It was at *Bluecoat* that my division first fought as integrated groups of armour and infantry, and it seems to me that we fought very much like the Americans that you describe. I think it is probably wrong to suggest that the Americans invented something – although they certainly did not learn from the British.[179]

The question is resolved by a contemporary source unremarked by Graham and all other historians: *Taurus Pursuant* confirms that the British learned from the Americans:

> For the advance, which was to start at 0700 on July 30th, fresh brigade groupings [in 11 BAD] were adopted. The experience of both Seventh Armoured *and the Americans in the bocage country* [this author's emphasis] had demonstrated the necessity for the closest cooperation of tanks and infantry. We now attempted a closer cooperation than had yet been tried within an armoured division. In this region of thick woods and narrow roads winding between impassable hedges and ditches 10 feet deep, numerous local engagements were anticipated and under these conditions reasonable progress could only be assured by the infantry accompanying the tanks on all routes and often actually riding upon them. The division therefore moved into brigade groups: 29th Armoured Brigade Group on the left consisting of two of their armoured regiments (23H and 3 R Tks), the motor battalion (8 RB) and one infantry battalion borrowed from 159 (3 Mon); and 159 Infantry Brigade Group on their right with their remaining two units (4 KSLI and 1 Hereford), one armoured regiment (2 FF Yeo) and the armoured reconnaissance regiment (2 N Yeo), now as usual employed as a normal tank unit. For the reconnaissance and contact which our role demanded we were again allotted an armoured car regiment; this time it was the Second Household Cavalry.[180]

And so without publicity the unthinkable happened, and 11 BAD and GAD reorganised themselves into what were in effect Mixed divisions, and in the way called for years earlier by Burnett-Stuart, Montgomery-Massingberd, Jumbo Wilson, Wavell, and Auchinleck. All the arguments of Hobart, Liddell Hart and Fuller were implicitly rejected and sanity at last began to prevail in the British Army. Note that Montgomery had nothing at all to do with this development and nothing to say about it. It was better late than never, but the terrible death rate in the infantry prior to this outbreak of realism was testament to the power of fashionable reputations to sell a faulty prospectus and then to resist change. When the shortcomings were revealed by the Americans, the resulting silence must have been deliberate to allow Churchill, Brooke, Montgomery, Richards, Hobart, Dempsey, Briggs and Roberts to save face. All talk of 'cracking about' was gone, and the armoured divisions became in effect infantry divisions with tanks. The face-saving formula that the change was only to cover the period while the divisions fought in the bocage was later quietly forgotten. Problems however remained. Nobody in the armoured divisions was trained in all-arms, and the unjustified feelings of superiority inculcated in the tank men were never addressed in the way Slim had done. The under-armoured Cruiser tanks were not changed for I-tanks, which resulted in the Churchills of 6 GTB time and again outperforming them.

The history of the British Army in NWE needs rewriting, but in the opposite direction of recent scholarship like the following:

179 Dominick Graham in a letter on 8 January 1995.

180 Anonymous, *Taurus Pursuant*, p. 30.

> Though the troops had to contend with initially imprecise battle doctrines, limitations on capability imposed by some equipment shortcomings, and operational methods that did not always yield the expected benefits, the performance of the British Army in 1944-5 was impressive. It matched resources with objectives, developed proficient fighting power sufficient to overcome the enemy, and delivered a victory to the British state that has for too long been downplayed by the passage of time.[181]

Such a view of history has been characterised as the easy demonstration of inevitability which works only retrospectively.[182]

Montgomery when he planned Overlord had no more knowledge about how to defeat the German field army than to send a reinforced all-tank 7 BAD to create 'deep penetration – early'. The British efforts to break through from 8 June to 18 July were seriously intended and not the feints subsequently portrayed. They were unsuccessful because of an absence of all-arms co-operation, especially between tanks and infantry but also between the ground and the air, and because of the lack of an I-tank with impenetrable frontal armour and accurate aircraft. Only 6 GTB possessed the required knowledge, training and imperfectly suitable equipment, but they were kept back out of spite by Montgomery until 20 July. Their abilities became public knowledge on the occasion of their spectacular debut in *Bluecoat.* Meanwhile the Americans had re-engineered their procedures and formed all-arms battle groups as we have seen, although their lack of I-tanks resulted in their later failure at Metz and in the Eifel. Progress in the bocage began as early as 11 July. News of the US success became known to the British, and the first sign of new thinking was O'Connor's request to convert Priests into APCs for *Goodwood.* However the growing successes of the Americans and the *Goodwood* disaster finally forced the conservative British to regroup into all-arms battle groups hastily and without training. The result was the spectacular success of 6 GTB operating with their old mixed-division partners, 15 BID and of significantly improved performance by 11 BAD in *Bluecoat.*

The story has not previously been presented in these terms, which bring no credit to the commanders. Neither Bradley, Eisenhower nor Montgomery were convinced on the first day of *Cobra* that anything had really changed, and the breakout came as a surprise to all of them. Bradley implicitly slandered his troops by ascribing success to Quesada's TAF, and Weigley copied Montgomery by pointing to 'concentration'. Montgomery had no interest in admitting, even to himself, that the Allied forces under his command had been committed to battle in Normandy unprepared, and that it was left to the Americans at divisional level and to 6 GTB to teach him and Bradley how it should have been done. So the myth of Montgomery's Plan and of the 'hinge strategy' became acceptable to the brass and to historians, even though its threadbare inconsistencies have been visible all along as an example of the fallacy of *post hoc ergo propter hoc.* It also contradicted the common sense view that he who wills the end (strategy) is bound to will the means (tactics). It was irresponsible of Montgomery and Bradley to insist that they were responsible for strategy while giving the task of developing the necessary tactics, or rather the operational methodology, to divisional commanders when it was the responsibility of corps commanders, as will be discussed below.

181 Buckley, *Monty's Men*, p. 303.
182 R Pipes, *Russia Under The Old Regime.* (London: Weidenfeld & Nicolson, 1974).

The Creation of an Incomplete All-Arms Operational Methodology

Partial all-arms operational methodology (infantry, artillery and tanks) was the closest the British Army ever came in the Second World War to complete all-arms (infantry, artillery, tanks and aircraft under integrated battlefield command). Furthermore, even this incomplete methodology occurred to this author's knowledge only on a few occasions when certain units of two specific tank brigades were involved with units in cooperative infantry divisions, such as 2 CID, 15 BID and some parts of 3 BID. The tank units were NIH in 25 BTB in Italy with its Dawnay Doctrine,[183] formulated by Lt Col David Dawnay of the NIH when 25 BTB was part of 43 and 1 Mixed IDs; and 3 SG in 6 GTB in NWE which developed its own culture under Brig Verney when part of Bullen-Smith's 15 Mixed ID, during the period 15 January to 9 September 1943. In its previous training within Guards Armoured Division, 6 GAB had practised independent action and limited co-operation with the Motor Bn. Such lessons were unlearned in 15 Mixed ID while an RTR officer, Lt-Col McLeod, was attached to 6 GTB as Umpire to ensure mechanical efficiency was not neglected.

Bullen-Smith was an infantryman from 3 BID and a protégé of Montgomery. He insisted that the fundamental objective was to create mutual confidence based upon personal acquaintance between all ranks in both tanks and infantry, and this also formed the basis of the Dawnay Doctrine. It had also been Monash's way of developing close cooperation between his Australian infantry and Brig Courage's tanks for the Battles of Hamel and Amiens in 1918. Bullen-Smith laid down the additional principle that neither arm was predominant, and that it was the duty of each to help the other. This was an improvement on previous thinking that armour should dominate; but the step that would have contributed most to effectiveness – namely subordinating armour to infantry – was never taken in the British Army in the Second World War, with the exceptions of the temporary Mixed divisional organisation and of Slim's command in Burma. Again it was Monash who had insisted with Courage that the tanks should be under Australian infantry command at Hamel and Amiens. Tanks were never under command in Europe in the Second World War but always 'in support'. However, Bullen-Smith went a long way towards placing 6 GTB 'under command' in 15 Mixed Division.

> It was during this period that most practical problems of co-operation were worked out, with the exception of communication between tanks and infantry. No satisfactory method was ever devised for this even when combat showed its necessity.
>
> To weld these two arms into one proved to be a long and difficult task. Perhaps the hardest problem was that of communication between the man on the tank and the man on the ground. The human voice was no good on account of the noise made by the tank engines, and hand or flag signals were unreliable because the various members of the tank crew were more or less blind. Later on, telephones were installed at the back of the tanks, but these were by no means as easy to work in practice as in theory. There was also a bell system, whereby the man outside pressed a button to attract the attention of the Tank Commander.
>
> Great efforts were made to develop the wireless technique of both Tanks and Infantry. Within the Tank unit, all communications were by wireless, and this was developed to such a high degree of efficiency that a Commanding Officer at times would have over 70 stations on his 'net' The weakness in using wireless for communicating with the Infantry lay in operating the Infantry sets in battle. They were cumbersome, their bearers offered a conspicuous target for enemy snipers. It was not easy for the Infantry Battalion and Company to

183 http://www.northirishhorse.net/articles/8.html

> maintain an adequate supply and reserve of trained and efficient operators, and the sets were not robust enough to stand the rough and violent movements to which they were inevitably subjected. Further, if reliance were placed on wireless it necessarily tied the Infantry Platoon and Company Commanders to their wireless sets, and the Infantry Commanding Officers to their carriers with the wireless, and was liable at times to prevent them moving about wherever they wished.
>
> Such was the chief problem, but there were many others. By continuous training, a close and invaluable bond was cemented with the Divisional Artillery. Their officers were made familiar with tanks and later on they were actually equipped with tanks of their own. Officers of the Brigade were trained to observe and direct Artillery fire, and this training was put to good use in the very first battle.[184]

6 GTB survived a proposal in June 1943 to break it up to provide infantry reinforcements for Italy, against a background of Montgomery's persistence in calling for the abolition of tank brigades and the phasing out of I-tanks. In September and October 1943, the brigade took part for ten days in 8 Corps' Exercise *Blackcock*. The Brigade left 15 Mixed Div on 9 September 1943 to become 8 Corps' troops where they stayed until 7 June 1944. Their performance was rated as outstanding. This was the only large-scale training exercise they ever undertook due to the absence of suitable training grounds. They were introduced to the staff of 8 Corps under whom they later fought *Bluecoat*/Caumont, and were able to practice communications with them and the other Divisions.

> The exercise was a remarkably accurate forecast of the first time the Brigade was to go into action. The difficult approach march, the close co-operation with 15th Division, and the dashing attack of the Coldstream Guards to the final objective – all were repeated on 30th July 1944 in Normandy. From this first action one lesson stands out above all others – the value of perfect understanding between the Tanks and the Infantry. As has been said already, the 6th Guards Tank Brigade and the 15th Scottish Division had lived and trained together for many months. Although the fighting of the previous weeks had sadly thinned the Scottish ranks, their reputation was higher than ever, and there were still many of all ranks who were well known to officers and men of the 6th Brigade. It was an act of providence which ordained that the 6th Guards Tank Brigade should go into their first battle with their old friends, and there can be no doubt whatever that it was this combination, rather than any other factor, that made the attack a success. Had the Infantry been strangers, the Tanks would not have advanced alone so far. It was this lone advance which turned a successful attack into a decisive victory, but it was the confidence felt by every tank man that the Scottish Infantry would follow up as fast as they could, regardless of difficulties, that made this advance possible, and it was the feeling of comradeship that fired the Scottish Infantry with the determination to get up to their tanks by nightfall, cost what it might. Beside that lesson all else pales – mechanical efficiency, perfect wireless communications, good shooting, use of ground.[185]

Such mutual confidence and obligation between infantry and tanks was also the key reason why Operation *Chesterfield* successfully penetrated the Hitler Line.

6 GTB were now Independent 8 Corps' troops available to any infantry division needing tank support. During January 1944 there were some short periods of training with the 51 BID, giving

184 Forbes, *6th Guards*, pp. 6-7.
185 Op. Cit., pp. 14-15.

them the chance to speak to soldiers who had seen battle in Sicily. In March 1944, another serious proposal, this time by Montgomery, was made to break up the brigade to provide infantry reinforcements. Representations were made to Churchill himself and words were said into the ear of the King when in that same month at Thoresby Park in Nottinghamshire, he reviewed a drive-past of 200 tanks. Churchill quashed the proposal and ruled that the RAF Regiment should provide reinforcements for the Guards. Montgomery was irate and transferred 6 GTB to 21 AG, where it remained from 8 June to 16 July, and from 17 July to 28 July they were 2 Army troops. Montgomery wrote to the Director of Staff Duties at the War Office:

> You cannot take line reinforcements and draft them into Guards units just like that. The two disciplines are quite different and it does not work. Meanwhile I have to do something very quickly and the action I have taken is as follows:
>
> I have withdrawn 6th Guards Tank Brigade into Army Group Reserve. This means that it is not in the build-up for Operation OVERLORD and will not be called to France for a long time.
>
> I have replaced it in 2nd Army by 31st Armoured Brigade which was in Army Group Reserve. [There was no 31 BAB. Montgomery meant 31 BTB which included 7 RTR's Crocodile flamethrowers]. One of the Regiments is a flame thrower regiment and it suits me very well. I suppose the Prime Minister is within his rights to disregard the considered advice of the Secretary of State for War, Chief of the Imperial General Staff and myself, but I cannot mess up my operations.
>
> I must have a tidy set-up. I know so well what happens when the set-up is not tidy and is unbalanced. I shall, therefore, not take the 6th Guards Tank Brigade to the war.[186]

Montgomery's strong reaction showed that more was involved than a theoretical concern about reinforcements. His decision to eliminate the Churchill tank and the tank brigades had been thwarted. They did not fit with his plans for pushing forward south of Villers Bocage with columns of interchangeable armoured brigades equipped with Sherman Capital or Universal Tanks. The unreality of his plan was not revealed publicly until 7 BAD failed at Villers Bocage soon after D-Day. The subject of the Churchill Tank grumbled on until the end of hostilities, with Montgomery still publicly arguing about it with Churchill in March 1945.

It is instructive to examine what Montgomery's chosen armoured brigades actually did in Normandy. On D-Day 3 BID landed with 27 BAB, but received virtually no support from its Shermans in the initial drive to seize Caen. By 6 July, however, support came nominally from 33 BAB. This formation had landed on June 14 under command of 7 BAD, and thereby doubled that division's armoured component for the push south, exactly as Montgomery intended. For a month 33 BAB saw plenty of action but no fighting, endlessly shifting its position to block a threatened German breakthrough or to exploit the British breakthrough that never came. While 6 GTB sat waiting in Kent for Montgomery's ire to abate, 3 BID attacked without armour time and again, always supposedly with 'tank support' but without tanks actually present on the battlefield. It happened again in Operation *Charnwood*, when 2 Lincolns seized Hérouville and defended itself with PIATs against counterattacking MkIV tanks. On this occasion the CO of 144 RAC wrote a first-hand account of the shambles that was Montgomery's command:

186 IWM 21AG/1065/CNC Montgomery Papers quoted in Farrell, *Reflections*, p.55.

> On the 6th of July we heard that we were to take part in the forthcoming attack on Caen in support of the 3rd Infantry Division. We were not, however, to be part of the main attack but were to be held in reserve for subsequent exploitation.
>
> About noon on the 8th of July we were ordered to move forward from Basly through Cazelle to a position about two miles north of Lebisey, from where we could quickly reach the battle if required. While we were on the move, the CO was called forward by the Brigadier to an 'O' Group near Bieville, which was being heavily shelled. Apart from the shelling, the situation was reminiscent of the more chaotic sort of manoeuvres. It was pouring with rain and the 'O' Group was held in a sort of dugout where there was not enough light to see one's map. No one seemed to know what was happening and the orders were vague. There had been no previous tie-up with the infantry whom we might have to support, nor had any liaison arrangements been made so as to give us a continuous up-to-the-minute picture of how the battle was going.
>
> However good progress had apparently been made and Lebisey Wood had been captured. The 1st Northamptonshire Yeomanry with a company of infantry were to move forward and occupy the 60-ring contour, while we followed on to the northern part of the feature. How two regiments of tanks were to deploy in such a restricted area was not clear, and the orders were changed later. But any tendency to seek further enlightenment at this moment was firmly discouraged by the brigadier.[187]

Were Montgomery alive to answer this stricture, he would no doubt say that the criticism is nonsense because he did send Churchill gun-tanks to Normandy and they also achieved nothing initially. This was 34 Independent Tank Brigade comprising 107, 147 and 153 Regts RAC under Brig Clarke. They landed on 15 June and did nothing except prepare for various actions until 9 July when they saw Caen being bombed but were not called upon for *Charnwood*. Stephen Dyson, the radio operator/loader in 107 Regt RAC, The King's Own, wrote that by this time they were 'disappointed that after getting all worked up it was like taking your harp to a party and not being asked to play.'[188] Their first round fired in anger was during the battle for Hill 112 on 14 July. The inability to find work for these Churchills while the infantry was fighting desperately without tank support demonstrates the ignorance about I-tanks of Montgomery and of the commanders of 1 and 12 Corps, Honest John Crocker, who had been mentored by Hobart, and Neil Ritchie, who had been sacked after Gazala as GOC 8 Army but re-employed.

Meanwhile 6 GTB had moved on 30 April to Charing in Kent as part of the *Fortitude* deception. It ceased, however, to be battle-worthy when a third of its REME workshop was destroyed by a flying bomb brought down by an RAF fighter on 24 June, killing 51 men and wounding 40. 6 GTB REME Workshop was at Newlands Stud Farm in Hurst Wood, Charing Heath near Lenham in Kent. War Diary entry: '4 June (0600 hours) – V1 shot down by the RAF bounced off the flat roof of the riding school and landed amongst the Nissen huts'. It was almost certainly shot down by F/L I StC Watson of 165 Squadron in a Spitfire at 0618 hrs.[189] At this time the Brigade adopted its badge of blue/red/blue stripes across a white shield superimposed with a gold sword, point upwards.

The month required to rebuild the workshop facility was well spent tactically. Verney sent Farrell to Normandy on D-Day for attachment to XXX Corps' advanced HQ. His orders were to collect 'lessons in tank fighting', and report back to each battalion in the brigade. Farrell observed 7

187 Jolly, *Blue Flash*.
188 Stephen Dyson. *Twins in Tanks* (London: Leo Cooper & IWM, 1994), p. 49.
189 Brian Cull. *Diver! Diver! Diver!* (London: Grub Street, 2008).

BAD's disaster at Villers Bocage and spoke to Hinde. He noticed how the tanks stuck to the roads and failed to go cross-country. He went out in a DUKW to fetch Macmillan, GOC of 15 BID, and realised that his Brigade should have been arriving with their friends. Later, when Farrell read John Keegan's account[190] of the lack of support given to their friends of 15 BID in Cheux during Operation *Epsom* by the Churchills of 9 RTR in 31 BTB, which was the formation Montgomery had sent in their stead, he became filled with sadness.

Farrell returned on or about 20 June. According to what he wrote in his book, Farrell told the units that the hull-down training they had been doing was irrelevant in the bocage, and the objective must now be to use the Churchill's superior cross-country capability to close unseen with the enemy. 3 SG then put on Exercise Sizzle[191] near Stone, and since there is no mention of it in Forbes, it would appear that it was interestingly a battalion and not a brigade exercise. It provided a realistic foretaste of the hedgerows of the bocage, and caused a great deal of damage to private property. Unlike Shermans, which could not scale the earth banks, the Churchills climbed and crashed over them as if on a steeplechase. This author asked Farrell whether Sizzle was a result of the lessons he had brought back from Normandy, but Farrell denied it, and his book ignores the exercise.

6 GTB landed near Arromanches on 20 July to assemble in orchards at Esquay. Visits to a tank graveyard led to hasty welding of track plates to turrets and hulls in a vain attempt to keep out 88 mm shot, although later they would act as a primitive form of spaced armour to detonate *Faustpatrone* prematurely. On 28 July they moved with great difficulty to the ridge of Caumont l'Eventé on the right flank of the British line, and prepared for the Battle of Caumont/Operation *Bluecoat*. On 30 July with little time for reconnaissance or planning, with normal artillery support and the assistance of 60 US medium bombers from the Ninth Air Force which bombed Les Loges and Dampierre through thick mist, and accompanied by their old friends, 15 BID, the Brigade's 170 Churchills advanced 6 miles in close bocage right through the heavily mined German defences and out the other side to occupy two hills. The German defenders were the 326 Infantry Division supported by Jagdpanthers of 654 GHQ Anti-tank Battalion.

The advance of the inexperienced 6 GTB in its first ever engagement compared well with the performance of experienced units such as 7 BAD and 11 BAD and the Churchills of 31 BTB. 50 BID and 8 BAB in 30 Corps advanced only 2,000 yards, while 43 BID managed 2 miles but after that made little progress. 11 BAD made much better progress due to Roberts reorganising two brigades with equal numbers of tank and infantry units. But they still had a lot to learn and much to unlearn in the matter of tank-infantry co-operation.

> The armoured divisions tried it but never really got hold of it, because, having always looked down on tank-infantry cooperation as being not quite the thing, they were a little slow in understanding what was wanted. Also their tanks weren't good enough, and couldn't stand up to heavy mortars.[192]

3 SG brought with them the techniques refined in Operation Sizzle which the Americans had taken over a month to develop for themselves.

> We advanced with the infantry right round us, to protect us from Bazooka men and snipers, and from hedge to hedge, making each hedge a bound. Each hedge was practically a tank

190 John Keegan. *Six Armies In Normandy* (London: Jonathan Cape, 1982).
191 Erskine, *The Scots Guards*.
192 Erskine, *The Scots Guards*, p. 346.

> obstacle anyway, as they were always on top of very high earth-banks. As we came through a hedge we made the infantry look first to see if there was a Panther in the next field. If not, we went through into the middle of the field, brought the supporting Troops up to the hedge behind, and then settled down to a quarter of an hour's speculative shooting up of the next hedge, HE into any likely looking places, and Besa everywhere, including the tree-tops. All this you must imagine happening under intense mortar fire and very considerable small arms fire, mostly Spandau, coming from all over the place but from nowhere where you could pinpoint it. Every house we brewed up with HE fire at once. This may sound a very slow method of advance but it paid time and time again. Of course, if there was no return fire against the infantry, we went straight on, so it was not really as slow as all that... This method was all based on our own carefully worked out technique of tank-infantry cooperation, and in the Bocage it was extremely successful.[193]

To resume; 6 GTB had taken risks in moving ahead without the infantry, and 3 SG lost 8 Churchills to Jagdpanthers. The fast ride had tested crews and machines to the limit. The Brigade believed it drew the right lessons from Caumont. Success in the final analysis depended on the degree of understanding achieved between the Tanks and the Infantry.

> The 15th Scottish Division had fought nobly; throughout the long and tiring day they had winkled out the enemy, mopped up his positions and succeeded, most of the time, in keeping up with the tanks. The many days and nights spent with them in 1943 [as members of the same Mixed division] practising just such an attack, had paid handsome dividends. Above all, the Churchill tank, reinforced with track plates welded around the hull and turret, had justified all the confidence placed in it.[194]

The Brigade also learned the fearful reality that although their pre-APDS 6pdr and 75 mms were incapable of knocking out a Tiger or Panther head-on, they were not extended the same courtesy by the Germans.

> Although the Churchill was the most heavily armoured tank yet produced by Britain or America, it was still incapable of withstanding a direct hit from an 88. Every member of the Brigade knew that his passport to heaven was engraved with a large 88 and that round every corner and over every hill it might be handed to him by a gunner of the German Army.[195]

6pdr Ammunition Performance at 1 km against 30° homogeneous armour[196]

Type	Weight of Shot (lbs)	Muzzle Velocity (fps)	Penetration mm/inch
HE	6	2,700	nil
AP	6	2,693	74 mm/3 in
APCBC	7	2,775	88 mm/3½ in
APCR	4	3,528	90 mm/3¾ in
APDS	3.2	4.050	146 mm/6 in

193 Op. Cit., p. 345.
194 Forbes, *6th Guards*, p. 24.
195 Op. Cit., p. 26.
196 http://www.canadiansoldiers.com/weapons/ordnance/6pounder.htm

Note: Tiger I had 100 mm/4 in, and Panther 80 mm/3¼ in. These figures vary considerably from, and are wildly optimistic compared with, those quoted above by Gerry Chester from trials by NIH in Italy. There the 6pdr with APDS achieved only 127 mm or 5 inches at 500 yards or half the distance. It was, however, still enough to penetrate the Tiger I and Panther.

The 6pdr's performance was in the process of being radically upgraded through deliveries of sabot (APDS) as 6 GTB landed in Normandy. This resulted from the concern and foresight of Andrew McNaughton working in a semi-unofficial capacity. Had McNaughton been given responsibility for the design and specification of all equipment, then the 10 inches of frontal armour required to withstand all anti-tank weapons would possibly have been made available by D-Day, adding between 3 and 4 tons to the all-up weight of 40 tons. Such armour could even have been salvaged from tank graveyards and welded over the existing 4 inch plate, or production panels sent out from the factory and applied in the field, provided something had been done to strengthen the front suspension. One might ask what more should have been needed than the support of W.S. Churchill for his eponymous tank, but he seems to have been ignored.

Montgomery failed to solve the problem of Allied armour. His first action as commander of 8 Army was to form a *Corps de Chasse*. He offered its command to Horrocks who declined after an uncomfortable experience commanding 6 BAD. Lumsden took command, but the abysmal performance led to the withdrawal of the *Corps de Chasse* on 28 October, deeply upsetting Churchill. Montgomery converted Alamein into an Australian infantry assault northwards supported by Valentine tanks and artillery. This ran into heavy resistance, so again he had to bring back Lumsden's armoured divisions to attack in the centre, after Ultra decrypts suggested that the German armour had been switched to the north and the coast was clear.[197] Again the armour failed.

Alamein was won by the resolution of the infantry, especially the Anzacs under Morshead and Freyberg. They used anti-tank guns, Valentines, Stuarts and especially artillery to wear out 90 Light and 21 Panzer Divisions on the coast road. Although given a second chance on 2 November, Lumsden's 10 Corps of 1 BAD and 7 BAD was unable to break out and cut off the enemy, although armoured cars managed it. The Afrika Korps escaped. The tanks were eventually led through the Axis lines by Wimberley's and Freyberg's infantry. Instead of the infantry not being able to keep up with the armour, events showed that the reverse was always the problem. At this point Montgomery could have grasped the bull by the horns and broken up the armoured divisions, placing the armoured brigades directly under the command of the infantry, and gone looking for a frontally invulnerable I-tank. The thought would never have crossed his mind, being kept out by fear of ridicule from the cult of the apostles and their supporters for giving in to the reactionary infantry.

As has been stated, Montgomery seemed unable to distinguish one tank from another. Two Daimler armoured cars of 11 Hussars captured one of the first Tigers at Wadi Akarit in April 1943, but 8 Army reported there was no need for its own heavily armoured tank. Instead Montgomery began to call for a universal or capital tank, which he identified as the Sherman with the 75 mm gun. The fine performance in Tunisia of the Churchills of 4 Mixed Division and of the six Churchills of Kingforce under his own command, seems to have entirely escaped Montgomery's attention. He decided to send only Shermans to Sicily and Italy.

1943 was the year when action on tank armour should have been implemented, but was not. While the new German Tigers, Panthers and Elefants battled at Prokharovka and Olkhovatka in the Kursk Salient, Montgomery was corresponding with Archie Nye, the Deputy Chief of the

197 Hamilton, *Monty, Master*, p. 18.

Imperial General Staff, about armour. On 7 June 1943[198] he stated that the armoured divisions needed only Shermans, which should be improved as soon as possible with the British high velocity 75 mm or the American 76.2 mm gun, and he asked for one troop per squadron to be upgunned with 17pdrs. He thought that the Tiger was a serious potential menace if it appeared in large numbers, and asked for research to continue to increase gun-power and armour without increasing weight and size to compromise mobility. He failed to realise that a 30 mph Cromwell that could not pass a roadblock or a town was less mobile than a 13 mph Churchill with that ability. He said there was no place for the 95 mm close support tank.

On 28 August 1943[199] Montgomery wrote to Nye that only two types of tank were needed; a capital tank, which would be either the Sherman or the Cromwell that he had never seen, and a light tank like the latest Honey. He stated categorically that a heavy infantry tank was not wanted. When he wrote this there was still time in the nine months before D-Day to procure an infantry tank with frontal immunity to the 88 mm provided by 9-10 inches (230-250 mm) of vertical armour, and to ensure that tanks were integrated under infantry command in the mixed division.

But Montgomery wanted no mixed division, insisting that all armoured brigades (with cruisers) must be identical and capable of working with infantry or armoured divisions. He wanted no tank brigades (with I-tanks). He rejected the argument that conditions in NW Europe were different from those in Italy. He suggested sloped armour as on the Panther, and was categorical that 100 mm of frontal armour was enough for any tank. The Churchill VII was meanwhile going into production with 152 mm frontal armour but required at least 230 mm to keep out the 88 mm. Montgomery expressed his concern that German guns were more powerful than our own, and believed that the lesson of history was that the gun always came out on top. In battle it was the gun that counted, he said, and the need was for a tank with a dual-purpose gun superior to the enemy's 88 mm. He argued that the tank must be designed around the gun and not the other way round. Britain's military future had been placed by Churchill and Brooke into the hands of a didactic RSM-type spouting simplicities from beneath a black beret.

On 7 October 1943[200] Nye replied to Montgomery, saying that there was a strong feeling in Britain that the army tank brigades were necessary and would become more vital the closer they got to Germany. There was also a need, said Nye, for an upgraded infantry tank for the assault rôle with armour sufficient to withstand all mobile anti-tank fire at almost point-blank range, a conclusion that Martel would have reinforced. The new heavily armoured Churchill Mk VII came within reach of meeting this rôle. He argued for the 95 mm CS tank because of its superior performance with HE and smoke. They were aiming by end-year, said Nye, for 6 inches (152 mm) of armour on the Churchill and 4 inches (100 mm) on the Cromwell. He agreed about the need for bigger guns and said they were examining the 3.7 inch (92 mm) high velocity gun. They were trying to improve the 17pdr's (76 mm) HE shell and might be forced to a dual range table with corresponding dual dials on the elevating wheel for HE and AP. Nye warned that the 17pdr would never have capable HE performance. He said attempts to get the 17pdr into the Sherman looked promising.

What is revealed in these exchanges was a long-standing conflict between the Apostles of Mobility, led by Montgomery the infantryman, and the rest of the Army. We have seen how Churchill was promoting the heaviest armour that the Churchill could carry. There was also Martel, who was feeding into the War Office the lessons from the Eastern Front that the Tiger, Panther and Elefant with their heavy frontal armour and outstanding guns were outclassing Russian tanks and Lend-Lease Churchills.

198 IWM: BLM 117: Montgomery Papers.
199 IWM: Private Papers of FM Montgomery: BLM 117/2.
200 IWM: Private Papers of FM Montgomery: BLM 117/3.

> We had been pressing all the time [by the end of 1942] for the development of the next model of infantry tank to replace the Churchill. This needed much heavier armour [emphasis added] and a powerful gun. Pilot models were under construction. We knew that the Germans were building more powerful tanks for the close fighting and the Panthers and Tigers appeared for the purpose in 1943. Unfortunately a decision was taken just after I left for Russia to concentrate on the more mobile type of tank and not to give any priority to the development of new models of heavy infantry tank. This was a most unfortunate decision. If we had produced these new models of heavy tanks, they would have blown the Tigers and Panthers off the battlefield, but without them we failed badly in the close fighting in Normandy, in the later stages of the war.[201]

The requirement for an Infantry tank with the 17pdr was stated in late 1941, but abandoned when the 75 mm Sherman appeared in 1942 to Montgomery's approval. It was revived in 1943 on Martel's prompting. The Director of Tank Design was then thinking of providing frontal immunity from the 88 mm through sloped frontal armour, which Martel stated should be 200 mm thick. Montgomery, with Brooke's support, rejected the requirement. Even so, design studies to fit a 17pdr gun, sloped armour and a 650 hp engine into the Churchill began in December 1943 as the Churchill Mk VII was in pre-production, but progress was dilatory given the resistance of Montgomery and Brooke, and the prototype British Tiger, called Black Prince, was not ready until January 1945. Even then it failed to meet the requirements of Churchill or Martel. Brooke and Montgomery argued that the gun would always predominate. It was pointless, they said, to try and defeat the gun with thicker armour because it was a race the gun would always win. The unspoken assumption was that the extra weight of armour would reduce the tank's mobility, which was unthinkable to people in thrall to Liddell Hart's concept of an 'expanding torrent'. No account was taken of the practical problem of placing and concealing on the battlefield a gun the size of the 88 mm. It was already a monster and at the upper end of what was practical. A towed or SP105 mm high velocity anti-tank gun supplied in volume was beyond German manufacturing capabilities in 1944, and too vulnerable. The single most effective way of defeating the Germans on the battlefield was, and had been since 1940, a tank with frontal immunity to the 88 mm handled by a mixed division.

In Normandy on 25 June 1944 Montgomery wrote a letter to the Secretary of State stating that the Allies had nothing to fear from Panthers or Tigers, which he said were unreliable. He argued that the 17pdr could shoot straight through either German tank and that the Panther in particular was vulnerable to flank attack. Montgomery wrote this on the same day that he closed down his network of officers at corps and divisional level, who had been instructed to report on the performance of Allied equipment. He rejected the negative reports that flooded in about allied tanks, labelling them alarmist, bellyaching, and bad for morale. They were also a serious threat to his reputation, since any cursory examination would reveal that 21 Army Group was ill equipped because of his continuing opposition to heavy armour.

The next letter in the file was a memorandum on British armour from Montgomery dated 6 July 1944.[202] In it he asked for a Churchill upgraded with a more powerful engine and the 17pdr gun. It was a good tank, he now had the gall to say, and with these improvements it would do well. Until it got the 17pdr Montgomery asked that all Churchill units be given an establishment of one Churchill per troop fitted with a 6pdr firing sabot. The users, however, argued that the 17pdr Archer and the 76 mm M10 Tank Destroyer provided all the necessary mobile anti-tank defences.

---

201 G LeQ Martel. The Russian Outlook (London: Michael Joseph, 1947), p. 63.
202 IWM: Private Papers of FM Montgomery: BLM 117/14.

Montgomery declined to accept either the 76 mm Sherman or the Cromwell since they both lacked the 17pdr, and he therefore preferred, he said, the 17pdr Challenger. In general, Montgomery wrote, he hoped the 17pdr would see them through the war, but they should not he said, repeating Brooke's argument, be complacent since the gun always won in the end.

On 10 July 1944[203] Weeks replied patiently to Montgomery that the Churchill could not receive the 17pdr until April 1945, and that that date could be met only by retaining the current engine, which was retained in the Black Prince. He corrected Montgomery, telling him that it was the sloping front plate of the Panther and not the turret front that was immune to the ordinary 17pdr APCBC shot, but that the new 17pdr sabot round would easily defeat it. He told Montgomery that only 200 Challengers would be produced because of its inadequate turret armour.

In his last wartime memorandum on armour on 21 February 1945,[204] and in public comment made in the same month, Montgomery restated his commitment to mobility at the expense of survivability, but added that the flame-throwing Crocodile was an unqualified success and that an increase in its range of 120 yds was desirable. He commented on the new Capital tank being readied for battlefield trials, saying it should weigh 45 tons with the 17pdr and be able to travel 100 miles in 7 hours. Inspired by the Panther, whose glacis it copied, this became the Centurion Mk I. It still lacked frontal immunity to the 88 mm, which had begun its tank-killing spree in 1937 in Spain. In Montgomery's view, with which Hobart disagreed, Centurion would replace both the Comet and the lighter Churchill, as the fallacy of mobility continued postwar.

In the days prior to the debacle in the Hochwald, Montgomery stated that the Ardennes Offensive would probably have succeeded had the Germans possessed British cruiser tanks, and that 21 Army Group could not have made the big advances from Normandy to Antwerp if equipped with Tigers and Panthers. Maj R.C. Crisp, MC reacted strongly to this nonsense, and spoke for many in a letter to The Times of 11 March 1945 addressed to Richard Stokes MP. Crisp had fought in seven different types of British and American cruiser tanks culminating in the Cromwell, and had lost seventeen of them. He had been wounded four times. He bitterly criticised the 'fast, lightly armoured and therefore more mobile' theory that had condemned the British to inferior tanks and horrendous losses. He envied the Red Army for its heavy tanks advancing on Berlin and destroying the Panthers and Tigers.

The military establishment closed ranks behind Montgomery and Brooke, giving priority to loyalty to the chain of command. Raymond Briggs, who had risen to DRAC in spite of abandoning Kippenberger's New Zealanders at El Mreir and failing to exploit in the *Corps de Chasse*, wrote to Montgomery a 'brown-nosed' comment about Crisp, and by inference dismissing Churchill:

> I am satisfied that we are better guided by compliance with the requirements of the Cs-in-C in the field than by the more frequent reiterations of persons less qualified to dictate policy on military weapons.[205]

The only effective institutional challenge of Churchill was the Parliamentary motion of censure on 1 July 1942 on the conduct of the war by the Minister of Defence. Churchill had always claimed to be a loyal servant of the House and to serve at the House's pleasure, which meant in any position the House should wish him to fill. There is little doubt that the House overwhelmingly wanted Churchill to remain as PM but to cease being Minister of Defence, which he had discharged incompetently. The motion called Churchill's bluff, and he chose to turn the motion

203 IWM: Private Papers of FM Montgomery: BLM 117/17.
204 IWM: Private Papers of FM Montgomery: BLM 117/20.
205 Fletcher, *The Universal Tank,* p.111.

into a vote of confidence in himself as PM by saying he would not continue as PM if he could not be Minister of Defence.

The proximate cause of the heavy defeat of the motion was John Wardlow-Milne's nomination of the Duke of Gloucester as military supremo, and Churchill's refusal to go along with it, making it clear that he would resign as PM if the MOD were removed from him. However, the cause-in-fact, or sine qua non cause, of the motion's defeat was the lack in the English-speaking armies of any analytical framework for developing a theory of operations and therefore of assessing alternative operational methodologies. The English language even lacked appropriate language, and it was believed that 'Tactics begins where strategy ends'.[206]

For Germans and Russians, by contrast, *Operativ, Operational Art* or *Operational Methodology* as it will be called here, fitted between strategy and tactics, and was the art of formulating a mix of divisions and equipment with men trained in their use to fulfill the operational goals set by minor strategy. Operational Methodology was the task of corps commanders.

Theoretical military organisation and allocation of responsibilities

Rank (* = General)	Unit/Formation commanded	Number commanded	Responsibility
Sergeant/Corporal	Section	11	Minor Tactics
Lieutenant/Sergeant	Platoon (3 sections)	33	Minor Tactics
Major/Captain	Company (3 platoons)	106	Minor Tactics
Lt Colonel	Battalion (6 companies)	800	Minor Tactics
Brigadier (*)	Brigade (3 battalions)	2,500	Tactics
Major-General (**)	Division (3 bdes & Arty)	18,000	Tactics
Lt-General (***)	**Corps (3 to 8 divisions)**	**55 – 150,000**	**Operational Methodology**
General (****)	Army (2 to 3 corps)	110 – 300,000	Minor Strategy
Field Marshal (*****)	Army Group (2 – 3 armies)	¼ – 1 million	Minor Strategy
General (*****)	Theatre (2 – 3 army groups)	½ – 3 million	Strategy
General Staff, War/ Defence Minister	National Forces	5 – 10 million	Grand Strategy
Combined Chiefs, Premier & President	Coalition Forces	10 – 20 million	Grand Strategy

Monash argued persuasively that military success depends on good staff work, adequate equipment and trained soldiery in that order of priority, and that despite commanding the best troops in the world at that time. Others, if they thought about it, fundamentally disagreed with him. Fuller believed success depended only on equipment without the need for staff work, arguing that, 'tools or weapons, if only the right ones can be invented, form 99 percent of victory.'[207] He claimed that the long years of apprenticeship and military experience required in an effective staff officer were detrimental to good performance. Fuller, together with Liddell Hart, called for the abolition of

206 OA Forsyth-Major. *Elements of Tactics* (Aldershot: Gale & Polden, 1916).
207 JFC Fuller. *The Application of Recent Developments in Mechanics and Other Scientific Knowledge to Preparation for Future War on Land* (Journal of the RUSI 65, May 1920).

military academies and the promotion to high rank of young and broadly educated university men possessing courage, creative intelligence and good health.

'Slosher' Martel (he had excelled at boxing) held similar ideas when he raised the Armoured Corps in 1941. He believed, however, that good soldiers were the priority, and that equipment would 'follow along' without a need for trained staff. In spite of bitter opposition, which he dismissed with contempt, he was allowed to remove the first-rate 7 BIB (Guards) from 3 BID and turn it into the pedestrian 5 GAB in GAD. Good equipment never followed along because there was no trained armoured corps staff to analyse the need and specify the equipment, and of course none to analyse the cause of British armour incompetence, and how to rectify it. The field was left to Montgomery to do as he wished through his Armoured Adviser, Maj Gen G.W. (Ricky) Richards – who had been Hobart's Adjutant in 4 RTC in 1928 – as figleaf. Martel wanted Richards's post, and was angered when Montgomery turned him down on the grounds that 'he had only commanded a few tanks in action south of Arras in 1940'.[208] No one dared to inform Montgomery, who in any case would not have listened, that but for Martel's 'few tanks in action south of Arras in 1940' Montgomery himself would probably have spent the rest of the war in a POW camp in Lower Saxony. Hobart and Martel did not get on, having no framework by which to sort out their differences.

Montgomery, the famous trainer and technical illiterate, also believed of course that trained soldiery were the priority. His official biographer opined that had Montgomery not been the son of a bishop and educated at public school, he would have made a career as an RSM,[209] for he loved imparting the minutiae of war to his men. For the Canadian Harry Foster,[210] Montgomery's idea of excellent staff work was the ability to create accurate movement tables for his entire army group, confusing military art with a mechanical facility required of a competent Brigadier General Staff (BGS), or a computer. Montgomery avoided the intellectual and creative give-and-take among intellectual equals that was common in German, Russian and the British staff before he took over. He avoided the company of his peers unless he was instructing them, preferring callow youth with whom, his critics claimed, the 'Master' wallowed in obtusity. Eric Dorman-Smith described how 'this silly, small man' behaved towards those threatening his authority:

> True Story.
> Time – 1927. Place – The Staff College.
> Dramatis Personae – teacher Montgomery (Lt Col), student Dorman-Smith (Capt).
>
> Scene I. The Junior Division has just done an exercise run by Monty. There an infantry division checked in advance by the very slight obstacle of the Blackwater stream and a built-up area beyond lightly held by an ill-defined enemy. What to do? Dorman-Smith solution, judged wrong; send over strong fighting patrols on a wide front – there may be nobody there. Montgomery's Directing Staff Solution; halt for 24 hours, bring up the divisional artillery, stage a divisional attack.
>
> Dorman-Smith comment, off-stage, 'Montgomery's only idea of tactics is to take a sledge-hammer to crack a nut'. This snide and undisciplined aside was reported later to Montgomery.

208 Macksey, *Armoured Crusader.*
209 Nigel Hamilton. *The Full Monty* (London: Allen Lane, 2001).
210 Foster, *Meeting of Generals.*

> Scene II. The Staff College ante room. Time – sherry before luncheon. Dorman-Smith on bum warmer drinking happily. Enter CO Montgomery who strides in his little man walk up to Dorman-Smith. Following dialogue.
>
> M. 'What's this I hear, Dorman-Smith; you think my idea of tactics is to take a sledgehammer to crack a nut? Is that true? Is that true?'
>
> D-S. 'Perfectly true, Colonel.'
>
> Montgomery strides to the door, slowly, 'Preposterous! Preposterous!'
>
> Dead silence among startled students. D-S finishes his sherry.
>
> Monty never really forgave. But what a silly small man he is. However, there is your genesis of the Rhine crossing. Monty remained absolutely true to form between 1927 and 1945.
>
> But why did it have to be me?[211]

A classic example of how operational methodology worked instinctively in the old British Army before Churchill destroyed its effectiveness, was Operation *Compass* under Maj Gen Richard O'Connor, who was in effect a corps commander. Wavell was Commander-in-Chief Middle East, effectively an Army Group commander covering nine countries and parts of two continents. He commanded three divisions and two brigade groups when the Italians declared war in June 1940 and threatened Egypt from their colony of Libya. Lt Gen Maitland (Jumbo) Wilson, effectively an army commander whose troops were spread from Abyssinia to Persia, had appointed Maj Gen Richard O'Connor, the GOC 7 BAD, to command the Western Desert Force. His task was to keep Egypt out of the hands of the Italians, and benefited from the farseeing decision of Elles and Montgomery-Massingberd to specify and order the Matilda II I-tank.

O'Connor commanded a small corps and established a small staff of Harding, Galloway and Beresford Peirse. He was reinforced with 4 Indian Div, parts of 6 Australian Div and of 4 NZ Div, and 7 RTR's 57 Matilda tanks. O'Connor found,

> the most able and thoroughly professional command and staff that any British Force enjoyed in the war, on a scale small enough to permit personal orders and an easy flexibility... O'Connor's expositions of his plans were modest and tentative. His plans spoke for him. O'Connor had the complete confidence of his troops. In contrast to Montgomery he had not been an able lecturer at staff college. His public manner was always reserved ... The difference between O'Connor and Montgomery was that O'Connor detested publicity and Monty lived on it, not only lived on it, but began it: and for very good reason.[212]

Under Wavell, O'Connor flourished. Later, under Montgomery, he did not. Montgomery did not expect Corps commanders to think, and novel suggestions were usually unwelcome. Montgomery in effect acted as commander right down to corps level, and decided which divisions should fight, where and how. For example, when O'Connor as corps commander was informed of the minor strategic objective of Operation *Goodwood*, he informed Dempsey, his army commander, of his plan to innovate the use of Kangaroo APCs to ensure infantry were up with the armour to suppress the Pakfront. Dempsey vetoed O'Connor's suggestion according to Carlo D'Este after, one would imagine, checking with Montgomery; O'Connor later wished he had been more insistent. Without a language, however, in which to discuss the corps commander's task, O'Connor was condemned for contravening Montgomery's doctrine and for importing confusion into Montgomery's tidy

211 LHCMA: Box 2/1 GB99 KCLMA Thompson, letter from Eric O'Gowan (né Dorman-Smith) on 2 April 1960 to RW Thompson.

212 Corelli Barnett. *The Desert Generals* (London: William Kimber, 1960), pp. 27-29.

albeit disastrous battle plans. Allied inability to think in operational terms had other serious consequences; John Campbell[213] mused that this inability may have proved a greater inhibition to the exploitation of Ultra than the allegedly excessive regard for its security.

Montgomery believed that having laid down the doctrine, all that remained was to implement the right strategy. Unfortunately he laid down the wrong doctrine on tank-infantry cooperation in February 1944, as we have seen, and the probable reason was his desire to eliminate detail without bothering to consider its precise meaning, believing such matters should be settled at divisional level or below.[214] This led to conflict both with corps commanders, whose job it was, and with Eisenhower.

> Doctrine is the officially sanctioned approach to military actions – the considered opinion as to the best way of doing things.[215]

Doctrine was a corpus of 'school solutions' imposed by a commander on his army. It was different from War Office 'policy', which was advice that the army group commander could take or leave, and different from Operational Research (OR). OR was the study of the optimization of systems such as convoy and the bomber stream, and the study of the application of new technology such as radar to old problems like the location of enemy mortars. Montgomery had his own OR team.

Operational Methodology was none of these things, but was rather the art of assembling a force combining the methodology, the equipment and sufficient trained troops to achieve the minor strategic objective. It required mastering enemy methods that were themselves changing as new equipment was introduced and the Germans countered allied methods that became familiar to them. Operational Methodology was therefore dynamic. Something that worked today might be neutralised days later. It was the art, not the science, of war.

In Hobart's 79 BAD, 21 AG had the rudiments of such a facility for studying Operational Methodology, but it was in the wrong place. Hobart controlled the specialised armour, and insisted his people be involved in its planning, its approval, and its use, killing any ideas he did not like, such as APCs in the first instance. Hobart, through his amanuensis, promoted himself:

> During its 2½ years of existence the 79th Armoured Division has carved out a unique position for itself. The decision made in 1943 by the CIGS to vest in one man the control and development of all specialist armoured devices, has paid a good dividend.
>
> The principle of advice and control has proved a success. Army Commanders when planning an operation, have taken advice from 79th Armoured Division and then submitted their requirements to Army Group. When approval has been given, mixed detachments of specialist units have been placed in support of the formations concerned. They remain under the command of the 79th Armoured Division Brigadier or Regimental Commander selected who also plays the rôle of adviser to the operating Commander.[216]

Hobart's valid responsibility was to prepare and make ready the specialised armour for use. His empire building and refusal to lose control of armour because only he 'understood' it was another mark of the cult leader, and added one more obstacle to ensure no new Monash could appear in 1944 in NWE to forge an updated all-arms operational methodology.

---

213 John Campbell. *Dieppe Revisited* (London: Routledge, 1993).
214 Place, *Military Training*, p. 152.
215 Paul Johnston. *Doctrine is not enough* (Parameters, Autumn 2000).
216 Anonymous, *The Story*.

The bitter scenes in Kervenheim between 4 CG in their Churchill Mk IVs and 141 Regiment RAC in their Churchill Mk VII Crocodiles, at a time when at least one hundred Mk VIIs were standing idle in tank parks for reasons known only to Hobart, undermined Hobart's self-satisfied paean to his empire building and monopoly control over the only tank that could reliably succeed, at least some of the time, against the Germans.

The lack of an allied mechanism for studying and countering German methods was the cause of significant weakness that has led some to condemn 'Montgomery's very mediocre leadership which cost his troops high casualties and almost lost him his command.'[217]

The problem was most acute at corps, described by Horrocks as, 'the highest formation which can be said to fight the day to day tactical battles.'[218]

The British corps comprised a permanent HQ and specialised units but without permanently assigned divisions. During planning periods it was without troops. This had not been true of Canadian, or Australian, corps ever since Currie and Monash had won their battle for independence in the First World War. Horrocks described 21 AG as Montgomery's personal fiefdom:

> I think it might be helpful if I made some remarks on how the higher formations of the Army worked in the campaign. Two facts must be stressed; first, that there did not, could not, exist any sort of manual setting out in precise terms the rôles and duties of organizations such as an Army Group, an Army or even a Corps; secondly, and this follows from the first point, that the quality of the personalities concerned and of their relationships with each other was of immense importance.[219]

This was self-serving and unhistorical, and raises questions how Horrocks could have passed staff college (psc) let alone entered Sandhurst, where he scored sixth-lowest of the 167 successful applicants for cadetships, even after adding bonus points for an OTC certificate. In the First World War, doctrine (not that the word was used) and tactics were widely disseminated at corps level through *SS* pamphlets, after action reports and informal communications between the corps commanders. The SS publications built on FSR 1 and at corps level were used to update the associated manuals.[220] The result was that 'from 1916 onwards, corps was the highest level of command concerned with the detail of operations, and success was crucially dependent on the planning of corps staffs.'[221] Operations were planned and executed at corps. Unfortunately in the Second World War the importance of the corps' rôle declined in the desert campaign of 1941-2, and was only patchily rebuilt since commanders like Horrocks were unable intellectually to handle the tasks, and relied on Montgomery, called 'Master'.

Horrocks did not think the Army Commander contributed much, writing that 'I have often been asked whether Dempsey was much involved in the higher planning of the Normandy campaign. I don't think so.'[222] Instead Montgomery controlled Second Army, and kept close personal tabs at the unit level through his LOs. He directed major operations personally and before Arnhem and again at Bremen went over Dempsey's head to Horrocks. The Canadian Maj-Gen Harry Foster thought Montgomery a 'bastard to deal with', but added that his 'relationships with most senior officers were more like an English housemaster with his sixth-form prefects than that of an army commander.'[223]

217 Heinz Magenheimer. *Hitler's War* (London: Cassell, 2002).
218 Horrocks, *Corps Commander.*
219 Ibid.
220 Andy Simpson. *Directing Operations* (Staplehurst: Spellmount, 2005).
221 Ibid.
222 Horrocks, *Corps Commander.*
223 Foster, *Meeting of Generals.*

The rôle of army and corps commanders was reduced to ensuring the mundane routine matters were looked after. 'Smelling the battlefield' was how Horrocks described this activity. It involved checking that the arrangements were holding, and 'maintaining morale'. Horrocks drove the divisions, and insisted commanders knew the exact location of every unit and what it was doing. It was control for the sake of maintaining a firm grip, and proxy for Montgomery.

Not satisfied with doing his inferiors' jobs, Montgomery famously made a bid to take over Eisenhower's strategic job as ground commander, while Eisenhower returned the compliment by involving himself in 'tactics' in which, according to de Guingand, he was Montgomery's superior as a field commander. Eisenhower left most of the administrative duties to Bedell Smith while he concentrated on operations in the field.[224]

Montgomery had no time for innovation, and did not expect it from 'his' people. Horrocks therefore had little of importance to do. Horrocks's book *Corps Commander* gives a measure of the man. 3 BID, whose Jimmy Stokes won a VC on March 1 at Kervenheim, was in Horrocks' XXX Corps, but the reader will find no mention of Stokes or of the battles described in this book. Instead, Horrocks and co-author Eversley Belfield covered in detail the doings of II Canadian Corps and their two VCs won by Tilston and Cosens. Horrocks ignored 3 BID probably because it was commanded by the successful Bolo Whistler, who saw through Horrocks and came to despise him. Ignoring 3 BID saved Horrocks from dealing with the tricky question of why the breakthrough at Winnekendonk was not reinforced by II Canadian Corps. In this case Horrocks was disloyal to those he commanded, which is a serious charge to level at a soldier. Instead of using feedback from the divisional commanders to seek ways of improving their battlefield performance, Horrocks saw his job as keeping a lid on discontent by making soothing noises to the harassed, and accepting no excuses. Horrocks developed man-management and control, rather than operations, into an art, describing himself as a 'subaltern general'.

Some of the feedback Horrocks got was quite crisp. Lt-Col Eddie Jones wrote:

> We first became aware of the Reichswald in the very early days of October 1944. The Battalion ...moved ... for Operation *Gatwick*. It was rumoured that Bolo replied that he was perfectly prepared to carry out this (*Gatwick*) order but they shouldn't expect to see him or his Division again until hostilities were over.[225]

Two consequences resulted from Horrocks's limitations. The quality of the operational plans was never debated, and there was no self-criticism. Montgomery conferred or didn't as he saw fit, worked out his plan in his head and then wrote the outline down for his planners to flesh out. He permitted no debate, which he called bellyaching, and insisted on the fiction that all outcomes were foreseen. If the operation failed tactically it was declared a strategic success by those for whom loyalty had turned into the obtuse sin of blind faith.

The second result was more serious. 21 AG persisted in practices that the Americans had abandoned, and seem to have been unaware of the American attempts to ameliorate the Sherman's vulnerability. Suggestions made on occasion by divisional and corps commanders were rejected. Michael Carver[226] recalled discussions prior to D-Day about reorganizing the armoured division into permanent tank-infantry groupings to improve co-operation. Montgomery vetoed the discussions because the requirement was thought to be limited to the bocage, and because his doctrine required tanks to lead as infantry could not keep up. In July 1944, after being denied permission to

224 F De Guingand. *Generals At War* (London: Hodder & Stoughton, 1964), p. 103.

225 Letter from Eddie Jones.

226 Michael Carver. *Out Of Step* (London: Hutchinson, 1989).

use APCs, O'Connor in his turn rejected Roberts's request to fight 11 BAD in mixed tank-infantry groups, mooted before D-Day and by then being implemented by the Americans. When Roberts demurred, O'Connor told him that if he didn't like his instructions then another armoured division would be found to lead the advance.[227]

Churchill and Brooke had foisted on the army in NWE a second-rate commander who instituted a personalised system that would have horrified the corps commanders of the First World War. Montgomery bullied everyone except Alan Brooke. The result of showing initiative could be an interview followed by a movement order to the UK. There was consequently a lack of openness.

> Intelligence reports were often misleading. An intelligence officer in 3rd Canadian Infantry Division attributes this to the climate of war in 1945. 'Senior staff only heard what they wanted to hear. They had already made the plan; what they wanted was substantive backup from the 'I' guys. If you didn't agree with them, you found yourself out in the field minding the transport echelon.[228]

Dempsey revealed to Chester Wilmot the degree of his blind faith in Montgomery, and the operational confusion underlying the persistent failure to break through:

> The attack we put in on July 18 [*Goodwood*] was not a very good operation of war tactically, but strategically it was a great success, even though we did get a bloody nose. I don't mind about that, I was prepared to lose a couple of hundred tanks. So long as I didn't lose men. If I had tried to achieve the same result with a conventional infantry attack, I hate to think what the casualties would have been.[229]

Lt Gen AGI McNaughton and Maj Gen Georges P Vanier inspecting the vehicles and equipment of 3 Battalion, RCE in England, 6 May 1943. (Lieut Dwight E Dolan/Canada. Dept of National Defence/Library & Archives Canada/PA-211277)

227 Delaforce, *The Black Bull.*
228 Whitaker, *Rhineland.*
229 Delaforce, *The Black Bull.*

Dempsey avoided the fact that neither O'Connor nor Roberts had proposed a 'conventional' infantry attack, whatever was meant by this phrase, and the idea of procuring a tank with frontal immunity to the 88 or putting the infantry into APCs would never have occurred to Dempsey.

Operational Methodology needed a champion and there was an excellent candidate for that rôle, combined with that of 'Weapons Supremo'. The first commander of the Canadian Corps, Lt-Gen Andrew McNaughton of Vimy Ridge fame and an artillery officer of greater ability than Alan Brooke, was interested, according to Walter Lippmann, in 'the relation of the design and manufacture of weapons to their use.'[230] Intellectually a giant, he combined scientific bent (he had a patent covering the use of cathode ray tubes for aircraft detection, the basis of radar) with deep knowledge of the military and artillery (he was well-known for promoting air-burst ranging, and sabot) and was acquainted with rising stars like Dempsey. He had been President of the National Research Council in Ottawa between 1935 and 1939, and had close connections with the Canadian Manufacturers' Association, with experience of North American arms procurement. His performance on 11 April 1942 at a meeting approved by the Director General of Weapons Procurement to overcome the inertia of the Ordnance Board, at which he presented his plans for sabot, was convincing. It inspired Sir Albert Stern to pursue what ended up as the vote of censure on Churchill on 1 July 1942 – see above – which, however, McNaughton had nothing to do with.

> Sir Albert Stern ...felt instinctively that McNaughton was the only person of stature who could save the Allies in the armament field. He suggested Canada should be approached for McNaughton's services. It was obvious to Stern that Professor Lindemann, Churchill's scientific advisor who supported the Ordnance Board, would have to go if McNaughton's services were to be effective; and Lindemann obviously would not go as long as Churchill remained Minister of Defence. Here, Stokes-Rees asserts, was the reason for the vote of censure of July 1942.[231]

Cdr Stokes-Rees was Superintendent of Armament (Guns) at the Ministry of Supply. McNaughton's sacking was engineered by Brooke and Paget for being 'unprofessional' and lacking in 'combat efficiency' during Exercise Spartan, 4 to 14, March 1943.[232] His replacement, Harry Crerar, could not hold a candle to McNaughton, but was judged by Brooke to have put on 'a real good show' and 'improved that Corps out of all recognition'. The sacking revealed more about Brooke than about MacNaughton. When Brooke's diary was published, McNaughton criticised it as 'egocentric bunk' for including a mendacious description of a meeting Brooke claimed he had with McNaughton in 1942 over Churchill's plan to invade Norway. The trouble between the two men can be traced to the Staff College in 1921, when Brooke was an artillery expert who lectured the students including McNaughton. Brooke lacked the training to make full use of the many scientific developments to aid gunnery in the field, and when he was seconded to the Canadian Corps he had shown no sympathy with McNaughton's counter-battery methods. Hastings Anderson, Commandant of the Staff College, asked McNaughton to give a lecture on 'The Organisation of Counter-Battery Work', which was given to both divisions. McNaughton excelled, and Brooke was put in his place.

Equipment inadequacies were a major cause of the difficulties experienced by the Western Allies throughout the war. Churchill, Brooke and Montgomery were responsible, and all three were quite out of their depth in such technicalities, with Brooke and Montgomery more so than Churchill

230 JL Granatstein. *The Generals* (Toronto: Stoddart, 1993).
231 Swettenham, *McNaughton*, p. 225.
232 John Nelson Rickard. *The Test Of Command* (Canadian Military History, Vol 8, No. 3, Summer 1999).

who at least recognised the need for a heavily armoured tank. McNaughton knew that what was needed to improve performance was not a spurious ability to put on a show, like Montgomery and Crerar, but equipment and systems for destroying the German army on the battlefield. His method of air-burst ranging to improve accuracy was never implemented.[233] Sabot was his successful answer to German tanks, and CAS, including dive-bombers, his answer to German anti-tank guns. McNaughton recognised this as early as 1940. 'The Germans', he pointed out, 'are using bombers as long-range artillery and the stronger we can get the air component closely associated with the ground troops the better'.[234]

Brooke and Montgomery never grasped the CAS problem which became, together with the cruiser tank debacle, a major reason for 21AG's ineffectiveness. They both insisted on unquestioning obedience and mundane methods, while stifling debate. Brooke harboured a grudge over McNaughton's insistence on keeping the Canadians together.[235] McNaughton must have made Brooke profoundly uneasy, and he was happy to get him out of the way. The widow of Brig Worthington, who established 1 Canadian Tank Brigade, and converted 4 CID into 4 CAD, questioned the results of exercises used to get rid of McNaughton:

> Spartan was not a success, and to this day (in 1961) it is a mystery to Worthy how the plans went so far astray. As outlined by the Army Commander, the original order of attack was good. Had it been executed in the manner General MacNaughton made clear to Worthy's ears, at least, the results would have been outstandingly successful. But the execution seemed to that observer incredibly contrary to what the Army Commander intended.[236]

Montgomery was fixated on training, and unsurprisingly organised 21 AG like his old school, St Paul's. He acted as High Master with his young LOs as prefects who actually referred to him as 'master'. Each curriculum subject, such as artillery or engineers, was in the hands of a 'senior master' CRA or CRE, while divisional commanders were the housemasters. Montgomery made all the important decisions after consultation with whomever he selected. In the important matter of special armour, but probably on all armour, he consulted Hobart and Richards.

> It is significant that from the time of their first meeting on the 12th (January, 1944) nothing is to be found in writing concerning the special relationship (between Montgomery and Hobart) ...Borthwick (GSO.2 (Ops)) noticed the significant manner in which Hobart's ideas often foreshadowed much of what came to pass ...There are very few records of what transpired between Montgomery and Hobart whenever they met in private, but it is inconceivable that a very considerable exchange of ideas by direct or indirect means did not take place. Clearly Montgomery sought advice and Hobart was the last man in the world to withhold it.[237]

Enquiries made at Bovington confirm that no records of their meetings are known to exist.

Horrocks was coy about naming Montgomery and Hobart; 'My superior commanders allotted me the divisions and specialist arms which, in their opinion, were required for the forthcoming battle.'[238] Officially Hobart held two positions; GOC 79 BAD and 'Specialised Armour Adviser'.

233 Swettenham, *McNaughton*, p. 143.
234 Op. cit., p. 42.
235 Op. cit., p. 167.
236 Larry Worthington. *Worthy* (Toronto: Macmillan, 1961), p. 189.
237 Macksey, *Armoured Crusader*.
238 Horrocks, Corps Commander.

He was one of Churchill's favourites and had Brooke's support. With no CRAC once the position held by Martel was abolished in 1942 without replacement, Hobart controlled the armour in 21 AG. He contracted directly with British industry, and by-passed the Directorate of Research at the War Office, dealing exclusively through the ACIGS(W), Gen Evetts, who used his own authority and that of Brooke to remove obstructions. Hobart lived side by side with Montgomery, and by mid-February 1944 had already, according to Macksey, established the rule that a senior member of 79 BAD was present during operations at every level of command down to Division. Macksey explained how the 'system whereby Hobart and his HQ staff were consulted by Montgomery or his staff ... guaranteed the observance of 79th Armoured Division control. Once the nature and scope of an operation had been formulated, Hobart decided in person on the exact composition of the force to be employed before sending one of his brigadiers to live with the formation charged with the whole show.'[239]

De Guingand described how Hobart got his way 'Some of the staff under me would become terrified when they knew General Hobo was about. He was such a go-getter that they never really knew until he had left what new commitment they had been persuaded to accept.'[240] Hobart never criticised Montgomery openly, even when they disagreed over the wisdom of replacing Infantry and Cruiser tanks with a Universal Tank. The Churchill was, ironically, important to 79 BAD.

Strategic decisions were made by Eisenhower at SHAEF about such things as whether to fight on a broad or narrow front, the composition of Army Groups, their boundaries, supply lines and where to concentrate, and liaison with the Russian ally. In February 1945 Eisenhower chose a broad front. His orders, including the transfer of 9 US Army into 21 AG, were issued to Montgomery and Bradley, who in their turn translated these strategic decisions into the minor strategy of hinges or pincer movements involving the three armies.

Montgomery ordered Crerar's 1 Canadian Army to strike east from Groesbeek to Wesel in *Veritable*; Simpson's 9 US Army to strike north from Julich to Düsseldorf and Wesel in *Grenade*; and Dempsey's 2 British Army to feint north while preparing for the Rhine crossing. Each army commander then gave geographical objectives to his corps commanders together with their boundaries, the identity of army troops they would receive (AGRAs, Tank Brigades, and units of 79 BAD), their timetable and the name of their operation: Crerar passed on *Veritable* to Horrocks, but later refined it, giving *Blockbuster* to Simonds with Wesel on the Rhine as objective, and *Leek* and *Heather* to Horrocks with Geldern and Wesel as objectives. Simpson interpreted his orders, giving Wesel as objective through Geldern and Rheinberg to Gillem's 13 US Corps, Orsoy on the Rhine as objective through Krefeld to Anderson's 16 US Corps, and Uerdingen on the Rhine as objective through München-Gladbach and Neuss to Crittenberger's 19 US Corps. These five corps commanders then wrote operational orders for each division by allocating centre lines and boundaries, setting timetables, splitting out the allocated army support, and sending corps transport where necessary to collect the allocated troops. Simonds opted for a replay of *Totalise/Tractable* without apparently understanding the reason for its failure, while Horrocks restricted himself to replacing most tired formations with fresh ones, and simply bashing on.

Success rested on the corps commander's ability to analyse the strategic task and create an operation which his men and equipment could achieve with minimal casualties. He needed to study the topography in which he would be operating; to master the intelligence about the strength and effectiveness of his enemy; and to imagine himself in his opponent's shoes. Then the various ways of achieving the task should be brainstormed, and their pluses and minuses assessed. Finally the best method would be chosen, and the second best developed as Plan B in case the enemy correctly

239 Macksey, *Armoured Crusader*.
240 De Guingand, *Generals at War*.

guessed and countered his intentions. Simonds seems to have undertaken much of this thinking although nothing was written down, while Horrocks, even when healthy, was constitutionally incapable on his own admission of doing any of it. Ironically, Simonds' plans came to nought, while Horrocks despite his superficiality, was successful solely because of the abilities and equipment of his troops which he inherited. Losses in both British Commonwealth corps were unnecessarily high, and their performance was pedestrian.

It is ironic that from June 1940 to February 1941 British arms won extraordinary victories solely because of the temporary existence of a set of conditions that were never repeated. The British Army, RAF and RN, for the first time since Cromwell, were able to fight under their own outstanding, home-grown leadership free from the constraint of needing to consider the needs of non-Commonwealth allies, and free from overweening interference from Churchill since he was preoccupied with other things during his first months of settling in as PM and MOD. But the itch to interfere that always governed Churchill's waking hours, and was unsatisfied by Gallipoli, Norway or Greece, soon came to the forefront and led Britain to perdition.

It began on 24 November 1940 when Churchill sacked the strategic genius and victor of the Battle of Britain, Air Chief Marshal Hugh Dowding, and removed all internal RAF opposition to Trenchard's bombing cult, making Portal the head of the RAF. Then on 9 February 1941 as the British approached El Agheila to complete the total defeat of the Italian Army and open the way to Tripoli, Churchill ordered the army sent to Greece. These two events marked the end of systematically disciplined British staff planning, and its replacement with an unregulated mass of undisciplined, ill-considered and impatient demands and instructions from Churchill. A victim of Churchill wrote:

> He bedevilled strategy for two years, then got out of the mess by scapegoating his field commanders and letting in the Americans.[241]

Dowding had developed his system of fighter defence against the active opposition of the Trenchardian Air Staff. He won the Battle of Britain without input from Churchill, although Churchill did delay implementation of the Trenchardian plot to sack Dowding until after the day Battle of Britain had been won. The result of the Battle would have been the same had Chamberlain or Halifax been PM. The Trenchardian bombing cult was deeply alarmed by Dowding's success because it disproved their contention that air defence came only from a powerful bomber force. They could obfuscate Churchill, but feared ridicule from Dowding. Churchill's mention to his crony Sinclair that Dowding should be considered a future Chief of the Air Staff was the final straw. The bombing cultists knew Dowding would downgrade Bomber Command from an independent strategic 'war-winning' force to one providing support to the RN and army. A conspiracy was hatched by Trenchard, Salmond, Sinclair, Portal, Douglas, Freeman and Leigh-Mallory to appoint Portal as CAS and persuade Churchill, who considered himself the creator and saviour of the RAF, that Dowding was the man for delivering the defensive victory but was no longer needed as the time had come for a strategy to take the battle to the enemy. The army, they said, was defeated and incapable of beating the Germans, but Bomber Command, they promised, would bomb German cities until morale collapsed and the war ended.[242] Churchill welcomed this nonsense as it chimed with his own strategy that he had borrowed from Fuller, who wrote, as we have seen above that

241 LHCMA: Thompson Papers, Box 2/1 GB99 KCLMA Thompson. O'Gowan to Thompson, 21 April 1960.
242 Dixon, *Dowding & Churchill.*

> Future war would be determined by the power of aircraft to strike at the civil will, the power of mechanised forces to strike at the military will, and the power of motorised guerillas to broadcast dismay and confusion.

To these nostra Churchill added one more; the need to make US industry the arsenal of democracy and so save FDR's New Deal and ensure his re-election with the hope that the USA would eventually declare war against Germany, which it never did.

Churchill went to Greece in order to keep its army in the field and give Eden a remote chance of creating a Balkan front against Hitler, which was a recurring obsession. Churchill said:

> If only I had sufficient force of character to swing the American C of S ... we should have had the whole Balkans ablaze by now and the war might have been finished by 1943.[243]

The question of why Wavell changed his mind and went to Greece became pressing in the 1960s for those who saw in hindsight that it was possibly the most fateful event of the war when at that point Wavell could have stopped Churchill's interference.

> Why Wavell gave in remains for most of us a mystery. John Connell's biography will doubtless supply the answer.[244]

The biography appeared in 1964 and was a damp squib, opining that it was a decision made by the British Empire in the persons of Churchill, Eden, Wavell, Menzies and Smuts.

> The Greek expedition makes no sense morally, intellectually or strategically, unless it is seen in terms of British imperial strategy and sentiment; for those were the terms in which those who launched it thought and felt about it.[245]

Connell failed to address the objection presented at the time by the DMO, Kennedy, that the Greek decision was improperly made because the Cabinet had never asked for, or received, a purely military view from the Chiefs of Staff or from Wavell:

> All the service advice given on this problem had been coloured by political considerations – a very dangerous procedure.[246]

RW Thompson opted to wait for Connell's (non)-explanation, but was already privy to speculation by 'Chink' Dorman-Smith, aka Dorman O'Gowan, that Wavell's decision was personal, seeing a personal benefit in accepting Churchill's Balkan myth.

> Wavell was a scholar and a gentleman, and should have been an Oxford don. In June 1915 Maj Wavell was BM 9 Infantry Brigade in which was Capt Dorman-Smith commanding a company in 1/5th Fusiliers. In the Railway Wood attack on June 25, 1915, Capt Dorman-Smith got his third wound and Maj Wavell lost an eye.

243 Arthur Bryant. *Triumph In The West* (London: Collins, 1959), p. 55.
244 RW Thompson. *The Yankee Marlborough* (London: Allen & Unwin, 1963), p. 314.
245 John Connell. *Wavell. Soldier and Scholar* (London: Collins, 1964), p. 342.
246 John Kennedy. *The Business Of War* (London: Hutchinson, 1957), p. 85.

> Wavell married an ambitious Irish woman, née Queenie Quirk of a protestantised O'Cuirk. Wavell had very small private means, two plain daughters and one son. Queenie wanted her daughters to marry well. So Wavell had to be cautious financially, especially as he had a fondness for hunters, so was prepared to compromise his integrity rather than lose promotion. He did this over a) the report of 6 Infantry Brigade experiments [probably a misprint for 7 Infantry Brigade that was involved in the 'Tidworth Affair' in 1927], and b) stopping O'Connor on February 7, 1941. He later excused himself by pleading logistical difficulties, which is the last thing to plead after a total victory. WSC definitely stopped him on February 12th, and reoriented him to the Balkans. Wavell was brainwashed by WSC and by the wooly optimism of Eden. WSC then got cold feet, but too late. Had I been DMO at GHQ in Feb/ March 1941, I'd have resisted this decision to the point of removal. But Archie [Wavell] had a dud C of S [Arthur Smith] and a (unrecognisable word) DMO [Whitely]. Archie would have listened to me, but I was not there.
>
> However it was NOT the going to Greece that mattered so much as NOT going to Tripoli. This was the disastrous decision for which Kennedy rightly blames Archie. The Planning Staff at GHQ M.E. was strongly opposed to Greece.[247]

It is worth emphasising that both Wavell and Dowding engineered overwhelming victories over the Axis without a contribution from, or even the involvement of, Churchill beyond the negative contribution of ensuring that Dowding stayed in post and Beaverbrook replaced Dowding's fighter losses, and the positive decision to send Wavell reinforcements including 50 Matilda I-tanks. The 'System' had worked triumphantly, but Churchill could not allow it to continue because of his urge to interfere and ensure future victories were to the glory of Marlborough reincarnate. The result was a series of mistakes listed by Dorman O'Gowan under two headings; military mistakes: not to take Tripoli, go to the Balkans instead, not to bring Malaya up to defensive standards, bomb Germany at the expense of using the air force in the Middle East and India, and demand *Acrobat* in the summer of 1942; and political mistakes: subjection to FDR and cringing to Stalin. By July 1942, Dorman-Smith concluded, Churchill had dissipated Britain's potential and squandered its strategic assets, making Britain bankrupt before FDR and Stalin, and joining the other bankrupts, Hitler, Mussolini and France.[248]

Had Churchill fallen under a bus in October 1940, Anthony Eden would likely have become PM and Maj Clement Atlee remained Deputy PM with Stafford Cripps as Minister of Defence. The Chiefs of Staff would probably have been Dill, Dowding and Pound. The result without a doubt would have seen O'Connor racing to Tripoli which was already blockaded by the strong British fleet. Tripoli would have fallen in February 1941 and Libya garrisoned with British soldiers exchanging pleasantries with Vichy French border-guards.

What would then have happened? Of course Churchill's Royal Flush, which he revealed on 15 February 1941, would never have existed:

> Do you play poker? Here is the hand that is going to win the war: A Royal Flush – Great Britain, the Sea, the Air, the Middle East, American aid.[249]

247 LHCMA: Thompson Papers, Box 2/1 GB99 KCLMA Thompson. O'Gowan to Thompson, 8 December 1960.

248 LHCMA: Thompson Papers, Box 2/1 GB99 KCLMA Thompson. O'Gowan to Thompson, 7 November 1960.

249 Kennedy, *The Business of War*, p. 79.

Churchill's strategy never revealed itself in a manner more glaring than this. Reliance on 'the Air' was a mistake that extraordinarily has been quantified only in the tentative pioneering work of John Fahey.[250] He has calculated that the cost to Britain of the strategic air offensive was £2.78 billion. This severe financial burden that Britain could not afford was a major cause of its post-war impoverishment. Churchill gambled the future of Britain on Rankin, which was a surrender by Germany out of the blue due to a collapse of morale as had happened, Churchill imagined falsely, in 1918 due to the blockade. To quote Kennedy concerning Churchill:

> For a long time, he continued to believe that the war would be won by aircraft. So sure was he of this that the bombing policy of the Air Staff was settled almost entirely by the Prime Minister himself in consultation with Portal, and was not controlled by the Chiefs of Staff.[251]

The Royal Flush excluded the Army except as defence and occupation troops, as Churchill explained in April 1941:

> The above considerations and the situation as a whole make it impossible for the Army, except in resisting invasion, to play a primary rôle in the defeat of the enemy. That task can only be done by the staying power of the Navy, and above all by the effect of air predominance. Very valuable and important services may be rendered overseas by the Army in operations of a secondary order, and it is for these special operations that its organization and character should be adopted.[252]

The Royal Flush contained the Middle East, for which Churchill had a hard and self-inflicted fight on his hands against Rommel. However, it had nothing to say about Malaya, which Churchill had dismissed by 1941 as a possible theatre of war and which subsequently became his greatest defeat and was, once again, self inflicted and signaled the end of the British Empire. Finally the Royal Flush included American aid, which Churchill's critics asserted should have been a last resort after building up the full potential of the Commonwealth. Churchill was a racist, which made him not only blind to India's industrial potential but led him to sabotage Stafford Cripps' attempt to negotiate Indian independence with FDR's strong support, which would have brought that enormous population on side and released its potential. Churchill has been charged with doing nothing to prevent parts of India from starving.[253]

In lieu of Churchill's Royal Flush, a strategy such as that proposed by Dorman-Smith in 1940 could have been implemented, and almost certainly would have been implemented in Churchill's absence. First priority was to secure the bases and their approaches: UK, Malaya, Egypt and India. Next was to secure the important channels of communication, with the RAF given as their priority the task of maintaining air supremacy over them with special reference to the English Channel and the Red Sea. It should be noted that under this strategic imperative the RAF would never have been permitted to delay the closing of the Atlantic 'air gap' that continued for years under Churchill and Portal. They diverted the available B24 Liberators with their revolutionary long-range wing design from closing the 'air gap' to ferrying VIPs and senior RAF officers. Having secured the fortresses, seaways and land corridors, the strategy should have turned to the offensive, whose objective would be the same as that adopted against Napoleon; to deprive Hitler of a quick

---

250 John T. Fahey. *The Economic Cost Of Strategic Bombing*.pdf (University of Sydney, http://hdl.handle.net/2123/664).

251 Kennedy, *The Business*, p. 97.

252 Ibid.

253 http://www.bbc.co.uk/blogs/thereporters/soutikbiswas/2010/10/how_churchill_starved_india.html

and final decision by stretching him to the limit of his resources. In Napoleon's day, Spain was the 'stretcher', but when Dorman-Smith wrote his strategic musings in 1940, and before Italy invaded Egypt, he saw the choice of 'stretcher' as being the Balkans, South Italy, the Mediterranean Islands and Libya, writing:

> Everywhere the sea lies between us and our enemy, we must make its shores an area of ever-present menace. ... So the next task is for our land forces to become amphibious... But before we can develop an amphibious strategy in the Mediterranean, it looks as if we ought to remove Libya from Italy... But since for some time to come initiative on land rests with the enemy, the trouble is to foretell from where the counter-attack on land will start. It may even start from Iraq, Southern Arabia or Central Africa.
>
> Without venturing too deeply into conjecture, we can, I think, see the broad lines of our return match taking shape into two main armies, west and east, both amphibious. The west to operate on the Atlantic coasts. The east to secure the Middle East, clear the North African coast and gradually mop up the northern Mediterranean coast until the Balkans, Italy and Spain detach themselves from Germany.[254]

It is therefore easy to see what would have happened after Libya had been removed from Italy by O'Connor and Wavell in 1941. Consolidation, and the raising and training of the western and eastern armies equipped with I-tanks immune to German anti-tank guns, would have been advanced when the picture changed unforeseeably with Operation *Barbarossa* in June 1941. On 4 September 1941, Stalin in his agony of defeat asked Britain either to open a second front in France or the Balkans to relieve the pressure on Leningrad and the Ukraine, or despatch a BEF to the Caucasus. Eden explained,

> Our difficulty throughout this period was that the Russians believed, or affected to believe, that it was possible for us to make an important diversion by landing at some point in sufficient strength to draw off the Germans, or alternatively to send 25 divisions to fight in Russia. October 10th. Harriman told me privately that Stalin had spoken of an alliance after the war and proposed it to Max [Beaverbrook who had just returned from Moscow].

On 16 October 194, Eden offered to send a brigade group of 5,000 men to the Caucasus but was turned down by Molotov who wanted an Army Group which could have the key Rostov-on-Don sector including Stalingrad.

> The PM suggested to Stalin on November 4th that Wavell and Gen Paget, C-in-C designate Far East, should visit Russia... Later the (Russian) Ambassador spoke again about the need for a final answer to Stalin's request for British forces to Russia. Would Wavell be able to discuss this? I replied that there should be no misunderstanding on this issue; Stalin had asked for twenty-five divisions to thirty divisions and the PM had made it plain that this was quite outside our powers... Maisky persisted, asking whether, if Stalin said he did not want a British force in the Caucasus but would welcome one, say, at Rostov, this was a matter the generals could discuss.[255]

254 Brig EE Dorman-Smith. *Land Warfare* (Journal of the USII, January 1941).
255 A Eden. *The Eden Memoirs; The Reckoning* (London: Cassell, 1965), pp. 277-279.

With the Axis excluded from North Africa; with Eden as PM; with Atlee as Deputy PM; and with Stafford Cripps at MOD, there can be little doubt that a BEF of about 30 British divisions or a million men would have been despatched to the Caucasus or Rostov on Don through Iran. The numbers could have been made available by maintaining the RAF at its actual establishment in March 1940 with Dowding as CAS disbanding BC with its fallacious plan to destroy Germany's will to continue the war without confronting the enemy's main force.

Redistribution of British manpower in December 1941 under alternative strategy

'000	Actual Manpower[1]			Alternative Manpower Distribution			of which in Russia
	Men	Women	Total	Men	Women	Total	
RN	449	22	471	449	22	471	Na
Army	2,340	85	2,425	2,903	184	3,085	1,000
RAF/RFC	813	98	911	250	10	262	100
Total	3,602	216	3,818	3,602	216	3,818	1,100

Note:
1. CSO, Fighting with *Figures*, Table 3.4.

The redistributed RAF manpower of 262,000 included a reconstituted RFC of 200,000, of which half would have been stationed in Russia.

If we are to believe Eden, he was aware that:

> Though Soviet Russia's immediate interests in the war were the same as ours, in the peace they might conflict with what we and much of the world thought right. It was this contingency that I wished to guard against, if I could. I was given to saying at this time that the failure of the British Empire and Russia to agree their policies in advance had made possible three great conflicts, the Napoleonic war and two world wars.[256]

All who dealt with Stalin agreed that he kept his agreements. His philosophy, he said, was that 'this war is not as in the past: whoever occupies a territory also imposes on it his own social system,'[257] which was not new but the same principle of *Cuius regio, eius religio*, in the Treaty of Westphalia that had ended the Thirty Years War in 1648. The implication, however, of an agreement between Russia and the British Commonwealth to send a BEF of a million men with all of their equipment to fight alongside the Red Army in exchange for a postwar alliance with protocols covering the freedom of Eastern Europe and the Baltics, with the whole sealed in blood on the battlefield of the defence of Moscow in December 1941, is wide ranging. It would have meant that Britain and the USSR together would have occupied Eastern Europe, and probably as early as 1944.

Such an agreement would have been momentous for British management of the war. Dowding as CAS would have closed down Bomber Command and split the RAF into a Fighter Command, Tactical Bomber Command for home and colonial, and particularly Malaysian, defence, and an RFC/army aviation. The superb Mosquito bomber would have been rushed into production instead of being long delayed by the RAF which wanted only heavy bombers, and used to destroy

256 Eden, *Reckoning*, p 317.
257 Milovan Djilas. *Conversations with Stalin* (London: Rupert Hart-Davis, 1962).

the electricity generating and distribution industry in Germany that BC never attacked and was described in the USSBS as Germany's Achilles' Heel.

The relationship between the Russian and British armies would have been the same as that between the BEF and the French Army in the First World War. Stalin, Shaposhnikov, Zhukov and Rokossovsky would have formed a working relationship with Wavell, (who spoke Russian), Dill, O'Connor, Maitland Wilson, Auchinleck and later Slim. Martel, who was well regarded in the Russian army, would have had the task of integrating the British and Russian armoured forces and pursuing the question of a heavily armoured Churchill Infantry Tank with frontal immunity to the 88 mm, which he recommended in Britain after his return from Russia. At corps and divisional level Russian-speaking officers such as Brian Horrocks and Bolo Whistler would have taken important liaison posts. The BEF would have learned first-hand of the quality of Russian staffwork and equipment – KV1 and T-34 tanks, Sturmovik ground-attack and Pe2 dive-bombers, Katyusha rockets, PPSH41 sub-machine guns – and all would have been made under license in Britain and used to re-equip the Army. The Russians would have been given Britain's secrets including the atom bomb, radar, enigma and the jet engine, which in fact they either received from traitors or openly bought postwar from Attlee.[258] These inventions would have been jointly developed and used, with more respect given to British ownership rights than was ever shown by the Americans. It should not be forgotten that the Americans refused to supply the details of the atom bomb to Britain, in violation of the Churchill-FDR agreement on the specious argument that Congress had not endorsed it. This was a repeat of their tricky refusal to join the League of Nations in 1919 after they had forced it on everybody else. Having been tricked once in this manner, it was sheer incompetence on Churchill's part to have allowed Britain to be tricked a second time over the Atom bomb and the peremptory and humiliating ending of Lend-Lease.

Despatch of the British Commonwealth Army to Russia would of course have moved the locus of *Heather* from an Anglo-Canadian-American army group in Winnekendonk in 1945 to an Anglo-Canadian-Russian Army Group in Berlin in 1944. The western presence would have caused beneficial turmoil in Russia as the closed society experienced a culture shock. The more significant difference for Britain would have been the absence of Americans from Europe and a postwar alliance with the Russians. The major area of conflict with the Russians was over Poland. It boiled over as early as 1943 with the discovery of Katyn, which Churchill never admitted publicly was Russia's doing. A treaty with Stalin in September/October 1941 guaranteeing the freedom of Poland and Czechoslovakia, would have drawn the venom from Katyn.

Churchill with his Royal Flush found himself at his wits' end in Cairo in December 1943 after the Tehran Summit. Despite being ill he kept telling Moran that he must go to Italy to see Alex. Moran refused on the grounds of his poor health at which, Moran wrote, Churchill lost his temper; 'You don't understand. You know nothing about these things. I am not going to see Alex for fun. He may be our last hope. We've got to do something with these bloody Russians.' Moran concluded that Churchill looked to Alex to get into Eastern Europe before the Russians.[259] It was, however, too late for Churchill to have regrets. He had acted in haste in January 1941 in sending the army to Greece against all good advice, and had the rest of his life to contemplate if not actually regret at leisure his reckless impetuosity and his distrust of the heads of the army, who knew better than he did how to win the war and maintain British independence.

Had an integrated Anglo-Russian army successfully resisted the Wehrmacht, the USA after Pearl Harbour would have concentrated on defeating Japan. They would have fought without the

---

258 V Kotelnikov & T Butler. *Early Russian Jet Engines* (Derby: RR Heritage Trust, 2003), Historical Series No.33.

259 Lord Moran. *Winston Churchil* (London: Constable, 1966), p. 144.

atom bomb, unless British and Russian traitors had given them its secrets. Singapore and Burma would not have fallen to the Japanese under a Dorman-Smith strategy since the RAF and the army would have been concentrated there in strength instead of sending too little too late and losing the territories to an inferior force. All told, the USA would therefore have had no opportunity of benefiting from the Second World War and becoming a Superpower at Britain's expense, or of imposing its mixture of idealism and realpolitik on Britain. Indeed, the combination of Russian and British forces and the absence of FDR's Declaration of unconditional surrender would have created turmoil in the German ranks, with the likelihood of Hitler's assassination in 1943 at the latest after the first failure of a German summer offensive at Kursk. The Russian Jewish Bolshevik bogeyman would have been less frightening for Germans if its armies had contained a British contingent, and if German cities had not been area-bombed. The German economy would have been wounded, and perhaps fatally, by the destruction by Mosquito bombers of the German electrical generating and distribution system, which would have included the Swiss generating stations supplying Germany if Switzerland had failed to adopt complete neutrality. Finally, close integration with Russia would have been widely supported among British factory workers and intelligentsia, including Beaverbrook, Eden and Cripps, and been seen as an implementation of their Second Front Now campaign. How Stalin would have been able in this scenario to maintain a closed society ruled by terror and the Gulags is beyond this author's powers of imagination.

The Reason why Elles' Tank ceased to be built.

In 1914 the British and German armies were similar in organization and equipment, although very different in size. The French army was like the German in size but had a different approach, based on constant infantry attack supported by the quick firing 75 mm gun. When both sides dug in and movement on the battlefield became lethal, all three armies developed new operational methodologies.

German methodology was based on two advantages. Their method of command called *Auftragstaktik,* which dated back to Frederick The Great, placed on soldiers at all levels the obligation of finding a way of fulfilling the mission. From this sprang the capability of implementing storm-troop infiltration tactics with 'long-distance tickets', as they called them. Germany also had most of the world's chemical industry including BASF, Hoechst, Bayer and Griesheim-Electron Chemische Fabrik. These companies used large amounts of toxic materials in the manufacture of synthetic dyes in which they had a global monopoly. It was therefore almost inevitable that in October 1914, as the British were beginning to look for a tank, the Chief of the Great German General Staff, von Falkenhayn, should establish a chemical warfare section of the war ministry to examine the employment of gas. Its head was Dr. Fritz Haber, who at once started experiments with chlorine. Haber was a distinguished scientist, benefactor of humanity and President of the Kaiser Wilhelm Institute in Berlin. He won the Nobel Prize for work on nitrogen and ammonia, which are the basis of fertilizers. He was also a Jew, friend of Einstein, and inventor of Zyklon B as a pesticide. As his descendant Fritz Stern put it; 'the horror of Haber's involvement with the gas that later murdered millions, including friends and distant relatives, beggars description'. Haber knew the Geneva Convention banned the use of gas in warfare. As Falkenhayn wrote; 'The ordinary weapons of attack often failed completely. A weapon had, therefore, to be found that was superior to them but would not tax the limited capacity of the German war industry. Such a weapon existed in gas.[260] They had it, so they used it, regardless of the Geneva Convention. The first gas was released on 22 April 1915 against French colonial troops in the Ypres Salient,

260 Quoted in: William Moore. *Gas Attack!* (London: Leo Cooper, 1987).

producing a breakthrough that was stopped by the Canadians. The British reacted quickly and in five months built an industrial base and retaliated in kind. The CIGS, Sir William Robertson, immediately appointed Col William Horrocks, a hygiene expert and father of Brian, head of an anti-gas committee of civilian and military members. They quickly designed a respirator bag containing hyposulphate of soda, supplies of which were rushed to France in May, and then worked on more advanced designs for protection against phosgene.

The Germans developed and improved their new weapons of gas and storm-troop infiltration, introducing a new machine pistol, and increasing the impact with heavy artillery concentrations combining gas and high explosive shells. Lt-Gen Oscar von Hutier and his artillery adviser, Lt-Col Georg Bruchmüller, refined these techniques in a victory at Riga in 1917. They transferred this *Operativ* to the West for the 1917 counterattack at Cambrai, when they recovered all Allied gains made by tanks. But although outwardly brilliant, their victory confirmed a belief that tanks were redundant, and that they could win by ending hostilities with Russia and concentrating their entire force on the western front using the new methods before the Americans arrived in strength. Operation *Michael* began on 9 March 1918, and was initially successful against the British, who fell back. On 28 March, Foch with the reserves assumed overall command. The French kept up with German chemistry, and in June introduced their own Yellow Cross gas.

The Germans were fought to a standstill and recognised their methods were not working. Quickly appreciating the danger of tanks, they began feverishly to copy British designs like the Whippet for production in 1919 as the light LKII, and a new version of their A7V. It was too late, and the British operational methodology of all-arms with tanks overwhelmed them. For although the British lacked the concept of operational methodology, random and exceptional forces had been at work during four years of trial and error. The results were available to the commander of the Australian Corps, who applied engineering principles to invent modern warfare.

The British were pragmatic, and started from the premise that the basic military problem was tactical in nature. Success belonged to the side that could turn the enemy out of his prepared positions and prevent him from doing likewise. This was the task of the 'the cutting edge of battle', as a later War Office Infantry Training Manual called the infantry. The document went on: 'Though battles are usually won by the close and effective co-operation of all arms, it is infantry that, in close combat, must finally decide the issue; in attack the infantryman must close with and complete the destruction of the enemy; in defence he must hold his position to the end'.

In order to survive, the infantry needed protection from enemy fire as they advanced in the open to the enemy line. In the ensuing 'dog-fight' they seized the position and defended against counter-attack. The key task in attack was therefore to neutralise or suppress the defenders' fire. This was achieved by destroying or frightening the enemy long enough to stop his firing and make him take cover. Such was the key doctrine of fire and movement; that no movement should take place without suppressive fire and no fire opened without movement to justify its expenditure. Fire not associated with movement was defined as waste of resources, and movement without fire was suicidal.

The development of armour and its correct use followed a process of 'random walk', pushed along in different directions by a few individuals like Swinton and Stern, and championed by Churchill in a relatively open environment neither aided nor successfully resisted by institutions and preconceptions. It was a case of the amateur getting it right by chance in a unique process that could not be replicated because it was neither understood nor formalised. The conditions were right for it in the First World War, when aircraft and tanks were subordinated to the infantry, and Haig permitted experimentation by his corps commanders. Monash and Currie were in any case foreign militia with open minds and the backing of an independent power base. By comparison in the Second World War conditions had changed for the worst. An independent RAF and autonomous Royal Armoured Corps formed an ad hoc alliance of the 'mobile' arms to refuse subordination to the 'immobile' infantry and artillery arms. Montgomery imposed stifling control on his corps commanders and selected the complaisant, while Brooke benefited from the self-destruction of the Canadian Army's independence.

Almost from the moment on 15 September 1916 when Lt-Col Bradley led the tanks of the Heavy Section of the Machine-Gun Corps into battle for the first time, until 8 May 1945 when the last German tank engine facing the British was turned off, two incompatible views about the rôle of armour and aircraft, and who should command them, fought an internecine war within the British Army, and even in the pages of the popular press. We will call them infantry doctrine, and armoured corps/RAF doctrine.

In the earliest days of the tank there was only *infantry doctrine.* General Hugh Elles, who replaced Bradley, insisted like Swinton that it was an infantry weapon designed to accompany the assaulting infantry as a mobile gun to suppress or destroy enemy weapons in order to break through the enemy's fixed defences. The tank replaced the horse artillery that had travelled with the infantry, firing their guns in support over open sights. Then Boer Mausers and the machine gun had driven the horse artillery back from the front line and out of sight, where howitzers applying the science of indirect fire replaced guns.

An urgent need therefore arose for an armoured gun to provide front-line fire support to the infantry over open sights during the assault. The French originally called the tank *une artillerie d'assaut,* although the earliest inspiration for it in 1914 was an armoured personnel carrier to straddle the enemy trench and drop a storming party of 50 men through trapdoors in its belly. By June 1915, however, its future rôle as a self-propelled gun had been settled, and the infantry again had a means of firing case shot over open sights, exactly like the horse artillery. 'They were doing what always paid with the First World War tanks, maintaining fire against all local targets. Case shot from the guns was a certain inducement to the enemy to go to earth or to cock their hands up.'[261] By contrast, until late 1942 no British tank had high explosive (HE) ammunition, let alone case shot. What had paid such dividends in the First World War could not be replicated until mid way through the Second World War.

Tactical employment of tanks was of course an infantry prerogative, and they were used for attacking fixed defences. Churchill, commanding 6 Royal Scots Fusiliers in Flanders, sent thoughts from the trenches on 3 December 1915 about the employment of caterpillars, although the code-name 'tank' had just been adopted.

> 3. *Caterpillars.* – The cutting of the enemy's wire and the general domination of his firing-line can be effected by machines of this character. About 70 are now nearing completion in England, and should be inspected. None should be used until all can be used at once. They should be disposed secretly along the whole attacking front two or three hundred yards apart. Ten or fifteen minutes before the assault these engines should move forward over the best line of advance open, passing through or across our trenches at prepared points. They are capable of traversing any ordinary obstacle, ditch, breastwork or trench. They carry two or three Maxims each, and can be fitted with flame apparatus. Nothing but a direct hit from a field-gun will stop them. On reaching the enemy's wire they turn to the left or right and run down parallel to the enemy's trench, sweeping his parapet with their fire, and crushing and cutting the barbed wire in lanes and in a slightly serpentine course. While doing this the Caterpillars will be so close to the enemy's line that they will be immune from his artillery. Through the gaps thus made the shield-bearing infantry will advance.

261 Hart. *The Tanks*, ref Maj Gerald Huntbach.

> If artillery is used to cut wire the direction and imminence of the attack is proclaimed days beforehand. But by this method the assault follows the wire-cutting almost immediately, i.e. before any reinforcements can be brought up by the enemy, or any special defensive measures taken.[262]

The job of the Tank Corps, as it became, was to maintain the new weapon and advance it according to the corps' set-piece plan. In theory during those early days the tank was expendable and discarded once infantry and cavalry had penetrated the enemy defences and regained freedom of movement.

The corps commanders controlled the tanks, and in planning set piece attacks felt no obligation to listen to their divisional commanders or to those officers who moved with the tanks. It was probably inevitable, therefore, that not long after their introduction the men who manned the tanks began to treat them as their property, to produce arguments why tanks were special due to their being motorised, and to develop a tank corps' doctrine. This stood infantry practice on its head by arguing that it was the greater rôle of cruiser and destroyer tanks to exploit the gap in the line created by infantry with their artillery, sappers and Infantry tanks. The cruiser tanks would then go for the 'Gee in Gap of which cavalrymen had so long dreamed', and 'crack about' in Montgomery's later phrase in Normandy, using their mobility to avoid the enemy's main force. Inspiration came from studying the cavalry raids of JEB Stuart in the Peninsula and Maryland Campaigns of 1862 when he navigated around the Army of the Potomac. A grand illusion was born in 1917. It took hold of men's minds to the exclusion of common sense and contrary facts on the ground, and gradually permeated the whole British Army, surviving intact although dented until well after 1945. In hindsight the cavalry created the illusion, and it was transferred to the tanks.

Until the introduction of the radically improved Mark V in June 1918, the tank was unreliable and difficult to operate, requiring four men to make a turn. It was tacked on to infantry attacks and used mostly in raids. The Germans learned to live with it, and even to find the means for infantry to destroy it, including the reversed K-Bullet of 1917 and the Mauser 1918 13.2 mm Tankgewehr, but to their ultimate undoing chose to rationalise their own lack of it. Its first great success came with the massed employment of 476 Mark IVs on good going at Cambrai in November 1917, when Fuller's adaptation of the vision of Churchill and Swinton together with the introduction by the artillery of firing off the map, led to penetration of the German line.

The development of Tank Corps' practice owed much to Fuller. He organised the fitment of 2 ton fascines by Central Workshops to make crossing-places in the wide trenches of the Hindenburg Line at Cambrai, and devised a way for tanks to work along each side of the trenches in conjunction with infantry, as envisaged by Churchill and Swinton. Third Army Headquarters approved these tactics, but Maj-Gen Harper of 51 Division refused to co-operate. He insisted 'his' tanks turn right instead of left, and that his troops remain 100 yards to their rear.[263] Fuller appealed to Corps and Army to discipline Harper but without success, leading him to investigate ways of bypassing obstructive infantry. After Cambrai, Allied doubts about tanks were set aside and a decision made to create a force of 10,000 tanks in 1919 including 4,000 British tanks to be manufactured in new factories with the Americans. In the event one-fifth of the number (23 battalions of 3 companies each with 10 tanks equalled 690 tanks) of new British machines handled in a radically different way by Monash sufficed to end the war a year earlier than the government had foreseen.

262 WS Churchill. *Thoughts & Adventures* (London: Thornton Butterworth, 1932).
263 Bryan Cooper. *The Ironclads of Cambrai* (London: Macmillan, 1970).

Monash replaced Birdwood in command of the Australian Corps on 30 May 1918 in a rise so rapid that he was soon tipped as Haig's replacement.[264] He knew his troops were thinking offensively and visited Elles, commander of the Tank Corps, to see a demonstration of the new Mark V and the troop-carrying Star version. These, he realized, gave him the means of capturing the Hamel re-entrant.

The British Commonwealth Army was suffering manpower reinforcement constraints imposed by Lloyd George, but had improved its detailed technique and solved most of its problems since the Somme. By the autumn of 1917 its tactical skill and potential had multiplied through mastering the use of gas, creeping barrages, lifting barrages, counter-battery fire with firing off the map, use of heavy and light machine guns, air superiority, aerial photography, mapping, sound location, signals, and communication. In most of these areas British expertise was the equal and usually superior to, German.

Monash was a civilian engineer by profession, who applied engineering methods to solving operational problems. A scientific approach is the basis of Operational Methodology. He considered it was the existence of the new tanks that gave promise of success. The Mark V had epicyclic drive, reducing the number of men required to steer the tank from four to one. There was a more powerful Ricardo engine (150 hp compared with the Daimler's 105 hp) without the telltale exhaust smoke, and the overall design had better balance and mechanical durability. Monash considered the Mark V as great an improvement over the Mark IV as the SMLE had been over the Brown Bess. Furthermore, the Tank Corps had been improved through training directed by Elles, Courage, Hankey, Hotblack and others, and now felt they had something to prove.

Mistrust of tanks by 4 Australian Division, dating from Bullecourt in April 1917, was remedied at Vaux in June 1918. The battalions were able 'to spend the day at play with the tanks', and got to know the crews personally, anticipating the Dawnay Doctrine of 1943. The new element introduced by Monash in his plan, submitted to Rawlinson on 21 June 1918, was intimate co-operation between tanks, infantry, machine guns, artillery and air. It subsequently became the winning formula in both wars, and was in effect storm-trooper tactics with tanks. An historian of the BEF's tactical achievement put it slightly differently by saying that the commander who coordinated all arms into his plan could normally guarantee success.[265] It would be more accurate to say that although it did not guarantee success against a first-class foe, the absence of integrated all-arms almost guaranteed failure, but not quite since the 9th Scottish Division, who were described as 'the finest and most 'tactical' of all divisions', claimed they won their many victories without the help of a single tank.[266] Monash wrote:

> I resolved to propose an operation for the recapture of Hamel, conditional upon being supplied with the assistance of tanks, a small increase in my artillery and an addition to my air resources. Approval to these proposals was given without delay; the additional resources were promised, and preparations for the battle were immediately put in hand.[267]

The difference between the positive response of the GOC 4 Army, Rawlinson to the request of the GOC Canadian Corps, Monash in June 1918, and the negative response of the GOC 2 Army, Dempsey to the request of the GOC VIII Corps, O'Connor for APCs in July 1944, epitomised the problem under examination; corps commanders exercising devolved power with open minds

264 FM Cutlack. *War Letters of General Monash* (Sydney: Angus & Robertson, 1935).
265 Paddy Griffiths. *Battle Tactics of the Western Front* (New Haven: Yale, 1996), p. 200.
266 Ibid.
267 Monash, *The Australian Victories*.

in 1918 compared with powerless corps commanders under the thumb of Montgomery's closed mind.

Monash arranged for the design of battalion set-piece exercises that were rehearsed with the tanks. Of particular importance was the agreed method whereby the infantry indicated a target by firing a rifle grenade at it. But the crucial innovation lay in the acceptance by Courage's 5 BTB of two radical and important innovations: they agreed to be under command of the infantry company commanders, and to advance on the same axis alongside them while leaning with them against the artillery barrage. It meant ignoring the tank experts who predicted the tall tanks would be at risk from shells falling short. It was the origin of the technique still used successfully at Winnekendonk. Another innovation was the use of four converted gun-carrier tanks, each of which replaced carrying parties of 300 men. They arrived within 30 minutes of the capture of the first objective with 24 tons of engineers' stores for its consolidation to resist counter-attack. Monash wrote:

> I can never be sufficiently grateful to Brigadier-General Courage for his loyal acceptance of the onerous conditions which the tactical methods that I finally decided upon imposed upon the tanks. These methods involved two entirely new principles. Firstly each tank was, for tactical purposes, to be treated as an infantry weapon; from the moment that it entered battle until the objective had been gained it was to be under the exclusive orders of the infantry commander to whom it had been assigned. Secondly the deployed line of tanks was to advance, level with the infantry, and pressing up to the barrage.[268]

Of Hamel Monash said that:

> No battle within my previous experience, not even Messines, passed so smoothly, so exactly to time-table, or was so free of any kind of hitch. It was all over in ninety-three minutes.[269]

The Hamel re-entrant was taken on 4 July 1918. Five companies of 13 Battalion with a total of 60 tanks were used together with 4 supply tanks under command of 10 Australian infantry battalions comprising some 8,000 troops on a frontage of 3½ miles. This was only 6 tanks per battalion and 125 men per tank compared with the 16 tanks and 25 men per tank at Winnekendonk in 1945. A similar ratio had been in effect five hundred years earlier, when 'Machiavelli believed that an army should contain 20 foot-soldiers to each cavalryman. A great deal of effort in the sixteenth century was devoted to establishing the correct mix.'[270]

The infantry led at Hamel but the tanks soon overtook them. At Winnekendonk the tanks stayed behind the front two rows of infantry, who defended against Panzerfausts. Losses at Hamel numbered 775 Australians, 134 Americans, and 13 tank crew with none killed. The 2.7% casualty rate for the tank crews – the Mark V having a crew of 8 compared with 5 in the Churchill – compared with 9.7% for the Australian infantry killed and injured, and showed one advantage of serving in tanks that never changed. At Winnekendonk infantry losses were 30% with 6% killed (25 killed and 95 wounded out of about 400) while tank crew losses were 3.7% killed, raised to 5% with the addition of the artillery FOO (4 out of 80). This was exceptionally high. At Hamel all save two tanks arrived on the objective. German losses are unknown, but prisoners numbered some 1,500 and 171 machine guns were captured.

268 Ibid.
269 Ibid.
270 John Keegan. *A History of Warfare* (London: Hutchinson, 1993).

On 4 September 1918 Monash sent a letter to his wife together with a box. He laid claim to inventing the system that won the First World War for the allies.

> The principal object in the box is a model of a Mark V Tank,[271] which I was the first to use in battle, namely at the Battle of Hamel on 4 July. The tactics of the employment of this new type of tank was my own invention and has now been adopted throughout the armies. I have had under my command since the middle of June, until a week ago, the whole of the 5th Tank Brigade, commanded by Brigadier-General Courage, consisting of three battalions, each of sixty tanks – a total personnel of 2,500 officers and men. My relations with this tank brigade have been of the very happiest and they have served me splendidly.[272]

For his next battle, Monash incorporated the engineering feature of fail-safe, so that the there was no knock-on effect from individual failure of the notoriously unreliable tanks:

> Each tank became definitely associated with a specified body of infantry, and acted during the actual battle under the immediate orders of the commander of that body; the working rule was 'one tank, one company'. To this was added the second working principle of 'one tank, one task', which rules meant that no individual tank was to be relied upon to serve more than one body of infantry, nor to carry out more than one phase of the battle. Elementary as this may sound, it involved this striking advantage that, in the event of one tank becoming disabled, its loss would impair no portion of the battle plan other than the fraction of it to which the tank had been allotted.[273]

On 21 July 1918 a complete reorganisation of the front was decided and the date for the offensive using the techniques of Hamel was fixed for 8 August. It was a disaster for Germany, prompting Ludendorff to call it the 'black day of the German Army'. He noted that it struck a part of the line he had deliberately strengthened and that the enemy attacked with no great superiority, apart from the tanks. Normally the Germans would have held their positions and seen off the attack, but on this occasion they were overwhelmed. 4 British Army with 414 tanks drove a hole 12 miles wide through the defences, capturing or destroying all the military resources contained within the area. Losses to Australians and Canadians were negligible.

The professional Germans now recognised that the Allies had a war winning Operational Methodology that could not be countered in the short term, and that all of the German eggs were in the wrong basket; it was over for them. On the other hand the British Army lacked the analytical framework to understand what they had invented, and indeed failed to replicate the technique in many subsequent battles. Few in Britain then or later understood the true cause of the Armistice. We have Churchill's word for it in a speech he gave in 1942:

> It is now the fashion to speak of the Lloyd George War Cabinet as if it gave universal satisfaction and conducted the war with unerring judgment and unbroken success. ... It made numerous serious mistakes. No one was more surprised than its members when the end of the War came suddenly in 1918.[274]

---

271 E-mail from curator Michael Cecil in July 2002 states that the model is relic RELAWM15132 in the Australian War Memorial, Canberra.

272 Cutlack, *War Letters.*

273 Monash, *The Australian Victories.*

274 Charles Eade. *The End of the Beginning: War Speeches by the Rt Hon Winston S. Churchill* (London: Cassell, 1943).

Ludendorff described some later attacks when, even though stretched thin with few reserves, the Commonwealth Army with its tanks was unstoppable in the set-piece attacks, and the Germans despaired in consequence:

> On August 21 the English (sic) attacked south of Arras between Boisieux and the Ancre; this was the first of a series of attacks which lasted almost uninterruptedly to the end of the war. During the following days the English, who had but few fresh reserves at their disposal, gained ground toward Bapaume after very severe fighting. The characteristic of their tactics was narrow but deep penetration by tanks after short but extremely violent artillery preparation, combined with artificial fog. Mass attacks by tanks and artificial fog remained hereafter our most dangerous enemies. The danger increased in proportion as the morale of our troops deteriorated and as our divisions grew weaker and more exhausted.[275]

The Germans had dismissed the tank with contempt as the weapon of an inferior military power without operational methodology. But now most Germans came to see that the tank and the way it was used were crucial elements in their downfall. General von Zwehl said 'Germany was not defeated by the genius of Marshal Foch, but by General Tank.'[276]

Haig said much the same in his final despatch, although he subsequently changed his mind; 'Since August 8, tanks have been employed on every battlefield, and the importance of the part played by them can scarcely be exaggerated.'[277] Such an opinion became unfashionable and has been denied with virtual unanimity by modern military historians. Seven examples out of many from 1919 to 1993 will suffice.

> Maj-Gen Sir Louis Jackson in a lecture at the Royal United Services Institution in November 1919: *Possibilities of the Next War.* 'The tank proper was a freak. The circumstances which called it into existence were exceptional and are not likely to recur. If they do, they can be dealt with by other means'.
>
> Brig-Gen Sir J.E. Edmonds: *History of the Great War* published in the 1930s, stated that the decisive effect of the tanks on August 8 was merely a legend put out since the war by the Germans to save their self-esteem as soldiers. 'Actually the infantry with machine-guns were the instrument of success, but their vital assistant was the artillery – not the tanks'.
>
> John Terraine: *To Win a War,* 1978. 'So it was demonstrated once more that the tanks of 1918 were not war-winners despite the mendacious alibi for defeat made by Major von dem Bussche. The Australians and their British tank crews made the disagreeable discovery that the Germans were now taking the measure of the tanks, and had devised various methods of dealing with them.'
>
> Len Deighton: *Blitzkrieg,* 1979. 'Whatever had brought an end to the war, it was not the tank. The Royal Navy had probably made the most vital contribution to Allied victory'.
>
> Shelford Bidwell & Dominick Graham: *Firepower,* 1982. 'But the dominant fact about the tank was that it was not durable. On the extended frontage on which the Army advanced during October and November 1918, the tanks were not the decisive factor that they had been earlier. The Germans held their front with marksmen, machine-gun detachments and field guns in the open. Tanks were seldom available to deal with either. After the war the impression remained among infantrymen that tanks were decisive in set-piece battles but only a

275 Erich von Ludendorff. *Ludendorff's Own Story* (New York: Harper, 1919).
276 FW von Mellenthin. *Panzer Battles* (Norman, Oklahoma University, 1955).
277 Hart, *The Tanks Vol I.*

> useful auxiliary in the extended fighting that followed. This led to the conclusion that tanks should be employed as auxiliary fire-support for infantry on specific occasions'.
>
> Lt-Col Carlo D'Este: *Decision in Normandy*, 1983. 'During the latter stages of the First World War tanks were first used on the battlefields of France and the results were less than spectacular'.
>
> Sir John Keegan: *A History of Warfare*, 1993: 'But the machines produced were too few in number, too slow and too cumbersome to impose a decisive alteration to tactical conditions. The First World War was eventually resolved not by any discovery or application of new military techniques by the high commands, but by the relentless attrition of manpower by industrial output. The fact that it was Germany which went down to defeat in the *Materialsschlacht* was almost fortuitous'.

What these historians missed was both the psychological impact on the Germans of the tank used as part of all-arms and the opportunity for endless repeatability. They focused rather on the tank's lack of durability and on the development of anti-tank forts and other counter-measures. It is true that on 8 August the British had 630 tanks, with only 145 runners on the second day, 85 on the third, 38 on the fourth and 6 on the fifth. Crews were exhausted.[278] This was irrelevant to Germans experiencing the devastating impact of the attack supported by tanks and promise of its repetition after a period for recuperation, which would reduce as tank numbers increased. Guderian's commanding officer summarised the German experience:

> To sum up, it may well be said that the importance of tanks was not at first estimated by our military leaders as highly as was proved necessary by later experience. When the construction of tanks was begun, the work was not organised efficiently enough or pressed on fast enough for the tanks to have been ready in large numbers in 1918. Our industries were capable of producing them. On the other hand, the great difficulties with regard to the provision of material and labour must not be underestimated. On the whole if we had recognised their importance early and acted with determination, we could have done more, even if we could not in any case have caught up with the enemy, who had the advantage of us, nor could hardly have produced tanks fit for service at the front before 1918.[279]

The British achieved success even when not employing tanks, due to improved technique as demonstrated by 9 Scottish Div. For those in the know, however, tanks were the key. Lt-Col Sir Albert Stern stated it clearly after the Armistice in describing the impetus generated by the arrival in London of Maj-Gen Sir Ernest Swinton in August 1915:

> It was largely owing to his efforts that the Army took up Tanks and developed the tactics rapidly enough to make it impossible for the German Army ever to catch us up.[280]

The Germans recognised an allied operational methodology for which the only answer was their own tank force. Too late for that, they despaired and asked for an armistice. Immobile in their anti-tank forts, and outfought in every department, they faced being chopped up like salami and defeated in detail. An army without the ability to manoeuvre is defeated, and the professional Germans knew it. Incontrovertible, unexpected, and worst of all grossly unjust since the

278 Bidwell & Graham. *Fire Power* (London: Harper Collins, 1982).
279 RH Lutz. *The Causes of the German Collapse in 1918* (Palo Alto, Stamford, 1934).
280 Hart, *The Tanks. Vol I.*

amateur British 'led by donkeys' without even the concept of operational methodology did not merit victory, defeat sowed the seeds of German revanchism.

Ludendorff described the causes of his despair after 8 August:

> We had to resign ourselves now to the prospect of a continuation of the enemy's offensive. Their success had been too easily gained. Their wireless was jubilant and announced – and with truth – that the morale of the German Army was no longer what it had been.[281]

A German study, just quoted, made in 1934 by Lutz into the causes of their defeat showed how they learned to counter the early use of tanks, but new operational methodology and the determination shown in its use shattered their complacency:

> In the fighting in Flanders in 1917 the use of tanks by the British did not have a decisive effect owing to the unsuitable ground. Ludendorff mentions that the tanks were not regarded as a special danger at that time, adding that the expression 'tank fright' met with no acceptance among the officers at the front.
>
> The first use of tanks in large numbers was near Cambrai on 20 November 1917. Several hundred tanks made a deep breach in our front without artillery preparation, which came as a complete surprise. The attack might have led to a complete breach of our front if the British had reserves to take full advantage of their success which came as a surprise to them.
>
> The French tanks achieved a great and decisive success on the occasion of General Foch's counter-attack from the forest of Villers Cotterêts on 18 July 1918, which was the turning point of the war [Gen Mangin's counterattack on the Marne]. Soon afterwards a large break was made in our positions on the Somme (by the British) [8 August], again with the use of tanks which decided the issue. From that time until the end of the war tanks played a decisive part in all the enemy's attacks. Thus, in the second part of the World War, tanks proved to be new and very effective weapons.[282]

Lutz speculated that if 600 tanks had supported Operation *Michael*, Germany would have won the war:

> Field Marshal Haig considers that if we had two or three cavalry divisions at our disposal it would have been possible for us to drive a wedge between the British and French armies. It is surely not saying too much to assert that we could have exercised this final pressure which was still lacking if six hundred tanks had paved the way more quickly for our infantry. After we had finally been forced to adopt the defensive, tanks, even if they are above all an offensive weapon, would have provided powerful moral support for our jaded troops and considerable assistance in counter-attacks. The shorter we were of men to replace casualties, the more we had to economise with regard to manpower and the more important became the greatest possible use of all mechanical means.[283]

The Germans learned their lesson and reconstituted their storm-troop army in the 1930's around a powerful and operationally integrated tank and air force. The British abandoned what they had invented and refined in battle, and exchanged it not for a theory that could not work, since the

281 Ludendorff, *Ludendorff's Own.*
282 Lutz, *The Causes.*
283 Ibid.

1935 redrafting of field regulations, FSRII, extolled all-arms, but for a practice in which infantry, artillery, armour and air acted independently of one another and pursued separate aims.

The British did not try to analyse the lessons of the war until the 1932 Kirke Report. By then the independent RTC and the RAF had developed and institutionalised their theories. These were still in vogue in February-March 1945, when BC nightly stirred over the ruins of the Ruhr or immolated Dresden, and 3 BID did not wait for GAD who took days to catch up and then squander the lead.

Even before the end of the First World War some on the British side began to play down the importance of tanks. In the despatches after the Battle of Cambrai, Maj-Gen Harper of 51 HD put out a false story to excuse his failure to support the tanks. He stated that the setback on the Flesquières Ridge was due to the bravery of one German officer who had knocked out 16 tanks. Arthur Conan Doyle repeated the story and it became widely accepted as true by the British, although not by the Germans. Seeking to identify the officer for a posthumous medal, they found he had never existed.

The vulnerability of tanks to well-sited anti-tank guns, which was a fact of life overcome only by infantry in close conjunction with I-tanks, artillery, and air, was used as an argument for keeping them away from the dangers of fixed defences where anti-tank guns were assumed to be. These it was suggested were the mundane responsibility of the infantry and I-tanks to overcome, while fast 'Cruiser' tanks would 'exploit' and 'crack about' in the enemy's rear areas far from anti-tank guns, destroying his nerve centres and bringing exciting victory. This was Fuller's thinking and adopted in Foch's Plan 1919. The reckoning was postponed by the Armistice until the Second World War when the Medium D was reincarnated as the Crusader, Sherman and Cromwell, and destroyed by the thousand.

The revanchist Germans studied their defeat and rearmed with two armies: a *schnell* mechanised and armoured army that was supported by Stuka flying artillery and was the First World War army of storm troopers with internal combustion engines. The other army was the traditional infantry that marched on its feet with horse-drawn artillery and supply trains. As soon as it became clear in Poland that the German soldier would attack only with armour support, they were supplied with StuG assault guns.

The Red Army, by contrast, studied the lessons of Monash's victory at Amiens and their own war with Poland. As Marxists they believed in the existence of social laws, and tried to discover and codify those governing warfare. They worked through the problem of deep penetration that had defeated them outside Warsaw, opting for a mobile army with masses of tanks and armoured aircraft built by an economy dedicated to helping the spread of the revolution they considered inevitable.

In Britain, the absence of operational methodology left the field open to the RAF, to the essay-writing skills of amateurs and to military politics. Fuller and Liddell-Hart followed the RAF's example and campaigned for the independence of the tank corps. The two arms then laid claim to the aircraft and tank in an absurd game of ideological finders-keepers. They ridiculed the conventional view contained in Haig's final dispatch, that the war should be seen as one long engagement:

> If the whole operations of the present war are regarded in correct perspective, the victories of the summer and autumn of 1918 will be seen to be as directly dependent upon the two years of stubborn fighting that preceded them.[284]

284 Earl Haig. *Dispatches* (London: Times, 1919), dispatch 8 of 21 March 1919.

Instead they suggested that the donkeys had resisted the tank and victory had been gained despite and not because of their policy of attrition.

Attrition, however, worked both ways, and Haig neglected to mention that the French and British Armies were also exhausted in June 1918. Fuller and Liddell Hart charged the Army with gross mismanagement and convicted the General Staff of murder. The RAF and the apostles of mobility in the Royal Tank Corps ridiculed the infantry and worked to establish themselves as independent institutions with attitudes precluding co-operation, and ensuring that any member proposing it was denounced and excluded as a traitor. They did not succeed, and a large element in the Royal Tank Corps including Elles recognised the need for close cooperation with infantry and the need for an I-tank. The integrity of the First World War armed forces, however, was destroyed.

The debate became personal and motivated shamelessly by military politics. In 1919, Fuller as S.D.4 in the War Office had been arguing for Plan 1919 to include:

> infantry tank units, to increase penetrative power, and independent tank units, to carry out the mobile rôle that cavalry had formerly played.[285]

What the 'apostles of mobility' never realised was that neither cavalry nor tanks could survive in the independent state once machine-guns and 88 mms were deployed on the battlefield. 'You can't make a cavalry charge until you have captured the enemy's last machine-gun', was an American comment quoted in the Official History by Liddell Hart. This should have been updated to, 'You can't make a tank charge until you have captured the enemy's last 88', or rather armoured your tank to withstand it. Mobility, however, became an end in itself. In 1920, Fuller said tanks would replace infantry, because, 'specialist corps, such as machine-gun, tank or infantry, do not tend towards efficient co-operation. Tanks, therefore, can replace infantry.'[286] In 1924 Lindsay, the Inspector of the Royal Tank Corps and an acquaintance of Montgomery, strongly opposed the inclusion in the Mechanised Force of any infantry with their obstructive regimental traditions, and he named the new tank the *Independent*.

> The real stumbling block in any reform or reorganisation is the present regimental system by which our army is divided into innumerable small packets each with different traditions and ideas. I feel that to perpetuate this in the new arm is only asking for trouble'.[287]

Indeed, he opposed the allocation of Mechanical Fighting Machines to any unit outside the RT.C, except the artillery, adopting the same chauvinist attitude as the RAF did towards aircraft. The result of these forceful words could only be an explosion of anger amongst officers of the other arms who saw it naturally as a bid to take over the army, and to deny any sort of prospect to the regiments. Liddell Hart and others pursued this debate publicly in the press with the underlying theme that old fogies like 'Uncle' Harper, who had been uncooperative at Cambrai, were resisting modernisation and wanting to repeat the conditions of the Somme and Paschendaele. This emotional charge does not stand up to examination. Montgomery-Massingberd was a progressive, mechanising CIGS who encouraged the work of the Tank Brigade. Military politics required him to be portrayed by Liddell Hart as a conservative.

285 Hart, *The Tanks Vol I.*

286 JFC Fuller. *The Application of Recent Developments in Mechanics & Other Scientific Knowledge to Preparation and Training for Future War on Land* (Journal of the RUSI 65, May 1920).

287 JP Harris. *Armoured Warfare* (London: St Martin's, 1990).

The 'apostles of mobility' dreamed of winning battles by 'attack against the rear and on no account to try and do so by direct attacks'. The gurus, Fuller, Liddell Hart and Hobart, pointed to the 'fact' that one man had destroyed 16 tanks as a reason for keeping armour away from fixed defences and creating for it an altogether independent and strategic rôle dependent on mobility. Liddell Hart could write of tanks having the 'power of recreating mobile warfare of a more dynamic nature and more rapidly decisive effect'. The British model became the Boer cavalry commandos of Denis Reitz and the Confederate Cavalry of General J.E.B. Stuart, operating in the enemy rear, vanishing and re-appearing unexpectedly and 'exploiting' through holes punched in the enemy lines by the infantry or after turning the enemy's flank. The object of exploitation was destruction of the enemy's advanced HQs, supply dumps and communications by putting a bullet into his brain.

In September 1925 all four divisions and the RTR held their first large-scale manoeuvre since the war, and on the third day Godley employed tanks as a true manoeuvre force for the first time in history. The lorry-borne infantry and artillery were left behind by the tanks that attacked the opposing HQ on their own. The new CIGS, Milne, encouraged tanks and established the EMF in 1927. He offered its command together with 7 BIB and the Tidworth Garrison to Fuller, reporting to Sir John Burnett-Stuart, GOC of 3 BID under Sir Archibald Montgomery-Massingberd. Fuller made difficulties and his appointment was cancelled, marking the end of his active career. Liddell Hart, who campaigned for Fuller, lost his privileged access to the War Office.

The EMF had tanks, armoured cars, tankettes, artillery, engineers and a machine gun battalion of infantry. They were all on tracks or wheels but their travel at different speeds was considered a problem. The final exercise in September involved cavalry, the EMF, the entire 3 BID and units from the RAF. The results were the subject of great interest in Britain and abroad but were marred by an inability to agree on the extent to which tanks were at risk from anti-tank guns. Burnett-Stuart stated that the exercise had convinced him that tanks should be regarded as more than an infantry-support weapon and that the time had come for them to move out 'as a principal, not merely as an assistant'. The result, he thought, meant a reduction in the importance of infantry and cavalry.

Fuller and Liddell Hart continued to press for tanks to be used to attack and paralyse the enemy's nerve centre, but a reaction had set in. Burnett-Stuart and Montgomery-Massingberd designed the exercises in September 1928 to hamper the Armoured Force and show its limitations, and in November it was stood down. It had succeeded in convincing many that tanks had an independent rôle, and discussion afterwards concentrated on whether that rôle should be dominant or subordinate to other arms. This issue was never resolved, and the British Army remained divided on the issue throughout the Second World War. The EAF had opened the way for two paths of development but could not resolve the issue of which one to choose. Public debate about tanks then ended and the subject seemed to disappear.

One major reason for its demise was the absence of armoured vehicles and the money to build them. A second was the lack of training areas while a third was a general lassitude in the 1930's and a feeling of marking time. The British introduced the Light Tank Mark VI and started on the long road to mechanising the Army as horses disappeared from the countryside. The Army thought it was going in the right direction. None of these factors limited the activities of Germans or Russians.

Charles Broad issued the Purple Primer, which was the first official manual on armoured warfare and spelled out the lessons of the exercises in 1927 and 1928. The Primer was immediately translated and studied in Germany and Russia. It contained valuable lessons in command and control and preached the all-tank theory of armoured warfare. The increasing importance of tanks was reflected in the 1929 Field Service Regulations, which did not, however, advocate all-tank operations. But the fateful dichotomy persisted and surfaced again officially in 1931 as the first tank brigade began its training. Broad wrote with lack of understanding that, 'The principal arm in the modern army may be either infantry or tanks', rather than insisting the two work together with air and artillery under a single integrated command.

In 1931 the Royal Tank Corps began practising 1 BAB under Broad in all-tank command and control. Their crystal wireless sets could not be linked with the infantry, who were now regarded as the enemy. Liddell Hart was ecstatic when the tanks attacked and destroyed a column of marching infantry. The Army dismissed this exercise as a trick. In 1932 tank exercised against tank and did a little infantry co-operation, but the different arms were now grown apart as the Ten Year Rule was officially abandoned. Fuller, the original 'Apostle of Mobility', now advocated élite mobile formations working ahead or to the flank of a firm base provided by the main infantry army. It revealed that the British Army was firmly and as it turned out, irreversibly, in the grip of a delusion.

In 1932 Liddell Hart published his book, *The British Way of Warfare.*[288] Its obscurantism perverted the thinking of a generation of British military minds including Churchill, Brooke and Montgomery. Hart's influence was as pervasive in its field as that of JM Keynes on Britain's economy. Both believed there was an unconventional way of succeeding, and both found their caveats ignored. Thus politicians encouraged by Keynes to run counter-cyclical deficits soon ran deficits in the good times as well. Generals like Ritchie, Auchinleck and Dorman-Smith read Hart's book and generalised its subtitle 'Adaptability and Mobility' (the subtitle of the Penguin edition of 1942). They perverted the Napoleonic doctrine of 'march dispersed, fight concentrated' by converting it into a policy of 'mobility and fluidity' at all times, even in the face of the enemy. But this is probably being too kind to Liddell Hart, who urged his readers to understand the causes and conduct of war. 'The historic British practice was based, above all, on mobility and surprise – apt to Britain's natural conditions and aptly used to enhance her relative strength while exploiting her opponent's weaknesses'. Talking of 'Speed in War', Liddell Hart believed that, 'The best hope of rapid progress lies in armoured vehicles, if there are enough of them. The aim of such moves will not be to strike the enemy in the back but to cut the communications on which they depend. The old proverb 'unity is strength' no longer holds good. The more concentrated a modern army is, the more vulnerable it will be; and the larger it is, the more liable to paralysis. The conscript armies of Europe, hugely swollen on mobilisation, invite more danger than they offer'. Clausewitz was dismissed by Hart as the 'Mahdi of Mass' (mobilisation). To this nonsense, Hart added the claim that Napoleon dispersed his forces, abhorred concentration and would have reshuffled his forces into fluidly assembled Jock Columns had the technology been available to him.

In the Epilogue, Liddell Hart gives 'The Concentrated Essence of War', which permitted him later to make the unfounded claim that only Rommel amongst his readers learned his lesson of the need for concentration after the enemy has been dispersed, which appears to have been a re-statement of 'march dispersed, fight concentrated'. Liddell Hart in his final lines advocated gambling with the forces, and the passage contains hints of future Arnhems.

> Occasionally a commander has eschewed the obvious and pursued the unexpected. He has won a decisive success – unless fortune has proved foul. For luck can never be divorced from war, as war is part of life. Hence the unexpected cannot guarantee success. But it guarantees the best chance of it. That is why the successes of history, if not won by exceptionally clever generalship, have been won by generalship that was astoundingly foolish. Perhaps this dual cause explains why Britain has had such a long run of success.

288 Liddell Hart. *The British Way of Warfare* (London: Faber & Faber, 1932).

This book was published in 1932, revised in 1935 as *When Britain Goes to War*, reprinted 1936 and published as a Penguin in 1942. There is little doubt that numbers of these Penguins were in the pockets of those in the desert who broke up the divisions into brigade boxes and Jock Columns and were defeated in detail by Rommel,

In 1933 Montgomery-Massingberd replaced Milne and established 1 BTB under Hobart, who trained it in the 'strategic and semi-independent rôle against some rearward enemy objective'. It attacked infantry columns with gusto, but in August 1934 was combined with 7 BIB, artillery and other support units under Lindsay into what was in effect, but not in name, an armoured division. It was given a tightly restricted task by Burnett-Stuart in which the infantry took their opportunity to get even. An armoured force operating behind enemy lines was shown to be vulnerable.

In 1935 rearmament started with the cavalry receiving light tanks, and forming with the Tank Brigade a Mobile Division influenced by the French *Division Lègére Mécanique*. It had reconnaissance but no infantry troops and was a type of mechanised cavalry division. The Army decided this would replace the old light cavalry while the RTC equipped with medium and heavy tanks would replace the heavy cavalry. This was the origin of the British Army's requirement for three tanks, soon to be increased to four; an Infantry or assault tank for the army tank battalions; a Cruiser, and a Medium tank for the Tank Brigades; and a Light tank with armoured cars for the cavalry. Cavalry officers remained on a separate list for promotion, but not the men who were amalgamated into the Tank Corps. The Mobile Division was in reality devoted to the traditional cavalry tasks of reconnaissance and pursuit, and omitted training in all-arms offensive operations.

In 1936 Cyril Deverell became CIGS. He continued the policy of complete mechanisation of the Army but resisted the tank advocates who called for the creation of an elite, mechanised element within the army without infantry. He ordered 2,030 tanks that would have given the British a higher proportion of tanks to its size than any other army including the Russian. However the lack of design teams and manufacturing facilities in an industrial environment where the needs of the RAF had priority, meant that the infantry was mechanised before the tanks were available.

Wavell and Martel visited the Russian manoeuvres and after watching the BT7 ordered a Christie prototype from the USA. They also saw the T.28 fitted with a 76.2 mm gun firing case, smoke, HE and AP, and they soon knew that the German Mk IV had a real 75 mm infantry gun. The Apostles' reaction was one of pity for foreign tank crews forced to carry these things, because a gun firing HE was regarded as a close support weapon rather than an anti-tank weapon, and code for being an old-fashioned servant of the infantry, instead of being allowed to run wild on their own.

In 1937, Hore-Belisha with Liddell Hart as his adviser pursued the blue-water policy of 'limited liability', placing continental involvement of the Army last in priority after defense of the home islands, maintenance of open seaways, and defense of overseas territories. In many ways they followed *The British Way of Warfare*. The Army resisted the policy that placed them at the end of the queue for rearmament, knowing the policy would not survive a declaration of war.

In 1938 the Mobile Division was reorganised into one motorised infantry battalion and over 600 tanks. The Matilda I-tank was entering production, and the class of medium tank was abolished in favour of the Cruiser. The result of the Christie redesign was the Mark III, but the Cruiser Mark I and Mark II continued in development in a proliferation of designs.

The Army was now living a nightmare. A dangerously angry bitterness developed against politicians who denied it resources in the name of appeasement, but in reality steered resources to the RAF. The War Office, knowing a conflict with Germany could not be limited, and that success could not come through manoeuvre and mobility, finally rejected Fuller and Liddell Hart as unrealistic. Instead, and at the last minute, the traditional arms were built up and tanks ordered for the rôles of infantry support and reconnaissance, arriving in time to prevent complete defeat.

In April 1939, a Ministry of Supply was created which took over the functions of research, design and experiment in connection with the stores which it would supply, and here the difficulties were institutionalised. The WO was emasculated by the decision to transfer tank design and procurement into a new Ministry of Supply.[289] Then in April 1940 the War Cabinet sealed the fate of British armour by decreeing that the tank programme:

> must not be interfered with either by the incorporation of improvements to the approved types, or by the production of newer models.[290]

This decision by Churchill in Cabinet precluded the copying of either enemy or Russian tank designs. Certainly until Rommel landed in North Africa the British had no captured German tanks to copy. One of the greatest what-ifs of the War was a proposal by General Pope in June 1940 to buy Russian tanks. Even a few of these in the desert would have opened military eyes to what they were missing, and possibly persuaded the Ministry of Supply that good tanks cost no more than inferior ones. The Russians shipped examples of the T-34 and KV1 to both Britain and the USA, who were unimpressed with their quality but liked the design. The Russians believed the UK was going to produce the tanks, but instead the UK favoured the USA.[291] Fletcher called Pope's suggestion fantastic and added that in the light of Britain's supplying tanks to Russia within a year it was probably just as well. This author disagrees.

Tank supply was the worst example of organisational chaos. The Ministry of Supply took the view that tank design was the responsibility of the tank producers, and their Department of Tank Design was restricted to modification of existing types. Thus Nuffield designed and built the Crusader, showing the prototype to the Department which issued an unfavourable report at the end of 1940. Nuffield then humiliated the Department by ignoring its report and as late as 1942 had failed to make any of the corrections asked for. But by 1943 this hubris had worked to the Department's advantage and it received authority for approving new types and finally became an actual source of designs.

Also a Tank Board which included the Ministry, the General Staff and the producing firms was set up in May 1940 and gradually brought some order into tank procurement. But the improvements in liaison were at the end of 1942 merely one point of anxiety among many. The whole subject of the tank was surrounded by the liveliest agitation and the gravest anxiety; the development career of Covenanter, Crusader and Churchill made it clear that something was wrong. There is indeed no doubt that more than one thing was wrong, and that some of the faults lay outside the MOS, principally in the failure of the General Staff to produce a forward policy for tanks up to the end of 1942. Within the Ministry, the fault lay in the organisational gap between design and production. User criticism – which arrived in a plentiful stream – had to be used by the design authorities in arguments with the production side over which, however, they had no authority. The production side, on the other hand, although under continuous pressure to improve quality at the expense of output, were unprovided with reliable information about design trends. In the summer of 1942 the situation had become so serious that the head of tank production felt constrained to warn the chairman of the Tank Board of the possibility of a complete breakdown in the supply of tanks to the army. In the following month three leading manufacturers also made a statement deploring the clash of interests within the Ministry. The Guy Report in 1942 made the

289 William Hornby. *History of The Second World War. Factories and Plants* (London: HMSO, 1958). Scott & Hughes, *History of the Second.*

290 Posten & Hay, *Design & Development.*

291 Fletcher, *The Great Tank Scandal,* p. 99.

necessary changes but the results were not visible until the Centurion appeared in 1945. Scientists were brought in to head up R&D and given high status, which was a great step towards making R&D of armaments professional and civilianised. The service expert became powerful and there was in effect a liberation of the talents, both civilian and military, as the Army through bitter experience came to realise what it lacked. But all this was too late to have very much impact on our story, and much responsibility for the deficiencies in the army's equipment must be placed squarely at Churchill's door. He was very ready to blame the Generals for the military disasters, but the chaos in the Ministry of Supply, which was certainly part of the problem, was his direct responsibility as Premier. His appointment of someone like Andy McNaughton in 1940 to take over weapon design and procurement would have produced a very different story.

The Mixed Divisional Organisation

A short-lived attempt to solve the command problem was made by Paget on Martel's recommendation on his return from the Middle East on 23 January 1942. Martel's ear had been bent with tales of armour shortcomings, and the infantry had demanded control over the Infantry tanks. The NZ Brig Kippenberger told Harding in June 1942; 'We would never get anywhere until the armour was placed under command of infantry brigadiers and advanced on the same axis as the infantry. Under command and on the same axis.' It was the principle that Swinton had expounded in 1916:

> It seems, as the tanks are an auxiliary to the infantry, that they must be counted as infantry and in operation be under the same command.[292]

It was the principle Monash adopted for Hamel, and a major reason for its success:

> These methods involved two entirely new principles. Firstly, each tank was to be treated as an infantry weapon under the exclusive orders of the infantry commander to whom it had been assigned. Secondly, the deployed line of tanks was to advance level with the infantry.[293]

It was, however, anathema to the RAC, and to those aspiring to be called a modern major general by the gurus of the armour cult, Liddell Hart, Fuller and Hobart.

The pressure was this time too great, especially as Churchill would do anything to appease the anger of the New Zealanders, who at any moment could decide they had been abused enough by Lumsden, Briggs and Richards, and go home. The result was a new infantry divisional organisation in which one of the three infantry brigades was replaced by a tank brigade.

> We now proposed that the time had come for the infantry divisions to absorb the army tank brigades that worked with them…we recommended that these tank brigades should replace one infantry brigade in each division. They could then become part and parcel of the division… 3rd Division to have 33rd Army Tank Brigade (Brigadier Jerram).[294]

First called a 'Division', and later a 'Mixed Division',[295] the intention was to end the internecine warfare between armour and infantry by placing both under a unified command. At the same

292 Ernest Swinton. *Notes on the Employment of Tanks* February 1916.
293 Monash, *The Australian Victories.*
294 Martel, *Our Armoured Forces.*
295 TNA: WO 20/Gen/6059(SDI): letters dated 1October 1942 and 24 April 1943.

time the armoured divisions were reorganised with one armoured and one infantry brigade, which halved the number of armoured battalions, in imitation of changed German practice. The 1941 armoured division had 6 armoured regiments, 2 infantry battalions and 1 field regiment of artillery. The 1942 armoured division had 3 armoured regiments, 4 infantry battalions and 2 field regiments. The mixed division had 3 armoured regiments, 6 infantry battalions and 3 field regiments, except the 2 NZ Mixed Division with 2 armoured regiments, 7 infantry battalions and 3 field regiments.

The number of mixed divisions was never large. Eight of the twenty-three British infantry divisions seeing active service out of 40 British infantry divisions which were raised, and a New Zealand division, were converted.

Infantry divisions converted to mixed divisions[296] (NC = Not Converted)

Division – Tank Brigade	Period as a mixed division	Division – Tank Brigade	Period as mixed division
1 – 34 TB/25TB*	June – Nov 1942	46	NC
2	NC	48 – 10 TB	Oct 1942 – Sept 43
3 – 33 TB	June 1942 – April 1943	49	NC
4 – 21 TB	June 1942 – April 1943	50	NC
5	NC	51	NC. Imprisoned
9	NC. Became 51 Div	52	NC
15 – 6 GTB	March – Sept 1943	53 – 31 TB	May 1942 – Oct 43
18	NC. Imprisoned	56	NC
36	NC	59	NC. Dispersed
42	Became 42 BAD	77 – 11 TB	Jan – Nov 1943
43 – 25 TB/34TB*	June 1942 – Sept 1943	78	NC
44	NC	2 NZ – 4AB	July 1942 – May 45

* 25 BTB and 34 BTB changed places on 3.9.1942.

2 NZID, whose GOC was Bernard Freyberg, converted to a Mixed Division for the duration by the novel method of putting 4 NZIB (18, 19 and 20 Inf Bns) into 150 Sherman tanks drawn from UK depots, and 22 (Motor) Bn into half tracks, and calling it 4 NZAB of four bns. Freyberg did not have to worry about getting 8 Army's agreement since Commonwealth armies had autonomy, but he always had good relations with Montgomery who thought highly of him. There is no record that Freyberg considered equipping with Churchill tanks which at that time lacked the 75 mm. 2 NZID was out of action for over a year before landing in Italy in September 1943.

> Here was potentially a most formidable engine of war, second to no other division in the weight of metal it could throw and the equal in fighting power of any two German divisions then in being. It was capable of moving fast, of hitting hard while it moved and, as an enemy that forced it to deploy would quickly discover, of hitting harder still when it halted. Its mixed character, neither a purely infantry nor a purely armoured division, fitted it for operations needing adaptability and some measure of independence for, where the terms of battle were at

296 Joslen, *Orders of Battle*.

> all equal, it possessed within itself the means of breaking into a defensive position, piercing it and exploiting its own success by flooding its armour through the gap.[297]

It was not as successful as it could have been. Although the command problem was solved, 2 NZID suffered from the related factors of faulty policy and vulnerable equipment. The task as always was to break into defensive positions repeatedly and with predictable success, and for that an invulnerable I-tank was needed. Instead 2 NZID was equipped and trained to flood armour through a gap with the vulnerable Sherman. They lacked a reliable means of penetration.

> At first the limitation of tanks in mud, on steep slopes, in close country and in fording rivers were not fully realised. If mobility was overestimated, vulnerability was underestimated. Casualties, however, soon demonstrated the hazards of sending tanks in to lead an attack, either alone or with infantry support, where there was no room for manoeuvre or where movement was confined to a single road. Anti-tank guns, well dug-in and concealed, remained the greatest menace. They could be countered to some extent by the use of smoke and by the skilful fire and movement of tanks in mutual support, but the method best attested by experience was a covering screen of infantry. In other words, success was gained rather by infantry attacks with tank support than by tank attacks with infantry support.[298]

In the absence of an effective tank, and in countryside where a mountain battery of howitzers carried on mules was more useful than a squadron of tanks, the almost static warfare and heavy fighting placed a premium on infantry numbers, leading to a conclusion that was reinforced by the experience of 2 NZ Mixed Division:

> positional as distinct from mobile warfare, in which the division would have to merge its identity into a larger mass, would rob it of these advantages and search out its latent weakness – a shortage of infantry.[299]

Nevertheless, the magnificent 2 NZ Div was assessed postwar by FM Kesselring for the US Historical Branch as outstanding. Freyberg had found a means of compensating for the Sherman's weakness while maximising the opportunities presented by the Mixed Divisional organisation. Kesselring wrote

> that the New Zealand Division was a formation of very high fighting value which 'always tried to take its opponents by surprise when it attacked. It was very inventive in the tactics it used, and not stereotyped. It attacked by day or night, either with or without a preliminary bombardment, sometimes on a wide front and sometimes in a very narrow spearhead, often trying to hit our positions where we did not expect it. Kesselring, however, was critical of junior leadership in the Division: 'At times the commanders of *smaller* formations failed to exploit opportunities which might have led to local successes, because they had been given no orders to cover this eventuality— contrary to German policy, which always strove to bring out initiative in junior commanders.' But he thought that the co-operation of the artillery and tanks with the infantry was always very good. The Division's most noticeable individual trait was its fondness for reconnaissance. 'As a rule both recce and fighting patrols were very

297 Phillips, *Official History*.
298 Ibid.
299 Ibid.

> active before an attack. This certainly made the German soldiers jittery, but on the other hand it enabled them to identify their opponents very quickly.' The New Zealand soldier 'was well trained in the use of his weapon and in the use of ground… brave and tough, very good in single combat and on patrols, equally fearless in attack and in the defence of newly-won ground.' Kesselring believed the Division 'had a large number of excellent snipers.[300]

Montgomery put Paget's organisation through its paces in Exercise Tiger in May 1942. He criticised the organisation on the theoretical and fallacious grounds that it made the corps inflexible, arguing that a commander might need to form a corps of two or even three armoured divisions for operations further afield, as he shortly attempted to do in Egypt with his unsuccessful *corps de chasse,* whose withdrawal after the hype lavished on it in the House of Commons turned Churchill incandescent with anger. Montgomery insisted that a corps commander must remain free to handle any type of division and any combination of armoured and infantry divisions. This argument bears the hallmark of Liddell Hart's support for armoured corps independence, and may well have been the result of direct contact between the two. Control of tanks by infantry was resisted by the tank lobby which argued, as Montgomery did, that it would cramp their ability to perform their 'expanding torrent' exploitation after the break-in. This was what Montgomery planned at Alamein, failed to achieve and let Rommel escape.

Montgomery told his officers that tanks alone were never the answer and success depended on intimate co-operation of all arms including the air force. The tanks must be used in concentrated force to seize vital ground which the enemy would then be forced to counter-attack to their loss. The basis of employing the armoured division offensively was, he said, to hold the battlefield with infantry and anti-tank guns and so free the armoured brigade for its independent and mobile role.[301] The armoured division was not to be squandered in infantry-style defence, Montgomery insisted, endorsing the insistence by tankers throughout the war that they leave the infantry at night to laager away from the front lines, instead of laagering in the front lines with the infantry. Cooperation was therefore never intimate, because for all his fine words Montgomery still viewed tanks and infantry as having separate rôles and echelons but required by circumstances to co-operate. He was incapable of making the mental jump of seeing his forces as an integrated whole, a cast of thousands putting on one battlefield-play comprising many parts. Instead, on Montgomery's battlefield many plays were acted out, some like the *corps de chasse* being slapstick comedy, while the Australian play, in which infantry, artillery and I-tanks acted as one on the northern flank, won the day in spite of Montgomery.

When it came to the new Mixed division, Montgomery worried how infantry could keep up with infantry tanks. In practice the problem was the reverse. Montgomery ordered that tanks be taken completely into the divisional 'fold' and made to feel welcome. He exhorted commanders to determine who would command when tanks were operating with infantry, which he obviously thought would be only part of the time, and he thought both infantry and tank battalion commanders should be in the same tank when fighting together and should exercise joint command. This injunction flew in the face of basic military common sense since the first casualty of joint command is individual responsibility. The logical step was to place tanks under infantry command, and if the armour brigadier was the better man, give him the command, but Montgomery failed to draw that conclusion then or ever. The exception proved the rule, and at Winnekendonk Maj Cathcart and Lt Col Firbank exercised joint command and thought as one. The tanks laagered that night

300 Kay, *Italy Volume II.*
301 Hamilton, *Monty: Master.*

in Winnekendonk with the infantry in the front lines. Two nights before at Kervenheim the Coldstream tanks and Norfolks did not act as one, and the result was a bloody disaster.

The reason given by G.W. Lambert, who was the secretary of the WO committee, for dismantling the mixed division was experience gained abroad. Both the WO[302] and Gerry Chester confirmed that the experience referred to occurred in 4 Mixed Division in Tunisia commanded by John Hawkesworth under Anderson.

> With the results of many field exercises upon which to form an opinion, it was decided that 21 Tank Brigade [comprising 12 RTR, 48 RTR, and 145 RAC], part of 4 Mixed Division, and 25 Army Tank Brigade [comprised the North Irish Horse, 51 RTR and 142 RAC], should be sent to North Africa, with the latter being the first to see action, to compare how each performed when committed to action.
>
> By any measure, 25 ATB's deployment was a success. However, for 21 TB it was less satisfactory. Simply put, on several occasions their AFVs were deployed unwisely. David Fletcher in *Mr. Churchill's Tank* summed it up well, writing about one action as being marred by 'bad planning and poor cooperation between tanks, infantry and artillery.'
>
> Being independent, 25 ATB, was not tied to any one division, and as a result squadrons were deployed wherever best needed. Another plus, the commander of 25 ATB although inferior in rank, when in conference with a divisional commander was considered an equal in the decision making process, and so it was down the line; regimental COs/infantry brigadiers, squadron leaders/battalion COs and troop leaders/company commanders.
>
> Summing up, the actions in Tunisia determined that the commitment of nearly 200 I-tanks for the sole use of one division was wasteful. By September 1943, the Mixed Divisions were no more.[303]

Subsequent events showed that this disastrous decision was based on shaky and unique circumstances. 25 ATB, that included Dawnay's enlightened command of NIH, shone in any situation, including the victory against all odds in the Hitler Line. Hawkesworth, however, was an old soldier, with all the strengths and weaknesses the term implied, including conservatism, as the events on 20 January 1944 on the River Rapido showed when his attempt at crossing it was repulsed. The burly Hawkesworth went to see Fred Walker, GOC 36 USID, to tell him it had failed because the river was running high and no further attempt was possible. He was sorry that Walker's flank would therefore be exposed during the Rapido attack that evening, but there it was, and he was sorry. Walker told his diary that the British were the world's greatest diplomats but could be counted on only to produce words.[304] The old soldier's caution was right on this occasion and saved his command from the disaster suffered by Walker's 36 USID, with 2,128 casualties from the 6,000 men involved in the two day assault, and for no gain.

The question of why the Mixed Division was scrapped, except for the NZ Mixed Div, was mulled over again a decade later by this author and Gerry Chester. To this author scrapping the Mixed Division, restricting the use of the Churchill tank, and failing to armour the Churchill to withstand all anti-tank guns were the three major reasons for the poor performance of 21 AG. The reasons given by Chester for scrapping the Mixed Division point the finger at the underperforming Hawkesworth. It was scrapped,

302 A verbal answer to an enquiry of the War Office in 2001.

303 E-mail from Gerry Chester on 29 November 2003.

304 Rick Atkinson. *The Day of Battle* (Boston: Henry Holt, 2007).

> Basically for two reasons. Being under command of infantry divisions the leaders of whom were poorly versed as to certain tank limitations; for example, ordering advances over terrain impossible for tracked vehicles to advance. Churchill/Infantry support was a mutual thing, the former being able to stay in action longer than infantry, they either had to continue without infantry support or withdraw.[305]

The biographer of 6 GTB, Erskine respected the decision to scrap the Mixed Division but lauded the great and lasting benefit derived from 6 GTB and 15 BID having been in a Mixed division. In this respect it was no 'luxury' but a necessity that was scrapped:

> The "mixed" division had been found to be an extravagant luxury, and in future tank brigades must be available to whatever Infantry Division needed them. But later when the 6th Brigade went into action, staffs took good care to put them in support of the 15th (Scottish) Division whenever that was possible; fortunately this proved to be the case in the Third Battalion's first battle.[306]

They were only a luxury given there were too few Churchill tank brigades to go round. The answer was to expand their number by dissolving the armoured divisions and converting their armoured brigades to tank brigades with Churchill tanks. Instead the infantry divisions, with the rare exception of 15 BID when supported by 6 GTB, were condemned to fighting without all-arms operational methodology, and for a month in Normandy without any effective tank support. The armoured brigades, like 2TAF, acted in support and independently, and never developed the close relationships of mutual trust characterised by 2 NZ Mixed Div.

Whatever the reason, on 1 September 1943 G.W. Lambert sent a letter recording the Army Council's decision to end the mixed division:

> Recent experience has shown that the Mixed Division is unlikely to prove a suitable organisation for operations on the continent of Europe.
>
> Commanders-in-Chief, both at home and abroad have endorsed this view and I am therefore commanded by the Army Council to inform you that it has been decided to abolish the organisation known as the Mixed Division with effect from the day of this letter.
>
> Instructions have already been issued for the conversion of Mixed Divisions to Infantry Divisions and for the retention as GHQ or Army troops of the tank brigades rendered surplus as a result of this reorganisation.[307]

The formation and the abolition of the mixed divisional organisation reflected conflicting requirements. If the most important ingredient in tank-infantry cooperation were intimacy between tank crews and infantry with mutual dedication, then only the mixed division could provide a guarantee of its occurrence. The model was infantry-artillery cooperation; field regiments were integral to the infantry division, with one field regiment permanently associated with each brigade, and a field battery with each battalion. That did not prevent them from supporting other brigades and other divisions, but they prided themselves on never letting their battalion or brigade go without artillery support. But if, as veterans argue, the need was to optimise the use

305 E-mail from Gerry Chester on 7 October 2013.
306 Erskine, *The Scots Guards*, p. 332.
307 TNA: WO204/4065:

of scarce armoured resources, then because tanks could stay in the field longer than infantry they were best organised independently and trained to support any infantry unit.

There are two comments. Firstly, neither the War Office nor Montgomery identified the lessons of the Mixed Divisions and then generalised them through training. The Dawnay Doctrine and 6 GTB's way of working with 15 BID were never written down and used to train tank brigades and infantry how to cooperate. Secondly, the ability of the armoured and tank brigades to go on and on without rest is not a given in all circumstances. Gerry Chester compares the exhaustion of 78 BID after eight days with the ability of 25 ATB to go on and on for three months:

> Just one instance as recorded in the story of the 78th (Battleaxe) Division:
>
> "The division had been in constant action for eight days and needed a pause..."
>
> The flexibility enjoyed by the Army Commander to deploy Churchills is illustrated by this extract:
>
> "The Regiment had now supported the following 'mixed bag' at various times throughout the winter [12th January to March 22nd 1945]: 1st Canadian Infantry Brigade, 2nd Canadian Infantry Brigade, 3rd Canadian Infantry Brigade, Cremona Gruppo (all six Battalions), 2nd Commando Brigade, 12th Royal Lancers, Jewish Brigade, 17th Indian Infantry Brigade, Garibaldi Brigade (Partigianis).[308]

The events of Operation *Heather*, however, showed that 6 GAB, the willing horse, had been in the field too long, and was visibly exhausted. It had supported 15 BID from 7 to 14 February, 2 CID to 18 February, 51 BID to 26 February and the fresh 3 BID to 4 March. Meanwhile until 2 March, GAD had sat on its hands in Pfalzdorf, and when called forward took four days to reach Bonninghardt. It need not have bothered. The GAD website states this about their action in *Veritable*, 'Due to the weather and the Germans flooding the area, only the (GAD's) infantry ended up playing an active part.'[309] The same thing happened in Italy in 1944 with lethal consequences for 1 BAD:

> In this period between the 25th August and the 4th of September, this intention (to break the Gothic Line) was achieved. Despite having informed Army Commander that the Division was ready, 1st Armoured took over 24 hours to commence their advance. The consequences of the delay were horrendous, it gave time for the Germans to deploy Tigers and 88 mm guns on Coriano Ridge which they had previously evacuated. From our vantage point, unable to do anything, we watched Shermans of the Queen's Bays being systematically destroyed. The headstones, in Coriano Ridge War Cemetery, of nearly 2,000 killed during the week-long battle to capture the Ridge, stand in their memory.[310]

Disbanding the armoured divisions and re-equipping them with Churchill I-tanks would have produced a sufficient number of brigades for each infantry division to increase its ORB with a fourth, armoured brigade, with each armoured regiment attached permanently to an infantry brigade and its battalions. If needed they could have been seconded to other divisions, as artillery would always divert to an Uncle target called by a neighbouring division in difficulties, but they

308 Gerry Chester in an e-mail on 21 December 2003.
309 http://en.wikipedia.org/wiki/Guards_Armoured_Division
310 Gerry Chester in an e-mail on 21 December 2003.

would have come to pride themselves on never leaving their division, brigade or battalion to hang out to dry without armour support.

In 1943, Paget[311] asked for the return of 21 and 25 BTBs from North Africa to become part of 21 AG in order to provide each of the five corps with a brigade of Churchill tanks as well as an armoured division, with three independent armoured brigades to be deployed as needed. Instead, Montgomery brought back 4 and 8 BABs, giving each corps an armoured brigade of Shermans and leaving three Churchill brigades to be deployed as needed. This ensured the presence of veteran 8 Army units in 21 AG, but showed that Montgomery believed the battle for France would involve mobile operations of exploitation more often than set-piece assaults.

Allied fortunes in Normandy depended largely on the Sherman tank and the way it was handled. On D-Day, 3 BID landed under orders to seize Caen with support from the Shermans of 27 BAB (13/18 Royal Hussars, 1 East Riding Yeomanry, and Staffordshire Yeomanry) under Brig Prior-Palmer. Never part of a mixed division, it had been part of Hobart's 79 AD from September 1942 to October 1943, experimenting with specialised armour. It was under command of 3 BID from October 1943 until disbandment in July 1944. They were delayed by tide and congestion on the beach, and 185 BIB pushed on without them towards Caen. The formation that had served with 8 and 9 BIBs in 3 Mixed Division from June 1942 to May 1943 was 33 BTB (43 R Tanks replaced by 1 Northamptonshire Yeomanry, 144, and 148 Regiments RAC). It had been re-equipped with Shermans as 33 BAB and was supporting 50 BID on landing on 16 June in fulfillment of Montgomery's belief that any armoured brigade could support any division. Shermans were, however, untrained in effective infantry support, as John English explained.

> 2 Canadian Corps Training Instruction No 12 dated 31 March 1944, directed that, 'the clear distinction between Sherman equipped and Churchill equipped armoured brigades be stressed'. The significance of this direction was that, despite Montgomery's decree that armoured and tank brigades should act the same, Sherman and Churchill brigades trained separately in infantry-tank cooperation. The characteristics of the lighter armoured Sherman, easy prey to the 50 mm Pak, 'made it clear that it could not carry out the infantry tank rôle in the deliberate attack'. The doctrine writers recommended accordingly that Sherman brigades remain 'backers-up to the assaulting troops and not, as infantry tanks, partners in the assault'. Shermans could best support infantrymen on foot by 'sitting back in hull or turret down positions' using their very effective high explosive guns and, to a limited extent, their machine guns' to gnaw through a defensive position. While admitting that 'gnawing was a slow methodical process', the authors insisted that this was, in 'fact and not opinion', the best way of handling Shermans in the infantry support rôle. This meant of course that the hapless infantryman was once again left setting the pace in the face of organised resistance.[312]

The armoured divisions could achieve nothing. Colonel Hans von Luck, commanding 21 Panzer Division, described the *Epsom* attack on 26 June by 11 BAD, calling Pip Roberts:

> probably the youngest but most experienced tank commander. As always with the British, they carried out their tank attacks without accompanying infantry; as a result, they were unable to eliminate at once any little anti-tank nests that were lying well camouflaged in woodland or behind hedges. The main attack broke down under our defensive fire.[313]

311 Place, *Military Training*.

312 John English. *The Canadian Army and the Normandy Campaign* (Mechanicsburg: Stackpole, 2009), p. 134.

313 Hans von Luck. *Panzer Commander* (New York: Praeger, 1989).

Armour and infantry were still separated for Operation *Goodwood* on 18 July as we have seen, although the consequences were becoming better understood, and rumours of American success with divisional all-arms battle groups circulated among O'Connor and Roberts, who wanted to introduce armoured personnel carriers for the infantry.

Ultimate responsibility for direction and oversight of the military and for this state of affairs belonged to Churchill as self-appointed Minister of Defence. But although one of the architects of the tank, Churchill was ignorant of the lessons of Hamel and Amiens, believing, he said, that De Gaulle had taught the world how to employ tanks; 'The idea of the tank was a British conception. The use of armoured forces as they are now being used was largely French, as General de Gaulle's book shows. It was left to the Germans to convert those ideas to their own use'.[314] He accepted the self-serving arguments of the various services for, although describing himself as a 'prod', he seldom over-ruled their autonomy. 'I have not found the need of defining formally or precisely the relationship between the office of Minister of Defence when held by a Prime Minister and the three service departments. There is of course no Ministry of Defence, and the three Service Departments remain autonomous'.[315] Nearly all the problems identified in Operation *Veritable* and in the central direction of the war, were debated in 1942 and 1943 when there was time enough before D-Day for them to be addressed and solved.

Churchill complained about the workload of being Leader of the House, so discharged it to Stafford Cripps in February 1942. But it had given him valuable input that he could have used to effect change. Instead he did those things that he ought not to have done, acting as the mouthpiece of the Services in justifying their parochialism and preventing all-arms. For example, he argued that co-operation between the Army and the RAF had been ensured in 1941 by his edict that the RAF in North Africa was to drop everything and help the Army 'when a battle is in prospect', which bizarrely implied aircraft types were interchangeable. 'We try to find the true and proper course between, on the one hand, not having aircraft attached to the infantry, which would be a misfortune, and, on the other hand, keeping large masses of aircraft which are required for major purposes standing by on specialized function'.[316] He rejected the army's need for dive-bombers, and ignorantly asserted that 8-gun fighters were due to the Air Marshals, when they had in fact opposed them. 'Most of the air-marshals think little of dive bombers, and they persist in their opinion. They are entitled to respect for their view, because it was from the same source that the 8-gun fighter was designed which destroyed so many hundreds of the dive bombers in the Battle of Britain and has enabled us to preserve ourselves free and unaided'.[317] He opposed effective CAS, ignorantly stating that there was an alternative to the accuracy of dive bombing and no need for an army aviation. 'There is no doubt at all that our ground strafing aircraft and fighter bombers are achieving results at least equal to those of the Stukas, without being vulnerable as the Stukas are when caught unprotected by their fighter escort'.[318] He was irresponsibly complacent. 'The manner in which in this Egyptian campaign the arrangements between the air and the military have been perfected has given a model which should be followed in all combined operations in the future'.[319] He arrogantly rejected the widespread doubts about area bombing that proved to be all too well-founded. 'And for my part, I hail it as an example of sublime and poetic justice that those who have loosed their horrors upon mankind will now in their homes and persons feel the shattering strokes of just retribution. We have a long list of German cities in which all the vital

314 *Parliamentary Debates 2 July 1942* (London: HMSO, 1942).
315 *Parliamentary Debates 24 February 1942* (London: HMSO, 1942).
316 *Parliamentary Debates 7 July 1942* (London: HMSO, 1942).
317 *Parliamentary Debates 2 July 1942* (London: HMSO, 1942).
318 *Parliamentary Debates 8 September 1942* (London: HMSO, 1942).
319 *Parliamentary Debates 11 November 1942* (London: HMSO, 1942).

industries of the German war machine are established. All these it will be our stern duty to deal with, as we have already dealt with Lübeck, with Rostock, and half-a-dozen important places. The civil population of Germany have, however, an easy way to escape from these severities. All they have to do is to leave the cities where munitions work is being carried on – abandon their work, and go out into the fields, and watch their home fires burning from a distance. In this way they may find time for meditation and repentance; there they may remember the millions of Russian women and children they have driven out to perish in the snows, and the mass executions of peasantry and prisoners-of-war which in varying scales they are inflicting upon so many ancient and famous peoples of Europe. There they may remember that it is the villainous Hitlerite regime which is responsible for dragging Germany through misery and slaughter to ultimate ruin, and learn that the tyrant's overthrow is the first step to world liberation'.[320] He persisted in believing bombing could end the war early. 'About bombing; I know there is a tendency to deride and disparage the bomber effort against Germany, but I think this is a very great mistake. It is going to get continually stronger until, in my view, it will play a great and perfectly definite part in abridging the course of this war, in taking the strain off our Russian Allies, and in reducing the construction of submarines and other weapons of war'.[321] He persevered despite BC's ineffectiveness. 'The Admiralty have pressed for their continued attack from the air in the hopes of disabling them [Scharnhorst, Gneisenau and Prinz Eugen] and preventing their being repaired. This process continued for more than ten months, during which time the ships were undoubtedly hit several times and repair work was made difficult. No less than 4,000 tons of bombs were dropped, and 3,299 bomber sorties were made upon them, with a loss of 247 Air Force personnel and 43 aircraft.'[322] Churchill failed to realize Germany's Achilles' heel, known to Hitler at the time. 'Hitler: One knows how significant it would have been if the enemy had attacked our power stations simultaneously'.[323] Dönitz promised victory with 300 submarines in 1940, but Hitler released the resources only after the opportunity had passed. Harris and Spaatz made the same promise to Churchill and Roosevelt but, although given the resources, they failed to deliver. The task which Churchill should have concentrated on, was to find a critical target that was within their capabilities without bankrupting Britain. The USAAF correctly identified three candidates; electricity, the railways, and petroleum in AWPD-1 of August 1941. The easiest and most critical was electricity, and that was the one both strategic air forces virtually ignored. The large rotors in generating stations were vulnerable to bombs, costly to repair, and knocking out a large station prevented electricity transmission and destabilised the entire system. Destruction of the five largest stations would have taken out 8% of installed capacity; destruction of 45 plants would have removed 33% and bombing 95 plants would have eliminated over 50%. As little as 0.2 of a ton of bombs (one 500-lb bomb) per acre of plant would have disrupted electricity generation for months, and 0.4 tons per acre put the plant out of operation for 6 months to a year or longer. As the Strategic Bombing Survey stated, 'all evidence indicates that the destruction of such installations would have a catastrophic effect on Germany's war production.' The means could have been the DH98 Mosquito, which first flew on 25 November 1940 with production starting in July 1941. If 1,000 had been ordered capable of carrying four 500-lb bombs, these could have been dropped accurately on the generating plants in the Ruhr by GEE, (which began service trials in July 1941), H2S (first trial at end 1941) and Oboe (first trial in the summer of 1942 and very accurate up to 270 miles from Britain but able to control only one bomber at a time. Oboe was

320 *Parliamentary Debates 10 May 1942* (London: HMSO, 1942).
321 *Parliamentary Debates 2 July 1942* (London: HMSO, 1942).
322 *Parliamentary Debates 27 February 1942* (London: HMSO, 1942).
323 Minutes of the Führer conference: 26 March 1945.

first used against a Dutch power station on December 20, 1942). From the Ruhr the destruction of electricity generation could have been generalised across Germany by following the transmission lines with an electro-magnetic detector. Bomber Harris ridiculed all targets as 'panaceas' except city centres, and Churchill let Harris get away with it. Churchill lied to the House about the *corps de chasse,* which was a dismal failure. 'For the purpose of turning the [Alamein] breach to the fullest account, an entirely new corps, the 10th, was formed consisting of two armoured divisions and the New Zealand Division. This very powerful force of between 40,000 and 50,000 men, including all the best tanks, the Grants and the Shermans, was withdrawn from the battle front and devoted itself entirely to extensive training exercises and preparation. It was this thunderbolt hurled through the gap which finished Rommel and his arrogant army'.[324]

Churchill was obscurantist in suggesting that victory would result from having the right tendencies rather than from battlefield success. 'The old wars were decided by their episodes rather than by their tendencies. In this war the tendencies are far more important than the episodes. Without winning any sensational victories we may win this war. Germany may be defeated more fatally in the second or third year of the war than if the Allied army had entered Berlin in the first.'[325] He told the miners in October 1942 that he sometimes had a strong feeling that the guiding hand of a guardian interfered in Britain's affairs, 'because we serve a great cause'.

Britain's obscurantist PM who was in thrall to the cult of bombing, foisted Montgomery onto the Army at Brooke's urging. Churchill disliked and nearly sacked Montgomery at Alamein and again in Normandy, probably suspecting that Montgomery lacked a war-winning method of the sort that made a solid reputation for Slim. Montgomery's strengths were in training, and in clarity of exposition. He was a doer, and no thinker, an ill educated and largely ignorant man, tactically competent only to the level of divisional command. He was pathologically vain, unpleasant and did not even try to get on with his American peers. The British Army did not deserve him.

His biographer has argued that Montgomery's 'homosocial' genius was to find a way of training and inspiring civilians, 'to transform the pathetic performance of democracy in war from humiliating defeat into victory'.[326] The thesis wilts when his achievements are compared with those of Bill Slim, who came from the Indian Army despised by Montgomery and Churchill. Slim was a thinker but no public speaker. He insisted on all-arms cooperation, and destroyed the independent pretensions of the armoured corps and the RAF that precluded it. The pre-Montgomery army was well trained to act independently, and this Montgomery never really changed. He correctly insisted that 8 Army fight in divisions rather than brigade groups, with concentrated artillery and under a clearly enunciated master plan that included the RAF. But he persisted with using armour independently in his *Corps de Chasse*, which fluffed all their chances provided by the hard fighting infantry, leaving the Anzacs and the tank brigades to win at Alamein in the same manner they had done under Auchinleck. Later Montgomery sacked the senior armour officer, Lumsden, but without resolving the problem. Montgomery remained a great trainer, but 'not a very good general', as Stephen Ambrose observed, and he rarely allowed experience to modify his views.

There were of course no tanks when Montgomery was wounded in November 1914. He returned in February 1915 as a staff officer and made his reputation training 104 BIB of Kitchener's new Army for use on the Somme without tanks. By 1917 he was GSO (2) Training in IX Corps, and issued a 60-page training document for Plumer's successful *Operativ* of all-arms 'bite and hold' on ground unsuitable for tanks. The document was remarkable not for 'the originality of

324 *Parliamentary Debates 11 November 1942* (London: HMSO, 1942).
325 *Parliamentary Debates, 24 February 1942* (London: HMSO, 1942).
326 Hamilton, *The Full Monty*.

ideas but their crystal-clear narrative presentation'.[327] Subsequently Montgomery became GSO (2) Operations in IX Corps, and in April 1918 was on Kemmel Ridge holding against the second German offensive, subsequently moving to the Lys where his corps was reduced to one division. He never used tanks. On 16 July Montgomery became chief of staff and deputy commander of 47 Div under Goringe in III Corps. As part of Rawlinson's 4 Army he must have been aware of Monash's successful operational innovation on 4 July at Hamel with tanks, but failed to see its significance.

It was not until 18 August, and ten days after the black day of the German Army, that Montgomery began to issue the aggressive instructions called for by allied battlefield domination, and ordered by Haig. Nigel Hamilton described the performance of 3 Corps as dilatory, poorly staffed and unsuccessful compared with the strong performance of the Australian and Canadian corps. Montgomery would have shared the general conclusion held by his biographer and most historians, that victory in 1918 came from superior numbers and attrition,[328] and from German social and political collapse[329] rather than from superior operational methodology based on the tank.

Montgomery revealed his inexperience with tanks when writing 49 Div's Tactical Notes in 1924, seeing them as a means of punching a gap in the enemy's lines before retiring to their 'rallying point'.[330] He believed, he said, in the future of tanks but saw them playing only a modest rôle. By 1930 he was acknowledging in his Infantry Training Manual cases where tanks would provide the primary arm of assault, but this was after considerable correspondence with Liddell Hart who strongly criticised his refusal to include in the Manual any reference to 'exploitation' as an 'expanding torrent' of armour supported by infantry. Hart's was the siren voice that mobility per se was sufficient to throw an enemy off-balance and force him to retire to protect his lines of communication. Montgomery rejected it as unrealistic rather than undesirable. Instead he seems to have internalized Hart's criticism, and returned constantly to practise it throughout the war, first at Wattrelos in 1940, then at Dieppe and Alamein in 1942, *Epsom, Goodwood* and Arnhem in 1944 and on the North German Plain in 1945.

Montgomery commanded 1 R Warwicks and was chief instructor at the Staff College at Quetta in the 1930s. In August 1937 he was appointed to command 9 BIB in 3 BID at Portsmouth. Here he trained them hard and included seaborne landings and secret gas trials, but significantly no tank-infantry co-operation. That was left to the period after he left for Palestine in October 1938 when 2 Lincolns gave an isolated demonstration of co-operation with a tank company at Bovington in early 1939 that was, 'viewed with surprise and some incredulity by spectators'.[331]

As commander of 3 BID in the retreat to Dunkirk, Montgomery tactically integrated infantry, artillery and engineers but had no occasion to work with air or armour. The Div had lost its armoured reconnaissance unit equipped with 44 Carriers and 28 Mark VI Light Tanks, but Montgomery sent 8 BIB with its organic carriers to undertake an 'expanding torrent' à la Liddell Hart at Wattrelos on 24 May. Montgomery believed that mobility was a state of mind alien to the First World War donkeys and Col Blimps, and the reason for German success, and he would demonstrate how modern he was. The result was disastrous, so Montgomery expunged it from history. Brooke was complicit and neglected to hold a board of enquiry.

Montgomery remained a true believer in mobility. No one, it must have seemed to him, doubted that mobility was the key to success. The only debate was whether the mobile formation should

327 Ibid.
328 Hamilton, *Monty: The Making*.
329 Hamilton, *The Full Monty*.
330 Ibid.
331 McNish, *Iron Division*.

comprise all arms or just armour, and that debate Montgomery had settled in favour of all-arms but never identified that it took a Dawnay Doctrine to achieve it. Montgomery failed to realise that all tanks and carriers were not alike, and that tanks vulnerable to Paks were immobile from fear of destruction. The burnt-out carriers and shrivelled corpses at Wattrelos were the first installment of the thousands of tanks that by war's end littered the fields of his passing through Alamein, Normandy and the Reichswald, where on 4 March 1945 Montgomery was still arguing with Churchill about the benefits of the heavily armoured Churchill tank and stating his undying opposition to it.

Montgomery argued with Auchinleck in 1940 about whether to concentrate armour and hold it back to attack the enemy after his landing, or rather to defend the beaches against a landing. In hindsight, the Germans would have landed their 88s first and destroyed the massed tanks whenever they attacked, free from attack by non-existent dive bombers. He then helped Brooke withstand the extreme teachings of Liddell Hart and Hobart for armoured independence, by arguing that the tank was the spearhead of a highly trained body of all arms acting as a mutually supporting team. His position was compromised by the vulnerable tanks chosen by the apostles of mobility, and by non-unified command which gave each arm its own echelon and self-interest.

In July 1940, two events occurred that decided the different outcomes in the Hochwald and at Winnekendonk. Martel's 50 BID came under Montgomery's command; and an order went to Vauxhall Motors for urgent production of the A22 Churchill Infantry Tank Mark IV, which could stand up to German anti-tank guns. In this respect Churchill was continuing Elles's vision of an immune tank. By December 1942 steps had been taken to stop production of the Churchill and replace it with the lightly-armoured Cromwell and Centaur, although Churchill had warned against this. For example, on 8 March 1942 he wrote to the Lord Privy Seal:

> I am not at all sure that speed is the supreme requirement of tanks, certainly not all tanks. Armour and gun-power decide the matter whenever tank meets tank. Anti-tank weapons are advancing fast in power, and thin-skinned vehicles will run ever-increasing risks.[332]

On Christmas day 1942 the British were thrown off Longstop Hill in Tunisia. Its recapture was achieved by the NIH in April 1943. Randolph Churchill was with the North Irish Horse, and wrote to WSC sometime in early 1943, 'that the Churchill tanks were proving a great success'.[333] In February 1943 Alexander sent a telegram to WSC about the Churchill tank:

> Its relatively heavy armour enables it to discharge tasks for which no other British tank at present seems equally fitted.[334]

A relieved Churchill took note, and wrote to Alexander on 24 February 1943:

> I am so glad that the much-abused Churchills acquitted themselves well. Of course my main idea in them was armour, and I believe they can take a lot of punishment.[335]

On 6 April 1943 The Secretary of State for War and the Ministry of Supply issued a joint memorandum on the subject of Tank Supply Policy. It stated that American tanks could fulfill the

332 W.S Churchill. *The Second World War Vol IV* (London: 1951), p. 756.
333 Churchill Papers: CHAR 1/375.42: Churchill College, per Gerry Chester.
334 Fletcher, *Mr Churchill's*.
335 Churchill, *The Hinge of Fate*, p. 660.

shortfall in British production of cruisers. This took pressure off British production facilities and particularly off a reluctant Vauxhall Motors to switch to Cromwell production. It recommended continuing production of Churchills through 1944 with improvements to reliability and armour protection.[336]

On 23 April 1943, just as the NIH prepared to storm Longstop Hill, Churchill replied presciently and full of concern that his reputation should not be risked by a failure to introduce a tank immune to anti-tank guns.

> PM to Sir Edward Bridges, and to Brigadier Jacob for Defence Committee (Supply) and others. Tank Supply Policy.
>
> Part I.
> Practically the whole of the tank production and arrivals for 1943 are beyond our control, and we should approve the figures set out.
>
> 2. It seems however of the highest importance to have some thicker armour on a proportion of our tanks. At least 200 and preferably 400 Churchills should be fitted with the *heaviest armour possible* [this authors emphasis, and NB this would mean 10 inches of frontal armour] at a sacrifice of speed down to eight or even six mile an hour or less. Let me have a definite programme for conversions of this kind, showing what is achieved, what must be paid in speed, how many will be treated, and when they will be finished. At least a hundred should be pushed forward as an emergency job.
>
> 3. We shall, I am sure, be exposed to criticism if we are found with a great mass of thin-skinned tanks of medium size, none of which can stand up to the German guns of 1943, still less those of 1944. The idea of having a spear-point, or battering-ram of heavily armoured vehicles to break the enemy's front and make a hole through which the lighter vehicles can be pushed has a very high military significance. A certain number of such vehicles should be attached to armies, and possibly even to corps, in each theatre. The wart-hog must play his part as well as the gazelle.
>
> 4. The experimental development of a heavy tank – 60, 70, or 80 tons – cannot be laid aside. Occasions will almost certainly arise when it would be a solution of particular problems. We shall be much to blame if the necessity appears and we are found to have fallen behind the enemy. Pray let me have a report on the Stern tank or any alternative that can be devised. What has happened to the amphibious tank? Surely a float or galosh can be made to take a tank of the larger size across the Channel under good conditions once a beach landing has been secured.
>
> Part II.
> 5. I was not convinced in favour of the widespread adoption of the 75 mm gun, and a further meeting of the Defence Committee on this subject must take place before any decision is taken. For us this gun, which is the same as that mounted in the Shermans, is a new weapon. I understand that preparations for manufacture have already started. Report to what point they have reached. What arrangements are made for the ammunition on the scale of the tank armament proposed? What amounts can be manufactured in the United Kingdom in 1943

336 Fletcher, *Mr Churchill's.*

> and 1944? Are we to rely upon supplies from America? Is it true that they are turning from the 75 mm medium velocity gun to the 76 mm high velocity gun? If so, will they not regard this class of ammunition as obsolescent?
>
> 6. The 95 mm tank howitzer, on the other hand, is already in production here. A detailed statement should be prepared, on one sheet of paper, showing the nature and qualities of both the 75 mm (Sherman type) and the 95 mm (British type). Also an estimate should be prepared by the ministry of Supply showing the relative deliveries of these weapons and their ammunition which would become effective in 1943 and 1944 if decisions were taken before the end of the month. These tables should be got ready for an early meeting of the Defence Committee.
>
> 7. Reports from the Middle East Army are of great interest so far as tactical operations in the Desert are concerned, and also generally. It must be remembered that they have not seen the alternatives to the 75 mm gun. They have only very recently had any HE ammunition for the 6pdr. They have never seen the 95 mm tank howitzer. We must be sure that this question is studied in all its bearings, or we may find ourselves lumbered up with obsolescent patterns, and thus be held most blameworthy.[337]

The Defence Committee endorsed the report. On 14 May 1943 the Ministry of Supply responded that it was impossible to increase turret armour because the ring would not take it, and the suspension could support only an additional half ton. The way was open to design the A22F or Churchill Mk VII as it came to be called. Testing started at the end of 1943 and there were units available before D-Day, but Churchill's suggestion that heavy armour be incorporated to withstand anti-tank guns was never pursued. Later events show he never forgot to remind Montgomery about this neglect. No one proposed all-or-nothing armouring.

The Churchill tank was saved by its performance in Tunisia. The appearance of the Tiger reinforced the decision, and WSC was always keen to promote his tank. Montgomery, however, like everyone in 8 Army thought 1 Army were amateurs, and all of their decisions automatically suspect. Support for the Churchill tank by 1 Army was enough to condemn it in Montgomery's eyes. As Sir Edgar Williams, Montgomery's head of intelligence, later reflected:

> (We) were a frightfully arrogant lot really. We'd had these successes and – 'there were these silly chaps making a balls of it' sort of attitude.[338]

7 BAD equipped with Shermans destroyed Rommel. This was the proven formula Montgomery took to Normandy to perform 'deep penetrations – early', with disastrous results.

Montgomery rationalised his rejection of the Churchill tank with the reasons given earlier. From 1942 to 1945 with Brooke's support he campaigned to abolish the Churchill and the army tank brigades that operated them. Had he succeeded then the outcomes at Winnekendonk and the Hochwald would have been identical.

Montgomery said the right thing, telling his officers that tanks alone were never the answer and that success depended on intimate co-operation of all arms including the air force. But this did not produce integration at the formation level. Instead the tanks, he said, must be used in concentrated force to seize vital ground to be held by infantry with anti-tank guns that the enemy would then be forced to counter-attack to their loss. The armoured division, he said, would then be withdrawn

337 Churchill, *The Hinge of Fate*, p. 850.
338 Hamilton, *Monty: Master*.

to be free for a further independent and mobile rôle.[339] The corps commander became a choreographer, who first chose vital ground, then sent in an armoured division to seize it, then replaced the armoured division with an infantry division that destroyed the enemy counter-attacks, and then repeated the exercise. It was a disastrous recipe that produced Operations *Epsom* and *Goodwood*. Montgomery never realized that in the end all that was required were mixed divisions equipped with frontally invulnerable infantry tanks that could seize ground and hold it *à la* Monash, and to do it reliably and repetitively for every one of the 753 miles from Hermanville to Berlin. History in 1945 would have repeated the events of 1918 when Ludendorff, recognising his fate was ineluctable, asked for an armistice.

The armoured division was not to be squandered in infantry-style defence, Montgomery insisted. He still viewed tanks and infantry as having separate rôles but required by circumstances to co-operate closely. When it came to the mixed division that included a tank brigade as described earlier, Montgomery worried how infantry could keep up with infantry tanks. In practice the problem was often the reverse with the Ghurkhas, for example, going ahead of Churchills crossing difficult terrain in Italy, and 2 Lincolns were first into Winnekendonk. Montgomery ordered that tanks be taken completely into the divisional fold and made to feel welcome. He exhorted commanders to determine who would command when tanks were operating with infantry, which he seemed to think would be only part of the time, and he ordered that both infantry and tank battalion commanders should be in the same tank when fighting together and should exercise joint command.

> Tank squadrons and infantry companies were similarly twinned. Because our two Grenadier Battalions fought as one group, command was exercised jointly by the two commanding officers, equals in rank. This did not alternate, like the Roman system of dual consulate, but depended on joint agreement on an overall plan, and executive orders to his own subordinates by each; sometimes there were combined 'Order Groups'.[340]

NIH found that after being under command of infantry in the UK, they came to exercise joint command in North Africa because the NIH's CO, Lt Col David Dawnay performed well when given command of five companies of infantry, two troops of anti-tank guns, and a detachment of RE for the defence of Le Kef. So impressed was Brig Maxwell by the result that higher command decreed that in future tank-infantry deployment would be the subject of joint decision except in cases of emergency.[341] This system became general except in the case of 4 Mixed Division and 21 ATB. The best compromise was the German insistence on unified command in all circumstances. Tanks or infantry were chosen to command, depending on the situation.

German military prestige has endured, based on the early overwhelming victories. Their *Operativ* was, however, flawed and relied on the elements of surprise and training. They had also been seduced by the mobility theory of Fuller and Liddell Hart, according to Heinz Guderian, who created the Panzerarmee:

> (We) were … trying to make of the tank something more than just an infantry support weapon … it was Liddell Hart who emphasised the use of armoured forces for long-range strokes, operations against the opposing army's communications, and also a type of armoured

339 Ibid.
340 David Fraser, *Wars and Shadows* (London: Allen Lane, 2002).
341 Gerry Chester in a letter to this author in December 2003.

> division combining panzer and panzer-grenadier units. Deeply impressed by these ideas I tried to develop them in a sense practicable for our own army.[342]

He argued that infantry and artillery should be under command of tanks, and this became inevitable when the Panzer Korps became a black-uniformed Nazi élite. Like Fuller, he believed the infantry were too set in their ways to understand the concept of speed. Therefore, rather than educate and equip an army it was easier for Guderian to build a specialist tank arm with its own infantry and artillery under command. This integrated all the arms in the Panzer army but left the infantry divisions without tanks since Germans also rejected the mixed divisional organization.

> In this year, 1929, I became convinced that tanks working on their own or in conjunction with infantry could never achieve decisive importance. My historical studies, the exercise carried out in England and our experiences with mock-ups had persuaded me that tanks would never be able to produce their full effect until the other weapons on whose support they must inevitably rely were brought up to their standard of speed and cross-country performance. In such a formation of all arms, the tanks must play the primary rôle, the other weapons being subordinated to the requirements of the armour. It would be wrong to include tanks in infantry divisions: what was needed were armoured divisions which would include all the supporting arms needed to allow the tanks to fight with full effect.[343]

Guderian became, ever increasingly preoccupied with the tactical and operational use of movement at division and corps. These studies in *Operativ* translated into a definition of the rôle the tanks should play and hence of their specifications: mobile tank-killing Mk IIIs with support from a more lightly armoured Mk IV equipped with a 75 mm firing HE.

The Germans knew the value of communications and all AFVs had radio. The resulting real-time command and control gave the Panzerarmee the edge over the French, British and Russians in 1940-41, achieving success despite inferior numbers and weapon quality.

Guderian never contemplated mechanising the infantry or giving them integral armour in a mixed division. Questions were raised at the time about relying on marching infantry. German industry could have built the necessary motor vehicles. After only a month in Russia on 4 August 1941, von Senger und Etterlin observed the problem:

> It is essential to fill the gap between attacking armour and the slower infantry. But how? More mechanization? More mechanized infantry and artillery within the armoured divisions? More concentration of armour with reserves held in rear to sustain their breakthrough? Perhaps, on the other hand, a shorter rein on the armoured divisions to keep them close to the infantry divisions. The same old problems are turning up for the new mechanized cavalry that their horsed forbears had.[344]

By October he could see the extent of the German armour's vulnerability.

> The real trouble is that both tanks and motorized infantry have a limited value in the attack as they offer too good a target for the defence. But the difference between the two is that when the armour gets enmeshed in the enemy's anti-tank defence, the infantry can dismount and

342 Heinz Guderian. *Panzer Leader* (London: Michael Joseph, 1970).

343 Ibid.

344 Frido von Senger & Etterlin, *Neither Fear Nor Hope* (London: Macdonald, 1963).

> maintain the momentum by pressing on foot as in a normal infantry attack. And a second important point: each main arm must be equally capable of defence and offence and to be able to change from one to the other as is so often demanded in warfare, at a moment's notice.[345]

On 7 December 1941 von Senger und Etterlin declared the problem insoluble with the means available, and the war lost.

The Russians, however, made no such mistake. Martel recognised that, 'the higher direction on the Russian front was excellent throughout the war. The Russians have a flair for warfare.'[346] They demonstrated the truth of Monash's axiom, for excellent staff, adequate equipment and poorly trained soldiery gave Russia victory over the mediocre staff, inadequate equipment but excellently trained soldiers of the Wehrmacht, and in spite of the latter's obtaining surprise and what appeared to be overwhelming victories in the first four months of Operation *Barbarossa*.

The excellence of Russian staff work resulted from extensive efforts in the 1920s and 1930s to develop a theory and practice of war. They studied foreign thinking, rejecting as frivolous the idea of a small but fast tank army proposed by Fuller and implemented by Guderian. Tukhachevsky imagined a war between Britain and the USA fought on the Canadian border with Fuller's cadres of 18 divisions with 5,000 tanks and 3,000 aircraft against US mass mobilization of 180 divisions with 50,000 tanks and 30,000 aircraft. His conclusion was that the British would be crushed because although it might reach and destroy Washington (Moscow), the Americans would withdraw and rebuild their army in Texas and supply it from California (beyond the Urals). Defeat for large countries was a state of mind, but for a small country like Germany it occurred when the enemy knocked on the door of Hitler's bunker. As Marxists the Russians considered the masses were there to be mobilized. In 1932 Varfolomeev studied the Battle of Amiens, and drew conclusions about how to employ shock armies in the offensive with mass armour and aviation, and how to overcome enemy operational reserves as they joined the engagement.

Marxism was a materialist historical theory claiming to have uncovered a deterministic relationship between the forces of production and governmental institutions. This predisposed Marxists to seek similar determinants in other areas such as warfare, given urgency by predictions of capitalist counter-attack in a futile attempt, as they saw it, to counter historical inevitability, and by their own desire to hasten that inevitability through calculated aggression and destabilisation. Trotsky called for an army based on military science, and Frunze for a unified military doctrine. To these ends an Academy of the General Staff was established.

The First World War and the Civil War gave Russian officers a rich fund of experience in modern war. Some who joined the Red Army as military specialists developed a theory of operational art to explain events such as Tukhachevsky's Vistula campaign of 1920, when ex-British Mk IVs and Mk Vs with ex-German A7Vs were employed. The Vistula campaign ended with the 'miracle of Warsaw' when Tukhachevsky over-reached himself and was defeated by the Poles. The problem of maintaining deep penetrations became a major subject of study in the Academy. The Germans outside Moscow suffered from a similar 'miracle' effect. They had not studied the problem and lacked a solution, famously neglecting the provision even of winter clothing.

Svechin, Frunze and Tukhachevsky conceptualised modern warfare. In 1923 Svechin invented the concept of 'operational art' to replace 'grand tactics' and 'lower strategy' as the:

345 Ibid.
346 Martel, *The Russian Outlook*.

> totality of maneuvers and battles in a given part of a theater of military action directed toward the achievement of the common goal, set as final in the given period of the campaign.[347]

Svechin proposed dedicating the entire state economy to supporting front operations. In 1924 a Chair in the Military Academy was established named 'Conduct of the Operation' and given to Varfolomeev. In 1929 the basic principle of 'combined arms' was established and evaluated in field exercises and command staff games, and this research into operational art succeeded in 'obviating the gap between theory and practice which plagued the development of armoured warfare in the West'.[348]

Tukhachevsky in 1927 proposed complete mechanization of the Red Army. Stalin accepted this plan in 1930 and started the brutal process of industrialization and forced collectivisation that were linked to national defence. Tukhachevsky in Leningrad had meanwhile developed his views about all-arms, sponsoring the development of tank, aviation and airborne forces. In 1930 he argued publicly for a mass, mechanised army as the means of implementing the new operational art. Between 1931 and 1937 he directed the mechanization of the Red Army and insisted on combined arms under integrated command. In 1936 he wrote the Field Regulations.

Stalin purged him and most of the staff and condemned their theories. Those who survived, however, such as Shaposhnikov, Zhukov, and Rokossovsky, had been exposed to the new thinking. Events in Manchuria, Poland, Finland and France forced reforms and design of the T34 and KV1, which were rushed out of fear that the Germans were developing similar machines. All was in hand before the German invasion.

From 1936 onwards and enshrined in Tukhachevsky's PU36, the Russians developed the concept of deep-counterattack by all-arms, which unnerved the Germans and von Senger und Etterlin outside Moscow in 1941. In that year with PU41, the Russians struck a better balance between tanks, infantry and artillery. Bagramyan recorded a most telling statement by Zhukov in September 1940 even before *Barbarossa.* 'We are now in great need of troop commanders who are well trained not only in combined-arms but in operational matters as well'.[349]

Zhukov could professionally criticise the German offensive against Moscow:

> The enemy's flank strike units were weak and were made up of an insufficient number of combined-arms units. To stake everything on the armour units under these specific conditions did not justify itself, as was shown in practice.[350]

The Russians knew their enemy. They had been closely involved with the Germans in the tank development and training establishment opened at Kazan in 1923 but closed by Hitler in 1933. By 1930 Tukhachevsky was forming the first mechanised brigades and in that year 60 British machines were bought including the 12 ton, the 6 ton from which the T26 was developed, and the Carden Lloyd that formed the basis of the turretless T27. But heavier tanks were also built in 1930, including the 29 ton T28 and the 45 ton T35 that were both armed with a 76.2 mm gun. Then in 1931 two Christie M-1931s were bought from the USA from which a series of BT (*bystrokhodnii*) fast tanks were developed. The BT-1 of 1931 had a 37 mm gun, the BT-3 of 1933 a 45 mm while the BT-8 of 1938 was fitted with the 76.2 mm. A feeling of inferiority with regard

347 Jacob W Kipp. Mass, *Mobility And The Red Army's Road to Operational Art* (Fort Leavenworth: US Army, 1987), ref Svechi. Strategiia.

348 Christopher Duffy. *Red Storm on the Reich* (New York: Atheneum, 1991).

349 OP Chaney. *Zhukov* (London: David & Charles, 1973), ref Ivan Khristoforovich Bagramyan. *Zapiski Nachalniki Operativnogo Otdela* (Voyenna-Istorichesky Zhurnal, January 1967).

350 Ibid.

to German equipment drove the Russians constantly to improve their tank designs. They refused to believe during a visit approved by Hitler to the German tank factories that the Mk IV was their heaviest tank.

In 1936 Martel was a celebrity in the Red Army due to wide dissemination of his translated book, *In the Wake of the Tank*. He watched Soviet manoeuvres near Minsk, and agreed with Tukhachevsky that the army needed two different types of tank for the infantry and reconnaissance rôles previously performed by the heavy and light cavalry. They debated armour thickness required for the infantry tank, and Martel gave his view that it must be enough to keep out all anti-tank projectiles. The Russians were still undecided and were operating cruiser tanks in support of infantry while experimenting with more heavily armoured tanks like the SMark and T100.

In spite of the purges, tank development continued. In 1939 Mikhail Ilyich Koshkin, who had been working in 1938 at the Kharkov Locomotive Works on an 18 ton A-20 running on either wheels or tracks, urged the Army to standardise on tracked tanks for production simplicity. With Alexander Morosov and Nikolai Kucherenko, a sick and dying Koshkin began the design of the T-34 in 1939. Prototypes were running in 1940 and the result made the Panzerarmee obsolete.

The T-34 weighed 28 tons, a similar weight to the Matilda. It was powered by a 500 hp diesel engine and could reach 32 mph. The sloped hull armour was about 40 mm thick and the cast turret was 45 mm. Armament was a 76.2 mm gun originally with a length of 30.5 calibres but soon increased to 41.2 giving it a muzzle velocity of 2,172 feet per second. It could penetrate 69 mm of armour at 500 yards, or 54 mm at a mile, which was enough to destroy any German tank. The T-34 carried 77 rounds, usually made up of 19 rounds of AP shot, 53 rounds of HE and 5 rounds of shrapnel. The design had several shortcomings.[351] It was in full production in 1941 and led Hitler to say that if he had known about Russian tanks he would never have invaded Russia. Through super-human effort the Germans countered the T34-76 with the MK V Panther, which was a heavy 45 ton cruiser. The Russians then cleverly matched the Panther's gun, but not its armour, in the T34-85 in 1943, allowing them to out-produce the Germans by a factor of three.

The combination of operational art and the interest of the head of state gave Russia the KV, or Klementi Voroshilov. This heavily armoured infantry tank with 75 mm armour, compared with 30 mm on the German Mk IV, upgraded to 50 mm in 1941, was called originally the Kotin-Stalin after the chief engineer of the Kirov-Zavod tank factory in Leningrad. In 1939 Stalin 'suggested' to Kotin those inspired changes to the flawed SMark and T100 tank designs which resulted in the fine KV design.

The Russians under Zhukov implemented an answer to the German *Blitzkrieg*[352] within three months of the outbreak of war, an extraordinary achievement of operational art and clarity of thought about combined-arms. This speed was matched historically only by the decision of Churchill and Swinton within three months of the beginning of the First World War to produce a tank, and the Germans to start gas warfare.

It would have been fitting for the British Army to have formed the left wing of this temporarily beaten Russian army, which had been written off in London and Washington, and then enjoyed participating in its renaissance. In Churchill's absence, this is surely what would have happened, as discussed above. The British Army would, once again, have measured itself against the main force of a triumphant enemy, as it did under Marlborough, Wellington and Monash, and not tried to win by avoiding the main force through *a guerre de course* based on trying to cow men by bombing their women and children.

351 Douglas Orgill. *T-34 Russian Armor* (London: Macdonald, 1971).
352 Geoffrey Jukes. *The Defence of Moscow* (London: Macdonald, 1970).

The young Russian commanders quickly learned how to implement Tukhachevsky's regulations, while industry, which had been on a war footing for a decade, was relocated and built the required weapons. The lack of trucks and railway locomotives was rectified through Lend-Lease. In the final phase of the war Soviet operations achieved what pre-war theory had promised.[353]

The damage done to the Wehrmacht by the Russians in 1941 was of such severity that the western allies were never again threatened with overwhelming German force. Yet the Wehrmacht rump in the west gave such an account of itself that in the winter of 1944 a retreating Bradley despaired, concluding that if the war was going to be finished the Russians would have to do it.

In the end the Allies never gave up their theory of two types of warfare and divisions, and of the primacy of mobility and exploitation devised by the apostles of mobility. The breakthrough at Winnekendonk was the signal for the GAD to tie up the roads for days, although 3 BID did not wait but pursued. The confusion in thought affected even a veteran infantryman such as Brig-Gen Whitaker:

> Ideally, then, tanks should be employed in massed formations, over hard, open country, to break through and disrupt the enemy in their rear areas.[354]

Most of the military's deficiencies were self-inflicted. By 1944 it should have been clear that only one type of warfare existed, and therefore only one type of division was required. Germany's defences in depth were in effect continuous right back to the Führerbunker in Berlin, with every town, village and farm in between a potential fortress manned by a hostile population. The task was to turn the Germans out of these defences, and to do it predictably and reliably and repeatedly with minimal loss of life and damage. For this only one type of division was required; a mixed division with two tank regiments equipped with frontally invulnerable infantry tanks, seven infantry battalions with a regiment of Kangaroo APCs on call to maintain momentum when the German line was broken, and four artillery regiments with SP artillery.

Montgomery showed his allegiance to the RAC by wearing its black beret. It is not surprising that he failed to recognise the systemic armour problem. But in Burma, Slim took the same material available to Montgomery and transformed it.

At exactly the same time that Major F.A. Tilston in the Hochwald and Private James Stokes at Kervenheim were winning the VC on 1 March 1945, Slim on the other side of the world was watching from a pagoda as 48 Brigade in Punch Cowan's 17 BID, part of Messervy's 4 Corps, attacked the prepared Japanese defences of General Kasuya around the North Lake at Meiktila in Burma. One Indian-manned Sherman was co-operating intimately with two platoons of Gurkhas as they methodically reduced the bunkers. Slim wrote that it was the closest as army commander he had come to real fighting, but it had also been one of the, 'neatest, most workmanlike bits of infantry and armoured minor tactics he had ever seen'.[355]

The contrast between Slim's paean to armour and the problems occurring on the same day half a world away in the Hochwald Gap became only more marked in the following days. In April Slim's army made an extraordinary advance of 300 miles in 30 days against strong opposition down the Sittang valley from Pyawbwe to Rangoon, while Montgomery had managed only 30 miles in 30 days from Groesbeek to Wesel. Slim's rapid advance was made possible by sending an integrated armoured infantry group down the single road, and air transporting a support brigade to airfields created every 50 miles, sometimes hacked out of the bush overnight. The airfield engineers

353 Kipp, Mass, *Mobility*.
354 Whitaker, *Rhineland*.
355 Slim, *Defeat into Victory*.

travelled with the tanks at the head of the column, and the airstrips were in use within hours of their arrival.

Such innovations were made in Slim's 'forgotten army' with only restricted material resources. His 18 divisions were spread out over a distance of 700 miles and faced in the Japanese defenders as fierce as and no less formidable defenders than the Fallschirmjäger. The Burmese terrain was generally less suited to tanks and more favourable to the defence than the area of the Niederrhein. Slim said he fought a 'kind of warfare more modern in essence than that fought by other British forces'.

It is worth wondering how Slim might have modernised 21 AG if he and not Montgomery had been in command. There would have been no cronyism, and Slim would have demanded more than loyalty from his subordinates. The in-fighting between infantry and armour would have been resolved by placing armour under command of infantry, and Slim would probably have retained the mixed divisional organization. He would have abolished the armoured divisions after categorizing them as special forces:

> The cult of special forces is as sensible as to form a Royal Corps of Tree Climbers and say that no soldier, who does not wear its green hat with a branch of oak leaves stuck in it, should be expected to climb a tree.[356]

Instead Slim would have expected the infantry to exploit their own breakthroughs with their own tanks, and to call on the RAF fleet of transport aircraft for movement and re-supply. He would have respected the need for a tank immune to the 88 mm, and insisted on its availability. The many shortcomings identified above would surely have been addressed, and best practices implemented. He would certainly have been working with the Americans in a joint effort to make an I-tank immune to the 88, when Montgomery, who liked to be isolated from his allies, was uninvolved and ignorant of such developments.

In the final advances of 1945 all attacking armies were in reality organised into mixed divisions, supported by a heavily armoured tank that nevertheless was still vulnerable to the 88 mm or 17pdr.; the Tiger II, IS-2, Sherman M4A3E2 Jumbo, and Churchill VII. Spearheads were infantry heavy, for when meeting the enemy in prepared positions and changing manoeuvre into engagement, the attacker had to be able to force a passage by immediately applying all arms in overwhelming strength before the enemy could reinforce or kill all the attacking troops, as could so easily have happened at Winnekendonk, and almost occurred at Kervenheim.

In 1945 the thinking of all armies had converged, with 21 AG the least able to comprehend the change. Dmitry Lelyushenko believed that, 'Two mechanised corps [lorried infantry divisions] and one tank corps [armoured division] – in my view that was the most advantageous organisation for a tank army [corps] at that time'. The Russian Mechanised Corps, the Russian name for an infantry division, had 16,000 troops, 180 T34-85 tanks, 60 SU-76 Assault Guns, 252 artillery pieces and mortars and 8 Katyusha rockets.[357] Similar in concept, but still operating without unified command, with a consequently degraded performance as we have seen in Operation *Heather*, 3 BID and 6 GAB together had 20,000 troops with 180 Churchill tanks, 12 M10s available but not being used as assault guns, and 323 artillery pieces and mortars with no rockets. The Americans, however, had gone much larger with the 'Big Red One', as 1 USID was known. In April 1945 it had under command the equivalent of an armoured division, giving it 25,000 men, 250 Sherman tanks, 36 M36 acting as assault guns, and 276 artillery pieces and mortars without rockets.

---

356 Slim, *Defeat into Victory*.
357 Duffy, *Red Storm*.

We have seen how Montgomery stared Churchill down and deprived 21 AG of a tank immune to the 88, leaving Churchill in the House to face Richard Stokes's criticism of the never ending British tank fiasco. The Americans, with their own serious tank problems that derived from Patton's preference in early 1944 for the Sherman over the new T28 Pershing, nevertheless showed how easy it would have been under anyone but Montgomery, Hobart and Richards to have fielded a Churchill at Winnekendonk that was frontally immune to the 88.

The Americans had their versions of the obscurantist Hobart and Richards in the persons of Gladeon M. Barnes and George S. Patton (who 'knew as little about tanks as anybody I know' according to Lesley McNair),[358] who always held that tanks did not fight tanks, and said in the autumn of 1943; 'Any attempt to armour and gun tanks so as to outmatch anti-tank guns is foredoomed to failure'.[359] There were also influential forward thinking generals such as Jacob Devers and Alvin Gillem, and even converts such as Patton himself later on, so that when the extent of the Sherman's vulnerability was revealed in Normandy, where the Panther appeared in numbers with its quasi frontal immunity, there were people able to find a solution in September 1944 with the M36 90 mm tank destroyer and with the 76 mm HVAP ammunition in the Sherman. Then in November 1944, 250 heavily armoured M4A3E2s were shipped to the ETO, which was the first American tank with frontal resistance to the 75 mm Pak 40. Its task became to lead the advance, and very quickly became indispensable. None was supplied to the British, who may not have been informed of its existence and no more were forthcoming even though Eisenhower demanded the maximum number that could be produced.

By the autumn of 1944 the Germans had concentrated their remaining tanks in the East, and left the west to be defended by StuGs, Mk IV Tank Destroyers, Paks, including the very large number of DP 88s that were diverted from their Flak employment, and heavily armed Fallschirmjägers. The formula worked in the Hochwald and was overcome in Operation *Heather* only by the exertions of exceptional men and somewhat less inadequate equipment.

The contrast between the lethargic do-nothing performance of 21 AG and the can-do 1 US Army, and later 12 AG, was first apparent, as we have seen, in Normandy when all-arms battlegroups were formed for Operation *Cobra* and that development was imitated without acknowledgment by the British armoured divisions. The British reacted well before D-Day to the threat of the Panther by introducing the Sherman Firefly. They also acted on Martel's recommendation and designed the Churchill VII to overcome the defensive techniques of defence-in-great-depth reported by Martel. Unfortunately, Montgomery permitted Hobart to sabotage the introduction of the Churchill VII into the Tank Brigades, who had to continue with the inadequate Churchill IV, onto which the crews welded tons of track links in a vain attempt to protect themselves against the 88 and Pak 40.

The American crews also tried to increase protection by piling sandbags attached to welded-on track links all over their Shermans. In February 1944 Chrysler had developed an appliqué armour kit for field installation, and a picture of its wooden mock-up exists,[360] but the programme was cancelled in that same month for reasons that Steven Zaloga could not discover. Other divisions used re-barred concrete on the front and sides of their Shermans. Patton, however, made amends for his crass error in rejecting the Pershing by ordering all 76 mm Shermans in 3rd Army to be retrofitted in February and March 1945 with additional front hull and turret armour, which is of course what 21 AG would have done for all of the Churchills. 3 US Army contracted with three factories near Bastogne to carry out the work of stripping armour plate from the tanks that littered

358 Zaloga, *Armored Thunderbolt*, p. 131.
359 Op. Cit., p. 24.
360 Op. Cit., p. 279.

the Ardennes battlefield and welding it to the fronts of 36 of the 168 Shermans in each of Patton's armoured divisions, 4th, 6th and 11th USADs. At the same time the co-axial .30 calibre machine gun was replaced with a .50 calibre.

This successful programme by 3 US Army was so popular with the crews that it was reported to Washington,[361] but news of it never reached either 1 Canadian Army or 2 British Army, according to two centres of expertise – LCMSDS and the Bovington Tank Museum.

Conclusion

This chapter is an inquest into whether the large number of deaths on the battlefields of *Heather* was avoidable. The conclusion is that the system put in place by Churchill made them unavoidable, but absent Churchill there was no reason why the success of 1918 with its low body count could not have been replicated and a more modest body count achieved.

The all-arms formula devised by Monash that brought victory with modest losses in 1918 was destroyed by Churchill and Smuts when they established the RAF as an independent strategic force, and created the environment for the Royal Armoured Corps to pretend likewise. These two strategic forces were taken over by cult leaders, Trenchard and Hobart, who updated the fallacy of the *guerre de course* to promise victory in a future war without the need to engage the main enemy force. When these two failed to deliver on their promises, the task of defeating the German field army devolved onto the infantry. The previous emphasis on giving the RAF and the RAC what they demanded resulted in the infantry being deprived of investment in the weapons needed for them to succeed without great losses.

In 1939/40 the traditional military leadership brought resounding victories at sea in the battles of the River Plate and Narvik, in the air in the Battle of Britain, and on land against the Italians in Libya. Unfortunately Churchill then took absolute control as PM and MOD and facilitated the cult leaders, being Trenchard, who had ruthlessly got rid of Dowding, and Hobart who he brought back after his rightful sacking. Churchill sent the victorious army to Greece rather than to Tunis in 1941 and thus allowed in Rommel's Afrika Korps, who dealt severely with the RAC cult which had no answer to Germans all-arms operational methodology. Auchinleck and Wavell had begun to retrain the army in all-arms when they were sacked by Churchill who wanted the cultic Strafer Gott but on his death had to settle for Alanbrooke's choice of the flawed Montgomery wearing his cultic black beret. Any improvement thereafter could occur only when Americans and Canadians started going their own ways militarily, such as American formation of all-arms teams in Normandy that were copied by the British, and the creation by the Canadians of the tracked APC that the British took over. The dead hand of Montgomery's total control of 21 AG prevented any new thinking of the type that brought victory to Haig's army in 1917-18.

3 BID therefore undertook *Heather* without integrated all-arms operational methodology with air and armour under infantry command, and without accurate aircraft-borne weapons or a tank with frontal immunity against the 88 mm. At Winnekendonk there was no air support at all, and the Lincolns were saved from annihilation only by the exceptional action of Jim Alldred who had not been subject to the RAC's way of thinking, just as during the previous day the Norfolks had been saved by the unconventional Alec Foucard's support of wild Jimmy Stokes. In these circumstances, in which the rank and file covered for the incompetence of the brass and the MOD, the large number of Norfolk and Lincoln dead were only to be expected, being similar to

361 Op. Cit., p. 284.

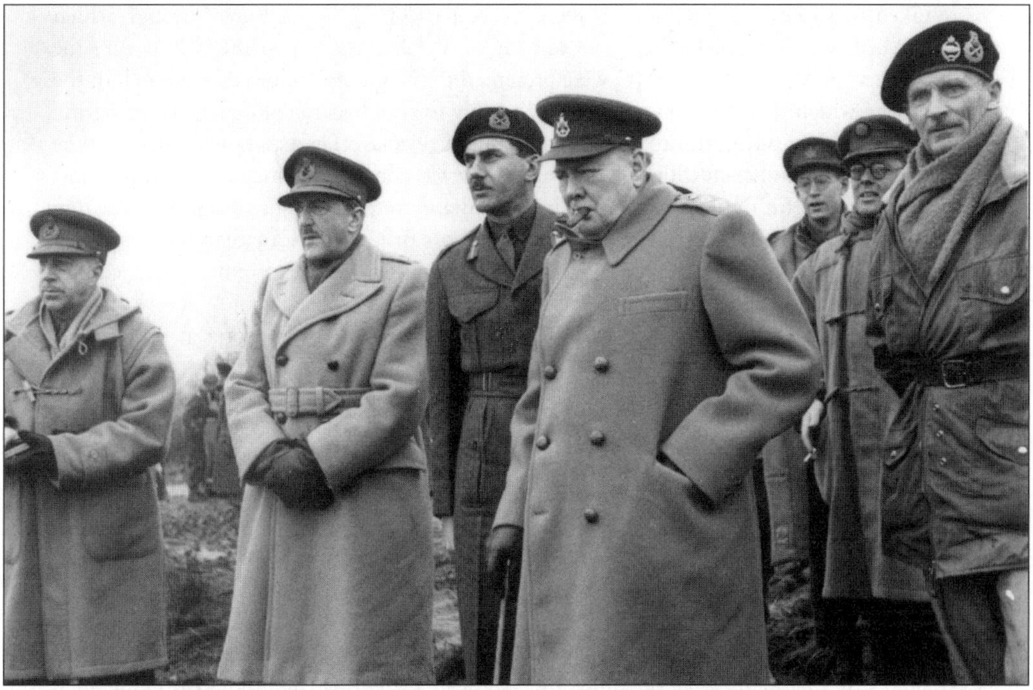

Near Kranenburg, 4 March 1945. Churchill's visit to 1 Canadian Army. Crerar, Brooke, Simonds, Churchill and Montgomery standing on the Brandenberg (81 m elev) in the Reichswald, 2 km south of Kranenburg. They were looking across the flooded Rhine valley from Kranenburg to German-occupied Millingen, 12 km away. (Barney J Gloster/Canada. Dept of National Defence/Library & Archives Canada/ PA-143952)

the Canadian experience in the nearby Hochwald where the butcher's bill failed even to produce a compensatory breakthrough.

All Second World War infantry, as the Germans discovered in 1939, needed armour for success. At Kervenheim the Norfolks were promised Churchill tanks that failed to appear because of the sodden ground, but such conditions would not have stopped a contemporary Russian assault with SU 152s and JS IIs, weighing the same as a Churchill but equipped with tracks twice its width. Under unified command the Russian armour would have rolled straight through Murmannshof, surrounded by infantry to ward off Panzerfausts, pounding the German StuGs and 88's with IL-2 Sturmoviks and Pe-2 divebombers with heavy shelling and mortaring. They would have taken Winnekendonk the same day and Wesel the next with a bridgehead over the Rhine on the third, for they understood the value of time like few armies before them.

Churchill would have been aware that his chickens were coming home to roost. Victory was assured but he foresaw a military showdown with Russia and therefore would want to understand first-hand why Montgomery's 21 AG was stuck in the Hochwald while again Russians and Americans were advancing quickly.

His opportunity came on 4 March 1945 when visiting II Canadian Corps at Materborn.

Guy Simonds War Diary:

> 4th March. Weather – rain. Corps Commander out visiting Divisions in early morning and at 1100 hrs received Prime Minister Winston Churchill at a rendezvous on RUBY route, who arrived with FM Sir Alan Brooke, FM BL Montgomery and Gen. HD Crerar. They

> were taken first to an OP vicinity E808537 to see part of the flooded area through which VERITABLE was launched. Then to Main HQ 2 Canadian Corps (E878531) where the senior officers of Main and Rear HQ were presented to the guests, followed by a lunch in the mess during which the PM's spirits rose considerably until it became quite a jovial gathering with some very interesting stories being told. Sir Alan Brooke related certain incidents in the 1940 campaign in France in which FM Montgomery was concerned which now would almost come under the definition of 'looting'. [The Canadians were notorious for looting, earning their reputation in the UK. Once on the continent most British and Canadian soldiers looted with abandon, even in the Netherlands, and the Canadians came to resent being singled out, and especially by Montgomery. Brooke was therefore playing to the gallery.] A picture of those at the lunch was taken in a tent before Mr. Churchill's departure for 30 Corps at 1400 hrs'.[362]

War correspondents reported on the visit.

> The tour took the party to one of the highest hills in the area where the British leader stared long and silently toward the Rhine obscured in the mists of this gloomy, cloudy day.[363]

The party then drove 6 km east to Corps HQ at Materborn near the present Reichswald War Cemetery. Charles Lynch, war correspondent, was there:

> Monty sent word ahead that whatever happened there was to be no liquor in Churchill's vicinity. Crerar's staff chose to spike the order and arranged a small bar in a room through which Churchill would have to pass on his way to the map room where he was to get a briefing. But when Montgomery, who was leading the way, spotted the bar, he reached in and slammed the door shut. Trouble was, just before Monty slammed the door, Churchill caught a glimpse of the bar. Winston Churchill never was one to enjoy early rising, so he was in a surly mood anyway, and the fact that Montgomery, the teetotaller, had denied him the chance of an eye-opener threw him into a sullen rage, which lasted through the briefing and during the morning's tour.
>
> Lunch was offered at the HQ of Gen Guy Simonds in the Hochwald [sic Reichswald]. It was not for nothing that Simonds was regarded as the keenest of the Canadian general officers. Quickly perceiving Churchill's mood, he told one of his junior officers to take one of the big tin mugs, fill it with whisky and place it in front of Churchill without comment.
>
> This was done and when Churchill took a sip of what looked like tea, his eyes brightened on the spot and he took two more long draughts. The effect was one of the sun breaking through dark clouds and there was a major change in mood, with Churchill becoming more and more ebullient as the lunch proceeded.[364]

Simonds referred above in his War Diary to stories told by Brooke about British army looting in France in 1940. He was playing to the gallery. The Canadians were notorious for looting, earning their reputation in the UK. Once on the continent most British and Canadian soldiers looted with abandon even in the Netherlands, and the Canadians came to resent being singled out, and especially by Montgomery.

362 LAC. RG 24 Series C3 Volume 13609, reel T-1867.
363 Ned Nordness for AP in *The Hamilton Spectator*, 6 March 1945.
364 Charles Lynch in *The Montreal Gazette*, 5 October 1983.

This lunch was the only social occasion that bore even a pale resemblance to the meeting at the Red (Delacour's) Château at Villers Bretonneux on 11 August 1918 when Rawlinson, Currie, Kavanagh, Godley, Monash, Montgomery (Massingberd), Budworth, Haig, Laurence, Wilson, Clemenceau and Klotz sat under a beech tree with the maps spread out on the grass as the politicians thanked the military of the British Commonwealth for decisively gaining the upper hand. At the 1945 lunch by contrast, Churchill, although well oiled and now enjoying himself with real friends, could not revel in the presence of a supremely successful military band of brothers as Clemenceau did in 1918 because 21 AG did not have the upper hand, except at Winnekendonk which those present did not know about, and the real movers and shakers speaking Russian and American were absent.

Many subjects came up at the lunch including the issue of the Churchill tank, which showed that Churchill was probing in the right area and forcing Montgomery to contradict him:

> During lunch under canvas, FM Montgomery told the PM in a jocular vein: 'I still don't like the Churchill tank'. 'And mark you', Mr. Churchill replied ruefully, 'The tank was not named after me until it had been marked with a few blemishes.'[365]

Montgomery was being disingenuous. Since 1942 he had been all for the Sherman Universal tank and against the Churchill, but by July 1944 was forced by reality, privately at least, to revise his opinion when its unique capabilities were demonstrated by 6 GTB. The Churchill 'is a good tank',[366] Montgomery then told the War Office, and later on that the Churchill Crocodile is 'an unqualified success'.[367]

> He (Churchill) granted us a press conference, and when Montgomery tried to cut in, Churchill waved him off.[368]

Churchill's dismissive treatment of Montgomery in public was telling. The question of the slow progress by 21 AG would have come up with the reporters, prompting Churchill to recycle Montgomery's old excuse.

> Mr. Churchill told war correspondents that FM Montgomery's north Rhine campaign was in effect a second Caen with British and Canadian troops drawing every power to it as the Americans slash through for resounding gains.[369]

This was also disingenuous because as Churchill spoke 3 BID with its 6 GAB Churchills was also making resounding gains towards the Bonninghardt Ridge and Wesel, but Montgomery and Crerar kept Churchill and the reporters ignorant of this momentous success. Instead Montgomery's moth-eaten hinge strategy in Normandy was used to rationalise the operational failure of II Canadian Corps as a strategic success. Montgomery would have wanted to keep from Churchill any knowledge that a reliable method of breakthrough and pursuit based on the Churchill tank had been operating unacknowledged in 21 AG since its introduction in *Bluecoat* in July 1944. It had been proved again at Overloon in September when 3 BID/6 GTB had succeeded where 7 USAD had failed and been withdrawn, and now again at Winnekendonk they

365 Ned Nordness, Hamilton Spectator.
366 IWM: Private Papers of FM Montgomery: BLM 117/14.
367 IWM: Private Papers of FM Montgomery: BLM 117/20.
368 Charles Lynch, The Montreal Gazette 5 October 1983.
369 Ned Nordness, Hamilton Spectator.

THE BRITISH PRIME MINISTER VISITS FIRST CANADIAN ARMY

In the front row of this photograph, taken at Headquarters 2nd Canadian Corps on 4 March 1945, are, from left to right, Field-Marshal Sir Alan Brooke, Chief of the Imperial General Staff; General Crerar; Mr. Churchill; Lieut.-General Simonds; and Field-Marshal Montgomery. In rear are staff officers and heads of services of the 2nd Corps. On the extreme left is Major-General T. G. Rennie, G.O.C. 51st (Highland) Division, who was killed three weeks later.

Churchill, now cheerful with half a bottle of whisky under his belt, was seated after lunch between his contented hosts with Brooke the raconteur at one end. At the other end was Montgomery, slouched, awkward and isolated, hands in pockets, staring into the distance with a mirthless grin beneath his silver RTR and gold General Officer badges. (Stacey, *Victory*, opposite p. 466.)

were through and 4 CAD was held in the Hochwald. Any recognition of these facts and their radical implications – such as breaking up the armoured divisions to provide reinforcements for the infantry divisions – would have raised unanswerable questions for Montgomery about his methods, and especially about his choice of tank. It would even have raised the question of why 3 CID had not been switched to reinforce 3 BID as had been agreed in advance. It is therefore likely that Montgomery's refusal to allow Churchill to visit the front line and his ban on drink were made to prevent any in his command from revealing anything to Churchill.

After the press conference Churchill left.

> Then the motorcade proceeded in the direction of the Rhine (sic Goch), with cheering troops lining the roadside and Churchill giving them the V-sign. That's not all he gave them, though. Having had so much to drink, the great man had to have a leak. In fact he had one every 20 minutes. Montgomery fumed. Monty must have known that Churchill was getting stimulants from somebody, but Simonds' battle-plan carried the day.[370]

370 Charles Lynch in *The Montreal Gazette*, 5 October 1983.

Reichswald 4 March 1945. Churchill's visit to 1 Canadian Army. After his lunch and press conference in Materborn, Churchill walked to the car acknowledging, by removing his cap, the warm reception from Canadian troops. (Barney J Gloster / Canada. Dept of National Defence / LAC / PA – 14572)

The cause of Churchill's earlier upset was not just the absence of drink, though that made things worse and provided a story reporters could understand, but Monty's veto of a visit by Churchill to the Hochwald where operations were bogged down. The excuse was the danger of mines and shelling. In the First World War Churchill when Minister of Munitions had taken Clemenceau dangerously close to the Germans. He now wanted the same consideration. The previous day he had visited Bill Simpson's 9 US Army in Jülich, and was reduced to pathetic begging.

> General Simpson had trouble convincing Mr. Churchill that it would be unsafe for him to visit the banks of the Rhine itself at Dusseldorf. "If they are shooting you can put me in a tank and I'll be alright", the PM urged. But General Simpson refused to risk the life of Britain's war leader. [371]

Horrocks expressed Montgomery's condescending view that Churchill was both an anachronism and a nuisance.

> Churchill's only failure was that he loved to become involved in the tactical battle and was never happier than when he had escaped Whitehall to the sharp end of battle, where his presence had a wonderful effect on the morale of the troops, but where he was a perfect nuisance to their immediate commanders, because he never seemed to realise that tactical methods had changed somewhat since he had charged at the Battle of Omdurman.[372]

371 Ross Munro in the *Globe & Mail*, Toronto, 6 March 1945.
372 Horrocks, *Corps Commander.*

Churchill wanted to observe the Anglo-Canadian Army. Increasingly concerned about the Russian threat, and puzzled as to why 21 AG was again outperformed by the Americans and Russians, he wanted to judge for himself the conduct of operations. Montgomery at first had tried to keep him away from his HQ but on 18 July 1944 Churchill had insisted on access through Brooke:

> With hundreds of war correspondents moving about freely this cannot be considered an unreasonable request from the Minister of Defence. If however General Montgomery disputes about it in any way the matter will be taken up officially, because I have a right and a duty to acquaint myself with the facts on the spot.[373]

The facts on the spot on 4 March 1945 in the Hochwald included Ben Dunkelman of D Coy the Queen's Own Rifles of Canada, 8 CIB, 3 CID, threatening to shoot an obdurate tank commander of 1 Canadian Hussars who refused to take his tank through a Schu minefield to create a safe path for his infantry because of the threat of anti-tank mines. The difference was that the infantry were terrified of being maimed or even killed by Schu mines and especially in the crutch, while the tank crews suffered only inconvenience when an anti-tank mine blew off a track or damaged the transmission, leaving the crew shaken but uninjured.

> I went ahead to see what was happening, and why the advance had halted. Unnerved by the mines, neither the tanks nor 'B' Company were prepared to move on. I ordered the tank commander to advance and blaze a trail for us; he had little to lose – at the very worst, a mine might blow off a tank's track. He refused to take orders from me, claiming that his tanks were not under the command of our battalion, but merely 'in support', which left him under no obligation to obey the orders of our officers. I contacted my CO, who backed my view, but the tank officer still refused to budge. Our CO contacted the tank officer's superior – to no avail. The dispute was long and bitter; at one point, I drew my pistol and threatened to shoot the tank commander unless he went ahead, but he had his own brand of courage and refused to be swayed by the threat. I consulted with our colonel again. It was getting late, our advance was being held up, throwing the timing of the whole assault out; the situation was critical. Almost inevitably, the colonel's answer was; 'I leave it up to you to find a way out.[374]

Dunkelman's 'way out' of his problem, which should in fairness have also been the shirking tank commander's problem, was to become fighting mad which brought him the DSO, but so easily could have resulted in his death. In a case that was quite rare, the citation written up by Dunkelman's CO, Stephen Lett for an immediate MC and forwarded on 9 March with counter-signature the same day by Brig JA Roberts, was upgraded by Ralph Keefler, GOC 3CID to a DSO on 19 April and passed by Simonds (May 4), Crerar (11 May) and Montgomery (as usual undated).

> **DSO. 8CIB, 3CID, 2 Cdn Corps, 1 Queen's Own Rifles of Canada (CIC), Acting Major Benjamin Dunkelman**
> Captain (Acting Major) Benjamin DUNKELMAN was Company Commander of 'D' Company, 1 Bn The Queen's Own Rifles of Canada on 5 (sic) March 1945. On that date this battalion was given the task of clearing the BALBERGER WALD, EAST of the NORTH SOUTH ROAD and SOUTH of the grid line 39. 'D' company, under the command of

373 Richard Lamb. *Churchill as War Leader* (London: Bloomsbury, 1993).
374 Ben Dunkelman. *Dual Allegiance* (Toronto: Macmillan, 1976), p. 137.

> Acting Major DUNKELMAN, had the task of clearing the SOUTHERN edges of the woods. Upon crossing the road which was the start line, the forward two platoons of 'D' Company were immediately pinned down by intense machine gun and 'bazooka' fire from the area of the edge of the clearing from 052382. The casualties suffered by these platoons were heavy, and due to the nature of the ground and the intense fire of the enemy, our troops were unable to press forward. DUNKELMAN picked up a PIAT gun, whose crew had been killed, and successfully silenced two of the enemy machine guns, then, rushing forward, led the remaining platoon into the attack upon the enemy positions.
>
> Acting Major DUNKELMAN personally killed ten of the enemy with his pistol and with his bare hands, all the time shouting to his men to press forward and to the enemy to "come out and fight". As a result of this gallant action and display of fearlessness, in the face of enemy fire, the platoon pressed home the attack and drove the enemy out of this area of the wood. 'D' Company was then able to proceed and fight on to their final objective.
>
> The display of leadership, the coolness under fire, and the fighting qualities shown by Acting Major DUNKELMAN, struck fear into the heart of the enemy, and those that could, fled from the scene of the action.
>
> This gallant action by Acting Major DUNKELMAN was directly responsible for 'D' Company successfully taking the objective, and the clearing of the final objective by the battalion.

Stacey identified the tank unit that refused to support Dunkelman as 1 Hussars, 6 Armd Regt, 2 BAB, and described what the tanks said had happened:

> Thickly-sown Schu-mines beset the path of the infantry, and the 1st Hussars, held up by numerous anti-tank mines, could only give supporting fire through the trees from stationary positions.[375]

Had Churchill witnessed this disgraceful scene, he might just have been led to wonder whether it was the consequence of his rescuing the sacked Hobart from the Home Guard in 1940. Churchill remembered how Haig, Robertson and Henry Wilson had concealed information from Lloyd George,[376] and would have been sure the same thing was recurring. He had always disliked Montgomery, and the excuses he heard on every side about the terrain and conditions were unconvincing. We now know what Churchill could not find out, that the recurring problem from Arras in 1940 to the Hochwald in 1945 was the lack of all-arms operational methodology with an immune Infantry tank and dive-bombers under infantry command.

Leaving the enthusiastic Canadians in Materborn, Churchill joined the Cleve to Goch road and to a very different reception from British troops. Lt Sidney Beck of 86 Fld Regt RA was waiting by that same road at Pfalzdorf to follow GAD in its tardy response to the breakthrough made by 2 Lincolns and 3 SG at Winnekendonk two days earlier. 86 Fld Regt had moved forward on 3 March into positions being vacated by 3 BID's 33 Fld Regt, but been recalled to support GAD's advance. The gunners were cold and bored after hanging about for over a day waiting for the Guards to reassemble, and were unhappy that the Americans

> had stolen all the headlines and still no credit had been given to the British troops who had just fought the most bitter and difficult battles of the whole campaign in atrocious weather against

375 Stacey, *Victory Campaign*, p. 513.
376 Richard Lamb: *Op cit.*

many natural obstacles. Such was the trend of our rather bitter thoughts as we stamped up and down to keep warm on that bleak and icy road. There was a diversion at 1600 hrs when a car passed with loudspeakers blaring, "Mr. Churchill will be passing through shortly". We could hardly believe our ears but decided to stay by the roadside and watch. Sure enough, about half an hour later, preceded by a number of Military Police on motor cycles, two large black saloon cars drove by, each carrying a small Union Jack over the bonnet. In the leading one were the Prime Minister and Sir Alan Brooke. The Prime Minister was clearly visible, cigar in one hand, hat in the other, moving it up and down rather mechanically. There was no cheering, everyone gave most correct and military salutes. Churchill looked just a little grim and serious. Probably he realised that no one was in a mood for cheering, still weary after a hard battle, still remembering our casualties, still remembering that the war was by no means over, still bitter about the newspaper reports and just a little puzzled why we had to wait hours and hours on a roadside in the cold while the Americans advanced all the time. There were more salutes for "Monty" as he drove past behind the Prime Minister's car. There was rather an ironical cheer, half suppressed, as another saloon boldly labelled "Press" quickly followed the leading two saloons. As we returned to our cold vigil we reflected "Winston gets around a bit", "Travels more than any other bloke in the world", "He must be feeling well satisfied to have set foot on German soil once again". "That will make Hitler eat another carpet when he knows" said a wag. We learned later that just beyond Goch, the Prime Minister fired a super-heavy gun into the German lines on the other side of the Rhine. Just before 1800 hrs the column began to move and we hurriedly packed up, stowed away our tents and cookhouses and moved off. Traffic jams in the ruined streets of Goch were frequent and progress was painfully slow. By now it was dark and the route difficult to follow. We remained on the road, moving forward slowly, for eleven weary hours and in that time we covered just less than eleven miles. Our route took us through Weeze, Kevelaer, and Wetten, all of which had seen bitter fighting.[377]

377 © Ben Beck. Personal war diary of 341 Bty 86 Fld Regt RA (Herts Yeomanry) 3 June 1944 to 9 April 1946 compiled by Lt Beck from the battery log and extracts from letters to his wife. The original is lodged in the IWM. http://benbeck.co.uk/fh/transcripts/sjb_war_diaries/batterydiary.htm

Appendix I

LAC:GOC-in-C 1-0-7/11 25 Feb 45 to Lt-Gen G.G. Simonds, Comd 2 Canadian Corps and Lt-Gen B.G. Horrocks, Comd 30 Corps.

1. In view of the determined enemy resistance 24/25 Feb, North of WEEZE, and consequent inability of 53 (W) Inf Div firmly to secure that town before Operation BLOCKBUSTER by 2 Canadian Corps commences, it will be necessary to reconsider the draft basic plan outlined to you in my memorandum of yesterday – in particular the proposals contained in para 5. The importance of 30 Corps clearing the WELL-WEEZE road at an early date, in order that WANSSUM-WELL bridge may be constructed, entails this consideration. On the above basis, the following Army plan will be discussed at our meeting this afternoon.

2. If possible, 2 Canadian Corps will complete BLOCKBUSTER as planned, and firmly secure the the general line KERVENHEIM-SONSBECK-XANTEN. It will then clean up all enemy remaining between this line and the R RHINE (see para 4 of yesterday's memo).

3. If by D plus 1 it is obvious that to complete BLOCKBUSTER a considerable regrouping, and a further deliberate attack is required, then a "partial" BLOCKBUSTER will terminate the operation – i.e. the completion of Phase III and the securing of the high ground East of the CALCAR-UDEM road.

4. Throughout either 'complete' or 'partial' BLOCKBUSTER, the principal responsibility of 30 Corps will be to secure the right (southern and western) flank of 2 Canadian Corps against enemy intervention, by keeping its left shoulder well up and to exploit any favourable situations (see para 3 of yesterday's memo).

5. In either of the alternative results given in para 2 and 3 above, the weight of the Canadian Army effort will then be transferred to 30 Corps – which, as a Canadian Army first priority, will then proceed to secure the WELL-WEEZE road, and eliminate any enemy remaining to the North of it.

HDC Crerar
CC Lt-Gen Sir John Crocker, Brig CC Mann.

Appendix II

This document is in this author's possession.

9 Brit Inf Bde
Points raised at Brigade Conference
1000 hrs 8 Mar 1945

Serial	Points Raised	Brigade Comd's remarks
1.	Are pre-arranged arty a good thing from inf point of view when fire is on call? (Gen feeling was against them)[1] (33 Fd Regt)	a) Numbered targets should be made known through RA channels to bty comd and FOOs b) Fire programmes on call should be made up by bn and bty cos concerned and notified to Bde HQ and FdRegt HQ.
2.	Is a barrage on a front of 2000 yds from one div arty possible?[2] (33 Fd Regt)	It might be required when opposition is slight and an adv on a broad front possible. Usually, however, other types of fire sp will be used.
3.	3 Can we help tks by securing a brhead across an obstacle before start of main op? Br can then be built and passage guaranteed.[3] (3 SG)	a) This WILL usually be done b) It was NOT done at the UDEM-WEEZE wood as this would have made success of major attack dependent upon success of minor preliminary one c) This course has many attractions but has often led to considerable failures.
4.	4 Inter-bde bdy with 8 Brit Inf Bde was unsound and caused confusion.[4] (3 SG)	a) Chief difficulty was caused by 8 Brit Inf Bde's failure to keep up with the barrage b) Reason for their failure was because they made their major attack dependent upon success of a minor brhead one which obtained partial success only (see para 3 above) c) It must be recognised that 8 Brit Inf Bde's task was more difficult than our own.
5.	For battle of WINNEKENDONK additional sqn of 3 SG might have watched right flank of 2 Lincolns. (3 SG)[5]	Agreed

Serial	Points Raised	Brigade Comd's remarks
6.	Tks should not be brought too far fwd by inf until actually needed. Proper recce required. Tks attract enemy fire. (3 SG)	Agreed in principle
7.	Smoke may be needed to cover flanks of tks when they adv. Must be available on call from RA. (3 SG)[6]	Agreed
8.	When tks are the assaulting[7] (as opposed to the supporting) arm, this will affect planning of op. (3 SG)	Agreed
9.	Sometimes an attack may have to be laid on at great speed and with little time for recce, in order to catch the daylt, so that tks can be used. This is a fair risk of war.[8] (2 LINCOLNS)	Agreed
10	Under 185 Bde, one coy of 2 Lincolns was put into KERVENHEIM battle, and doubt existed whether 2 LINCOLNS or 1 NORFOLK were fighting the battle.[9] (2 LINCOLNS)	Senior bn comd must assume responsibility if doubt exists, units are of similar str, and there is no time for bde decision.
11.	Crocodiles were of no value in KERVENHEIM. (2 LINCOLNS)	a) Crocodile sqn comd was killed b) Brig MATTHEWS considers close understanding between crocodiles and inf before start of op essential.
12.	Pre-arranged fire plan saved much time at WINNEKENDONK and was valuable. (2 LINCOLNS)	Noted
13.	We are still bad at street fighting. (2 LINCOLNS)	
14.	It takes too long to get craters in rds mended and fwd routes open. RE recce parties needed with fwd troops. (2 LINCOLNS)	a) Agreed b) Unit pnrs must also report existence of craters, etc.
15.	RE info not coming back properly from bns. RE recce party with each bn probably the answer provided it can use other people's commss. (253 Fd Coy)	Agreed
16.	RE sec under comd each inf bn usually wasted. Better to have one pl under comd Bde, moving well fwd on bde axis. (253 Fd Coy)	Agreed. In next battle of this type pl will be kept centralised.

Serial	Points Raised	Brigade Comd's remarks
17.	a) Rate of advance of inf in villages now approx 100 yards in 5 mins. b) Rate of advance of inf across open country for 1 KOSB first-lt attack was 100 yards in 2 1/2 mins. Fire plan was calculated on basis of 100 yards in 4 mins. c) Rate of adv of 2 RUR through woods was 100 yards in 5 mins. Fire plan should have catered for longer pause on main rd. (Various)	a) Noted b) Agreed. Fire plan must also allow for length of time it is estimated that fighting will last on any known or enemy posn. c) Pause of 15 mins was given. An additional pause had been omitted at request of 8 Brit Inf Bde
18.	a) Bde should have laid down report lines for woods. b) Danger of duplicated code-words. (1 KOSB)	Agreed. Bns must also inform Bde of code-words given by them for additional bounds.
19.	a) No 18 set is little use in woods. b) Kangaroos invaluable as comd vehs. (1 KOSB and 2 RUR)	Agreed
20.	Escorts for PW sent from fwd troops rarely rejoin pls. Need for unit collecting pt and special escorts detailed by bn. (1 KOSB and 2 RUR)	Agreed. Escorts must be forbidden by units to go beyond Bde HQ collecting pt.
21.	Advantage of fwd troops keeping right up close to the barrage and accepting some cas from odd gun firing short. (1 KOSB)	Agreed. This was extremely well done.
22.	Great advantage of sending 2ic to Bde HQ for orders on night before first lt attack. CO was meanwhile doing recce, having had outline plan by telephone from Bde HQ. (1 KOSB)	Noted
23.	FUP for tks was 2000 yards behind FUP for inf. This worked well. (1 KOSB)	Noted
24.	Moving in Kangaroos didn't save much time, but saved inf much fatigue in marching through deep mud. Forming up by Kangaroos well org by Kangaroo offrs. (1 KOSB)	Agreed that it is essential to put inf into battle fresh
25.	Bde failed to let 1 KOSB know that 2 LINCOLNS were attacking WINNEKENDONK. (1 KOSB)	Noted
26	Is it bn comd's decision whether arty concs are put on objective before attack or not. (2 RUR)	Bn fire plans will be built up inside any fire plans of higher formations.
27.	Attack by Typhoons. (2 RUR)	Error was at Corps or Army level.[10]
28.	a) Tks used wheeled tracks and destroyed them. b) RE must have parties in conc areas to cope with problems of tk tracks. (253 Fd Coy)	a) While battle is in progress tks must have freedom of all tracks. Later they must keep to tk tracks. b) Agreed.

Serial	Points Raised	Brigade Comd's remarks
29.	17 Pdr ATk guns are not strictly supposed to be deployed in fwd coy localities but in fact can be available if required. (45 ATk Bty)	Agreed
30.	Inf 6-pr ATk guns not very alert or battle-minded. (45 ATk Bty)	Agreed. Battle posns were often unsatisfactory.
31.	ADS needs proper accn in buildings. (9 Fd Amb)	Agreed
32.	a) Instead of one sec with each Inf bn, two CCPs successively leap-frogged behind narrow bde front and proved adequate. b) Additional SBs were sent fwd to reinforce bn med secs but were not required. (9 Fd Amb)	Noted
33.	Tks firing MMGs from directly behind inf are not popular. (1 KOSB)	Agreed. When firing Tks should be either level with inf, or in front of them or well to a flank.
34.	No really good way exists by which inf can indicate targets to tks. (3 SG)	Recognised

Notes
1. The infantry wanted flexibility.
2. This concerns the small weight of shell of the 25pdr. The division needed a 105 mm field piece.
3. The actual results of the battles were paradoxes. Renny was right in 3(c). Where everything was secured beforehand and a bridge laid at Wettermannshof on February 28, the result had been failure by Warwicks and CG. Where no bridgehead had been secured in advance there was success – 3 SG managed to negotiate the narrow causeway and bridge near Krüsbeckshof, the egg farm, during the battle. The explanation was surprise. The Germans neglected to blow the causeway only because they could not believe tanks would be committed amongst the bogs and woods. Had the causeway been destroyed, then the infantry would have been unsupported on the other side and vulnerable to counter-attack. Since in that event the major attack would have failed, it is difficult to follow Renny's logic about refusing to secure a bridgehead because this would make a major attack dependent on the success of a minor preliminary attack.
4. The inter-brigade boundary on the first day was through Babbe which was defended. The Suffolks and Grenadiers were delayed in the woods by swamps so 9 BIB found their right flank uncovered. It would have been better to have given Babbe to 9 BIB. The bridgehead was secured so Renny is wrong in 4(b) – see Renison's diary in which he records a rocket from Eddie Goulburn for being dilatory.
5. Memories were short. At Kervenheim a squadron of the CG was ordered to help the Warwicks secure the right flank. The Germans counter-attacked and stopped them.
6. The tanks seemed to place little reliance on their own ability to produce smoke.
7. The phrase 'assaulting arm' seems to refer to circumstance when infantry came under command of tanks.
8. The subject was Winnekendonk.
9. The reason for this observation has not come to light. Read in conjunction with Whistler's observation in his diary that the Lincolns were largely responsible for taking Kervenheim, it suggests that Firbank had direct contact with, and instructions from, Whistler concerning Kervenheim.
10. The fault belonged to neither. See above.

The conference covered a lot of ground. As far as the author knows this was the only conference held by 9 BIB. Each arm made positive suggestions about how it could do better. The artillery wanted greater accuracy (Serial 1) and bigger or more guns (2). The tanks wanted to improve punctuality (3), give a better service (5) to the infantry without causing them trouble (6) and to have better protection themselves (7). The infantry wanted better training (13) and more control over the artillery and Typhoons (17, 26, 27). The inadequate 6pdr anti-tank guns needed replacement by the 17pdr (29, 30). The medics wanted better protection for the wounded (31). But the big inadequacies were highlighted. Better communications between the arms, reflecting a true scandal in that war (15, 18, 19, 25, 27, 34) were desperately needed. The kangaroos had given the infantry a taste of what was possible and they wanted them as command vehicles (19). Better Royal Engineer support was asked for (14,15) but what, it was never asked, could truly have been expected when the decision had been made to fight in a bog against an enemy masterful in the use of explosives. Two participants who were criticised were absent; the Crocodiles of 79 BAD (11) and the Typhoons of 2 TAF (27).

The big deficiencies were not addressed. In item 9 Firbank stated rather than questioned the assumption that tanks could only be used in daylight when darkness was a real safeguard against the 88 mm. Mike Carver had shown how to fight with tanks at night on the Lincolns' left flank on the eve of the Yorkshire Bridge battle but that success did not enter the discussion even with reference to Barclay and Kervenheim. In Item 29, the representative of 45 Anti-tank Battery, RA, which might have been Lt-Col Thatcher, DSO, made a cute remark that although 17 Pdr ATk guns were not strictly supposed to be deployed in forward company localities they could be available if required, and he criticized the infantry's deployment of the 6pdr. The 17pdr was a potent weapon with the performance of an 88 mm and the idea may have been dawning that their place was in Brőnkshof engaging the 88 mm and StuGs instead of being used as an anti-tank screen against the non-existent threat of an enemy armoured offensive. This latter the infantry could not take seriously and so were careless about placement of the inadequate 6pdr. The bigger questions about the quality and survivability of tanks, guns and close-support aircraft and their control by the infantry were not touched upon.

After the conference, Douglas Renny also produced the following paper, whose only known copy came from the KOSB Archives, courtesy of Ian Martin. Its purpose and circulation list are unknown. The comments in square brackets were contributed by Lt Col Eddie Jones of 1 S Lancs, then a major.[1]

1 In a letter from Eddie Jones to this author on 19 March 2002.

Appendix III

Tactical points from the fighting in operation "HEATHER"

1. Introduction
   The aim of this paper is to place the lessons learned by the various battalions and supporting arms at the disposal of all. It will be divided into:
   a) Points produced by the enemy resistance.
   b) Lessons learned from the co-operation of our arms.
   c) Points for the future.

PART I – ENEMY

2. Enemy Morale
   a) The enemy morale was lowest in the UDEM-WEEZE woods where the shells from the five fd regts firing the barrage, burst in the trees. [Air-burst in woods had a marked effect on morale. We suffered it in reverse when shelled by 88s in the woods around Le Londel]. It was higher in the open and it was highest where the buildings gave overhead cover.
      This re-affirms the value of:
      i) Fd arty and Bofors in woods.
      ii) Air burst shells and plunging MG fire in the open.
      iii) Typhoons and medium arty in the villages.
   b) The readiness of the enemy to surrender at close quarters was significant of his national dislike of close combat.

   Troops must be made to realise that the closer they can get to the enemy the less hard he will fight. To give them additional confidence in themselves, training in close combat must continue.

3. Woods
   In woods, as might be expected, the enemy forward line of resistance was usually on the near side while the main line of resistance was on the far side. [This was certainly our experience in the Udem-Weeze woods where our infantry breaking through onto the main road came under MG fire in enfilade and the tanks were fired on by bazookas]. In addition, covering the exits from the far, i.e. enemy side of the wood, were further SP A tk guns and inf sited in tank proof localities. Our arrival at the far edge of the wood was the signal for the enemy to shell and heavily mortar that portion of the wood.
   It is therefore desirable that:
   a) Our tps should not show themselves on the far side of the wood unnecessarily
   b) Fire should neutralise the enemy defences covering the exits from the wood until our troops have made a good start in digging in
   c) The attacks should be continued as soon as possible, with full fire support, to capture the enemy defences dominating the far edge of the wood.

4. Buildings and villages
   a) Where buildings were held, there were often slit trenches both forward of them and to a flank. Allowance for their probable existence must be made when working out the fire plan with the tank and artillery commanders. [I am surprised that our troops were taken by surprise to find the enemy in slit-trenches nearby/around buildings, rather than in force in the buildings themselves. Our strict policy was to avoid buildings].
   b) For attacks against villages, the fire of heavier weapons is needed to supplement the field artillery. A useful sequence is:
      Typhoon attack.
      Medium guns and 4.2 in mortars.
      Field artillery (3 in mortars are better employed on the flanks).
   c) Further section and platoon street fighting training is required. One company commander considers that sections should be cut to six, bigger sections are very difficult to control among houses. [Our teaching prior to D-Day on house-clearing was more or less ineffectual. Use of the PIAT or anti-tank guns against occupied buildings was more effective].
   d) Full use must be made of surprise and the artillery fire to penetrate rapidly to the centre of the village. Methodical house to house fighting will be required when surprise has been lost.

5. Weight of fire
   Where a considerable weight of fire was used as in the UDEM-WEEZE woods, the enemy had not recovered when our troops went in. Where, as in KOSB bonus operation which followed, less intensive fire was requested, the enemy shot back with great spirit immediately the artillery fire had lifted.
   It is a waste of shell to be sparing with it on the frontage of attack.

6. Enemy flank defences
   The enemy's linear defences expose our attacks to flanking fire.
   Therefore we must protect our flanks with:
   Smoke screens. Advance information must be given to the artillery to enable the shell to be brought up. [We often wondered why (artillery) smoke was not used. Smoke grenades and 2/3" mortar smoke soon dispersed].
   Box barrages, the sides of which are stationary.
   MG's, SP A tk guns and tanks countering enemy flanking fire.
   Fixing the attention of the enemy flanking defences with diversions.

7. Enemy counter-attacks
   a) Enemy counter attacks took the form of:
      Intensive shelling and mortaring.
      Closer shelling by SP guns, which moved up during (i)
      Infiltration attacks carried out initially by small parties of infantry while the attention of our troops was taken up by (ii). These attacks were directed up covered approaches and against the flanks and rear.
   b) The first means of protecting oneself is the pre-arranged immediate consolidation plan. It must be put into action immediately the attack is ended.
   c) However, the best defence against counter attack is to avoid losing the initiative. To retain it, immediately one attack has ended, another one, threatening another enemy

vital point, should go in. When the plan of a higher command does not allow of further attacks, then fighting patrols must be sent out. Mental and physical fatigue must not blind commanders to the fact that a passive defence is always a dangerous one.

8 Attack with tanks

a) When both infantry and tanks attack on the same axis, the tanks must not engage the enemy from the rear of the leading infantry. [Definitely from a flank for the reasons mentioned. In addition we did have occasions when our own wounded were run over by our own tanks!]
b) Tanks require smoke to protect them against A tk fire. They accept smoke blowing towards them; we must do the same.
c) In planning an attack the infantry commander must discover the time the tanks will reach the FUP and the route thence to the SL.
d) Where possible a medium regiment FOO must accompany the tanks in addition to field regiment FOOs.

9. Attacks without tanks

Where tanks are not available, the enemy must not be allowed to engage our troops with aimed small arms fire. Smoke will usually be required in addition to strong HE shell support.

10. Crocodiles

An attempt was unsuccessfully made to use crocodiles at KERVENHEIM.
When they can be used their effect in villages is very great. To use them:

a) The ground must be firm
b) They must be shot in by tanks accompanying them. [Crocodiles have a relatively short range. Therefore they need other tanks to support them to within effective range].
c) Artillery fire and smoke is needed to see them in.

11. Artillery "shorts"

a) In the UDEM-WEEZE wood attack, where another division's artillery fired in the barrage, several guns fired persistently short, their first rounds falling in the FUPs of the res coys of the fwd bns.
   While everything is done to try and prevent these accidents, whenever a mass of artillery is used it is liable to happen.
   Troops must be trained to avoid the probable axis of the "short guns" and at all costs to keep with the remainder of the barrage.
   Furthermore, should, in spite of every effort being made, a gap develop between the troops and the barrage or timed concentration, then commanders must be prepared immediately to fill it with fire from:
   2 in mortar groups
   3 in mortars
   Superimposed arty on call
b) To decrease the number of shells bursting short in trees, the artillery should be asked to produce the steepest angle of descent for their shells that the need for accuracy allows.

12. Consolidation
    a) There is a marked tendency to dig in for protection against shells and weather rather than tactically. The importance of digging position to meet counter attack cannot be overemphasized. [We always tried to consolidate and site our slit trenches with a view to repelling the expected counter-attack and for no other reason].
    b) Troops having dug in, start wandering about and away from platoon localities. It is the platoon commander's responsibility to stop this. [I am surprised to learn about 'walk-abouts'. Once our soldiers got dug in they stayed put, often to the extent that they had to be urged to keep their heads up to watch out for enemy attack].
    c) 2 in mortars must be given DF tasks before the attack when consolidation plans are made from maps and air photographs.
    d) When the going permits the company carrier should move with the company and not move as a separate echelon.
    e) Men of the forward platoons were inclined to stop to search PWs instead of getting on with the battle.

    In one bn the following arrangement is being followed: No searching to take place forward of coy HQ [Normally enemy POW were told by a 'thumb jerk' to make their way back down the line. rarely did we stop to provide escort, unless a considerable body of enemy surrendered together].

    No man of a leading platoon is to escort prisoners further back than coy HQ where fresh escorts to Bn HQ will be arranged.

13. Movement
    a) Carriers get "bellied" on tracks reserved for tracks only. Carriers should always be treated as wheeled vehicles.
    b) Kangaroos are very useful over ground unfit for carriers, for:
       Moving up the mortar platoon
       Moving up Tac Bn HQ.
       Moving up the RAP.
       [Pros. Kangaroos enabled troops to get onto the objective whilst protected from small-arms fire. Cons; one anti-tank shell or mine could deprive the attack of a platoon's worth of infantry].
    c) It would be a very useful asset if kangaroos could be fitted to tow 6 prs. [6pdrs required to be towed. A big disadvantage, causing delay in getting the guns in position to repel enemy counter-attacks supported by tanks. Anti-tank guns should all have been self-propelled].

14. Adm [Agree on all points].

    The carriers provided a useful reserve of stretcher bearers.

    Each man should carry some biscuits as an emergency ration to be eaten only on order of coy comd.

    Coys should be given a time to expect a meal.

    On occasions, a hot meal might follow up the bn in containers carried by the carrier platoon.

    When vehicles become casualties drivers must remain with them.

15. Intercomn [We always had problems with the sets issued to the infantry. On occasions, we had to rely on the FOO's radio to communicate with Bde, and on one occasion ran out 1 – 2 miles of signal cable prior to a planned attack and this was our only means of communication between forward and rear-Bn HQ, and so to Bde].

a) 38 sets failed between the MFC and the mortar platoon. 18 sets would be better although not ideal.
b) Correspondence intended for Rear HQ went to the TAC HQ.
c) When there was only an 18 set at Tac Bn HQ communications with main bn HQ and Bde failed.

PART III – POINTS FOR THE FUTURE

16. The tackling of Huns dug in behind dykes requires further study.

17. Training in street fighting and close combat must be continued.

18. The idea to avoid shooting and giving away ones position during an attack must be killed. The Hun must NEVER be allowed to get the initiative.

19. 22 sets must accompany Tac Bn HQ. If necessary they must be carried on the man or else on the stretcher.

20. Another attempt will be made to get battalions scout cars.

GDR/WGD

Archive Sources and Bibliography

Archive Sources

Australian War Memorial, Canberra.
Geldern Stadtsarchiv, Geldern
Imperial War Museum, London
Library and Archives Canada, Ottawa
Liddell Hart Centre for Military Archives, London
National Archives, College Park, Maryland
RCAHMS, The Aerial Reconnaissance Archive, Edinburgh
The National Archives, Kew
U.S. Army War College Library, Carlisle Barracks, Carlisle
Weezer Stadtsarchiv, Weeze

Bibliography

HR Allen. *Who Won the Battle of Britain?* (London: Arthur Barker, 1974).
AK Altes & NKCA in't Veld. *The Forgotten Battle: Overloon & The Maas Salient 1944-45* (New York: Sarpedon, 1995).
Karl Alman. *Sprung in Die Hölle* (Rastatt: Erich Pabel, 1964).
Anonymous. *A Short History of the 8th Armoured Brigade* (Hanover: BAOR, 1945).
Anonymous. *Taurus Pursuant: A History of the 11th Armoured Brigade* (Germany: BAOR, 1945).
Anonymous. *From Mountain and Flood: History of the 52nd Lowland Division* (Glasgow: George Blake, 1950).
Anonymous. *By Air To Battle* (London: Ministry of Information, 1945).
Anonymous. *The Story of the 79th Armoured Division* (Hamburg: BAOR, 1945).
Anonymous. *Deutsches Soldatenjahrbuch 1980* (Munich: Schild-Verlag, 1980).
Rick Atkinson. *The Day of Battle: The War in Sicily and Italy* (Boston: Henry Holt, 2007).
Anonymous. Deutsches Soldatenjahrbuch 1980 (Munich: Schild-Verlag, 1980).
CN Barclay, *The History of the 53rd (Welsh) Division in the Second World War* (London: William Clowes, 1956).
Corelli Barnett. *The Desert Generals* (London: William Kimber, 1960).
Corelli Barnett. *Hitler's Generals* (London: Weidenfeld & Nicolson, 1990).
Bernard Baruch. *American Industry in the War* (New York: Prentice Hall, 1941).
The Battalion. *The History of the 1st Battalion the Royal Norfolk Regiment During the War* (Norwich: Jarrold & Sons, 1947).
Cajus Becker. *The Luftwaffe War Diaries* (New York: Ballantine, 1969).
Peter Beale. *Tank Tracks: The 9th Battalion RTR at War 1939-1945* (Stroud: Alan Sutton, 1995).
David Belchem. *Victory in Normandy* (London: Chatto & Windus, 1985).
PMH Bell. *The Origins of the Second World War* (London: Longman, 1997).
David Bercuson. *Maple Leaf Against the Axis* (Markham: Red Deer, 2004).
Shelford Bidwell. *Gunners at War: A Tactical Study of the Royal Artillery in the Twentieth Century* (London: Arms & Armour Press, 1970).

Shelford Bidwell and Dominick Graham. *Fire Power* (London: Harper Collins, 1982).
Jonathan Black. *The Face of Courage: Eric Kennington, Portraiture and the Second World War* (London: Philip Wilson, 2011).
Gregory Blaxland. *Destination Dunkirk* (London: Harper Collins, 1973).
Heinz Bliss and Bernd Bosshammer. *Das Fallschirmjäger-Lehr-Regiment*. (Witzenhausen: Im Auftrag des Verfasser, 1972).
Rudolf Böhmler and Werner Haupt. *Fallschirmjäger: Bildband und Chronik* (Dorheim: Podzun-Pallas, 1971).
Robert Boscawen. *Armoured Guardsmen: A War Diary* (Barnsley: Pen & Sword, 2000).
Heinz Bosch. *Der Zweite Weltkrieg Zwischen Maas und Rhein* (Geldern: des Hisrtorischen Vereins, 1977).
Leonard Bridgman. *Jane's All The World Aircraft 1945-6* (London: Jane's, 1946).
Stephen Broadberry and Mark Harrison. *The Economics of World War Two* (Cambridge: CUP, 2009).
Alan Brooke. *War* Diaries 1939-1945 (London: Weidenfeld & Nicolson, 2001).
Arthur Bryant. *Triumph in the West* (London: Collins, 1959).
William F Buckingham. *Arnhem 1944: A Reappraisal* (Stroud: Tempus, 2002).
John Buckley. *British Armour in the Normandy Campaign* (London: Routledge, 2004).
John Buckley. *Monty's Men: The British Army and the Liberation of Europe* (New Haven: Yale University Press, 2013).
Erich Busch. Die *Fallschirmjäger-Chronik* (Friedburg: Podzun-Pallas, 1983).
John Campbell. *Dieppe Revisited* (London: Routledge, 1993).
Humphrey Carpenter. *Robert Runcie: the Reluctant Archbishop* (London: Hodder & Stoughton, 1996).
William Carr. *A Time to Leave the Ploughshares* (London: Robert Hale, 1985).
Charles Carrington. *Soldier at Bomber Command* (London: Leo Cooper, 1987).
Michael Carver. *Second to None: The Royal Scots Greys 1919-1945* (Edinburgh: The Regiment, 1954).
Michael Carver. *The Apostles of Mobility: the Theory and Practice of Armoured Warfare* (London: Weidenfeld & Nicolson, 1979).
Michael Carver. *Out of Step: Memoirs of a Field Marshal* (London: Hutchinson, 1989).
Central Statistical Office. *Fighting with Figures* (London, HMSO, 1995).
Gregory Chaitin. *Conversations with a Mathematician: Math, Art and the Limits of Reason* (London: Springer, 2002).
Otto Preston Chaney. *Zhukov* (London: David & Charles, 1973).
Christopher Chant. *Ground Attack* (London: Almark, 1976).
WS Churchill. *Thoughts & Adventures: Plugstreet Wood* (London: Thornton Butterworth, 1932).
WS Churchill. *The Second World War, Vol II: Their Finest Hour* (London: Cassell, 1949).
WS Churchill. *The Second World War, Vol III: The Grand Alliance* (London: Cassell, 1950).
WS Churchill. *The Second World War, Vol IV: The Hinge of Fate* (London: Cassell, 1953).
Carl von Clausewitz. *Vom Kriege* (Berlin: Ferdinand Dümmler, 1832).
Pierre Clostermann. *The Big Show* (London: Chatto & Windus, 1951).
John Connell. *Wavell: Soldier and Scholar* (London: Collins, 1964).
Bryan Cooper. *The Ironclads of Cambrai* (London: Macmillan, 1970).
Belton Cooper. *Death Traps* (Novato: Presidio, 2008).
Terry Copp. *Montgomery's Scientists* (Waterloo: Laurier Centre, 2000).
Terry Copp and Mike Bechthold. *The Canadian Battlefields in Belgium, the Netherlands and Germany* (Waterloo, LCMSDS, 2011).

Terry Copp and Robert Vogel. *Anglo-Canadian Tactical Air Power in Normandy: A Re-assessment* (Virginia: American Military Institute, 2000).
Brian Cull. *Diver! Diver! Diver!* (London: Grub Street, 2008).
Bruce Culver. *Sturmgeschütz III in Action* (Warren: Squadron/Signal, 1979).
Marcus Cunliffe. *History of the Royal Warwickshire Regiment, 1818-1955* (London: Willam Clowes, 1956).
FM Cutlack. *War Letters of General Monash* (Sydney: Angus & Robertson, 1935).
Ian Daglish. *Over the Battlefield: Operation Goodwood* (Barnsley: Pen & Sword, 2005).
Francis de Guingand. *Generals at War* (London: Hodder & Stoughton, 1964).
Paul Deichmann. *Spearhead for Blitzkrieg* (Barnsley: Greenhill, 1996).
Paul Deichmann. *German Air Force Operations in Support of the Army* (North Stratford: Ayer, 1968).
Patrick Delaforce. *The Polar Bears* (Stroud: Fonthill Media, 2013).
Patrick Delaforce. *The Black Bull: From Normandy to the Baltic with the 11th Armoured Division* (Stroud: Alan Sutton, 1993).
Charles Demoulin. *Firebirds! Flying the Typhoon in Action* (Shrewsbury: Airlife, 1987).
Carlo D'Este. *Decision in Normandy* (New York: Dutton, 1983).
Carlo D'Este. *Patton: A Genius for War* (New York: Harper Collins, 1995).
John Dickson. *A Thoroughly Canadian General* (Toronto: U of T Press, 2007).
David Divine. *The Broken Wing* (London: Hutchinson, 1966).
Jack Dixon. *Dowding & Churchill: The Dark Side of the Battle of Britain* (Barnsley: Pen & Sword, 2008).
Milovan Djilas. *Conversations with Stalin* (London: Rupert Hart-Davis, 1962).
Colin Dobinson. *AA Command: Britain's Anti-Aircraft Defences of World War Two* (London, Methuen, 2001).
Michael Doubler. *Busting the Bocage: American Combined Arms Ops in France, 6 June-31 July 1944* (Fort Leavenworth: US General Staff College, 1988).
Michael Doubler. *Closing With the Enemy: How GIs Fought The War in Europe, 1944-45* (Lawrence: University of Kansas, 1994).
Christopher Duffy. *Red Storm on the Reich* (New York: Atheneum, 1991).
Margaret Duggan. *Runcie: the Making of an Archbishop* (London: Hodder & Stoughton, 1983).
Ben Dunkelman. *Dual Allegiance* (Toronto: Macmillan of Canada, 1976).
Stephen Dyson. *Tank Twins: East End Brothers in Arms 1943-45* (London: Leo Cooper & IWM, 1994). [Inside it is entitled *Twins in Tanks*].
Charles Eade. *The End of the Beginning: War Speeches of the Rt Hon Winston S Churchill* (London: Cassell, 1943).
Anthony Eden. *The Eden Memoirs: The Reckoning* (London: Cassell, 1965).
David Edwards. *Robert Runcie: A Portrait by his Friends.* (London: Harper Collins, 1990).
Roger Edwards. *German Airborne Troops* (London: Macdonald & Jane's, 1974).
John Eisenhower. *Bitter Woods* (London: Robert Hale, 1969).
WA Elliott. *Esprit de Corps: A Scots Guards' Officer on Active Service 1943-45* (Wilby: Michael Russell, 1969).
LF Ellis. *The War in France & Flanders 1939-40* (London: HMSO, 1953).
LF Ellis. *Victory in the West Vol I* (London: HMSO, 1962).
LF Ellis. *Victory in the West Vol II* (London: HMSO, 1968).
Peter Elstob. *Battle of the Reichswald* (London: Ballantine, 1970).
Vasily Emelianenko. *Red Star Against the Swastika* (London: Greenhill, 2005).
John English. *Patton's Peers* (Mechanicsburg: Stackpole, 2009).

John English. *The Canadian Army and the Normandy Campaign* (Mechanicsburg: Stackpole, 2009).
David Erskine. *The Scots Guards* 1919-55 (London: William Clowes, 1956).
Hubert Essame. *The Battle for Germany* (London: Batsford, 1959).
James Falkner. *Great and Glorious Days* (Staplehurst: Spellmount, 2002).
Brian P Farrell. *The Defence and Fall of Singapore* (Stroud: Tempus, 2005)
Charles Farrell. *Reflections 1939-45: A Scots Guards Officer in Training and War* (Bishop Auckland: Pentland Press, 2000).
Rex Fendick. *A Canloan Officer* (Nauwigewauk: Reginald F Fendick, 2000).
David Fletcher. *Vanguard of Victory* (London: HMSO, 1984).
David Fletcher. *Churchill Crocodile Flamethrower* (Botley: Osprey, 2007).
David Fletcher. *Mr Churchill's Tank: the British Infantry Tank Mk IV* (Atglen: Schiffer, 1999).
David Fletcher. *The Great Tank Scandal: British Armour in the Second World War, Part I* (London: HMSO, 1989).
David Fletcher, *The Universal Tank: British Armour in the Second World War, Part II.* (London: HMSO, 1993).
John Foley. *Mailed Fist* (St Albans: Mayflower, 1975).
Patrick Forbes. *6th Guards Tank Brigade* (London: Sampson Low, Marston, 1947).
Patrick Forbes. *The Grenadier Guards in the War of 1939-1945. Volume One* (Aldershot, Gale & Polden, 1949).
Ken Ford. *Battleaxe Division: From Africa to Italy with the 78th Division* (Stroud: History Press, 1999).
OA Forsyth-Major. *Elements of Tactics* (Aldershot: Gale & Polden, 1916).
Tony Foster. *Meeting of Generals* (London: Methuen, 1986).
Noble Frankland. *History at War* (London: Giles de la Mare, 1998).
Norman Franks. *Typhoon Attack* (London: William Kimber, 1984).
David Fraser. *Wars and Shadows* (London: Allen Lane, 2002).
Robert Frazer. *Black Yesterdays: The Argyll's War* (Hamilton: Argyll Regimental Foundation, 1996).
Stephen Fritz. *Frontsoldaten: The German Soldier in World War II* (Lexington: University Press of Kentucky, 1997).
JFC Fuller. *Memoirs of an Unconventional Soldier* (London: Nicholson & Watson, 1936).
JFC Fuller. *A Military History of the Western World.* (New York: Funk & Wagnalls, 1954).
JFC Fuller. *Armoured Warfare* (London: Eyre & Spottiswoode, 1943).
Adolf Galland. *The First and the Last* (London: Methuen, 1955).
LC Gates. *The History of the Tenth Foot* (Aldershot: Gale & Polden, 1953).
James Gavin. *On To Berlin* (London: Leo Cooper, 1979).
Ronald Gill and John Groves. *Club Route in Europe: The Story of 30 Corps in the European Campaign* (Hanover: 30 Corps, 1945).
Simon Godfrey. *British Army Communications in the Second World War* (London: Bloomsbury, 2013).
Chris Goss. *Luftwaffe Fighter-Bombers over Britain* (Manchester: Goodall, 2003).
Dominick Graham. *The Price of Command: A Biography of Gen Guy Simonds* (Toronto: Stoddart, 1993).
JL Granatstein. *The Generals* (Toronto: Stoddart, 1993).
Charles Graves. *The Royal Ulster Rifles* (Mexborough: RUR Committee, 1950).
Donald Graves. *The South Albertas: A Canadian Regiment at War* (Toronto: Robin Brass, 1998).
F Green and G Covell. *Medical Research* (London: HMSO, 1953).
Trevor Greenwood. *D-Day to Victory: the Diaries of a British Tank Commander* (London: Simon & Schuster, 2012).

Paddy Griffiths. *Battle Tactics of the Western Front* (New Haven: Yale University Press, 1996).
PJ Grigg. *Prejudice and Judgment* (London: Jonathan Cape, 1948).
Heinz Guderian. *Panzer Leader* (London: Michael Joseph, 1970).
Heinz Guderian. *From Normandy to the Ruhr with the 116th Panzer Division in World War II* (Bedford: Aberjona Press, 2001).
Hugh Gunning. *Borderers in Battle* (Berwick: Martin's, 1948).
Costas Hadjipateras and Maria Fafalios. *Crete 1941 Eyewitnessed* (Anixi Attikis: Efstathiadis Group, 1989).
Earl Haig. *Dispatches* (London: The Times, 1919).
Franz Halder. *The Halder Diaries* (Barnsley: Greenhill, 1988).
Nigel Hamilton. *Monty: The Making of a General* (London: Hutchinson, 1981).
Nigel Hamilton. *Monty: Master of the Battlefield 1942-4* (London: Hutchinson, 1983).
Nigel Hamilton. *Monty: The Field Marshal* (London: Hutchinson, 1986).
Nigel Hamilton. *The Full Monty Vol I* (London: Allen Lane, 2001).
JP Harris. *Men, Ideas and Tanks* (Manchester: University Press, 1995).
Mark Harrison. *The Economics of World War Two* (Cambridge: CUP, 2000).
Jack Harrod. *The History of the Second Battalion the Lincolnshire Regiment in North-West Europe* (Germany: 2 Lincolns, 1945).
Basil Liddell Hart. *The British Way of Warfare: Adaptability and Mobility* (London: Faber & Faber, 1932).
Basil Liddell Hart. *The Other Side of the Hill: Germany's Generals, their Rise and Fall* (London: Cassell, 1948).
Basil Liddell Hart. *The Tanks Vol I* (London: Cassell, 1959).
Adrian Hastings. *Robert Runcie: A Portrait by his Friends* (London: Mowbray, 1991).
Geoffrey W Hayes. *The Lincs: A History of the Lincoln & Welland Regiment at War* (Alma: Maple Leaf Route, 1986; Second Edition, 2007).
Hannes Heer and Klaus Neumann. *War of Extermination* (Hendon: Berghahn, 2000).
Ernst Heinkel. *Stormy Life* (Oberhaching: Aviatic, 1991).
William Hornby. *History of the Second World War: Factories and Plants* (London: HMSO, 1958).
Brian Horrocks. *Corps Commander* (New York: Scribners, 1977).
Richard Hough. *One Boy's War* (London: Heinemann, 1976).
Michael Howard and John Sparrow. *The Coldstream Guards 1920-46* (Oxford: OUP, 1951).
Montgomery Hyde. *British Air Policy Between the Wars* (London: Heinemann, 1976).
Harold Illing. *'No Better Soldier' 1939-45* (Warwick: Royal Warwickshire Museum, 2001).
David Irving. *Göring* (London: Focal Point, 1991).
Heinrich Janssen. *700 Jahre Winnekendonk: 1282-1982* (Winnekendonk: Geselligen Vereine, 1982).
Sidney Jary. *18 Platoon* (Carshalton Beeches, Sidney Jary, 1987).
Alan Jolly. *Blue Flash* (London: Alan Jolly, 1952).
HF Joslen. *Orders of Battle. Vol I* (London: HMSO, 1960).
Geoffrey Jukes. *The Defence of Moscow* (London: Macdonald, 1970).
Robin Kay. *The Official History of NZ in WW2: From Cassino to Trieste* (Wellington: Dept of Internal Affairs, 1967). Published online by NZETC.
John Keegan. *Six Armies in Normandy* (London: Jonathan Cape, 1982).
John Keegan. *Churchill's Generals* (London: Weidenfeld & Nicolson, 1991).
John Keegan. *A History of Warfare* (London: Hutchinson, 1993).
Heinrich Kempkes. *Die Kampfhandlungen und das Ende des Zweiten Weltkriegs im Bereich von Kervenheim* (Geldern: Heimatkalendar, 2001).
John Kennedy. *The Business of War* (London: Hutchinson, 1957).

Ludovic Kennedy. *Wicked Beyond Belief: the Luton Murder Case* (London: Granada, 1980).
Albert Kesselring. *The Memoirs of Field-Marshal Kesselring* (London: William Kimber, 1953).
Rudyard Kipling. *The Irish Guards in the Great War* (Garden City: Doubleday, 1923).
Rudyard Kipling. *Barrack Room Ballads* (London: Methuen, 1982).
Joseph Kipp. *Mass, Mobility and the Red Army's Road to Operational Art* (Fort Leavenworth: US Army Combined Arms Center, 1987).
Howard Kippenberger. *Infantry Brigadier* (Oxford: OUP, 1951).
Ben Kite. *Stout Hearts* (Solihull: Helion, 2014).
Vladimir Kotelnikov and Tony Butler. *Early Russian Jet Engines* (Derby: RR Heritage Trust, 2003).
John Lincoln. *Thank God and the Infantry* (Stroud: Alan Sutton, 1994).
Eric Linklater. *The Highland Division* (London: HMSO, 1942).
Robert Loeffel. *Family Punishment in Nazi Germany: Sippenhaft, Terror and Myth* (Basingstoke: Palgrave Macmillan, 2012).
Hans von Luck. *Panzer Commander* (New York: Praeger, 1989).
Erich von Ludendorff. *Von Ludendorff's Own Story; August 1914-November 1918* (New York: Harper, 1919).
Ralph Haswell Lutz. *The Cause of the German Collapse in 1918* (Palo Alta: Stanford, 1934).
Kenneth Macksey. *The Tank Pioneers* (London: Jane's, 1981).
Kenneth Macksey. *Armoured Crusader* (London: Hutchinson, 1967).
Heinz Margenheimer. *Hitler's War: Germany's Key Strategic Decisions, 1940-45* (London: Cassell, 2002).
Albert Mahan. *The Influence of Sea Power Upon History; 1660-1805* (Boston: Little Brown, 1894).
Richard Malone. *A World in Flames* (Toronto: Collins, 1984).
Philip Mansel. *Pillars of Monarchy: An Outline of the Political and Social History of Royal Guards* (London: Quartet, 1984).
Jonathan Mantle. *Archbishop* (London: Sinclair-Stevenson, 1991).
James Marsh. *The Canadian Encyclopedia* (Edmonton: Hurtig, 1985).
Gifford LeQ Martel. *In the Wake of the Tank* (London: Sifton Praed, 1931).
Gifford LeQ Martel. *Our Armoured Forces* (London: Faber & Faber, 1945).
Gifford LeQ Martel. *The Russian Outlook* (London: Michael Joseph, 1947).
HG Martin. *The History of the Fifteenth Scottish Division, 1939-45* (Edinburgh: William Blackwood, 1940).
Weston Martyr. *The Wandering Years* (Edinburgh: Blackwood, 1940).
Evan Mawdsley. *Thunder in the East* London: Bloomsbury, 2007).
Robin McNish. *Iron Division: The History of the 3rd Division* (Shepperton: Ian Allan, 1978).
FW von Mellenthin. *Panzer Battles* (Norman: University of Oklahoma, 1955).
Charles Messenger. *The Day We Won The War* (London: Weidenfeld and Nicolson, 2008).
Robert Michulec and Donald Caldwell. *Adolf Galland* (Sandomierz: MMP, 2003).
RB Moberley. *Second Battalion The Middlesex Regiment* (Cairo: R. Schindler, 1946).
John Monash. *The Australian Victories in France in 1918* (Sydney: Angus & Robertson, 1936).
Bernard L Montgomery. *Normandy to the Baltic* (London: Hutchinson, 1946).
Nigel Montgomery. *Churchill Tank: Owner's Workshop Manual* (Newbury Park: Haynes, 2013).
Charles Moore. *Margaret Thatcher* (London: Allen Lane, 2013).
William Moore. *Gas Attack!* (London: Leo Cooper, 1987).
Alan Moorehead. *Eclipse* (London: Hamish Hamilton, 1945).
Lord Moran. *Winston Churchill: The Struggle for Survival* (London: Constable, 1966).
BR Mullaly. *The South Lancashire Regiment: The Prince of Wales's Volunteers* (Bristol: White Swan, 1952).
Antonio Muñoz. *Göring's Grenadiers* (New York: Europa Books, 2002).

Sönke Neitzel. *Tapping Hitler's Generals: Transcripts of Secret Conversations 1942-45* (Barnsley: Frontline, 2007).
WN Nicholson. *The Suffolk Regiment 1928-46* (Ipswich: East Anglian Magazine, 1948).
GW Nicholson. *The Canadians in Italy; Vol II: 1943-5.* (Ottawa: Cloutier, 1958).
Gerald Nicholson. *The Gunners of Canada: The History of the Royal Regiment of Canadian Gunners* (Toronto: McClelland & Stewart, 1967).
Nigel Nicolson. *Alex* (London: Weidenfeld & Nicolson, 1973).
PR Nightingale. *The East Yorkshire Regiment, Duke of York's Own in the War 1939-45* (Goole: Mr Pye, 1998).
Dougas Orgill. *T34 Russian Armor* (London: Macdonald, 1971).
Richard Overy. *Goering: The Iron Man* (London: Routledge & Keegan Paul, 1987).
Richard Overy. *The Bombing War* (London: Allen Lane, 2013).
Jocelyn Pereira. *A Distant Drum; The War Memories of the Intelligence Officer of 5th Battalion Coldstream Guards* (Aldershot: Gale & Polden, 1948).
Bryan Perrett. *The Matilda* (London: Ian Allan, 1973).
Bryan Perrett. *Sturmartillerie and Panzerjäger* (London: Osprey, 1976).
Bryan Perrett. *The Churchill Tank* (London: Osprey, 1976).
Roland Perry. *Monash: The Outsider Who Won The War* (North Sydney: Random House, 2007).
NC Philips. *Official History of New Zealand in the Second World War: Italy, Vol I* (Wellington: Dept of Internal Affairs, 1957).
Richard Pipes. *Russia Under the Old Regime* (London: Weidenfeld & Nicolson, 1974).
Timothy Harrison Place. *Military Training in the British Army, 1940-44* (London: Routledge, 2000).
ISO Playfair. *Mediterranean and the Middle East, Vol 3* (London: HMSO. 1960).
Hermann Plocher. *The German Air Force Versus Russia 1942* (North Stratford: Ayer Co, 1968).
Jeffrey Plowman and Perry Rowe. *The Battles for Monte Cassino, Then and Now* (Old Harlow: Battle of Britain, 2011).
Martin Pöppel. *Heaven and Hell: The War Diary of a German Paratrooper* (Tunbridge Wells: Spellmount, 1988).
Karl Popper. *The Logic of Scientific Discovery* (London: Hutchinson, 1959).
MM Posten, D Hay and JD Scott. *Design and Development of Weapons* (London: HMSO, 1964).
Anthony Powell. *Faces in My Time, Vol III: The Memoirs of Anthony Powell* (London: Heinemann, 1980).
Jochen Prien and Gerhard Stemmer. *Jagdgeschwader 3 'Udet' in WWII* (Atglen: Schiffer, 2003).
Bruce Quarrie. *German Airborne Troops 1939-45* (London: Osprey, 1983).
GLY Radcliffe. *The King's Shropshire Light Infantry: History of the 2nd Battalion, 1944-5* (Oxford: Basil Blackwell, 1947).
Michael Reynolds. *Eagles and Bulldogs in Normandy 1944* (Havertown: History Press, 2003).
NW Routledge. *Anti-Aircraft Artillery 1914-55* (London: Brassey's, 1994).
Reginald Roy. *The Seaforth Highlanders of Canada, 1919-65* (Vancouver: Evergreen, 1969).
Hans Ulrich Rudel. *Stuka Pilot* (Dublin: Euphorian, 1952).
Kevin Ruffner. *Luftwaffe Field Divisions 1941-45* (London: Osprey, 1990).
John Sandars. *British 7th Armoured Division* (London: Osprey, 1977).
John Sandars. *Guards Armoured Division* (London: Osprey, 1979).
RA Saville-Sneath. *Aircraft of the United States* (Harmondsworth: Penguin, 1945).
Norman Scarfe. *Assault Division* (London: Collins, 1947).
Wolfgang Schneider. *Tigers in Combat, Vol II* (Mechanicsburg: Stackpole, 2005).
Walter Schwabedissen. *The Russian Air Force in the Eyes of German Commanders* (New York: Arno Press, 1968).

JD Scott and Richard Hughes. *History of the Second World War. The Administration of War Production* (London: HMSO, 1955).
Desmond Scott. *Typhoon Pilot* (London: Leo Cooper, 1982).
Frido Senger und Etterlin. *Neither Fear nor Hope* (London: Macdonald, 1963).
Geoffrey Serle. *John Monash: a Biography* (Carlton: Melbourne University Press, 1982).
William Shakespeare. *The Chronicle: History of Henry the fift* (London: Thomas Crede, 1600).
Ronald Sherbrooke-Walker. *Khaki and Blue* (London: Saint Catherine, 1952).
Christopher Shores. *Ground Attack Aircraft of WWII* (London: MacDonald & Jane's, 1977).
Christopher Shores. *2nd TAF* (Stroud: Osprey, 1970).
Christopher Shores and Chris Thomas. *2nd Tactical Airforce:Volume 3* (Hersham: Ian Allan, 2006).
Christopher Shores and Chris Thomas. *2nd Tactical Airforce:Volume 4* (Hersham: Ian Allan, 2008).
John Siborne. *The Waterloo Letters* (London: Cassell, 1891).
Hans Martin Simpel. *Die deutsche Fallschirmtruppe* (Hamburg: Mittler, 2001).
Andy Simpson. *Directing Operations: British Corps Command on the Western Front* (Staplehurst: Spellmount, 2005).
William Slim. *Defeat into Victory* (London: Cassell, 1956).
Wilfrid Smith. *Code Word Canloan* (Toronto: Dundurn Press, 1992).
John G Smith. *In at the Finish: North-West Europe 1944-5* (London: Minerva Press, 1995).
Peter C Smith. *Petlyakov Pe-2 Peschka* (Ramsbury: Crowood, 2003).
Peter C Smith. *Vengeance!* (Washington: Smithsonian, 1987).
Peter C Smith. *Close Air Support* (London: Orion, 1990).
John Smyth. *Bolo Whistler. The Life of General Sir Lashmer Whistler* (London: Frederick Muller, 1967).
Albert Speer. *Inside the Third Reich* (London: Macmillan, 1970).
Stephen Spender. *European Witness* (London: Hamish Hamilton, 1946).
Charles P Stacey. *The Victory Campaign* (Ottawa: DVD, 1960).
Roy Stanley. *World War II Photo Intelligence* (London: Sidgwick & Jackson, 1978).
John Swettenham. *McNaughton, Volume 3* (Toronto: Ryerson, 1969).
Charles Sydnor. *Soldiers of Destruction* (Princeton: Princeton University Press, 1977).
Tank Museum. *Churchill Tank: Vehicle History and Specification* (London: HMSO, 1983).
John Terraine. *The Right of the Line* (London: Hodder & Stoughton, 1985).
John Terraine. *To Win a War* (London: Sidgwick & Jackson, 1978).
RW Thompson. *Men Under Fire* (London: Macdonald, 1945).
RW Thompson. *The Battle for the Rhineland* (London: Hutchinson, 1958).
RW Thompson. *The Yankee Marlborough* (London: Allen & Unwin, 1963).
G Tornau and F Kurowski. *Sturmartillerie: Fels in der Brandung* (Hamburg: Maximilian-Verlag, 1965).
Francis Tuker. *Approach to Battle* (London: Cassell, 1963).
ES Turner. *Gallant Gentlemen: a Portrait of the British Officer, 1600-1956* (London: Michael Joseph, 1956).
John Vasco. *Bombsights over England* (Drayton: Jac, 1990).
GL Verney. *The Desert Rats* (Germany: BAOR, 1945).
Chris Vokes. *My Story* (Ottawa: Gallery Books, 1985).
Philip Warner. *The General Who Led from the Front* (London: Hamish Hamilton, 1984).
Evelyn Waugh. *Men At Arms* (London: Chapman & Hall, 1952).
Charles Webster and Noble Frankland. *Strategic Air Offensive Against Germany, 1939-45* (London: HMSO, 1961).
Russell Weigley. *Eisenhower's Lieutenants* (London: Sidgwick & Jackson, 1981).
Colin Welch. *The Odd Thing about the Colonel* (London: Bellew, 1997).

Denis and Shelagh Whitaker. *Rhineland: The Battle to End the War* (Toronto: Stoddart, 1989).
William Whitelaw. *The Whitelaw Memoirs* (London: Aurum, 1989).
Charles Whiting. *Hunters From the Sky* (London: Purnell, 1975).
Chester Wilmot. *The Struggle for Europe* (London: Collins, 1952).
WIG Wilson. *A Short History of the first Battalion KOSB in North West Europe* (Berwick-Upon-Tweed: Museum, 1945).
Andrew Wilson. *Flame Thrower* (London: William Kimber, 1984).
John Woods. *Peace In My Time! One Scouser's War* (Preston: Palatine, 1995).
Larry Worthington. *Worthy* (Toronto: Macmillan, 1961).
Steven Zaloga. *Armored Thunderbolt* (Mechanicsburg: Stackpole, 2008).
Frank Ziegler. *The Story of 609 Squadron* (London: Macdonald, 1971).
Solly Zuckerman. *From Apes to Warlords* (London: Hamish Hamilton, 1978).

Index

INDEX OF PEOPLE

INDEX OF PLACES

INDEX OF ALLIED MILITARY UNITS

INDEX OF GERMAN MILITARY UNITS

INDEX OF MISCELLANEOUS & GENERAL TERMS

A 4-colour battlefield map to accompany *The Noise of Battle* is available through eBay

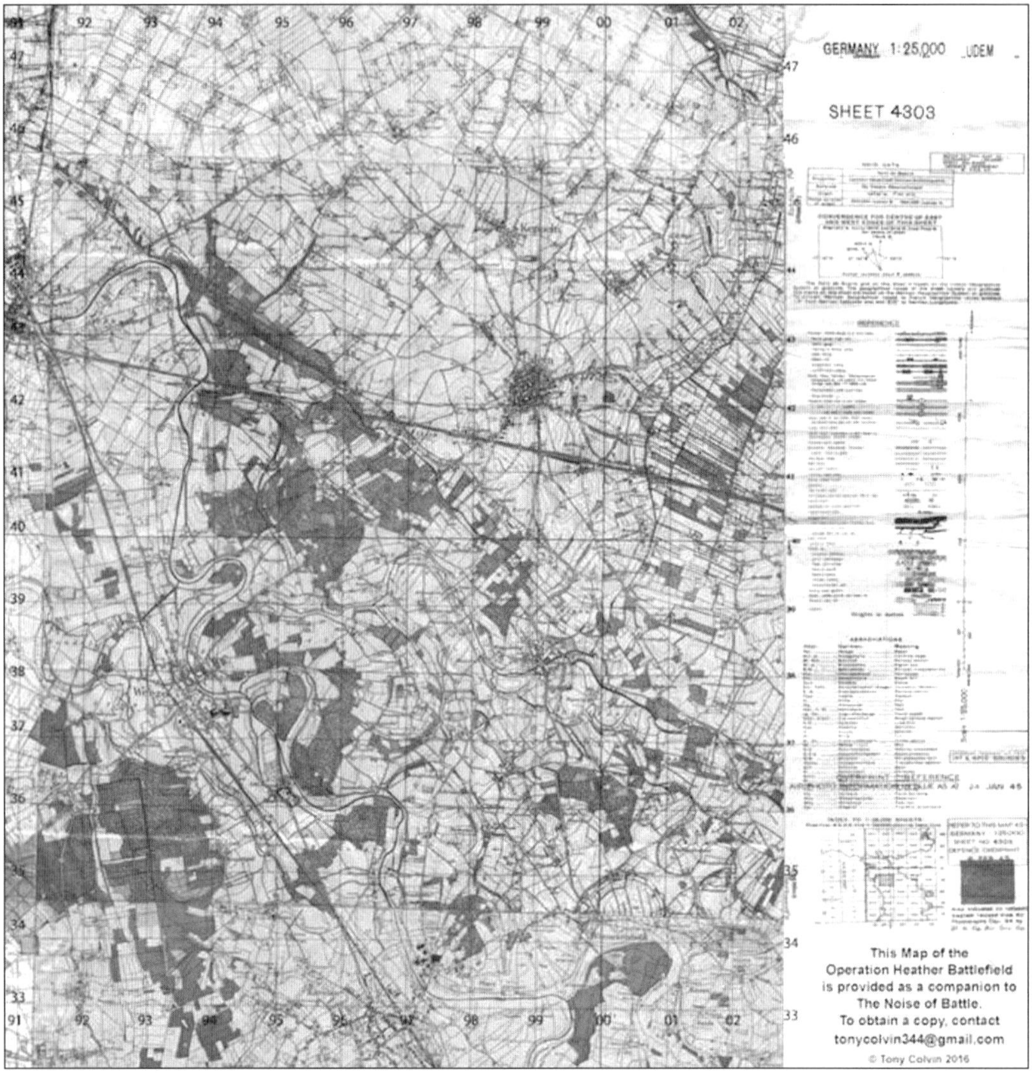

Period of availability: May 2016 to December 2017
Size: 600 mm × 600 mm (2 ft × 2 ft)
Folded dimension: 300 mm × 150 mm (1 ft × ½ ft)
How to buy: go to www.ebay.co.uk; search for
TNOB Map in *Collectables* > *Militaria* > *World War II (1939-1945)* > *Documents/Maps*
The unit price including delivery by 1st Class Mail to:

UK	£2.50
EU	£4.20
North America and RSA	£5.00
Australasia	£5.20

Prices may change to reflect the price of postage
Contact the author at tonycolvin344@gmail.com if you experience problems in ordering the map.